Contemporary Marketing

15th Edition

David L. Kurtz

CENGAGE
Learning·

Australia • Brazil • Japan • Korea • Mexico • Singapore • Spain • United Kingdom • United States

CENGAGE
Learning·

Contemporary Marketing: 15th Edition

Social Psychology and Human Nature, 15th Edition
David L. Kurtz

© 2012, 2010 Cengage Learning. All rights reserved.

ExamView® is a registered trademark of eInstruction Corp. Windows is a registered trademark of the Microsoft Corporation used herein under license. Macintosh and Power Macintosh are registered trademarks of Apple Computer, Inc. used herein under license.
© 2010 Cengage Learning. All rights reserved.

Cengage Learning WebTutor™ is a trademark of Cengage Learning.

Senior Project Development Manager:
Linda deStefano

Market Development Manager:
Heather Kramer

Senior Production/Manufacturing Manager:
Donna M. Brown

Production Editorial Manager:
Kim Fry

Sr. Rights Acquisition Account Manager:
Todd Osborne

For product information and technology assistance, contact us at
Cengage Learning Customer & Sales Support, 1-800-354-9706

For permission to use material from this text or product,
submit all requests online at **cengage.com/permissions**
Further permissions questions can be emailed to
permissionrequest@cengage.com

This book contains select works from existing Cengage Learning resources and was produced by Cengage Learning Custom Solutions for collegiate use. As such, those adopting and/or contributing to this work are responsible for editorial content accuracy, continuity and completeness.

Compilation © 2013 Cengage Learning
ISBN-13: 978-1-285-88012-9

ISBN-10: 1-285-88012-9

Cengage Learning
5191 Natorp Boulevard
Mason, Ohio 45040
USA

Cengage Learning is a leading provider of customized learning solutions with office locations around the globe, including Singapore, the United Kingdom, Australia, Mexico, Brazil, and Japan. Locate your local office at:

international.cengage.com/region.
Cengage Learning products are represented in Canada by Nelson Education, Ltd.
For your lifelong learning solutions, visit **www.cengage.com/custom.**
Visit our corporate website at **www.cengage.com.**

Printed in the United States of America

brief contents

Preface xxiv

1 Designing Customer-Oriented Marketing Strategies 1

Chapter 1   Marketing: The Art and Science of Satisfying Customers 2
Chapter 2   Strategic Planning in Contemporary Marketing 34
Chapter 3   The Marketing Environment, Ethics, and Social Responsibility 62
Chapter 4   E-Business: Managing the Customer Experience 100

2 Understanding Buyers and Markets 135

Chapter 5   Consumer Behavior 136
Chapter 6   Business-to-Business (B2B) Marketing 168
Chapter 7   Global Marketing 202

3 Target Market Selection 237

Chapter 8   Marketing Research and Sales Forecasting 238
Chapter 9   Market Segmentation, Targeting, and Positioning 274
Chapter 10   Relationship Marketing and Customer Relationship Management (CRM) 308

4 Product Decisions 341

Chapter 11   Product and Service Strategies 342
Chapter 12   Developing and Managing Brand and Product Categories 376

5 Distribution Decisions 411

Chapter 13   Marketing Channels and Supply Chain Management 412
Chapter 14   Retailers, Wholesalers, and Direct Marketers 448

6 Promotional Decisions 485

Chapter 15   Integrated Marketing Communications 486
Chapter 16   Advertising and Public Relations 526
Chapter 17   Personal Selling and Sales Promotion 564

7 Pricing Decisions 603

Chapter 18   Pricing Concepts 604
Chapter 19   Pricing Strategies 638

Appendix A   Your Career in Marketing A-1
Appendix B   Developing an Effective Marketing Plan A-19
Appendix C   Financial Analysis in Marketing A-33
Notes N-1
Glossary G-1
Name & Company Index I-1
Subject Index I-12
International Index I-28

contents

Preface   xxiv

PART 1

Designing Customer-Oriented Marketing Strategies

ch1   Marketing: The Art and Science of Satisfying Customers   2

OPENING VIGNETTE
Walmart Boosts Sustainability   2

CAREER READINESS
How to Network   12

SOLVING AN ETHICAL CONTROVERSY
Airport Scanners Raise Privacy Issues for the Government   25

MARKETING SUCCESS
Procter & Gamble Gets Future-Friendly   26

What Is Marketing?   5
A Definition of Marketing   7 | Today's Global Marketplace   7

Four Eras in the History of Marketing   9
The Production Era   9 | The Sales Era   10 | The Marketing Era   10 |
The Relationship Era   12 | Converting Needs to Wants   13

Avoiding Marketing Myopia   13

Extending the Traditional Boundaries of Marketing   14
Marketing in Not-for-Profit Organizations   14 | Characteristics of Not-for-Profit Marketing   15

Nontraditional Marketing   16
Person Marketing   17 | Place Marketing   17 | Cause Marketing   18 | Event Marketing   19 |
Organization Marketing   20

From Transaction-Based Marketing to Relationship Marketing   20
Using Interactive and Social Marketing to Build Relationships   21 | Developing Partnerships
and Strategic Alliances   22

Costs and Functions of Marketing   23

Ethics and Social Responsibility: Doing Well by Doing Good   24

Strategic Implications of Marketing in the 21st Century   28

Review of Chapter Objectives   28
Assessment Check: Answers   29 | Marketing Terms You Need to Know   30 |
Assurance of Learning Review   30 | Projects and Teamwork Exercises   31 |
Critical-Thinking Exercises   31 | Ethics Exercise   31 | Internet Exercises   32

Case 1.1   **Hewlett-Packard Reduces, Reuses, Recycles   32**

Video Case 1.2   **Marketing: Satisfying Customers at Flight 001   33**

Strategic Planning in Contemporary Marketing 34

Marketing Planning: The Basis for Strategy and Tactics 37
Strategic Planning versus Tactical Planning 39 | Planning at Different Organizational Levels 40

Steps in the Marketing Planning Process 41

Defining the Organization's Mission and Objectives 41
Assessing Organizational Resources and Evaluating Environmental Risks and Opportunities 42 | Formulating, Implementing, and Monitoring a Marketing Strategy 42

Successful Strategies: Tools and Techniques 42
Porter's Five Forces Model 43 | First Mover and Second Mover Strategies 45 | SWOT Analysis 46 | The Strategic Window 46

Elements of a Marketing Strategy 47
The Target Market 47 | Marketing Mix Variables 48 | The Marketing Environment 50

Methods for Marketing Planning 52
Business Portfolio Analysis 53 | The BCG Matrix 53

Strategic Implications of Marketing in the 21st Century 55

Review of Chapter Objectives 55
Assessment Check: Answers 56 | Marketing Terms You Need to Know 57 | Assurance of Learning Review 57 | Projects and Teamwork Exercises 57 | Critical-Thinking Exercises 58 | Ethics Exercise 58 | Internet Exercises 59

Case 2.1 **How a Stadium Becomes Part of a Marketing Strategy 59**

Video Case 2.2 **Strategic Planning and the Marketing Process at Preserve 60**

ch2

OPENING VIGNETTE
Ford's Dramatic Comeback: One Ford, One Team, One Plan, One Goal 34

CAREER READINESS
Plan the Most Effective Virtual Meeting 38

SOLVING AN ETHICAL CONTROVERSY
Tiger Woods Drives His Career into the Rough 43

MARKETING SUCCESS
In-N-Out Burgers Sell Themselves 48

The Marketing Environment, Ethics, and Social Responsibility 62

Environmental Scanning and Environmental Management 65

The Competitive Environment 66
Types of Competition 67 | Developing a Competitive Strategy 68 | Time-Based Competition 69

The Political-Legal Environment 70
Government Regulation 70 | Government Regulatory Agencies 73 | Other Regulatory Forces 74 | Controlling the Political-Legal Environment 75

The Economic Environment 76
Stages in the Business Cycle 76 | The Global Economic Crisis 77 | Inflation and Deflation 77 | Resource Availability 78 | The International Economic Environment 79

The Technological Environment 79
Applying Technology 80

ch3

OPENING VIGNETTE
At Nike, Corporate Responsibility Means Sustainable Business and Innovation 62

MARKETING SUCCESS
SC Johnson Committed to "Doing What's Right" 68

CAREER READINESS
Getting Employees to Go Green 78

SOLVING AN ETHICAL CONTROVERSY
In Search of Sparking Glassware 81

The Social-Cultural Environment 82
Consumerism 82

Ethical Issues in Marketing 84
Ethics in Marketing Research 86 | Ethics in Product Strategy 87 | Ethics in Distribution 87 | Ethics in Promotion 87 | Ethics in Pricing 88

Social Responsibility in Marketing 89
Marketing's Responsibilities 89 | Marketing and Ecology 90

Strategic Implications of Marketing in the 21st Century 93

Review of Chapter Objectives 93
Assessment Check: Answers 94 | Marketing Terms You Need to Know 95 | Assurance of Learning Review 95 | Projects and Teamwork Exercises 96 | Critical-Thinking Exercises 96 | Ethics Exercise 97 | Internet Exercises 97 | Ethics Questionnaire Answers 97

Case 3.1 **Dolores Labs Takes the Guesswork Out of Grunt Work 98**

Video Case 3.2 **The Marketing Environment, Ethics, and Social Responsibility at Scholfield Honda 99**

ch4 E-Business: Managing the Customer Experience 100

OPENING VIGNETTE
Net-à-Porter Knows What Luxury Shoppers Want 100

MARKETING SUCCESS
Craigslist Dominates in Classified Ads 110

SOLVING AN ETHICAL CONTROVERSY
Behavioral Targeting Raises Privacy Concerns 115

CAREER READINESS
Blogging on Your Best Behavior 120

The Digital World 103

E-Business and E-Marketing 104
Opportunities of E-Marketing 105 | Web Business Models 107

B2B E-Marketing 108
Proprietary B2B Transactions 108 | E-Procurement on Open Exchanges 109

B2C E-Marketing 109
Electronic Storefronts 110 | Benefits of B2C E-Marketing 111 | Online Buyers and Sellers 112

Challenges in E-Business and E-Marketing 113
Safety of Online Payment 113 | Privacy Issues 114 | Fraud and Scams 115 | Site Design and Customer Service 116 | Channel Conflicts and Copyright Disputes 117

Marketing and Web Communication 117
Online Communities and Social Networks 118 | Blogs and Podcasts 119 | Promotions on the Web 120

Building an Effective Web Presence 121
Successful Site Development 122 | Establishing Goals 122 | Implementation and Interest 122 | Pricing and Maintenance 123

Assessing Site Effectiveness 123

Strategic Implications of Marketing in the 21st Century 125

Review of Chapter Objectives 125

Assessment Check: Answers 127 | Marketing Terms You Need to Know 128 |
Assurance of Learning Review 128 | Projects and Teamwork Exercises 129 |
Critical-Thinking Exercises 129 | Ethics Exercise 129 | Internet Exercises 130

Case 4.1 Procter & Gamble's New Web Strategy 130

Video Case 4.2 E-Business at Evo 131

Greensburg, Inc. Continuing Video Case: Marketing Is Not a Dirty Word 133

Understanding
Buyers and Markets
2
PART 2

ch 5

Consumer Behavior 136

Interpersonal Determinants of Consumer Behavior 139

Cultural Influences 139 | Social Influences 143 | Family Influences 147

Personal Determinants of Consumer Behavior 148

Needs and Motives 148 | Perceptions 150 | Attitudes 152 | Learning 154 |
Self-Concept Theory 155

The Consumer Decision Process 156

Problem or Opportunity Recognition 158 | Search 158 | Evaluation of
Alternatives 159 | Purchase Decision and Purchase Act 159 | Postpurchase
Evaluation 160 | Classifying Consumer Problem-Solving Processes 160

Strategic Implications of Marketing in the 21st Century 161

Review of Chapter Objectives 162

Assessment Check: Answers 162 | Marketing Terms You Need to Know 163 |
Assurance of Learning Review 163 | Projects and Teamwork Exercises 164 |
Critical-Thinking Exercises 164 | Ethics Exercise 165 | Internet Exercises 165

Case 5.1 How Color Is Used in Marketing 166

Video Case 5.2 Consumer Behavior at Scholfield Honda 167

OPENING VIGNETTE
Paco Underhill: Hero to
Marketers 136

MARKETING SUCCESS
Marketers Cater to Penny–
Pinching Consumers 144

CAREER READINESS
Your Body Language Speaks
Volumes 153

SOLVING AN ETHICAL
CONTROVERSY
Facebook: Forced to Look in the
Mirror 157

Business-to-Business (B2B) Marketing   168

ch **6**

OPENING VIGNETTE
Corporate Customers Try
Zappos' Advice on for Size   168

**SOLVING AN ETHICAL
CONTROVERSY**
To Stuff Cookies, Or Not to
Stuff   174

MARKETING SUCCESS
Sysco Masters Logistics for
Food   178

CAREER READINESS
How to Work a Trade
Show   180

Nature of the Business Market 171
Components of the Business Market 172 | B2B Markets: The Internet Connection 173 | Differences in Foreign Business Markets 174

Segmenting B2B Markets 175
Segmentation by Demographic Characteristics 175 | Segmentation by Customer Type 175 | Segmentation by End-Use Application 176 | Segmentation by Purchase Categories 177

Characteristics of the B2B Market 177
Geographic Market Concentration 177 | Sizes and Numbers of Buyers 178 | The Purchase Decision Process 178 | Buyer–Seller Relationships 179 | Evaluating International Business Markets 180

Business Market Demand 181
Derived Demand 181 | Volatile Demand 182 | Joint Demand 182 | Inelastic Demand 182 | Inventory Adjustments 182

The Make, Buy, or Lease Decision 183
The Rise of Offshoring and Outsourcing 183 | Problems with Offshoring and Outsourcing 184

The Business Buying Process 185
Influences on Purchase Decisions 185 | Model of the Organizational Buying Process 187 | Classifying Business Buying Situations 189 | Analysis Tools 190

The Buying Center Concept 191
Buying Center Roles 191 | International Buying Centers 191

Developing Effective Business-to-Business Marketing Strategies 192
Challenges of Government Markets 192 | Challenges of Institutional Markets 194 | Challenges of International Markets 194

Strategic Implications of Marketing in the 21st Century 195

Review of Chapter Objectives 195
Assessment Check: Answers 197 | Marketing Terms You Need to Know 198 | Assurance of Learning Review 198 | Projects and Teamwork Exercises 199 | Critical-Thinking Exercises 199 | Ethics Exercise 199 | Internet Exercises 199

Case 6.1 **Peerless Pump Puts Customers First 200**

Video Case 6.2 **Business-to-Business Marketing at Flight 001 201**

Global Marketing   202

The Importance of Global Marketing 205
Service and Retail Exports 206 | Benefits of Going Global 207

The International Marketing Environment 209
International Economic Environment 209 | International Social-Cultural
Environment 210 | International Technological Environment 211 | International
Political-Legal Environment 212 | Trade Barriers 213 | Dumping 215

Multinational Economic Integration 215
GATT and the World Trade Organization 216 | The NAFTA Accord 217 | The Free Trade
Area of the Americas and CAFTA-DR 217 | The European Union 218

Going Global 219

Strategies for Entering Foreign Markets 220
Importing and Exporting 220 | Contractual Agreements 221 | International Direct
Investment 222

From Multinational Corporation to Global Marketer 222

Developing an International Marketing Strategy 223
International Product and Promotional Strategies 225 | International Distribution
Strategy 225 | Pricing Strategy 226 | Countertrade 226

The United States as a Target for International Marketers 227

Strategic Implications of Marketing in the 21st Century 228

Review of Chapter Objectives 228
Assessment Check: Answers 229 | Marketing Terms You Need to Know 230 |
Assurance of Learning Review 230 | Projects and Teamwork Exercises 231 |
Critical-Thinking Exercises 231 | Ethics Exercise 231 | Internet Exercises 232

Case 7.1 General Motors: Revved Up in China 232

Video Case 7.2 Global Marketing at Evo 233

Greensburg, Inc. Continuing Video Case: Rebuilding: They Didn't Ask for This 235

ch7

OPENING VIGNETTE
Pollo Campero: Flavor You Can't
"Campero" 202

MARKETING SUCCESS
I'm Lovin' It—Russian
Style 208

CAREER READINESS
Culture Tips for Marketing
Professionals 212

SOLVING AN ETHICAL
CONTROVERSY
Putting the Lid on Bottled
Water 216

PART 3

Target **Market Selection**

ch 8

OPENING VIGNETTE
Polaris Marketing Research
Shows the Way 238

SOLVING AN ETHICAL
CONTROVERSY
Looking into Census Bureau
Spending on Advertising 249

MARKETING SUCCESS
Mapping the Market 252

CAREER READINESS
Planning Effective Online
Surveys 257

Marketing Research and Sales Forecasting 238

The Marketing Research Function 240
Development of the Marketing Research Function 240 | Who Conducts Marketing Research? 242 | Customer Satisfaction Measurement Programs 243

The Marketing Research Process 244
Define the Problem 244 | Conduct Exploratory Research 245 | Formulate a Hypothesis 245 | Create a Research Design 246 | Collect Data 246 Interpret and Present Research Data 246

Marketing Research Methods 247
Secondary Data Collection 247 | Sampling Techniques 251 | Primary Research Methods 252 | Survey Methods 254

Conducting International Marketing Research 259

Interpretive Research 260
Ethnographic Studies 260

Computer Technology in Marketing Research 261
Marketing Information Systems (MISs) 261 | Marketing Decision Support Systems (MDSSs) 261 | Data Mining 261 | Business Intelligence 262 | Competitive Intelligence 262

Sales Forecasting 263
Qualitative Forecasting Techniques 264

Strategic Implications of Marketing in the 21st Century 266

Review of Chapter Objectives **266**
Assessment Check: Answers 268 | Marketing Terms You Need to Know 269 | Assurance of Learning Review 269 | Projects and Teamwork Exercises 269 | Critical-Thinking Exercises 270 | Ethics Exercise 270 | Internet Exercises 271

Case 8.1 **Oberto Sausage: A Recipe for Forecasting 271**

Video Case 8.2 **Marketing Research and Sales Forecasting at Ogden Publications 272**

Market Segmentation, Targeting, and Positioning 274

Types of Markets 277

The Role of Market Segmentation 277
Criteria for Effective Segmentation 278

Segmenting Consumer Markets 279

Geographic Segmentation 279
Using Geographic Segmentation 281 | Geographic Information Systems (GISs) 281

Demographic Segmentation 282
Segmenting by Gender 282 | Segmenting by Age 283 | The Cohort Effect: The Video Game Generation 287 | Segmenting by Ethnic Group 287 | Segmenting by Family Lifecycle Stages 289 | Segmenting by Household Type 290 | Segmenting by Income and Expenditure Patterns 291 | Demographic Segmentation Abroad 291

Psychographic Segmentation 292
What Is Psychographic Segmentation? 292 | VALS™ 293 | Psychographic Segmentation of Global Markets 294 | Using Psychographic Segmentation 295

Product-Related Segmentation 296
Segmenting by Benefits Sought 296 | Segmenting by Usage Rates 296 | Segmenting by Brand Loyalty 296 | Using Multiple Segmentation Bases 297

The Market Segmentation Process 297
Develop a Relevant Profile for Each Segment 297 | Forecast Market Potential 298 | Forecast Probable Market Share 298 | Select Specific Market Segments 298

Strategies for Reaching Target Markets 298
Undifferentiated Marketing 299 | Differentiated Marketing 299 | Concentrated Marketing 299 | Micromarketing 300

Selecting and Executing a Strategy 300

Strategic Implications of Marketing in the 21st Century 302

Review of Chapter Objectives 302
Assessment Check: Answers 303 | Marketing Terms You Need to Know 304 | Assurance of Learning Review 304 | Projects and Teamwork Exercises 305 | Critical-Thinking Exercises 305 | Ethics Exercise 305 | Internet Exercises 306

Case 9.1 Carrols Restaurant Group: Feeding a Hungry Public 306

Video Case 9.2 Targeting and Positioning at Numi Tea 307

ch9

OPENING VIGNETTE
Tween Brands "Gets" Tweens 274

CAREER READINESS
Communicating with Your Target Market 283

SOLVING AN ETHICAL CONTROVERSY
Taking Advantage of Seniors 286

MARKETING SUCCESS
LR Health and Beauty Helps Customers "Feel Good. Look Great." 294

ch 10

Relationship Marketing and Customer Relationship Management (CRM) 308

OPENING VIGNETTE
Airlines Are Uniting the
Skies 308

SOLVING AN ETHICAL
CONTROVERSY
Is Location-Based Advertising
Fair and Square? 315

CAREER READINESS
Establishing Relationships
through CRM 323

MARKETING SUCCESS
Google Partners for Android
Success 328

The Shift from Transaction-Based Marketing to Relationship Marketing 310
Elements of Relationship Marketing 312 | Internal Marketing 312

The Relationship Marketing Continuum 314
First Level: Focus on Price 314 | Second Level: Social Interactions 314 |
Third Level: Interdependent Partnership 316

Enhancing Customer Satisfaction 316
Understanding Customer Needs 316 | Obtaining Customer Feedback and Ensuring
Satisfaction 317

Building Buyer–Seller Relationships 318
How Marketers Keep Customers 318 | Database Marketing 319 |
Customers as Advocates 320

Customer Relationship Management 321
Benefits of CRM 321 | Problems with CRM 322 | Retrieving Lost Customers 323

Buyer–Seller Relationships in Business-to-Business Markets 324
Choosing Business Partners 325 | Types of Partnerships 325 | Cobranding and
Comarketing 326

Improving Buyer–Seller Relationships in Business-to-Business Markets 326
National Account Selling 327 | Business-to-Business Databases 327 | Electronic Data
Interchange and Web Services 327

Vendor-Managed Inventory 328
Managing the Supply Chain 328 | Business-to-Business Alliances 329

Evaluating Customer Relationship Programs 330

Strategic Implications of Marketing in the 21st Century 332

Review of Chapter Objectives 332
Assessment Check: Answers 334 | Marketing Terms You Need to Know 335 |
Assurance of Learning Review 335 | Projects and Teamwork Exercises 335 |
Critical-Thinking Exercises 335 | Ethics Exercise 336 | Internet Exercises 336

Case 10.1 **Microsoft Uses Partnership to Hedge Its Bet on Bing 336**

Video Case 10.2 **Relationship Marketing and CRM at Numi Tea 337**

Greensburg, Inc. **Continuing Video Case: This Isn't Your Father's Honda … or Is It? 339**

Product Decisions

PART 4

ch11 Product and Service Strategies 342

OPENING VIGNETTE
Massage Envy Builds a Following among the Stress-Weary 342

CAREER READINESS
Giving Helpful Feedback 357

SOLVING AN ETHICAL CONTROVERSY
Shelf-Space Wars: A Continuing Saga 364

MARKETING SUCCESS
Icebreaker Challenges the Synthetics 366

What Is a Product? 344

What Are Goods and Services? 345

Importance of the Service Sector 346

Classifying Goods and Services for Consumer and Business Markets 348
Types of Consumer Products 348 | Classifying Consumer Services 351 | Applying the Consumer Products Classification System 352 | Types of Business Products 353

Quality as a Product Strategy 356
Worldwide Quality Programs 357 | Benchmarking 358 | Quality of Services 358

Development of Product Lines 359
Desire to Grow 360 | Enhancing the Company's Market Position 360 | Optimal Use of Company Resources 360

The Product Mix 360
Product Mix Width 361 | Product Mix Length 361 | Product Mix Depth 361 | Product Mix Decisions 361

The Product Lifecycle 362
Introductory Stage 363 | Growth Stage 364 | Maturity Stage 365 | Decline Stage 365

Extending the Product Lifecycle 366
Increasing Frequency of Use 366 | Increasing the Number of Users 367 | Finding New Uses 367 | Changing Package Sizes, Labels, or Product Quality 368

Product Deletion Decisions 368

Strategic Implications of Marketing in the 21st Century 369

Review of Chapter Objectives **369**
Assessment Check: Answers 370 | Marketing Terms You Need to Know 371 | Assurance of Learning Review 371 | Projects and Teamwork Exercises 372 | Critical-Thinking Exercises 372 | Ethics Exercise 373 | Internet Exercises 373

Case 11.1 **New Balance "Experiences" China 373**

Video Case 11.2 **Product and Service Strategy at Preserve 374**

ch12 Developing and Managing Brand and Product Categories 376

OPENING VIGNETTE
Liz Claiborne and JCPenney:
A Marriage Made in
Heaven? 376

SOLVING AN ETHICAL
CONTROVERSY
Who Dat? Slogan Causes
Football Furor 384

CAREER READINESS
Using Jargon in Everyday
Communication 386

MARKETING SUCCESS
Swiffer Aims to Be Not
Just User-Friendly But
Pet-Friendly 392

Managing Brands for Competitive Advantage 378
Brand Loyalty 379 | Types of Brands 380 | Brand Equity 382 | The Role of Category and Brand Management 383

Product Identification 384
Brand Names and Brand Marks 385 | Trademarks 386 | Developing Global Brand Names and Trademarks 387 | Packaging 388 | Brand Extensions 390 | Brand Licensing 391

New-Product Planning 392
Product Development Strategies 392 | The Consumer Adoption Process 394 | Adopter Categories 395 | Identifying Early Adopters 396 | Organizing for New-Product Development 396 | The New-Product Development Process 398 | Idea Generation 399 | Screening 399 | Business Analysis 399 | Development 399 | Test Marketing 400 | Commercialization 400

Product Safety and Liability 400

Strategic Implications of Marketing in the 21st Century 402

Review of Chapter Objectives 402
Assessment Check: Answers 403 | Marketing Terms You Need to Know 404 | Assurance of Learning Review 404 | Projects and Teamwork Exercises 405 | Critical-Thinking Exercises 405 | Ethics Exercise 405 | Internet Exercises 406

Case 12.1 **Roy Choi Takes Gourmet Food to the Street 406**

Video Case 12.2 **Developing and Managing Brand and Product Categories at Maine Media Workshops 407**

Greensburg, Inc. **Continuing Video Case: Green: It's Not Just for Earth Day Anymore 409**

Distribution Decisions
PART 5

ch13 Marketing Channels and Supply Chain Management 412

OPENING VIGNETTE
Panama Canal Undergoes Extreme Makeover 412

CAREER READINESS
Anatomy of a Successful Sales Call 418

MARKETING SUCCESS
The Amazing Amazon 430

SOLVING AN ETHICAL CONTROVERSY
Guns on the High Seas? 437

The Role of Marketing Channels in Marketing Strategy 415

Types of Marketing Channels 416
Direct Selling 416 | Channels Using Marketing Intermediaries 418 | Dual Distribution 419 | Reverse Channels 420

Channel Strategy Decisions 421
Selection of a Marketing Channel 421 | Determining Distribution Intensity 422 | Who Should Perform Channel Functions? 424

Channel Management and Leadership 425
Channel Conflict 426 | Achieving Channel Cooperation 427

Vertical Marketing Systems 427
Corporate and Administered Systems 427 | Contractual Systems 428

Logistics and Supply Chain Management 429
Radio-Frequency Identification 430 | Enterprise Resource Planning 432 | Logistical Cost Control 432

Physical Distribution 432
The Problem of Suboptimization 433 | Customer Service Standards 433 | Transportation 434 | Major Transportation Modes 435 | Freight Forwarders and Supplemental Carriers 438 | Intermodal Coordination 439 | Warehousing 439 | Inventory Control Systems 440 | Order Processing 440 | Protective Packaging and Materials Handling 440

Strategic Implications of Marketing in the 21st Century 441

Review of Chapter Objectives 442
Assessment Check: Answers 443 | Marketing Terms You Need to Know 444 | Assurance of Learning Review 444 | Projects and Teamwork Exercises 444 | Critical-Thinking Exercises 445 | Ethics Exercise 445 | Internet Exercises 445

Case 13.1 **Carolyn Dorothy: Not Your Grandpa's Tugboat 446**

Video Case 13.2 **Marketing Channels and Supply Chain Management at Preserve 447**

ch14 Retailers, Wholesalers, and Direct Marketers 448

OPENING VIGNETTE
Wawa "Simplifies" for Customer
Convenience 448

MARKETING SUCCESS
Five Guys: Serving Up a
Gourmet Burger 452

SOLVING AN ETHICAL
CONTROVERSY
Hiring a Contingent
Workforce 456

CAREER READINESS
What Makes a Good
Supplier? 467

Retailing 450
Evolution of Retailing 451

Retailing Strategy 451
Selecting a Target Market 452 | Merchandising Strategy 454 | Customer Service
Strategy 455 | Pricing Strategy 456 | Location/Distribution Strategy 457 |
Promotional Strategy 458 | Store Atmospherics 460

Types of Retailers 460
Classification of Retailers by Form of Ownership 461 | Classification by Shopping
Effort 461 | Classification by Services Provided 462 | Classification by Product
Lines 462 | Classification of Retail Transactions by Location 464 | Retail Convergence
and Scrambled Merchandising 465

Wholesaling Intermediaries 465
Functions of Wholesaling Intermediaries 465 | Types of Wholesaling
Intermediaries 468 | Retailer-Owned Cooperatives and Buying Offices 472

Direct Marketing and Other Nonstore Retailing 472
Direct Mail 473 | Direct Selling 473 | Direct-Response Retailing 473 |
Telemarketing 474 | Internet Retailing 474 | Automatic Merchandising 474

Strategic Implications of Marketing in the 21st Century 475

Review of Chapter Objectives 476
Assessment Check: Answers 477 | Marketing Terms You Need to Know 477 |
Assurance of Learning Review 478 | Projects and Teamwork Exercises 478 |
Critical-Thinking Exercises 479 | Ethics Exercise 479 | Internet Exercises 479

Case 14.1 **Groupon: Finding Strength in Numbers 480**

Video Case 14.2 **Retailing at Flight 001 481**

Greensburg, Inc. **Continuing Video Case: A Little Hope for the Little Guy 482**

Promotional Decisions **6**

PART 6

ch15 Integrated Marketing Comunications 486

OPENING VIGNETTE
Denny's Gets the
Word Out   486

CAREER READINESS
Body Language: Watch What
You "Say"   494

SOLVING AN ETHICAL
CONTROVERSY
Should Companies Filter Their
Online Reviews?   496

MARKETING SUCCESS
Redbox Rules   498

Integrated Marketing Communications 489
Importance of Teamwork 490 | Role of Databases in Effective IMC Programs 491

The Communication Process 491

Objectives of Promotion 495
Provide Information 495 | Increase Demand 495 | Differentiate the
Product 497 | Accentuate the Product's Value 498 | Stabilize Sales 498

Elements of the Promotional Mix 499
Personal Selling 500 | Nonpersonal Selling 500 | Advantages and Disadvantages of Types
of Promotion 503

Sponsorships 504
How Sponsorship Differs from Advertising 504

Direct Marketing 505
Direct Marketing Communications Channels 506 | Direct Mail 506 | Catalogs 506 |
Telemarketing 507 | Direct Marketing via Broadcast Channels 508 | Electronic Direct
Marketing Channels 508 | Other Direct Marketing Channels 509

Developing an Optimal Promotional Mix 509
Nature of the Market 510 | Nature of the Product 510 | Stage in the Product Lifecycle 510 |
Price 511 | Funds Available for Promotion 511

Pulling and Pushing Promotional Strategies 512

Budgeting for Promotional Strategy 513

Measuring the Effectiveness of Promotion 515
Measuring Online Promotions 516

The Value of Marketing Communications 517
Social Importance 517 | Business Importance 518 | Economic Importance 518

Strategic Implications of Marketing in the 21st Century 519

Review of Chapter Objectives 519
Assessment Check: Answers 520 | Marketing Terms You Need to Know 521 |
Assurance of Learning Review 522 | Projects and Teamwork Exercises 522 |
Critical-Thinking Exercises 522 | Ethics Exercise 523 | Internet Exercises 523

Case 15.1 **Google Wants to Dominate in Display Ads** 523

Video Case 15.2 **Integrated Marketing Communications at Ogden Publications** 524

ch16

Advertising and Public Relations 526

OPENING VIGNETTE
Snickers: "You're Not You When
You're Hungry" 526

MARKETING FAILURE
Toyota Takes a Wrong
Turn 542

CAREER READINESS
How to Handle a Business
Crisis 551

SOLVING AN ETHICAL
CONTROVERSY
Should the Government Curb
Advertising That Targets
Children? 556

Advertising 529
Types of Advertising 529 | Objectives of Advertising 529

Advertising Strategies 531
Comparative Advertising 531 | Celebrity Testimonials 531 | Retail Advertising 533 |
Interactive Advertising 534

Creating an Advertisement 534
Translating Advertising Objectives into Advertising Plans 535

Advertising Messages 535
Advertising Appeals 536 | Developing and Preparing Ads 537 |
Creating Interactive Ads 538

Media Selection 539
Television 539 | Radio 541 | Newspapers 543 | Magazines 543 |
Direct Mail 544 | Outdoor Advertising 544 | Interactive Media 545 |
Other Advertising Media 545

Media Scheduling 546

Organization of the Advertising Function 547
Advertising Agencies 547

Public Relations 548
Marketing and Nonmarketing Public Relations 549
Publicity 549

Cross-Promotion 551

Measuring Promotional Effectiveness 552
Measuring Advertising Effectiveness 552 | Measuring Public Relations
Effectiveness 554 | Evaluating Interactive Media 554

Ethics in Nonpersonal Selling 555
Advertising Ethics 555 | Ethics in Public Relations 556

Strategic Implications of Marketing in the 21st Century 557

Review of Chapter Objectives 557
Assessment Check: Answers 558 | Marketing Terms You Need to Know 559 |
Assurance of Learning Review 559 | Projects and Teamwork Exercises 560 |
Critical-Thinking Exercises 560 | Ethics Exercise 560 | Internet Exercises 561

Case 16.1 **Politicians and "Their" Music** 561

Video Case 16.2 **Advertising and Public Relations at Ogden Publications** 562

Personal Selling and Sales Promotion 564

The Evolution of Personal Selling 567

The Four Sales Channels 568
Over-the-Counter Selling 568 | Field Selling 569 | Telemarketing 571 | Inside Selling 572
Integrating the Various Selling Channels 572

Trends in Personal Selling 572
Relationship Selling 573 | Consultative Selling 574 | Team Selling 574

Sales Tasks 576
Order Processing 576 | Creative Selling 577 | Missionary Selling 577

The Sales Process 578
Prospecting and Qualifying 578 | Approach 579 | Presentation 579 |
Demonstration 580 | Handling Objections 581 | Closing 581 | Follow-up 581

Managing the Sales Effort 582
Recruitment and Selection 582 | Training 583 | Organization 584 | Supervision 585 |
Motivation 585 | Compensation 586 | Evaluation and Control 586

Ethical Issues in Sales 588

Sales Promotion 588
Consumer-Oriented Sales Promotions 590 | Trade-Oriented Promotions 592

Strategic Implications of Marketing in the 21st Century 594

Review of Chapter Objectives 595
Assessment Check: Answers 596 | Marketing Terms You Need to Know 597 |
Assurance of Learning Review 597 | Projects and Teamwork Exercises 597 |
Critical-Thinking Exercises 598 | Ethics Exercise 598 | Internet Exercises 598

Case 17.1 **Private Jets: In Rarefied Air 599**

Video Case 17.2 **Personal Selling and Sales Promotion at Scholfield Honda 600**

Greensburg, Inc. **Continuing Video Case: A Town Rebounds 601**

ch17

OPENING VIGNETTE
Salesforce.com: Living It Up on a
Cloud 564

SOLVING AN ETHICAL
CONTROVERSY
Under-Age Sales Force: Using
Kids to Sell? 570

CAREER READINESS
Dressing Like a Sales
Professional 575

MARKETING SUCCESS
Toy Fair: Betting on
Tinseltown 592

Pricing Decisions

PART 7

ch18 Pricing Concepts 604

OPENING VIGNETTE
Microsoft Priced to Win 604

MARKETING SUCCESS
Super Bowl Ads Are a Win–Win 614

SOLVING AN ETHICAL CONTROVERSY
Revisiting Congestion Pricing 617

CAREER READINESS
Housing: Pricing to Sell in a Slow Economy 618

Pricing and the Law 607
Robinson-Patman Act 608 | Unfair-Trade Laws 608 | Fair-Trade Laws 609

Pricing Objectives and the Marketing Mix 609
Profitability Objectives 610 | Volume Objectives 612 | Prestige Objectives 614

Pricing Objectives of Not-for-Profit Organizations 616

Methods for Determining Prices 616

Price Determination in Economic Theory 619
Cost and Revenue Curves 620 | The Concept of Elasticity in Pricing Strategy 621 | Practical Problems of Price Theory 623

Price Determination in Practice 624
Alternative Pricing Procedures 624 | Breakeven Analysis 625

The Modified Breakeven Concept 627

Yield Management 628

Global Issues in Price Determination 629

Strategic Implications of Marketing in the 21st Century 631

Review of Chapter Objectives 632
Assessment Check: Answers 633 | Marketing Terms You Need to Know 634 | Assurance of Learning Review 634 | Projects and Teamwork Exercises 634 | Critical-Thinking Exercises 635 | Ethics Exercise 635 | Internet Exercises 635

Case 18.1 **The Cash for Clunkers Program 636**

Video Case 18.2 **Pricing Concepts at Evogear.com 637**

Pricing Strategies 638

Pricing Strategies 641

Skimming Pricing Strategy 641 | Penetration Pricing Strategy 642 | Competitive Pricing Strategy 644

Price Quotations 645

Reductions from List Price 645 | Geographic Considerations 648

Pricing Policies 649

Psychological Pricing 650 | Price Flexibility 651 | Product-Line Pricing 651 | Promotional Pricing 652 | Price–Quality Relationships 654

Competitive Bidding and Negotiated Prices 655

Negotiating Prices Online 656

The Transfer Pricing Dilemma 657

Global Considerations and Online Pricing 658

Traditional Global Pricing Strategies 658 | Characteristics of Online Pricing 659 Bundle Pricing 660

Strategic Implications of Marketing in the 21st Century 661

Review of Chapter Objectives 661

Assessment Check: Answers 662 | Marketing Terms You Need to Know 663 | Assurance of Learning Review 663 | Projects and Teamwork Exercises 664 | Critical-Thinking Exercises 664 | Ethics Exercise 665 | Internet Exercises 665

Case 19.1 **Holding the (Price) Line on Luxury Goods 665**

Video Case 19.2 **Pricing Strategy at Standard Renewable Energy 666**

Greensburg, Inc. **Continuing Video Case: Watt's the Deal? 668**

Appendix A

Your Career in Marketing A-1

Appendix B

Developing an Effective Marketing Plan A-19

Appendix C

Financial Analysis in Marketing A-33

Notes N-1

Glossary G-1

Name & Company Index I-1

Subject Index I-12

International Index I-28

ch**19**

OPENING VIGNETTE
JoS. A. Bank Tackles the Recession 638

CAREER READINESS
Communicating a Price Increase 650

SOLVING AN ETHICAL CONTROVERSY
Fast-Food Prices: Who Gets to Set Them? 653

MARKETING SUCCESS
Restaurants Serve Up Tasty Discounts 654

Continuing a Legacy of
Excellence—
Boone & Kurtz . . . In a Class by Itself!

Products often begin their lives as something extraordinary, and as they grow they continue to evolve. The most successful products in the marketplace are those that know their strengths and have branded and marketed those strengths to form a passionate emotional connection with loyal users and relationships with new users every step of the way. Just like the very best brands in the business world, Boone & Kurtz, *Contemporary Marketing*, continues to evolve, both as a product and as a brand. This 15th edition of *Contemporary Marketing* continues to develop and grow with new cases and examples, as well as a new emphasis on Sustainability. As with every good brand, though, the patterns of innovation and excellence established at the beginning remain steadfast. The goals and standards of Boone & Kurtz, *Contemporary Marketing*, remain intact and focused on excellence, as always. I present to you a text and supplement package that will not only show you why we've been the standard-bearer for so long but also prove to YOU and your STUDENTS why Boone & Kurtz remains . . . IN A CLASS BY ITSELF!

Putting Instructors in a Class by Themselves

This new edition's supplement package is designed to propel the instructor into the classroom with all the materials needed to engage students and help them understand text concepts. All the major teaching materials have been combined into one resource—the Instructor's Manual. While this might not sound revolutionary, good brands know that the heart of the product is in its core strengths. In the same way, our Instructor's Manual combines all of the most important teaching materials in one place. The lecture outline walks step-by-step through chapter content. And for your convenience, we've included references to the tables, figures, and PowerPoint slides throughout the lecture notes. Greensburg, Inc., our continuing case, is highlighted in part videos, while chapter videos showcase a stellar list of companies from a variety of industries, including Flight 001, Ogden Publications, and Numi Organic Tea.

We've heard your appreciation for our PowerPoint presentations and have once again tailored these to meet the needs of all instructors, offering two versions: our expanded collection and the basic collection. In addition, our CERTIFIED TEST BANK, which has been verified, gives instructors that extra edge needed to drive home key concepts, ignite critical thinking, and boost confidence and assurance when creating and issuing tests.

Finally, we've added a new online learning and teaching component to Boone & Kurtz *Contemporary Marketing*. CourseMate provides unmatched learning tools for students and provides instructors with a valuable assessment data-tracking tool to record student progress and achievement. More information on CourseMate and the Engagement Tracker is included later in this Preface, or contact your Cengage representative for more information or a demo.

The evolution of a brand or product can be a powerful and compelling undertaking involving every aspect of the marketing process. Understanding this evolution can be a student's best help in understanding how marketing is conducted every day. Every chapter begins with EVOLUTION OF A BRAND, which discusses the evolution of the company or product that is the focus of the opening vignette. We've focused our efforts on showing how stellar brands evolve and what this evolution means in the grander scheme of marketing and product management.

Helping Students Stand in a Class by Themselves

An intriguing series of continuing videos—Greensburg, Inc.—details the rebuilding of Greensburg, Kansas, following a devastating tornado that destroyed much of the town. Students will find the look into this town's "green" reconstruction efforts interesting and insightful. As always, every chapter is loaded with up-to-the-minute marketing issues and examples to liven up classroom discussion and debate. Processes, strategies, and procedures are brought to life through videos highlighting real companies and employees, an inventive business model, and collaborative learning exercises. And to further enhance the student learning process, a number of text-specific quizzes, games, and videos are available within the CourseMate and WebTutor platforms.

How Boone & Kurtz's *Contemporary Marketing* Evolved into the Leading Brand in the Market

For more than three decades, *Contemporary Marketing* has provided the latest in content and pedagogy. Our *current* editions have long been the model for our competitors' next editions. Consider Boone & Kurtz's proven record of providing instructors and students with pedagogical firsts:

- *Contemporary Marketing* was the first introductory marketing text written specifically for the student—rather than the instructor—featuring a conversational style that students readily understand and enjoy.

- *Contemporary Marketing* has always been based on marketing research, written the way instructors actually teach the course.

- *Contemporary Marketing* has always employed extensive pedagogy—such as opening vignettes and boxed features—to breathe life into the exciting concepts and issues facing today's marketers.

- *Contemporary Marketing* was the first business text to offer end-of-chapter video cases as well as end-of-part continuing video cases filmed by professional producers who include text concepts in each video.

- *Contemporary Marketing* was the first to use multimedia technology to integrate all ancillary components—videos, overhead transparencies, and PowerPoint CD-ROMs for both instructors and students—enabling instructors to customize lively lecture presentations.

- *Contemporary Marketing* received the William Holmes McGuffey Award for Excellence and Longevity, a testament to its many contributions to the field of marketing.

Sustainability

In addition to a continuing commitment to focus on brand evolution, this new edition of *Contemporary Marketing* takes a hard look at an important new topic in the marketing world—sustainability. Throughout the book, opening vignettes, boxed features, cases, and text references are dedicated to the discussion of how the trend to "go green" and create sustainability product has affected the world of marketing. A recycling icon is included throughout to signify "sustainability" topics. Plus, the book itself has gone "green" and is printed on recycled paper.

Environmental issues are prevalent in every industry, including publishing! Here is a sample look at the "green" scene, written in the style of an opening vignette:

Are You Consuming This Book in Paper or Plastic?...

You may be reading this book either in paper form, or in an e-book. One of the things that both consumers and businesses must address in today's environment is how their products,

processes, and consumption affect the environment. This edition of *Contemporary Marketing* has been printed on recycled paper and is also available in e-book form. Which of the versions—print or e-book—is the most ecologically sound?

You would think that reading an e-book would be more ecologically friendly than a traditional printed book, but when one compares the environmental costs for each medium, a traditional printed book or an e-book, interesting issues emerge. Overall, e-books win out for their reduced carbon footprint, but they still generate some potentially hazardous waste when the readers or PCs are thrown out. Greg Kozak was on the cutting edge four years ago when, for his master's degree thesis at the University of Michigan, he conducted a lifecycle assessment (LCA), comparing e-readers with paper college textbooks. An LCA is

sometimes called a cradle-to-grave analysis because it adds up all of the environmental impacts of a product or service from its manufacture to its disposal, including the use of energy, water, and natural resources. It's a great way to compare two products.

First, Kozak outlined all of the potential impacts of the e-book reader and the paper book for each phase of its lifecycle, starting with its manufacture from raw materials and continuing through its distribution to consumers, use, and disposal. For each stage, Kozak calculated the materials used, total energy consumed, air and water emissions, and total solid wastes on the basis of published values or through his own experiments if no published data existed.

In Kozak's analysis, e-textbooks won out overall for environmental friendliness. He found that over its lifecycle, a paper textbook created more

greenhouse gas emissions, ozone-depleting substances, and chemicals than an e-book reader. Conventional books also required more raw materials and water consumption than e-books. For e-book readers, most of the energy consumed is from the electricity used while reading. "Although [it was] the most significant contributor to the e-reader's LCA results, electricity generation for e-reader use had less of an environmental impact than did paper production for the conventional book system," Kozak writes. The paper book's biggest green advantage is that no electricity is needed to read it.

Sources: css.snre.umich.edu/css_doc/CSS03-04.pdf, Greg Kozak, LCA Analysis of Paper and e-Textbooks; Erica Engelhaupt, "Would you like that book in paper or plastic?" *Environmental Science and Technology* (May 7, 2008); "Paper versus Paperless: Which Makes Reading Greener?" LA Times online edition, June 2, 2008, http://latimesblogs.latimes.com/emeraldcity/2008/06/paper-vs-paperl.html.

Pedagogy

The reason Boone & Kurtz came together to write the first edition of *Contemporary Marketing* was revolutionary. They wanted to write a book about marketing that wasn't an encyclopedia: a text students would find interesting, a text filled with interesting examples and pedagogy. As with every edition of *Contemporary Marketing,* the 15th edition is packed with new pedagogical features to keep students interested and bring the text topics to life:

- **Assessment, Assessment, Assessment**: In every marketing department in the country, assessment and assurance of learning among students has become increasingly important. As a result, we've provided you with assessment checks after every main head in every chapter. In addition, the end-of-part video cases have been specifically designed to allow instructors to embed a signature assignment that not only can be used to assess the marketing competency and understanding of concepts by students but also has an associated rubric for assessing student communication ability, understanding of ethics, or application of technology that can then be used for a school's assurance of learning compliance.

- **Assurance of Learning Review**: Assurance of learning is further enhanced by end-of-chapter self-quizzes: in addition to ensuring that students are learning throughout the chapter, we've taken assessment one step further by incorporating self-quizzes called Assurance of Learning Review at the end of each chapter. These questions are designed to quickly assess whether students understand the basic concepts covered in the chapter.

- **Evolution of a Brand**: Products, brands, and people that evolve are the ones that succeed. The evolution of *Contemporary Marketing* is what has put BOONE & KURTZ . . . IN A CLASS BY ITSELF. Every chapter begins with a new Evolution of a Brand feature. This feature discusses the evolution of the company or product that is the focus of the opening vignette and what this evolution means in the larger picture of marketing strategy and product management.

- **Career Readiness**: Schools realize it has become increasingly important to understand proper business etiquette when entering the business world, so more and more schools are adding business etiquette to their curriculums. Every chapter of *Contemporary Marketing* contains a Career Readiness (formerly called Etiquette Tips for Marketing Professionals) box, addressing all aspects of proper behavior, including communications etiquette, business dinners, and even the most effective way to create customer relationships.

Continuing to Build the Boone & Kurtz Brand

Because the business world moves at an unprecedented pace today, the Principles of Marketing course must race to keep up. Trends, strategies, and practices are constantly changing, though a few things remain the same—the need for excellence and the necessity to evolve and innovate.

You've come to trust *Contemporary Marketing* to cover every aspect of marketing with a critical but fair eye. Let's face it: there are best practices and those we'd never want to repeat. However, both provide learning opportunities and we've always chosen to take a critical look at the way business is being done in the world and help students understand what they need to know in order to have a long and illustrious career in marketing. Keeping this in mind, here are just a few of the important trends and practices we've focused on for this edition:

- "Your Career in Marketing," which appeared as a prologue in the previous edition, has been moved to the end of the text as Appendix A. As in the previous edition, the section is chock full of practical advice for the student who is looking at career options in the field of marketing.

- Chapter 1 includes the American Marketing Association (AMA) definition of marketing and covers the most cutting-edge marketing technologies in use today, including an increased emphasis on social marketing and sustainability. As always, boxed features have been updated in Chapter 1, which now covers everything from Walmart to Procter & Gamble, and throughout the text.

- In-text examples in Chapter 2 are all new or updated from the previous edition. The appendix, "Developing an Effective Marketing Plan," which was previously placed just after Chapter 2, has been moved to the end of the text as Appendix B.

- Chapter 3 has a strong focus on green marketing practices, including coverage of Nike, SC Johnson, and getting employees to go green.

- Chapter 4 has been thoroughly updated with an expanded discussion of online communities and social networks.

- Chapter 8's section on government data has been heavily updated to include information on the 2010 Census. This chapter also includes an updated discussion of Internet-based methods of surveying participants, and coverage of interpretative research has been enhanced.

- A section title "Cohort Effect: The Video Game Generation" has been added to Chapter 9.

- Roy Choi, a leader in the new gourmet food truck category, is highlighted in the new case at the end of Chapter 12. All cases have been replaced or updated in this chapter.

- In Chapter 14, sections on pricing strategy, location and distribution strategy, and direct response retailing have been thoroughly updated.

- Chapter 16 includes new examples in the informative advertising, persuasive advertising, and reminder advertising sections.

- Each chapter includes new Internet exercises.

Greensburg, Inc. Continuing Video Case

You've come to expect only the best from us in choosing our continuing video case concepts, and we do not disappoint with our focus on a fresh, environmentally minded topic. Greensburg, Inc. is a series of videos that describes the rebuilding of Greensburg, Kansas, into a model green community following a tornado that destroyed much of the town. The rebuilding process has taken organization, coordination, determination, and a large amount of marketing. Students will hear from the town leaders instrumental in the rebuilding process as well as everyday people involved in the tragedy and reconstruction efforts. Students and instructors will see how the town is rebuilding from the ground up, brick by brick, focusing at each step on creating a sustainable community that can serve as an example to other communities—small and large—across the nation.

Written case segments at the end of each part of the text contain critical-thinking questions designed to provoke discussion and interaction in the classroom setting. Answers to the questions are in the Instructor's Manual, as well as a complete video synopsis, a list of text concepts covered in the videos, and even more critical-thinking exercises.

End-of-Chapter Video Cases

In addition to a stellar, continuing video case, we've produced video cases for each and every chapter, designed to exceed your every expectation. Students need to know the basics about life in the real world of marketing and how businesses succeed and grow—but they don't need a bunch of talking heads putting them to sleep. So although we admit that you will indeed see a few talking heads, they're just there because they really do know what they're talking about, and they have something important for students to hear. But trust us . . . the videos included in this edition of *Contemporary Marketing* contain so much more!

A complete set of written cases accompanies these chapter videos and are located at the end of each chapter. The written segments contain discussion questions. As with the Greensburg, Inc. cases, answers to the questions are in the Instructor's Manual, as well as a complete video synopsis, a list of text concepts covered in the videos, and even more critical-thinking exercises. The video cases are as follows:

Chapter 1: Marketing: Satisfying Customers at Flight 001

Chapter 2: Strategic Planning and the Marketing Process at Preserve

Chapter 3: The Marketing Environment, Ethics, and Social Responsibility at Scholfield Honda

Chapter 4: E-Business at Evo

Chapter 5: Consumer Behavior at Scholfield Honda

Chapter 6: Business-to-Business Marketing at Flight 001

Chapter 7: Global Marketing at Evo

Chapter 8: Marketing Research and Sales Forecasting at Ogden Publications

Chapter 9: Targeting and Positioning at Numi Tea

Chapter 10: Relationship Marketing and CRM at Numi Tea

Chapter 11: Product and Service Strategy at Preserve

Chapter 12: Developing and Managing Brand and Product Categories at Maine Media Workshops

Chapter 13: Marketing Channels and Supply Chain Management at Preserve

Chapter 14: Retailing at Flight 001

Chapter 15: Integrated Marketing Communications at Ogden Publications

Chapter 16: Advertising and Public Relations at Ogden Publications

Chapter 17: Personal Selling and Sales Promotion at Scholfield Honda

Chapter 18: Pricing Concepts at Evogear.com

Chapter 19: Pricing Strategy at Standard Renewable Energy

The Contemporary Marketing Resource Package

Since the first edition of this book was published, Boone & Kurtz has exceeded the expectations of instructors, and it quickly became the benchmark for other texts. With its precedent-setting learning materials, *Contemporary Marketing* has continued to improve on its signature package features—equipping students and instructors with the most comprehensive collection of learning tools, teaching materials, and innovative resources available. As expected, the 15th edition continues to serve as the industry benchmark by delivering the most extensive, technologically advanced, user-friendly package on the market.

For the Instructor

Instructor's Manual with Media Guide and Collaborative Learning Exercises

The 15th edition of *Contemporary Marketing* has a completely updated Instructor's Manual. This valuable tool integrates the various supplements and the text. A detailed lecture outline provides guidance about how to teach the chapter concepts. Collaborative learning exercises are included for each chapter, giving students a completely different way to apply chapter concepts to their own lives. References to the PowerPoint slides are included in the lecture outline. You'll also find answers to all of the end-of-chapter materials and various critical-thinking exercises. Full descriptions of all technology offerings can be found in the Media Guide along with complete video synopses, outlines, and extra questions. The Instructor's Manual is available on the Instructor's Resource CD-ROM or can be downloaded from the product support Web site.

Chapter Video Cases and Greensburg, Inc. Continuing Case on DVD (ISBN: 1-111-52816-0)

End-of-chapter video cases for every chapter of the text focus on successful real companies' processes, strategies, and procedures. Real employees explain real marketing situations with which they have been faced, bringing key concepts from the chapter to life. Also, the continuing video case details the "green" reconstruction of Greensburg, Kansas, after a devastating tornado destroyed much of the town. These videos examine the rebuilding efforts of companies and individuals as well as the formation of new organizations to deal with the disaster. Each piece of the reconstruction has taken organization, coordination, determination, and marketing. The written and video cases are divided into seven sections and are created to be used at the end of each part of the text.

Certified Test Bank

Containing more than 4,000 questions, this Test Bank has been thoroughly verified to ensure accuracy—with each question and answer read and reviewed. The Test Bank includes true/false, multiple-choice, essay, and matching questions. Each question in the Test Bank is labeled with text objective, text page reference, level of difficulty, and type. Each question is also tagged to AACSB, Marketing Discipline, and Dierdorff/Rubin guidelines. The Test Bank is available on the Instructor's Resource CD-ROM or can be downloaded from the product support Web site.

ExamView® Testing Software

Available on the Instructor's Resource CD-ROM, ExamView contains all of the questions in the Test Bank with all question tags described above. This program is easy-to-use test creation software and is compatible with Microsoft® Windows®. Instructors can add or edit questions, instructions, and answers, and select questions (randomly or numerically) by previewing them on the screen. Instructors can also create and administer quizzes online, whether over the Internet, a local-area network (LAN), or a wide-area network (WAN).

Basic and Expanded PowerPoint Presentations

After reviewing competitive offerings, we are convinced that our PowerPoint presentations are the best you'll find. We offer two separate collections. The Basic PowerPoint collection contains 10 to 20 slides per chapter. This collection is a basic outline of the chapter, with Web links that bring chapter concepts to life; it also includes figures and tables from the text. The Expanded PowerPoint collection includes 20 to 40 slides per chapter and provides a more complete overview of the chapter. The Expanded collection includes figures and tables from the chapter as well as Web links. The Basic and Expanded PowerPoint Presentations are available on the Instructor's Resource CD-ROM or can be downloaded from the product support Web site.

Instructor's Resource CD (ISBN: 0-538-48112-9)

The Instructor's Resource CD-ROM includes electronic versions of all of the instructor supplements: Instructor's Manual with Media Guide and Collaborative Learning Exercises, Test Bank, ExamView testing files and software, and Basic and Expanded PowerPoint Presentations.

CourseMate

Interested in a simple way to complement your text and course content with study and practice materials? Cengage Learning's Marketing CourseMate brings course concepts to life with interactive learning, study, and exam preparation tools that support the printed textbook. Watch student comprehension soar as your class works with the printed textbook and the textbook-specific Web site. Marketing CourseMate goes beyond the book to deliver what you need! Marketing CourseMate includes an interactive eBook as well as interactive teaching and learning tools, including quizzes, flashcards, homework videos cases, simulations, and more. Engagement Tracker monitors student engagement in the course.

CengageNOW (for WebCT® and Blackboard®)

Ensure that your students have the understanding they need of Marketing procedures and concepts they need to know with CengageNOW. This integrated, online course management and learning system combines the best of current technology to save time in planning and managing your course and assignments. You can reinforce comprehension with customized student learning paths and efficiently test and automatically grade assignments.

WebTutor™ (for WebCT® and Blackboard®)

Online learning is growing at a rapid pace. Whether you are looking to offer courses at a distance or in a Web-enhanced classroom, South-Western, a part of Cengage Learning, offers you a solution with WebTutor. WebTutor provides instructors with text-specific content that interacts with the two leading systems of higher education course management: WebCT and Blackboard.

WebTutor is a turnkey solution for instructors who want to begin using technology like Blackboard or WebCT but do not have Web-ready content available or do not want to be burdened with developing their own content. WebTutor uses the Internet to turn everyone in your class into a front-row student. WebTutor offers interactive study guide features, including quizzes, concept reviews, animated figures, discussion forums, video clips, and more. Instructor tools are also provided to facilitate communication between students and faculty.

Business & Company Resource Center (BCRC)

Available as an optional resource, BCRC puts a complete business library at your students' fingertips. BCRC is a premier online business research tool that allows students to seamlessly search thousands of periodicals, journals, references, financial information sources, market share reports, company histories, and much more. View a guided tour of the Business & Company Resource Center at gale.com/BusinessRC.

Contemporary Marketing, 15th Edition Web Site

Our text Web site is filled with a whole set of useful tools. Instructors will find all the key instructor resources in electronic format: Test Bank, PowerPoint collections, and Instructor's Manual with Media Guide and Collaborative Learning Exercises.

To access additional course materials and companion resources, please visit www.cengagebrain. com. At the CengageBrain.com home page, search for the ISBN of your title (from the back cover of your book) using the search box at the top of the page. This will take you to the product page where free companion resources can be found.

Resource Integration Guide (RIG)

The RIG is written to provide the instructor with a clear and concise guide to all of the ancillaries that accompany the text as well as how best to use these items in teaching a Principles of Marketing course. Not only are all of the book's ancillaries organized clearly for you, but we also provide planning suggestions, lecture ideas, and help in creating assignments. This guide will help instructors prepare for teaching the course, execute teaching plans, and evaluate student performance. The RIG can be found on the text Web site in the Instructor's Resource section.

Custom Solutions for *Contemporary Marketing,* 15th Edition

Cengage Learning Custom Solutions develops personalized solutions to meet your business education needs. Match your learning materials to your syllabus, and create the perfect learning solution. Consider the following when looking at your customization options for *Contemporary Marketing,* 15th edition:

- Remove chapters you do not cover or rearrange their order, creating a streamlined and efficient text students will appreciate.

- Add your own material to cover new topics or information, saving you time and providing students with a fully integrated course resource.

Cengage Learning Custom Solutions offers the fastest and easiest way to create unique customized learning materials delivered the way you want. Our custom solutions also include accessing on-demand cases from leading business case providers such as **Harvard Business School Publishing, Ivey, Darden,** and **NACRA;** building a tailored text online with www.textchoice2.com; and publishing your original materials. For more information about custom publishing options, visit cengage.com/custom/ or contact your local Cengage Learning representative.

For the Student

CourseMate

The more your students study, the better the results. They can make the most of their study time by accessing everything they need to succeed in one place. They can read the textbook, take notes, review flashcards, watch videos, and take practice quizzes—online with CourseMate. Marketing CourseMate includes an interactive eBook allowing students to take notes, highlight, bookmark, search the text, and use in-context glossary definitions. The interactive teaching and learning tools include quizzes, flashcards, homework video cases, simulations, and more.

CengageNOW (for both WebCT® and Blackboard®)

CengageNOW is an easy-to-use online resource that helps your students study in less time to get the grade they want. This integrated system helps the student efficiently manage and complete homework assignments from the text. Students can take pretests to determine the areas that require more practice, and they are directed to review tutorials, homework video cases and simulations, demonstration exercises, videos, eBook content, and fun marketing games to help them learn the material. They also get feedback on posttests that check their comprehension afterward.

WebTutor™ (for both WebCT® and Blackboard®)

This online learning system gives students a host of interactive study guide features including quizzes, concept reviews, animated figures, discussion forums, video clips, and more.

Acknowledgments

Over the years, *Contemporary Marketing* has benefited from the suggestions of hundreds of marketing instructors. I am most appreciative of their efforts and thoughts. These people provided valuable feedback for the current revision:

Steven Nichols
Metropolitan Community College

Daniel W. Biddlecom
Erie Community College North

Debbie Gaspard
Southeast Community College

John A. Grant
Ohio Dominican University

Charlane Held
Onondaga Community College

Larry T. Eiler
Eastern Michigan University

Gail H. Kirby
Santa Clara University

Jeffrey L. Goldberg
Massachusetts Bay Community College

Robert M. McMillen
James Madison University

Earlier reviewers and contributors include the following: Keith Absher, Kerri L. Acheson, Zafar U. Ahmed, Alicia T. Aldridge, M. Wayne Alexander, Bruce Allen, Linda Anglin, Allen Appell, Paul Arsenault, Dub Ashton, Amardeep Assar, Tom F. Badgett, Joe K. Ballenger, Wayne Bascom, Richard D. Becherer, Tom Becker, Richard F. Beltramini, Michael Bernacchi, Robert Bielski, Carol C. Bienstock, Roger D. Blackwell, David Blanchette, Jocelyn C. Bojack, Barbara Brown, Reginald E. Brown, Michele D. Bunn, Marvin Burnett, Scott Burton, James Camerius, Les Carlson, John Carmichael, Jacob Chacko, Robert Collins, Elizabeth Cooper-Martin, Deborah L. Cowles, Howard B. Cox, James Coyle, John E. Crawford, Elizabeth Creyer, Geoff Crosslin, Michael R. Czinkota, Kathy Daruty, Grant Davis, Gilberto de los Santos, William Demkey, Carol W. DeMoranville, Fran DePaul, Gordon Di Paolo, John G. Doering, Jeffrey T. Doutt, Michael Drafke, Sid Dudley, John W. Earnest, Joanne Eckstein, Philip E. Egdorf, Michael Elliot, Amy Enders, Bob Farris, Lori Feldman, Sandra M. Ferriter, Dale Fodness, Gary T. Ford, Michael Fowler, John Frankel, Edward Friese, Sam Fullerton, Ralph M. Gaedeke, G. P. Gallo, Nimish Gandhi, Sheryl A. Gatto, Robert Georgen, Don Gibson, David W. Glascoff, Robert Googins, James Gould, Donald Granbois, John Grant, Arlene Green, Paul E. Green, William Green, Blaine Greenfield, Matthew Gross, Robert F. Gwinner, Raymond M. Haas, John H. Hallaq, Cary Hawthorn, E. Paul Hayes, Hoyt Hayes, Joel Haynes, Betty Jean Hebel, Debbora Heflin-Bullock, John (Jack) J. Heinsius, Sanford B. Helman, Nathan Himelstein, Robert D. Hisrich, Mabre Holder, Ray S. House, Andrew W. Honeycutt, George Housewright, Dr. H. Houston, Donald Howard, John Howe, Michael D. Hutt, Gregory P. Iwaniuk, Don L. James, James Jeck, Tom Jensen, Candida Johnson, David Johnson, Eugene M. Johnson, James C. Johnson, Harold H. Kassarjian, Bernard Katz, Stephen K. Keiser, Michelle Keller, J. Steven Kelly, Marcella Kelly, James H. Kennedy, Charles Keuthan, Maryon King, Stephen C. King, Randall S. Kingsbury, Donald L. Knight, Linda S. Koffel, Philip Kotler, Kathleen Krentler, Terrence Kroeten, Russell Laczniak, Martha Laham, L. Keith Larimore, Edwin Laube, Ken Lawrence, Francis J. Leary, Jr., Mary Lou Lockerby, Laddie Logan, James Lollar, Paul Londrigan, David L. Loudon, Kent Lundin, Dorothy Maass, Patricia Macro, James C. Makens, Lou Mansfield, Frank Markley, Tom Marshall, Warren Martin, Dennis C. Mathern, James McCormick, Carl McDaniel, Lee McGinnis, Michael McGinnis, James McHugh, Faye McIntyre, H. Lee Meadow, Norma Mendoza, Mohan Menon, William E. (Gene) Merkle, John D. Milewicz, Robert D. Miller, Laura M. Milner, Banwari Mittal, Anthony Miyazaki, Harry J. Moak, J. Dale Molander, John F. Monoky, James R. Moore, Jerry W. Moorman, Linda Morable, Thomas M. Moran, Diane Moretz, Eugene Moynihan, Margaret Myers, Susan Logan Nelson, Colin F. Neuhaus, Robert T. Newcomb, Jacqueline Z. Nicholson, Thomas S. O'Connor, Robert O'Keefe, Nita Paden, Sukgoo Pak, George Palz, Eric Panitz, Dennis D. Pappas, Constantine Petrides, Barbara Piasta, Dennis D. Pitta, Barbara Pletcher, Carolyn E. Predmore, Arthur E. Prell, George Prough, Warren Purdy, Bill Quain, Salim Qureshi,

Rosemary Ramsey, Thomas Read, Thomas C. Reading, Joel Reedy, Gary Edward Reiman, Dominic Rella, Ken Ridgedell, Glen Riecken, Arnold M. Rieger, C. Richard Roberts, Patrick J. Robinson, William C. Rodgers, Fernando Rodriguez, William H. Ronald, Jack J. Rose, Bert Rosenbloom, Barbara Rosenthal, Carol Rowery, Lillian Roy, Ronald S. Rubin, Don Ryktarsyk, Arthur Saltzman, Rafael Santos, Elise T. Sautter, Duane Schecter, Buffie Schmidt, Dennis W. Schneider, Jonathan E. Schroeder, Larry J. Schuetz, Bruce Seaton, Howard Seigelman, Jack Seitz, Steven L. Shapiro, Farouk Shaaban, F. Kelly Shuptrine, Ricardo Singson, Norman Smothers, John Sondey, Carol S. Soroos, James Spiers, Miriam B. Stamps, William Staples, David Starr, Bob Stassen, David Steenstra, Bruce Stern, Robert Stevens, Kermit Swanson, G. Knude Swenson, Cathy Owens Swift, Clint B. Tankersley, Ruth Taylor, Sue Taylor, Donald L. Temple, Vern Terpstra, Ann Marie Thompson, Howard A. Thompson, Lars Thording, John E. Timmerman, Frank Titlow, Rex Toh, Dennis H. Tootelian, Fred Trawick, Pam Uhlenkamp, Richard Lee Utecht, Rajiv Vaidyanathan, Toni Valdez, Peter Vanderhagen, Dinoo T. Vanier, Sal Veas, Charles Vitaska, Cortez Walker, Roger Waller, Gayle D. Wasson, Mary M. Weber, Donald Weinrauch, Fred Weinthal, Susan B. Wessels, Vicki L. West, Elizabeth White, John J. Whithey, Debbora Whitson, David Wiley, William Wilkinson, James Williams, Robert J. Williams, Nicholas C. Williamson, Cecilia Wittmayer, Mary Wolfindarger, Joyce Wood, Van R. Wood, Julian Yudelson, and Robert J. Zimmer.

In Conclusion

I would like to thank Ingrid Benson and Susan Nodine of Elm Street Publishing Services. Their ability to meet tight deadlines is truly appreciated.

Let me conclude by mentioning that the new edition would never have become a reality without the superior efforts of the South-Western Cengage Learning production and marketing teams. My editors—Michael Roche, Erin Guendelsberger, Scott Dillon, and John Rich—produced another *Contemporary Marketing* winner.

Dave Kurtz

Designing
Customer-Oriented
Marketing Strategies

1

Chapter 1
Marketing: The Art
and Science of
Satisfying
Customers

Chapter 2
Strategic Planning
in Contemporary
Marketing

Chapter 3
The Marketing
Environment,
Ethics, and Social
Responsibility

Chapter 4
E-Business: Managing
the Customer
Experience

Marketing:
The Art and Science of Satisfying Customers

Walmart Boosts Sustainability • • • The actions of Walmart, the Arkansas-based retailer whose $400 billion plus revenues surpass the GDPs of 40 countries, have drawn criticism in the past. Now the low-price giant hopes to lead in a positive direction

1 Define *marketing,* explain how it creates utility, and describe its role in the global marketplace.

2 Contrast marketing activities during the four eras in the history of marketing.

3 Explain the importance of avoiding marketing myopia.

4 Describe the characteristics of not-for-profit marketing.

5 Identify and briefly explain each of the five types of nontraditional marketing.

6 Explain the shift from transaction-based marketing to relationship and social marketing.

7 Identify the universal functions of marketing.

8 Demonstrate the relationship between ethical business practices, social responsibility, sustainability, and marketplace success.

with its new Sustainability Index.

By leveraging Walmart's enormous buying power, the Index, which will ultimately provide millions of shoppers with a way to measure the environmental impact of each of the thousands of items it sells, could virtually remake the practice of retailing. To implement it—probably in the form of a scannable product label or packaging—the company will require its 60,000 consumer-products suppliers to reach back into their own supply chains and total the social and environmental impact of their offerings, from trampolines to flat-screen TVs to orange juice to greeting cards. For measuring up, suppliers can expect preferential treatment on the

shelves of Walmart's 8,000 stores in 15 countries around the world.

"We're on the cusp of a major transition in the marketplace of what consumers demand to know and producers have to tell," says the CEO of an independent consumer products sustainability guide. Walmart's senior vice president of sustainability adds that the Index is also about "creating a new level of competition in ways that, historically, manufacturers have not competed....it's going to be an algorithm that creates a score, and it will reward some suppliers better than others." That score will count four criteria: energy and greenhouse gas emissions, materials, natural resources, and social impact.

In addition to the pressure of competition, however, Walmart

is planning its own eventual departure from the Index project as an incentive to get suppliers, academics, government agencies like the EPA, nonprofits, and even competitors like Costco, Target, and Kroger to join the effort and pool sustainability data and ideas. It has created an independent Sustainability Consortium intended to carry out what Walmart has begun. "This has to be more than Walmart or it won't achieve standardization," says the Consortium's codirector. Says another observer, "They are willing to get the ball rolling, but they want to hand it off to someone else." Already on board, and making "green" improvements, are Frito-Lay, Monsanto, Unilever, Seventh Generation, Disney, and General

ave money. Live better.

© BETH HALL/LANDOV

Mills. The latter has reduced yogurt packaging 20 percent to save 1,200 tons of plastic a year.

The first step in the three-part process of creating the Index was to administer a 15-question survey to more than 1,000 of the firm's top suppliers, asking about their current sustainability efforts. Responses revealed big differences in how deeply invested firms are in community development and how carefully

they monitor use of natural resources. Next steps now under discussion include tests and feedback on the Index's labeling system in three product categories: electronics, food, and chemical-based products like household cleaning fluids.

"Imagine one day when every product on the shelf has behind it enough information from a life-cycle-thinking perspective that [it] allows us to be much, much more intelligent about how we're

buying," says Walmart's business strategy director. The company intends the Index also to weed out companies that engage in "green washing," making false or inflated claims of sustainability. "Can you have trackable, traceable supply chains that give you full visibility?" asks a manager at the Environmental Defense Fund, a Walmart partner. "It is extraordinarily difficult at this moment. But it can be done."[1]

evolution of a brand

Low prices and innovation have been at the heart of Walmart's marketing philosophy since the 1962 opening of its first store in Rogers, Arkansas. The company went public in 1970 and began a record of almost continuous growth. In the 1980s, Walmart added its innovative store "greeters," opened the first one-hour photo lab, installed barcode-scanning equipment, and linked its operating units with two-way voice and data communication via satellite. The

chain went international in 1991 with a store in Mexico City and introduced its own store brand the same year. In 1994, Walmart opened the first of its newly designed environmentally friendly buildings and expanded into Canada and Hong Kong. A program to conserve wildlife habitats was launched in 2005, and a $4 generic prescription drug program was introduced the following year. Meanwhile, Walmart stepped up efforts to design its stores to conserve energy and natural resources and reduce pollution.

- Walmart's vice president of energy says, "We absolutely are focused on doing things that are good for the planet, but it absolutely has to be good for profit as well." Why do you think Walmart links profit and sustainability?

- Some critics wonder how Walmart's Sustainability Index will choose whether, say, "greenhouse-gas emissions are more pressing than water conservation." How would you advise Walmart to make such choices?

chapter overview

> "I'll only drink caffeine-free Diet Pepsi."

> "I buy all my clothes at Macy's."

> "The next car I drive will be a Nissan Leaf."

> "I go to all the Philadelphia Eagles games at Lincoln Financial Field."

These words are music to a marketer's ears. They may echo the click of an online purchase, the ping of a cash register, the cheers of fans at a stadium. Customer loyalty is the watchword of 21st-century marketing. Individual consumers and business purchasers have so many goods and services from which to choose— and so many different ways to purchase them—that marketers must continually seek out new and better ways to attract and keep customers. It took a little while, but AT&T and Apple finally allow iPhone users to make voice over Internet protocol (VoIP) calls over the 3G network. Because such calls use data minutes instead of voice minutes, users can enjoy big savings on all their calls, both domestic and overseas. Applications for the phone offer different payment plans—free five-minute calls preceded by an ad, pay-per-call, or pay-per-month for unlimited calls and no ads.[2]

The technology revolution continues to change the rules of marketing in the 21st century and will continue to do so in years beyond. The combined power of telecommunications and computer technology creates inexpensive global networks that transfer voice messages, text, graphics, and data within seconds. These sophisticated technologies create new types of products and demand new approaches to marketing existing products. Newspapers are learning this lesson the hard way, as circulation continues to decline around the country, victim in large part to the rising popularity of blogs and auction and job-posting sites. Electronic reading devices like the Amazon Kindle, on the other hand, have been picking up speed, and enthusiastic fans.[3]

Communications technology also contributes to the globalization of today's marketplace where businesses manufacture, buy, and sell across national borders. You can bid at eBay on a potential bargain or eat a Big Mac or drink Coca-Cola almost anywhere in the world, and your MP3 player was probably manufactured in

briefly speaking

"A sign at Dell headquarters reads 'Think Customer.' A full 90 percent of employees deal directly with customers. What are the universal attributes of the Dell brand? Customer advocacy."

—Mike George
U.S. Consumer Vice President, Dell

China or South Korea. Both Mercedes-Benz and Hyundai SUVs are assembled in Alabama, while some Volkswagens are imported from Mexico. Finished products and components routinely cross international borders, but successful global marketing also requires knowledge to tailor products to regional tastes. A chain restaurant in the South might offer grits as an option to hash browns on its breakfast menu.

Rapidly changing business landscapes create new challenges for companies, whether they are giant multinational firms or small boutiques, profit-oriented or not-for-profit. Organizations must react quickly to shifts in consumer tastes, competitive offerings, and other market dynamics. Fortunately, information technologies give organizations fast new ways to interact and develop long-term relationships with their customers and suppliers. Such links have become a core element of marketing today.

Every company must serve customer needs—create customer satisfaction—to succeed. We call customer satisfaction an art because it requires imagination and creativity, and a science because it requires technical knowledge, skill, and experience. Marketing strategies are the tools that marketers use to identify and analyze customers' needs, then show that their company's goods and services can meet those needs. Tomorrow's market leaders will be companies that can make the most of these strategies to create satisfied customers.

This edition of *Contemporary Marketing* focuses on the strategies that allow companies to succeed in today's interactive marketplace. This chapter sets the stage for the entire text, examining the importance of creating satisfaction through customer relationships. Initial sections describe the historical development of marketing and its contributions to society. Later sections introduce the universal functions of marketing and the relationship between ethical business practices and marketplace success. Throughout the chapter—and the entire book—we discuss customer loyalty and the lifetime value of a customer.

What Is Marketing?

The production and marketing of goods and services—whether it's a new crop of organically grown vegetables or digital cable service—are the essence of business in any society. Like most business disciplines, marketing had its origins in economics. Later, marketing borrowed concepts from areas such as psychology and sociology to explain how people made purchase decisions. Mathematics, anthropology, and other disciplines also contributed to the evolution of marketing. These will be discussed in later chapters.

Economists contributed the concept of **utility**—the want-satisfying power of a good or service. Table 1.1 describes the four basic kinds of utility: form, time, place, and ownership.

Form utility is created when the company converts raw materials and component inputs into finished goods and services. Because of its appearance, gold can serve as a beautiful piece of jewelry, but because it also conducts electricity well and does not corrode, it has many applications in the manufacture of electronic devices like cell phones and global positioning satellite units. By combining glass, plastic, metals, circuit boards, and other components, Nikon makes a digital camera and Samsung produces an LED television. With fabric and leather, Prada manufactures its high-fashion line of handbags. With a ship and the ocean, a captain and staff, food and entertainment, Holland America Line creates a cruise. Although the marketing function focuses on influencing consumer and audience preferences, the organization's production function creates form utility.

1 **Define *marketing*, explain how it creates utility, and describe its role in the global marketplace.**

utility Want-satisfying power of a good or service.

table 1.1 Four Types of Utility

Type	Description	Examples	Organizational Function Responsible
Form	Conversion of raw materials and components into finished goods and services	Dinner at Red Lobster; iPod; jeans from American Eagle	Production*
Time	Availability of goods and services when consumers want them	Physician appointment; digital photographs; LensCrafters eyeglass guarantee; UPS Overnight	Marketing
Place	Availability of goods and services at convenient locations	Technicians available at an auto repair facility; on-site day care; banks in grocery stores	Marketing
Ownership (possession)	Ability to transfer title to goods or services from marketer to buyer	Retail sales (in exchange for currency, credit, or debit card payment)	Marketing

*Marketing provides inputs related to consumer preferences, but creating form utility is the responsibility of the production function.

NCR Corp. takes advantage of time and place utility, positioning the Blockbuster Express DVD rental kiosks in high-traffic convenience stores and pharmacy chains around the country. Marketing creates time, place, and ownership utilities. *Time and place utility* occur when consumers find goods and services available when and where they want to purchase them. Vending machines and convenience stores focus on providing place utility for people buying newspapers, snacks, and soft drinks. Several U.S. colleges are participating in a pilot program to test Gamefly G-box kiosks equipped with popular videogames at campus Barnes & Noble stores. "If it was just in the student union, like a lot of campuses, there wouldn't be anyone there to help or answer any questions, and so, by being in the bookstore, it really allows for a good customer experience," said Gamefly's cofounder Sean Spector.[4]

The transfer of title to goods or services at the time of purchase creates *ownership utility*. Signing up for a Sandals tropical vacation or buying a TV creates ownership utility. All organizations must create utility to survive. Designing and marketing want-satisfying goods, services, and ideas are the foundation for the creation of utility. But where does the process start? In the toy industry, manufacturers try to come up with items that children will want to play with—creating utility. But that's

> Crystal Cruises uses the components of ship, ocean, captain, staff, food, and entertainment to create its finished service—a cruise.

Celebrating
our
20th
ANNIVERSARY
with these gifts for you

• *New 2-for-1 fares*
• *$2,000 "All-Inclusive, As You Wish" spending credits*
• *Free Business or Economy air*
• *Price guarantee*

To learn more about our award-winning service, exotic worldwide destinations and special 20th Anniversary offers available on most voyages, visit crystalcruises.com. To book a voyage, contact your travel agent or call 877-465-5698.

CRYSTAL ❀ CRUISES

COURTESY OF CRYSTAL CRUISES, INC.

not as simple as it sounds. At the Toy Fair held each February in New York, retailers pore through the booths of manufacturers and suppliers, looking for the next Webkinz toys or Lego building blocks—trends that turn into classics and generate millions in revenues over the years. Marketers also look for ways to revive flagging brands. The classic yo-yo might be making a high-tech comeback, as an aerospace engineer from California working in his spare time has begun releasing a line of precision-engineered models with price tags that can run to $100. The limited-edition yo-yos have been selling out in a matter of days—and they have competitors.[5]

But how does an organization create a customer? Most take a three-step approach: identifying needs in the marketplace, finding out which needs the organization can profitably serve, and developing goods and services to convert potential buyers into customers. Marketing specialists are responsible for most of the activities necessary to create the customers the organization wants. These activities include the following:

- identifying customer needs;

- designing products that meet those needs;

- communicating information about those goods and services to prospective buyers;

- making the items available at times and places that meet customers' needs;

- pricing merchandise and services to reflect costs, competition, and customers' ability to buy; and

- providing the necessary service and follow-up to ensure customer satisfaction after the purchase.[6]

A Definition of Marketing

The word *marketing* encompasses such a broad scope of activities and ideas that settling on one definition is often difficult. Ask three people to define marketing, and three different definitions are likely to follow. We are exposed to so much advertising and personal selling that most people link marketing only to those activities. But marketing begins long before a product hits the shelf. It involves analyzing customer needs, obtaining the information necessary to design and produce goods or services that match buyer expectations, satisfying customer preferences, and creating and maintaining relationships with customers and suppliers. Marketing activities apply to profit-oriented businesses such as Apple and Overstock.com as well as not-for-profit organizations such as the Leukemia and Lymphoma Society and the Red Cross. Even government agencies such as the U.S. Postal Service engage in marketing activities. Today's definition takes all these factors into account. **Marketing** is an organizational function and a set of processes for creating, communicating, and delivering value to customers and for managing customer relationships in ways that benefit the organization and its stakeholders.[7]

The expanded concept of marketing activities permeates all functions in businesses and not-for-profit organizations. It assumes that organizations conduct their marketing efforts ethically and that these efforts serve the best interests of both society and the organization. The concept also identifies the marketing variables—product, price, promotion, and distribution—that combine to provide customer satisfaction. In addition, it assumes that the organization begins by identifying and analyzing who its potential customers are and what they need. At all points, the concept emphasizes creating and maintaining long-term relationships with customers and suppliers.

Today's Global Marketplace

Several factors have forced marketers—and entire nations—to extend their economic views to events outside their own national borders. First, international agreements are negotiated to expand trade among nations. Second, the growth of electronic business and related computer technologies allows previously isolated countries to enter the marketplace for buyers and sellers around the globe. Third, the interdependence of the world's economies is a reality because no nation produces all of the raw materials and finished goods its citizens need or consumes all of its output without exporting some

marketing
Organizational function and a set of processes for creating, communicating, and delivering value to customers and for managing customer relationships in ways that benefit the organization and its stakeholders.

While many airlines charge fees for checked bags, Southwest Airlines promotes its lack of fees.

COURTESY OF SOUTHWEST AIRLINES

to other countries. Evidence of this interdependence is illustrated by the introduction of the euro as a common currency to facilitate trade among the nations of the European Union and the creation of trade agreements such as the North American Free Trade Agreement (NAFTA) and the World Trade Organization (WTO).

Rising oil prices affect the price that U.S. consumers pay for just about everything—not just gasoline at the pump. Dow Chemical raised the prices of its products up to 20 percent to adjust to its rising cost for energy. The largest U.S. chemical company, Dow, supplies companies in industries from agriculture to health care, all of whom will be affected by the price hike. Airlines, too, are trying to respond to a near-doubling of the cost of jet fuel. Many have started charging customers for redeeming their reward miles, and Delta and Continental have raised fees to $25 for the first checked bag and $35 for the second.[8]

To remain competitive, companies must continually search for the most efficient manufacturing sites and most lucrative markets for their products. U.S. marketers now find tremendous opportunities serving customers not only in traditional industrialized nations but also in Latin America and emerging economies in central Europe, the Middle East, Asia, and Africa, where rising standards of living create increased customer demand for the latest products. Expanding operations beyond the U.S. market gives domestic companies access to 6.5 billion international customers. China is now the second-largest market in the world—only the United States is larger. And Chinese customers will soon purchase 11 to 12 million cars, trucks, and other vehicles a year, so automakers worldwide are extending their operations to China.[9] In addition, companies based in these emerging economies are beginning to compete in the global market. Over a recent two-year period, Chinese exports to the United States increased by more than 32 percent. In contrast, overall imports into the United States rose less than 17 percent during the same period.[10] Interestingly, however, signs are mounting that China's increasing prosperity may be reducing its attractiveness as a low-cost labor source. Rising costs already are driving some U.S. manufacturers out of the country, according to the American Chamber of Commerce. Mexico has taken the lead as the lowest-cost country for outsourced production, with India and Vietnam second and third; China stands in sixth place.[11]

Service firms also play a major role in today's global marketplace. Telecommunications firms like South Africa's MTN, Luxembourg's Millicom International, and Egypt's Orascom Telecom Holding have carved out new global markets for their products by following the lead of Finnish firm Nokia, among the first high-tech firms to create durable and affordable cell phones specifically designed for emerging markets. The opportunities for such telecom innovators will continue to grow as long as electricity-reliant personal computers remain out of reach for millions in the developing world. "Like a lot of people who made their first call on a mobile [phone], they will have their first experience with the Internet on a mobile," says one industry analyst.[12]

The United States is also an attractive market for foreign competitors because of its size and the high standard of living American consumers enjoy. Companies such as Nissan, Sony, and Sun Life of Canada operate production, distribution, service, and retail facilities in the United States. Foreign ownership of U.S. companies has increased also. Pillsbury and MCA are two well-known firms with foreign parents.

Although many global marketing strategies are almost identical to those used in domestic markets, more and more companies are tailoring their marketing efforts to the needs and preferences of consumers in foreign markets. It is often difficult to standardize a brand name on a global basis. The Japanese, for example, like the names of flowers or girls for their automobiles—names like Bluebird, Bluebonnet, Violet, and Gloria. Americans, on the other hand, prefer rugged outdoorsy names like Chevy Tahoe, Jeep Cherokee, and Dodge Challenger.

assessment check

1. Define *marketing*, and explain how it creates utility.
2. What three factors have forced marketers to embrace a global marketplace?

Four Eras in the History of Marketing

The essence of marketing is the **exchange process**, in which two or more parties give something of value to each other to satisfy perceived needs. Often, people exchange money for tangible goods such as groceries, clothes, a car, or a house. In other situations, they exchange money for intangible services such as a haircut or a college education. Many exchanges involve a combination of goods and services, such as dinner in a restaurant—where dinner represents the good and the wait staff represents the service. People also make exchanges when they donate money or time to a charitable cause such as Habitat for Humanity.

Although marketing has always been a part of business, its importance has varied greatly. Figure 1.1 identifies four eras in the history of marketing: (1) the production era, (2) the sales era, (3) the marketing era, and (4) the relationship era.

The Production Era

Before 1925, most firms—even those operating in highly developed economies in western Europe and North America—focused narrowly on production. Manufacturers stressed production of quality products and then looked for people to purchase them. The prevailing attitude of this era held that a high-quality product would sell itself. This **production orientation** dominated business philosophy for decades; business success often was defined solely in terms of production successes.

The production era reached its peak during the early part of the 20th century. Henry Ford's mass-production line exemplifies this orientation. Ford's slogan, "They [customers] can have any color they want, as long as it's black," reflected the prevalent attitude toward marketing. Production shortages and intense consumer demand ruled the day. It is easy to understand how production activities took precedence.

2 Contrast marketing activities during the four eras in the history of marketing.

exchange process Activity in which two or more parties give something of value to each other to satisfy perceived needs.

production orientation Business philosophy stressing efficiency in producing a quality product, with the attitude toward marketing that "a good product will sell itself."

figure 1.1

Four Eras of Marketing History

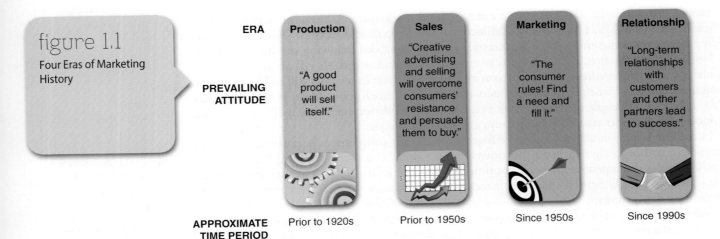

ERA	Production	Sales	Marketing	Relationship
PREVAILING ATTITUDE	"A good product will sell itself."	"Creative advertising and selling will overcome consumers' resistance and persuade them to buy."	"The consumer rules! Find a need and fill it."	"Long-term relationships with customers and other partners lead to success."
APPROXIMATE TIME PERIOD	Prior to 1920s	Prior to 1950s	Since 1950s	Since 1990s

sales orientation Belief that consumers will resist purchasing nonessential goods and services, with the attitude toward marketing that only creative advertising and personal selling can overcome consumers' resistance and persuade them to buy.

seller's market A market in which there are more buyers for fewer goods and services.

However, building a new product is no guarantee of success, and marketing history is cluttered with the bones of miserable product failures despite major innovations—more than 80 percent of new products fail. Inventing an outstanding new product is not enough because it must also fill a perceived marketplace need. Otherwise, even the best-engineered, highest-quality product will fail. Even Henry Ford's horseless carriage took a while to catch on. People were afraid of motor vehicles: they spat out exhaust, stirred up dust on dirt roads, got stuck in mud, and tied up horse traffic. Besides, at the speed of seven miles per hour, they caused all kinds of accidents and disruption. It took savvy marketing by some early salespeople—and eventually a widespread perceived need—to change people's minds about the product. Today, most of us could not imagine life without a car and have refined that need to preferences for certain types of vehicles, including SUVs, convertibles, trucks, and hybrids.

The Sales Era

As production techniques in the United States and Europe became more sophisticated, output grew from the 1920s into the early 1950s. As a result, manufacturers began to increase their emphasis on effective sales forces to find customers for their output. In this era, firms attempted to match their output to the potential number of customers who would want it. Companies with a **sales orientation** assume that customers will resist purchasing nonessential goods and services and that the task of personal selling and advertising is to persuade them to buy.

Although marketing departments began to emerge from the shadows of production and engineering during the sales era, they tended to remain in subordinate positions. Many chief marketing executives held the title of sales manager. But selling is only one component of marketing. As marketing scholar Theodore Levitt once pointed out, "Marketing is as different from selling as chemistry is from alchemy, astronomy from astrology, chess from checkers."

The Marketing Era

Personal incomes and consumer demand for products dropped rapidly during the Great Depression of the 1930s, thrusting marketing into a more important role. Organizational survival dictated that managers pay close attention to the markets for their goods and services. This trend ended with the outbreak of World War II, when rationing and shortages of consumer goods became commonplace. The war years, however, created only a pause in an emerging trend in business: a shift in the focus from products and sales to satisfying customer needs.

EMERGENCE OF THE MARKETING CONCEPT

The marketing concept, a crucial change in management philosophy, can be linked to the shift from a **seller's market**—one in which there were more buyers for fewer goods and services—to a **buyer's market**—one in which there were more goods and services than people willing to buy them. When World War II ended, factories stopped manufacturing tanks and ships and started turning out consumer products again, an activity that had, for all practical purposes, stopped in early 1942.

The advent of a strong buyer's market created the need for **consumer orientation** by businesses. Companies had to market goods and services, not just produce and sell them. This realization has been identified as the emergence of the marketing concept. Marketing would no longer be regarded as a supplemental activity performed after completing the production process. Instead, the marketer played a leading role in product planning. *Marketing* and *selling* would no longer be synonymous terms.

Today's fully developed **marketing concept** is a *companywide consumer orientation* with the objective of achieving long-run success. All facets—and all levels, from top to bottom—of the organization must contribute first to assessing and then to satisfying customer wants and needs. From marketing manager to accountant to product designer, every employee plays a role in reaching potential customers. Even during tough economic times, when companies tend to emphasize cutting costs and boosting revenues, the marketing concept focuses on the objective of achieving long-run success instead of short-term profits. Because the firm's survival and growth are built into the marketing concept, companywide consumer orientation should lead to greater long-run profits.

Apple exemplifies the marketing concept in every aspect of its business. Its products are consistently stylish and cutting edge but without overwhelming users with every possible feature. "A defining quality of Apple has been design restraint," says one industry consultant. That hallmark restraint is a characteristic of Apple's founder, Steven Jobs, and is reflected in the work of Apple's designers, managers, and engineers, whose contributions to the company's new products Jobs credits for the company's ability to constantly surprise the marketplace. Apple's latest release, the iPad, is being called a product that "may change the world." Says one business professor, "Real innovation in technology involves a leap ahead, anticipating needs that no one really knew they had and then delivering capabilities that redefine product categories. That's what Steve Jobs has done."[13]

A strong market orientation—the extent to which a company adopts the marketing concept—generally improves market success and overall performance. It also has a positive effect on new-product development and the introduction of innovative products. Companies that implement market-driven

buyer's market
A market in which there are more goods and services than people willing to buy them.

consumer orientation
Business philosophy incorporating the marketing concept that emphasizes first determining unmet consumer needs and then designing a system for satisfying them.

marketing concept
Companywide consumer orientation with the objective of achieving long-run success.

Apple exemplifies the marketing concept, creating consistently stylish and cutting-edge products. The iPad is a recent innovation.

career *readiness* (H)ow to Network

you may think only extroverts and social butterflies can build the personal networks that lead to business and career success. Not so! Networking is a skill anyone can learn. Here are some tips to get you started:

- Think of building your personal connections as making an investment in your future. It requires time and effort to become fruitful.

- Work on your network a little at a time. Start by attending one or two promising events a month or joining a professional networking service like LinkedIn or one or two professional groups you can find there, and stick with them.

- Be sure your online profile won't embarrass you with party photos or objectionable language.

- If you join a group or network that doesn't look immediately promising but you really enjoy it, keep going.

- Talk to new people everywhere, including social events like weddings and everyday places like checkout lines in stores.

- Don't hesitate to invite people to join you for coffee or a quick meal after work. Some of the most interesting contacts might just be shy.

- Carry information about yourself or your company to give out, such as an up-to-date brochure or business card.

- Remember, it's not all about you. Talk about relevant activities you've done, but be ready to ask questions that help others talk about themselves and their company or organization.

- Look for a few people who know a lot of other people, rather than many people in specific positions or types of businesses.

- Keep a record of people you want to stay in touch with, and don't wait for an occasion to get together. Follow-up and reciprocating are the keys to being remembered.

- Evaluate your results periodically. Which networking strategies are working best for you, and which can you improve?

Sources: Kristen Porter, "How to Grow Your Professional Networking," *eHow*, http://www.ehow.com, accessed February 4, 2010; Rob May, "How to Network: For Introverts," *Business Pundit*, www.businesspundit.com, accessed April 16, 2009; "How to Network Effectively," *eHow*, www.ehow.com, accessed April 16, 2009; C. J. Hayden, "Network Your Way to a New Job or Career, *About.com*, www.humanresources.about.com, accessed April 16, 2009.

---

strategies are better able to understand their customers' experiences, buying habits, and needs. Like Google, these companies can, therefore, design products with advantages and levels of quality compatible with customer requirements.

The Relationship Era

relationship marketing Development and maintenance of long-term, cost-effective relationships with individual customers, suppliers, employees, and other partners for mutual benefit.

The fourth era in the history of marketing emerged during the final decade of the 20th century and continues to grow in importance. Organizations now build on the marketing era's customer orientation by focusing on establishing and maintaining relationships with both customers and suppliers. **Relationship marketing** involves developing long-term, value-added relationships over time with customers and suppliers. Strategic alliances and partnerships among manufacturers, retailers, and suppliers often benefit everyone. The Boeing 787 Dreamliner, which has been under development and construction since 2004, is the result of an international team of companies working on the technology, design, and construction of the planes. Boeing and 43 global suppliers are working together to complete the planes. With orders for 876 planes, Boeing is proving that its long-term relationships are worth the effort.[14] The concept of relationship marketing, which is the current state of customer-driven marketing, is discussed in detail later in this chapter and in Chapter 10. On a personal level, see the "Career Readiness" feature for suggestions on creating your own personal network, a key to success in marketing and in business generally.

Converting Needs to Wants

Every consumer must acquire goods and services on a continuing basis to fill certain needs. Everyone must satisfy the fundamental needs for food, clothing, shelter, and transportation by purchasing items or, in some instances, temporarily using rented property and hired or leased transportation. By focusing on the benefits resulting from these products, effective marketing converts needs to wants. A need for a pair of pants may be converted to a desire for jeans—and further, a desire for jeans from Abercrombie & Fitch or Lucky Brand Jeans. The need for food may be converted to a desire for dinner at Pizzeria Uno or groceries from Trader Joe's. But if the need for transportation isn't converted to a desire for a Ford Focus or Mini Cooper, extra vehicles may sit unsold on a dealer's lot.

Consumers need to communicate. But converting that need to the desire for certain types of communication requires skill. It also requires listening to what consumers want. Consumers' demand for more cell phone and wireless services seems nearly unlimited, particularly with the surge in social networking sites—providing tremendous opportunities for companies. New products appear continually to feed that demand, such as increasingly popular broadband wireless services now offered by all cell phone carriers in a market currently dominated by Verizon Wireless and Sprint Nextel. Though many consumers who use Internet-friendly phones and other devices tend to be business travelers, the wireless broadband industry is intent on improving its appeal to the social networking mass market, perhaps with flexible service plans, new features, and lower fees. One industry analysis group predicts that very soon "for most consumers, the smartphone will be the norm and not the exception."[15]

 assessment check

1. What is the major distinction between the production era and the sales era?
2. What is the marketing concept?
3. Describe the relationship era of marketing.

Avoiding Marketing Myopia

The emergence of the marketing concept has not been devoid of setbacks. One troublesome problem led marketing scholar Theodore Levitt to coin the term **marketing myopia**. According to Levitt, marketing myopia is management's failure to recognize the scope of its business. Product-oriented rather than customer-oriented management endangers future growth. Levitt cites many service industries, such as dry cleaning and electric utilities, as examples of marketing myopia. But many firms have found innovative ways to reach new markets and develop long-term relationships.

Apple, for instance, has been working for a while on developing solar-powered devices, and in response to customer demand for longer battery life for its devices, the firm has restarted work on ways to use solar power for battery recharging. Such innovations also hold out the promise of greener and more sustainable manufacturing processes that might eliminate the use of some toxic or nonrecyclable parts in its products that have drawn criticism of Apple from such groups as Greenpeace.[16] Table 1.2 illustrates how firms in a number of industries have overcome myopic thinking by developing broader marketing-oriented business ideas that focus on consumer need satisfaction.

3 **Explain the importance of avoiding marketing myopia.**

marketing myopia
Management's failure to recognize the scope of its business.

 assessment check

1. What is marketing myopia?
2. Give an example of how a firm can avoid marketing myopia.

table 1.2 Avoiding Marketing Myopia

Company	Myopic Description	Company Motto—Avoiding Myopia
Audi	Automobile	Never follow
ClubMed	Resort vacations	Where Happiness Means the World
Mastercard	Credit card company	There are some things money can't buy. For everything else, there's Mastercard.
Allegra	Antihistamine	The relief goes on.
Goodyear	Tire manufacturer	The best tires in the world have Goodyear written all over them.
DHL	Express package	We move the world.

Extending the Traditional Boundaries of Marketing

Today's organizations—both profit oriented and not-for-profit—recognize universal needs for marketing and its importance to their success. During a television commercial break, viewers might be exposed to an advertisement for a Kia Spectra, an appeal to help feed children in foreign countries, a message by a political candidate, and a commercial for McDonald's—all in the space of about two minutes. Two of these ads are paid for by firms attempting to achieve profitability and other objectives. The appeal for funds to feed children and the political ad are examples of communications by not-for-profit organizations and individuals.

Marketing in Not-for-Profit Organizations

More than a quarter of all U.S. adults volunteer in one or more of the 1.5 million not-for-profit organizations across the country.[17] In total, these organizations generate hundreds of billions of dollars of revenues each year through contributions and from fund-raising activities. That makes not-for-profit organizations big business.

Not-for-profits operate in both public and private sectors. Federal, state, and local organizations pursue service objectives not keyed to profitability targets. The Federal Trade Commission oversees business activities; a state's department of motor vehicles issues car registrations and driver's licenses; a local school board is responsible for maintaining educational standards for its district. The private sector has an even greater array of not-for-profit organizations, including hospitals, libraries, the American Kennel Club, and the American Heart Association. Regardless of their size or location, all of these organizations need funds to operate. Adopting the marketing concept can make a great difference in their ability to meet their service objectives.

Conner Prairie in Fishers, Indiana, is an open-air re-creation of rural life in 1830s Indiana that features historic areas to explore, including a Lenape Indian camp, the Conner Homestead, a modern museum, and 800 acres of undeveloped land along with indoor play and learning areas for young children. Costumed staff host events that range from a festive wedding to the experience of slaves seeking freedom through the Underground Railroad. Thousands of families and school groups visit each year.[18]

Some not-for-profits form partnerships with business firms that promote the organization's cause or message. Target Stores funds a facility called Target House, which provides long-term housing for families with children treated at St. Jude Children's Research Hospital. The house has apartments and common areas where families can gather and children can play. Celebrities have also contributed to the house. Singer Amy Grant furnished a music room, and Olympic gold-medalist Scott Hamilton donated a fitness center and art room. Other "friends" of the organization include Olympic snowboarder Shaun White and "American Idol" runner-up Blake Lewis. Sponsors like Yahoo! and Brooks Brothers also support the house.[19]

Generally, the alliances formed between not-for-profit organizations and commercial firms and their executives benefit both. The reality of operating with multimillion-dollar budgets requires not-for-profit organizations to maintain a focused business approach. Consider some current examples:

- Feeding America (formerly known as America's Second Harvest) receives assistance from food manufacturers and grocery stores in distributing more than 2 billion pounds of food and grocery products to needy Americans. Participating businesses include Cott Beverages, Del Monte Foods Company, Heinz North America, the Kellogg Company, Pepperidge Farm, and Tropicana Products.[20]

- Corporate Angel Network works with the National Business Aviation Association to provide free transportation for cancer patients traveling to and from their treatments using empty seats on corporate jets.

- Donations from individuals, companies, and charitable organizations for the relief of victims of the 2010 earthquake in Haiti passed the $220 million mark within a week of the disaster. About half was donated online. Fund-raising was led by the American Red Cross and the U.S. Fund for UNICEF.[21]

The diversity of not-for-profit organizations suggests the presence of numerous organizational objectives other than profitability. In addition to their organizational goals, not-for-profit organizations differ from profit-seeking firms in several other ways.

Characteristics of Not-for-Profit Marketing

The most obvious distinction between not-for-profit organizations and for-profit—commercial—firms is the financial **bottom line**, business jargon that refers to the overall profitability of an organization. For-profit organizations measure profitability, and their goal is to generate revenues above and beyond their costs to make money for all stakeholders involved, including employees, shareholders, and the organization itself. Not-for-profit organizations hope to generate as much revenue as possible to support their causes, whether it is feeding children, preserving wilderness areas, or helping single mothers find work. Historically, not-for-profits have had less exact goals and marketing objectives than for-profit firms, but in recent years, many of these groups have recognized that, to succeed, they must develop more cost-effective ways to provide services, and they must compete with other organizations for donors' dollars. Marketing can help them accomplish these tasks. Some groups are finding, for instance, that online social network sites, such as Facebook and MySpace, can bring them increased attention. But they are also using specialized networks devoted to social causes like YourCause.com, and easy payment systems like Piryx, to generate funds.[22]

Other distinctions exist between for-profit and not-for-profit organizations as well, each of which influences marketing activities. Like profit-seeking firms, not-for-profit organizations may market tangible goods or intangible services. Pink products have long been important in raising both funds for and recognition of National Breast Cancer Awareness month in October every year. "Promotional items have been extremely important to the breast cancer awareness push," says the corporate relationship manager of the Susan G. Komen fund, a breast cancer fund-raising group. "Not only are they essential for fundraising to find a cure, they are also key to spreading life-saving messages to audience we might never reach without them. With the help of promotional items, it has finally become okay to talk about breast cancer."[23] But profit-seeking businesses tend to focus their marketing on just one public—their customers. Not-for-profit organizations, however, often must market to multiple publics, which complicates decision making about the correct markets to target. Many deal with at least two major publics—their clients and their sponsors—and often many

4 **Describe the characteristics of not-for-profit marketing.**

bottom line Reference to overall company profitability.

other publics as well. A college or university targets prospective students as recipients of its marketing program, but it also markets to current students, parents of students, major donors, alumni, faculty, staff, local businesses, and local government agencies.

A service user of a not-for-profit organization may have less control over the organization's destiny than customers of a profit-seeking firm. Not-for-profit organizations also often possess some degree of monopoly power in a given geographic area. An individual contributor might object to United Way's inclusion of a particular local agency, but that agency will receive a portion of any donor contribution.

 assessment check

1. What is the most obvious distinction between a not-for-profit organization and a commercial organization?
2. Why do for-profit and not-for-profit organizations sometimes form alliances?

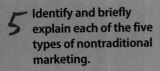 **5** Identify and briefly explain each of the five types of nontraditional marketing.

Nontraditional Marketing

As marketing evolved into an organization-wide activity, its application has broadened far beyond its traditional boundaries of for-profit organizations that create and distribute tangible goods and intangible services. In many cases, broader appeals focus on causes, events, individuals, organizations, and places. Table 1.3 lists and describes five major categories of nontraditional marketing: person marketing, place marketing, cause marketing, event marketing, and organization marketing. These categories can overlap—promotion for an organization may also encompass a cause or a promotional campaign may focus on both an event and a place.

table 1.3 **Categories of Nontraditional Marketing**

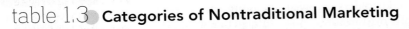

Type	Brief Description	Examples
Person marketing	Marketing efforts designed to cultivate the attention and preference of a target market toward a person	Athlete Peyton Manning, Indianapolis Colts quarterback; celebrity Toby Keith, country singer; political candidate James DeMint, U.S. Senate
Place marketing	Marketing efforts designed to attract visitors to a particular area; improve consumer images of a city, state, or nation; and/or attract new business	California: "Find Yourself Here." Colorado: "Enter a Higher State." Illinois: "Right Here. Right Now."
Cause marketing	Identification and marketing of a social issue, cause, or idea to selected target markets	"Click it or ticket." "Refill, not landfill."
Event marketing	Marketing of sporting, cultural, and charitable activities to selected target markets	London Olympics American Diabetes Association Tour de Cure
Organization marketing	Marketing efforts of mutual-benefit organizations, service organizations, and government organizations that seek to influence others to accept their goals, receive their services, or contribute to them in some way	American Red Cross: "Together, we can save a life." March of Dimes: "Saving babies, together" St. Jude Children's Research Hospital: "Finding Cures. Saving Children."

Person Marketing

Person marketing involves efforts designed to cultivate the attention, interest, and preferences of a target market toward a celebrity or authority figure. Celebrities can be real people or fictional characters. Political candidates engage in person marketing as they promote their candidacy for office. Authors such as Suze Orman of *The Road to Wealth* use person marketing to promote their books. Rachael Ray uses person marketing to promote her *Every Day with Rachael Ray* magazine, where she appears on every cover.

An extension of person marketing is *celebrity endorsements,* in which well-known athletes, entertainers, and experts or authority figures promote products for companies or social causes for not-for-profit organizations. NASCAR driver Tony Stewart takes a polygraph test to prove his devotion to Burger King Whoppers in a new ad series, and Target has signed an exclusive deal with the Black Eyed Peas. Actor William Shatner was seen in ads for Priceline.com, while his former "Star Trek" co-star Leonard Nimoy promoted the pain reliever Aleve. Athletes are the big winners in the celebrity endorsement arena—NBA star LeBron James has multi-million-dollar endorsement deals with Nike, Upper Deck, and The Coca-Cola Company. Olympic gold-medal swimmer Michael Phelps stars in TV ads for Subway, the sandwich chain. New York Giants quarterback Eli Manning has endorsement deals with Citizen Watch, Reebok, and Nabisco's Oreo brand, and with his brother, Indianpolis Colts' quarterback Peyton, faces off against Donald Trump in ads for Oreo cookies. Los Angeles Lakers coach Phil Jackson promotes the myTouch cell phone for T-Mobile.[24]

Tennis player Roger Federer provides a celebrity endorsement for Gillette.

My biggest problem should be my opponent, not sensitive skin.

Fusion, great performance even on sensitive skin.

Research recognised by

Gillette Fusion

Gillette
The Best a Man Can Get

IMAGE COURTESY OF THE ADVERTISING ARCHIVES

person marketing
Marketing efforts designed to cultivate the attention, interest, and preferences of a target market toward a person (perhaps a political candidate or celebrity).

Place Marketing

Another category of nontraditional marketing is **place marketing**, which attempts to attract customers to particular areas. Cities, states, regions, and countries publicize their tourist attractions to lure vacation travelers. They also promote themselves as good locations for businesses. Place marketing has become more important in the world economy—not only for tourism but also to recruit business and workers. Casino operator MGM is betting the house on its latest venture, the $8.5 billion CityCenter complex in Las Vegas, which is complete with four 61-story hotel towers, high-end stores, and dozens of bars and restaurants—and, of course, a casino. Like other hospitality businesses in the city, MGM is hoping to reverse Las Vegas's recently flagging status as a tourist draw, offering pricing deals to push the number of visitors up to nearly 40 million a year.[25]

Place marketing can be a showcase for ingenuity. Although commercial space travel remains a somewhat distant possibility, the New Mexico Spaceport Authority has already designed what it says will be the world's first public launch and landing site for space vehicles. Spaceport America, with a budget of $140 million in state tax dollars and more than $250 million more in private funding, will house seven spacecraft and includes a passenger terminal. It's planned to open by 2011 and will

place marketing
Marketing efforts to attract people and organizations to a particular geographic area.

Place marketing, such as this Explore Minnesota Web Site attempts to attract customers to a particular area.

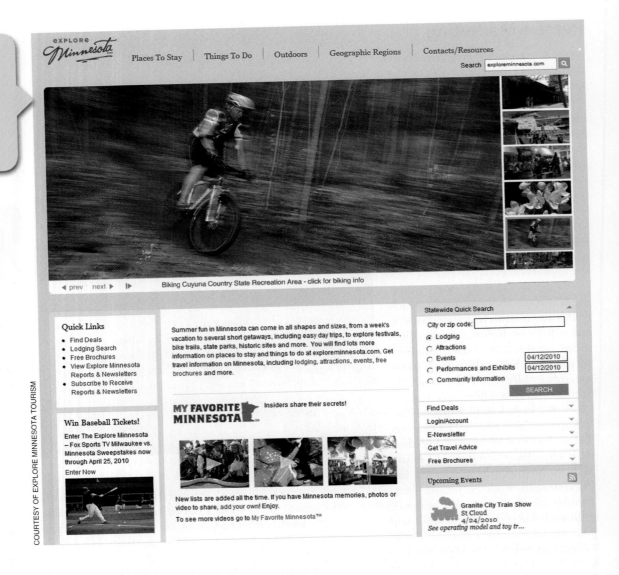

COURTESY OF EXPLORE MINNESOTA TOURISM

be home to Virgin Galactic, which is already accepting bookings online. The Spaceport Authority's executive director says the venture is "about the space powerhouse that New Mexico is."[26]

Minnesota Tourism, the state's Web site to promote its $11 billion travel and tourism industry, is backed by a strategic plan that details 16 separate programs and tactics to achieve its goals. They include traditional advertising, interactive marketing, partnership and group tour marketing, media relations, meetings and conventions, and the growth area of sports marketing, among others. Primary markets are the north central United States and Canada, Japan, China, the United Kingdom, Germany, and Scandinavia.[27]

In another area of the country, you wouldn't necessarily think of West Virginia as a hub for skiers. But the town of Davis is home to Timberline Four Seasons Ski Resort, which boasts up to 160 inches of snow per year on its Herz Mountain. Although often overlooked by skiers who routinely travel north and west, locals are convinced that their mountain, which recently upgraded the snowmaking capacity of its 37 slopes and trails, is about to be discovered. In addition to skiing, the area promotes mountain bike races and hiking in the summer.[28]

cause marketing
Identification and marketing of a social issue, cause, or idea to selected target markets.

Cause Marketing

A third category of nontraditional marketing, **cause marketing**, refers to the identification and marketing of a social issue, cause, or idea to selected target markets. Cause marketing covers a wide range of issues, including literacy, physical fitness, awareness of childhood obesity, environmental protection, elimination of birth defects, child-abuse prevention, and preventing drunk driving.

As mentioned earlier, an increasingly common marketing practice is for profit-seeking firms to link their products to social causes. Office supply giant Staples recently raised more than $630,000 in customer contributions for the national school supply drive set up by DoSomething.org. Staples donated the cash along with its own contribution of $125,000 worth of schools supplies and thousands of additional items given by customers. To leverage the power of social networking, the company also set up a Facebook page to raise awareness among teens about DoSomething.org, which is dedicated to inspiring young people to recognize a need and take positive action.[29]

Surveys show strong support for cause-related marketing by both consumers and company employees. In a recent survey, 92 percent of consumers had a more positive image of companies that support important social causes, and four of five respondents said that they would change brands to support a cause if the price and quality of the two brands remained equal. Cause marketing can help build relationships with customers.

Event Marketing

Event marketing refers to the marketing of sporting, cultural, and charitable activities to selected target markets. It also includes the sponsorship of such events by firms seeking to increase public awareness and bolster their images by linking themselves and their products to the events. Sports sponsorships have gained effectiveness in increasing brand recognition, enhancing image, boosting purchase volume, and increasing popularity with sports fans in demographic segments corresponding to sponsor business goals.

Some people might say that the premier sporting event is baseball's World Series. Others claim it's the Olympics or the World Cup. Still others might argue that it's the Super Bowl, which some consumers claim they watch only to see the debut of commercials. Those commercials are expensive, costing as much as $2.8 million for 30 seconds of airtime, or more than $93,000 a second.[30] But they reach an estimated 90 million viewers. Companies now also feed their commercials to Web sites and make them available for downloading to personal computers and video iPods. Experienced marketers caution that firms planning such a big expenditure should make it part of a larger marketing plan, not just a single shot at fame.

For those who prefer the international pageantry of the Olympics, marketers have plenty of plans. The promotion of upcoming Olympics—both summer and winter—begins years in advance. Before the end of each Olympics, hosts of the next games unveil their logo, and the marketing takes off from there. Corporate sponsors such as Adidas and Nike try to target the next Olympic gold medal winners, draping them in clothing and gear with company logos. The Vancouver Winter Olympics in 2010 afforded opportunities for hundreds of firms to provide wine and beer for hospitality events, frames and tents, jewelry, team uniforms, energy generation and temperature control systems, beds for the athletes' village, natural gas, cold and flu remedies, organic groceries, hand sanitizers, and computer and accounting services.[31]

event marketing
Marketing of sporting, cultural, and charitable activities to selected target markets.

Event marketing for the Olympics begins years in advance. Here is the logo for the 2012 Summer Olympics in London.

© AP IMAGES/PRNEWSFOTO/LONDON 2012

Organization Marketing

organization marketing Marketing by mutual-benefit organizations, service organizations, and government organizations intended to persuade others to accept their goals, receive their services, or contribute to them in some way.

Organization marketing attempts to persuade people to accept the goals of, receive the services of, or contribute in some way to an organization. Organization marketing includes mutual-benefit organizations such as Service Employees International Union and the Republican and Democratic political parties; service and cultural organizations such as DePaul University, Baylor College of Medicine, St. Louis's Barnes-Jewish Hospital, and Little Rock's Clinton Presidential Library; and government organizations such as the U.S. Coast Guard, the Newark Police Department, the Sacramento Fire Department, and the U.S. Postal Service. Colleges and universities use organizational marketing to help raise funds. The University of Texas now leads all colleges and universities in the sale of licensed merchandise—the school receives around $3.5 million a year from these sales.[32]

 assessment check

1. Identify the five major categories of nontraditional marketing.
2. Give an example of a way in which two or more of these categories might overlap.

6 Explain the shift from transaction-based marketing to relationship and social marketing.

From Transaction-Based Marketing to Relationship Marketing

transaction-based marketing Buyer and seller exchanges characterized by limited communications and little or no ongoing relationships between the parties.

As marketing progresses through the 21st century, a significant change is taking place in the way companies interact with customers. The traditional view of marketing as a simple exchange process, or **transaction-based marketing**, is being replaced by a different, longer-term approach that emphasizes building relationships with one customer at a time. Traditional marketing strategies focused on attracting customers and closing deals. Today's marketers realize that, although it's important to attract new customers, it's even more important to establish and maintain a relationship with them so they become loyal repeat customers. These efforts must expand to include suppliers and employees as well. Over the long term, this relationship may be translated to the lifetime value of a customer—the revenues and intangible benefits that a customer brings to an organization over an average lifetime, minus the investment the firm has made to attract and keep the customer.

Marketers realize that consumers are becoming more and more sophisticated. They quickly recognize marketing messages and may turn away from them if the messages don't contain information that consumers want and need. So marketers need to develop new techniques to establish and build trusting relationships between companies and their customers. As defined earlier in this chapter, relationship marketing refers to the development, growth, and maintenance of long-term, cost-effective exchange relationships with individual customers, suppliers, employees, and other partners for mutual benefit. It broadens the scope of external marketing relationships to include suppliers, customers, and referral sources. In relationship marketing, the term *customer* takes on a new meaning. Employees serve customers within an organization as well as outside it; individual employees and their departments are customers of and suppliers to one another. They must apply the same high standards of customer satisfaction to intradepartmental relationships as they do to external customer relationships. Relationship marketing recognizes the critical importance of internal marketing to the success of external marketing plans. Programs that improve customer service inside a company also raise productivity and staff morale, resulting in better customer relationships outside the firm.

Relationship marketing gives a company new opportunities to gain a competitive edge by moving customers up a loyalty ladder—from new customers to regular purchasers, then to loyal supporters of the firm and its goods and services, and finally to advocates who not only buy its products but recommend them to others, as shown in Figure 1.2.

Relationship building begins early in marketing. It starts with determining what customers need and want, then developing high-quality products to meet those needs. It continues with excellent customer service during and after purchase. It also includes programs that encourage repeat purchases and foster customer loyalty. Marketers may try to rebuild damaged relationships or rejuvenate unprofitable customers with these practices as well. Sometimes modifying a product or tailoring customer service to meet the needs of these customers can go a long way toward rebuilding a relationship.

Using Interactive and Social Marketing to Build Relationships

Today's technology allows people to transmit memos, reports, and drawings quickly and inexpensively over phone lines, cables, or wireless devices. People can subscribe to personalized news services that deliver article summaries on specified topics directly to their computers or cell phones. They can communicate via e-mail, voice mail, text messages, fax, videoconferencing, and computer networks; pay bills using online banking services; and use online resources to get information about everything from theater events to a local Ford dealer's special sale. As an increasing number of Internet users in the United States use wireless devices such as smartphones or notebook computers to access the Web and check their e-mail, the stage is set for **mobile marketing**—marketing messages transmitted via wireless technology.

Interactive media technologies combine computers and telecommunications resources to create software that users can control. Putting power into the hands of customers allows better communication, which can build relationships. **Interactive marketing** refers to buyer–seller communications in which the customer controls the amount and type of information received from a marketer. This technique provides immediate access to key product information when the consumer wants it, and it is increasingly taking place on social media sites like Facebook, Twitter, and blogs. **Social marketing** is the use of online social media as a communications channel for marketing messages. Social media is now the top online activity, and it's estimated that if Facebook were a country, it would be the fourth most populous in the world, right after the United States.[33] In one recent year, 50 million users posted 8 billion tweets on Twitter.[34] More than half the *Fortune* 100 companies have joined Twitter, and almost a third use Facebook and blogs. One Nielsen executive called social media "a catalyst for fresh thinking on how companies can improve customer service."[35]

Interactive marketing allows marketers and consumers to customize their communication. Customers may come to companies for information, creating opportunities for one-to-one marketing. They also can tell the company what they like or dislike about a product, and they can just as easily click the exit button and move on to another area. As interactive promotions grow in number and popularity, the challenge is to attract and hold consumer attention. "We can be more intimate with our marketplace customers and peers," says the president of the International Social Media Association. "Consumers are developing the expectation that companies are going to be more available and respond more quickly, that people are listening."[36]

One small business making good use of social media is Hansen's Cakes in Beverly Hills, whose cake decorator Suzi Finer uses Facebook and Twitter several times a day to tell thousands of "friends" and "followers" what she's up to at work. Finer says her posts have boosted sales 15 to 20 percent, even in an economic downturn. "People are still having birthday parties and weddings, and seeing these little bits about cakes on updates get them excited about the possibilities."[37] Kodak uses social media to accomplish what it calls "the 4 E's": engage, educate, excite, and evangelize. Says a company executive, "You have to create communication that engages the customer. Everyone talks about traditional ROIs [return on investment], but I talk about the new one, 'Return on Ignoring.' If you are ignoring this stuff, I can guarantee you are losing a fantastic business opportunity."[38]

Social media also allow larger exchanges in which consumers communicate with one another using e-mail or social networking sites. These electronic conversations can establish innovative relationships between users and the business, providing customized information based on users' interests and levels of understanding.

figure 1.2
Converting New Customers to Advocates

Advocate

Loyal Supporter

Regular Purchaser

New Customer

mobile marketing
Marketing messages transmitted via wireless technology.

interactive marketing
Buyer–seller communications in which the customer controls the amount and type of information received from a marketer through such channels as the Internet and virtual reality kiosks.

social marketing The use of online social media as a communications channel for marketing messages.

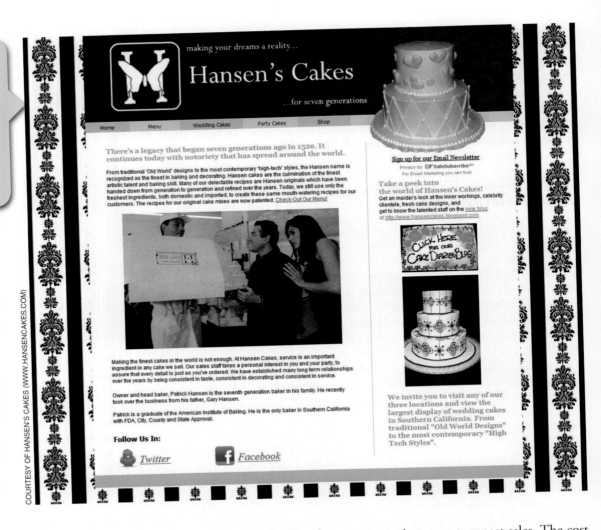

Cake decorator Suzi Finer of Hansen's Cakes uses Facebook and Twitter several times a day to tell thousands of followers what she is doing at work.

By converting indifferent customers into loyal ones, companies generate repeat sales. The cost of maintaining existing customers is far below the cost of finding new ones, and these loyal customers are profitable. Some of the best repeat customers are those who are also willing to spread the word—create a buzz—about a product. **Buzz marketing** can be very effective in attracting new customers by bridging the gap between a company and its products. Companies as diverse as Microsoft and KFC have tapped customers to create a buzz about their products. Firms that make the most efficient use of buzz marketing warn that it is not a "one-way" approach to building customer relationships.

Buzz can be purely visual, too. "Visual buzz," according to one marketing strategist, is "not only about telling, but more and more about showing. You see a Nike poster in a friend's dorm room; perhaps you don't even talk about it, but you noticed it." A prime example, the strategist says, is Lance Armstrong's Live Strong bracelet.[39]

Effective relationship marketing often relies heavily on information technologies such as computer databases that record customers' tastes, price preferences, and lifestyles. This technology helps companies become one-to-one marketers that gather customer-specific information and provide individually customized goods and services. The firms target their marketing programs to appropriate groups rather than relying on mass-marketing campaigns. Companies that study customer preferences and react accordingly gain distinct competitive advantages.

buzz marketing Word-of-mouth messages that bridge the gap between a company and its products.

Developing Partnerships and Strategic Alliances

Relationship marketing does not apply just to individual consumers and employees. It also affects a wide range of other markets, including business-to-business relationships with the firm's suppliers and distributors as well as other types of corporate partnerships. In the past, companies often have viewed their suppliers as adversaries against whom they must fiercely negotiate prices, playing one off against the other. But this attitude has changed radically as both marketers and their suppliers discover the benefits of collaborative relationships.

The formation of **strategic alliances**—partnerships that create competitive advantages—is also on the rise. Alliances take many forms, including product development partnerships that involve shared costs for research and development and marketing, and vertical alliances in which one company provides a product or component to another firm, which then distributes or sells it under its own brand. The Coca-Cola Company and PepsiCo (maker of Gatorade) have paid thousands of dollars to sponsor the University of Texas Longhorns football team, while Nike paid $1 million to have the players wear its famous "swoosh" on their jerseys.[40]

Not-for-profit organizations often use strategic alliances to raise awareness and funds for their causes. Nonni's Food Company sponsors the Susan G. Komen breast cancer fund, The Race for the Cure, by donating 55 or 75 cents for every UPC label customers submit from special packages of Old London products purchased in stores, and $1.50 for those redeemed online. The company has guaranteed a minimum donation of $100,000.[41]

strategic alliances
Partnerships in which two or more companies combine resources and capital to create competitive advantages in a new market.

 assessment check

1. How does relationship marketing give companies a competitive edge?
2. Why are interactive and social marketing important tools for marketers?
3. What is a strategic alliance?

Costs and Functions of Marketing

Firms must spend money to create time, place, and ownership utilities. Numerous attempts have been made to measure marketing costs in relation to overall product costs, and most estimates have ranged between 40 and 60 percent of total costs. On average, half of the costs involved in a product, such as a Subway sandwich, a Toyota Prius, or a financial planning lecture, can be traced directly to marketing. These costs are not associated with wheat, metal, or other raw materials nor are they associated with baking, welding, or any of the other production functions necessary for creating form utility. What functions does marketing perform, and why are they important in creating customer satisfaction?

As Figure 1.3 reveals, marketing is responsible for the performance of eight universal functions: buying, selling, transporting, storing, standardizing and grading, financing, risk taking, and securing

7 Identify the universal functions of marketing.

1. Buying
Ensuring that product offerings are available in sufficient quantities to meet customer demands

2. Selling
Using advertising, personal selling, and sales promotion to match products to customer needs

5. Standardizing and Grading
Ensuring that product offerings meet quality and quantity controls of size, weight, and other variables

6. Financing
Providing credit for channel members (wholesalers and retailers) and consumers

3. Transporting
Moving products from their point of production to locations convenient for purchasers

4. Storing
Warehousing products until needed for sale

7. Risk Taking
Dealing with uncertainty about future customer purchases

8. Securing Marketing Information
Collecting information about consumers, competitors, and channel members for use in making marketing decisions

figure 1.3
Eight Universal Marketing Functions

wholesalers
Intermediaries that operate between producers and resellers.

exchange functions
Buying and selling.

marketing information. Some functions are performed by manufacturers, others by retailers, and still others by marketing intermediaries called **wholesalers**.

Buying and selling represent **exchange functions**. Buying is important to marketing on several levels. Marketers must determine how and why consumers buy certain goods and services. To be successful, they must try to understand consumer behavior. In addition, retailers and other intermediaries must seek out products that will appeal to their customers. Marketers must also anticipate consumer preferences for purchases to be made several months later. Selling is the second half of the exchange process. It involves advertising, personal selling, and sales promotion in an attempt to match the firm's goods and services to consumer needs.

Transporting and storing are physical distribution functions. Transporting involves physically moving goods from the seller to the purchaser. Storing involves warehousing goods until they are needed for sale. Manufacturers, wholesalers, and retailers typically perform these functions.

The final four marketing functions—standardizing and grading, financing, risk taking, and securing marketing information—often are called facilitating functions because they help the marketer perform the exchange and physical distribution functions. Quality and quantity control standards and grades, frequently set by federal or state governments, reduce the need for purchasers to inspect each item. For example, if you request a certain size tire for your automobile, you expect to get it.

Financing is another marketing function because buyers often need access to funds to finance inventories prior to sales. Manufacturers often provide financing for their wholesale and retail customers. Some types of wholesalers perform similar functions for their markets. Finally, retailers frequently allow their customers to buy on credit with either store charge cards or major credit cards.

The seventh function, risk taking, is part of most ventures. Manufacturers create goods and services based on research and their belief that consumers need them. Wholesalers and retailers acquire inventory based on similar expectations of future consumer demand. Entrepreneurial risk takers accommodate these uncertainties about future consumer behavior when they market goods and services.

The final marketing function involves securing marketing information. Marketers gather information about potential customers: who they are, what they buy, where they buy, and how they buy. By collecting and analyzing marketing information, marketers can understand why consumers purchase some goods while passing others by. This information also helps determine what consumers want and need—and how to offer goods and services to satisfy them. So marketing is the direct connection between a firm and its customers, the link that helps build and maintain lasting relationships.

 assessment check

1. Which two marketing functions represent exchange functions?
2. Which two functions represent physical distribution functions?
3. Which four functions are facilitating functions?

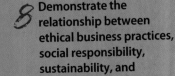 **8** **Demonstrate the relationship between ethical business practices, social responsibility, sustainability, and marketplace success.**

Ethics and Social Responsibility: Doing Well by Doing Good

Ethics are moral standards of behavior expected by a society. Most companies do their best to abide by an ethical code of conduct, but sometimes organizations and their leaders fall short. Several years ago, the Houston-based energy giant Enron collapsed, taking with it the retirement savings of its employees and investors. In another scandal, executives from Tyco were convicted of using millions of company dollars for their personal benefit. And chemical manufacturer Monsanto was convicted not only of polluting water sources and soil in a rural Alabama area for decades but of ignoring

ethics Moral standards of behavior expected by a society.

solving an ethical controversy

Airport Scanners Raise Privacy Issues for the Government

Full-body scanners, already fairly common in European airports and train stations, will soon come into wider use at security checkpoints in many U.S. airports. At a cost of $130,000 to $200,000 each, the machines blur facial images and project chalk-like outlines of the body to reveal plastic or chemical explosives and weapons hidden in clothing or on the body that would elude a metal detector.

No one argues that airline travel should not be as safe as airlines and governments can possibly make it. How to do so, however, is a question that brings security and privacy needs into apparent conflict for some.

Can governments encourage public support of full-body scans without endangering privacy rights?

PRO

1. Scanning requires only that passengers stand in the screening room, fully clothed, for about 15 seconds, and the machines can neither store images nor print them.

2. Because of the way tasks are assigned at screening locations, no security officer is able to both view the image and interact with the same passenger.

CON

1. Full-body scans are revealing, invasive, and undignified.

2. In addition to privacy concerns, scanning is a reactive move terrorists will quickly find their way around, and one that wastes millions of dollars better spent on preventive measures like better intelligence.

Summary

The U.S. Transportation Security Administration (TSA) is testing 40 full-body scanners at U.S. airports, mostly for secondary screening when a passenger sets off a metal detector. The TSA has 150 more scanners on the way and 300 more on order. It's unlikely the government will ever be able to scan passengers at every checkpoint in all the nation's 450 airports.

Sources: Aaron Ricadela, "Invasion of the Body Scanners," *Bloomberg BusinessWeek*, January 18, 2010, pp. 22–24; Steven Reinberg, "Airport Full Body Scanners Pose No Health Threat: Experts," *BusinessWeek*, http://www.businessweek.com, January 8, 2010; Joelle Tessler, "Airport Full-Body Scanners Have Benefits, and Limits," *DenverPost.com*, http://www.denverpost.com, December 31, 2009.

evidence its own scientists had gathered indicating the extent and severity of the pollution. Ethics matters in the public sector, too. Some see ethical concerns in the government's plans to widen the use of full-body scans at U.S. airports; see the "Solving an Ethical Controversy" feature for a discussion of the issues.

Most businesspeople follow ethical practices. More than half of all major corporations now offer ethics training to employees, and most corporate mission statements include pledges to protect the environment, contribute to communities, and improve workers' lives. This book encourages you to follow the highest ethical standards throughout your business and marketing career.

Social responsibility includes marketing philosophies, policies, procedures, and actions whose primary objective is to enhance society and protect the environment through sustainable products and practices. As the chapter opener pointed out, Walmart, for instance, has made great strides in reducing its use of energy in its stores. Social responsibility often takes the form of philanthropy,

social responsibility
Marketing philosophies, policies, procedures, and actions that have the enhancement of society's welfare as a primary objective.

making gifts of money or time to humanitarian causes. Many firms, both large and small, include social responsibility programs as part of their overall mission. These programs often produce such benefits as improved customer relationships, increased employee loyalty, marketplace success, and improved financial performance.

sustainable products
Products that can be produced, used, and disposed of with minimal impact on the environment.

Sustainable products, those that can be produced, used, and disposed of with minimal impact on the environment, are another goal of socially responsible firms. Many such firms have added annual sustainability reports and a top-level executive position to develop and promote their sustainability efforts. One such executive is DuPont's chief sustainability officer, Linda Fisher, who joined the firm after working for the U.S. Environmental Protection Agency (EPA) for 13 years. Says Fisher about the challenges DuPont faces in furthering its environmentally friendly efforts, "What our customers and their customers are looking for are products that are greener, more energy-efficient, but they'd like to keep the same price point. So they're demanding more.... Those are real cost issues and market issues.... It really is trying to balance the needs of industry and the economy with the needs of the environment. The two objectives tug at each other." But, says Fisher, given such basic factors as world population growth, "the fact is, we're going to have to become much more productive, and we need to do that in a sustainable way."[42]

What is the role of marketing in sustainability efforts? According to Fisher, "the folks we hire in marketing have a real interest in marketing around sustainability. Our public affairs and communications people are very involved.... No matter where you want to work, you can find an opportunity around sustainability."[43] Other sustainability and social responsibility officers agree that sustainability must permeate the firm's corporate strategy from the top down, so all areas in the firm can align their environmental goals in the same direction for the greatest effectiveness. As Apple's sustainability report acknowledges, "switching off lights and recycling office waste aren't enough."[44]

Firms stand to gain needed credibility from their efforts to protect the environment by reducing waste and pollution. Not only has the recent economic downturn made it important for them to cut waste and cost as never before, including the costs of damage to the environment, but consumers now are more aware of the real need for such drives—and ready to support them. According to a Canadian group called Network for Business Sustainability, customers are "typically willing to pay 10 percent [premium] for sustainable products."[45]

mktg: *success*

Procter & Gamble Gets Future-Friendly

Background. With 140 manufacturing facilities in more than 40 countries, Procter & Gamble (P&G) reaches about 4 billion people around the world with a wide variety of household products. In 2007, the company raised the bar on goals it had previously set for increasing "sustainable innovation" products (those that reduce energy, water, transportation, or packaging use by more than 10 percent), and for reducing waste and pollution from its manufacturing and transportation processes.

The Challenge. P&G's new goals call for it to sell at least $50 billion of sustainable products by 2012; to increase its reduction of carbon dioxide emissions by 20 percent; and to further decrease its water consumption, waste disposal, and reliance on trucks and planes. By 2015, it hopes to increase its use of rail transport to 30 percent.

The Strategy. The company has cut its waste disposal, water usage, and carbon dioxide emissions by more than 50 percent, and its energy use is down by almost half. It has sold more than $13 billion worth of sustainable products; cut its use

The "Marketing Success" feature describes Procter & Gamble's recent efforts toward achieving sustainability. Some other firms that have recently won praise for their efforts to eliminate dangerous or polluting ingredients in their products include Nokia and Sony Ericsson. Nokia, for instance, offers a recycling program with "takeback service" in 85 countries. "As we take our environmental responsibilities very seriously, it is of course rewarding to see our environmental efforts acknowledged in various rankings," said Nokia's head of sustainability. The environmental advocacy group Greenpeace recently gave high marks to Apple, which it has criticized in the past. "Apple beat all the other brands in removing polyvinyl chloride (PVC) and brominated flame retardants (BFRs) from all its products almost two years ahead of HP and the rest of the PC sector," the organization's report said. "Apple has demonstrated that there are no technical barriers to substituting PVC and BFRs with safer alternatives in smartphones, iPods, PCs, and TVs."[46]

The U.S. government recently undertook a massive effort to reduce the number of "clunkers," or older, gas-hungry cars on the road by offering drivers a rebate up to $4,500 (depending on various factors including the type of car) if they traded a working clunker in for a more fuel-efficient car. The program, whose other goal was to boost the nation's economy, was so successful that it not only reduced the number of polluting cars (the clunkers were disabled and then crushed or shredded so they could never be driven again), it ran through most of its allocated $1 billion in funding in a little over a week. An additional $2 billion was added to keep the program running a few weeks longer. Although it is considered a success, critics say the clunkers program should not have required consumers to buy another car, however fuel-efficient, or it should have mandated a big improvement in gas mileage for the new purchase.[47]

assessment check

8.1 Define *ethics*.

8.2 What is *social responsibility*?

8.3 What are *sustainable products*?

of packaging materials by 136,000 metric tons; and, through its Global Asset Recover Purchases program, found a profitable way to recycle shredded scrap metal from one of its European plants.

The Outcome. P&G continues to strive for higher sustainability goals and has launched "Future Friendly" programs in Canada and the United Kingdom to educate customers about its sustainable products and reassure them as to quality and value. Next up is a similar awareness program for the United States, supported by employee involvement. "Around the world, P&G employees have made sustainability a core part of their everyday work, developing innovative solutions and delivering meaningful results across the business," said the company's vice president of global sustainability.

Sources: Kevin Hagen, "Environmental Sustainability at Procter and Gamble," *Associated Content.com*, http://www.associatedcontent.com, accessed February 5, 2010; Alex Palmer, "P&G Touts Green Practices," *Brandweek*, http://www.brandweek.com, October 19, 2009; Anne Marie Mohan, "P&G 'Future-Friendly' Campaign to Educate Consumers on Green Products," *Greener Package*, http://www.greenerpackage.com, October 19, 2009.

strategic implications → f t 🛒 of marketing in the 21st century

nprecedented opportunities have emerged out of electronic commerce and computer technologies in business today. These advances and innovations have allowed organizations to reach new markets, reduce selling and marketing costs, and enhance their relationships with customers and suppliers. Thanks to the Internet and social media tools, business has grown into a global market.

Both profit-seeking and not-for-profit organizations must broaden the scope of their activities to prevent myopic results in their enterprises. If they fail to do so, they lose out on promising opportunities.

Marketers must constantly look for ways to create loyal customers and build long-term relationships with those customers, often on a one-to-one basis. They must be able to anticipate customer needs and satisfy them with innovative goods and services. They must do this faster and better than the competition. And they must conduct their business according to the highest ethical and sustainability standards.

Review of Chapter Objectives

 Define *marketing*, explain how it creates utility, and describe its role in the global marketplace.

Marketing is an organizational function and a set of processes for creating, communicating, and delivering value to customers and for managing customer relationships in ways that benefit the organization and its stakeholders. Utility is the want-satisfying power of a good or service. Four basic kinds of utility exist: form, time, place, and ownership. Marketing creates time, place, and ownership utilities. Three factors have forced marketers to embrace a global marketplace: expanded international trade agreements, new technologies that have brought previously isolated nations to the marketplace, and greater interdependence of the world's economies.

 Contrast marketing activities during the four eras in the history of marketing.

During the production era, businesspeople believed that quality products would sell themselves. The sales era emphasized convincing people to buy. The marketing concept emerged during the marketing era, in which there was a companywide focus on consumer orientation with the objective of achieving long-term success. The relationship era focuses on establishing and maintaining relationships between customers and suppliers. Relationship marketing involves long-term, value-added relationships.

 Explain the importance of avoiding marketing myopia.

Marketing myopia is management's failure to recognize a company's scope of business. It focuses marketers too narrowly on products and thus misses potential opportunities to satisfy customers. To avoid it, companies must broadly define their goals so that they focus on fulfilling consumer needs.

 Describe the characteristics of not-for-profit marketing.

Not-for-profit organizations operate in both public and private sectors. The biggest distinction between not-for-profits and commercial firms is the bottom line—whether the firm is judged by its profitability levels. Not-for-profit organizations may market to multiple publics. A customer or service user of a not-for-profit organization may have less control over the organization's destiny than customers of a profit-seeking firm. In addition, resource contributors to not-for-profits may try to influence the organization's activities. Not-for-profits and for-profits may form alliances that effectively promote each other's causes and services.

Identify and briefly explain each of the five types of nontraditional marketing.

Person marketing focuses on efforts to cultivate the attention, interest, and preferences of a target market toward a celebrity or noted figure. Place marketing attempts to attract visitors and businesses to a particular destination. Cause marketing identifies and markets a social issue, cause, or idea. Event marketing promotes sporting, cultural, charitable, or political activities. Organization marketing attempts to influence others to accept an organization's goals or services and contribute to it in some way.

 Explain the shift from transaction-based marketing to relationship and social marketing.

Relationship marketing represents a dramatic change in the way companies interact with customers. The focus on relationships gives a firm new opportunities to gain a competitive edge by moving customers up a loyalty ladder from new customers to regular purchasers and then to loyal supporters and advocates. Over the long term, this relationship may be translated to the lifetime value of a customer. Interactive technologies and social marketing (via Facebook, Twitter, and the like) allow marketers direct communication with customers, permit more meaningful exchanges, and put the customer in control. Organizations may form partnerships—called *strategic alliances*—to create a competitive advantage. These alliances may involve product development, raising awareness, and other activities.

 Identify the universal functions of marketing.

Marketing is responsible for eight universal functions, divided into three categories: (1) exchange functions (buying and selling); (2) physical distribution (transporting and storing); and (3) facilitating functions (standardization and grading, financing, risk taking, and securing market information).

 Demonstrate the relationship between ethical business practices, social responsibility, sustainability, and marketplace success.

Ethics are moral standards of behavior expected by a society. Companies that promote ethical behavior and social responsibility usually produce increased employee loyalty and a better public image. This image often pays off in customer growth, because many buyers want to associate themselves with—and be customers of—such firms. Social responsibility includes marketing philosophies, policies, procedures, and actions whose primary objectives are the enhancement of society and the protection of the environment through sustainable products and practices. These actions also generally promote a firm's public image.

 ## Assessment Check: Answers

1.1 Define *marketing*, and explain how it creates utility. Marketing is an organizational function and a set of processes for creating, communicating, and delivering value to customers and for managing customer relationships in ways that benefit the organization and its stakeholders. It creates time, place, and ownership utilities.

1.2 What three factors have forced marketers to embrace a global marketplace? International agreements are negotiated to expand trade among nations. The growth of technology is bringing previously isolated countries into the marketplace. The interdependence of the world's economies is now a reality.

2.1 What is the major distinction between the production era and the sales era? During the production era, businesspeople believed that quality products would sell themselves. But during the sales era, emphasis was placed on selling—persuading people to buy.

2.2 What is the marketing concept? The marketing concept is a companywide consumer orientation with the objective of achieving long-term success.

2.3 Describe the relationship era of marketing. The relationship era focuses on building long-term, value-added relationships over time with customers and suppliers.

3.1 What is marketing myopia? Marketing myopia is management's failure to recognize the scope of a company's business.

3.2 Give an example of how a firm can avoid marketing myopia. A firm can find innovative ways to reach new markets with existing goods and services.

4.1 What is the most obvious distinction between a not-for-profit organization and a commercial organization? The biggest distinction between for-profit and not-for-profit organizations is the bottom line—whether an organization is judged by its profitability.

4.2 Why do for-profit and not-for-profit organizations sometimes form alliances? For-profits and not-for-profits may form alliances to promote each other's causes and offerings. For-profits may do so as part of their social responsibility efforts.

5.1 Identify the five major categories of nontraditional marketing. The five categories of nontraditional marketing are person, place, cause, event, and organization marketing.

5.2 Give an example of a way in which two or more of these categories might overlap. Overlap can occur in many ways. An organization might use a person to promote its cause or event. Two organizations might use one marketing effort to promote an event and a place; for example, NBC Sports and the National Thoroughbred Racing Association combining to promote the Kentucky Derby at Churchill Downs.

6.1 How does relationship marketing give companies a competitive edge? Relationship marketing can move customers up a loyalty ladder, generating repeat sales and long-term relationships.

6.2 Why are interactive and social marketing important tools for marketers? Interactive marketing technologies create direct communication with customers, allow larger exchanges, and put the customer in control. Social marketing media (Facebook, Twitter, for example) let companies show customers they are listening and will respond quickly.

6.3 What is a strategic alliance? A strategic alliance is a partnership formed between two organizations to create a competitive advantage.

7.1 Which two marketing functions represent exchange functions? Buying and selling are exchange functions.

7.2 Which two functions represent physical distribution functions? Transporting and storing are physical distribution functions.

7.3 Which four functions are facilitating functions? The facilitating functions are standardization and grading, financing, risk taking, and securing market information.

8.1 Define *ethics*. Ethics are moral standards of behavior expected by a society.

8.2 What is *social responsibility*? Social responsibility involves marketing philosophies, policies, procedures, and actions whose primary objective is the enhancement of society.

8.3 What are *sustainable products*? Sustainable products are those that can be produced, used, and disposed of with minimal impact on the environment.

Marketing Terms You Need to Know

utility 5
marketing 7
exchange process 9
production orientation 9
sales orientation 10
seller's market 10
buyer's market 11
consumer orientation 11

marketing concept 11
relationship marketing 12
marketing myopia 13
bottom line 15
person marketing 17
place marketing 17
cause marketing 18
event marketing 19

organization marketing 20
transaction-based marketing 20
mobile marketing 21
interactive marketing 21
social marketing 21
buzz marketing 22
strategic alliances 23
wholesalers 24

exchange functions 24
ethics 24
social responsibility 25
sustainable products 26

Assurance of Learning Review

1. Identify the four types of utility, and give an example of each.
2. What condition in the marketplace gave rise to the need for a consumer orientation by businesses after World War II?
3. Define *relationship marketing*, and describe how it fits into the marketing concept.
4. Why do not-for-profit organizations need to engage in marketing efforts?
5. Give an example of how Big Apple Bagels could use one or more of the nontraditional marketing techniques to promote the opening of a new franchise.
6. What might be some of the benefits of mobile marketing for firms that use it to reach out to consumers?
7. Describe the significance of the shift from transaction-based marketing to relationship marketing. When does relationship building begin?
8. How have social media like Twitter and Facebook changed marketing communications?
9. How do ethics and social responsibility help a firm achieve marketplace success?
10. What motivates firms to develop sustainable products?

Projects and Teamwork Exercises

1. Consider each of the following firms and describe how the firm's goods and services can create different types of utility. If necessary, go online to the company's Web site to learn more about it. You can do this alone or in a team.
   a. American Express, Visa, or Mastercard
   b. Flickr or other online digital photo service
   c. Club Med
   d. Amazon.com
   e. SuperValu supermarkets

2. With a classmate, choose a U.S.-based company whose products you think will do well in certain overseas markets. The company can be anything from a music group to a clothing retailer—anything that interests you. Suggestions include Domino's Pizza, Jazzercise or Zumba, StubHub, Lady Gaga, or American Eagle Outfitters. Then write a plan for how you would target and communicate with overseas markets.

3. Choose a company that interests you from the following list or select one of your own. Research the company online, through business magazines, or through other sources to identify the scope of its business. Write a brief description of the company's current scope of business. Then describe strategies for avoiding marketing myopia, expanding the company's scope of business over the next ten years.
   a. United Parcel Service (UPS)
   b. Walt Disney World
   c. General Electric
   d. E*Trade
   e. Apple

4. With a classmate, choose one of the following not-for-profit organizations. Then come up with a for-profit firm with which you think your organization could form a strategic alliance. Create a presentation—an ad, a poster, or the like—illustrating and promoting the partnership.
   a. Humane Society
   b. Oxfam
   c. Habitat for Humanity
   d. American Cancer Society
   e. The Bill and Melinda Gates Foundation

5. Research one of the following electronics companies, or another of your choosing, and study its efforts to improve the sustainability of its products, particularly their safe disposal. What does the company do well in this area? What could it do better?
   a. Toshiba
   b. Nintendo
   c. Microsoft
   d. Fujitsu
   e. Samsung

Critical-Thinking Exercises

1. How does an organization create a customer?

2. How can marketers use interactive and social marketing to convert needs to wants and ultimately build long-term relationships with customers?

3. Why is utility such an important feature of marketing?

4. What benefits—monetary and nonmonetary—do social responsibility programs bring to a business?

5. Why is determining the lifetime value of a customer an important analysis for a company to make?

6. Why is it important for a firm to establish high ethical standards for sustainability? What role do you think marketers play in implementing these standards?

Ethics Exercise

You are having lunch with a friend who works for an advertising agency that competes with yours. Suddenly he remembers an errand he has to run before returning to work, and he rushes off with a hasty good-bye after giving you some money to cover his lunch. As you gather your things to leave a few minutes later, you realize your friend left his notebook computer on the table, open to a report about a client. Your company is very interested in doing some work for this client in the future.

1. Would you take a quick look at the report before you return it to your friend? Why or why not?

2. Would you share any information in the report with anyone in your office? Why or why not?

3. When you return the notebook to your friend, would you mention the contents and offer your own commentary on them? Why or why not?

Internet Exercises

1. **Marketing terminology.** Like many subjects, marketing appears to have a language of its own. Visit the Web site of the American Marketing Association. Click on "resource library" and then "dictionary." Define the following terms: A/B testing, dating, never out list, and will-call.
http://www.marketingpower.com

2. **Event marketing.** The Westminster Kennel Club runs the nation's largest dog show. Go to the event's Web site. Review the Web site and prepare a brief report relating what you learned to the material on event marketing in the chapter. Make sure to describe sponsor tie-ins and other joint marketing efforts.
http://www.westerminsterkennelclub.org

3. **Sustainability.** Johnson & Johnson engages in a major effort to incorporate sustainability into its wide-ranging business activities. Visit the Web site listed here and read about the firm's recent activities. How does Johnson & Johnson promote sustainability? What are some specific examples?
http://www.jnj.com/connect/caring/environment-protection/

Note: Internet Web addresses change frequently. If you don't find the exact site listed, you may need to access the organization's home page and search from there or use a search engine such as Google or Bing.

Case 1.1   *Hewlett-Packard Reduces, Reuses, Recycles*

Hewlett-Packard (HP), the world's largest information technology (IT) company, was founded in 1939 and makes its headquarters in Palo Alto, California. Ranking among the top 10 of the *Fortune* 500, HP operates in more than 170 countries and earned annual revenues

of more than $115 billion. Its products range from small, handheld devices to giant supercomputers and fall into three main business groups: Personal Systems, which includes PCs, workstations, and mobile computing devices; Enterprise Business, including storage devices, servers, and business software; and Imaging and Printing, encompassing inkjet and laser printers, commercial printing services, and printing supplies.

For its leadership role in reporting and reducing its greenhouse-gas emissions, HP was recently named the "Greenest Big Company in America" by *Newsweek* magazine. It has long been focused on contributing to each country and community in which it operates by reducing waste, raising standards among its global suppliers, and easing access to information technology around the world. Seeing itself as a "global steward," the firm recycles HP ink cartridges for free and accepts any brand of computer hardware and rechargeable batteries for recycling in the United States and Canada. In partnership with the National Cristina Foundation, HP also accepts used computer equipment for donation in the United States, as well as accepting equipment for trade-in and resale to reduce electronic waste.

"Recycling technology equipment is a win–win situation for everybody," HP believes. "It is good for the planet and good for business." In one recent year, the firm recycled more than 74,000 tons of hardware and print cartridges around the world, and it hopes soon to have recycled more than 900,000 tons of electronic products and supplies.

HP's scientists estimate that businesses' use of technology consumes more than 400 million tons of coal each year, emitting more than twice that amount in the form of carbon dioxide waste. "We cannot continue to consume energy at our current rates," the compa-

ny's website says. As part of its Design for the Environment strategy, HP's corporate phones and laptops use less energy thanks to displays that use ambient light, and soon the firm hopes to reduce the energy consumption and greenhouse-gas emissions of all its operations and products to 40 percent below their 2005 levels. It has already met its 2010 goal to reduce them to 25 percent below 2005 levels, and it is moving forward with plans to invest in renewable energy sources and to make it even easier to recycle every one of its products.

But HP isn't only cleaning up its own act; it's helping its customers too. It recently announced that its newest ProBook laptop models include a dedicated hardware circuit and "Power Assistant" software that can estimate and display the computers' energy use over time. With this feature, users can check bar charts or pie charts of energy use and reduce it, by customizing their power settings to reduce screen brightness, turn off certain networking features, run the processor at a lower speed, or squeeze out longer battery life. IT administrators can even manage a whole network of computers with Power Assistant, customizing the machines to go into energy-saving hibernate mode sooner, for instance. Future laptops and desktops from HP will boast the same innovative feature.

"The way we see it," says HP, "environmental responsibility and business success go hand in hand."

Questions for Critical Thinking

1. What kind(s) of marketing utility do you think Hewlett-Packard's sustainability efforts provide for its customers? Are there any downsides to these programs?

2. HP has entered a partnership with the National Cristina Foundation to accept used computer equipment for donation. What other partners, or types of partners, might help the company achieve its sustainability goals in the future?

Sources: Company Web site, http://www.hp.com, accessed February 23, 2010; "HP and the Environment," DestinationGreenIt, http://www.destinationgreenit. com, November 16, 2009; Agam Shah, "HP Green Laptops to Cut Power Usage," *TechWorld*, http://news.techworld.com, October 13, 2009; "Hewlett-Packard Sets New GHG Emission Reduction Target," *EcoSeed*, http://www.ecoseed.org, September 22, 2009; Daniel McGinn, "The Greenest Big Companies in America," *Newsweek*, http://www.newsweek.com, September 21, 2009.

Video Case 1.2
Marketing: Satisfying Customers at Flight 001

"We came up with this concept out of need," says Brad John, co-founder of Flight 001. John and fellow co-founder John Sencion had, until the late 1990s, worked in different aspects of the fashion industry in New York. Sencion was a menswear designer and John worked behind the scenes. Both did an enormous amount of travel between the United States, Europe, and Japan. No matter how many times they set out on a trip, the days and hours before hopping a cab for JFK were spent running from office supply store to bookstore to drugstore to boutique in a mad rush for the latest laptop bag. By the time they got to the airport, they were sweaty, stressed, and miserable—not exactly the glamorous existence they envisioned when they got into the fashion industry.

On May 5, 1998, somewhere high in the sky between New York and Paris, they came up with an idea for a one-stop travel shop targeted at fashion-forward globetrotters like themselves.

Not everyone got it. "Everyone would say, 'Well, there's luggage stores, Brad, what's the difference? You're gonna sell luggage,'" John recalls. "We were going to sell guidebooks, cosmetics, bags, passport covers. There's really no place in the world where you can buy all these items in one place."

"You can't just open another Mexican restaurant and think you're an entrepreneur," says Sencion. "Without innovation, there's no entrepreneurship." When it came to the design and concept, it was very important that Flight 001 not be just another luggage store. Sencion lent his design experience and John brought his talent for selecting product and merchandising to create a truly unique shopping experience.

The stores, shaped like airplane fuselages, are chock full of fun mid-century modern design, harkening back to a time when leg room didn't cost extra and when people dressed up to travel and actually looked forward to hanging out at the airport lounge. It's not all in the look, of course. Customer service at Flight 001 is key to the experience. Friendly and helpful staff members do whatever they can to start your trip on the right foot. Unfortunately, whatever happens once you reach the airport is out of their hands.

John and Sencion both know that a cool shop and nice people will only get you so far, so they put an enormous amount of thought into selecting and designing the products they sell. Looking back at the original inspiration for the store, Flight 001 created its own line of innovative space-saving packing bags called Space Pack.

Each Space Pack is designed for a specific garment and, once filled, can double the amount of space in your suitcase with the added bonus of keeping everything neat, clean, and organized. Future plans include an exclusive luggage line; ultimately, John would like for every product in his store to be a Flight 001 branded product.

Another important part of Flight 001's plan is careful marketing. While John and Sencion are not going to turn away business, it is important to the brand that they maintain the feeling of a small boutique, so they've never done any traditional paid advertising. Instead, they rely on partnerships with airlines such as Song, editorial spreads in magazines from *Lucky* to *Bloomberg Businessweek* and exclusive product deals and tie-ins with high fashion designers such as Yves Behar and automaker Mini Cooper. Unlike traditional paid advertising, they are in front of only those consumers most likely to purchase their products. Plus, it's free!

As Flight 001 celebrates its 10-year anniversary, it is clear that its success is based on more than a flashy design. With retail stores in Los Angeles, San Francisco, New York, and Chicago, it is clear that they aren't targeting your average big-box shopper. At the same time, they appeal to anyone who wants to make a statement at the baggage carousel. Stop by the Greenwich Village store on any given day and you may find yourself comparing guidebooks with celebs such as Rachael Ray, meeting a retired couple shopping for lightweight ergonomic carry-on approved luggage, or seeing a preteen in search of the cutest iPod protector and a vial of anti-bacterial "Cootie Spray"—just in case. As Sencion says, "We're trying to bring a little fun and glamour back in to travel."

Questions

1. How important are Flight 001's strategic alliances to their marketing?

2. What other companies or industries would be a good fit with Flight 001?

3. What role does the design of the store play in marketing Flight 001?

ch2 Strategic
Planning in Contemporary Marketing

1 Distinguish between strategic planning and tactical planning.

2 Explain how marketing plans differ at various levels in an organization.

3 Identify the steps in the marketing planning process.

4 Describe successful planning tools and techniques, including Porter's Five Forces model, first and second mover strategies, SWOT analysis, and the strategic window.

5 Identify the basic elements of a marketing strategy.

6 Describe the environmental characteristics that influence strategic decisions.

7 Describe the methods for marketing planning, including business portfolio analysis and the BCG matrix.

Ford's Dramatic Comeback: One Ford, One Team, One Plan, One Goal ... When Alan R. Mulally took over as Ford Motor Company's CEO, he had a single vision for the car company that seemed poised to drive off a cliff. His vision was so

simple and clear that its principles fit on a wallet-sized card: "One Ford … One Team … One Plan … One Goal." In fact, Mulally had the motto printed on thousands of cards and distributed to all Ford employees to carry in their wallets, pockets, and purses. Mulally's goal is to return Ford to its status as a global leader in the auto industry. His strategy involves developing the truly global car—a vehicle that is designed and engineered for consumers worldwide, sold under one brand and model name, with marketing campaigns tailored to diverse markets. "If we were going to be world-class, we needed to pull together and leverage and use our global assets around the world to create a powerhouse 'One Ford,'" Mulally explained in an interview about his initial plans. "It's exactly why we are here."

To achieve his goals, Mulally immediately arranged for Ford to borrow $24 billion—a strategy that would later prove to be brilliant. When the economy took a steep downturn, Ford had enough cash in its coffers to ward off bankruptcy and a bailout by the government. While its competitors, General Motors and Chrysler, were forced to ask for government aid, Ford continued to drive under its own power. In addition, Mulally insisted that Ford shift away from its signature vehicles—trucks and SUVs—a move that skeptics warned could lead to the firm's demise. Ford also dropped its luxury brands: Land Rover, Volvo, Jaguar, and Aston-Martin. Not only were they gas guzzlers, these brands were consuming Ford's resources. Meanwhile, under Mulally, the Ford bureaucracy had shrunk so the firm

could respond more quickly to market demands.

These decisions allowed the true Ford brand—with its blue oval logo—to emerge once again. They also cleared the way for the development and launch of a unified "world car." Mulally noted, "We made a strategic decision to move from a house of brands to a laser focus on Ford. That brand clarity was going to be absolutely essential and a competitive advantage." Ford then chose its first global car: a new version of the Ford Focus. The strategy made sense on several counts. The Focus is a small, light, fuel-efficient vehicle (although it is not a hybrid like the Fusion or Escape). While these attributes are easier to sell in Europe and Asia than they are in the United States, Ford marketers are committed to their prediction that even

Next-generation
Ford Focus

evolution of a
brand

U.S. consumers will begin to choose more economical, environmentally friendly vehicles over the next few years. "There's a tremendous amount of challenge in bringing small cars into [the U.S.] market," observes one analyst. But Mulally remains convinced that consumers around the world really all want the same things: safety, technology, fuel efficiency, and an attractive appearance. "You look at the reasons people buy vehicles,

and all those requirements [around the world] are coming together," he insists. Mulally concedes that marketing messages will have to be tailored to reach different audiences. "This is not a one-size-fits-all effort," he remarks. "But the diversity of the marketing is created by the customers we want to reach, and not by the differences in the vehicles."

The Focus, whose name reflects Mulally's vision for unifying Ford under a single

goal, is just one of several models that will eventually be redesigned and marketed as world cars. "The Focus represents the first tangible evidence of a global strategy," notes an auto industry consultant. "For the first time, Ford is executing it and not just talking about it." The strategy is working. Recently, Ford posted a $2.7 billion annual profit, its first in several years. It was the only U.S. automaker to declare itself in the black.[1]

Ford Motor Company began with a single focus: the black Model T. After more than a century in business, during which the company swelled to become a giant conglomerate of brands, Ford is returning to its roots. The company, which has for decades been known for its gas guzzling trucks and SUVs, is scaling back *and* expanding at the same time by marketing a single model—the Ford Focus—for sale around the world. In addition, Ford has made a commitment to producing more fuel-efficient vehicles in its lineup

(the Focus is one such vehicle). Within a few years, consumers will begin to think of Ford as a firm that offers global, environmentally friendly vehicles.

- Despite a 14 percent decline across the industry, Ford's hybrid vehicles, including the Escape and Fusion, have experienced a 73 percent increase in sales. "Hybrid customers are increasingly considering Ford," says David Finnegan, Ford hybrid marketing manager. Many of these customers are actually switch-

ing to Ford from Toyota and Honda. How does this strategy dovetail with the launch of the Ford Focus and the firm's commitment to a single vision?

- Ford has ventured into the use of social media to market its new vehicles, including Digital Snippets and Social Media Press Releases (SMPRs). How do you think social networking can help Ford get the message of "One Ford . . . One Team . . . One Plan . . . One Goal" across to consumers around the world?

chapter overview

> "More and more consumers are purchasing smaller, more fuel-efficient vehicles such as the Ford Focus, Fusion, and Escape. The market for large trucks and SUVs is dwindling. Are fuel-efficient vehicles the wave of the future? Should we commit to building more of them and feature them prominently in our marketing?"

> "We have fewer customers eating at our restaurant on weekends. Should we revamp our menu? Lower our prices? Use special promotions? Update the dining room décor?"

> "Recent marketing research shows that we are not reaching our customer target—consumers in their early to mid-20s. Should we consider another advertising agency?"

briefly speaking

" Those who look only to the past or present are certain to miss the future."

—John F. Kennedy
(1917–1963)
35th president of the United States

Marketers face strategic questions every day—planning strategy is a critical part of their job. The marketplace changes continually in response to changes in consumer tastes and expectations, technological developments, competitors' actions, economic trends, and political and legal events, as well as product innovations and pressures from suppliers and distributors. Although the causes of these changes often lie outside a marketer's control, effective planning can anticipate many of the changes.

When the price of gas and jet fuel soared recently, travelers opted to stay closer to home—taking "staycations" instead of booking vacations to exotic, faraway places. This represents an opportunity for places like Ocean City, Maryland, and Branson, Missouri. Local water parks and amusement parks, nearby lakes, indoor playgrounds or gyms, and restaurants can market themselves as potential alternatives. Any destination that promotes itself to potential vacationers within a short drive could find itself adding up the profits.

This chapter provides an important foundation for analyzing all aspects of marketing by demonstrating the importance of gathering reliable information to create an effective plan. These activities provide a structure for a firm to use its unique strengths. Marketing planning identifies the markets a company can best serve as well as the most appropriate mix of approaches to satisfy the customers in those markets. While this chapter focuses on planning, we will examine in greater detail the task of marketing research and decision making in Chapter 8.

Marketing Planning: The Basis for Strategy and Tactics

Everyone plans. We plan which academic courses we want to take, which movie we want to see, and which outfit to wear to a party. We plan where we want to live and what career we want to pursue. Marketers plan as well. **Planning** is the process of anticipating future events and conditions and determining the best way to achieve organizational objectives. Of course, before marketing planning can even begin, an organization must define its objectives. Planning is a continuous process that includes identifying objectives and then determining the actions through which a firm can attain those objectives. The planning process creates a blueprint for marketers, executives, production staff, and everyone else in the organization to follow for achieving organizational objectives. It also defines checkpoints so that people within the organization can compare actual performance with expectations to indicate whether current activities are moving the organization toward its objectives.

Planning is important for both large and small companies. For years, Sir Richard Branson—founder of the airline Virgin Galactic—dreamed of launching a spaceship designed for commer-

planning Process of anticipating future events and conditions and of determining the best way to achieve organizational objectives.

Virgin Galactic founder Sir Richard Branson has been looking toward commercial space travel for years. His planning has begun to pay off. After the successful launch of a prototype, the company is now working on a craft designed for commercial use.

© WENN/NEWSCOM

cial travel. The dream required complex design and engineering plans, including the launch of prototypes and rigorous rounds of safety testing. After one of the prototypes became the first privately owned, manned craft to reach space, the company's engineers went to work on a similar craft designed for commercial use, called SpaceShipTwo. Meanwhile, the idea of space travel has been marketed to wealthy clients, nearly 300 of whom have either made a deposit or paid the full $200,000 price to be among the first in line for the historic trip. If the idea catches on, Branson and Virgin Galactic will have positioned themselves strategically to become the first—and possibly the only—firm to offer commercial space travel for the near future.[2] Here on earth—and at the other end of the size spectrum—Shuttleworth, a small firm that manufactures conveyors, had to reevaluate its planning as its core business in electronics began to shrink. The company refocused its efforts on designing and building solar panel conveyors. Its new products have won acclaim, new customers, and a revitalized business.[3]

marketing planning
Implementing planning activities devoted to achieving marketing objectives.

Marketing planning—implementing planning activities devoted to achieving marketing objectives—establishes the basis for a marketing strategy. Product lines, pricing decisions, selection of appropriate distribution channels, and decisions relating to promotional campaigns all depend on plans formulated within the marketing organization. In today's boundaryless organizations, many planning activities take place over the Internet with *virtual conferences*—teleconferences with computer interfaces. These conferences represent a new way to build relationships among people who are in different geographic locations. The "Career Readiness" feature describes how effectively these meetings can work.

career readiness   Ⓟlan the Most Effective Virtual Meeting

many companies now encourage virtual meetings to save time and travel costs. The recent economic downturn made virtual meetings not just popular but essential. Virtual meetings offer the opportunity for people to gather from across the country or around the world, any time of day or night. While this may seem like the ideal way to bring people together, there can be some pitfalls. Holding a conference by phone or Internet can be most effective if you follow these guidelines:

- Schedule the meeting in advance, and be sure everyone is available to sign on at the appointed time and remind participants of the time and duration of the meeting ahead of time.

- Prepare for the conference just as you would for an in-person meeting. Set goals for the meeting. Circulate an agenda, including your contact information. Have all your facts and figures in front of you.

- Begin the meeting with a quick introduction or reintroduction of all participants and identify the goals. Request that anyone

who needs to leave the conversation because of prior commitments announce when she or he is doing so.

- If your meeting doesn't involve video, state your name, such as, "This is Emma," at the beginning of each time you speak. Speak clearly and slowly. Ask for agreement or disagreement from others, one by one.

- Do not engage in other tasks during the conference, regardless of whether other participants can see you. For example, don't read a memo or check your e-mail during the meeting. Keep your full attention on the conference at hand.

- At the conclusion of the conference, designate someone to prepare minutes highlighting discussion points of the meeting and any conclusions, and e-mail them to all participants.

Sources: Kate Harper, "Virtual Meetings That Work," *Kate Harper Coaching*, www. kateharper.com, accessed February 4, 2010; "Virtual Meeting Etiquette," *HR.com*, http://www.hr.com, accessed February 4, 2010; Cheryl Waters Likins, "The Best Practices for Facilitation of Virtual Meetings," *eHow*, http://www.ehow.com; "Virtual Meeting: Effective Meetings Enabled by Technology," *Persuasive Speeches Now*, http://www.persuasive-speechesnow.com, accessed January 12, 2010.

An important trend in marketing planning centers on relationship marketing, a firm's effort to develop long-term, cost-effective links with individual customers and suppliers for mutual benefit. Good relationships with customers can arm a firm with vital strategic weapons, and that's as true in business-to-business industries as anywhere else.

Many companies now include relationship-building goals and strategies in their plans. Relationship marketers frequently maintain databases to track customer preferences. These marketers may also manipulate product spreadsheets to answer what-if questions related to prices and marketing performance. At Procter & Gamble, the inspiration for new or better products often comes from customers themselves. The company operates in more than 150 countries with 138,000 employees, many of whom serve as the eyes and ears of the firm. Some P&G executives and marketers actually spend time in the homes of consumers, observing how they cook and eat meals, when they play, and where they shop. Other employees are trained simply to have conversations with friends and family about their lifestyles and the goods or services they use. All of this interaction helps build relationships, and the information helps develop products.[4]

Strategic Planning versus Tactical Planning

Planning often is classified on the basis of its scope or breadth. Some extremely broad plans focus on long-range organizational objectives that will significantly affect the firm for five or more years. Other more targeted plans cover the objectives of individual business units over shorter periods.

Strategic planning can be defined as the process of determining an organization's primary objectives and adopting courses of action that will achieve these objectives. This process includes, of course, allocation of necessary resources. The word *strategy* dates back to a Greek term meaning "the general's art." Strategic planning has a critical impact on a firm's destiny because it provides long-term direction for its decision makers.

Strategic planning is complemented by **tactical planning**, which guides the implementation of activities specified in the strategic plan. Unlike strategic plans, tactical plans typically address shorter-term actions that focus on current and near-future activities that a firm must complete to implement its larger strategies. Sometimes tactical planning requires swift decision making and actions. Although Toyota's long-range strategic planning involves maintaining its status at the number-one automaker in the world, when the firm was faced with growing reports of stuck accelerators, its officials had to devise and implement quick tactics. Toyota recalled more than 2.3 million vehicles in the United States alone, and offered a free repair on each vehicle. Then, Toyota had to work to regain the trust of its customers and restore its reputation for quality.[5]

1 Distinguish between strategic planning and tactical planning.

strategic planning
Process of determining an organization's primary objectives and adopting courses of action that will achieve these objectives.

tactical planning
Planning that guides the implementation of activities specified in the strategic plan.

Tactical planning can require swift decision making and actions. When Toyota was faced with growing reports of stuck accelerators, officials had to act quickly, recalling more than 2.3 million vehicles.

assessment check

1. Define *planning*.
2. Give an example of strategic planning and tactical planning.

Planning at Different Organizational Levels

Explain how marketing plans differ at various levels in an organization.

Planning is a major responsibility for every manager, so managers at all organizational levels devote portions of their workdays to planning. Top management—the board of directors, chief executive officers (CEOs), chief operating officers (COOs), and functional vice presidents, such as chief marketing officers—spend greater proportions of their time planning than do middle-level and supervisory-level managers. Also, top managers usually focus their planning on long-range strategic issues. In contrast, middle-level managers—such as advertising executives, regional sales managers, and marketing research directors—tend to focus on operational planning, which includes creating and implementing tactical plans for their own units. Supervisors often develop specific programs to meet goals in their areas of responsibility. Table 2.1 summarizes the types of planning undertaken at various organizational levels.

When it is most effective, the planning process includes input from a wide range of sources: employees, suppliers, and customers. Some marketing experts advocate developing a network of "influencers"—people who have influence over other people's opinions through authority, visibility, or expertise—to provide input and spread the word about company plans and products. According to a recent survey, 66 percent of responding marketers said that they plan to invest more heavily in social media marketing in the coming year, indicating that this method of communicating with potential customers is gaining rapidly in popularity.[6]

assessment check

1. How do marketing plans vary at different levels of the organization?
2. Why is it important to get input from others when planning?

table 2.1   Planning at Different Managerial Levels

Management Level	Types of Planning Emphasized at This Level	Examples
Top Management Board of directors Chief executive officer Chief operating officer Chief financial officer	Strategic planning	Organizationwide objectives; fundamental strategies; long-term plans; total budget
Middle Management General sales manager Team leader Director of marketing research	Tactical planning	Quarterly and semiannual plans; business unit budgets; divisional policies and procedures
Supervisory Management Regional sales manager Supervisor—telemarketing office	Operational planning	Daily and weekly plans; unit budgets; departmental rules and procedures

Steps in the Marketing Planning Process

The marketing planning process begins at the corporate level with the definition of a firm's mission. It then determines its objectives, assesses its resources, and evaluates environmental risks and opportunities. Guided by this information, marketers within each business unit then formulate a marketing strategy, implement the strategy through operating plans, and gather feedback to monitor and adapt strategies when necessary. Figure 2.1 shows the basic steps in the process.

3 Identify the steps in the marketing planning process.

Defining the Organization's Mission and Objectives

The planning process begins with defining the firm's **mission**, the essential purpose that differentiates the company from others. The mission statement specifies the organization's overall goals and operational scope and provides general guidelines for future management actions. Adjustments in this statement reflect changing business environments and management philosophies.

Although business writer Peter Drucker cautioned that an effective mission statement should be brief enough "to fit on a T-shirt," organizations typically define themselves with slightly longer statements. But they often condense their mission statement into a catchy slogan such as those that follow:

- Sephora: "The beauty authority."
- American Cancer Society: "The official sponsor of birthdays."
- Microsoft Office: "Real life tools."
- The Nature Conservancy: "Protecting nature. Preserving life."
- Infiniti: "Inspired performance."
- IBM: "Welcome to the decade of smart."

An organization lays out its basic objectives, or goals, in its complete mission statement. These objectives guide development of supporting marketing objectives and plans. Soundly conceived objectives should state specific intentions such as the following:

Generate a 15 percent profit over the next 24 months.

Add 25 new outlets within the next year.

Improve 5 products within the next 6 months.

Enter the Chinese market by the year 2015.

Cut manufacturing costs by 10 percent.

Reduce waste by 20 percent.

mission Essential purpose that differentiates one company from others.

briefly speaking

"Marketing and innovation produce results: All the rest are costs."

—Peter F. Drucker
(1909–2005)
U.S. management theorist

figure 2.1

The Marketing Planning Process

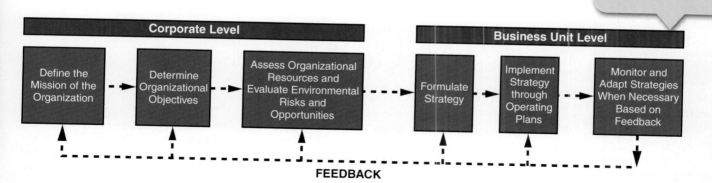

FEEDBACK

marketing strategy
Overall, companywide
program for selecting a
particular target market and
then satisfying consumers
in that market through the
marketing mix.

Assessing Organizational Resources and Evaluating Environmental Risks and Opportunities

The third step of the marketing planning process is to assess an organization's strengths, weaknesses, and available opportunities. Organizational resources include the capabilities of the firm's production, marketing, finance, technology, and employees. An organization's planners pinpoint its strengths and weaknesses. Strengths help them set objectives, develop plans for meeting those objectives, and take advantage of marketing opportunities.

Chapter 3 will discuss environmental factors that affect marketing opportunities. Environmental effects can emerge both from within the organization and from the external environment. For example, social media have transformed interpersonal communications as well as communications between companies and their customers.

Formulating, Implementing, and Monitoring a Marketing Strategy

Once a firm's marketers figure out their company's best opportunities, they can develop a marketing plan designed to meet the overall objectives. A good marketing plan revolves around an efficient, flexible, and adaptable marketing strategy.

A **marketing strategy** is an overall, companywide program for selecting a particular target market and then satisfying consumers in that market through a careful blending of the elements of the marketing mix—product, distribution, promotion, and price—each of which is a component of the overall marketing strategy.

In the two final steps of the planning process, marketers put the marketing strategy into action; then they monitor performance to ensure that objectives are achieved. Sometimes strategies need to be modified if the product's or company's actual performance is not in line with expected results. When cash was flowing and real estate prices were sky high, Tishman Speyer Properties and BlackRock Realty jointly purchased two large apartment complexes in New York City for a record $5.4 billion. They planned to convert several thousand rent-controlled apartments in the complex to luxury units that would command top dollar, earning them a hefty profit in the end. But the strategy backfired as New York's hot housing market cooled too quickly, tenants in the rent-controlled apartments fought back, and a state court ruled that $200 million in the proposed rent increases was illegal. Ultimately, the partnership was forced to turn the properties over to its creditors.[7]

Sometimes a marketing strategy backfires. This can happen rapidly in the case of celebrity endorsements, as described in the "Solving an Ethical Controversy" feature.

assessment check

1. Distinguish between an organization's mission and its objectives.
2. What is the importance of the final step in the marketing planning process?

4 **Describe successful planning tools and techniques, including Porter's Five Forces model, first and second mover strategies, SWOT analysis, and the strategic window.**

Successful Strategies: Tools and Techniques

We can identify a number of successful marketing planning tools and techniques. This section discusses four of them: Porter's Five Forces model, first and second mover strategies, SWOT analysis, and the strategic window. All planning strategies have the goal of creating a sustainable competitive advantage for a firm in which other companies simply cannot provide the same value to their customers that the firm does—no matter how hard they try.

solving an ethical controversy

Tiger Woods Drives His Career into the Rough

Hiring celebrities to endorse a line of products is common practice among marketers. When the celebrity is a popular entertainer or successful athlete, marketers are betting their products will enjoy the same popularity and success. But when the celebrity falls from grace—as Tiger Woods did when the scandal about his personal life made the news—the product sales can land in the weeds. Woods, who hid from the press as soon as the story broke, was accustomed to earning nearly $110 million in endorsements from companies including Nike, Gillette, AT&T, Accenture, and PepsiCo. One by one, these sponsors scratched Woods from their roster.

Should companies hold the celebrities who endorse their products accountable for their personal actions?

PRO

1. A celebrity who endorses a product is using his or her personal brand image to create a bond with consumers and boost sales. If a celebrity's image becomes tarnished, then consumers might abandon the product, costing the firm lost sales and—by association—a tarnished brand as well.

2. The high fees paid to a celebrity like Tiger Woods are marketing costs that are ultimately passed along to the consumer in the form of product price. So if the celebrity causes damage to the marketing campaign, the advertiser loses credibility and sales, and consumers don't get what they paid for.

CON

1. An endorsement is a marketing agreement dealing with a firm's goods and services—and does not apply to the celebrity's personal life. Woods's personal crisis is not related to how well he represents the game of golf or the products he endorses. Consumers are savvy enough to discriminate between the two.

2. One celebrity's mistakes are not powerful enough to cause an entire marketing campaign—or sport—to crumble. If a firm's products are of high quality, customers will continue to buy them anyway.

Summary

The Tiger Woods story created enough turmoil that marketers are now reevaluating their relationships with celebrities. "I don't think there's any question, at least in the short term, that advertisers will be more careful" about hiring athletes and other stars to endorse their products, observes Irving Rein, a professor at Northwestern University. In addition, marketers will likely insist on contract clauses or written statements prohibiting certain behaviors on the part of celebrity endorsers. "There might [even be] private investigators," notes one advertising executive. "These companies have the resources to do it." Meanwhile, Tiger Woods is out of the advertising game—at least for now.

Sources: Rhea Drysdale, "How Tiger Woods Can Rebuild His Image Online," *CNN*, March 1, 2010, http://www.cnn.com/2010/TECH/03/01/tiger.woods.online.image/ index.html?section=cnn_latest; James Surowiecki, "Branded a Cheat," *The New Yorker*, December 21, 2009, http://0-www.lexisnexis.com.library.uark.edu; Nancy Dillon, "Shocked Advertisers Will Be on the Prowl for a 'Boy Scout,'" *Daily News*, December 15, 2009, http://www.dailynews.com; Dan Shingler, "Feeling Cheated as a Tiger Customer," *Crain's Cleveland Business*, December 14, 2009, http://0-www. lexisnexis.com.library.uark.edu; Ed Smith, "Is This the Time to Buy into the Woods Brand?," *The Times*, December 11, 2009, http://0-www.lexisnexis.com.library.uark. edu; "Advertisers Put Tiger Woods on Hold," *Bloomberg News*, December 10, 2009, http://www.fptradingesk.com.

Porter's Five Forces Model

A number of years ago, renowned business strategist Michael E. Porter identified five competitive forces that influence planning strategies in a model called **Porter's Five Forces.** Porter later updated his model to include the impact of the Internet on the strategies that businesses use. As illustrated in Figure 2.2, the five forces are potential new entrants, bargaining power of buyers, bargaining power of suppliers, threat of substitute products, and rivalry among competitors.

Potential new entrants sometimes are blocked by the cost or difficulty of entering a market. It is a lot more costly and complicated to begin building aircraft than it is to start up an Internet

Porter's Five Forces Model developed by strategy expert Michael Porter that identifies five competitive forces that influence planning strategies: the threat of new entrants, the bargaining power of buyers, the bargaining power of suppliers, the threat of substitute products, and rivalry among competitors.

figure 2.2

Porter's Five Forces Model

• Internet reduces barriers to entry

Potential New Entrants

• Internet blurs differences among competitors

Rivalry Among Competitors

Threat of Substitute Products

• Internet creates new substitution threats

Bargaining Power of Buyers

• Internet shifts greater power to end consumers

Bargaining Power of Suppliers

• Internet tends to increase bargaining power of suppliers

consulting business. The Internet has reduced the barriers to market entry in many industries. In fact, most businesses now view an Internet presence as a requirement for success. If customers have considerable bargaining power, they can greatly influence a firm's strategy. The Internet can increase a customer's buying power by providing information that might not otherwise be easily accessible such as alternate suppliers and price comparisons. Firms continue to compete to develop the most effective Internet marketing, because they know that customers are savvy users of technology. Microsoft recently announced the launch of its AdECN online advertising exchange, to compete with Google's already successful venture, which allows ad sellers and buyers to negotiate in real time.[8]

The number of suppliers available to a manufacturer or retailer affects their bargaining power. If a seafood restaurant in the Midwest has only one supplier of Maine lobsters, that supplier has significant bargaining power. But seafood restaurants along the coast of Maine have many lobster suppliers, which gives their suppliers less bargaining power.

If customers have the opportunity to replace a company's products with goods or services from a competing firm or industry, the company's marketers may have to find a new market, change prices, or compete in other ways to maintain an advantage. McDonald's made what

When McDonald's started offering high-end coffee drinks, they entered into direct competition with Starbucks. The threat of a substitute product can create a need for a company's marketers to find new ways to compete.

© MATTHIAS SCHRADER/DPA/LANDOV

some considered a bold move when the firm announced that it would be offering lattes, cappuccinos, espressos, and other coffee drinks—in direct competition with Starbucks and Dunkin' Donuts. If McDonald's can serve premium beverages at a competitive price, it may become a major player in the coffee game. As McDonald's USA president Don Thompson says, "We want to be a beverage destination. For us, growing markets with great margins is the place to be."[9]

The four previous forces influence the rivalry among competitors. In addition, issues such as cost and differentiation or lack of differentiation of products—along with the Internet—influence the strategies that companies use to stand out from their competitors. With increased availability of information, which tends to level the playing field, rivalry heats up among competitors who try to differentiate themselves from the crowd.

First Mover and Second Mover Strategies

Some firms like to adopt a **first mover strategy**, attempting to capture the greatest market share and develop long-term relationships by being the first to enter the market with a good or service, as Virgin Galactic hopes to do by being the first to offer commercial space travel. Being first may also refer to entering new markets with existing products or creating significant innovations that effectively turn an old product into a new one. Naturally, this strategy has its risks—companies that follow can learn from mistakes by first movers. Some well-known first movers include Ford, IBM, Apple, Amazon.com, and MySpace. Each of these firms has stumbled at one time or another, but each is still in business. Ford is poised to make a remarkable comeback, and IBM has risen from the ashes several times.

Businesses often thrive on a **second mover strategy**, observing closely the innovations of first movers and then improving on them to gain advantage in the marketplace. Facebook appeared after MySpace. Target has followed in the footsteps of Walmart. Sometimes first movers are completely replaced by second movers and disappear from the marketplace altogether, such as Pan Am Airlines.

first mover strategy
Theory advocating that the company first to offer a product in a marketplace will be the long-term market winner.

second mover strategy Theory that advocates observing closely the innovations of first movers and then improving on them to gain advantage in the marketplace.

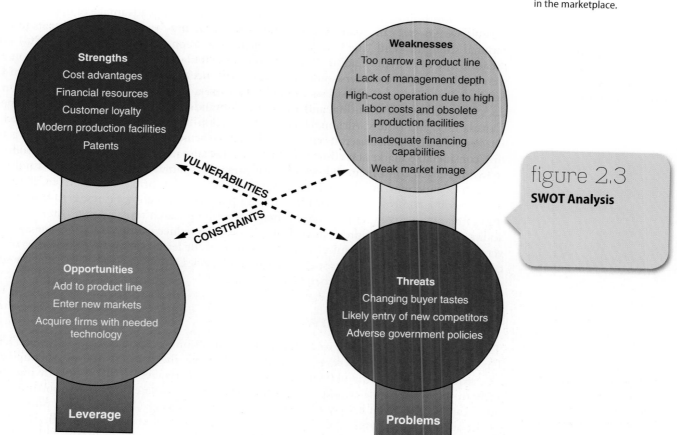

Strengths
Cost advantages
Financial resources
Customer loyalty
Modern production facilities
Patents

Weaknesses
Too narrow a product line
Lack of management depth
High-cost operation due to high labor costs and obsolete production facilities
Inadequate financing capabilities
Weak market image

VULNERABILITIES

CONSTRAINTS

Opportunities
Add to product line
Enter new markets
Acquire firms with needed technology

Threats
Changing buyer tastes
Likely entry of new competitors
Adverse government policies

Leverage

Problems

figure 2.3
SWOT Analysis

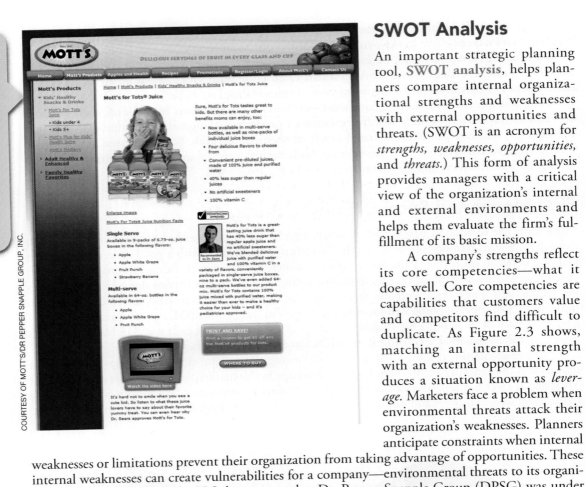

When marketing research revealed that parents were adding water to their children's juice drinks to reduce calories, DPSG departed from its core competencies and came up with Mott's for Tots, a new version of apple juice containing 40 percent less sugar.

COURTESY OF MOTT'S/DR PEPPER SNAPPLE GROUP, INC.

SWOT Analysis

An important strategic planning tool, **SWOT analysis**, helps planners compare internal organizational strengths and weaknesses with external opportunities and threats. (SWOT is an acronym for *strengths, weaknesses, opportunities,* and *threats.*) This form of analysis provides managers with a critical view of the organization's internal and external environments and helps them evaluate the firm's fulfillment of its basic mission.

A company's strengths reflect its core competencies—what it does well. Core competencies are capabilities that customers value and competitors find difficult to duplicate. As Figure 2.3 shows, matching an internal strength with an external opportunity produces a situation known as *leverage.* Marketers face a problem when environmental threats attack their organization's weaknesses. Planners anticipate constraints when internal

SWOT analysis
Review that helps planners compare internal organizational strengths and weaknesses with external opportunities and threats.

weaknesses or limitations prevent their organization from taking advantage of opportunities. These internal weaknesses can create vulnerabilities for a company—environmental threats to its organizational strength. While the U.S. beverage maker Dr. Pepper Snapple Group (DPSG) was under the umbrella of Britain's Cadbury, sales of its once popular drinks fizzled as distribution networks were neglected and marketers sometimes waited for weeks or months for decisions from Cadbury headquarters. But once DPSG successfully achieved a spin-off, it could concentrate on what it does best: making, distributing, and selling its 58 brands which include Dr. Pepper, Snapple, 7Up, Canada Dry, and others. Although soda consumption in the United States has dropped, sales of Dr. Pepper actually increased recently—and the firm's stock along with it. And DPSG is now putting considerable marketing effort into 7-Eleven, because no matter how good the products are, if they don't reach consumers they won't sell. "Strategy is fantastic," observes Tony English, DPSG director of supermarket sales in Texas. "But execution is what brings the results in."[10]

Even if a company focuses on its core competencies, sometimes it needs to broaden its offerings to maintain a competitive edge. When marketing research revealed that parents were actually adding water to their children's juice drinks in order to reduce calories, DPSG came up with a new version of its Mott's apple juice, containing 40 percent less sugar but a full serving of juice. It's called Mott's for Tots. Another success has been Canada Dry Green Tea Ginger Ale, for consumers who are looking for the health benefits of green tea.[11]

The Strategic Window

strategic window
Limited periods when key requirements of a market and a firm's particular competencies best fit together.

The success of products is also influenced by conditions in the market. Professor Derek Abell has suggested the term **strategic window** to define the limited periods during which the key requirements of a market and the particular competencies of a firm best fit together.[12] The view through a strategic window shows planners a way to relate potential opportunities to company capabilities. Such a view requires a thorough analysis of (1) current and projected external environmental conditions; (2) current and projected internal company capabilities; and (3) how, whether, and when the firm can feasibly reconcile environmental conditions and company capabilities by implementing one or more marketing strategies.

Large and small businesses can make the most of strategic windows. Despite its gargantuan size, Walmart finds ways to make the most of these opportunities. During the recent economic downturn, Walmart marketed its low prices and exceptional values at every opportunity—reassuring existing customers they were getting the best deal and attracting consumers who might not have considered buying their groceries, clothing, household items at Walmart in the past. The firm's updated slogan—"Save money. Live better."—champions the average consumer who is looking for value. Walmart's Web site provides tips for money-saving meals and the opportunity to sign up for e-mail alerts to price rollbacks and special offers. Marketers hope that when the economy rebounds, many of these shoppers will have become loyal Walmart customers.[13]

Small businesses can benefit from the same strategic window. As consumers tighten their belts, pawn shops and thrift stores often experience an increase in traffic. Instead of donating designer clothing to a not-for-profit organization like the Salvation Army, a well-dressed consumer might take those items to a local consignment shop—then make a few purchases while there. "More people are trying resale than may have done before," notes Adele Meyer of the National Association for Resale and Thrift Shops.[14]

assessment check

1. Briefly explain each of Porter's Five Forces.
2. What are the benefits and drawbacks of a first mover strategy?
3. What are the four components of the SWOT analysis? What is a strategic window?

Elements of a Marketing Strategy

Success for a product in the marketplace—whether it is a tangible good, a service, a cause, a person, a place, or an organization—depends on an effective marketing strategy. It's one thing to develop a great product, but if customers don't get the message about it, the product will die. An effective marketing strategy reaches the right buyers at the right time, persuades them to try the product, and develops a strong relationship with them over time. The basic elements of a marketing strategy consist of (1) the target market and (2) the marketing mix variables of product, distribution, promotion, and price that combine to satisfy the needs of the target market. The outer circle in Figure 2.4 lists environmental characteristics that provide the framework within which marketing strategies are planned.

> **5** Identify the basic elements of a marketing strategy.

The Target Market

A customer-driven organization begins its overall strategy with a detailed description of its target market: the group of people toward whom the firm aims its marketing efforts and ultimately its merchandise. Kohl's department stores serve a target market of consumers purchasing for themselves and their families. Other companies, such as Boeing, market most of their products to business buyers such as American Airlines and government purchasers. Still other firms provide goods and services to retail and wholesale buyers. In every instance, however, marketers pinpoint their target markets as accurately as possible. Although the concept of dividing markets into specific segments is discussed in more detail in Chapter 9, it's important to understand the idea of targeting a market from the outset.

Although it may be hard to imagine the classic Oreo cookie as anything other than two discs of chocolate with a white cream filling, Kraft Foods has reformulated the favorite to market it in China. The Chinese version is four layers of long, thin biscuits coated in chocolate, which is more appealing to consumers there. The move reflects Kraft Foods CEO Irene Rosenfeld's strategy of placing more authority in the hands of local business units around the world, trusting that people who live and work there know better what consumers want than the top Kraft Foods executives located at the firm's Illinois headquarters.[15] In addition to the Oreo reformulation, Kraft Foods has recently opened a new cookie factory in Russia named Bolshevik Biscuits.[16]

Diversity plays an ever-increasing role in targeting markets. According to the U.S. Census Bureau, the rapidly growing Hispanic population in the United States has surpassed African Americans as the largest minority group. The census reports more than 48 million Hispanics in America, or nearly 16 percent of the U.S. population.[17] With this phenomenal growth, marketers would be wise to pay attention to these and other markets—including women, seniors, and children of baby boomers—as they develop goods and services to offer consumers.

Targeting consumers in specific global markets also represents a challenge—and an opportunity. India is an enormous market that is culturally diverse within itself, containing 27 geographical states, numerous languages and religious practices, and a variety of lifestyles. Traditional Indian culture is infused with Western influences. And while nearly half of all Indian citizens earn less than $1 per day, there are still those consumers who long for—and can afford—brands like Baskin-Robbins, Tropicana, and even Louis Vuitton. Marketers make mistakes. Kellogg's failed in its introduction of crispy breakfast cereals because the company didn't realize that Indian consumers don't like cold milk. But marketers can be successful if they tailor their practices to Indian preferences. Using traditional Indian *kirana*-style markets (small shops), Walmart has made a successful entry into retailing with smaller shops in urban areas and low prices.[18]

Marketing Mix Variables

marketing mix
Blending of the four strategy elements—product, distribution, promotion, and pricing—to fit the needs and preferences of a specific target market.

After marketers select a target market, they direct their company's activities toward profitably satisfying that segment. Although they must manipulate thousands of variables to reach this goal, marketing decision making can be divided into four strategies: product, distribution, promotion, and pricing strategies. The total package forms the **marketing mix**—the blend of four strategic elements to fit the needs and preferences of a specific target market. While the fourfold classification is useful to study and analyze, remember that the marketing mix can—and should—be an ever-changing combination of variables to achieve success.

Figure 2.4 illustrates that the central focus of the marketing mix variables is the choice of the target market. In addition, decisions about product, distribution, promotion, and price are affected by the environmental factors in the outer circle of the figure. The environmental variables may play a major role in the success of a marketing program, and marketers must consider their probable effects.

PRODUCT STRATEGY

In marketing, the word *product* means more than a good, service, or idea. Product is a broad concept that also encompasses the satisfaction of all consumer needs in relation to a good, service, or

mktg: *success*

In-N-Out Burgers Sell Themselves

Background. In 1948, Harry and Esther Snyder opened the first drive-through burger stand in California. They named their new business after this novel idea: In-N-Out Burgers. The Snyders' marketing strategy was simple. "Give customers the freshest, highest quality foods you can buy and provide them with friendly service in a sparkling clean environment," said Harry. This product strategy remains in place today.

The Challenge. Consumers flocked to the first In-N-Out stand because the idea of a drive-through was new and because the burgers were hot and fresh. But 60 years later, In-N-Out faces competition from major players like McDonald's and Burger King. So the challenge is to continue enticing hungry customers.

The Strategy. While other fast-food chains have grown by offering franchises and expanded menus, In-N-Out Burger has done neither. Although there are now more than 230 locations in the chain, they are all company owned, ensuring tight control over

idea. So product strategy involves more than just deciding what goods or services the firm should offer to a group of consumers. It also includes decisions about customer service, package design, brand names, trademarks, patents, warranties, the lifecycle of a product, positioning the product in the marketplace, and new-product development.

The "Marketing Success" feature illustrates how California-based In-N-Out Burger relies on the high quality of a limited menu to attract hungry customers.

DISTRIBUTION STRATEGY

Marketers develop distribution strategies to ensure that consumers find their products in the proper quantities at the right times and places. Distribution decisions involve modes of transportation, warehousing, inventory control, order processing, and selection of marketing channels. Marketing channels are made up of institutions such as retailers and wholesalers—intermediaries that may be involved in a product's movement from producer to final consumer.

Technology continually opens new channels of distribution in many industries. The Internet has caused the biggest revolution in distribution since the mail-order catalog. Computer software and digital music files are obvious candidates, but everything from DVDs to motorcycles to houses can be found on the Web. For a fee, Amazon.com's Kindle allows consumers to download and read books and periodicals that were once the domain of the printed page. Some publications, like *BusinessWeek* and *The Wall Street Journal*, offer both online and print content, the online version often for free (although that is beginning to change).[19] But other publications have abandoned print altogether or were established entirely online in the first place.

PROMOTION STRATEGY

Promotion is the communications link between sellers and buyers. Organizations use varied ways to send messages about their goods, services, and ideas. They may communicate messages directly through salespeople or indirectly through advertisements and promotions. Promotions often offer a product at a reduced price for a limited time, bundle two or more products together, or give away a premium (such as a toy) with purchase. During one week, KFC gave away servings of its new grilled chicken in order to get consumers to try it. Over a period of months, Shaw's supermarkets gave

figure 2.4

Element of a Marketing Strategy and Its Environmental Framework

quality and management. And the menu features only four basic menu items: hamburgers, cheeseburgers, the Double-Double (two hamburger patties and two slices of cheese), and French fries. The food is made to order, and no microwaves, heat lamps, or freezers can be found at any In-N-Out Burger restaurant.

The Outcome. In-N-Out Burger is a favorite stop among Hollywood celebrities and average consumers. The food is fresh and people keep coming back for more. In addition, In-N-Out employees stay with the firm far longer than the norm in the fast-food business, because they are paid well and receive benefits. Workers who are dedicated

to serving the best burger and fries in town attract hungry consumers who become loyal customers.

Sources: In-N-Out Burger Web site, http://www.in-n-out.com, accessed February 5, 2010; "In-N-Out Burgers Company Profile," *Yahoo! Finance*, http://biz.yahoo.com, accessed February 5, 2010; Stacy Perman, "The Secret Sauce at In-N-Out Burger," *Business Week*, April 20, 2009, pp. 68–69.

© AP IMAGES/MARK LENNIHAN

Technology continually opens new channels of distribution. Amazon. com's Kindle allows consumers to download and read periodicals that were once available only in print, such as *The Wall Street Journal.*

shoppers points toward discounts at their local Irving gas stations. And in one six-week period, Dunkin' Donuts gave customers a chance to register their frequent-purchase DD Cards and receive a $2 rebate.[20]

In developing a promotional strategy, marketers blend the various elements of promotion to communicate most effectively with their target market. Many companies use an approach called integrated marketing communications (IMC) to coordinate all promotional activities so that the consumer receives a unified and consistent message.

Consumers might receive newsletters, e-mail updates, discount coupons, catalogs, invitations to company-sponsored events, and any number of other types of marketing communications about a product. Honda dealers mail maintenance and service reminders to their customers. Kroger supermarkets place discount coupons in local newspapers. A political candidate may send volunteer workers through a neighborhood to invite voters to a local reception.

PRICING STRATEGY

Pricing strategy deals with the methods of setting profitable and justifiable prices. It is closely regulated and subject to considerable public scrutiny. One of the many factors that influence a marketer's pricing strategy is competition. The computer industry has become all too familiar with price cuts by both current competitors and new market entrants. After years of steady growth, the market has become saturated with low-cost computers, driving down profit margins even farther. A good pricing strategy should create value for customers, building and strengthening their relationship with a firm and its products. But sometimes conditions in the external marketing environment cause difficulties in pricing strategies. Political unrest overseas, the soaring price of fuel, or a freeze that destroys crops could all affect the price of goods and services. If the economy is booming, consumers generally have more confidence and are willing to shop more often and pay more for discretionary goods. But when the economy takes a downturn, consumers look for bargains—they want high quality at low prices. It is a challenge for marketers to strike the right balance in order to make enough profits to survive and grow. Currently, sales at luxury retailers like Saks and Abercrombie & Fitch are down. But sales at local dollar stores, cheaper supermarkets, and the larger discount retailers are much stronger.[21]

assessment check

1. What are the two components of every marketing strategy?
2. Identify the four strategic elements of the marketing mix.

The Marketing Environment

6 Describe the environmental characteristics that influence strategic decisions.

Marketers do not make decisions about target markets and marketing mix variables in a vacuum. They must take into account the dynamic nature of the five dimensions of the marketing environment shown back in Figure 2.4: competitive, political-legal, economic, technological, and social-cultural factors. It's important to note that these five dimensions overlap, interact, and fluctuate.

Concerns about the natural environment have led to new and tighter regulations on air and water pollution, which affect the political-legal environment in which marketers operate. Efforts toward sustainability are now social-cultural factors as well because consumer awareness is turning

Automobile engineers have turned public concern and legal issues concerning the natural environment into opportunities by developing hybrid cars, biodiesel cars, and electric cars, such as this Nissan Leaf.

into consumer preference. Automobile engineers, for instance, have turned public concerns and legal issues into opportunities by developing hybrid cars, autos that run on biodiesel, and electric vehicles. In fact, the race to bring to market the most fuel-efficient vehicles for the future has become extremely competitive.

Businesses are increasingly looking to foreign shores for new growth markets. Of course, these opportunities represent economic, political-legal, and social-cultural challenges as well. The U.S. Department of Commerce provides resources, including contact lists and matching services for companies trying to enter the market in Mexico. Its Gold Key Matching Service helps develop partnerships between U.S. firms and local firms in Mexico. "Mexico has a high-context culture where personal relationships matter," says the department Web site. "Your competition is on the ground knocking on doors. Our industry specialists can put you face-to-face with prescreened companies that have expressed interest in working with you, enabling you to make the most efficient use of your time."[22]

Technology continually changes the marketing environment. Marketers are now increasing efforts to get their messages to consumers via smartphone. Although smartphone advertising still represents a small percentage of most firm's advertising budgets, the medium is receiving a lot of attention. Pizza Hut has launched an iPhone ordering app, and Victoria's Secret recently posted its Fashion Show app. During one campaign, Volkswagen offered a free iPhone racing app called Real Racing GTI, giving its target market (young customers) the first opportunity to test drive its newest model GTI. "Launching the all-new GTI via [iPhone app] allows us to connect with this savvy GTI consumer within his or her everyday life in a way that no 30-second spot ever could," said VW's marketing vice president Tim Ellis.[23]

In the competitive environment, some experts have coined the phrase *rule of three*, meaning that in any industry, the three strongest, most efficient companies dominate between 70 and 90 percent of the competitive market. Here are a few examples—all of which are household names:

Cereal manufacturers: General Mills, Kellogg's, Post

Running shoes: Nike, Fila USA, Reebok

Supermarkets: Walmart, Kroger, Supervalu

Pharmaceuticals: Merck, Pfizer, Bristol-Myers Squibb

Marketers are increasing efforts to get their messages to consumers via smartphone. Pizza Hut, for example, has launched an iPhone ordering app.

© J E BEAM PHOTOGRAPHY

While it may seem like an uphill battle for the remaining companies in any given industry, they can find a strategy for gaining competitive ground.

The social-cultural environment includes a variety of factors, including prevailing cultural norms. As the novelty of bidding for auction items on eBay has worn off for consumers who don't necessarily have the time or desire to wait several days or a week for auction results, eBay has begun to reshape itself. Fixed-price purchase items are becoming the new norm. The "Buy It Now" option on many auctions now accounts for more than 40 percent of all purchases made on eBay.[24] This new trend also reflects economic factors, including how much consumers are willing and able to spend.

The entire marketing environment provides a framework for all marketing activity. Marketers consider environmental dimensions when they develop strategies for segmenting and targeting markets and when they study consumer and organizational buying behavior.

 assessment check

1. What are the five dimensions of the marketing environment?
2. How is concern over the natural environment affecting the other dimensions?

Methods for Marketing Planning

7 Describe the methods for marketing planning, including business portfolio analysis and the BCG matrix.

As growing numbers of companies have discovered the benefits of effective marketing planning, they have developed planning methods to assist in this important function. This section discusses two useful methods: the strategic business unit concept and the market share/market growth matrix.

Business Portfolio Analysis

Although a small company may offer only a few items to its customers, a larger organization frequently offers and markets many products to widely diverse markets. Bank of America offers a wide range of financial products to businesses and consumers; Kraft Foods stocks supermarket shelves with everything from macaroni and cheese to mayonnaise. Top managers at these larger firms need a method for spotting product lines that deserve more investment as well as lines that aren't living up to expectations. So they conduct a portfolio analysis, in which they evaluate their company's products and divisions to determine the strongest and weakest. Much as securities analysts review their portfolios of stocks and bonds, deciding which to retain and which to discard, marketing planners must assess their products, the regions in which they operate, and other marketing mix variables. This is where the concept of an SBU comes in.

Strategic business units (SBUs) are key business units within diversified firms. Each SBU has its own managers, resources, objectives, and competitors. A division, product line, or single product may define the boundaries of an SBU. Each SBU pursues its own distinct mission and often develops its own plans independently of other units in the organization.

Strategic business units, also called categories, focus the attention of company managers so that they can respond effectively to changing consumer demand within limited markets. Companies may have to redefine their SBUs as market conditions dictate. International Business Machines Corp. (IBM) was once known as a manufacturer of high-quality clocks. Today, the firm markets everything from computer servers and systems, software, and Internet security to printing paper and toner. Its slogan, "Welcome to the Decade of Smart," conveys the firm's forward-thinking philosophy. People now compete for the old IBM clocks, which have become valuable collectibles.[25]

strategic business units (SBUs) Key business units within diversified firms.

The BCG Matrix

To evaluate each of their organization's strategic business units, marketers need some type of portfolio performance framework. A widely used framework was developed by the Boston Consulting

IBM, once known as a manufacturer of high-quality clocks, now markets everything from computer systems to global IT services and solutions.

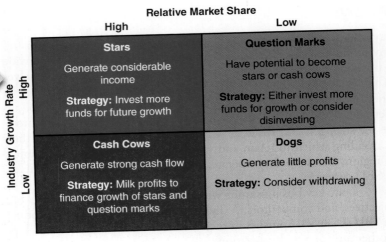

figure 2.5

BCG Market Share/Market Growth Matrix

Group (BCG). This market share/market growth matrix places SBUs in a four-quadrant chart that plots market share against market growth potential. Market share is the percentage of a market that a firm currently controls (or company sales divided by total market sales). The position of an SBU along the horizontal axis indicates its market share relative to those of competitors in the industry. Its position along the vertical axis indicates the annual growth rate of the market. After plotting all of a firm's business units, planners divide them according to the matrix's four quadrants. Figure 2.5 illustrates this matrix by labeling the four quadrants: stars, cash cows, question marks, and dogs. Firms in each quadrant require a unique marketing strategy.

Stars represent units with high market shares in high-growth markets. These products or businesses are high-growth market leaders. Although they generate considerable income, they need considerable inflows of cash to finance further growth. BlackBerry is the number-one selling smartphone in the United States, but in order to remain competitive the firm will have to continue offering new models to demanding and tech-savvy consumers.[26]

Cash cows command high market shares in low-growth markets. Marketers for such an SBU want to maintain this status for as long as possible. The business produces strong cash flows, but instead of investing heavily in the unit's own promotions and production capacity, the firm can use this cash to finance the growth of other SBUs with higher growth potentials. For instance, Microsoft uses the profits from sales of its Windows operating system to finance research and development for new Internet-based technologies.[27]

Question marks achieve low market shares in high-growth markets. Marketers must decide whether to continue supporting these products or businesses because question marks typically require considerably more cash than they generate. If a question mark cannot become a star, the firm should pull out of the market and target other markets with greater potential. Ford recently sold off its luxury brands Jaguar and Aston-Martin in order to concentrate on its more economical, fuel-efficient vehicles.

Dogs manage only low market shares in low-growth markets. SBUs in this category promise poor future prospects, and marketers should withdraw from these businesses or product lines as quickly as possible. In some cases, these products can be sold to other firms, where they are a better fit. Some firms build their entire business on other companies' dogs, purchasing recipes or manufacturing techniques. Blair Candy, an online candy retailer, specializes in hard-to-find favorites such as Mallo Cups, Necco Wafers, and Zagnut Candy Bars.[28]

✓ assessment check

1. What are SBUs?

2. Identify the four quadrants in the BCG matrix.

strategic implications
of marketing in the 21st century

ever before has planning been as important to marketers as the 21st century speeds ahead with technological
advances. Marketers need to plan carefully, accurately,
and quickly if their companies are to gain a competitive advantage in today's global marketplace. They need to define their
organization's mission and understand the different methods for
formulating a successful marketing strategy. They must consider
a changing, diverse population and the boundaryless business
environment created by the Internet. They must be able to evaluate when it's best to be first to get into a market and when it's best
to wait. They need to recognize when they've got a star and when
they've got a dog—when to hang on and when to let go. As daunting as this seems, planning can reduce the risk and worry of bringing new goods and services to the marketplace.

Review of Chapter Objectives

1 Distinguish between strategic planning and tactical planning.

Strategic planning is the process of identifying an organization's
primary objectives and adopting courses of action toward these
objectives. In other words, strategic planning focuses on the big
picture of which industries are central to a firm's business. Tactical
planning guides the implementation of the activities specified in the
strategic plan. Once a strategy is set, operational managers devise
methods (tactics) to achieve the larger goals.

2 Explain how marketing plans differ at various levels in an organization.

Top management spends more time engaged in strategic planning
than middle- and supervisory-level managers, who tend to focus
on narrower, tactical plans for their units. Supervisory managers are
more likely to develop specific plans designed to meet the goals
assigned to them, for example, streamlining production processes
so that they operate more efficiently.

3 Identify the steps in the marketing planning process.

The basic steps in the marketing planning process are defining the
organization's mission and objectives; assessing organizational
resources and evaluating environmental risks and opportunities;
and formulating, implementing, and monitoring the marketing
strategy.

4 Describe successful planning tools and techniques, including Porter's Five Forces model, first and second mover strategies, SWOT analysis, and the strategic window.

Porter's Five Forces are identified as the five competitive factors
that influence planning strategies: potential new entrants, bargaining power of buyers, bargaining power of suppliers, threat of substitute products, and rivalry among competitors. With a first mover
strategy, a firm attempts to capture the greatest market share by
being first to enter the market; with a second mover strategy, a
firm observes the innovations of first movers and then attempts
to improve on them to gain advantage. SWOT analysis (strengths,
weaknesses, opportunities, and threats) helps planners compare
internal organizational strengths and weaknesses with external
opportunities and threats. The strategic window identifies the limited periods during which the key requirements of a market and the
competencies of a firm best fit together.

5 Identify the basic elements of a marketing strategy.

Development of a marketing strategy is a two-step process:
(1) selecting a target market and (2) designing an effective marketing mix to satisfy the chosen target. The target market is the group
of people toward whom a company decides to direct its marketing
efforts. The marketing mix blends four strategy elements to fit the
needs and preferences of a specific target market: product strategy,
distribution strategy, promotion strategy, and pricing strategy.

Describe the environmental characteristics that influence strategic decisions.

The five dimensions of the marketing environment are competitive, political-legal, economic, technological, and social-cultural. Marketers must also address growing concern about the natural environment—including new regulations—and increasing cultural diversity in the global marketplace.

Describe the methods for marketing planning, including business portfolio analysis and the BCG matrix.

The business portfolio analysis evaluates a company's products and divisions, including strategic business units (SBUs). The SBU focuses the attention of company managers so that they can respond effectively to changing consumer demand within certain markets. The BCG matrix places SBUs in a four-quadrant chart that plots market share against market growth potential. The four quadrants are stars, cash cows, dogs, and question marks.

Assessment Check: Answers

1.1 Define *planning*. Planning is the process of anticipating future events and conditions and of determining the best way to achieve organizational objectives.

1.2 Give an example of strategic planning and tactical planning. To survive in a challenging environment that includes soaring fuel costs, several airlines have decided to combine as part of their strategic planning. Tactical plans include cutting the number of flights and charging passengers extra for checked baggage.

2.1 How do marketing plans vary at different levels of the organization? Top managers usually focus their planning activities on long-range strategic issues. In contrast, middle-level managers focus on operational planning, which includes creating and implementing tactical plans for their own units. Supervisors develop specific programs to meet the goals in their areas of responsibility.

2.2 Why is it important to get input from others when planning? Input from a variety of sources—other employees, suppliers, or customers—helps ensure that many ideas are considered. Involving those people in planning can also turn them into advocates for the plan.

3.1 Distinguish between an organization's mission and its objectives. The firm's mission is the essential purpose that differentiates the company from others. Its objectives guide development of supporting marketing objectives and plans. Avon's mission is to be "the company for women." One of its objectives might be to convert all its packaging to recycled materials.

3.2 What is the importance of the final step in the marketing planning process? In the final step of the marketing planning process, managers monitor performance to ensure that objectives are achieved.

4.1 Briefly explain each of Porter's Five Forces. Porter's Five Forces are the threats of potential new entrants, which increases competition in a market; bargaining power of buyers, which can depress prices; bargaining power of suppliers, which can increase costs or reduce selection; threat of substitute

products, which can lure customers to other products; and rivalry among competitors, which can bring about price wars or divert companies from their main goals.

4.2 What are the benefits and drawbacks of a first mover strategy? The benefits of a first mover strategy include capturing the greatest market share and developing long-term relationships with customers. Disadvantages include the possibility that companies that follow can learn from mistakes by first movers. Apple has been a first mover with its iPod products.

4.3 What are the four components of the SWOT analysis? What is a strategic window? SWOT analysis helps planners compare internal organizational strengths and weaknesses with external opportunities and threats. SWOT is an acronym for *strengths, weaknesses, opportunities,* and *threats.* A strategic window defines the limited periods when key requirements of a market and a firm's particular competencies best fit together.

5.1 What are the two components of every marketing strategy? The basic elements of a marketing strategy are (1) the target market and (2) the marketing mix variables.

5.2 Identify the four strategic elements of the marketing mix. The marketing mix consists of product, distribution, promotion, and pricing strategies.

6.1 What are the five dimensions of the marketing environment? The five dimensions of the marketing environment are competitive, political-legal, economic, technological, and social-cultural factors.

6.2 How is concern over the natural environment affecting the other dimensions? Concerns over the natural environment have led to new and tighter regulations on pollution, which affect the political-legal environment in which marketers operate. Efforts toward sustainability are now social-cultural factors as well because consumer awareness is turning into consumer preference.

7.1 What are SBUs? Strategic business units (SBUs) are key business units within diversified firms. Each SBU has its own managers, resources, objectives, and competitors.

7.2 Identify the four quadrants in the BCG matrix. The BCG matrix labels SBUs stars, cash cows, question marks, and dogs. Stars are the products with high market shares in high-growth markets; cash cows command high market shares in low-growth markets; question marks achieve low market shares in high-growth markets; and dogs manage only low market shares in low-growth markets.

Marketing Terms You Need to Know

planning 37
marketing planning 38
strategic planning 39
tactical planning 39

mission 41
marketing strategy 42
Porter's Five Forces 43
first mover strategy 45

second mover strategy 45
SWOT analysis 46
strategic window 46

marketing mix 48
strategic business units (SBUs) 53

Assurance of Learning Review

1. State whether each of the following illustrates strategic or tactical planning:
   a. Global automakers begin setting up manufacturing plants in India.
   b. The merging of Live Nation and Ticketmaster.
   c. The New England Patriots trade a backup quarterback to the Kansas City Chiefs.
   d. A regional airline looks for ways to expand to other areas of the country.

2. Imagine you had a chance to interview Google co-founders Larry Page and Sergey Brin. Page is now vice president and head of products. Brin is now vice president and head of technology. What questions might you ask each about strategic planning for his division and the firm overall?

3. What is the difference between a firm's mission and its objectives? Why is it important that both are conveyed clearly to employees and to customers?

4. Over which of Porter's Five Forces do consumers have the greatest influence? Over which do they have the least? How might these factors affect a firm's overall marketing strategy?

5. Why is it so important for a firm to identify its core competencies?

6. How might an understanding of diversity help formulate a firm's marketing strategy?

7. Suppose you have been hired as a marketer by online retailer Bluefly or eBay to help develop a new marketing mix. State one thing you would do to improve the retailer's position through each of the four strategic elements: product, distribution, promotion, and pricing.

8. What is the *rule of three?* Suppose you worked for a small firm in a large industry—such as a small manufacturer of furniture. How might you actually use the rule of three to enhance your firm's position in the marketplace?

9. What is a *portfolio analysis?* What purpose does it serve for marketers?

10. How does the BCG matrix help marketers decide which products to offer? According to the matrix, which types of products are most desirable, and why?

Projects and Teamwork Exercises

1. Choose one of the following companies, or select another one whose goods and services are familiar to you. On your own or with a classmate, formulate a mission statement for that company. Then create a list of objectives that reflect your company's mission.
   a. Old Navy
   b. Scottrade
   c. Taco Bell
   d. Verizon Wireless

2. Using a first mover strategy, Apple's iPod and iPhone have clearly established the lead in their markets. Research the products of another firm that produces either a digital music player or a smartphone to learn about its strategy. How has a second mover strategy benefited the firm? Has the second mover firm been able to catch Apple in sales?

3. When rivals Samsung and Sony each unveiled their new 3D TVs at a major electronics store, some consumers couldn't tell the difference between the two. But the firm's strategies

were very different. Sony now hires outside manufacturing firms to build its TVs, stating that the move will help cut costs and keep the company strong. In addition, Sony plans to add "Sony-unique applications," including Internet content and streaming Sony films before their DVD release. But Samsung insists on manufacturing its own TVs, including its own computer chips.[29] With a classmate, research these new offerings by both firms and evaluate their marketing strategy. Who is the target market for both of these TVs? How does product, distribution, promotion, and pricing fit into each firm's overall marketing strategy?

4. Select one of the following industries and research which firms might fall into the top three in the industry, creating a rule of three:
    a. online securities trading
    b. upscale hotels

c. electronics retailing
d. auto manufacturing

5. On your own or with a classmate, research one of the following large corporations. Select several product lines and classify each in the BCG matrix.
    a. Sears
    b. Johnson & Johnson
    c. Conde Nast Publications
    d. General Electric (GE)

Critical-Thinking Exercises

1. Suppose you are a marketer for a U.S. manufacturer of pet supplies. Two top executives have proposed expanding the company by opening retail stores and marketing pets on-site—puppies, kittens, rabbits, birds, fish, and the like. What are the potential benefits and drawbacks of making a move like this? How would you advise your company to proceed?

2. Netflix has made thousands of streaming videos available to its subscribers. How does this strategy demonstrate a strategic window for the company?

3. Choose one of the following products and describe how it may (or already has) become vulnerable to substitution. Then describe an overall strategy—with two or three tactics—for reducing this vulnerability.
    a. printed copies of periodicals or books
    b. television

c. telephone landlines
d. travel agencies

4. Research the Web site of one of the following retail firms to identify its target market. Then outline a strategy for expanding that target market.
    a. Quiznos
    b. Target
    c. Trader Joe's
    d. Nordstrom
    e. Dollar Tree

5. Research a company such as L.L. Bean or Kraft Foods that has a number of different successful SBUs. What factors do you think make these units—and this company—successful from a marketing standpoint?

Ethics Exercise

A recent news story reported a study whose results revealed that food at popular chain restaurants and in frozen-food packages at the supermarket contain more calories than advertised. Meals from restaurants including Ruby Tuesday and Wendy's were tested and found to be more than 18 percent higher in calories than listed on their menus. Frozen diet meals made by Lean Cuisine, Weight Watchers, and Healthy Choice, among others, averaged 8 percent higher in calories than listed on the package labels.[30] Imagine that you are a marketer for a food manufacturer that competes with these firms.

1. Create an advertisement for your firm's food. Decide on a strategy and tactics. Would you follow in the footsteps of some of your competition, or use accurate calorie counts? Would you refer to the study that found discrepancies in your competitors' numbers?

2. Would you price your own firm's food higher or lower than the competition's? Why?

Internet Exercises

1. **Business portfolio analysis.** Occasionally, companies sell parts of themselves to other firms. One stated motive for such divestitures is that the sold assets are a poor strategic fit for the rest of their business portfolios. One recent example is the sale of a controlling interest in NBC Universal by General Electric to cable giant Comcast. Using a major search engine, research the sale of NBC Universal. In the context of business portfolio analysis, why did GE decide to sell, and why did Comcast decide to buy, NBC Universal?

2. **Mission and objectives.** Visit the Web site of the Sara Lee Corporation (http://www.saralee.com), whose slogan is "the joy of eating." Define the firm's mission and objectives, and discuss how its brands and activities support both.

3. **SWOT analysis.** Visit the Web site of an organization whose goods and services interest you—such as Columbia Sportswear, Major League Baseball, Travelocity, Apple, or Urban Outfitters. Based on your research, create a SWOT analysis for your firm. Outline your own ideas for increasing the firm's strengths and reducing its weaknesses.

Note: Internet Web addresses change frequently. If you don't find the exact site listed, you may need to access the organization's home page and search from there or use a search engine such as Google or Bing.

Case 2.1 *How a Stadium Becomes Part of a Marketing Strategy*

A stadium isn't just the place where sports are played. Whether it's football, soccer, or baseball, a team's stadium is its home. It is where fans come to cheer and cry; it is where teams live and die each season. When team owners announce the construction of a new stadium—though it may be highly necessary in order to provide modern facilities and an increased number of seats—fans mourn the loss of an old favorite venue. The stadium has become one of the most important components of marketing strategy in professional sports.

It's not surprising that several National Football League (NFL) teams are competing not just on the field, but in the race to build bigger and better stadiums. The New Orleans Saints resurrected themselves with a 70,000-seat stadium post–Hurricane Katrina. The NY Jets and NY Giants have shared the reconstruction of their home field, Meadowlands Stadium. Dallas Cowboys owner Jerry Jones is going for the glitz and glamour—bigger, better, jazzier. Seating capacity at the new Dallas stadium tops 80,000, with another 20,000 available "standing room" slots. Club-level seats cost as much as a one-time hit of $50,000—and those aren't the luxury boxes, which house upholstered seats, business centers with video and Internet access, and entry to exclusive clubs. Food concessions offer a Kobe beef burger for $13 and pizza for $60. Of course, there's the gargantuan video screen, which hangs about 90 feet above the field. But the showpiece of the stadium is its retractable roof, supported by two enormous arches that soar nearly 300 feet above the playing field. It is the longest single-span roof in the world, making this the largest enclosed NFL stadium as well.

So, what do all these bells and whistles mean for a football team? Of course the team needs to win—if it doesn't, it won't matter how high the roof is or how big the video screen is. And if they lose, fans may be less likely to pay $13 for that burger. But if the home stadium conveys the team's image—particularly if it's a winner—then fans will pay to be associated with that image, or that brand. They'll buy tickets, food, T-shirts and caps. They'll bring friends and family. And they'll come back. At least, that's what marketers hope. It's part of the winning strategy.

Questions for Critical Thinking

1. How would you describe the target market for the Dallas Cowboys' new stadium? Do you think marketers are targeting the right consumers? Why or why not?

2. How does the new Dallas Cowboys' stadium fit into an overall marketing mix, in terms of product and pricing strategies?

Sources: Dallas Cowboys Stadium Web site, http://stadium.dallascowboys.com, accessed February 5, 2010; Football Parks Web site, http://www.footballparks. com, accessed February 5, 2010; Filip Bondy, "Locals' Stadium Won't Compare. Boys' New Home Towers," *Daily News*, September 22, 2009, http://www.dailynews. com; "Inside Cowboys Stadium," *Daily News*, September 20, 2009, http://www. dailynews.com.

Video Case 2.2
Strategic Planning and the Marketing Process at Preserve*

When Eric Hudson started the Massachusetts-based consumer products company, Preserve, in 1996, he wasn't necessarily trying to make a "green" company. Armed with an MBA, a love of the outdoors, and a desire to be his own boss, he came up with a product and

set out to find a way to make it. That product was the Preserve toothbrush. Made from recycled plastic, the brush was not only environmentally friendly, but featured a unique 45-degree angled head designed by his dad, an industrial designer specializing in automobiles and boats, and with help from several dentists. It is hard to believe today, with the popularity of green products and our increased environmental awareness, but in the late 1990s, green products were considered "fringe" and could be found mostly around college towns on both coasts. Most of the products were considered less effective and low quality. Many actually were. That's why, from the beginning, Hudson felt strongly that Preserve's mission would be to make it easy to be green by offering environmentally friendly products for the mass market—without sacrificing quality or performance.

For the first few years, the Preserve toothbrush was mostly available locally in natural food stores. Soon they were sold in Whole Foods, a national natural foods chain, and Trader Joe's, which specializes in unique and gourmet grocery items. Preserve was doing a lot of grassroots marketing. They were sampling products at an Earth Day celebration in Boston when an employee from Stonyfield Yogurt approached them with an idea. Stonyfield had a lot of scrap waste from the manufacture of their yogurt containers that was difficult for them to recycle. Preserve needed a reliable source of recycled plastic.

It was a match made in heaven. Stonyfield had a great piece of PR (public relations) to enhance its environmentally friendly reputation, and Preserve could benefit from an association with such a mainstream, well-respected product. The yogurt container toothbrushes hit the shelves in 2001 and have been doing well for both companies ever since. Stonyfield even encourages consumers to send Preserve used yogurt containers.

"We're a pretty scrappy, upstart company going up against some very big brands," says C. A. Webb, director of marketing at Preserve. Large retailers are unwilling or unable to devote large chunks of shelf space to an unknown brand, so Preserve put a lot of effort into refining its packaging and marketing to have more of a presence and appeal to a more sophisticated consumer. "Our marketing budget pales in comparison to our competitors," says Webb.

Even though they've been around for more than a decade, Preserve still relies heavily on sampling and grassroots marketing. Finally, in 2008, Webb persuaded the marketing department to do their first real advertising campaign. She and her small staff now work closely with a PR firm and smaller marketing agencies to keep the wheels turning.

With so little money and so few resources, Preserve relies heavily on publicity to market their brand. A magazine article or television appearance can reach an incredible number of unique consumers—plus, it's free. Because the green movement is hot right now, Preserve has received great press in *The New York Times Magazine, Gourmet,* and *Everyday* with *Rachael Ray* as well as on "Good Morning America," "The Today Show," and on Sundance Channel's "The Green."

"One thing you can be assured of is that some part of it won't work the way you'd hoped!" says Webb of her strategic marketing plans. She attributes many of the misses to the complexities of working with outside agencies on campaigns. Sometimes it's a failure to communicate or a firm's inability to deliver on the plan. No matter the reason, "sometimes you have to figure out a way to save that investment and then other times it just becomes a learning moment when you say, 'Okay, let's do the post mortem, let's understand what went wrong and let's just be sure we don't do that again.'"

Webb admits she hasn't performed a SWOT analysis, on paper at least, since business school. But when it comes to thinking about new channels, design decisions, bringing a product to market, or just looking at the marketplace in general, "I absolutely use that thinking on a daily basis . . . always," she says.

When Hudson started the company in 1998, he could have only dreamed that America's desire for green products would be as strong as it is today. Of course, all good trends eventually come to an end. "The interest in green products has just been incredible. The biggest thing I'm concerned about is whether it's going to kinda have a negative backlash." He is hoping that, like the dot-com trend that put a laptop on every desk and a BlackBerry in every palm, "We will all realize that we've incorporated these green activities in our lives."

Questions

1. Do you consider Preserve's strategy for the Preserve brand a first mover or second mover strategy? Explain.

2. Perform a SWOT analysis on Preserve. Identify their core competency and their weaknesses in the marketplace

"Preserve was previously called "Recycline." The Recycline brand has now stepped into the background as the parent company.

The Marketing
Environment, Ethics, and Social Responsibility

1 Identify the five components of the marketing environment.

2 Explain the types of competition marketers face and the steps necessary for developing a competitive strategy.

3 Describe how marketing activities are regulated and how marketers can influence the political-legal environment.

4 Outline the economic factors that affect marketing decisions and consumer buying power.

5 Discuss the impact of the technological environment on a firm's marketing activities.

6 Explain how the social-cultural environment influences marketing.

7 Describe the ethical issues in marketing.

8 Identify the four levels of the social responsibility pyramid.

At Nike, Corporate Responsibility Means Sustainable Business and Innovation ••• Flash back to the late 1990s: Nike was the Big Name in everything athletic—from shoes to apparel to equipment. Nike was also the subject of penetrating

global scrutiny and criticism for sweatshop conditions in Asian factories where its products were made—this at a time when company revenues were soaring off the charts.

The sweatshop scandal may have been the catalyst that propelled Nike into a comprehensive transformation of its corporate persona. Every facet of the global business—from workplace processes to business practices to supply chain to transparency—was put under the microscope. The result: a continuously evolving journey that, the company says, has positioned it to drive toward sustainability in all aspects of its operations.

Nike began its quest toward greater corporate responsibility by establishing a global compliance team charged with building a corporate function that would be

capable of constant reinvention as it also set standards, identified them, "put out fires," and charted Nike's course for the long term.

By 2001, the work of the Nike compliance team had evolved into what the company called its "second generation." During the ensuing five-year period, the team worked to articulate work processes that address environmental, health, and workplace safety concerns; create tools and methods for measuring their progress; and enforce the processes across the global firm. The Nike team also gathered and consolidated industry data and shared it widely, in an effort to create greater transparency not only inside the firm but also throughout the industry.

In 2006, Nike's efforts to create transparency helped move the compliance team into its next

generation, which it regards as its "transformation" stage. Since that time, the team has channeled its energy into creating a sustainability strategy for sourcing, building excellence in factory remediation, and forming industry coalitions based on best practices. During this phase, Nike has pushed what it calls "responsible competitiveness," taking a more holistic look at its supply chain and seeking to identify problems and find ways to drive systemic change.

According to a recently issued corporate responsibility report, Nike succeeded in cutting its 2009 greenhouse gas emissions across its global supply chain to 2007 levels. In addition, a program begun in 2008 to improve energy efficiency at its plants showed a 6 percent reduction in carbon emissions while production

increased 9 percent. With heavy investments in teleconference technology, Nike has significantly reduced corporate air travel—a move that keeps more executives off planes and, presumably, enhances productivity. Nike has also joined with other organizations to lobby Congress for legislation that

would reward businesses for significant investments in carbon reduction.

The corporate responsibility report helps Nike communicate its vision of a "closed loop" business model, in which a supply chain would generate zero waste and all products and materials would be continuously reused—in other words,

no pre- or post-consumer waste. As an example of this model, Nike points to its Air Jordan XX3, designed so that all of the shoe's pieces fit together like a jigsaw puzzle, with no waste. Today, Nike senior leadership calls sustainability the "key to Nike's growth and innovation" and continues to grow as a responsible corporate citizen.[1]

evolution of a brand

Nike co-founder Bill Bowerman may have said it best when he claimed, "If you have a body, you are an athlete." This statement—intended to encourage and motivate employees of the Beaverton, Oregon, company founded in 1972—has also inspired athletes of all abilities to aim for their personal best.

Today, Nike believes it can achieve its own personal best in a sustainable global economy by identifying ways for the company, its employees, consumers, and the planet to mutually thrive.

- Around the time that news stories broke regarding sweatshop conditions in Nike factories in Asia, the company established its corporate responsibility team. In your opinion, did the scandal cause Nike to launch this corrective initiative?

- Nike is not the only brand to come under fire for alleged sweatshop conditions in its plants.

Since then, many other brands have been similarly criticized. Does this type of charge cause you to rethink your decision to buy a company's product?

- By looking for ways to improve operations, is Nike doing enough to change how consumers think of the company and its products? What could it do differently?

chapter overview

> 1 **Identify the five components of the marketing environment.**

Change is a fact of life for all people, including marketers. Adapting to change in an environment as complex and unpredictable as the world's energy usage is perhaps the supreme challenge. In response to the rising cost of fuel, many airlines—including American, Delta, and United—are taking their less fuel-efficient aircraft out of service and eliminating flights.[2]

Although some change may be the result of sudden crises, more often it is the result of a gradual trend in lifestyle, income, population, and other factors. Consumers are increasingly interested in buying "green" products—goods that minimize their impact on the environment. Technology can trigger a sudden change in the marketplace: in one fell swoop, it appeared that Internet music downloads had replaced traditional CDs. And within mere months of offering its iPhone, Apple introduced the iPod touch MP3 player, which borrowed touch-screen technology from the iPhone.

Marketers must anticipate and plan for change. They must set goals to meet the concerns of customers, employees, shareholders, and the general public. Industry competi-

tion, legal constraints, the impact of technology on product designs, and social concerns are some of the many important factors that shape the business environment. All potentially have an impact on a firm's goods and services. Although external forces frequently are outside the marketer's control, decision makers must still consider those influences together with the variables of the marketing mix in developing, and occasionally modifying, marketing plans and strategies that take these environmental factors into consideration.

This chapter begins by describing five forces in marketing's external environment: competitive, political-legal, economic, technological, and social-cultural. Figure 3.1 identifies them as the foundation for making decisions that involve the four marketing mix elements and the target market. These forces provide the frame of reference within which all marketing decisions are made. The second focus of this chapter is marketing ethics and social responsibility. That section describes the nature of marketers' responsibilities both to business and to society at large.

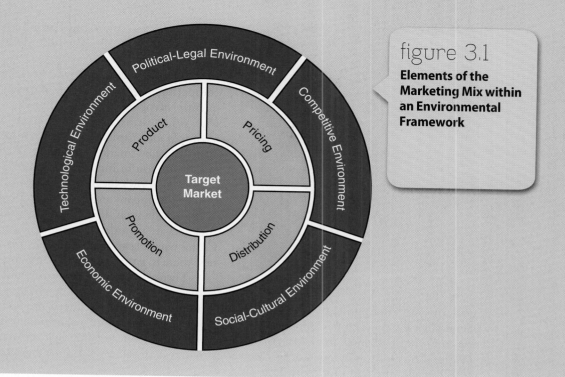

<figure 3.1

Elements of the Marketing Mix within an Environmental Framework

Environmental Scanning and Environmental Management

Marketers constantly monitor crucial trends and developments in the business environment. **Environmental scanning** is the process of collecting information about the external marketing environment to identify and interpret potential trends. The goal of this process is to analyze the information and decide whether these trends represent significant opportunities or pose major threats to the company. The firm can then determine the best response to a particular environmental change.

In the United States, the Consumer Product Safety Commission (CPSC) is responsible for keeping unsafe products out of the marketplace. It recently issued a recall of *The Princess and the Frog*-themed pendants, citing high levels of cadmium, a toxic metal, in the children's necklaces. The commission's announcement marked the first U.S. recall of a consumer product because of cadmium, a substance believed to harm brain development in children. Walmart pulled the merchandise from its shelves. In another recall, nearly 174,000 Papyrus brand greeting cards with painted wooden bead bracelets were pulled from store shelves. The paint on the beads was found to contain high levels of lead, another substance linked to brain damage and other serious health problems.[3]

Environmental scanning is a vital component of effective **environmental management**. Environmental management involves marketers' efforts to achieve organizational objectives by predicting and influencing the competitive, political-legal, economic, technological, and social-cultural environments. In the political-legal environment, managers who seek modifications of regulations, laws, or tariff restrictions may lobby legislators or contribute to the campaigns of sympathetic politicians. Consumer groups lobbying on behalf of credit card users persuaded Congress to create rules regarding credit cards—for example, barring banks from creating minimum interest rates, or "floors"; forbidding card issuers from arbitrarily picking dates with the highest prime rate

environmental scanning Process of collecting information about the external marketing environment to identify and interpret potential trends.

environmental management Attainment of organizational objectives by predicting and influencing the competitive, political-legal, economic, technological, and social-cultural environments.

In the United States, the Consumer Product Safety Commission is responsible for keeping unsafe products out of the marketplace.

© AP IMAGES/MEL EVANS

to apply to interest rates; and prohibiting them from automatically enrolling cardholders in over-the-limit protection.[4]

For many domestic and international firms, competing with established industry leaders frequently involves **strategic alliances**—partnerships with other firms in which the partners combine resources and capital to create competitive advantages in a new market. Strategic alliances are especially common in international marketing, in which partnerships with local firms provide regional expertise for a company expanding its operations abroad. Members of such alliances share risks and profits. Alliances are considered essential in a country such as China where laws require foreign firms doing business there to work with local companies.

Through successful research and development efforts, firms may influence changes in their own technological environments. A research breakthrough may lead to reduced production costs or a technologically superior new product. While changes in the marketing environment may be beyond the control of individual marketers, managers continually seek to predict their impact on marketing decisions and to modify operations to meet changing market needs. Even modest environmental shifts can alter the results of those decisions.

strategic alliance
Partnership in which two or more companies combine resources and capital to create competitive advantages in a new market.

 assessment check

1. Define *environmental scanning*.
2. How does environmental scanning contribute to environmental management?

The Competitive Environment

competitive environment
Interactive process that occurs in the marketplace among marketers of directly competitive products, marketers of products that can be substituted for one another, and marketers competing for the consumer's purchasing power.

monopoly Market structure in which a single seller dominates trade in a good or service for which buyers can find no close substitutes.

As organizations vie to satisfy customers, the interactive exchange creates the **competitive environment**. Marketing decisions by individual firms influence consumer responses in the marketplace. They also affect the marketing strategies of competitors. As a consequence, marketers must continually monitor their competitors' marketing activities: their products, distribution channels, prices, and promotional efforts.

Few organizations have **monopoly** positions as the sole supplier of a good or service in the marketplace. Utilities, such as natural gas, electricity, water, and cable TV service have traditionally accepted considerable regulation from local authorities who controlled such marketing-related factors as rates, service levels, and geographic coverage. In exchange, the utilities gained exclusive rights to serve a particular group of consumers. But the deregulation movement of the past three decades has ended total monopoly protection for most utilities. Many shoppers can choose from alternative cable TV and Internet providers, cell phone and traditional telephone carriers, and even gas and electric utilities. Some firms, such as pharmaceutical giants Merck and Pfizer, have *temporary* monopolies provided by patents on new drugs. When the U.S. Food and Drug Administration (FDA) approves a new drug for lowering cholesterol or improving sleep, its manufacturer typically is granted exclusive rights to produce and market the product during the life of the patent. This gives the manufacturer a chance to recoup the millions spent on developing and launching the drug. Once the patent expires, all bets are off, and competitors can flood the market with generic versions of the drug.

But what about professional sports teams who are part of a league? Is it lawful for their league to operate as a monopoly without violating U.S. **antitrust** laws? According to a case working its way through the court system, the 32 teams of the National Football League have operated as a monopoly in terms of licensed providers. For 20 years, apparel manufacturer American Needle had a contract to make team caps for the NFL, but it lost the business in 2000 after the league engaged Reebok as its exclusive provider. The suit brought by American Needle charges that the Reebok deal violates antitrust laws. The U.S. Supreme Court has agreed to hear the case.[5]

Rather than seeking sole dominance of a market, corporations increasingly prefer to share the pie with just a few rivals. Referred to by economists as an **oligopoly**, this structure of a limited number of sellers in an industry in which high start-up costs form barriers to keep out new competitors deters newcomers from breaking into markets while ensuring that corporations remain innovative. Commercial airplane manufacturers operate within an oligopolostic industry, currently dominated by Europe-based Airbus Industrie and U.S.-based Boeing. After earlier failures at building and marketing commercial airplanes, the Chinese government once again is attempting to enter this exclusive club. With the increasing numbers of Chinese air travelers, the government founded the Commercial Aircraft Corporation of China to build fuel-efficient jets domestically, in the hope that China can "buy local" and reduce its dependence on aircraft made in the West. China's "Big Plane" project for the C919 is scheduled to debut its first flight in 2014.[6]

Types of Competition

Marketers face three types of competition. The most *direct* form occurs among marketers of similar products, as when a competitive station like Marathon opens across the street from a Shell retail outlet. The cell phone market provides consumers with such alternative suppliers as Verizon, AT&T, and T-Mobile.

Costco, which sells everything from home generators to birthday cakes, also takes direct aim at luxury retailers. The largest U.S. warehouse club operator, Costco offers diamond jewelry, cashmere sweaters, Fendi handbags, and even Suzuki grand pianos.[7]

A second type of competition is *indirect,* involving products that are easily substituted. In the fast-food industry, pizza competes with chicken, hamburgers, and tacos. In entertainment, a movie could be substituted for a concert or a night at the bowling alley. Six Flags and Universal Studios amusement parks—traditional hot spots for family vacations—now compete with outdoor adventure trips. Many adults in the United States will decide not to make this year's vacation a tranquil week at the beach or a trip to Disney World. Instead, they'll choose to do something more adventurous—thrill-filled experiences such as skydiving, whitewater rafting, or climbing Mount Rainier. So marketers have to find ways to attract consumers to their specific brand as well as to their type of product.

A change such as a price increase or an improvement in a product's attributes can also affect demand for substitute products. As the prices for one type of energy soar, consumers look for cheaper, and more environmentally friendly, alternatives. Growing consumer interest in energy efficiency has led shoppers to look for products that have earned the ENERGY STAR. Administered jointly by the U.S. Environmental Protection Agency and the Department of Energy, the program awards the ENERGY STAR credential to appliances, building materials, computers, new homes, tools, and more.[8]

Advances in technology can give rise to other substitute products. Wireless fidelity, or Wi-Fi, makes the Internet available via radio waves and can be accessed at any number of public "hot spots" in a variety of locations, including airports, coffee shops, hotels, and libraries. The number of

antitrust Laws designed to prevent restraints on trade such as business monopolies.

oligopoly Market structure in which relatively few sellers compete and where high start-up costs form barriers to keep out new competitors.

2 **Explain the types of competition marketers face and the steps necessary for developing a competitive strategy.**

An improvement in a product's attributes can affect indirect competition, increasing demand for that product over substitutes. For example, growing consumer interest in energy efficiency has led shoppers to look for products with the ENERGY STAR.

© JUSTIN SULLIVAN/GETTY IMAGES

registered hot spots continues to grow worldwide, with more than 245,000 in existence.[9] While some hosts charge a fee, Wi-Fi increasingly is offered at no charge.

And as technology continues to advance, industry observers expect Wi-Fi eventually will be replaced as the wireless standard. Two possible "next-generation" successors, WiMax and LTE (an acronym for long-term evolution), offer enhanced capabilities for numerous applications. Both boast a stronger, more secure signal and significantly greater range than does Wi-Fi. Sprint's Nextel network currently uses WiMax in 27 cities; Verizon and AT&T are developing LTE networks.[10]

The final type of competition occurs among all organizations that compete for consumers' purchases. Traditional economic analysis views competition as a battle among companies in the same industry (direct competition) or among substitutable goods and services (indirect competition). But marketers know that *all* firms compete for a limited number of dollars that consumers can or will spend. In this broader sense, competition means that the purchase of a Honda Accord might compete with a Norwegian Cruise Line cruise.

Because the competitive environment often determines the success or failure of a product, marketers must continually assess competitors' marketing strategies. New products, updated features or technology, increased service, and lower prices are variations that marketers look for. When changes occur in the competition, marketers must decide how to respond. While some organizations assume a "wait and see" attitude on environmental issues, SC Johnson has taken steps toward sustainability, as the "Marketing Success" feature describes.

Developing a Competitive Strategy

competitive strategy
Methods through which a firm deals with its competitive environment.

Marketers at every successful firm must develop an effective strategy for dealing with the competitive environment. One company may compete in a broad range of markets in many areas of the world. Another may specialize in particular market segments, such as those determined by customers' geographic location, age, or income characteristics. Determining a **competitive strategy** involves answering the following three questions:

1. Should we compete?

2. If so, in what markets should we compete?

3. How should we compete?

mktg: *success*

SC Johnson Committed to "Doing What's Right"

Background. SC Johnson is a leading manufacturer of household cleaning products and other products for insect control, air fresheners, and home storage. The company's well-known brands are marketed in more than 110 countries around the world.

The Challenge. While the global debate continues on greenhouse gas emissions and climate change, SC Johnson faced a decision: should the company adopt a "wait and see" attitude on environmental issues, or act decisively now, doing what it believes is right?

The Strategy. SC Johnson's concern for the environment is nothing new. As far back as the 1930s, H.F. Johnson Jr. led an expedition to Brazil in search of a renewable resource for the wax used in Johnson's Wax. In the 1970s it eliminated harmful chlorofluorocarbons from its aerosol products—three years before the U.S. government mandate. The company published its first sustainability report in 1992, one of the first consumer packaged goods companies to do so, and well before the issue of sustainability became fashionable. In all its operations, the

The answer to the first question depends on the firm's resources, objectives, and expected profit potential. A firm may decide not to pursue or continue operating a potentially successful venture that does not mesh with its resources, objectives, or profit expectations. The board of directors at Accor SA voted to "demerge" the company's two divisions—prepaid services and hotels—saying each could grow more quickly as separate businesses. Cable & Wireless, a telecom carrier operating in the United Kingdom, split its two divisions, a global communication services business and another enterprise operating fixed-line and mobile services in Panama, Macau, and several Caribbean countries.[11]

Answering the second question requires marketers to acknowledge their firm's limited resources—sales personnel, advertising budgets, product development capability, and the like. They must allocate these resources to the areas of greatest opportunity. Some companies gain access to new markets or new expertise through acquisitions or mergers. Johnson & Johnson's $1 billion purchase of Cougar Biotechnology, a California-based developer of cancer drugs, was the latest in a string of leading biotech firms the company has acquired in recent years to broaden its in-house research capability.[12]

Answering the third question on the list requires marketers to make product, distribution, promotion, and pricing decisions that give the firm a competitive advantage in the marketplace. Firms can compete on a variety of bases, including product quality, price, and customer service. Stonyfield Farms, the world's largest maker of organic yogurt, competes on an environmental basis by using organic ingredients. And although it's higher priced, the Stonyfield Farms brand has risen to number three in the United States—behind Yoplait and Dannon—partially because customers support the company's commitment to organic foods.[13]

Time-Based Competition

With increased international competition and rapid changes in technology, a steadily growing number of firms use time as a strategic competitive weapon. **Time-based competition** is the strategy of developing and distributing goods and services more quickly than competitors. Although a video option on cell phones came late to the U.S. market, the new feature has been a big hit, attracting new customers to cell phone providers. The flexibility and responsiveness of time-based competitors enable them to improve product quality, reduce costs, and expand product offerings to satisfy new market segments and enhance customer satisfaction.

time-based competition Strategy of developing and distributing goods and services more quickly than competitors.

company exhorts its leadership, employees, suppliers, customers, and the communities in which it has operations, to "do what's right."

The Outcome. Today, SC Johnson is a founding member of the Team Earth sustainability project, sponsored by Conservation International, gathering businesses, not-for-profits, scientists, educators, and individuals in a global

campaign to address—and act on—the world's most pressing environmental problems. SC Johnson also imposes ambitious environmental goals on its own operations: the company succeeded in cutting greenhouse gas emissions firmwide by 27 percent—three years ahead of schedule. SC Johnson's wind energy pilot program is the latest in the company's

efforts to scale back its carbon footprint. "Doing what's right," the company claims, is not only good for business—it's what's best for the planet.

Sources: Company Web site, www.scjohnson.com, accessed February 17, 2010; "SC Johnson Continues to Push the Winds of Change," company press release, January 12, 2010, http://www.scjohnson.com; "SC Johnson Joins Conservation International Team Earth as a Founding Member," company press release, September 21, 2009, http://www.scjohnson.com.

In rapidly changing markets, particularly those that involve technology, time-based competition is critical to a firm's success. The Transportation Security Administration (TSA), partnering with Continental and Delta airlines, has begun using technology to move passengers through airports more quickly and to reduce the incidence of phony boarding passes. The solution? Paperless boarding passes. Traditionally, airlines issued paper boarding passes, but the electronic pass, with its encrypted barcode, is transmitted directly to a passenger's cell phone or PDA (personal digital assistant). At check-in, the passenger simply presents the phone or PDA to a TSA officer, who uses a handheld scanner to validate the barcode.[14]

assessment check

1. Distinguish between direct and indirect competition, and give an example of each.

2. What is time-based competition?

The Political-Legal Environment

political-legal environment
Component of the marketing environment consisting of laws and their interpretations that require firms to operate under competitive conditions and to protect consumer rights.

Before you play the game, learn the rules! You may find it hard to win a new game without first understanding the rules. Yet some businesspeople exhibit a lack of knowledge about marketing's **political-legal environment**—the laws and their interpretations that require firms to operate under competitive conditions and to protect consumer rights. Ignorance of laws, ordinances, and regulations or noncompliance with them can result in fines, negative publicity, and expensive civil damage suits.

The existing U.S. legal framework was constructed piecemeal, often in response to issues that were important when individual laws were enacted. Businesspeople must be diligent to understand the legal system's relationship to their marketing decisions. Numerous laws and regulations affect those decisions, many of them vaguely stated and inconsistently enforced by a multitude of different authorities.

Federal, state, and local regulations affect marketing practices, as do the actions of independent regulatory agencies. These requirements and prohibitions touch on all aspects of marketing decision making: designing, labeling, packaging, distributing, advertising, and promoting goods and services. To cope with the vast, complex, and changing political-legal environment, many large firms maintain in-house legal departments; small firms often seek professional advice from outside attorneys. All marketers, however, should be aware of the major regulations that affect their activities.

Government Regulation

3 Describe how marketing activities are regulated and how marketers can influence the political-legal environment.

The history of U.S. government regulation can be divided into four phases. The first phase was the *antimonopoly period* of the late 19th and early 20th centuries. During this era, major laws such as the Sherman Antitrust Act, Clayton Act, and Federal Trade Commission Act were passed to maintain a competitive environment by reducing the trend toward increasing concentration of industry power in the hands of a small number of competitors. Laws enacted more than 100 years ago still affect business in the 21st century.

The Microsoft case is a good example of antitrust legislation at work. The U.S. Department of Justice was successful in proving Microsoft guilty of predatory practices designed to crush competition. By bundling its own Internet Explorer browser with its Windows operating system—which runs 90 percent of the world's personal computers—Microsoft grabbed the majority of the market from rival Netscape. It also bullied firms as large as America Online to drop Netscape Navigator in favor of its browser. Microsoft's supporters countered that consumers have clearly benefited from the integrated features in Windows and that its bundling decisions were simply efforts to offer customer satisfaction through added value.

The second phase, aimed at *protecting competitors,* emerged during the Great Depression era of the 1930s, when independent merchants felt the need for legal protection against competition from larger chain stores. Among the federal legislation enacted was the Robinson-Patman Act. The third regulatory phase focused on *consumer protection.* The objective of consumer protection underlies most laws, with good examples including the Sherman Act, Federal Trade Commission Act, and Federal Food and Drug Act. Additional laws have been enacted over the past 40 years. The fourth phase, *industry deregulation,* began in the late 1970s and continues to the present. During this phase, government has sought to increase competition in such industries as telecommunications, utilities, transportation, and financial services by discontinuing many regulations and permitting firms to expand their service offerings to new markets.

The newest regulatory frontier is *cyberspace.* Federal and state regulators are investigating ways to police the Internet and online services. The Federal Trade Commission (FTC), along with private organizations and other government agencies, has created a site, **www.onguardonline.gov**, where consumers can take quizzes designed to educate them about ID theft, spam (junk e-mail), phishing (luring consumers to provide personal information), and online shopping scams. But cybercrime is spreading quickly. Attacks by malicious software that contain codes capable of stealing account logons, passwords, and other confidential data are on the rise. Numerous state laws as well as the federal Identity Theft Enforcement and Restitution Act enable victims of identity theft to seek restitution and make it easier for the government to prosecute phishing and those who threaten to steal or divulge information from a computer.[15]

Privacy and child protection issues are another important—but difficult—enforcement challenge. With the passage of the Children's Online Privacy Protection Act, Congress took the first step in regulating what children are exposed to on the Internet. The primary focus is a set of rules regarding how and when marketers need to get parental permission before obtaining marketing research information from children over the Web. Finally, the government's Do Not Call Registry, a list to which consumers can add their phone numbers, including cell phones, to avoid telemarketing calls, provides protection for consumers who do not want to be contacted by telemarketers. The law exempts callers representing not-for-profit organizations, companies with which the consumer has an existing relationship, and political candidates. Telemarketing firms must check the list quarterly, with fines of as much as $11,000 per occurrence. The government aggressively pursues offenders, resulting in settlements often totaling millions of dollars. Since the list was established, for example, DIRECTV has paid more than $7.6 million in fines.[16]

Table 3.1 lists and briefly describes the major federal laws affecting marketing. Legislation covering specific marketing practices, such as product development, packaging, labeling, product warranties, and franchise agreements, is discussed in later chapters.

The EPA, a federal regulatory agency, helped in monitoring and responding to the BP oil spill in the Gulf of Mexico.

© NEWSCOM

table 3.1 Major Federal Laws Affecting Marketing

Date	Law	Description
A. LAWS MAINTAINING A COMPETITIVE ENVIRONMENT		
1890	Sherman Antitrust Act	Prohibits restraint of trade and monopolization; identifies a competitive marketing system as a national policy goal.
1914	Clayton Act	Strengthens the Sherman Act by restricting such practices as price discrimination, exclusive dealing, tying contracts, and interlocking boards of directors where the effect "may be to substantially lessen competition or tend to create a monopoly;" amended by the Celler-Kefauver Antimerger Act to prohibit major asset purchases that would decrease competition in an industry.
1914	Federal Trade Commission Act (FTC)	Prohibits unfair methods of competition; establishes the Federal Trade Commission, an administrative agency that investigates business practices and enforces the FTC Act.
1938	Wheeler-Lea Act	Amends the FTC Act to outlaw additional unfair practices; gives the FTC jurisdiction over false and misleading advertising.
1998	Digital Millennium Copyright Act	Protects intellectual property rights by prohibiting copying or downloading of digital files.
B. LAWS REGULATING COMPETITION		
1936	Robinson-Patman Act	Prohibits price discrimination in sales to wholesalers, retailers, or other producers; prohibits selling at unreasonably low prices to eliminate competition.
1993	North American Free Trade Agreement (NAFTA)	International trade agreement between Canada, Mexico, and the United States and designed to facilitate trade by removing tariffs and other trade barriers among the three nations.
C. LAWS PROTECTING CONSUMERS		
1906	Federal Food and Drug Act	Prohibits adulteration and misbranding of food and drugs involved in interstate commerce; strengthened by the Food, Drug, and Cosmetic Act (1938) and the Kefauver-Harris Drug Amendment (1962).
1970	National Environmental Policy Act	Establishes the Environmental Protection Agency to deal with various types of pollution and organizations that create pollution.
1971	Public Health Cigarette Smoking Act	Prohibits tobacco advertising on radio and television.
1972	Consumer Product Safety Act	Created the Consumer Product Safety Commission, which has authority to specify safety standards for most products.
1998	Children's Online Privacy Protection Act	Empowers FTC to set rules regarding how and when marketers must obtain parental permission before asking children marketing research questions.
1998	Identity Theft and Assumption Deterrence Act	Makes it a federal crime to unlawfully use or transfer another person's identification with the intent to violate the law.
1999	Anticybersquatting Consumer Protection Act	Bans the bad-faith purchase of domain names that are identical or confusingly similar to existing registered trademarks.
2009	Credit Card Accountability, Responsibility and Disclosure (CARD) Act	Cracks down on questionable credit card industry practices by restricting retroactive rate increases, providing more advance notice of rate hikes, and increasing bill payment time, among other things.
2001	Electronic Signature Act	Gives electronic signatures the same legal weight as handwritten signatures.
2005	Real ID Act	Sets minimum standards for state driver's licenses and ID cards. To be phased in from 2010 through 2013.
2006	Consumer Telephone Records Act	Prohibits the sale of cell phone records.
2009	Fraud Enforcement and Recovery Act	Expands government's authority to investigate and prosecute mortgage fraud.
2009	Helping Families Save Their Homes Act	Helps homeowners avoid foreclosure and obtain sustainable, affordable mortgages.
2009	Credit Card Accountability, Responsibility and Disclosure Act	Provides new rules governing credit card rate increases, fees, billing, and other practices.

table 3.1 **Major Federal Laws Affecting Marketing** (continued)

Date	Law	Description
D. LAWS DEREGULATING SPECIFIC INDUSTRIES		
1978	Airline Deregulation Act	Grants considerable freedom to commercial airlines in setting fares and choosing new routes.
1980	Motor Carrier Act and Staggers Rail Act	Significantly deregulates trucking and railroad industries by permitting them to negotiate rates and services.
1996	Telecommunications Act	Significantly deregulates the telecommunications industry by removing barriers to competition in local and long-distance phone and cable and television markets.
2003	Amendments to the Telemarketing Sales Rule	Created the national Do Not Call Registry prohibiting telemarketing calls to registered telephone numbers. Restricted the number and duration of telemarketing calls generating dead air space with use of automatic dialers; cracked down on unauthorized billing; and required telemarketers to transmit their caller ID information.
2007	Do-Not-Call Improvement Act	Extends Telemarketing Sales Rule; allows registered numbers to remain on Do Not Call list permanently.
2007	Fee Extension Act	Extends Telemarketing Sales Rule; sets annual fees for telemarketers to access the Do Not Call Registry.

Marketers must also monitor state and local laws that affect their industries. Many states, for instance, allow hard liquor to be sold only in liquor stores while others prohibit the sale of alcoholic beverages on Sunday. California's stringent regulations for automobile emissions require special pollution control equipment on cars sold in the state.

Government Regulatory Agencies

Federal, state, and local governments have established regulatory agencies to enforce laws. At the federal level, the FTC wields the broadest powers of any agency to influence marketing activities. The FTC enforces laws regulating unfair business practices and stops false and deceptive advertising. It regulates communication by wire, radio, and television. Other federal regulatory agencies include the Consumer Product Safety Commission, the Federal Power Commission, the Environmental Protection Agency (EPA), the Food and Drug Administration (FDA), and the National Highway Traffic Safety Administration (NHTSA). But regulatory agencies aren't always known for strict oversight. The NHTSA came under fire for not investigating hundreds of complaints from Lexus and Toyota drivers who reported sudden or unintended acceleration that, in some cases, resulted in injuries and even death. After initial resistance, Toyota was compelled to recall millions of Camrys, Corollas, Priuses, and other popular models, reconfiguring the gas pedal, installing brake override software, and making other fixes. An ongoing government investigation of Toyota's handling of the problems could result in penalties totaling millions of dollars.[17]

The FTC uses several procedures to enforce laws. It may issue a consent order through which a business accused of violations can agree to voluntary compliance without admitting guilt. If a business refuses to comply with an FTC request, the agency can issue a cease-and-desist order, which gives a final demand to stop an illegal practice. Firms often challenge cease-and-desist orders in court. The FTC can require advertisers to provide additional information about products in their advertisements, and it can force firms using deceptive advertising to correct earlier claims with new promotional messages. In some cases, the FTC can require a firm to give refunds to consumers misled by deceptive advertising.

The FTC and U.S. Department of Justice can stop mergers if they believe the proposed acquisition will reduce competition by making it harder for new companies to enter the field. In recent years, these agencies have taken a harder line on proposed mergers, especially in the computer, telecommunications, financial services, and health-care sectors.

Removing regulations also changes the competitive picture considerably. Following deregulation of the telecommunications and utilities industries, suppliers no longer have exclusive rights to operate within a territory. Natural gas utilities traditionally competed with electric companies to supply homeowners and businesses with energy needs. Because of deregulation, they now also compete with other gas companies. The restructuring of the electricity industry by state took hold immediately in the Northeast, ranging from Maine to Virginia and reaching through the Midwest in Ohio, Michigan, and Illinois. Indiana and Vermont abstained. Texas, Arizona, and Oregon also jumped on the bandwagon. But several states delayed deregulation activities, and California actually suspended them altogether. Restructuring caused major headaches for some utilities, leading to shortages and an inability to coordinate service with needs, nonmaintenance of power lines, and lack of funds for operating or decommissioning nuclear power plants. Thus, while deregulation may be designed to promote competition and provide better service and prices for consumers, it doesn't always work as planned.

The latest round of deregulation began with the passage of the Telecommunications Act of 1996 and its 2003 amendment, the Do Not Call law mentioned earlier. The Telecommunications Act removed barriers between local and long-distance phone companies and cable companies. It allowed the so-called Baby Bells—the regional Bell operating companies—to offer long-distance service; at the same time, long-distance companies offered local service. Satellite television providers such as Dish Network and DIRECTV and cable companies such as Comcast can offer phone service, while phone companies can get into the cable business. The change promises huge rewards for competitive winners. Consumers can shop around for the best deals and packages as more companies compete for their business by packaging services at reduced prices.

Other Regulatory Forces

Public and private consumer interest groups and self-regulatory organizations are also part of the legal environment. Consumer interest organizations have mushroomed since the late 1970s, and today hundreds of groups operate at national, state, and local levels. These organizations seek to protect consumers in as many areas as possible. Citing the need for a standardized credit scoring system, the three major credit-reporting agencies—Equifax, Experian, and TransUnion—collaborated to create VantageScore. But consumer groups and other industry observers have criticized the system for being inconsistent and of questionable value to consumers.[18] The Coalition for Fire-Safe Cigarettes is working state-by-state to pressure tobacco companies to produce cigarettes that will not smolder and start fires if left unattended. Bills mandating fire-safe cigarettes have been passed in Canada and in 43 U.S. states as well as the District of Columbia.[19]

Other groups attempt to advance the rights of minorities, senior citizens, and other causes. The power of these groups has also grown. AARP (formerly known as the American Association of Retired Persons) wields political and economic power, particularly as more and more people reach retirement age.[20]

Self-regulatory groups represent industries' attempts to set guidelines for responsible business conduct. The Council of Better Business Bureaus is a national organization devoted to consumer service and business self-regulation. The council's National Advertising Division (NAD) promotes truth and accuracy in advertising. It reviews and advocates voluntary resolution of advertising-related complaints between consumers and businesses. If NAD fails to resolve a complaint, an appeal can be made to the National Advertising Review Board, composed of advertisers, ad agency representatives, and public members. In addition, many individual trade associations set business guidelines and codes of conduct and encourage members' voluntary compliance.

Toyota was one of the first automakers to commit to building hybrid cars. Toyota continues to reinvent the hybrid Prius.

The Direct Marketing Association (DMA) supports consumer rights through its Commitment to Consumer Choice. Under this principle, DMA's more than 3,600 member organizations are required to inform consumers of their right to modify or discontinue receiving solicitations.[21]

As mentioned earlier, regulating the online world poses a challenge. Favoring self-regulation as the best starting point, the FTC sponsored a privacy initiative for consumers, advertisers, online companies, and others as a way to develop voluntary industry privacy guidelines. The Interactive Services Association is also working on its own privacy standards.

Controlling the Political-Legal Environment

Most marketers comply with laws and regulations. Doing so not only serves their customers but also avoids legal problems that could ultimately damage a firm's image and hurt profits. But smart marketers get ahead of the curve by providing products that will meet customers' future needs while also addressing government goals. Showing remarkable forward thinking, Toyota was one of the first automakers to commit to building hybrid cars. Its efforts were supported by a government tax break for purchasers of the first hybrids.

Consumer groups and political action committees within industries may try to influence the outcome of proposed legislation or change existing laws by engaging in political lobbying or boycotts. Lobbying groups frequently enlist the support of customers, employees, and suppliers to assist their efforts.

 assessment check

1. Identify the four phases of U.S. government regulation of business. What is the newest frontier?
2. Which federal agency wields the broadest regulatory powers for influencing marketing activities?

4 Outline the economic factors that affect marketing decisions and consumer buying power.

The Economic Environment

The overall health of the economy influences how much consumers spend and what they buy. This relationship also works the other way. Consumer buying plays an important role in the economy's health; in fact, consumer spending accounts for nearly 70 percent of the nation's total **gross domestic product (GDP)**, the sum of all goods and services produced by a nation in a year.[22] Because marketing activities are directed toward satisfying consumer wants and needs, marketers must first understand how economic conditions influence the purchasing decisions consumers make.

Marketing's **economic environment** consists of factors that influence consumer buying power and marketing strategies. They include the stage of the business cycle, the global economic crisis, inflation and deflation, unemployment, income, and resource availability.

gross domestic product (GDP) Sum of all goods and services produced by a nation in a year.

economic environment Factors that influence consumer buying power and marketing strategies, including stage of the business cycle, inflation and deflation, unemployment, income, and resource availability.

business cycle Pattern of stages in the level of economic activity: prosperity, recession, depression, and recovery.

Stages in the Business Cycle

Historically, the economy has tended to follow a cyclical pattern consisting of four stages: prosperity, recession, depression, and recovery. Consumer buying differs in each stage of the **business cycle**, and marketers must adjust their strategies accordingly. In times of prosperity, consumer spending maintains a brisk pace, and buyers are willing to spend more for premium versions of well-known brands. Growth in services such as banking and restaurants usually indicates a strong economy. When economists predict such conditions as low inflation and low unemployment, marketers respond by offering new products, increasing their promotional efforts, and expanding distribution. They might even raise prices to widen profit margins. But high prices for some items, such as energy, can affect businesses and consumers alike. Skyrocketing gasoline prices have led many consumers to seek other forms of transportation, including the electric bicycle which, in less than a decade, has grown to an $11 billion industry. Especially in China, India, and Europe, an electric bike enables many to postpone the more costly purchase of a car.[23]

During economic slowdowns, consumers focus on more basic, functional products that carry lower price tags. They limit travel, restaurant meals, and entertainment. They skip expensive vacations and cook their own meals. During a recession, marketers consider lowering prices and increasing promotions that include special offers to stimulate demand. They may also launch special value-priced products likely to appeal to cost-conscious buyers.

Consumer spending sinks to its lowest level during a depression. The last true depression in the United States occurred during the 1930s. Although a severe depression could occur again, most experts see it as a slim possibility. Through its monetary and fiscal policies, the federal government attempts to control extreme fluctuations in the business cycle that lead to depression.

In the recovery stage, the economy emerges from recession and consumer purchasing power increases. But while consumers have money to spend, caution often restrains their willingness to buy. A family might buy a new car if no-interest financing is available. A couple might decide to book a trip through a discount travel firm such as Expedia.com or Travelocity. Companies like these can make the most of an opportunity and develop loyal customers by offering superior service at lower prices. Recovery still remains a difficult stage for businesses just climbing out of a recession because they must earn profits while trying to gauge uncertain consumer demand. Many cope by holding down costs. Some trim payrolls and close branch offices. Others cut back on business travel budgets, substituting teleconferencing and videoconferencing.

Business cycles, like other aspects of the economy, are complex phenomena that, despite the efforts of government, businesspeople, and others to control them, sometimes have a life of their own. Unforeseen natural disasters—such as the recent spate of tornadoes and flooding across the United States; narrowly averted terrorist attacks, like the one attempted on a Detroit-bound jet on Christmas Day 2009; and the effects of war or peace—all have an impact on business and the economy as a whole. The most effective marketers know how to recognize ways to serve their customers during the best (and worst) of times.

briefly speaking

"The most reliable way to forecast the future is to try to understand the present."

—John Naisbitt
(b. 1929)
American author

The Global Economic Crisis

Sometimes business cycles take a severe turn and affect consumers and businesses across the globe. That is the case with the recent recession, called the worst economic downturn since the Great Depression of the 1930s. Typically, nations' GDP rates grow—some modestly at 2 to 4 percentage points a year and some, such as rapidly expanding India and China, at or near double digits. With the crisis, economists predicted that the world economy might shrink for the first time in 60 years.

A struggling economy generates its own downward spiral: fearing worse days ahead, consumers and businesses become cautious about spending money and as they spend less, demand for many products also drops. Lessened demand forces employers to take extraordinary steps just to stay in business: institute a shortened workweek with reduced salaries or even slash the workforce. In the United States, layoffs resulted in double-digit unemployment during the recent recession.

Especially during a recession, marketers look to emphasize value in their offerings. Some slash prices or offer sales to help customers stretch their budget dollars. Automakers Ford and Hyundai recently assured new-car buyers that they would assist them with payments for a period of time if they lost their jobs or would take the cars back to avoid damaging consumers' credit. Retailers that emphasized affordable products, such as Walmart and McDonald's, saw their sales increase. With the severity of the recession, all marketers needed to reevaluate their strategies and concentrate on their most promising products. But it remains to be seen whether or how much consumers, now used to price reductions and special offers, will change their habits once they regain their economic footing in a recovery.

Inflation and Deflation

A major constraint on consumer spending, which can occur during any stage of the business cycle, is inflation—rising prices caused by some combination of excess demand and increases in the costs of raw materials, component parts, human resources, or other factors of production. **Inflation** devalues money by reducing the products it can buy through persistent price increases. These rising prices increase marketers' costs, such as expenditures for wages and raw materials, and the resulting higher prices may therefore negatively affect sales. U.S. inflation hit a heart-stopping high in 1979 of 13.3 percent. Recently, annual inflation hovered around 2.82 percent.[24]

> **inflation** Rising prices caused by some combination of excess consumer demand and increases in the costs of one or more factors of production.

If inflation is so bad, is its opposite, *deflation,* better? At first, it might seem so. Falling prices mean that products are more affordable. But deflation can be a long and damaging downward spiral, causing a freefall in business profits, lower returns on most investments, and widespread job layoffs. The last time the United States experienced significant deflation was in the Great Depression of the 1930s.

UNEMPLOYMENT

Unemployment is defined as the proportion of people in the economy who are actively seeking work but do not have jobs. Unemployment rises during recessions and declines in the recovery and prosperity stages of the business cycle. Like inflation, unemployment affects the way consumers behave. Unless unemployment insurance, personal savings, and union benefits effectively offset lost earnings, unemployed people have relatively little money to spend; they buy food, pay the rent or mortgage, and try to keep up with utility bills. Recently, unemployment stood near 10 percent nationally. Not surprisingly, job cuts have a direct effect on consumer spending.

> **unemployment** Proportion of people in the economy actively seeking work that do not have jobs.

INCOME

Income is another important determinant of marketing's economic environment because it influences consumer buying power. By studying income statistics and trends, marketers can estimate market potential and plan to target specific market segments. A rise in income represents potential for increasing overall sales. Many marketers are particularly interested in **discretionary income**, the amount of money people have to spend after buying necessities such as food, clothing, and housing. Those whose industry involves the necessities seek to turn those needs into preferences for their goods and services. With slowdowns in the U.S. economy, American consumers experienced a drop in their

> **discretionary income** Money available to spend after buying necessities such as food, clothing, and housing.

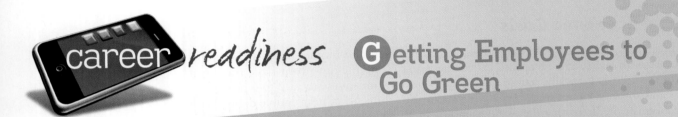

career *readiness*   **G**etting Employees to Go Green

As a marketing professional, you might expect to work long days or travel for the company on short notice. But you may be surprised if your employer asks you to think first before printing emails, or reminds you to turn off the lights when you leave for the night. When it comes to the environment, employers are paying increasing attention to becoming responsible citizens—and they're asking employees to help.

If you've been asked to develop or manage a "green" initiative, try these tips:

- *Identify champions.* Look for colleagues in your office who show an interest in environmental causes, then enlist their help. People who already care about the environment are often glad to help get the word out.

- *Communicate briefly, but often.* Employees are bombarded with information; if you want your messages to be read, keep them short and to the point. For example, a sign at the copier station can say "Do you *really* need color copies?" or "Save a tree; print duplex." Install recycling wastebaskets in workspaces. If your organization sponsors a "lunch-and-learn" program, invite engaging speakers to talk about recycling and related topics.

- *Grease the wheel.* Encourage employees in resource-saving behaviors: commuting via public transit or minimizing the use of paper and plastic. Include such gifts as a company-branded water bottle or coffee mug in the company's orientation of new hires. Hold random drawings for prizes like bus or train passes, pedometers, or thermal lunch bags.

- *Spread the fun.* Sponsor competitions to determine which department or work group is the greenest. Prizes can be small or substantial: green T-shirts for the winning team along with the privilege of wearing jeans on designated days all year, or an all-expenses-paid bus or bike tour—in a location of the winner's choice.

Sources: Kelly Spors, "How to Engage Employees in Workplace Greening," *Small Business Trends,* January 28, 2010, http://smallbiztrends.com; "Fairfield Companies Challenged to Go Green in 2010," *Acorn-Online,* January 11, 2010, http://www.acorn-online.com; "3,000 House Employees Learning to Go Green; Saving Energy and Money Takes Hold of Hill Culture," U.S. House of Representatives, January 8, 2010, http://cao.house.gov; Mary Tripsas, "Everybody in the Pool of Green Innovation," *The New York Times,* November 1, 2009, http://www.nytimes.com.

net worth because their homes and stock investments lost value. At the same time, Americans are spending less on nonessential items, and a greater proportion of their income goes toward food and other necessities.[25]

Changes in average earnings powerfully affect discretionary income. Historically, periods of major innovation have been accompanied by dramatic increases in living standards and rising incomes. Automobiles, televisions, telephones, and computers are just a few of the innovations that have changed consumers' lives—and standards of living. The Bureau of Economic Analysis, a division of the U.S. Department of Commerce, tracks personal income and discretionary income in the United States, then determines how much of that income is spent on personal consumption.[26] Marketers can use these figures to plan their approaches to everything from product development to the promotion of their goods and services.

Not only does income affect how much money individuals donate to not-for-profit organizations, but it can also affect the amount of time they're willing to spend on charitable efforts. The "Career Readiness" feature discusses how the most successful organizations structure their workplace greening programs.

Resource Availability

Resources are not unlimited. Shortages, temporary or permanent, can result from several conditions, including lack of raw materials, component parts, energy, or labor. The global financial crisis, coupled with extreme weather conditions such as drought and typhoons, signal the possibility of worldwide food shortages.[27]

One reaction to a shortage is **demarketing**, the process of reducing consumer demand for a product to a level that the firm can reasonably supply. Oil companies publicize tips for consumers on how to cut gasoline consumption, and utility companies encourage homeowners to install more insulation to reduce heating costs. Many cities promote mass transit and carpooling for consumers, and the federal government has created tax deductions for employers that subsidize their employees' transportation costs.[28] A shortage presents marketers with a unique set of challenges. They may have to allocate limited supplies, a sharply different activity from marketing's traditional objective of expanding sales volume. Shortages may require marketers to decide whether to spread limited supplies over all customers or limit purchases by some customers so that the firm can completely satisfy others.

Marketers have also devised ways to deal with increased demand for fixed amounts of resources. In its annual *Green Book,* the American Council for an Energy Efficient Economy (ACEEE) gives cars a "green score," rating vehicles on their manufacturers' use of scarce resources and attention to the environment in the production process. The recent winner? The ACEEE rated the Civic GX, powered by emission-friendly compressed natural gas, at the top.[29]

> **demarketing** Process of reducing consumer demand for a good or service to a level that the firm can supply.

The International Economic Environment

In today's global economy, marketers must also monitor the economic environment of other nations. Just as in the United States, a recession in Europe or Japan changes consumer and business buying habits. Changes in foreign currency rates compared with the U.S. dollar also affect marketing decisions. Labor costs and other factors affect firms' decisions to shift manufacturing operations overseas, decisions that may result in cutbacks in U.S. jobs and boosts to other nations' workforces. Although U.S. workers worry about the number of jobs sent overseas, some manufacturing remains strong in the United States. While workers in Asia assemble computers, production of computer chips often remains in the United States.

As China exports more and more goods to the world and to the United States in particular, some people voice concern over the widening trade gap. Only recently have broad economic reforms allowed China to play in the global marketplace. Some wonder if China's entry into world markets might help the West economically. However, with its gross domestic product still only a fraction of the U.S. GDP, economists say China cannot rescue the world economy—yet. But they point to China's rapidly expanding economy, fueled in part by a growing middle class with vast, untapped marketing potential.[30]

Politics in other countries affects the international economic environment as well. Elections in countries like Russia could result in a shift away from free-market policies. Turmoil in Venezuela affects the oil industry.

Hungary's long-time budget deficit drove the International Monetary Fund to orchestrate a financial bail-out for the nation, the first member of the European Union to require such aid. Economists are watching closely as Hungary's government works to manage its finances and reduce the gap.[31]

> **technological environment** Application to marketing of knowledge based on discoveries in science, inventions, and innovations.

 assessment check

1. Identify and describe briefly the four stages of the business cycle.
2. Explain how inflation and income affect consumer buying decisions.

The Technological Environment

The **technological environment** represents the application to marketing of knowledge based on discoveries in science, inventions, and innovations. Technology leads to new goods and services for consumers; it also improves existing products, offers better customer service, and often reduces prices through new, cost-efficient production and distribution methods. Technology can quickly make products obsolete—e-mail, for example, quickly eroded both letter writing and the market for fax

> **5** Discuss the impact of the technological environment on a firm's marketing activities.

machines—but it can just as quickly open new marketing opportunities sometimes in entirely new industries.

Pets have been wearing RFID—radio-frequency identification—transmitters for years, in case they got lost. Now RFID tags are used in many industries to locate everything from library books to laundry detergent. An RFID tag contains a computer chip with an antenna. A reader scans the tag and transmits the data from the tag to a computer. This innovation means that retailers, manufacturers, and others can locate and track inventory without opening packages. Dow AgroSciences, a division of Dow Chemical, uses RFID technology in its electronic system that detects and eliminates termites. When the system detects termite activity, it activates the RFID tag to send a signal to the exterminator. And to enhance life for the blind, students at Central Michigan University are at work on a robotic "guide dog" operated by RFID chips. But the use of RFID to track the movement of humans is controversial because of the privacy implications.[32]

Technology can address social concerns. In response to pressure from the World Trade Organization and the U.S. government, automakers used technology to develop more fuel-efficient vehicles and reduce dangerous emissions. Increased use of ethanol made from corn was another solution, but researchers have stepped up efforts to develop biofuels to replace gasoline. One such fuel, cellulosic ethanol, comes from cellulose—grass clippings, wood chips, yard waste—anything organic, even old tires. The biofuel emits significantly less greenhouse gases than gasoline and, if spilled, is less damaging to the environment. Scientists believe advances in technology eventually will make the fuel cost-effective to produce. Meanwhile, several start-up companies are working to create fuel from another organic source: algae. Low-cost, fast-growing, and carbon neutral, algae shows promise as a source of alternative energy.[33] See this chapter's "Solving an Ethical Controversy" feature for a debate concerning the use of phosphates.

Industry, government, colleges and universities, and other not-for-profit institutions all play roles in the development of new technology. The University of Delaware partners with private businesses like Allen Family Foods and Blue Skies Solar and Wind Power as it experiments with solar panels and other green technologies at the university's dairy farm, where researchers work to create a practical, sustainable dairy.[34]

Another major source of technology is the federal government, including the military. Air bags originated from Air Force ejection seats, digital computers were first designed to calculate artillery trajectories, and the microwave oven is a derivative of military radar systems. Even the Internet was first developed by the U.S. Department of Defense as a secure military communications system. Although the United States has long been the world leader in research, competition from rivals in Europe, Japan, and other Asian countries is intense.

Applying Technology

Marketers monitor the technological environment for a number of reasons. Creative applications of new technologies not only give a firm a definite competitive edge but can also benefit society. Marketers who monitor new technology and successfully apply it may also enhance customer service.

VoIP—voice over Internet protocol—is an alternative to traditional telecommunications services provided by telephone companies. The telephone is not connected to a traditional phone jack but instead is connected to a personal computer with any type of broadband Internet connection. Special software transmits phone conversations over the Internet, rather than through telephone lines. A VoIP user dials the phone as usual. Recipients can receive calls made using VoIP through regular telephone connections, land or wireless. Moreover, you can call another person who has VoIP using a regular landline or cell phone. Globally, VoIP continues to attract growing numbers of users—both consumers and businesses—mainly because of the cost savings. The VoIP business is also growing worldwide, with hundreds of service providers in the United States alone. One of the largest, Skype, has more than 500 million customers.[35]

As convenient as the Internet, cell phones, and Wi-Fi are for businesspeople and consumers, the networks that facilitate these connections aren't yet compatible with each other. So engineers are working on a new standard that would enable these networks to connect with each other, paving the way for melded services such as video exchanges between a cell phone and a computer. Called the Internet Protocol Multimedia Subsystem (IMS), the new standard is attempting to create a common

briefly speaking

"If you really care about the environment, you want to develop green technologies that are so inexpensive that it is profitable to be environmentally sensitive."

—Newt Gingrich
(b. 1943)
Professor, author, and former Speaker of the U.S. House of Representatives

VoIP (voice over Internet protocol) A phone connection through a personal computer with any type of broadband Internet connection.

solving an ethical controversy

In Search of Sparkling Glassware

Do you use a dishwasher? If so, chances are your detergent has contained phosphates, a compound that breaks down the grease and removes food.

But phosphates are bad for the environment. Phosphorus, an element in phosphates, pollutes the water supply, nourishing algae and ultimately killing fish. Washington was the first state to ban the sale of dishwasher detergents containing phosphates; more than a dozen states have followed, including the ban in Virginia, Maryland, and Washington, DC, to start in July 2010. Rather than sell different formulas in different states, some detergent marketers now distribute zero- or low-phosphate brands throughout the United States.

Consumers are unhappy; many say the eco-friendly alternatives don't get their dishes clean. Some Washington residents have even traveled to neighboring states in search of the traditional detergent formula.

Should states ban phosphates from dishwasher detergent?

PRO

1. Water treatment plants are ineffective at breaking down phosphates. When phosphates enter the water supply, they serve as food for algae. Dying algae consumes the oxygen in a lake or stream, destroying the ecosystem.

2. Consumers have a choice of several eco-friendly alternatives to the traditional detergent formula. Companies like Procter & Gamble continue to improve their products to assure sparkling-clean dishes.

CON

1. Banning dishwasher detergents containing phosphates is overkill. The amount of phosphorus in the water supply estimated to come from dishwashing is tiny compared to the amount that comes from farms and lawns, where fertilizers are used.

2. Automatic dishwashers are a time- and water-saver and get dishes cleaner because they use hotter water. Phosphate-free detergents leave glassware cloudy and silverware spotty. Having to wash those items by hand defeats the purpose.

Summary

Keeping lakes and rivers phosphate-free is an important goal. We need to find ways to reduce the phosphorus that comes from phosphates in other products.

Sources: Holly Martin, "Phosphate Ban May Make Cleaning Dishes More Difficult in Va., Md. And D.C.," *Manassas Environmental News Examiner,* January 27, 2010, http://www.examiner.com; Teresa F. Lindeman, "Phosphate Phaseout Has Dishwasher Soap Makers Scrambling for an Alternative," *Pittsburgh Post-Gazette,* November 29, 2009, http://www.post-gazette.com; Tom Avril, "The Dish on Phosphates," *Philadelphia Inquirer,* October 5, 2009, http://www.philly.com; Nicholas K. Geranios, "Spokane Residents Rebel over Dirty Dishes," *TheEagle.com,* March 28, 2009, http://www.theeagle.com.

interface so that data can be carried across networks between different devices. The implications for various communications providers are enormous—not only will they find new ways to cooperate, but they will also find new ways to compete. Subsequent chapters discuss in more detail how companies apply technologies—such as databases, blogs, and interactive promotional techniques—to create a competitive advantage.

 assessment check

1. What are some of the consumer benefits of technology?

2. Why must marketers monitor the technological environment?

The Social-Cultural Environment

social-cultural environment
Component of the marketing environment consisting of the relationship between the marketer, society, and culture.

consumerism Social force within the environment that aids and protects the consumer by exerting legal, moral, and economic pressures on business and government.

A rise in consumer activism has led retailers like Whole Foods to abandon plastic shopping bags in favor of reasonably priced, reusable cloth alternatives.

As a nation, the United States is becoming older, more affluent, and more culturally diverse. The birthrate is falling, and subculture populations are rising. People express concerns about the natural environment, buying ecologically friendly products that reduce pollution. They value their time with family and friends, cooking meals at home and exchanging vacation photos over the Internet. Marketers need to track these trends to be in tune with consumers' needs and desires. These aspects of consumer lifestyles help shape marketing's **social-cultural environment**—the relationship between marketing, society, and culture.

To remain competitive, marketers must be sensitive to society's demographic shifts and changing values. These variables affect consumers' reactions to different products and marketing practices. The baby boom generation—the 78 million Americans born between 1946 and 1964—represents a $2.1 trillion market. As boomers approach and enter retirement, marketers are scrambling to identify their needs and wants. With a longer life expectancy and the hope of more time and money to spend, baby boomers view retirement much differently than earlier generations did. Marketers already know that boomers feel young at heart and enjoy their leisure time, but they aren't playing canasta and shuffleboard—they're becoming "social media mavens" who spend a significant portion of their free time surfing the Web and connecting with friends and family on social networking sites like Facebook.[36] Some even launch a second career, starting their own small business. And boomers have a whole new take on the concept of grandparenting. More than past generations, boomer grandparents get actively involved in their grandchildren's daily lives and are more inclined to spend money on them. An estimated 20 percent of all travel involves grandchildren with grandparents, with or without their parents along. As they age, boomers will need health-care goods and services and, should they live longer, they may need everything from physical therapy for a repaired knee to a motorized scooter to get around.

Another social-cultural consideration is the increasing importance of cultural diversity. The United States is a mixed society composed of various submarkets, each with its unique values, cultural characteristics, consumer preferences, and purchasing behaviors. In an effort to attract the millions of Hispanic viewers in the United States, satellite and cable TV companies now offer more Spanish-language programming. Spanish-language networks Univision and Telemundo, which once dominated the Hispanic TV market, now face competition from Comcast, Cablevision, Time Warner Cable, Dish Network, and DIRECTV. Traditional media companies are creating networks that target online financial advertising and investment news to Latin American audiences. More than 340 Hispanic media outlets operate on the Web, with nearly 100 of the sites online only.[37]

© NEWSCOM

Marketers also need to learn about cultural and societal differences among countries abroad, particularly as business becomes more and more global. Marketing strategies that work in the United States often fail when used in other countries, and vice versa. In many cases, marketers must redesign packages and modify products and advertising messages to suit the tastes and preferences of different cultures. Chapter 7 explores the social-cultural aspects of global marketing.

Consumerism

Changing societal values have led to **consumerism**, defined as a social force within the environment that aids and protects the consumer by exerting legal, moral, and economic pressures on business and government. Today everyone—marketers, industry, government, and the public—is acutely aware of the impact of consumerism on the nation's economy and general well-being.

Marketers see a rise in consumer activism. Americans use an estimated 100 billion plastic shopping bags a year, accounting for 0.5 percent of the solid waste in landfills. Increasingly, however, retailers are trying to change that behavior. In 2009, Whole Foods discontinued the use of plastic shopping bags throughout its stores in the United States, Canada, and the United Kingdom. They and other retailers sell reasonably priced, reusable cloth alternatives. Other chains, like Target and CVS, offer a discount to shoppers for not using plastic bags.[38]

But firms cannot always adjust to meet the demands of consumer groups. The choice between pleasing all consumers and remaining profitable—thus surviving—defines one of the most difficult dilemmas facing business. Given these constraints, what do consumers have the right to expect from the companies from which they buy goods and services? The most frequently quoted answer to this question comes from a speech made by President John F. Kennedy more than four decades ago. Although this list does not amount to a definitive statement, it offers good rules of thumb that explain basic **consumer rights**:

1. *The right to choose freely.* Consumers should be able to choose from among a range of goods and services.

2. *The right to be informed.* Consumers should be provided with enough education and product information to enable them to be responsible buyers.

3. *The right to be heard.* Consumers should be able to express their legitimate displeasure to appropriate parties—that is, sellers, consumer assistance groups, and city or state consumer affairs offices.

4. *The right to be safe.* Consumers should be assured that the goods and services they purchase are not injurious with normal use. Goods and services should be designed so that the average consumer can use them safely.

These rights have formed the conceptual framework of much of the legislation enacted during the first five decades of the consumer rights movement. However, the question of how best to guarantee them remains unanswered. Sometimes local, state, or federal authorities step in. New York was the first city in the United States to require fast-food and casual-dining restaurants to post calorie counts of the various items displayed on their menu. Since then, similar mandates have been issued in New Jersey, the cities of Portland and Seattle, and in parts of California, all addressing the issue of obesity, fast becoming a nationwide health problem.[39]

Consumers' right to safety encompasses a vast range of products, from automobiles to children's toys. Sometimes it seems as though safety recalls are reported in the media too regularly. You might even receive a letter in the mail from a manufacturer informing you of a recall for a part on your refrigerator or car. To streamline the exchange of information among federal agencies and to make it more convenient for consumers to learn about product recalls, the U.S. government has established the Web site **www.Recalls.gov**. This Web site consolidates recall information

consumer rights List of legitimate consumer expectations suggested by President John F. Kennedy.

ARE YOU POURING ON THE POUNDS?

DON'T DRINK YOURSELF FAT.
Cut back on soda and other sugary beverages.
Go with water, seltzer or low-fat milk instead.

NYC Department of Health & Mental Hygiene
Michael R. Bloomberg, Mayor
Thomas Farley, M.D., M.P.H., Commissioner

COURTESY OF THE CITY OF NEW YORK; DEPARTMENT OF HEALTH & MENTAL HYGIENE

New York was the first city in the United States to require fast-food and casual-dining restaurants to post calorie counts for items on their menu. The city is now running a cautionary ad about drinking too much soda.

generated by the six federal agencies empowered to issue recalls, including the Consumer Product Safety Commission, the Food and Drug Administration, and others. The user-friendly site organizes information into broad categories: Boats, Consumer Products, Cosmetics, Environmental Products, Food, Medicine, and Motor Vehicles.[40]

Consumerism, along with the rest of the social-cultural environment for marketing decisions at home and abroad, is expanding in scope and importance. Today, no marketer can initiate a strategic decision without considering the society's norms, values, culture, and demographics. Understanding how these variables affect decisions is so important that some firms have created a new position—typically, manager of public policy research—to study the changing societal environment's future impact on their organizations.

 assessment check

1. Define *consumerism*.
2. Identify the four consumer rights.

Ethical Issues in Marketing

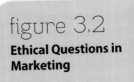 **Describe the ethical issues in marketing.**

The five environments described so far in this chapter do not completely capture the role that marketing plays in society and the resulting effects and responsibilities of marketing activities. Because marketing is closely connected with various public issues, it invites constant scrutiny. Moreover, because marketing acts as an interface between an organization and the society in which it operates, marketers often carry much of the responsibility for dealing with social issues that affect their firms.

Marketing operates outside the firm. It responds to that outside environment, and in turn is acted on by environmental influences. Relationships with employees, suppliers, the government, consumers, and society as a whole frame the social issues that marketers must address. The way that marketers deal with these social issues has a significant effect on their firm's eventual success. The diverse social issues that marketers face can be divided into two major categories: marketing ethics and social responsibility. While these two categories certainly overlap, this simple classification system provides a method for studying these issues.

marketing ethics
Marketers' standards of conduct and moral values.

Environmental influences have directed increased attention toward **marketing ethics**, defined as marketers' standards of conduct and moral values. Ethics concern matters of right and wrong: the responsibility of individuals and firms to do what is morally right. As Figure 3.2 shows, each element of the marketing mix raises its own set of ethical questions. Before any improvements to a firm's marketing program can be made, each element must be evaluated.

figure 3.2
Ethical Questions in Marketing

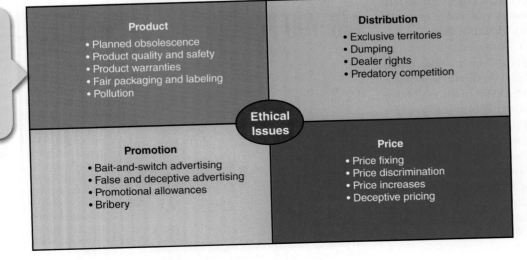

Product
- Planned obsolescence
- Product quality and safety
- Product warranties
- Fair packaging and labeling
- Pollution

Distribution
- Exclusive territories
- Dumping
- Dealer rights
- Predatory competition

Ethical Issues

Promotion
- Bait-and-switch advertising
- False and deceptive advertising
- Promotional allowances
- Bribery

Price
- Price fixing
- Price discrimination
- Price increases
- Deceptive pricing

Creating an ethics program may be complicated and time consuming, but worthwhile. Some firms take their cue from the U.S. Federal Sentencing Guidelines for Organizations, which provides a framework for evaluating misconduct in business activities such as fraud or price fixing. After discovering that similar cases had been resolved differently by courts, the U.S. Sentencing Commission developed guidelines in 1991 that rely on what legislators call the "stick-and-carrot approach" to corporate ethics: the financial penalties that the courts can impose for wrongdoing are the stick, while the existence of an effective ethics program can reduce the fines the courts can set, which serves as the carrot. Sentencing guidelines act as an incentive for corporations to implement effective ethics compliance programs—if they are hauled into court, the existence of such a program can help reduce penalties.

In some industries, organizations are required by law to maintain corporate-level positions responsible for ethics and legal compliance. Typically, ethics officers are responsible for creating and maintaining an ethical culture within the organization. They ensure that ethical protocols are established and enforced, and they serve as the chief source of information to all stakeholders inside and outside the organization regarding ethics.[41] Figure 3.3 presents a step-by-step framework for building an effective program.

Because ethical behavior is so important to business conduct, some firms and universities have taken an unusual step. They invite convicted corporate criminals to speak to employees and students about their mistakes and the consequences of their actions.[42]

Ensuring ethical practices means promising customers and business partners not to sacrifice quality and fairness for profit. In exchange, organizations hope for increased customer loyalty toward their brands. Yet issues involving marketing ethics are not always clear-cut. The issue of cigarette advertising, for example, has divided the ranks of advertising executives. Is it right for advertisers to promote a product that, while legal, has known health hazards?

For years, charges of unethical conduct plagued the tobacco industry. In the largest civil settlement in U.S. history, tobacco manufacturers agreed to pay $206 billion to 46 states. Four other states—Florida, Minnesota, Mississippi, and Texas—had separate settlements totaling another $40 billion. The settlement freed tobacco companies from state claims for the cost of treating sick smokers. For their part, cigarette makers could no longer advertise on billboards or use cartoon characters in ads, nor could they sell nontobacco merchandise containing tobacco brands or logos. Initially, states used settlement monies to fund tobacco prevention programs, but in recent years most states cut program funding well below the level recommended by the Centers for Disease Control and Prevention. As a result, tobacco use among adults—about 21 percent—has remained essentially unchanged since 2004.[43]

People develop standards of ethical behavior based on their own systems of values, which help them deal with ethical questions in their personal lives. However, the workplace may generate serious conflicts when individuals discover that their ethical beliefs are not necessarily in line with those of their employer. For example, employees may think that shopping online during a lunch break using an employer-owned computer is fine, but the company may decide otherwise. The questionnaire in Figure 3.4 highlights other everyday ethical dilemmas. (See page 97 for the answers.)

briefly speaking

"Thou shalt not use profanity.
Thou shalt not covet thy neighbor's putter.
Thou shalt not steal thy neighbor's ball.
Thou shalt not bear false witness in the final tally."

—Ground rules for a Grand Rapids, Michigan, ministers' golf tournament

1. Appoint a senior-level ethics compliance officer.

2. Set up an ethics code capable of detecting and preventing misconduct.

3. Distribute a written code of ethics to employees, subsidiaries, and associated companies and require all business partners to abide by it.

4. Conduct regular ethics training programs to communicate standards and procedures.

5. Establish systems to monitor misconduct and report grievances.

6. Establish consistent punishment guidelines to enforce standards and codes.

7. Encourage an open-door policy, allowing employees to report cases of misconduct without fear of retaliation.

8. Prohibit employees with a track record of misconduct from holding positions with substantial discretionary authority.

9. Promote ethically aware and responsible managers.

10. Continually monitor effectiveness of all ethics-related programs.

figure 3.3

Ten Steps for Corporations to Improve Standards of Business Ethics

Source: Adapted from O.C. Ferrell, John Fraedrich, and Linda Ferrell, *Business Ethics: Ethical Decision Making and Cases,* Eighth Edition, pp. 222–233. Copyright ©2011 by Cengage Learning. Reprinted with permission.

Office Technology

1. Is it wrong to use company e-mail for personal reasons?
   ❑ Yes ❑ No

2. Is it wrong to use office equipment to help your children or spouse do schoolwork?
   ❑ Yes ❑ No

3. Is it wrong to play computer games on office equipment during the workday?
   ❑ Yes ❑ No

4. Is it wrong to use office equipment to do Internet shopping?
   ❑ Yes ❑ No

5. Is it unethical to blame an error you made on a technological glitch?
   ❑ Yes ❑ No

6. Is it unethical to visit pornographic Web sites using office equipment?
   ❑ Yes ❑ No

Gifts and Entertainment

7. What's the value at which a gift from a supplier or client becomes troubling?
   ❑ $25 ❑ $50 ❑ $100

8. Is a $50 gift to a boss unacceptable?
   ❑ Yes ❑ No

9. Is a $50 gift from the boss unacceptable?
   ❑ Yes ❑ No

10. Of gifts from suppliers: Is it OK to take a $200 pair of football tickets?
    ❑ Yes ❑ No

11. Is it OK to take a $120 pair of theater tickets?
    ❑ Yes ❑ No

12. Is it OK to take a $100 holiday food basket?
    ❑ Yes ❑ No

13. Is it OK to take a $25 gift certificate?
    ❑ Yes ❑ No

14. Can you accept a $75 prize won at a raffle at a supplier's conference?
    ❑ Yes ❑ No

Truth and Lies

15. Due to on-the-job pressure, have you ever abused or lied about sick days?
    ❑ Yes ❑ No

16. Due to on-the-job pressure, have you ever taken credit for someone else's work or idea?
    ❑ Yes ❑ No

figure 3.4

Test Your Workplace Ethics
*Ethics questionnaire answers are on page 97.

Source: Ethics & Compliance Officer Association, Waltham, Massachusetts; Leadership Group, Wilmette, Illinois; survey sampled a cross-section of workers at large companies and nationwide; used with permission from Ethics & Compliance Officer Association.

How can these conflicts be resolved? In addition to individual and organizational ethics, individuals may be influenced by a third basis of ethical authority—a professional code of ethics that transcends both organizational and individual value systems. A professional peer association can exercise collective oversight to limit a marketer's individual behavior. Any code of ethics must anticipate the variety of problems marketers are likely to encounter. Promotional matters tend to receive the greatest attention, but ethical considerations also influence marketing research, product strategy, distribution strategy, and pricing.

Ethics in Marketing Research

Invasion of personal privacy has become a critical issue in marketing research. The proliferation of databases, the selling of address lists, and the ease with which consumer information can be gathered through Internet technology have increased public concern. The issue of privacy will be explored in greater detail in Chapter 4. One marketing research tool particularly problematic is the promise of cash or gifts in return for marketing information that can then be sold to direct marketers. Consumers commonly disclose their personal information in return for an e-mail newsletter or a favorite magazine.

Privacy issues have mushroomed with the growth of the Internet, with huge consequences to both consumers and marketers. A hacker break-in into the computer network of TJX, the parent of discount retail chains TJ Maxx and Marshalls, resulted in the theft of credit and debit card data for more than 40 million accounts. After apprehending the hacker, authorities learned he and his accomplices used the data to create fake credit and debit cards, then used the cards worldwide to make purchases and ATM withdrawals.[44] Managed health-care provider Health Net of the Northeast lost a hard drive containing medical information along with names, addresses, and Social Security numbers of 1.5 million customers. The unencrypted data comprised seven years' worth of patient information.[45] Incidents like these point to the importance of using encryption programs to safeguard data.

Several agencies, including the FTC, offer assistance to Internet consumers. Consumers can go to **ftc.gov/privacy** for information. The Direct Marketing Association also provides services, such as the Mail, Telephone, and E-Mail Preference Services, to help consumers get their names removed from marketers' targeted lists. Registration for the U.S. government's Do Not Call Registry is available at (888) 382–1222 and **www.donotcall.gov**. Unlistme.com and Junkbusters are free Web services that also help consumers remove their names from direct-mail and telemarketing lists.

Ethics in Product Strategy

Product quality, planned obsolescence, brand similarity, and packaging all raise ethical issues. Feeling the competition, some marketers have tried packaging practices that might be considered misleading, deceptive, or unethical. Larger packages take up more shelf space, and consumers notice them. An odd-sized package makes price comparisons difficult. Bottles with concave bottoms give the impression that they contain more liquid than they actually do. Are these packaging practices justified in the name of competition, or are they deceptive? Growing regulatory mandates appear to be narrowing the range of discretion in this area.

How do you evaluate the quality of a product like a beverage? By flavor or by ingredients? Citing several studies, some consumer advocates say that the ingredients in soft drinks—mainly the high sugar content—are linked to obesity in consumers, particularly children. Not surprisingly, the beverage industry disagrees, arguing that lack of exercise and a poor diet in general are greater contributors to weight gain than regular consumption of drinks.

Ethics in Distribution

Two ethical issues influence a firm's decisions regarding distribution strategy:

1. What is the appropriate degree of control over the distribution channel?
2. Should a company distribute its products in marginally profitable outlets that have no alternative source of supply?

The question of channel control typically arises in relationships between manufacturers and franchise dealers. For example, should an automobile dealership, a gas station, or a fast-food outlet be forced to purchase parts, materials, and supplementary services from the parent organization?

The second question concerns marketers' responsibility to serve unsatisfied market segments even if the profit potential is slight. Should marketers serve retail stores in low-income areas, serve users of limited amounts of the firm's product, or serve a declining rural market? These problems are difficult to resolve because often they involve individuals rather than broad segments of the general public. An important first step is to ensure that the firm consistently enforces its channel policies.

Ethics in Promotion

Promotion raises many ethical questions because it is the most direct link between a firm and its customers. Personal selling has always been a target of criticism—and jokes about untrustworthiness. Used-car dealers, horse traders, and purveyors of quack remedies have been the targets of such barbs. But promotion covers many areas, ranging from advertising to direct marketing, and it is vital for marketers to monitor their ethics in all marketing communications. Truth in advertising—representing accurately a product's benefits and drawbacks, warranties, price, and availability—is the bedrock of ethics in promotion.

briefly speaking

"Have the courage to say no. Have the courage to face the truth. Do the right thing because it is right. These are the magic keys to living your life with integrity."

—W. Clement Stone
(1902–2002)
Businessman, philanthropist, and motivational author

briefly speaking

"Character is doing what's right when nobody's looking."

—J. C. Watts Jr.
(b. 1957)
Former University of Oklahoma quarterback, politician, founder JC Watts Companies

Many organizations have modified how they advertise their products, pledging to emphasize the healthy benefits of snacks.

Marketing to children has been under close scrutiny for many years because children have not yet developed the skills to receive marketing messages critically. They simply believe everything they see and hear. With childhood obesity a serious concern in America, Kellogg Company announced it would change how it advertises its breakfast cereals to children worldwide, focusing solely on products that meet nutrition guidelines.[46] Other organizations like General Mills, Kraft Foods, McDonald's, and Quaker Oats pledged to also emphasize healthy choices. Yet, recent studies by Yale University and Children Now, a California–based child advocacy group, found that the food industry continues to target children in promoting the least nutritious products.[47] The Federal Trade Commission's Working Group on Food Marketed to Children recently suggested new nutritional standards for food advertising to children. Critics claim, however, that because the standards are guidelines and not regulations, they aren't enforceable.[48]

Promoting certain products to college students can raise ethical questions as well. College students are a prime market for firms that sell everything from electronics to beer. And although laws prohibit the sale of alcohol to anyone under 21, companies often advertise beer through popular items like hats, shirts, bar signs, and other collectibles. Critics have long claimed this practice supports underage drinking.

Another ethical issue involves paying universities for the use of their logo, team name, or mascot in advertising products and services to its students. Anheuser-Busch recently came under fire from colleges and universities across the nation for marketing Bud Light on campuses in "Fan Cans" specially designed in their school's colors. Citing concerns about alcohol use and trademark infringement, the schools contacted Anheuser-Busch to stop local distribution; some even threatened legal action.[49]

Ethics in Pricing

Pricing is probably the most regulated aspect of a firm's marketing strategy. As a result, most unethical price behavior is also illegal. Some aspects of pricing, however, are still open to ethics abuses. For example, should some customers pay more for merchandise if distribution costs are higher in their areas? Do marketers have an obligation to warn vendors and customers of impending price, discount, or return policy changes?

Some credit card companies target consumers with poor credit ratings and offer them what industry observers call "subprime" or "fee-harvesting" credit cards. Under such an arrangement, the company lures consumers to sign up for the card, promising to improve their credit rating. The cardholder is then charged exorbitant annual fees, leaving them in worse financial shape than before.[50]

While consumers are almost always informed of credit card terms in their agreements, the print often is tiny and the language may be hard to understand. For instance, a credit card issuer might advertise the benefits of its premium card, but the fine print explains that the firm is allowed to substitute a different plan—with a higher interest rate—if the applicant doesn't qualify for the premium card.

The Credit Card Accountability, Responsibility and Disclosure Act, enacted in 2009, curbs abuses in the credit-card industry and ends many questionable practices of credit card companies regarding interest rates, billing cycles, finance charges, and more.[51]

All these concerns must be dealt with in developing a professional ethic for pricing products. The ethical issues involved in pricing for today's highly competitive and increasingly computerized markets are discussed in greater detail in Chapters 18 and 19.

assessment check

1. Define *marketing ethics.*
2. Identify the five areas in which ethics can be a problem.

Social Responsibility in Marketing

Companies can do business in such a way that everyone benefits—customers, the companies themselves, and society as a whole. While ethical business practices are vital to a firm's long-term survival and growth, **social responsibility** raises the bar even higher. In marketing, social responsibility involves accepting an obligation to give equal weight to profits, consumer satisfaction, and social well-being in evaluating a firm's performance. In addition to measuring sales, revenues, and profits, a firm must also consider ways in which it contributes to the overall well-being of its customers and society.

Social responsibility allows a wide range of opportunities for companies to shine. If companies are reluctant, government legislation can mandate socially responsible actions. Government may require firms to take socially responsible actions in matters of environmental policy, deceptive product claims, and other areas. Also, consumers, through their power to repeat or withhold purchases, may force marketers to provide honest and relevant information and fair prices. The four dimensions of social responsibility—economic, legal, ethical, and philanthropic—are shown in Figure 3.5. The first two dimensions have long been recognized, but ethical obligations and the need for marketers to be good corporate citizens have increased in importance in recent years.

The locus for socially responsible decisions in organizations has always been an important issue. But who should accept specific accountability for the social effects of marketing decisions? Responses include the district sales manager, the marketing vice president, the firm's CEO, and even the board of directors. Probably the most valid assessment holds that all marketers, regardless of their stations in the organization, remain accountable for the social aspects of their decisions.

Marketing's Responsibilities

The concept of business's social responsibility has traditionally concerned managers' relationships with customers, employees, and stockholders. In general, managers traditionally have felt responsible for providing quality products at reasonable prices for customers, adequate wages and decent working environments for employees, and acceptable profits for stockholders. Only occasionally did the concept extend to relations with the government and rarely with the general public.

Today, corporate responsibility has expanded to cover the entire framework of society. A decision to temporarily delay the installation of a pollution-control device may satisfy the traditional sense of responsibility. Customers would continue to receive an uninterrupted supply of the plant's products, employees would not face layoffs, and stockholders would still receive reasonable returns

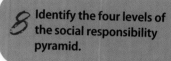

Identify the four levels of the social responsibility pyramid.

social responsibility
Marketing philosophies, policies, procedures, and actions that have the enhancement of society's welfare as a primary objective.

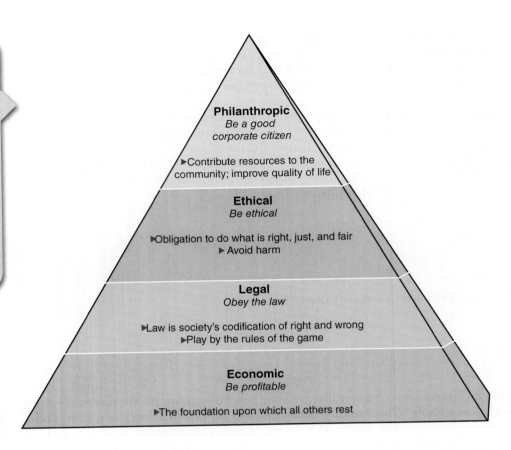

figure 3.5

The Four Step Pyramid of Social Responsibility

Source: The Four Step Pyramid of Corporate Social Responsibility from *Business Horizons*, Vol. 34, 1991, page 92, Freeman & Liedtka, "Corp. Social Responsibility." Reprinted from *Business Horizons* © 1991 with permission from Elsevier.

on their investments. Contemporary business ethics, however, would not accept this choice as socially responsible.

Contemporary marketing decisions must consider their global effect. Some clothing manufacturers and retailers have come under fire for buying from foreign suppliers who force employees, including children, to work long hours in dangerous conditions or pay less than a living wage. In some cases, workers who attempted to form a union have been threatened, fired, and even beaten.[52]

Marketers must also consider the long-term effects of their decisions and the well-being of future generations. Manufacturing processes that damage the environment or that use up natural energy resources are easy targets for criticism.

Marketers can use several methods to help their companies behave in socially responsible ways. Chapter 1 discussed cause marketing as one channel through which firms can promote social causes and at the same time benefit by linking their people and products to worthy undertakings. Socially responsible marketing involves campaigns that encourage people to adopt socially beneficial behaviors such as safe driving, eating more nutritious food, or improving the working conditions of people half a world away. And organizations that sponsor socially responsible programs not only help society but also develop goodwill for an organization, which could help the bottom line in the long run.

One way entire communities can benefit is through socially responsible investing. Many local banks and credit unions are committed to investing in their communities. When consumers purchase certificates of deposit or open money market accounts, the bank or credit union can use the money to finance loans for affordable housing or for small businesses. The U.S. Treasury Department has certified nearly 850 community development financial institutions that serve neighborhoods. These institutions might otherwise be overlooked and serve a second purpose to educate low-income borrowers.[53]

Marketing and Ecology

Ecology—the relationship between organisms and their natural environments—has become a driving force in influencing how businesses operate. Many industry and government leaders rank the protection of the environment as the biggest challenge facing today's corporations. Environmental issues such as water pollution, waste disposal, acid rain, depletion of the ozone layer, and global warming affect everyone. They influence all areas of marketing decision making, including product planning and public relations, spanning such topics as planned obsolescence, pollution control, recycling waste materials, and resource conservation.

In creating new-product offerings that respond to consumer demands for convenience by offering extremely short-lived products such as disposable diapers, ballpoint pens, razors, and cameras, marketers occasionally find themselves accused of intentionally offering products with limited durability—in other words, of practicing planned obsolescence. In addition to convenience-oriented items, other products become obsolete when rapid changes in technology create superior alternatives. In the computer industry, changes take place so quickly that lawmakers in several states have proposed legislation to force manufacturers to take back "e-waste"—used PCs and other technology products that contain toxic chemicals. For example, HP now supplies its printers with two cartridges—one for color and one for black. The replacement packs for each cartridge come with a self-addressed, postage-paid pouch to mail empty cartridges back to the company for reuse.

Public concern about pollution of such natural resources as water and air affects some industries, such as pharmaceuticals or heavy-goods manufacturing, more than others. Still, the marketing system annually generates billions of tons of packaging materials such as glass, metal, paper, and plastics that add to the world's growing piles of trash and waste. Recycling such materials, as HP does, is another important aspect of ecology. Recycling can benefit society by saving natural resources and energy as well as by alleviating a major factor in environmental pollution—waste disposal.

Unwanted and outdated electronic waste is the latest trash to overrun landfills as technology advances motivate Americans to ditch their old electronics for newer models. Increasingly, consumers wonder how to dispose of their old computers, monitors, printers, TVs, phones, cameras, and other gadgets, especially since many of the older models contain lead and other hazardous materials requiring special handling. Best Buy, the nation's largest electronics retailer, sponsors a recycling program under which customers can drop off a wide variety of unwanted electronics products—even if they weren't bought at Best Buy. There's a two-item-per-household-per-day limit, and while Best Buy imposes a $10 charge on certain recycled items like TVs and computer monitors, customers receive a $10 Best Buy gift card in return.[54]

Many companies respond to consumers' growing concern about ecological issues through **green marketing**—production, promotion, and reclamation of environmentally sensitive products. In the green marketing revolution of the early 1990s, marketers were quick to tie their companies and products to ecological themes. Consumers have responded by purchasing more and more of these goods, providing profits and opportunities for growth to the companies that make and sell them. The Sustainability Consortium, an independent organization dedicated to driving sustainability in

Timberland Earthkeepers:
Lightweight. Organic. Recycled.
Worship the ground you walk on.

Timberland Make it better.
www.timberlandonline.co.uk

In addition to measuring sales, revenues, and profits, a firm must consider ways in which it has contributed to the overall well-being of society. This ad shows Timberland's awareness of environmental issues.

© IMAGE COURTESY OF THE ADVERTISING ARCHIVES

green marketing
Production, promotion, and reclamation of environmentally sensitive products.

Unwanted and outdated electronics are the latest trash to overrun landfills. Increasingly, recycling programs are offered for these discarded items.

© PHOTOROLLER/SHUTTERSTOCK.COM

briefly speaking

"Air pollution is turning Mother Nature prematurely gray."

—Irv Kupcinet
(1912–2003)
American newspaper columnist

consumer goods, is working with Best Buy, Dell, HP, Intel, Toshiba, and Walmart to create standards to help consumers make green choices in electronics.[55] Accor North America, parent of hotel chain Motel 6 and the Sofitel and Studio 6 brands, is piloting a voluntary green rating program in some of its hotels. The Marriott chain is adding more green hotels to its portfolio. The recently opened Fairmont Pittsburgh, with 185 guestrooms, is one of the largest construction projects to be certified by the U.S. Green Building Council.[56]

Major League Baseball partnered with the Natural Resources Defense Council, an environmentalist group, to identify numerous ways to go green. Employees at Turner Field, home of the Atlanta Braves, wear shirts made, in part, from recycled soda bottles. The shirts evolved from an idea proposed by team sponsor The Coca-Cola Company. Night games at Yankee Stadium are illuminated by energy-efficient bulbs. The electricity savings could power an estimated 75 homes for a year. Fans who carpool to Tampa Bay Rays home games get free parking at the stadium in St. Petersburg. Pacific Gas & Electric, a sponsor of the San Francisco Giants, helped underwrite a green concession stand where the plates, napkins, and utensils are biodegradable; food fries in energy-efficient fryers and compact fluorescent bulbs light the way.[57]

✓ **assessment check**

1. Identify the four levels of the social responsibility pyramid.

2. What are the benefits of green marketing?

strategic implications → [f] [t] [🛒]

of marketing in the 21st century

arketing decisions that businesses make are influenced by changes in the competitive, political-legal, economic, technological, and social-cultural environments. Marketing ethics and social responsibility will continue to play important roles in business transactions in your hometown and around the globe.

As the Internet and the rapid changes in technology that it represents are fully absorbed into the competitive environment, competition is even more intense than before. Much of the competition results from innovations in technology and scientific discoveries. Business in the 21st century is propelled by information technolo-

gies but sustained by creative thinking and the willingness of marketers to meet challenges. Marketers face new regulations as the political and legal environment responds to changes in the United States and abroad. As the population ages and the social-cultural environment evolves, marketers will seek to meet the demands for new goods and services for consumers, such as increased health-related merchandise. As always, they will try to anticipate and make the most of every opportunity afforded by the business cycle.

Ethics and social responsibility must underlie everything that marketers do in the 21st century—those who find ways to "do well by doing good" will succeed.

Review of Chapter Objectives

1 Identify the five components of the marketing environment.

The five components of the marketing environment are (1) the *competitive environment*—the interactive process that occurs in the marketplace as competing organizations seek to satisfy markets; (2) the *political-legal environment*—the laws and interpretations of laws that require firms to operate under competitive conditions and to protect consumer rights; (3) the *economic environment*—environmental factors resulting from business fluctuations and variations in inflation rates and employment levels; (4) the *technological environment*—application to marketing of knowledge based on discoveries in science, inventions, and innovations; and (5) the *social-cultural environment*—the component of the marketing environment consisting of the relationship between the marketer and society and its culture.

2 Explain the types of competition marketers face and the steps necessary for developing a competitive strategy.

Three types of competition exist: (1) direct competition among marketers of similar products, (2) competition among goods or services that can be substituted for one another, and (3) competition among all organizations that vie for the consumer's purchasing power. To develop a competitive strategy, marketers must answer the following questions: (1) Should we compete? The answer depends on the firm's available resources and objectives as well as its expected profit potential. (2) If so, in what markets should we compete? This question requires marketers to make product, pricing, distribution, and promotional decisions that give their firm a competitive advantage. (3) How should we compete? This question requires marketers to make the technical decisions involved in setting a comprehensive marketing strategy.

3 **Describe how marketing activities are regulated and how marketers can influence the political-legal environment.**

Marketing activities are influenced by federal, state, and local laws that require firms to operate under competitive conditions and to protect consumer rights. Government regulatory agencies such as the Federal Trade Commission enforce these laws and identify and correct unfair marketing practices. Public and private consumer interest groups and industry self-regulatory groups also affect marketing activities. Marketers may seek to influence public opinion and legislative actions through advertising, political action committees, and political lobbying.

 4 **Outline the economic factors that affect marketing decisions and consumer buying power.**

The primary economic factors are (1) the stage in the business cycle, (2) inflation and deflation, (3) unemployment, (4) income, and (5) resource availability. All are vitally important to marketers because of their effects on consumers' willingness to buy and consumers' perceptions regarding changes in the marketing mix variables.

 5 **Discuss the impact of the technological environment on a firm's marketing activities.**

The technological environment consists of application to marketing of knowledge based on discoveries in science, inventions, and innovations. This knowledge can provide marketing opportunities: it results in new products and improves existing ones and it is a frequent source of price reductions through new production methods or materials. Technological applications also pose a threat because they can make existing products obsolete overnight. The technological environment demands that marketers continually adapt to change because its scope of influence reaches into consumers' lifestyles, competitors' offerings, and industrial users' demands.

 6 **Explain how the social-cultural environment influences marketing.**

The social-cultural environment is the relationship between marketing, society, and culture. To remain competitive, marketers must be sensitive to society's demographic shifts and changing values, which affect consumers' reactions to different products and marketing practices. Marketers must consider the increasing importance of cultural diversity, both in the United States and abroad. Changing societal values have led to consumerism, the social force within the environment designed to aid and protect the consumer by exerting legal, moral, and economic pressures on business. Consumer rights include the following: (1) the right to choose freely, (2) the right to be informed, (3) the right to be heard, and (4) the right to be safe.

 7 **Describe the ethical issues in marketing.**

Marketing ethics encompass the marketer's standards of conduct and moral values. Each element of the marketing mix raises its own set of ethical questions. Ethics in product strategy may involve quality and safety, packaging and labeling, and pollution. Ethics in distribution may involve territorial decisions. In promotion, ethical issues include honesty in advertising and promotion to children. Pricing may raise questions about price fixing and discrimination, increases deemed excessive, and deceptive pricing.

 8 **Identify the four levels of the social responsibility pyramid.**

The four levels of social responsibility are (1) *economic*—to be profitable, the foundation upon which the other three levels of the pyramid rest; (2) *legal*—to obey the law, society's codification of right and wrong; (3) *ethical*—to do what is right, just, and fair and to avoid wrongdoing; and (4) *philanthropic*—to be a good corporate citizen, contributing to the community and improving quality of life.

 ## Assessment Check: Answers

1.1 **Define *environmental scanning*.** Environmental scanning is the process of collecting information about the external marketing environment to identify and interpret potential trends.

1.2 **How does environmental scanning contribute to environmental management?** Environmental scanning contributes to environmental management by providing current information about the five different environments so marketers can predict and influence changes.

2.1 **Distinguish between direct and indirect competition, and give an example of each.** Direct competition occurs among marketers of similar products, such as supermarkets or gas stations. Indirect competition involves products that are easily substituted. Fried chicken could compete with pizza or tacos. A baseball game could compete with a trip to a water park.

2.2 **What is time-based competition?** Time-based competition is the strategy of developing and distributing goods and services more quickly than competitors.

3.1 Identify the four phases of U.S. government regulation of business. What is the newest frontier? The four phases of government regulation of business are the antimonopoly period, protection of competitors, consumer protection, and industry regulation. The newest frontier is cyberspace.

3.2 Which federal agency wields the broadest regulatory powers for influencing marketing activities? The Federal Trade Commission has the broadest regulatory authority.

4.1 Identify and describe briefly the four stages of the business cycle. The four stages of the business cycle are prosperity, recession, depression, and recovery.

4.2 Explain how inflation and income affect consumer buying decisions. Inflation devalues money and therefore may restrict some purchasing, particularly goods and services not considered necessary. Income also influences consumer buying power—the more discretionary income a household has, the more goods and services can be purchased.

5.1 What are some of the consumer benefits of technology? Technology can lead to new or improved goods and services, offer better customer service, and reduce prices. It can also address social concerns.

5.2 Why must marketers monitor the technological environment? Marketers need to monitor the technological environment to stay current with—and possibly ahead

of—competitors. If they don't, they may wind up with obsolete offerings.

6.1 Define _consumerism_. Consumerism is a social force within the environment that aids and protects the buyer by exerting legal, moral, and economic pressures on business.

6.2 Identify the four consumer rights. The four consumer rights are the right to choose freely, the right to be informed, the right to be heard, and the right to be safe.

7.1 Define _marketing ethics_. Marketing ethics refers to the marketer's standards of conduct and moral values.

7.2 Identify the five areas in which ethics can be a problem. The five areas of ethical concern for marketers are marketing research, product strategy, distribution, promotion, and pricing.

8.1 Identify the four levels of the social responsibility pyramid. The four levels of social responsibility are economic, legal, ethical, and philanthropic.

8.2 What are the benefits of green marketing? Green marketing, which responds to consumers' growing concerns about ecological issues, offers consumers high-quality products without health risks or damage to the environment. Many industries, including appliances, consumer electronics, construction, hospitality, and more, are finding that incorporating green practices rejuvenates their business.

Marketing Terms You Need to Know

environmental scanning 65
environmental management 65
strategic alliance 66
competitive environment 66
monopoly 66
antitrust 67
oligopoly 67

competitive strategy 68
time-based competition 69
political-legal environment 70
gross domestic product (GDP) 76
economic environment 76
business cycle 76
inflation 77

unemployment 77
discretionary income 77
demarketing 79
technological environment 79
VoIP—(voice over Internet protocol) 80
social-cultural environment 82

consumerism 82
consumer rights 83
marketing ethics 84
social responsibility 89
green marketing 91

Assurance of Learning Review

1. Why is environmental scanning an important activity for marketers?

2. What are the three different types of competition? Give an example of each.

3. What are the three questions marketers must ask before deciding on a competitive strategy?

4. What is the function of the Federal Trade Commission? The Food and Drug Administration?

5. Describe an industry or firm that you think might be able to weather an economic downturn and explain why.

6. Why do marketers monitor the technological environment?

7. How might marketers make the most of shifts in the social-cultural environment?

8. Describe the importance of consumer rights in today's marketing activities.

9. Why is it worthwhile for a firm to create an ethics program?

10. How can social responsibility benefit a firm as well as the society in which it operates?

Projects and Teamwork Exercises

1. With a classmate, choose two companies or brands that compete directly with each other. Select two of the following or choose your own. Then develop a competitive strategy for your firm while your partner develops a strategy for his or hers. Present the two strategies to the class. How are they similar? How are they different?
   a. Kmart and Target
   b. Verizon and T-Mobile
   c. Sea World and Universal Studios
   d. Visa and MasterCard
   e. Mazda and Hyundai
   f. Chili's and T.G.I. Friday's

2. Track your own consumer purchasing decisions as they relate to your income. Compare your decisions during the college year and the summer. Do you have a summer job that increases your income? How does that affect your decisions?

3. The U.S. Postal Service essentially enjoys a monopoly on the delivery of most mail. With a classmate, develop a strategy for a business that would compete with the USPS in areas that firms—such as UPS and FedEx—do not already address.

4. Choose one of the following products. Working in pairs or small groups, present arguments for and against having the United States impose certain regulations on the advertising of your product. (Note that some products already do have regulations—you can argue for or against them.)
   a. smokeless tobacco
   b. firearms
   c. state lottery
   d. prescription medications

5. With a classmate, research the recent trial of Bear Stearns' Matthew Tannin and Ralph Cioffi involving unethical and illegal activities. Describe the charges made against them and the outcome. Do you think they were fairly charged? Do you agree with the outcome? Why or why not?

Critical-Thinking Exercises

1. Suppose you and a friend want to start a company that markets frozen fish dinners. What are some of the questions about the competitive environment you would like to have answered before you begin production? How will you determine whom your customers are likely to be? How will you reach them?

2. Emissions standards for motorcycles took effect in 2006 under rules adopted by the Environmental Protection Agency. There were no previous emissions controls for motorcycles at all, but even under the new laws, "dirt" bikes for off-road use will be exempt. The new standards add about $75 to the average cost of a motorcycle according to the EPA, but $250 according to the Motorcycle Industry Council. Why do you think motorcycle makers did not adopt voluntary emissions standards? Should they have done so? Why or why not?

3. The social-cultural environment can have a strong influence on the decisions marketers must make. In recent years, animal rights groups have targeted the manufacture and sale of *foie gras,* a European food delicacy made from goose and duck liver. Activists cite the cruel treatment of these birds, while chefs and restaurant owners claim otherwise. Animal rights groups are pressuring restaurants to stop serving *foie gras.* Others argue that consumers should be allowed a choice. What aspects of the social-cultural environment are affecting the marketing of *foie gras?* Which of the other components of the marketing environment may come into play, and how?

4. Nearly 400 million rebates—worth about $6 billion—are offered to U.S. consumers by marketers every year. But do consumers like them? Often rebates require more effort than a consumer is willing to make to receive the cash back. Critics of the promotional effort say that marketers know this and are banking on consumers' not redeeming them, resulting in extra income for retailers and manufacturers. Do you think rebate programs are ethical? Why or why not?

5. The safe disposal of nuclear waste has been the topic of continuing public debate and an ongoing issue for marketers who work for nuclear power companies. This material is currently stored at 126 sites around the nation. To build a nuclear waste site, the U.S. Department of Energy must apply for and obtain a license. Supporters of such sites argue that they are important to building America's nuclear power capacity, while critics question their safety and usefulness. As a marketer, how would you approach this issue?

Ethics Exercise

Some retail firms protect their inventory against theft by locking their premises after hours even though maintenance and other workers are inside the stores working all night. Employees have charged that they are forbidden to leave the premises during these hours and that during an emergency, such as illness or injury, precious time is lost waiting for a manager to arrive who is authorized to unlock the doors. Although workers could open an emergency exit, in some cases they claim that they will be fired for doing so.

Employers assert that managers with keys are on the premises (or minutes away) and that locking employees in ensures their own safety as well as cutting down on costly "shrinkage."

1. Under what circumstances, if any, do you think locking employees in at night is appropriate?

2. If you feel this practice is appropriate, what safeguards do you think should be put into effect? What responsibilities do employers and employees have in such circumstances?

Internet Exercises

1. **Economic environment.** The U.S. Census Bureau projects what the U.S. population will look like in the next 15 to 25 years. Visit the Census Bureau's Web site and compare its projections of the U.S. population to current figures. What will the U.S. population look like in the future? How is it different from the current population? List two or three products or industries you feel will benefit from future population trends.

   http://www.census.gov/population/www/projections/index.html

2. **Fair trade coffee.** Go the Web site listed below to learn about so-called fair trade coffee. Prepare a brief report on the subject.

   How could a coffee manufacturer or retailer integrate fair trade products into its social responsibility efforts.

   http://www.globalexchange.org/campaigns/fairtrade/coffee/

3. **Building a brand.** Visit the Web site for footwear maker Ugg to learn about its efforts at building its brand. How has Ugg answered each of the five questions listed in the chapter concerning the development of a competitive strategy?

   http://www.uggaustralia.com/index.aspx

   Note: Internet Web addresses change frequently. If you don't find the exact site listed, you may need to access the organization's home page and search from there or use a search engine such as Google or Bing.

Ethics Questionnaire Answers

Questionnaire is on page 86.

1. 34% said personal e-mail on company computers is wrong.
2. 37% said using office equipment for schoolwork is wrong.
3. 49% said playing computer games at work is wrong.
4. 54% said Internet shopping at work is wrong.
5. 61% said it's unethical to blame your error on technology.
6. 87% said it's unethical to visit pornographic sites at work.
7. 33% said $25 is the amount at which a gift from a supplier or client becomes troubling, while 33% said $50, and 33% said $100.

8. 35% said a $50 gift to the boss is unacceptable.
9. 12% said a $50 gift from the boss is unacceptable.
10. 70% said it's unacceptable to take the $200 football tickets.
11. 70% said it's unacceptable to take the $120 theater tickets.
12. 35% said it's unacceptable to take the $100 food basket.
13. 45% said it's unacceptable to take the $25 gift certificate.
14. 40% said it's unacceptable to take the $75 raffle prize.
15. 11% reported they lied about sick days.
16. 4% reported they have taken credit for the work or ideas of others.

Case 3.1   *Dolores Labs Takes the Guesswork Out of Grunt Work*

Software developer Lukas Biewald had a problem at the office. He needed an army of temporary workers to tackle a simple but huge task that couldn't be automated. However, he had neither the time nor the budget to work with a conventional temp agency to engage the workers.

Instead, Biewald turned to Mechanical Turk, the online labor force operated by Amazon, for his temp workers. At Mechanical Turk, for about $2 an hour, employers can hire large numbers of freelancers (called "turkers") for a variety of menial tasks.

There was just one drawback, though: Biewald needed the work to be accurate, and he didn't have time to monitor the quality of the output he would receive.

Biewald's unmet need—for someone to assure an accurate, efficient labor force for his assignment—sparked the idea that eventually led him, in 2007, to found Dolores Labs: a business that, you could say, was born out of necessity.

San Francisco–based Dolores Labs serves as a middleman between the emerging cadre of "cloud labor"—the thousands of online moonlighters available to do simple tasks at bargain-basement hourly rates—and the organizations that want to hire them. The company fills the need by ensuring accountability and quality output from the cloud labor.

How is Dolores Labs able to deliver on its claim? Through its product, CrowdFlower, which consists of a set of statistical quality control algorithms devised to evaluate the accuracy and speed of cloud workers for a given task. The company emphasizes scalability: using CrowdFlower, clients can design a job to custom specifications. CrowdFlower provides the labor to deliver the work accurately and efficiently.

CrowdFlower screens candidates by giving them a dummy assignment and comparing their performance to that of veteran workers whose performance level is a known quantity. With increasing demand for inexpensive yet reliable labor to perform low-budget tasks where accuracy is important—such as medical transcription, content monitoring, marketing research, piracy policing, and others—the future looks bright for Dolores Labs. Already, the company has signed nearly two dozen clients since its founding. It received $5 million in venture capital in 2010.

Meanwhile, CrowdFlower's capabilities are being applied in other interesting ways. Leadership at Dolores Labs provided CrowdFlower's help following the earthquake in Haiti, where it was used to deploy volunteers to appropriate tasks throughout the devastated nation.

Questions for Critical Thinking

1. How does each of the five components of the marketing environment come into play for Dolores Labs?

2. Dolores Labs' involvement in helping to create a system for delivering humanitarian aid to the people of Haiti after the 2010 earthquake illustrates how a high-tech business can benefit society in a "high-touch" way. What other kinds of projects could a company like Dolores Labs undertake that would create similar impact?

Sources: Company Web site, http://www.doloreslabs.com, accessed February 23, 2010; Dave Foster, "Crowdsourcing the Haiti Relief," *Ashoka.org*, February 4, 2010, http://tech.ashoka.org; Leena Rao, "CrowdFlower Raises $5M for Cloud Sourced Labor," *TechCrunch.com*, January 20, 2010, http://techcrunch.com; Victoria Barret, "Dolores Labs Vets Web Sites on the Cheap," *Forbes*, March 30, 2009, http://www.forbes.com.

Video Case 3.2
The Marketing Environment, Ethics, and Social Responsibility at Scholfield Honda

When Al Gore won Best Documentary at the 2007 Academy Awards for his 2006 film, *An Inconvenient Truth*, the environment was still seen as an issue only for activists. Jokes were made. "Saturday Night Live" had a field day. Then, Gore won a Nobel Peace Prize.

Things started to change. By 2008, grocery stores around the country started filling up with organic and environmentally friendly products. Reusable bags showed up at checkout counters everywhere. More and more communities were providing curbside recycling pickup. The Discovery Channel even created a new cable network, Planet Green. Today, nearly every corporation from Frito-Lay to Ford has jumped on the green bandwagon.

Of course, there have always been companies ahead of the curve. Since the early 1970s, Honda had been producing the low-emission, fuel-efficient Civic. With so many auto manufacturers producing a dizzying line of makes and models, Honda is conscious about keeping up with the competition while staying true to its roots. The entire Honda line consists of four classes of vehicles: Good, Better, Best, and Ultimate. Their regular gas cars are Good, with about 30 mpg; hybrids are Better at about 45 mpg; and their Best solution is a natural, gas-powered Civic GX, which gets about 220 miles to a tank. Honda has Ultimate solutions in the works, including the new Honda FCX Clarity, a hydrogen fuel cell car in which hydrogen reacts with oxygen—both renewable resources—to create electricity. You can buy the natural gas Civic GX and Clarity today, but neither vehicle is practical for the average driver because the fueling stations are hard to come by.

Lee Lindquist, alternative fuels specialist at Scholfield Honda in Wichita, Kansas, had been researching alternative fuel vehicles for a presentation at a local Sierra Club meeting when he learned that, since 1998, the natural gas-powered Civic GX had been in use by municipalities and fleet customers in New York and California as a way to address air-quality issues.

Lindquist was aware that the Wichita market wasn't exactly teeming with green consumers but realized that everyone these days is looking for ways to combat rising fuel prices. Lindquist also saw the GX as a way to promote the use of local natural resources; Kansas produces much of the natural gas available in the United States today.

Lindquist's boss, owner Roger Scholfield, was skeptical about the Civic GX. While he was in search of a clever way to promote the dealership as more environmentally friendly, he didn't want to muddy the waters with this new, somewhat impractical, vehicle. He agreed to offer the car to his fleet and corporate customers and went back to work on a plan for the dealership.

They made a few small changes around the dealership—recycling the oil from oil changes to heat the shop, adding biodegradable and reusable cups at the coffee machine, and placing recycling bins everywhere. When the dealership made some renovations to its buildings, it created the Honda Green Zone—a rental space for organizations to hold meetings about green projects in the community. The space features a high-tech A/V (audio/visual) system and contains local and environmentally friendly furnishings.

Internally, Scholfield holds weekly meetings with his Green Team to brainstorm new environmentally friendly community projects, marketing, and products. They were at work on several other project ideas when a massive tornado hit the small town of Greensburg, Kansas, on May 4, 2007.

Scholfield and his family have always contributed to various causes, including a generous cash donation toward the rebuilding efforts in Greensburg. Once again, Lindquist approached Scholfield about the Honda Civic GX. He wanted to donate a GX to the town and a fueling station to go with it; Scholfield was skeptical but soon realized that the press the donation would receive could not only benefit his business but would raise awareness in the area about alternative fuels. The car would be made available to Greensburg residents to check out and try for themselves. The world would get to see the car in use by average people, and the town would have its own natural gas fueling station.

Scholfield is upfront about the decision to donate the car. It was a costly investment, and if he had done it solely for the PR, there are many more cost-effective ways of reaching his potential customers. When customers come into the dealership, they are more interested in alternative fuel and high-efficiency vehicles and recognize Scholfield Honda's commitment to the people of Greensburg and the green movement as a whole.

Questions

1. How does Scholfield Honda rate on the social responsibility pyramid? Do they meet all the criteria for a socially responsible company?

2. What social and cultural changes have affected the way car manufacturers design and market their products?

3. Should governmental regulations be placed on companies' claims that their products are green? Should official classifications for environmental friendliness be defined?

ch4 E-Business:
Managing the Customer Experience

Net-à-Porter Knows What Luxury Shoppers Want

••• The U.S. writer F. Scott Fitzgerald is supposed to have observed that "the rich are different," and that difference seems to apply to their online shopping habits as well. While they account for only a fraction

1 Describe the growth of Internet use worldwide.

2 Define *e-business* and *e-marketing*, and list the opportunities e-marketing presents.

3 Distinguish between a corporate Web site and a marketing Web site.

4 List the major forms of B2B e-marketing.

5 Explain business-to-consumer (B2C) e-marketing.

6 Identify online buyers and sellers.

7 Describe some of the challenges associated with online marketing and e-business.

8 Discuss how marketers use the communication function of the Web as part of their online marketing strategies.

9 Outline the steps involved in developing successful e-business Web sites, and identify methods for assessing Web site effectiveness.

of the $230 billion luxury goods market, online buyers of designer clothing form a highly desirable target for retailers trying to figure out what they want. These retailers are overcoming their initial skepticism about the power of online marketing, founded on fears of tarnishing stellar brand names, exposing them to disastrous counterfeiting scams, or appearing to reduce the value of their exclusivity through heavy discounts. Ironically, however, discretion is one big advantage of online luxury retailing. Nieman-Marcus and Bloomingdale's quietly e-mail customers with offers of limited-time markdowns up to 50 percent on selected luxury items. These promotions earn customer loyalty—and sales—but avoid angering those willing to buy designer brands at full price.

Net-à-Porter, an online retailer of high-end clothing, shoes, accessories, bags, and swimwear, is based in London. In a consumption-driven culture, part of its distinctive personality is the discrete black boxes in which its pricey dresses and shoes arrive. Customers can opt for even less noticeable brown packages. Speaking about the site's low-key profile and convenience, its founder said, "It just made a lot of sense to allow women to shop when they wanted to shop, how they wanted to shop—at work, at home, in the bedroom."

Net-à-Porter is not above discounting. It recently unveiled a Web site called outnet.com that offers past seasons' fashions at reduced prices. But the company was encouraged to note that only a few customers shop both sites, demonstrating that wealthy buyers

still want exclusive fashions, convenience, and quality more than low prices.

Another new venture for Net-à-Porter is its iPhone application, which lets iPhone users read fashion news stories from its Web site, view high-quality images of the fashions they like, zoom in, change viewing angles, and read product information before deciding whether to buy, add to a wish list, or keep shopping. The company's vice president of sales and marketing firmly believes in mobile technology: "We feel very strongly that third-generation technology is the new shop window. No one wants to be bound to their computer anymore.... Our customers love to shop from their homes or offices, but we want our customers to be able to shop from a cab or while waiting in line and really maximize what little free time they have."

Other luxury brands are overcoming reservations about online retailing as well. Hugo Boss, the German apparel designer, is following initial online efforts in Europe with Internet stores in the United States and Asia and hopes to sell about $70 million worth of luxury items within two years, a five-fold increase. Burberry launched a social networking site for owners of its legendary trench coats. The company wants to recreate online the lush environment of its physical stores. "Whether they are walking into our store on Bond Street or tapping in from India or China," says the company's chief creative officer, "it's about making sure the customer is getting the same experience." For brands like Valentino, Emilio Pucci, Bally, and Dolce & Gabbana, there is Yoox, an Italian firm that operates retailing sites for them.

According to Yoox founder Federico Marchetti, when luxury firms first thought of the Internet, "there was a lot of skepticism. Now it is the opposite."[1]

evolution of a brand

"Net-à-Porter has revolutionized the way we buy designer clothes." This comment by Vogue UK sums up Net-à-Porter's stylish accomplishments in the worlds of both fashion and online retailing. Calling itself "the world's premier online luxury fashion retailer," the company, founded in 2000 and based in London, made a quick recovery from the recent recession. With almost 2 million visitors a month, Net-à-Porter (the name is a pun on the fashion term "prêt-à-porter," meaning ready to wear) is back in

double-digit growth and expects sales to reach $168 million, about a 20 percent increase over past years. Its award-winning site is designed to look like a fashion magazine and offers editorial content, videos, e-mail alerts, and the hottest looks from hundreds of top designers, updated weekly. There is even a wedding boutique.

- What advantages do online retailers offer luxury buyers that store retailers can't provide? How big a role do you think such advantages will play in the future of online luxury retailing?

- "Social networking is very important among luxury buyers. . . . They are looking for reputation and testimonials from other customers." So said one auto industry ad executive. Do you think his comment applies to online fashion retailing as well? Do you think Net-à-Porter could improve sales or customer relationships if it followed Burberry's example and launched a social networking feature on its site?

chapter overview

e-business Conducting online transactions with customers by collecting and analyzing business information, carrying out the exchanges, and maintaining online relationships with customers.

During the past decade, marketing has become the cutting-edge tool for success on the Internet. Profit-seeking organizations are not the only benefactors of the Internet; organizations of all kinds are emphasizing marketing's role in achieving set goals. Colleges and universities, charities, museums, symphony orchestras, and hospitals now employ the marketing concept discussed in Chapter 1: providing customers the goods and services they want to buy when they want to buy them. Contemporary marketing continues to perform its function of bringing buyers and sellers together; it just does it faster and more efficiently than ever before. With just a few ticks of the clock and a few clicks of a mouse, the Internet revolutionizes every aspect of life. New terms have emerged such as *shopping blog, RSS, VoIP,* and *XML,* and old words have new meanings never imagined a few years ago: *Web, Net, surfer* and *server, banner* and *browser, tweet* and *twitter, online* and *offline.*

Electronic business or **e-business** refers to conducting business via the Internet and has turned virtual reality into reality. With a computer and Internet access, a virtual marketplace is open 24/7 to provide almost anything anywhere to anyone, including clothes, food, entertainment, medicine, and information. You can pay your cell phone bill, make travel reservations, do research for a term paper, post a résumé at an employment bulletin board, or buy a used car—perhaps at a lower price than you could in person.

Internet marketers can reach individual consumers or target organizations worldwide through a vast array of computer and communications technologies. In just a few short years, hundreds of thousands of companies large and small have been connected to electronic marketing channels. The size and scope of e-business is difficult to understate. For instance, according to the U.S. Census Bureau, online retail sales in the United States totaled $107 billion in a recent year during which online retail sales grew by 22 percent, or more than four times the overall growth rate in retail sales.[2]

E-business is much more than just buying and selling goods and services. Some surveys suggest that the Web is the number-one medium for new-product information, eclipsing catalogs, print ads, and trade shows. The Internet allows retailers and vendors to exchange vital information, improving the overall functioning of supply and distribution, lowering costs, and increasing profits. Moreover, an increasing number of Americans now get some of their news and information from *blogs* (online journals) rather than from traditional media such as television and newspapers. Consequently, a growing number of businesses use blogs to put human faces on their organizations and communicate directly with customers.

This chapter examines the current status and potential of e-business and online marketing. We begin by describing the growth of Internet use throughout the world. Next, we explore the scope of e-business and outline how marketers use the Internet to succeed, and then distinguish different types of Web business models. This discussion is followed by a review of the major types of B2B marketing online.

We then explore the types of goods and services most often traded in B2C marketing on the Internet, along with a profile of online buyers and sellers. We then describe some of the challenges associated with marketing on the Web, followed by a discussion of how marketers use the communication function of the Internet. We conclude the chapter by examining how to build an effective Web presence.

The Digital World

In the past decade, the number of Internet users in the United States and worldwide has grown dramatically. Today, an estimated 223 million U.S. citizens—almost three-quarters of the U.S. population—access the Internet at home, school, work, or public access sites. Worldwide, the number of Internet users exceeds 1.8 billion.[3] The map in Figure 4.1 shows the number of Internet users and Internet penetration for each of the world's continents and regions. Internet penetration is the percentage of a region's population who use the Internet.

Asia leads the world in the sheer number of users and the speed of growth in Internet use. Among individual countries with the highest number of Internet users, China ranks first; the next three countries are the United States, Japan, and India.[4] China's Internet audience has grown by 1,500 percent since 2000, while the United States' grew almost 140 percent for the same period.[5] South Korea has the fastest Internet service in the world, almost twice as fast as Japan and Hong Kong, the next fastest, and three or four times faster than in the United States. The United States recently ranked 18th in the world for Internet speed.[6]

What do people do online? Let's look at the two countries with the most Internet users—the United States and China. In the United States, Net usage is mostly about communication, information, and purchases. Nearly all North American users say they use e-mail; between 40 and 50 percent get news, send photos, shop for personal consumption items, pay bills, and use an instant messaging or social networking service.[7] Among U.S. users under the age of 35, almost a third in a recent survey said they check their Twitter or Facebook pages more than ten times a day, though the fastest-growing U.S. demographic group on Facebook is people 55 and over.[8] In China, where Internet users tend to be young (more than 80 percent are under 40) and low-wage earners, downloading and streaming music are the most popular activities, followed by online gaming, videogaming, and social networking. After a relatively slow start, online purchase transactions in China have doubled in value over the past year (to the equivalent of $36.5 billion), helped by the spread of local online payment systems.[9]

1 **Describe the growth of Internet use worldwide.**

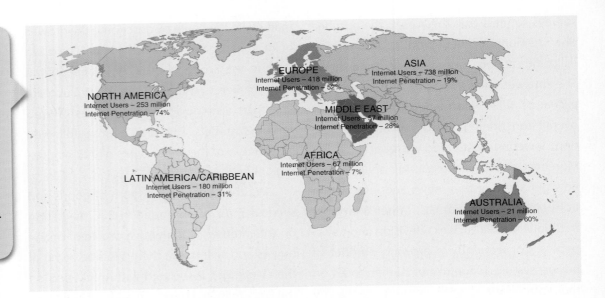

figure 4.1

Number of Internet Users and Internet Penetration Rate (by Region)

Source: Data from "Internet Usage Statistics," www. internetworldstats.com, accessed March 25, 2010.

So where is e-business going, and how can marketers capitalize on the digital links with consumers? In spite of the past success and future potential of the Internet, issues and concerns relating to e-business remain. Some highly touted e-business applications have proven less than successful, cost savings and profits have occasionally been elusive, and many privacy and security issues still linger. Nevertheless, the benefits and potential of e-business outweigh the concerns and problems.

 assessment check

1. How would you describe the growth of Internet use worldwide?
2. What do most U.S. consumers do online?

E-Business and E-Marketing

2 Define *e-business* and *e-marketing*, and list the opportunities e-marketing presents.

e-marketing Strategic process of creating, distributing, promoting, and pricing goods and services to a target market over the Internet or through digital tools.

Today, *e-business* describes the wide range of business activities taking place via Internet applications such as e-mail and virtual shopping carts. E-business can be divided into the following five broad categories: (1) *e-tailing* or virtual storefronts on Web sites; (2) business-to-business transactions; (3) electronic data interchanges (EDI), the business-to-business exchange of data; (4) e-mail, instant messaging, blogs, podcasts, and other Web-enabled communication tools and their use as media for reaching prospective and existing customers; and (5) the gathering and use of demographic, product, and other information through Web contacts.

The component of e-business of particular interest to marketers is *electronic marketing* or **e-marketing**, the strategic process of creating, distributing, promoting, and pricing goods and services to a target market over the Internet or through such digital tools as smartphones. E-marketing is the means by which e-business is achieved. It encompasses such activities as the following:

- viewing your favorite band's latest videos on YouTube;
- booking a flight to Atlanta on Expedia.com to attend a job fair;
- researching digital cameras on CNET.com and then placing an order on Newegg.com; and
- accessing research site LexisNexis through your college's network, allowing you to work on a paper, and then checking apartment rentals online.

The application of these electronic tools to contemporary marketing has the potential to greatly reduce costs and increase customer satisfaction by increasing the speed and efficiency of marketing interactions. Just as e-business is a major function of the Internet, e-marketing is an integral component of e-business.

A closely related but somewhat narrower term than e-marketing is *online marketing*. While electronic marketing can encompass digital technologies ranging from DVDs to interactive store kiosks that do not involve computers, online marketing refers to marketing activities that connect buyers and sellers electronically through interactive computer systems.

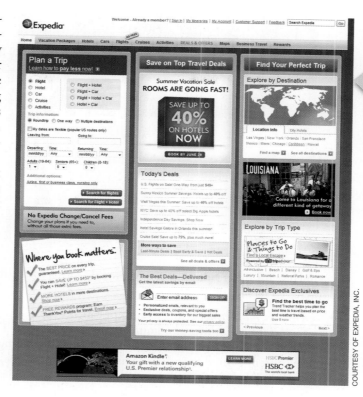

Booking a flight on Expedia.com is an example of e-marketing.

COURTESY OF EXPEDIA, INC.

Opportunities of E-Marketing

E-marketing offers countless opportunities to reach consumers. This radical departure from traditional brick-and-mortar operations provides the following benefits to contemporary marketers (summarized in Table 4.1).

- *Global reach.* The Net eliminates the geographic protections and limitations of local business and gives smaller firms a wider audience. Independent filmmakers often have a difficult time forging relationships with traditional distributors who buy the rights to films and promote

table 4.1 E-Marketing Capabilities

Capability	Description	Example
Global reach	The ability to reach anyone connected to the Internet anywhere in the world.	Independent filmmakers use the Internet to generate audiences and DVD sales for their films.
Personalization	Creating products to meet customer specifications.	Lululemon Athletica has a Web site feature that allows buyers to mix and match items to complete outfits to suit their individual tastes.
Interactive marketing	Buyer–seller communications through such channels as the Internet and interactive kiosks.	Dell maintains an IdeaStorm site where users trade ideas, information, and product feedback.
Right-time marketing	The ability to provide a product at the exact time needed.	The Southwest Airlines Web site lets customers make advance reservations, check-in online, check flight status, and sign up for the carrier's rewards program.
Integrated marketing	Coordination of all promotional activities to produce a unified, customer-focused promotional message.	Sony uses the slogan "Make. Believe." in both online and offline promotions.

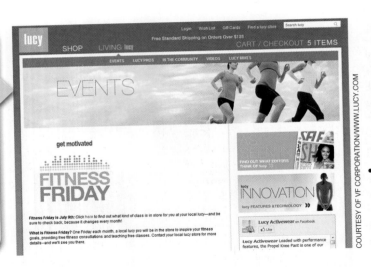

COURTESY OF VF CORPORATION/WWW.LUCY.COM

> An effective online presence can improve the performance of traditional marketing operations. For example, activewear provider Lucy.com advertises Fitness Friday on its Web site, drawing customers into the store.

them as they see fit. As a result, independent films sometimes have a limited audience. But the Internet is allowing filmmakers to organize their own screenings, send messages to interested online communities, and sell DVDs directly through their Web sites.[10]

- *Personalization*. Seven Cycles, a maker of customized bicycle frames, uses its Web site to introduce cyclists to its extensive Custom Kit data-gathering process, explain the required specifications and measurements, offer a timeline for order fulfillment, and provide forms for customers to print out and send to their preferred retailer.[11]

- *Interactive marketing*. Using a concept called **interactive marketing**, Bravo TV is partnering with social networking site Foursquare to integrate its TV shows including "Top Chef" and "The Real Housewives" with the site's real-world gaming features. "With Foursquare people leave content behind for others to find, like tips of the best drink at a bar," said the site's CEO. "With shows that are tied to real locations in real cities enhancing this with content from contestants and judges on 'Top Chef' or another Bravo show is going to make it even more interesting."[12]

- *Right-time marketing*. Online retailers, such as BN.com and REI.com, can provide products when and where customers want them.

- *Integrated marketing*. The Internet enables the coordination of all promotional activities and communication to create a unified, customer-oriented promotional message.

interactive marketing
Buyer–seller communications in which the customer controls the amount and type of information received from a marketer through such channels as the Internet and virtual reality kiosks.

In addition to the benefits listed here, an effective online presence can improve the performance of traditional marketing operations. Recent surveys of consumers found that, whether they purchase online or in person, well over half of shoppers do online product research before buying. In one recent survey, 60 percent of online shoppers said research would continue to be a critical factor in purchasing decisions over the next year, and a third were prepared to abandon store sites that did not perform well.[13] The Internet is thus a powerful force in shaping consumer behavior, even if it is seldom the only avenue most consumers pursue in their search for product information. Meanwhile, with online sales growing by well over 10 percent each year while retail stores remain flat, brick-and-mortar stores are fighting back with options online sellers can't deliver. Best Buy offers music lessons with the musical instruments it sells, and after purchasing its sports clothing, Lululemon athletica shoppers can take free yoga classes at the store.[14]

briefly speaking

"The Internet will help achieve 'friction free capitalism' by putting buyer and seller in direct contact and providing more information to both about each other."

—Bill Gates
(b. 1955)
Co-founder, Microsoft

✓ **assessment check**

1. Define *e-marketing*.

2. Explain the difference between e-business and e-marketing.

3. What are the major benefits of e-marketing?

Web Business Models

Virtually all businesses today have Web sites. They may offer general information, electronic shopping, and promotions such as games, contests, and online coupons. Type in the firm's Internet address, and the Web site's home page appears on your computer screen.

Two types of company Web sites exist. Many firms have established **corporate Web sites** to increase their visibility, promote their offerings, and provide information to interested parties. Rather than selling goods and services directly, these sites attempt to build customer goodwill and assist channel members in their marketing efforts. For example, Burger King's Web site offers menus and nutrition information, a store locator, and videos and other types of promotions.[15] In addition to using the Web to communicate product information and build relationships with customers, many companies also use their corporate Web sites for a variety of other purposes, including disseminating financial information to investors; giving prospective employees the opportunity to apply online for jobs; and providing a communication channel for customers and other interested parties via e-mail, blogs, and online forums.

Although **marketing Web sites** often include information about company history, products, locations, employment opportunities, and financial information, their goal is to increase purchases by visitors. For instance, the Dunkin' Donuts Web site contains all of the information traditionally found on a corporate Web site, but it also includes an online store selling everything from coffee beans to tea, mugs, coffee machines, and apparel.

Many marketing Web sites try to engage consumers in interactions that will move them closer to a demonstration, trial visit, purchase, or other marketing outcome. Some marketing Web sites, such as Canon.com, are quite complex. Visitors can compare the company's different models of digital cameras and other products, selecting three at a time for detailed feature comparisons as well as find product registration and support, sign up for news and promotions, and locate a Canon dealer.[16] But not all products lend themselves to sales on the Internet. Complex products or those requiring demonstration or trials may be better sold in person. And some companies have relationships with partners, such as dealers and franchisees, that sell their products, which we discuss later in the chapter.

3 Distinguish between a corporate Web site and a marketing Web site.

corporate Web site
Site designed to increase a firm's visibility, promote its offerings, and provide information to interested parties.

marketing Web site
Site whose main purpose is to increase purchases by visitors.

 assessment check

1. Explain the difference between a corporate Web site and a marketing Web site.
2. Why would companies *not* sell products on their Web sites?

© BALKIS PRESS/ABACAPRESS.COM/NEWSCOM

The Dunkin' Donuts Web site offers information traditionally found on a corporate Web site but also includes an online store for gift cards, merchandise, and coffee.

B2B E-Marketing

4 List the major forms of B2B e-marketing.

business-to-business (B2B) e-marketing
Use of the Internet for business transactions between organizations.

FedEx's Web site is not designed to be flashy. Although it contains some graphics and minimal video clips, its main purpose is not entertainment. Instead, it provides lots of practical information to help the firm's customers. The site enables customers to check rates, compare services, schedule package pickups and deliveries, track shipments, and order shipping supplies. This information is vital to FedEx's customers, most of whom are businesses. Customers access the site thousands of times a day.

Business-to-business (B2B) e-marketing is the use of the Internet for business transactions between organizations. Although most people are familiar with such online firms as Amazon.com and eBay, consumer transactions are dwarfed by their B2B counterparts. According to the U.S. Census Bureau, 92 percent of e-business activity consists of B2B transactions.[17]

In addition to generating sales revenue, B2B e-marketing also provides detailed product descriptions whenever needed. Payments and other information are exchanged on the Web, and B2B e-marketing can slash order-processing expenses. Business-to-business transactions, which typically involve more steps than consumer purchases, can be much more efficient on the Internet. Orders placed over the Internet usually contain fewer errors than handwritten ones, and when mistakes occur, the technology can quickly locate them. So the Internet is an attractive option for business buying and selling. In some industries, relying on the Internet to make purchases can reduce costs by almost 25 percent.

B2B e-marketing activity has become more varied in recent years. In addition to using the Web to conduct individual sales transactions and provide product information, companies use such tools as EDI, Web services, extranets, private exchanges, electronic exchanges, and e-procurement.

Proprietary B2B Transactions

One of the oldest applications of technology to business transactions is *electronic data interchange (EDI)*, computer-to-computer exchanges of price quotations, purchase orders, invoices, and other sales information between buyers and sellers. EDI requires compatible hardware and software systems to exchange data over a network. Use of EDI cuts paper flow, speeds the order cycle, and reduces errors. In addition, by receiving daily inventory status reports from vendors, companies can set production schedules to match demand.

Early EDI systems were limited due to the requirement that all parties had to use the same computer operating system. That changed with the introduction of *Web services*—Internet-based systems that allow parties to communicate electronically with one another regardless of the computer operating system they use. Web services rely on open source XML (Extensible Markup Language, a formatting language) standards. EDI and Web services are discussed further in Chapter 10.

The Internet also offers an efficient way for businesses to collaborate with vendors, partners, and customers through *extranets*, secure networks used for e-marketing and accessible through the firm's Web site by external customers, suppliers, or other authorized users. Extranets go beyond ordering and fulfillment processes by giving selected outsiders access to internal information. Like other forms of e-marketing, extranets provide additional benefits such as enhanced relationships with business partners. *Intranets* are secure internal networks that help companies share information among employees, no matter how many or how widespread they are. Accounting firm Schneider Downs & Co. has hundreds of employees working on dozens of different projects at two separate locations. Its intranet, nicknamed the Hub, lets each department create and post its own content for access by all the others. Says the company's technology officer, "We wanted something that, every day, when someone logs onto the network there is a bulletin board of announcements."[18]

Security and access authorization remain critical issues, and most companies create virtual private networks that protect information traveling over public communications media. These networks control who uses a company's resources and what users can access. Also, they cost considerably less than leasing dedicated lines.

The next generation of extranets is the *private exchange*, a secure Web site at which a company and its suppliers share all types of data related to e-marketing, from product design through order delivery. A private exchange is more collaborative than a typical extranet, so this type of arrangement

briefly speaking

"I have been quoted saying that, in the future, all companies will be Internet companies. I still believe that. More than ever, really."

—Andrew Grove
(b. 1936)
Co-founder, Intel Corporation

is sometimes called *e-business*. The participants can use it to collaborate on product ideas, production scheduling, distribution, order tracking, and any other functions a business wants to include. For example, Walmart Stores has a private exchange it calls *retail link*. The system permits Walmart employees to access detailed sales and inventory information. Suppliers such as Procter & Gamble and Nestlé, in turn, can look up Walmart sales data and forecasts to manage their own inventory and logistics, helping them better meet the needs of the world's largest retailer and its millions of customers worldwide.

E-Procurement on Open Exchanges

In the early stages of B2B transactions, marketers believed all types of products would be traded online. Entrepreneurs created electronic exchanges to bring buyers and sellers together in one electronic marketplace and cater to a specific industry's needs, but the performance of these sites was disappointing. Many suppliers weren't happy with the pressure to come in with the lowest bid each time, and buyers preferred to cultivate long-term relationships with their suppliers, even if those suppliers sometimes charged slightly more. Purchasing agents simply didn't see enough benefits from electronic exchanges to abandon suppliers they knew.

Evolving from electronic exchanges is **e-procurement**, Web-based systems that enable all types of organizations to improve the efficiency of their bidding and purchasing processes. Royal Dutch/Shell Group, a group of energy companies with operations in 140 countries, purchases millions of dollars of parts, components, supplies, and services every day. Recently the firm decided to replace its network of more than 100 different purchasing systems with a streamlined new system to unify procurement and reduce costs. "E-procurement enables us to make radical changes to the way we buy, the speed at which we buy, the way we and our suppliers work together, and the way we can use information to manage our business in the connected economy," said the company's strategic sourcing advisor.[19]

> **e-procurement** Use of the Internet by organizations to solicit bids and purchase goods and services from suppliers.

E-procurement also benefits the public sector. The City of Edinburgh, Scotland's capital and home to almost half a million people, wants to be northern Europe's "most successful city" by 2020. To help meet its goal, the City of Edinburgh Council now uses an automated procurement system from Oracle to run auctions for its large contracts, to rank suppliers, and to ensure transparent purchasing. It has reduced spending by 15 percent on a range of commodity purchases and has saved more than $8 million so far.[20] The state of Virginia maintains a Web site called eVay for its Web-based purchasing system. The site allows state and local agencies and government offices, as well as the state's colleges and universities, to invite bids, receive quotes, and place orders.[21]

 assessment check

1. What is B2B e-marketing? How large is it relative to consumer e-marketing?
2. Define *EDI* and *Web services*.
3. Briefly explain how e-procurement works.

B2C E-Marketing

One area of e-business that consistently grabs news headlines is Internet shopping. Known as **business-to-consumer (B2C) e-marketing**, it is selling directly to consumers over the Internet. Driven by convenience and improved security for transmitting credit card numbers and other financial information, online retail sales—sometimes called *e-tailing*—have grown rapidly in recent years. Daily e-tail sales topped $900 million for the first time in one recent holiday shopping period, and a MasterCard report called e-commerce "one of the stars of the season" in retail sales. Online retail sales in the same holiday season passed $850 million on several days before hitting the new high-water mark, helped by widespread offers of free shipping.[22]

> **5** Explain business-to-consumer (B2C) e-marketing.

> **business-to-consumer (B2C) e-marketing** Selling directly to consumers over the Internet.

With nearly one in five U.S. shoppers saying they expect to use mobile devices like smartphones for shopping in the near future, mobile retail may be poised to take off. Currently representing only about half of 1 percent of online sales, it has already attracted well over 100 retailers that now have mobile-commerce Web sites or applications. They include Toys "R" Us, Walgreens, Sears, Amazon, American Eagle, Best Buy, eBay, and Victoria's Secret. Mobile shoppers, especially in the 18 to 29 age range, plan to use their phones for finding store locations, researching prices, and finding coupons and other sales information. "People want to do their shopping when they want to do it," says the CEO of PriceGrabber, which has had a mobile retail site since 2004.[23]

Most people think of the Web as a giant cybermall of retail stores selling millions of goods online. However, service providers are also important participants in e-marketing, including providers of financial services. Brick-and-mortar banks such as PNC Financial and brokerage firms such as Charles Schwab have greatly expanded their online services. In addition, many new online service providers are rapidly attracting customers who want to do more of their own banking and investment trading at whatever time and day suits them. And where would individual buyers and sellers be without online classified ads? See the "Marketing Success" feature for the story of the Internet's dominant classified-ad site, Craigslist.

Electronic Storefronts

electronic storefronts
Company Web sites that sell products to customers.

Virtually all major retailers have staked their claims in cyberspace by setting up **electronic storefronts**, Web sites where they offer items for sale to consumers. Clothing retailer American Eagle sees e-retailing as a "significant growth opportunity" for all its brands and has been enjoying double-digit increases in electronic sales from year to year. The company's attractive Web site offers a store locator and wish list feature, gift card purchasing, a feedback link, and the opportunity to sign up for sales and other promotions. Clothing is organized by category—tops, bottoms, accessories, footwear, and so on—and the site has separate sections for sales and clearance items as well as for new arrivals and Web exclusives.[24]

electronic shopping cart   File that holds items the online shopper has chosen to buy.

Generally, online retailers—such as LLBean.com and BestBuy.com—provide an online catalog where visitors click on items they want to buy. These items are placed in a file called an **electronic shopping cart** or *shopping bag*. When the shopper indicates that he or she wants to complete the transaction, the items in the electronic shopping cart are listed on the screen, along with the total amount due, so the customer can review the whole order and make changes before paying.

One factor having a significant influence on the growth of online shopping is the increased capability of smartphones like the iPhone and Android. About 40 percent of smartphone

mktg: *success*

Craigslist Dominates in Classified Ads

Background. Craigslist, the online classified advertising service, was founded by Craig Newmark as a hobby in 1995; it accepts ads for cars, real estate, jobs, apartments, services, and almost everything in between. The site currently draws more than 90 percent of the traffic generated by online classified Web sites in the United States, and that traffic more than doubled between 2005 and 2009. About one in ten Internet users visit a classified Web site to buy or sell on any given day, also more than double the number in 2005. The rise in popularity of online classifieds has devastated newspaper revenues from this source, which crashed from a peak of nearly $20 billion in 1999 to less than $10 billion in 2008.

The Challenge. Although it was conceived as a community service rather than a profit generator and is still run that way, Craigslist wanted to lead in a medium that seemed a perfect fit for classified advertising, while retaining its

owners used their mobile device to purchase something in the last six months, according to a recent survey. Many bought books, DVDs, movie tickets, or videogames, while even more read product reviews or checked prices. The auction site eBay even reported the sale of a $350,000 Lamborghini and a boat selling for $150,000. Perhaps even more impressive than their capacity to connect to shopping sites, however, is smartphones' ability to influence consumers with deals and offers right in malls and stores, at the precise moment they are ready to buy. Such location-specific applications lead many observers to believe mobile commerce has yet to reach its full potential.[25]

Benefits of B2C E-Marketing

Many consumers prefer shopping online to the time needed to drive to a store and select purchases. Why do consumers shop online? Three main reasons are most often cited in consumer surveys: competitive pricing, access and convenience, and personalized service.

COMPETITIVE PRICING

Many of the best deals on products, such as airfares and hotels, can be found on the Internet. Expedia.com is just one of several sites that offer packages with combinations of flight, hotel, and car rental, plus special sales and last-minute flight specials at attractive prices organized by city and date of travel.[26] Though most airlines now charge passengers for checked baggage, most offer reduced rates for luggage checked online.[27] Bookseller Barnes & Noble's Web site offers member discounts up to 40 percent on hardcover best-sellers and other title-by-title price cuts.[28]

The Web is an ideal method for savvy shoppers to compare prices from dozens—even hundreds—of sellers. Online shoppers can compare features and prices at their leisure. Say, for instance, you're in the market for a new computer monitor. **Bots** aid consumers in comparison shopping. Bots—short for *robots*—are search programs that check hundreds of sites, gather and assemble information, and bring it back to the sender. For instance, at PriceGrabber.com, you can specify the type and size of monitor you're looking for, and the Web site displays a list of the highest-ranked monitors, along with the e-tailer offering the best price on each item and estimated shipping expenses. The Web site even ranks the e-marketers by customer experience and tells you whether a particular model is in stock.

bot (shopbot) Software program that allows online shoppers to compare the price of a particular product offered by several online retailers.

ACCESS AND CONVENIENCE

A second important factor in prompting online purchases is shopper convenience. Cybershoppers can order goods and services from around the world at any hour of the day or night. Most e-marketers

noncorporate culture and public service mission.

The Strategy. Most Craigslist ads are free (except for jobs and real estate), and the no-frills site is easy to use and self-policing. It currently operates in more than 700 cities across 70 countries, appearing in English and five other languages. In addition to buy-and-sell

opportunities, the site offers 100 discussion forums and countless opportunities to find advice, relationships, and local activities and entertainment.

The Outcome. The company receives about 20 billion page views a month, earns a profit (about $100 million in a recent year), and dominates online classifieds. Although

eBay holds a minority stake in the company and wants the right to elect a director to the board, Craigslist has so far held its only potential competitor at bay.

Sources: Company Web site, www.craigslist.org, accessed March 3, 2010; Olga Kharif, "EBay-Craigslist Court Clash Could Reprice Classifieds," *BusinessWeek*, www.businessweek.com, December 6, 2009; "Online Classifieds," Pew Internet & American Life Project, the Pew Research Center, May 2009.

Nike offers online customers personalized service, allowing shoppers the opportunity to customize a running shoe by personalizing features, including the outsole, amount of cushioning, and width.

© GETTY IMAGES FOR NIKE

allow customers to register their credit card and shipping information for quick use in making future purchases. Customers are required to select a user name and password for security. Later, when they place another order, registered customers are asked to type in their password. E-marketers typically send an e-mail message confirming an order and the amount charged to the buyer's credit card. Another e-mail is sent once the product is shipped, along with a tracking number, which the customer can use to follow the order through the delivery process. A new service provided by *Elle* magazine's British Web site is the ability to use online photos to conduct visual matches for desired shopping items. In other words, using a digital picture of what you want, say, a pair of shoes, you can locate similar items for sale online. In the United States, Like.com allows users to upload their own photos to find matches and follow links to sites where they can purchase the items.[29]

PERSONALIZED SERVICE

While online shopping transactions often operate with little or no human interaction, successful B2C e-marketing companies know how important personalization is to the quality of the shopping experience. Customer satisfaction is greatly affected by the marketer's ability to offer service tailored to many customers. But each person expects a certain level of customer service. Consequently, most leading online retailers offer customized features on their Web sites.

The early years of e-business saw Web marketers casting their nets broadly in an effort to land as many buyers as possible. Today, the emphasis has turned toward creating loyal customers likely to make repeat purchases. How does personalized marketing work online? Say you buy a book at Amazon.com and register with the site. The site welcomes you back for your next purchase by name. Using special software that analyzes your previous purchases, it also suggests several other books you might like. You even have the option of receiving periodic e-mails from Amazon.com informing you of new products. Many other leading e-marketers have adopted similar types of personalized marketing.

Some Web sites offer customized products to match individual consumer requirements. For instance, Nike offers online shoppers the opportunity to customize a running shoe, personalizing such features as the outsole, the amount of cushioning, and the width. The personalized shoe costs about $10 more than buying a product off store shelves. Some sites provide demonstrations and other product videos, and some, like Nordstroms, offer 3-D (three-dimensional) product images and allow shopping by cost and by feature.

assessment check

1. What is B2C e-marketing?
2. Explain the difference between a shopping Web site and an informational Web site.
3. Discuss the benefits of B2C e-marketing.

Online Buyers and Sellers

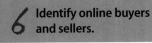
Identify online buyers and sellers.

A recent survey paints a picture of the characteristics of online users and buyers. Some of the key findings of the report are summarized in Figure 4.2. The typical Internet user is now likely to be between 18 and 64 years of age. More than half of all users make at least one purchase online each month, and more than six in ten research products online before buying them in a store. Many online shoppers are loyal and buy mostly from a single site; Amazon and eBay are the most popular. One in four online shoppers buys airline tickets, the most frequently purchased item. A broader range of Internet users now purchase products online compared with a few years

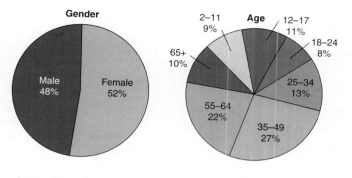

Average time online in a month (home and work) ≈ 54 hours
Average number of Web pages viewed per person in a month (home and work): 2,415

figure 4.2

Characteristics of U.S. Internet Users

Source: Data from Nielsen Online, "Nielsen Provides Topline U.S. Web Data for February 2010," http://blog. nielsen.com; Data from Nielsen Online, as cited in "Nielsen Online Reports Topline U.S. Data," *Market Wire*, accessed March 25, 2010.

ago. In 2000, men were the majority of online shoppers. Today, women make up 63 percent of online shoppers, with mothers being the fastest-growing group.[30]

Realizing that customers would have little or no opportunity to rely on many of the sense modes—smelling the freshness of direct-from-the-oven bread, touching the soft fabric of a new cashmere sweater, or squeezing fruit to assess its ripeness—early online sellers focused on offering products consumers were familiar with and tended to buy frequently, such as books and music. Other popular early online offerings included computer hardware and software and airline tickets.

Travel tops the list of top five products sold online during a recent year. Holiday packages and books are next. Close behind are concert and theater tickets, clothes and electrical goods (tied), CDs and movie tickets (tied), and DVDs and music downloads.[31]

Thanks to retailers' efforts, consumers' online shopping experiences have been steadily improving in quality and convenience. To keep up with rising expectations, some observers predict that e-businesses will have to continually update their offerings at an increasing rate; speed the checkout process by eliminating the need to click from page to page; add video segments to their online product catalogs; and implement advanced, intuitive, and easy-to-use search and navigation technologies. Finally, e-tailers might look to the socializing capabilities of networking sites like Facebook and MySpace and start capitalizing on customer loyalty to initiate conversations with and between their customers. One recent study of online shoppers found that more than half who use social networking sites like Facebook and Twitter already "friend" or "follow" up to five retailers online.[32]

 assessment check

1. Who shops online? Are the characteristics of online shoppers changing?

2. What are some of the capabilities e-marketers might add to their Web sites in the future?

Challenges in E-Business and E-Marketing

For all their advantages, e-business and e-marketing face some problems and challenges. Some of the most significant include developing safe online payment systems, protecting consumer privacy, preventing fraud and scams, improving site design and customer service, and reducing potential channel conflicts and copyright disputes.

7 Describe some of the challenges associated with online marketing and e-business.

Safety of Online Payment

In response to consumer concerns about the safety of sending credit card numbers over the Internet, companies have developed secure payment systems. Internet browsers, such as Microsoft Internet Explorer, contain sophisticated encryption systems to protect sensitive information. **Encryption** is the process of encoding data for security purposes. When such a system is active, users see a special icon that indicates they are at a protected Web site.

encryption The process of ecoding data for security purposes.

Online payment services such as Google Checkout expedite checkout and make shopping more secure.

COURTESY OF GOOGLE, INC.

To further increase consumer security, most companies involved in e-business—including all major credit card companies—use **Secure Sockets Layer (SSL)** technology to encrypt information and provide authentication. SSL consists of a public key and a private key. The public key is used to encrypt information and the private key is used to decipher it. When a browser points to a domain with an SSL certificate, the technology authenticates the server and the visitor and establishes an encryption method and a unique session key. Both parties can then begin a secure session that guarantees message privacy and integrity. VeriSign is one of the leading providers of SSL technology used by more than 95 percent of *Fortune* 500 companies and 96 of the nation's 100 largest banks.[33]

Secure Sockets Layer (SSL) Technology that secures a Web site by encrypting information and providing authentication.

Many online shoppers are switching to payment services such as Bill Me Later, Google Checkout, eBillme, and PayPal. Such services tend to speed checkout and make shopping more secure. They ensure that fewer merchants actually see the shopper's personal information and thus make it less vulnerable to hackers. These services benefit e-marketers, too, because they incur minimal marketing costs that then allow them to charge merchants lower transaction fees than credit card companies.[34]

Privacy Issues

Marketing research indicates privacy as one of the top concerns of many Internet users, although some recent studies suggest fears may be overstated. "There's far less information available about people on the Net than there is about anybody who uses a credit card," says one security expert. "The guy with the database has the same access to your information whether the data is sent through Amazon online or Barnes & Noble in the physical world."[35] Many consumers still have concerns, however; see the "Solving an Ethical Controversy" feature.

electronic signatures Electronic identification that allows legal contracts such as home mortgages and insurance policies to be executed online.

More recently, **electronic signatures** have become a way to enter into legal contract policies online. With an e-signature, an individual obtains a form of electronic identification and installs it in his or her Web browser. Signing the contract involves looking up and verifying the buyer's identity with this software.

Thanks to *cookies* and *spyware*—software used to automatically collect data from Internet browsers—online companies can track their customers' shopping and viewing habits. Amazon.com, for instance, has long employed sophisticated data collection systems to track customer preferences, and Google and other search engines gather users' search terms as a way to better target the ads that provide their revenue. The way companies use this technology has the potential both to make visits to the Web site more convenient and to invade computer users' privacy.

Most consumers want assurances that any information they provide won't be sold to others without their permission. In response to these concerns, online merchants take steps to protect consumer information. For example, many Internet companies have signed on with Internet privacy organizations such as TRUSTe. By displaying the TRUSTe logo on their Web sites, they indicate their promise to disclose how they collect personal data and what they do with the information. Prominently displaying a privacy policy is an effective way to build customers' trust.

Organizations, too, are concerned about the privacy of their data, and with good reason. Hackers were able to steal more than 100 million Visa, American Express, MasterCard, and other credit card records from Heartland Payment Systems, setting a new record for such thefts of information. "Our discussions with the Secret Service and Department of Justice give us a pretty good indication that this is part of a group that appears to have done security breaches at other financial institutions. This is a very sophisticated attack," said Heartland's president.

"The Internet is a telephone system that's gotten uppity."

—Clifford Stoll
U.S. astronomer, author, inventor

Behavioral Targeting Raises Privacy Concerns

solving an ethical controversy

Thanks to tracking technology such as cookies, online marketers can build profiles of Internet users, based on Web sites they've visited, articles they've read, products they've purchased, and even products they decided not to purchase. Using behavioral targeting, marketers use this information to precisely target ads and product offerings to individual users. While advertisers say they have no financial incentive to misuse personal information (and voluntary industry guidelines prevent doing so), many consumers are increasingly alarmed about privacy issues.

Should online marketers be allowed to use behavioral targeting to customize ads and promotions?

PRO

1. Behavioral targeting allows marketers to save time and money in reaching only those consumers likely to be receptive to their offers. "You get ads instead of paying subscription fees for services," says the executive director of the network Advertising Initiative.

2. Firms have no incentive to misuse information. "We're just trying to make an ad more relevant on a Web site to a consumer," says the CEO of an online ad company. "It's not worth . . . doing anything that could be adverse to a consumer's interest."

CON

1. Legal limits should be imposed to prevent information gathered online from being paired, even by accident, with names, addresses, and credit card information that can point to users' personal identity.

2. Databases of such personalized information represent a tempting target for hackers who can break into company files and steal sensitive and identifiable personal, medical, or financial information.

Summary

Despite marketers' assurances, recent studies found 50 percent to 70 percent of respondents were unhappy that advertising could see their browsing history, even when it wasn't personally identified with them. Yet in a National Retail Federation survey, the cost of shipping far outweighed privacy concerns among online shoppers.

Sources: "Behavioral Targeting to Grow," *Ad Week*, www.adweek.com, February 18, 2010; Mark David, "Behavioral Targeting of Online Ads Is Growing," *Kansas City Star*, www.kansascity.com, December 18, 2009; Jayne O'Donnell, "Are Retailers Going too Far Tracking Our Web Habits?" *USA Today*, www.usatoday.com, October 26, 2009; Stephen Baker, "The Web Knows What You Want," *BusinessWeek*, www.businessweek.com, July 27, 2009.

The company will likely pay millions of dollars to settle claims from the credit card issuers and clean up the damage.[36]

To prevent intrusions, companies install combinations of hardware and software called *firewalls* to keep unauthorized Net users from tapping into private corporate data. A **firewall** is an electronic barrier between a company's internal network and the Internet that limits access into and out of the network. However, an impenetrable firewall is difficult to find. A determined and skilled hacker often can gain access, so it is important for firms to test their Web sites and networks for vulnerabilities and back up critical data in case an intruder breaches security measures.

firewall Electronic barrier between a company's internal network and the Internet that limits access into and out of the network.

Fraud and Scams

Fraud is another impediment to the growth of e-business and e-marketing. The FBI, the National White Collar Crime Center, and the Bureau of Justice Assistance have formed a partnership called the Internet Crime Complaint Center (IC3) to receive and refer criminal complaints about cyber-fraud and other Internet crime.[37] A cybersecurity survey conducted by *CSO* magazine recently suggested that many attacks on corporate computer systems come from inside. "Although most of the top 15 security policies and procedures from the survey are aimed at preventing insider attacks," said one technical manager of a security firm, "51 percent of respondents who experienced a cyber-security event were still victims of an insider attack."[38]

One growing type of Internet fraud is called **phishing**. It is a high-tech scam that uses e-mail or pop-up messages that claim to be from familiar businesses or organizations such as banks, Internet service providers, or even government agencies. The message usually asks the reader to "update" or "validate" account information, often stating that some dire consequence will occur if the reader doesn't respond. The purpose of phishing is to get unsuspecting victims to disclose personal information such as credit card numbers, bank account numbers, Social Security numbers, or computer passwords. One recent phishing attack invited Twitter users to reset their passwords.[39] Phishing is also commonly used to distribute viruses and malicious spyware programs to computer users. In **vishing**, the voice equivalent of phishing, an e-mail or VoIP phone call requests the user to make a phone call to a voice response system that asks for the caller's credit card number. Three credit unions and two banks recently reported vishing attacks in Michigan, Wisconsin, Minnesota, and Mississippi. In one of these scams, a woman identifying herself as "Ashley" called customers about purported fraudulent use of their credit union checking accounts.[40]

Payment fraud is another growing problem for many e-marketers. Orders are placed online and paid for using a credit card, and the retailer ships the merchandise. Then the cardholder asks the credit card issuer for a chargeback to the e-tailer, claiming he or she never made the purchase or never received the merchandise. Some claims are legitimate, but many involve fraud. Because an online purchase doesn't require a customer's signature or credit card imprint, the merchant—not the card issuer—bears the liability in most fraud cases.

phishing High-tech scam that uses authentic-looking e-mail or pop-up messages to get unsuspecting victims to reveal personal information.

vishing Scam that collects personal information through voice response systems; stands for *voice phishing*.

Site Design and Customer Service

For firms to attract—and keep—customers, e-marketers must meet buyers' expectations. For instance, customers want to find products easily and have questions answered quickly. However, Web sites are not always well designed and easy to use. Competition and customer expectations will also drive more sites to include three-dimensional product photos and video demonstrations, because industry experts estimate better site design can quadruple the number of shoppers who actually buy what they put in their shopping carts. Product reviews, shopping information, pop-up discount offers, and instant messaging for customer questions are other features that can help online retailers to close sales.[41]

Another challenge to successful e-business is merchandise delivery and returns. Retailers sometimes have trouble making deliveries to on-the-go consumers. And consumers don't want to wait for packages to be delivered. Also, if customers aren't satisfied with products, then they have to arrange for pickup or send packages back themselves. Retailers are addressing these issues. Most have systems on their Web sites that allow customers to track orders from placement to delivery. E-marketers have also worked hard on a process known as *reverse logistics*. Detailed directions

Companies like Costco that combine their store and catalog operations with e-business have been more successful than many "pure-play" dot-com retailers with little or no brick-and-mortar experience.

COURTESY OF COSTCO WHOLESALE

on how to return merchandise, including preprinted shipping labels, are included in orders. A few, such as Nordstrom's and Zappos.com, even pay the shipping cost for returns.

Many of the so-called "pure-play" dot-com retailers—those without traditional stores or catalogs—didn't survive for very long. They had no history of selling and satisfying customers. Because of expertise in all parts of retailing, companies that combine their store and catalog operations with e-business, such as REI, generally have been more successful than those with little or no retail experience. That's probably part of the reason why seven of the top ten online retailers—like Target, Walmart, and Costco—are companies that have traditional brick-and-mortar stores. The three pure-play firms are eBay, Amazon, and Overstock.com, ranking first, second, and ninth, respectively. Online shoppers also exhibit a strong streak of loyalty; six in ten make most of their purchases from sites they are already familiar with.[42]

The same lesson also applies to other service industries. To be successful at e-business, firms must establish and maintain competitive standards for customer service. When it began offering customers the opportunity to check flight schedules and purchase tickets online, Southwest Airlines worked hard to make sure its Web site had the same high service standards the airline is known for. Southwest.com has proved very popular and profitable for the airline.

Channel Conflicts and Copyright Disputes

Companies spend time and money nurturing relationships with their partners. But when a manufacturer uses the Internet to sell directly to customers, it can compete with its usual partners. Retailers often have their own Web sites, so they don't want their suppliers competing with them for sales. As e-business broadens its reach, producers must decide whether these relationships are more important than the potential of selling directly on the Web. Conflicts between producers, wholesalers, and retailers are called **channel conflicts**.

Mattel, well known for producing toys such as Barbie, Cabbage Patch dolls, and Matchbox cars, sells most of its products in toy stores and toy departments of other retailers such as Target and Walmart. The company wants an Internet presence, but it would cut the retailers out of this important source of revenue if it sold toys online to consumers. Mattel cannot afford to lose the goodwill and purchasing power of major retailers such as Toys "R" Us, so the company sells only specialty products online, including pricey American Girl dolls.

Another conflict arises in the area of copyright law, usually when a site hosts content to which someone else holds the rights. Over the last several years, Google has scanned more than a million books from libraries at Oxford and Harvard Universities and the New York Public Library to make them searchable online. The Authors Guild filed a copyright infringement suit to stop the project, but it and Google have reached a settlement that gives Google the right to scan 12 million out-of-print titles. Said the Guild, "Protecting authors' interests has always been our top priority: in this case a timely harnessing of Google was the best way to do it."[43]

channel conflicts
Conflicts among manufacturers, wholesalers, and retailers.

 assessment check

1. What are the major challenges to growth in e-business and e-marketing?
2. Describe phishing and vishing.
3. Explain how e-marketing can create channel conflicts and copyright disputes.

Marketing and Web Communication

There are four main functions of the Internet: e-business, entertainment, information, and communication. Even though e-business is growing rapidly, communication still remains the most popular Web function. The volume of e-mail today exceeds regular mail (sometimes called *snail mail*) by something like ten to one. Contemporary marketers also use the communication function of the Internet to advance their organizational objectives.

8 Discuss how marketers use the communication function of the Web as part of their online marketing strategies.

Companies have long used e-mail to communicate with customers, suppliers, and other partners. Most companies have links on their Web sites that allow visitors to send e-mail directly to the most appropriate person or division within the company. For instance, if you have a question concerning an online order from Williams-Sonoma, you can click on a link on the retailer's Web site and send an e-mail to a customer service representative. Many online retailers have gone even further by offering their customers live help. Using a form of instant messaging, live help provides a real-time communication channel between customers and customer service representatives.

Firms also use e-mail to inform customers about events such as new products and special promotions. While using e-mail in this manner can be quite cost effective, companies have to be careful. A growing number of customers consider such e-mails to be **spam**, the popular name for junk e-mail. A recent study found as much as 95 percent of all e-mail is spam, up from 70 percent three years before and only 5 percent six years ago.[44] It is no wonder many Internet users employ *spam filters* that automatically eliminate junk e-mail from their in-boxes.

spam Popular name for junk e-mail.

Online Communities and Social Networks

In addition to e-mail, many firms use Internet forums, newsgroups, electronic bulletin boards, and social networks that appeal to people with common interests. All these sites take advantage of the communication power of the Internet. Members congregate online and exchange views and information on topics of interest. These communities may be organized for commercial or noncommercial purposes. JPMorgan Chase recently went to the Facebook community for input about which local charities should become recipients of $5 million in grants it planned to make. After collecting feedback, the bank was able to select 100 organizations from 31 states. Based on Facebook members' support, Chase plans to continue the community voting program.[45]

Online communities can take several forms, but all offer specific advantages to users and organizations alike. Online forums, for instance, are Internet discussion groups. Users log in and participate by sending comments and questions or receiving information from other forum members. Forums may operate as electronic bulletin boards, as libraries for storing information, or even as a type of classified ad directory. Firms often use forums to ask questions and exchange information with customers. Digg started as a community for technophiles, but its audience has since grown into millions of increasingly diverse users.

Newsgroups are noncommercial Internet versions of forums. Here, people post and read messages on specific topics. Tens of thousands of newsgroups are on the Internet, and the number continues to rise. **Electronic bulletin boards** are specialized online services that center on a specific topic or area of interest. For instance, mountain bikers might check online bulletin boards to find out about the latest equipment, new places to ride, or current weather conditions in popular biking locations. While newsgroups resemble two-way conversations, electronic bulletin boards are more like announcements.

electronic bulletin board Internet forum that allows users to post and read messages on a specific topic.

Social networking sites have grown dramatically. Facebook currently has in excess of 350 million enthusiastic members—more than the U.S. population—and is still growing fast around the world.[46] Twitter reportedly turned down an acquisition offer from Facebook and now boasts more than 6 million regular users, a staggering ten times the number a year earlier. Twitter plans to remain independent; its growth has been astronomical.[47]

Many observers believe marketers have quickly caught up to their customers in the savvy use of social networking communities, and that they will next become expert not only in exploiting their communication capabilities but also in tapping the huge and detailed databases they represent. Twitter, for instance, has been working on ways to let companies identify community members who might be interested in their products and also create profiles of those who follow these firms on the site. "We want to go for it and make a successful business out of this," says Twitter co-founder Biz Stone.[48] Some believe that adding search capabilities to Twitter's functions, for instance, would help unleash its marketing power. "There's a massive commercial opportunity here," says one online ad publisher.[49]

To get the most from social networking communities, marketers may want to consider their social marketing campaigns as if they were new products, complete with a launch phase, marketing support, and sales and customer service components.[50] Facebook already boasts hundreds of thousands of business pages, including those of large companies like The Coca-Cola Company, Starbucks, Adidas,

JCPenney, Eastman Kodak, and Pizza Hut, all of which have millions of Facebook fans. Acknowledging the extra power of such sites when accessed from mobile devices, Pizza Hut's director of digital marketing says its Facebook presence "makes us very relevant to the audience, and lets us communicate with them where they are, in a way that our Web site can't do."[51]

Marketers can also step up to advertising on sites like Facebook, which offers a variety of ad-buying options. Thanks to the public information members share on their profiles, advertisers can precisely target their Facebook ads. "You can literally find a book lover in New York who is a fan of Stephen King," says one analyst.[52]

Small companies, not to be outdone, make up about a third of the business with Facebook pages. One popular California nightspot asked its bartender to maintain its Facebook page as a way to offer discounts and specials and publicize special events. "It's one of the best ways we can reach a vast audience," the employee says. "After my shift, I can blast it to 650 friends in 30 seconds. I don't have to go around to each person, or call them up."[53] Sprinkles, a small bakery chain located in several cities across the country, which specializes in cupcakes, agrees. Co-owner Charles Nelson uses Facebook to run quizzes and contests and entice new customers and Facebook fans with offers of free cupcakes. "A Web site is you speaking out," Nelson explains. "But a Facebook page lets our customers come in and give their feedback. It generates business, and it's also a great community builder."[54]

Online communities are not limited to consumers. They also facilitate business-to-business marketing. Using the Internet to build communities helps companies find other organizations, including suppliers, distributors, and competitors, that may be interested in forming an alliance. Marketers wanting to expand internationally frequently seek advice from other members of their online community.

Social networking sites, such as Facebook, have grown dramatically.

© CJG - TECHNOLOGY/ALAMY

briefly speaking

"The new information technology, Internet and e-mail, have practically eliminated the physical costs of communications."

—Peter F. Drucker
(1909–2005)
Management author and educator

Blogs and Podcasts

Another popular online communication method is the **blog**. Short for *Web log*, a blog is a Web page that serves as a publicly accessible journal for an individual or organization. Typically updated daily or even more frequently, these hybrid diary-guide sites are read regularly by almost 30 percent of American Internet users. Using *RSS (Really Simple Syndication)* software, readers continually are kept up-to-date on new material posted on their favorite blogs whenever they are online. Unlike e-mail and instant messaging, blogs let readers post comments and ask questions aimed at the author, called a *blogger*. Some blogs also incorporate **wikis**. A wiki is a Web page anyone can edit so a reader can, in addition to asking questions or posting comments, actually make changes to the Web page. **Podcasts** are another emerging technology. Anyone from bloggers to traditional media sources can prepare an audio or video recording and then post it to a Web site from which it can be downloaded to any digital device that can play the file.

Given the growing interest in blogs and podcasts, it hasn't taken long for marketers to incorporate them into their e-business strategies. Of particular interest to marketers are blogs that focus on new-technology products, because they can prove effective at quickly forming public opinion. To try to reduce the damage from rumors and misinformation, some companies have decided to treat bloggers as members of the press and acknowledge their ability to spread news and influence. Other firms set up their own blogs. "A blog is a perfect way for us to share our experience and personalities," said the CEO of Quickoffice Inc., a leading provider of office productivity software. "We're excited to launch the Quickoffice corporate blog and provide a better way to share our opinions and insight with our worldwide customer, peer, and partner base."[55] Like Quickoffice, many believe that corporate blogs, if done properly, can also help build brand trust.

blog Short for *Web log*—an online journal for an individual or organization.

wiki Web page anyone can edit.

podcast Online audio or video file that can be downloaded to other digital devices.

career readiness Blogging on Your Best Behavior

The Internet is a very public place. That means writing a blog is like renting a billboard—anyone in the world can read what you write at any time, including family, friends, clients, colleagues, competitors, and current and future employers. Here are some guidelines for blogging that should help keep your online words from coming back to bite you.

- First, if you can't say something nice, don't say anything, especially not anonymously. If you can't accept responsibility for what you write, it's best not to write it. And while you can delete posts you later regret, others can copy and redistribute them first, ensuring they live forever.

- Avoid posting minute-by-minute details of your life. Such personal revelations seldom find a wide or loyal readership.

- Choose a specific area or subject you know something about or feel passionate about, and create your blog for a specific and interested audience.

- Ask the author's or creator's permission for everything you use that isn't yours, and use your own image-hosting site to avoid hogging others' bandwidth.

- Be honest but respectful if others comment on your blog. Everyone has an opinion, and you can have a healthy debate without having to change anyone's mind.

- Don't respond emotionally, or even at all, to inappropriate or irresponsible posts by others. You will only fan the fire.

- If you blog under a screen name, don't use it as a shield to hide behind. Remember it's always possible your real identity will become known.

- Never implicate or attack your employer, even if you think you've disguised it. Others have lost their jobs for this mistake, and the odds are against your getting away with it.

Sources: Scott Young, "Blog Etiquette: Ready, Set, Post!" www.platformmag. wordpress.com, February 3, 2010; Melanie Nelson, "5 Blogging Etiquette Tips for Beginning Bloggers," www.bloggingbasics101.com, August 17, 2009; "Blogging Etiquette," Deloitte, www.deloitte.com, accessed July 21, 2008; "The Social Etiquette of Blogging," September 14, 2007, www.customercrossroads.com; Zona Marie Tan, "Blogging Etiquette," *Suite 101*, May 28, 2007, blogs.suite101.com.

Many companies allow, and even encourage, employees to start their own blogs, believing employee blogs can serve useful functions. FastLane is the blog of General Motors' top executives. It attracts about 7,500 unique visitors every day with dozens of comments posted for each blog entry. Said the company's director of new media, who designed the blog, "I had been studying blogs for a few years and felt that a blog would have the potential to help humanize the company. And being able to hear customer feedback was important." Among other start-up issues, the blog had to educate its audience. "Our blog was a product blog, and we had to be clear that the blog was not going to respond to other issues such as policies or customer service issues." GM's blog is often considered an outstanding company blog.[56]

Some companies have strict policies about the content of employee blogs, and some employees have even been disciplined over what their employers thought was improper blogging. However, most companies today still have no official policies regarding employee blogs. The "Career Readiness" feature provides some hints on writing your own blog and keeping it trouble-free.

Promotions on the Web

banner ad Strip message placed in high-visibility areas of frequently visited Web sites.

pop-up ad Separate window that pops up with an advertising message.

Rather than rely completely on their Web sites to attract buyers, companies frequently expand their reach in the marketplace by placing ads on sites their prospective customers are likely to visit. **Banner ads**, the most common form of Internet advertising, are typically small, strip messages placed in high-visibility areas of frequently visited Web sites. **Pop-up ads** are separate windows that pop up with an advertising message. The effectiveness of pop-up ads, however, is questionable. First, scam artists use pop-ups. Second, many Internet users simply hate pop-up ads—even those from legitimate companies. Consequently, most ISPs now offer software that blocks pop-up ads. Google and Microsoft also offer free pop-up ad-blocking software.

Preroll video ads, marketing messages that play before an online video, are becoming more popular. Although users have shown some resistance, YouTube is one of the few sites to let viewers opt out of watching.[57] **Widgets** are tiny interactive applications Internet users can copy and add to their MySpace or Facebook pages or their personal Web sites to play music, video, or slide shows. Marketers are adopting the use of widgets at a rapid rate.[58]

Another type of online advertising is **search marketing**. This is considered one of the most effective forms of Web-based advertising. Companies pay search engines fees to have their Web sites or ads pop up after a user enters certain words into the search engine, or to make sure their firm's listing appears toward the top of the search results. Google and other search engines now include "Sponsored Links" on the right side of the search results page. A user who clicks on one of the sites listed under Sponsored Links is taken to that site, and the company pays the search engine a small fee. Google and Microsoft among others have made major investments in improving their search marketing services and capabilities.

Another way companies use the Web to promote their products is through online coupons. For instance, customers can visit a company's Web site—for example, Procter & Gamble (www.pg.com)—to learn about a new product and then print a discount coupon redeemable at participating retailers.

preroll video ad Brief marketing message that appears before expected video content.

widgets Tiny interactive applications that Internet users can copy and add to their own pages to play music, video, or slide shows.

search marketing Paying search engines, such as Google, a fee to make sure the company's listing appears toward the top of the search results.

 assessment check

1. What are online communities and social networks? Explain how online communities can help companies market their products and improve customer service.

2. What are blogs, wikis, and podcasts?

3. Explain the differences between a banner ad, a pop-up ad, preroll video ad, widget, and search marketing.

Building an Effective Web Presence

An e-business Web site can serve many purposes. It can broaden customer bases, provide immediate access to current catalogs, accept and process orders, and offer personalized customer service. As technology becomes increasingly easy to use, anyone with Internet access can open an account and place a simple Web site on the Internet. How people or organizations use their sites to achieve their goals determines whether their sites will succeed. Figure 4.3 lists some key questions to consider in developing a Web site.

9 Outline the steps involved in developing successful e-business Web sites, and identify methods for assessing Web site effectiveness.

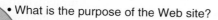

- What is the purpose of the Web site?
- How can we attract repeat visitors?
- What external links should be established to draw visitors to the site?
- What internal links to databases and other corporate resources are needed?
- What should the domain name be?
- What should the site contain?
- How should it work?
- Who should put the site on the Net—company or Web host?
- How much money should be spent to set up and maintain the site?
- How current does information on the site need to be?

figure 4.3

Questions to Consider in Developing a Web Site

Successful Site Development

Most Web experts agree: "It is easier to build a bad Web site than a good one." When judging Web sites, success means different things to different businesses. One firm might be satisfied by maintaining a popular site that conveys company information or reinforces name recognition—just as a billboard or magazine ad does—without requiring any immediate sales activity. Web sites like those of the *Los Angeles Times* and *USA Today* draw many visitors who want the latest news, and Yahoo!, Google, and ESPN.com are successful because they attract heavy traffic. As well as enhancing their brands, popular Web sites such as these add to their success by selling advertising space to other businesses.

Internet merchants need to attract customers who conduct business on the spot. Entrepreneurs are wise to clearly define their business goals, perhaps by creating a community of enthusiasts to build up sales in advance and to pay due attention to tried-and-true marketing tools that can complement Internet efforts, including television advertising. Listening to consumers is as important as talking to them via a company Web site or blog.

Establishing Goals

What is the company's goal for its Web site? Answering this question is the first and most important step in the Web site development process. For broadband telephone service provider Vonage, the primary objective is to sign up new customers. So the Web site designers put a link called "Sign Up Now" prominently in the upper portion of the home page.

Objectives for the Web site also determine the scope of the project. If the company's goal is to sell merchandise online, the site must incorporate a way for customers to place orders and ask questions about products, as well as links to the company's databases to track inventory and deliveries. The plan should include not only the appearance of the Web site but also the company's behind-the-scenes resources for making the Web site deliver on its promises.

Other key decisions include whether to create and maintain a site in-house or to contract with outside designers. Some companies prefer to retain control over content and design by producing their own sites. However, because acquiring the expertise to develop Web sites can be very time-consuming, hiring specialists may be more cost effective. Naming the Web site is another important early step in the planning process. A domain name should reflect the company and its products and be easy to remember. However, with millions of domain names already registered, the search for a unique, memorable, and easily spelled name can be difficult.

Web sites like Yahoo! are successful because they attract heavy traffic.

© NEWSCOM

Implementation and Interest

Implementing the goals of the site is the next stage, and content is one of the most important factors in determining whether visitors return to a site. People obviously are more inclined to visit a site that provides material that interests them. Many e-business Web sites try to distinguish themselves by offering additional features. For example, Williams-Sonoma's Web site lures traffic to the site with weekly menu planners; printer-ready recipes; and features that convert menus between metric and U.S. measurement systems, adjust measurements for different numbers of servings, and create shopping lists for menus. Many sites offer links to other sites that may interest visitors.

Standards for good content vary for every site, but available resources should be relevant to viewers; easy to access and understand; updated regularly; and written or displayed in a compelling, entertaining way. When the World Wide Web was a novelty, a page with a picture and a couple of paragraphs of text seemed entertaining. But such "brochureware" falls far short of meeting today's standards for interactivity, including the ability to accept customer data and orders, keep up-to-the-minute inventory records, and respond quickly to customer questions and complaints. Also, today's Internet users are less patient about figuring out how to make a site do what it promises. They won't wait ten minutes for a video clip to download or click through five different pages to complete a purchase. Revamping a site can help maintain interest and keep users on the site longer. Facebook recently rolled out a new design for its homepage that is more than just cosmetic. The changes are meant to improve site navigation and gather useful links and information in one part of the site.[59]

After making content decisions and designing the site, the next step is connecting to the Internet by placing the required computer files on a server. Companies can have their own dedicated Web servers or contract to place their Web sites on servers at Internet Service Providers (ISPs) or other host companies. Most small businesses lack the necessary expertise to set up and run their own servers; they are better off outsourcing to meet their hosting and maintenance needs. They also need to draw business to their site. This usually requires a listing with the major search engines, such as Google, Ask.com, and Microsoft Bing.

Pricing and Maintenance

As with any technological investment, Web site costs are an important consideration. The highly variable cost of a Web site includes not only development expenses but also the cost of placing the site on a Web server, maintaining and updating it, and promoting it. A reasonably tech-savvy employee with off-the-shelf software can create a simple piece of brochureware for a few hundred dollars. A Web site that can handle e-business will cost at least $10,000. Creating it requires understanding how to link the Web site to the company's other information systems.

Although developing a commercial Web site with interactive features can cost tens of thousands of dollars, putting it online can cost as little as $30 a month for a spot on the server of a Web host such as Yahoo! And Web hosts like GoDaddy deliver a huge audience.[60]

It's also important for a Web site to stay current. Visitors don't return to a site if they know that the information never changes or that claims about inventory or product selection are not relevant or current.[61] Consequently, updating design and content is another major expense. In addition, site maintenance should include running occasional searches to test that links to the company's Web site are still active.

Assessing Site Effectiveness

How does a company gauge the return from investing in a Web site? Measuring the effectiveness of a Web site is tricky, and the appropriate process often depends on the purpose of the Web site. Figure 4.4 lists some measures of effectiveness. Profitability is relatively easy to measure in companies that generate revenues directly from online product orders, advertising, or subscription sales. Southwest Airlines generates more than 74 percent of its bookings online at Southwest.com. However, what's not clear is how many of those tickets Southwest would have sold through other channels if Southwest.com did not exist. Also, evidence exists that so-called **Web-to-store shoppers**—a group that favors the Internet primarily as a research tool and time-saving device for retail purchases made in stores—are a significant consumer niche.

For many companies, revenue is not a major Web site objective. Most company Web sites are classified as corporate Web sites, not shopping sites, meaning that firms use their sites to

briefly speaking

" The Net is a waste of time, and that's exactly what's right about it."

—William Gibson
(b. 1948)
U.S. science fiction novelist

Web-to-store shoppers
Consumers who use the Internet as a tool to aid them at brick-and-mortar retailers.

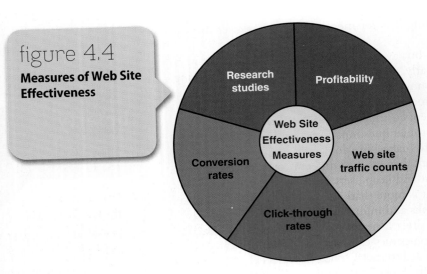

figure 4.4

Measures of Web Site Effectiveness

showcase their products and to offer information about their organizations. For such companies, online success is measured by increased brand awareness and brand loyalty, which presumably translates into greater profitability through offline transactions.

Some standards guide efforts to collect and analyze traditional consumer purchase data, such as how many Illinois residents purchased new Toyotas the previous year, watched "American Idol" on Fox, or tried the new Starbucks Gazebo Blend coffee. Still, the Internet presents several challenges for marketers. Although information sources are getting better, it is difficult to be sure how many people use the Internet, how often, and what they actually do online. Some Web pages display counters that measure the number of visits. However, the counters can't tell whether someone has spent time on the page or skipped over it on the way to another site, or whether that person is a first-time or repeat viewer.

click-through rate Percentage of people presented with a banner ad who click on it.

Advertisers typically measure the success of their ads in terms of **click-through rates**, meaning the percentage of people presented with a banner ad who click on it, thereby linking to a Web site or a pop-up page of information related to the ad. Recently, the average click-through rate has been declining to about 0.5 percent of those viewing an ad. This rate is much lower than the 1.0 to 1.5 percent response rate for direct-mail advertisements. Low click-through rates have made Web advertising less attractive than when it was new and people were clicking on just about anything online. Selling advertising has therefore become a less reliable source of e-business revenue.

conversion rate Percentage of visitors to a Web site who make a purchase.

As e-business gains popularity, new models for measuring its effectiveness are being developed. A basic measurement is the **conversion rate**, the percentage of visitors to a Web site who make purchases. A conversion rate of 3 to 5 percent is average by today's standards. A company can use its advertising cost, site traffic, and conversion rate data to find out the cost to win each customer. E-business companies are trying to boost their conversion rates by ensuring their sites download quickly, are easy to use, and deliver on their promises. Many are turning to one of several firms that help companies improve the performance of their Web sites. Nielsen/Net Ratings developed a new way to rate Web sites that measures **engagement**, or how much time users spend on sites, rather than counting how many pages of a site they view. Google Analytics is a tool for tracking the number of visitors to a site, which pages they visit, where they come from, and whether they buy, among other statistics.[62]

engagement Amount of time users spend on sites.

Webtrends' Mobile Analytics offers similar measurements of consumer wireless activity. Because many consumers download applications they never use, says Webtrends' vice president of marketing, "judging success purely by the number of downloads can overstate the success of your mobile objectives. Analytics shows where you are being successful and uncovers opportunities to tune your marketing tactics and improve customer experience."[63]

✓ **assessment check**

1. What are the basic questions a company should ask itself when planning a Web site?
2. How does the type of Web site affect measures of effectiveness?
3. Explain the difference between click-through rate, conversion rate, and engagement.

strategic implications → of marketing in the 21st century

he future is bright for marketers who continue to take advantage of the tremendous potential of e-business and e-marketing. Online channels, such as podcasts, that seem cutting edge today will be eclipsed within the next decade by newer technologies, some of which haven't even been invented yet. First and foremost, e-business empowers consumers. For instance, already a significant percentage of car buyers show up at a dealership armed with information on dealer costs and option packages—information they obtained online. And the percentage of informed buyers is only going to increase. This trend isn't about being market led or customer focused; it is about consumer control. Some argue that the Internet represents the ultimate triumph of consumerism.

Since the end of World War II, there has been a fundamental shift in the retailing paradigm from Main Street to malls to superstores.

Each time the framework shifted, a new group of leaders emerged. The old leaders often missed the early warning signs because they were easy to ignore. When the first Walmart and Home Depot stores appeared, how many people really understood what impact these large retailers would have on the marketing environment? Similarly, marketers must understand the potential impact of the Web. Initially, some experts predicted the death of traditional retailing. This hasn't happened and probably will never happen. Rather, a marketing evolution for organizations has occurred, one that embraces Internet technologies as essential parts of their marketing strategies. E-business is fueled by information; marketers who effectively use the wealth of data available will survive—and thrive—in cyberspace.

Review of Chapter Objectives

 Describe the growth of Internet use worldwide.

Worldwide, the number of Internet users has reached almost 1.5 billion. Among individual countries with the highest number of Internet users, the United States is first with 218 million users, and the next three countries are in Asia: China, Japan, and India. India's Internet audience grew by more than 25 percent in a recent year, while China's grew 14 percent.

maintaining online relationships with customers by means of computer networks such as the Internet. E-marketing is the strategic process of creating, distributing, promoting, and pricing goods and services to a target market over the Internet or through digital tools. The capabilities and benefits of e-business and e-marketing include the elimination of geographical boundaries, personalized marketing, interactive marketing, right-time marketing, and integrated marketing.

 Define *e-business* and *e-marketing*, and list the opportunities e-marketing presents.

E-business involves targeting customers by collecting and analyzing business information, conducting customer transactions, and

 Distinguish between a corporate Web site and a marketing Web site.

Virtually all businesses have Web sites. Generally, these sites can be classified as either corporate Web sites or marketing Web sites. Corporate Web sites are designed to increase the firms' visibility, promote their offerings, and provide information to interested parties. Marketing Web sites are also designed to communicate information and build customer relationships, but the main purpose of marketing Web sites is to increase purchases by site visitors.

 4   **List the major forms of B2B e-marketing.**

B2B e-marketing is the process of selling goods and services through online transactions. B2B e-marketing includes product information; ordering, invoicing, and payment processes; and customer service. In a B2B context, e-business uses Internet technology to conduct transactions between two organizations via electronic data interchange, Web services, extranets, private exchanges, electronic exchanges, and e-procurement.

 5   **Explain business-to-consumer (B2C) e-marketing.**

Business-to-consumer (B2C) e-marketing is maturing. B2C uses the Internet to connect companies directly with consumers. E-tailing and electronic storefronts are the major forms of B2C online sales channels. B2C Web sites are either shopping sites or informational sites. Products can be purchased on shopping sites, while informational sites provide product information along with links to sellers. Benefits of B2C e-marketing include competitive prices, increased access and convenience, and personalized service.

 6   **Identify online buyers and sellers.**

Today's typical Internet user is from 35 to 64 years of age and spends about 66 hours online in a month both at home and at work. Women now outnumber men online. The top products sold online are travel; computer hardware and software; autos and auto parts; apparel, accessories, and footwear; and home furnishings. Other fast-growing online product sales involve pet supplies, cosmetics and fragrances, gift cards, and movie and event tickets.

 7   **Describe some of the challenges associated with online marketing and e-business.**

One of the challenges to e-business is developing safe online payment methods. Most firms involved in e-business use Secure Sockets Layer technology to encrypt information and provide authentication. The growth of e-business has also been hampered by consumer security and privacy concerns and fraud. In addition,

poor Web site design and service, unreliability of delivery and returns, and lack of retail expertise has limited e-business success. The Internet can also generate conflict among manufacturers, wholesalers, and retailers and present another avenue for copyright disputes.

 8   **Discuss how marketers use the communication function of the Web as part of their online marketing strategies.**

Communication remains the most popular function of the Internet. Companies have long used e-mail to communicate with customers, suppliers, and other partners. Online communities are groups of people who share common interests. Companies use online communities, such as forums and electronic bulletin boards, and social networking sites to communicate with and obtain feedback from customers and other partners. Blogs are online journals that have gained popularity in recent years. Wikis are Web pages anyone can edit, and podcasts are audio and video files that can be downloaded from the Web to any digital device. Web-based promotions include advertising on other Web sites using banner ads and pop-up ads, preroll video ads, widgets, and search marketing. Banner ads are strip messages placed in high-visibility areas of frequently visited Web sites. A pop-up ad is a separate window that pops up with an advertising message. Preroll video ads appear before a selected video, and widgets are interactive applications users can add to their pages to play music, video, and slide shows. Search marketing is an arrangement by which a firm pays a search engine such as Google a fee to make sure the firm's listing appears toward the top of the search results.

 9   **Outline the steps involved in developing successful e-business Web sites, and identify methods for assessing Web site effectiveness.**

Businesses establish Web sites to expand their customer bases, increase buyer awareness of their products, improve consumer communications, and provide better service. Before designing a Web site, a company's decision makers must first determine what they want to achieve with the site. Other important decisions include who should create, host, and manage the site; how to promote it; and how much funding to allocate. Successful Web sites contain informative, up-to-date, and visually appealing content. Sites should also download quickly and be easy to use. Finally, management must develop ways of assessing how well a site accomplishes its objectives. Common methods of measuring the effectiveness of Web sites include profitability, click-through rates, conversion rates, and engagement.

Assessment Check: Answers

1.1 How would you describe the growth of Internet use worldwide? Worldwide, the number of Internet users has reached almost 1.5 billion. Among individual countries with the highest number of Internet users, the United States is first with almost three-quarters of the population online, but the next three countries are in Asia: China, Japan, and India. Growth in Asia has been rapid.

1.2 What do most U.S. consumers do online? Nearly three-quarters of U.S. users check their e-mail; between 26 and 40 percent get news, shop for personal consumption items, pay bills, and use an instant messaging service.

2.1 Define *e-marketing.* E-marketing is the strategic process of creating, distributing, promoting, and pricing goods and services to a target market over the Internet.

2.2 Explain the difference between e-business and e-marketing. E-business involves a wide range of activities that take place via the Internet. It is divided into five broad categories: (1) e-tailing; (2) business-to-business transactions; (3) electronic data interchanges; (4) e-mail, instant messaging, blogs, podcasts, and other Web-enabled communication; and (5) gathering and use of information through Web contacts. E-marketing transfers the traditional marketing functions of creating, distributing, promoting, and pricing goods and services to the Internet or through digital tools.

2.3 What are the major benefits of e-marketing? The major benefits of e-business include the elimination of geographical boundaries, personalized marketing, interactive marketing, right-time marketing, and integrated marketing.

3.1 Explain the difference between a corporate Web site and a marketing Web site. A corporate Web site is designed to increase a firm's visibility, promote its offerings, and provide information for interested parties. A marketing Web site generally includes the same information found on a corporate Web site but is also designed to increase sales by site visitors.

3.2 Why would companies *not* sell products on their Web sites? Their products might not lend themselves to online sales, or the firms may have relationships with partners, such as dealers or franchisees, that sell their products instead.

4.1 What is B2B e-marketing? How large is it relative to consumer e-marketing? B2B e-marketing is the use of the Internet for business transactions between organizations. By some estimates, 93 percent of all e-marketing activity consists of B2B transactions.

4.2 Define *EDI* and *Web services.* An EDI is a computer-to-computer exchange of invoices, purchase orders, price quotations, and other sales information between buyers and sellers. All parties must use the same computer operating system. Web services consist of Internet-based systems that allow parties to communicate and exchange data regardless of the computer operating system they used.

4.3 Briefly explain how e-procurement works. E-procurement systems are Web-based systems that enable all types of organizations to improve the efficiency of their bidding and purchasing processes.

5.1 What is B2C e-marketing? B2C e-marketing uses the Internet to connect companies directly with consumers through either shopping sites or informational sites.

5.2 Explain the difference between a shopping Web site and an informational Web site. Consumers can purchase products on shopping sites, while informational sites provide product information along with links to sellers. However, consumers cannot actually purchase products on informational sites.

5.3 Discuss the benefits of B2C e-marketing. Benefits of B2C e-marketing include competitive prices, increased access and convenience, and personalized service.

6.1 Who shops online? Are the characteristics of online shoppers changing? The typical Internet user now is likely to be between 35 and 64 years of age and spend an average of 66 hours a month viewing more than 2,300 Web pages, including home and office Internet use. While men used to shop more frequently online than women did, today women shoppers outnumber men.

6.2 What are some of the capabilities e-marketers might add to their Web sites in the future? E-marketers need to update their offerings at their Web sites at an increasing rate, speed the checkout process, add video segments to their online product catalogs, implement advanced and easy-to-use search and navigation technologies, and initiate network-type conversations with and between their customers.

7.1 What are the major challenges to growth in e-business and e-marketing? The major challenges include developing safe online payment, privacy concerns, and fraud and scams. In addition, poor site design and customer service, unreliability of delivery and returns, and lack of retail expertise have limited e-business success.

7.2 Describe phishing and vishing. Phishing is a scam that uses e-mail or pop-up messages that claim to be from familiar banks, Internet service providers, or other organizations asking for personal information. The purpose of phishing is to get unsuspecting victims to disclose personal information such as credit card numbers. Vishing is the voice equivalent of phishing, and consists of a voice message or e-mail telling the user to make a phone call designed to elicit credit card information.

7.3 Explain how e-marketing can create channel conflicts and copyright disputes. The Internet can generate conflict among manufacturers, wholesalers, and retailers—so-called channel conflicts. For instance, a channel conflict could be created when a manufacturer sells its products online and competes with its retail partners. Copyright disputes usually arise when a site hosts content to which someone else holds the rights.

8.1 What are online communities and social networks? Explain how online communities can help companies market their products and improve customer service. Online communities and social networks can take several forms and include Internet discussion groups and electronic bulletin boards, as well as networking sites like MySpace and Facebook. Users log in and participate by sending comments and questions or receiving information from other forum members. Companies use online communities to ask questions and exchange information with customers.

8.2 What are blogs, wikis, and podcasts? A blog, short for *Web log*, is a Web page that serves as a publicly accessible journal for an individual or organization. A wiki is a Web page anyone can edit. A podcast is an audio or video file that can be downloaded from a Web site to a digital device. Companies are starting to use blogs, wikis, and podcasts as tools to build and maintain customer relationships.

8.3 Explain the difference between a banner ad, pop-up ad, preroll video ad, widget, and search marketing. Banner ads are strip messages placed in high-visibility areas of frequently visited Web sites. A pop-up ad is a separate window that pops up with an advertising message. Preroll video ads are brief marketing messages that appear before expected video

content. Widgets are tiny interactive applications Internet users can copy and add to their own pages to play music, video, or slide shows. Search marketing is an arrangement by which a firm pays a search engine—such as Google—a fee to make sure the firm's listing appears toward the top of the search results.

9.1 What are the basic questions a company should ask itself when planning a Web site? The first question deals with the purpose of the Web site. The second deals with whether the firm should develop the site itself or outsource it to a specialized firm. The third question is determining the name of the site.

9.2 How does the type of Web site affect measures of effectiveness? For a shopping site, profitability is an important measure of effectiveness, though profitability can be difficult to measure given the presence of Web-to-store shoppers. For company Web sites, online success is measured by increased brand awareness and loyalty, which presumably translate into greater profitability through offline transactions.

9.3 Explain the difference between click-through rate, conversion rate, and engagement. The click-through rate is the percentage of viewers who, when presented with a banner ad, click on it. The conversion rate is the percentage of visitors to a Web site who actually make purchases. Engagement measures how long a user spends on a site instead of how many pages he or she views.

Marketing Terms You Need to Know

e-business 102
e-marketing 104
interactive marketing 106
corporate Web site 107
marketing Web site 107
business-to-business (B2B)
    e-marketing 108
e-procurement 109

business-to-consumer (B2C)
    e-marketing 109
electronic storefronts 110
electronic shopping cart 110
bot (shopbot) 111
encryption 113
Secure Sockets Layer (SSL) 114
electronic signatures 114
firewall 115

phishing 116
vishing 116
channel conflicts 117
spam 118
electronic bulletin board 118
blog 119
wiki 119
podcast 119
banner ad 120

pop-up ad 120
preroll video ad 121
widgets 121
search marketing 121
Web-to-store shoppers 123
click-through rate 124
conversion rate 124
engagement 124

Assurance of Learning Review

1. List the five e-business categories.

2. Explain how a Web presence can improve the performance of traditional brick-and-mortar operations.

3. Describe the type and purpose of information found on a corporate Web site.

4. Which is larger, B2B or B2C e-marketing?

5. How is wireless access changing e-marketing?

6. List the reasons consumers give for why they shop online.

7. Describe how firms can alleviate some of the privacy concerns of online shoppers.

8. What is purchase fraud?

9. How can companies benefit from blogs and avoid their downsides?

10. Describe the issues that go into developing a successful Web site. How does the purpose of the Web site affect its implementation and cost?

Projects and Teamwork Exercises

1. In small teams, research the benefits of purchasing the following products online:
   a. notebook computers
   b. hotel rooms in Orlando
   c. women's career clothes
   d. auto insurance

2. Assume your team is assigned to develop the Web site for a large online clothing retailer that also has traditional retail stores. Research the characteristics of Web users and online shoppers. What features would you want to incorporate into your Web site?

3. How can marketers use the concept of community to add value to their products? Give a real-world example of each of the types of communities discussed in the chapter.

4. Working with a small group, assume your group designs e-business Web sites. Identify a local company that operates with little or no online presence. Outline a proposal that explains the benefits to the firm of either going online or significantly expanding its online presence. Sketch out what the firm's Web site should look like and the functions it should perform.

5. Working with a partner, identify and visit ten different e-business Web sites. These can be either B2C or B2B sites. Which of these sites, in your opinion, have the highest and lowest conversion rates? Explain your choices and suggest some ways in which the conversion rates of all ten sites could be improved.

Critical-Thinking Exercises

1. Who are typical online buyers and sellers? What are some of the strategic implications of these facts to online marketers?

2. Some marketers argue that search marketing is a more effective means of using the Web to advertise than traditional pop-up or banner ads. Research the concept of search marketing. What are some of the benefits of using search marketing?

3. Assume you work for a U.S. company that markets its products throughout the world. Its current online presence outside the United States is limited. Outline some steps the company should take to expand its online presence internationally.

4. Visa offers a service called Verified by Visa. The purpose is to reduce Internet-related fraud (MasterCard and American Express have similar services). Research "Verified by Visa" and prepare a report summarizing the program and how it protects both buyers and sellers.

5. One factor that appears to impede growth in online sales is consumers' fear of receiving unsolicited e-mail after a purchase is made. Given that fear, should companies continue to use e-mail to communicate with customers? If so, how?

Ethics Exercise

One of the lingering impediments to e-business revolves around privacy concerns. Virtually all Web sites collect user data. Internet service providers, for example, can track where users go on the Web and store that information. Search engines keep detailed data on Internet searches by users. Those arguing that additional privacy laws and regulations are needed claim that users never know exactly what information is collected, nor when it is collected. Moreover, there is no means for determining whether Web sites follow their own privacy policies.

On the other hand, some say current laws and regulations are adequate because they make it illegal for firms to misrepresent their privacy policies or fail to disclose the type of information collected. Furthermore, there is no evidence that Internet companies are quietly passing on specific customer information to outside parties. Aside from the strictly legal issues, Web privacy raises a number of ethical issues as well.

Assume your company collects and stores personal information about its online customers. The company's privacy policy allows the company to give limited amounts of that information to "selected" third parties.

1.   Is this policy, in your opinion, appropriate and adequate? What ethical issues does your company's policy raise?

2.   How would you change the privacy policy to reflect your ethical concerns?

3.   From strictly an economic perspective, is the company's existing policy adequate and appropriate?

Internet Exercises

1.   **Online shopping.** Assume you're in the market for a new notebook computer. Visit at least two of the Web sites listed below and review shopping suggestions and model ratings. Next, list your top two models and, using a shopping site like Shopping.com (http://www.shopping.com), search for online retailers offering the best combination of price, user ratings, shipping, and other relevant criteria. Prepare a report summarizing your experience. What did this exercise teach you about the benefits and challenges of online retailing?
     http://www.pcmag.com
     http://www.notebookcomputer.com
     http://www.pcworld.com
     http://www.cnet.com

2.   **Marketing uses of social networking.** Choose two online retailers and two manufacturers. Go to each Web site. Compare and contrast how all four firms use social networking sites (such as Facebook and Twitter) to market their products. Which, in your opinion, uses social networking most effectively?

3.   **Search marketing.** Visit the Web site listed below. Prepare a brief report outlining how to optimize the use of search marketing. Be sure to include a discussion on measuring the effectiveness of search marketing.
     http://www.toprankblog.com/2009/03/charting-search-engine-optimization/

Note: Internet Web addresses change frequently. If you don't find the exact site listed, you may need to access the organization's home page and search from there or use a search engine such as Google or Bing.

Case 4.1   *Procter & Gamble's New Web Strategy*

Procter & Gamble (P&G), the global consumer products giant, earns about $79 billion a year from its portfolio of leading brands, including Pampers, Tide, Pantene, Bounty, Pringles, Charmin, Crest, Iams, Oral-B, Olay, Duracell, Gillette, Secret, Old Spice, Fusion, and many

others. Operating in 80 countries around the world, the firm employees about 135,000 people.

Currently P&G gets about $500 million a year from e-commerce sales, a fraction of its total annual revenues, and management is looking to increase that amount—perhaps as much as eight-fold to $4 billion or more. Given that fewer than one in three online buyers shop for consumer package goods, the company isn't expecting a lot of customers to go online just to buy toothpaste, but it's optimistic. Nielsen, the research firm, also expects this category of online purchases to grow as much as 20 to 25 percent in the next few years. "Some [product] categories see as much as 30 to 50 percent of their business in e-commerce," said P&G's digital business chief. "Our forecasts don't suggest consumer products will ever work like that. But it's not out of the realm of possibility e-commerce will be more than 1 percent of our sales. Getting north of 10 percent would be

an aggressive goal, but somewhere in between that would be, we think, within the realm of possibility." P&G already earns about that much of its sales from dollar stores and drugstores.

P&G isn't just sitting back waiting for more online sales to happen. It's increased its spending on marketing for digital media as well as on search, video, and behaviorally targeted ads (digital ads that rely on past online behavior to identify Internet users' interests). "Whether it's an investment in a banner ad, in a search-marketing ad, or in a shopping experience . . . we will look at all of those and their ability to drive revenue for our company," said the company's digital chief. And, while many of the firm's brands already have e-commerce sites of their own, such as Pampers. com (with 1.5 million unique visitors a month), the company is also opening a brand-new online store, called the eStore. For now, P&G views its eStore not so much as a potential source of increased revenue but as a kind of laboratory where it can research shoppers' buying behavior and habits. It plans later to share the resulting information with retailers like Walmart and Amazon that already sell P&G products. "We are very excited about the eStore's potential to reach more consumers and create new online experience and innovations that build our brands online," said P&G's vice president for North America.

To be owned and operated by an e-commerce service provider, the eStore will open as a pilot project with about 5,000 consumers and carry a selection of P&G branded products. Shipping fees on all orders are capped at a flat $5 rate. After the brief initial period the store will open to the public. "As the growth in consumer web commerce continues to evolve," said the CEO of the store's operating company, "we are seeing a strong trend toward the broadening of consumer purchase interests into more product categories. With each new product category comes the opportunity to develop and test marketing, selling, and retention concepts."

Questions for Critical Thinking

1. One of the things P&G already knows about online shoppers is that they expect brand Web sites like Pampers.com to offer the most information anywhere about a product line, including all its size, packaging, and product options. Do you think online outlets like P&G's eStore can convert more shoppers' needs for information like this into Internet sales? What other purposes can a pilot Web site like the eStore serve for retailers?

2. Do you think personalization, customization, or behavioral targeting can help Web sites like the eStore to succeed? What sort of personal information would you be willing to share online to improve a retailer's ability to meet your needs?

Sources: "P&G and PFSweb to Launch E-Commerce Learning Lab," *PR Newswire*, www.prnewswire.com, January 15, 2010; Anjali Cordeiro, "P&G To Test Online Sales," *The Wall Street Journal*, January 15, 2010, p. B7; Jack Neff, "Beyond Online Ads: P&G Sets $4 Bil E-Commerce Goal," *Advertising Age*, www.adage.com, September 7, 2009.

Video Case 4.2
E-Business at Evo

When professional skier Bryce Phillips began selling closeout ski equipment out of his garage in 2001, he was hoping to make a little extra money to fund his ski vacations. Things went well with the first garage sale, and soon he had a few employees and started selling snowboard, skateboard, and wakeboarding gear. Almost by accident, at age 20, Phillips had a company on his hands. He pulled some equity out of his house—and online retailer Evo was born. The company grew to 40 employees, then 60. Revenues came to nearly $6 million. Evogear.com became known worldwide by pros and amateurs alike looking for good deals on great stuff. They now offer all the top brands, closeouts, and used gear for every level and budget. All this success is quite surprising when you consider that buying skis or snowboards isn't the kind of thing generally done online or through a catalog. To get fully outfitted can cost $500 to $1,000, and most people need some expert help with their purchase. Through the design of the site and Phillips' desire to create a community for like-minded people, rather than simply another online discounter, Evogear.com is shredding the competition.

"Well, we want it to be functional, number one," says Molly Hawkins, affiliate program manager at Evo. "If you go to some of our competitors' sites, some of them look really cool" but, she says, "you try and navigate around their sites, they're not as intuitive."

Evogear.com is easy to use and does look cool, but adding value for the shopper is key to their business. The site offers product reviews, user accounts with all your past and current orders and preferences, tons of links to affiliate sites, events, blogs—pretty much everything you would want in a Web site, or a brick-and-mortar shop. "Aside from that," Hawkins says, "the About Us* page has played a huge role." Evo has, from the beginning, wanted to create a community for lovers of water and snow sports, and the About Us page really offers the customer an "in" to the company; their mission, values, personal pages and video clips by each employee. Customers love the idea that they can virtually "meet" their customer service person or buyer or Phillips himself. Hawkins believes this helped to legitimize the company in the beginning. "People would get excited to find that the person that they're talking to or the people that they're buying from are actual users of this gear that we're selling," she says.

Being seen as legit and trustworthy is paramount in the land of e-commerce. You spend weeks searching for the best price on that new digital camera or gaming system and when it arrives, if it arrives, it was not what you thought you were buying. Often, there is little you can do. The people at Evo know where you're coming from and want to make sure every purchase is stress-free. They have an easy return policy: just let them know what the problem is, from buyer's remorse to a box of splintered skis, and they'll make the switch.

Once an order is placed, Evo's distribution center jumps to attention. Most orders are shipped fast, within a day or two of the order. If you're not in a hurry, they'll ship it ground for free, or overnight via a partnership with FedEx.

Trust, value, and personal service are the key elements in Evo's success, but word of mouth only gets you so far. Advertising is difficult for an e-business such as Evo, where keeping it simple with low overhead and a no-frills annual budget is what makes them able to pass the discounts on to their customers. Like many Web sites, they offer an affiliate program that places ads or links on other Web sites to drive traffic back to Evo. An affiliate program or pay-per-click program pays owners of other sites every time a user clicks on an ad. In addition to paying for each click, Evo sends a "thank you" gift of 12 percent of each completed sale at evogear.com originating from the affiliate site. To protect their brand, remain authentic to their consumers, and remain in good standing with their suppliers, Molly Hawkins and her team lay out some ground rules for each potential affiliate. Their site must be well designed, easy to navigate, and, most importantly, must not contain any references to gambling, sexually explicit material, hate speech or racist content or any other inappropriate material. Sounds obvious, but being inadvertently connected with the most obscure, unseemly Web site could mean the end of their business.

Questions

1. Aside from offering good prices, how does evogear.com offer value to the consumer?

2. Evo has opened a large brick-and-mortar store/community art space in Seattle, Washington. Go to culture.evogear.com/category/seattle/ to learn more about what the store offers. Do you think this store will distract or enhance the Web site? Consider potential channel conflicts, pricing strategy, convenience, and consumer behavior in your answer.

* This is now found on Evo's Website under *Meet Evo/The Crew*.

Greensburg, Inc.

© CENGAGE LEARNING

Marketing Is Not a Dirty Word

May 4, 2007, started out more or less like any other spring day for the 1,500 residents of Greensburg, Kansas. There was talk of storms later in the day, but few paid much attention—the folks in this rural community had seen their share of storms and knew what to do. Around 9:20 p.m., the storm sirens went off and the residents gathered in their bathrooms and basements to ride out the storm. Minutes later, the town was gone.

"My town is gone," announced Town Administrator Steve Hewitt in the first press conference on the next morning. "I believe 95 percent of the homes are gone. Downtown buildings are gone, my home is gone, and we've got to find a way to make this work and get this town back on its feet." With 700 homes to rebuild, the town was essentially a clean slate. Hewitt rallied the town and, in the coming days and weeks, vowed to rebuild to the highest standard of energy efficiency and sustainability in accordance with the U.S. Green Building Council's *Leadership in Energy and Environmental Design* (LEED) rating system.

Thirty-five miles away, Daniel Wallach's wife Catherine Hart wept as he read the first words of his new business plan: "What if we turned this tragedy into something beautiful?" Wallach and Hart had long been interested in sustainable, green living. Their home was not impacted by the storm, but their hearts were. Wallach and Hart used their experience developing nonprofits to launch Greensburg GreenTown, an organization designed to support resident and business green building efforts through education and fund-raising as well as provide public and media relations for the town.

In the aftermath of the storm, the town received generous donations and media attention, but all too often today's tragedy quickly becomes tomorrow's old news. GreenTown must work every day to keep this unique town on the map and the much needed contributions flowing. "I don't think marketing is a dirty word," says Hart. "I think marketing is relationship building. That's what we strive to do."

One year later, as most of Greensburg is still operating out of temporary FEMA trailers, Greensburg GreenTown serves as the front line for those who want to help in the rebuilding efforts. Companies have given tremendous donations of goods and services for GreenTown to distribute on their behalf. They hand out everything from high-end, low-flow toilets to reusable grocery bags.

A large part of GreenTown's mission is to provide a green think-tank or "grink-tank" as Wallach calls it, for residents and businesses, the media and individuals interested in greening up their own lives. They host free seminars in green buildings and organic farmers organize a farmer's market, provide online resources and a place for residents still without electricity or computers to get online and do their own research. They are working closely with manufacturers, builders, and architects to create a series of green model homes throughout the town where residents and tourists can check out different techniques, products, technologies—and even spend the night. Wallach believes these partnerships work both ways. If successful, the model homes and eventually the town itself will become a living design magazine for all things green.

They've still got a long way to go in this very conservative town. Historically, the idea of green conjures up visions of politically radical, hippie tree-hugger types in Birkenstocks. While you may catch a glimpse of the ubiquitous footwear around the GreenTown office, Greensburg GreenTown strives to de-politicize green by making it easy and convenient for people to achieve. "If all you can do is build your deck out of recycled lumber, wonderful!" says Wallach. "We're gonna sing your praises as much as we will anybody else."

The long-term plans for Greensburg include a state of the art business incubator to help displaced businesses get back on their feet and bring new business to the town, a green industrial park, new highways, a green museum, green school system, wireless access throughout the city, and a community of green homes and businesses. While the city of Greensburg will take on the bulk of the financial responsibility for these projects, they will need GreenTown's help to continue to keep the cause on the radar of donors large and small to fund the gaps.

Questions

1. What is LEED, and how does adhering to LEED standards help create a story to market the town to the world?

2. What are the major challenges Greensburg GreenTown faces in gaining support for the green rebuilding efforts? What social and political views might they have to change?

3. Who is Greensburg GreenTown's "customer"?

4. Do you think Greensburg GreenTown's Web site (www.greensburggreentown.org) is an effective marketing tool?

5. Place yourself in the role of assisting Daniel Wallach and write a report (3 to 5 pages) that comments and provides recommendations on a specific product (i.e., low-flush toilet, solar or wind technology for power generation) and how to maximize the use of this technology.

Understanding
Buyers and Markets

2

Chapter 5
Consumer Behavior

Chapter 6
Business-to-Business (B2B)
Marketing

Chapter 7
Global Marketing

Consumer
Behavior

Paco Underhill: Hero to Marketers • • • Consumers are a mysterious bunch. Why do we walk into one store and not another? What makes us buy some products and walk past others? Do we take longer to make purchase decisions when we have less money to spend?

1. Define consumer behavior, and describe the role it plays in marketing decisions.

2. Describe the interpersonal determinants of consumer behavior: cultural, social, and family influences.

3. Explain each of the personal determinants of consumer behavior: needs and motives, perceptions, attitudes, learning, and self-concept theory.

4. Distinguish between high-involvement and low-involvement purchase decisions.

5. Outline the steps in the consumer decision process.

6. Differentiate among routinized response behavior, limited problem solving, and extended problem solving by consumers.

Do we respond more positively to certain words, images, and signs than others? Paco Underhill and his associates at Envirosell set out to answer questions such as these every day for retailers across the globe.

Underhill is a hero to marketers. He and his employees dig up all kinds of helpful information about the way consumers behave. In an economy where every sale—and every customer—counts, the insights provided by Envirosell's research are pure gold. Underhill and his team gather information about the habits of consumers for major retailers such as Walmart, Best Buy, and Gap, as well as smaller companies. Envirosell conducts research in three major ways: by observing consumers in real time as they shop, by interviewing shoppers about their attitudes toward buying, and by making qualitative assessments about consumer behavior using a

variety of techniques. Underhill and his associates evaluate all the data, transforming facts and figures into useful marketing information tailored to each client.

Here is how the team works. They videotape the actions of shoppers, learning which aisles they spend the most time in and which they tend to skip, what types of products they pick up, whether they spend time reading labels, how they respond to signs, and which items they actually purchase. (In all, the Envirosell team collects nearly 50,000 hours of video in a year.) Then the team interviews shoppers as soon as a purchase is made or when they leave the store. Later, the team might conduct traditional focus groups, leading consumers through a virtual shopping experience, or Web-based interviews. Finally, Envirosell researchers may collect further data on competing stores to compare against data from the

client's store. Envirosell sometimes uses mystery shoppers as well to track and measure customer service. Then the team analyzes all the data to create a cohesive set of information that a client can use.

One trend that Underhill and his group have noticed is that consumers generally make more purchase decisions when they are actually in a store than beforehand—even if they come armed with a shopping list. As a result, stores can take advantage of an opportunity to market products with signs and displays that are attractive and convey the right marketing messages. "It's all about in-store marketing," says Underhill. "It's making things occur to the shopper." Another trend is that shoppers are currently spending more time reading labels, comparing prices, and thinking about what they are buying. In grocery stores, consumers are removing items from their carts as they move along the check-out

line. "They are trading out or experiencing buyer's remorse," notes Underhill. In general, consumers are doing more with less. They are spending less money on nonessentials and substituting these purchases with free or inexpensive activities such as gardening, cooking, reading, watching TV, and volunteering.

If retailers observe and understand these trends, they can tailor their marketing to influence shoppers to make purchases. For example, if a retailer realizes that more than 60 percent of a shopper's time in the store may actually be spent waiting in line for a cashier, the retailer might put more effort into making attractive products available within reach from the line. One trend that Underhill has observed lately is that women have an even greater influence over all household purchases than they did in past years. This is partly because women now spend from their own income as well as from the total family income. Observing that women prefer an "experiential" shopping environment, Envirosell has helped some of its clients redesign their stores to reflect a comfortable, if chaotic atmosphere that entices female shoppers to spend more time—and ultimately more dollars. Walmart, Best Buy, and Anthropologie have followed this advice with success.

Underhill notes one important change in consumer behavior that has taken place in recent months. "Americans have started to re-open their wallets," he observes. "That's the good news. The challenge is that they are spending much more carefully." Underhill intends to help his clients compete for those carefully spent dollars.[1]

evolution of a brand

Envirosell offers marketing research services to help clients understand consumer behavior and increase retail sales. As the economy changes, Envirosell must monitor trends in consumer behavior. "The era of conspicuous consumption is over," observes Underhill. This doesn't mean that consumers aren't shopping at all; instead, it means that they are shopping more carefully. "We are a society of shoppers," acknowledges Underhill. In fact, Envirosell is based on the premise that the U.S. economy is fueled by consumer spending. As Underhill has worked to help his

clients strengthen their brands, his success in doing so has also strengthened the brand of Envirosell. Today, Envirosell is considered one of the top authorities on consumer behavior in the world.

- "Shopping isn't just about the acquisition of goods," says Underhill, "it's also about how we interact with each other." How does this statement relate to the study of consumer behavior?

- Retailers like Walmart and Best Buy rely on Envirosell to provide them with current, relevant information that will ultimately enhance their brands. What steps might Envirosell take to maintain the relevance of its own brand over the next decade?

chapter overview

1 **Define** *consumer behavior*, **and describe the role it plays in marketing decisions.**

consumer behavior
Process through which buyers make purchase decisions.

Why do you call for Papa John's Pizza whenever you have a craving for extra cheese and pepperoni? Why does your roommate stock Jones soda in the fridge? Why does your best friend drive five miles out of the way for Caribou Coffee—when the local coffee shop is much closer? The answers to these questions aren't obvious, and they directly affect every aspect of marketing strategy, including the development of a product, the level at which it is priced, and the way it is promoted. Developing a marketing strategy requires an understanding of the process by which individual consumers buy goods and services for their own use and organizational buyers purchase business products for their organizations.

A variety of influences affect both individuals buying items for themselves and personnel purchasing products for their firms. This chapter focuses on individual purchasing behavior, which applies to all of us as consumers. **Consumer behavior** is the process through which the ultimate buyer makes purchase decisions from toothbrushes to autos to vacations. Chapter 6 will shift the focus to business buying decisions.

The study of consumer behavior builds on an understanding of human behavior in general. As Paco Underhill of Envirosell states, shopping is "about how we interact with each other." In their efforts to understand why and how consumers make buying decisions, marketers borrow extensively from the sciences of psychology and sociology. The work of psychologist Kurt Lewin, for example, provides a useful classification scheme for influences on buying behavior. Lewin's proposition is

$$B = f(P, E)$$

This statement means that behavior (B) is a function (f) of the interactions of personal influences (P) and pressures exerted by outside environmental forces (E).

The statement usually is rewritten to apply to consumer behavior as follows:

$$B = f(I, P)$$

Consumer behavior (B) is a function (f) of the interactions of interpersonal influences (I)—such as culture, friends, classmates, coworkers, and relatives—and personal factors (*P*) such as attitudes, learning, and perception. In other words, inputs from others and an individual's psychological makeup affect his or her purchas-ing behavior. Before looking at how consumers make purchase decisions, we first consider how both interpersonal and personal factors affect consumers.

assessment check

1. Why is the study of consumer behavior important to marketers?
2. Describe Kurt Lewin's proposition.

Interpersonal Determinants of Consumer Behavior

You don't live in a bubble—and you don't make purchase decisions there. You might not be aware of it, but every buying decision you make is influenced by a variety of external and internal factors. Consumers often decide to buy goods and services based on what they believe others expect of them. They may want to project positive images to peers or satisfy the expectations of family members. They may buy a certain book because someone they respect recommended it. Or they may make res-ervations at a particular restaurant based on a good review in the newspaper. They may buy a home in a neighborhood they think will impress their family and friends. Students may even choose which college or university to attend based on where their parents went, how the school is ranked for certain features, or on their classmates' impression of the school. Marketers recognize three broad categories of interpersonal influences on consumer behavior: cultural, social, and family influences.

2 Describe the interper-sonal determinants of consumer behavior: cultural, social, and family influences.

Cultural Influences

Culture can be defined as the values, beliefs, preferences, and tastes handed down from one genera-tion to the next. Culture is the broadest environmental determinant of consumer behavior. Marketers need to understand their role in consumer decision making, both in the United States and abroad. They must also monitor trends in cultural values as well as recognize changes in these values. As attention to the environment becomes more prevalent in U.S. and other cultures, marketers are responding to this change by offering products that either contain environmentally friendly compo-nents or are made with energy-saving processes. Utah homebuilder Garbett Homes now focuses its marketing messages on potential homebuyers' desire for energy-efficient features by positioning itself as Utah's "greenest" builder. The firm is constructing medium-sized, affordable solar- and thermal-powered homes called the Solaris Collection. All of these homes are built to the 100-percent ENERGY STAR specification, which decreases monthly energy bills for their owners.[2]

Marketing strategies and business practices that work in one country may be offensive or ineffec-tive in another. Strategies may even have to be varied from one area of a country to another. Nowhere is that more true than the United States, where the population continues to diversify at a rapid rate. When you insert your bank card into an ATM, the first option on the screen often is what language you prefer for the transaction. Depending on where you live, you may choose between Spanish and English or French and English. The Las Vegas Convention and Visitors Authority has been advertis-ing in Spanish, placing commercials completely in Spanish on English-language programs on A&E, Bravo, Fox Sports Net, and Logo. Marketers believe this is an effective strategy because the strength of the Las Vegas brand is so great, and the images are so striking, that not everyone watching has to understand every word being broadcast.

culture Values, beliefs, preferences, and tastes handed down from one generation to the next.

Focusing on the core values of family and health, Stouffer's and The National Center on Addiction and Substance Abuse launched a joint marketing campaign called "Let's Fix Dinner," which encouraged families to eat dinner together.

CORE VALUES IN U.S. CULTURE

Some cultural values change over time, but basic core values do not. The work ethic and the desire to accumulate wealth are two core values in American society. Even though the typical family structure and family members' roles have shifted over the years, American culture still emphasizes the importance of family and home life. This value is strengthened during times of upheaval such as natural disasters—hurricanes, floods, wild fires, or tornadoes. Other core values include the importance of education, individualism, freedom, youth, health, volunteerism, and efficiency. You can probably recognize yourself in some of these core values. Each of these values influences consumer behavior, including your own. Focusing on the core values of family and health, Stouffer's and The National Center on Addiction and Substance Abuse (CASA) at Columbia University launched a joint marketing campaign called "Let's Fix Dinner," which encouraged families to eat dinner together. Marketing messages emphasized the benefits of families dining together at home, including a CASA study that found families who routinely eat together are "less likely to smoke, drink, or use drugs." The campaign featured Stouffer's prepared frozen meals and side dishes.[3]

Values that change over time also have their effects. As technology rapidly changes the way people exchange information, consumers adopt values that include communicating with anyone, anytime, anywhere in the world. The generation that includes older teens and young 20s is the most adept at learning and using rapidly changing communications technology, including smartphones. They regularly communicate via Facebook, Twitter, and other social media. Marketers are recognizing this, and in anticipation of more consumers adopting new communications technology, they are increasing their allocation of resources to reach consumers in this way. Shoppers at Target stores can now access their gift cards on smartphones and have the Target GiftCard barcode scanned by the checkout cashier. This is "one more way for [Target] to position itself as trendy," notes one industry analyst. "We're about to see a new wave of adoption for this technology, reaching out to non-technologically savvy shoppers."[4]

INTERNATIONAL PERSPECTIVE ON CULTURAL INFLUENCES

Cultural differences are particularly important for international marketers. Marketing strategies that prove successful in one country often cannot extend to other international markets because of cultural variations. Europe is a good example, with many different languages and a wide range of lifestyles and product preferences. Even though the continent is becoming a single economic unit as a result of the expansion of the European Union and the widespread use of the euro as currency, cultural divisions continue to define multiple markets.

McDonald's is known worldwide—its global business operations are now far greater than those in the United States and continue to grow faster. One reason for McDonald's success overseas is that the firm allows local managers to run

McDonald's worldwide business operations are larger and growing faster than those in the United States. One reason for their international success is that the company has worked to develop products that cater to the tastes of local consumers.

their own advertising campaigns tailored to the preferences of their customers—including language— although the traditional logo remains intact. Also, McDonald's has worked hard for years to develop products that cater to the tastes of its local customers. One of its most successful products, the Big Tasty burger, isn't even available in the United States. It was developed in Germany and now is a top seller on menus in Brazil, Italy, and Portugal. Australian foodies can order up an English muffin topped with Vegemite, a yeast-extract paste that is popular down under. And in Japan, customers can satisfy their hunger with an EBI Filet-O—a shrimp burger made of whole shrimp served on a bed of lettuce with spicy sauce on a Big Mac roll.[5]

SUBCULTURES

Cultures are not homogeneous groups with universal values, even though core values tend to dominate. Each culture includes numerous **subcultures**—groups with their own distinct modes of behavior. Understanding the differences among subcultures can help marketers develop more effective marketing strategies.

subcultures Groups with their own distinct modes of behavior.

The United States, like many nations, is composed of significant subcultures that differ by ethnicity, nationality, age, rural versus urban location, religion, and geographic distribution. The southwestern lifestyle emphasizes casual dress, outdoor entertaining, and active recreation. Orthodox Jews purchase and consume only kosher foods. Younger consumers are quicker to use new technology than older consumers. Immigrants from various nations often seek out spices, vegetables, and meats that are considered tasty or popular in their homelands. Understanding these and other differences among subcultures contributes to successful marketing of goods and services.

America's population mix is changing. According to the U.S. Census Bureau, the three largest and fastest-growing U.S. ethnic subcultures are Hispanics, African Americans, and Asians. Figure 5.1 shows the current makeup of U.S. society. By the year 2050, the U.S. population will total about 420 million, up from about 308 million today. Eighty-two percent of that increase will come from immigrants and their U.S.-born children and grandchildren. Today's minority groups will become the majority. By 2023, minorities will comprise more than half of all children in the United States.[6] The Hispanic population will triple, continuing to be the nation's largest minority group, representing more than 25 percent of the total U.S. population. The number of African Americans is expected to reach 61 million, or 14.6 percent of the population, and Asians will account for 8 percent. Women will continue to outnumber men, and the number of senior citizens will double.[7]

Marketers need to be sensitive to these shifts in population and to the differences in shopping patterns and buying habits of the members of different subcultures. Businesses must develop marketing messages that consider the needs of these different types of consumers. For example, members

figure 5.1

Ethnic and Racial Minorities as a Percentage of the Total U.S. Population

Note: Percentages do not total to 100 percent due to overlap of some racial and ethnic categories.

Source: Data from the U.S. Census Bureau, "Projected Population of the United States, by Race and Hispanic Origin: 2000 to 2050," www.census. gov, accessed February 25, 2010; "An Older and More Diverse Nation by Midcentury," U.S. Census Bureau News, http://www. census.gov, accessed February 25, 2010.

Hispanic American, 15.5%

African American, 13.1%

White Non-Hispanic 65.1%

Asian American, 4.6%

American Indian, Alaska Native, Native Hawaiian, Other Pacific Islander, and two or more races, 3.0%

of one subculture might be attracted to bargain offers while those of another might be offended by them. As important as differences in national origin may be, the differences in acculturation, or the degree to which newcomers have adapted to U.S. culture, plays a vital role in consumer behavior. Marketers should not assume that all Hispanics understand or speak Spanish—or the same dialect of Spanish. In addition, Asians come from a variety of countries, speak a wide range of languages, and eat different foods.

One thing that marketers must do is actually find where consumers of different subcultures live. The U.S. Census Bureau is now reporting that fewer Americans are relocating to different regions of the country, potentially making it easier to identify and develop relationships with groups of customers. Some of this trend has to do with a sluggish economy and housing market. "The mobility rate is lower than it has been in years," reports one demographer. California has actually experienced an influx of foreign immigrants and births.[8]

Hispanic American Consumers

Marketers face several challenges in appealing to Hispanic consumers. The nearly 48 million Hispanics in the United States are not a homogeneous group. They—or their parents and grandparents—come from a wide range of countries, each with its own culture. Nearly 30 million are from Mexico; more than 4 million are Puerto Rican, while about 1.6 million are Cuban. More than 1 million each are Salvadoran or Dominican. Guatemala, Columbia, Honduras, Ecuador, and Peru are also represented here in the United States.[9] Within the broad classification of Hispanic, there are many distinct segments. The greatest concentration of Hispanic residents—and consumers—occurs in California, Washington, Texas, Florida, and New York.[10]

The Hispanic population now accounts for more than 25 percent of all births in the United States.[11] As this population begins to include the second, third, and fourth generation, the attitudes and values of these consumers are likely to shift toward those of their age group and region. Still, it is important for marketers to be aware of subtle cultural differences as well as preferences in goods and services as well as media. For example, among those Hispanic consumers surveyed, 70 percent say they would rather spend time on the Internet than watching TV.[12] This statistic could have a huge impact on marketers who are trying to determine where and how to deliver their messages to this market. In addition, marketers should consider that Hispanics control more disposable income than any other minority group, a figure that has topped $1 trillion.[13]

African American Consumers

The continuously growing African American market offers a tremendous opportunity for marketers who understand its buying patterns. The African American population stands at more than 40 million people but is expected to grow to more than 61 million by 2050.[14] The buying power of these consumers is set to top $1 trillion, roughly equal to that of Hispanics.[15] A couple of trends that marketers should consider include the following:

- African American consumers spend about $39 billion a year on computers, cell phones, and other electronics.

- African Americans spend more time online (about 18 hours a week) than watching television (about 15 hours). In addition, more than 75 percent access the Web via their cell phones. They also update their social networking accounts on a regular basis.[16]

Despite these trends, as with any other subculture, marketers must avoid approaching all African American consumers in the same way; demographic factors such as income, age, language, and educational level must be considered. Most African Americans are descended from families who have lived in the United States for many generations, but some are recent immigrants. And they are members of every economic group.

Asian American Consumers

Marketing to Asian Americans presents many of the same challenges as reaching Hispanics. Like Hispanics, the country's more than 14 million Asian Americans are spread among culturally diverse groups, many retaining their own languages.[17] The Asian American subculture consists of more than two dozen ethnic groups, including Chinese, Filipinos, Indians, Japanese, Koreans, and Vietnamese.

Each group brings its own language, religion, and value system to purchasing decisions. Forty-eight percent of Asian Americans hold a college degree or higher, and 60 percent own their own homes. Asian American consumers wield nearly $700 billion in buying power. Marketers might keep the following trends in mind:

- The majority of these consumers prefer either in-language or bilingual advertisements.

- Nearly 90 percent spend time online, 70 percent of whom visit ethnic Web sites.

- Asian American consumers shop frequently at department stores—one to three times a week.[18]

> Sorabel Korean BBQ & Asian Noodles is the first Korean fast-food chain in the United States. Its mission is to make Korean food mainstream for all U.S. consumers, not just Asian Americans.

Sorabol Korean BBQ & Asian Noodles is the first Korean fast-food chain in the United States. Its mission is to make Korean food mainstream for all U.S. consumers, not just Asian Americans. While other restaurants are trying hard to add Asian items to their menus, Sorabol has actually "Americanized" its menu to appeal to a broader range of consumers while retaining a distinctly Asian foundation. Diners can order traditional *kabi* (barbequed short ribs) or *dak guyee* (barbequed chicken), stir-fried entrees or appetizers, or one of the many noodle dishes. In Korean culture, noodles are a symbol of long life and are served in a variety of ways. Noodles are a popular breakfast dish as well, because they are considered to be a healthy start to the day. Sorabol locates its restaurants in high-traffic retail locations, in financial districts, and on campuses. The restaurant chain seeks to offer an alternative to burgers and fries, making fast food "a pleasurable dining experience full of culture and flavor."[19]

Social Influences

As a consumer, you belong to a number of social groups. Your earliest group experience came from membership in a family. As you began to grow, you might have joined a group of friends in elementary school or in the neighborhood. Later, you might have played on a soccer team, sang in a chorus, or volunteered in the community. By the time you became an adult, you had already been a member of many social groups—as you are now.

Group membership influences an individual consumer's purchase decisions and behavior in both overt and subtle ways. Every group establishes certain norms of behavior. Norms are the values, attitudes, and behaviors a group deems appropriate for its members. Group members are expected to comply with these norms. Members of such diverse groups as the Harley Owners Group (H.O.G.), Volunteers of America, and the local swim club tend to adopt their organization's norms of behavior. Norms can even affect nonmembers. Individuals who aspire to membership in a group may adopt its standards of behavior and values.

Differences in group status and roles can also affect buying behavior. Status is the relative position of any individual member in a group; roles define behavior that members of a group expect of individuals who hold specific positions within that group. Some groups (such as the American Medical Association) define formal roles, and others (such as a book club among friends) impose informal expectations. Both types of groups supply each member with both status and roles; in doing so, they influence that person's activities—including his or her purchase behavior. A neighborhood may have formal or informal rules governing pet ownership—especially rules about cleaning up after pets. One company considers these rules an opportunity to create a competitive advantage for itself. Like other pet care businesses, DogSmith offers a full range of dog care services, from boarding to training to daily dog walks. But DogSmith goes the extra block—its employees will remove any waste left by dogs during their walk. "We take care of both ends of the leash," says DogSmith founder Niki Tudge with pride.[20] Customers are grateful for the extra service, which helps them abide by the rules

Pet care business DogSmith offers extra waste-removal services that help customers abide by neighborhood rules and norms.

© THE DOGSMITH NATIONAL TRAINING CENTER

and norms, fulfilling their roles as conscientious dog owners and neighbors.

People often make purchases designed to reflect their status within a particular group, particularly when the purchase is considered expensive by society. In the past few years, affluent consumers have spent money on home renovations and exotic trips. Loyal customers of Apple products are willing to pay top dollar for the latest gadgets, apps, and upgrades, not only because of their high quality, but because of the status they reflect.[21]

As the economy fluctuates, affluent shoppers actually achieve status by joining warehouse clubs or shopping at discount stores and consignment shops. Searching for the best value becomes the new norm—and status symbol.[22] But these consumers are willing to spend more on fresh or organic produce, often found at upscale grocery markets. And they like to tout the health and environmental benefits of these foods. Over the past several years, as the economy has dipped and adjusted itself, a new norm has emerged for most U.S. consumers, regardless of their economic standing—restrained spending and an emphasis on value. In fact, a certain amount of frugality has become chic. Businesses like those described in the "Marketing Success" feature are finding new ways to attract value-conscious consumers.

THE ASCH PHENOMENON

Groups influence people's purchase decisions more than they realize. Most people adhere in varying degrees to the general expectations of any group they consider important, often without conscious

mktg: *success*

Marketers Cater to Penny-Pinching Consumers

Background. When the economy dove into a recession several years ago, consumers stopped spending. Those who lost their jobs couldn't spend. Those who were afraid of losing their jobs cinched their belts so tight they could hardly breathe, let alone buy new clothes or electronics. As a result, many retailers and manufacturers of consumer goods faltered.

The Challenge. Marketers had to find a way to reassure consumers and entice them back into stores. They had to convey an understanding of new norms and values among consumers. "It's not so much [that we have] a different audience, but an audience that's acting different," observed John Lansing of Scripps Networks Interactive. "Their value system is shifting from aspiring to material wealth to aspiring to a life better lived."

The Strategy. Companies like Timberland, Walmart, Hyundai, and many others are taking these new consumer norms seriously. Hyundai made a special offer stating that consumers who bought a new car and subsequently lost their jobs could return the car; alternatively, if they wanted to keep the car, Hyundai would cover several months of payments. Timberland has gone back to producing its basic work boots instead of

awareness. The surprising impact of groups and group norms on individual behavior has been called the Asch phenomenon, named after social psychologist S. E. Asch, who first documented characteristics of individual behavior. Through his research, Asch found that individuals conformed to majority rule, even if it went against their beliefs. The Asch phenomenon can be a big factor in many purchase decisions, from major choices such as buying a car to deciding whether to buy a pair of shoes on sale.

REFERENCE GROUPS

Discussion of the Asch phenomenon raises the subject of **reference groups**—groups whose value structures and standards influence a person's behavior. Consumers usually try to coordinate their purchase behavior with their perceptions of the values of their reference groups. The extent of reference group influence varies widely among individuals. Strong influence by a group on a member's purchase requires two conditions:

1. The purchased product must be one that others can see and identify.

2. The purchased item must be conspicuous; it must stand out as something unusual, a brand or product that not everyone owns.

Reference group influence would significantly affect the decision to buy a luxury home in an upscale neighborhood but probably wouldn't have an impact on the decision to buy a loaf of bread, unless that loaf of bread was purchased at a gourmet bakery. Reference group influence can create what some marketers call "elastic consumers"—consumers who make decisions to save or splurge in the same economy. During a slow economy, a consumer might purchase generic brands at the supermarket but, because of reference group influence, spend those savings on designer jeans or a flat-screen TV. Banking on the fact that grandparents like to show off their grandchildren to friends—and are willing to spend the money to do so, even if they skimp on themselves—BabyGap recently launched a premium denim line for infants and toddlers. Five-pocket jeans for baby boys retail for $19.50 a pair, while a skirt-all for the girls runs $29.50. Matching denim jackets go for $29.50. Keeping in mind that babies and toddlers outgrow clothing quickly, these tags translate to luxury prices.[23]

Children are especially vulnerable to the influence of reference groups. They often base their buying decisions on outside forces such as what they see on television and the Internet (including social networking sites) or the opinion of friends. Understanding this phenomenon, marketers sometimes take a step back so that older children, preteens, and teens can shop—even if they don't have their own money to spend. More retailers now welcome teens who browse but don't buy. These retailers know they are still developing loyal customers—the teens will return when they have their own or their parents' money.

reference groups
People or institutions whose opinions are valued and to whom a person looks for guidance in his or her own behavior, values, and conduct, such as a spouse, family, friends, or celebrities.

---

trendy new styles. Walmart continues to offer lower prices, store brands, and special programs like discount prescriptions under a slogan that is now considered fashionable: "Save money. Live better."

The Outcome. Consumers are responding to messages that convey value. "People are moving toward a simpler, less materialistic lifestyle," remarks pollster John Zogby.

This doesn't mean that consumers aren't buying—but they are more thoughtful about their purchases. In a recent survey of more than 40,000 consumers, respondents were asked if they would choose to purchase a $500 jewelry item from Tiffany in its signature blue box or a similar item for $250 at Walmart. Seventy-eight percent said they would choose the Walmart item.

Sources: "Study Just Published: Remote Shopping 2010," *PR Log*, February 11, 2010, http://www.prlog.org; "Nielsen Predicts 2010 Top Consumer Spending Trends," *Convenience Store News*, December 17, 2009, http://www.csnews.com; Lisa Bannon and Bob Davis, "Beyond the Bubble: America's New Economy," *The Wall Street Journal*, December 17, 2009, http://wsj.com; Simon Houpt and Marina Strauss, "Frugality Fatigue," *Globe and Mail*, December 12, 2009, http://0-www.lexisnexis.com.library.uark.edu; "Less Materialistic U.S. Chooses Wal-Mart Over Tiffany: Poll," *Reuters*, September 7, 2009, http://news.yahoo.com.

Banking on the fact that grandparents like to show off their grandchildren to friends (their reference group), BabyGap recently launched a premium denim line for infants and toddlers.

In addition, marketers are recognizing the power of the Internet, including smartphones and social networking sites, as a tool for reaching children and teens—not just to market new or existing goods and services, but to learn more about reference groups and upcoming trends. More than 90 percent of consumers ages 12 to 17 are online, and at least 60 percent are making purchases. They visit social networking sites on a regular basis, get information, and form opinions from these interactions.[24]

SOCIAL CLASSES

W. Lloyd Warner's research identified six classes within the social structures of both small and large U.S. cities: the upper-upper, lower-upper, upper-middle, and lower-middle classes, followed by the working class and lower class. Class rankings are determined by occupation, income, education, family background, and residence location. Note that income is not always a primary factor; pipe fitters paid at union scale earn more than many college professors, but their purchase behavior may be quite different. Still, the ability to make certain purchases, such as a private jet or an ocean-view home, is an important factor in determining class.

Family characteristics, such as the occupations and incomes of one or both parents, have been the primary influences on social class. As women's careers and earning power have increased over the past few decades, marketers have begun to pay more attention to their position as influential buyers.

People in one social class may aspire to a higher class and therefore exhibit buying behavior common to that class rather than to their own. Middle-class consumers often buy items they associate with the upper classes. Marketers of certain luxury goods appeal to these consumers. Coach, Tiffany, and Bloomingdale's—all traditionally associated with high-end luxury goods—now offer their items in price ranges and locations attractive to middle-class consumers. Saks Fifth Avenue, one of the nation's most well-known luxury retailers, recently unveiled a private-label collection of men's clothing priced less than some of its premier brands. The new collection features Italian wool suits for $1,000 and $135 dress shirts—but the retailer's marketers consider that a bargain when compared to the typical $8,000 price tag for its designer suits.[25]

Marketers use language in their marketing messages designed to appeal to certain social classes—or to those who aspire to them. Here are a few examples:

- Aria Resort & Casino: "The rest of the world will seem so ordinary."
- Giorgio Armani: "Handmade to measure."
- Virtuoso Travel: "Expert advice for extraordinary experiences."
- JetPass Select: "Not all Jet Cards are created equal."[26]

OPINION LEADERS

opinion leaders
Trendsetters who purchase new products before others in a group and then influence others in their purchases.

In nearly every reference group, a few members act as **opinion leaders**. These trendsetters are likely to purchase new products before others in the group and then share their experiences and opinions via word of mouth. As others in the group decide whether to try the same products, they are influenced by the reports of opinion leaders. Generalized opinion leaders are rare; instead, individuals tend to act as opinion leaders for specific goods or services based on their knowledge of and interest in those products. Their interest motivates them to seek out information from mass media, manufacturers, and other sources and, in turn, transmit this information to associates through interpersonal communications. Opinion leaders are found within all segments of the population.

Information about goods and services may flow from the Internet, television, or other mass media to opinion leaders, and then from opinion leaders to others. Sometimes information flows

directly from media sources to all consumers. In still other instances, a multi-
step flow carries information from mass
media to opinion leaders and then on
to other opinion leaders before dissemination to the general public.

Some opinion leaders influence
purchases by others merely through
their own actions. Oprah Winfrey is
one such individual. Through her on-
air book club, she encouraged millions
of viewers to read. And through many
on-air wellness programs, she motivated
viewers to commit to a more healthful lifestyle through diet and exercise.

Opinion leader Oprah
Winfrey has launched a
"No Phone Zone" cam-
paign urging viewers to
sign an online pledge
to refrain from texting
or talking on their cell
phones while driving.

Viewers followed Winfrey and she took part in these activities herself. Recently, Winfrey launched
her "No Phone Zone" campaign, urging viewers to sign an online pledge to refrain from texting or
talking on their cell phones while driving. Celebrity designer Nate Berkus and his office staff took the
pledge on air during an episode of Winfrey's TV show. And although Winfrey has announced the
conclusion of her TV talk show, her production studio and other pursuits will continue.[27]

Family Influences

Most people are members of at least two families during their lifetimes—the ones they are born into
and those they eventually form later in life. The family group is perhaps the most important determinant of consumer behavior because of the close, continuing interactions among family members.
Like other groups, each family typically has norms of expected behavior and different roles and status
relationships for its members.

According to the U.S. Census Bureau, the structure of families has changed greatly over the last
century. Today, only about half of all households are headed by married couples. Many couples are
separated or divorced, so single heads of households are more common. In addition, there has been
an increase in households headed by same-sex couples. Women are having fewer children, giving
birth later in life, and spacing their children farther apart. More women are choosing to live alone,
with or without children. And more senior citizens are living alone or without younger generations
present in their homes. Still, to target a market for their goods and services, marketers find it useful to
describe the role of each spouse in a household in terms of the following four categories:

1. Autonomic role is seen when the partners independently make equal numbers of decisions.
   Personal-care items would fall into the category of purchase decisions each would make for
   himself or herself.

2. Husband-dominant role occurs when the husband usually makes certain purchase decisions.
   Buying a generator or woodstove for the home is a typical example.

3. Wife-dominant role has the wife making most of certain buying decisions. Children's clothing
   is a typical wife-dominant purchase.

4. Syncratic role refers to joint decisions. The purchase of a house follows a syncratic pattern.

Numbers 2 and 3 on this list have changed dramatically over the years. The increasing occur-
rence of the two-income family means that women have a greater role in making large family
purchases, such as homes, vacations, and automobiles. And studies show that women take the lead
in choosing entertainment, such as movies and restaurants. Women now outspend men in the purchase of electronics. Conversely, as more highly educated women begin to out-earn their spouses,
men are appearing more frequently at the grocery store because their wives are still at the office.[28]
In addition, men are taking a more active role in child care. Both of these shifts in family life mean
that marketers must consider both genders as potential consumers when creating their marketing

messages. For example, although men still do most of the automobile buying in the U.S., women tend to buy more energy-efficient models.[29]

Studies of family decision making have also shown that households with two wage earners are more likely than others to make joint purchasing decisions. Members of two-income households often do their shopping in the evening and on weekends because of the number of hours spent at the workplace. Shifting family roles have created new markets for a variety of products. Goods and services that save time, promote family togetherness, emphasize safety, or encourage health and fitness appeal to the family values and influences of today.

CHILDREN AND TEENAGERS IN FAMILY PURCHASES

Children and teenagers represent a huge market—more than 50 million strong—and they influence what their parents buy, from cereal to automobiles. These consumers are bombarded with messages from a variety of media. They are presented with a wide array of choices. Preteens and teens now wield nearly $200 billion of their own spending power.[30] They also have significant influence over the goods and services their families purchase. As teens obtain their driver's licenses, they put pressure on their families to purchase more vehicles. While parents tend to focus on safety features and cost, teens lean toward style and performance. But teens don't necessarily shy away from practicality—in fact, marketing research shows that they want fuel-efficient cars that are environmentally friendly and cheaper to fill with gas.[31]

Children and teens are wired. Most teens and even some preteens make their own purchases online. Girls tend to make more online purchases than boys. Both genders download music, play games, and participate in interactive marketing online.[32] Firms like Apple and Toyota—both of which have Facebook pages—demonstrate that they understand how teens receive information and communicate.

 assessment check

1. List the interpersonal determinants of consumer behavior.
2. What is a subculture?
3. Describe the Asch phenomenon.

Personal Determinants of Consumer Behavior

3 Explain each of the personal determinants of consumer behavior: needs and motives, perceptions, attitudes, learning, and self-concept theory.

Consumer behavior is affected by a number of internal, personal factors in addition to interpersonal ones. Each individual brings unique needs, motives, perceptions, attitudes, learned responses, and self-concepts to buying decisions. This section looks at how these factors influence consumer behavior.

Needs and Motives

need Imbalance between a consumer's actual and desired states.

Individual purchase behavior is driven by the motivation to fill a perceived need. A **need** is an imbalance between the consumer's actual and desired states. A person who recognizes or feels a significant or urgent need then seeks to correct the imbalance. Marketers attempt to arouse this sense of urgency by making a need "felt" and then influencing consumers' motivation to satisfy their needs by purchasing specific products.

motive Inner state that directs a person toward the goal of satisfying a need.

Motives are inner states that direct a person toward the goal of satisfying a need. The individual takes action to reduce the state of tension and return to a condition of equilibrium.

MASLOW'S HIERARCHY OF NEEDS

Psychologist Abraham H. Maslow developed a theory that characterized needs and arranged them into a hierarchy. Maslow identified five levels of needs, beginning with physiological needs and progressing to the need for self-actualization. A person must at least partially satisfy lower-level needs, according to Maslow, before higher needs can affect behavior. In developed countries, where relatively large per-capita incomes allow most people to satisfy the basic needs on the hierarchy, higher-order needs may be more important to consumer behavior. Table 5.1 illustrates products and marketing themes designed to satisfy needs at each level.

Physiological Needs

Needs at the most basic level concern essential requirements for survival, such as food, water, shelter, and clothing. Pur promotes its water filtration system with the slogan, "Your water should be Pur." Its ads emphasize the need for clean water: "When you realize how often water touches your family's life, you discover just how important healthy, great-tasting water is."

Safety Needs

Second-level needs include financial or lifestyle security, protection from physical harm, and avoidance of the unexpected. To gratify these needs, consumers may buy life insurance, alarm systems, or retirement plans. In one of its ads Fidelity asks, "Will you be ready for the retirement you have in mind?" The answer to the question is, "Let Fidelity be your guide."

Social/Belongingness Needs

Satisfaction of physiological and safety needs leads a person to attend to third-level needs—the desire to be accepted by people and groups important to that individual. To satisfy this need, people may join organizations and buy goods or services that make them feel part of a group. Chase offers its

table 5.1 Marketing Strategies Based on Maslow's Hierarchy of Needs

Physiological needs	Products	Food, water, medicines, vitamins, exercise equipment and gym memberships, health care and cleansing products, sleep aids and mattresses, food for pets
	Marketing themes	Fresh Express salads: "Consistently, deliciously, fresh." GNC vitamins and supplements: "Be a better you." Colgate Total: "#1 recommended by dentists and hygienists." Purina pet food: "A difference you can see."
Safety needs	Products	Health and life insurance, computer antivirus software, smoke and carbon monoxide detectors, antibacterial cleaners, business protection, auto safety features
	Marketing themes	Progressive Insurance: "Helping you save money. That's Progressive." Lysol household cleaners: "Disinfect to protect." Better Business Bureau: "Start with trust." Chevrolet trucks: "You have a right to know the truth."
Belongingness	Products	Cosmetics, food, entertainment, fashion, appliances and home furnishings, clubs and organizations, cars
	Marketing themes	Avon Walk for Breast Cancer: "In it to end it." Lowe's: "Let's build something together." Lee: "Get what fits." Payless shoes: "Save now. Feel good." Olay: "Love the skin you're in." Hershey's Special Dark: "Not fancy, just deliciously special." Ford: "Drive one."
Esteem needs	Products	Fashion, jewelry, gourmet foods, electronics, cosmetics, luxury cars, credit cards, investments, sports and hobbies, travel, spas
	Marketing themes	Rolex watches: "A crown for every achievement." Lincoln automobiles: "Reach higher." L'Oreal Paris: "Because you're worth it." Visa Black Card: "The world awaits."
Self-actualization	Products	Education, cultural events, sports and hobbies, motivational seminars, technology, travel, investments
	Marketing themes	University of Findlay: "Be a champion." Fidelity Investments: "Let Fidelity be your guide." Tony Robbins: "Unleash the power within." Canyon Ranch: "The power of possibility."

Owning jewelry created by leading Italian jewelry designer Roberto Coin might satisfy a consumer's esteem needs.

CapriPlus Collection   ◆ ROBERTO COIN

Blueprint program, "a new set of free features only for Chase customers."

Esteem Needs

People have a universal desire for a sense of accomplishment and achievement. They also wish to gain the respect of others and even exceed others' performance once lower-order needs are satisfied. Pandora's jewelry ads encourage consumers to buy its pieces because "Life has its moments...make them unforgettable."

Self-Actualization Needs

At the top rung of Maslow's ladder of human needs is people's desire to realize their full potential and find fulfillment by expressing their unique talents and capabilities. Companies that run exotic adventure trips aim to satisfy consumers' needs for self-actualization. Not-for-profit organizations that invite paying volunteers to assist in such projects as archaeological digs or building homes for the needy appeal to these needs as well. Four Seasons resorts advertises one of its African locations by showing two of its guests riding elephants through the mist. "It's said they never forget," reads the tag line. "Neither will you."

Maslow believed that a satisfied need no longer has to be met. Once the physiological needs are met, the individual moves on to pursue satisfaction of higher-order needs. Consumers periodically are motivated by the need to relieve thirst and hunger, but their interests soon return to focus on satisfaction of safety, social, and other needs in the hierarchy. But people may not always progress through the hierarchy; they may fixate on a certain level. For example, consumers who live through an economic downturn may always be motivated to save money in order to avoid financial insecurity—a second-level need. Marketers who understand this can create opportunities for their firms by offering money-saving goods and services.

Critics have pointed out a variety of flaws in Maslow's reasoning. For example, some needs can be related to more than one level, and not every individual progresses through the needs hierarchy in the same order; some bypass social and esteem needs and are motivated by self-actualization needs. But the hierarchy of needs can offer an effective guideline for marketers who want to study consumer behavior.

Perceptions

perception Meaning that a person attributes to incoming stimuli gathered through the five senses.

Perception is the meaning that a person attributes to incoming stimuli gathered through the five senses—sight, hearing, touch, taste, and smell. Certainly a buyer's behavior is influenced by his or her perceptions of a good or service. Researchers now recognize that people's perceptions depend as much on what they want to perceive as on the actual stimuli. For this reason, Bloomingdale's and Target are perceived differently, as are Godiva chocolates and M&Ms. A person's perception of an object or event results from the interaction of two types of factors:

1. *stimulus factors*—characteristics of the physical object such as size, color, weight, and shape
2. *individual factors*—unique characteristics of the individual, including not only sensory processes but also experiences with similar inputs and basic motivations and expectations.

PERCEPTUAL SCREENS

The average American consumer constantly is barraged with marketing messages. A typical supermarket now carries 30,000 different packages, each serving as a miniature billboard vying to attract consumers' attention. More than 6,000 commercials are aired on network TV each week. As marketers compete for attention—and dollars—they get more creative about where they place their messages. Consumers might find a carton of eggs stamped with the name of a television show, or takeout cartons emblazoned with the name of a major airline. Old-fashioned billboards—once thought to be obsolete—have made a comeback as large digital advertising screens.

The overnight test drive.

Only at BMW of Bridgeport.

NED GERARD, HEARST CONNECTICUT MEDIA GROUP, © 2010

In an attempt to break through perceptual screens and be noticed, a BMW dealer in Connecticut installed a billboard that featured a life-sized mannequin with pajamas and a teddy bear perched dangerously on top of the advertisement.

The problem with all of these messages is they create clutter in the minds of consumers, causing them to ignore many promotional messages. People respond selectively to messages that break through their **perceptual screens**—the mental filtering processes through which all inputs must pass. Doubling the size of an ad, using certain colors or graphics, or developing unique packaging are some techniques that marketers use to elicit a positive response from consumers. For example, color is so suggestive that its use on product packaging and logos often is the result of a long and careful selection process. Red grabs the attention, and orange has been shown to stimulate appetite. Blue is associated with water—you'll find blue on cleaning products. Green connotes low-fat or healthful food products. The psychological concept of closure also helps marketers create messages that stand out. Closure is the human tendency to perceive a complete picture from an incomplete stimulus. Advertisements that allow consumers to do this often succeed in breaking through perceptual screens.

But as marketers get more and more creative in an effort to break through the barrier of clutter, sometimes these efforts backfire. When a BMW dealer in Connecticut installed a billboard that featured a life-sized mannequin wearing pajamas and clutching a teddy bear perched precariously top of the billboard, worried motorists called 911 to report the dangerous situation. Emergency dispatchers had to reassure callers that the figure wasn't real—and wasn't about to fall off the billboard. While there was some initial criticism about the advertisement, the general sales manager reported that the dealership actually got more people asking to take test drives because of it.[33]

perceptual screens
The mental filtering processes through which all inputs must pass.

Word of mouth is probably the oldest marketing technique in existence. It is also one of the most effective. If one satisfied customer tells a friend, relative, neighbor, or coworker about a positive experience with a product, that message quite often breaks through the listener's perceptual screen because trust between the two already exists.

On the other end of the scale lie newer, high-tech marketing tools. These include virtual reality (in which a consumer can test drive a car or tour a resort) and social media such as Facebook, Twitter, and LinkedIn. While investment in these new tools is increasingly rapidly, it is interesting to note that the old methods remain strong—with modification—as in the case of the billboard. Although some marketers predicted the certain demise of the traditional 30-second television commercial, that prediction has not come true. "[The TV commercial] is still the best way to reach a mass audience," notes Bill Duggan, executive vice

Stand up straight. Don't chew gum in school.
Always say please and thank you. Walk. Don't run.

There are rules we all have to live by.

Thankfully, there is a place we can go
where 'no rules' is always the rule of the day.

A place that yells 'go for it' up, down and all around.

A place where 3,288 miles of
freshwater freedom is Pure Michigan.

PURE MICHIGAN®
Your trip begins at michigan.org

© PURE MICHIGAN (WWW.MICHIGAN.ORG)

Travel Michigan's successful "Pure Michigan" marketing campaign relied on a combination of print, outdoor, and broadcast media, including national television advertising, to attract visitors to the state.

president of the Association of National Advertisers. But the effectiveness of commercials will have to be more selectively measured.[34] One recently successful marketing campaign that relied heavily on TV advertising was Travel Michigan's "Pure Michigan," in which commercials were aired nationally in an effort to attract tourists to the state. At the conclusion of the campaign, Michigan reported 680,000 first-time trips to the state from tourists who lived outside the region. Those new visitors spent $250 million at Michigan businesses in one summer as a result of the campaign.[35]

With selective perception at work screening competing messages, it is easy to see the importance of marketers' efforts in developing brand loyalty. Satisfied customers are less likely to seek information about competing products. Even when competitive advertising is forced on them, they are less apt than others to look beyond their perceptual filters at those appeals. Loyal customers simply tune out information that does not agree with their existing beliefs and expectations.

SUBLIMINAL PERCEPTION

subliminal perception
The subconscious receipt of incoming information.

More than 50 years ago, a New Jersey movie theater tried to boost concession sales by flashing the words "Eat Popcorn" and "Drink Coca-Cola" between frames of actress Kim Novak's image in the movie *Picnic*. The messages flashed on the screen every five seconds for a duration of one three-hundredth of a second each time. Researchers reported that these messages, though too short to be recognizable at the conscious level, resulted in a 58 percent increase in popcorn sales and an 18 percent increase in Coke sales. After the findings were published, advertising agencies and consumer protection groups became intensely interested in **subliminal perception**—the subconscious receipt of incoming information.

Subliminal advertising is aimed at the subconscious level of awareness to circumvent the audience's perceptual screens. The goal of the original research was to induce consumer purchases while keeping consumers unaware of the source of the motivation to buy. All later attempts to duplicate the test findings were unsuccessful. Although subliminal advertising is considered manipulative, it is exceedingly unlikely to induce purchasing except by people already inclined to buy. There are three reasons for this:

1. Strong stimulus factors are required just to get a prospective customer's attention.

2. Only a very short message can be transmitted.

3. Individuals vary greatly in their thresholds of consciousness. Messages transmitted at the threshold of consciousness for one person will not be perceived at all by some people and will be all too apparent to others. The subliminally exposed message "Drink Coca-Cola" may go unseen by some viewers, while others may read it as "Drink Pepsi-Cola," "Drink Cocoa," or even "Drive Slowly."

Despite the findings about subliminal advertising, however, neuroscientists know that thoughts and emotions, including those a person may not be consciously aware of, play a vital role in decision making, and marketers are looking to find ways to elicit emotions that motivate people toward a purchase. Neuromarketing has already taken some concrete forms. Firms such as Yahoo!, Hyundai, and Microsoft are using EEGs and MRIs—which measure brain activity—to study consumers' responses to certain stimuli associated with their products. Frito-Lay used brain imaging to determine that the matte beige packaging that pictures potatoes and other natural ingredients on a bag of potato chips doesn't trigger activity in the area of the brain associated with guilt. On the other hand, those shiny, brightly colored bags loaded with pictures of chips do elicit brain activity associated with guilt feelings. The company's chief marketing officer insists that this type of measurement is much more accurate and "honest" than responses from focus group participants.[36]

Attitudes

attitudes Person's enduring favorable or unfavorable evaluations, emotions, or action tendencies toward some object or idea.

Perception of incoming stimuli is greatly affected by attitudes. In fact, a consumer's decision to purchase an item is strongly based on his or her attitudes about the product, store, or salesperson. **Attitudes** are a person's enduring favorable or unfavorable evaluations, emotions, or action tendencies toward some object or idea. As they form over time through individual experiences and group contacts, attitudes become highly resistant to change. New fees, a reduction in service hours, or a change in location can be difficult for customers to accept. Because favorable attitudes likely affect brand preferences, marketers are interested in determining consumer attitudes toward their offerings. Numerous attitude-scaling devices have been developed for this purpose.

career readiness **Y**our Body Language Speaks Volumes

consumer's attitude toward goods and services can determine whether or not a purchase will be made. As a marketer, you can influence that attitude through your own body language. "You can go from a thumbs down to a thumbs up," counsels Richard Newman, a professional body-language coach hired by firms to train their sales and marketing staffs. In addition, you can "read" and interpret the customer's body language to understand his or her attitude toward the product you are offering. Here are a few tips for using body language to communicate successfully:

- Make eye contact with the person to whom you are speaking, but in a relaxed manner—don't stare or glare.

- Lean slightly forward in order to indicate interest in what the other person is saying—but don't crowd that person's space.

- Sit or stand with shoulders open—hunched shoulders or crossed arms indicate that you are already negating what the other person wants to say.

- Remain calm—avoid fidgeting gestures, such as cracking your knuckles or crossing and recrossing your legs.

- Genuinely smile and nod in agreement, if smiling is appropriate to the situation. Don't plaster a false smile on your face, and don't laugh nervously or inappropriately.

As you interpret the body language of your customer, watch for signs of nervousness (such as irregular breathing, stammering, or fidgeting) or potential combativeness (glaring, arms crossed, stiff posture). By using your own body language effectively, you can potentially turn the other person's attitude from a negative one to a positive one—or simply reinforce a positive attitude that was already there.

Sources: "Body Language in Sales," Effective Communication.com, http://www. effective-communicating.com, accessed February 19, 2010; Dennis Kyle, "Reading Body Language for Sales Professionals," Selfgrowth.com, http://www.selfgrowth. com, accessed February 19, 2010; Anita Raghavan, "Watch Your Body Language," *Forbes*, March 16, 2009, pp. 92–93.

Marketers can influence their customers' attitudes through the messages they create, including body language when communicating in person, as described in the "Career Readiness" feature.

ATTITUDE COMPONENTS

An attitude has cognitive, affective, and behavioral components. The cognitive component refers to the individual's information and knowledge about an object or concept. The affective component deals with feelings or emotional reactions. The behavioral component involves tendencies to act in a certain manner. For example, in deciding whether to shop at a specific retailer for a laptop computer, a consumer might gather information about what the store offers from advertising, visits to the store, and input from family, friends, and coworkers—the cognitive component. The consumer might also receive affective input by listening to others about their shopping experiences at this store. Affective input might cause the consumer to make a judgment about people who shop at the store, and whether those people represent a group with which the consumer wants to be associated. Finally, the consumer might decide to buy his or her new laptop at that store—the behavioral component. All three components maintain a relatively stable and balanced relationship to one another. Together, they form an overall attitude about an object or idea.

CHANGING CONSUMER ATTITUDES

A favorable consumer attitude is vital to the success of a marketing effort. Marketers can approach this in one of two ways:

1. by attempting to produce consumer attitudes that will lead to the purchase of an existing product.

2. by evaluating existing consumer attitudes and creating or modifying products to appeal to these attitudes.

It's always easier to create and maintain a positive attitude toward a product than it is to change an unfavorable one to favorable. But if consumers view a product unfavorably, all is not lost. The seller might redesign the product, offer new or desired options, or enhance service. Sometimes an attitude isn't unfavorable, but consumers just don't feel a need for the product—they aren't motivated to make the purchase. So marketers must find a way to change shoppers' attitude to include the desire to buy. For example, although most consumers don't necessarily have a negative attitude toward sweet potatoes, they might not have a strong enough positive attitude to cause them to add sweet potatoes to their grocery list. In order to boost sales, marketers recently began to provide more information about sweet potatoes, including their high content of vitamins, antioxidants, and dietary fiber. This information addressed the cognitive component of consumers' attitude toward sweet potatoes, pushing it enough toward the positive that shoppers began to buy them more often.[37]

MODIFYING THE COMPONENTS OF ATTITUDE

Attitudes frequently change in response to inconsistencies among the three components. The most common inconsistencies result when new information changes the cognitive or affective components of an attitude. Marketers can modify attitudes by providing evidence of product benefits and by correcting misconceptions. Marketers may also change attitudes by engaging buyers in new behavior. Free samples might change attitudes by getting consumers to try a product.

Sometimes new technologies can encourage consumers to change their attitudes. Consumers who sign up to receive Internet coupons for goods and services might be more likely to try these products without knowing a lot about them. Personalized shopping alerts from firms such as Amazon.com might encourage consumers to purchase a new book or CD by making shoppers feel as though the retailer cares about their individual reading or listening preferences.

Learning

learning Knowledge or skill acquired as a result of experience, which changes consumer behavior.

Marketing is concerned as seriously with the process by which consumer decisions change over time as with the current status of those decisions. **Learning**, in a marketing context, refers to immediate or expected changes in consumer behavior as a result of experience. The learning process includes the component of drive, which is any strong stimulus that impels action. Fear, pride, greed, jealousy, hunger, thirst, comfort, and rivalry are examples of drives. Learning also relies on a cue—any object or signal in the environment that determines the nature of the consumer's response to a drive. Cues include a flashing neon sign in the window of a bakery (a cue for a hungry person) and a commercial for a get-rich-quick sales seminar (a cue for someone who wants more money). A response is the individual's reaction to a set of cues and drives. The hungry person might duck into the bakery to buy a pastry, while the person who wants more money might sign up for the seminar.

Reinforcement is the reduction in drive that results from a proper response. As a response becomes more rewarding, it creates a stronger bond between the drive and the purchase of the product, likely increasing future purchases by the consumer. Reinforcement is the rationale that underlies frequent-buyer programs that reward repeat purchasers for their loyalty. These programs may offer points for premiums or discounts, frequent-flyer miles, and the like. However, so many companies now offer these programs that marketers must find ways to differentiate

Learning relies on a cue, such as a neon sign in the window of a bakery, which acts as a cue for a hungry person.

© NEWSCOM

them. And firms that don't offer the programs quickly learn that consumers will bypass their products and move on to those of competitors.

Customization is the latest trend toward attracting reward card users. Chase Sapphire card users can choose points or cash rewards, which never expire. In addition, they have access to live customer service representatives around the clock, personal concierge services, and premier travel services that include booking any flights with points they choose, without being subject to blackout dates.[38]

APPLYING LEARNING THEORY TO MARKETING DECISIONS

Learning theory has some important implications for marketing strategists, particularly those involved with consumer packaged goods. Marketers must find a way to develop a desired outcome such as repeat purchase behavior gradually over time. **Shaping** is the process of applying a series of rewards and reinforcements to permit more complex behavior to evolve.

Both promotional strategy and the product itself play a role in the shaping process. Marketers want to motivate consumers to become regular buyers of certain merchandise. Their first step in getting consumers to try the product might be to offer a free-sample package that includes a substantial discount coupon for the next purchase. This example uses a cue as a shaping procedure. If the item performs well, the purchase response is reinforced and followed by another inducement—the coupon. The reason a sample works so well is that it allows the consumer to try the product at no risk. Supermarket shoppers have the opportunity to sample products on a regular basis—crackers, cheese, appetizers, salad dressings, cookies, and the like. Generally a display is set up near the aisle where the item is sold, staffed by a person who dispenses the sample along with a coupon for future purchase.

The second step is to entice the consumer to buy the item with little financial risk. The discount coupon enclosed with the free-sample prompts this action. Suppose the package that the consumer purchases has another, smaller discount coupon enclosed. Again, satisfactory product performance and the second coupon provide reinforcement.

The third step is to motivate the person to buy the item again at a moderate cost. A discount coupon accomplishes this objective, but this time the purchased package includes no additional coupon. The only reinforcement comes from satisfactory product performance.

The final test comes when the consumer decides whether to buy the item at its true price without a discount coupon. Satisfaction with product performance provides continuing reinforcement. Repeat purchase behavior literally is shaped by effective application of learning theory within a marketing strategy context.

Self-Concept Theory

Our **self-concept**—our multifaceted view of ourselves—plays an important role in our consumer behavior. Perhaps you see yourself as a creative person, someone who thinks outside the box. You pride yourself on keeping up with the latest trends—in fact, you like to think of yourself as a trendsetter, ahead of the wave. You might express this

shaping The process of applying a series of rewards and reinforcements to permit more complex behavior to evolve.

self-concept Person's multifaceted picture of himself or herself.

Customers might express self-concept by wearing certain clothes, such as those offered by the Ed Hardy brand, who experts agree has established a new trend in "street fashion."

© MATT CROSSICK/PA PHOTOS /LANDOV

self-concept by wearing certain clothes, such as those offered by the Ed Hardy brand. Ed Hardy was created by designer Christian Audigier and tattoo artist Don Ed Hardy. The cooperation of these two creative people brought to market jeans, jackets, sweatshirts, sunglasses, hats, and other items bearing tattoo art. Fashion industry experts acknowledge that the Ed Hardy line established a new trend in "street fashion."[39]

The concept of self emerges from an interaction of many of the influences—both personal and interpersonal—that affect buying behavior. A person's needs, motives, perceptions, attitudes, and learning lie at the core of his or her conception of self. In addition, family, social, and cultural influences affect self-concept.

A person's self-concept has four components: real self, self-image, looking-glass self, and ideal self. The real self is an objective view of the total person. The self-image, the way an individual views himself or herself, may distort the objective view. The looking-glass self, the way an individual thinks others see him or her, may also differ substantially from self-image because people often choose to project different images to others than their perceptions of their real selves. The ideal self serves as a personal set of objectives, because it is the image to which the individual aspires.

When making purchasing decisions, consumers likely will choose products that move them closer to their ideal self-images. For example, suppose your ideal self-image is one of a trendsetter, but you generally have a hard time wearing anything other than conventional clothes. You might buy one Ed Hardy purse or jacket in an effort to break out of the box and bring you closer to your ideal self-image. Social network media such as Facebook appeal to people's ideal self-image—users are often likely to post pictures and entries that paint themselves in a flattering light. But Facebook itself has come under fire recently for changes in the way it saves and stores its members' information, as described in the "Solving an Ethical Controversy" feature.

assessment check

1. Identify the personal determinants of consumer behavior.
2. What are the human needs categorized by Abraham Maslow?
3. How do perception and learning differ?

The Consumer Decision Process

4 **Distinguish between high-involvement and low-involvement purchase decisions.**

Although we might not be aware of it, as consumers we complete a step-by-step process in making purchasing decisions. The time and effort devoted to a particular purchasing decision depend on how important it is.

Purchases with high levels of potential social or economic consequences are said to be **high-involvement purchase decisions**. Buying a car or deciding where to go to college are examples of high-involvement decisions. Routine purchases that pose little risk are **low-involvement purchase decisions**. Buying a loaf of bread or a pint of ice cream at the corner grocery store is a good example.

Consumers generally invest more time and effort in buying decisions for high-involvement products than in those for low-involvement products. A home buyer will visit a number of listings, compare asking prices, apply for a mortgage, have the selected house inspected, and even ask close friends or family members to visit the home before signing the final papers. Few buyers invest that much effort in choosing a brand of orange juice at the supermarket. Believe it or not, though, they will still go through the steps of the consumer decision process—but on a more compressed scale.

Figure 5.2 shows the six steps in the consumer decision process. First, the consumer recognizes a problem or unmet need, searches for appropriate goods or services, and evaluates the alternatives before making a purchase decision. The next step is the actual purchase. After buying the item, the

high-involvement purchase decisions Purchases with high levels of potential social or economic consequences.

low-involvement purchase decisions Routine purchases that pose little risk to the consumer.

Facebook: Forced to Look in the Mirror

Facebook now boasts more than 350 million users worldwide. That's approximately the entire population of the United States and Canada. The social networking site, first popular among college students, is now the virtual meeting place of high school students, adults, and even businesspeople. And although Facebook was once touted as a much more secure site for users than its predecessor, MySpace, recently the site has come under fire for instituting new privacy settings that aren't so private at all. Whereas the new settings have been marketed as designed to make it easier and simpler for users to control the flow of information about themselves, critics charge that the changes may not be as secure as users think they are.

Should social networking sites like Facebook do a better job of explaining changes in privacy settings, give users more options, and disclose the true intention of the changes?

PRO

1. Under the Facebook changes, users no longer have the option of hiding their profile picture, which has angered users as well as digital rights consumer groups. This gives third parties—including businesses and individuals—open access to users' identity, including age and race. "These new privacy changes are clearly intended to push Facebook users to publicly share even more information than before. Even worse, the changes will actually reduce the amount of control that users have over some of their personal data," warns the Electronic Frontier Foundation.

2. "Facebook is nudging the settings toward the 'disclose everything' position. That's not fair from the privacy perspective," says Marc Rotenberg of the Electronic Privacy Information Center. Ironically, this is exactly the opposite of Facebook's original stance.

CON

1. Facebook has done nothing unusual. "When you look at what's really visible, it's not a whole lot. Assuming one isn't a digital hermit, most of this information can be easily found in a Google search anyway," notes Dary Tay, a business analyst for marketing firm Blue Singapore.

2. Facebook argues that its new settings, along with its process of instituting them, are "consistent with user expectations, and within the law."

Summary

The Privacy Commissioner of Canada is now investigating complaints from Facebook users about the new privacy settings. In the U.S., the Electronic Privacy Information Center along with several other organizations have filed a joint complaint with the Federal Trade Commission. Meanwhile, perhaps the best advice to Facebook users would be to make sure they fully understand the changes, monitor their settings, and be careful about what kinds of information they post.

Sources: "Canada Privacy Office Launches New Facebook Probe," SFgate.com, January 27, 2010, http://www.sfgate.com; Ian Paul, "Facebook's Privacy Settings: 5 Things You Should Know," *ABC News*, December 12, 2009, http://abcnews.go.com; Joyce Hooi, "Where Everybody Knows Your Name," *The Business Times Singapore*, December 12, 2009, http://0-www.lexisnexis.com.library.uark.edu; Edward C. Baig, "Users: Facebook's Getting Grabby With Our Data," *USA Today*, February 18, 2009, http://www.usatoday.com.

consumer evaluates whether he or she made the right choice. Much of marketing involves steering consumers through the decision process in the direction of a specific product.

Consumers apply the decision process in solving problems and taking advantage of opportunities. Such decisions permit them to correct differences between their actual and desired states. Feedback from each decision serves as additional experience in helping guide subsequent decisions.

5 Outline the steps in the consumer decision process.

Problem or Opportunity Recognition

During the first stage in the decision process, the consumer becomes aware of a gap between the existing situation and a desired situation. You have experienced this yourself. Perhaps you open the refrigerator door and find a slice of cheese and a cup of yogurt. You are really hungry for a sandwich. By identifying the problem—not enough food in the refrigerator—you can resolve it with a trip to the grocery store. Sometimes the problem is more specific. You might have a full refrigerator, but no mustard or mayonnaise for sandwiches. This problem requires a solution as well.

Suppose you are unhappy with a particular purchase, say, a brand of cereal. The cereal might be too sweet or too crunchy. Or maybe you just want a change from the same old cereal every morning. This is the recognition of another type of problem or opportunity—the desire for change.

What if you just got a raise at work? You might decide to splurge on dinner at a restaurant. Or you might want to try a gourmet, prepared take-home dinner from the supermarket. Both dinners are more expensive than the groceries you have always bought, but now they are within financial reach. The marketer's main task during this phase of the decision-making process is to help prospective buyers identify and recognize potential problems or needs. This task may take the form of advertising, promotions, or personal sales assistance. A supermarket employee might suggest appetizers or desserts to accompany a gourmet take-home dinner.

Search

During the second step in the decision process, a consumer gathers information about the attainment of a desired state. This search identifies different ways to solve the problem. A high-involvement purchase might mean conducting an extensive search for information, whereas a low-involvement purchase might require much less research.

The search may cover internal or external sources of information. An internal search is simply a mental review: Is there past experience with the product? Was it good or bad? An external

figure 5.2

Integrated Model of the Consumer Decision Process

Source: Roger Blackwell, Paul W. Miniard, and James F. Engel, *Consumer Behavior*, 10th ed. (Mason, OH: South-Western, 2006).

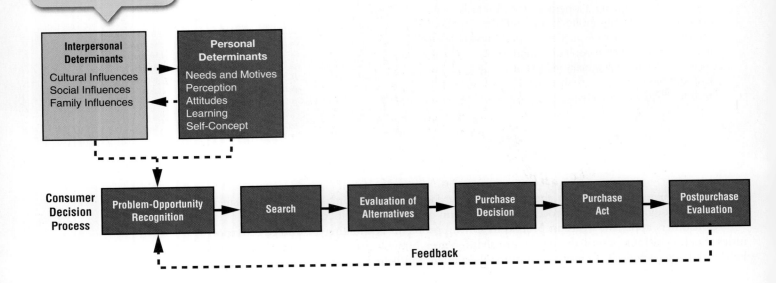

search involves gathering information from all kinds of outside sources—for instance, family, friends, coworkers or classmates, advertisements or salespeople, online reviews, and consumer magazines. Because conducting an external search requires time and effort, it usually is done for high-involvement purchases.

The search identifies alternative brands or models for consideration and possible purchase. The collection of alternatives a consumer actually considers in making a purchase decision is known in marketing as the **evoked set**. In some cases, consumers already know which brands merit further consideration; in others, consumers make external searches to develop such information. The number of brands that are included in the evoked set may vary, depending on the situation and the person. An immediate need, such as filling a nearly empty gas tank, might limit the evoked set. But a driver with half a tank of gas, with more time to make a decision, might expand the evoked set to choose from a broader range of options that include lower prices or certain brands.

Consumers now choose among more alternative products than ever before. This variety can confuse and complicate the analysis that narrows the range of choices. Instead of comparing one or two brands, a consumer often faces a wide array of brands and sub-brands. Products that once included only regular and decaffeinated coffee now are available in many different forms—flavored coffee, latte, mocha, cappuccino, espresso, and iced coffee, to name a few. Researchers have conducted studies showing that too many choices—and resulting decisions—can cause anxiety and stress.[40]

Recognizing this, and wanting to help consumers find their way through the maze of choices, some firms have set up online sites where shoppers can compare products. The Biz Rate Web site allows shoppers to compare everything from air conditioners to GPS devices to barbecue grills and sunglasses. They can compare features, prices, and reviews of all the products listed.[41]

evoked set Number of alternatives a consumer actually considers in making a purchase decision.

Evaluation of Alternatives

The third step in the consumer decision process is to evaluate the evoked set of options. Actually, it is difficult to completely separate the second and third steps because some evaluation takes place as the search progresses; consumers accept, distort, or reject information as they receive it. For example, knowing that you are looking for a new pair of boots, your roommate might tell you about this great online site for shoes she visited recently. But you don't particularly like her taste in shoes or boots, so you reject the information, even though the site might have a pair of boots that you would have bought.

The outcome of the evaluation stage is the choice of a brand or product within the evoked set, or possibly a decision to keep looking for alternatives. To complete this analysis, the consumer must develop a set of evaluative criteria to guide the selection. **Evaluative criteria** are the features a consumer considers in choosing among alternatives. These criteria can either be objective facts (a washing machine's energy rating) or subjective impressions (a favorable view of Free People clothing). Common criteria include price, brand name, and country of origin. Evaluative criteria can vary with the consumer's age, income level, social class, and culture; what's important to a senior citizen might not matter at all to a college student. When it comes to dining out, an affluent senior might look for a restaurant with an upscale atmosphere and high-quality food; a budget-conscious college student might choose a place that's inexpensive and fast to accommodate study hours or class.

Marketers attempt to influence the outcome of this stage in three ways. First, they try to educate consumers about attributes they view as important in evaluating a particular class of goods. They also identify which evaluative criteria are important to an individual and attempt to show why a specific brand fulfills those criteria. Finally, they try to induce a customer to expand the evoked set to include the marketed product.

evaluative criteria Features a consumer considers in choosing among alternatives.

Purchase Decision and Purchase Act

The search and alternative evaluation stages of the decision process result in the purchase decision and the actual purchase. At this stage, the consumer has evaluated each alternative in the evoked set based on his or her personal set of evaluative criteria and narrowed the alternatives down to one.

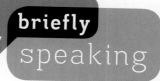

briefly speaking

"Indecision may or may not be my problem."

—Jimmy Buffett
*(b. 1946)
American singer and songwriter*

The consumer then decides where—or from whom—to make the purchase. Sometimes this decision is part of the evaluation; perhaps one seller is offering a better price or better warranty than another. The purchase may be made online or in person at a retail store. The delivery options might also influence the decision of where to purchase an item. For example, a local electronics store might deliver your HDTV for free, whereas an online retailer might charge $50 for delivery.

Postpurchase Evaluation

The purchase act produces one of two results. The buyer feels either satisfaction at the removal of the discrepancy between the existing and desired states or dissatisfaction with the purchase. Consumers are generally satisfied if purchases meet—or exceed—their expectations.

cognitive dissonance
Imbalance among knowledge, beliefs, and attitudes that occurs after an action or decision, such as a purchase.

Sometimes, however, consumers experience postpurchase anxiety called **cognitive dissonance**. This anxiety results from an imbalance among a person's knowledge, beliefs, and attitudes. You might experience some dissonance about your purchase of a TV if you can't figure out how to use it, if it doesn't have the features you thought it had, or if you see an ad the next week for the same model at a discount.

Dissonance is likely to increase (1) as the dollar value of a purchase increases, (2) when the rejected alternatives have desirable features that the chosen alternatives do not provide, and (3) when the purchase decision has a major effect on the buyer. In other words, dissonance is more likely with high-involvement purchases than with those that require low involvement. If you buy a diet soda and don't like the flavor, you can toss it and buy a different one. But if you have spent more than $1,000 on a TV and you aren't satisfied with it, you will most likely experience dissonance. You might try to reduce the dissonance by focusing on good reviews about your choice. Or you might show a friend all the neat features on your TV—without pointing out anything you find dissatisfactory.

Marketers can help buyers reduce cognitive dissonance by providing information that supports the chosen item. Automobile dealers recognize the possibility of "buyer's remorse" and often follow up purchases with letters or telephone calls from dealership personnel offering personal attention to any customer questions or potential problems. Advertisements that stress customer satisfaction also help reduce cognitive dissonance.

A final method of dealing with cognitive dissonance is to change products. The consumer may ultimately decide that one of the rejected alternatives would have been the best choice, and vow to purchase that item in the future. Marketers may capitalize on this with advertising campaigns that focus on the benefits of their products or with tag lines that say something like, "If you're unhappy with them, try us." But making a different choice isn't always an option, particularly if the item requires a large investment in time and money. If you decide you aren't happy with your TV, you could try to selling it, perhaps on a Web site like eBay or Craigslist, before purchasing another one.

 assessment check

1. List the steps in the consumer decision process.
2. What is meant by the term *evoked set*?
3. What are evaluative criteria?

Classifying Consumer Problem-Solving Processes

 6 Differentiate among routinized response behavior, limited problem solving, and extended problem solving by consumers.

As mentioned earlier, the consumer decision processes for different products requires varying amounts of problem-solving efforts. Marketers recognize three categories of problem-solving behavior: routinized response, limited problem solving, and extended problem solving. The classification of a particular purchase within this framework clearly influences the consumer decision process.

ROUTINIZED RESPONSE BEHAVIOR

Consumers make many purchases routinely by choosing a preferred brand or one of a limited group of acceptable brands. This type of rapid consumer problem solving is referred to as routinized response behavior. A routine purchase of the same brand of dog food or the renewal of a magazine subscription are examples. The consumer has already set evaluative criteria and identified available options. External search is limited in such cases, which characterize extremely low-involvement products.

LIMITED PROBLEM SOLVING

Consider the situation in which the consumer previously set evaluative criteria for a particular kind of purchase but then encounters a new, unknown brand. The introduction of a new shampoo is an example of a limited problem-solving situation. The consumer knows the evaluative criteria for the product but has not applied these criteria to assess the new brand. Such situations demand moderate amounts of time and effort for external searches. Limited problem solving is affected by the number of evaluative criteria and brands, the extent of external search, and the process for determining preferences. Consumers making purchase decisions in this product category will likely feel involvement in the middle of the range.

EXTENDED PROBLEM SOLVING

Extended problem solving results when brands are difficult to categorize or evaluate. The first step is to compare one item with similar ones. The consumer needs to understand the product features before evaluating alternatives. Most extended problem-solving efforts involve lengthy external searches. High-involvement purchase decisions—cars, homes, and colleges—usually require extended problem solving.

 assessment check

1. What is routinized response behavior?
2. What does limited problem solving require?
3. Give an example of an extended problem-solving situation.

strategic implications
of marketing in the 21st century

arketers who plan to succeed with today's consumers need to understand how their potential market behaves. Cultural influences play a big role in marketers' relationships with consumers, particularly as firms conduct business on a global scale but also as they try to reach diverse populations in the United States. In addition, family characteristics are changing—more women are in the workforce, more senior citizens are living alone—which forecasts a change in the way families make purchasing decisions. One of the biggest shifts in family spending involves the amount of power that children and teens wield in the marketplace. These young consumers are more and more involved, in some cases know more about certain products—such as electronics—than their parents do, and very often influence purchase decisions. This holds true even with high-involvement purchases such as autos and computers.

Marketers constantly work toward changing or modifying components of consumers' attitudes about their products to gain a favorable attitude and purchase decision. Finally, they refine their understanding of the consumer decision process and use their knowledge to design effective marketing strategies.

Review of Chapter Objectives

Define consumer behavior, and describe the role it plays in marketing decisions.

Consumer behavior refers to the buyer behavior of individual consumers. Consumer behavior plays a huge role in marketing decisions, including what goods and services to offer, to whom, and where. If marketers can understand the factors that influence consumers, they can develop and offer the right products to those consumers.

Describe the interpersonal determinants of consumer behavior: cultural, social, and family influences.

Cultural influences, such as the general work ethic or the desire to accumulate wealth, come from society. Core values may vary from culture to culture. Group or social influences include social class, opinion leaders, and reference groups with which consumers may want to be affiliated. Family influences may come from spouses, parents, grandparents, or children.

Explain each of the personal determinants of consumer behavior: needs and motives, perceptions, attitudes, learning, and self-concept theory.

A need is an imbalance between a consumer's actual and desired states. A motive is the inner state that directs a person toward the goal of satisfying a need. Perception is the meaning that a person attributes to incoming stimuli gathered through the five senses. Attitudes are a person's enduring favorable or unfavorable evaluations, emotions, or action tendencies toward something. In self-concept theory, a person's view of himself or herself plays a role in purchasing behavior. In purchasing goods and services, people will likely choose products that move them closer to their ideal self-images.

Distinguish between high-involvement and low-involvement purchase decisions.

Purchases with high levels of potential social or economic consequences are called high-involvement purchase decisions. Examples include buying a new car or home. Routine purchases that pose little risk to the consumer are called low-involvement purchase decisions. Choosing a candy bar or a newspaper are examples.

Outline the steps in the consumer decision process.

The consumer decision process consists of six steps: problem or opportunity recognition, search, alternative evaluation, purchase decision, purchase act, and postpurchase evaluation. The time involved in each stage of the decision process is determined by the nature of the individual purchases.

Differentiate among routinized response behavior, limited problem solving, and extended problem solving by consumers.

Routinized response behavior refers to repeat purchases made of the same brand or limited group of items. Limited problem solving occurs when a consumer previously set criteria for a purchase but then encounters a new brand or model. Extended problem solving results when brands are difficult to categorize or evaluate. High-involvement purchase decisions usually require extended problem solving.

✓ Assessment Check: Answers

1.1 Why is the study of consumer behavior important to marketers? If marketers can understand the behavior of consumers, they can offer the right products to consumers who want them.

1.2 Describe Kurt Lewin's proposition. Kurt Lewin proposed that behavior (B) is the function (f) of the interactions of personal influences (P) and pressures exerted by outside environmental forces (E). This research sheds light on how consumers make purchase decisions.

2.1 List the interpersonal determinants of consumer behavior. The interpersonal determinants of consumer behavior are cultural, social, and family influences.

2.2 What is a subculture? A subculture is a group within a culture that has its own distinct mode of behavior.

2.3 Describe the Asch phenomenon. The Asch phenomenon is the impact of groups and group norms on individual behavior.

3.1 Identify the personal determinants of consumer behavior. The personal determinants of consumer behavior are needs and motives, perceptions, attitudes, learning, and self-concept theory.

3.2 What are the human needs categorized by Abraham Maslow? The human needs categorized by Abraham Maslow are physiological, safety, social/belongingness, esteem, and self-actualization.

3.3 How do perception and learning differ? Perception is the meaning that a person attributes to incoming stimuli. Learning refers to immediate or expected changes in behavior as a result of experience.

4.1 Differentiate between high-involvement decisions and low-involvement decisions. High-involvement decisions have high levels of potential social or economic consequences, such as selecting an Internet service provider. Low-involvement decisions pose little financial, social, or emotional risk to the buyer, such as a magazine or gallon of milk.

4.2 Categorize each of the following as a high- or low-involvement product: toothpaste, notebook computer, apartment, cup of coffee, cell phone service. High-involvement products are the notebook, apartment, and cell phone service. Low-involvement products are the toothpaste and cup of coffee.

5.1 List the steps in the consumer decision process. The steps in the consumer decision process are problem or opportunity recognition, search, alternative evaluation, purchase decision, purchase act, and postpurchase evaluation.

5.2 What is meant by the term *evoked set*? The evoked set is the number of alternatives a consumer actually considers in making a purchase decision.

5.3 What are evaluative criteria? Evaluative criteria are the features a consumer considers in choosing among alternatives.

6.1 What is routinized response behavior? Routinized response behavior is the repeated purchase of the same brand or limited group of products.

6.2 What does limited problem solving require? Limited problem solving requires a moderate amount of a consumer's time and effort.

6.3 Give an example of an extended problem-solving situation. An extended problem-solving situation might involve the purchase of a car or a college education.

Marketing Terms You Need to Know

consumer behavior 138	*motive 148*	*shaping 155*	*evoked set 159*
culture 139	*perception 150*	*self-concept 155*	*evaluative criteria 159*
subcultures 141	*perceptual screens 151*	*high-involvement purchase*	*cognitive dissonance 160*
reference groups 145	*subliminal perception 152*	*decisions 156*	
opinion leaders 146	*attitudes 152*	*low-involvement purchase*	
need 148	*learning 154*	*decisions 156*	

Assurance of Learning Review

1. What are core values? Describe what you think are three core values of American society. Do you consider these your core values as well?

2. Why is the concept of acculturation important to marketers who want to target such groups as Hispanic, Asian, or African American consumers?

3. Describe a purchase that a consumer might make that would reflect his or her status within a particular group. If that person's status increased, how might the purchase selection change?

4. What are the four role categories that describe each spouse in a household? Which role has changed the most in recent years, and why?

5. According to Maslow, what is the difference between needs and motives? How can marketers make use of these two concepts to lead consumers toward purchases?

6. What are the two factors that interact to create a person's perception of an object? How is this important for marketers?

7. What are the three reasons that subliminal perception is unlikely to result in a purchase? Despite these findings, what role is neuroscience now playing in the creation of marketing messages?

8. What are the components of attitude? Explain the two ways in which marketers can try to change consumer attitudes toward their products.

9. What is learning as it relates to marketing? Explain the four steps in the learning process and give examples as they relate to marketing.

10. For each of the following products, what steps might marketers take to transform them from a limited problem-solving situation for a consumer to a routinized response situation?

a. gym membership
b. magazine or newspaper subscription
c. appointment at a hair salon
d. office supplies
e. oil change for a car

Projects and Teamwork Exercises

1. Choose a person whom you believe to be a true opinion leader. It might be a media celebrity, a political leader, a sports figure, or someone in another category entirely. Research ways in which the person has possibly shaped consumer attitudes toward various goods and services. Present your findings in class.

2. Consider your own participation in family purchases. How much influence did you have on your family's decisions as a child? As a teenager? Over what types of products did you have an influence—or not? Compare your answers with those of classmates.

3. One major trend in consumer spending that is likely to last for the next several years is a focus on value. "The Dollar Stores of the world are winning," notes Envirosell's Paco Underhill.[42] While consumers search for bargains, manufacturers and retailers of luxury goods are struggling to change consumer attitudes toward their products. On your own or with a classmate, choose one of the following luxury brands (or select one of your own) and create an advertisement for the product that seeks to change consumer attitudes about your product would make a good purchase.

a. Mercedes-Benz automobiles
b. Louis Vuitton leather goods
c. Tiffany jewelry
d. Four Seasons Hotels and Resorts
e. flightOptions jet ownership

4. Consider a purchase decision involving one of the following types of products. Develop an evoked set of three alternatives for your purchase decision. Then create a list of evaluative criteria that you would use to choose among the alternatives. Research your alternatives in more detail—online, at a store, at a friend's apartment, and the like. Finally, make your purchase decision. Describe to the class how you made your decision—and why.

5. Choose a partner and select a low-involvement, routinized consumer product such as toothpaste, a jar of spaghetti sauce, laundry detergent, or kitchen trash bags. Create an ad you think could stimulate consumers to change their preferred brand to yours.

Critical-Thinking Exercises

1. Describe a group to which you belong—it might be a team, a club, or your dorm suite. Outline the norms of the group, the major roles that different members play, and your own status within the group. Have you ever sought to change your status? Why or why not?

2. What are the two conditions that must exist for a consumer to be influenced by a reference group? Have you ever made a purchase based on reference group influence? If so, what was the purchase and how did you come to the decision to make it? If not, why not?

3. Marketers point out that the five levels in Maslow's hierarchy of needs are sometimes combined or even bypassed by consumers making purchase decisions. Explain how each of the following could fulfill more than one need:

a. A download of "We Are the World"
b. A retirement investment account
c. Philosophy body wash
d. Dinner at a restaurant

4. What are some of the ways marketers can break through consumers' perceptual screens? If you were a marketer for a line of pet food for cats and dogs, what method might you use?

5. Suppose you are employed by a large electronics retailer, and a customer comes to you with cognitive dissonance over the purchase of an expensive computer system from your store the previous week. How would you work with the customer to help dispel that dissonance?

Ethics Exercise

Marketers of online news content are struggling to change consumer attitudes about whether or not it is fair to charge for this content. While consumers are already willing to pay for movies, music, and games, they don't want to pay for news—whether it is from online versions of newspapers and magazines or online feeds of radio and talk shows. "Much of their content has basically become a commodity, readily available elsewhere for free," notes a Nielsen study. Yet these news formats are created by paid professionals, and can be expensive to produce.[43]

1. Express your own view. Is it ethical for marketers of online news content to begin charging consumers for their services? If so, under what circumstances? If not, why or why not?

2. Go online to research different news sources—those that are free (such as the headlines offered on Yahoo!) and those for which there is a charge (such as online magazine or newspaper subscriptions). Is there a difference in features or the extent of services offered?

3. Based on your research and your knowledge of consumer behavior, what steps do you think news marketers might take to change consumer attitudes about whether news should be offered for free?

Internet Exercises

1. **Marketing to children**. Advertising and other marketing efforts directed toward children have long been controversial. Visit the Web site of Children's Advertising Review Unit (CARU)—an organization created by the advertising industry to address issues associated with marketing to children. What is the purpose of CARU? What are the major issues regarding marketing to children? What have been some of its recent actions? Why have some prominent marketers, such as The Coca-Cola Company, decided to end advertising aimed at children? In your opinion, can industry self-regulation ever be an effective substitute for government regulation? http://www.caru.org

2. **Consumer decision making**. Assume you're in the market for both a new cell phone and cell phone provider. Follow the beginning stages in the consumer decision model described in the chapter—recognition of problem or opportunity, search, and evaluation of alternatives. Use the Internet to aid in your consumer decision process. Prepare a report summarizing your experience. Compare and contrast your experience with an actual consumer purchase decision you recently made.

3. **Marketing strategies and Maslow's Hierarchy of Needs**. Visit the Web sites listed here. Review the marketing strategies shown in each site. Which level of Maslow's Hierarchy of Needs does each site emphasize? Be prepared to defend your answers.
   http://www.michelin-us.com
   http://www.starbucks.com
   http://shop.nordstrom.com
   http://www.hollandamerica.com
   http://www.unilever.com

Note: Internet Web addresses change frequently. If you don't find the exact site listed, you may need to access the organization's home page and search from there or use a search engine such as Google or Bing.

Case 5.1   *How Color Is Used in Marketing*

Everyone has a favorite color. When someone asks us what it is, we usually answer without hesitation. As consumers, we gravitate toward that color in just about everything—clothing, room décor, automobiles, and the like. (Do you have a friend who *always* wears black? Or a roommate who insists on decorating entirely in purple?) We're also drawn to our favorite color when we see it in packaging. Marketers know this. They do a great deal of research to determine greater complexities in the perception of color, as well as cultural determinants of color preferences. To break through consumers' perceptual screens so they are attracted to the products being offered, marketers need to understand how color is perceived in order to use it effectively.

Scientists know that color literally affects the body and mind. Colors stimulate the nervous system and create emotional states. For example, red increases the heart and breathing rate. It also represents danger or caution. Advertisements that display words or product details—such as tooth decay prevention—against a red background may cause consumers to respond with a purchase in order to avoid getting cavities. McDonald's use of red in its color scheme subliminally encourages consumers to order and eat their food quickly—the whole idea of fast food.

On the other hand, blue has a calming influence on the nervous system and evokes peace, freedom, optimism, trustworthiness, and creativity. If marketers want to emphasize the teeth-whitening properties of the toothpaste described earlier, using advertisements or packaging with a blue background would likely be most effective. The color blue also suggests intelligence. IBM has always been known as "Big Blue." For a firm that develops and promotes high-tech products, the link to trustworthiness, creativity, and intelligence helps create a positive attitude among consumers. Green is another positive marketing color, commonly representing nature, freshness, health, abundance, and money. General Mills has a green "G" as part of its logo. Freshness, health, nature, and abundance are all qualities that consumers would like to find in the food they buy.

Color has certain meanings in different cultures—in the U.S., white signifies cleanliness and purity; but in China, white is associated with funerals and mourning. So, a U.S. manufacturer of bedding or tablecloths would not want to try to market its crisp white linens to Chinese consumers. And whereas yellow signifies happiness in the U.S., the color symbolizes sadness in Greece and jealousy in France. This presents a difficulty for global marketers such as McDonald's, whose signature brand colors are red and yellow. Although the golden arches remain their true color at the restaurants themselves, visitors to the McDonald's France Web site will find that pale blue and pale yellow are the predominant colors that appear on the site.

Understanding the psychology of color—the way it can be used to affect perception and shape consumer attitudes toward goods and services—is an important tool for marketers. The next time you find yourself reaching for the green bottle of vitamins or asking to test drive the blue car, at least you'll know why.

Questions for Critical Thinking

1. Choose one of the following companies. What colors does it use predominantly in its logo or packaging? How do these colors affect the perception of its products?
   a. Wendy's
   b. Microsoft
   c. L.L. Bean
   d. Starbucks

2. Should a global firm like McDonald's or General Mills change the colors of its logo or packaging depending on the country in which it is marketing? Why or why not? How might this affect consumer attitudes toward the company and its products?

Sources: "Strategic Use of Color in Marketing Materials," Keysteps Internet Marketing, http://www.keysteps.com, accessed February 23, 2010; Darrell Zahorsky, "What Color Is Your Business?," Small Business Information, *About. com*, http://sbinformation.about.com, accessed February 23, 2010; Elaine Love, "Psychology of Colors Marketing," *Golden Nuggets for Entrepreneurs*, February 4, 2010, http://leloveforlife.blogspot.com; "Internet Marketing and the Psychology of Color," *Money Easy Tips*, January 30, 2010, http://moneyeasytips.com; "Marketing and the Psychology of Color," *ArticleBase.com*, November 20, 2009, http://www.articlesbase.com; Nancy Pekala, "Color Me Creative: New Study Analyzes the Psychology of Color," *Marketing Power.com*, February 27, 2009, http://www.marketingpower.com.

Video Case 5.2
Consumer Behavior at Scholfield Honda

If you want to study consumer behavior, probably the best place to start would be a car dealership. Cars are a big investment. Most people spend upwards of $20,000 on a new car and $6,000 or more on a preowned vehicle. In the United States, where we drive pretty much

everywhere, your car is your first contact with the world. One look at someone's car and you might get an idea of their politics, bank account, occupation, education, musical tastes, and favorite weekend activities. It's the ultimate fashion accessory. Does it have a lot of cup holders and a DVD player in the headrest? Family car. Cute little convertible? Twenty-five-year old with her first real job. That Italian sports car? Retail therapy for the mid-life crisis. That person in the 2010 Honda Fit hybrid who just stole your parking space? Likely some smug, 20-something activist.

But looks can be deceiving.

When the Honda Insight, Honda's first consumer hybrid car, hit the market in 2000, Roger Scholfield, owner of Scholfield Honda in Wichita, Kansas, thought he had it all figured out. For one thing, Wichita isn't exactly known as the epicenter of eco-consumerism. He'd probably sell a handful of the hybrid cars to a couple of single, 20-somethings. The car only had two seats and seemed pretty flimsy with its lightweight aluminum body. And with a sticker price of $20,000, it was pretty pricey.

The first Insight he sold went to a 63-year-old.

The second person to buy one was 65.

As it turns out, Scholfield's experience was consistent with Honda's marketing research. They determined that the typical Insight customer was older, highly educated, probably with an engineering or science background—a person who tended to be very research-driven.

Vinnie Koc, a sales consultant at Scholfield Honda, relies more on his experience than the data to sell cars. "The vehicle pretty much sells itself," says Koc. "Most of my customers are previous owners or someone in their family owns a Honda that wants them to buy a Honda." Koc's customers don't just show up and hop in the first car

they see. Most of them have spent time on the Scholfield and Honda Web sites, researching and comparing models before they come in. They know what they want, are unlikely to be upsold on additional bells and whistles, and are clear on how much they are willing to pay. "Our job is to present the vehicle," says Koc. It usually takes a few test drives to complete the sale, but he is patient. It is all part of Scholfield Honda's low-pressure environment.

"I love my Scholfield Honda" is the tagline on many of the dealership's television and radio ads. "The Scholfield reputation is 100 percent why the customers are here," says Koc. In a market where the anonymous experience of shopping online is the norm for so many consumers, providing opportunities for customers to feel special and paid attention to can really make a difference, especially in car sales, an industry where trust so often is lacking. Owner and general manager Scholfield takes the time to meet with customers, and consultants like Koc take the time to follow up on every meeting—from test drive to final sale. "If they see that you are able to provide the information they need, they feel comfortable with you and that makes them happy." It is not unusual for Koc's customers to drop by on their lunch hour just to say "thanks" and gush about how much they are enjoying their new Honda.

Questions

1. Name the top influence(s) impacting a consumer's decision to buy a car from Scholfield Honda.

2. Go to www.honda.com and view the different Hondas to select the car you would be most likely to purchase. Carefully consider all the determinants discussed in the chapter and their impact on your decision.

Business-to-

Business (B2B) Marketing

1 Explain each of the components of the business-to-business (B2B) market.

2 Describe the major approaches to segmenting business-to-business (B2B) markets.

3 Identify the major characteristics of the business market and its demand.

4 Discuss the decision to make, buy, or lease.

5 Describe the major influences on business buying behavior.

6 Outline the steps in the organizational buying process.

7 Classify organizational buying situations.

8 Explain the buying center concept.

9 Discuss the challenges of and strategies for marketing to government, institutional, and international buyers.

Corporate Customers Try Zappos' Advice on for Size • • • How many corporate CEOs have more Twitter followers than the whole NFL? Anthony Hsieh does. Hsieh (pronounced "shay") is the 30-something leader of the Zappos family of companies, which

operate the quirky and wildly popular online retailer (Zappos.com) that carries more than 3 million items and boasts annual sales of more than $1 billion. (The Zappos family was recently purchased by Amazon.com for more than $800 million but will remain its own brand as a subsidiary of Amazon.)

The Zappos family has grown fast since its 1999 founding, mostly through word of mouth about its passionate devotion to customer service. While more than 95 percent of its retail transactions occur online, Zappos.com boasts free delivery and free returns with a 24-hour customer hotline staffed by well-trained employees. In addition to doing whatever it takes

to make customers satisfied, one ad executive who visited the firm's Nevada headquarters said, "They would stay on the line for as long as you wanted to talk. They would talk about anything." The director of brand marketing agrees, "Our customer loyalty team is not scripted and is not measured on time of calls."

Friendly customer service is so important to the firm, in fact, that its new multi-million-dollar TV and Internet ad campaign celebrates real Zappos family employees, with Muppet-like representations of them shown helping cronically difficult or emotional customers get through simple product exchanges. Customers "may only call once in

their life," says Hsieh, "but that is our chance to wow them."

And that's why Zappos.com has more to offer the world than just shoes. With a unique and successful business model that focuses on making employees happy—the firm is listed on *Fortune*'s list of Best American Companies to Work For—it also serves as an intriguing and informative benchmark for other firms. So, by popular request, Zappos Insights Inc. was created to offer insights into its unconventional corporate culture to organizations ranging from competing Internet retailers to entrepreneurial start-ups, software providers, heating and air conditioning specialists, and even the Girl Scouts.

There are two main ways to learn from the zany company's management savvy. The first is to sign up for Zappos Insights, a special company Web site that provides management tips, video interviews with Zappos family managers, a discussion forum, and articles about the company's core values, employee training, and mind-body-technology balance for a monthly fee of $39.95. The second is to attend a two-day seminar held at headquarters several times a year, at a cost of $4,000 to $5,000 per participant, observing call center workers in action and hearing frank talk about hiring, customer service, and the employee-friendly work environment directly from Tony Hsieh, the company's chief financial officer, and more than 20 other employees.

While the goal is to help build the Zappos brand, "We're not really trying to position ourselves as management gurus," says Hsieh. "Not everything we do is going to make sense for their company. It's really just about sharing what we do and they take away whatever they want to take away."[1]

evolution of a brand

Zappos.com was founded by Nick Swinmurn after an unsuccessful shoe shopping trip. Swinmurn soon brought in Tony Hsieh to apply his extensive Internet start-up experience to the then-fledgling retailer. The Zappos family of companies currently employs about 1,300 people, split between its Nevada headquarters and its Kentucky fulfillment center.

The firm's offbeat attitude is on display several times a week, when guests touring the headquarters building—whose cafeteria offers free food and an open mike—are

evolution of a **brand**

treated to raucous greetings from employees wielding horns and cowbells. The playful yet hard-working spirit of the firm is also evident in its ten core values, including "Create fun and a little weirdness" and "Build a positive team and family spirit" along with "Do more with less" and "Deliver WOW through service."

- "It's a brand about happiness," says Hsieh, "whether to customers or employees or even vendors." Do you agree with Hsieh that keeping employees happy can affect customer and supplier relationships? Why or why not?

- Focus on the team is so strong at the Zappos family headquarters that janitorial services, once outsourced, were recently brought back inside. What could this management decision suggest to corporate customers of the Zappos family's management advice?

chapter overview

business-to-business (B2B) marketing
Organizational sales and purchases of goods and services to support production of other products, to facilitate daily company operations, or for resale.

We are all aware of the consumer marketplace. As consumers, we're involved in purchasing needed items almost every day. In addition, we can't help noticing the barrage of marketing messages aimed at us through a variety of media. But the business-to-business marketplace is, in fact, significantly larger. U.S. companies pay more than $300 billion each year just for office and maintenance supplies. Government agencies contribute to the business-to-business market even further; for example, the Department of Defense budget for one recent year was over $533 billion.[2] U.S. business-to-business commerce conducted over the Internet now totals nearly $3 trillion.[3]

Whether through face-to-face transactions, via telephone, or over the Internet, business marketers each day deal with complex purchasing decisions involving multiple decision makers. They range from simple reorders of previously purchased items to complex buys for which materials are sourced from all over the world. They often involve the steady building of relationships between companies and customers as well as the ability to respond to changing circumstances in existing markets.

Customer satisfaction and customer loyalty are major factors in the development of these long-term relationships.

This chapter discusses buying behavior in the business or organizational market. **Business-to-business (B2B) marketing** deals with organizational sales and purchases of goods and services to support production of other products, to facilitate daily company operations, or for resale. But you ask, "How do I go about distinguishing between consumer purchases and B2B transactions?" Actually, it's pretty simple. Just ask yourself two questions:

1. Who is buying the good or service?
2. Why is the purchase being made?

Consumer buying involves purchases made by individuals. We purchase items for our own use and enjoyment—and not for resale. By contrast, B2B purchases are made by businesses, government, and marketing intermediaries to be resold, combined with other items to create a finished product for resale, or used up in the day-to-day operations of the organization. So answer the two questions—"Who is buying?" and "Why?"—and you have the answer.

Nature of the Business Market

Firms usually sell fewer standardized products to organizational buyers than to ultimate consumers. Although you might purchase a cell phone for your personal use, a company generally has to purchase an entire communications system from a supplier such as AT&T, whose OneNet Service offers digital voice and Internet technology in a single business network.[4] Purchases such as this require greater customization, more decision making, and usually more decision makers. So the buying and selling process becomes more complex, often involving teams and taking an average of 6 to 36 months to make decisions. Because of the complexity of the purchases, customer service is extremely important to B2B buyers. Advertising plays a much smaller role in the business market than in the consumer market, although advertisements placed in business magazines or trade publications are common. Business marketers advertise primarily to announce new products, to enhance their company image and presence, and to attract potential customers who would then deal directly with a salesperson. Personal selling plays a much bigger role in business markets than in consumer markets, distribution channels are shorter, customer relationships tend to last longer, and purchase decisions can involve multiple decision makers. Table 6.1 compares the marketing practices commonly used in both B2B and consumer marketing.

Like final consumers, an organization purchases products to fill needs. However, its primary need—meeting the demands of its own customers—is similar from firm to firm. A manufacturer buys raw materials such as wood pulp, fabric, or grain to create the company's product. A wholesaler or retailer buys the manufactured products—paper, clothing, or cereal—to resell. Mattel buys everything from plastic to paints to produce its toys; FAO Schwartz buys finished toys to sell to the public. And passenger airlines buy and lease aircraft from manufacturers such as Boeing and Airbus. Wilson Sporting Goods supplies the National Football League with its official game ball, "The Duke." Institutional purchasers such as government agencies and nonprofit organizations also buy products to meet the needs of their constituents, whether it is global positioning system (GPS) mapping devices or meals ready to eat (MRE) for troops in the field.

Companies also buy services from other businesses. A firm may purchase legal and accounting services, an office-cleaning service, a call center service, or a recruiting service. Jan-Pro is a commercial cleaning service company in business since 1991. The chain has more than 75 master franchise

table 6.1 Comparing Business-to-Business Marketing and Consumer Marketing

	Business-to-Business Marketing	Consumer Marketing
Product	Relatively technical in nature; exact form often variable; accompanying services very important	Standardized form; service important but less than for business products
Promotion	Emphasis on personal selling	Emphasis on advertising
Distribution	Relatively short, direct channels to market	Product passes through a number of intermediate links en route to consumer
Customer Relations	Relatively enduring and complex	Comparatively infrequent contact; relationship of relatively short duration
Decision-making Process	Diverse group of organization members makes decision	Individual or household unit makes decision
Price	Competitive bidding for unique items; list prices for standard items	List prices

Intel's digital and wireless computer technology is found in business computing systems and personal computers. In the campaign that's featured, they partnered with Dell.

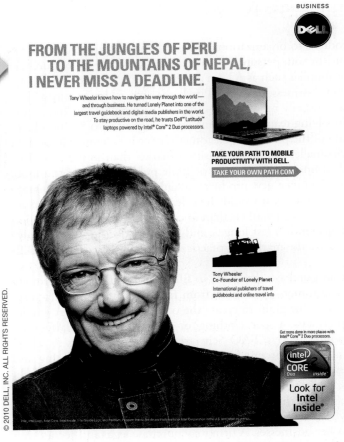

FROM THE JUNGLES OF PERU TO THE MOUNTAINS OF NEPAL, I NEVER MISS A DEADLINE.

Tony Wheeler knows how to navigate his way through the world — and through business. He turned Lonely Planet into one of the largest travel guidebook and digital media publishers in the world. To stay productive on the road, he trusts Dell™ Latitude™ laptops powered by Intel® Core™ 2 Duo processors.

TAKE YOUR PATH TO MOBILE PRODUCTIVITY WITH DELL.
TAKE YOUR OWN PATH.COM

Tony Wheeler
Co-Founder of Lonely Planet
International publishers of travel guidebooks and online travel info

Get more done in more places with Intel® Core™ 2 Duo processors.

Look for Intel Inside®

offices throughout the United States and Canada and more than 10,000 individual franchise operations in the United States alone.[5]

Environmental, organizational, and interpersonal factors are among the many influences in B2B markets. Budget, cost, and profit considerations all play parts in business buying decisions. In addition, the business buying process typically involves complex interactions among many people. An organization's goals must also be considered in the B2B buying process. Later sections of the chapter will explore these topics in greater detail.

Some firms focus entirely on business markets. For instance, DuPont sells materials such as polymers, coatings, and color technologies to manufacturers that use them in a variety of products. Caterpillar makes construction and mining equipment, diesel and natural gas engines, and industrial gas turbines. SAP America provides collaborative business software that allows companies to work with customers and business partners using databases and other applications from every major software vendor. Other firms sell to both consumer and business markets. Herman Miller makes award-winning office furniture as well as stylish furniture for the home, and Intel's digital and wireless computer technology is found in business computing systems and personal computers. Note also that marketing strategies developed in consumer marketing often are appropriate for the business sector, too. Final consumers often are the end users of products sold into the business market and, as explained later in the chapter, can influence the buying decision.

The B2B market is diverse. Transactions can range from orders as small as a box of paper clips or copy machine toner for a home-based business to transactions as large as thousands of parts for an automobile manufacturer or massive turbine generators for an electric power plant. As mentioned earlier, businesses are also big purchasers of services such as telecommunications, computer consulting, and transportation services. Four major categories define the business market: (1) the commercial market, (2) trade industries, (3) government organizations, and (4) institutions.

Components of the Business Market

1 | Explain each of the components of the business-to-business (B2B) market.

commercial market
Individuals and firms that acquire products to support, directly or indirectly, production of other goods and services.

The **commercial market** is the largest segment of the business market. It includes all individuals and firms that acquire products to support, directly or indirectly, production of other goods and services. When Dell buys computer chips from Intel, when Sara Lee purchases wheat to mill into flour for an ingredient in its breads, and when a plant supervisor orders light bulbs and cleaning supplies for a factory in Tennessee, these transactions take place in the commercial market. Some products aid in the production of other items (the computer chips). Others are physically used up in the production of a good or service (the wheat). Still others contribute to the firm's day-to-day operations (the maintenance supplies). The commercial market includes manufacturers, farmers, and other members of resource-producing industries; construction contractors; and providers of such services as transportation, public utilities, financing, insurance, and real-estate brokerage.

The second segment of the organizational market, **trade industries**, includes retailers and wholesalers, known as **resellers**, who operate in this sector. Most resale products such as clothing, appliances, sports equipment, and automobile parts are finished goods that buyers sell to final consumers. Acco supplies paper clips, ring binders, vinyl envelopes, sheet protectors, and fasteners to Office Depot.[6] In other cases, the buyers may complete some processing or repackaging before reselling the products. A retail meat market may purchase a side of beef and then cut individual pieces for its customers. Lumber dealers and carpet retailers may purchase in bulk and then provide quantities and sizes to meet customers' specifications. In addition to resale products, trade industries buy computers, display shelves, and other products needed to operate their businesses. All of these goods—as well as maintenance items and specialized services such as scanner installation, newspaper inserts, and radio advertising—represent organizational purchases.

The government category of the business market includes domestic units of government—federal, state, and local—as well as foreign governments. This important market segment makes a wide variety of purchases, ranging from highways to Internet services. The primary motivation of government purchasing is to provide some form of public benefit such as national defense or pollution control. But government agencies have also become creative when it comes to selling; local police departments and state and federal agencies sell unclaimed shipments, confiscated goods, and unclaimed items found in safe-deposit boxes on eBay. Lucky bidders might be able to buy a custom yacht for their business, a sausage grinder for their restaurant, or an auto transmission for their delivery truck through an Internet auction.[7]

Institutions, both public and private, are the fourth component of the business market. This category includes a wide range of organizations such as hospitals, churches, skilled care and rehabilitation centers, colleges and universities, museums, and not-for-profit agencies. Some institutions—such as in public higher education—must rigidly follow standardized purchasing procedures, but others have less formal buying practices. Business-to-business marketers often benefit by setting up separate divisions to sell to institutional buyers.

The Seam survived the Internet boom and bust and now brings together global buyers of commodities like cotton, peanuts, and grain.

© THE SEAM. LLC

trade industries
Retailers or wholesalers that purchase products for resale to others.

resellers Marketing intermediaries that operate in the trade sector.

B2B Markets: The Internet Connection

While consumers' use of Internet markets receives the bulk of public attention, about 93 percent of all Internet sales are B2B transactions.[8] Many business-to-business marketers have set up private portals that allow their customers to buy needed items. Service and customized pages are accessed through passwords provided by B2B marketers. Online auctions and virtual marketplaces offer other ways for buyers and vendors to connect with each other over the Internet.

During the early Internet boom, start-up companies rushed to connect buyers and sellers without considering basic marketing principles such as targeting their customers and making sure to fulfill their needs. As a result, many of these companies failed. But the companies that survived—and new firms that have learned lessons from others' mistakes—have established a much stronger marketing presence. For instance, they recognize their business customers have a lot at stake and expect greater value and utility from the goods and services they purchase as well as streamlined marketing communications such as e-mail, blogs, and podcasts.[9] Another way for marketers to connect with each other online is through affiliate marketing. See the "Solving an Ethical Controversy" feature for some of the rewards and pitfalls of this strategy for driving Web traffic and sales.

To Stuff Cookies, Or Not to Stuff

solving an ethical controversy

Many people want to make quick money online. One legitimate B2B method of doing so is affiliate marketing. This strategy relies on the use of cookies (a small piece of text stored on a user's computer) to allow a Web site owner, the "affiliate," to earn commissions by helping drive traffic to a marketer's Web site when certain ads are clicked or products sold. Some describe affiliate marketing as an easy way for marketers to "hire" a commissioned sales force. However, unethical affiliates can collect extra commissions by "stuffing" site visitors' computers with cookies for sites and products they aren't promoting. When these cookies result in site visits or sales, the affiliates get commissions they haven't earned.

Should cookie stuffing be illegal?

PRO

1. Web site owners who unethically stuff cookies on the computers of those who visit their site are in effect stealing commissions from the merchants they charge.

2. Cookie stuffing loads Internet users' computers with hidden tags that many consider an invasion of their privacy.

CON

1. It is up to Internet merchants to do business with honest affiliates and monitor their behavior.

2. Cookie stuffing allows affiliate marketers to increase profits without hurting anyone.

Summary

Federal officials recently charged a Las Vegas man with selling cookie-stuffing software to defraud eBay. It's believed some of those who bought the software and participated in the scheme may have received as much as $10,000 a month in referral fees "despite the fact that no eBay advertising or link on the affiliate Web site or Web page had actually been clicked." While not illegal, cookie stuffing and other questionable methods of driving Internet traffic do risk the ire of powerful Internet companies like eBay and Google. Legitimate online networks and marketers may be less willing to work with a marketer who has earned a reputation for using these tools.

Sources: Jeff D. McQueen, "Black and White Affiliate Marketing Methods: What You Need to Know," *ArticleSnatch.com*, www.articlesnatch.com, accessed March 11, 2010; Kundan Pandey, "Free Affiliate Marketing," *Buzzle.com*, www.buzzle.com, February 18, 2010; "Unethical? Or Just Smart Marketing?" *FreeAffiliateMarketingInfo.com*, www.freeaffiliatemarketinginfo.com, February 13, 2010; David Kravets, "Feds Bust Cookie-Stuffing Code Seller," *Wired.com*, www.wired.com, February 9, 2010.

The Internet also opens up foreign markets to sellers. One such firm, which began as a cotton exchange called The Seam, survived the Internet boom and bust and is now bringing together global buyers of commodities like cotton, peanuts, and grain.[10]

Differences in Foreign Business Markets

When The Seam first moved into other countries, its marketers had to consider the fact that foreign business markets may differ due to variations in government regulations and cultural practices. Some business products need modifications to succeed in foreign markets. In Australia, Japan, and Great Britain, for instance, motorists drive on the left side of the road. American-made automobiles must be modified to accommodate such differences.

Business marketers must be willing to adapt to local customs and business practices when operating abroad. They should also research cultural preferences. Factors as deceptively simple as the time of a meeting and methods of address for associates can make a difference. A company even needs to consider what ink colors to use for documents because colors can have different meanings in different countries.

Segmenting B2B Markets

Business-to-business markets include wide varieties of customers, so marketers must identify the different market segments they serve. By applying market segmentation concepts to groups of business customers, a firm's marketers can develop a strategy that best suits a particular segment's needs. The overall process of segmenting business markets divides markets based on different criteria, usually organizational characteristics and product applications. Among the major ways to segment business markets are demographics (size), customer type, end-use application, and purchasing situation.

> **2** Describe the major approaches to segmenting business-to-business (B2B) markets.

Segmentation by Demographic Characteristics

As in consumer markets, demographic characteristics define useful segmentation criteria for business markets. For example, firms can be grouped by size, based on sales revenues or number of employees. Marketers may develop one strategy to reach *Fortune* 500 corporations with complex purchasing procedures and another strategy for small firms in which decisions are made by one or two people. According to one study, many firms are actually increasing their outreach to small and midsize businesses. Microsoft, for instance, targets small-business customers online but also recently partnered with a user-contributed Web site called Kirtsy.com that focuses on female small-business owners.

Together Microsoft and Kirtsy offered free, informal hands-on instruction to groups around the United States and Canada in using social media as marketing tools. Said a senior marketing manager for Microsoft Office Live, "Today, there are lots of options for small business owners looking to leverage the Web to bring down marketing costs and connect with customers. . . . By holding these sessions, we hope to help entrepreneurs gain some valuable insights they can take back and immediately use to grow their businesses."[11]

Segmentation by Customer Type

Another useful segmentation approach groups prospects according to type of customer. Marketers can apply this concept in several ways. They can group customers by broad categories—manufacturer, service provider, government agency, not-for-profit organization, wholesaler, or retailer—and by industry (see the "Marketing Success" feature on page 178 for an example). These groups may be further divided using other segmentation approaches discussed in this section.

Customer-based segmentation is a related approach often used in the business-to-business marketplace. Organizational buyers tend to have much more precise—and complex—requirements for goods and services than ultimate consumers do. As a result, business products often fit narrower market segments than consumer products, which leads some firms to design business goods and services to meet detailed buyer specifications. Pasadena-based Tetra Tech provides a variety of environmental services, including technology development, design, engineering, and pollution remediation for organizations around the world. Because the company's customers include government agencies as well as private firms—and because customers' needs are different—Tetra Tech has 280 offices worldwide that offer a range of programs to suit each type of customer. For instance, the firm provides consulting services for utilities, helps communities clean up polluted water sources, and even conducts programs to clear public and private sites of unexploded military supplies.[12]

customer-based segmentation Dividing a business-to-business market into homogeneous groups based on buyers' product specifications.

NORTH AMERICAN INDUSTRY CLASSIFICATION SYSTEM (NAICS)

In the 1930s, the U.S. government set up a uniform system for subdividing the business marketplace into detailed segments. The Standard Industrial Classification (SIC) system standardized efforts to collect and report information on U.S. industrial activity.

SIC codes divided firms into broad industry categories: agriculture, forestry, and fishing; mining and construction; manufacturing; transportation, communication, electric, gas, and sanitary services; wholesale trade; retail trade; finance, insurance, and real-estate services; public administration; and nonclassifiable establishments. The system assigned each major category within these classifications its own two-digit number. Three-digit and four-digit numbers further subdivided each industry into smaller segments.

North American Industry Classification System (NAICS)
Classification used by NAFTA countries to categorize the business marketplace into detailed market segments.

For roughly 70 years, B2B marketers used SIC codes as a tool for segmenting markets and identifying new customers. The system, however, became outdated with implementation of the North American Free Trade Agreement. Each NAFTA member—the United States, Canada, and Mexico—had its own system for measuring business activity. NAFTA required a joint classification system that would allow marketers to compare business sectors among the member nations. In effect, marketers required a segmentation tool they could use across borders. The **North American Industry Classification System (NAICS)** replaced the SIC and provides more detail than previously available. The NAICS created new service sectors to better reflect the economy of the 21st century. They include information; health care and social assistance; and professional, scientific, and technical services.

Table 6.2 demonstrates the NAICS system for wholesale stationery and office supplies. The NAICS uses six digits, compared with the four digits used in the SIC. The first five digits are fixed among the members of NAFTA. The sixth digit can vary among U.S., Canadian, and Mexican data. In short, the sixth digit accounts for specific data needs of each nation.[13]

Segmentation by End-Use Application

end-use application segmentation
Segmenting a business-to-business market based on how industrial purchasers will use the product.

A third basis for segmentation, **end-use application segmentation**, focuses on the precise way in which a business purchaser will use a product. For example, a printing equipment manufacturer may serve markets ranging from a local utility to a bicycle manufacturer to the U.S. Department of Defense. Each end use of the equipment may dictate unique specifications for performance, design, and price. Praxair, a supplier of industrial gases, for example, might segment its markets according to user. Steel and glass manufacturers might buy hydrogen and oxygen, while food and beverage manufacturers need carbon dioxide. Praxair also sells krypton, a rare gas, to companies that produce lasers, lighting, and thermal windows. Many small and medium-sized companies also segment markets according to end-use application. Instead of competing in markets dominated by large firms, they concentrate on specific end-use market segments. The approximately two dozen companies that manufacture wooden baseball bats for Major League Baseball focus on specific end users who are very different from the youth and high-school players using aluminum bats.

table 6.2 **NAICS Classification for Stationery and Office Supplies Merchant Wholesalers**

42	Merchant wholesalers
424	Merchant wholesalers; nondurable goods
4241	Paper and paper product merchant wholesalers
42412	Stationery and office supplies merchant wholesalers
424120	Stationery and office supplies merchant wholesalers in the U.S. industry

Source: NAICS, U.S. Census Bureau, www.census.gov, accessed February 17, 2010.

Segmentation by Purchase Categories

Firms have different structures for their purchasing functions, and B2B marketers must adapt their strategies according to those organizational buyer characteristics. Some companies designate centralized purchasing departments to serve the entire firm, and others allow each unit to handle its own buying. A supplier may deal with one purchasing agent or several decision makers at various levels. Each of these structures results in different buying behavior.

When the buying situation is important to marketers, they typically consider whether the customer has made previous purchases or this is the customer's first order, offering special rates or programs for valued clients. Verizon Wireless offers government customers cell phone discounts as either credits or reimbursements.[14]

Increasingly, businesses that have developed **customer relationship management (CRM)** systems—strategies and tools that reorient an entire organization to focus on satisfying customers— can segment customers in terms of the stage of the relationship between the business and the customer. A B2B company, for example, might develop different strategies for newly acquired customers than it would for existing customers to which it hopes to sell new products. Similarly, building loyalty among satisfied customers requires a different approach than developing programs to "save" at-risk customer relationships. CRM will be covered in more depth in Chapter 10.

customer relationship management (CRM) Combination of strategies and tools that drives relationship programs, reorienting the entire organization to a concentrated focus on satisfying customers.

assessment check

1. What are the four major ways marketers segment business markets?
2. What is the NAICS?

Characteristics of the B2B Market

3 Identify the major characteristics of the business market and its demand.

Businesses that serve both B2B and consumer markets must understand the needs of their customers. However, several characteristics distinguish the business market from the consumer market:

1. geographic market concentration
2. the sizes and numbers of buyers
3. the purchase decision process
4. buyer–seller relationships.

The next sections consider how these traits influence business-to-business marketing.

Geographic Market Concentration

The U.S. business market is more geographically concentrated than the consumer market. Manufacturers converge in certain regions of the country, making these areas prime targets for business marketers. For example, the Midwestern states that make up the East North Central region— Ohio, Indiana, Michigan, Illinois, and Wisconsin—lead the nation in manufacturing concentration, followed by the South and the Northeast regions.[15]

Certain industries locate in particular areas to be close to customers. Firms may locate sales offices and distribution centers in these areas to provide more attentive service. It makes sense that the Washington, DC, area is favored by companies that sell to the federal government.

In the automobile industry, suppliers of components and assemblies frequently build plants close to their customers. Volkswagen plans a supplier park near its Chattanooga assembly plant. The campus allows suppliers to produce or assemble products close to the plant, reducing costs, controlling parts

briefly speaking

"No matter what your product is, you are ultimately in the education business. Your customers need to be constantly educated about the many advantages of doing business with you, trained to use your products more effectively, and taught how to make never-ending improvement in their lives."

—Robert G. Allen
Author of the One-Minute Millionaire

inventory, and increasing flexibility.[16] As Internet-based technology continues to improve, allowing companies to transact business even with distant suppliers, business markets may become less geographically concentrated. Much of government spending, for example, is now directed through the Internet.

Sizes and Numbers of Buyers

In addition to geographic concentration, the business market features a limited number of buyers. Marketers can draw on a wealth of statistical information to estimate the sizes and characteristics of business markets. The federal government is the largest single source of such statistics. Every five years, it conducts both a Census of Manufacturers and a Census of Retailing and Wholesaling, which provide detailed information on business establishments, output, and employment. Many government units and trade organizations also operate Web sites that contain helpful information.

Many buyers in limited-buyer markets are large organizations. The international market for jet engines is dominated by three manufacturers: United Technology's Pratt & Whitney unit, General Electric, and Rolls-Royce. These firms sell engines to Boeing and the European consortium, Airbus Industries. These aircraft manufacturers compete for business from passenger carriers such as American Airlines, British Airways, Emirates Air Lines, and Singapore Airlines, along with cargo carriers such as Federal Express and UPS.

Trade associations and business publications provide additional information on the business market. Private firms such as Dun & Bradstreet publish detailed reports on individual companies. These data serve as a useful starting point for analyzing a business market. Finding data in such a source requires an understanding of the NAICS, which identifies much of the available statistical information.

Having an enormous number of business customers with varying needs can pose quite a logistical challenge to a firm. See the "Marketing Success" feature for an example of how one supplier to the restaurant industry copes with 400,000 customers around the United States.

The Purchase Decision Process

To market effectively to other organizations, businesses must understand the dynamics of the organizational purchase process. Suppliers who serve business-to-business markets must work with multiple buyers, especially when selling to larger customers. Decision makers at several levels may influence final orders, and the overall process is more formal and professional than the consumer purchasing process. Purchasers typically require a longer time frame because B2B involves more complex deci-

mktg: *success*

Sysco Masters Logistics for Food

Background. A *Fortune* 500 firm, Sysco is a leading food distributing company based in Houston. It ships almost 22 million tons of fresh food and food-related products like cooking oil and cleaning supplies to chain restaurants, school and institutional cafeterias, and stadiums around the country every year. Among its 400,000 customers are McDonald's, Wendy's, the Kroger grocery chain, and hundreds of regional restaurant chains.

The Challenge. Sysco must not only race to take receipt of fresh fruit, meat, and vegetables from suppliers and deliver them in prime condition to customer locations all over the United States, it must also manage a complex set of logistics that include properly handling and delivering nonperishables and stored foods as different as caviar, flour, and frozen onion rings. The company also has to limit costs by avoiding sending out half-full trucks and by reducing the time it takes to load and unload them at each of its sorting centers.

The Strategy. The company relies on custom logistics tools and software to create

sions. Suppliers must evaluate customer needs and develop proposals that meet technical requirements and specifications. Also, buyers need time to analyze competing proposals. Often decisions require more than one round of bidding and negotiation, especially for complicated purchases.

Buyer–Seller Relationships

An especially important characteristic of B2B marketing is the relationship between buyers and sellers. These relationships often are more complex than consumer relationships, and they require superior communication among the organizations' personnel. Satisfying one major customer may mean the difference of millions of dollars to a firm.

Relationship marketing involves developing long-term, value-added customer relationships. A primary goal of business-to-business relationships is to provide advantages that no other vendor can provide—lower price, quicker delivery, better quality and reliability, customized product features, more favorable financing terms, and so on. For the business marketer, providing these advantages means expanding the company's external relationships to include suppliers, distributors, and other organizational partners. CDW, for instance, relies on a variety of vendors to meet its own business, government, and education customers' technology needs with hardware, software, networking, and data storage. It has developed a CDW Supplier Diversity Program to increase and improve relationships with small-business suppliers owned by minorities, women, and veterans and thus must manage its supplier as well as its customer relationships successfully.[17]

Close cooperation, whether through informal contacts or under terms specified in contractual partnerships and strategic alliances, enables companies to meet buyers' needs for quality products and customer service. This holds true both during and after the

© BRAD WHITSITT/SHUTTERSTOCK.COM

briefly speaking

"I would rather have a million friends than a million dollars."

—Edward V. Rickenbacker
(1890–1973)
American aviator

The international market for jet engines, a limited-buyer market, is dominated by three manufacturers—United Technology's Pratt & Whitney unit, General Electric, and Rolls-Royce.

and help execute daily logistical plans, making sure, for instance, that Fuji apples ordered by a restaurant chain aren't delivered to a school district that wants Macintoshes. Its warehouse workers use wireless scanners and portable printers to manage forklift loads based on the weight, location, and destination of each item, and a centralized Sysco group consolidates incoming deliveries from suppliers (sometimes prepacking pallets by customer) so Sysco trucks are fewer and more full when they hit the road.

The Outcome. Sysco leads the industry with 17 percent of a $200 billion market and recently clocked record sales of $1.1 billion. As recession threatened many of its restaurant customers, the firm created a free consulting service to help them stay afloat with improved training and marketing methods.

"We felt if we could improve their business," said Sysco's vice chair, "that would improve our business with them."

Sources: Sham Gad, "Sysco Delivers the Goods," *Investopedia*, http://stocks.investopedia.com, February 3, 2010; Dimitra Defotis, "Food Giant Sysco Keeps on Trucking," *Barrons*, www.smartmoney.com, December 2, 2009; Jia Lynn Yang, "Veggie Tales," *Fortune*, June 8, 2009, pp 25–30; Chrisopher Palmeri, "Sysco's Hands-on Way of Keeping Restaurants Going," *BusinessWeek*, www.businessweek.com, May 7, 2009.

career readiness How to Work a Trade Show

epresenting your company at a trade show is a challenging but rewarding experience. It takes some planning to put your best foot forward when meeting prospective clients. Here are some tips for avoiding common mistakes in the booth:

- Make sure there is always one person in the booth with expertise in your company's offerings and who can answer questions from the most casual to the most interested.

- Prepare a script for everyone in the booth to ensure they all greet visitors quickly and pleasantly, with a competent one-minute introduction to the company and the benefits your goods or services offer.

- Show respect for your company, its mission, and its offerings.

- Remain standing to greet visitors. If you need a seat, get a tall stool so that you can stay at eye level with attendees.

- Keep the booth neat, clean, and well stocked at all times. Always leave the booth to eat or use your cell phone.

- Invite current customers to visit the booth and thank them for their loyalty. These customers are worth five to seven times the value of new ones.

- Don't use the trade show as an opportunity to catch up or gossip with your coworkers or the folks in the next booth. Nothing turns off potential visitors faster than the appearance that *they* are not the reason you're there.

- Remember that every impression you make during a show or convention is important, and first impressions count. Spend time listening to your visitors.

- Ask whether you can help answer any particular questions, and if you can, follow up by ensuring you've satisfied the potential customer and given them any appropriate literature or contact information.

- Always thank your visitors for stopping by.

Sources: Rob Hard, "Trade Show Booth Etiquette Can Attract or Repel Attendees," *About.com*, Event Planning, eventplanning.about.com, accessed January 23, 2010; "Trade Show Staffing Strategies," *Trade-Show-Advisor.com*, www.trade-show-advisor.com, accessed January 23, 2010; "Boothmanship: The Etiquette to Man a Trade Show Booth," Catalyst Exhibits, www.catalystexhibit.com, accessed January 23, 2010; Susan Friedmann, "Good News on the (Trade Show) Marketing Budget: Trends 2010," http://thetradeshowcoach.com, January 7, 2010.

purchase process. Tetra Tech, mentioned earlier, has formal Client Service Quality and Shared Vision programs, designed to engage customers in continuous communication leading to customer satisfaction. For some tips on developing good relationships with potential customers at trade shows, see the "Career Readiness" feature.

Relationships between for-profit and not-for-profit organizations are just as important as those between two commercial organizations. Walmart is a longtime corporate sponsor of Children's Miracle Network, an international organization that helps improve children's health and welfare by raising funds for state-of-the-art care, cutting-edge research, and education. In one recent year Walmart raised and donated a record-breaking $33.5 million to 170 children's hospitals in the network.[18]

Evaluating International Business Markets

Business purchasing patterns differ from one country to the next. Researching these markets poses a particular problem for B2B marketers. Of course, as explained earlier, the NAICS has corrected this problem in the NAFTA countries.

In addition to assessing quantitative data such as the size of the potential market, companies must also carefully weigh its qualitative features. This process includes considering cultural values, work styles, and the best ways to enter overseas markets in general. Nokia is supporting its push into cell phone markets in emerging economies by establishing nine satellite studios in China, India, and Brazil. There its designers can customize products and approaches to each market. The firm also has a chief anthropologist who travels around the world with a team to study how people in different countries use mobile phones. In the last few years, Nokia has sold more than 750 million basic mobile phones in emerging markets.[19]

In today's international marketplace, companies often practice **global sourcing**, purchasing goods and services from suppliers worldwide. This practice can result in substantial cost savings, although product quality must be carefully monitored. India, China, and Malaysia are the world's top destinations for global IT sourcing, while Egypt, Jordan, and Vietnam recently moved up to make the top ten list.[20]

Global sourcing requires companies to adopt a new mindset; some must even reorganize their operations. Among other considerations, businesses sourcing from multiple multinational locations should streamline the purchase process and minimize price differences due to labor costs, tariffs, taxes, and currency fluctuations.

global sourcing
Purchasing goods and services from suppliers worldwide.

 assessment check

1. Why is geographic segmentation important in the B2B market?
2. In what ways is the buyer–seller relationship important in B2B marketing?
3. What is global sourcing?

Business Market Demand

The previous section's discussion of business market characteristics demonstrated considerable differences between marketing techniques for consumer and business products. Demand characteristics also differ in these markets. In business markets, the major categories of demand include derived demand, volatile demand, joint demand, inelastic demand, and inventory adjustments. Figure 6.1 summarizes these different categories of business market demand.

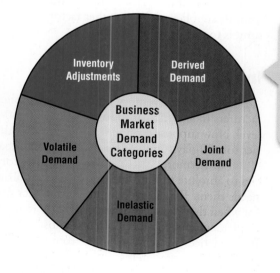

figure 6.1

Categories of Business Market Demand

Derived Demand

Derived demand refers to the linkage between demand for a company's output and its purchases of resources such as machinery, components, supplies, and raw materials. The demand for computer microprocessor chips is *derived* from the demand for personal computers. If more businesses and individuals buy new computers, the demand for chips increases; if fewer computers are sold, the demand for chips decreases. Michigan-based Lear Corporation, for instance, supplied auto seats and other interior parts to companies like Ford and General Motors. In the wake of the car makers' recent plant closings and reduced production plans, demand for Lear products declined.[21]

Organizational buyers purchase two general categories of business products: capital items and expense items. Derived demand ultimately affects both. Capital items are long-lived business assets that must be depreciated over time. *Depreciation* is an accounting term that refers to charging a portion of a capital item's cost as a deduction against the company's annual revenue for purposes of determining its net income. Examples of capital items include major installations such as new manufacturing plants, office buildings, and computer systems.

derived demand
Demand for a resource that results from demand for the goods and services produced by that resource.

Expense items, in contrast, are items consumed within short time periods. Accountants charge the cost of such products against income in the year of purchase. Examples of expense items include the supplies necessary to operate the business, ranging from copy paper to machine lubricants.

Volatile Demand

Derived demand creates volatility in business market demand. Assume the sales volume for a gasoline retailer is increasing at an annual rate of 5 percent. Now suppose the demand for this gasoline brand slows to a 3 percent annual increase. This slowdown might persuade the firm to keep its current gasoline pumps and replace them only when market conditions improve. In this way, even modest shifts in consumer demand for a gasoline brand would greatly affect the pump manufacturer.

Joint Demand

joint demand Demand for a product that depends on the demand for another product used in combination with it.

Another important influence on business market demand is **joint demand**, which results when the demand for one business product is related to the demand for another business product used in combination with the first item. Both lumber and concrete are required to build most homes. If the lumber supply falls, the drop in housing construction will most likely affect the demand for concrete. Another example is the joint demand for electrical power and large turbine engines. If consumers decide to conserve power, demand for new power plants drops, as does the demand for components and replacement parts for turbines.

Inelastic Demand

inelastic demand Demand that, throughout an industry, will not change significantly due to a price change.

Inelastic demand means that demand throughout an industry will not change significantly due to a price change. If the price of lumber drops, a construction firm will not necessarily buy more lumber from its suppliers unless another factor—such as lowered mortgage interest rates—causes more consumers to purchase new homes.

Inventory Adjustments

Adjustments in inventory and inventory policies can also affect business demand. Assume manufacturers in a particular industry consider a 60-day supply of raw materials at the optimal inventory level. Now suppose economic conditions or other factors induce these firms to increase their inventories to a 90-day supply. The change will bombard the raw-materials supplier with new orders.

just-in-time (JIT)/ JIT II Inventory practices that seek to boost efficiency by cutting inventories to absolute minimum levels. With JIT II, suppliers' representatives work at the customer's facility.

sole sourcing Purchasing a firm's entire stock of an item from just one vendor.

Furthermore, **just-in-time (JIT)** inventory policies seek to boost efficiency by cutting inventories to absolute minimum levels and by requiring vendors to deliver inputs as the production process needs them. JIT allows companies to better predict which supplies they will require and the timing for when they will need them, markedly reducing their costs for production and storage. Widespread implementation of JIT has had a substantial impact on organizations' purchasing behavior. Firms that practice JIT tend to order from relatively few suppliers. In some cases, JIT may lead to **sole sourcing** for some items, that is, buying a firm's entire stock of a product from just one supplier. Electronic data interchange (EDI) and quick-response inventory policies have produced similar results in the trade industries. The latest inventory trend, **JIT II**, leads suppliers to place representatives at the customer's facility to work as part of an integrated, on-site customer–supplier team. Suppliers plan and order in consultation with the customer. This streamlining of the inventory process improves control of the flow of goods.

Although inventory adjustments are critical in manufacturing processes, they are equally vital to wholesalers and retailers. Perhaps nowhere is inventory management more complex than at Walmart, the largest retailer in the world, with sales topping $400 billion per year. With no signs of slowing down, suppliers such as Procter & Gamble and Unilever—giants themselves—work closely with Walmart to monitor and adjust inventory as necessary. Other suppliers such as Mega Toys, Parkway Imaging and Graphics, and Ruiz Foods generate a large portion of their total income from Walmart, so inventory management is critical for those companies as well.[22]

assessment check

1. How does derived demand create volatile demand?
2. Give an example of joint demand.
3. How might JIT II strengthen marketing relationships?

The Make, Buy, or Lease Decision

Before a company can decide what to buy, it should decide whether to buy at all. Organizational buyers must figure out the best way to acquire needed products. In fact, a firm considering the acquisition of a finished good, component part, or service has three basic options:

> **4** Discuss the decision to make, buy, or lease.

1. Make the good or provide the service in-house.

2. Purchase it from another organization.

3. Lease it from another organization.

If the company has the capability to do so, manufacturing the product itself may be the best route. It may save a great deal of money if its own manufacturing division does not incur costs for overhead that an outside vendor would otherwise charge.

On the other hand, most firms cannot make all the business goods they need. Often it would be too costly to maintain the necessary equipment, staff, and supplies. As a result, purchasing from an outside vendor is the most common choice. Xerox manufactures more than 50 different types of color printers to meet nearly any business need—from affordable color laser printers to high-performance ink-jet printers. Its wide array of products, coupled with its track record of a century of supplying businesses, has made it a leader in the B2B printer market.[23] Companies can also look outside their own plants for goods and services formerly produced in-house, a practice called *outsourcing*, that the next section will describe in more detail.

In some cases, however, a company may choose to lease inputs. This option spreads out costs compared with lump-sum costs for up-front purchases. The company pays for the use of equipment for a certain time period. A small business may lease a copier for a few years and make monthly payments. At the end of the lease term, the firm can buy the machine at a prearranged price or replace it with a different model under a new lease. This option can provide useful flexibility for a growing business, allowing it to easily upgrade as its needs change.

Companies can also lease sophisticated computer systems and heavy equipment. For example, some airlines prefer to lease airplanes rather than buy them outright because short-term leases allow them to adapt quickly to changes in passenger demand.

The Rise of Offshoring and Outsourcing

Chances are, if you dial a call center for a firm such as Dell, GE, American Express, or Nestlé, your call may be answered by someone in India. In recent years, a firestorm has been ignited by the movement of U.S. jobs to lower-cost overseas locations, a business practice referred to as **offshoring**. When Hugo Boss, the high-end clothing maker, announced it would close its Cleveland plant and lay off 400 workers, picketers including company employees, union organizers, and local community leaders braved freezing temperatures outside a local department store where Hugo Boss was sold to draw attention to the loss of local jobs.[24] This relocation of business processes to a lower-cost location can involve production offshoring or services offshoring. China has emerged as the preferred destination for production offshoring, while India has emerged as the dominant player in services offshoring.

offshoring Movement of high-wage jobs from one country to lower-cost overseas locations.

nearshoring Moving jobs to vendors in countries close to the business's home country.

outsourcing Using outside vendors to provide goods and services formerly produced in-house.

Some U.S.-based firms want to remain closer to home but take advantage of the benefits of locating some of their operations overseas. Mexico and Canada are attractive locations for these **nearshoring** operations. In today's highly competitive marketplace, firms look outside the United States to improve efficiency and cut costs on just about everything including customer service, human resources, accounting, information technology, manufacturing, and distribution. **Outsourcing**, using outside vendors to produce goods and services formerly produced in-house, is a trend that continues to rise. Businesses outsource for several reasons: (1) they need to reduce costs to remain competitive, (2) they need to improve the quality and speed of software maintenance and development, and (3) outsourcing has begun to offer greater value than ever before.

Outsourcing allows firms to concentrate their resources on their core business. It also allows access to specialized talent or expertise that does not exist within the firm. The most frequently outsourced business functions include information technology (IT) and human resources, with other white-collar service jobs such as accounting, drug research, technical research and development (R&D), and film animation. Although most outsourcing is done by North American–based companies, the practice is rapidly becoming commonplace in Asia, Europe, and Central America.

China has been leading the way in offshore manufacturing, making two-thirds of the world's copiers, microwaves, DVD players, and shoes, and virtually all the world's toys. The size of its manufacturing workforce in the Guangdong province is estimated to rival that of the entire United States. In recent years, however, China's very success and the resulting rise of an increasingly wealthy middle class have pushed up its labor and management costs and may have helped shift many companies to suppliers in Vietnam and India, where such costs are still low.[25]

Outsourcing can be a smart strategy if a company chooses a vendor that can provide high-quality products and perhaps at a lower cost than could be achieved by the company itself. This priority allows the outsourcer to focus on its core competencies. Successful outsourcing requires companies to carefully oversee contracts and manage relationships. Some vendors now provide performance guarantees to assure their customers they will receive high-quality services that meet their needs.

Problems with Offshoring and Outsourcing

Offshoring and outsourcing are not without their downsides. Many companies discover their cost savings are less than vendors sometimes promise. Also, companies that sign multiyear contracts may find their savings drop after a year or two. When proprietary technology is an issue, outsourcing raises security concerns. Similarly, if companies are protective of customer data and relationships they may think twice about entrusting functions such as customer service to outside sources.

In some cases, outsourcing and offshoring can reduce a company's ability to respond quickly to the marketplace, or they can slow efforts in bringing new products to market. Suppliers that fail to deliver goods promptly or provide required services can adversely affect a company's reputation with its customers.

Outsourcing and offshoring are controversial topics with unions, especially in the auto industry, as the percentage of component parts made in-house has steadily dropped. These practices can create conflicts between nonunion outside workers and in-house union employees, who fear job loss. Management initiatives to outsource jobs can lead to strikes and plant shutdowns. Even if they do not lead to disruption in the workplace, outsourcing and offshoring can have a negative impact on employee morale and loyalty.

 assessment check

1. Identify two potential benefits of outsourcing.

2. Identify two potential problems with outsourcing.

The Business Buying Process

Suppose that MyMap Inc., a hypothetical manufacturer of GPS devices for automakers, decides to upgrade its manufacturing facility with $5 million in new automated assembly equipment. Before approaching equipment suppliers, the company must analyze its needs, determine goals the project should accomplish, develop technical specifications for the equipment, and set a budget. Once it receives vendors' proposals, it must evaluate them and select the best one. But what does *best* mean in this context? The lowest price or the best warranty and service contract? Who in the company is responsible for such decisions?

The business buying process is more complex than the consumer decision process. Business buying takes place within a formal organization's budget, cost, and profit considerations. Furthermore, B2B and institutional buying decisions usually involve many people with complex interactions among individuals and organizational goals. To understand organizational buying behavior, business marketers require knowledge of influences on the purchase decision process, the stages in the organizational buying model, types of business buying situations, and techniques for purchase decision analysis.

5 **Describe the major influences on business buying behavior.**

Influences on Purchase Decisions

B2B buying decisions react to various influences, some external to the firm and others related to internal structure and personnel. In addition to product-specific factors such as purchase price, installation, operating and maintenance costs, and vendor service, companies must consider broader environmental, organizational, and interpersonal influences.

ENVIRONMENTAL FACTORS

Environmental conditions such as economic, political, regulatory, competitive, and technological considerations influence business buying decisions. MyMap may wish to defer purchases of the new equipment in times of slowing economic activity. During a recession, sales to auto companies might drop because households hesitate to spend money on a new car. The company would look at the derived demand for its products, possible changes in its sources of materials, employment trends, and similar factors before committing to such a large capital expenditure.

Environmental factors can also include natural disasters such as the freezing weather that recently hit Florida, creating "one of the longest stretches of chilly weather that Florida has ever seen," according to one meteorologist. The cold was expected to have damaged about 5 percent of the crops readied by the state's famed orange industry, which employs some 76,000 people.[26]

Political, regulatory, and competitive factors also come into play in influencing purchase decisions. Passage of a privacy law that restricted GPS tracking would affect demand, as would competition from smartphones and other devices containing map features. Finally, technology plays a role in purchase decisions. When GPS systems were first introduced, many customers bought separate units to install in their cars. But as more new cars come factory equipped with the units, the market for standalone boxes naturally decreases.

ORGANIZATIONAL FACTORS

Successful business-to-business marketers understand their customers' organizational structures, policies, and purchasing systems. A company with a centralized procurement function operates differently from one that delegates purchasing decisions to divisional or geographic units. Trying to sell to the local store when head office merchandisers make all the decisions would clearly waste salespeople's time. Buying behavior also differs among firms. For example, centralized buying tends to emphasize long-term relationships, whereas decentralized buying focuses more on short-term results. Personal selling skills and user preferences carry more weight in decentralized purchasing situations than in centralized buying.

Environmental factors can include natural disasters such as the freezing weather that recently hit Florida, damaging orange crops.

© AP IMAGES/CHRIS O'MEARA

How many suppliers should a company patronize? Because purchasing operations spend more than half of each dollar their companies earn, consolidating vendor relationships can lead to large cost savings. However, a fine line separates maximizing buying power from relying too heavily on a few suppliers. Many companies engage in **multiple sourcing**—purchasing from several vendors. Spreading orders ensures against shortages if one vendor cannot deliver on schedule. However, dealing with many sellers can be counterproductive and take too much time. Each company must set its own criteria for this decision.

multiple sourcing
Purchasing from several vendors.

INTERPERSONAL INFLUENCES

Many people may influence B2B purchases, and considerable time may be spent obtaining the input and approval of various organization members. Both group and individual forces are at work here. When committees handle buying, they must spend time to gain majority or unanimous approval. Also, each individual buyer brings to the decision process individual preferences, experiences, and biases.

Business marketers should know who in an organization will influence buying decisions for their products and should know each of their priorities. To choose a supplier for an industrial press, for example, a purchasing manager and representatives of the company's production, engineering, and quality control departments may be involved in deciding on a supplier. Each of these principals may have a different point of view that the vendor's marketers must understand.

To effectively address the concerns of all people involved in the buying decision, sales personnel must be well versed in the technical features of their products. They must also interact well with employees of the various departments involved in the purchase decision. Sales representatives for medical products—traditionally called "detailers"—frequently visit hospitals and doctors' offices to discuss the advantages of their products and leave samples with clinical staff.

THE ROLE OF MERCHANDISERS AND CATEGORY ADVISORS

Many large organizations attempt to make their purchases through systematic procedures employing professional buyers. In the trade industries, these buyers, often referred to as **merchandisers**, secure needed products at the best possible prices. Nordstrom has buyers for shoes and clothing that will ultimately be sold to consumers. Ford has buyers for components that will be incorporated into its cars and trucks. A firm's purchasing or merchandising unit devotes all of its time and effort in determining needs, locating and evaluating alternative suppliers, and making purchase decisions.

merchandisers Trade sector buyers who secure needed products at the best possible prices.

Purchase decisions for capital items vary significantly from those for expense items. Firms often buy expense items routinely with little delay. Capital items, however, involve major fund commitments and usually undergo considerable review.

One way a firm may attempt to streamline the buying process is through **systems integration**, or centralization of the procurement function. One company may designate a lead division to handle all purchasing. Another firm may choose to designate a major supplier as the systems integrator. This vendor then assumes responsibility for dealing with all of the suppliers for a project and for presenting the entire package to the buyer. In trade industries, this vendor is sometimes called a **category advisor** or **category captain**.

systems integration
Centralization of the procurement function within an internal division or as a service of an external supplier.

category advisor (category captain)
Trade industry vendor who develops a comprehensive procurement plan for a retail buyer.

A business marketer may set up a sales organization to serve national accounts that deal solely with buyers at corporate headquarters. A separate field sales organization may serve buyers at regional production facilities.

Corporate buyers often use the Internet to identify sources of supplies. They view online catalogs and Web sites to compare vendors' offerings and obtain product information. Some use Internet exchanges to extend their supplier networks.

 assessment check

1. Identify the three major factors that influence purchase decisions.
2. What are the advantages and disadvantages of multiple sourcing?

Model of the Organizational Buying Process

An organizational buying situation takes place through a sequence of activities. Figure 6.2 illustrates an eight-stage model of an organizational buying process. Although not every buying situation requires all these steps, this figure provides a good overview of the whole process.

> **6** Outline the steps in the organizational buying process.

STAGE 1: ANTICIPATE OR RECOGNIZE A PROBLEM/NEED/OPPORTUNITY AND A GENERAL SOLUTION

Both consumer and business purchase decisions begin when the recognition of problems, needs, or opportunities triggers the buying process. Perhaps a firm's computer system has become outdated or an account representative demonstrates a new service that could improve the company's performance. Companies may decide to hire an outside marketing specialist when their sales stagnate.

The problem may be as simple as needing to provide a good cup of coffee to a firm's employees. The founders of Keurig Incorporated, which supplies about 2.5 million individually brewed cups of coffee to U.S. homes and offices each day, started by asking themselves, "Why do we brew coffee a pot at a time when we drink it a cup at a time?"[27]

STAGE 2: DETERMINE THE CHARACTERISTICS AND QUANTITY OF A NEEDED GOOD OR SERVICE

The coffee problem described in stage 1 translated into a service opportunity for Keurig. The small firm was able to offer a coffee system that would brew one perfect cup of coffee at a time, according to the preferences of each employee. After finding success in the offices of many accounting, law, and medical practices, the company developed a single-cup brewer for home use and has most recently introduced a unique full-color touch screen that allows coffee lovers to readily customize each cup's temperature and strength.[28]

STAGE 3: DESCRIBE CHARACTERISTICS AND THE QUANTITY OF A NEEDED GOOD OR SERVICE

After determining the characteristics and quantity of needed products, B2B buyers must translate these ideas into detailed specifications. Customers told Keurig they wanted a foolproof, individual coffee maker. The Keurig system supplies a plastic K-Cup® portion pack, containing ground coffee

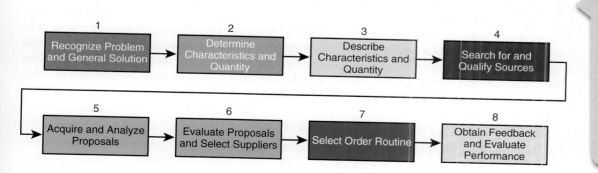

figure 6.2

Stages in the B2B Buying Process

Source: Based on Michael D. Hutt and Thomas W. Speh, *Business Marketing Management: B2B,* 10th ed. (Mason, OH: South-Western, 2010).

The founders of Keurig Incorporated asked themselves, "Why do we brew coffee a pot at a time when we drink it a cup at a time?"

© HANDOUT/MCT/NEWSCOM

that the individual simply places in the coffee maker—no measuring of water or coffee is required. Out comes the perfect cup of coffee. Firms could easily base the quantity requirements of the Keurig system on the number of coffee-drinking employees they have or the amount of space they occupy.

STAGE 4: SEARCH FOR AND QUALIFY POTENTIAL SOURCES

Both consumers and businesses search for good suppliers of desired products. The choice of a supplier may be relatively straightforward—because there was no other machine like it, its early adopters had no trouble selecting the Keurig coffee system. Other searches may involve more complex decision making. A company that wants to buy a group life or health insurance policy, for example, must weigh the varying provisions and programs of many different vendors.

STAGE 5: ACQUIRE AND ANALYZE PROPOSALS

The next step is to acquire and analyze suppliers' proposals, often submitted in writing. If the buyer is a government or public agency, this stage of the purchase process may involve competitive bidding. During this process, each marketer must develop its bid, including a price that will satisfy the criteria determined by the customer's problem, need, or opportunity. While competitive bidding is less common in the business sector, a company may follow the practice to purchase nonstandard materials, complex products, or products made to its own specifications.

STAGE 6: EVALUATE PROPOSALS AND SELECT SUPPLIERS

Next in the buying process, buyers must compare vendors' proposals and choose the one that seems best suited to their needs. Proposals for sophisticated equipment, such as a large computer networking system, can include considerable differences among product offerings, and the final choice may involve trade-offs.

Price is not the only criterion for the selection of a vendor. Relationship factors such as communication and trust may also be important to the buyer. Other issues include reliability, delivery record, time from order to delivery, quality, and order accuracy. These are particularly important in the package delivery business. FedEx recently concluded a unique deal with ProFlowers that allowed the package company to deliver Valentine's Day flowers on a Sunday for the first time in its history. "FedEx has been working with ProFlowers since its launch more than ten years ago," said a FedEx senior vice president. "We were able to leverage our existing supply chain expertise, our extensive flexible network, and their distribution facility locations to create a cost-effective solution that would fit ProFlowers' business needs during this busy time of year."[29]

STAGE 7: SELECT AN ORDER ROUTINE

Once a supplier has been chosen, buyer and vendor must work out the best way to process future purchases. Ordering routines can vary considerably. Most orders will, however, include product descriptions, quantities, prices, delivery terms, and payment terms. Today, companies have a variety of options for submitting orders: written documents, phone calls, faxes, or electronic data interchange (EDI).

STAGE 8: OBTAIN FEEDBACK AND EVALUATE PERFORMANCE

At the final stage, buyers measure vendors' performances. Sometimes this judgment may involve a formal evaluation of each supplier's product quality, delivery performance, prices, technical knowledge, and overall responsiveness to customer needs. At other times, vendors may be measured according to whether they have lowered the customer's costs or reduced its employees' workloads. In general, bigger firms are more likely to use formal evaluation procedures, while smaller companies lean toward informal evaluations. Regardless of the method used, buyers should tell vendors how they will be evaluated.

Sometimes firms rely on independent organizations to gather quality feedback and summarize results. J.D. Power and Associates conducts research and provides information to a variety of firms so they can improve the quality of their goods and services.

assessment check

1. Why does the organizational buying process contain more steps than the consumer buying process?
2. List the steps in the organizational buying process.

Classifying Business Buying Situations

As discussed earlier, business buying behavior responds to many purchasing influences such as environmental, organizational, and interpersonal factors. This buying behavior also involves the degree of effort the purchase decision demands and the levels within the organization where it is made. Like consumer behavior, marketers can classify B2B buying situations into three general categories, ranging from least to most complex: (1) straight rebuying, (2) modified rebuying, and (3) new-task buying. Business buying situations may also involve reciprocity. The following sections look at each type of purchase.

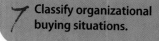
7 Classify organizational buying situations.

STRAIGHT REBUYING

The simplest buying situation is a **straight rebuy**—a recurring purchase decision in which a customer reorders a product that has satisfied its needs in the past. The buyer already likes the product and terms of sale, so the purchase requires no new information. The buyer sees little reason to assess competing options and so follows a routine repurchase format. A straight rebuy is the business market equivalent of routinized response behavior in the consumer market. Purchases of low-cost items such as paper clips and pencils for an office are typical examples of straight rebuys. Reorders of coffee from Keurig would also be straight rebuys. Marketers who maintain good relationships with customers by providing high-quality products, superior service, and prompt delivery can go a long way toward ensuring straight rebuys.

straight rebuy Recurring purchase decision in which a customer repurchases a good or service that has performed satisfactorily in the past.

MODIFIED REBUYING

In a **modified rebuy**, a purchaser is willing to reevaluate available options. Buyers may see some advantage in looking at alternative offerings within their established purchasing guidelines. They might take this step if their current supplier has let a rebuy situation deteriorate because of poor service or delivery performance. Price, quality, and innovation differences can also provoke modified rebuys. Modified rebuys resemble limited problem solving in consumer markets.

modified rebuy Situation in which a purchaser is willing to reevaluate available options for repurchasing a good or service.

B2B marketers want to induce current customers to make straight rebuys by responding to all of their needs. Competitors, on the other hand, try to lure those buyers away by raising issues that will persuade them to reconsider their decisions.

NEW-TASK BUYING

new-task buying
First-time or unique purchase situation that requires considerable effort by decision makers.

The most complex category of business buying is **new-task buying**—first-time or unique purchase situations that require considerable effort by the decision makers. Many companies decide, for instance, that they want to buy a customized data center rather than try to build their own. Companies like Procter & Gamble, Nokia, Ericsson, Unilever, and Pfizer and organizations like Indiana University have contracted with Hewlett-Packard (HP) to outsource their data center or information technology functions.[30] These one-time purchases require customers and HP to work closely together to determine which functions to outsource, which to keep in house (if any), and which hardware and software configurations best meet their needs. The consumer market equivalent of new-task buying is extended problem solving.

A new-task buy often requires a purchaser to carefully consider alternative offerings and vendors. A company entering a new field must seek suppliers of component parts that it has never before purchased. This new-task buying would require several stages, each yielding a decision of some sort. These decisions would include developing product requirements, searching out potential suppliers, and evaluating proposals. Information requirements and decision makers can complete the entire buying process, or they may change from stage to stage.

RECIPROCITY

reciprocity Buying from suppliers who are also customers.

Reciprocity—a practice of buying from suppliers who are also customers—is a controversial practice in a number of procurement situations. An office equipment manufacturer may favor a particular supplier of component parts if the supplier has recently made a major purchase of the manufacturer's products. Reciprocal arrangements traditionally have been common in industries featuring homogeneous products with similar prices such as the chemical, paint, petroleum, rubber, and steel industries.

Reciprocity suggests close links among participants in the organizational marketplace. It can add to the complexity of B2B buying behavior for new suppliers trying to compete with preferred vendors. Although buyers and sellers enter into reciprocal agreements in the United States, both the Department of Justice and the Federal Trade Commission view them as attempts to reduce competition. Outside the United States, however, governments may take more favorable views of reciprocity. In Japan, close ties between suppliers and customers are common.

Analysis Tools

value analysis
Systematic study of the components of a purchase to determine the most cost-effective approach.

vendor analysis
Assessment of supplier performance such as price, back orders, timely delivery, and attention to special requests.

Two tools that help professional buyers improve purchase decisions are value analysis and vendor analysis. **Value analysis** examines each component of a purchase in an attempt to either delete the item or replace it with a more cost-effective substitute. Airplane designers have long recognized the need to make planes as light as possible. Value analysis supports using composite materials such as Kevlar in airplane construction because it weighs less than the metals it replaces. The resulting fuel savings are significant for buyers in this marketplace.

Vendor analysis carries out an ongoing evaluation of a supplier's performance in categories such as price, EDI capability, back orders, delivery times, liability insurance, and attention to special requests. In some cases, vendor analysis is a formal process. Some buyers use a checklist to assess a vendor's performance. A checklist quickly highlights vendors and potential vendors that do not satisfy the purchaser's buying requirements.

 assessment check

1. What are the four classifications of business buying situations?

2. Differentiate between value analysis and vendor analysis.

The Buying Center Concept

The buying center concept provides a model for understanding B2B buying behavior. A company's **buying center** encompasses everyone involved in any aspect of its buying activity. A buying center may include the architect who designs a new research laboratory, the scientist who works in the facility, the purchasing manager who screens contractor proposals, the chief executive officer who makes the final decision, and the vice president of research who signs the formal contracts for the project. Buying center participants in any purchase seek to satisfy personal needs, such as participation or status, as well as organizational needs. A buying center is not part of a firm's formal organizational structure. It is an informal group whose composition and size vary among purchase situations and firms.

8 **Explain the buying center concept.**

buying center Participants in an organizational buying decision.

Buying Center Roles

Buying center participants play different roles in the purchasing decision process. **Users** are the people who will actually use the good or service. Their influence on the purchase decision may range from negligible to extremely important. Users sometimes initiate purchase actions by requesting products, and they may also help develop product specifications. Users often influence the purchase of office equipment.

user Individual or group that actually uses a business good or service.

Gatekeepers control the information that all buying center members will review. They may exert this control by distributing printed product data or advertisements or by deciding which salespeople may speak to which individuals in the buying center. A purchasing agent might allow some salespeople to see the engineers responsible for developing specifications but deny others the same privilege. The office manager for a medical group may decide whether to accept and pass along sales literature from a pharmaceutical detailer or sales representative.

gatekeeper Person who controls the information that all buying center members will review.

Influencers affect the buying decision by supplying information to guide evaluation of alternatives or by setting buying specifications. Influencers typically are technical staff such as engineers or quality-control specialists. Sometimes a buying organization hires outside consultants such as architects who influence its buying decisions.

The decider chooses a good or service, although another person may have the formal authority to do so. The identity of the decider is the most difficult role for salespeople to pinpoint. A firm's buyer may have the formal authority to buy, but the firm's chief executive officer may actually make the buying decision. Alternatively, a decider might be a design engineer who develops specifications that only one vendor can meet.

influencer Typically, technical staff such as engineers who affect the buying decision by supplying information to guide evaluation of alternatives or by setting buying specifications.

The buyer has the formal authority to select a supplier and to implement the procedures for securing the good or service. The buyer often surrenders this power to more influential members of the organization, though. The purchasing manager often fills the buyer's role and executes the details associated with a purchase order.

decider Person who chooses a good or service, although another person may have the formal authority to complete the sale.

B2B marketers face the task of determining the specific role and the relative decision-making influence of each buying center participant. Salespeople can then tailor their presentations and information to the precise role an individual plays at each step of the purchase process. Business marketers have found their initial—and in many cases, most extensive—contacts with a firm's purchasing department often fail to reach the buying center participants who have the greatest influence, because these people may not work in that department at all.

buyer Person who has the formal authority to select a supplier and to implement the procedures for securing a good or service.

Consider the selection of meeting and convention sites for trade or professional associations. The primary decision maker could be an association board or an executive committee, usually with input from the executive director or a meeting planner; these individuals might choose meeting locations, sometimes with input from members; finally, the association's annual meeting committee or program committee might make the meeting location selection. Because officers change periodically, centers of control may change frequently. As a result, destination marketers and hotel operators must constantly assess how an association makes its decisions on conference locations.

International Buying Centers

Two distinct characteristics differentiate international buying centers from domestic ones. First, marketers may have trouble identifying members of foreign buying centers because of cultural differences in decision-making methods. Second, a buying center in a foreign company often includes more participants than U.S. companies involve. International buying centers employ from 1 to 50 people, with 15 to 20 participants commonplace. Global B2B marketers must recognize and accommodate this greater diversity of decision makers.

International buying centers can change in response to political and economic trends. Many European firms once maintained separate facilities in each European nation to avoid tariffs and customs delays. When the European Union lowered trade barriers between member–nations, however, many companies closed distant branches and consolidated their buying centers. The Netherlands has been one of the beneficiaries of this trend.

assessment check

1. Identify the five roles of people in a buying center decision.
2. What are some of the problems that U.S. marketers face in dealing with international buying centers?

Developing Effective Business-to-Business Marketing Strategies

 Discuss the challenges of and strategies for marketing to government, institutional, and international buyers.

A business marketer must develop a marketing strategy based on a particular organization's buying behavior and on the buying situation. Clearly, many variables affect organizational purchasing decisions. This section examines three market segments whose decisions present unique challenges to B2B marketers: units of government, institutions, and international markets. Finally, it summarizes key differences between consumer and business marketing strategies.

Challenges of Government Markets

Government agencies—federal, state, and local—together make up the largest customer group in the United States. Almost 90,000 government units buy a wide variety of products, including office supplies, furniture, concrete, vehicles, grease, military aircraft, fuel, and lumber, to name just a few.[31]

To compete effectively, business marketers must understand the unique challenges of selling to government units. One challenge results because government purchases typically involve dozens of interested parties who specify, evaluate, or use the purchased goods and services. These parties may or may not work within the government agency that officially handles a purchase.

Government purchases are also influenced by social goals, such as "Buy American" provisions and minority subcontracting programs. Government entities such as the U.S. Postal Service strive to maintain diversity in their suppliers by making a special effort to purchase goods and services from small firms and companies owned by minorities and women. The Postal Service has developed a Supplier Diversity Corporate Plan to show its commitment to ensuring "a continued focus on—and improvement in—our relationships with small, minority-owned, and women-owned businesses."[32] The government also relies on its prime suppliers to subcontract to minority businesses.

Contractual guidelines create another important influence in selling to government markets. The government buys products under two basic types of contracts: fixed-price contracts, in which seller and buyer agree to a set price before finalizing the contract, and cost-reimbursement contracts, in which the government pays the vendor for allowable costs, including profits, incurred during performance of the contract. Each type of contract has advantages and disadvantages for B2B marketers. Although the fixed-price contract offers more profit potential than the alternative, it also carries greater risks from unforeseen expenses, price hikes, and changing political and economic conditions.

GOVERNMENT PURCHASING PROCEDURES

Many U.S. government purchases go through the General Services Administration (GSA), a central management agency involved in areas such as procurement, property management, and information resources management. The GSA buys goods and services for its own use and for use by other government agencies. In its role as, essentially, the federal government's business manager, it purchases billions of dollars' worth of products. The Defense Logistics Agency (DLA) serves the same function for the Department of Defense.

By law, most federal purchases must be awarded on the basis of bids, or written sales proposals, from vendors. As part of this process, government buyers develop specifications—detailed descriptions of needed items—for prospective bidders. U.S. government purchases must comply with the Federal Acquisition Regulation (FAR), an approximately 30,000-page set of standards originally designed to cut red tape in government purchasing. FAR standards have been further complicated by numerous exceptions issued by various government agencies. Because they provide services to various federal government agencies such as the Department of Energy, Environmental Protection Agency, and Department of Defense, large environmental engineering firms such as MACTEC, Tetra Tech, and Weston Solutions typically have procurement and contract specialists on staff. These specialists stay current with FAR standards and conduct internal quality-assurance and quality-control programs to make sure the standards are followed by their companies.

State and local government purchasing procedures resemble federal procedures. Most states and many large cities have created buying offices similar to the GSA. Detailed specifications and open bidding are common at this level as well. Many state purchasing regulations give preference to in-state bidders.

Government spending patterns may differ from those in private industry. Because the federal government's fiscal year runs from October 1 through September 30, many agencies spend much of their procurement budgets in the fourth quarter, from July 1 to September 30. They hoard their funds to cover unexpected expenditures, and if they encounter no such problems, they find themselves with money to spend in late summer. Companies understand this system and keep their eyes on government bulletins so that they can bid on the listed agency purchases, which often involve large amounts of money.

ONLINE WITH THE FEDERAL GOVERNMENT

Like their colleagues in the private sector, government procurement professionals are streamlining purchasing procedures with new technology. Rather than paging through piles of paper catalogs and submitting handwritten purchase orders, government buyers now prefer online catalogs that help them compare competing product offerings. In fact, vendors find doing business with the government almost impossible unless they embrace electronic commerce.

Vendors can sell products to the federal government through three electronic options. Web sites provide a convenient method of exchanging information for both parties. Government buyers locate and order products, paying with a federally issued credit card, and the vendors deliver the items within about a week. Another route is through government-sponsored electronic ordering systems, which help standardize the buying process. GSA Advantage allows federal employees to order more than 11 million products and services directly over the Internet at the preferred government price and logs about 2,500 orders every day. "We were already operational while Amazon was still beta-testing its site," recalls the e-business director of GSA's Federal Supply Service.[33] The Phoenix Opportunity System, set up by the Department of Commerce, provides a similar service for minority-owned companies. A pilot program at the Treasury is testing an electronic check-payment system to speed up the settling of vendor invoices.

Despite these advances, many government agencies remain less sophisticated than private-sector businesses. The Pentagon, for instance, is still coping with procurement procedures that were developed over the past 50 years. However, it is introducing a streamlined approach to defense contracting that reduces the time necessary to develop specifications and select suppliers.

© THE MINORITY BUSINESS DEVELOPMENT AGENCY (MBDA), WWW.MBDA.GOV

The Phoenix Opportunity System, set up by the Department of Commerce, provides a government-sponsored electronic ordering system for minority-owned companies.

Challenges of Institutional Markets

Institutions constitute another important market. Institutional buyers include a wide variety of organizations such as schools, hospitals, libraries, foundations, clinics, churches, and not-for-profit agencies.

Institutional markets are characterized by widely diverse buying practices. Some institutional purchasers behave like government purchasers because laws and political considerations determine their buying procedures. Many of these institutions, such as schools and prisons, may even be managed by government units.

Buying practices can differ between institutions of the same type. In a small hospital, the chief dietitian may approve all food purchases, while in a larger medical facility, food purchases may go through a committee consisting of the dietitian and a business manager, purchasing agent, and cook. Other hospitals may belong to buying groups, perhaps health maintenance organizations or local hospital cooperatives. Still others may contract with outside firms to prepare and serve all meals.

Within a single institution, multiple buying influences may affect decisions. Many institutions, staffed by professionals such as physicians, nurses, researchers, and instructors, may also employ purchasing managers or even entire purchasing departments. Conflicts may arise among these decision makers. Professional employees may prefer to make their own purchase decisions and resent giving up control to the purchasing staff. This conflict can force a business marketer to cultivate both professionals and purchasers. A detailer for a pharmaceutical firm must convince physicians of the value to patients of a certain drug while simultaneously convincing the hospital's purchasing department that the firm offers competitive prices, good delivery schedules, and prompt service.

Group purchasing is an important factor in institutional markets because many organizations join cooperative associations to pool purchases for quantity discounts. Universities may join the Education and Institutional Purchasing Cooperative; hospitals may belong to regional associations; and chains of profit-oriented hospitals such as HCA Healthcare can also negotiate quantity discounts. Central headquarters staff usually handles purchasing for all members of such a chain.

Diverse practices in institutional markets pose special challenges for B2B marketers. They must maintain flexibility in developing strategies for dealing with a range of customers, from large cooperative associations and chains to midsize purchasing departments and institutions to individuals. Buying centers can work with varying members, priorities, and levels of expertise. Discounts and effective distribution functions play important roles in obtaining—and keeping—institutions as customers.

Challenges of International Markets

remanufacturing
Efforts to restore older products to like-new condition.

To sell successfully in international markets, business marketers must consider buyers' attitudes and cultural patterns within areas where they operate. In Asian markets, a firm must maintain a local presence to sell products. Personal relationships are also important to business deals in Asia. Companies that want to expand globally often need to establish joint ventures with local partners. International marketers must also be poised to respond to shifts in cultural values.

Local industries, economic conditions, geographic characteristics, and legal restrictions must also be considered in international marketing. Many local industries in Spain specialize in food and wine; therefore, a maker of forklift trucks might market smaller vehicles to Spanish companies than to German firms, which require bigger, heavier trucks to serve the needs of that nation's large automobile industry.

Remanufacturing—efforts to restore worn-out products to like-new condition—can be an important marketing strategy in a

Buying practices can differ among institutions of the same type. In a small school cafeteria, the chief dietician may approve food purchases, while in a larger facility, food purchases may go through a committee.

© STEVE MCCONNELL

nation that cannot afford to buy new products. Developing countries often purchase remanufactured factory machinery, which costs 35 to 60 percent less than new equipment.

Foreign governments represent another important business market. In many countries, government or state-owned companies dominate certain industries such as construction and other infrastructure sales. Additional examples include airport and highway construction, telephone system equipment, and computer networking equipment. Sales to a foreign government can involve an array of regulations. Many governments, like that of the United States, limit foreign participation in their defense programs. Joint ventures and countertrade are common, as are local content laws, which mandate domestic production of a certain percentage of a business product's components.

assessment check

1. What are some influences on government purchases?
2. Why is group purchasing important in institutional purchases?
3. What special factors influence international buying decisions?

strategic implications
of marketing in the 21st century

 o develop marketing strategies for the B2B sector, marketers must first understand the buying practices that govern the segment they are targeting, whether it is the commercial market, trade industries, government, or institutions. Similarly, when selling to a specific organization, strategies must take into account the many factors that influence purchasing. B2B marketers must identify people who play the various roles in the buying decision and understand how these members interact with one another, other members of their own organizations, and outside vendors. Marketers must be careful to direct their marketing efforts to their organization, to broader environmental influences, and to individuals who operate within the constraints of the firm's buying center.

Review of Chapter Objectives

 Explain each of the components of the business-to-business (B2B) market.

The B2B market is divided into four segments: the commercial market, trade industries, governments, and institutions. The commercial market consists of individuals and firms that acquire products to be used, directly or indirectly, to produce other goods and services. Trade industries are organizations such as retailers and wholesalers that purchase for resale to others. The primary purpose of government purchasing at federal, state, and local levels is to provide some form of public benefit. The fourth segment, institutions, includes a diverse array of organizations such as hospitals, schools, museums, and not-for-profit agencies.

Describe the major approaches to segmenting business-to-business (B2B) markets.

Business markets can be segmented by (1) demographics, (2) customer type, (3) end-use application, and (4) purchasing situation. The North American Industry Classification System (NAICS), instituted after the passage of NAFTA, helps further classify types of customers by the use of six digits.

 Identify the major characteristics of the business market and its demand.

The major characteristics of the business market are geographic concentration, size and number of buyers, purchase decision procedures, and buyer–seller relationships. The major categories of demand are derived demand, volatile demand, joint demand, inelastic demand, and inventory adjustments.

 Discuss the decision to make, buy, or lease.

Before a company can decide what to buy, it must decide whether to buy at all. A firm has three options: (1) make the good or service in-house, (2) purchase it from another organization, or (3) lease it from another organization. Companies may outsource goods or services formerly produced in-house to other companies either within their own home country or to firms in other nations. The shift of high-wage jobs from the home country to lower-wage locations is known as *offshoring*. If a company moves production to a country close to its own borders, it uses a *nearshoring* strategy. Each option has its benefits and drawbacks, including cost and quality control.

 Describe the major influences on business buying behavior.

B2B buying behavior tends to be more complex than individual consumer behavior. More people and time are involved, and buyers often seek several alternative supply sources. The systematic nature of organizational buying is reflected in the use of purchasing managers to direct such efforts. Major organizational purchases may require elaborate and lengthy decision-making processes involving many people. Purchase decisions typically depend on combinations of such factors as price, service, certainty of supply, and product efficiency.

 Outline the steps in the organizational buying process.

The organizational buying process consists of eight general stages: (1) anticipate or recognize a problem/need/opportunity and a general solution, (2) determine characteristics and quantity of needed good or service, (3) describe characteristics and quantity of needed good or service, (4) search for and qualify potential sources, (5) acquire and analyze proposals, (6) evaluate proposals and select supplier(s), (7) select an order routine, and (8) obtain feedback and evaluate performance.

 Classify organizational buying situations.

Organizational buying situations differ. A straight rebuy is a recurring purchase decision in which a customer stays with an item that has performed satisfactorily. In a modified rebuy, a purchaser is willing to reevaluate available options. New-task buying refers to first-time or unique purchase situations that require considerable effort on the part of the decision makers. Reciprocity involves buying from suppliers who are also customers.

 Explain the buying center concept.

The buying center includes everyone who is involved in some fashion in an organizational buying action. There are five buying center roles: users, gatekeepers, influencers, deciders, and buyers.

 Discuss the challenges of and strategies for marketing to government, institutional, and international buyers.

A government purchase typically involves dozens of interested parties. Social goals and programs influence government purchases. Many U.S. government purchases involve complex contractual guidelines and often require detailed specifications and a bidding process. Institutional markets are challenging because of their diverse buying influences and practices. Group purchasing is an important factor because many institutions join cooperative associations to get quantity discounts. An institutional marketer must be flexible enough to develop strategies for dealing with a range of customers. Discounts and effective distribution play an important role. An effective international business marketer must be aware of foreign attitudes and cultural patterns. Other important factors include economic conditions, geographic characteristics, legal restrictions, and local industries.

Assessment Check: Answers

1.1 Define B2B marketing. Business-to-business, or B2B, marketing deals with organizational purchases of goods and services to support production of other products, to facilitate daily company operations, or for resale.

1.2 What is the commercial market? The commercial market consists of individuals and firms that acquire products to be used, directly or indirectly, to produce other goods and services.

2.1 What are the four major ways marketers segment business markets? Business markets can be segmented by (1) demographics, (2) customer type, (3) end-use application, and (4) purchasing situation.

2.2 What is the NAICS? The North American Industry Classification System (NAICS) is a unified system for Mexico, Canada, and the United States to classify B2B market segments and ease trade.

3.1 Why is geographic segmentation important in the B2B market? Certain industries locate in particular areas to be close to customers. Firms may choose to locate sales offices and distribution centers in these areas to provide more attentive service. For example, the Washington, DC, area is favored by companies that sell to the federal government.

3.2 In what ways is the buyer–seller relationship important in B2B marketing? Buyer–seller relationships often are more complex than consumer relationships, and they require superior communication among the organizations' personnel. Satisfying one major customer may mean the difference of millions of dollars to a firm.

3.3 What is global sourcing? Global sourcing involves contracting to purchase goods and services from suppliers worldwide.

3.4 How does derived demand create volatile demand? Business demand often is derived from consumer demand. Even modest shifts in consumer demand can produce disproportionate—and volatile—shifts in business demand.

3.5 Give an example of joint demand. Both lumber and concrete are required to build most homes. If the lumber supply falls, the drop in housing construction will most likely affect the demand for concrete.

3.6 How might JIT II strengthen marketing relationships? Under JIT II, suppliers place representatives at the customer's facility to work as part of an integrated, on-site customer–supplier team. Suppliers plan and take orders in consultation with the customer. This streamlining of the inventory process improves control of the flow of goods.

4.1 Identify two potential benefits of outsourcing. Outsourcing allows firms to concentrate their resources on their core business. It also allows access to specialized talent or expertise that does not exist within the firm.

4.2 Identify two potential problems with outsourcing. Many companies discover their cost savings are less than vendors sometimes promise. Also, companies that sign multiyear contracts may find their savings drop after a year or two.

5.1 Identify the three major factors that influence purchase decisions. In addition to product-specific factors such as purchase price, installation, operating and maintenance costs, and vendor service, companies must consider broader environmental, organizational, and interpersonal influences.

5.2 What are the advantages and disadvantages of multiple sourcing? Spreading orders ensures against shortages if one vendor cannot deliver on schedule. However, dealing with many sellers can be counterproductive and take too much time.

6.1 Why does the organizational buying process contain more steps than the consumer buying process? The additional steps arise because business purchasing introduces new complexities that do not affect consumers.

6.2 List the steps in the organizational buying process. The steps in organizational buying are (1) anticipate or recognize a problem/need/opportunity and a general solution, (2) determine characteristics and quantity of a needed good or service, (3) describe characteristics and quantity of needed good or service, (4) search for and qualify potential sources, (5) acquire and analyze proposals, (6) evaluate proposals and select supplier(s), (7) select an order routine, and (8) obtain feedback and evaluate performance.

7.1 What are the four classifications of business buying situations? The four classifications of business buying are (1) straight rebuying, (2) modified rebuying, (3) new-task buying, and (4) reciprocity.

7.2 Differentiate between value analysis and vendor analysis. Value analysis examines each component of a purchase in an attempt to either delete the item or replace it with a more cost-effective substitute. Vendor analysis carries out an ongoing evaluation of a supplier's performance in categories such as price, EDI capability, backorders, delivery times, liability insurance, and attention to special requests.

8.1 Identify the five roles of people in a buying center decision. There are five buying center roles: users (those who use the product), gatekeepers (those who control the flow of information), influencers (those who provide technical information or specifications), deciders (those who actually choose the product), and buyers (those who have the formal authority to purchase).

8.2 What are some of the problems that U.S. marketers face in dealing with international buying centers? International buying centers pose several problems. First, there may be cultural differences in decision-making methods.

Second, a buying center in a foreign company typically includes more participants than is common in the United States. Third, international buying centers can change in response to political and economic conditions.

9.1 What are some influences on government purchases? Social goals and programs often influence government purchases.

9.2 Why is group purchasing important in institutional purchases? Group purchasing is an important factor because many institutions join cooperative associations to get quantity discounts.

9.3 What special factors influence international buying decisions? An effective international business marketer must be aware of foreign attitudes and cultural patterns. Other important factors include economic conditions, geographic characteristics, legal restrictions, and local industries.

Marketing Terms You Need to Know

business-to-business (B2B) marketing 170
commercial market 172
trade industries 173
resellers 173
customer-based segmentation 175
North American Industry Classification System (NAICS) 176
end-use application segmentation 176

customer relationship management (CRM) 177
global sourcing 181
derived demand 181
joint demand 182
inelastic demand 182
just-in-time (JIT)/just-in-time II (JIT II) 182
sole sourcing 182
offshoring 183

nearshoring 184
outsourcing 184
multiple sourcing 186
merchandisers 186
systems integration 186
category advisor (category captain) 186
straight rebuy 189
modified rebuy 189
new-task buying 190

reciprocity 190
value analysis 190
vendor analysis 190
buying center 191
user 191
gatekeeper 191
influencer 191
decider 191
buyer 191
remanufacturing 194

Assurance of Learning Review

1. Which is the largest segment of the business market? What role does the Internet play in the B2B market? What role do resellers play in the B2B market?

2. How is customer-based segmentation beneficial to B2B marketers? Describe segmentation by purchasing situation.

3. How do the sizes and numbers of buyers affect B2B marketers? Why are buyer–seller relationships so important in B2B marketing?

4. Give an example of each type of demand.

5. For what reasons might a firm choose an option other than making a good or service in-house? Why is outsourcing on the rise? How is offshoring different from outsourcing?

6. What are some of the environmental factors that may influence buying decisions? Identify organizational factors that may influence buying decisions. Describe the role of the professional buyer.

7. Why are there more steps in the organizational buying process than in the consumer buying process? Explain why feedback between buyers and sellers is important to the marketing relationship.

8. Give an example of a straight rebuy and a modified rebuy. Why is new-task buying more complex than the first two buying situations?

9. What buying center participant is a marketer likely to encounter first? In the buying center, who has the formal authority to make a purchase?

10. Describe some of the factors that characterize U.S. government purchases. Why are institutional markets particularly challenging?

Projects and Teamwork Exercises

1. As a team or individually, choose a commercial product—such as computer chips, flour for baking, paint, or equipment—and research and analyze its foreign market potential. Report your findings to the class.

2. In pairs, select a business product in one of two categories—capital or expense—and determine how derived demand will affect the sales of the product. Create a chart showing your findings.

3. Imagine you and your teammates are buyers for a firm such as Olive Garden, Dick's Sporting Goods, Marriott, or another company you like. Map out a logical buying process for a new-task purchase for your organization.

4. Form a team to conduct a hypothetical team selling effort for the packaging of products manufactured by a food company such as Kraft or General Mills. Have each team member cover a certain concern such as package design, delivery, and payment schedules. Present your marketing effort to the class.

5. Conduct research into the U.S. government's purchasing process. Select a federal agency or department such as the Environmental Protection Agency, National Aeronautics and Space Administration (NASA), or the Department of Health and Human Services. What types of purchases does it make? What is the range of contract amounts? Who are the typical suppliers? What type of process is involved in buying?

Critical-Thinking Exercises

1. Imagine you are a wholesaler for dairy products such as yogurt and cheese, which are produced by a cooperative of small farmers. Describe what steps you would take to build relationships with both the producers—farmers—and retailers such as supermarkets.

2. Describe an industry that might be segmented by geographic concentration. Then identify some of the types of firms that might be involved in that industry. Keep in mind that these companies might be involved in other industries as well.

3. Imagine you are in charge of making the decision to lease or buy a fleet of automobiles for the limousine service for which you work. What factors would influence your decision and why?

4. Do you think online selling to the federal government benefits marketers? What might be some of the drawbacks to this type of selling?

Ethics Exercise

Suppose you work for a well-known local restaurant, and a friend of yours is an account representative for a supplier of restaurant equipment. You know the restaurant owner is considering upgrading some of the kitchen equipment. Although you have no purchasing authority, your friend has asked you to arrange a meeting with the restaurant owner. You have heard unflattering rumors about this supplier's customer service.

1. Would you arrange the meeting between your friend and your boss?

2. Would you mention the customer service rumors either to your friend or your boss?

3. Would you try to influence the purchase decision in either direction?

Internet Exercises

1. **Marketing to airlines.** Boeing and Airbus are the two major manufacturers of commercial aircraft. Visit the Web sites of both firms. After you review the Web sites, prepare a report that compares and contrasts the marketing strategies employed by both firms.
www.boeing.com/commercial/
www.airbus.com/index.php?id=1217

2. **Marketing to small businesses.** According to some experts, there are important differences between marketing to large businesses compared with small businesses. Go to the Web sites listed here and review the material. Prepare a summary you can use in a class discussion on the topic.
http://www.entrepreneurslife.com/thoughts/channel/b2b-marketing/

http://www.score.org/sell_business_12_steps.html
http://smallbiztrends.com/2007/02/five-mistakes-when-selling-to-small-business-owners.html

3. **Selling to the federal government.** The General Services Administration (GSA) purchases billions of dollars worth of goods and services for various federal agencies. Visit the GSA's Web site to learn more about selling to the federal government.

What products does the GSA purchase? Who may sell products to the federal government? What are the requirements to become a federal government vendor?
http://www.gsa.gov/Portal/gsa/ep/home.do?tabId=0

Note: Internet Web addresses change frequently. If you don't find the exact site listed, you may need to access the organization's home page and search from there or use a search engine such as Google or Bing.

Case 6.1 *Peerless Pump Puts Customers First*

Pumps are the world's second most commonly used machines. They supply almost a quarter of global demand for electric motor energy. Peerless Pump Co. of Indianapolis has been providing reliable pumps for high-value applications in the industrial, municipal, agriculture, and

fire protection segments since 1923. By focusing on safety, quality, schedule, and cost—in that order—the firm has enjoyed steady growth and even increased its revenue expectations for the future. "Continued enthusiasm and management commitment make our future growth ambitions very attainable," says Fred Bock, Peerless vice president of marketing and business planning.

A company initiative called "One Peerless" focused the attention of the company's 430 employees, who work in many different global locations, on improving teamwork, communication, leadership, and continuous improvement (growth). "It is very easy to focus on needs, One Peerless takes a proactive approach to focusing on what our customers—both internal and external—truly want," Bock says. "One Peerless is a well-rounded operations, sales, and marketing plan that involves everyone associated with our company, from suppliers to employees to distributors to end users."

The company, with $120 million in annual sales, was acquired in 2007 from a private equity firm by Danish pump giant Grundfos, which has been expanding rapidly in eastern Europe and Asia, as well as a significant commitment to North America, where they see "significant growth potential."

"The synergies and similarities in corporate culture are significant and will allow for the acceleration of the growth that Peerless Grundfos have enjoyed over the past five years," added Bock, who also holds the position of North American Marketing Director for Grundfos.

Originally founded in California to supply agricultural irrigation pumps for orange growers, the company now counts water treatment facilities, stadiums, airports, and many of the world's tallest skyscrapers among its many clients. With energy costs increasing, such customers continue to increase their focus on saving money on operations wherever possible. Peerless assists its partners by applying a "life cycle cost" approach to its design and sales strategies by examining costs—in both time and resources—of repair rather versus replacement of less efficient equipment.

Looking at the costs associated with installation, maintenance, and especially energy consumption over the long term—some pumps are in service for more than 50 years—allows Peerless to compare all possible solutions, from which the customer can evaluate the best solution. The company identifies the particular pump features and specifications in each option that will best improve reliability and minimize energy consumption, even in pump systems that move large volumes of water 24 hours a day. Market growth for new equipment far exceeds repairs as a source of revenue; however, in order to minimize downtime from potential breakdowns and help customers make the right repair/replace decision, Peerless advocates and offers ongoing training of its engineers and customers in preventive maintenance and repair as well as recommending spare parts inventories. This strategic approach makes the continuous and open line of communication between the company and end user a necessity.

Questions for Critical Thinking

1. Do you think Peerless focuses on safety, quality, schedule, and cost in the right order to meet its customers' and distributors' needs? Why or why not? How do you think a B2B company can most accurately determine what its business customers need and want?

2. What benefits does Peerless gain from helping its customers evaluate system repair as a potential alternative to costly replacement of a pump system? What strategies and business tools do you think the company must have in place to fulfill this customer need? Why is it important for Peerless to address it, if it is not as profitable for the firm as selling a new system?

Sources: Personal communication with Fred Bock, Peerless Pump, April 2010; company Web site, www.peerlesspump.com, accessed April 15, 2010; "Grundfos Pumps Opens New Facility in Houston," *The Air Conditioning/Heating/Refrigeration News*, March 16, 2010; "Andrew Warrington Named Peerless Pump Company's New President," *CONTRACTORmag.com*, November 16, 2009.

Video Case 6.2
Business-to-Business Marketing at Flight 001

By the time each of us retires, we will probably have acquired thousands of useless gifts from our employers, clients, and vendors. Teeny staplers, space pens, solar desk clocks, binders, cheap calculators, and, of course, the ubiquitous tote bag emblazoned

with logos and slogans for products you don't want and will never own.

The folks at Flight 001 appreciate the work we do and want our employers to reward us with some better swag, so they offer a corporate gifting program to help big business say thank you with a little more style. "Everything is for travel, everything is useful," says Brad John of his travel boutique, Flight 001. "At all these big companies, everyone travels and we're useful, so we're really the perfect item for a corporate gift." To guard against re-gifting, Flight 001's consultant works one-on-one with corporate clients to find just the right gift.

It's nice that Flight 001 is looking out for the workers of America, but they get a return as well from the corporate gifting program. While Flight 001 has been very successful in its first 10 years in business and has plans to open at least 20 new shops in the next few years, it is important to the brand that it maintain its local, independent boutique feel. Part of that is resisting the lure of splashy paid advertising. With that off the table, the company uses programs like corporate gifting to get their products in the hands of their ultimate retail customer, the business traveler. The online travel search engine, Orbitz, recently placed a huge order for Flight 001's passport and document folder. Flight 001 agreed to print the Orbitz name on it, and Orbitz gave the folder away to its best customers. The program was a huge success, and Flight 001 saw an increase in requests for similar sales.

In the wholesale market, Flight 001 has been successful in identifying like-minded customers such as Northwest and Song airlines. One of their more successful partnerships has been with Jet Blue, an airline known for serving a younger, hipper traveler. Flight 001 offers some of their travel gear branded with both the Jet Blue and Flight 001 name via the airline's store.

Flight 001 hopes to start selling its products wholesale to boutique and luxury hotel chains. While they have sold to hotels in the past, they haven't had much success. An emerging trend in boutique hotels is an expanded mini-bar offering high-end cosmetics and other travel products for that late-night impulse buy. John is hoping to see Flight 001 products next to the macadamia nuts and Toblerone bars soon.

In comparing Flight 001's consumer retail market with its business-to-business market, John says, "Is it the most exciting part? No. But it's a very easy business."

Questions

1. How does marketing Flight 001's products to give as gifts to companies such as Orbitz affect sales at Flight 001's retail stores?

2. What potential conflicts might arise between Flight 001's wholesale business to Jet Blue and Northwest and Flight 001 retail business? Do you think their wholesale/retail strategy is sound? Why or why not?

ch7

Global
Marketing

1 Describe the importance of global marketing from the perspectives of the individual firm and the nation.

2 Identify the major components of the environment for global marketing.

3 Outline the basic functions of GATT, WTO, NAFTA, FTAA, CAFTA-DR, and the European Union.

4 Identify the alternative strategies for entering foreign markets.

5 Differentiate between a global marketing strategy and a multi-domestic marketing strategy.

6 Describe the alternative marketing mix strategies used in global marketing.

7 Explain the attractiveness of the United States as a target market for foreign marketers.

Pollo Campero: Flavor You Can't "Campero"...

Pollo Campero, in Spanish, means "country chicken." And, according to a growing population of devoted fans, the taste of this native Guatemalan dish is mouth-watering and incomparable. Today, Pollo Campero ranks as the world's largest Latin American chicken restaurant chain, serving more than 85 million customers a year and generating a whopping $400 million in global revenues.

The company was founded during the 1970s by Juan Bautista Gutiérrez, a Guatemalan poultry farmer who was looking for a distribution channel for his poultry. Gutierrez opened the first Pollo Campero restaurant in Guatemala City in 1971.

While many businesses grow through word of mouth, Pollo Campero seemed to grow by "word of nose." According to popular legend, news of the popular restaurant spread to the United States during the late 1990s because visitors to Guatemala would board airplanes for their flight home armed with Pollo Campero carryout boxes. The tantalizing aroma of Pollo Campero chicken would waft through the plane and engulf the cabin, creating such a stir that company management became aware of it and began to think seriously about entering the U.S. market.

When the company introduced its first U.S. store in Los Angeles, thousands of customers lined up outside the restaurant in the early-morning hours on Day One. Since then, Pollo Campero has opened more than 50 U.S. locations in 14 states and the District of Columbia, particularly in large cities like Chicago, Dallas, Houston, Miami, New York, and Phoenix.

In all, Pollo Campero and its franchisees operate more than 300 restaurants on four continents, in such countries as Andorra, Costa Rica, Ecuador, El Salvador, Honduras, Mexico, Nicaragua, Spain, and the United States in the West to Bahrain, China, India, and Indonesia in the East. Pollo Campero's first outlet in India opened in the food court of a New Delhi shopping mall, and the company expects to open 50 additional restaurants in India before 2012.

With its drive-thru window and restaurant layout, Pollo Campero may look and feel like a fast-food establishment, but it considers itself a family restaurant. And in terms of quality, the food is arguably several cuts above fast-food fare. In addition to its signature marinated and pressure-cooked fried chicken, Pollo Campero's authentic Latin American menu features such traditional side

© NEWSCOM

dishes as black beans and rice, yucca fries, fried plaintains, corn tortillas, and a selection of fresh salsas. For dessert, diners may choose caramel flan (a baked custard) or tres leches (a Spanish sponge cake). To make its menu more appealing to non-Hispanic customers in the United States, Pollo Campero broadened its fare with more common North American–style dishes, such as grilled chicken, chicken sandwiches, mashed potatoes, french fries, dinner rolls, Caesar salad, and cole slaw. Also in the United States, Pollo Campero restaurants offer a wide-ranging catering menu. Capitalizing on consumer interest in healthy eating, Pollo Campero has also introduced complete meals totaling no more than 505 calories.

Walt Disney World Resort recently announced that a Pollo Campero restaurant would replace McDonald's in the resort's Downtown Disney Marketplace. Pollo Campero predicts it will open 300 U.S. restaurants by 2014.

From a single restaurant in Central America, Juan Bautista Gutiérrez' business has grown into a global empire.[1]

evolution of a brand

A tasty fried chicken recipe has helped vault Pollo Campero to worldwide success. The combination of high-quality food served efficiently has proved to be a winning combination for this family-owned organization.

- Compared to fast-food competitors, Pollo Campero's offerings are generally more expensive. How does it manage to increase business despite its higher prices?

- Pollo Campero attracted non-Hispanic customers in the United States by adding traditional American foods, like french fries and mashed potatoes, to its menu. What should the company do to gain a foothold in the Middle East and Asia?

chapter overview

Global trade now accounts for nearly 30 percent of the U.S. gross domestic product (GDP), compared with 10 percent 30 years ago.[2] Figure 7.1 shows the top ten nations with which the United States trades. Those ten countries account for nearly 67 percent of U.S. imports and 62 percent of U.S. exports.

Global trade can be divided into two categories: **exporting**, marketing domestically produced goods and services abroad, and **importing**, purchasing foreign goods and services. Global trade is vital to a nation and its marketers for several reasons. It expands markets, makes production and distribution economies possible, allows companies to explore growth opportunities in other nations, and makes them less dependent on economic conditions in their home nations. Many also find that global marketing and trade can help them meet customer demand, reduce costs, and provide valuable information on potential markets around the world.

For North American marketers, trade with foreign markets is especially important because the U.S. and Canadian economies represent a mature market for many products. Outside North America, however, it is a different story. Economies in many parts of sub-Saharan Africa, Asia, Latin America, central Europe, and the Middle East are growing rapidly. This opens up new markets for U.S. products as consumers in these areas have more money to spend and as the need for American goods and services by foreign companies expands.

Global trade also builds employment. The United Nations estimates that 82,000 transnational corporations are operating today, employing about 77 million workers directly and through subsidiaries.[3] Many of these companies and their subsidiaries represent **related party trade**, which includes trade by U.S. companies with their subsidiaries overseas as well as trade by U.S. subsidiaries of foreign-owned firms with their parent companies. According to the U.S. Department of Commerce, related party trade in a recent year accounted for nearly 40 percent of total goods traded.[4] Because importing and exporting of so many goods and services play such an important role in the U.S. economy, your future job might very well involve global marketing, either here in the United States or overseas.

Global marketers carefully evaluate the marketing concepts described in other chapters. However, transactions that cross national borders involve additional considerations. For example, different laws, varying levels of technological capability, economic conditions, cultural and business norms, and consumer preferences often require new strategies. Companies that want to market their products worldwide must reconsider each of the marketing variables—product, distribution, promotion, and price—in terms of the global marketplace. To succeed in global marketing, today's marketers answer questions such as these:

- How do our products fit into a foreign market?
- How can we turn potential threats into opportunities?
- Which strategic alternatives will work in global markets?

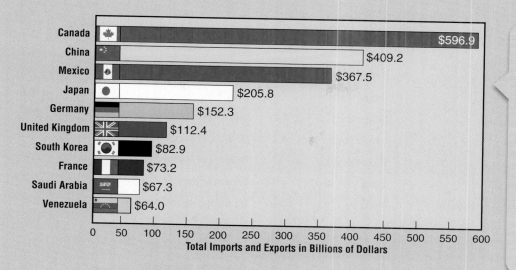

figure 7.1

Top U.S. Trading Partners—Total Trade Including Exports and Imports

Source: Data from U.S. Census Bureau, "Top Trading Partners—Total Trade, Exports, Imports," Foreign Trade Division, census.gov/foreign-trade/statistics, accessed February 25, 2010.

Many of the answers to these questions can be found by studying techniques used by successful global marketers. This chapter first considers the importance and characteristics of foreign markets. It then examines the international marketing environment, the trend toward multinational economic integration, and the steps that most firms take to enter the global marketplace. Next, the importance of developing a global marketing mix is discussed. The chapter closes with a look at the United States as a target market for foreign marketers.

The Importance of Global Marketing

As the list of the world's ten largest corporations shown in Table 7.1 reveals, half of these companies are headquartered in the United States. For most U.S. companies—both large and small—global marketing is rapidly becoming a necessity. The demand for foreign products in the fast-growing economies of the Pacific Rim and other Asian nations offers one example of the benefits of thinking globally. U.S. exports to China, Hong Kong, and Indonesia continue to rise year over year.[5] This increase was due partly to a weak American dollar, but also because Asian consumers believe American goods are higher quality than those made in their own countries. International marketers recognize how the slogan "Made in the USA" yields tremendous selling power.

Over the past decade, U.S. goods and services exports have increased more than 90 percent.[6] In a recent year, the United States exported more than $1.4 trillion in goods and services, making it the world's third-largest exporter behind Germany and China.[7] Among the leading U.S. firms in revenues generated from exports are Boeing, Intel, Motorola, and Caterpillar.

Walmart currently ranks as the world's largest private employer—with about 2.1 million employees—and the largest retailer; its annual sales are more than double those of Target, Sears, Costco, and Kmart combined. If Walmart were a country, industry observers estimate, it would rank seventh among China's trading partners, spending upwards of $18 billion per year in goods. The retail giant also allocates billions of dollars in expansion efforts abroad in China, Central America, India, Japan, South America, and the United Kingdom.[8]

The rapid globalization of business and the boundless nature of the Internet have made it possible for every marketer to become an international marketer. And while it isn't easy to be a successful marketer on the Web and larger firms have the advantage of more resources and wider distribution systems, smaller companies can build Web sites for as little as a few hundred dollars and

1 Describe the importance of global marketing from the perspectives of the individual firm and the nation.

table 7.1   World's Ten Largest Marketers (Ranked by Annual Sales)

Rank	Company	Country	Industry	Sales (in billions of dollars)
1	Walmart Stores	United States	Retailing	$408
2	Royal Dutch Shell	Netherlands	Oil and gas operations	278
3	ExxonMobil	United States	Oil and gas operations	276
4	BP	United Kingdom	Oil and gas operations	239
5	Toyota Motor	Japan	Consumer durable	211
6	Sinopec-China Petroleum	China	Oil and gas operations	208
7	ING Group	Netherlands	Insurance	167
8	Total	France	Oil and gas operations	161
9	Chevron	United States	Oil and gas operations	159
10	PetroChina	China	Oil and gas operations	157

Source: Data from "The Global 2000," *Forbes*, http://www.forbes.com, accessed April 21, 2010.

can bring products to market quickly. Coverity, a developer of tools that help companies uncover bugs in their software with its headquarters in San Francisco, has seen profits skyrocket beyond $20 million in Year 5 of its existence. Small companies like Coverity succeed by being nimble and identifying the unmet needs of prospective customers.[9]

Just as some firms depend on foreign and Internet sales, others rely on purchasing raw materials abroad as input for their domestic manufacturing operations. A North Carolina furniture manufacturer may depend on purchases of South and Central American teak, while 21st-century furniture retailers take advantage of increased Chinese-made styling and quality and their traditionally low prices. Among the top U.S. imports are crude oil, computers and computer accessories, medicinal and pharmaceutical preparations, and passenger cars.[10]

Service and Retail Exports

The United States has seen great shifts in the sources of its annual production over the years. In the 1800s, more than 90 percent of Americans worked in farming; today, less than 1.5 percent do. Likewise, manufactured goods no longer account for the lion's share of U.S. production output; today, only about 10 percent of the workforce works in manufacturing. Despite these shifts in the work population, the United States continues to produce record volumes of agricultural and manufactured goods.

The service industry has seen steady growth, with nearly 90 percent of Americans now working in services. Nearly four of every five dollars in the nation's gross domestic product comes from services such as banking, entertainment, business and technical services,

Walmart currently ranks as the world's largest employer, with about 2.1 million employees. The firm is devoting billions of dollars to expansion efforts abroad.

© IMAGINECHINA VIA AP IMAGES

retailing, and communications.[11] These figures represent a profound change from a largely manufacturing economy to a largely service economy. Still, manufacturers as diverse as Ford and Procter & Gamble strive to serve growing markets such as China. Ford's Focus compact and Fiesta subcompact models have sold well in China. P&G is the leading consumer products marketer in China, offering a number of its popular brands, including Crest, Olay, Safeguard, and Tide.[12]

In addition to agricultural products and manufactured goods, the United States is the world's largest exporter of services and retailing. Of the approximately $508 billion in annual U.S. service exports, about one-fifth of it comes from travel and tourism—money spent by foreign nationals visiting the United States.[13] But China is expected to become the number-one tourist destination in the world by 2020, as well as the fourth-largest source of tourists, with 100 million tourists projected per year. Already, an estimated 51 million Chinese travel outside their country each year. Hong Kong, the United States, and the United Kingdom account for the bulk of overseas investment in China's tourism industry.[14]

Profitable U.S. service exports include business and technical services such as engineering, financial, computing, legal services, insurance, and entertainment. The financial services industry, already a major presence outside North America, is expanding globally via the Internet. Today, even the most novice Web users visit finance Web sites to pay bills, do their banking, or trade stocks online. And, according to a recent survey, nearly four out of five U.S. households with Web access use online banking services.[15] A glance at the increasing number of foreign companies listed on the New York Stock Exchange illustrates the importance of global financial services. A number of global service exporters are household names in the United States: American Express, AT&T, Citigroup, Disney, and Allstate Insurance. Many earn a substantial percentage of their revenues from international sales. Others are smaller firms, such as the many software firms that have found overseas markets receptive to their products. Still others are nonprofit organizations such as the U.S. Postal Service, which is attempting to increase overall revenues by operating a worldwide delivery service. The USPS competes with for-profit firms such as UPS and Federal Express.

The entertainment industry is another major service exporter. Movies, TV shows, and music groups often travel to the ends of the earth to entertain their audiences. Almost a century of exposure to U.S.-made films, television programs and, more recently, music video clips has made international viewers more familiar with American culture and geography than that of any other nation on earth. The growing popularity of mixed martial arts led six TV networks in Australia, Europe, Latin America, and the United Kingdom to buy Strikeforce programming for broadcasting in their markets.[16]

U.S. retailers, ranging from Foot Locker and The Gap to Office Depot and Costco, have opened stores around the world. Abercrombie & Fitch, which operates more than 1,000 stores in the United States and major international cities like London, Milan, Tokyo, and Toronto, continues its global expansion with a store in Copenhagen.[17]

Benefits of Going Global

Besides generating additional revenue, firms expand operations outside their home country to gain other benefits, including new insights into consumer behavior, alternative distribution strategies, and advance notice of new products. By setting up foreign offices and production facilities, marketers may encounter new products, new approaches to distribution, or clever new promotions that they may apply successfully in their domestic market or in other international markets.

Global marketers typically are well positioned to compete effectively with foreign competitors. A major key to achieving success in foreign markets is the ability to adapt products to local preferences and culture. As discussed earlier, McDonald's succeeded outside the United States by paying attention to local tastes and modifying its menu. Similarly, Yum! Brands, parent of KFC and Pizza Hut, successfully launched KFC in 1987 by catering to Chinese tastes. China's first fast-food chain, KFC augmented its familiar chicken-based menu with such Chinese staples as fish, porridge, fried dough, beef rice, bean curd, and egg tarts. Today, the company looks to repeat its success as it targets the Indian market.[18]

briefly speaking

"Globalization and free trade do spur economic growth, and they lead to lower prices on many goods."

—Robert Reich
(b. 1946)
Former U.S. Secretary of Labor

Papa John's has more than 3,400 pizza shops worldwide. As local tastes differ, so do pizza toppings.

© IMAGINECHINA VIA AP IMAGES

A product as seemingly universal as pizza must be localized as well. Papa John's has more than 3,400 pizza shops in 30 countries. Expansion plans continue in Asia, where the company intends to open 50 restaurants across China and South Korea as well as additional stores in India, Ireland, Mexico, and Russia. But buying behaviors differ around the globe. While Americans tend to prefer carryout or home delivery, customers in China and Russia like to eat their pizza in a restaurant, so Papa John's built attractive seating areas and added soups and salads to the menu. In addition, as local tastes differ, so does Papa John's menu. In Egypt, the menu includes pasta and soups containing lentils, and the pizzas have exotic names: "Fisherman's Catch" includes shrimp and alfredo sauce; "Indian Splendor" features a topping of tandoori chicken.[19]

mktg: success

I'm Lovin' It—Russian Style

Background. McDonald's began dishing up burgers to a hungry public in the mid-1950s. After opening its first international restaurants in 1967—in Canada and Puerto Rico—the company was hungry for further expansion.

The Challenge. An opportunity presented itself in 1976 at the Winter Olympics in Montreal, when a McDonald's executive became acquainted with members of the Soviet Union's delegation. It was at the height of the Cold War: across the eastern border of Europe, the Iron Curtain was still in place, creating an ideological and physical boundary between East and West. Under communist rule, private business ownership in the Soviet Union was all but nonexistent. McDonald's business model called for a sophisticated supply chain for the 300+ ingredients required for the menu.

The Strategy. McDonald's built McComplex, a factory outside Moscow where every menu item was made from scratch—the hamburgers, the fries, the apple pies, and more. About 80 percent of the ingredients had to be imported, and

Because companies must perform the marketing functions of buying, selling, transporting, storing, standardizing and grading, financing, risk taking, and obtaining market information in both domestic and global markets, some may question the wisdom of treating global marketing as a distinct subject. But as this chapter will explain, there are similarities and differences that influence strategies for both domestic and global marketing.

assessment check

1. Define *importing* and *exporting*.
2. What is the largest category of exports from the United States?
3. What must global marketers do effectively to reach foreign markets?

The International Marketing Environment

As in domestic markets, the environmental factors discussed in Chapter 3 have a powerful influence on the development of a firm's global marketing strategy. Marketers must pay close attention to changing demand patterns as well as competitive, economic, social-cultural, political-legal, and technological influences when they venture abroad. The need for energy has hit the global market, so search for new, clean energy sources is a worldwide phenomenon, as the "Marketing Success" feature describes.

> **2** Identify the major components of the environment for global marketing.

International Economic Environment

A nation's size, per-capita income, and stage of economic development determine its prospects as a host for international business expansion. Nations with low per-capita incomes may be poor markets for expensive industrial machinery but good ones for agricultural hand tools. These nations cannot afford the technical equipment that powers an industrialized society. Wealthier countries may offer prime markets for many U.S. industries, particularly those producing consumer goods and services and advanced industrial products.

But some less industrialized countries are growing fast. India and China, for example, may rival the United States in world economic importance in a generation or two. Although the U.S. per-capita GDP of $46,400 ranks way above China's $6,500 and India's $2,900, these nations have far larger populations and thus more potential human capital to develop in the future.[20] Their ability to import

finding private local suppliers became a painstaking, decades-long process.

The Outcome. After a mind-boggling 14 years of negotiation, the first Russian McDonald's opened its doors on January 31, 1990. Located in Moscow's famed Pushkin Square, the restaurant served a record 30,000 customers on its first day in business. By this time, the Berlin Wall had toppled, the Soviet Union had started to come undone, and capitalism began to take root. Today, Western Russia is McDonald's fastest-growing European market, serving nearly a million customers per day. Private businesses in Russia now provide 80 percent of the menu ingredients. The Pushkin Square restaurant is the busiest McDonald's on the globe. McDonald's Russia has 245 stores in 60 cities, employing more than 25,000 people; an additional 45 outlets are planned.

Sources: Company Web site, http://www.mcdonalds. com, accessed February 27, 2010; Andrew E. Kramer, "Russia's Evolution, Seen through Golden Arches," *The New York Times*, February 2, 2010, http://www.nytimes. com; Nataliya Vasilyeva, "McMoscow Their Kind of Place," *Arkansas Democrat Gazette*, February 2, 2010, pages 1D, 6D; "McDonald's Celebrates 20th Anniversary in Russia," *Chain Leader*, February 1, 2010, http://www. chainleader.com.

technology and foreign capital, as well as to train scientists and engineers and invest in research and development, ensures that their growth will be rapid and their income gaps with the United States will close quickly. Most recently, India's GDP rose 6.6 percent and China's rose 10.1 percent, but the United States' GDP grew only 2.1 percent.[21]

infrastructure A nation's basic system of transportation networks, communications systems, and energy facilities.

Infrastructure—the underlying foundation for modern life and efficient marketing that includes transportation, communications, banking, utilities, and public services—is another important economic factor to consider when planning to enter a foreign market. An inadequate infrastructure may constrain marketers' plans to manufacture, promote, and distribute goods and services in a particular country. People living in countries blessed by navigable waters often rely on them as inexpensive, relatively efficient alternatives to highways, rail lines, and air transportation. Thai farmers use their nation's myriad rivers to transport their crops. Their boats even become retail outlets in so-called floating markets, like the one located outside Bangkok. Often the population in rural areas begins to shift to where the infrastructure is more developed. This change is happening in both China and India. In 15 years, China's cities are projected to have an additional 350 million people—more than the total population of the United States today. And in India, which claims one-sixth of the world's population, 42 cities have a population of 1 million or more, up from 32 such cities just two years ago.[22] Marketers expect developing economies to have substandard utility and communications networks. China encountered numerous problems in establishing a 21st-century communications industry infrastructure. The Chinese government's answer was to bypass the need for landline telephone connections by leapfrogging technologies and moving directly to cell phones.

exchange rate Price of one nation's currency in terms of another country's currency.

Changes in exchange rates can also complicate international marketing. An **exchange rate** is the price of one nation's currency in terms of another country's currency. Fluctuations in exchange rates can make a nation's currency more or less valuable compared with those of other nations. In today's global economy, imbalances in trade, dependence on fossil fuels, and other conditions affect the currencies of many countries, not just one or two. The rising cost of energy and raw materials, stricter business standards, and a faltering U.S. dollar contributed to price increases for most goods produced in China.[23]

At the beginning of the 21st century, most members of the European Union (EU) switched to the euro as the replacement to their traditional francs and liras. The long-range idea behind the new currency is that switching to a single currency will strengthen Europe's competitiveness in the global marketplace. Russian and many eastern European currencies are considered *soft currencies* that cannot be readily converted into such hard currencies as the dollar, euro, or Japanese yen.

International Social-Cultural Environment

Before entering a foreign country, marketers should study all aspects of that nation's culture, including language, education, religious attitudes, and social values. The French love to debate and are comfortable with frequent eye contact. In China, humility is a prized virtue, colors have special significance, and it is insulting to be late. Swedes value consensus and do not use humor in negotiations. Navigating these rules that are commonly understood among the citizens of a foreign country takes time, patience, and a willingness to learn about other cultures. The "Career Readiness" feature offers a few tips on doing business globally.

Language plays an important role in global marketing. Table 7.2 lists the world's ten most frequently spoken languages. Marketers must make sure not only to use the appropriate language or languages for a country but also to ensure the message is correctly translated and conveys the intended meaning.

Firms that rely on call centers located in India and staffed by Indian nationals have discovered an occasional language gap. But these employees do speak English, the worldwide language of commerce. Despite some glitches, the call centers, along with other outsourced operations, are booming—creating jobs and a new middle class in India. The country's economy has benefited hugely from the influx of foreign direct investment that came after the country loosened restrictions on foreign ownership. India now boasts the fastest-growing market for wireless services; mobile-phone sales tripled in a two-year period recently. IBM plans to recruit an additional 5,000 employees in India in an effort to expand its business process outsourcing (BPO) operations there.[24]

table 7.2 The World's Most Frequently Spoken Languages

Rank	Language	Number of Speakers
1	Mandarin (Chinese)	1.2 billion
2	Spanish	329 million
3	English	328 million
4	Arabic	221 million
5	Hindi	182 million
6	Bengali	181 million
7	Portuguese	178 million
8	Russian	144 million
9	Japanese	122 million
10	German	90 million

Source: Data from "Most Widely Spoken Languages in the World," www.infoplease.com, accessed February 27, 2010.

International Technological Environment

More than any innovation since the telephone, Internet technology has made it possible for both large and small firms to connect to the entire world. The Internet transcends political, economic, and cultural barriers, reaching every corner of the globe. It has made it possible for marketers to add new business channels. It also helps developing nations compete with industrialized nations. However, a huge gap still exists between the regions with the greatest Internet usage and those with the least. Asia, Europe, and North America together account for about 81 percent of the world's total Internet usage. Latin America and the Caribbean follow with 10 percent, while Africa accounts for nearly 4 percent, the Middle East 3 percent, and Oceania/Australia just below 2 percent. Despite those numbers, usage in the Middle East jumped more than 1,600 percent since 2000, and Africa's usage grew almost 1,400 percent.[25]

Technology presents challenges for global marketers that extend beyond the Internet and other telecommunications innovations. A major issue involving food marketers is genetic reengineering. Although U.S. grocery shelves are filled with foods grown with genetically modified organisms (GMOs), most Americans are unaware they are eating GMO foods because no labeling disclosures are required. In Europe, a number of countries—including Austria, Bulgaria, France, Germany, and Hungary—have banned the cultivation of GMO crops, but the European Court of Justice has yet to issue a ruling that would ban GMOs throughout the European Union.

A major issue involving food marketers is genetic reengineering. Although U.S. grocery shelves are filled with foods grown with genetically modified organisms (GMOs), most Americans are unaware they are eating GMO foods.

© ISTOCKPHOTO.COM/VALENTYN VOLKOV

career readiness Culture Tips for Marketing Professionals

When working with people in other countries, remember: one size does *not* fit all. Study up on a country's culture in advance. Though the differences can be subtle, you ignore them at your own peril.

- **Greetings vary by culture.** Americans shake hands, gripping firmly and pumping twice while looking the other person in the eye. In France and Germany, expect to pump only once. In the Middle East, the handshake may continue during introductions. The traditional Japanese greeting was a bow, not a handshake, but these days, you're likely to get a handshake with a lighter grip and possibly including a bow. Muslim women in traditional attire don't shake hands with men.

- **Be careful with humor.** Americans regard a smile and a joke as appropriate icebreakers, but not so in Russia, where lightheartedness is reserved for social settings. The mood is also serious in Germany. Expect to engage in small talk in China before getting down to business, but keep it impersonal.

- **"Here's my card."** Most cultures regard the business card as a representation of the person himself, so exchanging cards is not only practical but symbolic. Generally, present your card only after introductions have been made, and make sure it's face-up so the recipient can read it. To people from China, Hong Kong, Japan, or Singapore, present your card with both hands. Show respect by taking time to look at a business card offered to you, and place it carefully in front of you during a meeting. Put cards away deliberately and respectfully; never jam them into your pocket, particularly a back pocket.

- **Watch your hands.** The "OK" sign conveys different, sometimes obscene, meanings in other countries. In France, Germany, Sweden, and Switzerland, keep your hands out of your pockets unless you're reaching for your wallet. Belgians consider it rude to crack one's knuckles. Pointing is impolite in any country.

Sources: Edward Chalmers, "Business Etiquette in Europe," *AskMen.com*, http://www.askmen.com, accessed February 19, 2010; Armando Gomez, "Business Travel Etiquette," *AskMen.com*, http://www.askmen.com, accessed February 19, 2010; Lydia Ramsey, "International Business Etiquette Tips," *The Sideroad*, http://www.sideroad.com, accessed February 19, 2010; Emily Maltby, "Expanding Abroad? Avoid Cultural Gaffes," *The Wall Street Journal*, January 19, 2010, http://online.wsj.com.

With soaring food prices and global grain shortages, governments the world over are rethinking their position on foods made from crops that are engineered to resist pests and drought.[26] This complex issue affects almost every marketer in the global food industry.

International Political-Legal Environment

political risk assessment (PRA)
Units within a firm that evaluate the political risks of the marketplaces in which they operate as well as proposed new marketplaces.

Global marketers must continually stay abreast of laws and trade regulations in each country in which they compete. Political conditions often influence international marketing as well. Political unrest in places such as the Middle East, Africa, eastern Europe, Spain, Greece, and South America sometimes results in acts of violence such as destruction of a firm's property or even deaths from bombings or other violent acts. As a result, many Western firms have set up internal **political risk assessment (PRA)** units or turned to outside consulting services to evaluate the political risks of the marketplaces in which they operate.

The political environment also involves labor conditions in different countries. For decades, Chinese laborers have suffered workplace abuses including forced labor, withholding of pay, and other unfair practices. But that may be changing with the recent passage of a labor law that gives workers more rights.[27]

friendship, commerce, and navigation (FCN) treaties International agreements that deal with many aspects of commercial relations among nations.

The legal environment for U.S. firms operating abroad results from three forces: (1) international law, (2) U.S. law, and (3) legal requirements of host nations. International law emerges from treaties, conventions, and agreements among nations. The United States has many **friendship, commerce, and navigation (FCN) treaties** with other governments. These agreements set terms for various aspects of commercial relations with other countries such as the right to conduct business in the treaty partner's domestic market. Other international business agreements concern worldwide standards for various products, patents, trademarks, reciprocal tax treaties, export control, international air travel, and international communications. Since the 1990s, Europe has pushed for mandatory **ISO (International Organization for Standardization) certification**—internationally recognized standards that ensure a company's goods, services, and operations meet established quality levels. The organization has two sets of standards: the ISO 9000 series of standards sets requirements for quality in goods and services, and the ISO 14000 series sets standards for operations that minimize harm to the environment. Today, many U.S. companies follow these certification standards as well. Currently, organizations in 159 countries participate in both series.[28] The International Monetary Fund (IMF), another major player in the international legal environment, lends foreign exchange to nations that require it to conduct international trade. These agreements facilitate the entire process of world marketing.

The second dimension of the international legal environment, U.S. law, includes various trade regulations, tax laws, and import and export requirements affecting international marketing. One important law, the Export Trading Company Act of 1982, exempts companies from antitrust regulations so they can form export groups that offer a variety of products to foreign buyers. The law seeks to make it easier for foreign buyers to connect with U.S. exporters. The controversial Helms-Burton Act of 1996 strengthened international trade sanctions against the Cuban government. More than a decade later, argument still raged over whether the law should remain on the books or be repealed.

Another important law is the Foreign Corrupt Practices Act, which makes it illegal to bribe a foreign official in an attempt to solicit new or repeat sales abroad. This act has had a major impact on international marketing and mandates that adequate accounting controls be installed to monitor internal compliance. Violations can result in a $1 million fine for the firm and a $10,000 fine and five-year imprisonment for the individuals involved. This law has been controversial, mainly because it fails to clearly define what constitutes bribery. The 1988 Trade Act amended the law to include more specific statements of prohibited practices.

Finally, legal requirements of host nations affect foreign marketers. Despite China's many advances in recent years—and even as it attempts to build a modern economy—the Chinese government continues to censor the Internet. More than 338 million Chinese currently use the Internet—more than the entire population of the United States—and an active cadre of Chinese "hacktivists" works to outwit the government's firewall and help fellow citizens gain unfettered access.[29]

> **ISO (International Organization for Standardization) certification** Internationally recognized standards that ensure a company's goods, services, and operations meet established quality levels and its operations minimize harm to the environment.

Trade Barriers

Assorted trade barriers also affect global marketing. These barriers fall into two major categories: **tariffs**—taxes levied on imported products—and administrative, or nontariff, barriers. Some tariffs impose set taxes per pound, gallon, or unit; others are calculated according to the value of the imported item. Administrative barriers are more subtle than tariffs and take a variety of forms such as customs barriers, quotas on imports, unnecessarily restrictive standards for imports, and export subsidies. Because the GATT and WTO agreements (discussed later in the chapter) eliminated tariffs on many products, countries frequently use nontariff barriers to boost exports and control the flows of imported products.

The United States and other nations continually negotiate tariffs and other trade agreements. In 2010, China entered into a free trade agreement with the Association of Southeast Asian Nations (ASEAN). The agreement created the China–ASEAN Free Trade Area, or CAFTA, and represents the largest free trade area of developing nations, covering a total population of 1.9 billion with trade volume equivalent to $4.5 trillion. The agreement reduces the average tariff on goods from ASEAN nations to China from 9.8 percent 0.1 percent. In addition, the average tariff on Chinese goods to ASEAN nations dropped from 12.8 percent to 0.6 percent.[30]

> **tariff** Tax levied against imported goods.

TARIFFS

Tariffs can be classified as either revenue or protective tariffs. **Revenue tariffs** are designed to raise funds for the importing government. For years, most U.S. government revenue came from this source. **Protective tariffs**, usually higher than revenue tariffs, are designed to raise the retail price of an imported product to match or exceed that of a similar domestic product. Some countries use tariffs in a selective manner to discourage certain consumption practices and thereby reduce access to their local markets. For example, the United States has tariffs on luxury items such as Rolex watches and Russian caviar. In 1988, the United States passed the Omnibus Trade and Competitiveness Act

> **revenue tariffs** Taxes designed to raise funds for the importing government.
>
> **protective tariffs** Taxes designed to raise the retail price of an imported product to match or exceed that of a similar domestic product.

to remedy what it perceived as unfair international trade conditions. Under the so-called Super 301 provisions of the law, the United States can single out countries that unfairly impede trade with U.S. domestic businesses. If these countries do not open their markets within 18 months, the law requires retaliation in the form of U.S. tariffs or quotas on the offenders' imports into this country.

Governments sometimes use tariffs to retaliate for real or perceived threats by a trading partner. After Congress shut down a pilot program that permitted some Mexican truckers to operate on U.S. highways, Mexico protested by announcing tariffs on 90 U.S.-made goods ranging from produce and toiletries to sunglasses and curtain rods. Trade officials said they were careful not to place duties on U.S.-made goods for which local demand is great, to avoid hurting Mexican consumers. Meanwhile, U.S. truckers and other industries have felt significant impact from the tariffs.[31]

OTHER TRADE BARRIERS

In addition to direct taxes on imported products, governments may erect a number of other barriers, ranging from special permits and detailed inspection requirements to quotas on foreign-made items in an effort to stem the flow of imported goods—or halt them altogether. In one of the longest-running trade disputes, European shoppers paid about twice as much for bananas as did North Americans. Through a series of import license controls, Europe had limited the importation of bananas from Latin American countries in an effort to protect producers in former European colonies in Africa and the Caribbean, who pay no tariff. The World Trade Organization ruled that the European tariffs on imported bananas unfairly discriminated against Latin American banana growers. After 16 years of wrangling, the European Union reached an agreement with Latin American growers, which will make them subject to lower tariffs—and likely lower the cost of bananas in Europe.[32]

import quotas Trade restrictions limiting the number of units of certain goods that can enter a country for resale.

Other forms of trade restrictions include import quotas and embargoes. **Import quotas** limit the number of units of products in certain categories that can cross a country's border for resale. The quota is supposed to protect domestic industry and employment and preserve foreign exchange, but it doesn't always work that way. For more than 50 years, the United States imposed quotas on apparel from China and other countries. However, companies often found loopholes in the quota systems and wound up not only with huge profits but also plenty of jobs for their own workers. For years, global trade experts claimed the quotas did nothing to benefit the U.S. economy. Since then the United States has lifted import quotas on garments from China and Vietnam.[33]

embargo Complete ban on the import of specified products.

subsidies Government financial support of a private industry.

The ultimate quota is the **embargo**—a complete ban on the import of a product. In 1960, the United States instituted an embargo against Cuba in protest of Fidel Castro's dictatorship and the expropriation of property and disregard for human rights. Not only do the sanctions prohibit Cuban exports—cigars and sugar are the island's best-known products—to enter the country, but they also apply to companies that profit from property that Cuba's communist government expropriated from Americans following the Cuban Revolution. Some years ago, the discovery of mad cow disease and the potential for contaminated beef resulted in a number of embargoes. South Korea banned the importation of beef from the United States and the European Union. Later, South Korea

Thanks to a recent WTO ruling on banana importation, European shoppers are likely to see more bananas from Latin America in their supermarkets—along with a more affordable price.

modified the ban and agreed to accept beef products from U.S.-raised cattle under 30 months old, the age at which animals are believed to be at greater risk for mad cow disease.[34]

Other trade barriers include **subsidies**. China has long subsidized the cost of many products, such as gasoline, to boost consumption. When Chinese wireless carriers recently subsidized the cost of 3G (third-generation) handsets, they projected a six-fold increase

© SAUL LOEB/AFP/GETTY IMAGES

in sales.[35] Some nations also limit foreign ownership in the business sectors. And still another way to block international trade is to create so many regulatory barriers that it is almost impossible to reach target markets. China has a maze of regulations controlling trade, and while the government continues to lift the barriers, experienced businesspeople agree that it's important to have personal connections, or *guanxi*, to help navigate the bureaucratic challenges.[36]

Foreign trade can also be regulated by exchange control through a central bank or government agency. **Exchange control** means that firms that gain foreign exchange by exporting must sell foreign currencies to the central bank or other foreign agency, and importers must buy foreign currencies from the same organization. The exchange control authority can then allocate, expand, or restrict foreign exchange according to existing national policy.

Dumping

The practice of selling a product in a foreign market at a price lower than it commands in the producer's domestic market is called **dumping**. Critics of free trade often argue that foreign governments give substantial support to their own exporting companies. Government support may permit these firms to extend their export markets by offering lower prices abroad. In retaliation for this interference with free trade, the United States adds import tariffs to products that foreign firms dump on U.S. markets to bring their prices in line with those of domestically produced products. However, businesses often complain that charges of dumping must undergo a lengthy investigative and bureaucratic procedure before the government assesses import duties. U.S. firms claiming that dumping threatens to hurt their business can file a complaint with the U.S. International Trade Commission (ITC), which—on average—rejects about half the claims it receives.

China recently fined the United States for dumping chicken feet into the Chinese market. Poultry processors in the United States see China an attractive destination for the item, considered virtually worthless in America but regarded as a delicacy in southern China.[37]

exchange control
Method used to regulate international trade among importing organizations by controlling access to foreign currencies.

dumping Controversial practice of selling a product in a foreign market at a price lower than what it receives in the producer's domestic market.

free-trade area Region in which participating nations agree to the free trade of goods among themselves, abolishing tariffs and trade restrictions.

 assessment check

1. What are the three criteria that determine a nation's prospects as a host for international business expansion?

2. What is an FCN treaty?

3. What are the two major categories of trade barriers?

Multinational Economic Integration

A noticeable trend toward multinational economic integration has developed over the nearly seven decades since the end of World War II. Multinational economic integration can be set up in several ways. The simplest approach is to establish a **free-trade area** in which participating nations agree to the free trade of goods among themselves, abolishing tariffs and trade restrictions. A **customs union** establishes a free-trade area plus a uniform tariff for trade with nonmember nations, and a **common market** extends a customs union by seeking to reconcile all government regulations affecting trade. Despite the many factors in its favor, not everyone is enthusiastic about free trade. For more than a decade, Americans have lost jobs when employers outsourced their work to countries like Mexico, where wages are lower. Now, workers in Mexico face the same outsourcing threat as their employers begin outsourcing work to China, where wages are even lower. Although productivity and innovation are said to grow more quickly with free trade, workers often find themselves working longer and for reduced pay as operations move overseas. But many firms view the change as a way to offer superior service. The "Solving an Ethical Controversy" feature debates another issue related to trade: the pros and cons of banning the sale of bottled water in a community.

3 Outline the basic functions of GATT, WTO, NAFTA, FTAA, CAFTA-DR, and the European Union.

customs union
Establishment of a free-trade area plus a uniform tariff for trade with nonmember unions.

common market
Extension of a customs union by seeking to reconcile all government regulations affecting trade.

solving an ethical controversy

ⓟutting the Lid on Bottled Water

Bottled water is big business. In a recent year, Americans consumed nearly 9 billion gallons of the stuff. But many people believe bottled water is also an environmental nuisance. Environmentalists say it takes more than 17 million barrels of oil to produce the plastic bottles for just one year's consumption in the United States—enough to power a million cars in a year.

The bottles are also an environmental hazard. According to a recent estimate, less than one-fifth of them are properly recycled, with the rest ending up as litter or in landfills. Many municipalities—from San Francisco to Takoma Park, Maryland—have laws limiting the sale of bottled water. Though Vancouver officials voted in 2009 to phase out the sale of bottled water in government buildings, the city was obliged to honor earlier contracts that permitted sales of bottled water at the 2010 Winter Olympics. Little Bundanoon, Australia—population 2,000—is believed to be the first city to ban the sale of bottled water altogether.

Should the sale of bottled water be banned?

PRO

1. Bottled water is too expensive. In most cases, it's merely tap water sold at highly inflated prices.

2. Plastic bottles are bad for the environment and manufacturing them requires oil, a scarce resource.

3. Scientists have discovered health hazards connected with the plastic in bottles.

CON

1. Bottled water is a 21st-century convenience.

2. In underdeveloped countries and in areas hit by natural disaster (such as earthquakes in Haiti and Chile), the absence of potable water can be life-threatening. Bottled water becomes a necessity.

3. Bottled-water marketers are redesigning bottles to use less plastic, and many sponsor recycling programs.

Summary

Many consumers stopped buying bottled water during the recession; meanwhile, the environmental outcry continues to pick up steam. Watch for more developments on this hot issue.

Sources: Tiffany Crawford, "Vancouver's Push to Ban Plastic Bottles Won't Hold during Olympics," *Vancouver Sun*, January 29, 2010, http://www.vancouversun.com; Isobel Drake, "Asia Boosts Global Bottled Water Market," *Australian Food News*, January 15, 2010, http://www.ausfoodnews.com; "Bottle Ban," *Sunday Herald Sun*, October 11, 2009, http://www.heraldsun.com.au; Kathy Marks, "The Australian Town That Kicked the Bottle; Drinking Fountains Replace Shop-Bought Mineral Water in Environmental Initiative," *Independent*, September 28, 2009, http://www.independent.co.uk; Nadia Jamal, "Bottler of Idea as Town Doesn't Go with the Flow," *Sunday Herald Sun*, September 27, 2009, http://www.heraldsun.com.au; "Australian Town in 'World-First' Bottled Water Ban," *Space & Earth*, September 26, 2009, http://www.physorg.com; "Aussie Town Votes to Ban Bottled Water," *Toronto Star*, September 8, 2009, http://www.thestar.com; Ylan Q. Mui, "Bottled Water Boom Appears Tapped Out," *Washington Post*, August 13, 2009, http://www.washingtonpost.com.

GATT and the World Trade Organization

General Agreement on Tariffs and Trade (GATT) International trade accord that has helped reduce world tariffs.

The **General Agreement on Tariffs and Trade (GATT)**, a trade accord that has sponsored several rounds of major tariff negotiations, substantially reducing worldwide tariff levels, has existed for six decades. In 1994, a seven-year series of GATT conferences, the Uruguay Round, culminated in one of the biggest victories for free trade in decades. The Uruguay Round reduced average tariffs by one-third, or more than $700 billion. Among its major victories:

- reduced farm subsidies, which opened vast new markets for U.S. exports;

- increased protection for patents, copyrights, and trademarks;

- included services under international trading rules, creating opportunities for U.S. financial, legal, and accounting firms; and

- phased-out import quotas on textiles and clothing from developing nations, a move that cost textile workers thousands of jobs when their employers moved many of these domestic jobs to lower-wage countries, but benefited U.S. retailers and consumers.

A key outcome of the GATT talks was establishment of the **World Trade Organization (WTO)**, a 153-member organization that succeeds GATT. The WTO oversees GATT agreements, serves as a forum for trade negotiations, and mediates trade disputes. It also monitors national trade policies and works to reduce trade barriers throughout the world. Unlike GATT, WTO decisions are binding. Countries that seek to become members of the WTO must participate in rigorous rounds of negotiations that can last several years. Russia holds the record: having applied for membership in 1993, its application is still in negotiations.[38]

To date, the WTO has made slow progress toward its major policy initiatives: liberalizing world financial services, telecommunications, and maritime markets. Trade officials have not agreed on the direction for the WTO. Big differences between developed and developing nations create a major roadblock to its progress, and its activities thus far have focused more on dispute resolution through its Dispute Settlement Body than on reducing trade barriers. But the WTO also provides important technical assistance and training for the governments of developing countries.[39]

The NAFTA Accord

More than a decade after the passage of the **North American Free Trade Agreement (NAFTA)**, an agreement between the United States, Canada, and Mexico that removes trade restrictions among the three nations, negotiations among the nations continue. The three countries insist that they will not create a trade bloc similar to the European Union, that is, they will not focus on political integration but instead on economic cooperation. NAFTA is particularly important to U.S. marketers because Canada and Mexico are two of its largest trading partners.

But NAFTA is a complex issue, and from time to time groups in one or more of the three countries chafe under the agreement. In Mexico, farm workers have charged that NAFTA puts their industry at a disadvantage. In Canada, some observers claim NAFTA has compromised their country's oil reserves. And in the United States, critics argue that U.S. workers lose jobs to cheap labor south of the border. Yet since NAFTA's passage, these three countries daily conduct more than $2 billion in trade with each other and have experienced GDP growth as a result.[40]

The Free Trade Area of the Americas and CAFTA-DR

NAFTA was the first step toward creating a **Free Trade Area of the Americas (FTAA)**, stretching the length of the entire Western Hemisphere, from Alaska's Bering Strait to Cape Horn at South America's southern tip, encompassing 34 countries, a population of 800 million, and a combined gross domestic product of more than $11 trillion. The FTAA would be the largest free-trade zone on earth and would offer low or nonexistent tariffs; streamlined customs; and no quotas, subsidies, or other barriers to trade. In addition to the United States, Canada, and Mexico, countries expected to become members of the proposed FTAA include Argentina, Brazil, Chile, Colombia, Ecuador, Guatemala, Jamaica, Peru, Trinidad and Tobago, Uruguay, and Venezuela. The United States is a staunch supporter of the FTAA, which still has many hurdles to overcome as countries wrangle for conditions most favorable to them.

As FTAA negotiations continue, the United States entered into an agreement with the Dominican Republic and Central American nations known as the **Central American Free Trade Agreement-DR (CAFTA-DR)**. Some of its provisions took effect immediately, while others will phase in over the next two decades. Supporters of the agreement say it will help American workers, farmers, and small businesses thrive and grow; critics worry that more American agricultural and manufacturing jobs will be lost. However, both sides agree that CAFTA's economic impact is likely to be relatively small compared with NAFTA.[41]

World Trade Organization (WTO) Organization that replaces GATT, overseeing GATT agreements, making binding decisions in mediating disputes, and reducing trade barriers.

North American Free Trade Agreement (NAFTA) Accord removing trade barriers among Canada, Mexico, and the United States.

Free Trade Area of the Americas (FTAA) Proposed free-trade area stretching the length of the entire Western Hemisphere and designed to extend free trade benefits to additional nations in North, Central, and South America.

Central American Free Trade Agreement–DR (CAFTA-DR) Trade agreement among the United States, Central American nations, and the Dominican Republic.

The European Union

European Union (EU)
Customs union that is moving in the direction of an economic union by adopting a common currency, removing trade restrictions, and permitting free flow of goods and workers throughout the member nations.

The best-known example of a multinational economic community is the **European Union (EU)**. As Figure 7.2 shows, 27 countries make up the EU: Austria, Belgium, Bulgaria, Cyprus, the Czech Republic, Denmark, Estonia, Finland, France, Germany, Greece, Hungary, Ireland, Italy, Latvia, Lithuania, Luxembourg, Malta, the Netherlands, Poland, Portugal, Romania, Slovakia, Slovenia, Spain, Sweden, and the United Kingdom. Three countries—Croatia, Macedonia, and Turkey—are candidates for membership. With a total population of more than 492 million people, the EU forms a huge common market.[42]

The goal of the EU, headquartered in Belgium, is eventually to remove all barriers to free trade among its members, making it as simple and painless to ship products between Sweden and Hungary as it is between New Mexico and Ohio. Also involved is the standardization of currencies and regulations that businesses must meet. Introduced in 1999, the EU's euro is the common currency in 16 member-countries, with eight other EU countries planning to phase it in over time. Only Denmark, Sweden, and the United Kingdom have declined to use the euro.

In addition to simplifying transactions among members, the EU looks to strengthen its position in the world as a political and economic power. Its recently ratified Treaty of Lisbon is designed to further streamline operations and enables the EU to enter into international agreements as a political entity.[43]

In some ways, the EU is making definite progress toward its economic goals. It is drafting standardized eco-labels to certify that products are manufactured according to certain environmental standards, as well as creating guidelines governing marketers' uses of customer information. Marketers can also protect some trademarks throughout the entire EU with a single application and registration process through the Community Trademark (CTM), which simplifies doing business and eliminates having to register with each member-country. Yet marketers still face challenges when selling their products in the EU. Customs taxes differ, and no uniform postal system exists. Using one toll-free phone number for several countries will not work, either, because each country

figure 7.2
The 27 Members of the European Union

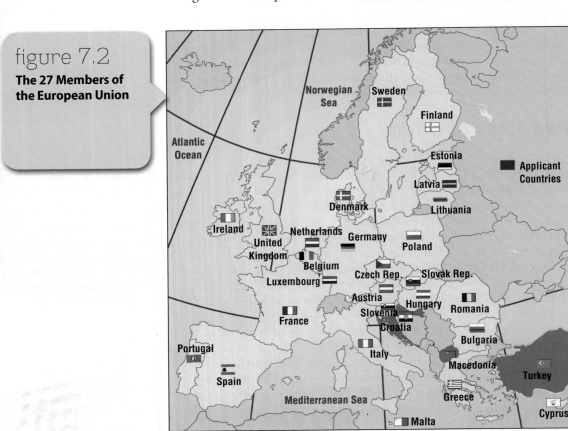

has its own telephone system for codes and numbers. Mexico negotiated a trade agreement with the EU that makes it easier for European companies to set up operations in Mexico. The agreement gives EU companies the same privileges enjoyed by the United States and Canada and brings new investors to Mexico.

assessment check

1. What is the World Trade Organization?
2. What countries are parties to the NAFTA accord?
3. What is the goal of the European Union?

Going Global

Globalization affects almost every industry and individual throughout the world, at least in some way. Traditional marketers who take their firms global may do so because they already have strong domestic market shares or their target market is too saturated to offer any substantial growth. Sometimes, by evaluating key indicators of the marketing environment, marketers can move toward globalization at an optimal time. The German footwear firm Adidas made a big jump into the global market after its successful "Impossible Is Nothing" ad campaign, announcing it would purchase rival Reebok in an effort to overtake number-one competitor Nike.

Using the benefits of the EU while also making a play for the Asian market, Adidas marketers believe they have a good chance at winning the global game. Making deals with athletes, such as British soccer legend David Beckham and Italian tennis star Flavia Pennetta, and licensing agreements for major U.S. sports leagues have helped Adidas strengthen its brand in major markets around the world. Recently, the firm scored one of its biggest coups to date: introducing the official match ball for soccer's 2010 World Cup.[44]

Most large firms—and many smaller businesses—already participate in global commerce, and virtually every domestic marketer, large or small, recognizes the need to investigate whether to market its products overseas. It is not an easy step to take, requiring careful evaluation and preparation of a

German footwear firm Adidas made a big jump into the global market after its successful "Impossible Is Nothing" ad campaign.

© COURTESY OF ADIDAS

strategy. Common reasons that marketers cite for going global include globalization of customers, new customers in emerging markets, globalization of competitors, reduced trade barriers, advances in technology, and enhanced customer responsiveness.

Strategies for Entering Foreign Markets

Successful global marketing starts at the top. Without the enthusiasm and support of senior managers, an initiative is likely to fail. Once marketers have researched and identified markets for expansion and won the support of leadership, they may choose from three basic strategies for entering foreign markets: importing and exporting; contractual agreements such as franchising, licensing, and subcontracting; and international direct investment. As Figure 7.3 shows, the level of risk and the firm's degree of control over international marketing increase with greater involvement. Firms often use more than one of these entry strategies.

Importing and Exporting

An importer is a firm that brings in goods produced abroad to sell domestically or to be used as components in its products. In making import decisions, the marketer must assess local demand for the product, taking into consideration factors such as the following:

- ability of the supplier to maintain agreed-to quality levels;
- flexibility in filling orders that might vary considerably from one order to the next;
- response time in filling orders; and
- total costs—including import fees, packaging, and transportation—in comparison with costs of domestic suppliers.

Exporting, another basic form of global marketing, involves a continuous effort in marketing a firm's merchandise to customers in other countries. Many firms export their products as the first step in reaching foreign markets. Furniture manufacturer IKEA has built an entire exporting strategy around its modular furniture. Because IKEA's furniture is lightweight, packs flat, and comes in components that customers can assemble, the firm can ship its goods almost anywhere in the world at a low cost, unlike manufacturers of traditional furniture.[45]

First-time exporters can reach foreign customers through one or more of three alternatives: export-trading companies, export-management companies, or offset agreements. An export-trading company (ETC) buys products from domestic producers and resells them abroad. While manufacturers lose control over marketing and distribution to an ETC, it helps them export through a relatively simple and inexpensive channel, in the process providing feedback about the overseas market potential of their products.

The second option, an export-management company (EMC), provides the first-time exporter with expertise in locating foreign buyers, handling necessary paperwork, and ensuring that its goods

Degree of Control

Low · Moderate · High

Exporting and Importing	Contractual Agreements Franchising Foreign Licensing Subcontracting	International Direct Investment Acquisitions Joint Ventures Overseas Divisions

Low · Moderate · High

Degree of Risk

meet local labeling and testing laws. However, the manufacturer retains more control over the export process when it deals with an EMC than if it were to sell the goods outright to an export-trading company. Smaller firms can get assistance with administrative needs such as financing and preparation of proposals and contracts from large EMC contractors.

The final option, entering a foreign market under an offset agreement, teams a small firm with a major international company. The smaller firm essentially serves as a subcontractor on a large foreign project. This entry strategy provides new exporters with international experience, supported by the assistance of the primary contractor, in such areas as international transaction documentation and financing.

Contractual Agreements

As a firm gains sophistication in global marketing, it may enter contractual agreements that provide several flexible alternatives to exporting. Both large and small firms can benefit from these methods. Franchising and foreign licensing, for example, are good ways to take services abroad. Subcontracting agreements may involve either production facilities or services.

FRANCHISING

A **franchise** is a contractual arrangement in which a wholesaler or retailer (the franchisee) agrees to meet the operating requirements of a manufacturer or other franchiser. The franchisee receives the right to sell the products and use the franchiser's name as well as a variety of marketing, management, and other services. Fast-food companies such as McDonald's have been active franchisers around the world.

One advantage of franchising is risk reduction by offering a proven concept. Standardized operations typically reduce costs, increase operating efficiencies, and provide greater international recognizability. However, the success of an international franchise depends on its willingness to balance standard practices with local customer preferences. McDonald's, Pizza Hut, and Domino's are expanding into India with special menus that feature lamb, chicken, and vegetarian items, in deference to Hindu and Muslim customers who do not eat beef and pork.

> **franchise** Contractual arrangement in which a wholesaler or retailer agrees to meet the operating requirements of a manufacturer or other franchiser.

FOREIGN LICENSING

A second method of going global through the use of contractual agreements is **foreign licensing**. Such an agreement grants foreign marketers the right to distribute a firm's merchandise or to use its trademark, patent, or process in a specified geographic area. These arrangements usually set certain time limits, after which agreements are revised or renewed.

Licensing offers several advantages over exporting, including access to local partners' marketing information and distribution channels and protection from various legal barriers. Because licensing does not require capital outlays, many firms, both small and large, regard it as an attractive entry strategy. Like franchising, licensing allows a firm to quickly enter a foreign market with a known product. The arrangement may also provide entry into a market that government restrictions close to imports or international direct investment. Entertainment software producer Electronic Arts entered into licensing agreements with consumer electronics accessory manufacturers to create and distribute accessories for iPod, Nintendo DS, and Wii under its EA SPORTS brand.[46]

> **foreign licensing** Agreement that grants foreign marketers the right to distribute a firm's merchandise or to use its trademark, patent, or process in a specified geographic area.

SUBCONTRACTING

A third strategy for going global through contractual agreements is **subcontracting**, in which the production of goods or services is assigned to local companies. Using local subcontractors can prevent mistakes involving local culture and regulations. Manufacturers might subcontract with a local company to produce their goods or use a foreign distributor to handle their products abroad or provide customer service. Manufacturing within the country can provide protection from import duties and may be a lower-cost alternative that makes it possible for the product to compete with local offerings. But it can also have a downside if local suppliers don't make the grade or if a manufacturer imposes an unrealistically tight timeframe on a supplier to deliver the product, leading to long hours or sweatshop conditions in the factory.[47]

> **subcontracting** Contractual agreements that assign the production of goods or services to local or smaller firms.

International Direct Investment

Another strategy for entering global markets is international direct investment in foreign firms, production, and marketing facilities. Because the United States is the world's largest economy, its foreign direct investment inflows and outflows—the total of American investments abroad and foreign investments in the United States—are more than double France's and two and a half times more than the United Kingdom's, its two largest competitors. U.S. direct investment abroad is nearly $3.2 trillion, with its greatest presence in Canada, the Netherlands, and the United Kingdom. On the other hand, foreign direct investment in the United States in a recent year totaled almost $2.3 trillion and originated chiefly through investors in Europe, the United Kingdom, and Japan.[48]

Although high levels of involvement and high risk potential are characteristics of investments in foreign countries, firms choosing this method often have a competitive advantage. Direct investment can take several forms. A company can acquire an existing firm in a country where it wants to do business, or it can set up an independent division outside its own borders with responsibility for production and marketing in a country or geographic region. Chinese firms have been seeking to purchase U.S. businesses, mostly in industries involving natural resources such as oil, natural gas, metals, and coal. However, they have been making inroads in industrial, technology, and finance companies as well. Chinese investment in U.S. companies now outstrips U.S. investment in China.[49] U.S. technology is attractive to many would-be acquirers. Multinational conglomerate AREVA, a leading nuclear power firm, recently bought U.S.-based Ausra, a provider of solar-power solutions for electricity generation and industrial steam production. AREVA made the acquisition to solidify its position in the renewable energy sector. The company relocated its world headquarters to Ausra's former headquarters in Mountain View, California.[50]

Companies may also engage in international marketing by forming joint ventures in which they share the risks, costs, and management of the foreign operation with one or more partners. These partnerships join the investing companies with nationals of the host countries. While some companies choose to open their own facilities overseas, others share with their partners. Because India puts limits on foreign direct investment, Walmart formed a partnership with Indian conglomerate Bharti Enterprises to open wholesale cash-and-carry stores in India. The stores do business under the name BestPrice Modern Wholesale.[51]

Although joint ventures offer many advantages, foreign investors have encountered problems in several areas throughout the world, especially in developing economies. Lower trade barriers, new technologies, lower transport costs, and vastly improved access to information mean that many more partnerships will be involved in international trade.

 assessment check

1. What are the three basic strategies for entering foreign markets?
2. What is a franchise?
3. What is international direct investment?

From Multinational Corporation to Global Marketer

A multinational corporation is a firm with significant operations and marketing activities outside its home country. Examples of multinationals include General Electric, Siemens, and Mitsubishi in heavy electrical equipment, and Timex, Seiko, and Citizen in watches. Since they first became a force in international business in the 1960s, multinationals have evolved in some important ways. First, these companies are no longer exclusively U.S.–based. Today, it is as likely for a multinational to be based in Japan, Germany, or Great Britain as in the United States. Second, multinationals no longer think of their foreign operations as mere outsourcing appendages that carry out the design, production, and engineering ideas conceived at home. Instead, they encourage constant exchanges of ideas, capital, and technologies among all the multinational operations.

Multinationals often employ huge foreign workforces relative to their American staffs. More than half of all Ford and IBM personnel are located outside the United States. These workforces are no longer seen merely as sources of cheap labor; on the contrary, many multinationals center technically complex activities in locations throughout the world. Texas Instruments does much of its research, development, design, and manufacturing in East Asia. It is increasingly common for U.S. multinationals to bring product innovations from their foreign facilities back to the States.

Multinationals have become global corporations that reflect the interdependence of world economies, the growth of international competition, and the globalization of world markets. However, many people worry that this globalization means that U.S. dominance in many markets will decline and disappear. Sixty percent of households in Hong Kong get their television services through ultra-high-speed broadband connections that turn their TVs into computers, a concept still catching on slowly in the United States. European and Asian consumers now use smart cards with embedded memory chips instead of traditional credit cards or cash for retail purchases. Chile has emerged as a highly attractive destination for multinational firms seeking to expand their "global footprint" by outsourcing some functions, particularly if the firms serve both English- and Spanish-speaking customers. Swiss engineering and technology giant ABB recently chose Chile as the site of its first remote service center. The center provides real-time monitoring, diagnostics, and technical assistance for a number of ABB's businesses.[52]

briefly speaking

"Learn Chinese. There's going to be a lot of action in China."

—Lakshmi Narayanan
CEO, Cognizant Technologies

---

assessment check

1. What is a multinational corporation?
2. What are two ways in which multinationals have changed since the 1960s?

Developing an International Marketing Strategy

In developing a marketing mix, international marketers may choose between two alternative approaches: a global marketing strategy or a multidomestic marketing strategy. A **global marketing strategy** defines a standard marketing mix and implements it with minimal modifications in all foreign markets. This approach brings the advantage of economies of scale to production and marketing activities. Procter & Gamble marketers follow a global marketing strategy for Pringles potato chips, a leading export brand. P&G began by selling one product with a consistent formulation in every country and meets 80 percent of worldwide demand with only six flavors of Pringles and one package design. This standardized approach saves money because it allows large-scale production runs and reinforces the brand's image. In addition, a global strategy can foster collaborative innovation, as with the development of Pringles Stixx, a recent extension of the popular product line.[53]

A global marketing perspective can effectively market some goods and services to segments in many nations that share cultures and languages. This approach works especially well for products with strong, universal appeal such as McDonald's, luxury items such as Rolex watches, and high-tech brands such as Microsoft. Global advertising outlets such as international editions of popular consumer and business magazines and international transmissions of TV channels such as

5 Differentiate between a global marketing strategy and a multidomestic marketing strategy.

global marketing strategy Standardized marketing mix with minimal modifications that a firm uses in all of its domestic and foreign markets.

A global marketing strategy can be highly effective for luxury products like diamonds that target upscale consumers. These ads typically have little copy, just a beautiful photo of the product.

Fox, CNN, MTV, and the CNBC financial network help marketers deliver a single message to millions of global viewers. DIRECTV recently became the exclusive satellite TV provider of RTVi, an independent Russian-language TV network reaching more than 50 million viewers across the globe.[54]

A global marketing strategy can also be highly effective for luxury products that target upscale consumers everywhere. Marketers of diamonds and luxury watches, for instance, typically use advertising with little or no copy—just a picture of a beautiful diamond or watch with the name discreetly displayed on the page.

But a global strategy doesn't always work, as Domino's discovered after it opened stores in Asia during the late 1990s. With its "30-minutes-or-it's-free" policy, the pizza purveyor has been known for the fastest pizzas rather than the best-tasting ones. Apparently for Asians, the 30-minute guarantee wasn't attractive enough to offset how the food tasted, and Domino's ended up closing more than 50 stores in Hong Kong, Indonesia, Singapore, and Thailand from 1997 to 2001. Recently, Domino's threw out its 50-year-old recipe and underwent a pizza makeover. Armed with a bold, new taste, Domino's reentered Singapore, with plans to open a total of nine stores there.[55]

A major benefit of a global marketing strategy is its low cost to implement. Most firms, however, find it necessary to practice market segmentation outside their home markets and tailor their marketing mixes to fit the unique needs of customers in specific countries. This **multidomestic marketing strategy** assumes that differences between market characteristics and competitive situations in certain nations require firms to customize their marketing decisions to effectively reach individual marketplaces. Many marketing experts believe that most products demand multidomestic marketing strategies to give them realistic global marketing appeal. Cultural, geographic, language, and other differences simply make it difficult to send the same message to many countries. Specific situations may allow marketers to standardize some parts of the marketing process but customize others.

multidomestic marketing strategy Application of market segmentation to foreign markets by tailoring the firm's marketing mix to match specific target markets in each nation.

 assessment check

1. What is the difference between a global marketing strategy and a multidomestic marketing strategy?

International Product and Promotional Strategies

Global marketers can choose from among five strategies for selecting the most appropriate product and promotion strategy for a specific foreign market: straight extension, promotion adaptation, product adaptation, dual adaptation, and product invention. As Figure 7.4 indicates, the strategies center on whether to extend a domestic product and promotional strategy into international markets or adapt one or both to meet the target market's unique requirements.

A firm may follow a one-product, one-message straight extension strategy as part of a global marketing strategy. This strategy permits economies of scale in production and marketing. Also, successful implementation creates universal recognition of a product for consumers from country to country. FedEx's global advertising campaign, "FedEx Delivers to a Changing World," has run in Brazil, China, Germany, India, Japan, Mexico, South Korea, and the United Kingdom. The campaign highlights how FedEx helps businesses reach new markets and connect in sustainable ways.[56]

Other strategies call for product adaptation, promotion adaptation, or both. Marketers in the greeting-card industry adapt their product and messaging to cultural differences. For example, Russians are unlikely to send a card to a man on his 40th birthday. Reason: a common superstition in Russia that says big parties for a man celebrating that milestone attract "the Death." In Japan, where the parent–child relationship is formal, cards intended for a parent are also formal and express less sentimentality. And most cultures outside the United States don't resonate to images of Santa Claus and the Easter Bunny.[57]

Finally, a firm may select product invention to take advantage of unique foreign market opportunities. To match user needs in developing nations, an appliance manufacturer might introduce a hand-powered washing machine even though such products became obsolete in industrialized countries years ago. Although Chapter 12 discusses the idea of branding in greater detail, it is important to note here the value of a company's recognizable name, image, product, or even slogan around the world.

International Distribution Strategy

Distribution is a vital aspect of overseas marketing. Marketers must set up proper channels and anticipate extensive physical distribution problems. Foreign markets may offer poor transportation systems and warehousing facilities—or none at all. Global marketers must adapt promptly and efficiently to these situations to profit from overseas sales.

A distribution decision involves two steps. First, the firm must decide on a method of entering the foreign market. Second, it must determine how to distribute the product within the foreign market through that entry channel. Daimler AG had been marketing its subcompact car, the smart

6 Describe the alternative marketing mix strategies used in global marketing.

Product Strategy

		Same Product	Product Adaptation	New Product
Promotion Strategy	**Same Promotion**	**Straight Extension** General Mills Cheerios Coca-Cola Mars Snickers candy bar	**Product Adaptation** Campbell's soup Exxon gasoline	**Product Invention** Nonelectric sewing machines Manually operated washing machines
	Different Promotion	**Promotion Adaptation** Bicycles/motorcycles Outboard motors	**Dual Adaptation** Coffee Some clothing	

figure 7.4

Alternative International Product and Promotional Strategies

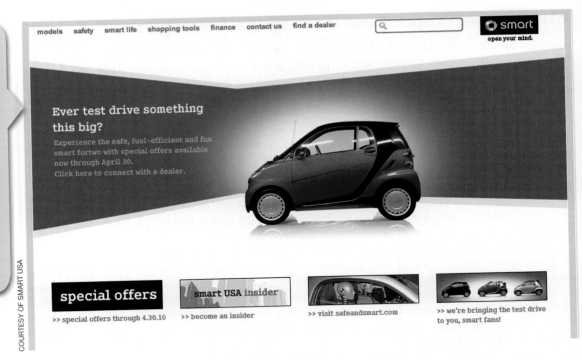

Daimler AG has been marketing its subcompact car, the smart fortwo, for at least a decade in Europe. Seeing Americans' growing interest in fuel-efficient cars, Daimler entered the U.S. market with this product in 2008 through a distributorship with smart USA.

fortwo, through its Mercedes-Benz division for at least a decade in Europe. Seeing Americans' growing interest in fuel-efficient cars, Daimler decided to enter the U.S. market, establishing smart USA, the only authorized U.S. smart fortwo distributor, with headquarters in a Detroit suburb. The cars are shipped to 77 dealerships across the country. Since the arrival of the fortwo in America, nearly 40,000 have been sold.

Pricing Strategy

Pricing can critically affect the success of an overall marketing strategy for foreign markets. Considerable competitive, economic, political, and legal constraints often limit pricing decisions. Global marketers can succeed if they thoroughly understand these requirements.

Companies must adapt their pricing strategies to local markets and change them when conditions change. In India, Unilever's partner Hindustan Lever offers "penny packets" of shampoo to lower-income consumers who typically cannot afford to buy an entire bottle of shampoo. Although local firms follow the same practice, Hindustan Lever wants to develop loyalty among these consumers so that when they move up the income scale, they will be more apt to buy the firm's higher-priced products as well.

An important development in pricing strategy for international marketing has been the emergence of commodity marketing organizations that seek to control prices through collective action. The Organization of Petroleum Exporting Countries (OPEC) is a good example of this kind of collective export organization.

Countertrade

countertrade Form of exporting whereby goods and services are bartered rather than sold for cash.

In a growing number of nations, the only way a marketer can gain access to foreign markets is through **countertrade**—a form of exporting in which a firm barters products rather than selling them for cash. Less-developed nations sometimes impose countertrade requirements when they lack sufficient foreign currency to attain goods and services they want or need from exporting countries. These nations allow sellers to exchange their products only for domestic products as a way to control their balance-of-trade problems.

Countertrade became popular two decades ago, when companies wanted to conduct business in eastern European countries and the former Soviet Union. Those governments did not allow exchanges of hard currency, so this form of barter facilitated trade. PepsiCo made one of the largest countertrades ever when it exchanged $3 billion worth of Pepsi-Cola for Russian Stolichnaya vodka, a cargo ship, and tankers from the former Soviet Union.

assessment check

1. What are the five strategies for selecting the most appropriate product and promotion strategy for a specific foreign market?

2. What is countertrade?

The United States as a Target for International Marketers

Foreign marketers regard America as an inviting target. It offers a large population of more than 308 million people. In addition, U.S. consumers have a high level of discretionary income, with a GDP per capita estimated at more than $38,600 and a median gross family income of about $52,000.[58] Risks to foreign marketers are also low due to the United States's political stability, generally favorable attitude toward foreign investment, and growing economy.

For South Korean consumer electronics giant LG Electronics, the United States is a hugely profitable market. Since establishing a North American headquarters in the United States, sales top $10 billion annually. LG markets a broad array of home appliances as well as consumer electronics products, including Blu-ray players, cell phones, computers, MP3 players, TVs, and other digital media.[59] As mentioned earlier in the chapter, Cuba would benefit from trade with the United States, but the U.S. embargo prohibits any trade with that country.

Among the best-known industries in which foreign manufacturers have established U.S. production facilities is automobiles. Most of the world's leading auto companies have invested heavily in assembly facilities in the United States: Honda, Hyundai, Mercedes-Benz, and Toyota in Alabama; Kia in Georgia; BMW in South Carolina; Nissan in Mississippi and Tennessee; and Honda in Ohio.[60] As we discussed earlier, foreign investment continues to grow in the United States. Increasingly, foreign multinationals will invest in U.S. assets as they seek to produce goods locally and control distribution channels.

> **7** Explain the attractiveness of the United States as a target market for foreign marketers.

assessment check

1. What characteristics of the United States make it an inviting target for foreign marketers?

2. Why would U.S. automobile manufacturing be a target for foreign companies?

strategic implications →
of marketing in the 21st century

he first decade of the new century has marked a new era of truly global marketing, in which the world's marketplaces are accessible to nearly every firm. Marketers in both small, localized firms and giant businesses need to reevaluate the strengths and weaknesses of their current marketing practices and realign their plans to meet the new demands of this era.

Marketers are the pioneers in bringing new technologies to developing nations. Their successes and failures will determine the direction global marketing will take and the speed with which it will be embraced. Actions of international marketers will influence every component of the marketing environment: competitive, economic, social-cultural, political-legal, and technological.

The greatest competitive advantages will belong to marketers who capitalize on the similarities of their target markets and adapt to the differences. In some instances, the actions of marketers today help determine the rules and regulations of tomorrow.

Marketers need flexible and broad views of an increasingly complex customer. Goods and services will likely become more customized as they are introduced in foreign markets—yet some recognizable brands seem to remain universally popular just as they are. New and better products in developing markets will create and maintain relationships for the future.

Review of Chapter Objectives

1 Describe the importance of global marketing from the perspectives of the individual firm and the nation.

Global marketing expands a company's market, allows firms to grow, and makes them less dependent on their own country's economy for success. For the nation, global trade provides a source of needed raw materials and other products not available domestically in sufficient amounts, opens up new markets to serve with domestic output, and converts countries and their citizens into partners in the search for high-quality products at the lowest possible prices. Companies find that global marketing and international trade can help them meet customer demand, reduce certain costs, provide information on markets around the world, and increase employment.

2 Identify the major components of the environment for global marketing.

The major components of the international environment are economic, social–cultural, technological, political–legal, and

competitive. A country's infrastructure also plays an important role in determining how effective marketers will be in manufacturing, promoting, and distributing their goods and services.

3 Outline the basic functions of GATT, WTO, NAFTA, FTAA, CAFTA-DR, and the European Union.

The General Agreement on Tariffs and Trade is an accord that has substantially reduced tariffs. The World Trade Organization oversees GATT agreements, mediates disputes, and tries to reduce trade barriers throughout the world. The North American Free Trade Agreement removes trade restrictions among Canada, Mexico, and the United States. The proposed Free Trade Area of the Americas seeks to create a free-trade area covering the entire Western hemisphere. As another step in that direction, the United States has made an agreement with the Dominican Republic and Central American nations known as the Central American Free Trade Agreement–DR (CAFTA-DR). The European Union is a customs union whose goal is to remove all barriers to free trade among its members.

Identify the alternative strategies for entering foreign markets.

Several strategies are available to marketers, including exporting, importing, franchising, foreign licensing, subcontracting, and direct investment. This progression moves from the least to the most involvement by a firm.

 Differentiate between a global marketing strategy and a multidomestic marketing strategy.

A global marketing strategy defines a standard marketing mix and implements it with minimal modifications in all foreign markets. A multidomestic marketing strategy requires firms to customize their marketing decisions to reach individual marketplaces.

 Describe the alternative marketing mix strategies used in global marketing.

Product and promotional strategies include the following: straight extension, promotion adaptation, product adaptation, dual adaptation, and product invention. Marketers may also choose among distribution, pricing, and countertrade strategies.

 Explain the attractiveness of the United States as a target market for foreign marketers.

The United States has a large population, high levels of discretionary income, political stability, a favorable attitude toward foreign investment, and a steadily growing economy.

Assessment Check: Answers

1.1 Define _importing_ and _exporting_. Importing involves purchasing foreign goods and services. Exporting refers to marketing domestically produced goods and services abroad.

1.2 What is the largest category of exports from the United States? The largest category of exports from the United States is services.

1.3 What must global marketers do effectively to reach foreign markets? Global marketers must adapt their goods and services to local preferences.

2.1 What are the three criteria that determine a nation's prospects as a host for international business expansion? A nation's size, per-capita income, and stage of economic development determine its prospects as a host for international business expansion.

2.2 What is an FCN treaty? FCN stands for friendship, commerce, and navigation. These treaties set terms for various aspects of commercial relations with other countries.

2.3 What are the two major categories of trade barriers? The two categories of trade barriers are tariffs and nontariffs.

3.1 What is the World Trade Organization? The World Trade Organization (WTO) oversees GATT agreements and mediates disputes. It also continues efforts to reduce trade barriers around the world.

3.2 What countries are parties to the NAFTA accord? The United States, Canada, and Mexico are members of NAFTA.

3.3 What is the goal of the European Union? The European Union (EU) seeks to remove all barriers to free trade among its members and strengthen its position in the world as an economic and political power.

4.1 What are the three basic strategies for entering foreign markets? The three basic strategies are importing and exporting, contractual agreements, and international direct investment.

4.2 What is a franchise? A franchise is a contractual agreement in which a wholesaler or retailer (the franchisee) agrees to meet the operating requirements of a manufacturer or other franchiser.

4.3 What is international direct investment? International direct investment is direct investment in foreign firms, production, and marketing facilities.

4.4 What is a multinational corporation? A multinational corporation is a firm with significant operations and marketing activities outside the home country.

4.5 What are two ways in which multinationals have changed since the 1960s? Two ways these firms have changed are that they are no longer exclusively U.S. based, and they no longer think of their foreign operations as mere outsourcing appendages.

5.1 What is the difference between a global marketing strategy and a multidomestic marketing strategy? A global marketing strategy defines a marketing mix and implements it with minimal modifications in all foreign markets. A multidomestic marketing strategy requires that firms customize their marketing decisions to reach individual marketplaces.

6.1 What are the five strategies for selecting the most appropriate product and promotion strategy for a specific foreign market? The five strategies are straight extension, promotion adaptation, product adaptation, dual adaptation, and product invention.

6.2 What is countertrade? Countertrade is a form of exporting in which a firm barters products rather than selling them for cash.

7.1 What characteristics of the United States make it an inviting target for foreign marketers? The characteristics making the United States an attractive target for foreign marketers are a large population to sell products to and high levels of discretionary income that make purchases possible. In addition, it has low risks to foreign marketers due to a stable political environment, favorable attitude toward foreign investment, and a growing economy.

7.2 Why would U.S. automobile manufacturing be a target for foreign companies? Because the United States has a large population and high income levels, foreign car manufacturers would find the country an attractive and lucrative market. The size and weight of cars make them bulky to transport long distances, so firms might find local manufacturing a profitable alternative to exporting.

Marketing Terms You Need to Know

exporting 204
importing 204
related party trade 204
infrastructure 210
exchange rate 210
political risk assessment (PRA) 212
friendship, commerce, and
    navigation (FCN) treaties 212
ISO (International Organization
    for Standardization)
    certification 213

tariff 213
revenue tariffs 213
protective tariffs 213
import quotas 214
embargo 214
subsidies 214
exchange control 215
dumping 215
free-trade area 215
customs union 215
common market 215

General Agreement on Tariffs
    and Trade (GATT) 216
World Trade Organization
    (WTO) 217
North American Free Trade
    Agreement (NAFTA) 217
Free Trade Area of the Americas
    (FTAA) 217
Central American Free Trade
    Agreement–DR
    (CAFTA-DR) 217

European Union (EU) 218
franchise 221
foreign licensing 221
subcontracting 221
global marketing strategy 223
multidomestic marketing
    strategy 224
countertrade 226

Assurance of Learning Review

1. What are the benefits to firms that decide to engage in global marketing?

2. Why is a nation's infrastructure an important factor for global marketers to consider?

3. What are the two different classifications of tariff? What is each designed to do?

4. How does an import quota restrict trade?

5. What are two major victories achieved by the Uruguay Round of GATT conferences?

6. Why has the progress of the WTO been slow?

7. What are the three alternatives for first-time exporters to reach foreign customers?

8. Define and describe the different types of contractual agreements that provide flexible alternatives to exporting.

9. In what conditions is a global marketing strategy generally most successful?

10. What type of nation benefits most from countertrade? Why?

Projects and Teamwork Exercises

1. Imagine you and a classmate are marketers for one of the following companies: Apple Inc., Burger King, General Mills, or Mattel Toys. Choose one of the following markets into which your company could expand: Mexico, India, or China. Research the country's infrastructure, social–cultural environment, technological environment, and any possible trade barriers your firm might encounter. Then present your findings to the class, with a conclusion on whether or not you think the expansion would be beneficial.

2. Assume you work for Domino's Pizza, which already has more than 3,200 outlets in more than 55 overseas markets. With a classmate, identify a country that Domino's has not yet reached and write a brief plan for entering that country's market. Then create a print ad for that market (you can write the ad copy in English). It may be helpful to visit Domino's Web site for some ideas.

3. London is hosting the 2012 Summer Olympics. By yourself or with a classmate, identify a company that might benefit from promoting its goods or services at the London Olympics. In a presentation, describe which strategy you would use: straight extension, product or promotion adaptation, dual adaptation, or product invention. Consider the fact that England is a member of the European Union.

4. Suppose you work for a firm that is getting ready to introduce its brand of MP3 player to the Chinese marketplace. With a classmate, decide which strategies your firm could use most effectively for entering this market. Present your ideas either in writing or to the class.

5. Chinese automaker Geely (pronounced *jeely*) recently announced plans to enter the U.S. market. With a classmate, research Geely to find out more about its cars, then create an ad for the firm, targeting U.S. consumers.

Critical-Thinking Exercises

1. Few elements in the global marketing environment are more difficult to overcome than the unexpected, such as natural disasters or outbreaks of disease such as the avian flu. Travel may be curtailed or halted by law, by a breakdown in infrastructure, or simply by fear on the part of consumers. Suppose you work for a firm that has resorts on several continents. As a marketer, what kinds of contingency plans might you recommend for your firm in the event of an unexpected disaster?

2. Zippo lighters have been around for more than 75 years. But as the number of smokers in the United States continues to decline, Zippo has spent the last half-century scouting the world for new markets. Today, Zippo is a status symbol among Chinese consumers, who prefer U.S. products. To reduce the sale of made-in-China knockoffs, Zippo's ads show Chinese consumers how to identify a real Zippo. In addition, Zippo has worked with U.S. government officials to find a safe way to package its lighters for air travel. Both of these examples demonstrate a firm adapting to requirements of a new marketplace. Do you think a global marketing strategy or a multidomestic strategy would work best if Zippo decided to enter other markets? Explain the reasons for your choice.

3. Do you agree with the goals and ideas of the proposed FTAA? Why or why not?

4. Do you agree with countertrade as a legitimate form of conducting business? Why or why not? Describe a countertrade agreement that Microsoft might make in another country.

5. Foreign investment continues to grow in the United States. Do you think this is a positive trend for U.S. businesses and consumers? Why or why not?

Ethics Exercise

Cheap—and illegal—copies of pirated popular movies, video games, and music often are available for sale in Asia within days of their worldwide release. The entertainment industry has so far had little success in stopping the flow of these copies into consumers' hands. Do you think multinational economic communities should be more effective at combating piracy? Why or why not? What actions could they take?

Internet Exercises

1. **Chinese currency policy.** Critics contend that the Chinese government pursues policies that keep the value of the Chinese currency artificially low relative to other currencies such as the U.S. dollar and euro. Using Google News and other online news sources, research the current state of Chinese currency policy. Why would the Chinese government engage in such efforts? What impact do these efforts have on global trade? Assume you work for a U.S. based firm that engages in extensive trading operations with China. What impact would a major revaluation of the Chinese currency have on your firm? http://news.google.com

2. **Global marketing strategies.** Samsung—the Korean-based electronics company—has been quite successful over the past ten years at marketing its products worldwide. Visit the Samsung Web site and note two or three elements of the firm's global marketing strategy. Next visit the Web sites of two other global electronics company, such as Sony or Philips. Compare and contrast the marketing strategies used by all three companies.

http://www.samsung.com
http://www.philips.com
http://www.sony.com

3. **World statistics.** The *CIA World Factbook* contains a wide range of information and statistics on individual countries. Go to the Web site listed below. Click on "Guide to Country Comparisons." Then click on the relevant section to obtain the top five countries in each of the following:
   a. Per-capita GDP
   b. Real growth rate in GDP
   c. Inflation rate
   d. Exports
   e. Population growth rate

https://www.cia.gov/library/publications/the-world-factbook/

Note: Internet Web addresses change frequently. If you don't find the exact site listed, you may need to access the organization's home page and search from there or use a search engine such as Google or Bing.

Case 7.1   *General Motors: Revved Up in China*

For General Motors, 2009 was a year to remember. A global recession—triggering massive layoffs, widespread unemployment, and faltering consumer confidence—sent car sales plummeting. Recognizing that GM's demise would create a catastrophic ripple effect in the

American economy, the federal government provided a $50 billion bailout to keep the giant automaker afloat.

But 2009 also had one bright spot: GM's performance in China. GM China is on a tear. The world's largest and mostly untapped market for automobiles, China saw continued economic growth despite a worldwide recession—a claim few nations can make.

GM has had operations in China for decades. Over time, the business grew to comprise nine joint ventures, two wholly owned firms, and 32,000 employees making automobiles, trucks, and vans for a burgeoning Chinese middle class.

In addition to its Chinese brands Wuling and Jiefang, GM markets some names familiar to American consumers: Buick, Cadillac, and Chevrolet. But a number of its best-selling models are currently made and sold only in Asia, including a group of fuel-efficient Chevys: the Spark, a mini-car; the Cruze, a small sedan; the Epica, a mid-size sedan; and the Aveo hatchback. The Cruze and the Spark are to be introduced in the United States later.

GM sales in China have expanded in high double digits year over year. Recently the company reported 67 percent growth in sales overall, with Chevy and Cadillac brands enjoying triple-digit sales increases from the prior year. The Buick line also did well, reporting a 60 percent increase in sales from the previous year—more than triple the U.S. figure.

GM China's sales were aided by a Chinese government stimulus program, now ended. Nonetheless, the company predicts continued double-digit revenue as demand remains strong.

For years, GM has invested heavily in China, to the tune of about $1 billion annually. Today, it holds a 13 percent market share, trailing Volkswagen, Changan, Shanghai Automotive, and Hyundai.

Most recently, the company entered into a $300 million joint venture with state-owned FAW Group to build light-duty trucks and vans. An estimated 200,000 vehicles are expected to roll off the assembly line after the first year of production, with future plans to export from the Chinese assembly plants.

In some respects, GM's success in China helped blunt the pain of the near-collapse of the U.S. auto market that same year. However, with the cars GM sells in China priced considerably less—pickups and vans range from $4,000 to $7,000—revenues from U.S. sales remain higher.

Questions for Critical Thinking

1. Through overseas expansion, General Motors takes advantage of untapped markets. But that strategy came under criticism after the company received bailout money from the U.S. government. Do you think the criticism was warranted? Why?

2. GM plans to introduce the Chevy Spark and the Chevy Cruze, two fuel-efficient models made in China, in the United States.

How do you think the cars will be received? What advice would you give management about this strategy?

Sources: General Motors Web site, "General Motors Sets February Sales Record in China," press release, March 4, 2010, http://media.gm.com; GM China Web site, http://www.gmchina.com, accessed March 4, 2010; Joseph Szczesny, "Buick Drives up Big Sales in China," *Morning Sun*, February 7, 2010, http://www.themorningsun.com; Elaine Kurtenbach, "GM's China Sales Nearly Double in January," *Globe and Mail*, February 4, 2010, http://www.theglobeandmail.com; Peter Whoriskey, "GM Sales in China Surge 67 Percent in 2009," *Washington Post*, January 5, 2010, http://www.washingtonpost.com; Alison Leung, "GM Sees China Sales Growth Slowing in 2010," *Reuters*, November 22, 2009, http://www.reuters.com; Norihiko Shirouzu and Patricia Jiayi Ho, "GM Launches Truck Venture in China," *The Wall Street Journal*, August 31, 2009, http://online.wsj.com; Norihiko Shirouzu, "GM China Set to Expand Reach," *pbs.org*, August 14, 2009, http://www.pbs.org; Peter Whoriskey, "GM Emerges from Bankruptcy after Landmark Government Bailout," *Washington Post*, July 10, 2009, http://www.washingtonpost.com.

Video Case 7.2
Global Marketing at Evo

The ski and snowboard community is relatively small, so Evo—the Seattle-based snowboard, ski, skateboard, and wakeboard store—is always looking to maximize their exposure, and that means crossing borders and going global. The company started as an online outlet, selling closeouts and used gear to bargain hunters. Over the years, they have expanded their offerings to include first-quality new stuff, trips to exotic locales, and a retail store in Seattle. "There's a ton of really exciting things that happen here at a regional level that have an impact on the global community," says Molly Hawkins, in charge of brand and events marketing at Evo. One of the most effective ways they reach their consumers is through advertisements and editorial pieces in the top snow sports magazines. Publications such as *Freeskier Magazine, Powder,* and *The Ski Journal* all have international circulations.

International exposure is nice, but selling the gear keeps the lights on. Their expertise in e-commerce makes for a fairly easy transition into the global marketplace. Canada, not surprisingly, is one of Evo's largest international markets. "Our daily unique [visitors] for example, from July 2008, we have like, 64,000 from Canada," notes Hawkins. The United Kingdom, Germany, Australia, and Korea are also quite big for Evo with daily visitors to their Web sites in the 20,000 range—and that's in July!

But, here's the rub: all of the products Evo sells are name brand items that are for sale in local shops overseas. These brands often restrict the sales of their products to licensed resellers within a particular geographical zone. With the Internet, these rules become quite complicated. Evo can't stop someone in Japan from placing an order. They are working with their resellers to come up with a way to honor the contracts, but still be able to serve customers everywhere.

The world of business is becoming increasingly borderless, but there are still cultural issues to grapple with. Marketing and advertising is a particularly difficult thing to do globally. If language were the only hurdle, it would be fairly simple to translate. Unfortunately, even among English-speaking nations, cultural subtleties and colloquialisms can turn an innocent euphemism into a deeply offensive word. "I work with a lot of our vendors in marketing, looking for ways to co-promote their products through Evo," says Hawkins. "Like Rossignol, they're based out of Europe. Their business style and their designs and branding and marketing ideas are definitely, ah, different." Hawkins and her staff tend to leave the marketing of the company pretty generic. Their main propositions: best brands, best prices, and a top-notch knowledge base really know no boundaries.

Evo has extended its commitment to a boundaryless world by offering extreme skiing and boarding expeditions to some of the world's most incredible destinations. "EvoTrip is such a natural extension of the Evo brand," says Bryce Phillips, Evo's founder, "and we're doing it with great activities—skiing, snowboarding, surfing."

"EvoTrip is definitely unique," says Hawkins. "There are other companies that are doing something similar, but our product is a little different in that we really take people on these extreme trips that people like Bryce and people here at Evo would actually go on. They know the intricacies of getting around these areas and so I think without them, for someone who just wanted to go down there on their own, they wouldn't have the same kind of experience. These guys have that insider info, that connection."

"The reason why I get so excited about this concept is that it is near and dear to what all of us value," says Phillips. "It's just like, getting out there, learning more about different cultures, doing the activities in different parts of the world and seeing beautiful locations you might never have seen before." Through a partnership with online travel site JustFares.com—and local guides and professional athletes in each country—they will offer trips to South America, Japan, Indonesia, Switzerland, and many more locations. It's not all about the adventure, of course; sound business is behind it all. Every trip allows Evo's "ambassadors" to get in front of their actual potential customers in each of the countries they visit. No translations. No miscommunications. No boundaries.

Questions

1. Why doesn't Evo need to tailor its marketing to different countries? Do you agree with their decision to present one marketing message? Why or why not?

2. What challenges do U.S. e-commerce companies face when selling their products overseas? Do you believe brands have the right to limit a company's right to sell internationally?

Greensburg, Inc.

© CENGAGE LEARNING

Rebuilding: They Didn't Ask for This

On May 4, 2007, the Green Acres Bed & Breakfast at 122 W. Iowa in Greensburg, Kansas, was destroyed by an F5 tornado. To innkeepers Janice and John Haney, this wasn't just the loss of a business, but also of their home. The brick, split-level house was built in 1926 by a high school shop teacher. It was tidy, charming, and filled with period detail and Janice's hand-made quilts. "We had never had any intentions of ever building a new house, we were just very happy with the house we had," Janice said. As inviting as the home was, Janice admits that it was drafty and in need of some energy-efficient upgrades. "This was an opportunity for us to want to do something bigger and better and a once-in-a-lifetime opportunity to make it as green as possible," she said. The Haneys did not decide to rebuild right in town, instead choosing to build a larger, more energy-efficient home on some family land about eight miles out of town. For the most part, Janice left the construction to contractors and kept the decorating for herself.

Farrell Allison lived right off Route 54 in a beautiful 100-year-old Victorian with stained glass and elaborate woodwork artfully restored by Allison and his wife. It was a lifelong labor of love, but when the tornado seriously damaged the home and plans were announced to reroute a new highway right through the Allisons' backyard, it was time to move on. Never one to shy from a challenge, Allison hit the books and set out to build the greenest house in Greensburg. His new home is truly state-of-the-art, even for the new Greensburg. Unlike the Haneys, Allison, a soil consultant, is acting as his own contractor, sourcing his own materials, hiring crews and subcontractors and, of course, managing the budget.

"Contractors are a different breed," says Allison. "I had one, the heating and air guy say, 'You know you are really particular!' and

I said, 'I'm payin' the bills, I'm the one who's gonna be living in this house, you're not, and this is the way we're gonna build it.'"

Allison has become such an expert in green building that contractors and even government agencies such as the USDA's Rural Development arm have come to him for advice on building green.

Mike Boyles, owner of Calmarc Construction, had been building homes in the Wichita, Kansas, area for years, but when the tornado destroyed 700 houses in Greensburg, he knew exactly what he had to do.

He went home.

"We couldn't be here by ourselves," says Boyles, speaking about B&B Lumber, their regular lumber vendor in Wichita. Even before the tornado, Greensburg residents had a tough time getting contractors, repair services, and supplies. After the tornado, it was impossible to source materials locally, especially the environmentally friendly products Greensburg residents are demanding.

Calmarc's ability to serve these customers relies on the existing relationships with vendors like B&B. Randy Mude, a sales representative with B&B, doesn't mind going the extra mile. "Every stick you move and every piece of plywood you sell is a benefit to your company," says Mude, adding that if the tragedy hadn't happened, he'd probably be doing the same volume of work with Calmarc in Wichita. "If we give Mike and the homeowners out here some extra attention and time, we have to [do it] to make things right." Mude even takes their Greensburg clients to his own home to get ideas and see what some of the products will look like. In turn, Mude gets the opportunity to learn about and try new green materials, which he hopes someday to sell to larger developers.

While the town provides residents with a list of reliable contractors, most are not from the area and don't understand the needs of the people the way Boyles does. "They didn't ask for this, and we have to understand that," he says. Those who choose to build back green are constantly researching and bringing questions and ideas to Boyles and Mude. Boyles often incorporates pieces from the old homes into the new homes he builds, and spends a lot of extra time working with his Greensburg clients, adding, "if this was a different place and I didn't know the people, it wouldn't be worth it."

When it comes to buyers and sellers, regardless of whether you're talking business-to-consumer or business-to-business, the same principles apply; caveat emptor, buyer beware! The Haneys, like most homeowners, put their trust and dollars in an outside contractor and luckily for them, their new home came out beautifully. Sadly, not all Greensburg residents have been this lucky. A few homeowners have fallen victim to shady contractors who have overcharged or left them with half-finished homes.

Allison's do-it-yourself plan saves him money by not paying the markup an outside contractor would charge, and he gets ultimate control over the project. On the other hand, he lacks the leverage and buying power companies like Calmarc have with B&B.

Boyles lives in the best (or worst) of both worlds. He's got all the power and none of it, depending on whether he's dealing with a client or dealing with a supplier.

Questions

1. How are the Haneys, Allison, and Boyles similar in terms of their consumer behavior? How are they different?

2. Would you consider Allison a regular consumer or a B2B buyer?

3. Why is it important that Calmarc maintain a good buyer–seller relationship with B&B? What does Calmarc get out of it and what's in it for B&B?

4. Write a report on the advantages and disadvantages of working with customers who want to act as their own contractors.

Target
Market Selection

3

PART 3

Chapter 8
Marketing Research
and Sales Forecasting

Chapter 9
Market Segmentation,
Targeting, and
Positioning

Chapter 10
Relationship
Marketing and
Customer Relationship
Management (CRM)

Marketing
Research and Sales Forecasting

Polaris Marketing Research Shows the Way · · ·
How do companies know whether to change their online marketing strategy? What processes help them identify the right features to ensure the success of a new service or product? Where can they find out which

1 **Describe the development of the marketing research function and its major activities.**

2 **Explain the steps in the marketing research process.**

3 **Distinguish between primary and secondary data, and identify the sources of each type.**

4 **Explain the different sampling techniques used by marketing researchers.**

5 **Identify the methods by which marketing researchers collect primary data.**

6 **Explain the challenges of conducting marketing research in global markets.**

7 **Outline the most important uses of computer technology in marketing research.**

8 **Identify the major types of forecasting methods.**

global markets offer the best opportunities for expanding sales or market share overseas?

Marketing research helps provide many of the answers, and Polaris Marketing Research, named for the night sky's guiding North Star, is one of the firms that companies in need of such information turn to. Based in Atlanta, Polaris was founded in 1989 and has grown steadily since then, undertaking six major expansions and adding to its already long list of business clients. It offers its customers marketing research in five key areas: customer satisfaction and loyalty, brand research, employee research, customer retention and win-back, and new-product development.

Polaris is a full-service firm. It collects marketing research—through telephone interviews, mail surveys, personal interviews, brainstorming, mystery shoppers, and focus groups, as well as online surveys—designs and manages research projects, and provides full reports and recommendations for its clients. The company's services span many different areas intended to help customers identify, understand, and retain current and future customers—including their employees, who are often considered internal customers of a firm. Polaris's researchers pursue both accuracy of their information and clarity in their reporting.

Its expertise in brands and brand strategy, for instance, covers six separate research areas for

Polaris clients: "creating a new brand strategy, understanding how far your brand can stretch, brand architecture, brand management, revitalizing brands, and brand positioning." The firm also conducts customer surveys and loyalty measurement programs and lost customer and customer win-back analysis. Its new-product team can assist with every stage of product launch, from identifying market needs all the way to developing marketing strategies for new offerings.

Polaris recently revamped its Web site to provide even more information about conducting brand and new product research and keeping and retrieving customers. It also introduced a new service called SurveyTrac™, an

online survey package that lets companies design and conduct one or more of their own online surveys, but with expert personal assistance via live access to a Polaris professional, and easy-to-read results in the form of online graphs and charts. Users of the package can get as deeply involved in designing and administering the survey as they want, or they can just write the questions, describe the sample population, and let Polaris take it from there.

One satisfied Polaris customer that sought the firm's help in measuring employee performance is the National Basketball Association (NBA), whose manager of player development comments, "Polaris was instrumental in helping us develop and launch our annual player development end-of-season assessments. The results have allowed us to use honest organizational feedback to set standards and enhance program offerings. Their reporting is detailed and user-friendly, which is critical for us to be able to share it with the entire organization."[1]

evolution of a brand

Polaris has produced a series of four reports on measuring customer satisfaction, and its newly expanded Web site offers a complete free guide to marketing research. Called the Marketing Research Education Center, this online area includes common research errors to avoid, sample survey questions, sample size and statistical testing calculators, and a glossary of marketing research terms among other helpful features.

- What benefits do you think Polaris offers its current and potential customers?

- For several years Polaris has partnered with Western Wats, the largest data collection firm in the United States, to provide telephone

interviewing services (both incoming and outgoing calls). Polaris chose Western Wats for its dedication to quality. How does the partners' dedication to quality translate into results for Polaris's customers?

chapter overview

marketing research
Process of collecting and using information for marketing decision making.

Collecting and managing information about what customers need and want is a challenging task for any marketer. **Marketing research** is the process of collecting and using information for marketing decision making. Data comes from a variety of sources. Some results come from well-planned studies designed to elicit specific information. Other valuable information comes from sales force reports, accounting records, and published reports. Still other data emerges from controlled experiments and computer simulations. Thanks to new database technologies, some data companies collect are compiled for them by research specialists, and some are collected and compiled by in-house staff. Marketing research, by presenting pertinent information in a useful format, aids decision makers in analyzing data and in suggesting possible actions.

This chapter discusses the marketing research function. Marketers use research to understand their customers, target customer segments, and develop long-term customer relationships—all keys to profitability. Information collected through marketing research underlies much of the material on market segmentation discussed in the following chapter. Clearly, the marketing research function is the primary source of information needed to make effective marketing decisions. The use of technology to mine data and gather business and competitive intelligence is also discussed, as is technology's vast impact on marketing research decision making and planning. This chapter also explains how marketing research techniques are used to make accurate sales forecasts, a critical component of marketing planning.

The Marketing Research Function

Describe the
development of the
marketing research
function and its major
activities.

Before looking at how marketing research is conducted, we must first examine its historical development, the people and organizations it involves, and the activities it entails. Because an underlying purpose of research is to find out more about consumers, research is clearly central to effective customer satisfaction and customer relationship programs. Media technologies such as the Internet and virtual reality are opening up new channels through which researchers can tap into consumer information.

Development of the Marketing Research Function

It has been more than 130 years since advertising pioneer N. W. Ayer conducted the first organized marketing research project in 1879. A second important milestone in the development of marketing research occurred 32 years later, when Charles C. Parlin organized the nation's first commercial research department at Curtis Publishing, publisher of *The Saturday Evening Post*.

Parlin got his start as a marketing researcher by counting soup cans in Philadelphia's garbage. Here is what happened. Parlin, an ad salesman, was trying to persuade the Campbell Soup Company to advertise in *The Saturday Evening Post*. Campbell Soup resisted, believing that the *Post* reached primarily working-class readers, who they thought preferred to make their own soup. Campbell Soup marketers were targeting higher-income people who could afford to pay for the convenience of soup in a can. To prove Campbell wrong, Parlin began counting soup cans in the garbage collected from different neighborhoods. His research revealed that working-class families bought more canned soup than wealthy households, who had servants to cook for them. Campbell Soup soon became a regular

Early on, Campbell Soup marketers targeted higher-income people who could afford to pay for the convenience of soup in a can, until marketing research revealed that working-class families bought more canned soup than wealthy households.

Post client. It is interesting to note that garbage remains a good source of information for marketing researchers even today. Prior to the current cutbacks in food service, some airlines studied the leftovers from onboard meals to determine what to serve passengers.

Most early research gathered little more than written testimonials from purchasers of firms' products. Research methods became more sophisticated during the 1930s as the development of statistical techniques led to refinements in sampling procedures and greater accuracy in research findings.

In recent years, advances in computer technology have significantly changed the complexion of marketing research. Besides accelerating the pace and broadening the base of data collection, computers have aided marketers in making informed decisions about problems and opportunities. Simulations, for example, allow marketers to evaluate alternatives by posing what-if questions. Marketing researchers at many consumer goods firms simulate product introductions through computer programs to determine whether to risk real-world product launches or even to subject products to test marketing.

Who Conducts Marketing Research?

The size and organizational form of the marketing research function usually are tied to the structure of the company. Some firms organize research units to support different product lines, brands, or geographic areas. Others organize their research functions according to the types of research they need to perform such as sales analysis, new-product development, advertising evaluation, or sales forecasting.

Many firms outsource their research needs and depend on independent marketing research firms. These independent organizations might specialize in handling just part of a larger study such as conducting consumer interviews. Firms can also contract out entire research studies.

Marketers usually decide whether to conduct a study internally or through an outside organization based on cost. Another major consideration is the reliability and accuracy of the information collected by an outside organization. Because collecting marketing data is what these outside organizations do full-time, the information they gather often is more thorough and accurate than that collected by less experienced in-house staff. Often an outside marketing research firm can provide technical assistance and expertise not available within the company's marketing department. Interaction with outside suppliers also helps ensure that a researcher does not conduct a study only to validate a favorite viewpoint or preferred option.

Marketing research companies range in size from sole proprietorships to national and international firms such as ACNielsen, Information Resources, and Arbitron. They can be classified as syndicated services, full-service suppliers, or limited-service suppliers depending on the types of services they offer to clients. Some full-service organizations are also willing to take on limited-service activities.

syndicated service
Organization that provides standardized data on a periodic basis to its subscribers.

Marketers usually decide whether to conduct a study internally or externally based on cost as well as reliability and accuracy of the information collected by an outside organization. This ad touts the firm's global reach.

SYNDICATED SERVICES

An organization that regularly provides a standardized set of data to all customers is called a **syndicated service**. Mediamark Research, for example, operates a syndicated product research service based on personal interviews with adults regarding their exposure to advertising media. Clients include advertisers, advertising agencies, magazines, newspapers, broadcasters, and cable TV networks.

Another syndicated service provider is J.D. Power and Associates, a global marketing information firm headquartered in California that specializes in surveying customer satisfaction, product quality, and buyer behavior. Among its customers are companies in the telecommunications, travel and hotel, marine, utilities, health care, building, consumer electronics, automotive, and financial services industries.[2]

FULL-SERVICE RESEARCH SUPPLIERS

An organization that contracts with clients to conduct complete marketing research projects is called a **full-service research supplier**. Brain Research Group, a Mexican marketing research firm, provides quantitative and qualitative research and various field studies, including face-to-face and telephone interviews, online interviews, multinational studies, B2B interviews, and even "mystery shopper" research to collect information about retail outlets. The company also studies public opinion and buyer behavior and evaluates Web pages and work environments. Its editing department reviews questionnaires before they are used, under strict supervision, by Brain Research's staff in interviews, focus groups, and other types of observation techniques, including video.[3] A full-service supplier becomes the client's marketing research arm, performing all of the steps in the marketing research process (discussed later in this chapter).

full-service research supplier Marketing research organization that offers all aspects of the marketing research process.

LIMITED-SERVICE RESEARCH SUPPLIERS

A marketing research firm that specializes in a limited number of activities, such as conducting field interviews or performing data processing, is called a **limited-service research supplier**. Nielsen Media Research specializes in tracking what people watch on TV, and who watches what, in more than 30 countries.[4] The firm also prepares studies to help clients develop advertising strategies and to track awareness and interest. Syndicated services can also be considered a type of limited-service research supplier.

limited-service research supplier Marketing research firm that specializes in a limited number of research activities such as conducting field interviews or performing data processing.

Customer Satisfaction Measurement Programs

In their marketing research, firms often focus on tracking the satisfaction levels of current customers. Austin, Texas–based Bazaarvoice charges a monthly fee to clients and does everything from designing and managing a firm's customer feedback area on its Web site to moderating online discussion groups and analyzing comments.[5] Some marketers have also gained valuable insights by tracking the dissatisfaction that led customers to abandon certain products for those of competitors. Some customer defections are only partial; customers may remain somewhat satisfied with a business but not completely satisfied. Such attitudes could lead them to take their business elsewhere. Studying the underlying causes of customer defections, even partial defections, can be useful for identifying problem areas that need attention. The annual Airline Quality Rating survey scores specific carriers, and the airline industry in general, on such measures as on-time performance, baggage handling, diverted and cancelled flights, overbooking, and number of customer complaints. The national study, a joint effort by faculty at Saint Louis University and Wichita State University, recently reported that Hawaiian Airlines had the best on-time performance while U.S. Airways was "the most improved airline."[6]

Some organizations conduct their own measurement programs through online polls and surveys. California Pizza Kitchen's servers point out to customers a special code number printed on their check. Entering the code number on the company Web site brings up a customer satisfaction survey that offers respondents a chance to participate in a sweepstakes.[7]

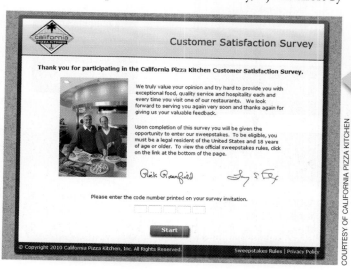

Some organizations, such as California Pizza Kitchen, conduct their own measurement programs through online polls and surveys.

COURTESY OF CALIFORNIA PIZZA KITCHEN

The Marketing Research Process

Explain the steps in the marketing research process.

As discussed earlier, business executives rely on marketing research to provide the information they need to make effective decisions regarding their firm's current and future activities. The chances of making good decisions improve when the right information is provided at the right time during decision making. To achieve this goal, marketing researchers often follow the six-step process shown in Figure 8.1. In the initial stages, researchers define the problem, conduct exploratory research, and formulate a hypothesis to be tested. Next, they create a design for the research study and collect needed data. Finally, researchers interpret and present the research information. The following sections take a closer look at each step of the marketing research process.

Define the Problem

A popular anecdote advises that well-defined problems are half solved. A well-defined problem permits the researcher to focus on securing the exact information needed for the solution. Clearly defining the question that the researcher needs to answer increases the speed and accuracy of the research process.

Researchers must carefully avoid confusing symptoms of a problem with the problem itself. A symptom merely alerts marketers that a problem exists. For example, suppose that a maker of frozen pizzas sees its market share drop from 8 to 5 percent in six months. The loss of market share is a symptom of a problem the company must solve. To define the problem, the firm must look for the underlying causes of its market share loss.

A logical starting point in identifying the problem might be to evaluate the firm's target market and marketing mix elements. Suppose, for example, a firm has recently changed its promotional strategies. Research might then seek to answer the question, "What must we do to improve the effectiveness of our marketing mix?" The firm's marketers might also look at possible environmental changes. Perhaps a new competitor entered the firm's market. Decision makers will need information to help answer the question, "What must we do to distinguish our company from the new competitor?"

Target recently saw a sales increase of more than $4.5 million from the addition of its new P-Fresh concept,

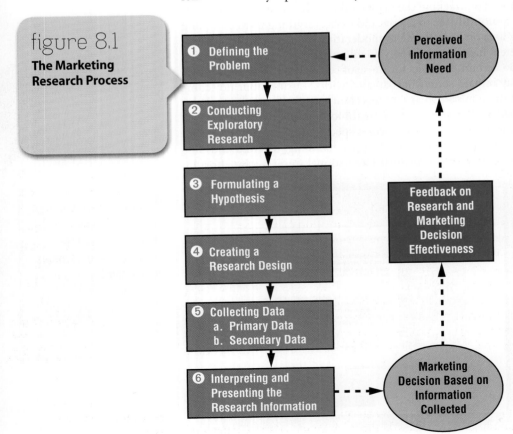

figure 8.1
The Marketing Research Process

introducing grocery departments to 108 reformatted stores around the United States. These stores were an expansion of the chain's first two-year test of the concept at two locations. Their success has encouraged the chain to invest $1 billion in additional remodels of 350 more stores in "high-priority markets." The goal is to broaden the chain's product categories and reduce its reliance on purchase of discretionary items.[8]

Conduct Exploratory Research

Once a firm has defined the question it wants to answer, researchers can begin exploratory research. **Exploratory research** seeks to discover the cause of a specific problem by discussing the problem with informed sources both within and outside the firm and by examining data from other information sources. Marketers at Romano's Macaroni Grill, part of Dallas-based Brinker International, might talk with their customers, suppliers, and retailers. Executives at Brinker might also ask for input from the sales force or look for overall market clues. In addition, exploratory research can include evaluation of company records, such as sales and profit analyses, and available competitive data. Marketing researchers often refer to internal data collection as situation analysis. The term *informal investigation* is often used for exploratory interviews with informed people outside the researchers' firms.

exploratory research
Process of discussing a marketing problem with informed sources both within and outside the firm and examining information from secondary sources.

USING INTERNAL DATA

Marketers can find valuable data in their firm's own internal records. Typical sources of internal data are sales records, financial statements, and marketing cost analyses. Marketers analyze sales performance records to gain an overall view of company efficiency and to find clues to potential problems. Prepared from company invoices or a computer database system, this **sales analysis** can provide important details to management. The study typically compares actual and expected sales based on a detailed sales forecast by territory, product, customer, and salesperson.

sales analysis In-depth evaluation of a firm's sales.

Once the sales quota—the level of expected sales to which actual results are compared—has been established, it is a simple process to compare actual results with expected performance. SuperPharm Limited, a chain of retail pharmacy superstores operating in Trinidad and Tobago, recently installed a new centralized software system to track and analyze sales trends for the 15,000 items it stocks and the 10,000 customer transactions it logs every day. Reports trigger restocking and inventory decisions as well as provide information for financial statements and reporting, and a backup system provides for uninterrupted operations in case of Internet access problems in individual stores.[9]

Other possible breakdowns for sales analysis separate transactions by customer type, product, sales method (Internet, mail, telephone, or personal contact), type of order (cash or credit), and order size. Sales analysis is one of the least expensive and most important sources of marketing information available to a firm.

Accounting data, as summarized in the firm's financial statements, can be another good tool for identifying financial issues that influence marketing. Using ratio analysis, researchers can compare performance in current and previous years against industry benchmarks. These exercises may hint at possible problems, but only more detailed analysis would reveal specific causes of indicated variations.

A third source of internal information is *marketing cost analysis*—evaluation of expenses for tasks such as selling, warehousing, advertising, and delivery to determine the profitability of particular customers, territories, or product lines. Firms often examine the allocation of costs to products, customers, and territories. Marketing decision makers then evaluate the profitability of particular customers and territories on the basis of the sales produced and the costs incurred in generating those sales. Sometimes internal data can produce remarkably detailed customer profiles.

Like sales analysis and financial research, marketing cost analysis is most useful when it provides information linked to other forms of marketing research. A later section of this chapter will address how computer technologies can accomplish these linkages and move information among a firm's units.

Formulate a Hypothesis

After defining the problem and conducting an exploratory investigation, the marketer needs to formulate a **hypothesis**—a tentative explanation for some specific event. A hypothesis is a statement

hypothesis Tentative explanation for a specific event.

about the relationship among variables that carries clear implications for testing this relationship. It sets the stage for more in-depth research by further clarifying what researchers need to test. For example, Olive Garden restaurants might want to see whether good customer service is related to its increased sales, so its marketers would conduct a survey of customers to test this hypothesis.

Not all studies test specific hypotheses, however, a carefully designed study can benefit from the rigor introduced by developing a hypothesis before beginning data collection and analysis.

Create a Research Design

research design Master plan for conducting market research.

To test hypotheses and find solutions to marketing problems, a marketer creates a **research design**, a master plan or model for conducting marketing research. In planning a research project, marketers must be sure the study will measure what they intend to measure. A second important research design consideration is the selection of respondents. Marketing researchers use sampling techniques (discussed later in the chapter) to determine which consumers to include in their studies.

Test kitchens and willing palates are indispensable in the fast-food business. At McDonald's test kitchen, "We guesstimate 1,800 new ideas a year we're exposed to," says the company's director of culinary innovation. After input from the business research and marketing teams about where the firm is looking to pick up business, the company's four chefs and suppliers' chefs get together for brainstorming. "When we're in that environment," says the culinary director, "I say, 'Look, we close the door, there are no bad ideas in this kitchen.'" About 30 ideas each year get a closer look, and about half of those are presented to the fast-food chain's management team. Between three and five are actually launched in a given year.[10]

Collect Data

3 Distinguish between primary and secondary data, and identify the sources of each type.

Marketing researchers gather two kinds of data: secondary data and primary data. **Secondary data** are information from previously published or compiled sources. Census data is an example. **Primary data** refers to information collected for the first time specifically for a marketing research study. An example of primary data is statistics collected from a survey that asks current customers about their preferences for product improvements. Global research firm Synovate collects primary data in the Americas, Asia, Europe, and the Middle East for its clients. The company has no physical headquarters and operates in 60 countries around the world, conducts thousands of projects and focus groups and millions of interviews, and employs nearly 6,000 people with "one thing in common: boundless curiosity."[11]

secondary data Previously published information.

primary data Information collected for a specific investigation.

Secondary data offer two important advantages: (1) such data are almost always less expensive to gather than primary data, and (2) researchers usually spend less time to locate and use secondary data. A research study that requires primary data may take three to four months to complete, while a researcher often can gather secondary data in a matter of days.

Secondary data have limitations that primary data do not. First, published information can quickly become obsolete. A marketer analyzing the population of various areas may discover that even the most recent census figures already are out of date because of rapid growth and changing demographics. Second, published data collected for an unrelated purpose may not be completely relevant to the marketer's specific needs. For example, census data do not reveal the brand preferences of consumers.

Although research to gather primary data can cost more and take longer, the results can provide richer, more detailed information than secondary data offer. The choice between secondary and primary data is tied to cost, applicability, and effectiveness. Many marketing research projects combine secondary and primary data to fully answer marketing questions. This chapter examines specific methods for collecting both secondary and primary data in later sections.

Interpret and Present Research Data

The final step in the marketing research process is to interpret the findings and present them to decision makers in a format that allows managers to make effective judgments. Possible differences in interpretations of research results may occur between marketing researchers and their audiences due to differing backgrounds, levels of knowledge, and experience. Both oral and written reports should be presented in a manner designed to minimize such misinterpretations.

Marketing researchers and research users must cooperate at every stage in the research process. Too many studies go unused because management fears that the results are of little use, once they hear lengthy discussions of research limitations or unfamiliar terminology. Marketing researchers must remember to direct their reports toward management and not to other researchers. They should spell out their conclusions in clear and concise terms that can be put into action. Reports should confine technical details of the research methods to an appendix, if they are included at all. By presenting research results to all key executives at a single sitting, researchers can ensure that everyone will understand the findings. Decision makers can then quickly reach consensus on what the results mean and what actions need to be taken.

assessment check

1. What are the six steps in the marketing research process?
2. What is the goal of exploratory research?

Marketing Research Methods

Clearly, data collection is an integral part of the marketing research process. One of the most time-consuming parts of collecting data is determining what method the marketer should use to obtain the data. This section discusses the most commonly used methods by which marketing researchers find both secondary and primary data.

Secondary Data Collection

Secondary data come from many sources. The overwhelming quantity of secondary data available at little or no cost challenges researchers to select only data relevant to the problem or issue studied.

Secondary data consist of two types: internal and external data. Internal data, as discussed earlier, include sales records, product performance reviews, sales force activity reports, and marketing cost reports. External data come from a variety of sources, including government records, syndicated research services, and industry publications. Computerized databases provide access to vast amounts of data from both inside and outside an organization. The following sections on government data, private data, and online sources focus on databases and other external data sources available to marketing researchers.

GOVERNMENT DATA

The federal government is the nation's most important source of marketing data. Census data provide the most frequently used government statistics. A census of population is conducted every ten years and is made available at no charge in local libraries, on computer disks, and via the Internet. Because of problems implementing a computerized system, the U.S. Census Bureau recently abandoned plans to go high-tech with handheld computers for data collection. Instead, it will count the country's more than 300 million residents by training workers to collect data with pen and paper from those who don't respond to its mailed survey.[12] The Census Bureau also conducts a periodic census of housing, population, business, manufacturers, agriculture, minerals, and governments.

THE 2010 U.S. CENSUS

The U.S. Census of Population contains a wealth of valuable information for marketers. It breaks down the U.S. population of more than 300 million people by very small geographic areas, making it possible to determine population traits by city block or census tract in large cities. It also divides the populations

briefly speaking

" When you are drowning in numbers, you need a system to separate the wheat from the chaff."

—Anthony Adams
(b. 1940)
Fortune 500 marketing consultant

U.S. census data help the government properly allocate federal funding. It is also used by marketing researchers.

HELP OUR CHILDREN RECEIVE THEIR SHARE OF $400 BILLION

Now is your chance to help ensure that your community gets its fair share of over $400 billion per year in federal funds. By taking just 10 minutes to answer 10 simple questions, you can help provide better roads, schools and healthcare for your community. Help create positive change for yourself, your children and your nation. Responses are confidential and will not be shared with immigration or third parties. 2010CENSUS.GOV

WE CAN'T MOVE FORWARD UNTIL YOU MAIL IT BACK.

United States Census 2010   IT'S IN OUR HANDS

of nonmetropolitan areas into census tracts, which are important for marketing analysis because they highlight small groups of about 1,500 to 8,000 people with similar traits. Census data, collected every ten years since 1790 as required by the U.S. Constitution and most recently completed in 2010, help the government properly allocate states' seats in the U.S. House of Representatives. Also at stake in 2010 were more than $400 billion of federal funding earmarked for hospitals, schools, senior centers, job training and public works projects, and emergency services. "If the community needs a firetruck, or training for EMTs, or they need a senior center, small communities are more aware now than ever before that the amount of [government] funds is based on the number of people in a community," said a state labor official in Alaska, where the 2010 count began.[13]

The cost of the 2010 Census was estimated at more than $11 billion; see the "Solving an Ethical Controversy" feature for a discussion of the costs of marketing decisions about the project. This Census featured a shortened version of the household questionnaire and was the first Census to use handheld computing devices with GPS functions (to verify respondents' addresses), but, unlike the preceding count, it could be completed only by mail and did not offer the option of responding online.[14]

Marketers, such as local retailers and shopping center developers, can readily access Census data to gather vital information about customers in an immediate neighborhood without spending time or money to conduct comprehensive surveys. Marketing researchers have found even more valuable resources in the government's computerized mapping database originally called the TIGER system, for Topographically Integrated Geographic Encoding and Referencing system. This system overlays topographic features such as railroads, highways, and rivers with census data such as household income figures. Recently updated with an Oracle relational database, the new TIGER/Line Shapefiles are downloadable and cover all 50 states, the District of Columbia, and Puerto Rico.[15]

Marketers often get other information from the federal government, such as the following:

- *Monthly Catalog of United States Government Publications* and *Statistical Abstract of the United States*, published annually and available online as the *Catalog of U.S. Government Publications (CGP)*;

- *Survey of Current Business*, updated monthly by the Bureau of Economic Analysis; and

- *County and City Data Book*, typically published every three years and available online, providing data on all states, counties, and cities of more than 25,000 residents.

State and city governments serve as additional important sources of information on employment, production, and sales activities. In addition, university bureaus of business and economic research frequently collect and disseminate valuable information.

PRIVATE DATA

Many private organizations provide information for marketing decision makers. A trade association may be an excellent source of data on activities in a particular industry. Thomson Gale's

solving an ethical controversy

Looking into Census Bureau Spending on Advertising

Officials of the 2010 U.S. Census balanced their Constitutional mandate to reach the country's 308 million residents against record levels of government debt. Before it even began, the Census, which is used to allocate seats in the House of Representatives and distribute billions of federal aid dollars, was criticized for wasteful spending, including $4.5 million to train 10,000 employees who either worked for a single day or quit or were let go before performing any work. A SuperBowl spot costing $2.5 million was also scorned.

Should the government buy expensive advertising?

PRO

1. Awareness-raising is critical to completing an accurate count. "We have a very limited window of opportunity to achieve our goals," said the Census Bureau, "and therefore need programming that delivers high ratings. We did not choose the SuperBowl at the expense of some other programming. We went where the audience was."

2. Its SuperBowl deal with CBS gave the Census Bureau "added value" in the form of extra 30-second spots before and during the game and several on-air mentions during the pregame show. "We think this is a pretty good deal for taxpayers," said the Bureau's associate communications director.

CON

1. Senator John McCain commented on the SuperBowl ad, seen by nearly 100 million people, calling it "symptomatic of the spending practices of the federal government and the Congress in a way that is completely out of touch with what's going on out there in the real world."

2. A federal audit warned that Census costs could continue to rise unless spending controls were tightened.

Summary

Census promotions included television, radio, print, Web advertisements, and videos on Facebook, MySpace, Twitter, and YouTube. Census director Robert Groves predicted that such efforts, by motivating residents to respond on time, would avoid costly in-person follow-up and help the department return millions of dollars to the federal government.

Sources: "Census Bureau Wasted Millions on 2010 Headcount Preparations, Audit Finds," *Fox News.com*, www.foxnews.com, February 16, 2010; Hope Yen, "Gov't Buys $2.5M in Super Bowl Ads to Boost Census," *Yahoo! News*, http://news.yahoo.com, February 5, 2010; Ed O'Keefe, "Census's Super Bowl Ad Draws a Flag from McCain," *The Washington Post*, http://voices.washingtonpost.com, February 4, 2010; Aaron Smith, "Census Bureau Counts on Super Bowl Ad," *CNNMoney.com*, http://money.cnn.com, January 26, 2010.

Encyclopedia of Associations, available in many libraries, can help marketers track down trade associations that may have pertinent data. Also, the advertising industry continuously collects data on audiences reached by various media.

Business and trade magazines also publish a wide range of valuable data. *Ulrich's Guide to International Periodicals*, another common library reference, can point researchers in the direction of trade publications that conduct and publish industry-specific research. General business magazines can also be good sources. *Sales & Marketing Management*, for instance, publishes an annual *Survey of Media Markets* that combines statistics for population, effective buying income (EBI), and retail sales into buying power indexes that indicate each geographic market's ability to buy.

Because few libraries carry specialized trade journals, the best way to gather data from them is either directly from the publishers or through online periodical databases such as ProQuest Direct's ABI/Inform, available at many libraries. Increasingly, trade publications maintain Web home pages that allow archival searches. Larger libraries can often provide directories and other publications that

Scanning technology is widely used by grocers and other retailers. Marketing research companies, such as ACNielsen and Information Resources, store these data in commercially available databases.

can help researchers find secondary data. For instance, Guideline's *FindEx: The Directory of Market Research Reports, Studies, and Surveys* lists a tremendous variety of completed research studies available for purchase.

Several national firms offer information to businesses by subscription. RoperASW is a global database service; its Roper Reports Worldwide provides continuing data on consumer attitudes, life stages, lifestyle, and buying behavior for more than 30 developed and developing countries. Wright Investors produces research reports and quality ratings on more than 31,000 companies from 55 countries.

Electronic systems that scan UPC (Universal Product Code) bar codes speed purchase transactions and provide data used for inventory control, ordering, and delivery. Scanning technology is widely used by grocers and other retailers, and marketing research companies such as ACNielsen and Information Resources store this data in commercially available databases. These scanner-based information services track consumer purchases of a wide variety of UPC-coded products. Retailers can use this information to target customers with the right merchandise at the right time.

Newer techniques that rely on radio-frequency identification (RFID) technology are in growing use. American Apparel, a rapidly growing chain of U.S.-made clothing with more than 200 retail stores in 18 countries, tested RFID tags for stocking and inventory replenishment in its New York City store. The company found the tags improved stock keeping and thus helped customers find more items in the right size and color in the right place on the selling floor, thus increasing sales and freeing salespeople from restocking chores so they could spend more time assisting shoppers. In addition, inventory counts that used to occupy several salespeople for an entire day were done by two people in a couple of hours, and more accurately. The company has already decided to roll the RFID technology out across all its U.S. store locations.[16]

ACNielsen SalesNet uses the Internet to deliver scanner data quickly to clients. Data are processed as soon as they are received from supermarkets and are then forwarded to marketing researchers so they can perform more in-depth analysis. At the same time, Nielsen representatives summarize the data in both graphic and spreadsheet form and post the data on the Internet for immediate access by clients.

ONLINE SOURCES OF SECONDARY DATA

The tools of cyberspace sometimes simplify the hunt for secondary data. Hundreds of databases and other sources of information are available online. A well-designed, Internet-based marketing research project can cost less yet yield faster results than offline research.

The Internet has spurred the growth of research aggregators—companies that acquire, catalog, reformat, segment, and then resell premium research reports that have already been published. Aggregators put valuable data within reach of marketers who lack the time or the budget to commission custom research. Because Web technology makes their databases easy to search, aggregators such as Datamonitor and eMarketer can compile detailed, specialized reports quickly and cost-effectively.[17] Social networking sites also yield valuable marketing information. Social networks may also provide secondary private data. Google Analytics is a business tool for measuring online sales, tracking e-mail and ad campaigns, and benchmarking key measures against competitors. Marketers are beginning to use it to collect information from sites mentioned on Twitter, while Facebook has partnered with Nielsen Co. to poll users about their reactions to ads on the site in an effort to demonstrate the ads' effectiveness.[18] YouTube now offers a service called YouTube Insight that gives its video-uploading account holders an array of statistics, graphs, and maps about the audiences they attract, far more specific than just the number of views it used to collect.[19]

sampling Process of selecting survey respondents or research participants.

population (universe) Total group that researchers want to study.

Researchers must, however, carefully evaluate the validity of information they find on the Internet. People without in-depth knowledge of the subject matter may post information in a newsgroup. Similarly, Web pages might contain information gathered using questionable research methods. The phrase *caveat emptor* ("let the buyer beware") should guide evaluation of secondary data on the Internet.

probability sample
Sample that gives every member of the population a chance of being selected.

 assessment check

1. Distinguish between primary and secondary data.
2. What are the major methods of collecting secondary data?
3. What are the major methods of collecting primary data?

Sampling Techniques

 Explain the different sampling techniques used by marketing researchers.

Before undertaking a study to gather primary data, researchers must first identify which participants to include in the study. **Sampling** is the process of selecting survey respondents or research participants. Sampling is important because, if a study fails to involve consumers who accurately reflect the target market, the research is likely to yield misleading conclusions.

The total group of people the researcher wants to study is called the **population** or **universe**. For a political campaign study, the population would be all eligible voters. For research about a new lipstick line, it might be all women in a certain age bracket. The sample is a representative group chosen from this population. Researchers rarely gather information from a study's total population, resulting in a census. Unless the total population is small, the costs of a census are simply too high. Sometimes limitations can reduce the size of the sample. Online surveys, for instance, often draw large but self-selected, rather than random, groups of respondents who don't usually represent the total population. Vague questions and surveys that are too long further reduce the number of respondents and can skew the results even further. [20]

Samples can be classified as either probability samples or nonprobability samples. A **probability sample** is one that gives every member of the population a chance of being selected. Types of probability samples include simple random samples, stratified samples, and cluster samples.

In a **simple random sample**, every member of the relevant universe has an equal opportunity of selection. The draft lottery of the Vietnam era is an example. The days of the year were drawn and set into an array. The placement of a person's birthday in this list determined his likelihood of being called for service. In a **stratified sample**, randomly selected subsamples of different groups are represented in the total sample. Stratified samples provide efficient, representative groups that are relatively homogeneous for a certain characteristic for such studies as opinion polls in which groups of individuals share various divergent viewpoints. In a **cluster sample**, researchers select a sample of subgroups (or clusters) from which they draw respondents. Each cluster reflects the diversity of the whole population being sampled. This cost-efficient type of probability sample is widely used when the entire population cannot be listed or enumerated.

In contrast, a **nonprobability sample** relies on personal judgment somewhere in the selection process. In other words, researchers decide which particular groups to study. Types of nonprobability samples are convenience samples and quota samples. A **convenience sample** is a nonprobability sample selected from among readily available respondents; this sample often is called an *accidental sample* because those included just happen to be in the place where the study is being conducted. Mall intercept surveys and TV call-in opinion polls are good examples. Marketing researchers sometimes use convenience samples in exploratory research but not in definitive studies. A **quota sample** is a nonprobability sample divided to maintain the proportion of certain characteristics among different segments or groups seen in the population as a whole. In other words, each field worker is assigned a quota that specifies the number and characteristics of the people to contact. It differs from a stratified sample in which researchers select subsamples by some random process; in a quota sample, they handpick participants.

simple random sample
Basic type of probability sample in which every individual in the relevant universe has an equal opportunity of being selected.

stratified sample
Probability sample constructed to represent randomly selected subsamples of different groups within the total sample; each subgroup is relatively homogeneous for a certain characteristic.

cluster sample
Probability sample in which researchers select a sample of subgroups (or clusters) from which they draw respondents; each cluster reflects the diversity of the whole population sampled.

nonprobability sample
Sample that involves personal judgment somewhere in the selection process.

convenience sample
Nonprobability sample selected from among readily available respondents.

quota sample Nonprobability sample divided to maintain the proportion of certain characteristics among different segments or groups seen in the population as a whole.

✓ assessment check

1. What is sampling?
2. Explain the different types of probability samples.
3. Identify the types of nonprobability samples.

5   Identify the methods by which marketing researchers collect primary data.

Primary Research Methods

Marketers use a variety of methods for conducting primary research, as Figure 8.2 shows. The principal methods for collecting primary data are observation, surveys, and controlled experiments. The choice among these methods depends on the issues under study and the decisions that marketers need to make. In some cases, researchers may decide to combine techniques during the research process.

OBSERVATION METHOD

In observational studies, researchers view the overt actions of subjects being studied. Marketers trying to understand how consumers behave in certain situations find observation a useful technique. Observation tactics may be as simple as counting the number of cars passing by a potential site for a fast-food restaurant or checking the license plates at a shopping center near a state line to determine where shoppers live.

Technological advances provide increasingly sophisticated ways for observing consumer behavior. The television industry relies on data from people meters, electronic remote-control devices that record the TV viewing habits of individual household members to measure the popularity of TV shows. Traditional people meters require each viewer to press a button each time he or she turns on the TV, changes channels, or leaves the room.

Some observers expect that communications technology will also change the way consumers respond to advertising. Internet users are more willing than ever to use real money for purchases that arise during their social gaming and social networking sessions, for instance, including on Facebook. "It surprised a lot of people," said *Adweek*'s digital editor. "It's an activity that showed up first in Asia and many people thought, 'Oh well, people will never do that here.'"[21] Technology is also yielding new ways to observe people. Read the "Marketing Success" feature to learn about the marketing implications of software that maps consumers' movements around cities.

mktg: *success*

Mapping the Market

Background. Just as Internet marketers can track the number of visitors to their Web sites, so do marketers in the physical world want to be able to understand where consumers go, when, how often, and who else is there. Discovering what similarly located people have in common can help them target advertising with pinpoint accuracy.

The Challenge. Collecting highly detailed mapping information is easier than

ever thanks to Wi-Fi and smartphones like the iPhone and BlackBerry, used by millions of consumers. Hundreds of applications for these mobile devices already tap the user's physical location to offer walking or driving directions, locate friends, and recommend nearby stores and restaurants. "The phone in your hand is the bridge between the virtual and real worlds," said a Web executive at Nokia. Remaining marketing challenges are

overcoming consumers' resistance to unsolicited ads on their cell phones and working out privacy issues inherent in the highly specific mapping capabilities that now are possible.

The Strategy. A New York City startup called Sense Networks is developing software that pinpoints real-time consumer activity around different city neighborhoods. After shying away from selling

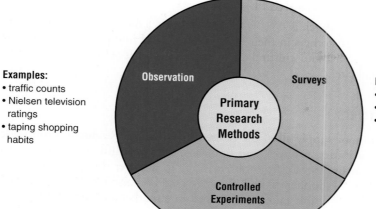

figure 8.2

Types of Primary Research

Examples:
• traffic counts
• Nielsen television ratings
• taping shopping habits

Observation

Surveys

Primary Research Methods

Examples:
• focus group interviews
• telephone surveys
• online surveys

Controlled Experiments

Example:
• test market

Videotaping consumers in action is also gaining acceptance as a research technique. Cookware manufacturers may videotape consumers cooking in their own kitchens to evaluate how they use their pots and pans. A toothbrush manufacturer asked marketing research firm E-Lab to videotape consumers brushing their teeth and using mouthwash in its quest to develop products that would leave behind the sensation of cleanliness and freshness.

In an effort to understand what makes younger consumers tick, a trend-forecasting firm called Teenage Research Unlimited has auditioned and hired a panel of more than 300 "diverse, trend-setting, savvy teens" to participate in focus groups and research queries for its Trendwatch Panel. The company has also interviewed more than 2 million teens and "twenty-somethings" in 20 countries around the world for its annual TRU Study report.[22]

© TERRI MILLER/E-VISUAL COMMUNICATIONS, INC.

Observation methods may be as simple as counting the number of cars passing by a potential site for a fast-food restaurant.

services directly to these spotlighted consumers because of privacy concerns, the firm started looking into ways to allow marketers to make use of its mapping data, organized by "tribes" or people with similar behavior. While Sense could collect personal data too, "It's not worth the risk," says the firm, "and we don't need that information."

The Outcome. Some say the new cartography heralds the arrival of the "Next Net," and Sense recently raised $6 million in new venture capital. While its pure marketing possibilities are still being explored, mapping software like Sense Networks' also has the potential to improve transit systems and traffic patterns, ease workers' commutes, pinpoint the occurrence and spread of crime,

slow the transmission of disease, and even guide some investment decisions.

Sources: Company Web site, Sense Networks Inc., www.sensenetworks.com, accessed March 2, 2010; Matt Marshall, "Sense Networks Gets $6M in Hotly Contested Deal for 'Tribe' Advertising," *DigitalBeat*, http://digital.venturebeat.com, June 26, 2009; Kate Greene, "Mapping a City's Rhythm," *Technology Review*, www.technologyreview.com, March 13, 2009; Stephen Baker, "The Next Net," *BusinessWeek*, March 9, 2009, pp. 42–45.

INTERPRETATIVE RESEARCH

Another type of primary research is **interpretative research**, a method in which a researcher observes a customer or group of customers in their natural setting and interprets their behavior based on an understanding of the social and cultural characteristics of that setting. We discuss interpretative research in more detail later.

Survey Methods

Observation alone cannot supply all of the desired information. Researchers must ask questions to get information on attitudes, motives, and opinions. It is also difficult to get exact demographic information, such as income levels, from observation. To discover this information, researchers can use either interviews or questionnaires. Philadelphia-based Dorland Healthcare Information provides marketing research for the health care and managed care market and relies heavily on mail, phone, and fax surveys as well as interviews with knowledgeable sources.[23]

TELEPHONE INTERVIEWS

Telephone interviews are a quick and inexpensive method for obtaining a small quantity of relatively impersonal information. Simple, clearly worded questions are easy for interviewers to pose over the phone and are effective at drawing appropriate responses. Telephone surveys have relatively high response rates, especially with repeated calls; calling a number once yields a response rate of 50 to 60 percent, but calling the same number five times raises the response rate to 85 percent. To maximize responses and save costs, some researchers use computerized dialing and digitally synthesized voices that interview respondents.

However, phone surveys have several drawbacks. Most important, many people refuse to take part in them. Their reasons include lack of time, the nuisance factor, negative associations of phone surveys with telemarketing, and poorly designed surveys or questions that are difficult to understand. The Do Not Call Registry, which regulates telemarketing, excludes calls made for research purposes.[24]

Many respondents hesitate to give personal characteristics about themselves over the telephone. Also, results may be biased by the omission of typical households in which adults are working during the day. Other households, particularly market segments such as single women and physicians, are likely to have unlisted numbers. While computerized random dialing can give access to unlisted numbers, it is restricted in several states.

The popularity of Caller ID systems to screen unwanted calls is another obstacle for telephone researchers. State laws on Caller ID vary. Some require vendors to offer a blocking service to callers who wish to evade the system. Marketers face other problems in obtaining responses from a representative sample of respondents using phone surveys: consumer perception of intrusion into their privacy and the number of consumers in the Do Not Call Registry.

Other obstacles restrict the usefulness of telephone surveys abroad. In areas where telephone ownership is rare, survey results will be highly biased. Telephone interviewing is also difficult in countries that lack directories or charge landline telephone customers on a per-minute basis, or where call volumes congest limited phone line capacity.

Telephone interviews are a quick and inexpensive method for obtaining a small quantity of relatively impersonal information.

© ISTOCKPHOTO.COM/NEUSTOCKIMAGES

PERSONAL INTERVIEWS

The best means for obtaining detailed information about consumers usually is the personal interview because the interviewer can establish rapport with respondents and explain confusing or vague questions. In addition to contacting respondents at their homes or workplaces, marketing research firms can conduct interviews in rented space in shopping centers where they gain wide access to potential buyers of the merchandise they are studying. These locations sometimes feature private interviewing space, videotape equipment, and food preparation facilities for taste tests. As mentioned earlier, interviews conducted in shopping centers typically are called **mall intercepts**. Downtown retail districts and airports provide other valuable locations for marketing researchers.

FOCUS GROUPS

Marketers also gather research information through the popular technique of focus group interviews. A **focus group** brings together 8 to 12 individuals in one location to discuss a subject of interest. Unlike other interview techniques that elicit information through a question-and-answer format, focus groups usually encourage a general discussion of a predetermined topic. Focus groups can provide quick and relatively inexpensive insight into consumer attitudes and motivations.

In a focus group, the leader, or moderator, typically begins by explaining the purpose of the meeting and suggesting an opening topic. The moderator's main purpose, however, is to stimulate interaction among group members to encourage their discussion of numerous points. The moderator may occasionally interject questions as catalysts to direct the group's discussion. The moderator's job is difficult, requiring preparation and group facilitation skills.

Focus group sessions often last one or two hours. Researchers usually record the discussion on tape, and observers frequently watch through a one-way mirror. Some research firms also allow clients to view focus groups in action through videoconferencing systems.

Focus groups are a particularly valuable tool for exploratory research, developing new-product ideas, and preliminary testing of alternative marketing strategies. They can also aid in the development of well-structured questionnaires for larger-scale research.

Focus groups have a few drawbacks. For instance, one argumentative participant can intimidate everyone else in the group, just as one person who won't open up in the discussion can hold others back. In addition, some group members may say what they think researchers want to hear, offer ideas and opinions for which they have no supporting evidence or experience, or assume everyone feels the same way they do.[25]

Researchers are finding ways to re-create the focus group environment over the Internet. With experienced moderators who have the technical skills to function fluently online, it is possible to gain valuable qualitative information at a fraction of the cost of running a traditional focus group session. Online focus groups can be both cost and time efficient, with immediate results in the form of chat transcripts. The convenience of online conversations tends to improve attendance as well, particularly among those who are otherwise difficult to include, such as professionals and people who travel frequently, and the problem of peer pressure is virtually eliminated. Some drawbacks include the lack of ability to see body language and nonverbal cues, the difficulty of testing any products in which taste or smell is relevant, and the potential for samples to be nonrepresentative because they are limited to those who have Internet access and a certain comfort level with technology.

MAIL SURVEYS

Although personal interviews can provide very detailed information, cost considerations usually prevent an organization from using personal interviews in a large-scale study. A mail survey can be a cost-effective alternative. Mail surveys can provide anonymity that may encourage respondents to give candid answers. They can also help marketers track consumer attitudes through ongoing research and sometimes provide demographic data that may be helpful in market segmentation.

Mail questionnaires do, however, have several limitations. First, response rates are typically much lower than for personal interviews. Second, because researchers must wait for respondents to complete and return questionnaires, mail surveys usually take a considerably longer time to conduct. A third limitation is that questionnaires cannot answer unanticipated questions that occur to respondents as they complete the forms. In addition, complex questions may not be suitable for a mail questionnaire. Finally, unless they gather additional information from nonrespondents through other means, researchers must worry about possible bias in the results stemming from differences between respondents and nonrespondents.

mall intercepts
Interviews conducted inside retail shopping centers.

focus group
Simultaneous personal interview of a small group of individuals that relies on group discussion about a certain topic.

Researchers try to minimize these limitations by carefully developing and pretesting questionnaires. Researchers can boost response rates by keeping questionnaires short and by offering incentives—typically, discount coupons or a dollar bill.

FAX SURVEYS

The low response rates and long follow-up times associated with mail surveys have spurred interest in the alternative of faxing survey documents. In some cases, faxes may supplement mail surveys; in others, they may be the primary method for contacting respondents. Because millions of households do not have fax machines, securing a representative sample of respondents is a difficult undertaking in fax surveys of final consumers. As a result, most of these surveys focus on business-related research studies.

The federal junk fax law prohibits the sending by fax of "any material advertising the commercial availability or quality of any property, goods, or services which is transmitted to any person without that person's prior express invitation or permission, in writing or otherwise." The first page of any fax solicitation must now include information for the recipient about how to opt out of similar messages in the future.[26]

ONLINE SURVEYS AND OTHER INTERNET-BASED METHODS

The growing population of Internet users has spurred researchers to conduct online surveys. Using the Web, they are able to speed the survey process, increase sample sizes, ignore geographic boundaries, and dramatically reduce costs. While a standard research project can take up to eight weeks to complete, a thorough online project may take two weeks or less. Less intrusive than telephone surveys, online research allows participants to respond at their leisure. The novelty and ease of answering online may even encourage higher response rates. For some tips on creating online surveys, see the "Career Readiness" feature.

Businesses and other organizations are increasingly including questionnaires on their Web pages to solicit information about consumer demographics, attitudes, and comments and suggestions for improving goods and services or improving marketing messages. Online polling is also increasingly popular. Social networking sites, on which consumers around the world now spend an average of five and a half hours a month (up from just three hours a year ago), show no sign of slowing down. Facebook has the highest on-site time (nearly six hours a month), and the largest number of unique users—nearly 210 million worldwide.[27] While companies have struggled for ways to measure the impact of social media, more tools than ever exist for tracking which ones drive traffic to any particular site or sites and thus which would be the best sites on which to post polls or questionnaires.

The Georgia Aquarium took a more direct approach to measuring the Internet's effect on ticket sales, offering deep discounts off admission prices to those who either followed it on Twitter or became Aquarium fans on MySpace or Facebook. Using a separate URL with which to track the promotion, the Aquarium found it reaped an additional $42,000 in ticket sales (or 2,500 admissions) during the four-month promotion. Though officials weren't able to determine how many of those tickets were due to the discount and how many people would

A YouTube video called "Dancing Otters" provided indirect online marketing for the Georgia Aquarium.

© DM GORDON/SHUTTERSTOCK.COM

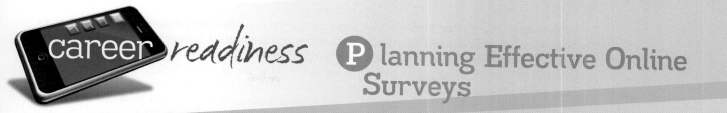

career readiness 🅟 lanning Effective Online Surveys

nline surveys are significantly less expensive than paper questionnaires and telephone interviews. They offer respondents anonymity, which helps most people speak more freely, and the chance to answer questions at their own pace. They do require a bit of planning, however, to make sure that you get the results you want and don't waste respondents' time. Here are some tips for creating successful online surveys.

- Find out what you want to know. List items you want customers to tell you, and prioritize them. Then create and rank a list of your own questions about your business, its goals, or its products. Write a third list of recent customer complaints or suggestions. Compare the lists. Issues appearing on two or more lists are those you'll want to ask about.

- Decide how to organize the results. This will help you determine whether to ask about category breakdowns like age, sex, income bracket, geographic location, and educational attainment.

- Determine how much effort you want to spend analyzing write-in comments, as opposed to easy-to-tabulate multiple-choice and yes/no responses.

- Recognize that people won't spend a long time answering questions. Keep the survey and its instructions short and to the point.

- Word questions carefully. Avoid complex constructions like double negatives, keep questions neutral (don't lead respondents to the answer), and weed out acronyms and abbreviations.

- Make sure the survey is professional looking, and have at least two people proofread it carefully.

- Test the survey on people in different departments of your firm. You may get valuable insights from their different points of view.

- Tabulate the test surveys to make sure there won't be any technical glitches in the live survey.

- Edit once more to make sure each question will provide you with information that's really useful to your business.

- Motivate your sample to respond by explaining the purpose of your survey and how the information you gather can benefit them. Consider e-mail reminders, or even an incentive like a gift certificate or raffle, to boost your response rate.

Sources: "Guidelines for Conducting an Online Survey," *Survey-Hosting.com*, www.survey-hosting.com, accessed March 31, 2010; Sharon Long, "5 Survey Tips to Decrease Survey Abandonment and Non-Response," *Survey.Cvent.com*, http://survey.cvent.com, February 4, 2010; "How to Conduct an Online Survey and Engage Customers in a Dialogue," *SurveyPro*, www.surveyspro.com, accessed May 5, 2009; "How to Conduct an Online Customer Survey," *EHow*, www.ehow.com, accessed May 5, 2009.

---

have come anyway, they are optimistic. "We had zero sales through social media last year," said the Aquarium's marketing vice president, "so it's infinite growth." Aquarium officials were even able to make an indirect online measure of the Aquarium's appeal thanks to a YouTube video called "Dancing Otters," shot and posted by an Aquarium visitor. It doesn't mention the Georgia Aquarium's name, but it drew nearly 1 million YouTube visitors. What the Aquarium staff would still like to be able to do is figure out how online videos and chat about the Aquarium translate into actual ticket sales. "I've been a big proponent of being able to measure and using measurements to drive decisions," says the Aquarium's vice president for information technology. "And we're making progress."[28]

At present, no industrywide standards define techniques for measuring Web use. Some sites ask users to register before accessing the pages; others merely keep track of the number of "hits," or number of times a visitor accesses a page. Marketers have tried to place a value on a site's "stickiness"—longer-lasting site visits—as a means of measuring effectiveness. Others use "cookies," which, as Chapter 4 explained, are electronic identifiers deposited on viewers' computers, to track click-through behavior—the paths users take as they move through the site. However, because some consumers change their Internet service providers frequently and special software is available to detect and remove them, cookies have lost some of their effectiveness.

Research suggests that about 50 percent of marketing executives are unsure of the return they are getting for their online marketing efforts. Meanwhile some observers believe the traditional measure of ROI, or return on investment, must evolve into one or more other results that are easier for online marketers to actually measure, such as the sales success rate, the ability to build self-moderating customer service programs within social networks, or the creation of brand advocates, perhaps tracked with click-through sales or promotional codes. Others look to turn the often intangible effects of social media into new measures like user time spent interacting with others, degree of user involvement, and level of user attention.[29]

Certainly observing consumers online, where users spend more time than with any other medium including TV, offers marketers the opportunity to monitor the buying decision process, understand what turns a browser into a buyer, see how shoppers compare product features, and grasp the relative impacts on purchase decisions of marketing and price. Details like these help advertisers grow increasingly accurate about where they place their messages.

EXPERIMENTAL METHOD

controlled experiment
Scientific investigation in which a researcher manipulates a test group (or groups) and compares the results with those of a control group that did not receive the experimental controls or manipulations.

test marketing
Marketing research technique that involves introducing a new product in a specific area and then measuring its degree of success.

The third—and least-used—method for collecting primary data is the **controlled experiment**. A marketing research experiment is a scientific investigation in which a researcher controls or manipulates a test group (or groups) and compares the results with those of a control group that did not receive the experimental controls or manipulations.

The most common use of this method by marketers is **test marketing**, or introducing a new product in a specific area and then observing its degree of success. Up to this point, a product development team may have gathered feedback from focus groups. Other information may have come from shoppers' evaluations of competing products. Test marketing is the first stage at which the product performs in a real-life environment.

The Coca-Cola Company and Procter & Gamble have used streaming ads in a section of MySpace to invite users to try free samples of new products or incentives. (The soft-drink giant offered a free music download.)[30] Some firms omit test marketing and move directly from product development to full-scale production. These companies cite three problems with test marketing:

1. Test marketing is expensive. A firm can spend more than $1 million depending on the size of the test market city and the cost of buying media to advertise the product.

2. Competitors quickly learn about the new product. By studying the test market, competitors can develop alternative strategies.

3. Some products are not well suited to test marketing. Few firms test market long-lived, durable goods such as cars because of the major financial investments required for their development, the need to establish networks of dealers to distribute the products, and requirements for parts and servicing.

Companies that decide to skip the test-marketing process can choose several other options. A firm may simulate a test-marketing campaign through computer-modeling software. By plugging in data on similar products, it can develop a sales projection for a new product. Another firm may offer an item in just one region of the United States or in another country, adjusting promotions and advertising based on local results before going to other geographic regions. Another option may be to limit a product's introduction to only one retail chain to carefully control and evaluate promotions and results.

assessment check

1. What are the principal methods for collecting primary data?
2. Identify the different types of survey methods.

Conducting International Marketing Research

As corporations expand globally, they need to gather correspondingly more knowledge about consumers in other countries. Although marketing researchers follow the same basic steps for international studies as for domestic ones, they often face some very different challenges.

U.S. organizations can tap many secondary resources as they research global markets. One major information source is the U.S. government, which offers a wealth of information through its dedicated Web site, Export.gov. Here, marketers can find marketing research, business leads, and other data on international trade and intellectual property protection drawn from sources across the U.S. government. The site's trove of international marketing research is organized by country (more than 120 countries) and by industry (more than 110 business sectors). Personalized counseling and customized research are available (the latter for a fee), as well as guidance on improving international business strategy, targeting markets overseas, evaluating international business partners, and increasing brand awareness around the world. U.S. trade show organizers can get help attracting foreign visitors.[31] The U.S. Department of Commerce offers one-click access to business, trade, and economic information through its STAT-USA® Web site, which features more than 200,000 trade releases, international research reports, country analyses, and trade and procurement leads.[32]

When conducting international studies, companies must be prepared to deal with both language issues—communicating their message in the most effective way—and cultural issues, or capturing local citizens' interests while avoiding missteps that could unintentionally offend them. Companies also need to take a good look at a country's business environment, including political and economic conditions, trade regulations affecting research studies and data collection, and the potential for short- and long-term growth. Many marketers recommend tapping local researchers to investigate foreign markets.

Businesses may need to adjust their data collection methods for primary research in other countries because some methods do not easily transfer across national frontiers. Face-to-face interviewing, for instance, remains the most common method for conducting primary research outside the United States.

While mail surveys are a common data collection method in developed countries, they are useless in many other nations because of low literacy rates, unreliable mail service, and a lack of address lists. Telephone interviews may also not be suitable in other countries, especially those where many people do not have phones. Focus groups can be difficult to arrange because of cultural and social factors. In Latin American countries, for example, highly educated consumers make up a sought-after and opinionated minority, but they have little time to devote to lengthy focus group discussions. Middle- to lower-income Latin Americans may not be accustomed to articulating their opinions about products and grow reticent in the presence of others, whereas in some countries where violence and kidnapping are common, affluent consumers are reluctant to attend meetings with strangers. To help with such difficulties, a growing number of international research firms offer experience in conducting global studies.

> 6 Explain the challenges of conducting marketing research in global markets.

assessment check

1. What are some U.S. organizations that can serve as sources of international secondary marketing data?
2. What is the most common method of primary data collection outside the United States?

Interpretive Research

As mentioned earlier, interpretative research is a method that observes a customer or group of customers in their natural settings and then interprets their behavior based on an understanding of social and cultural characteristics of that setting.

Interpretative research has attracted considerable interest in recent years. Developed by social anthropologists as a method for explaining behavior that operates below the level of conscious thought, interpretative research can provide insights into consumer behavior and the ways in which consumers interact with brands.

Ethnographic Studies

In interpretive research, the researcher first spends an extensive amount of time studying the culture, and for that reason, the studies often are called *ethnographic* studies. The word *ethnographic* means that a researcher takes a cultural perspective of the population being studied. For that reason, interpretative research often is used to interpret consumer behavior within a foreign culture where language, ideals, values, and expectations are subject to different cultural influences. After experiencing a number of product failures in low-income markets in Latin America, Procter & Gamble (P&G) began an "immersion research" program called "Living It," in which P&G managers and executives spent time with low-income families around the world living in their homes to develop a better understanding of their needs and desires. P&G's subsequent sales suggest that the effort was worthwhile. Among the mistakes the firm corrected was a low sudsing detergent it introduced in Mexico, unaware that most of its customers there were manual laborers who associated suds with cleaning power.[33]

Interpretative research focuses on understanding the meaning of a product or the consumption experience in a consumer's life. Its methods capture consumers interacting with products in their environment—in other words, capturing what they actually do, not what they say they do. Typically, subjects are filmed in specific situations, such as socializing with friends in a bar for research into beverage consumption, or for extended periods of time for paid participants. Paid participants may be followed by a videographer who records their day-to-day movements and interactions, or they may film themselves. Some companies even pay consumers to wear mini video cameras attached to visors and linked to a sound recorder. These systems record consumer behavior while participants are shopping or doing chores.

An iPhone application developed by Everyday Lives, a British research agency, allows ethnographic researchers to take photos, notes, and audio and video clips of subjects while conducting their studies. Users can organize the material by theme and send it to their e-mail account to review it later. A BlackBerry version of the app is under development. "We expect word of mouth to play a hugely important part in promoting the app," said Everyday Lives' founder.[34]

An iPhone application developed by Everyday Lives allows ethnographic researchers to take photos, notes, and audio and video clips of subjects while conducting their studies.

assessment check

1. How is interpretative research typically conducted?

2. When should ethnographic research be employed?

Computer Technology in Marketing Research

The ability to quickly gather and analyze business intelligence can create a substantial strategic advantage. Computer databases provide a wealth of data for marketing research, whether they are outside the company or designed specifically to gather important facts about its customers. Chapter 10 explores how companies use internal databases and customer relationship management technology. This section addresses important uses of computer technology related to marketing research: marketing information systems (MISs), marketing decision support systems (MDSSs), data mining, business intelligence, and competitive intelligence.

Marketing Information Systems (MISs)

In the past, many marketing managers complained that their information problems resulted from too much rather than too little information. Reams of data were difficult to use and not always relevant. At times, information was almost impossible to find. Modern technological advances have made constraints like these obsolete.

A **marketing information system (MIS)** is a planned, computer-based system designed to provide decision makers with a continuous flow of information relevant to their areas of responsibility. A component of the organization's overall management information system, a marketing information system deals specifically with marketing data and issues.

A well-constructed MIS serves as a company's nerve center, continually monitoring the market environment—both inside and outside the organization—and providing instantaneous information. Marketers can store data for later use, classify and analyze that data, and retrieve it easily when needed.

Marketing Decision Support Systems (MDSSs)

A **marketing decision support system (MDSS)** consists of software that helps users quickly obtain and apply information in a way that supports marketing decisions. Taking MIS a step further, it allows managers to explore and connect such varying information as the state of the market, consumer behavior, sales forecasts, competitors' actions, and environmental changes. MDSSs consist of four main characteristics: they are interactive, investigative, flexible, and accessible. An MDSS can create simulations or models to illustrate the likely results of changes in marketing strategies or market conditions.

While an MIS provides raw data, an MDSS develops this data into information useful for decision making. For example, an MIS might provide a list of product sales from the previous day. A manager could use an MDSS to transform this raw data into graphs illustrating sales trends or reports estimating the impact of specific decisions, such as raising prices or expanding into new regions.

Data Mining

Data mining is the process of searching through computerized data files to detect patterns. It focuses on identifying relationships not obvious to marketers—in a sense, answering questions that marketing researchers may not even have thought to ask. The data is stored in a huge database called a *data warehouse*. Software for the marketing decision support system often is associated with the data warehouse and is used to mine data. Once marketers identify patterns and connections, they use this intelligence to check the effectiveness of different strategy options.

Data mining is an efficient way to sort through huge amounts of data and to make sense of that data. It helps marketers create customer profiles, pinpoint reasons for customer loyalty or the lack thereof, analyze potential returns on changes in pricing or promotion, and forecast sales. Data mining offers considerable advantages in retailing, the hotel industry, banking, utilities, and many other areas and holds the promise of providing answers to many specific strategic questions.

San Diego research firm Strategic Vision conducted a data-mining study of car sales to link motivation to purchase. It found that all vehicle segments, including luxury buyers, were affected by a carmaker's longstanding reputation for the reliability and durability of its vehicles, leading other

marketing information system (MIS) Planned, computer-based system designed to provide managers with a continuous flow of information relevant to their specific decisions and areas of responsibility.

marketing decision support system (MDSS) Marketing information system component that links a decision maker with relevant databases and analysis tools.

data mining Process of searching through customer databases to detect patterns that guide marketing decision making.

> 7 Outline the most important uses of computer technology in marketing research.

firms to work harder to catch up. "Durability alone and simply satisfying customers is not enough for buyers who demand both immediate and long-term value," said Strategic Vision's president.[35]

Business Intelligence

Business intelligence is the process of gathering information and analyzing it to improve business strategy, tactics, and daily operations. Using advanced software tools, marketers gather information from within and outside the organization. Business intelligence can thus tell the firm how its own sales operation is doing or what its top competitors are up to.

The key is not only gathering the information but also getting it into a form that employees can make sense of and use for decision making and strategizing. Software can help users collect, aggregate, and create reports with outside information available on the Web from such databases as, say, Dun & Bradstreet. SmartOrg, based in Menlo Park, California, is one firm that specializes in helping firms like Boeing and Hewlett-Packard identify and manage information. "SmartOrg systems and processes give us the ability to evaluate uncertainty and gives the project teams the freedom to drive towards the upside," says Hewlett-Packard's director of new business creation.[36]

Competitive Intelligence

Competitive intelligence is a form of business intelligence that focuses on finding information about competitors using published sources, interviews, observations by salespeople and suppliers in the industry, government agencies, public filings such as patent applications, and other secondary sources, including the Internet. Its aim is to uncover the specific advantages a competitor has, such as new-product launches, new features in existing goods or services, or new marketing or promotional strategies. Even a competitor's advertising can provide clues. Marketers use competitive intelligence to make better decisions that strengthen their own competitive strategy in turn.

 assessment check

1. Distinguish between an MIS and an MDSS.
2. What is data mining?
3. Describe the process of collecting business and competitive intelligence.

table 8.1 A Sampling of Sales Forecasting Software Programs

Forecast Pro
- Input historical data and then the software analyzes the data, selects the appropriate forecasting technique, and makes its statistical calculations.
- Adjust the information and save the new changes.
- The software creates reports and graphs for presenting results.
- There are three editions available: Forecast Pro Unlimited, Forecast Pro TRAC, and Forecast Pro XE.

Right90
- Includes a four-step forecasting process: Capture, Vet, Analyze, Drive.
- Integrates with existing company IT applications.
- Available forecasting applications include: Right90 Sales Forecast Capture, Right90 Statistical Forecasting, Right90 Change Analytics, Right90 Trust Analytics.

SAS
- SAS/ETS Time Series Forecasting uses the following techniques: time series and econometric.
- SAS Forecast Server creates several forecasts quickly to allow a company to plan their future.

Sales Forecasting

A basic building block of any marketing plan is a **sales forecast**, an estimate of a firm's revenue for a specified future period. Sales forecasts play major roles in new-product decisions, production scheduling, financial planning, inventory planning and procurement, distribution, and human resources planning. An inaccurate forecast may lead to incorrect decisions in each of these areas. There are a number of software programs that offer companies sales forecasting applications to help automate the forecasting process. Table 8.1 outlines three of those programs.

Marketing research techniques are used to deliver effective sales forecasts. A sales forecast is also an important tool for marketing control because it sets standards against which to measure actual performance. Without such standards, no comparisons can be made.

Planners rely on short-run, intermediate, and long-run sales forecasts. A short-run forecast usually covers a period of up to one year, an intermediate forecast covers one to five years, and a long-run forecast extends beyond five years. Although sales forecasters use an array of techniques to predict the future—ranging from computer simulations to studying trends identified by futurists—their methods fall into two broad categories: qualitative and quantitative forecasting.

Qualitative forecasting techniques rely on subjective data that reports opinions rather than exact historical data. **Quantitative forecasting** methods, by contrast, use statistical computations such as trend extensions based on past data, computer simulations, and econometric models. As Table 8.2 shows, each method has benefits and limitations. Consequently, most organizations use a combination of both techniques.

> ### 8 Identify the major types of forecasting methods.

> **sales forecast** Estimate of a firm's revenue for a specified future period.
>
> **qualitative forecasting** Use of subjective techniques to forecast sales, such as the jury of executive opinion, Delphi technique, sales force composite, and surveys of buyer intentions.
>
> **quantitative forecasting** Use of statistical forecasting techniques such as trend analysis and exponential smoothing.

table 8.2 Benefits and Limitations of Various Forecasting Techniques

Techniques	Benefits	Limitations
Qualitative Methods		
Jury of executive opinion	Opinions come from executives in many different departments; quick; inexpensive	Managers may lack background knowledge and experience to make meaningful predictions
Delphi technique	Group of experts may predict long-term events such as technological breakthroughs	Time-consuming; expensive
Sales force composite	Salespeople have expert customer, product, and competitor knowledge; quick; inexpensive	Inaccurate forecasts may result from low estimates of salespeople concerned about their influence on quotas
Survey of buyer intentions	Useful in predicting short-term and intermediate sales for firms that serve selected customers	Intentions to buy may not result in actual purchases; time-consuming; expensive
Quantitative Methods		
Test market	Provides realistic information on actual purchases rather than on intent to buy	Alerts competition to new-product plans; time-consuming; expensive
Trend analysis	Quick; inexpensive; effective with stable customer demand and environment	Assumes the future will continue the past; ignores environmental changes
Exponential smoothing	Same benefits as trend analysis, but emphasizes more recent data	Same limitations as trend analysis, but not as severe due to emphasis on recent data

Qualitative Forecasting Techniques

Planners apply qualitative forecasting methods when they want judgmental or subjective indicators. Qualitative forecasting techniques include the jury of executive opinion, Delphi technique, sales force composite, and survey of buyer intentions.

JURY OF EXECUTIVE OPINION

jury of executive opinion Qualitative sales forecasting method that assesses the sales expectations of various executives.

The technique called the **jury of executive opinion** combines and averages the outlooks of top executives from such areas as marketing, finance, and production. Top managers bring the following capabilities to the process: experience and knowledge about situations that influence sales, open-minded attitudes toward the future, and awareness of the bases for their judgments. This quick and inexpensive method generates good forecasts for sales and new-product development. It works best for short-run forecasting.

DELPHI TECHNIQUE

Delphi technique Qualitative sales forecasting method that gathers and redistributes several rounds of anonymous forecasts until the participants reach a consensus.

Like the jury of executive opinion, the **Delphi technique** solicits opinions from several people, but it also gathers input from experts outside the firm, such as academic researchers, rather than relying completely on company executives. It is most appropriately used to predict long-run issues, such as technological breakthroughs, that could affect future sales and the market potential for new products.

The Delphi technique works as follows: A firm selects a panel of experts and sends each a questionnaire relating to a future event. After combining and averaging the answers, the firm develops another questionnaire based on these results and sends it back to the same people. The process continues until it identifies a consensus. Although firms have successfully used Delphi to predict future technological breakthroughs, the method is both expensive and time-consuming.

SALES FORCE COMPOSITE

sales force composite Qualitative sales forecasting method based on the combined sales estimates of the firm's salespeople.

The **sales force composite** technique develops forecasts based on the belief that organization members closest to the marketplace—those with specialized product, customer, and competitive knowledge—offer the best insights concerning short-term future sales. It typically works from the bottom up. Management consolidates salespeople's estimates first at the district level, then at the regional level, and finally nationwide to obtain an aggregate forecast of sales that reflects all three levels.

The sales force composite approach has some weaknesses, however. Because salespeople recognize the role of their sales forecasts in determining sales quotas for their territories, they are likely to make conservative estimates. Moreover, their narrow perspectives from within their limited geographic territories may prevent them from considering the impact on sales of trends developing in other territories, forthcoming technological innovations, or the major changes in marketing strategies. Consequently, the sales force composite gives the best forecasts in combination with other techniques.

SURVEY OF BUYER INTENTIONS

survey of buyer intentions Qualitative sales forecasting method that samples opinions among groups of present and potential customers concerning their purchase intentions.

A **survey of buyer intentions** gathers input through mail-in questionnaires, online feedback, telephone polls, and personal interviews to determine the purchasing intentions of a representative group of present and potential customers. This method suits firms that serve limited numbers of customers but often proves impractical for those with millions of customers. Also, buyer surveys gather useful information only when customers willingly reveal their buying intentions. Moreover, customer intentions do not necessarily translate into actual purchases. These surveys may help a firm predict short-run or intermediate sales, but they employ time-consuming and expensive methods.

Quantitative Forecasting Techniques

Quantitative techniques attempt to eliminate the subjectiveness of the qualitative methods. They include such methods as test markets, trend analysis, and exponential smoothing.

TEST MARKETS

One quantitative technique, the test market, frequently helps planners assess consumer responses to new-product offerings. The procedure typically begins by establishing one or more test markets to gauge consumer responses to a new product under actual marketplace conditions. These tests also permit experimenters to evaluate the effects of different prices, alternative promotional strategies, and other marketing mix variations by comparing results among different test markets.

The primary advantage of test markets is the realism they provide for the marketer. On the other hand, these expensive and time-consuming experiments may also communicate marketing plans to competitors before a firm introduces a product to the total market.

TREND ANALYSIS

Trend analysis develops forecasts for future sales by analyzing the historical relationship between sales and time. It implicitly assumes the collective causes of past sales will continue to exert similar influences in the future. When historical data are available, planners can quickly and inexpensively complete trend analysis. Software programs can calculate the average annual increment of change for the available sales data. This average increment of change is then projected into the future to come up with the sales forecast. So if the sales of a firm have been growing $15.3 million on average per year, this amount of sales could be added to last year's sales total to arrive at next year's forecast.

Of course, trend analysis cannot be used if historical data are not available, as in new-product forecasting. Also, trend analysis makes the dangerous assumption that future events will continue in the same manner as the past. Any variations in the determinants of future sales will cause deviations from the forecast. In other words, this method gives reliable forecasts during periods of steady growth and stable demand. If conditions change, predictions based on trend analysis may become worthless. For this reason, forecasters have applied more sophisticated techniques and complex, new forecasting models to anticipate the effects of various possible changes in the future.

EXPONENTIAL SMOOTHING

A more sophisticated method of trend analysis, the **exponential smoothing** technique, weighs each year's sales data, giving greater weight to results from the most recent years. Otherwise, the statistical approach used in trend analysis is applied here. For example, last year's sales might receive a 1.5 weight, while sales data from two years ago could get a 1.4 weighting. Exponential smoothing is considered the most commonly used quantitative forecasting technique.

trend analysis
Quantitative sales forecasting method that estimates future sales through statistical analyses of historical sales patterns.

exponential smoothing Quantitative forecasting technique that assigns weights to historical sales data, giving the greatest weight to the most recent data.

assessment check

1. Describe the jury of executive opinion.

2. What is the Delphi technique?

3. How does the exponential smoothing technique forecast sales?

strategic
implications of marketing in the 21st century

arketing research can help an organization develop effective marketing strategies. Most new products eventually fail to attract enough buyers to remain viable. Why? A major reason is the seller's failure to understand market needs.

Consider, for example, the hundreds of dot-com companies that went under. A characteristic shared by all of those failing businesses is that virtually none of them was founded on sound marketing research. Very few used marketing research techniques to evaluate sales potential, and even fewer studied consumer responses after the ventures were initiated. While research might not have prevented every dot-com meltdown, it may have helped a few of those businesses survive.

Marketing research ideally matches new products to potential customers. Marketers also conduct research to analyze sales of their own and competitors' products, to gauge the performance of existing products, to guide the development of promotional campaigns and product enhancements, and to develop and refine products. All of these activities enable marketers to fine-tune their marketing strategies and reach customers more effectively and efficiently.

Marketing researchers have at their disposal a broad range of techniques with which to collect both quantitative and qualitative data on customers, their lifestyles, behaviors, attitudes, and perceptions. Vast amounts of data can be rapidly collected, accessed, interpreted, and applied to improve all aspects of business operations. Because of customer relationship management technology, that information is no longer generalized to profile groups of customers—it can be analyzed to help marketers understand every customer.

Review of Chapter Objectives

 Describe the development of the marketing research function and its major activities.

Marketing research, or the collection and use of information in marketing decision making, began when Charles C. Parlin, an ad salesman, counted empty soup cans in Philadelphia's trash in an effort to persuade the Campbell Soup Company to advertise in *The Saturday Evening Post*. Today, the most common marketing research activities are (1) determining market potential, market share, and market characteristics and (2) conducting sales analyses and competitive product studies. Most large consumer goods companies now have internal marketing research departments. However, outside suppliers still remain vital to the research function. Some perform the complete research task, while others specialize in a limited area or provide specific data services.

 Explain the steps in the marketing research process.

The marketing research process can be divided into six specific steps: (1) defining the problem, (2) conducting exploratory research, (3) formulating hypotheses, (4) creating a research design, (5) collecting data, and (6) interpreting and presenting the research information. A clearly defined problem focuses on the researcher's search for relevant decision-oriented information. Exploratory research refers to information gained outside the firm. Hypotheses, tentative explanations of specific events, allow researchers to set out specific research designs—that is, the series of decisions that, taken together, comprise master plans or models for conducting the investigations. The data collection phase of the marketing research process can involve either or both primary (original) and secondary (previously published) data. After the data are collected, researchers must interpret and present them in a way that is meaningful to management.

 ### Distinguish between primary and secondary data, and identify the sources of each type.

Primary data can be collected by the firm's own researchers or by independent marketing research companies. Three principal methods of primary data collection are observation, survey, and experiment. Secondary data can be classified as either internal or external. Sources of internal data include sales records, product evaluation, sales force reports, and records of marketing costs. Sources of external data include the government and private sources such as business magazines. Both external and internal data can also be obtained from computer databases.

 ### Explain the different sampling techniques used by marketing researchers.

Samples can be categorized as either probability samples or nonprobability samples. A probability sample is one in which every member of the population has a known chance of being selected. Probability samples include simple random samples, in which every item in the relevant universe has an equal opportunity to be selected; stratified samples, in which randomly selected subsamples of different groups are represented in the total sample; and cluster samples, in which geographic areas are selected from which respondents are drawn. A nonprobability sample is arbitrary and does not allow application of standard statistical tests. Nonprobability sampling techniques include convenience samples, in which readily available respondents are picked, and quota samples, divided so that different segments or groups are represented in the total sample.

 ### Identify the methods by which marketing researchers collect primary data.

Observation data are gathered by observing consumers via devices such as people meters or videotape. Survey data can be collected through telephone interviews, mail or fax surveys, personal interviews, focus groups, or a variety of online methods. Telephone interviews provide more than half of all primary marketing research data. They give the researcher a fast and inexpensive way to get small amounts of information but generally not detailed or personal information. Personal interviews are costly but allow researchers to get detailed information from respondents. Mail surveys are a means of conducting national studies at a reasonable cost; their main disadvantage is potentially inadequate response rates. Focus groups elicit detailed, qualitative information that provides insight not only

into behavior but also into consumer attitudes and perceptions. Online surveys can yield fast responses but face obstacles such as the adequacy of the probability sample. The experimental method creates verifiable statistical data through the use of test and control groups to reveal actual benefits from perceived benefits.

 ### Explain the challenges of conducting marketing research in global markets.

Many resources are available to help U.S. organizations research global markets. Government resources include the Department of Commerce, state trade offices, small-business development centers, and foreign embassies. Private companies, such as marketing research firms and companies that distribute research from other sources, are another resource. Electronic networks offer online international trade forums, in which marketers can establish global contacts.

 ### Outline the most important uses of computer technology in marketing research.

Important uses of computer technology in marketing research include (1) a marketing information system (MIS)—a planned, computer-based system designed to provide managers with a continuous flow of information relevant to their specific decision-making needs and areas of responsibility; (2) a marketing decision support system (MDSS)—a marketing information system component that links a decision maker with relevant databases and analysis tools; (3) data mining—the process of searching through consumer information files or data warehouses to detect patterns that guide marketing decision making; (4) business intelligence—the process of gathering information and analyzing it to improve business strategy, tactics, and daily operations; and (5) competitive intelligence—the form of business intelligence that focuses on finding information about competitors using published sources, interviews, observations by salespeople and suppliers in the industry, government agencies, public filings such as patent applications, and other secondary methods including the Internet.

 ### Identify the major types of forecasting methods.

There are two categories of forecasting methods. Qualitative methods are more subjective because they are based on opinions rather than exact historical data. They include the jury of executive opinion, the Delphi technique, the sales force composite, and the survey of buyer intentions. Quantitative methods include more factual and numerical measures such as test markets, trend analysis, and exponential smoothing.

Assessment Check: Answers

1.1 Identify the different classifications of marketing research suppliers, and explain how they differ from one another. Marketing research suppliers can be classified as syndicated services, which regularly send standardized data sets to all customers; full-service suppliers, which contract to conduct complete marketing research projects; or limited-service suppliers, which specialize in selected activities.

1.2 What research methods can be used to measure customer satisfaction? Some companies look at feedback from existing customers, for instance, hiring marketing research firms to collect and analyze customer feedback at their Web sites. Other firms collect feedback about customer defections—why a customer no longer uses a product. Other organizations conduct research through online polls and surveys.

2.1 What are the six steps in the marketing research process? The marketing research process can be divided into six specific steps: (1) defining the problem, (2) conducting exploratory research, (3) formulating hypotheses, (4) creating a research design, (5) collecting data, and (6) interpreting and presenting the research information.

2.2 What is the goal of exploratory research? Exploratory research seeks to discover the cause of a specific problem by discussing the problem with informed sources within and outside the firm and examining data from other information sources.

3.1 Distinguish between primary and secondary data. Primary data are original; secondary data have been previously published.

3.2 What are the major methods of collecting secondary data? Sources of internal data include sales records, product evaluations, sales force reports, and records of marketing costs.

3.3 What are the major methods of collecting primary data? Three principal methods of primary data collection are observation, survey, and experiment.

4.1 What is sampling? Sampling is the process of selecting representative survey respondents or research participants from the total universe of possible participants.

4.2 Explain the different types of probability samples. Types of probability samples include simple random samples, stratified samples, and cluster samples.

4.3 Identify the types of nonprobability samples. Nonprobability samples are convenience samples and quota samples.

5.1 What are the principal methods for collecting primary data? The principal methods for collecting primary data are observation, surveys, and controlled experiments.

5.2 Identify the different types of survey methods. Different survey methods may include telephone interviews, personal interviews, focus groups, mail surveys, fax surveys, and online or other Internet-based methods.

6.1 What are some U.S. organizations that can serve as sources of international secondary marketing data? The Departments of Commerce and State offer reports and guides to many countries. Other sources include state trade offices, small-business development centers, and U.S. embassies in various nations.

6.2 What is the most common method of primary data collection outside the United States? Face-to-face interviewing remains the most common method for conducting primary research outside the United States.

6.3 How is interpretative research typically conducted? Interpretative research observes a customer or group of customers in their natural setting and interprets their behavior based on social and cultural characteristics of that setting.

6.4 When should ethnographic research be employed? Ethnographic research is used to look at the consumer behavior of different groups of people.

7.1 Distinguish between an MIS and an MDSS. A marketing information system (MIS) is a planned, computer-based system designed to provide managers with a continuous flow of information relevant to their specific decision-making needs and areas of responsibility. A marketing decision support system (MDSS) is a marketing information system component that links a decision maker with relevant databases and analysis tools to help ask what-if questions.

7.2 What is data mining? Data mining is the process of searching through huge consumer information files or data warehouses to detect patterns that can help marketers ask the right questions and guide marketing decision making.

7.3 Describe the process of collecting business and competitive intelligence. Business intelligence is the process of gathering information and analyzing it to improve business strategy, tactics, and daily operations. Competitive intelligence focuses on finding information about competitors using published sources, interviews, observations by salespeople and suppliers in the industry, government agencies, public filings such as patent applications, and other secondary methods including the Internet.

8.1 Describe the jury of executive opinion. The jury of executive opinion combines and averages the outlooks of top executives from areas such as marketing, finance, production, and purchasing.

8.2 What is the Delphi technique? The Delphi technique solicits opinions from several people but also includes input from experts outside the firm.

8.3 How does the exponential smoothing technique forecast sales? Exponential smoothing weighs each year's sales data, giving greater weight to results from the most recent years.

Marketing Terms You Need to Know

marketing research 240
syndicated service 242
full-service research supplier 243
limited-service research
 supplier 243
exploratory research 245
sales analysis 245
hypothesis 245
research design 246
secondary data 246

primary data 246
sampling 250
population (universe) 250
probability sample 251
simple random sample 251
stratified sample 251
cluster sample 251
nonprobability sample 251
convenience sample 251
quota sample 251

interpretative research 254
mall intercepts 255
focus group 255
controlled experiment 258
test marketing 258
marketing information
 system (MIS) 261
marketing decision support system
 (MDSS) 261
data mining 261

sales forecast 263
qualitative forecasting 263
quantitative forecasting 263
jury of executive opinion 264
Delphi technique 264
sales force composite 264
survey of buyer intentions 264
trend analysis 265
exponential smoothing 265

Assurance of Learning Review

1. Outline the development and current status of the marketing research function.

2. What are the differences between full-service and limited-service research suppliers?

3. List and explain the steps in the marketing research process. Trace a hypothetical study through the stages in this process.

4. Distinguish between primary and secondary data. When should researchers collect each type of data?

5. What is sampling? Explain the differences between probability and nonprobability samples and identify the various types of each.

6. Distinguish among surveys, experiments, and observational methods of primary data collection. Cite examples of each method.

7. Define and give an example of each of the methods of gathering survey data. Under what circumstances should researchers choose a specific approach?

8. Describe the experimental method of collecting primary data and indicate when researchers should use it.

9. Describe business intelligence.

10. Contrast qualitative and quantitative sales forecasting methods.

Projects and Teamwork Exercises

1. ACNielsen offers data collected by optical scanners from the United Kingdom, France, Germany, Belgium, the Netherlands, Austria, Italy, and Finland. This scanner data tracks sales of UPC-coded products in those nations. In small teams, imagine you are Nielsen clients in the United States. One team might be a retail chain, another an Internet company, and still another a toy manufacturer. Discuss the types of marketing questions these data might help you answer. Share your list with other teams.

2. Discuss some of the challenges Pizza Hut might face in conducting marketing research in potential new international markets. What types of research would you recommend the company use in choosing new countries for expansion?

3. Working alone or with a partner, choose a new-product idea, or a variation on an existing product, that you think would appeal to your classmates, such as yogurt or an energy drink in a new flavor, and devise a test marketing plan for it. Determine where you will test your product and which variables you will assess, such as price and promotional activities. Be prepared to present your plan to the class and include a description of the information you hope your test market will provide.

4. Interpretative research offers marketing researchers many possibilities, including the opportunity to improve product features such as packaging for food or over-the-counter medication that is difficult for seniors or the disabled to open. List some other ways in which you think this observation method can help make existing product offerings more appealing or more useful to specific users. What kind of products would you choose, and how would you test them?

5. McDonald's conducts extensive marketing research for all its new products, including new menu items for its overseas

stores. Because of cultural and other differences and preferences, the company cannot always extrapolate its results from one country to another. For instance, Croque McDo fried ham-and-cheese sandwiches are unlikely to be as popular in the United States as they are in France, which invented the *croque* *monsieur* sandwich on which the McDonald's product is based. Can you think of any other kinds of firms that share this limitation on global applications of their research? In contrast, what sorts of questions *could* multinational firms answer on a global basis? Why?

Critical-Thinking Exercises

1. Some companies are broadening their markets by updating classic products to appeal to younger people's tastes and preferences. What primary and secondary marketing information would you want to have if you were planning to reinvigorate an established brand in each of the following categories? Where and how would you obtain the information?
   a. household cleaner
   b. moist packaged cat food
   c. spray starch
   d. electrical appliances

2. Marketers sometimes collect primary information by using so-called mystery shoppers who visit stores anonymously (as if they were customers) and note such critical factors as store appearance and ambiance, items in stock, and quality of service including waiting time and courtesy of employees. (The CEO of Staples has gone on mystery shopper trips and sometimes asked his mother to make similar trips.) Prepare a list of data you would want to obtain from a mystery shopper surveying a chain of gas stations in your area. Devise a format for gathering the information that combines your need to compile the data electronically and the researcher's need to remain undetected while visiting the stores.

3. Select a sales forecasting method (or combination of methods) for each of the following information needs and explain your pick(s).
   a. prediction of next year's sales based on last year's figures
   b. prediction of next year's sales based on weighted data from the last five years
   c. expected sales categorized by district and by region
   d. estimated product usage for the next year by typical consumers
   e. probable consumer response to a new product

4. The Internet provides ready access to secondary information but is also a portal to an almost limitless store of primary information via social networking sites, message boards, chat rooms, e-mail questionnaires, newsgroups, and Web site registration forms. What are some specific drawbacks of each of these methods for obtaining primary information from customers?

Ethics Exercise

Consumer groups sometimes object to marketers' methods of collecting primary data from customers. They object to such means as product registration forms; certain types of games, contests, or product offers; and "cookies" and demographic questionnaires on company Web sites. Marketers believe that such tools offer them an easy way to collect market data. Most strictly control the use of such data and never link identifying information with consumers' financial or demographic profiles. However, the possibility of abuse or error always exists.

Research the code of ethics of the American Marketing Association (AMA). Note especially the guidelines for use of the Internet in marketing research.

1. Check the Web sites of a few large consumer products companies. How effectively do you think these sites are at informing visitors about the use of "cookies" on the sites? Do you think marketers could or should improve their protection of visitors' privacy? If so, how?

2. Do you think the AMA's code of ethics would be violated if marketers compiled a mailing list from information provided on warranty and product registration cards and then used the list to send customers new-product information? Why or why not? Does your opinion change if the company also sends list members special discount offers and private sale notices?

Internet Exercises

1. **Focus groups.** Visit each of the Web sites listed below. Each discusses the proper way to organize and conduct a focus group. After reviewing the material, prepare a brief report on the subject.

   http://www.businessweek.com/magazine/content/09_70/s0910027439027.htm?campaign_id=rss_smlbz_bulgaria
   http://managementhelp.org/evaluatn/focusgrp.htm
   http://www.ehow.com/how_4393027_conduct-focus-group.html

2. **Marketing research firm services.** Nielsen is one of the world's largest marketing research firms. Go to the firm's U.S. Web site (http://en-us.nielsen.com/). Assume you run a small online retailer. What types of marketing research services could a firm like Nielsen provide to your company? What are some of the benefits?

3. **Data analysis.** The Census Bureau publishes the Statistical Abstract of the U.S. each year. Visit the Web site shown below. Collect the following data by state: per-capita income, percent of population living in urban areas, median age, percent of population with college degrees. Analyze the relationships between income and urban population, age, and education.

   http://www.census.gov/compendia/statab/

Note: Internet Web addresses change frequently. If you don't find the exact site listed, you may need to access the organization's home page and search from there or use a search engine such as Google or Bing.

Case 8.1 *Oberto Sausage: A Recipe for Forecasting*

How does a food company forecast demand for its meat snack and sausage products? Oberto Sausage, an 85-year-old family business in Washington State, sells beef jerky and other packaged meat products, such as pork rinds and smoked sausage sticks, directly

to mass merchandisers and supermarket chains. Oberto has been enjoying double-digit growth. The company has also been expanding its consumer marketing efforts into the digital realm; it recently concluded a successful sweepstakes promotion that invited participants to text in their entries from their cell phones.

Growing demand means accurate forecasting is critical to Oberto's ability to provide a steady supply of fresh products to the right places at the right time. Forecasting also ensures Oberto has the necessary ingredients and packaging available to fill orders on time. In its recent search for a new computer-based forecasting system, the company looked for a way to create a model of routine and ongoing "base" demand, incorporate and keep track of changes it made to the model, forecast general demand and demand for specific market segments, input human judgment, and finally keep costs for the new system in line with the quality of forecasting the company desired.

The company chose a suite of software programs from a forecasting software company called Forecast Pro headquartered in Massachusetts. The programs serve as "the main foundation of our demand forecasting process," says the company's director of forecasting and planning. "It's where the forecast is generated and

maintained. After we establish the forecast, it is fed into our ERP [enterprise resource planning] system where it drives procurement, planning/scheduling, and plant execution. One of our biggest forecasting challenges is really understanding what our true baseline demand is. We start by creating a relatively conservative base forecast that's statistically driven off history. ... To accommodate abnormal conditions in history, things that happened that aren't expected to happen again in the future—promotions, weather, outliers—we use event models. That's our starting point."

Despite its reliance on computer models, however, Oberto still brings a big dose of human judgment into its forecasting process at critical points. The company's demand manager, as well as its customer service representatives, review the computer-generated forecast and make changes their experience and information suggest. "The forecast team interfaces directly with the sales team and often has knowledge of unusual conditions, things that wouldn't be reflected in the history," says Oberto's forecasting director. "Their job is to make sure the forecasting process captures this 'business as usual.' ... We use our sales team to provide intelligence only when history doesn't tell us what's happening—and this approach has worked well."

Next, Oberto's forecast analysts look at what they know about important customers and add available consumption data to the model. They also add unusual events like the sweepstakes promotion. "The forecast analysts concentrate on the 20% of our customers and events that drive 80% of our volume," says Oberto's forecasting director.

Oberto is getting full value from its forecasting process. Its forecasting director reports, "We've been able to sustain years of double-digit growth while inventory value has remained constant. We've also been able to strategically identify potential gaps in our plans where we may have shortfalls with important customers and move proactively to fill those gaps. Our forecasts are used for everything from planning/scheduling all the way up to revenue projection by the executive team."

Questions for Critical Thinking

1. Why do you think it was important for Oberto to have a computer-based forecasting program that could accept human input and even overrides?

2. What other factors in the company's external environment, in addition to the ones mentioned in the case, should its executives consider in preparing their demand forecasts?

Sources: Company Web site, Oberto Sausage Company, www. obertosausagecompany. com, accessed March 11, 2010; "Oberto Sausage Finds the Right Recipe for Forecasting," company Web site, Forecast Pro, www.forecastpro.com, accessed February 19, 2010; Christopher Heine, "Jerky Taunts Fuel Beef Jerky Mobile Push," *BrandWeek*, www. brandweek.com, June 3, 2009.

Video Case 8.2
Marketing Research and Sales Forecasting at Ogden Publications

"One thing we do differently here than people do in most businesses is we don't budget, we forecast," claims Bryan Welch, publisher and editorial director of Ogden Publications. Ogden Publications is a small publishing house based in Tulsa, Oklahoma. They publish

13 magazines, including *Mother Earth News, Natural Home*, and *Utne Reader*. A few years ago, these titles and others from their catalog were only available in specialty bookstores, often those with a more eco-conscious clientele. The green movement has done wonders for Ogden in the past few years. Now, many of their titles are sold at the local Barnes & Noble bookstore or at hardware stores.

"I will tell you, without a shadow of a doubt, that the five-year forecast is accurate six months out. Beyond that, it is wildly inaccurate," says Welch. So why bother? "The reason you do it is because it is a strategic tool. It makes everyone think about 'what will we need to do to be successful in five years?'" Welch is a big proponent of being open and flexible enough to make what he calls "wise course corrections." He always reminds his staff that just because they assigned money to a project doesn't mean they have to do the project. "Because the world is changing so rapidly, we need to be able to not make an investment we planned nine months ago," says Welch, so they can "make an investment we never thought of nine months ago."

"We work together with advertising sales and editorial," explains Cherilyn Olmsted, circulation and marketing director at Ogden Publications. One of their most valuable tools is an online survey system called Survey Monkey that collects and stores all the data from the many online surveys they present to their readers. "We like to try to find out various things from an editorial perspective and an advertising sales perspective that will help improve the content we are providing to our readers and to make sure we are reaching the audience that our advertisers would like to reach." Much of the information is what one might expect—demographics, age, income, and psychographic information. Of course, without a good magazine, there are no readers to count, so they also perform surveys asking for more subjective feedback on covers, style, and content. This information is reported back to the editorial staff of each magazine.

Olmsted and her team use information from past sales and the reception from various new marketing projects to forecast future sales, both at the subscription and newsstand level and with advertisers. Like most, if not all, magazines, revenue is almost exclusively from ad sales, so they have to continually track reader and advertiser responses in everything they do.

While surveys have been invaluable to Ogden's marketing research, one of the best and most valuable tools has been the Web companions to their magazines. This passive form of marketing research asks nothing of the reader except that he or she visits the site. Every visit, mouse click, advertising link, and download is tracked. With a few simple clicks, Olmsted can even see how many minutes a user spent on each page. With a traditional magazine, they would have to wait six months or more to get all the sales returns and reader and advertiser feedback and to compile new subscription rates. Now, with the companion sites, they can instantly see if they need to include more political articles or home improvement projects, or recipes or technical articles about geothermal heating systems. They can make adjustments to the next editions of the print and Web products.

Ask anyone working in marketing today, and they will agree that a good portion of their lives is spent spotting trends. The editors and marketers at Ogden are no exception. Welch cautions, however, that "a lot of trends are short-lived and have no real impact in the economy." His skepticism extends to a particularly hot trend in the magazine industry today: the digital magazine. "There hasn't been good evidence, in spite of the fact that it is a cool idea, that a lot of people will pay for it." But, Welch adds, "if someone suddenly came up with a formula that allowed us to make money doing it, it would only take us a couple of months to gear up and do it."

Questions

1. Now that so many companies have Web companions and/or e-commerce components to their business, do you think more traditional methods such as telephone surveys, focus groups, response cards, and analyzing sales data will become obsolete? Why or why not?

2. What are some of the limitations to forecasting at Ogden Publications?

ch 9 Market
Segmentation, Targeting, and Positioning

1 Identify the essential components of a market.

2 Outline the role of market segmentation in developing a marketing strategy.

3 Describe the criteria necessary for effective segmentation.

4 Explain the geographic approach to segmenting consumer markets.

5 Discuss the demographic approach to segmenting consumer markets.

6 Outline the psychographic approach to segmenting consumer markets.

7 Describe product-related segmentation.

8 Identify the steps in the market segmentation process.

9 Discuss four basic strategies for reaching target markets.

10 Summarize the types of positioning strategies, and explain the reasons for positioning and repositioning products.

Tween Brands "Gets" Tweens • • • For the past 20 years, the New Albany, Ohio—based specialty retailer has been in the business of understanding and serving a special market segment—the "tween." The company describes this demographic—the 7- to 14-year-old girl—as

someone who's "caught somewhere between Barbie and a driver's license," who has become increasingly aware of fashion since entering elementary school, and is interested in defining a style of her own.

Today, with more than 900 stores in the United States, Puerto Rico, Russia, and the Middle East, Tween Brands is the world's largest premier tween specialty retailer. Its holdings include the Justice retail chain and Limited Too, which it acquired after the retailer was spun off from The Limited. Both Tween Brands chains offer a full line of apparel, footwear, and accessories— in short, everything a "tween" would want to make a fashion statement.

Marketers at Tween Brands study 7- to 14-year-old girls and understand what makes them tick, as reflected by the company's merchandising strategy. They know that girls become fashion-conscious during their tween years; many aspire to look as cool as their older sister or their babysitter. The company appeals to the tween lifestyle and carries a broad array of apparel, shoes, and accessories, aiming to make shopping a unique, exciting fashion experience for their customers.

Tween Brands believes organizational culture is important to its success and hires customer-focused individuals who know how to "have

fun and enjoy life." Salespeople at the Justice stores, for example, are encouraged to be outgoing and creative in relating to their young customers. The stores themselves are positioned as an "everything for her" experience offering fashion and fun—and are even promoted as a destination venue for tween birthday parties.

Tween Brands uses direct mail and its signature "catazine"—a cross between a catalog and a magazine—to reach its market. The company also hosts a colorful, user-friendly e-commerce site geared to its adolescent shoppers.

A few years ago, Tween Brands launched the transformation of

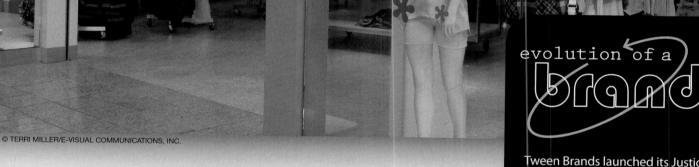

© TERRI MILLER/E-VISUAL COMMUNICATIONS, INC.

its two chains, working to gradually combine the higher-priced Euro-styled Limited Too and the lower-priced Justice brands into a single, slightly more upscale Justice brand. Historically, Justice stores have been located in strip centers or "off the mall" shopping centers, while Limited Too stores are typically located inside malls. While the transformation continued, Tween Brands was acquired by Dress Barn, a leading national specialty retailer known for women's career and casual apparel. Though some industry observers questioned the "marriage" of Dress Barn and Tween Brands, Dress Barn has a track record of successful acquisitions, including its purchase of the Maurices chain, another women's apparel retailer. With the acquisition, Dress Barn announced that the Tween Brands leadership team would continue to operate the company as an independent subsidiary.[1]

evolution of a brand

Tween Brands launched its Justice retail chain (and later acquired the Limited Too brand) because it saw significant potential in marketing to 7- to 14-year-old girls. However, serving this demographic can be challenging because it requires managers to be able to spot trends and stay on top of the likes and dislikes of what can be a fickle consumer population, where "what's hot" and "what's not" can change, literally, overnight.

- When Tween Brands announced it would rebrand Justice and Limited Too to a single, unified brand, some industry observers

thought the strategy was risky. Then, an economic downturn curbed consumer spending.
How do you think the rebranding strategy
helped Tween Brands? Its consumers?

- Among Tween Brands' competitors are other
  specialty retailers like The Gap and numerous
  department stores. How might the Tween

Brands marketing strategy differ from that of
its competitors?

- Later, Tween Brands was acquired by Dress
  Barn, a retailer of women's fashion. Do you
  think this change of ownership will affect
  Tween Brands' strategy going forward? Why or
  why not?

chapter overview

Each of us is unique. We come from different
backgrounds, live in different households, and
have different interests and goals. You and your
best friend may shop at different stores, listen to
different music, play different sports, and take
different courses in college. Suppose you like
country music, but your best friend prefers rock.
Marketers for all kinds of music-related products,
ranging from digital songs to live concerts, want
to capture your interest as well as that of your
friends. Do you play an instrument or sing, or
are you a fan who goes to clubs and downloads
music? Marketers at Tween Brands, for example,
look at customers and potential customers to
figure out what their characteristics are, whether
they can identify certain subgroups, and how
they can best offer products to meet their needs.
Your interests and needs, your lifestyle and
income, the town where you live, and your age
all contribute to the likelihood that you will listen to and buy certain types of music—say, Lady
Gaga or the score to *Billy Elliot*. All of these factors make up a market. A **market** is composed
of people with sufficient purchasing power,
authority, and willingness to buy. Marketers
must use their expertise to understand the market for a good or service, whether it's a room for a
business traveler at a Marriott Hotel or a vacation
timeshare at Disney World.

Many markets include consumers with different lifestyles, backgrounds, and income levels. Nearly everyone buys toothpaste, but that
does not mean every consumer has the same
lifestyle, background, or income. So it is unusual
for a single marketing mix strategy to attract all
sectors of a market. By identifying, evaluating,
and selecting a target market to pursue, such as
consumers who prefer toothpaste made with
all-natural ingredients or those who want an
extra-whitening formula—marketers develop
more efficient and effective marketing strategies. On the other hand, some products, such
as luxury sports cars and fly-fishing supplies,
are intended for a more specific market. In
either case, the **target market** for a product is
the specific segment of consumers most likely
to purchase a particular item.

Marketing now takes place on a global
basis more than ever, incorporating many target markets. To identify those markets, marketers must determine useful ways for segmenting
different populations and communicating with
them successfully. This chapter discusses useful
ways to accomplish this objective, explaining
the steps of the market segmentation process
and surveying strategies for reaching target
markets. Finally, it looks at the role of positioning in developing a marketing strategy.

market Group of people
with sufficient purchasing
power, authority, and
willingness to buy.

target market Group
of people to whom a firm
decides to direct its marketing
efforts and ultimately its
goods and services.

Types of Markets

Products usually are classified as either consumer products or business products. **Consumer products** are bought by ultimate consumers for personal use, for example, cell phones, sports tickets, or fashion magazines. **Business products** are goods and services purchased for use either directly or indirectly in the production of other goods and services for resale. Most goods and services purchased by individual consumers, such as DVDs and restaurant meals, are considered consumer products. Rubber and raw cotton are examples of items generally purchased by manufacturers and therefore classified as business products. B. F. Goodrich buys rubber to manufacture tires; textile manufacturers such as Burlington Industries convert raw cotton into cloth.

However, in many cases, a single product can serve different uses. Tires purchased for the family car constitute consumer products, but tires purchased by Ford Motor Company to be mounted on its Ford Focus are business products because they become part of another product destined for resale. Or, a product that was once a business product might be modified for consumer use, and vice versa. A line of professional cookware sold to restaurants—a business product—could be adapted by its manufacturer to become a line of cookware for home use—a consumer product. If you want to determine the classification of an item, just think about who is going to buy the product, who will use it, and how or why the product will be used. The bottle of mouthwash you buy at the supermarket is a consumer product, but if a large hotel chain purchases large quantities of the same mouthwash from a wholesaler, it becomes a business product.

1 **Identify the essential components of a market.**

consumer products
Products bought by ultimate consumers for personal use.

business products
Goods and services purchased for use either directly or indirectly in the production of other goods and services for resale.

 assessment check

1. Define *target market*.
2. Distinguish between a consumer product and a business product.

The Role of Market Segmentation

There are 6.8 billion people in the world today; more than 308 million live in the United States.[2] In today's business world, too many variables exist in consumer needs, preferences, and purchasing power to attract all consumers with a single marketing mix. That's not to say that firms must actually change products to meet the needs of different market segments—although they often do—but they must attempt to identify the factors that affect purchase decisions and then group consumers according to the presence or absence of these factors. Finally, they adjust marketing strategies to meet the needs of each group.

Consider motor vehicles. Unlike a century ago, when Henry Ford pronounced that customers could order any color of car they liked—as long as it was black—today there is a make, model, and color for every taste and budget. But auto manufacturers need to adjust their messages for different markets. And savvy marketers look toward markets that show growth, such as the U.S. Hispanic population—now the largest ethnic group in the country—and aging baby boomers, whose needs for goods and services are changing.

The division of the total market into smaller, relatively homogeneous groups is called **market segmentation**. Both profit-oriented and not-for-profit organizations practice market segmentation.

2 **Outline the role of market segmentation in developing a marketing strategy.**

market segmentation
Division of the total market into smaller, relatively homogeneous groups.

 assessment check

1. Define *market segmentation*.
2. Describe the role of market segmentation.

Criteria for Effective Segmentation

Segmentation doesn't automatically guarantee success in the marketing arena; instead, it is a tool for marketers to use. Its effectiveness depends on four basic requirements.

First, the market segment must present measurable purchasing power and size. With jobs, incomes, and decision-making power, female consumers represent a hefty amount of purchasing power, approaching $1 trillion, or 60 percent of the nation's wealth.[3] Women control or influence the purchase of 80 percent of all consumer goods, including such items as stocks for investment, personal computers, and family vehicles.[4] With this information in mind, car manufacturers and dealers now market directly to women. In addition, Web sites like AskPatty.com offer advice to women on making car purchases—and certify "female-friendly" dealers and automotive centers that provide the kind of service that builds loyalty among female consumers.[5]

Second, marketers must find a way to effectively promote and serve the market segment. Because women now wield purchasing power in the technology market, marketers need to find different ways to appeal to them. Some companies have taken this advice to heart. T-Mobile and BlackBerry have created ads featuring working moms.

Third, marketers must then identify segments large enough to give them good profit potential. Because women significantly influence 80 to 90 percent of home purchases, homebuilders have turned their marketing efforts to them. Nebraska-based Design Basics, the largest home-plan design company in the country, now focuses on designs aimed at women. Its guidelines include improving storage options, creating multipurpose rooms, and emphasizing the practicality of the back-door entry—with space for muddy boots and school backpacks, car keys, mail, and a plug to recharge cell phones. Using its research data, the firm's Women-Centric Matters division has even been able to create four distinct personality profiles of female home buyers:

1. Margo wishes to impress her visitors with the uniqueness of her home.

2. Elise is more traditional in her design tastes.

3. Claire demands perfection.

4. Maggie has some trouble staying focused on the design details.[6]

Fourth, the firm must aim for segments that match its marketing capabilities. Targeting a large number of small markets can be an expensive, complex, and inefficient strategy, so smaller firms may decide to stick with a particular niche, or target market. But Harley-Davidson, once thought

IMAGE COURTESY OF THE ADVERTISING ARCHIVES

EXPECT HIGH-FASHION HANDBAG ENVY AT A STREET-SMART PRICE CARLOS FALCHI FOR TARGET

EXPECT MORE. PAY LESS.

to be the exclusive domain of men, has experienced a surge in purchases by women, who represent the fastest-growing segment of the motorcycle business and currently account for nearly one in four motorcyclists. So Harley-Davidson runs targeted ads in women's magazines and annually hosts "Garage Party" events throughout the United States, geared specifically for women and featuring demonstrations, social gatherings, and an "intimidation-free zone" where female riders can meet and network.[7]

✓ assessment check

1. Identify the four criteria for effective segmentation.

2. Give an example of a market segment that meets these criteria.

Segmenting Consumer Markets

Market segmentation attempts to isolate the traits that distinguish a certain group of consumers from the overall market. An understanding of the group's characteristics—such as age, gender, geographic location, income, and buying patterns—plays a vital role in developing a successful marketing strategy. In most cases, marketers seek to pinpoint a number of factors affecting buying behavior in the target segment. Marketers in the travel industry consider employment trends, changes in income levels and buying patterns, age, lifestyle, and other factors when promoting their goods and services. To boost flagging attendance at its theme parks, Disney World advertises to "empty nesters" and groups of friends instead of focusing entirely on families with young children. Marketers rarely identify totally homogeneous segments, in which all potential customers are alike; they almost always encounter some differences among members of a target group but must be careful to ensure their segments accurately reflect consumers.

In the next sections, we discuss the four common bases for segmenting consumer markets: geographic segmentation, demographic segmentation, psychographic segmentation, and product-related segmentation. These segmentation approaches offer important guidance for marketing strategies, provided they identify significant differences in buying behavior.

geographic segmentation Division of an overall market into homogeneous groups based on their locations.

Geographic Segmentation

Marketers have long practiced **geographic segmentation**—dividing an overall market into homogeneous groups based on their locations. Geographic location does not ensure all consumers in a location will make the same buying decisions, but this segmentation approach helps identify some general patterns.

4 **Explain the geographic approach to segmenting consumer markets.**

The approximately 308 million people living in the United States are not scattered evenly across the country. For instance, many are concentrated in major metropolitan areas; New York is the largest U.S. city, with more than 8.4 million citizens, but the metropolitan area surrounding it includes more than 19 million people. Los Angeles ranks second, with 3.8 million, and a surrounding area of nearly 13 million.[8] Figure 9.1 shows populations of the ten largest cities in the United States and the ten states with the largest populations. California tops the list at 38 million residents. Wyoming is the least-populated state, with 520,000. In addition to total population, marketers need to look at the *fastest-growing* states to plan their strategies for the future. Nevada and Arizona are the fastest-growing states, but Louisiana is rebounding from its population loss after Hurricane Katrina.[9]

figure 9.1

The Ten Largest Cities and Ten Most Populous States in the United States

10. San Jose; .9 million
2. Los Angeles; 3.8 million
8. San Diego; 1.3 million
5. Phoenix; 1.5 million
3. Chicago; 2.9 million
9. Dallas; 1.2 million
4. Houston; 2.1 million
7. San Antonio; 1.3 million
1. New York; 8.2 million
6. Philadelphia; 1.4 million

38 million
10.4 mil.
12.6 mil.
11.6 mil.
12.9 mil.
19.4 mil.
24.6 million
9.6 million
19.3 mil.

Ranking State Populations

1.	California	38.0 mil.
2.	Texas	24.6 mil.
3.	New York	19.4 mil.
4.	Florida	19.3 mil.
5.	Illinois	12.9 mil.
6.	Penn.	12.6 mil.
7.	Ohio	11.6 mil.
8.	Michigan	10.4 mil.
9.	Georgia	9.6 mil.
10.	New Jersey	9.0 mil.

Sources: "United States of America: Largest Cities and Towns and Statistics of Their Population" and "United States of America: Administrative Divisions," *World Gazetteer*, http://world-gazetteer.com, accessed March 21, 2010.

A look at the worldwide population distribution illustrates why so many firms pursue customers around the globe. China has the most citizens, with more than 1.3 billion people, and India is second with nearly 1.2 billion. The United States is third with 308 million, and Indonesia is fourth with 240 million. Japan is a distant tenth with 127 million.[10] As in the United States, much of the world's population lives in urban environments. The two largest cities in the world are Shanghai, China, with 16.3 million and Bombay, India, with 13.8 million. The two largest metropolitan areas are Tokyo, Japan, with more than 37.7 million and Mexico City with 23.6 million.[11]

Population size alone, however, may not be reason enough for a business to expand into a specific country. Businesses also need to look at a wide variety of economic variables. Some businesses may decide to combine their marketing efforts for countries that share similar population and product-use patterns instead of treating each country as an independent segment. This grouping is taking place with greater frequency throughout the European Union as the currency and trade laws of the member nations become more unified.

While population numbers indicate the overall size of a market, other geographic indicators such as job growth give useful guidance to marketers, depending on the type of products they sell. Automobile manufacturers might segment geographic regions by household income because it is an important factor in the purchase of a new car.

Geographic areas also vary in population migration patterns. Job transfer and retirement are two circumstances that cause people to move. Major natural disasters may affect population migration, as in the case of Hurricane Katrina, which devastated New Orleans. It's also important for marketers to observe who is moving where: people who leave the East Coast aren't necessarily jumping to the West, and vice versa. New Yorkers tend to gravitate to the South or even to Connecticut or New Jersey. Californians often move to other western states instead of coming farther east. The recession has caused other migration changes: whereas healthy economic times saw greater migration to New England's small towns and resort areas, the states of Maine, Massachusetts, New Hampshire, and Vermont have seen a falloff in recent years. Similarly, states like Michigan and Ohio, whose economy depends heavily on the auto industry, saw migration out of those states as jobs disappeared.[12]

The move from urban to suburban areas after World War II created a need to redefine the urban marketplace. This trend radically changed cities' traditional patterns of retailing and led to decline in many downtown shopping areas. Subsequently, traditional city boundaries become almost meaningless for marketing purposes. However, marketers now observe a trend toward the revitalization of some downtown urban areas.

In an effort to respond to these changes, the government now classifies urban data using the following categories:

- The category of **core based statistical area (CBSA)** became effective in 2000 and refers collectively to metropolitan and micropolitan statistical areas. Each CBSA must contain at least one urban area with a population of 10,000 or more. Each metropolitan statistical area must have at least one urbanized area of 50,000 or more inhabitants. Each micropolitan statistical area must have at least one urban cluster with a population of at least 10,000 but less than 50,000. There are 362 metropolitan and 560 micropolitan statistical areas in the United States. Of the 362 metropolitan statistical areas, 178 are classified as large, meaning they contain more than 250,000 people.[13]

- A **metropolitan statistical area (MSA)** is a freestanding urban area with a population in the urban center of at least 50,000 and a total metropolitan statistical area population of 100,000 or more. Buyers in metropolitan statistical areas exhibit social and economic homogeneity and usually border on nonurbanized counties. Examples include Little Rock, Arkansas; Kalamazoo–Battle Creek, Michigan; and Rochester, New York. Figure 9.2 identifies the ten largest metropolitan areas in the United States.

- A **micropolitan statistical area** has at least one town of 10,000 to 49,999 people—it can have several such towns—and proportionally few of its residents commuting outside the area. Recently, the government counted 560 such areas in the continental United States. Examples of micropolitan statistical areas include Corning, New York; Kalispell, Montana; Kahului-Wailuku, Hawaii; and Key West, Florida.

core based statistical area (CBSA) Collective term for metropolitan and micropolitan statistical areas.

metropolitan statistical area (MSA) Freestanding urban area with a population in the urban center of at least 50,000 and a total MSA population of 100,000 or more.

micropolitan statistical area Area with at least one town of 10,000 to 49,999 people with proportionally few of its residents commuting to outside the area.

- The category of **consolidated metropolitan statistical area (CMSA)** includes the country's 25 or so urban giants such as Detroit–Ann Arbor–Flint, Michigan; Los Angeles–Riverside–Orange County, California; and Philadelphia–Wilmington–Atlantic City. (Note in the third example, three states are involved: Pennsylvania, Delaware, and New Jersey.) A CMSA must include two or more primary metropolitan statistical areas, discussed next.

Bar chart: values by metropolitan area

New York 18.8; Los Angeles 12.9; Chicago 9.5; Dallas–Ft. Worth 6.1; Philadelphia 5.8; Houston 5.6; Miami–Ft. Lauderdale 5.4; Washington, D.C. 5.3; Atlanta 5.3; Boston–Cambridge 4.5

figure 9.2

The Ten Largest Metropolitan Areas in the United States

Source: "Large Metropolitan Statistical Areas—Population: 1990 to 2008," *Statistical Abstract of the United States 2009*, U.S. Census Bureau, http://www.census.gov, accessed April 17, 2010.

- A **primary metropolitan statistical area (PMSA)** is an urbanized county or set of counties with social and economic ties to nearby areas. PMSAs are identified within areas of 1-million-plus populations. Olympia, Washington, is part of the Seattle–Tacoma–Bremerton PMSA. Bridgeport, Connecticut, is part of the New York–northern New Jersey–Long Island PMSA, and Riverside–San Bernardino, California, is a PMSA within the Los Angeles–Riverside–Orange County PMSA.[14]

consolidated metropolitan statistical area (CMSA) Urban area that includes two or more PMSAs.

primary metropolitan statistical area (PMSA) Urbanized county or set of counties with social and economic ties to nearby areas.

core region Region from which most major brands get 40 to 80 percent of their sales.

Using Geographic Segmentation

Demand for some categories of goods and services can vary according to geographic region, and marketers must be aware of how these regions differ. Marketers of major brands are particularly interested in defining their **core regions**, the locations where they get 40 to 80 percent of their sales.

Residence location *within* a geographic area is an important segmentation variable. City dwellers often rely on public transportation and may get along fine without automobiles, whereas those who live in the suburbs or rural areas depend on their own cars and trucks. Also, those who live in the suburbs spend more on lawn and garden care products than city dwellers. Climate is another important segmentation factor; for example, at 41.7 quarts per person per year, consumers in cold northern states eat the most ice cream in America. A recent survey named Tampa, Florida, as the number-one city in overall caffeine consumption (including the consumption of coffee, tea, chocolate, and caffeinated energy drinks). However, Seattle and New York top the list in their consumption of coffee and tea, respectively. Marketers can use this information to determine where their products are most likely to be successful.[15]

Geographic segmentation provides useful distinctions when regional preferences or needs exist. A consumer may not want to invest in a snow blower or flood insurance but may *have* to because of the location of his or her home. But it's important for marketers not to stop at geographic location as a segmentation method because distinctions among consumers also exist within a geographic location. Consider those who relocate from one region to another for work or family reasons. They may bring with them their preferences from other parts of the country. Using multiple segmentation variables is probably a much better strategy for targeting a specific market.

Geographic Information Systems (GISs)

Super Bowl Sunday is more than a sporting event—it is also the single biggest sales day of the year for pizza companies like Domino's. On a recent Super Bowl Sunday, Domino's delivered more than 1.3 million pizzas around the nation. The firm built its reputation as the number-one pizza delivery company in the world, which means its delivery system must be as streamlined and efficient

> To achieve its objectives, Domino's invested in new technology systems like its "pizza tracker."

COURTESY OF DOMINO'S PIZZA, INC.

geographic information systems (GISs) Software packages that assemble, store, manipulate, and display data by their location.

as possible. To achieve its objectives, Domino's invested in new technology systems like its "pizza tracker," which allows football fans to order their favorite pizzas ahead of time online with their computers or mobile phones via Domino's and track the delivery status of their pies.[16] This new feature is part of the firm's geographic information system.

Once used mainly by the military, **geographic information systems (GISs)** are computer systems that assemble, store, manipulate, and display data by their location. GISs simplify the job of analyzing marketing information by relating data to their locations. The result is a geographic map overlaid with digital data about consumers in a particular area. A growing number of companies benefit from using a GIS to locate new outlets, assign sales territories, plan distribution centers—and map out the most efficient delivery routes. Google Earth is a recent application of GIS technology that allows computer users to view different parts of the country up close. Users simply type in an address and zoom into it, whether it's a house, a theme park, a school, or a store.

 assessment check

1. Under what circumstances are marketers most likely to use geographic segmentation?
2. What are the five main categories for classifying urban data?

Demographic Segmentation

5 Discuss the demographic approach to segmenting consumer markets.

demographic segmentation Division of an overall market into homogeneous groups based on variables such as gender, age, income, occupation, education, sexual orientation, household size, and stage in the family lifecycle; also called *socioeconomic segmentation*.

The most common method of market segmentation—**demographic segmentation**—defines consumer groups according to demographic variables such as gender, age, income, occupation, education, sexual orientation, household size, and stage in the family lifecycle. This approach is also called *socioeconomic segmentation*. Marketers review vast quantities of available data to complete a plan for demographic segmentation. One of the primary sources for demographic data in the United States is the Census Bureau. Marketers can obtain many of the Census Bureau's statistics online at www.census.gov.

The following discussion considers the most commonly used demographic variables. Keep in mind, however, that while demographic segmentation is helpful, it can also lead to stereotyping—a preconception about a group of people—which can alienate a potential market or cause marketers to miss a potential market altogether. The idea is to use segmentation as a starting point, not as an endpoint. Demographic segmentation can help marketers communicate effectively with their target markets, as described in the "Career Readiness" feature.

Segmenting by Gender

Gender is an obvious variable that helps define the markets for certain products, but segmenting by gender can be tricky. In some cases, the segmenting is obvious—lipstick for women, facial shaving products for men. However, in recent years, the lines have increasingly blurred. Some men wear

as a marketer, you learn to create and communicate messages for the people you want to purchase your firm's goods and services. The messages you send can have a major impact on potential customers' decisions to buy your products or those offered by a competitor. Understanding the needs and preferences of your target market will help you communicate effectively with the right people. The following suggestions will help you succeed:

- Develop an understanding of your target market before attempting to market products to them. This way, you will gain credibility among your consumers.

- Tailor your message directly to the group of consumers you want to reach. Don't try to sell your products to everyone.

- Use appropriate language for the recipients of your message. Become familiar with the conventional sayings, wording, and tone suitable for your audience.

- Use images that illustrate to your market segment that you understand their culture, beliefs, and lifestyle. This will also communicate that you understand their needs and preferences.

- Create messages that provide clear solutions to specific problems or needs consumers may have.

- Always be respectful of the consumers you intend to serve. Address their needs and preferences seriously.

Sources: Laura Lake, "In Marketing You Must Know Your Target," *About.com Marketing*, http://www.marketing.about.com, accessed April 18, 2010; Greg Beverly, "12 Great Reasons to Know Your Target Market," *Info Central Online*, February 21, 2010, http://www.infocentralonline.com; Chelsea Nicole, "The Best Ways to Communicate with Your Target Market," *QViews.com*, January 28, 2010, http://www.qviews.com.

earrings and use skin-care products, once both the province of women. Some of today's women purchase power tools and pickup trucks, once considered traditionally male purchases. So marketers of cars and trucks, power tools, jewelry, and skin-care products have had to change the way they segment their markets. Nivea, well known for its skin-care products for women and babies, created an entire line of men's skin-care products called Nivea for Men. Some companies successfully market the same—or similar—products to both men and women. Visa markets its small-business credit card services to firms owned by both men and women.

As purchasing power in many households has shifted toward women, marketers learned that female consumers who regularly use the Internet make most of the decisions about retail items. Based on this information, Yahoo! recently launched Shine, a site specifically for women. The site offers content in a variety of areas ranging from entertainment to finance and provides opportunities for advertisers to reach a targeted female audience. Bank of America, Bertolli, and E*TRADE are among the brands advertised on the site.[17]

Segmenting by Age

Age is another variable marketers use to segment their markets. As with gender, age seems an easy distinction to make—baby food for babies, retirement communities for seniors. But the distinctions become blurred as consumers' roles and needs change, and as age distribution shifts and changes in each group take place. St. Joseph's baby aspirin is no longer marketed just to parents for their infants; now it is also marketed to adults to help prevent heart disease.

SCHOOL-AGE CHILDREN

School-age children—and those even younger—exert considerable influence over family purchases, as marketers are keenly aware, particularly in the area of food. Children as young as 2 make choices about what they want to eat, play with, and wear. The food industry reportedly spends $10 billion each year marketing to children. Its advertisements for such products as breakfast cereals, snack foods, and beverages are designed to attract the attention of children under the age of 12—who in turn persuade their families to purchase them. With childhood obesity on the rise, nutritionists and pediatricians are concerned about the nutritional value of foods marketed to children. In fact, a recent study by the University of California at Los Angeles revealed that the advertising of junk food plays a key role in childhood obesity.[18]

TWEENS AND TEENS

Tweens—sometimes also called *preteens*—and teens are a rapidly growing market. This group is 71 million strong and packs a wallop when it comes to spending—some researchers estimate as much as $200 billion. But they also influence billions of dollars' worth of purchases made by their families. Although members of this group don't fall into a single category—they reflect the diversity of the U.S. population in general—the most popular purchases include candy and snacks, soft drinks, clothing, music, and electronics. If marketers could describe this group with one characteristic, it would likely be *interactive*. They grew up with the Internet, and they expect to be actively involved in their own entertainment. They might rather determine the outcome of a video game than watch to see who won a football game on TV. Even the TV shows they watch—like "American Idol"—provide opportunities for input. They are completely comfortable in a digital world, and many cannot imagine life without their cell phones and iPods. When they want to communicate with friends—or parents—they send text messages. They expect a vast array of choices when it comes to programming, media alternatives, and interactive experiences. The big challenge for marketers is keeping up with them—let alone staying a step ahead. Phone companies and car companies have increased their spending on advertising to older teens, while snacks, clothing, and video games claim the attention of the younger set.[19]

Some companies have expanded their product lines to include specific offerings to tweens and teens. Pottery Barn devotes an entire catalog to this group, PBteen. Teen consumers—both boys and girls—can decorate their bedrooms or dorm rooms with coordinating furniture, bedding, pillows, curtains, corkboards, and even retro-styled telephones from PBteen.[20]

GENERATION X

The group born between 1968 and 1979, now generally in their early 30s to early 40s, often are referred to as *Generation X*. This group of an estimated 41 million faced some economic and career challenges as they began their adult lives and started families: housing costs were high and debt associated with college loans and credit cards was soaring. But their financial squeeze should ease as they enter their prime earning years. This group is very family oriented—not defining themselves by their careers as much as previous generations—well educated, and optimistic. Like their younger counterparts, Gen Xers are comfortable with the Internet; even if they make a purchase at a retail store, they are likely to have researched their choices online. But like their elders, they were raised on television—so the TV is still an important marketing tool.[21]

As this generation matures, they are growing more concerned about social issues and protecting the natural environment, both of which they view as affecting the well-being of their children. As a result, they are turning to goods and services that support certain causes. Singer-songwriter Jack Johnson, in his mid-30s, recorded an album using solar energy. He requires his concert promoters to recycle and launched an online social networking site, All At Once, where fans can support environmental

> Some companies have expanded their product lines to include specific offerings to tweens and teens, such as Pottery Barn's PBteen.

© NEWSCOM

not-for-profit organizations. Johnson, a member of Generation X, appeals both to his own age group and older teens.[22]

BABY BOOMERS

Baby boomers—those born between 1946 and 1964—are a popular segment to target because of their numbers and income levels. Approximately 78 million people were born during this period in the United States.[23] The values of this age group were influenced both by the Vietnam War era and the career-driven era that followed. They also came of age with early television and with TV commercials serving as a backdrop to most of their lives. They tried new breakfast cereals, ate TV dinners, and recall when cigarettes were advertised on television.

Not surprisingly, baby boomers are a lucrative segment for many marketers. Baby boomers wield spending power estimated at $3 trillion, which is why businesses try to woo this group.[24] Different subgroups within this generation complicate segmentation and targeting strategies. Some boomers put off having children until their 40s, while others their age have already become grandparents. Boomers tend to value health and quality of life—a fact not lost on marketers for products such as organic foods, financial investments, travel, and fitness. But boomers are also quick to embrace new technology, even as they age. While boomers make up slightly less than one-third of the U.S. population, according to a recent Pew Research Center study they represent 36 percent of Internet users. In addition, nearly half of all boomers maintain a Facebook page.[25]

The motorcycle industry has boomers clearly in its sights. As a group, baby boomers are significantly more physically active than their counterparts in previous generations. However, boomers are beginning to experience the wide range of health problems that typically come with age—arthritis, back pain, chronic joint and muscle issues, and more—making it difficult for them to continue to ride their two-wheelers. With baby boomers comprising more than 40 percent of the motorcycling population, several manufacturers have introduced trikes—that is, three-wheeled motorcycles. The trikes even include luxury features like GPS navigation, cruise control, and stereo speakers.[26]

SENIORS

As baby boomers age and Americans continue to live longer, the median age of the U.S. population has dramatically increased. Today, more than 55 million people are now over age 65. With discretionary income and rates of home ownership higher than those of other age groups, they also account for a major proportion of new-car sales and travel dollars spent. Many marketers have found that seniors are a group worth targeting. Although many seniors live on modest, fixed incomes, those who are well off financially have both time and money to spend on leisure activities and luxury items. Knowing this, some unethical marketers try to take advantage of seniors, as discussed in the "Solving an Ethical Controversy" feature.

Other important characteristics of this group include the following:

- Families experienced economic hardship during this group's childhood.

Baby boomers are a lucrative segment for many marketers. Verizon Wireless often targets older customers with advertising for phones that are easier to use.

- They built the suburbs.
- They value hard work.
- They like to associate with people who have similar views and backgrounds.
- They are concerned with personal safety.
- They spend money conservatively, but have reached a level of financial comfort where they like to indulge in some luxury.
- They are not likely to be the first to try new products.[27]

Understanding just a few of these characteristics helps marketers develop goods and services and create marketing messages that will reach this group. When it was founded, Overseas Adventure Travel offered trekking, mountaineering, safari, and kayaking trips geared toward younger travelers. Today, OAT is part of the Grand Circle Travel Company and focuses on outdoor travel experiences for people ages 50 and older. The trips are less rigorous than the original itineraries, but still provide access to places off the beaten path. The company knows its customers have both the time and income for such excursions and appreciate the adventure experience.[28]

solving an ethical controversy

ⓣaking Advantage of Seniors

In a recent year, about 25 million seniors in the United States were victims of fraud. As baby boomers age, industry observers predict the number of financial scams targeting this group will increase dramatically. Seniors are vulnerable to unethical, sometimes illegal, practices, particularly involving insurance, mortgages, and investments. The recent economic downturn has intensified seniors' need to preserve their assets, making them prime targets for financial scams. Consumer and elder advocacy groups as well as the Securities and Exchange Commission (SEC) are working to stop such practices.

Should special laws be enacted to protect seniors from marketing abuses?

PRO

1. Investing events target seniors with "no-obligation" lunch or dinner seminars are nothing more than a high-pressure sales pitch masquerading as an educational workshop. Seniors are coerced into making investments immediately, without full disclosure of the risks involved.

2. Preying on fear or taking advantage of their lack of understanding, some companies induce seniors to buy products they don't need or can't afford, such as reverse-equity mortgages, prepaid funerals, annuities, and prescription drug plans. While some products are outright scams, others are legitimate products wholly unsuitable for the buyer.

CON

1. Seniors are consumers. Marketers should be allowed to gather information on them and target them for purchases just like any other group of consumers in a free-enterprise economy.

2. All consumers can be targets of fraud. Seniors do not need special protection from the SEC or other agencies.

Summary

Regulators, marketers, and advocacy groups agree there is no place for unethical behavior in the marketplace. However, they may not agree about what action to take. Meanwhile, like all consumers, seniors should remember two things: If they're being told they must "act now" to "get in on" a good deal, that message should serve as a red flag. And if the claim sounds too good to be true, it probably is.

Sources: Terry Cettina, "Fraud: 5 Scams Aimed at the Elderly," *Bankrate.com*, http://www.bankrate.com, accessed March 23, 2010; Ken and Daria Dolan, "Top Scams That Target Seniors," *WalletPop.com*, December 11, 2009, http://www.walletpop.com; Jennifer Levitz, "Laws Take on Financial Scams against Seniors," *The Wall Street Journal*, May 19, 2009, http://online.wsj.com.

The Cohort Effect: The Video Game Generation

Marketers can learn from a sociological concept called the **cohort effect**, the tendency of members of a generation with common characteristics—like an interest in sustainability—to be influenced and bound together by significant events occurring during their key formative years, roughly ages 17 to 22. These events help define the core values of the age group that eventually shape consumer preferences and behavior. For seniors, the events would be the Great Depression, World War II, and Korea because many were in this age bracket at that time. Later groups were influenced by the Cold War, the civil rights movement, and the assassination of John F. Kennedy. For older baby boomers, it would be the Vietnam War and the women's movement.

The current cohort—generally consisting of those born during the late 1970s to the early 1990s—may be the most cohesive to date. Marketers have called this group by several names: *Generation Y*, the *Millennial Generation, Generation Next*, and *Echo Boomers* (an echo of baby boomers). Others called it the *9–11 Generation* because its members were in their formative years during the terrorist attacks of September 11, 2001.

But something else happened during this group's formative years to shape its preferences and behaviors: while they were coming of age, so too were video games. For this reason, we call this cohort the **Video Game Generation**.

The early versions of video games were developed during the 1950s and 1960s and were displayed on oscilloscopes, mainframe computers, and television screens. Atari and Magnavox were the first commercial entrants on the scene, with Atari introducing its Pong game and Magnavox launching the Odyssey home video game system. During the late 1970s and 1980s, other competitors entered the market: Activision, Commodore, Nintendo, Sega, and more. As the technology improved, the games and systems became more sophisticated, with 3-D, realistic graphics, laser disks, and handheld consoles. The industry has continued to evolve, with the introduction of PlayStation, the Nintendo DS, Microsoft's Xbox, and the Wii. Today, more consumers regularly play video games—at home, on their mobile phone, on the beach, anywhere—than go to the movies.

Members of the Video Game Generation are highly visual and are generally comfortable with all forms of technology. They gravitate to activities that provide constant entertainment and immediate gratification. They get their information from social media like Facebook and MySpace as opposed to traditional media, and they prefer instant messaging and texting to e-mails.

The significance of the cohort effect for marketers lies in understanding the general characteristics of the Video Game Generation as it responds to its life-defining events. The social and economic influences it experiences help form members' long-term beliefs and goals in life—and can have a lasting effect on their buying habits and the product choices they make.[29]

cohort effect Tendency of members of a generation to be influenced and bound together by events occurring during their key formative years—roughly ages 17 to 22.

Video Game Generation During this cohort's formative years, while their preferences and behaviors were being shaped, so too were video games.

Segmenting by Ethnic Group

According to the Census Bureau, America's racial and ethnic makeup is constantly changing. The three largest and fastest-growing racial/ethnic groups are Hispanics, African Americans, and Asian Americans. From a marketer's perspective, it is important to note that spending by these groups is rising at a faster pace than for U.S. households in general.

HISPANICS AND AFRICAN AMERICANS

Hispanics and African Americans are currently the largest racial/ethnic minority groups in the United States, with Hispanics surpassing African Americans at nearly 48 million, according to the most recent census data.[30] The Hispanic population is growing much faster than the African American population.[31] The population growth has created *majority-minority counties*—that is, places where more than half the population is a single racial or ethnic group other than non-Hispanic white. Majority-minority counties exist in several states.[32] Just as important for marketers, although U.S. Hispanics' disposable income is still significantly less than that of non-Hispanic whites, a recent study found that Hispanic buying power is rising at a rate nearly triple that of the national average.[33]

Many marketers have focused their efforts on the Hispanic population in the United States. Procter & Gamble, The Coca-Cola Company, and Walmart are among the largest advertisers to target this group of consumers. Still, many companies find it a challenge to reach Hispanic consumers and turn them into customers. Consorte Media specializes in gathering and analyzing data about the

Hispanic market for clients such as Best Buy and Dealix. Founder and CEO Alicia Morga focuses on the online habits of Hispanic consumers, more than 26 million of whom visit the Internet regularly. She helped Best Buy build a better recruitment site for Hispanic job candidates and used her research to assist BuenaMusica.com in developing a more effective ad campaign.[34]

Like Hispanics, who originate from a variety of countries, the more than 41 million African Americans in the United States—who make up nearly 14 percent of the population—do not comprise a single category.[35] Instead, they represent broad diversity ranging from country of origin to income, age, education, and geographic location. Studies show that affluent African Americans are creating a significant impact on the consumer economy. The number of African American households earning $75,000 or more continues to grow; in a recent five-year period, it increased 47 percent and now represents an estimated $87.3 billion in buying power.[36] This growing segment represents an opportunity for advertisers, few of whom currently target African Americans in national campaigns. However, PepsiCo recently tapped into the African American mom demographic with the launch of a digital community carrying the tagline "We inspire."[37]

ASIAN AMERICANS

Although Asian Americans represent a smaller segment than either the African American or Hispanic populations, with more than 14 million in the United States, they are the second-fastest-growing segment of the population. The Census Bureau estimates this group will grow to 18 million by the year 2020, representing more than 5 percent of the U.S. population.[38] Asian Americans are an attractive target for marketers because they also have the fastest-growing income.

The Asian American population is concentrated in fewer geographic areas than other ethnic markets. Half of Asians live in California, Texas, and New York. The population is diverse, however, because it represents numerous cultures and its members speak a wide variety of languages, including Bengali, Cantonese, Hawaiian, Hindi, Hmong, Japanese, Korean, Laotian, Mandarin, Tagalog, Tamil, Telugu, Thai, Urdu, and Vietnamese. As a result, demographics differ widely by Asian group. For example, the median household income for Asian Indians in a recent year totaled nearly $91,000 while median income for Vietnamese Americans during the same period was just under $56,000.[39]

NATIVE AMERICANS

Another important minority group is Native Americans, whose current population numbers nearly 5 million, or 1.6 percent of the total U.S. population, including both American Indians and Alaska natives. In addition to tribes located in the continental United States, such as Cherokee, Apache, Navaho, Pueblo, and Iroquois, the Census Bureau includes Alaska native tribes such as Aleut and Eskimo. The Native American population grew 1.7 percent in a recent year, faster than the U.S. population in general.[40]

In addition to population growth, Native American businesses are growing. In a recent year, more than 201,000 non-farm Native American firms operated in the United States, with nearly $27 billion in receipts and primarily representing the construction, maintenance and repair, retail, and services industries.[41] Reservation-based casinos and related gaming activities make up a multi-billion-dollar industry. The Native American Business Alliance Fund fosters relationships between Native American–owned firms and other corporations. A recent NABA-hosted conference and golf outing featured such sponsors as Avis, Denny's, Kellogg Co., Starwood Hotels & Resorts Worldwide, and UPS.[42]

Asian Americans, the second fastest growing segment of the U.S. population, are an attractive target for marketers because they also have the fastest rising income. This ad features actress Lucy Liu, who is of Chinese descent.

IMAGE COURTESY OF THE ADVERTISING ARCHIVES

Rez-Biz, a magazine published by the Navajo nation, is aimed at Native American entrepreneurs and includes blogs from other entrepreneurs, business stories, advertisements, and contacts. The magazine encourages entrepreneurial ventures and economic development on reservations and other locations where Native Americans are concentrated.[43]

PEOPLE OF MIXED RACE

U.S. residents completing census forms now have the option of identifying themselves as belonging to more than one racial category. According to the Census Bureau, about 7 million U.S. residents classify themselves this way, and their numbers are growing.[44] Marketers need to be aware of this change. On one hand, it benefits marketers by making racial statistics more accurate; on the other hand, marketers may find it difficult to compare the new statistics with data from earlier censuses. In some cases, people of mixed race prefer to emphasize one part of their heritage over another; in other cases, they prefer not to make a choice. Recent estimates place nearly 60 percent of the U.S. mixed-race population under the age of 25, and these consumers are having their own families.[45] Forward-thinking marketers should keep tabs on this group, identifying their needs and preferences.

Segmenting by Family Lifecycle Stages

Still another form of demographic segmentation employs the stages of the **family lifecycle**—the process of family formation and dissolution. The underlying theme of this segmentation approach is that life stage, not age per se, is the primary determinant of many consumer purchases. As people move from one life stage to another, they become potential consumers for different types of goods and services.

family lifecycle Process of family formation and dissolution.

An unmarried person setting up an apartment for the first time is likely a good prospect for inexpensive furniture and small home appliances. This consumer must probably budget carefully, ruling out expenditures on luxury items. Alternatively, a young single person still living at home will probably have more money to spend on products such as a car, entertainment, and clothing. As couples marry, their consumer profiles change. Couples without children are frequent buyers of personalized gifts, power tools, furniture, and homes. Eating out and travel may also be part of their lifestyles.

The birth or adoption of a first child changes any consumer's profile considerably; parents must buy cribs, changing tables, baby clothes, baby food, car seats, and similar products. Parents usually spend less on the children who follow because they have already bought many essential items for the first child. Today, the average woman gives birth to fewer children than she did a century ago and usually waits until she is older to have them. Although the average age for American women to have their first child is 25, many women wait much longer, often into their 30s and even 40s. This means that, if they work outside the home, older women are likely more established financially with more money to spend. However, if a woman chooses to stay home after the birth of a child, income can drop dramatically.

Families typically spend the most during the years their children are growing—on everything including housing, food, clothing, braces, and college. Thus, they often look to obtain value wherever they can. Marketers can create satisfied and loyal customers among this group by giving them the best value possible.

Once children are on their own—or at least off to college—married couples enter the "empty nest" stage. Empty nesters may have the disposable incomes necessary to purchase premium products once college tuitions and mortgages are paid off. They may travel more, eat out more often, redecorate the house, or go back to school themselves. They may treat themselves to a new and more luxurious car or buy a vacation home. In later years, empty nesters may decide to sell their homes and become customers for retirement or assisted-living communities. They may require home-care services or more health care products as well. However, more older adults report they have not saved enough for retirement, which may include this type of care. People currently in this stage of life now say they would advise younger adults to address issues of a lifetime income, the cost of health care, and less reliance on Social Security benefits for income. Whether to meet expenses or for intellectual stimulation, many retired adults are returning to work at least part-time—as Walmart greeters, as consultants in their field of expertise, or something completely different, such as a paid fellowship with a not-for-profit organization.[46]

One trend noted by researchers in the past decade is an increase in the number of grown children, or "boomerangs," who return home to live with their parents. A recent Pew Research Center study found that one in seven parents with grown children had boomerangs, some of them bringing along pets or families of their own.[47] Another trend is the growing number of grandparents who care for grandchildren on a regular basis—making them customers all over again for baby and child products such as toys, food, and safety devices.[48]

Segmenting by Household Type

The first U.S. census in 1790 found an average household size of 5.8 people. Today, that number is below 3, due in part to a declining birth rate.[49] Sociologists attribute the decline to couples' reluctance to take on the added expense of a child.[50] The U.S. Department of Commerce cites several other reasons for the trend toward smaller households: lower fertility rates (including the decision to have fewer children or no children at all), young people's tendency to postpone marriage, the frequency of divorce, and the ability and desire of many people to live alone.

Today's U.S. households represent a wide range of diversity. They include households with a married couple and their children; households blended through divorce or loss of a spouse and remarriage; those headed by a single parent, same-sex parents, or grandparents; couples without children; groups of friends; and single-person households.

Couples without children may be young or old. If they are seniors, their children may have already grown and be living on their own. Some older couples choose to live together without marriage because they prefer to keep their finances separate and because they could lose valuable health or pension benefits if they married. Younger couples without children are considered attractive to marketers because they often have high levels of income to spend. These couples typically eat out often, take expensive vacations, and buy luxury cars.

Same-sex couples who share households—with or without children—are on the rise. More than 400,000 U.S. children are raised by same-sex couples. While the social debate over same-sex marriage and civil unions continues, marketers recognize these households as important customers. Walmart has introduced a line of wedding cards and commitment rings designed for same-sex couples. Companies such as American Airlines, Best Buy, and Hewlett-Packard have also created ad campaigns aimed at gay and lesbian households.[51]

People live alone for a variety of reasons—sometimes by choice and sometimes by necessity, such as divorce or widowhood. In response, marketers have modified their messages and their products to meet the needs of single-person households. Food industry manufacturers are downsizing products, offering more single-serving foods, ranging from soup to macaroni and cheese.

Marketers have modified their messages and their products to meet the needs of single-person households, offering items such as single-serving foods.

Segmenting by Income and Expenditure Patterns

Part of the earlier definition of *market* described people with purchasing power. Not surprisingly, then, a common basis for segmenting the consumer market is income. Marketers often target geographic areas known for the high incomes of their residents. Or they might consider age or household type when determining potential buying power.

ENGEL'S LAWS

How do expenditure patterns vary with income? Over a century ago, Ernst Engel, a German statistician, published what became known as **Engel's laws**—three general statements based on his studies of the impact of household income changes on consumer spending behavior. According to Engel, as household income increases, the following will take place:

1. A smaller percentage of expenditures goes for food.

2. The percentage spent on housing, household operations, and clothing remains constant.

3. The percentage spent on other items (such as recreation and education) increases.

Are Engel's laws still valid? Recent studies say yes, with a few exceptions. Researchers note a steady decline in the percentage of total income spent on food, beverages, and tobacco as income increases. Although high-income families spend greater absolute amounts on food items, their purchases represent declining percentages of their total expenditures compared with low-income families.[52] In addition, that percentage has declined over the last century.[53] But as food prices become inflated, consumers change how they shop—they may spend the same to buy fewer items, spend more to buy the same items, or try to spend less and buy as many items as possible within the new budget. Marketers note that consumers are more selective, on the alert for bargains at the supermarket. One other recent finding splits the food dollar according to meals cooked and eaten at home versus meals eaten out at restaurants. Over the years, the proportion of food U.S. consumers ate away from home gradually increased, to nearly half their food dollar. However, with the belt-tightening that accompanies an economic downturn, the restaurant industry has seen a sustained dip in sales. Currently, U.S. consumers reportedly spend 48 percent of their food dollar on meals eaten away from home.[54]

The second law remains partly accurate. However, the percentage of fixed expenditures for housing and household operations has increased over the past 30 years. And the percentage spent on clothing rises with increased income. Also, expenditures may vary from region to region. In general, residents of the Northeast and West spend more on housing than people who live in the Midwest and South.

The third law remains true, with the exception of medical and personal-care costs, which appear to decline as a percentage of increased income.

Engel's laws can help marketers target markets at all income levels. Regardless of the economic environment, consumers still buy luxury goods and services. One reason is some companies now offer their luxury products at different price levels. Mercedes-Benz has its lower-priced C-class models, while Tiffany sells a $100 sterling silver heart pendant with chain. Both of these firms continue to offer their higher-priced items but have broadened their market by serving other consumers.

Demographic Segmentation Abroad

Marketers often face a difficult task in obtaining the data necessary for demographic segmentation abroad. Many countries do not have scheduled census programs. Germany skipped counting from 1970 to 1987, and France conducts a census about every seven years. By contrast, Japan and Canada conduct censuses every five years; however, the mid-decade assessments are not as complete as the end-of-decade counts.

Also, some foreign data include demographic divisions not found in the U.S. census. Canada collects information on religious affiliation, for instance. On the other hand, some of the standard

Engel's laws Three general statements about the impact of household income on consumer spending behavior: as household income increases, a smaller percentage of expenditures goes for food; the percentage spent on housing, household operations, and clothing remains constant; and the percentage spent on other items (such as recreation and education) increases.

segmentation data for U.S. markets are not available abroad. Many nations do not collect income data. Great Britain, Japan, Spain, France, and Italy are examples. Similarly, family lifecycle data are difficult to apply in global demographic segmentation efforts. Ireland acknowledges only three marital statuses—single, married, and widowed—while Latin American nations and Sweden count their unmarried cohabitants.

One source of global demographic information is the International Programs Center (IPC) at the U.S. Census Bureau. The IPC provides a searchable online database of population statistics for many countries on the Census Bureau's Web page. Another source is the United Nations, which sponsors national statistical offices that collect demographic data on a variety of countries.

In addition, private marketing research firms can supplement government data. Firms like Boston Consulting Group gather data on income of consumers around the world, focusing in particular on millionaire households. While a global economic crisis caused worldwide wealth to decline, the country with the most millionaire households remains the United States, with nearly 4 million, followed by Japan, China, Germany, and Great Britain. Countries with the highest *density* of millionaire households are Singapore, followed by Switzerland, Kuwait, United Arab Emirates, and the United States.[55]

assessment check

1. What is demographic segmentation?

2. What are the major categories of demographic segmentation?

Psychographic Segmentation

Outline the psychographic approach to segmenting consumer markets.

Marketers have traditionally referred to geographic and demographic characteristics as the primary bases for dividing consumers into homogeneous market segments. Still, they have long recognized the need for fuller, more lifelike portraits of consumers in developing their marketing programs. As a result, psychographic segmentation can be a useful tool for gaining sharper insight into consumer purchasing behavior.

What Is Psychographic Segmentation?

psychographic segmentation Division of a population into groups having similar attitudes, values, and lifestyles.

Psychographic segmentation divides a population into groups with similar values and lifestyles. Lifestyle refers to a person's mode of living and describes how an individual operates on a daily basis. Consumers' lifestyles are composites of their individual psychological profiles, including their needs, motives, perceptions, and attitudes. A lifestyle also bears the mark of many other influences such as family, job, social activities, and culture.

AIO statements Items on lifestyle surveys that describe various activities, interests, and respondents' opinions.

The most common method for developing psychographic profiles of a population is to conduct a large-scale survey asking consumers to agree or disagree with a collection of several hundred AIO statements. These **AIO statements** describe various activities, interests, and opinions. The resulting data allow researchers to develop lifestyle profiles. Marketers can then develop a separate marketing strategy that closely fits the psychographic makeup for each lifestyle segment.

Marketing researchers have conducted psychographic studies on hundreds of goods and services, such as beer and air travel. Hospitals and other health care providers use such studies to assess consumer behavior and attitudes toward health care in general, to learn the needs of consumers in particular marketplaces, and to determine how consumers perceive individual institutions. Many businesses turn to psychographic research to learn what consumers in various demographic and geographic segments want and need.

VALS™

A quarter-century ago, research and consulting firm SRI International developed a psychographic segmentation system it called VALS, an acronym for *VAlues and LifeStyles*. Initially, VALS categorized consumers by their social values—how they felt about issues such as legalization of marijuana or abortion, for example. Today, VALS is owned and managed by SRI Consulting Business Intelligence (SRIC-BI), an SRI spin-off that has revised the system to link it more closely with consumer buying behavior. The revised VALS system categorizes consumers by characteristics that correlate with purchase behavior. It is based on two key concepts: resources and self-motivation. **VALS** divides consumers into eight psychographic categories: innovators, thinkers, achievers, experiencers, believers, strivers, makers, and survivors. Figure 9.3 details the profiles for these categories and their relationships.

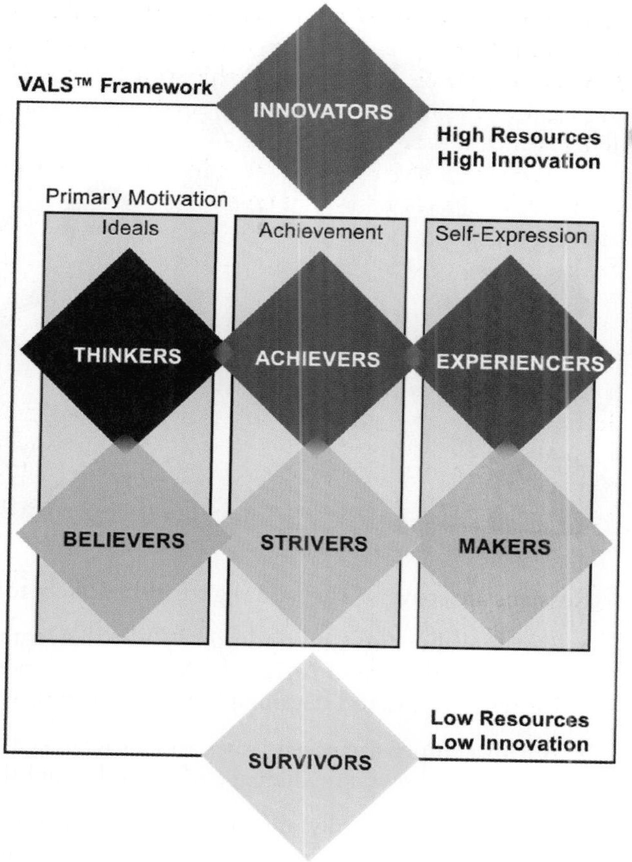

The VALS framework in the figure displays differences in resources as vertical distances, and primary motivation is represented horizontally. The resource dimension measures income, education, self-confidence, health, eagerness to buy, and energy level. Primary motivations divide consumers into three groups: principle-motivated consumers who have a set of ideas and morals—principles—they live by; achievement-motivated consumers, influenced by symbols of success; and action-motivated consumers who seek physical activity, variety, and adventure. Marketers of new lines of eco-friendly fragrances and beauty aids are likely to create appeals for principle-motivated consumers who want to wear their environmental commitment—literally—as described in the "Marketing Success" feature.

SRIC-BI has created several specialized segmentation systems based on this approach. GeoVALS™, for instance, estimates the percentage of each VALS type in a U.S. residential Zip code. Marketers can identify Zip codes with the highest concentrations of the segment they want to reach, they can use the information to choose locations for retail outlets, and they can tailor marketing messages for a local audience. For example, a GeoVALS study can tell a marketer the percentage of consumers in Kettering, Ohio, who fall into each of the eight psychographic categories. Japan-VALS segments the Japanese marketplace with an emphasis on early adopters of new ideas and products. With a questionnaire of 49 items, marketers using Japan-VALS zero in on consumer needs, differentiate their brands, and develop more targeted tools and strategies.[56]

Other tools available include LifeMatrix, offered by marketing research firm GfK Roper Consulting. LifeMatrix is a consumer segmentation system that crunches the numbers on hundreds of personal variables that include political views, religious affiliations, and social attitudes and comes up with ten psychographic categories reflecting today's lifestyles. Participants are asked to indicate how many hours each week they spend on certain activities, which helps shape the overall picture of their lives.[57]

figure 9.3
The VALS Network

Source: SRI Consulting Business Intelligence (SRIC-BI); www.strategicbusinessinsights.com/vals.

VALS Segmentation system that divides consumers into eight psychographic categories: innovators, thinkers, achievers, experiencers, believers, strivers, makers, and survivors.

> Intimates, who value family and personal relationships, are divided almost equally between males and females. One American or European in four would be categorized as an intimate.

© ANDRESR/SHUTTERSTOCK.COM

Psychographic Segmentation of Global Markets

As Japan-VALS suggests, psychographic profiles can cross national boundaries. RoperASW, now part of Germany-based GfK NOP, surveyed 7,000 people in 35 nations. From the data, Roper identified six psychographic consumer segments that exist in all 35 nations, although to varying degrees:

- *Strivers*, the largest segment, value professional and material goals more than the other groups. One-third of the Asian population and one-fourth of Russians are strivers. They are slightly more likely to be men than women.

- *Devouts* value duty and tradition. While this segment comprises 22 percent of all adults, they are most common in Africa, the Middle East, and developing Asia. They are least common in western Europe and developed Asian countries. Worldwide, they are more likely to be female.

- *Altruists* emphasize social issues and societal well-being. Comprising 18 percent of all adults, this group shows a median age of 44 and a slightly higher percentage of women.

- *Intimates* value family and personal relationships. They are divided almost equally between males and females. One American or European in four would be categorized as intimates, but only 7 percent of consumers in developing Asia fall into this category.

- *Fun seekers*, as you might guess from their name, focus on personal enjoyment and pleasurable experiences. They comprise 12 percent of the world's population, with a male–female ratio of 54 to 46. Many live in developed Asia.

mktg: *success*

LR Health and Beauty Helps Customers "Feel Good. Look Great."

Background. LR Health and Beauty Systems was founded in Germany to help customers get and stay healthy—and look good at the same time. The company manufacturers fragrances, skin-care products, and nutritional supplements. All of its products are eco-friendly.

The Challenge. All of the markets targeted by the fledgling company—

fragrances, beauty aids, and supplements—are highly competitive. What's more, many of the players have been in operation for decades. So it was especially important for the company to successfully differentiate its offerings.

The Strategy. LR uses only natural ingredients in its products. All are manufactured in Germany under strict testing for

purity and quality. Product packaging is also eco-friendly. The company introduced a line of celebrity fragrances that showcase supermodel Heidi Klum, British R&B and pop artist Leona Lewis, former tennis star Boris Becker, racer Michael Schumacher, and others. The Grammy-nominated Lewis, a vegetarian and animal lover, says she decided to partner with LR Health and Beauty because of its

- *Creatives*, the smallest segment, account for just 10 percent of the global population. This group seeks education, technology, and knowledge; their male–female ratio is roughly equal.

Roper researchers note that some principles and core beliefs—such as protecting the family—apply to more than one psychographic segment. In addition to Roper, GfK operates 115 companies in more than 100 countries, generating a wide range of marketing research. A recent venture involves a partnership between GfK's Mediamark Research & Intelligence and the Media Behavior Institute to build a U.S. database of consumer activity that will help marketers identify when and where consumers are most receptive to marketers' messages.[58]

Using Psychographic Segmentation

No one suggests that psychographic segmentation is an exact science, but it does help marketers quantify aspects of consumers' personalities and lifestyles to create goods and services for a target market. Psychographic profile systems such as those of Roper and SRIC-BI can paint useful pictures of the overall psychological motivations of consumers. These profiles produce much richer descriptions of potential target markets than other techniques can achieve. The enhanced detail aids in matching a company's image and product offerings with the types of consumers who use its products.

Identifying which psychographic segments are most prevalent in certain markets helps marketers plan and promote more effectively. Often, segments overlap; however, in a recent study of mobile phone users, consumer-research firm Experian Simmons discovered five distinct segments, which they named basic planners, mobile professionals, pragmatic adopters, social connectors, and mobirati. Mobile phones have become so prevalent that the user population is large enough to be studied—and segmented.[59]

Psychographic segmentation is a good supplement to segmentation by demographic or geographic variables. For example, marketers may have access to each consumer type's media preferences in network television, cable television, Internet use, radio format, magazines, and newspapers. Psychographic studies may then refine the picture of segment characteristics to give a more elaborate lifestyle profile of the consumers in the firm's target market. A psychographic study could help marketers of goods and services in Philadelphia, Grand Rapids, or Las Vegas predict what kinds of products consumers in those cities would be drawn to and eliminate those that are not attractive.

---

ethical production standards. The company also markets its FiguAktiv instant drinks, a line of health tonics laced with restorative aloe vera and available in three flavors: peach, honey, and freedom. The drinks are said to be especially effective for those experiencing high blood pressure, high cholesterol, stress, diabetes, arthritis, gout, and even simple aches and pains. Independent sales consultants called "LR Partners" sell the products.

The Outcome. Today, LR Health and Beauty Systems has expanded well beyond Germany. More than 300,000 LR Partners work throughout Europe, in Saudi Arabia and Oman, and the Philippines, Australia, and New Zealand. Most recently LR debuted its "Desperate Housewives" line of fragrances with scents named for the characters of the ABC series. Latest revenue figures totaled $22 billion.

Sources: Company Web site, "The Secret behind LR Health and Beauty's Success," http://www.lrworld.com, accessed March 23, 2010; "Beauty Secret Is in the Aloe Vera," *Kalgoorlie Miner*, September 12, 2009, http://www.URL.com; Susan Stone, "LR Health & Beauty Adds Celebrity Muscle," *Women's Wear Daily*, August 18, 2009, http://0-proquest.umi.com.

assessment check

1. What is psychographic segmentation?
2. Name the eight psychographic categories of the U.S. VALS.

Product-Related Segmentation

Product-related segmentation involves dividing a consumer population into homogeneous groups based on their relationships to the product. This segmentation approach can take several forms:

1. segmenting based on the benefits people seek when they buy a product;
2. segmenting based on usage rates for a product; or
3. segmenting according to consumers' brand loyalty toward a product.

product-related segmentation Division of a population into homogeneous groups based on their relationships to a product.

Segmenting by Benefits Sought

This approach focuses on attributes people seek and benefits they expect to receive from a good or service. It groups consumers into segments based on what they want a product to do for them. Consumers who drink Starbucks premium coffees are not just looking for a dose of caffeine. They are willing to pay extra to savor a pleasant experience, one that makes them feel pampered and appreciated. Women who work out at Curves want to look their best and feel healthy. Pet owners who feed their cats and dogs Science Diet believe they are giving their animals a great-tasting, healthful pet food.

Even if a business offers only one product line, however, marketers must remember to consider product benefits. Two people may buy the same product for very different reasons. A box of Arm & Hammer baking soda could end up serving as a refrigerator freshener, a toothpaste substitute, an antacid, or a deodorizer for a cat's litter box.

Segmenting by Usage Rates

Marketers may also segment a total market by grouping people according to the amounts of a product they buy and use. Markets can be divided into heavy-, moderate-, and light-user segments. The **80/20 principle** holds that a big percentage of a product's revenues—maybe 80 percent—comes from a relatively small, loyal percentage of total customers, perhaps 20 percent. The 80/20 principle is sometimes referred to as *Praedo's law*. Although the percentages need not exactly equal these figures, the general principle holds true: relatively few heavy users of a product can account for the bulk of its consumption.

80/20 principle Generally accepted rule that 80 percent of a product's revenues come from 20 percent of its customers.

Depending on their goals, marketers may target heavy, moderate, or light users as well as nonusers. A company may attempt to lure heavy users of another product away from their regular brands to try a new brand. Nonusers and light users may be attractive prospects because other companies are ignoring them. Usage rates can also be linked to other segmentation methods such as demographic and psychographic segmentation.

Segmenting by Brand Loyalty

A third product-related segmentation method groups consumers according to the strength of the brand loyalty they feel toward a product. A classic example of brand loyalty segmentation is the frequent-purchase program—it might be frequent flyer, frequent stay, or frequent purchase of books or gasoline. Other companies attempt to segment their market by developing brand loyalty over a period of time, through consumers' stages of life. Reebok launched a collection of toddler and children's shoes featuring Mr. and Mrs. Potato Head (characters in the "Toy Story" movies). K-Swiss offers sneakers for infants and toddlers: tiny replicas of the famous tennis shoes for adults. Marketers for these companies are intent on

briefly speaking

"Define your business goals clearly so that others can see them as you do."

—George Burns
(1896–1996)
American comedian

creating brand loyalty for their shoes at the earliest stages of life.[60]

Companies spar for loyalty on just about every front. After McDonald's rolled out its McCafé line of coffee drinks, Burger King announced it would begin serving Seattle's Best Coffee in its restaurants. Adding Seattle's Best to its menu—a brand that Starbucks acquired—enables Burger King to take direct aim at McDonald's on yet another front.[61]

Using Multiple Segmentation Bases

Segmentation can help marketers increase their accuracy in reaching the right markets. Like other marketing tools, segmentation is probably best used in a flexible manner—for instance, combining geographic and demographic segmentation techniques or dovetailing product-related segmentation with segmentation by income and expenditure patterns. An important point to keep in mind is that segmentation is a tool to help marketers get to know their potential customers better and ultimately satisfy their needs with the appropriate goods and services.

Segmenting by benefits focuses on the attributes that people seek and the benefits they expect to receive from a good or service. This ad focuses on the healthy benefits of milk.

 assessment check

1. List the three approaches to product-related segmentation.
2. What is the 80/20 principle?

The Market Segmentation Process

To this point, the chapter has discussed various bases on which companies segment markets. But how do marketers decide which segmentation base—or bases—to use? Firms may use a management-driven method, in which segments are predefined by managers based on their observation of the behavioral and demographic characteristics of likely users. Or they may use a market-driven method, in which segments are defined by asking customers for the attributes important to them. Then, marketers follow a four-stage process.

 Identify the steps in the market segmentation process.

Develop a Relevant Profile for Each Segment

After identifying promising segments, marketers should understand the customers in each one. This in-depth analysis of customers helps managers accurately match buyers' needs with the firm's marketing offers. The process must identify characteristics that both explain the similarities among customers within each segment and account for differences among segments.

The task at this stage is to develop a profile of the typical customer in each segment. Such a profile might include information about lifestyle patterns, attitudes toward product attributes and brands, product-use habits, geographic locations, and demographic characteristics.

Forecast Market Potential

In the second stage, market segmentation and market opportunity analysis combine to produce a forecast of market potential within each segment. Market potential sets the upper limit on the demand competing firms can expect from a segment. Multiplying by market share determines a single firm's maximum sales potential. This step should define a preliminary go or no-go decision from management because the total sales potential in each segment must justify resources devoted to further analysis. For example, in deciding whether to market a new product to teens, electronics firms need to determine the demand for it and the disposable income of that group.

Forecast Probable Market Share

Once market potential has been estimated, a firm must forecast its probable market share. Competitors' positions in targeted segments must be analyzed, and a specific marketing strategy must be designed to reach these segments. These two activities may be performed simultaneously. Moreover, by settling on a marketing strategy and tactics, a firm determines the expected level of resources it must commit, that is, the costs it will incur to tap the potential demand in each segment.

Apple's iPod took the marketplace by storm, followed by the iPhone, and analysts believe these two products helped boost sales of the iMac computer as well. Most recently, Apple's introduction of the iPad was met with a flood of orders: an estimated $75 million were sold on the first day alone.[62]

Select Specific Market Segments

The information, analysis, and forecasts accumulated throughout the entire market segmentation decision process allow management to assess the potential for achieving company goals and to justify committing resources in developing one or more segments. Demand forecasts, together with cost projections, determine the profits and the return on investment the company can expect from each segment. Marketing strategy and tactics must be designed to reinforce the firm's image, yet keep within its unique organizational capabilities.

At this point in the analysis, marketers weigh more than monetary costs and benefits; they also consider many difficult-to-measure but critical organizational and environmental factors. The firm may lack experienced personnel to launch a successful attack on an attractive market segment. Similarly, a firm with 60 percent of the market faces possible legal problems with the Federal Trade Commission if it increases its market concentration. This assessment of both financial and nonfinancial factors is a difficult but vital step in the decision process.

✓ **assessment check**

1. Identify the four stages of market segmentation.
2. Why is forecasting important to market segmentation?

Strategies for Reaching Target Markets

9 Discuss four basic strategies for reaching target markets.

Marketers spend a lot of time and effort developing strategies that will best match their firm's product offerings to the needs of particular target markets. An appropriate match is vital to the firm's marketing success. Marketers have identified four basic strategies for achieving consumer satisfaction: undifferentiated marketing, differentiated marketing, concentrated marketing, and micromarketing.

Undifferentiated Marketing

A firm may produce only one product or product line and promote it to all customers with a single marketing mix; such a firm is said to practice **undifferentiated marketing**, sometimes called *mass marketing*. Undifferentiated marketing was much more common in the past than it is today.

While undifferentiated marketing is efficient from a production viewpoint, the strategy also brings inherent dangers. A firm that attempts to satisfy everyone in the market with one standard product may suffer if competitors offer specialized alternatives to smaller segments of the total market and better satisfy individual segments. In fact, firms that implement strategies of differentiated marketing, concentrated marketing, or micromarketing may capture enough small segments of the market to defeat another competitor's strategy of undifferentiated marketing. The golden arches of McDonald's have always stood for quick, inexpensive meals. Consumers could count on the same food and same dining experience at every McDonald's they visited. But McDonald's marketers are changing the firm's strategy somewhat in response to a trend that says consumers want a little luxury with their burger and fries and a more varied dining experience from restaurant to restaurant. Some stores feature wall-mounted televisions, a color scheme featuring earth tones, wood fixtures, pendant lighting, and video game stations for children.[63]

undifferentiated marketing Strategy that focuses on producing a single product and marketing it to all customers; also called *mass marketing*.

Differentiated Marketing

Firms that promote numerous products with differing marketing mixes designed to satisfy smaller segments are said to practice **differentiated marketing**. By providing increased satisfaction for each of many target markets, a company can produce more sales by following a differentiated marketing strategy than undifferentiated marketing would generate. Oscar Mayer, a marketer of a variety of meat products, practices differentiated marketing. It increased its sales by introducing Lunchables, aimed at children. The original Lunchables were so successful that Oscar Mayer introduced more choices in the line, including snack versions. In general, however, differentiated marketing also raises costs. Production costs usually rise because additional products and variations require shorter production runs and increased setup times. Inventory costs rise because more products require added storage space and increased efforts for record keeping. Promotional costs also rise because each segment demands a unique promotional mix.

Despite higher marketing costs, however, an organization may be forced to practice differentiated marketing to diversify and reach new customers. The travel industry now recognizes the need to target smaller groups of travelers with specialized interests. History buffs can attend special events at Colonial Williamsburg or at George Washington's estate, Mount Vernon.[64] The Sierra Club and other environmental organizations—in addition to commercial travel operators—offer hikes, kayaking expeditions, and birdwatching trips for outdoor enthusiasts.[65] Luxury travel company Tauck now offers a series of guided, all-inclusive trips called Tauck Bridges, designed with traveling families or grandparents and their grandchildren in mind.[66]

differentiated marketing Strategy that focuses on producing several products and pricing, promoting, and distributing them with different marketing mixes designed to satisfy smaller segments.

concentrated (or niche) marketing Focusing marketing efforts on satisfying a single market segment.

Concentrated Marketing

Rather than trying to market its products separately to several segments, a firm may opt for a concentrated marketing strategy. With **concentrated marketing** (also known as **niche marketing**), a firm focuses its efforts on profitably satisfying a single market segment. This approach can appeal to a small firm lacking the financial resources of its competitors and to a company offering highly specialized goods and services. American Express, a large firm with many financial products, recently introduced two new credit cards designed for very specific markets: The Knot, for engaged couples, and The Nest, for newlyweds.

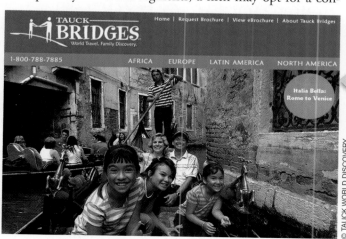

Luxury travel company Tauck now offers a series of trips called Tauck Bridges, designed with traveling families or grandparents and their grandchildren in mind.

© TAUCK WORLD DISCOVERY

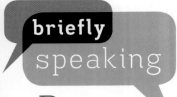

"Put all your eggs in one basket, and watch the basket."

—Mark Twain
(1835–1910)
American author

Peanut Butter & Co. appeals to the world's peanut butter lovers with its proprietary brand of gourmet, natural peanut butter flavors including Smooth Operator, Crunch Time, and Dark Chocolate Dreams. Its Mighty Maple is intended for pancake fans, and The Bee's Knees can replace a humdrum jar of honey. Fans visiting the flagship store in New York City can sample favorites such as "ants on a log" or grilled peanut butter, banana, honey, and bacon sandwiches; or they can shop for their favorite blends online.[67] But along with its benefits, concentrated marketing has its dangers. Because the strategy ties a firm's growth to a specific segment, sales can suffer if new competitors appeal successfully to the same target. If another firm targets peanut butter lovers in the same manner, Peanut Butter & Co. may face a struggle. In addition, errors in forecasting market potential or customer buying habits can lead to severe problems, particularly if the firm has spent substantially on product development and promotion. If more people—children in particular—continue to develop peanut allergies, sales of Peanut Butter & Co.'s products may begin to decline. Anticipating this, the company could begin to diversify product offerings to include nonallergenic foods.

Micromarketing

micromarketing
Targeting potential customers at very narrow, basic levels such as by Zip code, specific occupation, or lifestyle—possibly even individuals themselves.

The fourth targeting strategy, still more narrowly focused than concentrated marketing, is **micromarketing**—targeting potential customers at a very basic level, such as by Zip code, specific occupation, or lifestyle. Ultimately, micromarketing can target even individuals. A salesperson at your favorite clothing boutique may contact you when certain merchandise she thinks you might like arrives at the store. The Internet allows marketers to make micromarketing even more effective: by tracking specific demographic and personal information, marketers can send e-mail directly to individual consumers most likely to buy their products.

Best Buy, known for its broad appeal to what it refers to as "Middle America," altered its marketing strategy to focus on specific customer segments at certain stores. Although the retailer's "Planagans"—store layouts—are determined at headquarters, local managers have the authority to move products around to appeal to the needs of their customers.

But micromarketing, like niche marketing, can become too much of a good thing if companies spend too much time, effort, and marketing dollars to unearth a market too small and specialized to be profitable. In addition, micromarketing may cause a company to lose sight of other, larger markets. So it's important for marketers to assess the situation and pursue the most profitable markets.

 assessment check

1. Explain the difference between undifferentiated and differentiated marketing strategies.
2. What are the benefits of concentrated marketing?

Selecting and Executing a Strategy

 Summarize the types of positioning strategies, and explain the reasons for positioning and repositioning products.

Although most organizations adopt some form of differentiated marketing, no single choice suits all firms. Any of the alternatives may prove most effective in a particular situation. The basic determinants of a market-specific strategy are (1) company resources, (2) product homogeneity, (3) stage in the product life cycle, and (4) competitors' strategies.

A firm with limited resources may have to choose a concentrated marketing strategy. Small firms may be forced to select small target markets because of limitations in their sales force and advertising budgets. On the other hand, an undifferentiated marketing strategy suits a firm selling items perceived by consumers as relatively homogeneous. Marketers of grain, for example, sell standardized grades of generic products rather than individual brand names. Some petroleum companies implement undifferentiated marketing to distribute their gasoline to the mass market.

The firm's strategy may also change as its product progresses through the stages of the lifecycle. During the early stages, undifferentiated marketing might effectively support the company's effort to build initial demand for the item. In the later stages, however, competitive pressures may force modifications in products and in the development of marketing strategies aimed at segments of the total market.

The strategies of competitors also affect the choice of a segmentation approach. A firm may encounter obstacles to undifferentiated marketing if its competitors actively cultivate smaller segments. In such instances, competition usually forces each firm to adopt a differentiated marketing strategy.

Having chosen a strategy for reaching their firm's target market, marketers must then decide how best to position the product. The concept of **positioning** seeks to put a product in a certain position, or place, in the minds of prospective buyers. Marketers use a positioning strategy to distinguish their firm's offerings from those of competitors and to create promotions that communicate the desired position. Restaurants that position themselves as "fast-casual" continue to outperform most other categories of restaurants. Top menu choices in this segment include Mexican, bakery café, pizzas, Asian, chicken, and hamburgers. Analysts believe fast-casual restaurants provide consumers with the chance to sit down to a dinner priced lower than what is offered at an upscale restaurant yet of higher quality than a fast-food restaurant. Fast-casual provides good value in the minds of many consumers. Many fast-casual restaurants currently are trying to upgrade their menu with new premium offerings, redesigning their interior to make it more inviting, and using Facebook and Twitter to attract even more customers.[68]

To achieve the goal of positioning, marketers follow a number of positioning strategies. Possible approaches include positioning a product according to the following categories:

1. *Attributes*—eBay, "Buy it. Sell it. Love it."

2. *Price/quality*—Omega watches, "We measure the 100th of a second that separates winning from taking part."

3. *Competitors*—Walmart, "Save money. Live better."

4. *Application*—Blue Cross Blue Shield health insurance, "Experience. Wellness. Everywhere."

5. *Product user*—Crane's stationery, "for the writer somewhere in each of us."

6. *Product class*—BMW, the "ultimate driving machine."

Whatever strategy they choose, marketers want to emphasize a product's unique advantages and differentiate it from competitors' options. A **positioning map** provides a valuable tool in helping managers position products by graphically illustrating consumers' perceptions of competing products within an industry. Marketers can create a competitive positioning map from information solicited from consumers or from their accumulated knowledge about a market. A positioning map might present two different characteristics—price and perceived quality—and show how consumers view a product and its major competitors based on these traits. The hypothetical positioning map in Figure 9.4 compares selected retailers based on possible perceptions of the prices and quality of their offerings.

Restaurants that position themselves as "fast-casual," such as Corner Bakery, continue to outperform most other categories of restaurants.

© CORNER BAKERY CAFE

positioning Placing a product at a certain point or location within a market in the minds of prospective buyers.

positioning map Tool that helps marketers place products in a market by graphically illustrating consumers' perceptions of competing products within an industry.

figure 9.4

Hypothetical Positioning Map for Selected Retailers

repositioning Changing the position of a product within the minds of prospective buyers relative to the positions of competing products.

Sometimes changes in the competitive environment force marketers to **reposition** a product—changing the position it holds in the minds of prospective buyers relative to the positions of competing products. Repositioning may even be necessary for already successful products or firms in order to gain greater market share. After General Motors sold its Saab division to Netherlands-based automaker Spyker, the new owner announced it would reposition the brand as "a performance-oriented niche car with an industry-leading environmental strategy."[69]

assessment check

1. What are the four determinants of a market-specific strategy?
2. What is the role of positioning in a marketing strategy?

strategic implications
of marketing in the 21st century

o remain competitive, today's marketers must accurately identify potential customers. They can use a variety of methods to accomplish this, including segmenting markets by gender and by geographic location. The trick is to figure out the best combination of methods for segmentation to identify the most lucrative, long-lasting potential markets. Marketers must also remain flexible, responding to markets as they change—for instance, following a generation as it ages or reaching out to new generations by revamping or repositioning products.

The greatest competitive advantage will belong to firms that pinpoint and serve markets without segmenting them to the point at which they are too small or specialized to garner profits. Marketers who reach and communicate with the right customers have a greater chance of attracting and keeping those customers than marketers who search for the wrong buyers in the wrong place.

Review of Chapter Objectives

 Identify the essential components of a market.

A market consists of people and organizations with the necessary purchasing power, willingness, and authority to buy. Consumer products are purchased by the ultimate consumer for personal use. Business products are purchased for use directly or indirectly in the production of other goods and services. Certain products may fall into both categories.

 Outline the role of market segmentation in developing a marketing strategy.

Market segmentation is the process of dividing a total market into several homogeneous groups. It is used in identifying a target market for a good or service. Segmentation is the key to deciding a marketing strategy.

 Describe the criteria necessary for effective segmentation.

Effective segmentation depends on these four basic requirements: (1) the segment must have measurable purchasing power and size, (2) marketers can find a way to promote to and serve the market, (3) marketers must identify segments large enough for profit potential, and (4) the firm can target a number of segments that match its marketing capabilities.

Explain the geographic approach to the segmentation of consumer markets.

Geographic segmentation divides the overall market into homogeneous groups according to population locations.

 Discuss the demographic approach to segmenting consumer markets.

Demographic segmentation classifies the market into groups based on characteristics such as age, gender, and income level.

 Discuss the psychographic approach to segmenting consumer markets.

Psychographic segmentation uses behavioral profiles developed from analyses of consumers' activities, opinions, interests, and lifestyles to identify market segments.

 Describe product-related segmentation.

Product-related segmentation can take three basic forms: segmenting based on the benefits people seek when buying a product, segmenting based on usage rates for a product, and segmenting according to consumers' brand loyalty toward a product.

 Identify the steps in the market segmentation process.

Market segmentation is the division of markets into relatively homogeneous groups. Segmentation follows a four-step sequence:

(1) developing user profiles, (2) forecasting the overall market potential, (3) estimating market share, and (4) selecting specific market segments.

 Discuss four basic strategies for reaching target markets.

Four strategies are (1) undifferentiated marketing—uses a single marketing mix; (2) differentiated marketing—produces numerous products, each with its own mix; (3) concentrated marketing—directs all the firm's marketing resources toward a small segment; and (4) micromarketing—targets potential customers at basic levels, such as zip code or occupation.

 Summarize the types of positioning strategies, and explain the reasons for positioning and repositioning products.

Positioning strategies include positioning a good or service according to attributes, price/quality, competitors, application, product user, and product class. Positioning helps distinguish a firm's products from those of competitors and provides a basis for marketing communications. Repositioning a product—changing the position it holds in consumers' minds—may be necessary to gain greater market share.

 Assessment Check: Answers

1.1 Define *target market*. A target market is the specific segment of consumers most likely to purchase a particular product.

1.2 Distinguish between a consumer product and a business product. A consumer product is purchased by the ultimate buyer for personal use. A business product is purchased for use directly or indirectly in the production of other goods and services.

2.1 Define *market segmentation*. Market segmentation is the process of dividing a total market into several homogeneous groups.

2.2 Describe the role of market segmentation. The role of market segmentation is to identify the factors that affect purchase decisions and then group consumers according to the presence or absence of these factors.

3.1 Identify the four criteria for effective segmentation. The four criteria for effective segmentation are (1) the market segment must present measurable purchasing power and size, (2) marketers must find a way to promote effectively and serve the market segment, (3) marketers must identify segments sufficiently large to give them good profit potential, and (4) the firm must aim for segments that match its marketing capabilities.

3.2 Give an example of a market segment that meets these criteria. Examples might include women, teenagers, Hispanics, empty nesters, and NASCAR enthusiasts.

4.1 Under what circumstances are marketers most likely to use geographic segmentation? Marketers usually use geographic segmentation when regional preferences exist and when demand for categories of goods and services varies according to geographic region.

4.2   **What are the five main categories for classifying urban data?** The five categories are core based statistical area (CBSA), metropolitan statistical area (MSA), micropolitan statistical area, consolidated metropolitan statistical area (CMSA), and primary metropolitan statistical area (PMSA).

5.1   **What is demographic segmentation?** Demographic segmentation defines consumer groups according to demographic variables such as gender, age, income, occupation, household, and family lifecycle.

5.2   **What are the major categories of demographic segmentation?** The major categories of demographic segmentation are gender, age, ethnic group, family lifecycle, household type, income, and expenditure patterns.

6.1   **What is psychographic segmentation?** Psychographic segmentation divides a population into groups with similar values and lifestyles.

6.2   **Name the eight psychographic categories of VALS.** The eight categories are innovators, thinkers, achievers, experiencers, believers, strivers, makers, and survivors.

7.1   **List the three approaches to product-related segmentation.** The three approaches are segmenting by benefits sought, segmenting by usage rates, and segmenting by brand loyalty.

7.2   **What is the 80/20 principle?** The 80/20 principle states that a big percentage (80 percent) of a product's revenues comes from a relatively small number (20 percent) of loyal customers.

8.1   **Identify the four stages of market segmentation.** The four stages are developing user profiles, forecasting the overall market potential, estimating market share, and selecting specific market segments.

8.2   **Why is forecasting important to market segmentation?** Forecasting is important because it can define a preliminary go or no-go decision based on sales potential. It can help a firm avoid a disastrous move or point out opportunities.

9.1   **Explain the difference between undifferentiated and differentiated marketing strategies.** Undifferentiated marketing promotes a single product line to all customers with a single marketing mix. Differentiated marketing promotes numerous products with different marketing mixes designed to satisfy smaller segments.

9.2   **What are the benefits of concentrated marketing?** Concentrated marketing can allow a firm to focus on a single market segment, which is especially appealing to smaller firms and those that offer highly specialized goods and services.

10.1   **What are the four determinants of a market-specific strategy?** The four determinants are company resources, product homogeneity, stage in the product lifecycle, and competitors' strategies.

10.2   **What is the role of positioning in a marketing strategy?** Positioning places a product in a certain position in the minds of prospective buyers so marketers can create messages that distinguish their offerings from those of competitors.

Marketing Terms You Need to Know

market 276
target market 276
consumer products 277
business products 277
market segmentation 277
geographic segmentation 279
core based statistical area (CBSA) 280
metropolitan statistical area (MSA) 280

micropolitan statistical area 280
consolidated metropolitan statistical area (CMSA) 281
primary metropolitan statistical area (PMSA) 281
core region 281
geographic information systems (GISs) 282
demographic segmentation 282

cohort effect 287
Video Game Generation 287
family lifecycle 289
Engel's laws 291
psychographic segmentation 292
AIO statements 292
VALS 293
product-related segmentation 296
80/20 principle 296

undifferentiated marketing 299
differentiated marketing 299
concentrated (or niche) marketing 299
micromarketing 300
positioning 301
positioning map 301
repositioning 302

Assurance of Learning Review

1. Classify each of the following as a business product or a consumer product:
   a. laptop computer
   b. bottle of hairspray
   c. fleet of delivery trucks
   d. bulk order of flour
   e. digital camera
   f. Kenny Chesney music CD

2. What are core regions? Why do marketers try to identify these regions?

3. What is the cohort effect? This chapter suggested that the rise of video games was sufficiently significant to have influenced and bound a generation together. Do you agree?

4. What is the fastest-growing racial/ethnic minority group in the United States? What types of things do marketers need to know about this group to market successfully to these consumers?

5. How is segmentation by family lifecycle and household type useful to marketers? Briefly describe your own family in these terms, identifying characteristics that might be helpful to marketers for a firm selling HDTVs.

6. What are AIO statements? How are they used by marketers?

7. Identify a branded product to which you are loyal, and explain why you are loyal to this item. What factors might cause your loyalty to change?

8. Choose another branded product. Create a relevant profile for the marketing segment this product serves.

9. What are the six categories generally used to position a product?

10. How does a positioning map work? What are its benefits?

Projects and Teamwork Exercises

1. On your own or with a partner, choose one of the following consumer products and think about how it could be used as a business product. Then create a business advertisement for your product.
   a. lawn care products
   b. microwave oven
   c. tennis balls
   d. bottled water
   e. smartphone
   f. vacuum cleaner

2. With a classmate, choose one of the following products you believe is generally targeted for either men or women and create an advertisement for the product aimed at the opposite gender.
   a. barbeque grill and accessories
   b. hunting or fishing supplies
   c. nail salon
   d. minivan
   e. large-screen TV

3. Create a chart showing how your family's income and expenditure patterns have changed over the years as the family lifecycle changed. You don't need exact figures, just the general picture. If possible, interview other family members for additional information.

4. With a classmate, choose a product and come up with a slogan representing each of the six positioning approaches for the product.

5. On your own or with a classmate, select one of the following products. Visit the firm's Web site to see how the product is positioned, then create an advertisement showing how you think marketers could reposition the product to gain greater market share.
   a. Gatorade
   b. Dove soap
   c. Barilla pasta
   d. Fiskars scissors
   e. Hallmark cards

Critical-Thinking Exercises

1. Create a profile of yourself as part of a market segment. Include the following:
   a. geographic location
   b. gender and age
   c. household type
   d. income and spending habits

2. Select one of the following products and explain how you would use segmentation by income and expenditure patterns to determine your targeted market.
   a. Busch Gardens theme parks
   b. Sony Cyber-shot camera
   c. Healthy Choice frozen entrées
   d. Smart fortwo car

3. How do you think the Internet has affected differentiated marketing techniques?

4. Choose one of the following products and describe a marketing approach that segments the target market by benefits sought:
   a. Kryptonite bicycle lock
   b. A private college or university
   c. Pella windows and doors
   d. Vacation Village water park
   e. Edy's Grand Ice Cream

5. Visit the Web site for a large company such as Kraft Foods, Sony, or Campbell Soup. Look for ways the firm practices differentiated marketing. How do you think this approach benefits the firm?

Ethics Exercise

Marketers are making a new pitch to men—at the risk of political incorrectness. Marketers for firms such as Unilever and Wendy's were frustrated at their inability to reach young male consumers with their messages. After searching for clues about what this crowd likes, these firms created marketing campaigns designed to grab their attention—perhaps at the expense of other consumers. Some advertising is designed to appeal to "bad boy" attitudes, lowbrow humor, and sex.

1. What are some of the pitfalls of this kind of segmentation?

2. Do you think these ads will be successful in the long run? Why or why not?

3. Should marketers be concerned about offending one market segment when trying to reach another? Why or why not?

Internet Exercises

1. **Psychographic segmentation.** Visit the Web sites of Caterpillar, Hilton Hotels, and PepsiCo. How does each firm employ psychographic segmentation (such as the VALS approach) to the marketing of its products? Is there a relationship between the use of psychographic segmentation and the types of products sold by each firm?
http://www.cat.com
http://www.hilton.com
http://www.pepsico.com

2. **Market segmentation.** Go to the Web site of Siemens. How does Siemens segment its markets, such as geographical, product

related, demographic, or brand loyalty? Does the firm use more than one method of product segmentation? Why or why not?
http://www.siemens.com/entry/cc/en/

3. **Target market.** Visit the Web site of Philips. What strategy or strategies does the firm employ for reaching its target markets? Does it rely more on undifferentiated or differentiated marketing?
http://www.philips.com

Note: Internet Web addresses change frequently. If you don't find the exact site listed, you may need to access the organization's home page and search from there or use a search engine such as Google or Bing.

Case 9.1   *Carrols Restaurant Group: Feeding a Hungry Public*

Syracuse, New York–based Carrols Restaurant Group is one of the largest restaurant companies in the nation. With more than 16,000 employees and annual sales of about $750 million, the company owns, operates, and franchises three distinct restaurant concepts across 16 states:

- **Burger King.** Carrols operates 312 Burger King restaurants as a franchise in Indiana, Kentucky, Maine, Massachusetts, Michigan, New Jersey, New York, North Carolina, Ohio, Pennsylvania, South Carolina, and Vermont. They employ more than 10,000 people.

- **Pollo Tropical.** This regional "quick-serve" restaurant chain features fresh, grilled chicken prepared with a special blend of spices and without oil or breading. The menu emphasizes dishes made from scratch using fresh, nutritious ingredients with a strongly Caribbean flavor. Restaurants include free table service, a children's menu, and a complimentary salsa bar. Pollo Tropical began operations in 1988 in Miami. Today, more than 2,700 employees work in the more than 90 company-owned Pollo Tropical stores in Connecticut, Florida, New Jersey, and New York. Carrols has opened franchised locations at Florida colleges and universities and has expanded its reach to the Caribbean and South America. Currently, about 30 Pollo Tropical franchises operate in the Bahamas, Ecuador, Honduras, Puerto Rico, Trinidad and Tobago, with plans for franchises under way in Panama.

- **Taco Cabana.** Another company-owned brand, Taco Cabana is a regional quick-serve chain that offers such Tex-Mex fare as homemade tortillas, salsa, and grilled fajitas. The restaurant began as a taco stand in San Antonio in 1978. Today, it comprises more than 150 restaurants with more than 4,000 employees in New Mexico, Oklahoma, and Texas. Carrols positions Taco

Cabana as an alternative to traditional Mexican restaurants or fast-food taco joints, with a festive Mexican theme, indoor and patio dining, and generous portions.

The Carrols Restaurant Group was established in 1960 as Carrols Systems, a business division of a midwestern company. Under the arrangement, division leader Herbert N. Slotnick was licensed to operate Carrols Drive-In Restaurants in New York. The drive-in chain grew up at a time when the fast-food sector was gaining in popularity, and under Slotnick's leadership, Carrols expanded and prospered, building awareness and capturing significant share in the New York fast-food market. In 1975, the company entered into a franchise agreement with Burger King, simultaneously converting many of its Carrols locations and phasing out others. Carrols bought Pollo Tropical in 1998 and Taco Cabana in 2000. The company is known for community outreach. Under its "Dollars for Doers" program, employees who actively volunteer for a charitable organization can request a company contribution to the charity (up to two gifts of $250 each per year). The company also encourages its workforce to register with the National Marrow Donor Program, covering the cost of the medical test for employees.

Questions for Critical Thinking

1. Carrols Restaurant Group operates three very different restaurant chains. Imagine that you work in the company's marketing department. How would you segment the market for those different businesses?

2. Today, many restaurants offering Mexican or Caribbean fare appeal to a predominantly Hispanic audience. Two of the Carrols holdings—Pollo Tropical and Taco Cabana—feature those types of cuisines. Since Hispanics are the fastest-growing minority segment in the United States, would you concentrate your marketing efforts on this segment or work to expand the market for Pollo Tropical and Taco Cabana?

Sources: Company Web site, http://carrols.com, accessed April 21, 2010; Peter Romeo, "BK Franchisee Speaks Out," *QSR Magazine*, March 2010, http://www.qsrmagazine.com; "Hillsborough Pollo Tropical Restaurant Remodel Will Serve up a Change, for a Great Cause!" press release, January 22, 2010, http://www.pollotropical.com; Bob Niedt, "Syracuse's Carrols Corp. Gets a Shout-Out—But Not for the Burger Kings We're Familiar With," *Syracuse.com*, January 5, 2009, http://blog.syracuse.com.

Video Case 9.2
Targeting and Positioning at Numi Tea

Numi Tea founders, siblings Ahmed and Reem Rahim, immigrated to the United States when they were young children and grew up in Cleveland, Ohio. Reem became a biomedical engineer. Ahmed traveled the world as a photographer and settled for a time in Prague where he opened two tea shops. Reem eventually left her career to pursue life as an artist. In 1999, the two reconnected in Oakland, California, and started Numi Tea in Reem's apartment.

"I think in the positioning of our brand, we wanted to target a certain type of customer base, from the natural health food stores, to fine dining and hotels, to universities and coffee shops, gourmet stores," says Ahmed. "What I've been most surprised about in our growth is the mass market consumer." In recent years, demand by the average American consumer for organic and ethically produced products has exploded. At the same time, economic influences have driven the more affluent and natural foods consumers to large discounters such as Target, supersize grocery chains, warehouse clubs, and online shopping.

Today, explains Jennifer Mullin, vice president of marketing for Numi Tea, the average Numi consumer is female, college educated, and buys two to three boxes of tea per month, usually green tea. She also buys organic products whenever possible. All of these details, while not surprising, are fairly new. Until Mullin joined the team and formalized their marketing department, Numi assumed its customers fit the same profile as the staff—young, cool, and urban. While many of Numi tea drinkers are all these things, Mullin's findings proved that the company needed to put some additional energy toward targeting the younger, college market. They launched an initiative to raise awareness of the product on campuses where people are more inclined to be interested in issues of sustainability, fair trade, and organics. Because Numi teas are considered a premium product, they do have an affordable but still higher price point than conventionally produced teas. College students in general have less money to spend, so Numi approached the food service departments of universities such as Stanford to serve the tea as part of their prepaid meal plans. Not only does the food service contract represent a giant account, it encourages trial. Sampling is Numi's most successful marketing activity for attracting new users. Students can learn to love the product, essentially for free.

The most compelling reason for drinking Numi tea is its health benefits. The company found that it doesn't need to spend much time talking up the organic aspect of its product. In the premium and natural foods space where Numi operates, organic is expected. There is the threat that as the terms "organic" and "natural" invade the mainstream marketplace, a lack of trust or cynicism may arise as some products will inevitably fail to live up to their labels' claims. This is why Numi relies heavily on educating its consumers about the product. When targeting women, their most valued consumer, says Mullin, "We have an in-house PR team that works a lot with editors [of women's magazines] to educate them on tea and make sure they understand the healthy properties of tea." They follow up with sampling at Whole Foods or events targeted toward environmentally conscious moms. Numi rounds out the education efforts on its Web site with more health information as well as in-depth articles on the benefits of specific teas.

Although still young, the Numi brand is expanding rapidly and has enjoyed success overseas as well. Whatever the marketing and PR teams do—store sampling, environmental events, or partnerships with like-minded companies such as Clif Bar—they continue to survey and assess the demographic and psychographic profiles of their consumer.

Questions

1. Which of the four basic targeting strategies does Numi Tea employ when reaching its markets?

2. Would you classify Numi Tea's marketing strategy as "concentrated"? If so, what are the plusses and minuses of using such a strategy in today's market?

ch10

1 Contrast transaction-based marketing with relationship marketing.

2 Identify and explain the four basic elements of relationship marketing, as well as the importance of internal marketing.

3 Identify the three levels of the relationship marketing continuum.

4 Explain how firms can enhance customer satisfaction.

5 Describe how companies build buyer–seller relationships.

6 Explain customer relationship management (CRM) and the role of technology in building customer relationships.

7 Describe the buyer–seller relationship in business-to-business marketing, and identify the four types of business partnerships.

8 Describe how business-to-business marketing incorporates national account selling; electronic data interchange and Web services; vendor-managed inventories; collaborative planning, forecasting, and replenishment; managing the supply chain; and creating alliances.

9 Identify and evaluate the most common measurement and evaluation techniques within a relationship marketing program.

Relationship
Marketing and Customer Relationship Management (CRM)

Airlines Are Uniting the Skies • • • Pressured by economic recession, government regulation, reduced business travel, and rising fuel costs, passenger airlines around the world have looked for innovative ways to keep themselves afloat. One potential solution that many have

embraced is global partnerships with other carriers—helping companies that are otherwise competitors to share resources and reduce costs.

There are three major alliances in the airline industry today. The Star Alliance is the largest, with 26 members operating in almost 1,100 airports in 175 countries. The Star Alliance includes Lufthansa, Singapore Airlines, Thai Airways, Air Canada, Air China, Air New Zealand, United, Continental, and Brussels Airlines, among others. Together, the Star members employ almost half a million people and carry about 6 million passengers a year.

The SkyTeam alliance includes Delta, Air France, KLM, Alitalia, Korean Air, and China Southern. The third partnership, Oneworld,

consists of Qantas, British Airways, American Airlines, Cathay Pacific, and Japan's JAL.

What all three have in common is the ability to offer passengers more destinations, better and easier connections in common terminal areas, streamlined ticketing and check-in technology, and shared (and thus better and more comfortable) airport facilities. They also offer travelers the opportunity to earn and redeem frequent-flier points across all members of a given partnership. As the consumer affairs director of the International Airline Passengers Association (IAPA) describes them, airline alliances "are becoming more and more like de facto mergers. Only government rules prevent member airlines from

forming even closer operational and marketing ties. . . . As alliances grow and more airlines join, the result will be competition between alliances (not airlines) and dominance at major international hubs."

Whether this result will be good for airline customers is something critics debate. As the IAPA director points out, "Our basic view is that airline alliances are an overall benefit to flyers—when they work the way they are touted. However, if the ultimate goal is to reduce competition and dominate a market or airport, then buyer beware."

Governments so far have not seen cause for antitrust or other worries in SkyTeam, Oneworld, or Star Alliance. The U.S. Department of Transportation recently approved a partnership between British Airways and American Airlines, both members of Oneworld, that allows them to jointly price, market, and schedule international flights between the United States, Mexico, and Canada and the European Union, Switzerland, and Norway, linking about 500 destinations in 100 countries. The partners are working out a response to objections raised by the European Union's competition commissioner, but they have already agreed to give competitors four takeoff and landing slots at London's Heathrow Airport. British Airways and Spain's Iberia Airlines have completed a separate merger deal.

Qantas, another Oneworld partner, has agreed to share intellectual property and no-frills expertise with JAL to help the struggling Japanese airline improve its bottom line. Qantas gains too—it will add about $500 million a year in revenue from routes between Australia and Japan. "Strategically and philosophically we think that is a logical way to go," said Qantas' commercial chief.[1]

evolution of a brand

Though alliance members currently retain their separate corporate identities, ironically, airline alliances may in fact spell the end of airline brands. Says IAPA's consumer affairs director, "We may reach a day when the individual airline brands become secondary, or even disappear, and passengers will simply fly Oneworld, Star, or SkyTeam."

- Richard Branson, the flamboyant founder and owner of Virgin Atlantic describes the alliance

between British Airways and American Airlines as "a real kick in the teeth for consumers" for which they will be "paying the price . . . for years to come" via higher fares. What could explain Branson's view of airline partnerships?

- Lufthansa's chief takes a different view. "We are responsible for the connectivities of

mobile societies, he says. "Passengers want and are demanding more from those connectivities; the airline alliances know that they must move to ensure it." Do you agree with this statement? Which view do you think most airline passengers take?

chapter overview

transaction-based marketing Buyer and seller exchanges characterized by limited communications and little or no ongoing relationship between the parties.

relationship marketing Development, growth, and maintenance of long-term, cost-effective relationships with individual customers, suppliers, employees, and other partners for mutual benefit.

Marketing revolves around relationships with customers and with all the business processes involved in identifying and satisfying them. The shift from **transaction-based marketing**, which focuses on short-term, one-time exchanges, to customer-focused relationship marketing is one of the most important trends in marketing today. Companies know they cannot prosper simply by identifying and attracting new customers; to succeed, they must build loyal, mutually beneficial relationships with both new and existing customers, suppliers, distributors, and employees. This strategy benefits the bottom line because retaining customers costs much less than acquiring new ones. Building and managing long-term relationships between buyers and sellers are the hallmarks of relationship marketing. **Relationship marketing** is the development, growth, and maintenance of cost-effective, high-value relationships with individual customers, suppliers, distributors, retailers, and other partners for mutual benefit over time.

Relationship marketing is based on promises: the promise of low prices, the promise of high quality, the promise of prompt delivery, the promise of superior service. A network of promises—within the organization, between the organization and its supply chain, and between buyer and seller—determines whether or not a relationship will grow. A firm is responsible for keeping or exceeding the agreements it makes, with the ultimate goal of achieving customer satisfaction.

This chapter examines the reasons organizations are moving toward relationship marketing and customer relationship management, explores the impact this move has on producers of goods and services and their customers, and looks at ways to evaluate customer relationship programs.

1 Contrast transaction-based marketing with relationship marketing.

The Shift from Transaction-Based Marketing to Relationship Marketing

Since the Industrial Revolution, most manufacturers have run production-oriented operations. They have focused on making products and then promoting them to customers in the hope of selling enough to cover costs and earn profits. The emphasis has been on individual sales or transactions. In transaction-based market-ing, buyer and seller exchanges are character-ized by limited communications and little or no ongoing relationships. The primary goal is to entice a buyer to make a purchase through such inducements as low price, convenience, or packaging. The goal is simple and short term: sell something—now.

Some marketing exchanges remain largely transaction based. In residential real estate sales, for example, the primary goal of the agent is to make a sale and collect a commission. While the agent may seek to maintain the appearance of an ongoing buyer–seller relationship, in most cases, the possibility of future transactions is fairly limited. The best an agent can hope for is to represent the seller again in a subsequent real estate deal that may be several years down the line or, more likely, gain positive referrals to other buyers and sellers.

Today, many organizations have embraced an alternative approach. Relationship marketing views customers as equal partners in buyer–seller transactions. By motivating customers to enter a long-term relationship in which they repeat purchases or buy multiple brands from the firm, mar-keters obtain a clearer understanding of customer needs over time. This process leads to improved goods or customer service, which pays off through increased sales and lower marketing costs. In addition, marketers have discovered it is less expensive to retain satisfied customers than it is to attract new ones or to repair damaged relationships.

The move from transactions to relationships is reflected in the changing nature of the inter-actions between customers and sellers. In transaction-based marketing, exchanges with custom-ers are generally sporadic and, in some instances, disrupted by conflict. As interactions become relationship-oriented, however, conflict changes to cooperation, and infrequent contacts between buyers and sellers become ongoing exchanges.

As Figure 10.1 illustrates, relationship marketing emphasizes cooperation rather than conflict between all of the parties involved. This ongoing collaborative exchange creates value for both parties and builds customer loyalty. Customer relationship management goes a step further and integrates the customer's needs into all aspects of the firm's operations and its relationships with suppliers, dis-tributors, and strategic partners. It combines people, processes, and technology with the long-term goal of maximizing customer value through mutually satisfying interactions and transactions.

Twenty-first-century marketers now understand they must do more than simply create prod-ucts and then sell them. With so many goods and services to choose from, customers look for added value from their marketing relationships. PetSmart not only charges lower prices than gro-cery stores for pet products but also offers a huge selection—everything from premium and national brands of food, toys and bedding, leashes, and other supplies to comprehen-sive services like dog training, grooming, day and overnight boarding and even veterinary care and hospitalization. You can even buy your pet there. These offerings help build cus-tomer loyalty in the pet owner-ship market, where the number of consumers and the level of spending per pet are both rising.[2]

figure 10.1

Forms of Buyer–Seller Interactions from Conflict to Integration

Customer Relationship Management — Integration

Relationship Marketing — Cooperation

Transaction-based Marketing — Conflict

PetSmart offers a huge selection of pet supplies as well as services such as dog training, grooming, boarding, and veterinary care. These offerings help build customer loyalty.

© AP IMAGES/GERRY BROOME

In general, the differences between the narrow focus of transaction marketing and the much broader view of relationship marketing can be summarized as follows:

Relationship marketing:

- focuses on the long term rather than the short term;
- emphasizes retaining customers over making a sale;
- ranks customer service as a high priority;
- encourages frequent customer contact;
- fosters customer commitment with the firm;
- bases customer interactions on cooperation and trust; and
- commits all employees to provide high-quality products.

As a result, the buyer–seller bonds developed in a relationship marketing partnership last longer and cover a much wider scope than those developed in transaction marketing.

 assessment check

1. What are the major differences between transaction-based marketing and relationship marketing?

Elements of Relationship Marketing

> **2** Identify and explain the four basic elements of relationship marketing, as well as the importance of internal marketing.

To build long-term customer relationships, marketers need to place customers at the center of their efforts. When a company integrates customer service and quality with marketing, the result is a relationship marketing orientation.

But how do firms achieve these long-term relationships? They build them with four basic elements.

1. They gather information about their customers. Database technology, discussed later in this chapter, helps a company identify current and potential customers with selected demographic, purchase, and lifestyle characteristics.

2. They analyze the data collected and use it to modify their marketing mix to deliver differentiated messages and customized marketing programs to individual consumers.

3. Through relationship marketing, they monitor their interactions with customers. They can then assess the customer's level of satisfaction or dissatisfaction with their service. Marketers can also calculate the cost of attracting one new customer and figure out how much profit that customer will generate during the relationship. Information is fed back, and they then can seek ways to add value to the buyer–seller transaction so the relationship will continue.

4. With customer relationship management (CRM) software, they use intimate knowledge of customers and customer preferences to orient every part of the organization—including both its internal and external partners—toward building a unique company differentiation based on strong, unbreakable bonds with customers. Sophisticated technology and the Internet help make that happen.

external customers
People or organizations that buy or use a firm's goods or services.

internal customers
Employees or departments within an organization that depend on the work of another employee or department to perform tasks.

Internal Marketing

The concepts of customer satisfaction and relationship marketing usually are discussed in terms of **external customers**—people or organizations that buy or use a firm's goods or services. But marketing in organizations concerned with customer satisfaction and long-term relationships must also address **internal customers**—employees or departments within the organization whose success depends on the work of other employees or departments. A person processing an order for a new piece of equipment is the internal customer of the salesperson who completed the sale, just as the person who bought the product is the salesperson's external customer. Although the order processor might never directly encounter an external customer, his or her performance can have a direct impact on the overall value the firm is able to deliver.

Internal marketing depends on managerial actions that enable all members of an organization to understand, accept, and fulfill their respective roles in implementing a marketing strategy. Good internal customer satisfaction helps organizations attract, select, and retain outstanding employees who appreciate and value their role in the delivery of superior service to external customers. At General Mills, employees in all areas of the company on cross-functional teams enroll in week-long, hands-on "Brand Champions" training programs designed to teach the fine points of building and maintaining the company's brands. The programs are among the "best in class" training sessions that have placed the company in *Training* magazine's Top 10 Hall of Fame.[3]

Employee knowledge and involvement are important goals of internal marketing. Companies that excel at satisfying customers typically place a priority on keeping employees informed about corporate goals, strategies, and customer needs. Employees must also have the necessary tools to address customer requests and problems in a timely manner. Companywide computer networks aid the flow of communications between departments and functions. Several companies also include key suppliers in their networks to speed and ease communication of all aspects of business from product design to inventory control.

Employee satisfaction is another critical objective of internal marketing. Employees seldom, if ever, satisfy customers when they themselves are unhappy. Dissatisfied employees are likely to spread negative word-of-mouth messages to relatives, friends, and acquaintances, and these reports can affect purchasing behavior. Satisfied employees buy their employer's products, tell friends and families how good the customer service is, and ultimately send a powerful message to customers. One recommended strategy for offering consistently good service is to attract good employees, hire good employees, and retain good employees. Upscale hotel chain Four Seasons pampers its customers and generates a loyal following. But the company relates its high service standards directly to its hiring policies and to maintaining satisfied employees. "Our goal has always been to treat our staff the way we would like them to treat guests," said the company's executive vice president for human resources, "with intelligence, kindness, and respect for the value of their time. We thank them for their support and their commitment to creating exceptional guest experiences." Four Seasons was recently named one of *Fortune* magazine's 100 best companies to work for, making the list for the 13th year in a row and placing higher than any other hotel company.[4]

internal marketing
Managerial actions that help all members of the organization understand, accept, and fulfill their respective roles in implementing a marketing strategy.

employee satisfaction
Employee's level of satisfaction in his or her company and the extent to which that loyalty—or lack thereof—is communicated to external customers.

Upscale hotel chain Four Seasons pampers its customers but also relates its high service standards directly to maintaining satisfied employees. This Florida Four Seasons employee is a restaurant hostess.

© JEFF GREENBERG/ALAMY

 assessment check

1. What are the four basic elements of relationship marketing?
2. Why is internal marketing important to a firm?

table 10.1 Three Levels of Relationship Marketing

Characteristic	Level 1	Level 2	Level 3
Primary bond	Financial	Social	Structural
Degree of customization	Low	Medium	Medium to high
Potential for sustained competitive advantage	Low	Moderate	High
Examples	Fast-food dollar-menu items	TiVo-YouTube partnership	Southwest Airlines business traveler program

Source: Adapted from Leonard L. Berry, "Relationship Marketing of Services—Growing Internet, Emerging Perspectives," *Journal of the Academy of Marketing Science*, Fall 1995, p. 240.

The Relationship Marketing Continuum

3 Identify the three levels of the relationship marketing continuum.

Like all other interpersonal relationships, buyer–seller relationships function at a variety of levels. As an individual or firm progresses from the lowest level to the highest level on the continuum of relationship marketing, as shown in Table 10.1, the strength of commitment between the parties grows. The likelihood of a continuing, long-term relationship grows as well. Whenever possible, marketers want to move their customers along this continuum, converting them from level 1 purchasers, who focus mainly on price, to level 3 customers, who receive specialized services and value-added benefits that may not be available from another firm.

First Level: Focus on Price

Interactions at the first level of relationship marketing are the most superficial and the least likely to lead to a long-term relationship. In the most prevalent examples of this first level, relationship marketing efforts rely on pricing and other financial incentives to motivate customers to enter into buying relationships with a seller. Fast-food chains, for instance, regularly use value- and dollar-menu promotions, offering more food for less, to attract fickle customers. In a difficult economy, lower prices are especially attractive. "It's a tough economic situation out there," said one fast-food industry consultant, "and the fast-food pie has shrunk."[5] Service providers offer price savings, too. Verizon's unlimited calling plans offer new and existing customers low flat rates for unlimited calls anytime, anywhere in the United States.[6]

Although these programs can be attractive to users, they may not create long-term buyer relationships. Because the programs are not customized to the needs of individual buyers, they are easily duplicated by competitors. The lesson? It takes more than a low price or other financial incentives to create a long-term relationship between buyer and seller.

As buyers and sellers reach the second level of relationship marketing, their interactions develop on a social level, one that features deeper and less superficial links than the financially motivated first level.

© AP IMAGES/PRNEWSFOTO/VERIZON WIRELESS

Second Level: Social Interactions

As buyers and sellers reach the second level of relationship marketing, their interactions develop on a social level, one that features deeper and less superficial links than the financially

Is Location-Based Advertising Fair and Square?

The rapid rise of GPS-enabled smartphones offers unparalleled convenience—with services like Loopt, Foursquare, Twitter, Buzz, and Facebook's new mobile service, users can learn where their friends are and broadcast their own location. For marketers, mobile GPS offers huge potential: the ability not only to track users' geographic locations but also to reach them with targeted mobile advertising at the precise moment they're in a retail location and ready to buy. But some worry that such pinpoint accuracy exposes social networkers to the risk of intrusive, unwanted messages and threats to privacy.

Does allowing location-based advertising abuse customer relationships?

PRO

1. Users should not have to face a constant stream of unwanted advertising in order to take advantage of GPS capabilities in social networking applications.

2. Marketers' ability to know where consumers are and to act on this information poses a threat to privacy.

CON

1. Most GPS-enabled services require the user to actively check in to enable tracking ability. "I only share my location with people I am comfortable meeting up with, and when I want to be found," said a visitor to the recent South by Southwest technology conference.

2. User benefits include discounts, special offers, and suggestions about nearby places of interest that services like Pulse (from Loopt) and Foursquare provide.

Summary

Apple's iPhone, one of the most popular GPS-enabled devices, does not allow location-tracking apps like Loopt to run in the background, so it's not possible for marketers to do continuous monitoring. Apple has also taken a strong lead in ensuring that user benefits, not advertising, drive the development of future apps accepted by the App Store. It's telling developers that features based on location must provide a benefit to the user and not be designed just to carry ads.

Sources: Kevin Nakao, "5 Things You Need to Know about Location-Based Social Media," *Mashable.com*, http://mashable.com, March 19, 2010; Jenna Wortham, "Telling Friends Where You Are (or Not)," *The New York Times*, www.nytimes.com, March 14, 2010; Kit Eaton, "Facebook Really Wants to Know Where You Are, Considers Buying Loopt," *Fast Company*, www.fastcompany.com, February 25, 2010; Rene Ritchie, "Apple: No Location-Based Ads for Non Location-Based Apps," *Tipb.com*, www.tipb.com, February 5, 2010.

motivated first level. Sellers have begun to learn that social relationships with buyers can be very effective marketing tools. Customer service and communication are key factors at this stage.

Social interaction can take many forms. The owner of a local shoe store or dry cleaner might chat with customers about local events. A local wine shop may host a wine-tasting reception. The service department of an auto dealership might call a customer after a repair to see whether or not the customer is satisfied or has any questions. An investment firm might send holiday cards to all its customers. Even television watching, once passive, is getting more social: TiVo and YouTube have partnered to bring Web videos to users' televisions, enhancing the social interaction characteristics of the Web site by featuring the most widely seen, and talked about, videos on the Internet.[7] Marketers are beginning to see the potential for more precise targeting through the use of social networking sites like Facebook and MySpace, but are still finding their way. The "Solving an Ethical Controversy" feature looks at the potential pitfalls of marketing through social networking sites.

Third Level: Interdependent Partnership

At the third level of relationship marketing, relationships are transformed into structural changes that ensure buyer and seller are true business partners. As buyer and seller work more closely together, they develop a dependence on one another that continues to grow over time. Southwest Airlines is a leader in customer satisfaction in the airline industry, but the company is reaching out to business travelers with service changes and upgrades to its normally frills-free waiting areas. Airport lounges now feature comfortable leather seats and plug-ins for computers and cell phone rechargers, and planes offer in-flight media and new international connections. Using new interactive voice-response technology, the airline gives customers who are on hold more than two minutes the option to hang on or request a callback. Since implementing the system, Southwest reports, it has cut time-to-answer almost in half (to about three minutes) and prevented about half a million customers from hanging up. It cites its Twitter and Facebook pages as evidence that customers are pleased with the change, which has saved the airline telecom dollars too—it now pays for almost 25 million fewer toll minutes.[8]

assessment check

1. Identify the three levels of the marketing relationship.
2. Which level is the most complicated? Why?

Enhancing Customer Satisfaction

4 **Explain how firms can enhance customer satisfaction.**

Marketers monitor customer satisfaction through various methods of marketing research. As part of an ongoing relationship with customers, marketers must continually measure and improve how well they meet customer needs. As Figure 10.2 shows, three major steps are involved in this process: understanding customer needs, obtaining customer feedback, and instituting an ongoing program to ensure customer satisfaction.

Understanding Customer Needs

customer satisfaction
Extent to which customers are satisfied with their purchases.

Knowledge of what customers need, want, and expect is a central concern of companies focused on building long-term relationships. This information is also a vital first step in setting up a system to measure **customer satisfaction**. Marketers must carefully monitor the characteristics of their product that really matter to customers. They also must remain constantly alert to new elements that might affect satisfaction.

Satisfaction can be measured in terms of the gaps between what customers expect and what they perceive they have received. Such gaps can produce favorable or unfavorable impressions. Goods or services may be better or worse than expected. If they are better, marketers can use the opportunity to create loyal customers. If goods or services are worse than expected, a company may start to lose customers. The American Customer Satisfaction Index (ACSI) is a nationwide tool to provide information about customer satisfaction with product quality. Based on more than 65,000 telephone interviews a year, it tracks customer responses to

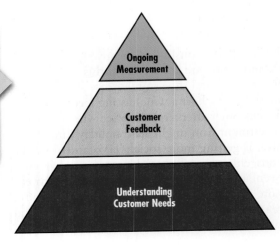

figure 10.2

Three Steps to Measure Customer Satisfaction

more than 5,000 brands produced by about 300 companies and 100 federal agencies. Some of the firms ACSI rates are 1-800-FLOWERS, Amazon.com, Kraft Foods, Levi Strauss, Marriott International, AOL, Nissan, Netflix, Charles Schwab, Outback Steakhouse, The Coca-Cola Company, Overstock. com, and Quaker Foods. Each rating is based on 250 customer interviews.[9] Marketers at the companies profiled can use such rankings to measure how well they satisfy customer needs.

To avoid unfavorable service gaps, marketers need to keep in touch with the needs of current and potential customers. They must look beyond traditional performance measures and explore the factors that determine purchasing behavior to formulate customer-based missions, goals, and performance standards.

Obtaining Customer Feedback and Ensuring Satisfaction

The second step in measuring customer satisfaction is to compile feedback from customers regarding present performance. Increasingly, marketers try to improve customers' access to their companies by including toll-free phone numbers or Web site addresses in their advertising. Most firms rely on reactive methods of collecting feedback. Rather than solicit complaints, they might, for example, monitor Usenet, other online discussion groups, and popular blogs to track customer comments and attitudes about the value received. Marketers at cable company Comcast review postings on blogs, message boards, and social networking sites. Dell learned the hard way that ignoring negative blog posts annoyed customers and failed to solve the underlying problems. The company has since created its own social media site (Direct2Dell) for the "Dell community" and an idea-sharing site at Ideastorm.com. The turnaround Dell made to achieve customer service excellence is now legendary.[10] Even Apple's CEO, Steven Jobs, occasionally answers customer e-mails, creating waves of excitement among Apple users around the world.[11] Some companies hire mystery shoppers who visit or call businesses posing as customers to evaluate the service they receive. Their unbiased appraisals usually are conducted semiannually or quarterly to monitor employees, diagnose problem areas in customer service, and measure the impact of employee training.

Because unhappy customers typically talk about their buying experiences more than happy customers do, the cost of dissatisfaction can be high. One instance of poor complaint handling at an upscale fitness club, for instance, could cost the gym thousands of dollars in lost membership fees; the fee is $1,000 for membership and, if the disgruntled customer tells seven people, the club could lose $7,000. So it makes sense to try to resolve problems quickly. In addition to training employees to resolve complaints, firms can benefit from providing several different ways for customers to make their dissatisfaction known, including prepaid mail questionnaires, telephone help lines, comment cards, and face-to-face exit surveys as people leave the premises. Any method that makes it easier for customers to complain actually benefits a firm. Customer complaints offer firms the opportunity to overcome problems and prove their commitment to service. People often have greater loyalty to a company after a conflict has been resolved than if they had never complained at all.

Many organizations also use proactive methods to assess customer satisfaction, including visiting, calling, or mailing out surveys to clients to find out their level of satisfaction. Nokia has an ambitious online experiment to draw user feedback on new products that actually lead to product innovation. A cell phone application, Sports Tracker, lets runners and cyclists tap into the global positioning functions of some Nokia phones to plot their routes as well as record their speed and distance traveled. When the company posted a work-in-progress version of the application on its Web site for downloading, more than a million people used it, sometimes in ways Nokia never imagined, including hot-air ballooning and paragliding. Best of all, they provided enthusiastic feedback that helped Nokia add improvements like online groups for sharing text and photos. The award-winning program has been downloaded millions of times.[12]

assessment check

1. How is customer satisfaction measured?

2. Identify the ways marketers may obtain customer feedback.

Building Buyer–Seller Relationships

5 Describe how companies build buyer–seller relationships.

Marketers of consumer goods and services have discovered they must do more than simply create products and then sell them. With a dizzying array of products to choose from, many customers seek ways to simplify both their business and personal lives, and relationships provide a way to do this.

One reason consumers form continuing relationships is their desire to reduce choices. Through relationships, they can simplify information gathering and the entire buying process as well as decrease the risk of dissatisfaction. They find comfort in brands that have become familiar through their ongoing relationships with companies. Such relationships may lead to more efficient decision making by customers and higher levels of customer satisfaction. A key benefit to consumers in long-term buyer–seller relationships is the perceived positive value they receive. Relationships add value because of increased opportunities for frequent customers to save money through discounts, rebates, and similar offers; via special recognition from the relationship programs; and through convenience in shopping.

Marketers should also understand why consumers end relationships. Computerized technologies and the Internet have made consumers better informed than ever before by giving them unprecedented abilities to compare prices, merchandise, and customer service. If they perceive a competitor's product or customer service is better, customers may switch loyalties. Many consumers dislike feeling locked into a relationship with one company, and that is reason enough for them to try a competing item the next time they buy. Some customers simply become bored with their current providers and decide to sample the competition.

How Marketers Keep Customers

One of the major forces driving the push from transaction-based marketing to relationship marketing is the realization that retaining customers is far more profitable than losing them. Some banking industry analysts estimate that banks acquire new customers at the rate of about 13.5 percent per year, only 1 percentage point faster than they lose them. Meanwhile, it costs five times as much to acquire a new customer as it does to keep a loyal one. This **customer churn**, or turnover, is expensive. Some estimate that banks can increase their net profits 20 percent by eliminating just 5 percent of their customer churn.[13] In the telecom industry, wireless services in the United States and Europe replace about a third of their customer base each year. That number could rise to 50 percent, according to some industry observers, based on customers' desire for the latest and most attractive handset with the most sophisticated features and impatience with any billing or service problems or gaps in network coverage. "If you can keep a customer from getting angry at you," says one telecom consultant, "they probably will never bother to check other plans." But if they do, they are up to eight times as likely to churn again.[14]

Also, customers usually enable a firm to generate more profits with each additional year of the relationship. For example, the Marriott Rewards program now boasts more than 17 million members who spend an average of 2.5 times as much at Marriott hotels as nonmembers and account for 40 percent of Marriott's total sales. They have more than 250 reward options, earning airline miles or points toward hotel stays and merchandise. They can receive 33 percent savings through Marriott Rewards Pointsavers, and during certain time periods, may earn double Marriott rewards or double upgrade points with rental car firm Hertz. Now they can also use points to ship their luggage door to door.[15]

customer churn
Turnover in a company's customer base.

The Marriott Rewards program, an example of frequency marketing, offers more than 250 reward options.

Programs like Marriott's are an example of **frequency marketing**. These programs reward top customers with cash, rebates, merchandise, or other premiums. Buyers who purchase an item more often earn higher rewards. Frequency marketing focuses on a company's best customers with the goal of increasing their motivation to buy even more of the same or other products from the seller.

Many different types of companies use frequency programs: fast-food restaurants, retail stores, telecommunications companies, and travel firms. Popular programs include airline frequent-flyer programs, such as Continental's OnePass, and retail programs, such as Hallmark's Gold Crown Card.

About 80 percent of credit card purchases (by value) now include some sort of reward, such as cash back, frequent-flyer miles, price rebates, and other offerings. Eighty million U.S. consumers use such cards, although credit counselors caution that their rewards aren't strictly free. Most companies charge higher interest payments and fees to finance the give-backs, making some cards more costly to consumers than the "rewards" they offer.[16]

In addition to frequency programs, companies use **affinity marketing** to retain customers. Each of us holds certain things dear. Some may feel strongly about Eastern Michigan University, while others admire the New Orleans Saints or the Atlanta Braves. These examples, along with an almost unending variety of others, are subjects of affinity programs. An affinity program is a marketing effort sponsored by an organization that solicits involvement by individuals who share common interests and activities. With affinity programs, organizations create extra value for members and encourage stronger relationships. And sometimes those relationships are geared toward eternity: the University of Florida is one of a handful of colleges that allow alumni to have their ashes buried on campus grounds after paying for the upkeep. The Universities of Richmond, Notre Dame, Virginia, and North Carolina-Chapel Hill are some of the others.[17]

Avid sports fans are another logical target for affinity programs. The U.S. Olympic Committee offered an affinity program linked to the Vancouver Winter Games that matched each rewards dollar fans earned with a donation to the Committee and Team USA. Hundreds of online retailers participated in the 15 percent cash-back offer.[18]

Not all affinity programs involve credit cards. WNET, the New York public television station, thanks members who contribute more than $40 a year with a card that entitles them to discounts at participating restaurants, museums, theaters, hotels, and car rental companies.[19]

Database Marketing

The use of information technology to analyze data about customers and their transactions is referred to as **database marketing**. The results form the basis of new advertising or promotions targeted to carefully identified groups of customers. Database marketing is a particularly effective tool for building relationships because it allows sellers to sort through huge quantities of data from multiple sources on the buying habits or preferences of thousands or even millions of customers. Companies can then track buying patterns, develop customer relationship profiles, customize their offerings and sales promotions, and even personalize customer service to suit the needs of targeted groups of customers. Properly used, databases can help companies in several ways, including:

- identifying their most profitable customers;
- calculating the lifetime value of each customer's business;
- creating a meaningful dialogue that builds relationships and encourages genuine brand loyalty;
- improving customer retention and referral rates;
- reducing marketing and promotion costs;
- boosting sales volume per customer or targeted customer group; and
- expanding loyalty programs.[20]

Where do organizations find all the data that fill these vast marketing databases? Everywhere! Credit card applications, software registration, and product warranties all provide vital statistics of individual customers. Point-of-sale register scanners, customer opinion surveys, and sweepstakes entry forms may offer not just details of name and address but information about preferred brands

---

frequency marketing
Frequent-buyer or -user marketing programs that reward customers with cash, rebates, merchandise, or other premiums.

affinity marketing
Marketing effort sponsored by an organization that solicits responses from individuals who share common interests and activities.

database marketing
Use of software to analyze marketing information, identifying and targeting messages toward specific groups of potential customers.

and shopping habits. Web sites offer free access in return for personal data, allowing companies to amass increasingly rich marketing information.

Google Personalized Search is a new platform that can track users' past online history and use it to improve and tailor the results of future searches. Real Time Search uses not just past Google history for this purpose but also recent public updates on Twitter, Facebook, and MySpace. The goal of these features is to make Google search experiences better based on the user's preferences, without the customer having to enter any additional information. Some see personalized search results as a breakthrough that allows the company to target its ads to those who will be most interested in them. Others have privacy concerns, however, and some simply prefer the open-ended nature of searches without personalization.[21]

CBS and the Nielsen Co. carefully track Super Bowl viewership each year to help the network and other football broadcasters determine ad rates for the following year, among other results. Of the record-shattering audience that saw the New Orleans Saints beat the Indianapolis Colts, the CEO of CBS said, "For anyone who wants to write that broadcasting is dead, 106 million people watched this program. You can't find that anywhere else."[22]

Newer technologies such as radio-frequency identification (RFID) allow retailers to identify shipping pallets and cargo containers, but most observers anticipate that, in the near future, RFID will be cost-effective enough to permit tagging of individual store items, allowing retailers to gather information about the purchaser as well as managing inventory and deterring theft, but also raising privacy concerns.

interactive television delivers even more valuable data—information on real consumer behavior and attitudes toward brands. Linked to digital television, sophisticated set-top boxes already collect vast amounts of data on television viewer behavior, organized in incredible detail. As the technology makes its way into more homes, marketers receive firsthand knowledge of the kind of programming and products their targeted customers want. In addition, rather than using television to advertise to the masses, they can talk directly to the viewers most interested in their products. At a click of a button, viewers can skip ads, but they can also click to a full-length infomercial on any brand that captures their interest. Sales of Internet video devices are expected to soon increase 80 percent, and, in just a few years, industry experts anticipate that half a billion households will be able to watch Internet videos on their televisions.[23]

New technologies like widgets—small software applications, such as games, easily passed from friend to friend on sites like Facebook—are becoming popular marketing tools. One California job search site, Doostang, attracted 1,200 new members in three days with a game widget. Cell phone advertising is increasing, and with it the prospect that it can become highly targeted because telecom companies already have access to users' personal and credit card information, and even their current location. Discount offers can be sent to users passing a particular store, for instance. Marketers can even build their own social networking sites, perhaps using a program like Ning, rather than relying on MySpace or Facebook.[24]

As database marketing becomes more complex, a variety of software tools and services enable marketers to target consumers more and more narrowly while enriching their communications to selected groups. After all, a huge repository of data is not valuable unless it can be turned into information useful to a firm's marketers. **Application service providers (ASPs)** assist marketers by providing software when it is needed to capture, manipulate, and analyze masses of consumer data. One type of software collects data on product specifications and details that marketers can use to isolate products best meeting a customer's needs. This feature would be particularly important in selling expensive business products that require high involvement in making a purchase decision. Texas-based Convio provides such database services to nonprofit organizations trying to cultivate a wider base of members and supporters. Convio also supplies software and online services designed to help groups such as Easter Seals, the American Diabetes Association, the Jewish National Fund, Feeding America, museums, and other organizations identify and communicate with contributors.[25]

Customers as Advocates

Recent relationship marketing efforts focus on turning customers from passive partners into active proponents of a product. **Grassroots marketing** involves connecting directly with existing and

---

interactive television
Television service package that includes a return path for viewers to interact with programs or commercials by clicking their remote controls.

application service providers (ASPs) Outside companies that specialize in providing both the computers and the application support for managing information systems of business clients.

grassroots marketing Efforts that connect directly with existing and potential customers through nonmainstream channels.

potential customers through nonmainstream channels. The grassroots approach relies on marketing strategies that are unconventional, nontraditional, and extremely flexible. Grassroots marketing sometimes is characterized by a relatively small budget and lots of legwork, but its hallmark is the ability to develop long-lasting, individual relationships with loyal customers.

With **viral marketing**, firms let satisfied customers get the word out about products to other consumers—like a spreading virus. PepsiCo saw a great response to its viral Pepsi Refresh Project, created by the company's Social Media Marketing team. Through a special Web site, the company invites individuals, firms, and communities to suggest up to 1,000 "refreshing," socially responsible, and achievable ideas per month, in fields ranging from health and the arts to education and the environment. Site visitors vote to select up to 32 winners a month to receive thousands of dollars in funding from PepsiCo. Traffic to the site has grown steadily. According to a firm that has been tracking the project, "This release alone is a perfect example of the secondary gains and branding that viral marketing can achieve. The Pepsi Refresh Project has been receiving a tremendous amount of free publicity every week. However, it's also for a great cause."[26]

Buzz marketing gathers volunteers to try products and then relies on them to talk about their experiences with friends and colleagues. "Influencers," or early adopters of products, are ideal carriers of buzz marketing messages because their credibility makes their choices valuable among their peers. They often are recruited online through chat rooms, blogs, and instant messaging. Word-of-mouth—the idea behind buzz marketing—isn't new, but by accelerating communication, technology has made many more applications possible. Procter & Gamble's Tremor division relies on the buzz created by 250,00 recruited teens, while its Vocalpoint site does the same with 450,000 mothers.[27] Techniques in this area are still evolving, and the Word of Mouth Marketing Association is developing rules and standards for buzz marketing it hopes will prevent fraud and preserve the value of buzz marketing.[28]

> **viral marketing** Efforts that allow satisfied customers to spread the word about products to other consumers.

> **buzz marketing** Marketing that gathers volunteers to try products and then relies on them to talk about their experiences with their friends and colleagues.

assessment check

1. Describe two ways marketers keep customers.
2. List three efforts that turn customers into advocates for products.

Customer Relationship Management

Emerging from—and closely linked to—relationship marketing, **customer relationship management (CRM)** is the combination of strategies and technologies that empowers relationship programs, reorienting the entire organization to a concentrated focus on satisfying customers. Made possible by technological advances, it leverages technology as a means to manage customer relationships and to integrate all stakeholders into a company's product design and development, manufacturing, marketing, sales, and customer service processes.

CRM represents a shift in thinking for everyone involved with a firm—from the CEO down and encompassing all other key stakeholders, including suppliers, dealers, and other partners. All recognize that solid customer relations are fostered by similarly strong relationships with other major stakeholders. Because CRM goes well beyond traditional sales, marketing, or customer service functions, it requires a top-down commitment and must permeate every aspect of a firm's business. Technology makes that possible by allowing firms—regardless of size and no matter how far-flung their operations—to manage activities across functions, from location to location, and among their internal and external partners.

> **6** Explain customer relationship management (CRM) and the role of technology in building customer relationships.

> **customer relationship management (CRM)** Combination of strategies and tools that drives relationship programs, reorienting the entire organization to a concentrated focus on satisfying customers.

Benefits of CRM

CRM software systems are capable of making sense of the vast amounts of customer data that technology allows firms to collect. B2B firms benefit just as much as retailers. With software from

SAP, Spy Optic, a California wholesale maker of high-performance goggles, sunglasses, and other trendy accessories, improved its tracking of sales and inventory data so the firm could better keep up with fads, help its dealers restock fast-selling items, and boost sales. Before implementing the software, "We didn't have good data about regional tastes, sales, or even our own inventory. We were making design, stock, and marketing decisions based on gut feel and assumptions," says the company's vice president of marketing. Now, however, "the whole company operates off the same set of data, which eliminates confusion and redundancy and speeds customer service. ... We can now tell dealers which product models they should carry, in what quantities. We can help them see that if they replenish their top-10 sellers every week, and even increase the space devoted to sunglasses, they can increase sales. It's completely changed the way we sell to dealers." [29]

Another key benefit of customer relationship management systems is they simplify complex business processes while keeping the best interests of customers at heart. Working with Capgemini, a consulting company with offices across the country, Kimberly-Clark developed a new query-management system for its customer service centers across Europe. The new system eliminated the need to rekey customer information, provided better tracking of unanswered queries, and allowed easier access to information to resolve queries so they could be dealt with faster. [30]

Selecting the right CRM software system is critical to the success of a firm's entire CRM program. CRM can be used at two different levels: on-demand, accessed via the Internet as a Web-based service, and on-premises, installed on a company's computer system on site. A firm may choose to buy a system from a company such as SAP or Oracle or rent hosted CRM applications through Web sites such as Salesforce.com or Salesnet. Purchasing a customized system can cost millions of dollars and take months to implement, while hosted solutions—rented through a Web site—are cheaper and quicker to get up and running. But purchasing a system allows a firm to expand and customize, whereas hosted systems are more limited. Experienced marketers also warn that it is easy to get mired in a system too complicated for staff to use.

Software solutions are just one component of a successful CRM initiative. The most effective companies approach customer relationship management as a complete business strategy in which people, processes, and technology are organized around delivering superior value to customers. See the "Career Readiness" feature for some specific strategies you can apply.

Successful CRM systems share the following qualities:

- They create partnerships with customers in ways that align with the company's mission and goals.
- They reduce costs by empowering customers to find the information they need to manage their own orders.
- They improve customer service by centralizing data and help sales representatives guide customers to information.
- They reduce response time and thus increase customer satisfaction.
- They improve customer retention and loyalty, leading to more repeat business and new business from word of mouth.
- They can provide a complete picture of customers.
- Their results are measurable. [31]

Once the groundwork has been laid, technology solutions drive firms toward a clearer understanding of each customer and his or her needs.

Problems with CRM

CRM is not a magic wand. The strategy needs to be thought out in advance, and everyone in the firm must be committed to it and understand how to use it. If no one can put the system to work, it is an expensive mistake.

Experts explain that failures with CRM often result from failure to organize—or reorganize—the company's people and business processes to take advantage of the benefits the CRM system offers. For instance, it might be important to empower salespeople to negotiate price with their

career readiness — Establishing Relationships through CRM

relationship marketing doesn't happen by chance. It's a deliberate, and profitable, strategy that focuses more on satisfying current customers than finding new ones. What are some ways to deepen relationships with your most valuable customers?

- Make sure you have the right tools. By adopting a customer care software tool that unified many scattered applications, Overstock.com boosted customer satisfaction 10 percent and jumped onto the National Retail Federation's list of 150 highest-rated companies for customer service at fourth place.

- Know who your customers are. Readily available customer relationship management software can help you get a clear picture of their preferences, likes, and dislikes.

- Share customer information with all staff members who work directly with customers, so they can use it to deepen the loyalty that leads to sales.

- Train employees to share your customer-oriented outlook, and show them the same loyalty and consideration you want them to extend to your customers.

- Consider connecting with customers via a blog about products, services, innovations, sales, and special events. Keep your posts relevant to their needs, update frequently, and read and respond to legitimate customer comments.

- Whether you blog or not, maintain regular communication with a brief mailed or online newsletter. Keep it professional-looking, and supplement it with personal greeting cards or service reminders for special customers.

- Offer incentives for special customers. A restaurant might serve regulars an occasional free dessert, a retailer could offer a simple frequent-buyer reward program, and even a dentist might do a free cleaning to acknowledge a new referral.

- Be flexible. If you insist on always sticking to policy, you'll lose customers whose problems you might otherwise have solved.

Sources: "Ten Tips to Build Customer Loyalty," *AllBusiness.com*, www.allbusiness.com, accessed March 7, 2010; Gail Goodman, "5 Key Ways to Build Customer Relationships," company Web site, Microsoft Corp., www.microsoft.com, accessed March 7, 2010; "Overstock.com," company Web site, www.rightnow.com, accessed March 7, 2010; Jim Blasingame, "Small Business Advocate: Build, Grow Customer Relationships with a Blog," *The Commercial Appeal*, February 22, 2010, www.commercialappeal.com; Michael Harris, "How to Build Enduring Customer Relationships!" *PRLog*, www.prlog.org, accessed February 9, 2010.

customers to close more sales with CRM, but if a company does not adapt its centralized pricing system, its CRM efforts will be hampered. Second, if sales and service employees do not have input in the CRM process during its design phase, they might be less willing to use its tools—no matter how much training is offered. "It is important to clearly communicate the benefits of the CRM, train employees how to use it, and have an onsite, dedicated 'go-to' person they can call on for help," says one marketing manager who managed four CRM implementations.[32] A third factor is some CRM "failures" are actually at least partially successful, but companies or their executives have set their expectations too high. Having a realistic idea what CRM can accomplish is as important to success as properly implementing the program. Finally, truly understanding customers, their needs, and the ways they differ from customers of the past is a critical element in any successful CRM project. One of the easiest ways to lose a customer, or to damage any business relationship, is rudeness. But good manners are a two-way street.

Retrieving Lost Customers

Customers defect from an organization's goods and services for a variety of reasons. They might be bored, they might move away from the region, they might not need the product anymore, or they might have tried—and preferred—competing products. Figure 10.3 illustrates the yearly defection rates for some industries. An increasingly important part of an effective CRM strategy is **customer win-back**, the process of rejuvenating lost relationships with customers.

customer win-back
Process of rejuvenating lost relationships with customers.

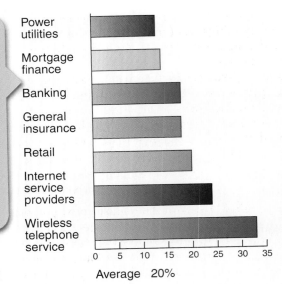

figure 10.3

Annual Customer Defection Rates

Source: Data from Andrew Greenyer, "The Danger of Defection," *CRM Today*, www. crm2day.com, accessed April 6, 2010.

In many cases, a relationship gone sour can be sweetened again with the right approach. When some customers complained about its pizza in hidden camera focus groups, Domino's rolled out a preemptive ad campaign that took those customers' words like "totally devoid of flavor" and "like cardboard" from the hidden camera footage and used it in the campaign. Domino's head chef then goes to their homes to offer them a taste of the new, improved pizza and watches them change their minds.[33] A good rule for service providers is to anticipate where problems will arise and figure out how to prevent them in the first place. The second part of this strategy is to accept that mistakes will occur in even the best system and to, consequently, have a high-quality recovery effort in place that employees are empowered to enact.

Sometimes, however, the missteps are so great that it is almost impossible for a company to repair the damage until enough time has passed for attention to simply turn elsewhere. This may prove to be the case for British Petroleum (BP), the energy company whose reputation suffered a severe blow following the recent explosion of its offshore oil rig that sent tens of thousands of barrels of oil into the Gulf of Mexico every day for weeks until the spill was contained. Many observers feel the company's public response compounded the damage, which included threats to plant and animal life in the Gulf and the widespread loss of residents' livelihoods from an uncontrolled flow of oil that eventually grew to 5 million barrels. BP is thought to have hurt its credibility by issuing initial reports far below the actual volume of oil spewing out; by appearing to blame its contractors for the spill; and by entrusting its communications about the crisis to CEO Tony Hayward, whose public gaffes included his statement that he wanted his life back and his mid-crisis departure for a vacation. "It was one of the worst PR approaches that I've seen in my 56 years of business," said a noted public relations specialist. "Right away they [BP] should have accepted responsibility and recognized what a disaster they faced. They basically thought they could spin their way out of catastrophe. It doesn't work that way." Although BP rushed out a series of ads expressing its concern and the leak was eventually closed, Hayward soon resigned as CEO.[34]

business-to-business (B2B) marketing Organizational sales and purchases of goods and services to support production of other products, for daily company operations, or for resale.

✓ assessment check

1. Define *customer relationship management.*
2. What are the two major types of CRM systems?
3. Describe two steps a firm can take to rejuvenate a lost relationship.

Buyer–Seller Relationships in Business-to-Business Markets

7 Describe the buyer–seller relationship in business-to-business marketing, and identify the four types of business partnerships.

Customer relationship management and relationship marketing are not limited to consumer goods and services. Building strong buyer–seller relationships is a critical component of business-to-business marketing as well.

Business-to-business (B2B) marketing includes an organization's purchase of goods and services to support company operations or the production of other products. Buyer–seller relationships between companies involve working together to provide advantages that benefit both parties. These advantages might include lower prices for supplies, quicker delivery of inventory, improved quality and reliability, customized product features, and more favorable financing terms.

A **partnership** is an affiliation of two or more companies that help each other achieve common goals. Partnerships cover a wide spectrum of relationships from informal cooperative purchasing arrangements to formal production and marketing agreements. In business-to-business markets, partnerships form the basis of relationship marketing.

A variety of common goals motivate firms to form partnerships. Companies may want to protect or improve their positions in existing markets, gain access to new domestic or international markets, or quickly enter new markets. Expansion of a product line—to fill in gaps, broaden the product line, or differentiate the product—is another key reason for joining forces. Other motives include sharing resources, reducing costs, warding off threats of future competition, raising or creating barriers to entry, and learning new skills.

Choosing Business Partners

How does an organization decide which companies to select as partners? The first priority is to locate firms that can add value to the relationship—whether through financial resources, contacts, extra manufacturing capacity, technical know-how, or distribution capabilities. The greater the value added, the greater the desirability of the partnership. In many cases, the attributes of each partner complement those of the other; each firm brings something to the relationship the other party needs but cannot provide on its own. Other partnerships join firms with similar skills and resources to reduce costs. Organizations must share similar values and goals for a partnership to succeed in the long run.

Types of Partnerships

Companies form four key types of partnerships in business-to-business markets: buyer, seller, internal, and lateral partnerships. This section briefly examines each category.

In a **buyer partnership**, a firm purchases goods and services from one or more providers. AT&T, for example, is selling data connectivity services on its wireless network to providers of electronic readers including the Amazon Kindle, the Sony Reader Daily Edition, and the Barnes & Noble Nook. It also provides Internet connectivity for the iPad.[35]

When a company assumes the buyer position in a relationship, it has a unique set of needs and requirements vendors must meet to make the relationship successful. Although buyers want sellers to provide fair prices, quick delivery, and high quality levels, a lasting relationship often requires more effort. To induce a buyer to form a long-term partnership, a supplier must also be responsive to the purchaser's unique needs. AT&T had to move quickly to add the Kindle, for instance, after Amazon dropped Sprint as its carrier. The new partnership brought the number of e-readers supported by AT&T to more than 1 million.[36]

Seller partnerships set up long-term exchanges of goods and services in return for cash or other considerations. Sellers, too, have specific needs as partners in ongoing relationships. Most prefer to develop long-term relationships with their partners. Sellers also want prompt payment.

The importance of **internal partnerships** is widely recognized in business today. The classic definition of the word *customer* as the buyer of a good or service is now more carefully defined in terms of external customers. However, customers within an organization also have their own needs. Internal partnerships are the foundation of an organization and its ability to meet its commitments to external entities. If the purchasing department selects a parts vendor that fails to ship on the dates required by manufacturing, production will

partnership Affiliation of two or more companies that help each other achieve common goals.

buyer partnership Relationship in which a firm purchases goods and services from one or more providers.

seller partnership Relationship involving long-term exchanges of goods or services in return for cash or other valuable consideration.

internal partnership Relationship involving customers within an organization.

When customers complained about its pizza, Domino's remade its product and then rolled out an ad campaign to show off the new, improved taste.

COURTESY OF DOMINO'S PIZZA, INC.

© AP IMAGES/PRNEWSFOTO/BERRY CHILL

Chicago yogurt shop Berry Chill used cobranding to create new specialty toppings for its products and attract customers who already enjoyed the offerings of local firms like Sarah's Candies. Here is Berry Chill's pumpkin spice dessert.

lateral partnership Strategic relationship that extends to external entities but involves no direct buyer–seller interactions.

cobranding Cooperative arrangement in which two or more businesses team up to closely link their names on a single product.

comarketing Cooperative arrangement in which two businesses jointly market each other's products.

halt and products will not be delivered to customers as promised. As a result, external customers will likely seek other more reliable suppliers. Without building and maintaining internal partnerships, an organization will have difficulty meeting the needs of its external partnerships.

Lateral partnerships include strategic alliances with other companies or with not-for-profit organizations and research alliances between for-profit firms and colleges and universities. The relationship focuses on external entities—such as customers of the partner firm—and involves no direct buyer–seller interactions. Strategic alliances are discussed later in this chapter.

Cobranding and Comarketing

Two other types of business marketing relationships include cobranding and comarketing. **Cobranding** joins two strong brand names, perhaps owned by two different companies, to sell a product. Berry Chill, a Chicago yogurt shop, used cobranding to create new specialty toppings for its products and attract customers who already enjoyed the offerings of local firms like Sarah's Candies, Milk & Honey Granola, and Leonard's Bakery. The toppings include Dark Chocolate Delight, Rocky Road Clusters, and Smiley Face Cookies and are proving to be a big hit with Berry Chill's customers.[37]

In a **comarketing** effort, two organizations join to sell their products in an allied marketing campaign. Elemé Medical Inc. (a body shaping aesthetics company) and Osyris Medical USA (a medical laser company) created a comarketing alliance to target dermatologists, plastic surgeons, and medical spa staff with marketing, public relations, and trade show events. Said Eleme's president, "Combining the expertise of both teams is a strategic move to serve our physician partners more completely and increase revenues by offering one-stop shopping for body-shaping techniques that grow practices."[38]

assessment check

1. What are the four key types of business marketing partnerships?
2. Distinguish between cobranding and comarketing.

8 **Describe how business-to-business marketing incorporates national account selling; electronic data interchange and Web services; vendor-managed inventories; collaborative planning, forecasting, and replenishment; managing the supply chain; and creating alliances.**

Improving Buyer–Seller Relationships in Business-to-Business Markets

Organizations that know how to find and nurture partner relationships, whether through informal deals or contracted partnerships, can enhance revenues and increase profits. Partnering often leads to lower prices, better products, and improved distribution—resulting in higher levels of customer satisfaction. Partners who know each other's needs and expectations are more likely to satisfy them and forge stronger long-term bonds. Often partnerships can be cemented through personal relationships, no matter where firms are located.

In the past, business relationships were conducted primarily in person, over the phone, or by mail. Today, businesses use the latest electronic, computer, and communications technology to link up. E-mail, the Internet, and other telecommunications services allow businesses to communicate any time and any place. Chapter 4 discussed the business role of the Internet in detail. The following sections explore other ways buyers and sellers cooperate in business-to-business markets.

National Account Selling

Some relationships are more important than others due to the large investments at stake. Large manufacturers such as Procter & Gamble and Clorox pay special attention to the needs of major retailers such as Walmart and Target. Manufacturers use a technique called **national account selling** to serve their largest, most profitable customers. The large collection of supplier offices in northwest Arkansas—near Walmart's home office—suggests how national account selling might be implemented. These offices are usually called *teams* or *support teams*.

The advantages of national account selling are many. By assembling a team of individuals to serve just one account, the seller demonstrates the depth of its commitment to the customer. The buyer–seller relationship is strengthened as both collaborate to find mutually beneficial solutions. Finally, cooperative buyer–seller efforts can bring about dramatic improvements in both efficiency and effectiveness for both partners. These improvements find their way to the bottom line in the form of decreased costs and increased profits.

national account selling Promotional effort in which a dedicated sales team is assigned to a firm's major customers to provide sales and service.

Business-to-Business Databases

As noted earlier, databases are indispensable tools in relationship marketing. They are also essential in building business-to-business relationships. Using information generated from sales reports, scanners, and many other sources, sellers can create databases that help guide their own efforts and those of buyers who resell products to final users.

Electronic Data Interchange and Web Services

Technology has transformed the ways companies control their inventories and replenish stock. Gone are the days when a retailer would notice stocks were running low, call the vendor, check prices, and reorder. Today's **electronic data interchanges (EDIs)** automate the entire process. EDI involves computer-to-computer exchanges of invoices, orders, and other business documents. It allows firms to reduce costs and improve efficiency and competitiveness. Retailers such as Dillard's and Lowe's all require vendors to use EDI as a core **quick-response merchandising** tool. Quick-response merchandising is a just-in-time strategy that reduces the time merchandise is held in inventory, resulting in substantial cost savings. At Blue C Sushi restaurant chain in Seattle, an RFID tag is attached to the bottom of each sushi plate on the store's conveyor belt. It tracks the time that elapses from the moment it leaves the chef's cutting board until it is picked up by a customer, when it triggers a signal to chefs to update the inventory. The RFID tags also automate the restaurant's billing process and help it track inventory. "We now have the ability to track customers' preferences at certain times of the day to indicate what should be circulating on the conveyor belt," says the chain's co-founder.[39] An added advantage of EDI is it opens new channels for gathering marketing information helpful in developing long-term business-to-business relationships.

Web services provide a way for companies to communicate even if they are not running the same or compatible software, hardware, databases, or network platforms. Companies in a customer–supplier relationship, or a partnership such as airlines and car rental firms, may have difficulty getting their computer systems to work together or exchange data easily. Web services are platform-independent information exchange systems that use the Internet to allow interaction between the firms. They usually are simple, self-contained applications that handle functions from the simple to the complex.

electronic data interchange (EDI) Computer-to-computer exchanges of invoices, orders, and other business documents.

quick-response merchandising Just-in-time strategy that reduces the time a retailer must hold merchandise in inventory, resulting in substantial cost savings.

Web services Platform-independent information exchange systems that use the Internet to allow interaction between the firms.

Vendor-Managed Inventory

vendor-managed inventory (VMI) Inventory management system in which the seller—based on an existing agreement with a buyer—determines how much of a product is needed.

The proliferation of electronic communication technologies and the constant pressure on suppliers to improve response time have led to another way for buyers and sellers to do business. **Vendor-managed inventory (VMI)** has replaced buyer-managed inventory in many instances. It is an inventory management system in which the seller—based on an existing agreement with the buyer—determines how much of a product a buyer needs and automatically ships new supplies to that buyer.

"We were hitting our desired customer service performance metrics," says the national sales manager at Velvac, a Wisconsin parts manufacturer and supplier, "but at a cost of carrying high inventory or scrambling on the manufacturing side to expedite specific items. VMI gives us the visibility to gauge market conditions and allows for a much more disciplined and orderly process. Rush and fill-in orders are now the exception. Our overall efficiency has been improved, and service levels have also increased—including distributor order fill rates and on-time deliveries."[40]

collaborative planning, forecasting, and replenishment (CPFaR) Planning and forecasting approach based on collaboration between buyers and sellers.

Some firms have modified VMI to an approach called **collaborative planning, forecasting, and replenishment (CPFaR)**—a planning and forecasting technique involving collaborative efforts by both purchasers and vendors. TruServ, a wholesale hardware cooperative located in Chicago and owned by 6,200 independent True Value retailers, relies on its more than 50 trading partners to use computer-assisted ordering. At the company's 12 distribution centers, inventory has been reduced 41 percent, while service levels have climbed above 97 percent. Shorter lead times, more accurate forecasting, and faster reactions to marketplace trends are other benefits TruServ has realized from its CPFaR program.[41]

Managing the Supply Chain

supply chain Sequence of suppliers that contribute to the creation and delivery of a product.

Good relationships between businesses require careful management of the **supply chain**—sometimes called the *value chain*—the entire sequence of suppliers that contribute to the creation and delivery of a product. This process affects both upstream relationships between the company and its suppliers and downstream relationships with the product's end users. The supply chain is discussed in greater detail in Chapter 13.

mktg: *success*

Google Partners for Android Success

Background. Google, which already dominates the field of Internet search, decided to challenge Apple's preeminence in the smartphone industry by developing its own smartphone, powered by Google's new Android operating system.

The Challenge. As an Internet search company, Google couldn't jump into the mobile business alone. It needed to find partners to manufacture phones that would carry the Android software. To directly challenge Apple, it also wanted to offer customers more choices of service providers than Apple's original reliance on AT&T for its popular iPhone.

The Strategy. Google formed partnerships with both HTC and Samsung, leading smartphone manufacturers, to build the new phone, the Nexus One. It also partnered with wireless service providers T-Mobile, Verizon, and Vodaphone to offer users in the United States and the United Kingdom their choice of service plan. The Nexus One is available only at Google's Web site, where customers can purchase it with or without a service contract. The phone offers voice control,

Effective supply chain management can provide an important competitive advantage for a business marketer that results in:

- increased innovation;

- decreased costs;

- improved conflict resolution within the chain; and

- improved communication and involvement among members of the chain.

Good relationships between businesses require careful management of the supply chain—the entire sequence of suppliers that contribute to the creation and delivery of a product.

© SCPHOTOS/ALAMY

By coordinating operations with the other companies in the chain, boosting quality, and improving its operating systems, a firm can improve speed and efficiency. Because companies spend considerable resources on goods and services from outside suppliers, cooperative relationships can pay off in many ways.

Business-to-Business Alliances

Strategic alliances—the ultimate expression of relationship marketing—are partnerships formed to create a competitive advantage. These more formal long-term arrangements improve each partner's supply chain relationships and enhance operating flexibility in today's complex and rapidly changing marketplace. The size and location of strategic partners are not important. Strategic alliances include businesses of all sizes, of all kinds, and in many locations; it is what each partner can offer the other that is important. When it launched its Nexus One smartphone, for instance, Internet search giant Google needed business partners that could manufacture mobile devices for its Android operating system and provide customers with wireless telecom service. See the "Marketing Success" feature for details.

Companies can structure strategic alliances in two ways. Alliance partners can establish a new business unit in which each takes an ownership position. In such a joint venture, one partner might own 40 percent, while the other owns 60 percent. Alternatively, the partners may decide to form

strategic alliance
Partnership in which two or more companies combine resources and capital to create competitive advantages in a new market.

noise canceling, thousands of apps, GPS, and Internet access, all with ease of use. "We look forward to working with handset manufacturers and operators to bring more phones to market ... worldwide," said Google's vice president of engineering.

The Outcome. Calling the mobile phone "fundamental to everything you do

and ... the extension of everything we are," Google's CEO announced at a recent Mobile World Congress that "we are now shipping more than 60,000 Andoid devices ... per day and that number has doubled over the last quarter. The growth rate is accelerating and we hope the growth rate, as well as the demand, will continue for a very long time."

Sources: "Google Flaunts Android Sales Growth," *The New Zealand Herald*, www.nzherald.co.nz, February 18, 2010; "Google Offers New Model for Consumers to Buy a Mobile Phone," *Drug Week*, www.drugweek.com, January 22, 2010; "The Nexus Big Step Forward," *The Daily Telegraph* (Australia), www.dailytelegraph.com.au, January 20, 2010; Andrew Walmsley, "Google's Value Nexus," *Marketing*, www.marketingmagazine.co.uk, January 13, 2010; "Google Reveals Nexus One 'Super Phone,'" *TechWeb*, www.techweb.com, January 5, 2010.

a less formal cooperative relationship that does not involve ownership—for example, a joint new-product design team. The cooperative alliance can operate more flexibly and change more easily as market forces or other conditions dictate. In either arrangement, the partners agree in advance on the skills and resources each will bring into the alliance to achieve their mutual objectives and gain a competitive advantage. Resources typically include patents; product lines; brand equity; product and market knowledge; company and brand image; and reputation for product quality, innovation, or customer service. Relationships with customers and suppliers are also desirable resources as are a convenient manufacturing facility, economies of scale and scope, information technology, and a large sales force. Alliance partners can contribute marketing skills, such as innovation and product development; manufacturing skills, including low-cost or flexible manufacturing; and planning and research and development expertise.

Companies form many types of strategic alliances. Some create horizontal alliances between firms at the same level in the supply chain; others define vertical links between firms at adjacent stages. The firms may also serve the same or different industries. NBC Sports and the Kentucky Derby shared a partnership alliance that allowed NBC to broadcast exclusive coverage of the annual horse race through 2010.[42] Alliances can also involve cooperation among rivals who are market leaders or between a market leader and a follower.

assessment check

1. Name four technologies businesses can use to improve buyer–seller relationships in B2B markets.
2. What are the benefits of effective supply chain management?

Evaluating Customer Relationship Programs

9 Identify and evaluate the most common measurement and evaluation techniques within a relationship marketing program.

One of the most important measures of relationship marketing programs, whether in consumer or business-to-business markets, is the **lifetime value of a customer**. This concept can be defined as the revenues and intangible benefits, such as referrals and customer feedback, a customer brings to the seller over an average lifetime of their relationship, less the amount the company must spend to acquire, market to, and serve the customer. Long-term customers are usually more valuable assets than new ones because they buy more, cost less to serve, refer other customers, and provide valuable feedback. The "average lifetime" of a customer relationship depends on industry and product characteristics. Customer lifetime for a consumer product such as microwave pizza may be very short, while that for an automobile or computer will last longer.

For a simple example of a lifetime value calculation, assume a Chinese takeout restaurant's typical customer buys dinner twice a month at an average cost of $25 per order over a lifetime of five years. That business results in revenues of $600 per year and $3,000 for five years. The restaurant can calculate and subtract its average costs for food, labor, and overhead to arrive at the per-customer profit. This figure serves as a baseline against which to measure strategies to increase the restaurant's sales volume, customer retention, or customer referral rate.

Another approach is to calculate the payback from a customer relationship, or the length of time it takes to break even on customer acquisition costs. Assume an Internet service provider spends $75 per new customer on direct mail and enrollment incentives. Based on average revenues per subscriber, the company takes about three months to recover that $75. If an average customer stays with the service 32 months and generates $800 in revenues, the rate of return is nearly 11 times the original investment. Once the customer stays past the payback period, the provider should make a profit on that business.

lifetime value of a customer Revenues and intangible benefits such as referrals and customer feedback a customer brings to the seller over an average lifetime of their relationship, less the amount the company must spend to acquire, market to, and service the customer.

In addition to lifetime value analysis and payback, companies use many other techniques to evaluate relationship programs, including:

- tracking rebate requests, coupon redemption, credit card purchases, and product registrations;

- monitoring complaints and returned merchandise and analyzing why customers leave;

- reviewing reply cards, comment forms, and surveys; and

- monitoring click-through behavior on Web sites to identify why customers stay and why they leave.

These tools give the organization information about customer priorities so managers can make changes to their systems—if necessary—and set appropriate, measurable goals for relationship programs.

One writer suggests that, in developing the kind of loyalty that makes lifetime customers valuable, attracting the right buyers is just as important as treating them well. Lexus, for example, targets former owners of Mercedes and Cadillac cars, while Infiniti, with its focus on fashion and high performance, looks for younger drivers of sporty BMWs and Jaguars. Because these younger drivers are less loyal to car companies in general, the Infiniti repurchase rate is about 42 percent compared with 63 percent for the Lexus. Lexus is marketed to older drivers more attracted to long-term values such as service and reliability.[43]

A hotel chain may set a goal of improving the rate of repeat visits from 44 to 52 percent. A mail-order company may want to reduce time from 48 to 24 hours to process and mail orders. If a customer survey reveals late flight arrivals as the number-one complaint of an airline's passengers, the airline might set an objective of increasing the number of on-time arrivals from 87 to 93 percent.

Companies large and small can implement technology to help measure the value of customers and the return on investment from expenditures developing customer relationships. They can choose from a growing number of software products, many tailored to specific industries or flexible enough to suit companies of varying sizes.

For a simple example of lifetime value calculation, imagine the spending of a Chinese takeout restaurant's average customer.

© ISTOCKPHOTO.COM/ETHAN MYERSON

assessment check

1. Define lifetime value of a customer.

2. Why are customer complaints valuable in evaluating customer relationship programs?

strategic implications
of marketing in the 21st century

focus on relationship marketing helps companies create better ways to communicate with customers and develop long-term relationships. This focus challenges managers to develop strategies that closely integrate customer service, quality, and marketing functions. By leveraging technology—both through database marketing and through customer relationship management applications—companies can compare costs of acquiring and maintaining customer relationships with profits received from these customers. This information allows managers to evaluate the potential returns from investing in relationship marketing programs.

Relationships include doing business with consumers as well as partners such as vendors, suppliers, and other companies. Partners can structure relationships in many different ways to improve performance, and these choices vary for consumer and business markets. In all marketing relationships, it is important to build shared trust. For long-term customer satisfaction and success, marketers must make promises they can keep.

Review of Chapter Objectives

Contrast transaction-based marketing with relationship marketing.

Transaction-based marketing refers to buyer–seller exchanges characterized by limited communications and little or no ongoing relationships between the parties. Relationship marketing is the development and maintenance of long-term, cost-effective relationships with individual customers, suppliers, employees, and other partners for mutual benefit.

Identify and explain the four basic elements of relationship marketing, as well as the importance of internal marketing.

The four basic elements are database technology, database marketing, monitoring relationships, and customer relationship management (CRM). Database technology helps identify current and potential customers. Database marketing analyzes the information provided by the database. Through relationship marketing, a firm monitors each relationship. With CRM, the firm orients every part of the organization toward building a unique company with an unbreakable bond with customers. Internal marketing involves activities within the company designed to help all employees understand, accept, and fulfill their roles in the marketing strategy.

Identify the three levels of the relationship marketing continuum.

The three levels of the relationship marketing continuum are (1) focus on price, (2) social interaction, and (3) interdependent partnership. At the first level, marketers use financial incentives to attract customers. At the second level, marketers engage in social interaction with buyers. At the third level, buyers and sellers become true business partners.

Explain how firms can enhance customer satisfaction and how they build buyer–seller relationships.

Marketers monitor customer satisfaction through various methods of marketing research. They look to understand what customers want—including what they expect—from goods or services. They also obtain customer feedback through means such as toll-free phone numbers and Web sites. Then they use this information to improve.

Describe how companies build buyer–seller relationships.

Marketers of consumer goods and services have discovered they must do more than simply create products and then sell them. One reason consumers form continuing relationships is their desire to reduce choices. Through relationships, they can simplify information gathering and the entire buying process as well as decrease the risk of dissatisfaction. One of the major forces driving the push from transaction-based marketing to relationship marketing is the realization that retaining customers is far more profitable than losing them. Database marketing is a particularly effective tool for building relationships because it allows sellers to sort through huge quantities of data from multiple sources on the buying habits or preferences of thousands or even millions of customers.

Explain customer relationship management (CRM) and the role of technology in building customer relationships.

Customer relationship management is the combination of strategies and technologies that empowers relationship programs, reorienting the entire organization to a concentrated focus on satisfying customers. Made possible by technological advances, it leverages technology as a means to manage customer relationships and to integrate all stakeholders into a company's product design and development, manufacturing, marketing, sales, and customer service processes. CRM allows firms to manage vast amounts of data from multiple sources to improve overall customer satisfaction. The most effective companies approach CRM as a complete business strategy in which people, processes, and technology are organized around delivering superior value to customers. A recent outgrowth of CRM is virtual relationships, in which buyers and sellers rarely, if ever, meet face-to-face.

Describe the buyer–seller relationship in business-to-business marketing, and identify the four types of business partnerships.

By developing buyer–seller relationships, companies work together for their mutual benefit. Advantages may include lower prices for supplies, faster delivery of inventory, improved quality or reliability, customized product features, or more favorable financing terms. The four types of business partnerships are buyer, seller, internal, and lateral. Regardless of the type of partnership, partners usually share

similar values and goals that help the alliance endure over time. Two other types of business marketing relationships are cobranding and comarketing.

Describe how business-to-business marketing incorporates national account selling; electronic data interchange and Web services; vendor-managed inventories; collaborative planning, forecasting, and replenishment; managing the supply chain; and creating alliances.

National account selling helps firms form a strong commitment with key buyers, resulting in improvements in efficiency and effectiveness for both parties. The use of electronic data interchanges allows firms to reduce costs and improve efficiency and competitiveness. Web services are software applications that allow firms with different technology platforms to communicate and exchange information over the Internet. Vendor-managed inventory (VMI) is a system in which sellers can automatically restock to previously requested levels. The collaborative planning, forecasting, and replenishment (CPFaR) approach bases plans and forecasts on collaborative seller–vendor efforts. Managing the supply chain provides increased innovation, decreased costs, conflict resolution, and improved communications. Strategic alliances can help both partners gain a competitive advantage in the marketplace.

Identify and evaluate the most common measurement and evaluation techniques within a relationship marketing program.

The effectiveness of relationship marketing programs can be measured using several methods. In the lifetime value of a customer, the revenues and intangible benefits a customer brings to the seller over an average lifetime—less the amount the company must spend to acquire, market to, and service the customer—are calculated. With this method, a company may determine its costs to serve each customer and develop ways to increase profitability. The payback method calculates how long it takes to break even on customer acquisition costs. Other measurements include tracking rebates, coupons, and credit card purchases; monitoring complaints and returns; and reviewing reply cards, comment forms, and surveys. These tools give the organization information about customer priorities so managers can make changes to their systems and set measurable goals.

Assessment Check: Answers

1.1 What are the major differences between transaction-based marketing and relationship marketing? Transaction-based marketing refers to buyer–seller exchanges involving limited communications and little or no ongoing relationships between the parties. Relationship marketing is the development and maintenance of long-term, cost-effective relationships with individual customers, suppliers, employees, and other partners for mutual benefit.

2.1 What are the four basic elements of relationship marketing? The four basic elements are database technology, database marketing, monitoring relationships, and customer relationship management (CRM).

2.2 Why is internal marketing important to a firm? Internal marketing enables all members of the organization to understand, accept, and fulfill their respective roles in implementing a marketing strategy.

3.1 Identify the three levels of the marketing relationship. The three levels of the relationship marketing continuum are (1) focus on price, (2) social interaction, and (3) interdependent partnership.

3.2 Which level is the most complicated? Why? The third level is most complex because the strength of commitment between the parties grows.

4.1 How is customer satisfaction measured? Marketers monitor customer satisfaction through various marketing research methods.

4.2 Identify the ways marketers may obtain customer feedback. Marketers can include a toll-free phone number or Web site address in their advertising; monitor Usenet, other online discussion groups, and blogs; and hire mystery shoppers to personally check on products.

5.1 Describe two ways marketers keep customers. Through frequency marketing—frequent-buyer or -user marketing programs that reward customers with cash, rebates, merchandise, or other premiums. A second way is through affinity marketing—a marketing effort sponsored by an organization that solicits responses from individuals who share common interests and activities.

5.2 List three efforts that turn customers into advocates for products. Relationship marketing efforts that turn customers from passive partners into advocates include grassroots marketing, viral marketing, and buzz marketing.

6.1 Define *customer relationship management*. Customer relationship management is the combination of strategies and technologies that empowers relationship programs, reorienting the entire organization to a concentrated focus on satisfying customers.

6.2 What are the two major types of CRM systems? The two major types of CRM systems are purchased and customized.

6.3 Describe two steps a firm can take to rejuvenate a lost relationship. Marketers can rejuvenate a lost relationship by changing the product mix, if necessary, or changing some of their processes.

7.1 What are the four key types of business marketing partnerships? The four key types of business partnerships are buyer, seller, internal, and lateral.

7.2 Distinguish between cobranding and comarketing. Cobranding joins two strong brand names—perhaps owned by two different companies—to sell a product. In a comarketing effort, two organizations join to sell their products in an allied marketing campaign.

8.1 Name four technologies businesses can use to improve buyer–seller relationships in B2B markets. The use of electronic data interchanges allows firms to reduce costs and improve efficiency and competitiveness. Web services provide a way for companies to communicate even if they are not running the same or compatible software, hardware, databases, or network platforms. In a vendor-managed inventory (VMI) system, sellers can automatically restock to previously requested levels. The collaborative planning, forecasting, and replenishment (CPFaR) approach bases plans and forecasts on collaborative seller–vendor efforts.

8.2 What are the benefits of effective supply chain management? Managing the supply chain provides increased innovation, decreased costs, conflict resolution, and improved communications.

9.1 Define *lifetime value of a customer*. In the lifetime value of a customer, the revenues and intangible benefits a customer brings to the seller over an average lifetime—less the amount the company must spend to acquire, market to, and service the customer—are calculated.

9.2 Why are customer complaints valuable in evaluating customer relationship programs? Customer complaints give the organization information about customer priorities so managers can make changes to their systems, if necessary, and set appropriate, measurable goals for relationship programs.

Marketing Terms You Need to Know

transaction-based marketing 310
relationship marketing 310
external customers 312
internal customers 312
internal marketing 313
employee satisfaction 313
customer satisfaction 316
customer churn 318
frequency marketing 319
affinity marketing 319

database marketing 319
interactive television 320
application service providers
  (ASPs) 320
grassroots marketing 320
viral marketing 321
buzz marketing 321
customer relationship management
  (CRM) 321
customer win-back 323

business-to-business (B2B)
  marketing 324
partnership 325
buyer partnership 325
seller partnership 325
internal partnership 325
lateral partnership 326
cobranding 326
comarketing 326
national account selling 327

electronic data interchange
  (EDI) 327
quick-response merchandising 327
Web services 327
vendor-managed inventory (VMI) 328
collaborative planning, forecasting,
  and replenishment (CPFaR) 328
supply chain 328
strategic alliance 329
lifetime value of a customer 330

Assurance of Learning Review

1. Describe the benefits of relationship marketing. How does database technology help firms build relationships with customers?
2. What types of factors might the firm monitor in its relationships?
3. What is an affinity marketing program?
4. Distinguish among grassroots marketing, viral marketing, and buzz marketing.
5. Describe at least four qualities of a successful CRM system.
6. Explain how marketers can turn customers into advocates.
7. Describe each of the four types of business partnerships.
8. Why is it important for a firm to manage the relationships along its supply chain?
9. What is the most important factor in a strategic alliance?
10. Explain how a firm goes about evaluating the lifetime value of a customer.

Projects and Teamwork Exercises

1. With a teammate, choose one of the following companies. Create a plan to attract customers at the first level of the relationship marketing continuum—price—and move them to the next level with social interactions. Present your plan to the class.
   a. dog-grooming service
   b. health spa
   c. surfboard or snowmobile manufacturer
   d. pizza parlor
2. With a teammate, select a business you are familiar with and design a frequency marketing program for the firm. Now design a grassroots, viral marketing, or buzz marketing campaign for the company you selected. Present your campaign to the class.
3. A hotel chain's database has information on guests, including demographics, number of visits, and room preferences. Describe how the chain can use this information to develop several relationship marketing programs. How can it use a more general database to identify potential customers and personalize its communications with them?
4. Select a local business enterprise. Find out as much as you can about its customer base, marketing strategies, and internal functions. Consider whether a customer relationship management focus would sharpen the enterprise's competitive edge. Argue your position in class.
5. Choose a company that makes great stuff—something you really like, whether it is designer handbags, electronics, the tastiest ice cream flavors, or the best jeans. Now come up with a partner for your firm that you think would make a terrific strategic alliance. Write a plan for your alliance, explaining why you made the choice, what you want the two firms to accomplish, and why you think the alliance will be successful.

Critical-Thinking Exercises

1. Suppose you were asked to be a marketing consultant for a restaurant specializing in a regional cuisine such as Tex-Mex, Cuban dishes, or New England clambake. The owner is concerned about employee satisfaction. When you visit the restaurant, what clues would you look for to determine employee satisfaction? What questions might you ask employees?
2. What types of social interaction might be appropriate—and effective—for a local bank to engage in with its customers?

3. What steps might a clothing store take to win back its lost customers?

4. Explain why a large firm such as General Mills might use national account selling to strengthen its relationship with a major supermarket chain.

5. Why is it important for a company to calculate the lifetime value of a customer?

Ethics Exercise

Suppose you work for a firm that sells home appliances such as refrigerators, microwaves, and washers and dryers. Your company has been slowly losing customers, but no one seems to know why. Employee morale is sliding as well. You believe the company is run by honest, dedicated owners who want to please their customers. One day, you overhear an employee quietly advising a potential customer to shop at another store. You realize your firm's biggest problem may be lack of employee satisfaction—which is leading to external customer loss.

1. Would you approach the employee to discuss the problem?

2. Would you ask the employee why he or she is turning customers away?

3. What steps do you think your employer could take to turn the situation around?

Internet Exercises

1. **Cobranding.** Use a search engine such as Google or Bing to find three examples of cobranding similar to the Delta Skymiles credit card from American Express.
http://www.201.americanexpress.com/getthecard/home?source=prosphp_inav-personalcards

2. **CRM software.** ACT! is a type of customer relationship management software. Visit the Web site shown here and prepare a brief report about ACT! software and how it can improve marketing relationships.
http://www.act.com/

3. **Rewards programs.** Virtually all hotels and airlines have customer loyalty rewards programs. Go to the Web sites listed here to learn more about the rewards programs offered by Southwest Airlines and Starwood hotels. Prepare a brief report comparing the two programs.
http://www.southwest.com/rapid_rewards/?int=GNAVRPDRWDS&disc=&ss=0
http://www.starwoodhotels.com/preferredguest/index.html

Note: Internet Web addresses change frequently. If you don't find the exact site listed, you may need to access the organization's home page and search from there or use a search engine such as Google or Bing.

Case 10.1   *Microsoft Uses Partnership to Hedge Its Bet on Bing*

When Microsoft recently unveiled its own search engine, Bing, skeptics said it would have a tough time making inroads on Google's dominance of the search industry, where revenue is generated by advertising. It's true that Bing has struggled to become a viable contender.

Microsoft has already invested more than $5 billion trying to build an online business that can make money, and its online services business is still losing millions of dollars. But Bing has managed so far to gain a little more than 11 percent of the search market, and Microsoft is pinning its hopes for the infant search engine on a new ten-year partnership with Yahoo!, which holds about 17 percent of the market. Google claims an intimidating 65 percent and earns overall annual revenues of more than $23 billion.

"As soon as we close and implement the Yahoo! deal, we have achieved a milestone: for advertisers, we are a credible No. 2," says Microsoft's senior vice president of online audience business.

"Really, now, the goal is about share gain. If we grow share, we will grow our way into profitability, and we have confidence we can do that."

Once approved by U.S. regulators, the deal will give Microsoft effective control of a nearly 30 percent share of the search market by making it Yahoo!'s underlying search engine. "At 30 points we are now a credible option, so that number matters," says Microsoft's senior vice president. "The nice thing is we can say [to advertisers], you can be close to 30 percent share in one easy buy. That 30 percent carries a lot of weight in the marketplace. . . . There's no question we intend to make a profit. . . . Clearly there's a huge return in the search marketplace that can more than make up for the investments we've put in to this point. . . . Every day that we grow a tenth of point of share, that moves us further up the curve."

Bing is already a successful application for Apple's iPhone, but Microsoft isn't saying whether it will add a partnership with Apple to its Yahoo! agreement. Meanwhile Google's share of the search market adds up to ad revenues of more than $23 billion a year. "Ultimately we want to be a major player at scale, so we're going to have to grow against Google at some point," Microsoft's vice president acknowledged.

Some observers looking at Yahoo!'s prospects are concerned that the Bing-Yahoo! partnership may lower Yahoo!'s stock value, at least in the short term, and possibly complicate Microsoft's attempts to buy Yahoo!. Adding Bing may also hurt Yahoo!, they say, in its

own continuing challenge to Google's increasing online dominance. Other problems that still face Bing are related to Microsoft's decreasing dominance of the Internet browser market. Its Internet Explorer no longer dominates the scene, and newer browsers like Safari, Mozilla, Opera, and Chrome have taken share. Users of these programs don't have to rely on Bing, cutting the new search engine's potential audience.

Microsoft is undeterred, however. It recently unwrapped a new feature that lets Bing users looking for travel, health, leisure, and shopping view images of their search results instead of poring over pages of text-based links. It's also planning ways to tailor Bing for international audiences.

Questions for Critical Thinking

1. Which partner do you think has more to gain from the Microsoft-Yahoo! partnership, Microsoft or Yahoo!? Why?

2. What possible disadvantages could the partnership have for the two firms? Which one do you think has more to lose, and why?

Sources: G. Garza, "Bing Success! But Online Services Failure," http://windows7news.com, February 13, 2010; Doug Caverly, "Microsoft Exec Talks Bing Success/Profitability," *WebProNews*, www.webpronews.com, February 3, 2010; Bill Rigby, "Microsoft's Bing Will Make Money: Executive," *Reuters*, www.reuters.com, February 2, 2010; Mike Harvey, "Bing Looms Larger in Google's Rear-View Mirror in Race for Search Supremacy," *The Times* (London), www.timesonline.co.uk, September 17, 2009.

Video Case 10.2
Relationship Marketing and CRM at Numi Tea

Chances are, if you've heard of Numi Tea, you heard about it from someone else. Jennifer Mullin, vice president of marketing for the company, explains that this is by design. "That person really believes in the tea and is sharing the tea," she says. "It's far more credible than us saying,

'Hey, try our tea,' because, obviously, we're Numi Tea." Numi Tea was started in 1999 by brother and sister team Ahmed and Reem Rahim. Keeping it in the family is big at Numi. Reem's artwork adorns every box of tea. Their childhood friend, Hammad Atassi, is their director of food service. Every member of the Tea'm, as they call it, is committed to the company's core values of sustainability, creativity, and quality organics. This extends to their corporate customers and their producers, as well. Like their teas, every relationship is carefully cultivated and maintained.

"We focus on sampling versus the traditional marketing methods such as print or TV advertising because, for us, the conversion

happens when people taste Numi Tea," explains Mullin. Numi has found that few remember their print ads, but they remember the taste of the tea and Reem's artwork on the package. Sampling has become a very popular marketing tactic. It is big business, too. An entire industry has popped up to place products in gift bags for events ranging from local events to the Oscars. Aware that most of their best marketing is done friend to friend, Numi started a Tea Champions program. Numi sends thank-you packages to fans and provides them with free tea and educational literature on their fair-trade producers and the health benefits of natural and organic teas they can share with their friends.

Maintaining a close relationship with their end-users has been relatively easy. Free stuff goes a long way toward winning over the average consumer. "The food service customer tends to really just have one provider that they want to partner with," says Hammad. "You're either in or you're out. So marketing to the food service customer is unique. You've gotta really make it a program that's easy for them to execute and you have to have the support to drive sales—whether it's signage, customized menu cards, a big poster."

Numi has been fortunate to be the tea of choice in high-end restaurants, hotel chains, and cruise lines. The food service industry in total makes up about 40 percent of their business. Along with that comes added pressure to deliver on price, quality, and customer service. While they clearly lead in quality, it is hard for any small company to compete with the giant food service companies on price. An important part of Numi Tea is their story. To tell that story, they need to forge very hands-on, personal relationships with restaurant food and beverage managers, giving them a natural competitive advantage. A regular teabag may be cheaper, but there's not much else to say about it. When Hammad can conduct a private cupping (tea tasting) for the kitchen staff and explain all the different exotic teas, talk about the farms and farmers, their commitment to sustainability, organic farming and events in their local community, it's pretty much a slam dunk before the tea is even steeped. Turnover is notoriously high in the food service industry, so there's always a chance that a new chef or buyer will go another direction. Luckily for Numi, this hasn't been the case. Due in part to their excellent customer relationships, it is more common for them to keep the old client and follow the chef or buyer to his new restaurant.

Their success in the food service industry has driven retail business. While there are countless testimonials about customers experiencing Numi tea at a friend's house for the first time, a surprising number of Numi converts come from restaurants. As the requests from consumers wanting to know where to get Numi in their area have rolled in, Numi has needed to expand to their retail customers. Once available only at natural food stores and cafés, Numi has begun to sell teas in stores, including Target, large grocery chains, and even some warehouse club stores. While good for the consumer, this poses a tricky proposition to the Hammads' carefully maintained fine dining customer relationships. It could present a problem if the same premium tea served at a restaurant is also available at a local Target. Luckily, so far the two channels have co-existed peacefully.

As the company grows, one of the biggest challenges to its marketing model will be maintaining the family feel on a global scale. Jennifer Mullin and her team have begun tailoring e-mail communications to newsletter subscribers to inform them about local events and are hoping to add some regional sales and marketing teams in the near future. They've also added Numi fan sites on Facebook and Twitter. The sites are monitored by a staffer to address any questions or concerns about the products. Most importantly, no matter how busy they may get, founders Ahmed and Reem will always be there, lending their personal touch through their art, personal stories, and experiences.

Questions

1. How do marketing activities such as gift with purchase, samples by mail, and product community blogs affect your purchasing decisions and loyalty? What was the last product you purchased because of sampling?

2. Do you consider Numi's relationships with its producers as important to their marketing as the relationships with its customers?

© CENGAGE LEARNING

This Isn't Your Father's Honda ... or Is It?

When you think about the kind of people who buy hybrid and alternative fuel cars, you're probably picturing a handful of smug, hipster vegetarians tooling around Seattle or San Francisco or Vermont. There's probably a lot of political bumper stickers on the back of the car. Maybe there's a kayak or mountain bike on the roof.

A few years ago, you'd probably be right.

When the Honda Insight, the carmaker's first consumer hybrid car hit the market in 2000, Roger Schofield, owner of Schofield Honda in Wichita, Kansas, thought he had it all figured out. For one thing, Wichita isn't exactly known as the epicenter of eco-consumerism. He'd probably sell a handful of the combination Nickel-Metal Hydride rechargeable cell/internal combustion-engine, gas-powered cars to a couple of single 20-somethings. The thing only had two seats and seemed pretty flimsy with its lightweight aluminum body. With a sticker price of $20,000, it was pretty pricey, too.

The first Insight Scholfield sold went to a 63-year-old.

The second person to buy one was 65.

As it turns out, Scholfield's experience was consistent with Honda's marketing research. They determined that the typical Insight customer was older, highly educated, probably with an engineering or science background—people who tend to be very research-driven. Nearly a decade later, almost every auto manufacturer has a hybrid car, SUV, or truck on the showroom floor.

Lee Lindquist, an employee at Schofield Honda, had always been interested in technology and the environment. As a member of the Sierra Club, an environmental group, he would often speak about the environmental impact of automobiles. He found that audiences were really interested not just in the fuel-efficient hybrids, but in alternative fuels as well. Lindquist did some research and learned that Honda had been selling a natural gas car to the City of Los Angeles since 1998. Because this car ran exclusively on natural gas, it was considered by the EPA to be the cleanest internal combustion motor in the market. Everything about the car was the same as a traditional Honda Civic—except the polluting emissions.

Lindquist asked Scholfield if he could try to bring a Natural Gas Civic GX to Wichita with the intention of selling the idea to large companies as a fleet car and to Los Angeles for municipal use. His pitch was simple. Once the municipality or company invested in the natural gas fueling station, fill-ups would be incredibly cheap—the equivalent of about $1.00 a gallon with the added plus of limiting their impact on the environment. It was a great value proposition. Selling the car to the Average Joe was another matter entirely. The fueling stations cost thousands but, even with the lower prices at the pump, it would be hard to justify that kind of expense.

When Scholfield heard the news that a tornado wiped out the small town of Greensburg, Kansas, he knew he had to help. Initially, the dealership made a generous cash donation to the relief efforts. When the news broke that the town had decided to rebuild green, Lindquist saw an opportunity to reintroduce the Civic GX to the people of Kansas. His thinking was simple. In rural farming communities, people are naturally greener than their city cousins; the environment is their livelihood, and the notion of conserving and recycling resources is a necessity, not a fad or a slogan on a T-shirt. It is not uncommon for farmers—large and small—to have propane or other sources of fuel to power their farming equipment. Kansas, and Greensburg in particular, provide a large percentage of the country's natural gas. About 100 of the county's residents lease parts of their land to gas companies to put in pumps and pipelines.

For Scholfield, it took a little more convincing. In the end, he decided to go for it. As he drove the Civic GX two hours west on Highway 54 to Greensburg, he started to have second thoughts. Wouldn't the $25,000 the car was going to set him back be better spent on a few prime-time local ads? What's a farmer going to do with a little Honda? In the end, he figured, at the very least, with all the media attention Greensburg was getting, their name would be out there.

In a well-attended ceremony, Roger Scholfield handed the keys to the natural gas Civic to Daniel Wallach of Greensburg GreenTown. Residents came to check it out. No sales were made that day, but the story broadcast on KAKE, Wichita's ABC affiliate, and was picked up nationwide. Before long, city and fleet managers from around the region, not just the city, were looking for the GX.

Questions

1. What are the primary market(s) for the Honda Civic GX?

2. Does it make sense for Scholfield Honda to market their alternative fuel cars to a mass audience? What are the upsides and downsides to this practice?

3. How important is marketing research in promoting a new product?

4. How might the Scholfield Honda brand have suffered if the Greensburg promotion was a flop?

5. Go to a few automobile dealerships and record the sticker prices of some hybrid and conventional vehicles for similar classes (sedans, SUVs). Conduct a survey of ten people from one demographic group and construct a survey to determine at what price they would purchase a hybrid over a traditional vehicle. Write a memo to Schofield about the strategies that he should use to market hybrid vehicles to the market segment you've targeted and support your conclusions with the data from your research.

Product
Decisions

PART 4

Chapter 11
Product and Service Strategies

Chapter 12
Developing and Managing Brand and Product Categories

1 Define *product*, and distinguish between goods and services and how they relate to the goods–services continuum.

2 Outline the importance of the service sector in today's marketplace.

3 List the classifications of consumer goods and services, and briefly describe each category.

4 Identify each of the types of business goods and services.

5 Discuss how quality is used by marketers as a product strategy.

6 Explain why firms develop lines of related products.

7 Describe the way marketers typically measure product mixes and make product mix decisions.

8 Explain the concept of the product lifecycle.

9 Discuss how a firm can extend a product's lifecycle, and explain why certain products may be deleted.

ch11 Product
and Service Strategies

Massage Envy Builds a Following among the Stress-Weary • • • Consider it a sign of the times, or think of it as a society that's suddenly burning the candle at both ends. Either way, according to the American Massage Therapy Association, these days

Americans in unprecedented numbers are seeking the therapeutic benefits of massage. Whether for simple relaxation, to reduce stress, ease muscle strain, manage pain, or rehabilitate from earlier injuries, American consumers of all ages are finding relief in massage therapy. And the provider of millions of those therapeutic treatments is an entrepreneurial start-up known as Massage Envy.

Founded in Scottsdale, Arizona, Massage Envy has quickly risen to become the largest therapeutic massage provider in the nation. Its credentialed massage professionals practice the full range of massage types, including Swedish massage, trigger point therapy, deep muscle massage, sports massage, prenatal massage for expectant mothers, and reflexology. Massage Envy is structured as a franchise operation. Today, nearly 500 franchisees currently operate one or more of the 600 Massage Envy outlets located in 42 states.

The entrepreneurs behind Massage Envy thought about the reasons people don't indulge in massage more often, and the two main reasons they identified were time and price. This conclusion led them to structure their business differently—on a membership basis, making the services more convenient and affordable while also ensuring appropriate service delivery from a massage therapy professional. Under the terms of the program, customers can book their first massage at a special introductory price of $39; thereafter, they can purchase a membership. This arrangement includes a monthly fee that entitles members to one prepaid 50-minute massage each month (unused massages roll over to the next month). Membership benefits also include discounts on additional monthly massages, reduced monthly rates for family members, and guest passes. What's more, members can use their membership at any Massage Envy location nationwide.

And despite recent turbulence in the U.S. economy, which saw consumers become cautious in their discretionary spending habits, Massage Envy's popularity continues to grow. It recently reported performing its 20-millionth massage and is recorded in the *Guinness Book*

COURTESY OF MASSAGE ENVY

evolution of a brand

Massage Envy has managed to build a successful franchise operation across the United States, offering a service that many would characterize as a "nice to have" rather than a necessity.

- In the midst of its growth, Massage Envy expanded to include spa services and established a partnership with Murad to offer skin-care treatments using the Murad product line. Why would the company expand its service offerings?

of World Records for having the most individuals receiving a massage under the same roof at the same time (167).

With a business philosophy that includes an emphasis on wellness and healthy lifestyle, it may seem only natural that Massage Envy recently expanded into the spa business, opening new locations as full-service spas and converting some of its existing outlets into spas. Massage Envy is also the largest spa chain in America, opening its 100th spa, in Minneapolis, and promoting the belief that massage can restore life balance and enhance well-being. In addition, Massage Envy entered into an exclusive partnership with Murad Inc., pioneers in the skin-care industry, to provide skin-care treatments at their locations.

Massage Envy was recently named a top franchise by AllBusiness.com, Dun & Bradstreet's comprehensive online business aggregator. In addition, *Entrepreneur* magazine recognized Massage Envy as one of the nation's 20 fastest-growing franchise operations.[1]

• Massage Envy has differentiated itself as a chain in a market consisting primarily of small, independent businesses. Do you

think this feature works to the company's advantage? Why or why not?

chapter overview

briefly speaking

"Brand awareness is built by a thousand different inter-actions over time, where each one slightly builds or weakens [the customer's] impressions."

—Shelly Lazarus
(b. 1947)
CEO of Ogilvy & Mather
advertising agency

We've discussed how marketers conduct research to determine unfilled needs in their markets, how customers behave during the purchasing process, and how firms expand their horizons overseas. Now our attention shifts to a company's **marketing mix**, the blend of four elements of a marketing strategy—product, distribution, promotion, and price—to satisfy the target market. This chapter focuses on how companies like Massage Envy select and develop the goods and services they offer, starting with planning which products to offer. The other variables of the marketing mix—distribution channels, promotional plans, and pricing decisions—must accommodate the product strategy selected.

Marketers develop strategies to promote both tangible goods and intangible services. Any such strategy begins with investigation, analysis, and selection of a particular target market, and it continues with the creation of a marketing mix designed to satisfy that segment. Tangible goods and intangible services both intend to satisfy consumer wants and needs, but the marketing efforts supporting them may be vastly different. Many firms sell both types of products, offering innovative goods and ongoing service to attract and retain customers for the long term. Doing so can be profitable, as you'll see in this chapter.

This chapter examines the similarities and differences in marketing goods and services. It then presents basic concepts—product clas-sifications, development of product lines, and the product lifecycle—marketers apply in developing successful products. Finally, the chapter discusses product deletion and prod-uct mix decisions.

What Is a Product?

1 Define *product,* and distinguish between goods and services and how they relate to the goods–services continuum.

At first, you might think of a product as an object you hold in your hand, such as a baseball or a toothbrush. You might also think of the car you drive as a product. But this doesn't take into account the idea of a service as a product. Nor does it consider the idea of what the product is used for. So a television is more than a box with a screen and a remote control. It's really a means of providing entertainment—your favorite movies, news programs, or reality shows. Marketers acknowledge this broader conception of product; they realize that people buy *want satisfaction* rather than objects.

You might feel a need for a television to satisfy a want for entertainment. You might not know a lot about how the device itself works, but you understand the results. If you are entertained by watching TV, then your wants are satisfied. If, however, the television is working just fine but you don't like the programming offered, you may need to satisfy your desire for entertainment by changing your service package to include premium channels. The service—and its offerings—is a product.

Marketers think in terms of a product as a compilation of package design and labeling, brand name, price, availability, warranty, reputation, image, and customer service activities that add value for the customer. Consequently, a **product** is a bundle of physical, service, and symbolic attributes designed to satisfy a customer's wants and needs.

product Bundle of physical, service, and symbolic attributes designed to satisfy a customer's wants and needs.

 assessment check

1. Define *product*.
2. Why is the understanding of want satisfaction so important to marketers?

What Are Goods and Services?

Services are intangible products. A general definition identifies **services** as intangible tasks that satisfy the needs of consumer and business users. But you can't hold a service in your hand the way you can **goods**—tangible products customers can see, hear, smell, taste, or touch. Most service providers cannot transport or store their products; customers simultaneously buy and consume these products such as haircuts, car repairs, and visits to the dentist. One way to distinguish services from goods is the **goods–services continuum**, as shown in Figure 11.1.

This spectrum helps marketers visualize the differences and similarities between goods and services. A car is a pure good, but the dealer may also offer repair and maintenance services or include the services in the price of a lease. The car falls at the pure good extreme of the continuum because the repair or maintenance services are an adjunct to the purchase. A dinner at an exclusive restaurant is a mix of goods and services. It combines the physical goods of gourmet food with the intangible services of an attentive wait staff, elegant surroundings, and perhaps a visit to your table by the chef or restaurant owner to make sure your meal is perfect. At the other extreme, a dentist provides pure service—cleaning teeth, filling cavities, taking X-rays. The dentist's office may also sell items such as night guards, but it's the service that is primary in patients' minds.

You can begin to see the diversity of services. Services can be distinguished from goods in several ways:

1. *Services are intangible.* Services do not have physical features buyers can see, hear, smell, taste, or touch prior to purchase. Service firms essentially ask their customers to buy a promise—the haircut will be stylish, the insurance will cover injuries, the lawn will be mowed, and so on.

2. *Services are inseparable from the service providers.* Consumer perceptions of a service provider become their perceptions of the service itself. The name of a doctor, lawyer, or hair stylist is synonymous with the service they provide. A bad haircut can deter customers, while a good one will attract more to the salon. A house-cleaning service such as Merry Maids depends on its workers to leave each house spotless, because its reputation is built on this service.

services Intangible tasks that satisfy the needs of consumer and business users.

goods Tangible products customers can see, hear, smell, taste, or touch.

goods–services continuum Spectrum along which goods and services fall according to their attributes, from pure good to pure service.

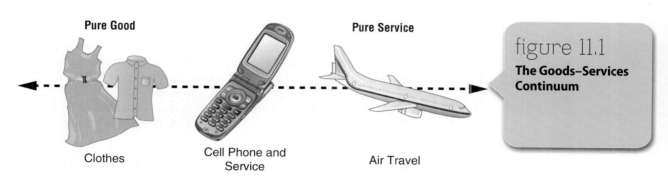

Pure Good

Pure Service

Clothes

Cell Phone and Service

Air Travel

figure 11.1
The Goods–Services Continuum

Service transactions, like a car rental, require interaction between buyer and seller.

© AP IMAGES/CARLOS OSORIO

3. *Services are perishable.* Providers cannot maintain inventories of their services. A day spa can't stockpile facials or pedicures. A travel agent can't keep quantities of vacations on a shelf. For this reason, some service providers such as airlines and hotels may raise their prices during times of peak demand—such as during spring break from school—and reduce them when demand declines.

4. *Companies cannot easily standardize services.* However, many firms are trying to change this. Most fast-food chains promise you'll get your meal within a certain number of minutes and it will taste the way you expect it to. A hotel chain may have the same amenities at each location—a pool, fitness room, free breakfast, and HBO movies.

5. *Buyers often play important roles in the creation and distribution of services.* Service transactions frequently require interaction between buyer and seller at the production and distribution stages. When a traveler arrives at the airport to pick up a rental car, he or she may have a choice of vehicle and additional amenities such as a GPS unit or car seat for a child. If the car is ready to go immediately, the customer will likely be satisfied. If the desired car is not available or is not clean or doesn't have a full tank of gas, the customer may not book with this company again.

6. *Service standards show wide variations.* New York City's posh Le Cirque and your local Pizza Hut are both restaurants. Depending on your expectations, both can be considered good restaurants. But the service standards at each vary greatly. At Le Cirque, you'll experience finely prepared cuisine served by a highly trained wait staff. At Pizza Hut, you may serve yourself fresh pizza from the buffet. If you receive your dinner from attentive wait staff at Le Cirque, you will be satisfied by the service standards. If the pizza at Pizza Hut is hot and fresh, and the buffet is replenished frequently, you will be satisfied by those standards as well.

Keep in mind that a product often blurs the distinction between services and goods. U-Haul is a service that rents trucks and moving vans, which are goods. LensCrafters provides eye examinations—services from optometrists—while also selling eyeglasses and contact lenses, which are goods.

 assessment check

1. Describe the goods–services continuum.
2. List the six characteristics distinguishing goods from services.

Importance of the Service Sector

2 Outline the importance of the service sector in today's marketplace.

You would live a very different life without service firms to fill many needs. You could not place a phone call, log on to the Internet, flip a switch for electricity, or even take a college course if organizations did not provide such services. During an average day, you probably use many services without much thought, but these products play an integral role in your life.

The service sector makes a crucial contribution to the U.S. economy in terms of products and jobs. Yet, only one of *Fortune*'s top ten most admired U.S. companies is a pure service firm—Google (two other service firms, Southwest Airlines and FedEx, rank 12th and 13th, respectively). But the other nine firms in the top ten, all listed in Figure 11.2, provide highly regarded services in conjunction with the goods they sell.[2]

The U.S. service sector now makes up more than two-thirds of the economy, as the shift from a goods-producing economy to a service-producing economy continues. According to the U.S. Department of Labor, service industries are expected to account for 4.1 million new jobs by the year 2018.[3]

Services also play a crucial role in the international competitiveness of U.S. firms. While the United States runs a continuing trade deficit in goods, it has maintained a trade surplus in services every year since 1992.[4] However, although some economists believe more precise measurements of service exports would reveal an even larger surplus, others worry about the effect of offshoring service jobs such as customer service call centers to nations such as India.

While some firms have found success with offshoring their call centers, others such as Transamerica Asset Management and United Airlines have decided to return much of their call center work to this country after receiving complaints from customers that they did not get the quality of support or service they needed.[5] Termed *backshoring,* this trend is growing and actually becoming a marketing tool for firms. "Foreign call centers feed into the perception that companies aren't interested in their customers," notes one marketing researcher. And some companies bringing their call centers back to the United States are taking another approach using home-based hourly workers, often managed by a private firm.[6]

An emerging trend, **homeshoring** enables firms to save on office space, furnishings, and supplies. In addition, most also save on health-care and other benefits. JetBlue is one well-known firm to practice homeshoring, with 900 home-based reservations agents based near Salt Lake City. Similarly, Miramar, Florida–based Arise Virtual Solutions supplies home-based employees to other companies, much the way an employment agency does. The practice is becoming so popular that some estimates expect the number of home-based call agents to exceed 300,000 by the year 2013.[7] Firms that practice homeshoring are experiencing another benefit: a reduction in the use of energy and other natural resources, which decreases these firms' impact on the environment. Because employees are not commuting to work every day, and because an office does not have to be heated, cooled, and supplied with electricity and water every day, firms not only experience reduced costs but also a drop in emissions. These companies can highlight their green practices in marketing messages to customers.[8]

Observers cite several reasons for the growing importance of services, including consumer desire for speed and convenience and technological advances that allow firms to fulfill this demand. Services involving wireless communications, data backup and storage, and even meal preparation for busy families are on the rise. Grocery chain Trader Joe's is benefiting from this need for quick meals by offering partially cooked, fully cooked, and

figure 11.2

America's Most Admired Companies

Source: "World's Most Admired Companies 2010," *Fortune,* March 22, 2010, http://money.cnn.com.

1. Apple
2. Google
3. Berkshire Hathaway
4. Johnson & Johnson
5. Amazon.com
6. Procter & Gamble
7. Toyota Motor
8. Goldman Sachs
9. Walmart
10. The Coca-Cola Company

homeshoring Hiring workers to do jobs from their homes.

Consumers are looking to advisors to help plan for a financially secure future.

help²achieve

Merrill Lynch Wealth Management
Bank of America Corporation

flash-frozen entrées that can be picked up and prepared in less time than meals made from scratch. Many traditional supermarkets offer prepared entrées and side dishes shoppers can buy at the store and heat quickly in the microwave at home. Consumers are also looking to advisors to help plan for a financially secure future and insurance to protect their homes and families.

Most service firms emphasize marketing as a significant activity for two reasons. First, the growth potential of service transactions represents a vast marketing opportunity. Second, the environment for services is changing. For instance, increased competition is forcing traditional service industries to differentiate themselves from their competitors. Providing superior service is one way to develop long-term customer relationships and compete more effectively. As we discussed earlier, relationship marketing is just one of the ways service firms can develop and solidify their customer relationships.

 assessment check

1. Identify two reasons services are important to the U.S. economy and business environment.
2. Why do service firms emphasize marketing?

Classifying Goods and Services for Consumer and Business Markets

consumer (B2C) product Product destined for use by ultimate consumers.

business-to-business (B2B) product Product that contributes directly or indirectly to the output of other products for resale; also called industrial or organizational product.

A firm's choices for marketing a good or service depend largely on the offering itself and on the nature of the target market. Product strategies differ for consumer and business markets. **Consumer (B2C) products** are those destined for use by ultimate consumers, while **business (B2B) products** (also called *industrial* or *organizational products*) contribute directly or indirectly to the output of other products for resale. Marketers further subdivide these two major categories into more specific categories, as discussed in this section.

Some products fall into both categories. A case in point is prescription drugs. Traditionally, pharmaceutical companies marketed prescription drugs to doctors, who then made the purchase decision for their patients by writing the prescription. These medications would be classified as a business product. However, many drug companies now advertise their products in consumer-oriented media, including magazines, television, and the Internet. This direct-to-consumer advertising tops $4.5 billion each year.[9]

Types of Consumer Products

unsought products Products marketed to consumers who may not yet recognize a need for them.

The most widely used product classification system focuses on the buyer's perception of a need for the product and his or her buying behavior. However, **unsought products** are marketed to consumers who may not yet recognize any need for them. Examples of unsought products are long-term-care insurance and funeral services.

However, relatively few products fall into the unsought category. Most consumers recognize their own needs for various types of consumer purchases and actively seek them, so the customer buying-behavior variations are key in distinguishing the various categories. The most common classification scheme for sought products divides consumer goods and services into three groups based on customers' buying behavior: convenience, shopping, and specialty. Figure 11.3 illustrates samples of these categories, together with the unsought classification.

convenience products Goods and services consumers want to purchase frequently, immediately, and with minimal effort.

CONVENIENCE PRODUCTS

Convenience products refer to goods and services consumers want to purchase frequently, immediately, and with minimal effort. Milk, bread, and toothpaste are convenience products. Convenience services include 24-hour quick-stop stores, walk-in hair or nail salons, copy shops, and dry cleaners.

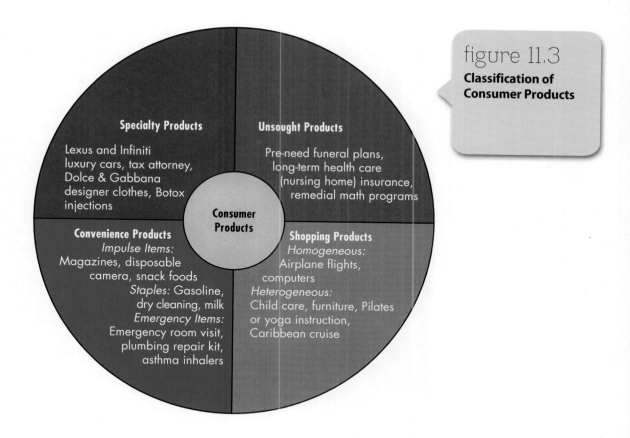

figure 11.3
Classification of Consumer Products

Marketers further subdivide the convenience category into impulse items, staples, or emergency items. **Impulse goods and services** are purchased on the spur of the moment—for example, a visit to a car wash or a pack of gum picked up at the supermarket register. Some marketers have even come up with ways to make impulse shopping on the Internet attractive. Last-minute shoppers can use ArtTownGifts.com's last-minute and emergency gifts service to choose and ship gifts quickly, even for same-day delivery. They can select balloon bouquets, flowers, fruit or wine baskets, and more. Emergency gifts don't come cheap—they range in price from about $40 to $215—but they fulfill an immediate need for goods and services. Shoppers can also sign up for the firm's reminder service, which sends them e-mail reminders of loved ones' birthdays, anniversaries, and any other occasion that might require a gift.[10]

Staples are convenience goods and services consumers constantly replenish to maintain a ready inventory: gasoline, shampoo, and dry cleaning are good examples. Marketers spend many hours and dollars creating messages for consumers about these products, partly because there are so many competitors.

Emergency goods and services are bought in response to unexpected and urgent needs. A snow blower purchased during a snowstorm and a visit to a hospital emergency room to treat a broken ankle are examples. Depending on your viewpoint, the products offered by ArtTownGifts.com's emergency service could also fall into this category.

Because consumers devote little effort to convenience product purchase decisions, marketers must strive to make these exchanges as simple as possible. Store location can boost a convenience product's visibility. Marketers compete vigorously for prime locations, which can make all the difference between a consumer choosing one gas station, vending machine, or dry cleaner over another.

In addition, location *within* a store can make the difference between success and failure of a product, which is why manufacturers fight so hard for the right spot on supermarket shelves. Typically, the largest grocery manufacturers such as Sara Lee, Kellogg, and General Mills get the most visible spots. But visibility to consumers sometimes comes at a price, often through a practice called *slotting allowances,* or *slotting fees*—money paid by producers to retailers to guarantee display of their merchandise. According to retailers, the purpose of slotting allowances is to cover their

impulse goods and services Products purchased on the spur of the moment.

staples Convenience goods and services consumers constantly replenish to maintain a ready inventory.

emergency goods and services Products bought in response to unexpected and urgent needs.

IMAGE COURTESY OF THE ADVERTISING ARCHIVES

> Staples are convenience goods and services that consumers constantly replenish to maintain a ready inventory. Marketers spend a significant amount of money creating messages for consumers about these products.

losses if products don't sell. But the Federal Trade Commission (FTC) investigated the practice of slotting allowances and found these fees vary greatly across product categories. In addition, a new trend regarding slotting allowances is emerging: growth in the private-label goods category has been so great over the past few years that retailers are willing to forfeit allowances they might receive so they can get into the manufacturing end themselves. This is particularly true of private-label organic and ethnic foods.

SHOPPING PRODUCTS

In contrast to the purchase of convenience items, consumers buy **shopping products** only after comparing competing offerings on such characteristics as price, quality, style, and color. Shopping products typically cost more than convenience purchases. This category includes tangible items such as clothing, furniture, electronics, and appliances as well as services such as child care, auto repairs, insurance, and hotel stays. The purchaser of a shopping product lacks complete information prior to the buying trip and gathers information during the buying process.

shopping products Products consumers purchase after comparing competing offerings.

Several important features distinguish shopping products: physical attributes, service attributes such as warranties and after-sale service terms, prices, styling, and places of purchase. A store's name and reputation have considerable influence on people's buying behavior. The personal selling efforts of salespeople also provide important promotional support.

Buyers and marketers treat some shopping products, such as refrigerators and washing machines, as relatively homogeneous products. To the consumer, one brand seems largely the same as another. Marketers may try to differentiate homogeneous products from competing products in several ways. They may emphasize price and value, or they may attempt to educate buyers about less obvious features that contribute to a product's quality, appeal, and uniqueness.

Other shopping products seem heterogeneous because of basic differences among them. Examples include furniture, physical-fitness training, vacations, and clothing. Differences in features often separate competing heterogeneous shopping products in the minds of consumers. Perceptions of style, color, and fit can all affect consumer choices.

SPECIALTY PRODUCTS

specialty products Products with unique characteristics that cause buyers to prize those particular brands.

Specialty products offer unique characteristics that cause buyers to prize those particular brands. They typically carry high prices, and many represent well-known brands. Examples of specialty goods include Hermès scarves, Kate Spade handbags, Ritz-Carlton resorts, Tiffany jewelry, and Lexus automobiles. Specialty services include professional services such as financial advice, legal counsel, and cosmetic surgery.

Purchasers of specialty goods and services know exactly what they want—and they are willing to pay accordingly. These buyers begin shopping with complete information, and they refuse to accept substitutes. Because consumers are willing to exert considerable effort to obtain specialty products, producers can promote them through relatively few retail locations. In fact, some firms intentionally limit the range of retailers carrying their products to add to their cachet. Both highly personalized service by sales associates and image advertising help marketers promote specialty items. Because these products are available in so few retail outlets, advertisements frequently list their locations or give toll-free telephone numbers that provide customers with this information.

In recent years, makers of some specialty products, such as Coach handbags and Donna Karan clothing, have broadened their market by selling some of their goods through company-owned discount outlets. The stores attract consumers who want to own specialty items but who cannot or do not wish to pay their regular prices. The goods offered, however, usually are last season's styles. Tiffany has taken a different approach—broadening its base within its own store. Shoppers who visit the store on Fifth Avenue in New York City can take the elevator to the second floor, where they may purchase a variety of items in sterling silver at prices significantly lower than those for gold and gemstone jewelry. A number of these items are also available in Tiffany's mail-order catalog.

Specialty products like those associated with Lexus offer unique characteristics that cause buyers to prize them, typically carry high prices, and represent well-known brands.

IMAGE COURTESY OF THE ADVERTISING ARCHIVES

Classifying Consumer Services

Like tangible goods, services are also classified based on the convenience, shopping, and specialty products categories. But added insights can be gained by examining several factors unique to classifying services. Service firms may serve consumer markets, business markets, or both. A firm offering architectural services may design either residential or commercial buildings or both. A cleaning service may clean houses, offices, or both. In addition, services can be classified as equipment based or people based. A car wash is an equipment-based service, whereas a law office is people based. Marketers may ask themselves any of these five questions to help classify certain services:

1. What is the nature of the service?

2. What type of relationship does the service organization have with its customers?

3. How much flexibility is there for customization and judgment on the part of the service provider?

4. Do demand and supply for the service fluctuate?

5. How is the service delivered?[11]

A person attempting to classify the activities of a boarding kennel would answer these questions in one way; a person evaluating a lawn-care service would come up with different answers. For example, customers would bring their pets to the kennel to receive service, while the lawn-care staff would travel to customers' homes to provide service. Workers at the kennel are likely to have closer interpersonal relationships with pet owners—and their pets—than lawn-care workers, who might not meet their customers at all. Someone assessing demand for the services of a ski resort or a food concession at the beach is likely to find fluctuations by season. And a dentist has flexibility in making decisions about a patient's care, whereas a delivery service must arrive with a package at the correct destination, on time.

3 List the classifications of consumer goods and services, and briefly describe each category.

Applying the Consumer Products Classification System

The three-way classification system of convenience, shopping, and specialty goods and services helps guide marketers in developing a successful marketing strategy. Buyer behavior patterns differ for the three types of purchases. For example, classifying a new food item as a convenience product leads to insights about marketing needs in branding, promotion, pricing, and distribution decisions. Table 11.1 summarizes the impact of this classification system on the development of an effective marketing mix.

The classification system, however, also poses a few problems. The major obstacle to implementing this system results from the suggestion that all goods and services must fit within one of the three categories. Some fit neatly into one category, but others share characteristics of more than one category. How would you classify the purchase of a new automobile? Before classifying the expensive good, which is handled by a few exclusive dealers in the area as a specialty product, consider other characteristics. New-car buyers often shop extensively among competing models and dealers before deciding on the best deal. And there is a wide range of models, features, and prices to consider. At one end of the spectrum is a basic car like a Kia Forte or a Chevrolet Aveo that could be purchased for less than $15,000. At the other end is what people are calling European supercars, such as the Lamborghini Murcielago, at $450,000, or the Aston Martin One-77, priced at more than $1 million. These cars are fast, powerful, and hard to find—which boosts their value.[12]

So it's a good idea to think of the categorization process in terms of a continuum representing degrees of effort expended by consumers. At one end of the continuum, they casually pick up convenience items; at the other end, they search extensively for specialty products. Shopping products fall between these extremes. In addition, car dealers may offer services, both during and after the sale, which play a big role in the purchase decision. On this continuum, the new car purchase might appear between the categories of shopping and specialty products but closer to specialty products.

A second problem with the classification system emerges because consumers differ in their buying patterns. One person may walk into a hair salon and request a haircut without an appointment, while another may check references and compare prices before selecting a stylist. But the first consumer's impulse purchase of a haircut does not make hair styling services a convenience item. Marketers classify goods and services by considering the purchase patterns of the majority of buyers.

table 11.1 Marketing Impact of the Consumer Products Classification System

	Convenience Products	Shopping Products	Specialty Products
Consumer Factors			
Planning time involved in purchase	Very little	Considerable	Extensive
Purchase frequency	Frequent	Less frequent	Infrequent
Importance of convenient location	Critical	Important	Unimportant
Comparison of price and quality	Very little	Considerable	Very little
Marketing Mix Factors			
Price	Low	Relatively high	High
Importance of seller's image	Unimportant	Very important	Important
Distribution channel length	Long	Relatively short	Very short
Number of sales outlets	Many	Few	Very few; often one
Promotion	Advertising and promotion by producer	Personal selling and advertising by producer and retailer	Personal selling and advertising by producer and retailer

assessment check

1. What are the three major classifications of consumer products?
2. Identify five factors marketers should consider in classifying consumer services.

Types of Business Products

Business buyers are professional customers. Their job duties require rational, cost-effective purchase decisions. For instance, General Mills applies much of the same purchase decision process to buying flour that Kellogg's does.

The classification system for business products emphasizes product uses rather than customer buying behavior. B2B products generally fall into one of six categories for product uses: installations, accessory equipment, component parts and materials, raw materials, supplies, and business services. Figure 11.4 illustrates the six types of business products.

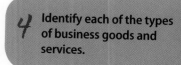

4 **Identify each of the types of business goods and services.**

INSTALLATIONS

The specialty products of the business market are called **installations**. This classification includes major capital investments for new factories and heavy machinery and for telecommunications systems. Purchases of new Boeing 787 Dreamliner airplanes by Qantas and Kenya Airways are considered installations for those airlines.

Because installations last for long periods of time and their purchases involve large sums of money, they represent major decisions for organizations. Negotiations often extend over several months and involve numerous decision makers. Vendors often provide technical expertise along with tangible goods. Representatives who sell custom-made equipment work closely with buying firms' engineers and production personnel to design the most satisfactory products possible.

installations Major capital investments in the B2B market.

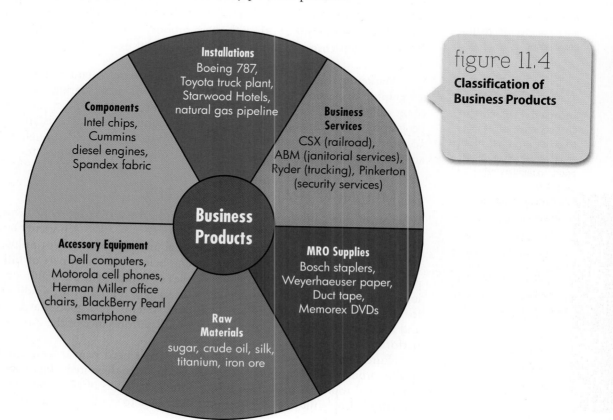

figure 11.4

Classification of Business Products

Installations
Boeing 787,
Toyota truck plant,
Starwood Hotels,
natural gas pipeline

Components
Intel chips,
Cummins
diesel engines,
Spandex fabric

Business Services
CSX (railroad),
ABM (janitorial services),
Ryder (trucking), Pinkerton
(security services)

Business Products

Accessory Equipment
Dell computers,
Motorola cell phones,
Herman Miller office
chairs, BlackBerry Pearl
smartphone

MRO Supplies
Bosch staplers,
Weyerhaeuser paper,
Duct tape,
Memorex DVDs

Raw Materials
sugar, crude oil, silk,
titanium, iron ore

Purchases of new Boeing 787 Dreamliner airplanes by Qantas and Kenya Airways are considered installations for those airlines.

Price typically does not dominate purchase decisions for installations, although two recent orders for Airbus 350 XWB aircraft—by United Airlines and US Airways—were valued at a total of $10 billion.[13] A purchasing firm buys such a product for its efficiency and performance over its useful life. The firm also wants to minimize breakdowns. Downtime is expensive because the firm must pay employees while they wait for repairs on a machine. In addition, customers may be lost during downtime; in this case, travelers might choose to fly with another airline. Installations are major investments often designed specifically for the purchasers. Training of the buyer's workforce to operate the equipment correctly, along with significant after-sale service, usually is also involved. As a result, marketers of these systems typically focus their promotional efforts on employing highly trained sales representatives, often with technical backgrounds. Advertising, if the firm uses it at all, emphasizes company reputation and directs potential buyers to contact local sales representatives.

Most installations are marketed directly from manufacturers to users. Even a one-time sale may require continuing contacts for regular product servicing. Some manufacturers prefer to lease extremely expensive installations to customers rather than sell the items outright, and they assign personnel directly to the lessees' sites to operate or maintain the equipment.

ACCESSORY EQUIPMENT

accessory equipment Capital items such as desktop computers and printers that typically cost less and last for shorter periods than installations.

Only a few decision makers may participate in a purchase of **accessory equipment**—capital items that typically cost less and last for shorter periods than installations. Although quality and service exert important influences on purchases of accessory equipment, price may significantly affect these decisions. Accessory equipment includes products such as power tools, computers, smartphones, and cell phones. Although these products are considered capital investments and buyers depreciate their costs over several years, their useful lives generally are much shorter than those of installations.

Marketing these products requires continuous representation and dealing with the widespread geographic dispersion of purchasers. To cope with these market characteristics, a wholesaler—often called an **industrial distributor**—might be used to contact potential customers in its own geographic area. Customers usually do not require technical assistance, and a manufacturer of accessory equipment can often distribute its products effectively through wholesalers. Advertising is an important component in the marketing mix for accessory equipment.

industrial distributor Channel intermediary that takes title to goods it handles and then distributes these goods to retailers, other distributors, or business or B2B customers; also called a *wholesaler*.

COMPONENT PARTS AND MATERIALS

component parts and materials Finished business products of one producer that become part of the final products of another producer.

Whereas business buyers use installations and accessory equipment in the process of producing their own final products, **component parts and materials** represent finished business products of one producer that become part of the final products of another producer. Some materials—for example, flour—undergo further processing before becoming part of finished products. Textiles, paper pulp, and chemicals are also examples of component parts and materials. Bose supplies its luxury sound systems to auto manufacturers such as Audi, Infiniti, Cadillac, and Ferrari. Marketers for the auto manufacturers believe that Bose systems are a good match between premium sound and their top-line vehicles, comparing the high performance of the Bose sound systems to the high performance of their cars.[14]

Purchasers of component parts and materials need regular, continuous supplies of uniform-quality products. They generally contract to purchase these items for set periods of time. Marketers commonly emphasize direct sales, and satisfied customers often become regular buyers. Wholesalers sometimes supply fill-in purchases and handle sales to smaller purchasers.

RAW MATERIALS

Farm products such as beef, cotton, eggs, milk, poultry, and soybeans, and natural resources such as coal, copper, iron ore, and lumber constitute **raw materials**. These products resemble component parts and materials in that they become part of the buyers' final products. Cargill supplies many of the raw materials for finished food products—dry corn ingredients, flour, food starch, oils and shortenings, soy protein and sweeteners, and beef and pork. Food manufacturers then take and turn these materials into finished products, including cake and bread.[15]

Most raw materials carry grades determined according to set criteria, assuring purchasers of the receipt of standardized products of uniform quality. As with component parts and materials, vendors commonly market raw materials directly to buying organizations. Wholesalers are increasingly involved in purchasing raw materials from foreign suppliers.

Price is seldom a deciding factor in a raw materials purchase since the costs often are set at central markets, determining virtually identical transactions among competing sellers. Purchasers buy raw materials from the firms they consider best able to deliver the required quantities and qualities.

> **raw materials** Natural resources such as farm products, coal, copper, or lumber that become part of a final product.

SUPPLIES

If installations represent the specialty products of the business market, operating supplies are its convenience products. **Supplies** constitute the regular expenses a firm incurs in its daily operations. These expenses do not become part of the buyer's final products.

Supplies are also called **MRO items** because they fall into three categories: (1) maintenance items, such as brooms, filters, and lightbulbs; (2) repair items, such as nuts and bolts used in repairing equipment; and (3) operating supplies, such as printer paper and cartridges, mouse batteries, and pens. Office Max sells all kinds of supplies to small, medium, and large businesses. Companies can purchase everything from paper and labels to filing cabinets, lighting, computers, and copiers. The firm also offers printing and binding services, downloadable forms, and more.[16]

A purchasing manager regularly buys operating supplies as a routine job duty. Wholesalers often facilitate sales of supplies because of the low unit prices, the small order size, and the large number of potential buyers. Because supplies are relatively standardized, heavy price competition frequently keeps costs under control. However, a business buyer spends little time making decisions about these products. Exchanges of products frequently demand simple telephone, Web or EDI orders, or regular purchases from a sales representative of a local wholesaler.

> **supplies** Regular expenses a firm incurs in its daily operations.
>
> **MRO items** Business supplies that include maintenance items, repair items, and operating supplies.

BUSINESS SERVICES

The **business services** category includes the intangible products firms buy to facilitate their production and operating processes. Examples of business services are financial services, leasing and rental services that supply equipment and vehicles, insurance, security, legal advice, and consulting. As mentioned earlier, many service providers sell the same services to both consumers and organizational buyers—telephone, gas, and electricity, for example—although service firms may maintain separate marketing groups for the two customer segments.

Organizations also purchase many adjunct services that assist their operations but are not essentially a part of the final product. Cisco Systems offers its TelePresence Meeting service to businesses seeking to link people in a single interactive conference. The service combines voice, data, and video on the same network, providing an interactive and collaborative experience for participants.[17]

> **business services** Intangible products firms buy to facilitate their production and operating processes.

> Office Max sells MRO products to small, medium, and large businesses.

© JUSTIN SULLIVAN/GETTY IMAGES

table 11.2   Marketing Impact of the Business Products Classification System

Factor	Installations	Accessory Equipment	Component Parts and Materials	Raw Materials	Supplies	Business Services
Organizational Factors						
Planning time	Extensive	Less extensive	Less extensive	Varies	Very little	Varies
Purchase frequency	Infrequent	More frequent	Frequent	Infrequent	Frequent	Varies
Comparison of price and quality	Quality very important	Quality and price important	Quality important	Quality important	Price important	Varies
Marketing Mix Factors						
Price	High	Relatively high	Low to high	Low to high	Low	Varies
Distribution channel length	Very short	Relatively short	Short	Short	Long	Varies
Promotion method	Personal selling by producer	Advertising	Personal selling	Personal selling	Advertising by producer	Varies

Price may strongly influence purchase decisions for business services. The buying firm must decide whether to purchase a service or provide that service internally. This decision may depend on how frequently the firm needs the service and the specialized knowledge required to provide it. In the case of TelePresence, firms may decide the cost of the service is offset by savings in travel expenses for meeting participants. In addition, the service offers convenience.

Purchase decision processes vary considerably for different types of business services. A firm may purchase window-cleaning services through a routine and straightforward process similar to buying operating supplies. By contrast, a purchase decision for highly specialized environmental engineering advice requires complex analysis and perhaps lengthy negotiations similar to purchases of installations. This variability of the marketing mix for business services and other business products is outlined in Table 11.2.

The purchase of the right business services can make a difference in a firm's competitiveness. The Regus Group provides businesses with facilities for meetings and conferences in 450 cities across 75 countries. The more than 1,000 facilities are fully furnished and equipped with every electronic medium and amenity a business could possibly need and are staffed by trained support personnel. Regus serves large and small companies, including those relying on mobile and home-based workers. The firm's services allow businesses to customize their office and meeting needs while saving money during periods when office space is not necessary.[18]

 assessment check

1. What are the six main classifications of business products?
2. What are the three categories of supplies?

Quality as a Product Strategy

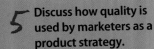

5 Discuss how quality is used by marketers as a product strategy.

No matter how a product is classified, nothing is more frustrating to a customer than having a new item break after just a few uses or having it not live up to expectations. The cell phone that hisses static at you unless you stand still or the seam that rips out of your new jacket aren't life-altering experiences, but they do leave an impression of poor quality that likely will lead you

career readiness Giving Helpful Feedback

All consumers have positive and negative experiences with the goods and services they purchase. When companies ask for feedback, they are looking for information that will help them improve the products they offer, either by enhancing the items themselves or the services that support them. You can use your training as a marketer to provide valuable feedback to companies. When doing so, keep in mind the following tips:

- *Be honest.* Describe clearly and accurately your experience with the company and its products, including salespeople, tech support, and anyone else with whom you have contact. If you were dissatisfied, avoid engaging in an angry tirade; instead, calmly outline the facts.

- *Be concise.* Include only the details most relevant to the product's performance. In that way, the company can concentrate on exactly what needs improvement. Don't go into a long description unless you are asked for more information.

- *Be polite.* Avoid rude language or comments. The point is to find a solution to a problem, if one exists, not to offend those asking for your views.

- *Be positive.* Don't forget to tell the firm what *does* work and what you like about its products. Positive feedback lets a company know what it is doing right. Try to give specific examples—features of the products, results you've had, and so on.

- *Offer suggestions.* You might not be able to give a design engineer the specs to improve your car's interior, but you could say, "It would be great if I had a place to store my iPod," or "I wish the cup holder was easier to reach."

- *Thank the company for listening.* Even if you are taking an online survey, offer a thank-you to the firm if there is space for additional comments. The company's marketers will know you appreciate the opportunity to give feedback, and they might contact you for further insights.

Sources: eBay, "Feedback Etiquette," http://reviews.ebay.com, accessed April 30, 2010; IBM, "Forum Use and Etiquette," http://www.ibm.com, accessed April 30, 2010; Amy Gallo, "How to Give Your Boss Feedback," *Harvard Business Review*, March 24, 2010, http://blogs.hbr.org.

---

to make different purchases in the future. Then there's the issue of service quality—the department store that seems to have no salespeople or the computer help line that leaves you on hold for 20 minutes.

Quality is a key component to a firm's success in a competitive marketplace. The efforts to create and market high-quality goods and services have been referred to as **total quality management (TQM)**. TQM expects all of a firm's employees to continually improve products and work processes with the goal of achieving customer satisfaction and world-class performance. This means engineers design products that work, marketers develop products people want, and salespeople deliver on their promises. Managers are responsible for communicating the goals of total quality management to all staff members and for encouraging workers to improve themselves and take pride in their work. Of course, achieving maximum quality is easier said than done, and the process is never complete. Many companies solicit reviews or feedback from customers to improve their goods and services. As a customer, you can provide valuable insight to marketers by providing honest feedback, as described in the "Career Readiness" feature.

total quality management (TQM) Continuous effort to improve products and work processes with the goal of achieving customer satisfaction and world-class performance.

Worldwide Quality Programs

Although the movement began in the United States in the 1920s as an attempt to improve product quality by improving the manufacturing process, it was during the 1980s when the quality revolution picked up speed in U.S. corporations. The campaign to improve quality found the leaders at large manufacturing firms—such as Ford, Xerox, and Motorola—had lost market share to Japanese competitors. Smaller companies that supplied parts to large firms then began to recognize quality as a requirement for success. Today, commitment to quality has spread to service industries, not-for-profit organizations, government agencies, and educational institutions.

Congress established the Malcolm Baldrige National Quality Award to recognize excellence in quality management. Named after the late secretary of commerce Malcolm Baldrige, the award is the highest national recognition for quality a U.S. company can receive. The award works toward promoting quality awareness, recognizing quality achievements of U.S. companies, and publicizing successful quality strategies.

The quality movement is also strong in European countries. The European Union's ISO 9001:2000 standards define international, generic criteria for quality management and quality assurance. Originally developed by the International Organization for Standardization in Switzerland to ensure consistent quality among products manufactured and sold throughout the European Union (EU), the standards now include criteria for systems of management as well. Although most other ISO standards are specific to particular products or processes, ISO 9001 applies to any organization, regardless of the goods or services it produces. Many European companies require suppliers to achieve ISO certification, a rigorous process that takes several months to complete, as a condition of doing business with them. The U.S. member body of ISO is the National Institute of Standards and Technology (NIST).[19]

ISO 9001:2000 Standards developed by the International Organization for Standardization in Switzerland to ensure consistent quality management and quality assurance for goods and services throughout the European Union (EU).

Benchmarking

Firms often rely on an important tool called **benchmarking** to set performance standards. The purpose of benchmarking is to achieve superior performance that results in a competitive advantage in the marketplace. A typical benchmarking process involves three main activities: identifying manufacturing or business processes that need improvement, comparing internal processes to those of industry leaders, and implementing changes for quality improvement. The practice of benchmarking has been around for a long time. Henry Ford is known to have developed his own version of the assembly line—an improvement to gain competitive advantage—by observing the way meat-packing plants processed their meat products.[20]

Benchmarking requires two types of analyses: internal and external. Before a company can compare itself with another, it must first analyze its own activities to determine strengths and weaknesses. This assessment establishes a baseline for comparison. External analysis involves gathering information about the benchmark partner to find out why the partner is perceived as the industry's best. A comparison of the results of the analysis provides an objective basis for making improvements. Large firms engaged in benchmarking include 3M, Bank of America, DuPont, General Mills, and Kraft Foods. These firms conduct formal, complex programs, but smaller firms may decide to use benchmarking as well.[21]

benchmarking Method of measuring quality by comparing performance against industry leaders.

Quality of Services

Everyone has a story about bad and good service—the waiter who forgot a dinner order, a car mechanic who offered a ride to and from the repair shop. As a consumer, your perception of the quality of the service you have purchased usually is determined during the **service encounter**—the point at which the customer and service provider interact. Employees such as bank tellers, cashiers, and customer service representatives have a powerful impact on their customers' decision to return or not. You might pass the word to your friends about the friendly staff at your local breakfast eatery, the slow cashiers at a local supermarket, or the huge scoops of ice cream you got at the nearby ice cream stand. Those words form powerful marketing messages about the services you received.

Service quality refers to the expected and perceived quality of a service offering, and it has a huge effect on the competitiveness of a company. Online retailer Zappos.com (now part of Amazon) built its business on delivering exceptional customer service—for example, providing free shipping, maintaining a 365-day return policy, and paying rigorous attention to hiring only those whose passion for customer service matches the company's high standards. The decision

service encounter Point at which the customer and service provider interact.

service quality Expected and perceived quality of a service offering.

to focus on customer service rather than on marketing enabled Zappos to grow to a billion-dollar company. In fact, in a recent consumer survey on customer service, respondents gave Zappos the highest score: 88 of 100.[22]

Unfortunately, poor service can cut into a firm's competitiveness. When Salesforce.com experienced a software outage on a recent business day, cloud-computing customers throughout North America were momentarily stopped in their tracks. Although the system was restored less than 30 minutes later (along with an apology), the company offered no explanation for the outage.[23] Such glitches in customer service often lead consumers to switch to a competitor.

Service quality is determined by five variables:

1. *Tangibles,* or physical evidence. A tidy office and clean uniforms are examples.

2. *Reliability,* or consistency of performance and dependability. "The right technology. Right away," asserts software solutions provider CDW.

3. *Responsiveness,* or the readiness to serve. "Citi never sleeps," say the ads for the banking giant.

4. *Assurances,* or the confidence communicated by the service provider. "Let your worries go," reassures Northwestern Mutual, an investment and insurance firm.

5. *Empathy,* which shows the service provider understands customers' needs and is ready to fulfill them. "Clear your mind. Relax your soul," says Hotel Nikko San Francisco.

If a gap exists between the level of service customers expect and the level they think they received, it can be favorable or unfavorable. If you get a larger steak than you expected or your plane arrives ahead of schedule, the gap is favorable, and you are likely to try that service again. But if your steak is tiny, overcooked, and cold or your plane is two hours late, the gap is unfavorable, and you may seek out another restaurant or decide to drive the next time.

© ISTOCKPHOTO.COM/GENE CHUTKA

As a consumer, your perception of the quality of the service you have purchased is usually determined during the service encounter—the point at which the customer and the service provider interact.

briefly speaking

"If you can't smile, don't open a store."

—Chinese proverb

product line Series of related products offered by one company.

 assessment check

1. What is TQM?

2. What are the five variables of service quality?

Development of Product Lines

Few firms today market only one product. A typical firm offers its customers a **product line**—that is, a series of related products. The motivations for marketing complete product lines rather than concentrating on a single product include the desire to grow, enhancing the company's position in the market, optimal use of company resources, and exploiting the product lifecycle. The following subsections

6 Explain why firms develop lines of related products.

examine each of the first three reasons. The final reason, exploiting the stages of the product lifecycle, is discussed in the section that focuses on strategic implications of the product lifecycle concept.

Desire to Grow

A company limits its growth potential when it concentrates on a single product, even though the company may have started that way, as retailer L.L.Bean did with its single style of boots called Maine Hunting Shoes. Now the company sells boots for men, women, and children, along with apparel, outdoor and travel gear, home furnishings, and even products for pets. The company, which has grown into a large mail-order and online retailer with a flagship store in Freeport, Maine, is nearly a century old. It is unlikely the company would have grown to its current size if the successors of Leon Leonwood Bean had stuck to manufacturing and selling a single style of his original Maine Hunting Shoes.[24]

Enhancing the Company's Market Position

A company with a line of products often makes itself more important to both consumers and marketing intermediaries than a firm with only one product. A shopper who purchases a tent often buys related camping items. For instance, L.L.Bean now offers a wide range of products with which consumers can completely outfit themselves for outdoor activities or travel. They can purchase hiking boots, sleeping bags and tents, fishing gear, duffel bags, kayaks and canoes, bicycles, snowshoes and skis, as well as clothing for their adventures. In addition, the firm offers Outdoor Discovery Schools programs that teach customers the basics of kayaking, fly fishing, and other sports directly related to the products they purchase from the retailer. L.L.Bean also offers many of its products sized to fit children—from fleece vests to school backpacks.[25] If children grow up wearing L.L.Bean clothes and skiing on L.L.Bean skis, they are more likely to continue as customers when they become adults.

Servicing the variety of products a company sells can also enhance its position in the market. Bean's Outdoor Discovery Schools programs are a form of service, as are its policy to accept returns—no matter what. Schoolchildren who purchase the firm's backpacks can return them anytime for a new one—even if the child has simply outgrown the pack. Policies like this make consumers feel comfortable about purchasing many different products from L.L.Bean.

Optimal Use of Company Resources

product mix
Assortment of product lines and individual product offerings a company sells.

By spreading the costs of its operations over a series of products, an organization may reduce the average production and marketing costs of each product. Hospitals have taken advantage of idle facilities by adding a variety of outreach services. Many now operate health and fitness centers that, besides generating profits themselves, also feed customers into other hospital services. For example, a blood pressure check at the fitness center might result in a referral to a staff physician.

assessment check

1. List the four reasons for developing a product line.
2. Give an example of a product line with which you are familiar.

7 | Describe the way marketers typically measure product mixes and make product mix decisions.

The Product Mix

A company's **product mix** is its assortment of product lines and individual product offerings. The right blend of product lines and individual products allows a firm to maximize sales opportunities within the limitations of its resources. Marketers typically measure product mixes according to width, length, and depth.

Product Mix Width

The *width* of a product mix refers to the number of product lines the firm offers. As Table 11.3 shows, Johnson & Johnson offers a broad line of retail consumer products in the U.S. market as well as business-to-business products to the medical community. Consumers can purchase over-the-counter medications, nutritional products, dental care products, and first-aid products, among others. Health-care professionals can obtain prescription drugs, medical and diagnostic devices, and wound treatments. LifeScan, one of the firm's subsidiaries, offers an entire suite of products designed to help diabetes patients manage their condition. DePuy, another subsidiary, manufactures orthopedic implants and joint replacement products. At the drugstore, consumers can pick up some of J&J's classic products, such as Motrin and Visine.[26]

Product Mix Length

The *length* of a product mix refers to the number of different products a firm sells. Table 11.3 also identifies some of the hundreds of health-care products offered by Johnson & Johnson. Some of J&J's most recognizable brands are Band-Aid, Tylenol, and Listerine.

Product Mix Depth

Depth refers to variations in each product the firm markets in its mix. Johnson & Johnson's Band-Aid brand bandages come in a variety of shapes and sizes, including Finger-Care Tough Strips, Comfort-Flex and Activ-Flex for elbows and knees, and Advance Healing Blister bandages.

Product Mix Decisions

Establishing and managing the product mix have become increasingly important marketing tasks. Adding depth, length, and width to the product mix requires careful thinking and planning; otherwise, a firm can end up with too many products, including some that don't sell well. To evaluate a firm's product mix, marketers look at the effectiveness of its depth, length, and width. Has the firm ignored a viable consumer segment? It may improve performance by increasing product line depth to offer a product variation that will attract the new segment. Can the firm achieve economies in its sales and distribution efforts by adding complementary product lines to the mix? If so, a wider product mix may seem appropriate. Does the firm gain equal contributions from all items in its portfolio? If not, it may decide to lengthen or shorten the product mix to increase revenues. Geox

table 11.3 Johnson & Johnson's Mix of Health-Care Products

Over-the-Counter Medicines	Nutritionals	Skin and Hair Care	Oral Care	Medical Devices and Diagnostics
Motrin pain reliever	Lactaid digestive aid	Aveeno lotions	Listerine oral rinse	Ethicon surgical instruments and systems
Tylenol pain reliever	Splenda artificial sweetener	Clean & Clear facial cleansers and toners	REACH dental floss	Lifescan diabetes management products
Benadryl antihistamine	Viactiv calcium supplement	Johnson's Baby Shampoo	Rembrandt whitening toothpaste	Orthopedic joint replacement products
Mylanta antacid	Sun Crystals	Neutrogena soaps and shampoos	Efferdent	Veridex diagnostic tests

Source: Company Web site, www.jnj.com, accessed May 4, 2010.

...like a second skin.

© GEOX S.P.A.

> Italian shoe manufacturer Geox is known for its patented breathable fabric that keeps feet cool and comfortable. With growing sales, Geox is expanding in width and length, offering new styles and lines.

is an Italian shoe manufacturer known for its patented breathable fabric that keeps feet cool and comfortable. With sales of more than $1.2 billion, Geox is expanding both ways—in width and length. The firm offers trendy shoe styles, including strappy sandals and retro-inspired bowling shoes. In addition, Geox has launched apparel and shoe lines for men and children, made of similar breathable fabrics that help keep consumers cool and dry.[27]

Another way to add to the mix is to purchase product lines from other companies. Or a firm can acquire entire companies through mergers or acquisitions. Prime Line, a Connecticut–based supplier to the promotional products industry, recently acquired the Leeman New York product line from another industry supplier, Leeman Designs. The acquisition enabled Prime Line to expand its offerings of fine-quality leather and glass items.[28]

A firm should assess its current product mix for another important reason: to determine the feasibility of a line extension. A **line extension** adds individual offerings that appeal to different market segments while remaining closely related to the existing product line. Florida-based SunnyRidge Farm recently added organic blueberries to its existing product mix of blackberries, blueberries, raspberries, and strawberries. The move will enable SunnyRidge, which supplies supermarkets and club stores, to enter the growing organics market.[29]

The marketing environment also plays a role in a marketer's evaluation of a firm's product mix. In the case of SunnyRidge Farm, consumers' increased interest in learning about growing methods and in purchasing foods grown organically inspired the company's decision to extend its product line.

Careful evaluation of a firm's current product mix can also help marketers make decisions about brand management and new-product introductions. Chapter 12 examines the importance of branding, brand management, and the development and introduction of new products.

line extension
Development of individual offerings that appeal to different market segments while remaining closely related to the existing product line.

---

assessment check

1. Define *product mix*.
2. How do marketers typically measure product mixes?

The Product Lifecycle

 Explain the concept of the product lifecycle.

Products, like people, pass through stages as they age. Successful products progress through four basic stages: introduction, growth, maturity, and decline. This progression, known as the **product lifecycle**, is shown in Figure 11.5.

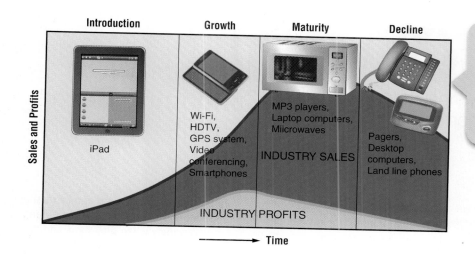

Introduction   Growth   Maturity   Decline

figure 11.5
Stages in the Product Lifecycle

Sales and Profits

iPad

Wi-Fi, HDTV, GPS system, Video conferencing, Smartphones

MP3 players, Laptop computers, Miicrowaves

INDUSTRY SALES

Pagers, Desktop computers, Land line phones

INDUSTRY PROFITS

Time

The product lifecycle concept applies to products or product categories within an industry, not to individual brands. For instance, camera cell phones are moving rapidly from the introductory stage to the growth stage. Digital cameras are still in the growth stage but moving toward maturity. Film cameras have declined so much that it is difficult for consumers to purchase film for their old cameras. There is no set schedule or time frame for a particular stage of the lifecycle. CDs have been around for more than a quarter of a century but are declining, in part, due to the increase in digital music downloads.[30] Additionally, retailers can shorten a product's lifecycle for other reasons as the "Solving an Ethical Controversy" feature explores.

product lifecycle
Progression of a product through introduction, growth, maturity, and decline stages.

Introductory Stage

During the **introductory stage** of the product lifecycle, a firm works to stimulate demand for the new-market entry. Merchandise in this stage might bring new technology to a product category. Because the product is unknown to the public, promotional campaigns stress information about its features. Additional promotions try to induce distribution channel members to carry the product. In this phase, the public becomes acquainted with the item's merits and begins to accept it.

A product whose introductory stage has been successful is the GPS mapping device. Although global positioning systems have been around for a number of years, their introduction to the consumer market was recent. By promoting its practical applications and making the devices easy to use, marketers have seen GPS sales increase rapidly, moving the products quickly toward the growth stage. Garmin now holds more than 50 percent of the U.S. consumer market for GPS devices, followed by Magellan and Mio.[31]

Technical problems and financial losses are common during the introductory stage as companies fine-tune product design and spend money on advertising. Many users remember early problems with the Internet—jammed portals, order fulfilling glitches, dot-coms that went bust. But DVD players and camera phones experienced few of these setbacks. Users of GPS devices reported some glitches but also conceded that some problems stem from learning how to operate the devices correctly.

introductory stage
First stage of the product lifecycle, in which a firm works to stimulate sales of a new-market entry.

The GPS mapping device has had a successful introductory stage. By promoting its practical applications and making the devices easy to use, marketers have seen GPS sales increase rapidly, moving the product toward the growth stage.

solving an ethical controversy

Ⓢhelf-Space Wars: A Continuing Saga

During the recent economic downturn, when large retailers like CVS and Walmart trimmed the number of product brands displayed on their shelves, they were focused on hunkering down and enhancing profits. Eliminating those brands that don't move as quickly gives retailers a double benefit: they can provide shelf space to the best-selling, fastest-moving national brands while also increasing space for their house brand, typically lower in cost. Shelf space represents an ongoing battle for consumer products companies, who spend millions of dollars in advertising and promotion to keep their brands present in the consumer's mind.

Is it ethical for retailers to drop national brands in order to provide more space for their house brand?

PRO

1. Merchants have the right to alter their product assortment as it suits them. Moreover, retailers are under no obligation to offer every brand (and every product) indefinitely.

2. To survive during an economic downturn, many businesses look for ways to offer goods that customers perceive as affordable.

CON

1. The prospect of eliminating shelf space may be a way for a large retailer to coerce companies into offering more-attractive pricing agreements.

2. Cutting popular brands and increasing the amount of shelf space designated for a house brand is risky. Consumers want variety when they shop, and they may decide to shop elsewhere rather than switch brands—a habit that results in decreased sales and lost customers for the retailer.

Summary

Retailers need to tread carefully when readjusting shelf space and eliminating some national brands, particularly when the winner is the house brand. Even in tougher economic times, consumers have proved to be brand-loyal. When Walmart dropped several well-known national brands, customers turned to several competitors for their shopping needs—a fact borne out by Walmart's reported decline in foot traffic and sales during a recent period. As a result, the company reinstated products in several product categories, including health and beauty, cereal, and laundry detergent.

Sources: Jason Notte, "Retailers Get Push-Back as Brands Disappear," *TheStreet.com*, March 17, 2010, http://www.thestreet.com; Chris Burritt, "Wal-Mart Brings Back Goods as Shoppers Turn to Lowe's," *Bloomberg.com*, March 8, 2010, http://www.bloomberg.com; Parija Kavilanz, "Dumped! Brand Names Fight to Stay in Stores," *CNNMoney.com*, February 16, 2010, http://www.money.cnn.com; "Wal-Mart Cuts Food Storage Bag Brands," *Store Brand Decisions*, February 9, 2010, http://www.storebranddecisions.com; Zoe Wood, "Brands Fighting for Shelf Space Now That Wal-Mart Believes Less Is More," *The Observer*, August 16, 2009, http://www.observer.guardian.co.uk.

Growth Stage

growth stage Second stage of the product lifecycle that begins when a firm starts to realize substantial profits from its investment in a product.

Sales volume rises rapidly during the **growth stage** as new customers make initial purchases and early buyers repurchase the product, such as camera phones and GPS devices. The growth stage usually begins when a firm starts to realize substantial profits from its investment. Word-of-mouth reports, mass advertising, and lowered prices all encourage hesitant buyers to make trial purchases of new products. In the case of big-screen TVs, low prices generally have not been a factor—many cost several thousand dollars. "Big-screen" now refers to a TV that is about 60 inches. As sales volume rises, competitors enter the marketplace, creating new challenges for marketers. As plasma technology is gradually replaced by LCD and LED-LCD models, companies with competing technologies vied for dominance, the TVs themselves grew larger, and prices continued to range widely. Shoppers can purchase a 55-inch Samsung 3D LED-LCD HDTV for $7,000, a 60-inch Sony Bravia LCD HDTV for $2,250, or opt for the less-expensive 42-inch Panasonic Viera at just under $700.[32]

Maturity Stage

Sales of a product category continue to grow during the early part of the **maturity stage** but—eventually reach a plateau as the backlog of potential customers dwindles. By this time, many competitors have entered the market, and the firm's profits begin to decline as competition intensifies.

At this stage in the product lifecycle, differences between competing products diminish as competitors discover the product and promotional characteristics most desired by customers. Available supplies exceed industry demand for the first time. Companies can increase their sales and market shares only at the expense of competitors, so the competitive environment becomes increasingly important. In the maturity stage, heavy promotional outlays emphasize any differences still separating competing products, and brand competition intensifies. Some firms try to differentiate their products by focusing on attributes such as quality, reliability, and service. Others focus on redesign or other ways of extending the product lifecycle. Nike athletic shoes could be said to be in the maturity stage. With hundreds of athletic shoes on the market, it is difficult to differentiate competing products. But a Nike innovation has enabled the manufacture of shoes that weigh less than one ounce apiece yet are able to take the pounding of a professional athlete. The innovation is Flywire, a lightweight thread made of Vectran fibers. Most recently, the company has applied Flywire technology to athletic shoes for professional soccer players. Flywire shoes are so simple and inexpensive to manufacture that Nike could be looking at a whole new lifecycle for its time-honored shoes.[33]

maturity stage Third stage of the product lifecycle, in which industry sales level out.

Decline Stage

In the **decline stage** of a product's life, innovations or shifts in consumer preferences bring about an absolute decline in industry sales. Dial telephones became touch-tone phones, which evolved to portable phones, which are now being replaced with conventional cell phones, which in turn are being replaced with camera phones. Thirty-five-millimeter home-movie film was replaced with videotape, which is now being replaced with DVD technology.

decline stage Final stage of the product lifecycle, in which a decline in total industry sales occurs.

Some manufacturers refuse to give up in the decline stage. Young consumers, accustomed to CDs and digital downloads, are beginning to turn their attention to vinyl records. They have discovered their parents' and grandparents' collections of LPs and have hauled old record turntables out of the attic. If curiosity led them to the discovery, the sound and graphics of a record seems to be holding their interest. Marketers in the music industry have taken notice, and some bands have begun to issue limited numbers of records

JONATHAN FERREY/GETTY IMAGES FOR NIKE

Nike athletic shoes could be classified in the maturity stage, but the company's innovative lightweight thread, Flywire, has led to a new generation of athletic shoes. Nike may be looking at a new lifecycle for its shoes.

along with CDs and MP3 formats. They don't expect vinyl to become the primary medium for music—but are happy to resurrect a classic product for a new generation of listeners.[34] Sheep farmers in New Zealand have devised a new use for wool: in performance garments designed to challenge those fashioned of Lycra and other synthetic fibers, as the "Marketing Success" feature discusses. The next section of this chapter discusses more specific strategies for extending the lifecycle of a product.

It is important to remember that the traditional product lifecycle differs from fad cycles. Fashions and fads profoundly influence marketing strategies. Fashions are currently popular products that tend to follow recurring lifecycles. For example, bell-bottom pants popular in the 1960s and 1970s have returned as flares or boot-cut pants. In contrast, fads are products with abbreviated life-cycles. Most fads experience short-lived popularity and then quickly fade, although some maintain residual markets among certain segments. Webkinz (the stuffed animals that have their own online Webkinz World) are an example of a fad.

assessment check

1. Identify the four stages of the product lifecycle.
2. During which stage or stages are products likely to attract the most new customers?

Extending the Product Lifecycle

9 Discuss how a firm can extend a product's lifecycle, and explain why certain products may be deleted.

Marketers usually try to extend each stage of the lifecycles for their products as long as possible. Product lifecycles can stretch indefinitely as a result of decisions designed to increase the frequency of use by current customers; increase the number of users for the product; find new uses; or change package sizes, labels, or product quality.

Increasing Frequency of Use

During the maturity stage, the sales curve for a product category reaches a maximum point if the competitors exhaust the supply of potential customers who previously had not made purchases.

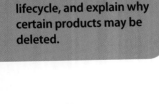

mktg: *success*

Icebreaker Challenges the Synthet

Background. New Zealand is home to approximately 40 million merino sheep that produce some of the softest wool in the world. Traditionally, merino wool has been used mostly in dress suits and sweaters, but merino's merits were recently rediscovered. Merino wool is a natural fiber that feels soft against the skin. It "breathes" and doesn't

retain odors. In other words, thought entre-preneur Jeremy Moon, it would be a perfect fiber for apparel for skiers, runners, hikers, and cyclists.

The Challenge. Moon founded his company, Icebreaker, to manufacture tops, leggings, gloves, scarves, socks, and underwear out of merino wool, using sustainable,

environmentally friendly practices. But he knew the wool had become a commodity in New Zealand, with unpredictable quality and incon-sistent yields from year to year. In addition, he faced stiff competition from existing apparel manufacturers, who used synthetic fibers.

The Strategy. Moon offered New Zealand sheep farmers multiyear contracts,

However, if current customers buy more frequently than they formerly did, total sales will rise even though no new buyers enter the market.

For instance, consumers buy some products during certain seasons of the year. Marketers can boost purchase frequency by persuading these people to try the product year-round. For decades, most people used sunscreen only during warm and sunny seasons of the year. With greater warnings about the risks of sun damage and skin cancer, however, companies now advertise the benefits of using sunscreen year-round. In another change, Hershey now offers its famous Hershey's Kisses with personalized messages such as "Congratulations," "It's a Boy," and "Happy Birthday" to celebrate personal events.

Increasing the Number of Users

A second strategy for extending the product lifecycle seeks to increase the overall market size by attracting new customers who previously have not used the product. Marketers may find their products in different stages of the lifecycle in different countries. This difference can help firms extend product growth. Items that have reached the maturity stage in the United States may still be in the introductory stage somewhere else.

In Australia, the Australian Broadcasting Company recently announced plans to start a 24-hour news channel. Programming will feature major breaking news in Australia and around the globe and will also include regular programming focusing on world news, Australian politics, and business. The new channel, to be broadcast in 44 countries, hopes to gain additional viewers.[35]

Finding New Uses

Finding new uses for a product is an excellent strategy for extending a product's lifecycle. New applications for mature products include oatmeal as a cholesterol reducer, antacids as a calcium supplement, and aspirin for promoting heart health.

Marketers sometimes conduct contests or surveys to identify new uses for their products. They may post the results or their own new ideas on their Web sites. Arm & Hammer's Web site lists a variety of alternative uses throughout the house for its baking soda. Consumers can use baking soda to clean crayon off walls, as an antacid to settle an upset stomach, and as an agent to balance the pH in swimming pool water. The firm has even developed a new product—a waterproof resealable pouch—that consumers can use for poolside storage of their Arm & Hammer baking soda.[36]

paying them a guaranteed price for their wool as long as it met Icebreaker's rigorous quality standards. In addition to its sustainable, manufacturing practices, the company created a traceability program under which customers can learn the origins of a garment through a unique code stitched inside it.

The Outcome. Athletes have embraced the woolen apparel and, with revenues now exceeding $100 million, Icebreaker merchandise is now sold in more than 2,000 stores in 24 countries. The company also operates retail stores in the United States and France, and it outfitted

the New Zealand Olympic team for the 2010 Games in Vancouver.

Sources: Bill Saporito, "Global Business," *Time*, March 22, 2010, pp. 1–2; "First US Factory Outlet Store for NZ-Based Icebreaker," *Fibre2Fashion.com*, February 2, 2010, http://www.fibre2fashion.com; "Icebreaker Bodyfit to Keep Olympians Warm in Vancouver Winter," *Fibre2Fashion.com*, January 11, 2010, http://www.fibre2fashion.com.

Procter & Gamble is rejuvenating several of its product lines through the introduction of its Future Friendly campaign.

Changing Package Sizes, Labels, or Product Quality

Many firms try to extend their product life-cycles by introducing physical changes in their offerings. Alternatively, new packaging and labels with updated images and slogans can help revitalize a product. Procter & Gamble is rejuvenating several of its product lines through the introduction of its Future Friendly campaign to heighten consumer awareness of green practices. Bottles of Procter & Gamble's Tide Coldwater detergent, for example, carry the Future Friendly label to remind consumers that they conserve energy when they wash clothes using cold water.[37]

Changes in packaging can lengthen a product's lifecycle. Food marketers have brought out small packages designed to appeal to one-person households and extra-large containers for customers who want to buy in bulk. Other firms offer their products in convenient packages for use away from home or at the office. When international grocer ALDI changed to a fancy, expensive-looking bottle for its Carlini Olive Oil, the product took on a new, upscale look—presumably better able to compete with the myriad of high-priced olive oils in a crowded sector. Despite the new bottle, however, the price stayed the same.[38]

Product Deletion Decisions

To avoid wasting resources promoting unpromising products, marketers must sometimes prune product lines and eliminate marginal products. Marketers typically face this decision during the late maturity and early decline stages of the product lifecycle. Periodic reviews of weak products should justify either eliminating or retaining them. After battling it out with Sony in the DVD player arena, Toshiba finally conceded defeat and announced it would stop making its HD DVD player. That left Sony the winner in the marketplace with its Blu-ray format.

A firm may continue to carry an unprofitable item to provide a complete line for its customers. For example, most grocery stores may lose money on bulky, low-unit-value items such as salt, they continue to carry these items to meet shopper demand.

Shortages of raw materials sometimes prompt companies to discontinue production and marketing of previously profitable items. A firm may even drop a profitable product that fails to fit into its existing line or fails to fit the direction in which the firm wants to grow. Some of these "orphan brands" return to the market when other firms purchase and relaunch them. In the largest relaunch in hotel history, InterContinental Hotels Group recently undertook a $1 billion relaunch of its Holiday Inn chain. Over a three-year period, 3,300 Holiday Inns will reemerge with a redesigned logo; upgraded lobbies and guest bathrooms; and new signage, landscaping, lighting, and bedding. What's more, all employees will be retrained under the chain's new "Stay Real" program.[39]

 assessment check

1. Describe the four strategies for extending a product's lifecycle.
2. Under what circumstances do firms decide to delete a product from their line?

strategic implications
of marketing in the 21st century

arketers who want their businesses to succeed continue to develop new goods and services to attract and satisfy customers. They engage in continuous improvement activities, focusing on quality and customer service. And they continually evaluate their company's mix of products.

Marketers everywhere are constantly developing new and better products that fit their firm's overall strategy. Technological innovations are one area in which new products quickly replace old ones. Marketers are sometimes faced with the dilemma of lagging sales for formerly popular products. They must come up with ways to extend the lives of certain products to extend their firms' profitability and sometimes must recognize and delete those that no longer meet expectations.

Review of Chapter Objectives

 1 **Define *product*, and distinguish between goods and services and how they relate to the goods–services continuum.**

Marketers define a product as the bundle of physical, service, and symbolic attributes designed to satisfy customers' wants and needs. Goods are tangible products customers can see, hear, smell, taste, or touch. Services are intangible tasks that satisfy the needs of customers. Goods represent one end of a continuum, and services represent the other.

 2 **Outline the importance of the service sector in today's marketplace.**

The service sector makes a crucial contribution to the U.S. economy in terms of products and jobs. The U.S. service sector now makes up more than two-thirds of the economy. Services have grown because of consumers' desire for speed, convenience, and technological advances.

3 **List the classifications of consumer goods and services, and briefly describe each category.**

Consumer products—goods and services—are classified as convenience products (frequently purchased items), shopping products (products purchased after comparison), and specialty products (those offering unique characteristics that consumers prize).

 4 **Identify each of the types of business goods and services.**

Business products are classified as installations (major capital investments), accessory equipment (capital items that cost less and last for shorter periods than installations), component parts and materials (finished business products of one producer that become part of the final products of another producer), raw materials (natural resources such as lumber, beef, or cotton), supplies (regular expenses a firm incurs in daily operations), and business services (the intangible products firms buy to facilitate their production and operating processes).

 5 **Discuss how quality is used by marketers as a product strategy.**

Many companies use total quality management (TQM) in an effort to encourage all employees to participate in producing the best goods and services possible. Companies may also participate in ISO 9001:2000 certification or benchmarking to evaluate and improve quality. Consumers often evaluate service quality on the basis of tangibles, reliability, responsiveness, assurance, and empathy, so marketers of service firms strive to excel in all of these areas.

6   Explain why firms develop lines of related products.

Companies usually produce several related products rather than individual ones to achieve the objectives of growth, optimal use of company resources, and increased company importance in the market, and to make optimal use of the product lifecycle.

7   Describe the way marketers typically measure product mixes and make product mix decisions.

Marketers must decide the right width, length, and depth of product lines. Width is the number of product lines. Length is the number of products a company sells. Depth refers to the number of variations of a product available in a product line. Marketers evaluate the effectiveness of all three elements of the product mix. They may purchase product lines from other companies or extend the product line, if necessary. Firms may also acquire entire companies and their product lines through mergers and acquisitions.

8   Explain the concept of the product lifecycle.

The product lifecycle outlines the stages a product goes through, including introduction, growth, maturity, and decline. During the introductory stage, marketers work to stimulate demand for the new product. New customers make initial purchases and repurchases of the product in the growth stage. Sales continue to grow during the maturity stage but eventually level off. In the decline stage, sales are reduced due to innovations or a shift in consumer preferences.

9   Describe how a firm can extend a product's lifecycle, and explain why certain products may be deleted.

Marketers can extend the product lifecycle by increasing frequency of use or number of users; finding new uses for the product; or changing package size, label, or quality. If none of these is successful, or if the product no longer fits a firm's line, the firm may decide to delete it from its line.

Assessment Check: Answers

1.1 Define the term *product*. A product is a bundle of physical, service, and symbolic attributes designed to satisfy a customer's wants and needs.

1.2 Why is the understanding of want satisfaction so important to marketers? The understanding of want satisfaction is important to marketers because it helps them understand why people purchase certain goods and services.

1.3 Describe the goods–services continuum. The goods–services continuum is a spectrum that helps marketers visualize the differences and similarities between goods and services.

1.4 List the six characteristics distinguishing services from goods. The six characteristics distinguishing services from goods are the following: (1) services are intangible, (2) services are inseparable from the service providers, (3) services are perishable, (4) companies cannot easily standardize services, (5) buyers often play important roles in the creation and distribution of services, and (6) service standards show wide variations.

2.1 Identify two reasons services are important to the U.S. economy and business environment. The service sector makes an important contribution to the economy in terms of

products and jobs. Services also play a vital role in the international competitiveness of U.S. firms.

2.2 Why do service firms emphasize marketing? The growth of potential service transactions represents a vast marketing opportunity, and the environment for services is changing—so marketers need to find new ways to reach customers.

3.1 What are the three major classifications of consumer products? The three major classifications are convenience products, shopping products, and specialty products.

3.2 Identify five factors marketers should consider in classifying consumer services. Five factors are the following: (1) the nature of the service, (2) the relationship between the service organization and its customers, (3) flexibility for customization, (4) fluctuation of supply and demand, and (5) the way the service is delivered.

4.1 What are the six main classifications of business products? The six main classifications of business products are the following: (1) installations, (2) accessory equipment, (3) component parts and materials, (4) raw materials, (5) supplies, and (6) business services.

4.2 What are the three categories of supplies? The three categories of supplies are maintenance items, repair items, and operating supplies.

5.1 What is TQM? TQM stands for total quality management, a process that expects all of a firm's employees to continually improve its products and work processes.

5.2 What are the five variables of service quality? The five variables of service quality are tangibles, reliability, responsiveness, assurances, and empathy.

6.1 List the four reasons for developing a product line. The four reasons firms want to develop product lines are the following: (1) a desire to grow, (2) enhancing the company's position in the market, (3) optimal use of company resources, and (4) exploiting the stages of the product lifecycle.

6.2 Give an example of a product line with which you are familiar. Product lines could include salad dressings, hybrid automobiles, sporting equipment, hotel chains, and so on.

7.1 Define *product mix*. The product mix is a company's assortment of product lines and individual product offerings.

7.2 How do marketers typically measure product mixes? The product mix is measured by width, length, and depth.

8.1 Identify the four stages of the product lifecycle. The four stages of the product lifecycle are introduction, growth, maturity, and decline.

8.2 During which stage or stages are products likely to attract the most new customers? Products usually attract the most new customers during the introductory and growth stages.

9.1 Describe the four strategies for extending a product's lifecycle. The four strategies are increasing frequency of use, increasing the number of users, finding new users, and changing packaging or quality.

9.2 Under what circumstances do firms decide to delete a product from their line? Firms may decide to delete a product if none of their strategies work, if raw materials become unavailable, or if the product no longer fits the existing or future product line.

Marketing Terms You Need to Know

marketing mix 344
product 345
services 345
goods 345
goods–services continuum 345
homeshoring 347
consumer (B2C) product 348
business-to-business (B2B) product 348
unsought products 348

convenience products 348
impulse goods and services 349
staples 349
emergency goods and services 349
shopping products 350
specialty products 350
installations 353
accessory equipment 354
industrial distributor 354
component parts and materials 354

raw materials 355
supplies 355
MRO items 355
business services 355
total quality management (TQM) 357
ISO 9001:2000 358
benchmarking 358
service encounter 358
service quality 358

product line 359
product mix 360
line extension 362
product lifecycle 363
introductory stage 363
growth stage 364
maturity stage 365
decline stage 365

Assurance of Learning Review

1. Choose one of the following products and explain how it blurs the distinction between goods and services.
   a. knee replacement surgery
   b. dinner at a popular restaurant
   c. purchase and installation of new roof
   d. live concert
   e. custom-made suit

2. What are the differences between consumer products and B2B products? Describe a product that could be used as both.

3. What are unsought products? Give an example of an unsought product, and explain how it might be marketed.

4. What important features distinguish shopping products from one another?

5. How does marketing for installations and accessory equipment differ?

6. How do firms use benchmarking?

7. Describe briefly how L.L.Bean achieved each of the objectives for developing a product line. Why do you think the firm has been successful?

8. What is a line extension? Describe how *one* of the following might create a line extension:
   a. Viva paper towels
   b. Kellogg's Frosted Flakes
   c. Starbucks Via coffee
   d. Gain laundry detergent

9. What steps do marketers take to make the introductory stage of the product lifecycle successful enough to reach the growth stage? What are some of the challenges they face?

10. Arm & Hammer extended the lifecycle of its baking soda by coming up with new uses for the product. Think of a product whose lifecycle you believe could be extended by finding new uses. Describe the product and your ideas for new uses.

Projects and Teamwork Exercises

1. On your own or with a classmate, choose one of the following goods (or choose one of your own). Visit the company's Web site to learn as much as you can about your product and the way it is marketed. Then create a marketing strategy for developing the services to support your product and make it stand out from others.
   a. Lucky Brand jeans
   b. BlackBerry smartphone
   c. Sephora makeup
   d. HP laptop
   e. Mini Cooper car

2. On your own or with a classmate, create an advertisement for an unsought product such as a remedial reading or math course, a warranty for a big-screen TV, a first-aid kit, or the like. How can your ad turn an unsought product into one actually desired by consumers?

3. Consider a customer service experience you have had in the last month or so. Was it positive or negative? Describe your experi-

ence to the class and then discuss how the firm might improve the quality of its customer service—even if it is already positive.

4. With a classmate, choose one of the following firms or another that interests you. Visit the firm's Web site and measure its product mix. Then create a chart like the one for Johnson & Johnson in Table 11.3 (on page 361), identifying the company's major product lines, along with a few specific examples.
   a. Champion athletic clothing
   b. Condé Nast magazines
   c. Wyndham Hotels
   d. Panasonic
   e. Audi

5. With the same classmate, create a plan for further extending one of the firm's product lines. Describe the strategy you would recommend for extending the line as well as new products that might be included.

Critical-Thinking Exercises

1. Draw a line representing the goods–services continuum. Then place each of the following along the continuum. Briefly explain your decision.
   a. Skype
   b. Teleflora.com
   c. Kohl's department stores
   d. Kia dealership
   e. Netflix

2. Make a list of all the convenience products you buy in a week. Does the list change from week to week based on need or your budget? What would it take to make you switch from one product to another?

3. Imagine your favorite restaurant. List as many installations, raw materials, and supplies as you can that you think the restaurant owner or manager must be responsible for purchasing.

4. Why is it important for even a small firm to develop a line of products?

5. Choose one of the following goods and services and describe your strategy for taking it to the next stage in its product lifecycle. For products in the maturity or decline stage, describe a strategy for extending their lifecycle.
   a. Satellite radio (growth)
   b. MP3 players (maturity)
   c. Text messaging (growth)
   d. Pressure cookers (decline)
   e. Duct tape (maturity)

6. Describe a fad that has come and gone during your lifetime, such as Beanie Babies or Pokemon. Did you take part in the fad? Why or why not? How long did it last? Why do you think it faded?

Ethics Exercise

The airline industry has suffered recent setbacks, such as the high cost of fuel, that have forced the major carriers to cut back on many of their services. Some airlines, like American and United, have started charging passengers fees for checked baggage. Another, Spirit Air, announced it would also charge for carry-on bags. Most airlines charge for in-flight snacks or don't serve any at all. Airlines have reduced the number of flights they operate to certain destinations, packing planes full to overflowing; and recent restrictions on the use of frequent-flyer miles make it difficult to cash them in. Then there are the record-setting delays and lost luggage claims. All of these factors add up to less-than-enjoyable flying experiences for most travelers, many of whom are opting to find other modes of transportation or

just staying home.[40] Suppose you are a marketer for one of the major airlines. Your company is facing difficulty providing acceptable service to the passengers on its flights, but you need to find a way to emphasize the positive features of your airline's service.

1. Using the five variables of service quality as your guideline, what steps would you take—within your realm of control—to close the gap between the level of service passengers expect and the level they have been receiving?

2. How might you attract business customers? Would you give them a level of service that is different from families and other consumers who are flying for pleasure?

Internet Exercises

1. **Product classifications.** Visit the Web site of a company such as Reckitt Benckiser, Colgate, or Unilever. Choose at least five different products and classify each as a convenience or shopping product. Explain your reasoning.
    http://www.rb.com
    http://www.colgate.com
    http://www.unilever.com

2. **ISO certification.** The International Organization for Standardization (ISO) is responsible for the development and implementation of product standards. Go to the ISO's Web site (http://www.iso.org) and answer the following questions:

    a. Who belongs to ISO and how is it administered?
    b. How are ISO standards developed?
    c. What are some of the advantages of ISO certification?

3. **Product lifecycle.** Arm & Hammer baking soda was first sold more than 100 years ago. Visit the Arm & Hammer Web site (http://www.armhammer.com). Review the history of the product and then prepare a brief report outlining how the makers of Arm and Hammer baking soda have been able to extend the product's lifecycle.

Note: Internet Web addresses change frequently. If you don't find the exact site listed, you may need to access the organization's home page and search from there or use a search engine such as Google or Bing.

Case 11.1 *New Balance "Experiences" China*

Boston-based New Balance has invaded China. The 103-year-old company got its start manufacturing and selling arch supports to people like police officers and waiters, whose work kept them on their feet all day. During the 1970s, the company switched its focus to

designing and marketing athletic shoes for "the everyday athlete," with proper fit being its key selling point. Over time, New Balance added an apparel line and has become a leading name in the industry. The company's family of brands also includes Dunham, Aravon, Warrior, Brine, and the classic American sneaker, PF Flyers.

The first New Balance retail stores in China, called "Experience Stores," opened in Beijing and Shanghai in 2010, with hundreds more planned for the near future. The stores' décor emphasizes the company's century-long heritage and accomplishments. Walk in the front door and you'll swear you've just entered a shoe store from the

1950s. The space evokes all five of the senses: comfortable, well-worn leather couches; framed archival photographs, advertisements, and other paraphernalia from the company's early days; an oak scent in the air, reminiscent of the smell of an old-time shoe store; and piped-in sounds from the "be-bop" era, including such artists as the Everly Brothers, Little Richard, Fats Domino, Jerry Lee Lewis, and Bill Haley and the Comets. A "DNA ribbon" in each Experience Store— underscoring the company's unique Performance DNA concept— traces the company's history and accomplishments and hints at the future as it extends from the first floor to the second floor.

Programmed in-store messaging promotes the Performance DNA concept and draws shoppers to the second floor, where the merchandise is displayed in a decidedly 21st-century setting. (Recent consumer research suggests that up to 40 percent of consumers are influenced by such in-store messaging.)

To plan for its entry into China, New Balance engaged leading Asian branding consultants Equal Strategy to create a "total sensory experience." The Experience Stores exemplify the concept of "sensory branding": that is, the process of creating a brand experience that calls upon all of the senses in reflecting a company's brand.

Consistent with the company's Total Fit campaign, the store openings include healthy running tips, pointers on foot care, and inspirational stories from some of China's most well-known runners. The Beijing launch included an American-style street carnival reminiscent of the 1960s. To further celebrate the openings, New Balance sponsored an international marathon in Hong Kong, featuring 88 Chinese entrants and 6K runs in the cities of Nanjin and Hangzhou.

New Balance has 4,000 employees worldwide and recently posted revenues of $1.64 billion.

Questions for Critical Thinking

1. Do you think opening retail stores in China is a good move for New Balance? Why or why not?

2. New Balance calls its new retail stores "Experience Stores." In your opinion, what does the company mean by "experience," and how does that experience translate to sales?

Sources: Company Web site, http://www.newbalance.com, accessed April 6, 2010; George Kiel III, "New Balance Experience Store in Shanghai," *NiceKicks,* February 11, 2010, http://www.nicekicks.com; "The World's First New Balance Experience Store Brought to Life through a Sensory Approach," *Newswire,* August 23, 2009, http://www.i-newswire.com; Rosemary Feitelberg, "New Balance to Open Experience Unit in Beijing," *Women's Wear Daily,* August 14, 2009, http://www.wwd.com.

Video Case 11.2
*Product and Service Strategy at Preserve**

When Eric Hudson graduated from business school with his MBA, he did what most people do. He went out and got a real job. After about six years, the daily grind in corporate America had gotten old. "My family was a bit crunchy and had been known to actually hug trees," recalls Hudson, "but it wasn't until the early '90s that I decided I wanted to marry my professional career with my love of nature."

As a teenager, he remembered his dentist reminding him to hold his toothbrush at a 45-degree angle, but he was always surprised that few toothbrushes were actually shaped for that angle. When it came time to start his own business, he enlisted his father—an industrial designer specializing in automobiles and boats—to help him design a better-shaped toothbrush. Once they came up with a design they liked, they sought the approval of several dentists.

At the same time, Hudson became aware of how few environmentally friendly products there were in the marketplace. The products available may have been made of recycled or recyclable materials, but they were more expensive and usually didn't work as well. He also noticed that while more communities in his native Massachusetts were starting recycling programs, much of what people were throwing in the bins was food containers made from #5 plastic. At the time, few companies reused that type of plastic, and it often ended up in the landfill. Hudson knew there had to be a clever way to reuse that plastic for his toothbrush.

He brought the idea to a plastics lab at the University of Massachusetts and, after a lot of experimenting, finally figured out a way to turn all that plastic into a material suitable for the toothbrush. The Preserve toothbrush hit the market in 1998.

Sales in the beginning were slow, but the product was well received. Green products had yet to hit the shelves of stores like Target and Walmart, but Hudson definitely was on top of the emerging trend. As sales improved and consumers started asking for more environmentally friendly products, he developed a recyclable razor, a children's toothbrush, and a tongue cleaner—all made from recycled plastic. Not wanting their products to end up in the trash, Preserve takes back used toothbrushes and razors to be melted down and used again.

In late 2007, Preserve announced an exclusive deal with the Austin-based Whole Foods natural and gourmet grocery chain to partner on a new product line for the kitchen. The Preserve Kitchen line includes a Preserve Colander, Preserve Cutting Board, Preserve Mixing Bowls, and Preserve Food Storage Containers—all made from #5 plastic. They also added a Preserve 100% Post-Consumer Recycled Paper Cutting Board. Priced competitively, but slightly higher than similar conventionally produced products, Preserve marketers knew that if they were to compete against the likes of Tupperware and Rubbermaid, they would need more than a good story. Until then, they were able to get by designing their products in-house with little help from the outside. It was time to call for backup.

Industrial design firm Evo Design was the perfect solution. Their offices were nearby in Connecticut, so Hudson and his team could just hop in his "grease car"—a Volkswagen Hudson modified to run on French fry grease collected from a local Wendy's. Evo's team of designers, engineers, and business experts have earned a reputation for making really cool looking (and functioning) stuff for the competition: Crate & Barrel, Cuisinart, Kimberly-Clark, Schick, and Waring.

For Preserve to make its mark in the CPG (consumer packaged goods) arena, it will need to continue to come up with new products in new categories. Demand by new parents for environmentally friendly toys and products present a perfect opportunity for Preserve. The company has plans to launch its first toy line in the near future.

Questions

1. Why is the development of an entire product line critical to Preserve's growth and success?

2. At which stage are most "green" products in the product lifecycle? As these products mature, what can be done to extend their product lifecycles?

* "Preserve" was previously called "Recycline." The Recycline brand has now stepped into the background as the parent company.

ch12 Developing
and Managing Brand and Product Categories

Liz Claiborne and JCPenney: A Marriage Made in Heaven? • • • For years, the name "Liz Claiborne" has been synonymous with classic American sportswear for women. The popular brand was carried in many of the nation's best department stores, such

1. Determine how to define a brand.

2. Identify the different types of brands.

3. Explain the strategic value of brand equity.

4. Explain the benefits of category and brand management.

5. Discuss how companies develop a strong identity for their product or brand.

6. Identify and briefly describe each of the new-product development strategies.

7. Describe the consumer adoption process.

8. List the stages in the new-product development process.

9. Explain the relationship between product safety and product liability.

as Marshall Field, Dillard's, and Bon Ton.

Now, however, department stores nationwide are struggling. In recent years, stores were consolidated. Many famous chains were sold or closed; Marshall Field stores, for example, were renamed Macy's. In the process, some of the most sought-after brands lost their footing. As a result, certain brands have decided to sever ties with retailers that carried their product lines for years and, instead, are tying their future to exclusive contracts with a single department store chain. Such was the case with Liz Claiborne. Just recently, the company discontinued selling its men's, women's and home lines at Macy's and moved to an exclusive ten-year deal with JCPenney. Under

the arrangement, JCPenney also has the option of buying the brand in five years.

What's in it for the brand? In Liz Claiborne's case, the exclusive arrangement means the company will continue to provide the design for its product lines, but JCPenney will be responsible for procurement, production, marketing, and distribution. This shifting of roles is expected to save Liz Claiborne a bundle in fixed costs because they won't need to hold inventory or have working capital. In addition, the company's bottom line will no longer be stung by department stores' end-of-season markdowns of pricey merchandise—a common problem for fashion houses when dealing with retailers. Under the new arrangement, Liz Claiborne

will receive a percentage of net sales as well as a portion of the profit. What's more, the company's exclusive relationship with JCPenney means the national chain is likely to provide optimal shelf space for the Liz Claiborne lines and feature it prominently in advertising and promotions.

JCPenney had already demonstrated success marketing Liz Claiborne's Liz & Co. line. Being the exclusive retailer of a respected brand like Liz Claiborne brings cachet and can be expected to attract a new, different customer segment—in this case, the brand-loyal Liz Claiborne shoppers, many of whom shop JCPenney rarely or not at all. Carrying Liz Claiborne accessories, shoes, and home goods in addition to the men's and women's apparel lines will give JCPenney a powerful new marketing tool.

According to industry observers, when a brand exits a long-time relationship with a retailer, the departure often confuses shoppers for a time, because they have been accustomed to finding that brand in the stores they frequent. In some cases, shoppers will remain loyal to the retailer and will try the store's other brands. Sometimes, however, shoppers are brand-loyal and will seek out their favorite brand in other stores even if they're unfamiliar to the stores. Once there, shoppers may take time to discover the other brands the "new" retailer carries. However, marketers say the brand confusion eventually evens out.

Liz Claiborne Inc. got its start in 1976, when fashion designer Liz Claiborne helped found the company bearing her name. Success came almost overnight. By 1985, Liz Claiborne Inc. had made the *Fortune* 500—the only firm on the list with a woman at the helm. The company continued to grow after Claiborne retired in 1989, adding such labels as Juicy Couture, Lucky Brands, DKNY Jeans, and Kate Spade to its family of brands.[1]

evolution of a brand

The Liz Claiborne brand, an icon in women's fashion, was known for consistently high quality and a classic look. In addition to women's apparel, the company eventually expanded its product lines to include accessories, shoes, home goods, and apparel for men.

- For decades, JCPenney has had a reputation for selling moderately priced merchandise. Yet, Liz Claiborne Inc. has been known for more upscale brands. In your opinion, will the exclusive relationship between JCPenney and

Liz Claiborne Inc. Change the image of JCPenney or the brand? Why?

- Liz Claiborne isn't the first brand to undergo a makeover. Its Dana Buchman brand, previously a fixture at Saks Fifth Avenue, was reconfigured for Kohl's shoppers. Whereas a Dana Buchman pantsuit at Saks would have sold for as much as $600, at Kohl's the Dana Buchman apparel—offered as separates— are priced at $12 to $116. How do such brand transformations benefit a retailer? The brand?

chapter overview

Brands play a huge role in our lives. We try certain brands for all kinds of reasons: on recommendations from friends, because we want to associate ourselves with the images certain brands possess, or because we remember colorful advertisements. We develop loyalty to certain brands and product lines for varying reasons as well—quality of a product, price, and habit are a few examples. This chapter examines the way companies make decisions about developing and managing the products and product lines they hope will become consumer necessities. Developing and marketing a product and product line and building a desired brand image are costly propositions. To protect its investment, a specialized marketer called a *category manager* must carefully nurture both existing and new products. The category manager is responsible for an entire product line.

This chapter focuses on two critical elements of product planning and strategy. First, it looks at how firms build and maintain identity and competitive advantage for their products through branding. Second, it focuses on the new-product planning and development process. Effective new-product planning and meeting the profit responsibility a category manager has for a product line require careful preparation. The needs and desires of consumers change constantly, and successful marketers manage to keep up with—or stay just ahead of—those changes.

briefly speaking

" The man who uses Calloway golf clubs, drives a Jaguar, and wears Ralph Lauren apparel makes a statement about his identity. He is a man separate and apart from the man who uses a Penn fishing reel, drives a Dodge Durango, and wears Levi's."

—Laurence Vincent
American author and brand consultant

Managing Brands for Competitive Advantage

1 Determine how to define a brand

Think of the last time you went shopping for groceries. As you moved through the store, chances are your recognition of various brand names influenced many of your purchasing decisions. Perhaps you chose Colgate toothpaste over competitive offerings or loaded Heinz ketchup into your cart instead of the store brand. Walking through the snack food aisle, you might have reached for Orville Redenbacher popcorn or Lay's potato chips without much thought.

Marketers recognize the powerful influence products and product lines have on customer behavior, and they work to create strong identities for their products and protect them. Branding is the process of creating that identity. A **brand** is a name, term, sign, symbol, design, or some combination that identifies the products of one firm while differentiating these products from competitors' offerings. The tradition of excellence created by the Gucci Group is carried through in all the brands in its lineup—Gucci, Yves Saint Laurent, Boucheron, Stella McCartney, and Balenciaga, to name a few.

As you read this chapter, consider how many brands you are aware of, both those you are loyal to and those you have never tried or have tried and abandoned. Table 12.1 shows some selected brands, brand names, and brand marks. Satisfied buyers respond to branding by making repeat purchases of the same product because they identify the item with the name of its producer. One buyer might derive satisfaction from an ice cream bar with the brand name Dove; another might derive the same satisfaction from one with the name Ben & Jerry's.

> **brand** Name, term, sign, symbol, design, or some combination that identifies the products of one firm while differentiating them from that of the competition.

Brand Loyalty

Brands achieve widely varying consumer familiarity and acceptance. A snowboarder might insist on a Burton snowboard, but the same consumer might show little loyalty to particular brands in another product category such as bath soap. Marketers measure brand loyalty in three stages: brand recognition, brand preference, and brand insistence.

Brand recognition is a company's first objective for newly introduced products. Marketers begin the promotion of new items by trying to make them familiar to the public. Advertising offers one effective way for increasing consumer awareness of a brand. Glad is a familiar brand in U.S. kitchens, and it drew on customers' recognition of its popular sandwich bags and plastic wraps when it introduced a new plastic food wrap that seals around items with just the press of a finger. Other tactics for creating brand recognition include offering free samples or discount coupons for purchases. Once consumers have used a product, seen it advertised, or noticed it in stores, it moves from the unknown to the known category, increasing the probability that some of those consumers will purchase it.

> **brand recognition** Consumer awareness and identification of a brand.

At the second level of brand loyalty, **brand preference**, buyers rely on previous experiences with the product when choosing it, if available, over competitors' products. You may prefer Steve Madden shoes or Juicy Couture clothes to other brands and buy their new lines as soon as they are offered. If so, those products have established brand preference.

> **brand preference** Consumer reliance on previous experiences with a product to choose that item again.

table 12.1 Selected Brands, Brand Names, and Brand Marks

Brand type	Dr Pepper or A&W root beer
Private brand	Craftsman tools (Sears) or Trader Jacques French soap (Trader Joe's)
Family brand	RAID insect sprays or Progresso soups
Individual brand	Purex or Clorox
Brand name	Kleenex or Cheetos
Brand mark	Colonel Sanders for KFC or the gecko for Geico insurance

Glad, a familiar brand, drew on customers' recognition of its popular sandwich bags and plastic wraps when it introduced a new plastic food wrap that seals with the press of a finger.

Brand insistence, the ultimate stage in brand loyalty, leads consumers to refuse alternatives and to search extensively for the desired merchandise. A product at this stage has achieved a monopoly position with its consumers. Although many firms try to establish brand insistence with all consumers, few achieve this ambitious goal. Companies that offer specialty or luxury goods and services, such as Rolex watches or Lexus automobiles, are more likely to achieve this status than those offering mass-marketed goods and services.

 assessment check

1. What is a brand?
2. Differentiate among brand recognition, brand preference, and brand insistence.

Types of Brands

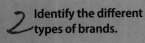 **Identify the different types of brands.**

Brands are classified in many ways: private, manufacturer's or national, family, and individual brands. In making branding decisions, firms weigh the benefits and drawbacks of each type of brand. Some firms, however, sell their goods without any efforts at branding. These items are called **generic products**. They are characterized by plain labels, little or no advertising, and no brand names. Common categories of generic products include food and household staples. These no-name products were first sold in Europe at prices as much as 30 percent below those of branded products. This product strategy was introduced in the United States three decades ago. The market shares for generic products increase during economic downturns but subside when the economy improves. However, many consumers request generic substitutions for brand-name prescriptions at the pharmacy whenever they are available.

brand insistence
Consumer refusal of alternatives and extensive search for desired merchandise.

generic products
Products characterized by plain labels, no advertising, and the absence of brand names.

manufacturer's brand
Brand name owned by a manufacturer or other producer.

private brand Brand offered by a wholesaler or retailer.

MANUFACTURERS' BRANDS VERSUS PRIVATE BRANDS

Manufacturers' brands, also called *national brands*, define the image most people form when they think of a brand. A **manufacturer's brand** refers to a brand name owned by a manufacturer or other producer. Well-known manufacturers' brands include Hewlett-Packard, Sony, Pepsi-Cola, Dell, and French's. In contrast, many large wholesalers and retailers place their own brands on the merchandise they market. The brands offered by wholesalers and retailers usually are called **private brands** (or *private labels*). Although some manufacturers refuse to produce private-label goods, most regard such production as a way to reach additional market segments. Supervalu offers many private-label products in its retail grocery stores, including Equaline over-the-counter pharmaceuticals, Homelife household goods, and President's Choice foods.

The growth of private brands has paralleled chain stores in the United States. Manufacturers not only sell their well-known brands to stores but also put the store's own label on similar products. Such leading manufacturers as Westinghouse, Armstrong Rubber, and Heinz generate ever-increasing percentages of their total incomes by producing goods for sale under retailers' private labels. In U.S. grocery stores, one of every five items sold is a private brand. Private brands account for more than $85 billion in retail sales and are especially popular in western European countries such as Germany and the United Kingdom.[2]

Consistent with its corporate goal to buy and sell green products, office supply retailer Office Depot launched Office Depot Green, a private-label line of environmentally sound products. The line includes recycled paper and paper products, ink and toner cartridges, compact fluorescent light bulbs, and other items that create minimal impact on the environment.[3]

CAPTIVE BRANDS

The nation's major discounters—such as Walmart, Target, and Kmart—have come up with a spinoff of the private-label idea. So-called **captive brands** are national brands sold exclusively by a retail chain. Captive brands typically provide better profit margins than private labels. Target's captive brands include housewares and apparel by Michael Graves and Mossimo Giannulli; paper collections, including party supplies such as napkins, tablecloths, and paper plates by Belgian designer Isabelle de Borchgrave; Liz Lange maternity wear; furniture collections by Sean Conway; and moderately priced clothing by Isaac Mizrahi.[4]

captive brand National brand sold exclusively by a retail chain.

FAMILY AND INDIVIDUAL BRANDS

A **family brand** is a single brand name that identifies several related products. For example, KitchenAid markets a complete line of appliances under the KitchenAid name, and Johnson & Johnson offers a line of baby powder, lotions, plastic pants, and baby shampoo under its name. All Pepperidge Farm products, including bread, rolls, and cookies, carry the Pepperidge Farm brand. Frito-Lay markets both chips and salsa under its Tostitos family brand.

family brand Single brand name that identifies several related products.

Alternatively, a manufacturer may choose to market a product as an **individual brand**, which uniquely identifies the item itself, rather than promoting it under the name of the company or under an umbrella name covering similar items. Unilever, for example, markets Knorr, Bertolli, Lipton, and Slim-Fast food products; Pond's and Sunsilk beauty products; and Lifebuoy, Lux, and Dove soaps. PepsiCo's Quaker Oats unit markets Aunt Jemima breakfast products, Life and Cap'n Crunch cereals, and Rice-a-Roni side dishes along with Quaker oatmeal. Its Frito-Lay division makes Lays, Ruffles, and Doritos chips and Smartfood popcorn, while the Pepsi-Cola brands include Mountain Dew, Sierra Mist, Sobe juices and teas, and Aquafina water. Individual brands cost more than family

individual brand Single brand that uniquely identifies a product.

brands to market because the firm must develop a new promotional campaign to introduce each new product. Distinctive brands are extremely effective aids in implementing market segmentation strategies, however.

On the other hand, a promotional outlay for a family brand can benefit all items in the line. Family brands also help marketers introduce new products to both customers and retailers. Because supermarkets stock thousands of items, they hesitate to add new products unless they are confident they will be in demand.

Family brands should identify products of similar quality, or the firm risks harming its overall product image. If Rolls-Royce marketers were to place the Rolls name on a low-end car or a line of discounted clothing, they would severely tarnish the image of the luxury car line. Conversely,

© JEFF HAYNES/AFP/GETTY IMAGES

A family brand is a single brand name that identifies several related products. KitchenAid markets a complete line of appliances under its name.

Lexus, Infiniti, and Porsche put their names on luxury sport-utility vehicles to capitalize on their reputations and to enhance the acceptance of the new models in a competitive market.

Individual brand names should, however, distinguish dissimilar products. Kimberly-Clark markets two different types of diapers for infants under its Huggies and Pull-Ups names. Procter & Gamble offers shaving products under its Gillette name; laundry detergent under Cheer, Tide, and other brands; and dishwasher detergent under Cascade.

assessment check ✓

1. Identify the different types of brands.
2. How are generic products different from branded products?

Brand Equity

3 Explain the strategic value of brand equity.

As individuals, we often like to say our strongest asset is our reputation. The same is true of organizations. A brand can go a long way toward making or breaking a company's reputation. A strong brand identity backed by superior quality offers important strategic advantages for a firm. First, it increases the likelihood that consumers will recognize the firm's product or product line when they make purchase decisions. Second, a strong brand identity can contribute to buyers' perceptions of product quality. Branding can also reinforce customer loyalty and repeat purchases. A consumer who tries a brand and likes it will probably look for that brand on future store visits. All of these benefits contribute to a valuable form of competitive advantage called *brand equity.*

brand equity Added value that a respected, well-known brand name gives to a product in the marketplace.

Brand equity refers to the added value a certain brand name gives to a product in the marketplace. Brands with high equity confer financial advantages on a firm because they often command comparatively large market shares and consumers may pay little attention to differences in prices. Studies have also linked brand equity to high profits and stock returns. Service companies are also aware of the value of brand equity.

In global operations, high brand equity often facilitates expansion into new markets. Currently, Walmart and Google are the most valuable—and most recognized—brands in the world.[5] Similarly, Disney's brand equity allows it to market its goods and services in Europe and Japan—and now China. What makes a global brand powerful? According to Interbrand, which measures brand equity in dollar values, a strong brand has the power to increase a company's sales and earnings. A global brand generally is defined as one that sells at least 20 percent outside its home country.

Global advertising agency Young & Rubicam developed another brand equity system called the BrandAsset Valuator. Y&R's database of consumers' brand perceptions contains more than 400,000 consumer interviews and information on 20,000 brands across 44 countries. According to Y&R, a firm builds brand equity sequentially on four dimensions of brand personality. These four dimensions are differentiation, relevance, esteem, and knowledge:

briefly speaking

" The right name is an advertisement in itself."

—Claude C. Hopkins
(1866–1932)
American advertising pioneer

- *Differentiation* refers to a brand's ability to stand apart from competitors. Brands such as Porsche and Victoria's Secret stand out in consumers' minds as symbols of unique product characteristics.

- *Relevance* refers to the real and perceived appropriateness of brand to a big consumer segment. A large number of consumers must feel a need for the benefits offered by the brand. Brands with high relevance include Microsoft and Hallmark.

Most customers have knowledge, or awareness and understanding, of the Band-Aid brand.

© AP IMAGES/PHIL COALE

- *Esteem* is a combination of perceived quality and consumer perceptions about a brand's growing or declining popularity. A rise in perceived quality or in public opinion about a brand enhances a brand's esteem. But negative impressions reduce esteem. Brands with high esteem include General Mills and Honda.

- *Knowledge* refers to the extent of customers' awareness of the brand and understanding of what a good or service stands for. Knowledge implies that customers feel an intimate relationship with a brand. Examples include Jell-O and Band-Aid.[6]

 assessment check

1. What is brand equity?
2. What are the four dimensions of brand personality?

The Role of Category and Brand Management

Because of the tangible and intangible value associated with strong brand equity, marketing organizations invest considerable resources and effort in developing and maintaining these dimensions of brand personality. Traditionally, companies assigned the task of managing a brand's marketing strategies to a **brand manager**. Today, because they sell about 80 percent of their products to national retail chains, major consumer goods companies have adopted a strategy called **category management**. In this strategy, a manufacturer's *category manager* maximizes sales for the retailer by overseeing an entire product line, often tracking sales history with data from the retail checkout point and aggregating it with sales data for the entire category (obtained from third-party vendors) and qualitative data such as customer surveys.[7]

Unlike traditional product managers, category managers have profit responsibility for their product group and help the retailer's category buyer maximize sales for the whole category, not just the particular manufacturer's product. These managers are assisted by associates usually called *analysts*. Part of the shift to category management was initiated by large retailers, who realized they could benefit from the marketing muscle of large grocery and household goods producers such as Kraft and Procter & Gamble. As a result, producers began to focus their attention on in-store merchandising instead of mass-market advertising. Some manufacturers that are too small to dedicate a category manager to each retail chain assign a category manager to each major channel such as convenience stores, drugstores, grocery stores, and so on.[8]

Some of the steps companies follow in the category management process include defining the category based on the target market's needs, scoping out a consumer's decision process when shopping the category, identifying consumer groups and the store clusters with the greatest sales potential, creating a marketing strategy and performance goal for each cluster and using a scorecard to measure progress, defining and executing the tactics, and tracking progress.[9] Hershey's vending division offers category management services to its institutional customers, providing reduced inventory costs, improved warehouse efficiency, and increased sales.[10]

 Explain the benefits of category and brand management.

brand manager
Marketer responsible for a single brand.

category management
Product management system in which a category manager—with profit and loss responsibility—oversees a product line.

 assessment check

1. Define *brand manager*.
2. How does category management help retailers?

Product Identification

Organizations identify their products in the marketplace with brand names, symbols, and distinctive packaging. Almost every product distinguishable from another gives buyers some means of identifying it. Sunkist Growers, for instance, stamps its oranges with the name Sunkist. Iams stamps a paw print on all of its pet food packages. For well over a century, Prudential Financial has used the Rock of Gibraltar as its symbol. In the "Solving an Ethical Controversy" feature, the NFL wants to protect its product identification.

Choosing how to identify a firm's output represents a major strategic decision for marketers. Produce growers have another option besides gummed paper stickers for identifying fruits and vegetables: laser coding. This technology marks fruits and vegetables with their name, identification number, and country of origin. The food tattoo is visible but also edible—good news for consumers who

solving an ethical controversy

Who Dat? Slogan Causes Football Furor

fter decades of bravely chanting "Who Dat Say Dey Gonna Beat Dem Saints?" New Orleans Saints fans finally got the answer they hoped for when their team won Super Bowl XLIV. The team's fan base, which calls itself Who Dat Nation, appropriated the chant during the 1980s and used it regularly despite a run of losing seasons.

But 2009–2010 proved to be different, as the Saints defeated all but one of their competitors during the regular season and took the big prize, beating the Indianapolis Colts 31–17 in the Super Bowl. In fact, it was not until the Saints became a serious contender that the National Football League told New Orleans it had no claim to the "Who Dat?" slogan. Furthermore, the NFL announced it had issued cease-and-desist orders against all sellers of Saints memorabilia bearing the slogan.

Does the NFL own the rights to "Who Dat?"

PRO

1. Everything a football franchise does is governed by the NFL.

2. Merchandise that carries a slogan could confuse customers into thinking the products are official NFL products.

CON

1. The saying "Who Dat?" is embedded in New Orleans culture and history and, as such, the "Who Dat?" cheer belongs to New Orleans.

2. To prevent a merchant from engaging in business could be considered restraint of trade.

Summary

After a flood of protest from Louisianans—including the state's chief executive Governor Bobby Jindal—the NFL backed down. Spokespersons claimed the whole matter was merely a "misunderstanding," saying the NFL only wanted to be sure souvenir manufacturers didn't pair the "Who Dat?" slogan with an NFL or Saints logo, thus implying that their products constituted official merchandise. What this experience taught sports fans everywhere: don't mess with New Orleans.

Sources: Jacqui Goddard, "Reason on Side of the Saints in Slogan Row with Football Chiefs; United States," *London Times,* February 3, 2010, http://timesonline.co.uk; Neely Tucker, "Who Dat Messing with the Saints' Who Dat Cheer?" *Washington Post,* February 2, 2010, http://www.washingtonpost.com; Jennifer Levitz, "Who Dat Owns 'Who Dat?' Dat's Us, Sez da NFL—League Moves against Vendors of T-Shirts with New Orleans Chant," *The Wall Street Journal,* January 30, 2010, http://online.wsj.com.

tire of peeling tiny stickers from their apples and tomatoes. While the stickers provide important information in the form of four- or five-digit price look-up (PLU) codes that a supermarket cashier enters into the computer system to retrieve pricing information, the stickers must also be removed from the produce before it can be eaten. The laser codes include the PLU code and eliminate sticky labels.[11]

© AP IMAGES/PRNEWSFOTO/MICHELIN NORTH AMERICA

> A brand mark is a symbol or pictorial design that distinguishes a product, such as the Michelin Man, a symbol for the Michelin tire company.

Brand Names and Brand Marks

A name plays a central role in establishing brand and product identity. The American Marketing Association defines a **brand name** as the part of a brand that can be spoken. It can consist of letters, numbers, or words and forms a name that identifies and distinguishes the firm's offerings from those of its competitors. Firms can also identify their brands by brand marks. A **brand mark** is a symbol or pictorial design that distinguishes a product, such as the Jolly Green Giant for Green Giant Vegetables.

Effective brand names are easy to pronounce, recognize, and remember. Short names, such as Nike, Ford, and Bounty, meet these requirements. Marketers try to overcome problems with easily mispronounced brand names by teaching consumers the correct pronunciations. For example, early advertisements for the Korean carmaker Hyundai explained that the name rhymes with *Sunday*. Sensitivity to clear communication doesn't end with the choice of brand name; marketers should also be aware of how well they get their point across in interpersonal communications. The "Career Readiness" feature provides some tips for avoiding jargon in marketing communications.

A brand name should also give buyers the correct connotation of the product's image. Nissan's X-Terra connotes youth and extreme sports to promote the off-road SUV, while Kodak's EasyShare tells consumers how simple printing digital pictures can be. ConAgra's Healthy Choice food line presents an alternative to fast foods that may be high in sodium or fat, and the iPod Nano uses a name that aptly suggests its tiny size. A brand name must also qualify for legal protection. The Lanham Act of 1946 states that registered trademarks must not contain words or phrases in general use, such as *automobile* or *suntan lotion*. These generic words actually describe particular types of products, and no company can claim exclusive rights to them.

Marketers feel increasingly hard-pressed to coin effective brand names, as multitudes of competitors rush to stake out names for their own products. Some companies register names before they have products to fit them to prevent competitors from using them. Few, however, have found as memorable a name for their product as Louisiana pharmacist George Boudreaux, whose highly successful diaper rash cream is called Boudreaux's Butt Paste. The Butt Paste line has been extended with products for chapped lips, razor burn, bedsores, and other conditions, but nothing keeps the Butt Paste name in front of the public like its NASCAR sponsorships.[12]

When a class of products becomes generally known by the original brand name of a specific offering, the brand name may become a descriptive generic name. If this occurs, the original owner loses exclusive claim to the brand name. The generic names nylon, aspirin, escalator, kerosene, and zipper started as brand names. Other generic names that were once brand names include cola, yo-yo, linoleum, and shredded wheat.

Marketers must distinguish between brand names that have become legally generic terms and those that seem generic only in many consumers' eyes. Consumers often adopt legal brand names as descriptive names. Jell-O, for instance, is a brand name owned exclusively by Kraft Foods, but many

brand name Part of a brand, consisting of letters, numbers, or words, that can be spoken and that identifies and distinguishes a firm's offerings from those of its competitors.

brand mark Symbol or pictorial design that distinguishes a product.

career *readiness* ⓤsing Jargon in Everyday Communication

Wireless technology has supercharged the pace of everyday life, and with it comes the temptation to use the shorthand common to text messaging in other everyday communications. But consider these facts:

- When you use abbreviations like "btw" and "p&c" in your communication, you're using jargon. And by its very definition, jargon can be confusing and misleading. For example, while it might be obvious to you that "btw" stands for "by the way," to another person it may mean "between." You may interpret "p&c" to mean "private and confidential," but to people in the insurance industry, it stands for "property and casualty." And think of the potential danger in using "jk" when you mean "just kidding": your reader may skip right past those two letters or mistake them for someone's initials.

- Jargon excludes. When you use jargon and people don't understand your message, they may peg you as someone who's not open or friendly. In fact, recent studies reveal that jargon users are perceived as less likable. Would you really want a client or customer to feel that way about you?

- Using jargon in business communication could be a deal breaker. Although the jargon of text-messaging has become increasingly common, it's too casual for business correspondences and creates a poor impression as you search for—or try to succeed at—that new job. And if your manager is older than you—say, a member of the baby boom generation—he or she is unlikely to be impressed.

Sources: Tim Burress, "Abbreviations Used in E-Mail," *Videojug.com*, http://www.videojug.com, accessed May 11, 2010; Todd Hicks, "Why Business Jargon and Acronyms Must Be Avoided in Communication," *Associated Content.com*, January 14, 2010; "How to Write an Effective Business Communication Email," *eHow.com*, July 10, 2009, http://www.ehow.com.

---

consumers casually apply it as a descriptive name for gelatin desserts. Similarly, many people use the term Kleenex to refer to facial tissues. English and Australian consumers use the brand name Hoover as a verb for vacuuming. One popular way to look something up on the Internet is now to "Google it." Xerox is such a well-known brand name that people frequently—though incorrectly—use it as a verb to mean photocopying. To protect its valuable trademark, Xerox Corporation has created advertisements explaining that Xerox is a brand name and registered trademark and should not be used as a verb.

Trademarks

Businesses invest considerable resources in developing and promoting brands and brand identities. The high value of brand equity encourages firms to take steps in protecting the expenditures they invest in their brands.

A **trademark** is a brand for which the owner claims exclusive legal protection. A trademark should not be confused with a trade name, which identifies a company. The Coca-Cola Company is a trade name, but Coke is a trademark of the company's product. Some trade names duplicate companies' brand names.

PROTECTING TRADEMARKS

trademark Brand for which the owner claims exclusive legal protection.

Trademark protection confers the exclusive legal right to use a brand name, brand mark, and any slogan or product name abbreviation. It designates the origin or source of a good or service. Frequently, trademark protection is applied to words or phrases, such as *Bud* for Budweiser or *the Met* for the New York Metropolitan Opera. Robert Burck, better known as the Naked Cowboy—a New York street performer who plays guitar in Times Square wearing nothing but white cowboy boots, cowboy hat, and underpants—registered his likeness and the words "Naked Cowboy" as a trademark. Burck sued Mars, the makers of M&Ms, for trademark infringement after they erected a video billboard showing a blue M&M playing the guitar and clad only in white boots, hat, and underpants.[13]

Firms can also receive trademark protection for packaging elements and product features such as shape, design, and typeface. U.S. law has fortified trademark protection in recent years. The Federal Trademark Dilution Act of 1995 gives a trademark holder the right to sue for trademark infringement even if other products using its brand are not particularly similar or easily confused in the minds of consumers. The infringing company does not even have to know it is diluting another's trademark. The act also gives a trademark holder the right to sue if another party imitates its trademark.

The Internet is the next battlefield for trademark infringement cases. Some companies are attempting to protect their trademarks by filing infringement cases against companies using similar Internet addresses or using unauthorized versions of the same name. Such was the case when a St. Louis–based technology firm called Bing! Information Design sued Microsoft for naming its search engine "Bing." The suit claims the design firm has been using the "Bing!" name since before 2000 while Microsoft's use of the word "Bing" did not surface until mid-2009. The suit claims the duplication erodes the design firm's efforts to differentiate itself and causes confusion in the marketplace.[14]

TRADE DRESS

Visual cues used in branding create an overall look sometimes referred to as **trade dress**. These visual components may be related to color selections, sizes, package and label shapes, and similar factors. For example, the McDonald's "golden arches," Merrill Lynch's bull, and the yellow of Shell's seashell are all part of these products' trade dress. Owens Corning has registered the color pink to distinguish its insulation from the competition. A combination of visual cues may also constitute trade dress. Consider a Mexican food product that uses the colors of the Mexican flag: green, white, and red.

Trade dress disputes have led to numerous courtroom battles but no apparent consensus from the Supreme Court. Apparel and accessories designer Marc Jacobs recently filed a lawsuit against another firm for allegedly copying the design of its Marc Jacobs Pretty Nylon tote bag and affixing marks that look "confusingly similar" to the Marc Jacobs logo.[15]

trade dress Visual components that contribute to the overall look of a brand.

Developing Global Brand Names and Trademarks

Cultural and language variations make brand-name selection a difficult undertaking for international marketers; an excellent brand name or symbol in one country may prove disastrous in another. An advertising campaign for E-Z washing machines failed in the United Kingdom because the British pronounce *z* as "zed." A firm marketing a product in multiple countries must also decide whether to use a single brand name for universal promotions or

Shell's yellow seashell is part of the product's trade dress.

© AP IMAGES/PRNEWSFOTO/SHELL OIL COMPANY

tailor names to individual countries. Most languages contain *o* and *k* sounds, so *okay* has become an international word. Most languages also have a short *a,* so Coca-Cola, Kodak, and Texaco work as effective brands abroad.

In a recent dispute, two global companies recently squared off, with distiller Maker's Mark winning a judgment against Jose Cuervo International. As part of the manufacturing process of its Maker's Mark bourbon, the company seals the bottles by hand-dipping the tops in red wax, creating a free-form red seal. Makers of Jose Cuervo tequila had recently begun affixing a red wax seal on its bottles. The court agreed that the red wax seal was part of Maker's Mark's trademark and barred Jose Cuervo International from its further use.[16]

Packaging

A firm's product strategy must also address questions about packaging. Like its brand name, a product's package can powerfully influence buyers' purchase decisions.

Marketers apply increasingly scientific methods to their packaging decisions. Rather than experimenting with physical models or drawings, more and more package designers work on special computer graphics programs that create three-dimensional images of packages in thousands of colors, shapes, and typefaces. Another software program helps marketers design effective packaging by simulating the displays shoppers see when they walk down supermarket aisles.

Companies conduct marketing research to evaluate current packages and to test alternative package designs. Marketers at Sara Lee identified convenience, value, and flavor as significant trends for convenience stores. For this reason, Sara Lee offers these retailers special programs that exploit those trends, including "on-the-go" packaging of several Sara Lee products, such as individually wrapped bakery items and handheld sandwiches.[17]

A package serves three major objectives: (1) protection against damage, spoilage, and pilferage; (2) assistance in marketing the product; and (3) cost effectiveness. Let's briefly consider each of these objectives.

PROTECTION AGAINST DAMAGE, SPOILAGE, AND PILFERAGE

The original objective of packaging was to offer physical protection for the merchandise. Products typically pass through several stages of handling between manufacturing and customer purchases, and a package must protect its contents from damage. Furthermore, packages of perishable products must protect the contents against spoilage in transit and in storage until purchased by the consumer. Fears of product tampering have forced many firms to improve package designs. Over-the-counter medicines are sold in tamper-resistant packages covered with warnings informing consumers not to purchase merchandise without protective seals intact. Many grocery items and light-sensitive products are packaged in tamper-resistant containers as well. Products in glass jars, such as spaghetti sauce and jams, often come with vacuum-depressed buttons in the lids that pop up the first time the lids are opened.

Even prescription medicine packaging can be revolutionized for the consumer's benefit, as Target found. Its ClearRx prescription dispensing system offers bottles with easy-to-read labels, in a shape designed to fit in the palm of the hand. An information card tucked into a sleeve on the back of the bottle provides a brief summary of the medication's uses and side effects. For households where several people are taking medication, color-coded rings on the neck of the bottle help family members identify their medication at a glance.[18]

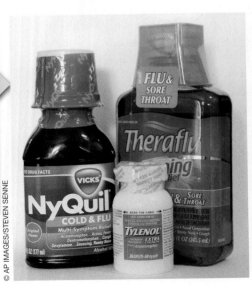

Over-the-counter medicines are sold in tamper-resistant packages covered with warnings informing consumers not to purchase merchandise without protective seals intact.

© AP IMAGES/STEVEN SENNE

Many packages offer important safeguards against pilferage for retailers. Shoplifting and employee theft cost retailers several billion dollars each year. To limit this activity, many packages feature oversized cardboard backings too large to fit into a shoplifter's pocket or purse. Efficient packaging that protects against damage, spoilage, and theft is especially important for international marketers, which must contend with varying climatic conditions and the added time and stress involved in overseas shipping.

ASSISTANCE IN MARKETING THE PRODUCT

The proliferation of new products, changes in consumer lifestyles and buying habits, and marketers' emphasis on targeting smaller market segments have increased the importance of packaging as a promotional tool. Many firms address consumer concerns about protecting the environment by designing packages made of biodegradable and recyclable materials. To demonstrate serious concern regarding environmental protection, Procter & Gamble, Coors, McDonald's, and other firms created ads that describe their efforts in developing environmentally sound packaging.

In a grocery store where thousands of different items compete for notice, a product must capture the shopper's attention. Marketers combine colors, sizes, shapes, graphics, and typefaces to establish distinctive trade dress that sets their products apart from the products of competitors. Packaging can help establish a common identity for a group of items sold under the same brand name. Like the brand name, a package should evoke the product's image and communicate its value. The design features of Folgers' AromaSeal container include a flexible cap, special handle, and concave bottom to improve freshness and make the canister easier to use. After Kraft Foods introduced its Maxwell House coffee in a canister that Procter & Gamble, makers of Folgers, claimed was patent infringement, the two companies instituted a series of lawsuits. The suits have since been settled.[19]

Other packages also enhance convenience. Pump dispensers, for example, facilitate the use of products ranging from mustard to insect repellent. Squeezable bottles of honey and ketchup make the products easier to use and store. Packaging provides key benefits for convenience foods such as meals and soups packaged in microwavable containers, juice drinks in aseptic packages, and frozen entrées and vegetables packaged in single-serving portions.

Some firms increase consumer utility with packages designed for reuse. Empty jelly jars have long doubled as drinking glasses. Parents can buy bubble bath in animal-shaped plastic bottles suitable for bathtub play. Packaging is a major component in Avon's overall marketing strategy. The firm's decorative, reusable bottles have even become collectibles.

COST-EFFECTIVE PACKAGING

Although packaging must perform a number of functions for the producer, marketers, and consumers, it must do so at a reasonable cost. Sometimes changes in the packaging can make packages both cheaper and better for the environment. A redesign of the standard gallon milk jug has cut shipping costs and lessened its environmental impact. And a design student's recent redesign of a classic icon, the Coke bottle, has yielded a squared-off container with an off-center cap that makes drinking easier. The container is also stackable and able to be nested, saving space and enabling easier shipping.[20]

LABELING

Labels were once a separate element applied to a package; today, they are an integral part of a typical package. Labels perform both promotional and informational functions. A **label** carries an item's brand name or symbol, the name and address of the manufacturer or distributor, information about the product's composition and size, and recommended uses. The right label can play an important role in attracting consumer attention and encouraging purchases.

Consumer confusion and dissatisfaction over such descriptions as giant economy size, king size, and family size led to the passage of the Fair Packaging and Labeling Act in 1966. The act requires

label Branding component that carries an item's brand name or symbol, the name and address of the manufacturer or distributor, information about the product, and recommended uses.

that a label offer adequate information concerning the package contents and that a package design facilitate value comparisons among competing products.

The Nutrition Labeling and Education Act of 1990 imposes a uniform format in which food manufacturers must disclose nutritional information about their products. In addition, the Food and Drug Administration (FDA) has mandated design standards for nutritional labels that provide clear guidelines to consumers about food products. The FDA has also tightened definitions for loosely used terms such as *light, fat free, lean,* and *extra lean,* and it mandates that labels list the amounts of fat, sodium, dietary fiber, calcium, vitamins, and other components in typical servings. The latest ruling requires food manufacturers to include on nutritional labels the total amount of trans fats—hydrogenated oils that improve texture and freshness but contribute to high levels of cholesterol—in each product.

The new Food Allergen Labeling and Consumer Protection Act requires that food labeling disclose all major food allergens in terms the average consumer can understand. According to the Food and Drug Administration, eight allergens account for most documented allergic reactions to food, and all must be identified. They are milk, eggs, peanuts, tree nuts (such as almonds, cashews, and walnuts), fish (such as bass, cod, and flounder), shellfish (such as crab, lobster, and shrimp), soy, and wheat.[21]

Labeling requirements differ elsewhere in the world. In Canada, for example, labels must provide information in both English and French. The type and amount of information required on labels also vary among nations. International marketers must carefully design labels to conform to the regulations of each country in which they market their merchandise.

The **universal product code (UPC)** designation is another important aspect of a label or package. Introduced in 1974 as a method for cutting expenses in the supermarket industry, UPCs are numerical bar codes printed on packages. Optical scanner systems read these codes, and computer systems recognize items and print their prices on cash register receipts. Although UPC scanners are costly, they permit both considerable labor savings over manual pricing and improved inventory control. The universal product code is also a major asset for marketing research. However, many consumers feel frustrated when only a UPC is placed on a package without an additional price tag, because they do not always know how much an item costs if the price labels are missing from the shelf.

Radio-frequency identification (RFID) tags—electronic chips that carry encoded product identification—may replace some of the functions of UPC codes, such as price identification and inventory tracking. But consumer privacy concerns about the amount of information RFID tracking can accumulate may limit their use to aggregate packaging such as pallets, rather than units sized for individual sale. When the FDA decided to require drug makers and marketers to place a scannable code on all drugs sold to U.S. hospitals at the level of patient unit doses, it chose UPC codes.

universal product code (UPC) Numerical bar code system used to record product and price information.

Brand Extensions

Some brands become so popular that marketers may decide to use them on unrelated products in pursuit of instant recognition for the new offerings. The strategy of attaching a popular brand name to a new product in an unrelated product category is known as **brand extension**. This practice should not be confused with **line extensions**, which refers to new sizes, styles, or related products. A brand extension, in contrast, carries over from one product nothing but the brand name. In establishing brand extensions, marketers hope to gain access to new customers and markets by building on the equity already established in their existing brands. This is the strategy behind Nautica's brand extension from fashion to furniture and bedding. Nintendo extended its participative Wii videogame line with Wii Fit Plus, an expansion on its popular Wii Fit fitness software.[22]

Targeting the 7- to 12-year-old age group, Mattel extended its Barbie fashion doll brand in an effort to sustain older children's interest. It launched the "Barbie Girls" experience, which includes a free interactive Web site and a subscription-based "VIP" version, both with opportunities for children to create a virtual world where they can design their own room, cruise a cyber-mall, and more. A Barbie-inspired handheld MP3 device interacts with the sites. Mattel also offers a free Web site for parents, with tools and resources for cyberspace safety. The flagship Barbie Store in Shanghai offers a "fashion-tainment" experience complete with a playroom also available

brand extension Strategy of attaching a popular brand name to a new product in an unrelated product category.

line extension Development of individual offerings that appeal to different market segments while remaining closely related to the existing product line.

Mattel has extended its Barbie fashion doll brand to include a Web site as well as a Barbie Store, where visitors can buy Barbie-branded apparel, mostly in shades of pink.

I'm a Barbie Girl!

© AP IMAGES/NATACHA PISARENKO

for parties, a kid-sized salon, and a café. Visitors to the Barbie Store can also buy Barbie-branded apparel—mostly in shades of pink.[23]

Brand Licensing

A growing number of firms authorize other companies to use their brand names. Even colleges license their logos and trademarks. Known as **brand licensing**, this practice expands a firm's exposure in the marketplace, much as a brand extension does. The brand name's owner also receives an extra source of income in the form of royalties from licensees, typically 8 to 12 percent of wholesale revenues.[24]

Brand experts note several potential problems with licensing, however. Brand names do not transfer well to all products. The PetSmart PetsHotel was a winner, as was *American Idol* camp, but recent losers were Precious Moments coffins, Donald Trump steaks, and Girls Gone Wild apparel. If a licensee produces a poor-quality product or an item ethically incompatible with the original brand, the arrangement could damage the reputation of the brand. Consider the failure of two odd brand extensions: Cheetos lip balm and Bic disposable underwear.[25]

Brand overextension is another risk. Starbucks extended its coffee brand to a "lifestyle" brand by marketing coffee beans in supermarkets and selling CDs, books, and a broad food menu in its retail outlets. By moving away from the qualities that helped make it successful, the brand suffered and market share declined, resulting in the closing of nearly 1,000 Starbucks stores. The company's latest brand extension—an instant coffee called Via, sold in single-serving packets—seems to fly in the face of the traditional Starbucks image of a barista carefully brewing an individual cup of coffee for an appreciative customer who savors the experience.[26]

brand licensing
Practice that expands a firm's exposure in the marketplace.

 assessment check

1. Distinguish between a brand name and a trademark.
2. What are the three purposes of packaging?
3. Describe brand extension and brand licensing.

New-Product Planning

6 **Identify and briefly describe each of the new-product development strategies.**

As its offerings enter the maturity and decline stages of the product lifecycle, a firm must add new items to continue to prosper. Regular additions of new products to the firm's line help protect it from product obsolescence.

New products are the lifeblood of any business, and survival depends on a steady flow of new entries. Some new products may implement major technological breakthroughs. Other new products simply extend existing product lines. In other words, a new product is one that either the company or the customer has not handled before.

Product Development Strategies

A firm's strategy for new-product development varies according to its existing product mix and the match between current offerings and the firm's overall marketing objectives. The current market positions of products also affect product development strategy. Figure 12.1 identifies four alternative development strategies as market penetration, market development, product development, and product diversification.

A **market penetration strategy** seeks to increase sales of existing products in existing markets. Firms can attempt to extend their penetration of markets in several ways. They may modify products, improve product quality, or promote new and different ways to use products. Packaged-goods marketers often pursue this strategy to boost market share for mature products in mature markets. Product positioning often plays a major role in such a strategy.

Product positioning refers to consumers' perceptions of a product's attributes, uses, quality, and advantages and disadvantages relative to competing brands. Marketers often conduct marketing research studies to analyze consumer preferences and to construct product positioning maps that plot their products' positions in relation to those of competitors' offerings.

Hyundai Motors has repositioned its Hyundai brand in the United States. Although the Hyundai entered the U.S. market as an inexpensive alternative to other cars, the company

market penetration strategy Strategy that seeks to increase sales of existing products in existing markets.

product positioning Consumers' perceptions of a product's attributes, uses, quality, and advantages and disadvantages relative to competing brands.

mktg: *success*

Swiffer Aims to Be Not Just User-Friendly But Pet-Friendly

Background. Cincinnati–based Procter & Gamble, the world's largest consumer products company, markets dozens of brands. Each of its top 23 brands tallies more than $1 billion in annual sales. Eleven years ago, the company introduced Swiffer, a line of dusters, brooms, and mops that use electrostatically charged disposable cloths to get the job done. While Swiffer

hasn't yet reached the elite billion-dollar ranks, it brought in $325.4 million in a recent year.

The Challenge. Sales of Procter & Gamble's many products represent the equivalent of a $12 spend by every human being on earth. Arguably, however, Swiffer is one of those items that people don't really need. After all, for centuries homemakers

have used other tools—brooms, brushes, mops, rags—to clean. Some observers assert that cleaning can be accomplished without electrostatically charged disposable cloths.

The Strategy. Procter & Gamble seeks to expand its global customer base beyond its current 4 billion. Besides targeting women as their primary consumer, they have turned

has ratcheted up the look and feel of its sedans to emphasize quality and safety as well as eco-friendliness: Hyundai leads the industry in fuel economy.[27]

A **market development strategy** concentrates on finding new markets for existing products. Market segmentation, discussed in Chapter 9, provides useful support for such an effort. New Jersey–based supermarket chain Asian Food Markets once targeted chiefly Asian shoppers from China, Taiwan, Korea, and Japan to the Phillippines, Southeast Asia, and India. Today, however, the family-owned enterprise has expanded its reach beyond Asian customers by offering a wide selection of fresh produce, meat and poultry, and fresh baked goods as well as authentic Chinese-inspired dishes for take-out.[28] Procter & Gamble searches for a new market of pet owners for its Swiffer products, described in the "Marketing Success" feature.

The strategy of **product development** refers to the introduction of new products into identifiable or established markets. Responding to moviegoers' recently revived interest in 3-D, Panasonic introduced the world's first 3-D home entertainment system. The system includes a pair of special 3-D eyewear as well as a Blu-ray disk player for playing movies at home in 3-D format.[29]

Firms may also choose to introduce new products into markets in which they have already established positions to try to increase overall market share. These new offerings are called *flanker brands*. The fragrance industry uses this strategy extensively when it develops scents related to their most popular products. The flanker scents are related in both their smell and their names. Coty has built a family of flanker brands around its popular Stetson fragrance. The flanker brands include All American Stetson, Lady Stetson, Stetson Black, Stetson Sierra, Stetson Untamed, and the latest in the line, Stetson Fresh.[30]

Finally, a **product diversification strategy** focuses on developing entirely new products for new markets. Some firms look for new target markets that complement their existing markets; others look in completely new directions. PepsiCo's CEO, Indra Nooyi, regards obesity as one of the world's most significant public-health issues—and wants her company to be part of the solution,

figure 12.1
Alternative Product Development Strategies

market development strategy Strategy that concentrates on finding new markets for existing products.

product development Introduction of new products into identifiable or established markets.

product diversification strategy Developing entirely new products for new markets.

their focus to pet owners. Research reveals that about half of all American households includes a cat or dog. In addition, pets today are more likely to be regarded as a member of the family.

The Outcome. To engage this consumer segment, Procter & Gamble hired Cesar Millan, animal behaviorist and host of the TV program "Dog Whisperer," to appear in Swiffer ads. A Swiffer user himself, Millan will appear in online marketing opportunities, providing dog tips on the Swiffer Web site and Facebook page, to promote the SweeperVac, a rechargeable vacuum cleaner that uses Swiffer cloths. In the ads, Millan will demonstrate how to use Swiffer products without upsetting household pets. He will also promote the SweeperVac on his own Facebook page, which numbers more than 195,000 followers.

Sources: Bruce Horovitz, "Consumer Products Giant Looks beyond U.S. Borders," *USA Today,* March 18, 2010, http://www.usatoday.com; Stephen Treffinger, "Saluting Mops That Can," *The New York Times,* March 18, 2010, http://www.nytimes.com; Andrew Adam Newman, "Teaching Pet-Friendly Homes New Cleaning Tricks," *The New York Times,* February 16, 2010, http://www.nytimes.com.

In addition to the classic Stetson scent, customers can choose flanker brands like Lady Stetson and Stetson Black. Flanker brands are common in the fragrance industry.

IMAGE COURTESY OF THE ADVERTISING ARCHIVES

cannibalization Loss of sales of an existing product due to competition from a new product in the same line.

not the problem. In 2006, PepsiCo began diversifying its product lines beyond items that are "fun for you" to items that are "good for you," including juices, nuts, and oatmeal. Today, the company's growing family of "good for you" products accounts for $10 billion in annual revenues—nearly 20 percent of sales.[31]

In selecting a new-product strategy, marketers should keep in mind an additional potential problem: **cannibalization**. Any firm wants to avoid investing resources in a new-product introduction that will adversely affect sales of existing products. A product that takes sales from another offering in the same product line is said to cannibalize that line. A company can accept some loss of sales from existing products if the new offering will generate sufficient additional sales to warrant its investment in its development and market introduction.

 assessment check

1. Distinguish between market penetration and market development strategies.

2. What is product development?

3. What is product diversification?

The Consumer Adoption Process

Describe the consumer adoption process.

In the **adoption process**, consumers go through a series of stages from first learning about the new product to trying it and deciding whether to purchase it regularly or reject it. These stages in the consumer adoption process can be classified as follows:

adoption process Stages consumers go through in learning about a new product, trying it, and deciding whether to purchase it again.

1. *Awareness.* Individuals first learn of the new product, but they lack full information about it.

2. *Interest.* Potential buyers begin to seek information about it.

3. *Evaluation.* They consider the likely benefits of the product.

4. *Trial.* They make trial purchases to determine its usefulness.

5. *Adoption/Rejection.* If the trial purchase produces satisfactory results, they decide to use the product regularly.

Marketers must understand the adoption process to move potential consumers to the adoption stage. Once marketers recognize a large number of consumers at the interest stage, they can take steps to stimulate sales by moving these buyers through the evaluation and trial stages. To introduce its new cupcake line, Cinnabon bakeries sponsored a massive giveaway promotion. Customers who visited a Cinnabon outlet in a shopping mall received a free bite-sized portion of the new cupcakes. The promotion included an online essay contest on the subject "why my life needs Cinnabon frosting," with a $100 gift card as the prize.[32]

Cinnabon bakeries sponsored a massive giveaway promotion to introduce its new cupcake line.

Adopter Categories

First buyers of new products, the **consumer innovators**, are people who purchase new products almost as soon as these products reach the market. Later adopters wait for additional information and rely on the experiences of initial buyers before making trial purchases. Consumer innovators welcome innovations in each product area. Some computer users, for instance, rush to install new software immediately after each update becomes available.

A number of studies about the adoption of new products have identified five categories of purchasers based on relative times of adoption. These categories, shown in Figure 12.2, are consumer innovators, early adopters, early majority, late majority, and laggards.

While the adoption process focuses on individuals and the steps they go through in making the ultimate decision of whether to become repeat purchasers of the new product or reject it as a failure to satisfy their needs, the **diffusion process** focuses on all members of a community or social system. The focus here is on the speed at which an innovative product is accepted or rejected by all members of the community.

Figure 12.2 shows the diffusion process as following a normal distribution from a small group of early purchasers *(innovators)* to the final group of consumers *(laggards)* to make trial purchases of the new product. A few people adopt at first and then the number of adopters increases rapidly as the value of the product becomes apparent. The adoption rate finally diminishes as the number of potential consumers who have not adopted, or purchased, the product diminishes. Typically, innovators make up the first 2.5 percent of buyers who adopt the new product; laggards are the last 16 percent to do so. Figure 12.2 excludes those who never adopt the product.

consumer innovators
People who purchase new products almost as soon as the products reach the market.

diffusion process
Process by which new goods or services are accepted in the marketplace.

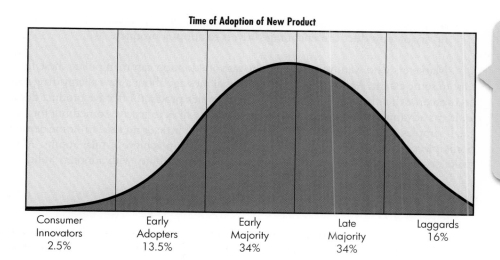

Time of Adoption of New Product

| Consumer Innovators 2.5% | Early Adopters 13.5% | Early Majority 34% | Late Majority 34% | Laggards 16% |

figure 12.2

Categories of Adopters Based on Relative Times of Adoption

Identifying Early Adopters

It's no surprise that identifying consumers or organizations most likely to try a new product can be vital to a product's success. By reaching these buyers early in the product's development or introduction, marketers can treat these adopters as a test market, evaluating the product and discovering suggestions for modifications. Because early purchasers often act as opinion leaders from whom others seek advice, their attitudes toward new products quickly spread to others. Acceptance or rejection of the innovation by these purchasers can help forecast its expected success. New-car models are multiplying, for instance, and many are sporting a dizzying variety of options such as ports to accommodate—and integrate—the driver's iPod, wireless phone, and laptop. Improved stability controls, collision warnings, and "smart engines" that save fuel are also available.

A large number of studies have established the general characteristics of first adopters. These pioneers tend to be younger, are better educated, and enjoy higher incomes than other consumers. They are more mobile than later adopters and change both their jobs and addresses more often. They also rely more heavily than later adopters on impersonal information sources; more hesitant buyers depend primarily on company-generated promotional information and word-of-mouth communications.

RATE OF ADOPTION DETERMINANTS

Frisbees progressed from the product introduction stage to the market maturity stage in a period of six months. By contrast, the U.S. Department of Agriculture tried for 13 years to persuade corn farmers to use hybrid seed corn, an innovation capable of doubling crop yields. Five characteristics of a product innovation influence its adoption rate:

1. *Relative advantage.* An innovation that appears far superior to previous ideas offers a greater relative advantage—reflected in terms of lower price, physical improvements, or ease of use—and increases the product's adoption rate.

2. *Compatibility.* An innovation consistent with the values and experiences of potential adopters attracts new buyers at a relatively rapid rate. Consumers already comfortable with the miniaturization of communications technology may be attracted to smartphones, for instance, and the iPhone's 2- by 3-inch screen.

3. *Complexity.* The relative difficulty of understanding the innovation influences the speed of acceptance. In most cases, consumers move slowly in adopting new products they find difficult to understand or use. Farmers' cautious acceptance of hybrid seed corn illustrates how long an adoption can take.

4. *Possibility of trial use.* An initial free or discounted trial of a good or service means adopters can reduce their risk of financial loss when they try the product. A coupon for a free item or a free night's stay at a hotel can accelerate the rate of adoption.

5. *Observability.* If potential buyers can observe an innovation's superiority in a tangible form, the adoption rate increases. In-store demonstrations or even advertisements that focus on the superiority of a product can encourage buyers to adopt a product.

Marketers who want to accelerate the rate of adoption can manipulate these five characteristics at least to some extent. An informative promotional message about a new allergy drug could help consumers overcome their hesitation in adopting this complex product. Effective product design can emphasize an item's advantages over the competition. Everyone likes to receive something for free, so giving away small samples of a new product lets consumers try it at little or no risk. In-home demonstrations or trial home placements of items such as furniture or rugs can achieve similar results. Marketers must also make positive attempts to ensure the innovation's compatibility with adopters' value systems.

Organizing for New-Product Development

A firm needs to be organized in such a way that its personnel can stimulate and coordinate new-product development. Some companies contract with independent design firms to develop new products. Many assign product-innovation functions to one or more of the following entities: new-product committees, new-product departments, product managers, and venture teams.

NEW-PRODUCT COMMITTEES

The most common organizational arrangement for activities in developing a new product is to center these functions in a new-product committee. This group typically brings together experts in such areas as marketing, finance, manufacturing, engineering, research, and accounting. Committee members spend less time conceiving and developing their own new-product ideas than reviewing and approving new-product plans that arise elsewhere in the organization. The committee might review ideas from the engineering and design staff or perhaps from marketers and salespeople who are in constant contact with customers.

Because members of a new-product committee hold important jobs in the firm's functional areas, their support for any new-product plan likely foreshadows approval for further development. However, new-product committees in large companies tend to reach decisions slowly and maintain conservative views. Sometimes members compromise so they can return to their regular responsibilities.

NEW-PRODUCT DEPARTMENTS

Many companies establish separate, formally organized departments to generate and refine new-product ideas. The departmental structure overcomes the limitations of the new-product committee system and encourages innovation as a permanent full-time activity. The new-product department is responsible for all phases of a development project within the firm, including screening decisions, developing product specifications, and coordinating product testing. The head of the department wields substantial authority and typically reports to the chief executive officer, chief operating officer, or a top marketing executive.

PRODUCT MANAGERS

A **product manager** is another term for a brand manager, a function mentioned earlier in the chapter. This marketer supports the marketing strategies of an individual product or product line. Procter & Gamble, for instance, assigned its first product manager in 1927, when it made one person responsible for Camay soap.

Product managers set prices, develop advertising and sales promotion programs, and work with sales representatives in the field. In a company that markets multiple products, product managers fulfill key functions in the marketing department. They provide individual attention for each product and support and coordinate efforts of the firm's sales force, marketing research department, and advertising department. Product managers often lead new-product development programs, including creation of new-product ideas and recommendations for improving existing products.

However, most consumer-goods companies such as Procter & Gamble and General Mills have either modified the product manager structure or done away with it altogether in favor of a category management structure. Category managers have profit and loss responsibility, which is not characteristic of the product management system. This change has largely come about because of customer preference, but it can also benefit a manufacturer by avoiding duplication of some jobs and competition among the company's own brands and its managers.

product manager
Marketer responsible for an individual product or product line; also called a brand manager.

VENTURE TEAMS

A **venture team** gathers a group of specialists from different areas of an organization to work together in developing new products. The venture team must meet criteria for return on investment, uniqueness of product, serving a well-defined need, compatibility of the product with existing technology, and strength of patent protection. Although the organization sets up the venture team as a temporary entity, its flexible lifespan may extend over a number of years. When purchases confirm the commercial potential of a new product, an existing division may take responsibility for that product, or it may serve as the nucleus of a new business unit or of an entirely new company. Some marketing organizations differentiate between venture teams and task forces. A new-product task force assembles an interdisciplinary group working on temporary assignment

venture team Associates from different areas of an organization who work together in developing new products.

through their functional departments. Its basic activities center on coordinating and integrating the work of the firm's functional departments on a specific project.

Unlike a new-product committee, a venture team does not disband after every meeting. Team members accept project assignments as major responsibilities, and the team exercises the authority it needs to both plan and implement a course of action. To stimulate product innovation, the venture team typically communicates directly with top management but functions as an entity separate from the basic organization.

assessment check

1. Who are consumer innovators?
2. What characteristics of a product innovation can influence its adoption rate?

The New-Product Development Process

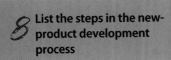

List the steps in the new-product development process

Once a firm is organized for new-product development, it can establish procedures for moving new-product ideas to the marketplace. Developing a new product often is time-consuming, risky, and expensive. Usually, firms must generate dozens of new-product ideas to produce even one successful product. In fact, the failure rate of new products averages 80 percent. Products fail for a number of reasons, including inadequate market assessments, lack of market orientation, poor screening and project evaluation, product defects, and inadequate launch efforts. And these blunders cost a bundle: firms invest nearly half of the total resources devoted to product innovation on products that become commercial failures.

A new product is more likely to become successful if the firm follows the six-step development process shown in Figure 12.3: (1) idea generation, (2) screening, (3) business analysis, (4) development, (5) test marketing, and (6) commercialization. Of course, each step requires decisions about whether to proceed further or abandon the project. And each step involves a greater financial investment.

Traditionally, most companies developed new products through phased development, which follows the six steps in an orderly sequence. Responsibility for each phase passes first from product planners to designers and engineers, then to manufacturers, and finally to marketers. The phased development method can work well for firms that dominate mature markets and can develop variations on existing products. But with rapid changes in technology and markets, many companies feel pressured to speed up the development process.

This time pressure has encouraged many firms to implement accelerated product development programs. These programs generally consist of teams with design, manufacturing, marketing, and sales personnel who carry out development projects from idea generation to commercialization. This method can reduce the time needed to develop products because team members work on the six steps concurrently rather than in sequence.

Whether a firm pursues phased development or parallel product development, all phases can benefit from planning tools and scheduling methods such as the program evaluation and review technique (PERT) and the critical path method (CPM). These techniques, originally developed by the U.S. Navy in connection with construction of the Polaris missile and submarine, map out the sequence of each step in a process and show the time allotments for each activity. Detailed PERT and CPM flowcharts help marketers coordinate all activities in the development and introduction of new products.

figure 12.3

Steps in the New-Product Development Process

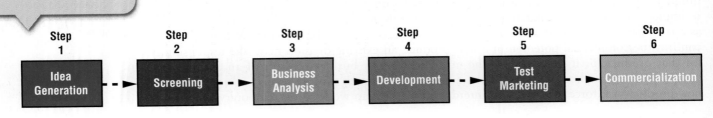

Step 1	Step 2	Step 3	Step 4	Step 5	Step 6
Idea Generation	Screening	Business Analysis	Development	Test Marketing	Commercialization

Idea Generation

New-product development begins with ideas from many sources: suggestions from customers, the sales force, research and development specialists, competing products, suppliers, retailers, and independent inventors. Bose Corporation has built its brand by staying at the forefront of technology. Spending an estimated $100 million a year on research, the company leads the market for products using advanced technology: sound systems for businesses, cars, and consumer home use and the award-winning Wave radio and Wave and Acoustic wave music systems.[33] Hallmark, the world's largest producer of greeting cards, maintains a massive, world-class design studio at its Kansas City headquarters, where a creative staff of 800 comes up with 19,000 new cards and other products each year.[34] Similarly, ongoing research by scientists at lawn-care industry leader ScottsMiracle-Gro helps the company fine-tune its understanding of consumer needs as it develops products and incorporates environmentally responsible behavior throughout its operations.[35]

Screening

Screening separates ideas with commercial potential from those that cannot meet company objectives. Some organizations maintain checklists of development standards in determining whether a project should be abandoned or considered further. These checklists typically include factors such as product uniqueness, availability of raw materials, and the proposed product's compatibility with current product offerings, existing facilities, and present capabilities. The screening stage may also allow for open discussions of new-product ideas among different parts of the organization.

Business Analysis

A product idea that survives the initial screening must then pass a thorough business analysis. This stage consists of assessing the new product's potential market, growth rate, and likely competitive strengths. Marketers must evaluate the compatibility of the proposed product with organizational resources.

Concept testing subjects the product idea to additional study prior to its actual development. This important aspect of a new product's business analysis represents a marketing research project that attempts to measure consumer attitudes and perceptions about the new-product idea. Focus groups and in-store polling can contribute effectively to concept testing. The Eclipse 500 Very Light Jet, a six-passenger airplane about the size of an SUV, weighs under 10,000 pounds and can fly faster and higher than other aircraft in its class. Before manufacturing the plane, Eclipse Aviation spent years testing its concept. During its research phase, the company sought input from small- and large-plane pilots as well as experts from both inside and outside the aviation industry.[36] The screening and business analysis stages generate extremely important information for new-product development because they (1) define the proposed product's target market and customers' needs and wants and (2) determine the product's financial and technical requirements. Firms willing to invest money and time during these stages tend to be more successful at generating viable ideas and creating successful products.

concept testing
Method for subjecting a product idea to additional study before actual development by involving consumers through focus groups, surveys, in-store polling, and the like.

Development

Financial outlays increase substantially as a firm converts an idea into a visible product. The conversion process is the joint responsibility of the firm's development engineers, who turn the original concept into a product, and its marketers, who provide feedback on consumer reactions to the product design, package, color, and other physical features. Many firms implement computer-aided design and manufacturing (CAD/CAM) systems to streamline the development stage, and prototypes may go through numerous changes before the original mock-up becomes a final product. Southern California–based sports eyewear and apparel marketer Oakley uses a design approach called *sculptural physics,* which it views as the discipline of wrapping science with art. The company's ideas are born using CAD/CAM engineering and are given form as three-dimensional prototypes. New products are evaluated and field-tested by the world's top athletes. Once finalized, they are released to the general public.

briefly speaking

"Product testing should not be the basis for introducing a new product because 90 percent of the failures have had successful product test results."

—Richard H. Buskirk
(1927–1994)
American marketing educator

Test Marketing

As discussed in Chapter 8, many firms test market their new-product offerings to gauge consumer reaction. After a company develops a prototype, it may decide to test market it to measure consumer reactions under normal competitive conditions. Test marketing's purpose is to verify that the product will perform well in a real-life environment. If the product does well, the company can proceed to commercialization. If it flops, the company can fine-tune certain features and reintroduce it or pull the plug on the project altogether. Industries that rely heavily on test marketing are snack foods, automobiles, and movies. Of course, even if a product tests well and reaches the commercialization stage, it may still take a while to catch on with the general public.

Commercialization

When a new-product idea reaches the commercialization stage, it is ready for full-scale marketing. Commercialization of a major new product can expose the firm to substantial expenses. It must establish marketing strategies, fund outlays for production facilities, and acquaint the sales force, marketing intermediaries, and potential customers with the new product.

 assessment check

1. Where do ideas for new products come from?
2. What is concept testing?
3. What happens in the commercialization stage?

Product Safety and Liability

Explain the relationship between product safety and product liability.

product liability Responsibility of manufacturers and marketers for injuries and damages caused by their products.

A product can fulfill its mission of satisfying consumer needs only if it ensures safe operation. Manufacturers must design their products to protect users from harm. Products that lead to injuries, either directly or indirectly, can have disastrous consequences for their makers. **Product liability** refers to the responsibility of manufacturers and marketers for injuries and damages caused by their products. Chapter 3 discussed some of the major consumer protection laws that affect product safety. These laws include the Flammable Fabrics Act of 1953, the Fair Packaging and Labeling Act of 1966, the Poison Prevention Packaging Act of 1970, and the Consumer Product Safety Act of 1972.

Federal and state legislation play a major role in regulating product safety. The Poison Prevention Packaging Act requires drug manufacturers to place their products in packaging that is child resistant yet accessible to all adults, even ones who have trouble opening containers. The Consumer Product Safety Act created a powerful regulatory agency—the Consumer Product Safety Commission (CPSC). This agency has assumed jurisdiction over every consumer product category except food, automobiles, and a few other products already regulated by other agencies. The CPSC has the authority to ban products without court hearings, order recalls or redesigns of products, and inspect production facilities. It can charge managers of negligent companies with criminal offenses. The CPSC is especially watchful of products aimed at infants and young children.

The federal Food and Drug Administration must approve food, medications, and health-related devices such as wheelchairs. The Food Allergen Labeling and Consumer Protection Act mentioned earlier increased the requirements for food labeling. The FDA can also take products off the market if concerns arise about the safety of these products. The number of product liability lawsuits filed against manufacturers skyrocketed in recent years. Marketers' exposure to potential liability and litigation is also on the rise in many overseas markets. Many of these claims reach settlements out of court. For example, Louisiana recently became the 11th state in the country to settle a lawsuit against pharmaceuticals manufacturer Eli Lilly over the inappropriate marketing of Zyprexa, its drug for schizophrenia and bipolar disorder.[37] However, juries settle many other suits,

> Volvo is well known for the safety features it designs into its automobiles, and consumers recognize that fact when they decide to purchase one.

sometimes awarding multi-million-dollar settlements to individuals or their families. This threat has led most companies to step up efforts to ensure product safety. Safety warnings appear prominently on the labels of such potentially hazardous products as cleaning fluids and drain cleaners to inform users of the dangers of these products, particularly to children. Changes in product design have reduced the hazards posed by such products as lawn mowers, hedge trimmers, and toys. Product liability insurance has become an essential element for any new or existing product strategy. Premiums for this insurance have risen alarmingly, however, and insurers have almost entirely abandoned some kinds of coverage.

Regulatory activities and the increased number of liability claims have prompted companies to sponsor voluntary improvements in safety standards. Many companies, including Walmart and Mattel, have worked with the Consumer Product Safety Commission to improve their safety protocols. Walmart uses its Retailer Reporting Model to provide CPSC with detailed weekly reports about customer product safety complaints and concerns. Safety planning is now a vital element of product strategy, and many companies now publicize the safety planning and testing that go into the development of their products. Volvo, for example, is well known for the safety features it designs into its automobiles, and consumers recognize that fact when they decide to purchase a Volvo.

Due in part to companies' voluntary policing efforts, the tide may be turning on some liability lawsuits. In a huge decision for the medical device industry, the U.S. Supreme Court ruled that patients injured by medical devices could not sue the manufacturer. However, in another recent ruling, the Court said pharmaceuticals companies could be sued in state court over their product's alleged defects, even if the Food and Drug Administration had approved use of the medication.[38]

 assessment check

1. What is the role of the Consumer Product Safety Commission (CPSC)?

2. What safety issues come under the jurisdiction of the Food and Drug Administration (FDA)?

strategic implications
of marketing in the 21st century

arketers who want to see their products reach the marketplace successfully have a number of options for developing them, branding them, and developing a strong brand identity among consumers and business customers. The key is to integrate all of the options so they are compatible with a firm's overall business and marketing strategy and, ultimately, the firm's mission. As marketers consider ideas for new products, they need to be careful not to send their companies in so many differ-ent directions as to dilute the identities of their brands, making it nearly impossible to keep track of what their companies do well. Category management can help companies develop a consistent product mix with strong branding, while at the same time meeting the needs of customers. Looking for ways to extend a brand with-out diluting it or compromising brand equity is also an important marketing strategy. Finally, marketers must continue to work to produce high-quality products that are safe for all users.

Review of Chapter Objectives

 1 Determine how to define a brand.

Marketers recognize the powerful influence products and product lines have on customer behavior, and they work to create strong identities for their products and protect them. Branding is the pro-cess of creating that identity. A brand is a name, term, sign, symbol, design, or some combination that identifies the products of one firm while differentiating these products from competitors' offerings.

 2 Identify the different types of brands.

A generic product is an item characterized by a plain label, no advertising, and no brand name. A manufacturer's brand is a brand name owned by a manufacturer or other producer. Private brands are brand names placed on products marketed by a wholesaler or retailer. A family brand is a brand name that identifies several related products. An individual brand is a unique brand name that identifies a specific offering within a firm's product line to avoid grouping it under a family brand.

 3 Explain the strategic value of brand equity

Brand equity provides a competitive advantage for a firm because consumers are more likely to buy a product that carries a respected, well-known brand name. Brand equity also smoothes the path for global expansion.

 4 Explain the benefits of category and brand management.

Category management is beneficial to a business because it gives direct responsibility for creating profitable product lines to category managers and their product group. Consumers respond to branding by making repeat purchases of favored goods and services. Therefore, managing brands and categories of brands or product lines well can result in a direct response from consumers, increasing profits and revenues for companies and creating consumer satisfaction. Brand and category manag-ers can also enhance relationships with business customers such as retailers.

5 Discuss how companies develop a strong identity for their product or brand.

Effective brands communicate to a buyer an idea of the prod-uct's image. Trademarks, brand names, slogans, and brand icons create an association that satisfies the customer's expec-tation of the benefits that using or having the product will yield.

Identify and briefly describe each of the new-product development strategies.

The success of a new product can result from four product development strategies: (1) market penetration, in which a company seeks to increase sales of an existing product in an existing market; (2) market development, which concentrates on finding new markets for existing products; (3) product development, the introduction of new products into identifiable or established markets; and (4) product diversification, which focuses on developing entirely new products for new markets.

 Describe the consumer adoption process.

In the adoption process, consumers go through a series of stages from learning about the new product to trying it and deciding whether to purchase it again. The stages are called awareness, interest, evaluation, trial, and adoption/rejection.

 List the stages in the new-product development process.

The stages in the six-step process are (1) idea generation, (2) screening, (3) business analysis, (4) development, (5) test marketing, and (6) commercialization. These steps may be performed sequentially or, in some cases, concurrently.

 Explain the relationship between product safety and product liability.

Product safety refers to the goal of manufacturers to create products that can be used safely and will protect consumers from harm. Product liability is the responsibility of marketers and manufacturers for injuries and damages caused by their products. Major consumer protection laws are in place to protect consumers from faulty products.

 Assessment Check: Answers

1.1 What is a brand? A brand is a name, term, sign, symbol, design, or some combination that identifies the products of one firm while differentiating these products from competitors' offerings.

1.2 Differentiate among brand recognition, brand preference, and brand insistence. Brand recognition is a company's first objective for newly introduced products and aims to make these items familiar to the public. Brand preference means buyers rely on previous experiences with the product when choosing it over competitors' products. Brand insistence leads consumers to refuse alternatives and to search extensively for the desired merchandise.

2.1 Identify the different types of brands. The different types of brands are manufacturer's (or national) brands, private brands, captive brands, family brands, and individual brands.

2.2 How are generic products different from branded products? Generic products are characterized by plain labels, little or no advertising, and no brand names.

3.1 What is brand equity? Brand equity refers to the added value a certain brand name gives to a product in the marketplace.

3.2 What are the four dimensions of brand personality? The four dimensions of brand personality are differentiation, relevance, esteem, and knowledge.

4.1 Define brand manager. The person at a company with the task of managing a brand's marketing strategies.

4.2 How does category management help retailers? Category management helps retailers by providing a person—a category manager—to oversee an entire product line and maximize sales for that retailer. It teams the consumer goods producer's marketing expertise with the retailer's in-store merchandising efforts to track and identify new opportunities for growth.

5.1 Distinguish between a brand name and a trademark. A brand name is the part of the brand consisting of letters, numbers, or words that can be spoken and that forms a name distinguishing a firm's offerings from competitors. A trademark is a brand for which the owner claims exclusive legal protection.

5.2 What are the three purposes of packaging? A package serves three major objectives: (1) protection against damage, spoilage, and pilferage; (2) assistance in marketing the product; and (3) cost effectiveness.

5.3 Describe brand extension and brand licensing. Brand extension is the strategy of attaching a popular brand name to a new product in an unrelated product category. Brand licensing is the strategy of authorizing other companies to use a brand name.

6.1 Distinguish between market penetration and market development strategies. In a market penetration strategy, a company seeks to increase sales of an existing product in an existing market. In a market development strategy, the company concentrates on finding new markets for existing products.

6.2 What is product development? Product development refers to the introduction of new products into identifiable or established markets.

6.3 What is product diversification? A product diversification strategy focuses on developing entirely new products for new markets.

7.1 Who are consumer innovators? Consumer innovators are the first buyers of new products—people who purchase new products almost as soon as these products reach the market.

7.2 What characteristics of a product innovation can influence its adoption rate? Five characteristics of a product innovation influence its adoption rate: relative advantage, compatibility, complexity, possibility of trial use, and observability.

8.1 Where do ideas for new products come from? New-product development begins with ideas from many sources: suggestions from customers, the sales force, research and development specialists, assessments of competing products, suppliers, retailers, and independent inventors.

8.2 What is concept testing? Concept testing subjects the product idea to additional study prior to its actual development.

8.3 What happens in the commercialization stage? When a new-product idea reaches the commercialization stage, it is ready for full-scale marketing.

9.1 What is the role of the Consumer Product Safety Commission (CPSC)? The Consumer Product Safety Commission is a powerful regulatory agency with jurisdiction over every consumer product category except food, automobiles, and a few other products already regulated by other agencies.

9.2 What safety issues come under the jurisdiction of the Food and Drug Administration (FDA)? The Food and Drug Administration must approve food, medications, and health-related devices such as wheelchairs.

Marketing Terms You Need to Know

brand 379
brand recognition 379
brand preference 379
brand insistence 380
generic products 380
manufacturer's brand 380
private brand 380
captive brand 381
family brand 381

individual brand 381
brand equity 382
brand manager 383
category management 383
brand name 385
brand mark 385
trademark 386
trade dress 387
label 389

universal product code (UPC) 390
brand extension 390
line extension 390
brand licensing 391
market penetration strategy 392
product positioning 392
market development strategy 393
product development 393
product diversification strategy 393

cannibalization 394
adoption process 394
consumer innovators 395
diffusion process 395
product manager 397
venture team 397
concept testing 399
product liability 400

Assurance of Learning Review

1. What are the three stages marketers use to measure brand loyalty?

2. Identify and briefly describe the different types of brands.

3. Why is brand equity so important to companies?

4. What are the characteristics of an effective brand name?

5. What role does packaging play in helping create brand loyalty and brand equity?

6. What is category management, and what role does it play in the success of a product line?

7. Describe the different product development strategies.

8. What are the five stages of the consumer adoption process?

9. Describe the different ways companies can organize to develop new products.

10. List the six steps in the new-product development process.

Projects and Teamwork Exercises

1. Locate an advertisement for a product that illustrates an especially effective brand name, brand mark, packaging, and overall trade dress. Explain to the class why you think this product has a strong brand identity.

2. With a classmate, search a grocery store for a product you think could benefit from updated or new package design. Then sketch out a new package design for the product, identifying and explaining your changes as well as your reasons for the changes. Bring the old package and your new package design to class to share with your classmates.

3. What category of consumer adopter best describes you? Do you follow the same adoption pattern for all products, or are you an early adopter for some and a laggard for others? Create a graph or chart showing your own consumer adoption patterns for different products.

4. Which product labels do you read? Over the next several days, keep a brief record of the labels you check while shopping. Do you read nutritional information when buying food products? Do you check care labels on clothes before you buy them? Do you read the directions or warnings on a product you haven't used before? Make notes about what influenced your decision to read or not read the product labels. Did you think they provided enough information, too little, or too much?

5. Some brands achieve customer loyalty by retaining an air of exclusivity and privilege, even though that often comes with high pricetags. Louis Vuitton, the maker of luxury leather goods, is one such firm. What kind of brand loyalty is this, and how does Vuitton achieve it?

Critical-Thinking Exercises

1. In this chapter, you learned that Mattel has launched a "Barbie Girls" experience in an attempt to sustain the interest of older girls in the Barbie brand. Do you think this strategy will work for Mattel? Why or why not? Identify another well-known product that appeals to a specific age group. Do you think a similar strategy would be successful? Why or why not?

2. General Mills and several other major food makers have begun producing organic foods. But they have deliberately kept their brand names off the packaging of these new products, thinking that the kind of customer who goes out of his or her way to buy organic products is unlikely to trust multinational brands. Other companies, however, such as Heinz, PepsiCo, and Tyson Foods, are betting that their brand names will prove to be persuasive in the $11 billion organic foods market. Which strategy do you think is more likely to be successful? Why?

3. After the terrorist attacks of 9/11, an ad hoc task force of DDB Worldwide advertising professionals in 17 countries set out to discover what people abroad thought of the United States. In the course of their research, they developed the concept of "America as a Brand," urged U.S. corporations with overseas operations to help "restore" positive impressions of Brand America around the world, and urged the United States to launch Alhurra as an alternative to the popular Al Jazeera network. Do you think foreigners' perception of a country and its culture can be viewed in marketing terms? Why or why not?

4. Brand names contribute enormously to consumers' perception of a brand. One writer has argued that alphanumeric brand names, such as the Toyota RAV4, Jaguar's X-Type sedan, the Xbox game console, and the GTI from Volkswagen, can translate more easily overseas than "real" names like Golf, Jetta, Escalade, and Eclipse. What other advantages and disadvantages can you think of for each type of brand name? Do you think one type is preferable to the other? Why?

Ethics Exercise

As mentioned in the chapter, some analysts predict bar codes may soon be replaced by a wireless technology called *radio-frequency identification (RFID)*. RFID is a system of installing tags containing tiny computer chips on, say, supermarket items. These chips automatically radio the location of the item to a computer network where inventory data are stored, letting store managers know not only where the item is at all times but also when and where it was made and its color and size. Proponents believe RFID will cut costs and simplify inventory tracking and reordering. It may also allow marketers to respond quickly to shifts in demand, avoid under- and overstocking, and reduce spoilage by automatically removing outdated perishables from the shelves. Privacy advocates, however, think the chips provide too much product-preference information that might be identified with individual consumers. In the meantime, Walmart is requiring its major suppliers to begin using the new technology on products stocked by the giant retailer.

1. Do you think RFID poses a threat to consumer privacy? Why or why not?

2. Do you think the technology's possible benefits to marketers outweigh the potential privacy concerns? Are there also potential benefits to consumers, and, if so, what are they?

3. How can marketers reassure consumers about privacy concerns if RFID comes into widespread use?

Internet Exercises

1. **Ferrari brand.** Visit the Ferrari Web site. Review the material and prepare a report outlining how Ferrari—a company that produces products that only a handful of consumers can afford—has been able to build such a strong, recognizable brand.
http://www.ferrari.com

2. **Trademark disputes.** Search an Internet news site, such as Google News (http://news.google.com), and the U.S. Patent & Trademark Office (http://www.uspto.gov) for recent trademark dispute cases. Select two of these cases and prepare a summary of each. Do the number of trademark dispute cases appear to be growing? If so, what is one possible explanation for this increase?

3. **Brand equity.** Several sources compile lists each year of the world's most valuable brands. Two are *BusinessWeek* magazine and a consulting firm called Brand Finance. Visit both Web sites and review the most recent lists of the world's most valuable brands. How many firms are represented on both lists? Where are these firms located? What criteria do *BusinessWeek* and Brand Finance use in determining brand equity? Which brands have improved their values the most over the past couple of years?
http://www.businessweek.com
http://www.brandfinance.com

Note: Internet Web addresses change frequently. If you don't find the exact site listed, you may need to access the organization's home page and search from there or use a search engine such as Google or Bing.

Case 12.1   *Roy Choi Takes Gourmet Food to the Street*

Ah, the food truck! Long ago, food trucks parked outside a factory or office building or on a college campus were dubbed "ptomaine trailers" and "roach coaches" because they dispensed eats that only the brave—or the seriously famished—would consume. But today,

the food truck concept has morphed into a valuable channel for delivering high-quality food at affordable prices to people in neighborhoods that can't support gourmet restaurants and where healthful eating isn't always the norm.

Helping to change the food truck's image and introduce gourmet cuisine to the masses is Los Angeles chef Roy Choi, the son of Korean immigrants, who grew up on the streets of Koreatown. A law-school dropout, Choi became inspired to enroll in culinary school while watching chef Emeril Lagasse on TV. Preparing delicious, healthy food for people of modest means has become something of a calling for Choi. He gets passionate when he talks about it: "It's convenient to eat horrible food, and it's so difficult to eat great

food. It's O.K. to eat flaming-hot Cheetos and never read books or eat vegetables."

After working as a hotel and restaurant chef, Choi borrowed a truck from a friend and began serving a mix of Korean and Mexican cuisine—short-rib tacos and kimchi quesadillas—to targeted neighborhoods. Another friend created visibility for Choi's enterprise, Kogi BBQ, through Twitter and a Web site. The first couple of months, the venture simply broke even, but by the end of Year One, Kogi BBQ had generated $2 million in sales, with the average tab around $13. Today, Kogi BBQ operates four trucks in Los Angeles.

For aspiring restaurateurs and entrepreneurial chefs, a food truck represents an opportunity for those who lack the capital to open a restaurant. The trucks are like rolling warming kitchens that can fit into empty niches or park on a corner, revitalizing street life or providing some sense of community where none existed before. Choi's business has led to numerous "copycat" food truckers and helped build momentum for the food-truck enterprise in Los Angeles. Now, a nondescript corner in Santa Monica serves as a gathering place for a number of trucked-in food stops serving a wide variety of eats, from sushi to grilled cheese.

Food & Wine magazine recently named Choi one of the best new chefs in America. The annual award recognizes ten new chefs who are "changing the landscape of eating." But success hasn't changed Roy Choi: his goals remain intact. His most recent endeavor: a sit-down restaurant in an old strip mall. Choi didn't spend money beautifying the space, however; the fare includes rice bowls for $7 to $9 and, he points out, the plates are mismatched.

Questions for Critical Thinking

1. What did Roy Choi do to build the Kogi BBQ brand? What measures has he taken to extend the brand? In your opinion, would further expansion hurt Roy Choi's efforts? Why?

2. The introduction of Kogi BBQ has led to several other food truck businesses in and around Los Angeles. Does this competition help or hurt Choi's mission?

Sources: Ben Leventhal, "Roy Choi Named 2010 *Food & Wine* Best New Chef," *NBC Los Angeles,* April 6, 2010, http://www.nbclosangeles.com; Joel Stein, "Gourmet on the Go," *Time,* March 29, 2010, 47–48; Antoinette Bruno, "Community Award Winner Chef Roy Choi," *StarChefs.com,* March 2010, http://www.starchefs.com; Hayley Richardson and Greg Smith, "Atlanta Missing out on Gourmet Street Food and a Hot New Brand," *Atlanta Journal-Constitution,* March 22, 2010, http://www.ajc.com; Betty Hallock, "One Corner, Many Trucks: The Debut of Gourmet Food Truck Corner; Kogi, the Restaurant," *Los Angeles Times,* January 4, 2010, http://latimes.blogs.latimes.com.

Video Case 12.2
Developing and Managing Brand and Product Categories at Maine Media Workshops

Since 1973, Maine Media Workshops has seen some of the most talented filmmakers, photographers, and writers pass through its doors. The program started as a summer camp of sorts for amateurs and professionals wanting to hone their creative arts skills

while enjoying a week along the beautiful coast of Rockport, Maine. Over the years, students have had the opportunity to work with and learn from Hollywood's heavy hitters: Vilmos Zsigmond, cinematographer on "Close Encounters," "The Black Dahlia," and "The Deer Hunter"; Alan Myerson, Emmy-winning director of everything from "The Love Boat" to "The Larry Saunders Show" to "Boston Public"; and actor Gene Wilder. The names are impressive, but what has always set the program apart is its intensity and quality. The family style lobster dinner at the end doesn't hurt, either.

Sadly, in recent years, the workshops had lost their way and the school was in danger of closing. "When it fell on hard times, and there was the possibility of it not surviving, it was hard to imagine being here anymore," says Charles Altschul, Rockport resident and current executive director of the school. Something had to be done to revitalize this gem along the rocky Maine coast.

In a recent year, the family-owned school became a non-profit educational institution. The school underwent all of the infrastructure and management changes one might expect from this kind of transition, but the biggest challenges lay ahead. While

the school had always enjoyed an excellent reputation within the industry, it was losing ground. More and more universities were providing excellent opportunities for students in the creative arts. These schools had deep pockets, were able to attract top-notch faculty, and more importantly, could afford superior facilities and equipment. No longer operating as a for-profit business, the Maine Workshops could now reach out to private and corporate donors to keep things afloat. This was especially critical when it came to equipment. There would be little gained by students working in outdated facilities. The reputation of the school was at stake. Companies like Canon, Sony, and Apple could now partner with the school by donating equipment. The workshops could attach these sponsors' cutting-edge products and technologies to their marketing materials to attract students, and the equipment manufacturers could advertise their association with the school to attract customers.

One of their most valuable relationships is with Canon. As the Maine Workshops brands itself as a leader in digital arts, Canon desires the same thing. There isn't one product—from still film camera to HD video camera to office printer to professional printing press—in Canon's product line that isn't relevant to the Workshops' offerings.

The partnership with Canon is a great first step toward repositioning the school as a leader in digital media and arts, but it has been a challenge to rally the troops and get a unified message together. Traditionally, the departments worked independently, marketing photography to photographers, writing to writers, and filmmaking to the film students. "We felt it was important, after the transition, to publish a catalog that contains all of the programs we offer," says Altschul. "It's 162 pages, we printed 165,000 copies of it, it cost most of our marketing budget to do."

Moving forward, they'll do much less of the paper catalogs, which is an obvious cash-sucker. More importantly, Altschul believes that to present themselves as a leader in digital media, they need to walk the walk in everything they do. The school's Web site recently underwent a major overhaul to better communicate that, "We're back and better than before." The site contains all the standard information one might need along with a complete course catalog and school blog, as well as a place to pay tuition, take a placement test, register for classes, or donate to the school. Links to technology partners also serve as a showcase for student work.

This new interdisciplinary approach has served the school well. Enrollment is up from past years, and the phone is ringing off the hook with professionals wanting to teach a workshop. The school has also added a degree program. The full-time, one- to five-year program at Maine Media College is fully accredited to offer an MFA in Maine and is expected to receive national accreditation in the next few years.

Questions

1. What are the main elements of the Maine Media Workshops brand equity? Analyze the workshop's brand equity using the Young & Rubicam "dimensions of brand personality."

2. Would you consider the Maine Media College an extension of the Maine Media Workshops brand or a new-product development strategy—or both? Explain.

3. How can the Maine Media Workshops benefit from consumers' brand recognition, preference, and insistence with companies such as Canon. Can Canon benefit from the association with the Workshops?

Greensburg, Inc.

© CENGAGE LEARNING

Green: It's Not Just for Earth Day Anymore

Honda has always enjoyed a reputation as being a fuel-efficient economical brand. As early as 1974, Honda has been changing the way we look at cars with the low-emission/fuel-efficient Civic CVCC. In the years since, Honda's commitment to the environment has spawned a line of Good, Better, Best, and Ultimate vehicles. Regular gas cars are Good, with about 30 mpg; hybrids are Better at about 45 mpg; and their Best solution is a natural gas-powered Civic GX that gets about 220 miles to a tank. Honda has Ultimate solutions in the works, including the new Honda FCX Clarity, a hydrogen fuel cell car in which hydrogen reacts with oxygen, both renewable resources, to create electricity. The only emissions you get are a little steam. You can buy the natural gas Civic GX and Clarity today, but neither vehicle is practical for the average driver because the fueling stations are hard to come by.

Roger Schofield of Schofield Honda in Wichita, Kansas, has been promoting Honda as a good and good-for-you vehicle for years. Gas mileage, safety, and brand loyalty are all important parts of Schofield's marketing. Unfortunately, despite the increasing interest in the environment, alternative fuel vehicles make up a very small part of his business. Even the Civic hybrid, a car with a lot of buzz, only makes up about 4 percent of his annual sales.

Sales figures on alternative fuel cars as they were, Schofield wanted to reposition the Schofield *brand* in the green marketplace, rather than focus on particular products. When the dealership did some renovations to their buildings, they created the Honda Green Zone, a rental space for organizations to hold meetings about green projects. Internally, Schofield holds weekly meetings with his

Green Team to brainstorm new projects, marketing, and products. They were at work on several other project ideas when an F5 tornado hit Greensburg on May 4, 2007. At that moment, the idea of going green at Schofield Honda took on a whole new life.

The news of the green rebuilding initiative in Greensburg really drove home the need to become a leader in promoting more environmentally friendly technology. With any new technology, it takes a few early adopters to help lay the infrastructure for the rest of us. Well aware of the media attention surrounding Greensburg, Schofield decided to donate a natural gas Honda Civic GX to the town and a fueling station to go with it. The car would be made available to the residents to check out and try for themselves. The world would get to see the car in use by average people, and the town would have its own natural gas fueling station.

He admits questioning his decision even as he was driving into Greensburg on the day of the presentation, but when all was said and done, it was the right thing to do. When customers come into the dealership, they are more interested in alternative-fuel and high-efficiency vehicles and recognize Schofield Honda's commitment to the people of Greensburg and the green movement as a whole.

Visit Schofield Honda today, and you're going green—regardless of which type of vehicle you purchase. Employees will be drinking from ceramic coffee mugs "sponsored" by other local businesses. When you clean out your trade-in, you can use the recycling bins and take your important stuff with you in a Schofield Honda reusable shopping bag. If you're just there for an oil change, your old oil will be recycled to heat the shop.

Despite the media coverage on Greensburg and Schofield's green marketing efforts, sales are still slow on the alternative fuel vehicles, but Schofield is okay with that. Making the products available to those on the cutting edge will earn him a reputation as cutting edge himself. When Wichita is ready for a change, Schofield Honda will be there and waiting.

Questions

1. Do you think repositioning the dealership as a green business will have a positive impact on their products' lifecycles?

2. What impact, if any, will going green have on brand loyalty? Discuss the Honda brand as well as the Schofield Honda brand.

3. Would you consider "green" to be a line extension at Schofield Honda? Why or why not?

4. Write a memo (3 to 5 pages) about which "businesses" on your campus (i.e., the food court, the bookstore, athletic center) could incorporate some of the initiatives that Schofield has taken with his dealership.

Distribution Decisions

Chapter 13
Marketing Channels
and Supply Chain
Management

Chapter 14
Retailers, Wholesalers,
and Direct Marketers

ch13 Marketing
Channels and Supply Chain Management

1 Describe the types of marketing channels and the roles they play in marketing strategy.

2 Outline the major channel strategy decisions.

3 Describe the concepts of channel management, conflict, and cooperation.

4 Identify and describe the different vertical marketing systems.

5 Explain the roles of logistics and supply chain management in an overall distribution strategy.

6 Identify the major components of a physical distribution system.

7 Compare the major modes of transportation.

8 Discuss the role of transportation intermediaries, combined transportation modes, and warehousing in improving physical distribution.

Panama Canal Undergoes Extreme Makeover · · ·

The Panama Canal is one of the world's most famous examples of engineering know-how. Built in 1914, this 48-mile-long "ditch" dug by the U.S. Army Corps of Engineers and thousands of laborers made it

possible for ships to cross the Isthmus of Panama, a thin strip of land that separates the Atlantic and Pacific oceans. Over its ten decades of operation, the canal has served as a critical artery for global trade. In recent times, the canal welcomed 14,000 ships passing through each year, carrying about 5 percent of the world's ocean cargo—280 million tons.

Shipping companies once designed their ocean-going vessels to fit the Panama Canal's locks—100 feet long and 110 feet wide—and these vessels, which came to be known as "Panamax" ships, still carry much of the world's cargo. During the 1970s, however, ships began to be built longer and wider. These days, for example, some of the ships moving through

the Panama Canal are three times longer than a football field. Even for some vessels that regularly make the journey, passage through the canal's narrow Miraflores Locks is a tense, nerve-wracking exercise, with barely a couple of feet to spare on either side. Today, the newest breed of ship, known as "post-Panamax," cannot navigate the canal at all.

With the canal now too narrow for more than one-third of the world's cargo ships, Panamanian government officials saw the writing on the wall: unless they took action to upgrade it, the canal would become obsolete. As a result, voters in Panama approved a $5.25 billion expansion project. The new locks will be 60 percent longer and 40 percent wider. When

it reopens in 2014, the remodeled canal will be able to handle more than double its current shipping capacity, including tankers that hold as much as 1 million barrels of oil as well as container ships that carry up to 12,500 cargo containers. The canal's expansion will make it easier and less costly to ship goods from Asia to the Eastern Seaboard of the United States. It will also provide China with better access to Latin America markets.

The 1999 transfer of the Panama Canal from the United States to Panama has proved to be a game-changer for the tiny tropical nation. Whereas the U.S. government had administered the canal as a federal agency—for example, maintaining a toll

© AP IMAGES/JIM MONE

schedule just high enough to cover operating costs—the Panama Canal Authority operates the canal like a commercial enterprise. The canal authority introduced a tariff schedule scaled to different-sized cargoes and charges extra for certain services. Under Panamanian management, shipping traffic in the canal increased significantly, from 200,000 ships in 1995 to more than 4.6 million in a recent year. Today, the canal represents 14 percent of Panama's gross domestic product.

The expansion plan, which is reportedly on time and on budget, is being financed chiefly through retained earnings from the canal; the rest is underwritten by global lenders. The predicted surge in shipping from the expanded canal is likely to spill over to U.S. ports, many of whom are currently taking steps to upgrade their own facilities.

The Panama Canal Authority predicts that the expanded canal will double the country's economy, create jobs, and ease poverty.[1]

evolution of a brand

When it opened to transoceanic ships in 1914, the Panama Canal quickly became an icon, changing the face of trade between the East and West. And a century later—when its current expansion project is complete—the Panama Canal will once again change the face of trade, not only in terms of the increased number of ships passing through but also in terms of its implications for other businesses and other major modes of transportation.

In a typical day, the Panama Canal's original locks used about 2 billion gallons of water. Although the locks in the expanded canal will hold 65 percent more water, the new design aims for sustainability. Thus, the locks will ultimately use less water than the original locks and will recycle more than half the water used.

Do you think this green practice is important for the Panama Canal? How could the Panama Canal Authority use the practice to enhance the brand?

- Can an expanded Panama Canal affect marketing strategy for businesses worldwide? How?

chapter overview

distribution Movement of goods and services from producers to customers.

marketing (distribution) channel System of marketing institutions that enhances the physical flow of goods and services, along with ownership title, from producer to consumer or business user.

logistics Process of coordinating the flow of information, goods, and services among members of the distribution channel.

supply chain management Control of the activities of purchasing, processing, and delivery through which raw materials are transformed into products and made available to final consumers.

physical distribution Broad range of activities aimed at efficient movement of finished goods from the end of the production line to the consumer.

Distribution—moving goods and services from producers to customers—is the second marketing mix variable and an important marketing concern. Firms depend on waterways like the Panama Canal to be able to move their goods from one destination to another. A distribution strategy has two critical components: (1) marketing channels and (2) logistics and supply chain management.

A **marketing channel**—also called a **distribution channel**—is an organized system of marketing institutions and their interrelationships that enhances the physical flow and ownership of goods and services from producer to consumer or business user. The choice of marketing channels should support the firm's overall marketing strategy. By contrast, **logistics** refers to the process of coordinating the flow of information, goods, and services among members of the marketing channel. **Supply chain management** is the control of activities of purchasing, processing, and delivery through which raw materials are transformed into products and made available to final consumers. Efficient logistical

systems support customer service, enhancing customer relationships—an important goal of any marketing strategy.

A key aspect of logistics is physical distribution, which covers a broad range of activities aimed at efficient movement of finished goods from the end of the production line to the consumer. Although some marketers use the terms *transportation* and *physical distribution* interchangeably, these terms do not carry the same meaning. **Physical distribution** extends beyond transportation to include such important decision areas as customer service, inventory control, materials handling, protective packaging, order processing, and warehousing.

Well-planned marketing channels and effective logistics and supply-chain management provide ultimate users with convenient ways for obtaining the goods and services they desire. This chapter discusses the activities, decisions, and marketing intermediaries involved in managing marketing channels and logistics. Chapter 14 looks at other players in the marketing channel: retailers, direct marketers, and wholesalers.

The Role of Marketing Channels in Marketing Strategy

A firm's distribution channels play a key role in its overall marketing strategy because these channels provide the means by which the firm makes the goods and services available to ultimate users. Channels perform four important functions. First, they facilitate the exchange process by reducing the number of marketplace contacts necessary to make a sale. Suppose you've had a Nintendo DS handheld game player in the past and been satisfied with it, so when you see an ad for the Nintendo Wii, you are interested. You visit the Nintendo Web site where you learn more about the Wii and its unique features. You are particularly drawn to the games "NCAA Football All-Play" and "The Beatles: Rock Band." But you want to see the game console in person, so you locate a dealer near enough for you to visit.[2] The dealer forms part of the channel that brings you—a potential buyer—and Nintendo—the seller—together to complete the exchange process. It's important to keep in mind that all channel members benefit when they work together; when they begin to disagree or—worse yet—compete directly with each other, everyone loses.

Distributors adjust for discrepancies in the market's assortment of goods and services via a process known as *sorting*, the second channel function. A single producer tends to maximize the quantity it makes of a limited line of goods, while a single buyer needs a limited quantity of a wide selection of merchandise. Sorting alleviates such discrepancies by channeling products to suit both the buyer's and the producer's needs.

The third function of marketing channels involves standardizing exchange transactions by setting expectations for products, and it involves the transfer process itself. Channel members tend to standardize payment terms, delivery schedules, prices, and purchase lots, among other conditions. Standardization helps make transactions efficient and fair.

The final marketing channel function is to facilitate searches by both buyers and sellers. Buyers search for specific goods and services to fill their needs, while sellers attempt to learn what buyers want. Channels bring buyers and sellers together to complete the exchange process. Hundreds of distribution channels exist today, and no single channel best serves the needs of every company. Instead of searching for the best channel for all products, a marketing manager must analyze alternative channels in light of consumer needs to determine the most appropriate channel or channels for the firm's goods and services.

Marketers must remain flexible because channels may change over time. Today's ideal channel may prove inappropriate in a few years, or the way a company uses that channel may have to change. Two decades ago, Michael Dell came up with a revolutionary way to sell computers: by telephone, directly to consumers. Later, Dell added Internet sales to its operations. Next, the firm added another channel for making its computers available to consumers: Best Buy, one of the nation's largest electronics retailers. Selected models of Dell's PCs became available at Best Buy stores around the United States. Today, Dell is exploiting another channel to sell computers: reaching its consumers through Twitter. By continuing to identify new channels for distribution, Dell stays engaged with current and prospective customers.[3]

If you are interested in learning more about the Nintendo Wii, you may want to see the game console in person by visiting a local dealer.

© AP IMAGES/PAUL SAKUMA

Keep up with Dell on Twitter!

Breaking news • 24/7 updates • Deals and discounts

Follow us, tweet us, and retweet us to all your friends. We'll see you on Twitter!

Marketers must remain flexible because channels change over time. Dell products, originally available only through direct-to-customer selling, are now sold at Best Buy, and Dell is exploring another channel to sell computers: reaching its consumers through Twitter.

The following sections examine the diverse types of channels available to marketers and the decisions marketers must make to develop an effective distribution strategy that supports their firm's marketing objectives.

Types of Marketing Channels

The first step in selecting a marketing channel is determining which type of channel will best meet both the seller's objectives and the distribution needs of customers. Figure 13.1 depicts the major channels available to marketers of consumer and business goods and services.

Most channel options involve at least one marketing intermediary. A **marketing intermediary** (or **middleman**) is an organization that operates between producers and consumers or business users. Retailers and wholesalers are both marketing intermediaries. A retail store owned and operated by someone other than the manufacturer of the products it sells is one type of marketing intermediary. A **wholesaler** is an intermediary that takes title to the goods it handles and then distributes these goods to retailers, other distributors, or sometimes end consumers. Although some analysts believed that the Internet would ultimately render many intermediaries obsolete, that hasn't happened. Instead, it has enabled many such businesses to enhance customer service. To manage their large corporate accounts, airlines typically use the services of intermediaries, such as global distribution systems, online travel agents, or travel management companies, paying them a regular fee for service. But with the high cost of fuel, airlines are looking for ways to trim their costs. American Airlines is aiming to cut out the middleman by promoting its Direct Connect program, enabling customers to access the airline's Web site and book their own flights without having to use an intermediary.[4]

A short marketing channel involves few intermediaries. By contrast, a long marketing channel involves several intermediaries working in succession to move goods from producers to consumers. Business products usually move through short channels due to geographic concentrations and comparatively fewer business purchasers. Service firms market primarily through short channels because they sell intangible products and need to maintain personal relationships within their channels. Haircuts, manicures, and dental cleanings all operate through short channels. Not-for-profit organizations also tend to work with short, simple, and direct channels. Any marketing intermediaries in such channels usually act as agents, such as independent ticket agencies or fund-raising specialists.

Direct Selling

The simplest and shortest marketing channel is a direct channel. A **direct channel** carries goods directly from a producer to the business purchaser or ultimate user. This channel forms part of **direct selling**, a marketing strategy in which a producer establishes direct sales contact with its product's final users. Direct selling is an important option for goods requiring extensive demonstrations

marketing intermediary (or **middleman**) Wholesaler or retailer that operates between producers and consumers or business users.

wholesaler Channel intermediary that takes title to the goods it handles and then distributes these goods to retailers, other distributors, or business or B2B customers.

direct channel Marketing channel that moves goods directly from a producer to the business purchaser or ultimate user.

direct selling Strategy designed to establish direct sales contact between producer and final user.

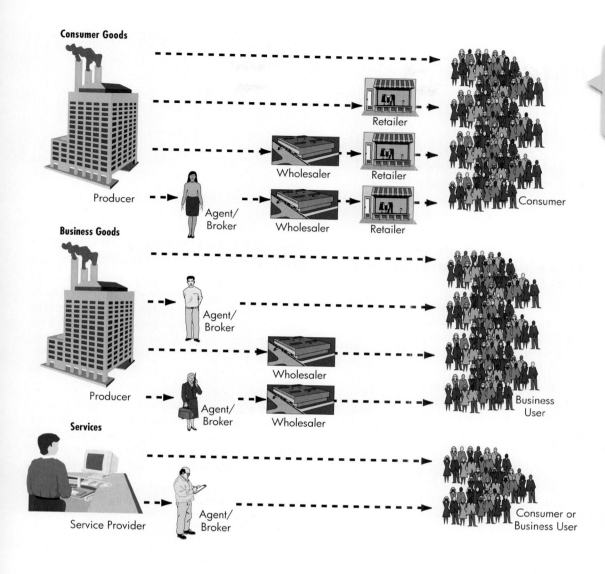

figure 13.1
Alternative Marketing Channels

in persuading customers to buy. The "Career Readiness" feature contains suggestions for making successful sales calls.

Direct selling plays a significant role in business-to-business marketing. Most major installations, accessory equipment, and even component parts and raw materials are sold through direct contacts between producing firms and final buyers. Many people in business enjoy successful sales careers. According to the *Occupational Outlook Handbook* published by the U.S. Department of Labor, about 2 million people are employed as sales representatives in manufacturing and wholesaling industries.[5]

Direct selling is also important in consumer-goods markets. Direct sellers such as Avon, Pampered Chef, and Tastefully Simple sidestep competition in store aisles by developing networks of independent representatives who sell their products directly to consumers. Many of these companies practice a direct selling strategy called the *party plan*, originally popularized by Tupperware. Jewelry boutique company Stella & Dot is one such business. Launched by entrepreneur Jessica Herrin, Stella & Dot jewelry is sold at home-based parties, or "trunk shows," by independent sales representatives. The jewelry, which appeals to women of all ages, is accessible and affordable—and is often worn by TV celebrities. Stella & Dot recently topped $30 million in sales.[6]

The Internet provides another direct selling channel for both B2B and B2C purchases. Consumers who want to sport designer handbags, but don't want to pay full price for them, can rent

career readiness　Ⓐnatomy of a Successful Sales Call

When you make a sales call to a prospective or current customer, you represent the face and voice of your firm. The way people perceive you is the way they perceive your company, so you want to make a good first impression as well as a positive lasting impression. Most likely, you will receive training—either by your supervisor or someone else in your company—in the fine art of a successful sales call. Here are a few additional tips to help you:

- *Do your homework.* Be sure you know the correct spelling and pronunciation of the company you are visiting—and the person you are scheduled to meet. Familiarize yourself with the company's goods or services and past history with your company.

- *Assess the company's potential needs.* Don't launch into a "data dump" about your products before learning what the customer needs. If you have familiarized yourself with the customer's business, you should be able to ask a few intelligent questions and really listen to the answers. Then, you can offer a few ideas of solutions.

- *Dress appropriately and arrive on time.* Wear the proper business attire for your industry, whether it's a business suit or business casual clothing. Cover any tattoos or body piercings and wear conservative jewelry. In other words, play it safe. Always arrive a few minutes before the scheduled time. Doing

so shows respect for your customer's time and indicates you are serious about doing business.

- *Be conservative in your behavior.* Always stand to greet your customer. Smile, shake hands, and follow the customer to wherever the meeting will take place. Address him or her with the title "Mr." or "Ms.," and do not assume the person wishes to be called by first name until you are invited to do so.

- *Turn off your cell phone.* If possible, turn off your cell phone before entering the building for your meeting. At least, turn it off when you enter the meeting. Never take a call during a meeting, and only make one if it will help the progress of the meeting. For example, a customer might have a question only your supervisor can answer. A successful sales call requires your total attention on the customer.

- *Follow up the meeting with a thank-you.* After the sales call, be sure to follow up with a phone call, e-mail, or note to thank the person—regardless of the outcome. Even if the call did not produce a sale or other immediate results, it could possibly have laid the groundwork for a future relationship.

Sources: Dan Seidman, "Practice What You Preach in Sales," *Monster Career Advice*, career-advice.monster.com, accessed April 18, 2010; Robert Estupinian, "Three Successful Sales Call Strategies for Entrepreneurs," *Bay Area Mastermind*, April 1, 2010, http://www.bayareamastermind.com; Geoffrey James, Sales Calls: Four Key Rules to Make Them More Effective," *BNet.com*, March 25, 2010, http://blogs.bnet.com.

them from Avelle, an e-commerce business. For those who like to change purses often but can't or won't pay the hundreds or thousands of dollars for Chanel's, Prada's, or Gucci's latest, Avelle may be a real bargain. By paying an optional monthly membership fee of $5 to $10, customers receive discounts and special deals. In addition to designer handbags, shoppers can find sunglasses and jewelry to complete their look.[7]

Direct mail can also be an important part of direct selling—or it can encourage a potential customer to contact an intermediary such as a retailer. Either way, it is a vital communication piece for many marketers.

Channels Using Marketing Intermediaries

Although direct channels allow simple and straightforward marketing, they are not practical in every case. Some products serve markets in different areas of the country or world, or have large numbers of potential end users. Other categories of goods rely heavily on repeat purchases. The producers of these goods may find more efficient, less expensive, and less time-consuming alternatives to direct channels by using marketing intermediaries. This section considers five channels that involve marketing intermediaries.

PRODUCER TO WHOLESALER TO RETAILER TO CONSUMER

The traditional channel for consumer goods proceeds from producer to wholesaler to retailer to user. This method carries goods between thousands of small producers with limited lines and local retailers. A firm with limited financial resources will rely on the services of a wholesaler that serves as an immediate source of funds and then markets to hundreds of retailers. On the other hand, a small retailer can draw on a wholesaler's specialized distribution skills. In addition, many manufacturers hire their own field representatives to service retail accounts with marketing information. Wholesalers may then handle the actual sales transactions.

PRODUCER TO WHOLESALER TO BUSINESS USER

Similar characteristics in the organizational market often attract marketing intermediaries to operate between producers and business purchasers. The term *industrial distributor* commonly refers to intermediaries in the business market that take title to the goods.

PRODUCER TO AGENT TO WHOLESALER TO RETAILER TO CONSUMER

In markets served by many small companies, a unique intermediary—the agent—performs the basic function of bringing buyer and seller together. An agent may or may not take possession of the goods but never takes title. The agent merely represents a producer by seeking a market for its products or a wholesaler, which does take title to the goods, by locating a supply source.

PRODUCER TO AGENT TO WHOLESALER TO BUSINESS USER

Like agents, brokers are independent intermediaries who may or may not take possession of goods but never take title to these goods. Agents and brokers also serve the business market when small producers attempt to market their offerings through large wholesalers. Such an intermediary, often called a **manufacturers' representative**, provides an independent sales force to contact wholesale buyers. A kitchen equipment manufacturer may have its own manufacturer's representatives to market its goods, for example.

manufacturers' representative Agent wholesaling intermediary that represents manufacturers of related but noncompeting products and receives a commission on each sale.

PRODUCER TO AGENT TO BUSINESS USER

For products sold in small units, only merchant wholesalers can economically cover the markets. A merchant wholesaler is an independently owned wholesaler that takes title to the goods. By maintaining regional inventories, this wholesaler achieves transportation economies, stockpiling goods and making small shipments over short distances. For a product with large unit sales, however, and for which transportation accounts for a small percentage of the total cost, the producer-agent-business user channel is usually employed. The agent in effect becomes the producer's sales force, but bulk shipments of the product reduce the intermediary's inventory management function.

Dual Distribution

Dual distribution refers to the movement of products through more than one channel to reach the firm's target market. Nordstrom, for instance, has a three-pronged distribution

dual distribution Network that moves products to a firm's target market through more than one marketing channel.

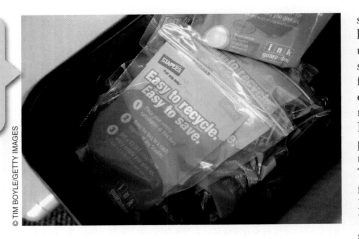

> Staples collects empty ink and toner cartridges at its stores, so customers can recycle them instead of throwing catridges away.

system, selling through stores, catalogs, and the Internet. Marketers usually adopt a dual distribution strategy either to maximize their firm's coverage in the marketplace or to increase the cost-effectiveness of the firm's marketing effort. Nintendo and Netflix recently partnered to offer entertainment through more than one channel. Traditionally, customers order their favorite movies online and have the DVDs delivered to their mailboxes. Under the new agreement, Netflix subscribers with at least an $8.99 monthly subscription can stream movies and TV programs and view them on their Wii console at no extra cost.[8]

Reverse Channels

reverse channel
Channel designed to return goods to their producers.

While the traditional concept of marketing channels involves the movement of goods and services from producer to consumer or business user, marketers should not ignore **reverse channels**—channels designed to return goods to their producers. Reverse channels have gained increased importance with rising prices for raw materials, increasing availability of recycling facilities, and passage of additional antipollution and conservation laws. Purchase a new set of tires, and you'll find a recycling charge for disposing of the old tires. The intent is to halt the growing litter problem of illegal tire dumps. Automotive and marine batteries contain potentially toxic materials, including 25 pounds of lead, plastic, and sulfuric acid. Yet, 99 percent of the elements in a spent battery can be reclaimed, recycled, and reused in new batteries. Thirty-nine states now require consumers to turn in their old batteries when they purchase new ones. To help in this effort, the American Automobile Association (AAA) holds an annual AAA Great Battery Roundup in the United States and Canada, during which consumers can drop off their dead batteries.[9]

Some reverse channels move through the facilities of traditional marketing intermediaries. In states that require bottle deposits, retailers and local bottlers perform these functions in the soft-drink industry. For other products, manufacturers establish redemption centers, develop systems for rechanneling products for recycling, and create specialized organizations to handle disposal and recycling. Staples collects empty ink and toner cartridges at its stores, rewarding customers who recycle rather than dispose of the items. Nike's Reuse-A-Shoe program collects people's cast-off athletic shoes and recycles virtually the entire shoe. These recycling efforts are likely to help build customer loyalty and enhance the brands' reputations.[10]

Reverse channels also handle product recalls and repairs. An appliance manufacturer might send recall notices to the buyers of a washing machine. An auto manufacturer might send notices to car owners advising them of a potential problem and offering to repair the problem at no cost through local dealerships.

   assessment check

1. Distinguish between a marketing channel and logistics.
2. What are the different types of marketing channels?
3. What four functions do marketing channels perform?

Channel Strategy Decisions

Marketers face several strategic decisions in choosing channels and marketing intermediaries for their products. Selecting a specific channel is the most basic of these decisions. Marketers must also resolve questions about the level of distribution intensity, assess the desirability of vertical marketing systems, and evaluate the performance of current intermediaries.

> **2** Outline the major channel strategy decisions.

Selection of a Marketing Channel

Consider the following questions: What characteristics of a franchised dealer network make it the best channel option for a company? Why do operating supplies often go through both agents and merchant wholesalers before reaching their actual users? Why would a firm market a single product through multiple channels? Marketers must answer many such questions in choosing marketing channels.

A variety of factors affect the selection of a marketing channel. Some channel decisions are dictated by the marketplace in which the company operates. In other cases, the product itself may be a key variable in picking a marketing channel. Finally, the marketing organization may base its selection of channels on its size and competitive factors. Individual firms in a single industry may choose different channels as part of their overall strategy to gain a competitive edge. Book publishers, for instance, may sell books through bookstores, directly to consumers on their own Web sites, or through nontraditional outlets including specialty retailers such as craft stores or home improvement stores.

MARKET FACTORS

Channel structure reflects a product's intended markets, for either consumers or business users. Business purchasers usually prefer to deal directly with manufacturers (except for routine supplies or small accessory items), but most consumers make their purchases from retailers. Marketers often sell products that serve both business users and consumers through more than one channel.

Other market factors also affect channel choice, including the market's needs, its geographic location, and its average order size. To serve a concentrated market with a small number of buyers, a direct channel offers a feasible alternative. But in serving a geographically dispersed potential trade area in which customers purchase small amounts in individual transactions—the conditions that characterize the consumer goods market—distribution through marketing intermediaries makes sense.

PRODUCT FACTORS

Product characteristics also guide the choice of an optimal marketing channel strategy. Perishable goods, such as fresh fruit and vegetables, milk, and fruit juice, move through short channels. Trendy or seasonal fashions, such as swimsuits and skiwear, are also examples.

Vending machines represent another short channel. Typically, you can buy Skittles, SunChips, or a bottle of Dasani water from a vending machine. But how about bike parts? By installing a vending machine that sells basic bike parts like patch kits, pumps, inner tubes, and brake pads, bicycle retailer Traif Bike Gesheft offers 24-hour service to bicyclists in and around Brooklyn, New York.[11]

Complex products, such as custom-made installations and computer equipment, are often sold directly to ultimate buyers. In general, relatively standardized items that are also nonperishable pass through comparatively long channels. Products with low unit costs, such as cans of dog food, bars of soap, and packages of gum, typically travel through long channels. Perishable items—fresh flowers, meat, and produce—require much shorter channels.

ORGANIZATIONAL AND COMPETITIVE FACTORS

Companies with strong financial, management, and marketing resources feel less need for help from intermediaries. A large, financially strong manufacturer can hire its own sales force, warehouse

Instead of selling directly to customers, entrepreneur Sara Blakely relies on big retail partners to get her product, Spanx, into consumers' hands.

© LEE CELANO/WIREIMAGE FOR SILVER SPOON/GETTY IMAGES

its own goods, and extend credit to retailers or consumers. But a small firm with fewer resources may do better with the aid of intermediaries. Entrepreneur Sara Blakely knew she had a unique idea when she cut the feet off her pantyhose and created the first pair of Spanx underwear. Blakely says she wants her power shapers to empower women, and scores of women—including celebrities such as Gwyneth Paltrow and Tyra Banks—are loyal customers. Consumers write to Spanx thanking the company for giving them the confidence to wear the form-fitting clothes they always wanted to wear. But Blakely doesn't sell her shapers directly to customers. Instead, she relies on big retail partners such as Neiman Marcus, Nordstrom, and Saks to get her product into consumers' hands.[12]

A firm with a broad product line can usually market its products directly to retailers or business users because its own sales force can offer a variety of products. High sales volume spreads selling costs over a large number of items, generating adequate returns from direct sales. Single-product firms often view direct selling as unaffordable.

The manufacturer's desire for control over marketing its products also influences channel selection. Some manufacturers sell their products only at their own stores. Manufacturers of specialty or luxury goods, such as scarves from Hermès and watches from Rolex, limit the number of retailers that can carry their products.

Businesses that explore new marketing channels must be careful to avoid upsetting their channel intermediaries. Conflicts frequently arose as companies began to establish an Internet presence in addition to traditional outlets. Today, firms look for new ways to handle both without damaging relationships. NBC and Apple struck a deal in which NBC would sell its television programs through the iTunes store, but the agreement turned sour over issues of price and piracy (the unauthorized use or reproduction of copyrighted material). However, the two resumed their alliance after figuring out a way to add antipiracy features (or countermeasures against copyright infringement) and rework the price agreement for NBC's programming.[13]

Table 13.1 summarizes the factors that affect the selection of a marketing channel and examines the effect of each factor on the channel's overall length.

Determining Distribution Intensity

Another key channel strategy decision is the intensity of distribution. *Distribution intensity* refers to the number of intermediaries through which a manufacturer distributes its goods in a particular market. Optimal distribution intensity should ensure adequate market coverage for a product. Adequate market coverage varies depending on the goals of the individual firm, the type of product, and the consumer segments in its target market. In general, however, distribution intensity varies along a continuum with three general categories: intensive distribution, selective distribution, and exclusive distribution.

table 13.1 Factors Influencing Marketing Channel Strategies

	Characteristics of Short Channels	Characteristics of Long Channels
Market Factors	Business users	Consumers
	Geographically concentrated	Geographically dispersed
	Extensive technical knowledge and regular servicing required	Little technical knowledge and regular servicing not required
	Large orders	Small orders
Product Factors	Perishable	Durable
	Complex	Standardized
	Expensive	Inexpensive
Organizational Factors	Manufacturer has adequate resources to perform channel functions	Manufacturer lacks adequate resources to perform channel functions
	Broad product line	Limited product line
	Channel control important	Channel control not important
Competitive Factors	Manufacturer feels satisfied with marketing intermediaries' performance in promoting products	Manufacturer feels dissatisfied with marketing intermediaries' performance in promoting products

INTENSIVE DISTRIBUTION

An **intensive distribution** strategy seeks to distribute a product through all available channels in a trade area. Because Campbell Soup practices intensive distribution for many of its products, you can pick up a can from its microwavable line just about anywhere—the supermarket, the drugstore, and even Sears. Usually, an intensive distribution strategy suits items with wide appeal across broad groups of consumers.

intensive distribution
Distribution of a product through all available channels.

SELECTIVE DISTRIBUTION

In another market coverage strategy, **selective distribution**, a firm chooses only a limited number of retailers in a market area to handle its line. Italian design firm Gucci sells its merchandise only through a limited number of select boutiques worldwide. By limiting the number of retailers, marketers can reduce total marketing costs while establishing strong working relationships within the channel. Moreover, selected retailers often agree to comply with the company's strict rules for advertising, pricing, and displaying its products. *Cooperative advertising*—in which the manufacturer pays a percentage of the retailer's advertising expenditures and the retailer prominently displays the firm's products—can be used for mutual benefit, and marginal retailers can be avoided. Where service is important, the manufacturer usually provides training and assistance to the dealers it chooses.

selective distribution
Distribution of a product through a limited number of channels.

© TERRI MILLER/E-VISUAL COMMUNICATIONS, INC.

Because Campbell Soup practices intensive distribution for many of its products, you can pick up a can of its microwavable line just about anywhere—the supermarket, the drugstore, or even Sears.

EXCLUSIVE DISTRIBUTION

exclusive distribution
Distribution of a product
through a single wholesaler
or retailer in a specific
geographic region.

When a producer grants exclusive rights to a wholesaler or retailer to sell its products in a specific geographic region, it practices **exclusive distribution**. The automobile industry provides a good example of exclusive distribution. A city with a population of 40,000 probably has a single Ford dealer. Exclusive distribution agreements also govern marketing for some major appliance and apparel brands.

Marketers may sacrifice some market coverage by implementing a policy of exclusive distribution. However, they often develop and maintain an image of quality and prestige for the product. If it's harder to find a Free People silk dress, the item seems more valuable. In addition, exclusive distribution limits marketing costs because the firm deals with a smaller number of accounts. In exclusive distribution, producers and retailers cooperate closely in decisions concerning advertising and promotion, inventory carried by the retailers, and prices.

Legal Problems of Exclusive Distribution

Exclusive distribution presents potential legal problems in three main areas: exclusive dealing agreements, closed sales territories, and tying agreements. Although none of these practices is illegal per se, all may break the law if they reduce competition or tend to create monopolies.

As part of an exclusive distribution strategy, marketers may try to enforce an exclusive dealing agreement, which prohibits a marketing intermediary (a wholesaler or, more typically, a retailer) from handling competing products. Producers of high-priced shopping goods, specialty goods, and accessory equipment often require such agreements to ensure total concentration on their own product lines. Such contracts violate the Clayton Act only if the producer's or dealer's sales volumes represent a substantial percentage of total sales in the market area. While exclusive distribution is legal for companies first entering a market, such agreements violate the Clayton Act if used by firms with a sizable market share seeking to bar competitors from the market.

closed sales
territory Exclusive
geographic selling region
of a distributor.

Producers may also try to set up **closed sales territories** to restrict their distributors to certain geographic regions, reasoning that the distributors gain protection from rival dealers in their exclusive territories. Some beverage distributors have closed territories, as do distributors of plumbing fixtures.[14] But the downside of this practice is that the distributors sacrifice opportunities to open new facilities or market the manufacturers' products outside their assigned territories. The legality of a system of closed sales territories depends on whether the restriction decreases competition. If so, it violates the Federal Trade Commission Act and provisions of the Sherman and Clayton Acts.

The legality of closed sales territories also depends on whether the system imposes horizontal or vertical restrictions. Horizontal territorial restrictions result from agreements between retailers or wholesalers to avoid competition among sellers of products from the same producer. Such agreements consistently have been declared illegal. However, the U.S. Supreme Court has ruled that vertical territorial restrictions—those between producers and wholesalers or retailers—may meet legal criteria. The ruling gives no clear-cut answer, but such agreements likely satisfy the law in cases in which manufacturers occupy relatively small parts of their markets. In such instances, the restrictions may actually increase competition among competing brands; the wholesaler or retailer faces no competition from other dealers carrying the manufacturer's brand, so it can concentrate on effectively competing with other brands.

tying agreement
Arrangement that requires
a marketing intermediary to
carry items other than those
they want to sell.

The third legal question of exclusive distribution involves **tying agreements**, which allow channel members to become exclusive dealers only if they also carry products other than those they want to sell. In the apparel industry, for example, an agreement might require a dealer to carry a comparatively unpopular line of clothing to get desirable, fast-moving items. Tying agreements violate the Sherman Act and the Clayton Act when they reduce competition or create monopolies that keep competitors out of major markets.

Who Should Perform Channel Functions?

A fundamental marketing principle governs channel decisions. A member of the channel must perform certain central marketing functions. Responsibilities of the different members may vary,

**briefly
speaking**

"You can do away with
middlemen, but you can't do
away with the functions they
perform."

—American business
saying

however. Although independent wholesalers perform many functions for manufacturers, retailers, and other wholesaler clients, other channel members could fulfill these roles instead. A manufacturer might bypass its wholesalers by establishing regional warehouses, maintaining field sales forces, serving as sources of information for retail customers, or arranging details of financing. For years, auto manufacturers have operated credit units that offer new car financing; some have even established their own banks.

An independent intermediary earns a profit in exchange for providing services to manufacturers and retailers. This profit margin is low, however, ranging from 1 percent for food wholesalers to 5 percent for durable goods wholesalers. Manufacturers and retailers could retain these costs, or they could market directly and reduce retail prices—but only if they could perform the channel functions and match the efficiency of the independent intermediaries.

To grow profitably in a competitive environment, an intermediary must provide better service at lower costs than manufacturers or retailers can provide for themselves. In this case, consolidation of channel functions can represent a strategic opportunity for a company.

 assessment check

1. Identify four major factors in selecting a marketing channel.
2. Describe the three general categories of distribution intensity.

Channel Management and Leadership

Distribution strategy does not end with the choice of a channel. Manufacturers must also focus on channel management by developing and maintaining relationships with the intermediaries in their marketing channels. Positive channel relationships encourage channel members to remember their partners' goods and market them. Manufacturers also must carefully manage the incentives offered to induce channel members to promote their products. This effort includes weighing decisions about pricing, promotion, and other support efforts the manufacturer performs.

Increasingly, marketers are managing channels in partnership with other channel members. Effective cooperation allows all channel members to achieve goals they could not achieve on their own. Keys to successful management of channel relationships include the development of high levels of coordination, commitment, and trust between channel members.

Not all channel members wield equal power in the distribution chain, however. The dominant member of a marketing channel is called the **channel captain**. This firm's power to control a channel may result from its control over some type of reward or punishment to other channel members such as granting an exclusive sales territory or taking away a dealership. Power might also result from contractual arrangements, specialized expert knowledge, or agreement among channel members about their mutual best interests.

In the grocery industry, food producers once were considered channel captains. Today, retail giants like Kroger, SuperValu, and Safeway face competition from all quarters: discounters like ALDI and Save-A-Lot, club stores like Costco and Sam's Club, and even dollar stores. To survive in the competitive grocery industry, supermarket owners are diversifying their retail formats from traditional stores to include natural and organic and upscale specialty stores to satisfy a wider variety of customers, and to compete with such chains as Whole Foods Market and Trader Joe's.[15] But the pressure on traditional chains is coming from another strategy: supercenters like Walmart and Target. Walmart is continuing its expansion in the grocery market; in fact, its grocery receipts now account for a whopping 51 percent of its U.S. sales.[16]

3 Describe the concepts of channel management, conflict, and cooperation.

channel captain
Dominant and controlling member of a marketing channel.

briefly speaking

"All things being equal, people will do business with a friend. All things being unequal, people will still do business with a friend."

—Mark McCormack
(1930–2003)
American sports agent and founder, IMG Sports Management

Channel Conflict

Marketing channels work smoothly only when members cooperate in well-organized efforts to achieve maximum operating efficiencies. Yet channel members often perform as separate, independent, and even competing forces. Two types of conflict—horizontal and vertical—may hinder the normal functioning of a marketing channel.

HORIZONTAL CONFLICT

Horizontal conflict sometimes results from disagreements among channel members at the same level, such as two or more wholesalers or two or more retailers, or among marketing intermediaries of the same type, such as two competing discount stores or several retail florists. More often, horizontal conflict causes problems between different types of marketing intermediaries that handle similar products. In an effort to resolve such a situation, Europe and the United States initiated an "open skies" agreement, lifting restrictions on U.S. and European air carriers and clearing the path for increased competition. Airlines from Europe and the United States will be allowed to choose routes based on demand within government limitations and will be able to set prices and capacity without interference. Airlines such as American, British Airways, and Virgin Atlantic will be affected. Negotiators on both sides predict more cooperative marketing arrangements among the carriers.[17]

VERTICAL CONFLICT

Vertical relationships may result in frequent and severe conflict. Channel members at different levels find many reasons for disputes, as when retailers develop private brands to compete with producers' brands or when producers establish their own retail stores or create mail-order operations that compete with retailers. Producers may annoy wholesalers and retailers when they attempt to bypass these intermediaries and sell directly to consumers. After years of conflict, cable companies have reached an agreement with the electronics industry so that manufacturers can produce TVs and other electronic devices that will work—regardless of the cable provider. Comcast and Time Warner are participating in the initiative, called "tru2way," which will allow devices to receive *and send* digital information. The new standardization across the cable networks should foster the development of two-way communication from TVs to set-top boxes to PCs and other devices.[18]

gray goods Products manufactured abroad under license from a U.S. firm and then sold in the U.S. market in competition with that firm's own domestic output.

The resolution of vertical conflict between cable companies and electronics manufacturers paved the way for "tru2way," an initiative that will allow devices not only to receive but to also send digital information.

© AP IMAGES/PRNEWSFOTO/PANASONIC

THE GRAY MARKET

Another type of channel conflict results from activities in the so-called gray market. As U.S. manufacturers license their technology and brands abroad, they sometimes find themselves in competition in the U.S. market against versions of their own brands produced by overseas affiliates. These **gray goods**, goods produced for overseas markets often at reduced prices, enter U.S. channels through the actions of unauthorized foreign distributors. While licensing agreements usually prohibit foreign licensees from selling in the United States, no such rules inhibit their distributors. Other countries also have gray markets. For example, while Amazon is not licensed to sell its Kindle in China, the product is available on China's gray market.

Similarly, even before the iPad's official global release, enterprising individuals had bought them up in the United States for resale at an inflated price in Hong Kong.[19]

Achieving Channel Cooperation

The basic antidote to channel conflict is effective cooperation among channel members. Cooperation is best achieved when all channel members regard themselves as equal components of the same organization. The channel captain is primarily responsible for providing the leadership necessary to achieve this kind of cooperation.

Imax, Sony, and Discovery Communications formed a joint venture to create a 3-D television channel. The new channel, to be distributed by Discovery, will include a programming mix that includes sports, entertainment, and some natural-history shows.[20]

vertical marketing system (VMS) Planned channel system designed to improve distribution efficiency and cost-effectiveness by integrating various functions throughout the distribution chain.

assessment check

1. What is a channel captain? What is its role in channel cooperation?
2. Identify and describe the three types of channel conflict.

Vertical Marketing Systems

Efforts to reduce channel conflict and improve the effectiveness of distribution have led to the development of vertical marketing systems. A **vertical marketing system (VMS)** is a planned channel system designed to improve distribution efficiency and cost effectiveness by integrating various functions throughout the distribution chain.

A vertical marketing system can achieve this goal through either forward or backward integration. In **forward integration**, a firm attempts to control downstream distribution. For example, a manufacturer might set up a retail chain to sell its products. **Backward integration** occurs when a manufacturer attempts to gain greater control over inputs in its production process. A manufacturer might acquire the supplier of a raw material the manufacturer uses in the production of its products. Backward integration can also extend the control of retailers and wholesalers over producers that supply them.

A VMS offers several benefits. First, it improves chances for controlling and coordinating the steps in the distribution or production process. It may lead to the development of economies of scale that ultimately saves money. A VMS may also let a manufacturer expand into profitable new businesses. However, a VMS also involves some costs. A manufacturer assumes increased risk when it takes control of an entire distribution chain. Manufacturers may also discover they lose some flexibility in responding to market changes.

Marketers have developed three categories of VMSs: corporate systems, administered systems, and contractual systems. These categories are outlined in the following sections.

Corporate and Administered Systems

When a single owner runs an organization at each stage of the marketing channel, it operates a **corporate marketing system**. Phillips Auctioneers runs a corporate marketing system. An **administered marketing system** achieves channel coordination when a dominant channel member exercises its power. Even though Goodyear sells its tires through independently owned and

4 Identify and describe the different vertical marketing systems.

forward integration Process through which a firm attempts to control downstream distribution.

backward integration Process through which a manufacturer attempts to gain greater control over inputs in its production process, such as raw materials.

corporate marketing system VMS in which a single owner operates the entire marketing channel.

administered marketing system VMS that achieves channel coordination when a dominant channel member exercises its power.

operated dealerships, it controls the stock these dealerships carry. Another example of channel captains leading administered channels is McKesson.

Contractual Systems

contractual marketing system
VMS that coordinates channel activities through formal agreements among participants.

Instead of common ownership of intermediaries within a corporate VMS or the exercising of power within an administered system, a **contractual marketing system** coordinates distribution through formal agreements among channel members. In practice, three types of agreements set up these systems: wholesaler-sponsored voluntary chains, retail cooperatives, and franchises.

WHOLESALER-SPONSORED VOLUNTARY CHAIN

Sometimes an independent wholesaler tries to preserve a market by strengthening its retail customers through a wholesaler-sponsored voluntary chain. The wholesaler adopts a formal agreement with its retailers to use a common name and standardized facilities and to purchase the wholesaler's goods. The wholesaler may even develop a line of private brands to be stocked by the retailers. This practice often helps smaller retailers compete with rival chains—and strengthens the wholesaler's position as well.

IGA (Independent Grocers Alliance) Food Stores is a good example of a voluntary chain. Other wholesaler-sponsored chains include Associated Druggists, Sentry Hardware, and Western Auto. Because a single advertisement promotes all the retailers in the trading area, a common store name and similar inventories allow the retailers to save on advertising costs.

RETAIL COOPERATIVE

retail cooperative
Group of retailers that establish a shared wholesaling operation to help them compete with chains.

In a second type of contractual VMS, a group of retailers establishes a shared wholesaling operation to help them compete with chains. This is known as a **retail cooperative**. The retailers purchase ownership shares in the wholesaling operation and agree to buy a minimum percentage of their inventories from this operation. The members typically adopt a common store name and develop common private brands.

FRANCHISE

franchise Contractual arrangement in which a wholesaler or retailer agrees to meet the operating requirements of a manufacturer or other franchiser.

A third type of contractual vertical marketing system is the **franchise**, in which a wholesaler or dealer (the franchisee) agrees to meet the operating requirements of a manufacturer or other franchiser. Franchising is a huge and growing industry—more than 1,500 U.S. companies distribute goods and services through systems of franchised dealers, and numerous firms also offer franchises in international markets. Nationwide, more than 750,000 retail outlets represent franchises.[21] Table 13.2 shows the 20 fastest-growing franchises in the United States, with Jan-Pro, Subway, and Stratus Building Solutions topping the list.

Franchise owners pay anywhere from several thousand to more than a million dollars to purchase and set up a franchise. Typically, they also pay a royalty on sales to the franchising company. In exchange for these initial and ongoing fees, the franchise owner receives the right to use the company's brand name as well as services such as training, marketing, advertising, and volume discounts. Major franchise chains justify the steep price of entry because it allows new businesses to sell winning brands. But if the brand enters a slump or the corporation behind the franchise makes poor strategic decisions, franchisees often are hurt.

assessment check

1. What are vertical marketing systems? Identify the major types.
2. Identify the three types of contractual marketing systems.

table 13.2 The Top 20 Fastest-Growing Franchises

Rank	Company and Product
1	Jan-Pro Franchising International; commercial cleaning
2	Subway; sandwiches and salads
3	Stratus Building Solutions; commercial cleaning
4	Dunkin' Donuts; coffee and doughnut
5	Anago Cleaning Systems; commercial cleaning
6	McDonald's; hamburgers, chicken, salads
7	CleanNet USA Inc.; commercial cleaning
8	Bonus Building Care; commercial cleaning
9	Liberty Tax Service; income-tax preparation
10	Vanguard Cleaning Systems; commercial cleaning
11	Pizza Hut; pizza, pasta, buffalo wings
12	Anytime Fitness; fitness centers
13	Sonic Drive-In Restaurants; drive-in restaurants
14	ampm Mini Market; convenience stores and gas stations
15	Long John Silver's Restaurants; fish and chicken
16	System4; commercial cleaning
17	Jazzercise Inc.; dance fitness classes
18	InterContinental Hotels Group; hotels
19	Choice Hotels International; hotels
20	Snap Fitness Inc.; 24-hour fitness centers

Source: "2010 Fastest-Growing Franchise Rankings," *Entrepreneur*, http://www.entrepreneur.com, accessed April 18, 2010.

Logistics and Supply Chain Management

Pier 1 imports its eclectic mix of items from vendors in more than 50 countries, most representing small companies. If high-demand items or seasonal products are late into its six North American distribution centers or are shipped in insufficient quantities, the company may miss opportunities to deliver popular shopping choices to its more than 1,000 retail stores and could lose ground to such competitors as Pottery Barn and Crate & Barrel. The situation facing Pier 1 illustrates the importance of logistics. Careful coordination of Pier 1's supplier network, shipping processes, and inventory control is the key to its continuing success. In addition, the store's buyers develop relationships with suppliers in all participating countries.[22]

Effective logistics requires proper supply chain management, control of the activities of purchasing, processing, and delivery through which raw materials are transformed into products and made available to final consumers. The **supply chain**, also known as the *value chain*, is the complete sequence of suppliers and activities that contribute to the creation and delivery of goods and services. The supply chain begins with the raw material inputs for the manufacturing process of a product and then proceeds to the actual production activities. The final link in the supply chain is the movement of finished products through the marketing channel to customers. Each link of the

> **5** Explain the roles of logistics and supply chain management in an overall distribution strategy.

supply chain Complete sequence of suppliers and activities that contribute to the creation and delivery of merchandise.

© AMY T. ZIELINSKI/NEWSCAST/NEWSCOM

Careful coordination of Pier 1's supplier network, shipping process, and inventory control is the key to its continuing success.

upstream management
Controlling part of the supply chain that involves raw materials, inbound logistics, and warehouse and storage facilities.

downstream management
Controlling part of the supply chain that involves finished product storage, outbound logistics, marketing and sales, and customer service.

radio-frequency identification (RFID)
Technology that uses a tiny chip with identification information that can be read by a scanner using radio waves from a distance.

chain benefits the consumers as raw materials move through manufacturing to distribution. The chain encompasses all activities that enhance the value of the finished goods, including design, quality manufacturing, customer service, and delivery. Customer satisfaction results directly from the perceived value of a purchase to its buyer.

To manage the supply chain, businesses must look for ways to maximize customer value in each activity they perform. Supply chain management takes place in two directions: upstream and downstream, as illustrated in Figure 13.2. **Upstream management** involves managing raw materials, inbound logistics, and warehouse and storage facilities. **Downstream management** involves managing finished product storage, outbound logistics, marketing and sales, and customer service.

Companies choose a variety of methods for managing the supply chain. They can include high-tech systems such as radio-frequency identification (discussed in the next section) and regular person-to-person meetings. Arizona-based JDA Software Group helps other businesses track and manage their global supply chains. Using its proprietary software solutions, JDA helps its clients enhance customer service and improve inventory management.[23]

Logistics plays a major role in giving customers what they need when they need it, and thus is central in the supply chain. Another important component of this chain, *value-added service*, adds some improved or supplemental service that customers do not normally receive or expect. The following sections examine methods for streamlining and managing logistics and the supply chain as part of an overall distribution strategy. See the "Marketing Success" feature to read about Amazon.com's supply chain process.

Radio-Frequency Identification

One tool marketers use to help manage logistics is **radio-frequency identification (RFID)** technology. With RFID, a tiny chip with identification information that can be read by a radio-frequency

mktg: *success*

The Amazing Amazon

Background. CEO Jeff Bezos founded Amazon.com in 1995 as a place where book lovers could shop online for books.

The Challenge. From the outset, Bezos correctly identified Amazon's competition as not only other e-commerce sites but also brick-and-mortar stores. To be successful, he reasoned, Amazon customers would need to have a shopping experience that far surpassed what they could get at brick-and-mortar stores or at other e-commerce sites. They would need to find the best variety of merchandise at the lowest prices, with the fastest delivery. To provide that excellent shopping experience, Amazon needed a superior supply chain.

The Strategy. One of Amazon's strengths is its ability to ship an unprecedented number of products: currently about 10 million, compared to Walmart's 500,000. Unlike brick-and-mortar stores, Amazon doesn't stock all the items it sells. Instead, it created a huge supply chain, setting up real-time connections with hundreds of manufacturers. As a customer places an order, it is relayed to the manufacturer, who fills the order on Amazon's behalf. By contrast,

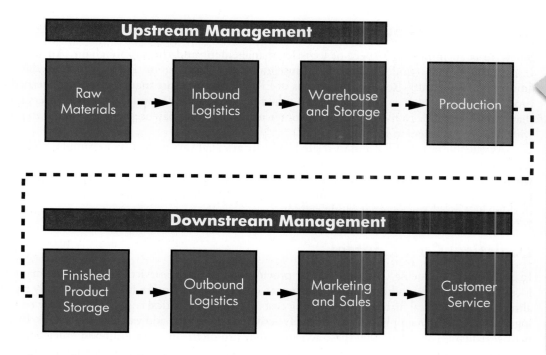

figure 13.2

The Supply Chain of a Manufacturing Company

Source: Adapted from Figure 2.2, Ralph M. Stair and George W. Reynolds, *Principles of Information Systems: A Managerial Approach*, 9th ed., Boston: Course Technology. ©2010 South-Western, a part of Cengage Learning, Inc. Reproduced by permission. www.cengage.com/permissions.

scanner from a distance is placed on an item. These chips are already widely used in tollway pass transmitters, allowing drivers to zip through tollbooths without stopping or rolling down their windows to toss change into baskets.

They are also embedded in employee ID cards workers use to open office doors without keys. But businesses such as retail giant Walmart, manufacturer Procter & Gamble, credit card firms MasterCard and American Express, and German retailer Metro AG are eagerly putting the technology to wider use; they say it will speed deliveries, make consumer bar codes obsolete, and provide marketers with valuable information about consumer preferences. Walmart requires its biggest suppliers to attach RFID tags to pallets and cases of products such as Coca-Cola and Dove soap, saying the technology vastly improves its ability to track inventory and keep the right amount of products in stock.

Boeing Company manufactures airplanes at its plant in Everett, Washington—a 100-acre complex said to be the largest building in the world. A Boeing plane is made up of 2 to 3 million individual parts, and by using RFID tags and Wi-Fi technology to track and locate those parts throughout the supply chain process, Boeing saves time and paperwork.[24] Industry insiders say Apple will soon introduce a new generation of iPhone that works as both an RFID tag—enabling it to be used as a payment device, such as a credit card—and an RFID reader—which would permit the phone to interact with objects bearing an RFID tag.[25]

briefly speaking

"Be prepared for all possible instances of demand, whenever and wherever they may occur."

—Michael Dell
(b. 1965)
Founder, Dell Inc.

brick-and-mortar stores place orders out of their own inventory, typically working with relatively few vendors.

Where Amazon does hold inventory, it uses huge warehouses where order fulfillment is computerized—and speedy. Some of its largest facilities fill 16 orders per second—as many as 1.4 million orders a day.

The Outcome. Amazon has built a supply chain focused on responsiveness and customer service. Same-day shipping is available in seven major U.S. cities. Today, Amazon is the world's largest online retailer, offering books, CDs, shoes, and a myriad of other merchandise. It numbers its active customer accounts at more than 98 million.

Sources: Company Web site, http://phx.corporate-ir.net, accessed May 29, 2010; Michael S. Hopkins, "Your Next Supply Chain," *MIT Sloan Management Review*, January 1, 2010, http://sloanreview.mit.edu; Robin Turner, "Amazon's Vast Depot in Wales," *Western Mail*, December 4, 2009, http://www.walesonline.co.uk; "Fit for the Holidays: Amazon Is Shaping Up and Shipping Out," *Knoweldge@Wharton*, November 11, 2009, http://knowledge.wharton.upenn.edu; Heather Green, "How Amazon Aims to Keep You Clicking," *BusinessWeek*, March 2, 2009, 34.

Enterprise Resource Planning

enterprise resource planning (ERP) system Software system that consolidates data from among a firm's various business units.

Software is an important aspect of logistics management and the supply chain. An **enterprise resource planning (ERP) system** is an integrated software system that consolidates data from among the firm's units. Roughly two-thirds of ERP system users are manufacturers concerned with production issues such as sequencing and scheduling. German software giant SAP offers systems that allow businesses to manage their customer relations. And eBay uses an SAP system to interact with its top customers in Europe.[26]

As valuable as it is, ERP and its related software aren't always perfect. For example, ERP failures were blamed for Hershey's inability to fulfill all of its candy orders during one Halloween period when a fall-off in sales was blamed on a combination of shipping delays, inability to fill orders, and partial shipments while candy accumulated in warehouses. The nation's major retailers were forced to shift their purchases to other candy vendors.

Logistical Cost Control

In addition to enhancing their products by providing value-added services to customers, many firms focus on logistics for another important reason: to cut costs. Distribution functions currently represent almost half of a typical firm's total marketing costs. To reduce logistical costs, businesses are reexamining each link of their supply chains to identify activities that do not add value for customers. By eliminating, reducing, or redesigning these activities, they can often cut costs and boost efficiency. As just described, new technologies such as RFID can save businesses millions—or even billions—of dollars.

Because of increased security requirements in recent years, businesses involved in importing and exporting have faced a major rise in logistical costs. The U.S. Transportation Security Administration (TSA) is charged with screening cargo on passenger planes, which increases the cost of transporting goods even more.[27]

THIRD-PARTY LOGISTICS

third-party (contract) logistics firm Company that specializes in handling logistics activities for other firms.

Some companies try to cut costs and offer value-added services by outsourcing some or all of their logistics functions to specialist firms. **Third-party (contract) logistics firms** (3PL firms) specialize in handling logistical activities for their clients. Third-party logistics is a huge industry, estimated at more than $126 billion in the United States alone.[28]

Through outsourcing alliances, producers and logistical service suppliers cooperate in developing innovative, customized systems that speed goods through carefully constructed manufacturing and distribution pipelines. Although many companies have long outsourced transportation and warehousing functions, today's alliance partners use similar methods to combine their operations.

assessment check

1. What is upstream management? What is downstream management?
2. Identify three methods for managing logistics.

Physical Distribution

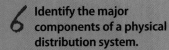

6 Identify the major components of a physical distribution system.

A firm's physical distribution system is an organized group of components linked according to a plan for achieving specific distribution objectives. It contains the following elements:

1. *customer service*—level of customer service the distribution activities support;
2. *transportation*—how the firm ships its products;
3. *inventory control*—quantity of inventory the firm maintains at each location;

4. *protective packaging and materials handling*—how the firm packages and efficiently handles goods in the factory, warehouse, and transport terminals;

5. *order processing*—how the firm handles orders; and

6. *warehousing*—the distribution system's location of stock and the number of warehouses the firm maintains.

All of these components function in interrelated ways. Decisions made in one area affect efficiency in others. The physical distribution manager must balance each component so the system avoids stressing any single aspect to the detriment of overall functioning. A firm might decide to reduce transportation costs by shipping its products by less costly—but slow—water transportation. But slow deliveries would likely force the firm to maintain higher inventory levels, raising those costs. This mismatch between system elements often leads to increased production costs. So balancing the components is crucial.

The general shift from a manufacturing economy to a service economy in the United States has affected physical distribution in two key ways. First, customers require more flexible—yet reliable—transportation service. Second, the number of smaller shipments is growing much faster than the number of large shipments. Although traditional, high-volume shipments will continue to grow, they will represent a lower percentage of the transportation industry's revenues and volume.

The Problem of Suboptimization

Logistics managers seek to establish a specified level of customer service while minimizing the costs of physically moving and storing goods. Marketers must first decide on their priorities for customer service and then figure out how to fulfill those goals by moving goods at the least cost. Meshing together all the physical distribution elements is a huge challenge that firms don't always meet.

Suboptimization results when the managers of individual physical distribution functions attempt to minimize costs, but the impact of one task leads to less than optimal results on the others. Imagine a hockey team composed of star players. Unfortunately, despite the individual talents of the players, the team fails to win a game. This is an example of suboptimization. The same thing can happen at a company when each logistics activity is judged by its own accomplishments instead of the way it contributes to the overall goals of the firm.

Suboptimization often happens when a firm introduces a new product that may not fit easily into its current physical distribution system.

Effective management of the physical distribution function requires some cost trade-offs. By accepting relatively high costs in some functional areas to cut costs in others, managers can minimize their firm's total physical distribution costs. Of course, any reduction in logistical costs should support progress toward the goal of maintaining customer service standards.

suboptimization
Condition that results when individual operations achieve their objectives but interfere with progress toward broader organizational goals.

Customer Service Standards

Customer service standards state the goals and define acceptable performance for the quality of service a firm expects to deliver to its customers. Internet retailers such as Giftbaskets.com thrive because of their ability to ship within hours of receiving an order. 1-800-FLOWERS.com offers same-day delivery, every day of the week, nationwide, with a 100 percent guarantee of satisfaction. The firm's fulfillment system includes a network of more than 9,000 florists—one reason why the company can guarantee its deliveries.[29] A pizza restaurant might set a standard to deliver customers' pizzas hot and fresh within 30 minutes. An auto repair shop might set a standard to complete all oil changes in a half hour. All are examples of customer service standards.

Designers of a physical distribution system begin by establishing acceptable levels of customer service. These designers then assemble physical distribution components in a way that will achieve this standard at the lowest possible total cost. This overall cost breaks down into five components: (1) transportation, (2) warehousing, (3) inventory control, (4) customer service/order processing, and (5) administrative costs.

© GETTY IMAGES

1-800-FLOWERS.com strives for high customer service standards, offering same-day delivery, every day of the week, nationwide, with a 100 percent guarantee of satisfaction.

Transportation

The transportation industry was largely deregulated a number of years ago. Deregulation has been particularly important for motor carriers, railroads, and air carriers. Today, an estimated 15.5 million trucks are transporting goods throughout the United States; 2 million of these are tractor-trailers. It is estimated that more than 500,000 trucking companies and nearly 3.5 million truck drivers operate in the country.[30] Railroads are enjoying a new boom: once hauling mostly commodities like corn and grain, they now transport cross-country the huge loads of goods coming from China through West Coast ports. Railroads can move a greater amount of freight for less fuel than trucks. In North America, more than 1.5 million rail cars carry freight on 173,000 miles of track, with the industry generating $42 billion in annual revenues.[31]

Typically adding about 10 percent to the cost of a product, transportation and delivery expenses represent the largest category of logistics-related costs for most firms. Also, for many items—particularly perishable ones such as fresh fish or produce—transportation makes a central contribution to satisfactory customer service.

Many logistics managers have found that the key to controlling their shipping costs is careful management of relationships with shipping firms. Freight carriers use two basic rates: class and commodity rates. A class rate is a standard rate for a specific commodity moving between any pair of destinations. A carrier may charge a lower commodity rate, sometimes called a *special rate*, to a favored shipper as a reward for either regular business or a large-quantity shipment. Railroads and inland water carriers frequently reward customers in this way. In addition, the railroad and motor carrier industries sometimes supplement this rate structure with negotiated, or contract, rates. In other words, the two parties finalize the terms of rates, services, and other variables in a contract.

CLASSES OF CARRIERS

Freight carriers are classified as common, contract, and private carriers. **Common carriers**, often considered the backbone of the transportation industry, provide transportation services as for-hire carriers to the general public. The government still regulates their rates and services, and they cannot conduct their operations without permission from the appropriate regulatory authority. Common carriers move freight via all modes of transport. FedEx is a major common carrier serving businesses and consumers. One way the firm remains competitive is by developing new methods for enhancing customer service. FedEx has a service called InSight, a free online service that essentially reverses the package-tracking process—instead of following a package from shipment to delivery, customers can go online to find out what will be delivered to them that day. One FedEx customer that has benefited greatly from this new service is Nashville–based Holtkamp Greenhouses, which ships perishable goods—begonias, miniature poinsettias, and other plants—to florists and nursery departments of such big-box stores as Home Depot, Lowe's, and Walmart. With InSight, the company can easily track the status of its shipments.[32]

briefly speaking

"Our country's prosperity depends on its having an efficient and well-maintained rail system."

—Warren Buffett
(b. 1930)
American investor

common carriers
Businesses that provide transportation services as for-hire carriers to the general public.

Contract carriers are for-hire transporters that do not offer their services to the general public. Instead, they establish contracts with individual customers and operate exclusively for particular industries, such as the motor freight industry. These carriers operate under much looser regulations than common carriers.

Private carriers do not offer services for hire. These carriers provide transportation services solely for internally generated freight. As a result, they observe no rate or service regulations. The Interstate Commerce Commission (ICC), a federal regulatory agency, permits private carriers to operate as common or contract carriers as well. Many private carriers have taken advantage of this rule by operating their trucks fully loaded at all times.

contract carriers For-hire transporters that do not offer their services to the general public.

private carriers Transporters that provide service solely for internally generated freight.

 assessment check

1. What are the six major elements of physical distribution?
2. What is suboptimization?

Major Transportation Modes

Logistics managers choose among five major transportation alternatives: railroads, motor carriers, water carriers, pipelines, and air freight. Each mode has its own unique characteristics. Logistics managers select the best options by matching these features to their specific transportation needs.

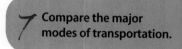 **7** Compare the major modes of transportation.

RAILROADS

Railroads continue to control the largest share of the freight business as measured by ton-miles. The term *ton-mile* indicates shipping activity required to move one ton of freight one mile. Rail shipments quickly rack up ton-miles because this mode provides the most efficient way for moving bulky commodities over long distances. Rail carriers generally transport huge quantities of coal, chemicals, grain, nonmetallic minerals, lumber and wood products, and automobiles. The railroads have improved their service standards through a number of innovative concepts such as unit trains, run-through trains, **intermodal operations**, and double-stack container trains. Unit trains carry much of the coal, grain, and other high-volume commodities shipped. They run back and forth between single loading points (such as a mine) and single destinations (such as a power plant) to deliver a commodity. Run-through trains bypass intermediate terminals to speed up schedules. They work similarly to unit trains, but a run-through train may carry a variety of commodities.

In piggyback operations, one of the intermodal operations, highway trailers and containers ride on railroad flatcars, thus combining the long-haul capacity of the train with the door-to-door flexibility of the truck. A double-stack container train pulls special rail cars equipped with bathtub-shaped wells so they can carry two containers stacked on top of one another. By nearly doubling train capacity and slashing costs, this system offers enormous advantages to rail customers.

As mentioned earlier, the railroad industry is enjoying a resurgence—this also means it must build a better infrastructure to handle the increase in demand. California, Florida, and Illinois have launched plans for high-speed rail corridors, with the Federal Railroad Administration agreeing to help fund those projects. There are also rail infrastructure projects in other states, including North Carolina, Ohio, Oregon, Vermont, and Washington.[33]

intermodal operations Combination of transport modes, such as rail and highway carriers (piggyback), air and highway carriers (birdyback), and water and air carriers (fishyback), to improve customer service and achieve cost advantages.

MOTOR CARRIERS

The trucking industry is also an important factor in the freight industry—the American Trucking Association reports that trucks haul about 10.2 billion tons of freight each year, making deliveries to areas railroads simply can't reach.[34]

Trucking offers some important advantages over the other transportation modes, including relatively fast shipments and consistent service for both large and small shipments. Motor carriers concentrate on shipping manufactured products while railroads typically haul bulk shipments of raw materials. Motor carriers therefore receive greater revenue per ton shipped, because the cost for shipping raw materials is higher than shipping manufactured products.

Technology has also improved the efficiency of trucking. Many trucking firms now track their fleets via satellite communications systems. In-truck computer systems allow drivers and dispatchers to make last-minute changes in scheduling and delivery. The Internet is also adding new features to motor carrier services.

Even so, the trucking industry must adjust to changes in the marketing environment. Trucking firms report a shortage of long-haul drivers, causing delays in some deliveries and higher costs, along with the rising cost of fuel, to customers. Some firms offer drivers regional runs and dedicated routes for more predictable work hours, as well as better pay. They also recruit husband-and-wife teams for the long-haul routes, which is becoming a popular practice.[35]

WATER CARRIERS

Two basic types of transport methods move products over water: inland or barge lines and oceangoing, deepwater ships. Barge lines efficiently transport bulky, low-unit-value commodities such as grain, gravel, lumber, sand, and steel. A typical lower Mississippi River barge line may stretch more than a quarter mile across.

Large ships also operate on the Great Lakes, transporting materials such as iron ore from Minnesota and harvested grain for market. These lake carrier ships range in size from roughly 400 feet to more than 1,000 feet in length.

Oceangoing supertankers from global companies such as Maersk Line are the size of three football fields, almost doubling the capacity of other vessels. At full capacity, the ships can cut the cost by a fifth of shipping a container across the Pacific Ocean. Shippers that transport goods via water carriers incur very low costs compared with the rates for other transportation modes. Standardized modular shipping containers maximize savings by limiting loading, unloading, and other handling.

Ships often carry large refrigerated containers called "reefers" for transporting everything from fresh produce to medical supplies. These containers, along with their nonrefrigerated counterparts, improve shipping efficiency because they can easily be removed from a ship and attached to trucks or trains. Although shipping by water has traditionally been less expensive than other modes of transportation, as explained earlier, costs for this mode have increased dramatically because of tightened security measures. Freight rates are based on the size of the vessel, the cost of fuel, and security measures. Industry experts predict these costs will continue to climb over the next several years.[36]

FedEx is now offering an alternative shipping method that allows customers to move their cargo from Asia to varying U.S. destinations via one integrated process. The FedEx Trade Networks system combines its ocean freight forwarding and customs brokerage services with its U.S. transportation and delivery services: FedEx Freight, FedEx Ground, and FedEx Express. Customers can initiate and track the entire process through one FedEx point of contact, reducing costs and the chance for error.[37]

The "Solving an Ethical Controversy" feature discusses a recent issue involving ocean-going vessels: the issue of piracy.

The FedEx Trade Networks system combines its ocean freight forwarding and customs brokerage services with its U.S. transportation and delivery services.

© AP IMAGES/MARK LENNIHAN

PIPELINES

Although the pipeline industry ranks third after railroads and motor carriers in ton-miles transported, many people scarcely recognize its existence. More than 2.5 million miles of pipelines crisscross the United States in an extremely efficient network for transporting energy products—enough to circle the planet 100 times. The pipelines are operated by more than 3,000 large and small firms.[38] Oil pipelines carry two types of commodities: crude (unprocessed) oil and

Guns on the High Seas?

solving an ethical controversy

It was once the stuff of swashbuckling novels and adventure movies: piracy on the high seas. Lately, however, pirates' attacks on oceangoing cargo vessels has become a reality. Not long ago, Somali pirates attacked the *Maersk Alabama*, a container ship sailing under the U.S. flag, and took its captain, Richard Phillips, hostage. With the world watching, the stand-off ended five days later as U.S. Navy snipers aboard the *USS Bainbridge* killed three of his captors and took a fourth prisoner. The *Maersk Alabama* story is just one in a long string of recent attacks by Somali pirates, who have stepped up their activities in the Gulf of Aden.

Should crews of ocean-going vessels be permitted to bear arms?

PRO

1. Pirates have become increasingly sophisticated in their tactics. By training and arming senior officers or bringing aboard highly trained military veterans, civilian ships can defend themselves. The knowledge alone that ships are armed would serve as a deterrent to piracy.

2. A ship that travels unarmed into regions known to be dangerous is arguably an unsafe workplace and an unseaworthy vessel.

CON

1. Piracy is rare. In a recent year, of the 33,000 ships that sailed the Gulf of Aden, only 122 sustained an attempted attack, and just 42 of those attacks were successful.

2. Knowing that a crew is armed would encourage pirates to resort to even more dangerous tactics, leading to an escalating situation merchant sailors aren't trained to handle.

Summary

The U.S. Coast Guard recently issued an advisory confirming that merchant ships are permitted to defend themselves. Months later, the *Maersk Alabama* was fired upon—again—by Somali pirates. This time, however, a private security force was onboard and fired back, causing the pirates to retreat. Providing a security force is costly, and arming merchant sailors is fraught with legal issues, so one thing is clear: this issue is not yet resolved.

Sources: "Pirates Hijack Ship with Indian Crew," *Independent Online*, April 12, 2010, http://www.iol.co.za; Kelly Sweeney, "In Pirate Zone, an Unarmed Ship Is an Unseaworthy Ship," *Professional Mariner*, March 2010, http://professionalmariner.com; Gordon Lubold, "With Piracy Odds in Their Favor, Ships Shun Armed Guards," *Christian Science Monitor*, May 6, 2009, http://www.esmonitor.com; Peter Chalk, "Keep Arms off Ships," *USA Today*, May 4, 2009, http://www.usatoday.com; Andrea Stone, "Sea Captain Calls for Arming Ship Officers," *USA Today*, May 1, 2009, http://www.usatoday.com.

refined products such as gasoline, jet fuel, and kerosene. In addition, one so-called slurry pipeline carries coal in suspension after it has been ground up into a powder and mixed with water. The Black Mesa Pipeline, owned by Union Pacific, moves the coal mined by Peabody Coal from northern Arizona 290 miles south into southern Nevada.

Although pipelines offer low maintenance and dependable methods of transportation, a number of characteristics limit their applications. They have fewer locations than water carriers, and they can accommodate shipments of only a small number of products. Finally, pipelines represent a relatively slow method of transportation; liquids travel through this method at an average speed of only three to four miles per hour.

AIR FREIGHT

Although the air freight industry grew steadily for many years, recently that growth has dropped off—at least in certain market sectors such as overnight delivery service. But firms are adapting. UPS recently revamped its services, now offering an expanded international express service called UPS

table 13.3 Comparison of Transport Modes

Mode	Speed	Dependability in Meeting Schedules	Frequency of Shipments	Availability in Different Locations	Flexibility in Handling	Cost
Rail	Average	Average	Low	Low	High	Average
Water	Very slow	Average	Very low	Limited	Very high	Very low
Truck	Fast	High	High	Very extensive	Average	High
Pipeline	Slow	High	High	Very limited	Very low	Low
Air	Very fast	High	Average	Average	Low	Very high

Express Freight. The service provides guaranteed time-definite, overnight to three-day door-to-door delivery, including customs clearance, to large global metropolitan areas. UPS is also offering two less-expensive, nonguaranteed services: UPS Air Freight Direct and UPS Air Freight Consolidated. Both are available worldwide and provide package pickup, delivery, and customs clearance.[39]

COMPARING THE FIVE MODES OF TRANSPORT

Table 13.3 compares the five transportation modes on several operating characteristics. Although all shippers judge reliability, speed, and cost in choosing the most appropriate transportation methods, they assign varying importance to specific criteria when shipping different goods. For example, while motor carriers rank highest in availability in different locations, shippers of petroleum products frequently choose the lowest-ranked alternative, pipelines, for their low cost. Examples of types of goods most often handled by the different transports include:

- *railroads*—lumber, iron, steel, coal, automobiles, grain, and chemicals;
- *motor carriers*—clothing, furniture, fixtures, lumber, plastic, food, leather, and machinery;
- *water carriers*—fuel, oil, coal, chemicals, minerals, and petroleum products; automobiles and electronics from foreign manufacturers; and low-value products from foreign manufacturers;
- *pipelines*—oil, diesel fuel, jet fuel, kerosene, and natural gas; and
- *air freight*—flowers, medical testing kits, and gourmet food products sent directly to consumers.

✓ assessment check

1. Identify the five major modes of transport.
2. Which mode of transport is currently experiencing a resurgence, and why?

Freight Forwarders and Supplemental Carriers

 Discuss the role of transportation intermediaries, combined transportation modes, and warehousing in improving physical distribution.

Freight forwarders act as transportation intermediaries, consolidating shipments to gain lower rates for their customers. The transport rates on less-than-truckload (LTL) and less-than-carload (LCL) shipments often double the per-unit rates on truckload (TL) and carload (CL) shipments. Freight forwarders charge less than the highest rates but more than the lowest rates. They profit by consolidating shipments from multiple customers until they can ship at TL and CL rates. The customers gain two advantages from these services: lower costs on small shipments and faster delivery service than they could achieve with their own LTL and LCL shipments.

In addition to the transportation options reviewed so far, a logistics manager can ship products via a number of auxiliary, or supplemental, carriers that specialize in small shipments. These carriers include UPS, FedEx, and the U.S. Postal Service.

Intermodal Coordination

Transportation companies emphasize specific modes and serve certain kinds of customers, but they sometimes combine their services to give shippers the service and cost advantages of each. *Piggyback* service, mentioned in the section on rail transport, is the most widely used form of intermodal coordination. *Birdyback* service, another form of intermodal coordination, sends motor carriers to pick up a shipment locally and deliver that shipment to local destinations; an air carrier takes it between airports near those locations. *Fishyback* service sets up a similar intermodal coordination system between motor carriers and water carriers.

Intermodal transportation generally gives shippers faster service and lower rates than either mode could match individually because each method carries freight in its most efficient way. However, intermodal arrangements require close coordination between all transportation providers.

Recognizing this need, multimodal transportation companies have formed to offer combined activities within single operations. Piggyback service generally joins two separate companies: a railroad and a trucking company. A multimodal firm provides intermodal service through its own internal transportation resources. Shippers benefit because the single service assumes responsibility from origin to destination. This unification prevents disputes over which carrier delayed or damaged a shipment.

Warehousing

Products flow through two types of warehouses: storage and distribution warehouses. A storage warehouse holds goods for moderate to long periods in an attempt to balance supply and demand for producers and purchasers. For example, controlled-atmosphere—also called *cold storage*—warehouses in Yakima and Wenatchee, Washington, serve nearby apple orchards. By contrast, a distribution warehouse assembles and redistributes goods, keeping them moving as much as possible. Many distribution warehouses or centers physically store goods for less than 24 hours before shipping them to customers.

Logistics managers have attempted to save on transportation costs by developing central distribution centers. A manufacturer might send a single, large, consolidated shipment to a break-bulk center—a central distribution center that breaks down large shipments into several smaller ones and delivers them to individual customers in the area. Many Internet retailers use break-bulk distribution centers.

As part of a multiyear expansion program, Caterpillar Logistics Services is building a $65 million parts distribution center near Dayton, Ohio. The new facility will cover more than 1 million square feet and employ 500 to 600 people. The new warehousing facility is intended to replace a regional distribution center in Indiana and will perform some of the work done at another parts distribution center in Illinois. The facility will serve as a convenient inbound receiving center close to suppliers and provide improved delivery of parts to Caterpillar dealers and customers.[40]

AUTOMATED WAREHOUSE TECHNOLOGY

Logistics managers can cut distribution costs and improve customer service dramatically by automating their warehouse systems. Although automation technology represents an expensive investment, it can provide major labor savings for high-volume distributors such as grocery chains. A computerized system might store orders, choose the correct number of cases, and move those cases in the desired sequence to loading docks. This kind of warehouse system reduces labor costs, worker injuries, pilferage, fires, and breakage.

WAREHOUSE LOCATIONS

Every company must make a major logistics decision when it determines the number and locations of its storage facilities. Two categories of costs influence this choice: (1) warehousing

© DMITRY KALINOVSKY/SHUTTERSTOCK.COM

Products flow through two types of warehouses—storage and distribution warehouses. A storage warehouse holds goods for a moderate to long period of time while a distribution warehouse assembles and redistributes goods quickly.

and materials handling costs and (2) delivery costs from warehouses to customers. Large facilities offer economies of scale in facilities and materials handling systems; per-unit costs for these systems decrease as volume increases. Delivery costs, on the other hand, rise as the distance from warehouse to customer increases.

Warehouse location also affects customer service. Businesses must place their storage and distribution facilities in locations from which they can meet customer demands for product availability and delivery times. They must also consider population and employment trends. For example, the rapid growth of metropolitan areas in the southern and western United States has caused some firms to open more distribution centers in these areas. Nike's distribution center in Memphis, an eco-friendly facility, represents a $135 million investment in the Nike supply chain network. Using barcode scanners, RFID tag technology, and a voice-based management system to scan, sort, store, and ship Nike merchandise, the distribution center occupies more than 1 million square feet and employs 450 full-time and 100 to 300 temporary workers.[41]

Inventory Control Systems

Inventory control captures a large share of a logistics manager's attention because companies need to maintain enough inventory to meet customer demand without incurring unneeded costs for carrying excess inventory. Some firms attempt to keep inventory levels under control by implementing just-in-time (JIT) production. Others, as discussed earlier in this chapter, are beginning to use RFID technology.

vendor-managed inventory (VMI) Inventory management system in which the seller—based on an existing agreement with a buyer—determines how much of a product is needed.

Retailers often shift the responsibility—and costs—for inventory from themselves back to individual manufacturers. **Vendor-managed inventory (VMI)** systems like this are based on the assumption that suppliers are in the best position to spot understocks or surpluses, cutting costs along the supply chain that can be translated into lower prices at the checkout. Hubbell Inc., which manufactures electrical products for commercial and industrial customers, found that using a VMI system tightened the procurement cycle and generated cost savings. VMI also enables Hubbell to serve its distribution partners more efficiently, enhancing the supply chain relationship.[42]

Order Processing

Like inventory control, order processing directly affects the firm's ability to meet its customer service standards. A company may have to compensate for inefficiencies in its order-processing system by shipping products via costly transportation modes or by maintaining large inventories at many expensive field warehouses.

Order processing typically consists of four major activities: (1) conducting a credit check; (2) keeping a record of the sale, which involves tasks such as crediting a sales representative's commission account; (3) making appropriate accounting entries; and (4) locating orders, shipping them, and adjusting inventory records. A stockout occurs when an order for an item is not available for shipment. A firm's order-processing system must advise affected customers of a stockout and offer a choice of alternative actions.

As in other areas of physical distribution, technological innovations improve efficiency in order processing. Many firms are streamlining their order-processing procedures by using e-mail and the Internet. Outdoor-gear retailer REI, for example, pushes customers toward Web ordering—its least costly fulfillment channel—in its catalogs, store receipts, signs, mailers, and membership letters.

Protective Packaging and Materials Handling

materials handling system Set of activities that move production inputs and other goods within plants, warehouses, and transportation terminals.

Logistics managers arrange and control activities for moving products within plants, warehouses, and transportation terminals, which together compose the **materials handling system**. Two important concepts influence many materials handling choices: unitizing and containerization.

Unitizing combines as many packages as possible into each load that moves within or outside a facility. Logistics managers prefer to handle materials on pallets (platforms, generally made of wood, on which goods are transported). Unitizing systems often lash materials in place with steel bands or shrink packaging. A shrink package surrounds a batch of materials with a sheet of plastic that shrinks after heating, securely holding individual pieces together. Unitizing promotes efficient materials handling because each package requires minimal labor to move. Securing the materials together also minimizes damage and pilferage. Imperial Sugar uses an efficient process in distributing its products as *unitized pallets*—that is, a pallet holding merchandise ready for in-store display. To create these pallets, the company invested in a unitizer, a machine that stacks 495 bags of sugar more quickly—and more exactly—than human hands can. Customers like Sam's Club and Costco receive the pallets and move them directly to the selling floor.[43]

Logistics managers extend the same concept through **containerization**—combining several unitized loads. A container of oil rig parts, for example, can be loaded in Tulsa and trucked to Kansas City, where rail facilities place the shipment on a high-speed run-through train to New York City. There, the parts are loaded on a ship headed to Saudi Arabia.

In addition to the benefits outlined for unitizing, containerization also markedly reduces the time required to load and unload ships. Containers limit in-transit damage to freight because individual packages pass through fewer handling systems en route to purchasers.

> **containerization**
> Process of combining several unitized loads into a single, well-protected load for shipment.

assessment check

1. What are the benefits of intermodal transportation?
2. Identify the two types of warehouses, and explain their function.

strategic implications
of marketing in the 21st century

everal factors, including the e-business environment, security issues, and the cost of fuel, are driving changes in channel development, logistics, and supply chain management. As the Internet continues to revolutionize the ways manufacturers deliver goods to ultimate consumers, marketers must find ways to promote cooperation between existing dealer, retailer, and distributor networks while harnessing the power of the Web as a channel. This system demands not only delivery of goods and services faster and more efficiently than ever before, it also provides superior service to Web-based customers.

In addition, increased product proliferation—grocery stores typically stock almost 50,000 different items—demands logistics systems that can manage multiple brands delivered through multiple channels worldwide. Those channels must be finely tuned to identify and rapidly rectify problems such as retail shortfalls or costly overstocks. The trend toward leaner retailing, in which the burden of merchandise tracking and inventory control is switching from retailers to manufacturers, means that to be effective, logistics and supply chain systems must result in cost savings.

Review of Chapter Objectives

 Describe the types of marketing channels and the roles they play in marketing strategy.

Marketing (distribution) channels are the systems of marketing institutions that enhance the physical flow of goods and services, along with ownership title, from producer to consumer or business user. In other words, they help bridge the gap between producer or manufacturer and business customer or consumer. Types of channels include direct selling, selling through intermediaries, dual distribution, and reverse channels. Channels perform four functions: facilitating the exchange process, sorting, standardizing exchange processes, and facilitating searches by buyers and sellers.

 Outline the major channel strategy decisions.

Decisions include selecting a marketing channel and determining distribution intensity. Selection of a marketing channel may be based on market factors, product factors, organizational factors, or competitive factors. Distribution may be intensive, selective, or exclusive.

 Describe the concepts of channel management, conflict, and cooperation.

Manufacturers must practice channel management by developing and maintaining relationships with the intermediaries in their marketing channels. The channel captain is the dominant member of the channel. Horizontal and vertical conflict can arise when disagreement exists among channel members. Cooperation is best achieved when all channel members regard themselves as equal components of the same organization.

 Identify and describe the different vertical marketing systems.

A vertical marketing system (VMS) is a planned channel system designed to improve distribution efficiency and cost-effectiveness by integrating various functions throughout the distribution chain. This coordination may be achieved by forward integration or backward integration. Options include a corporate marketing system, operated by a single owner; an administered marketing system, run by a dominant channel member; and contractual marketing systems, based on formal agreements among channel members.

 Explain the roles of logistics and supply chain management in an overall distribution strategy.

Effective logistics requires proper supply chain management. The supply chain begins with raw materials, proceeds through actual production, and then continues with the movement of finished products through the marketing channel to customers. Supply chain management takes place in two directions: upstream and downstream. Tools that marketers use to streamline and manage logistics include radio-frequency identification (RFID), enterprise resource planning (ERP), and logistical cost control.

 Identify the major components of a physical distribution system.

Physical distribution involves a broad range of activities concerned with efficient movement of finished goods from the end of the production line to the consumer. As a system, physical distribution consists of six elements: (1) customer service, (2) transportation, (3) inventory control, (4) materials handling and protective packaging, (5) order processing, and (6) warehousing. These elements are interrelated and must be balanced to create a smoothly functioning distribution system and to avoid suboptimization.

 Compare the major modes of transportation.

The five major modes of transport are railroads, motor carriers, water freight, pipelines, and air freight. Railroads rank high on flexibility in handling products; average on speed, dependability in meeting schedules, and cost; and lower on frequency of shipments. Motor carriers are relatively high in cost but rank high on speed, dependability, shipment frequency, and availability in different locations. Water carriers balance their slow speed, low shipment frequency, and limited availability with lower costs. The special nature of pipelines makes them rank relatively low on availability, flexibility, and speed, but they are also lower in cost. Air transportation is high in cost but offers very fast and dependable delivery schedules.

 Discuss the role of transportation intermediaries, combined transportation modes, and warehousing in improving physical distribution.

Transportation intermediaries facilitate movement of goods in a variety of ways, including piggyback, birdyback, and fishyback services—all forms of intermodal coordination. Methods such as unitization and containerization facilitate intermodal transfers.

Assessment Check: Answers

1.1 Distinguish between a marketing channel and logistics. A marketing channel is an organized system of marketing institutions and their interrelationships designed to enhance the flow and ownership of goods and services from producer to user. Logistics is the actual process of coordinating the flow of information, goods, and services among members of the marketing channel.

1.2 What are the different types of marketing channels? The different types of marketing channels are direct selling, selling through intermediaries, dual distribution, and reverse channels.

1.3 What four functions do marketing channels perform? The four functions of marketing channels are (1) facilitating the exchange process by reducing the number of marketplace contacts necessary for a sale, (2) sorting, (3) standardizing exchange transactions, and (4) facilitating searches by buyers and sellers.

2.1 Identify four major factors in selecting a marketing channel. The four major factors in selecting a marketing channel are market, product, organizational, and competitive.

2.2 Describe the three general categories of distribution intensity. Intensive distribution seeks to distribute a product through all available channels in a trade area. Selective distribution chooses a limited number of retailers in a market area. Exclusive distribution grants exclusive rights to a wholesaler or retailer to sell a manufacturer's products.

3.1 What is a channel captain? What is its role in channel cooperation? A channel captain is the dominant member of the marketing channel. Its role in channel cooperation is to provide the necessary leadership.

3.2 Identify and describe the three types of channel conflict. Horizontal conflict results from disagreements among channel members at the same level. Vertical conflict occurs when channel members at different levels disagree. The gray market causes conflict because it involves competition in the U.S. market of brands produced by overseas affiliates.

4.1 What are vertical marketing systems? Identify the major types. Vertical marketing systems are planned channel systems designed to improve the effectiveness of distribution,

including efficiency and cost. The three major types are corporate, administered, and contractual.

4.2 Identify the three types of contractual marketing systems. The three types of contractual systems are wholesale-sponsored voluntary chains, retail cooperatives, and franchises.

5.1 What is upstream management? What is downstream management? Upstream management involves managing raw materials, inbound logistics, and warehouse and storage facilities. Downstream management involves managing finished product storage, outbound logistics, marketing and sales, and customer service.

5.2 Identify three methods for managing logistics. Methods for managing logistics include RFID technology, enterprise resource planning (ERP) systems, and logistical cost control.

6.1 What are the six major elements of physical distribution? The major elements of physical distribution are customer service, transportation, inventory control, materials handling and protective packaging, order processing, and warehousing.

6.2 What is suboptimization? Suboptimization occurs when managers of individual functions try to reduce costs but create less than optimal results.

7.1 Identify the five major modes of transport. The five major modes of transport are railroads, motor carriers, water carriers, pipelines, and air freight.

7.2 Which mode of transport is currently experiencing a resurgence, and why? Railroad transport is currently experiencing a resurgence because of the cost of fuel and its efficiency in transporting large amounts of freight for less fuel.

8.1 What are the benefits of intermodal transportation? Intermodal transportation usually provides shippers faster service and lower rates than a single mode could offer.

8.2 Identify the two types of warehouses, and explain their function. The two types of warehouses are storage and distribution. Storage warehouses hold goods for moderate to long periods of time to balance supply and demand. Distribution warehouses assemble and redistribute goods as quickly as possible.

Marketing Terms You Need to Know

distribution 414

marketing (distribution) channel 414

logistics 414

supply chain management 414

physical distribution 414

*marketing intermediary
  (middleman) 416*

wholesaler 416

direct channel 416

direct selling 416

manufacturers' representative 419

dual distribution 419

reverse channel 420

intensive distribution 423

selective distribution 423

exclusive distribution 424

closed sales territory 424

tying agreement 424

channel captain 425

gray goods 426

*vertical marketing system
  (VMS) 427*

forward integration 427

backward integration 427

corporate marketing system 427

administered marketing system 427

contractual marketing system 428

retail cooperative 428

franchise 428

supply chain 429

upstream management 430

downstream management 430

*radio-frequency identification
  (RFID) 430*

*enterprise resource planning (ERP)
  system 432*

*third-party (contract) logistics
  firm 432*

suboptimization 433

common carriers 434

contract carriers 435

private carriers 435

intermodal operations 435

*vendor-managed inventory
  (VMI) 440*

materials handling system 440

containerization 441

Assurance of Learning Review

1. What is a marketing intermediary? What is the intermediary's role?

2. Explain why the following firms might choose a dual distribution strategy:
   a. Netflix
   b. Home Shopping Network
   c. Target

3. Describe the three levels of distribution intensity. Give an example of a product in each level.

4. Compare and contrast the two types of channel conflict. Why is channel conflict damaging to all parties?

5. What are the benefits of owning a franchise? What are the drawbacks?

6. Why do firms choose to streamline their supply chains? Describe two or three ways a firm might go about streamlining their supply chains.

7. What are the five components associated with the cost of achieving customer service standards in a physical distribution system?

8. Which mode of transport would probably be selected for the following goods?
   a. diesel fuel
   b. chain-link fencing
   c. locally grown blueberries
   d. automobiles made in South Korea
   e. T-shirts manufactured in Honduras
   f. grain grown in North Dakota

9. Which two categories of costs influence the choice of how many storage facilities a firm might have and where they are located?

10. Describe the two concepts that influence materials handling choices. Give an example of a product that would be appropriate for each.

Projects and Teamwork Exercises

1. The traditional channel for consumer goods runs from producer to wholesaler to retailer to user. With a classmate, select a product from the following list (or choose one of your own) and create a chart that traces its distribution system. You may go online to the firm's Web site for additional information.
   a. kayak from the Orvis catalog or Web site
   b. tickets to a Major League baseball game
   c. DVD recorder/player from Best Buy

2. On your own or with a classmate, identify, draw, and explain a reverse channel with which you are familiar. What purpose does this reverse channel serve to businesses? To the community? To consumers?

3. With a classmate, choose a product you think would sell best through a direct channel. Then create a brief sales presentation for your product and present it to class. Ask for feedback.

4. With a classmate, choose one of the franchises listed in Table 13.2 (on page 429) or another franchise that interests you. Visit the Web site of the company to learn more about how its goods and services are distributed. Create a chart outlining the firm's physical distribution system.

5. It takes a lot to move an elaborate stage performance like Cirque du Soleil, Big Apple Circus, or a rock band from one location to another while it is on tour. With a classmate, choose a touring performance that interests you—a music group, a circus, a theater performance, a NASCAR race, or the like—and imagine you are in charge of logistics. Create a chart showing what modes of transportation you would select to move the performance, how you would warehouse certain items during downtime, and what methods you would use to control costs.

Critical-Thinking Exercises

1. Imagine a vending machine that would charge more for hot drinks—coffee, tea, and cocoa—during cold weather. What is your opinion of a temperature-sensitive vending machine? Consumers who live in colder climates might pay more over a longer time period each year than consumers who live in warmer climates. Would your opinion change if alternatives were nearby, say, a convenience store or a vending machine that is not temperature sensitive? Do you think such a machine would be successful? Why or why not?

2. Auto dealerships typically have exclusive distribution rights in their local markets. How might this affect the purchase choices consumers make? What problems might a dealership encounter with this type of distribution?

3. Choose one of the following firms and identify which marketing channel or channels you think would be best for its goods or services. Then explain the market factors, product factors, and organizational and competitive factors contributing to your selection.

   a. Barnes & Noble
   b. Outback Steakhouse
   c. *Sports Illustrated* magazine
   d. SeaWorld
   e. Banana Republic

4. In their most basic form, RFID tags track the progress of products from warehouse to retail shelf to checkout counter. But they have great potential to provide marketers with more information about consumers' purchase patterns. In what ways might RFID technology be used to serve customers better? What problems might arise?

5. After a trip to India, where you were inspired by the craftsmanship of artisans who make jewelry and decorative artifacts, you decide to establish an import business focusing on their work. How would you determine distribution intensity for your business? What mode or modes of transportation would you use to get the goods to the United States? How and where would you warehouse the goods? Explain your answers.

Ethics Exercise

As more and more firms do business globally, transporting goods from one part of the world to another, there has been a surge in piracy—criminals making off with cargo shipments filled with everything from component parts to finished goods. A tractor-trailer loaded with electronics might be stolen from a truck stop; a warehouse stacked with pallets of new clothing, TVs, or just about anything else might be susceptible to theft. Large, sophisticated cargo theft gangs have been identified by law enforcement authorities in California, New Jersey, New York, and Texas and in cities such as Atlanta, Chicago, and Miami. However, members of the supply chain can work together to close the net around would-be thieves, developing stronger relationships with each other and law enforcement.[44]

1. What steps might manufacturers take to achieve the kind of channel cooperation that could reduce or prevent cargo theft?

2. How might transportation firms use security measures to build trust with customers and strengthen their position in the marketplace?

Internet Exercises

1. **Channel conflicts**. Garmin produces a wide range of GPS devices for a variety of applications. Garmin uses several channels to sell its products, including its own Web store. Visit the Garmin USA Web site. How does Garmin avoid channel conflict? Explain your answer.

   http://www.garmin.com/garmin/cms/site/us

2. **RFID developments**. Go to the Web site of the *RFID Journal*. Review the material and prepare a report outlining some of the more significant developments in RFID technology.

   http://www.rfidjournal.com

3. **Barge transportation statistics**. Visit the Web site of the American Waterways Operators (http://www.americanwaterways.com/). Click on "Facts About the Industry" and answer the following questions:
   a. How many barges are in operation in the U.S.?
   b. What commodities are typically shipped by barge in the U.S.?
   c. Compared to railroads and trucks, why are barges a more economical way to ship certain types of commodities?

Note: Internet Web addresses change frequently. If you don't find the exact site listed, you may need to access the organization's home page and search from there or use a search engine such as Google or Bing.

Case 13.1   *Carolyn Dorothy: Not Your Grandpa's Tugboat*

While it may *look* like a standard tugboat, the *Carolyn Dorothy* is anything but. In fact, this tenth vessel in the line of Dolphin-class tugs operated by Seattle-based Foss Maritime is a hybrid tug, the first of its kind in the world. Its power system includes two

diesel generators and two diesel engines; electric motor-generators; and 126 12-volt lead-acid batteries weighing 18,000 pounds. The boat can operate off the batteries only, off the power of one or more generators or engines, or a mix of sources. This highly variable combination allows the *Carolyn Dorothy* to match the power needed to the task at hand.

Founded in 1889, Foss Maritime began with a single used rowboat and grew into a global maritime empire whose services play an important role in the supply chains of numerous industries, from bridge construction to logging. In the spirit of continuous improvement, Foss has long desired to build a cleaner, more fuel-efficient tugboat—one that helps the company minimize toxic emissions and energy use. Recently, in collaboration with an engineering firm, it devised a way to adapt a standard, "off-the-shelf" power system and combine it with battery technology to create a hybrid tugboat.

Foss began by analyzing how tugs typically operate. It discovered that 60 percent of the time, tugs need less than a fifth of their power, and 95 percent of the time, less than two-thirds of their power. What's more, their diesel engines operate at fuel efficiency only when used at the top of their range. After considering (and rejecting) several alternatives, Foss consulted with Aspin Kemp & Associates, a Canadian engineering firm that builds specialized systems for oceangoing vessels, drill ships, and semi-submersibles.

Together, the firms fashioned a new methodology. Like a typical tug, the *Carolyn Dorothy* has four engines—two big ones for heavy loads and two smaller ones for auxiliary power. However, unlike a typical tug—where both large engines must operate simultaneously to balance the ship's load—it can use a single small engine to power the whole boat at low speeds. A computerized system allows the captain to switch seamlessly between hybrid and conventional power.

Foss has not yet calculated the exact return on its investment, but it knows one thing: the hybrid performs better. Using about 30 percent less fuel, its greenhouse gas emissions are also reduced. Early tests suggest its nitrous oxide emissions are cut nearly in half, with carbon-dioxide and sulfur-dioxide emissions reduced by as much as 30 percent. The boat is quieter, too. And because the main engines work less than those of standard tugs—about half the number of hours per year—the hybrid tug has lower lifecycle costs. Another plus: while Foss expects to replace the *Carolyn Dorothy*'s batteries three to five years from now, it believes that advances in battery technology will provide a greater choice of replacement options. Meanwhile, the company is giving serious thought to retrofitting its other Dolphin-class tugs with the hybrid technology.

Questions for Critical Thinking

1. Foss Maritime earned ISO 14001 certification for its commitment to such environmental goals as reducing fuel consumption and vessel emissions. Does this credential offer a differentiator for the company? How should Foss use this information in marketing its services?

2. With other firms' expressing interest in the hybrid technology, Foss and Aspin Kent are considering a joint venture to sell the technology, and have a patent pending. What other applications, besides tugboats, may be feasible?

Sources: Bruce Buls, "Crossbreed: Foss Maritime's Carolyn Dorothy: World's First Hybrid Tug," *Western Mariner*, June 2010, 39–44; Company Web site, http://www.foss.com, accessed May 31, 2010; "Foss Maritime Environmental Milestone," *Marinelink.com*, March 31, 2010, http://marinelink.com; "America Cargo Transport and Foss Maritime Providing Aid to Haiti Following Earthquake," *Maritime Executive*, January 18, 2010, http://www.maritime-executive.com; Clark Williams-Derry, "Give a Toot, Don't Pollute," *Daily Score*, October 22, 2009, http://www.daily.sightline.org.

Video Case 13.2
Marketing Channels and Supply Chain Management at Preserve*

"Our company was born in the natural channel—natural grocery stores, Whole Foods Market, Wild Oats, and Trader Joe's," says C. A. Webb, director of marketing for Preserve. It's a channel the company knows well. For over a decade, Preserve has been selling its line of toothbrushes and razors to eco-friendly consumers across the country.

"Whole Foods is our number one customer," says Webb. "Not only do they do an amazing job of telling our story in-store, they are the ultimate retail partner for us because they are so trusted." Customers have a sense that when they enter a Whole Foods market, every product has been carefully hand selected in accordance with Whole Foods' mission to sell organic and locally produced food and to present responsibly sourced and manufactured products.

One unique opportunity that came out of the relationship between Whole Foods and Preserve was the development of the Preserve line of kitchenware. Preserve was looking for a way to expand its recycled and recyclable product line, and Whole Foods was looking for an exclusive housewares line. "Together, we did the competitive research, we speced out the products, we developed the pricing strategy, designs," says Webb. The line of colanders, cutting boards, mixing bowls, and storage containers hit the shelves in 2007. "It created less risk on both sides," remarks Webb. The relatively tiny Preserve was able to take an untested product and put it in the nation's largest and most respected natural foods store, which in turn used its experience and resources in the channel to do all the legwork to ensure the product sold well. "We gave Whole Foods a 12-month exclusive on the line," says Webb, "which in turn gave them a great story to tell." That story was told everywhere. The "Today Show," *The New York Times Magazine,* "Everyday with Rachael Ray," *Gourmet* magazine, and many other natural and mainstream lifestyle publications covered the product. Today, in addition to Whole Foods, you can find the entire Preserve product line at thousands of retailers around the United States and Canada, including Target, Crate & Barrel, Trader Joe's, and large regional grocery chains such as Shaws, Hannaford's, and Stop and Shop.

With the recent increase in demand for green products by the average U.S. consumer, mainstream grocery and drug stores have been knocking on the doors of companies like Preserve to stock their shelves. It is a difficult space to work in, admits Webb. It's hard to make an impact on a shelf with one or two items when companies like Gillette or Rubbermaid offer 15 or 20 products in the same category.

One of the great benefits of working with Whole Foods in the beginning was that even though they are the largest chain in the natural foods channel, in the grocery and discount chain area, they are really quite small. "The quantities that we were needing to provide them were manageable for a small company like ours and it just gave us time together to assess demand, to keep inventory levels steady," says Webb. "It was much more of a 'bump-free' launch than we would have seen if we launched in other channels."

"Heading up the sales department, I think that every single day what we are working with here is supply chain management," notes Jon Turcotte, vice president of sales at Preserve.

Large supermarkets and stores like Target have entire Plan-o-gram departments that schedule and stock the shelves on a very tight schedule. If the plans include a turnover to a Fourth of July holiday special, Preserve needs to be able to supply them with exact quantities and selection of Preserve Picnic Ware to fit the Plan-o-gram for the aisle. "There aren't a lot of people in the process. Everything is controlled by computers," laments Turcotte. Just-in-time inventory systems have saved retailers millions of dollars, but as a result, there is little room for exceptions and do-overs. Failure to deliver could result in losing a tremendous opportunity to present products to literally hundreds of thousands of shoppers. "The old adage that time is money holds very true in today's world," Turcotte says. For a company like Preserve, with limited resources and very tight marketing budgets, this missed chance could spell disaster for the line.

Questions

1. As Preserve makes more headway into the larger retail chains, what challenges will it face?

2. What type of marketing channel would be best to support Preserve's growth over the next five years?

*"Preserve" was previously called "Recycline." The Recycline brand has now stepped into the background as the parent company.

ch14 Retailers, Wholesalers, and Direct Marketers

1 Explain the wheel of retailing.

2 Discuss how retailers select target markets.

3 Show how the elements of the marketing mix apply to retailing strategy.

4 Explain the concepts of retail convergence and scrambled merchandising.

5 Identify the functions performed by wholesaling intermediaries.

6 Outline the major types of independent wholesaling intermediaries and the appropriate situations for using each.

7 Compare the basic types of direct marketing and nonstore retailing.

8 Describe how much the Internet has altered the wholesaling, retailing, and direct marketing environments.

Wawa "Simplifies" for Customer Convenience ...

It's 2 a.m., your car's running on empty, and so are you. Where can you go for a quick pick-me-up? If you happen to be in Delaware, Maryland, New Jersey, Pennsylvania, or Virginia, chances are the answer is "Wawa."

To millions of people along the Eastern Seaboard, Wawa is a 24/7 haven for freshly brewed coffee, hot breakfast items, built-to-order hoagies, ready-to-eat salads, and more. Wawa stores are like mini-supermarkets, selling more than 6,000 items. Super Wawa stores also sell gasoline.

Wawa is one of the largest privately held convenience-store chains in the United States. Majority-owned and -operated by the Wood family, Wawa traces its roots to enterprising Wood ancestors who built a foundry (1803), a dairy farm (1902) and, finally, Wawa Food Markets. The first store opened in 1964 in Folsom, Pennsylvania. The Wawa name comes from the Pennsylvania town in which the dairy was located. "Wawa" means "goose" in the language of the Lenni Lenape Indians, the region's original residents. The Wawa corporate logo includes the image of a goose in flight.

With more than 570 stores and 16,000 employees, Wawa recently posted revenues of $5.83 billion—an increase of 15 percent over the prior year—and ranked 55th on a recent Forbes list of largest private companies. It pours more than 195 million cups of coffee per year and serves more than 400 million customers.

As Wawa leadership sees it, they're in business to simplify their customers' lives. The company adopted its "155-second rule"—referring to the length of the average store visit—as a guideline in assessing all of its systems and processes. To enable customers to order sandwiches the way they want them (and keep errors to a minimum), Wawa installed an automated ordering system at the deli counter. To give customers easy access to their cash, in the 1970s Wawa piloted a paperless cash-access system, moving to surcharge-free ATMs in all of its stores. Later, Wawa adopted "contactless technology," which enables a card reader to register a sales transaction when a customer passes a credit or debit card within two inches of the reader.

OPEN 24 HOURS

Wawa

evolution of a brand

Wawa has a broad range of competitors, from stand-alone convenience stores (the independent, "mom-and-pop" stores as well as regional and national chains) to gasoline stations with built-in convenience stores. Yet, Wawa has managed to differentiate itself; for example, unlike its competitors, Wawa declines to sell lottery tickets. And, as early as the 1980s, it began to focus on sustainability, launching an initiative to eliminate harmful chlorofluorocarbons by replacing or converting its walk-in coolers and dairy cases.

Wawa's e-commerce site features customized Web pages and sells gift cards, coffee packs, and a line of Wawa-logoed merchandise. To stay close to its public, Wawa also maintains a page on Facebook.[1]

Wawa has achieved success in a competitive marketplace by staying true to its mission: to simplify life for its customers. Stores are designed to help customers get in and out quickly, with "stations" strategically placed so that foot traffic flows smoothly. Although in-store displays in aisles and on countertops are known to increase sales through impulse buying, it's unlikely that a shopper will encounter them in a Wawa store as they slow down the shopping experience.

• Some years ago, Wawa closed its stores in Connecticut, Florida, the New York metropolitan area,

and New England, citing oversaturated markets. How can too much competition affect a retailer's strategy?

- Wawa defines its core purpose as simplifying their customers' lives. What makes that strategy successful?

chapter overview

In exploring how today's retailing sector operates, this chapter introduces many examples that explain the combination of activities involved in selling goods to ultimate consumers. Then the chapter discusses the role of wholesalers and other intermediaries who deliver goods from the manufacturers into the hands of retailers or other intermediaries. Finally, the chapter looks at nonstore retailing.

Direct marketing, a channel consisting of direct communication to consumers or business users, is a major form of nonstore retailing. It includes not just direct mail and telemarketing but also direct-response advertising, infomercials, and Internet marketing. The chapter concludes by looking at a less pervasive but growing aspect of nonstore retailing—automatic merchandising.

---

1 Explain the wheel of retailing.

Retailing

retailing Activities involved in selling merchandise to ultimate consumers.

Retailers are the marketing intermediaries in direct contact with ultimate consumers. **Retailing** describes the activities involved in selling merchandise to these consumers. Retail outlets serve as contact points between channel members and ultimate consumers. In a very real sense, retailers represent the distribution channel to most consumers because a typical shopper has little contact with manufacturers and virtually no contact with wholesaling intermediaries. Retailers determine locations, store hours, number of sales personnel, store layouts, merchandise selections, and return policies—factors that often influence the consumers' images of the offerings more strongly than consumers' images of the products themselves. Both large and small retailers perform the major channel activities: creating time, place, and ownership utilities.

Retail outlets such as Von Maur serve as contact points between channel members and ultimate consumers.

© TERRI MILLER/E-VISUAL COMMUNICATIONS, INC.

Retailers act as both customers and marketers in their channels. They sell products to ultimate consumers, and at the same time, they buy from wholesalers and manufacturers. Because of their critical location in the marketing channel, retailers often perform a vital feedback role. They obtain information from customers and transmit that information to manufacturers and other channel members.

Evolution of Retailing

The development of retailing illustrates the marketing concept in operation. Early retailing in North America can be traced to the establishment of trading posts, such as the Hudson Bay Company, and to pack peddlers who carried their wares to outlying settlements. The first type of retail institution, the general store, stocked a wide range of merchandise that met the needs of an isolated community or rural area. Supermarkets appeared in the early 1930s in response to consumers' desire for lower prices. In the 1950s, discount stores delivered lower prices in exchange for reduced services. The emergence of convenience food stores in the 1960s satisfied consumer demand for fast service, convenient locations, and expanded hours of operation. The development of off-price retailers in the 1980s and 1990s reflected consumer demand for brand-name merchandise at prices considerably lower than those of traditional retailers. In recent years, Internet-enabled retailing has increased in influence and importance.

A key concept, known as the **wheel of retailing**, attempts to explain the patterns of change in retailing. According to the wheel of retailing, a new type of retailer gains a competitive foothold by offering customers lower prices than current outlets charge and maintains profits by reducing or eliminating services. Once established, however, the innovator begins to add more services, and its prices gradually rise. It then becomes vulnerable to new low-price retailers that enter with minimum services—and so the wheel turns. The retail graveyard is littered with the likes of Gottschalks, Sharper Image, Linens 'n Things, KB Toys, Circuit City, Harold's, and Levitz Furniture.

Many major developments in the history of retailing appear to fit the wheel's pattern. Early department stores, chain stores, supermarkets, discount stores, hypermarkets, and catalog retailers all emphasized limited service and low prices. Most of these retailers gradually increased prices as they added services.

Some exceptions disrupt this pattern, however. Suburban shopping centers, convenience food stores, and vending machines never built their appeals around low prices. Still, the wheel pattern has been a good indicator enough times in the past to make it an accurate indicator of future retailing developments.

The wheel of retailing suggests that retailing is always changing. From Walmart's beginnings in the 1960s, founder Sam Walton held mandatory weekly Saturday morning meetings for Walmart executives. It was at these legendary assemblies that managers planned strategy, debated business philosophy, and built competitive advantage—in short, where the company culture was formed. Today, those meetings convene monthly, not weekly. Why the change? Some observers speculate the meetings no longer served their purpose. Whatever the reason, Walmart's change from weekly to monthly Saturday morning meetings signals the end of an era.[2]

wheel of retailing
Hypothesis that each new type of retailer gains a competitive foothold by offering lower prices than current suppliers charge; the result of reducing or eliminating services.

briefly speaking

" W hen I walk into a grocery store and look at all the products you can choose, I say, 'My God! No king ever had anything like I have in my grocery store today.' "

—Bill Gates
(b. 1955)
Cofounder, Microsoft

assessment check

1. What is retailing?
2. Explain the wheel-of-retailing concept.

Retailing Strategy

Like manufacturers and wholesalers, a retailer develops a marketing strategy based on the firm's goals and strategic plans. The organization monitors environmental influences and assesses its own strengths and weaknesses in identifying marketing opportunities and constraints. A retailer bases its key decisions on two fundamental steps in the marketing strategy process:

1. selecting a target market and
2. developing a retailing mix to satisfy the chosen market.

The retailing mix specifies merchandise strategy, customer service standards, pricing guidelines, target market analysis, promotion goals, location/distribution decisions, and store atmosphere choices. The combination of these elements projects a desired retail image. Retail

Components of Retail Strategy

Target Market · Merchandising · Customer Service · Promotion · Pricing · Location/Distribution · Store Atmospherics

image communicates the store's identity to consumers. Kohl's, for instance, counts on its trendy, contemporary image to attract consumers. As Figure 14.1 points out, components of retailing strategy must work together to create a consistent image that appeals to the store's target market.

Offering high-quality local produce at low prices is the strategy of Sunflower Farmers Market, a growing chain of supermarkets in six states in the West and Southwest. Launched a few years ago under the slogan "Serious food...silly prices," Sunflower targets consumers who look for quality but can't afford to pay boutique prices. In the face of an ongoing economic downturn, Sunflower emphasizes affordable organic produce, meats, and poultry. Recent sales figures show a 50 percent increase over the previous year.[3] Serving a gourmet hamburger that's never been frozen is part of the retailing strategy of Five Guys Burgers, profiled in the "Marketing Success" feature.

Selecting a Target Market

2 Discuss how retailers select target markets.

A retailer starts to define its strategy by selecting a target market. Factors that influence the retailer's selection are the size and profit potential of the market and the level of competition for its business.

mktg: *success*

Five Guys: Serving Up a Gourmet Burger

Background. It was 1986, and Jerry and Janie Murrell had a problem: their five sons were growing up. Pretty soon, the Virginia couple realized, the boys would leave home, go off to college, maybe even settle down far away. So the Murrells had a brainstorm: open a family business and employ the kids. They named their business—a take-out hamburger stand in Arlington, Virginia—Five Guys Burgers and Fries after their five sons.

Challenge. The fast-food market is one of the largest segments in the restaurant industry and also highly competitive. For Five Guys to succeed against the big chains

Retailers pore over demographic, geographic, and psychographic profiles to segment markets. In the end, most retailers identify their target markets in terms of certain demographics.

The importance of identifying and targeting the right market is dramatically illustrated by the erosion of department store retailing. While mall anchor stores struggle to attract customers, stand-alone store Target makes a memorable splash with edgy advertising that incorporates its signature red doughnut-shaped logo in imaginative ways. And although Target can be categorized as a discount retailer, it has differentiated itself from competitors like Walmart and Kmart by offering trendy, quality merchandise at low prices.[4]

Deep-discount chains like Deal$, Dollar General, Dollar Tree, Family Dollar Stores, and 99¢ Only, with their less glamorous locations and low-price merchandise displayed in narrow aisles, target lower-income bargain hunters. Attracted by cents-off basics such as shampoo, cereal, and laundry detergent, customers typically pick up higher-margin goods—toys or chocolates—on their way to the checkout.

By creating stores with wide aisles and clean presentation and offering friendly service and high-end product lines like Laura Ashley paints, home improvement chain Lowe's competes with archrival Home Depot. Lowe's ambiance helps make the store more appealing to female shoppers, who account for half of all home improvement store customers.[5]

After identifying a target market, a retailer must then develop marketing strategies to attract these chosen customers to its stores or Web site. The following sections discuss tactics for implementing different strategies.

 assessment check

1. How does a retailer develop a marketing strategy?
2. How do retailers select target markets?

in Arlington as well as the independent local burger joints, the Murrells realized they had to differentiate it from the pack.

The Strategy. The Murrells kept the menu simple, serving only hamburgers, hot dogs, and french fries. Because they couldn't afford to advertise, they decided to "let the food do the talking." Serving the very best burgers, dogs, and fries meant buying only top-grade ingredients. The burgers, for example, are made from a mixture of ground sirloin and ground chuck. And all menu items would be made fresh, never frozen: the french fries are fresh-cut and cooked in peanut oil. In addition to bacon and

cheese, guests could choose from 15 free toppings ranging from the traditional (mustard, ketchup, onions) to a tad more exotic (jalapeño peppers, grilled mushrooms, hot sauce). Five Guys' gourmet burgers aren't cheap: they range from about $4 to over $6.

The Outcome. By sticking to its original strategy—the company still doesn't spend money on advertising, for example—Five Guys has expanded well beyond its first burger stand in Arlington. Today the company boasts more than 560 outlets in 38 states and Canada. Latest annual sales figures report a 59 percent increase from the prior year. That's a lotta burgers.

Sources: Steve Ginsburg, "Five Guys Burgers Prepares to Munch into New Mexico," *Sacramento Business Journal,* February 19, 2010, http://www.bizjournals.com; "Five Guys Burgers and Fries Selects MICROS RES for Rapid Expansion Plans," *Forbes,* February 8, 2010, http://www.forbes.com; Peter Saltsman, "Go North, Beef Patty; Five Guys Burgers and Fries: Good Enough for Obama, Good Enough for Us," *National Post,* November 25, 2009, http://www.nationalpost.com; Emily Bryson York, "Five Guys: An America's Hottest Brands Case Study," *Advertising Age,* November 16, 2009, http://www.advertisingage.com; Bruce Horovitz, "Fast-Food Joints Upscale Burgers; New Sandwiches Get Premium Prices," *USA Today,* September 18, 2009, http://www.usatoday.com; Roger Yu, "Five Guys Is Simply Successful," *USA Today,* June 3, 2009, p. 3B.

Merchandising Strategy

A retailer's merchandising strategy guides decisions regarding the items it will offer. A retailer must decide on general merchandise categories, product lines, specific items within lines, and the depth and width of its assortments. Shoe retailer DSW characterizes its product assortment as "very broad and shallow," with high-fashion, high-quality footwear.[6] Big-box electronics retailer Best Buy recently expanded its product offerings to include a full line of musical instruments.[7]

To develop a successful merchandise mix, a retailer must weigh several priorities. First, it must consider the preferences and needs of its previously defined target market, keeping in mind that the competitive environment influences these choices. The retailer must also consider the overall profitability of each product line and product category.

CATEGORY MANAGEMENT

As mentioned in Chapter 12, a popular merchandising strategy is *category management,* in which a category manager oversees an entire product line and is responsible for the profitability of the product group. Both vendors and retailers use this strategy. Category management seeks to improve the retailer's product category performance through more coordinated buying, merchandising, and pricing. Rather than focusing on the performance of individual brands, such as Flex shampoo or Kleenex tissue, category management evaluates performance according to each product category. Laundry detergent, skin-care products, and paper goods, for example, are each viewed as individual profit centers, and different category managers supervise each group. Those that underperform are at risk of being dropped from inventory, regardless of the strength of individual brands. To improve their profitability, for example, some department stores have narrowed their traditionally broad product categories to eliminate high-overhead, low-profit lines such as toys, appliances, and furniture.

THE BATTLE FOR SHELF SPACE

As discussed in Chapter 13, large-scale retailers are increasingly taking on the role of channel captain within many distribution networks. Some have assumed traditional wholesaling functions, while others dictate product design and specifications to manufacturers. The result is a shift in power from the manufacturers of top-selling brands to the retailer who makes them available to customers.

A retailer must decide on the depth and width of merchandise assortments. Shoe retailer DSW characterizes its product assortment as "very broad and shallow," with high-fashion, high-quality footwear.

© JEFF GREENBERG/ALAMY

Adding to the pressure is the increase in the number of new products and variations on existing products. To identify the varying items within a product line, retailers refer to a specific product offering as a **stock-keeping unit (SKU)**. Within the skin-care category, for example, each facial cream, body moisturizer, and sunscreen in a variety of sizes and formulations is a separate SKU. The proliferation of new SKUs has resulted in a fierce battle for space on store shelves.

Increasingly, major retailers such as JCPenney make demands in return for providing shelf space. They may, for example, seek pricing and promotional concessions from manufacturers as conditions for selling their products. Retailers, such as Walmart, also require that manufacturers participate in their electronic data interchange (EDI) and quick-response systems. Manufacturers unable to comply may find themselves unable to penetrate this marketplace.

Slotting allowances are just one of the range of nonrefundable fees grocery retailers receive from manufacturers to secure shelf space for new products. Manufacturers may pay a national retailer thousands of dollars to get their new product displayed on store shelves.[8] Other fees include failure fees that are imposed if a new product does not meet sales projections; annual renewal fees, a "pay to stay" inducement for retailers to continue carrying brands; trade allowances; discounts on high-volume purchases; survey fees for research done by the retailers; and even fees to allow salespeople to present new items.

stock-keeping unit (SKU) Offering within a product line such as a specific size of liquid detergent.

Customer Service Strategy

Some stores build their retailing strategy around heightened customer services for shoppers. Gift wrapping, alterations, return privileges, bridal registries, consultants, interior design services, delivery and installation, and perhaps even electronic shopping via store Web sites are all examples of services that add value to the shopping experience. A retailer's customer service strategy must specify which services the firm will offer and whether it will charge customers for these services. Those decisions depend on several conditions: store size, type, and location; merchandise assortment; services offered by competitors; customer expectations; and financial resources. The "Solving an Ethical Controversy" feature discusses what it's like to be a part-time employee.

The basic objective of all customer services focuses on attracting and retaining target customers, thus increasing sales and profits. Some services—such as convenient restrooms, lounges, and complimentary coffee—enhance shoppers' comfort. Other services are intended to attract customers by making shopping easier and faster than it would be without the services. Some retailers, for example, offer child-care services for customers.

Consumers can also get "virtual assistance" from companies like Virtuosity and CallWave, which manage phone calls by allowing users to switch between voice mail, e-mail, and real-time cell and landline calls using voice commands. Virtuosity's Virtual Assistant software can answer, screen, and route calls much like a living, breathing administrative assistant. Similarly, CallWave's Voicemail-to-Text service screens mobile calls, converts voice mail to text, and helps users manage their time.[9]

Home Depot assures customers with its familiar slogan, "More saving. More doing."

A beautifully updated kitchen is now more doable than ever before, with new lower prices on special-order cabinets and countertops. This includes our exclusive Thomasville Cabinetry, like Blakely Maple shown in Cranberry and River Rock finishes, and Silestone countertop in Sierra Madre. The bigger your kitchen project, the more money you'll save. Get started in-store with our free kitchen design services or at homedepot.com/cabinets. **That's the power of The Home Depot.**

Member NKBA
National Kitchen & Bath Association

More saving. **More doing.**

© THE HOME DEPOT U.S.A. INC.

Hiring a Contingent Workforce

The recent recession generated widespread layoffs and caused soaring unemployment. Traditionally, as the economy begins to improve, employers start hiring again; but this time, most hiring is for contingent, or temporary, workers. As organizations regroup, they're recasting many formerly full-time permanent jobs as part-time or temporary. As a result, employment for contract workers has grown: nearly 166,000 jobs in less than a year's time. Many employers believe hiring temps is a safer way to go because, in most cases, temps are ineligible for health insurance, the retirement plans, paid vacation, and other benefits.

Is it ethical to replace full-time employees with contract workers?

PRO

1. Hiring contract workers may be the only way a business can stay afloat. If the business fails, not only does everyone lose their jobs, the business disappears from the economy.

2. Recent events show that having a full-time job on the company payroll is no guarantee of permanence. While most people prefer a job with benefits, many realize they're better off staying nimble in case of layoffs.

CON

1. Holding down a contract position when what you really need is full-time employment has a chilling effect on a household's disposable income and consumer confidence, which in turn affects how quickly an economy can lift itself out of recession.

2. The recession flooded the job market with experienced workers who apply for many temporary jobs typically filled by younger, less experienced candidates. Employers get an unfair advantage when they can slot a more experienced employee into a lower-paying job.

Summary

During a recession, hiring becomes a buyer's market: a disproportionate number of candidates—many of them overqualified—are vying for a handful of jobs. Reconfiguring the work into contract positions can be a risky strategy because it disrupts the organization's culture and creates feelings of mistrust among the regular workforce who survived the layoffs.

Sources: "You're Hired. For Now," *Kiplinger's Personal Finance*, March 2010, pp. 13–14; Chris Zappone, "Full-Time Worries for Part-Time Workers," *WAtoday.com*, February 12, 2010, http://www.watoday.com; "Employment-Population Ratio, Part Time Workers, Temporary Workers," *Calculated Risk.com*, February 5, 2010, http://www.calculatedrisk.com; Phil Villareal, "Target Employee Says 8K Full Timers Will Be Part-Time," *Consumerist.com*, February 3, 2010, http://consumerist.com; Jessica Dickler, "Battle Brews over Hourly Jobs," *CNNMoney.com*, February 2, 2010, http://money.cnn.com.

A customer service strategy can also support efforts in building demand for a line of merchandise. Despite the trend toward renovation, redecorating, and do-it-yourself home projects, Home Depot was experiencing slowing sales until it decided to revamp its stores, improve customer service, offer a decorating service, and upgrade its marketing efforts. Home Depot experienced solid growth with the strategy, assuring its customers with its familiar slogan, "More saving. More doing."

Pricing Strategy

Prices reflect a retailer's marketing objectives and policies. They also play a major role in consumer perceptions of a retailer. Consumers realize, for example, that when they enter a Hermes boutique, they will find such expensive merchandise as leather handbags priced at $2,450 and up, along with belts at $400 and up. By contrast, customers of Tuesday Morning or Big Lots expect totally different merchandise and prices.

MARKUPS AND MARKDOWNS

The amount a retailer adds to a product's cost to set the final selling price is the **markup**. The amount of the markup typically results from two marketing decisions:

1. *Services performed by the retailer.* Other things being equal, stores that offer more services charge larger markups to cover their costs.

2. *Inventory turnover rate.* Other things being equal, stores with a higher turnover rate can cover their costs and earn a profit while charging a smaller markup.

A retailer's markup exerts an important influence on its image among present and potential customers. In addition, the markup affects the retailer's ability to attract shoppers. An excessive markup may drive away customers; an inadequate markup may not generate sufficient revenue to cover costs and return a profit. Retailers typically state markups as percentages of either the selling prices or the costs of the products.

Marketers determine markups based partly on their judgments of the amounts that consumers will pay for a given product. When buyers refuse to pay a product's stated price, however, or when improvements in other items or fashion changes reduce the appeal of current merchandise, a retailer must take a **markdown**. The amount by which a retailer reduces the original selling price—the discount typically advertised for a sale item—is the markdown. Markdowns are sometimes used to evaluate merchandisers. For example, a department store might base its evaluations of merchandise buyers partly on the average markdown percentages for the product lines for which they are responsible.

The formulas for calculating markups and markdowns are provided in the "Financial Analysis in Marketing" appendix at the end of the text.

markup Amount a retailer adds to the cost of a product to determine its selling price.

markdown Amount by which a retailer reduces the original selling price of a product.

Location/Distribution Strategy

Retail experts often cite location as a potential determining factor in the success or failure of a retail business. A retailer may locate at an isolated site, in a central business district, or in a planned shopping center. The location decision depends on many factors, including the type of merchandise, the retailer's financial resources, characteristics of the target market, and site availability.

In recent years, many localities have become saturated with stores. As a result, some retailers have reevaluated their location strategies. A chain may close individual stores that do not meet sales and profit goals. Other retailers have experimented with nontraditional location strategies. For instance, Starbucks is now found in some Macy's and Target stores.

LOCATIONS IN PLANNED SHOPPING CENTERS

Over the past several decades, retail trade has shifted away from traditional downtown retailing districts and toward suburban shopping centers. A **planned shopping center** is a group of retail stores designed, coordinated, and marketed to shoppers in a geographic trade area. Together, the stores provide a single convenient location for shoppers as well as free parking. They facilitate shopping by maintaining uniform hours of operation, including evening and weekend hours.

There are five main types of planned shopping centers. The smallest, the *neighborhood shopping center,* is likely to consist of a group of smaller stores such as a drugstore, a dry cleaner, a card and gift shop, and perhaps a hair salon. This kind of center provides convenient shopping for 5,000 to 50,000 shoppers who live within a few minutes' commute. It contains 5 to 15 stores, and the product mix usually is confined to convenience items and some limited shopping goods.

A *community shopping center* serves 20,000 to 100,000 people in a trade area extending a few miles from its location. It contains anywhere from 10 to 30 retail stores, with a branch of a local department store or some other large store as the primary tenant. In addition to the stores found in a neighborhood center, a community center probably encompasses more stores featuring shopping goods, some professional offices, a branch bank, and perhaps a movie theater or supermarket.

planned shopping center Group of retail stores planned, coordinated, and marketed as a unit.

Community shopping centers typically offer ample parking, and tenants often share some promotion costs. With the advent of stand-alone, big-box retailers, some community shopping centers have declined in popularity. Some department stores are also moving away from the strategy of locating in shopping centers and opting for freestanding stores.

A *regional shopping center* is a large facility with at least 300,000 square feet of shopping space. Its marketing appeal usually emphasizes major department stores with the power to draw customers, supplemented by as many as 200 smaller stores. A successful regional center needs a location within 30 minutes' driving time of at least 250,000 people. A regional center like Indianapolis' Fashion Mall at Keystone or a superregional center such as Xanadu in New Jersey provides a wide assortment of convenience, shopping, and specialty goods, plus many personal service facilities. Some shopping centers are going green, working to reduce their carbon footprint with mandatory recycling programs, maximizing the use of natural light, and installing heat-reflecting roofing that reduces the need for air conditioning.[10]

A *power center,* usually located near a regional or superregional mall, brings together several huge specialty stores, such as Sports Authority, Home Depot, and Bed Bath & Beyond, as stand-alone stores in a single trading area. Rising in popularity during the 1990s, power centers offered value because they underpriced department stores while providing a huge selection of specialty merchandise. Heated competition from cost-cutter Walmart and inroads from more upscale discounters such as Target and Kohl's are currently hurting the drawing power of these centers.

A fifth type of planned center, the *lifestyle center,* is a retailing format offering a combination of shopping, movie theaters, stages for concerts and live entertainment, decorative fountains and park benches in greenways, and restaurants and bistros in an attractive outdoor environment. At around 300,000 to 1 million square feet, the centers are large, but they seek to offer the intimacy and easy access of neighborhood village retailing with a fashionable cachet. Convenience and pleasant ambiance are also part of the appeal. Here, shoppers find a mix of just the right upscale tenants—Williams-Sonoma, Banana Republic, Ann Taylor, Pottery Barn, and Restoration Hardware, for instance. Some lifestyle centers include office parks, townhouses, and condominiums. Customers visit such lifestyle centers as Santana Row in San Jose, California; Kierland Commons in Scottsdale, Arizona; Oak Brook Promenade in Oak Brook, Illinois; and St. John's Town Center in Jacksonville, Florida.[11]

To fill the empty spaces in malls and attract shoppers, malls are increasingly adding businesses that offer entertainment and experiences. Today, many shopping centers include movie theatre complexes, indoor playgrounds, arcade games, bowling alleys, and more. The White Flint Mall in North Bethesda, Maryland, hosts a Discovery Zone and a Dave & Buster's. In Dallas, Grapevine Mills Mall has added a Lego Discovery Centre and a miniature-golf course built from Legos.[12]

Promotional Strategy

To establish store images that entice more shoppers, retailers use a variety of promotional techniques. Through its promotional strategy, a retailer seeks to communicate to consumers information about its stores—locations, merchandise selections, hours of operation, and prices. If merchandise selection changes frequently to follow fashion trends, advertising is typically used to promote current styles effectively. In addition, promotions help retailers attract shoppers and build customer loyalty.

Innovative promotions can have interesting results. Blu Dot, a Minneapolis-based furniture maker, left several of its popular "Real Good" chairs—an item that

Lifestyle centers offer a combination of shopping, movie theaters, restaurants, and other forms of entertainment.

© AP IMAGES/JAY LAPRETE

retails at $129—on curbs throughout New York City. Embedded in each chair was a GPS device that enabled Blu Dot to track chairs as passersby noticed them and carried them off. Marketers posted a Google map and a Twitter feed to update followers on each chair's journey. Next, teams were deployed to locate the chairs and interview the individuals who had rescued them from the street.[13]

National retail chains often purchase advertising space in newspapers, on radio, and on television. Other retailers promote their goods over the Internet or use wireless technology to send marketing messages to customers' cell phones. Consumers are increasingly using their smartphones to surf the Web. To promote its bands, Warner Music Group launched a Wireless Application Protocol (WAP)–based site designed specifically for mobile browsing. Special analysis software enables Warner to analyze the browsing data by the user's device, origin of the session, and other criteria.[14]

Retailers also try to combine advertising with in-store merchandising techniques that influence buyer behavior at the point of purchase. Spain-based Zara stores offer fast fashion—inexpensive but trendy apparel that changes frequently. Merchandise arrives directly from the factory on plastic shipping hangers and already tagged. Clerks move items immediately to the selling floor, later switching out the plastic hangers for Zara's traditional wooden ones. Items typically sell out before they need to be marked down, creating a sense of exclusivity. Zara shoppers tend to visit often, sometimes even daily, to check out the new arrivals on the plastic hangers. Meanwhile, store managers wielding handheld computers pay close attention to what shoppers consider hot—or not—and alert Zara's designers, reordering best-selling merchandise in minutes instead of the hours it once required.[15]

A friendly, well-trained, and knowledgeable salesperson plays a vital role in conveying the store's image to consumers and in persuading shoppers to buy. To serve as a source of information, a salesperson must possess extensive knowledge regarding credit policies, discounts, special sales, delivery terms, layaways, and returns. To increase store sales, the salesperson must persuade customers that the store sells what those customers need. To this end, salespeople should receive training in selling up and suggestion selling.

By *selling up,* salespeople try to persuade customers to buy higher-priced items than originally intended. For example, an automobile salesperson might persuade a customer to buy a more expensive model than the car the buyer had initially considered. Of course, the practice of selling up must always respect the constraints of a customer's real needs. If a salesperson sells customers something they really do not need, the potential for repeat sales dramatically diminishes.

Another technique, *suggestion selling,* seeks to broaden a customer's original purchase by adding related items, special promotional products, or holiday or seasonal merchandise. Here, too, the salesperson tries to help a customer recognize true needs rather than unwanted merchandise. Beauty advisors in upscale department stores are masters of suggestion selling. Beauty retail chain Sephora creates a spa mood by treating customers like royalty. Sephora employees, called "cast members," receive special training before they hit the sales floor. Customers are encouraged to take their time, sample the wares, and indulge their senses in a stress-free environment.[16]

Just as knowledgeable and helpful sales personnel can both boost sales and set retailers apart from competitors, poor service influences customers' attitudes toward a retailer. Increasing customer complaints about unfriendly, inattentive, and uninformed salespeople have prompted many retailers to intensify their attention to training and motivating salespeople. Older training methods are giving way to online learning in many firms.

Sephora creates a spa mood by treating customers like royalty. Customers are encouraged to take their time in a stress-free environment.

NEWSCOM

Store Atmospherics

atmospherics
Combination of physical characteristics and amenities that contribute to a store's image.

While store location, merchandise selection, customer service, pricing, and promotional activities all contribute to a store's consumer awareness, stores also project their personalities through **atmospherics**—physical characteristics and amenities that attract customers and satisfy their shopping needs. Atmospherics include both a store's exterior and interior décor.

A store's exterior appearance, including architectural design, window displays, signs, and entryways, helps identify the retailer and attract its target market shoppers. The Saks Fifth Avenue script logo on a storefront and McDonald's golden arches are exterior elements that readily identify these retailers. Other retailers design eye-catching exterior elements aimed at getting customers' attention. Colorful, lifelike recreations of jungle animals flank the theatrically lit entrances of the popular Rainforest Cafés, and the tropical motif carries over to the interiors, decorated with wall-sized aquariums.

The interior décor of a store should also complement the retailer's image, respond to customers' interests, and, most importantly, induce shoppers to buy. Interior atmospheric elements include store layout, merchandise presentation, lighting, color, sounds, scents, and cleanliness. By strategically positioning the sections where aroma or fragrance are key—the flower shop, the bakery, and the deli where table-ready fried chicken or pizza are sold—supermarkets can boost impulse sales. Some retailers, like women's apparel store Bebe, even use hidden devices to waft a fragrance throughout their stores.[17]

When designing the interior and exterior of a store, marketers must remember that many people shop for reasons other than just purchasing needed products. Other common reasons for shopping include escaping the routine of daily life, avoiding weather extremes, fulfilling fantasies, and socializing with family and friends. Retailers expand beyond interior design to create welcoming and entertaining environments that draw shoppers. Some retailers offer a "store within a store" to sell selected merchandise in a more intimate setting—for example, the Peet's Coffee & Tea stands inside California-based Raley's supermarkets, Mango ministores selling trendy Euro-styled clothing within JCPenney stores, and Sunglass Hut stores within Macy's.[18]

✓ assessment check

1. What is an SKU?
2. What are the two components of a markup?
3. What are store atmospherics?

Types of Retailers

figure 14.2

Bases for Categorizing Retailers

Shopping Effort Expended by Customers
Convenience Retailers
Shopping Stores
Specialty Outlets

Services Provided for Customers
Self-Service
Self-Selection
Limited Service
Full-Service

Form of Ownership
Corporate Chain
Independent Retailer

Product Lines
Specialty Retailer
Limited-Line Retailer
General Merchandise Retailer

Location of Retail Transactions
Retail Stores
Nonstore and Internet Retailing

Because new types of retailers continue to evolve in response to changes in consumer demand, a universal classification system for retailers has yet to be devised. Certain differences do, however, define several categories of retailers: (1) forms of ownership, (2) shopping effort expended by customers, (3) services provided to customers, (4) product lines, and (5) location of retail transactions.

As Figure 14.2 points out, most retailing operations fit in different categories. A 7-Eleven outlet may be classified as a convenience store (category 2) with self-service (category 3) and a relatively broad product line (category 4). It is both a store-type retailer (category 5) and a member of a chain (category 1).

Classification of Retailers by Form of Ownership

Perhaps the easiest method for categorizing retailers is by ownership structure, distinguishing between chain stores and independent retailers. In addition, independent retailers may join wholesaler-sponsored voluntary chains, band together to form retail cooperatives, or enter into franchise agreements with manufacturers, wholesalers, or service provider organizations. Each type of ownership has its own unique advantages and strategies.

Apple's freestanding stores have long been known for their innovative design.

© DBIMAGES/ALAMY

CHAIN STORES

Chain stores are groups of retail outlets that operate under central ownership and management and handle the same product lines. Chains have an advantage over independent retailers in economies of scale. Volume purchases allow chains to pay lower prices than their independent rivals must pay. Because a chain may have hundreds of retail stores, it can afford extensive advertising, sales training, and computerized systems for merchandise ordering, inventory management, forecasting, and accounting. Also, the large sales volume and wide geographic reach of a chain may enable it to advertise in a variety of media.

INDEPENDENT RETAILERS

The second-largest industry in the United States by number of establishments as well as number of employees, the retailing structure supports a large number of small stores, many medium-size stores, and a small number of large stores. It generates about $4.5 trillion in retail sales every year and accounts for more than 12 percent of all business establishments in the United States.[19]

Independent retailers compete with chains in a number of ways. The traditional advantage of independent stores is friendly, personalized service. Cooperatives offer another strategy for independents. For instance, cooperatives like Best Western Hotels and Valu-Rite Pharmacies help independents compete with chains by providing volume buying power as well as advertising and marketing programs.

Classification by Shopping Effort

Another classification system is based on the reasons consumers shop at particular retail outlets. This approach categorizes stores as convenience, shopping, or specialty retailers.

Convenience retailers focus their marketing appeals on accessible locations, extended store hours, rapid checkout service, and adequate parking facilities. Local food stores, gasoline stations, and dry cleaners fit this category. GreenStop, Canada's chain of alternative-fuel stations, features convenience stores that sell solar-roasted coffee and organic veggie wraps instead of candy and cigarettes.

Shopping stores typically include furniture stores, appliance retailers, clothing outlets, and sporting goods stores. Consumers usually compare prices, assortments, and quality levels at competing outlets before making purchase decisions. Consequently, managers of shopping stores attempt to differentiate their outlets through advertising, in-store displays, well-trained and knowledgeable salespeople, and appropriate merchandise assortments.

Specialty retailers combine carefully defined product lines, services, and reputations in attempts to persuade consumers to expend considerable effort to shop at their stores. Examples include Bergdorf Goodman, Neiman Marcus, Nordstrom, and Dillard's.

convenience retailer Store that appeals to customers on accessible location, long hours, rapid checkout, and adequate parking.

specialty retailer Store that combines carefully defined product lines, services, and reputation to persuade shoppers to spend considerable shopping effort there.

Classification by Services Provided

Another category differentiates retailers by the services they provide to customers. This classification system consists of three retail types: self-service, self-selection, or full-service retailers.

The AM PM Mini-Mart is classified as a self-service store, while Safeway and Kroger grocery stores are examples of self-selection stores. Both categories sell convenience products people can purchase frequently with little assistance. In the clothing industry, catalog retailer Lands' End is a self-selection store. Full-service retailers such as Macy's focus on fashion-oriented merchandise, backed by a complete array of customer services.

Classification by Product Lines

Product lines also define a set of retail categories and the marketing strategies appropriate for firms within those categories. Grouping retailers by product lines produces three major categories: specialty stores, limited-line retailers, and general-merchandise retailers.

SPECIALTY STORES

A *specialty store* typically handles only part of a single product line. However, it stocks this portion in considerable depth or variety. Specialty stores include a wide range of retail outlets, including fish markets, grocery stores, men's and women's shoe stores, and bakeries. Although some specialty stores are chain outlets, most are independent, small-scale operations. They represent perhaps the greatest concentration of independent retailers who develop expertise in one product area and provide narrow lines of products for their local markets.

Specialty stores should not be confused with specialty products. Specialty stores typically carry convenience and shopping goods. The label *specialty* reflects the practice of handling a specific, narrow line of merchandise. For example, Lady Foot Locker is a specialty store that offers a wide selection of name-brand athletic footwear, apparel, and accessories made specifically for women. Gloria Jean's Coffees sells whole-bean coffees, beverages, and gifts.[20]

LIMITED-LINE RETAILERS

limited-line store
Retailer that offers a large assortment within a single product line or within a few related product lines.

category killer Store offering huge selections and low prices in single product lines.

Customers find a large assortment of products within one product line or a few related lines in a **limited-line store**. This type of retail operation typically develops in areas with a large enough population to sufficiently support it. Examples of limited-line stores are IKEA (home furnishings and housewares) and Rubensteins of New Orleans (men's clothing). These retailers cater to the needs of people who want to select from complete lines in purchasing particular products.

A unique type of limited-line retailer is known as a **category killer**. These stores offer huge selections and low prices in single product lines. Stores within this category—such as Best Buy, Bed Bath & Beyond, and Home Depot—are among the most successful retailers in the nation. Category killers at first took business away from general merchandise discounters, which were not able to compete in selection or price. Recently, however, expanded merchandise and aggressive cost cutting by warehouse clubs and Walmart have turned the tables. Competition from Internet companies that can offer unlimited selection and speedy delivery has also taken customers away. While they still remain a powerful force in retailing, especially for local businesses, category killers are not invulnerable.

Category killer Bed Bath & Beyond offers home goods at low prices.

© KRISTOFFER TRIPPLAAR/ALAMY

GENERAL MERCHANDISE RETAILERS

General merchandise retailers, carrying a wide variety of product lines stocked in some depth, distinguish themselves from limited-line and specialty retailers by the large number of product lines they carry. The general store described earlier in this chapter was an early form of a general merchandise retailer. This category includes variety stores, department stores, and mass merchandisers such as discount houses, off-price retailers, and hypermarkets.

general merchandise retailer Store that carries a wide variety of product lines, stocking all of them in some depth.

Variety Stores

A retail outlet that offers an extensive range and assortment of low-price merchandise is called a *variety store*. Less popular today than they once were, many of these stores have evolved into or given way to other types of retailers such as discount stores. In recent years, many pharmacies have become drugstore–variety store combinations. Walgreens, for example, has nearly 7,200 stores nationwide and fills more than a million prescriptions a year.[21] The nation's variety stores now account for less than 1 percent of all retail sales. However, variety stores remain popular in other parts of the world. Many retail outlets in Spain and Mexico are family-owned variety stores.

Department Stores

In essence, a **department store** is a series of limited-line and specialty stores under one roof. By definition, this large retailer handles a variety of merchandise, including men's, women's, and children's clothing and accessories; household linens and dry goods; home furnishings; and furniture. It serves as a one-stop shopping destination for almost all personal and household products.

Department stores such as Bloomingdale's built their reputations by offering wide varieties of services such as charge accounts, delivery, gift wrapping, and liberal return privileges. As a result, they incur relatively high operating costs, averaging about 45 to 60 percent of sales.

Department stores have faced intense competition over the past several years. Relatively high operating costs have left them vulnerable to retailing innovations such as discount stores, Internet retailers, and hypermarkets. In addition, department stores' traditional locations in downtown business districts have suffered from problems associated with limited parking, traffic congestion, and population migration to the suburbs.

Department stores have fought back in a variety of ways. Many have closed certain sections, such as electronics, in which high costs kept them from competing with discount houses and category killers. They have added bargain outlets, expanded parking facilities, and opened major branches in regional shopping centers. Marketers have attempted to revitalize downtown retailing in many cities by modernizing their stores, expanding store hours, making special efforts to attract the tourist and convention trade, and serving the needs of urban residents. Over the years, U.S. department stores have also undergone massive consolidation, with only a handful of companies owning many department-store chains that were once freestanding.[22]

department store Large store that handles a variety of merchandise, including clothing, household goods, appliances, and furniture.

briefly speaking

"Our attitude is that if you hire good people and pay them a fair wage, then good things will happen for the company."

—Jim Sinegal
(b. 1936)
CEO, Costco

Mass Merchandisers

Mass merchandising has made major inroads into department store sales by emphasizing lower prices for well-known brand-name products, high product turnover, and limited services. A **mass merchandiser** often stocks a wider line of items than a department store but usually without the same depth of assortment within each line. Discount houses, off-price retailers, hypermarkets, and catalog retailers are all examples of mass merchandisers.

mass merchandiser Store that stocks a wider line of goods than a department store, usually without the same depth of assortment within each line.

Discount Houses

A **discount house** charges low prices and offers fewer services. Early discount stores sold mostly appliances. Today, they offer soft goods, drugs, food, gasoline, and furniture.

By eliminating many of the "free" services provided by traditional retailers, these operations can keep their markups 10 to 25 percent below those of their competitors. Some of the early discounters have since added services, stocked well-known name brands, and boosted their prices. In fact, many now resemble department stores.

A discount format gaining strength is the *warehouse club*. Costco, BJ's, and Sam's Club are the largest warehouse clubs in the United States. These no-frills, cash-and-carry outlets offer consumers access to name-brand products at deeply discounted prices. Selection at warehouse

discount house Store that charges low prices but may not offer services such as credit.

Off-price retailers such as Loehmann's keep their prices below those of traditional retailers by offering fewer services.

clubs includes gourmet popcorn, fax machines, peanut butter, luggage, and sunglasses sold in vast warehouselike settings. Attracting business away from almost every retailing segment, warehouse clubs now even offer fresh food and gasoline. Customers must be members to shop at warehouse clubs.

Off-Price Retailers

Another version of a discount house is an *off-price retailer*. This kind of store stocks only designer labels or well-known brand-name clothing at prices equal to or below regular wholesale prices and then passes the cost savings along to buyers. While many off-price retailers are located in outlets in downtown areas or in freestanding buildings, a growing number are concentrating in *outlet malls*—shopping centers that house only off-price retailers.

Inventory at off-price stores changes frequently as buyers take advantage of special price offers from manufacturers selling excess merchandise. Off-price retailers such as Loehmann's, Marshalls, Ross, Stein Mart, and T.J. Maxx also keep their prices below those of traditional retailers by offering fewer services. Off-price retailing has been well received by today's shoppers. France-based retailer Vente-privée.com sells high-fashion overstock merchandise through invitation-only clearance sales conducted solely on the Web.[23]

Hypermarkets and Supercenters

hypermarket Giant one-stop shopping facility offering wide selections of grocery items and general merchandise at discount prices, typically filling up 200,000 or more square feet of selling space.

Another innovation in discount retailing is the creation of **hypermarkets**—giant, one-stop shopping facilities that offer wide selections of grocery and general merchandise products at discount prices. Store size determines the major difference between hypermarkets and supercenters. Hypermarkets typically fill up 200,000 or more square feet of selling space, about a third larger than most **supercenters**. Midwest-based Meijer stores offer a vast array of items in dozens of departments, including housewares, groceries, apparel, drugs, hardware, electronics, and photo finishing in more than 180 stores in five states.[24]

supercenter Large store, usually smaller than a hypermarket, that combines groceries with discount store merchandise.

Walmart is testing a new type of hypermarket in the metropolitan Chicago area. Online shoppers at Walmart.com can choose to have their order shipped free to a local Walmart store, then pick it up at a drive-through window. So far, management says shoppers seem to appreciate the convenience.[25]

Showroom and Warehouse Retailers

These retailers send direct mail to their customers and sell the advertised goods from showrooms that display samples. Backroom warehouses fill orders for the displayed products. Low prices are important to catalog store customers. To keep prices low, these retailers offer few services; store most inventory in inexpensive warehouse space; limit shoplifting losses; and handle long-lived products such as luggage, small appliances, gift items, sporting equipment, toys, and jewelry.

Classification of Retail Transactions by Location

Although most retail transactions occur in stores, nonstore retailing serves as an important marketing channel for many products. In addition, both consumer and business-to-business marketers rely on nonstore retailing to generate orders or requests for more information that may result in future orders.

Direct marketing is a broad concept that includes direct mail, direct selling, direct-response retailing, telemarketing, Internet retailing, and automatic merchandising. The last sections of this chapter consider each type of nonstore retailing.

Retail Convergence and Scrambled Merchandising

Many traditional differences no longer distinguish familiar types of retailers, rendering any set of classifications less useful. **Retail convergence**, whereby similar merchandise is available from multiple retail outlets distinguished by price more than any other factor, is blurring distinctions between types of retailers and the merchandise mix they offer. A few years ago, a customer looking for a fashionable coffeepot might have headed straight for Williams-Sonoma or Starbucks. Today, she's just as likely to pick one up at Target or her neighborhood Sam's Club, where she can check out new spring fashions and stock up on paper goods. The Gap is no longer pitted only against American Eagle Outfitters or L.L.Bean but against designer-label brands at department stores and Kohl's, too. Grocery stores compete with Walmart Supercenter, Sam's Club, and Costco. Walmart has beefed up its already robust product mix to include VUDU broadband streaming services for the consumer electronics products it sells alongside the apparel, housewares, fine jewelry, and more.[26]

Scrambled merchandising—in which a retailer combines dissimilar product lines in an attempt to boost sales volume—has also muddied the waters. Drugstores not only fill prescriptions but sell cameras, cards, housewares, magazines, and even small appliances. In addition, Walgreens, CVS, Target, and other stores have discovered another consumer need: in-store health clinics that diagnose and treat minor illnesses and injuries quickly and affordably.[27]

4 Explain the concepts of retail convergence and scrambled merchandising.

retail convergence
Situation in which similar merchandise is available from multiple retail outlets, resulting in the blurring of distinctions between types of retailers and merchandise offered.

scrambled merchandising
Retailing practice of combining dissimilar product lines to boost sales volume.

assessment check

1. How do we classify retailers by form of ownership?
2. Categorize retailers by shopping effort and by services provided.
3. List several ways to classify retailers by product line.

Wholesaling Intermediaries

Recall from Chapter 13 that several distribution channels involve marketing intermediaries called **wholesalers**. These firms take title to the goods they handle and sell those products primarily to retailers or to other wholesalers or business users. They sell to ultimate consumers only in insignificant quantities, if at all. **Wholesaling intermediaries**, a broader category, include not only wholesalers but also agents and brokers who perform important wholesaling activities without taking title to the goods.

Functions of Wholesaling Intermediaries

As specialists in certain marketing functions, as opposed to production or manufacturing functions, wholesaling intermediaries can perform these functions more efficiently than producers or consumers. The importance of these activities results from the utility they create, the services they provide, and the cost reductions they allow.

CREATING UTILITY

Wholesaling intermediaries create three types of utility for consumers. They enhance time utility by making products available for sale when consumers want to purchase them. They create place utility by helping deliver goods and services for purchase at convenient locations. They create ownership (or possession) utility when a smooth exchange of title to the products from producers or intermediaries to final purchasers is complete. Possession utility can also result from transactions in which actual title does not pass to purchasers, as in rental car services.

wholesaler Channel intermediary that takes title to goods it handles and then distributes these goods to retailers, other distributors, or B2B customers.

wholesaling intermediary
Comprehensive term that describes wholesalers as well as agents and brokers.

5 Identify the functions performed by wholesaling intermediaries.

PROVIDING SERVICES

Table 14.1 lists a number of services provided by wholesaling intermediaries. The list clearly indicates the marketing utilities—time, place, and possession utility—that wholesaling intermediaries create or enhance. These services also reflect the basic marketing functions of buying, selling, storing, transporting, providing marketing information, financing, and risk taking.

Of course, many types of wholesaling intermediaries provide varying services, and not all of them perform every service listed in the table. Producer-suppliers rely on wholesaling intermediaries for distribution and selection of firms that offer the desired combinations of services. In general, however, the critical marketing functions listed in the table form the basis for any evaluation of a marketing intermediary's efficiency. The risk-taking function affects each service of the intermediary.

Ingram Micro is a leading technology distributor with business clients in more than 150 countries and vendors all over the world. Ranking number 67 in the *Fortune* 100, it offers a wide range of information technology services for order management and fulfillment, contract manufacturing and warehousing, transportation management, and credit and collection management, as well as distributing and marketing information technology products to businesses worldwide.[28]

The "Career Readiness" feature discusses how to identify and work with a wholesale distributor.

table 14.1 **Wholesaling Services for Customers and Producer-Suppliers**

Service	Customers	Producer-Suppliers
Buying Anticipates customer demands and applies knowledge of alternative sources of supply; acts as purchasing agent for customers.	Yes	No
Selling Provides a sales force to call on customers, creating a low-cost method for servicing smaller retailers and business users.	No	Yes
Storing Maintains warehouse facilities at lower costs than most individual producers or retailers could achieve. Reduces risk and cost of maintaining inventory for producers.	Yes	Yes
Transporting Customers receive prompt delivery in response to their demands, reducing their inventory investments. Wholesalers also break bulk by purchasing in economical carload or truckload lots, then reselling in smaller quantities, thereby reducing overall transportation costs.	Yes	Yes
Providing Marketing Information Offers important marketing research input for producers through regular contacts with retail and business buyers. Provides customers with information about new products, technical information about product lines, reports on competitors' activities and industry trends, and advisory information concerning pricing changes, legal changes, and so forth.	Yes	Yes
Financing Grants credit that might be unavailable for purchases directly from manufacturers. Provides financing assistance to producers by purchasing products in advance of sale by promptly paying bills.	Yes	Yes
Risk Taking Evaluates credit risks of numerous, distant retail customers and small-business users. Extends credit to customers that qualify. By transporting and stocking products in inventory, the wholesaler assumes risk of spoilage, theft, or obsolescence.	Yes	Yes

Beneficiaries of Service

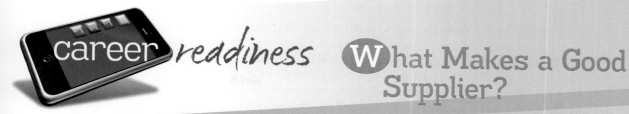

career readiness — What Makes a Good Supplier?

o be a successful retailer, you need good rapport with your customers. But did you know you also need to build a solid relationship with the vendors who supply your merchandise and other goods? How you identify and work with suppliers can make or break your business. Here are some tips:

- *Get acquainted.* You can't tell much about a business if you're dealing exclusively online or by phone. Try to meet for a cup of coffee: perhaps you'll be at the same trade show or in each other's city. Ask questions; you're trying to ascertain whether the supplier's business is legit and financially sound.

- *Visit the warehouse.* Ask to see the vendor's distribution center. Is it clean and in good condition? Are goods housed properly and safely? Ask about your vendor's inventory system. How does it work?

- *Do a price-check.* Are the vendor's prices competitive? If not, why? Is there some compelling reason to favor a more costly supplier? Those higher prices impact your bottom line.

- *Know the policies.* Is there a minimum order and if so, what is it? How are goods shipped and when will they arrive? What happens if they arrive damaged? Late? Not at all? What are the terms of payment: cash or credit? What will that credit cost you? Make sure you know about the policies up-front—and any guarantees offered.

- *Be a good customer.* It may sound like a no-brainer, but be the kind of customer you want your customers to be. Pay your bills on time and don't squeeze your supplier; you're not the only one with a payroll to meet and bills to pay.

Sources: Danny J. Vanguard, "How to Build a Good Business Relationship with Your Wholesale Supplier," *Ezinearticles.com,* http://ezinearticles.com, accessed February 27, 2010; Trevor Marshall, "What to Look for in a Wholesale Distributor," http://articles.rsorange.com, accessed February 27, 2010; Paris Burstyn, "Wholesale Doesn't Cannibalize Sales But Opens up New Revenue," *Telecoms Europe,* September 21, 2009, http://www.telecomseurope.net; "The Best of the Fresh: This Wholesale Distributor Is a Dominant Force in Several Western Regions of the Country," *American Executive,* September 1, 2009, http://www.americanexecutive.com.

LOWERING COSTS BY LIMITING CONTACTS

When an intermediary represents numerous producers, it often cuts the costs of buying and selling. The transaction economies are illustrated in Figure 14.3, which shows five manufacturers marketing their outputs to four different retail outlets. Without an intermediary, these exchanges create a total of 20 transactions. Adding a wholesaling intermediary reduces the number of transactions to nine.

United Stationers is a wholesale distributor of business products ranging from paper clips to technology equipment and office furniture. It serves

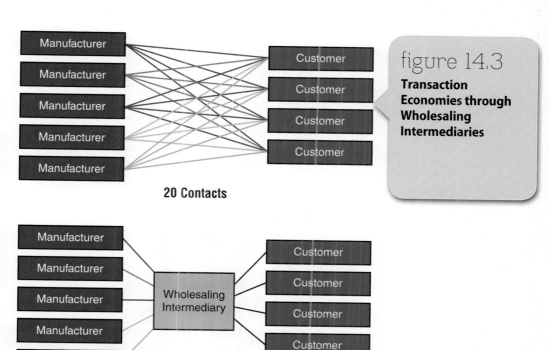

20 Contacts

9 Contacts

figure 14.3

Transaction Economies through Wholesaling Intermediaries

discount chains, independent stores, and Internet resellers. While big-box retailers buy in bulk directly from manufacturers, they can order low-volume specialty goods faster and more efficiently from United Stationers. By ordering online, mom-and-pop stores have access to about 100,000 items from more than 1,000 manufacturers, delivered either to the store or directly to customers overnight. A one-stop warehousing, logistics, and distribution network, United Stationers' product mix even includes industrial products and janitorial and breakroom supplies.[29]

✓ assessment check

1. What is a wholesaler? How does it differ from a wholesaling intermediary?
2. How do wholesaling intermediaries help sellers lower costs?

Types of Wholesaling Intermediaries

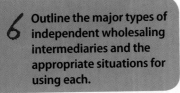

6 Outline the major types of independent wholesaling intermediaries and the appropriate situations for using each.

Various types of wholesaling intermediaries operate in different distribution channels. Some provide wide ranges of services or handle broad lines of goods, while others specialize in individual services, goods, or industries. Figure 14.4 classifies wholesaling intermediaries by two characteristics: ownership and title flows—whether title passes from manufacturer or wholesaling intermediary. The three basic ownership structures are as follows: (1) manufacturer-owned facilities, (2) independent wholesaling intermediaries, and (3) retailer-owned cooperatives and buying offices. The two types of independent wholesaling intermediaries are merchant wholesalers, which take title of the goods, and agents and brokers, which do not.

Several reasons lead manufacturers to distribute their goods directly through company-owned facilities. Some perishable goods need rigid control of distribution to avoid spoilage; other goods require complex installation or servicing. Some goods need aggressive promotion. Goods with high unit values allow profitable sales by manufacturers directly to ultimate purchasers. Manufacturer-owned facilities include sales branches, sales offices, trade fairs, and merchandise marts.

A *sales branch* carries inventory and processes orders for customers from available stock. Branches provide a storage function like independent wholesalers and serve as offices for sales representatives

figure 14.4

Major Types of Wholesaling Intermediaries

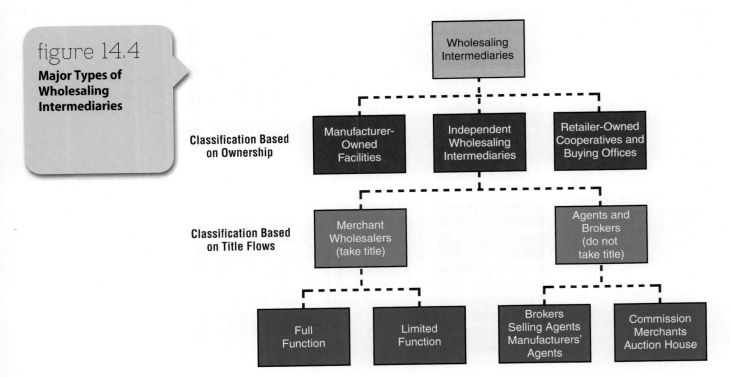

in their territories. They are prevalent in marketing channels for chemicals, commercial machinery and equipment, and petroleum products.

A *sales office,* in contrast, does not carry inventory, but it does serve as a regional office for a manufacturer's sales personnel. Locations close to the firm's customers help limit selling costs and support effective customer service. For example, numerous sales offices in the Detroit area serve the domestic automobile industry.

A *trade fair* (or trade exhibition) is a periodic show at which manufacturers in a particular industry display their wares for visiting retail and wholesale buyers. The world's largest consumer technology trade show and the largest trade show of any kind in America, the annual International Consumer Electronics Show (CES), takes place in January in Las Vegas. CES typically attracts more than 110,000 attendees and features 2,700 exhibitors in nearly 40 product categories.[30]

A *merchandise mart* provides space for permanent showrooms and exhibits, which manufacturers rent to market their goods. One of the world's largest merchandise marts is Chicago's Merchandise Mart Center, a 7-million-square-foot complex with its own Zip code that hosts more than 30 seasonal buying markets each year.

The International Consumer Electronics Show (CES) in Las Vegas is the world's largest consumer technology trade show.

© ROBYN BECK/AFP/GETTY IMAGES

INDEPENDENT WHOLESALING INTERMEDIARIES

Many wholesaling intermediaries are independently owned. These firms fall into two major categories: merchant wholesalers and agents and brokers.

Merchant Wholesalers

A **merchant wholesaler** takes title to the goods it handles. Merchant wholesalers account for roughly 60 percent of all sales at the wholesale level. Further classifications divide these wholesalers into full-function or limited-function wholesalers, as indicated in Figure 14.4.

A full-function merchant wholesaler provides a complete array of services for retailers and business purchasers. Such a wholesaler stores merchandise in a convenient location, allowing customers to make purchases on short notice and minimizing inventory requirements. The firm typically maintains a sales force that calls on retailers, makes deliveries, and extends credit to qualified buyers. Full-function wholesalers are common in the drug, grocery, and hardware industries. In the business-goods market, full-function merchant wholesalers—often called *industrial distributors*—sell machinery, inexpensive accessory equipment, and supplies.

A **rack jobber** is a full-function merchant wholesaler that markets specialized lines of merchandise to retailers. A rack jobber supplies the racks, stocks the merchandise, prices the goods, and makes regular visits to refill shelves. Sometimes rack jobbers are the exclusive supplier of a retailer—as in the case of Anderson Merchandisers, a rack jobber in the entertainment sector, which grew by being the supplier to Walmart stores' consumer electronics departments.[31]

Limited-function merchant wholesalers fit into four categories: cash-and-carry wholesalers, truck wholesalers, drop shippers, and mail-order wholesalers. Limited-function wholesalers serve the food, coal, lumber, cosmetics, jewelry, sporting goods, and general merchandise industries.

A *cash-and-carry wholesaler* performs most wholesaling functions except for financing and delivery. Although feasible for small stores, this kind of wholesaling generally is unworkable for large-scale grocery stores. Today, cash-and-carry operations typically function as departments within regular full-service wholesale operations. Cash-and-carry wholesalers are commonplace outside the United States, such as in the United Kingdom.

merchant wholesaler Independently owned wholesaling intermediary that takes title to the goods it handles; also known as an industrial distributor in the business goods market.

rack jobber Full-function merchant wholesaler that markets specialized lines of merchandise to retail stores.

truck wholesaler (or truck jobber) Limited-function merchant wholesaler that markets perishable food items.

drop shipper Limited-function merchant wholesaler that accepts orders from customers and forwards these orders to producers, which then ship directly to the customers who placed the orders.

mail-order wholesaler Limited-function merchant wholesaler that distributes catalogs instead of sending sales personnel to contact customers.

commission merchant Agent wholesaling intermediary who takes possession of goods shipped to a central market for sale, acts as the producer's agent, and collects an agreed-upon fee at the time of the sale.

A **truck wholesaler (or truck jobber)** markets perishable food items such as bread, tobacco, potato chips, candy, and dairy products. Truck wholesalers make regular deliveries to retailers, perform sales and collection functions, and promote product lines. Regional wholesale distributor S. Abraham & Sons delivers brand-name groceries, health and beauty aids, and other merchandise to convenience, drug, and grocery stores in the Midwest.[32]

A **drop shipper** such as ONE Inc., of Tampa, Florida, accepts orders from customers and forwards these orders to producers, which then ship the desired products directly to customers. Although drop shippers take title to goods, they never physically handle or even see the merchandise. These intermediaries often operate in industries selling bulky goods, such as coal and lumber, that customers buy in large lots.

A **mail-order wholesaler** is a limited-function merchant wholesaler that distributes physical or online catalogs as opposed to sending sales representatives to contact retail, business, and institutional customers. Customers then make purchases by mail, by phone, or online. Such a wholesaler often serves relatively small customers in outlying areas. Mail-order operations mainly exist in the hardware, cosmetics, jewelry, sporting goods, and specialty food lines as well as in general merchandise. Some popular mail-order products are pharmaceuticals, roasted bean coffee, Christmas trees and wreaths, and popcorn.

Table 14.2 compares the various types of merchant wholesalers and the services they provide. Full-function merchant wholesalers and truck wholesalers rank as relatively high-cost intermediaries because of the number of services they perform, while cash-and-carry wholesalers, drop shippers, and mail-order wholesalers provide fewer services and set lower prices because they incur lower operating costs.

Agents and Brokers

A second group of independent wholesaling intermediaries, agents and brokers, may or may not take possession of the goods they handle, but they never take title. They normally perform fewer services than merchant wholesalers, working mainly to bring together buyers and sellers. Agents and brokers fall into five categories: commission merchants, auction houses, brokers, selling agents, and manufacturers' representatives (reps).

Commission merchants, which predominate in the markets for agricultural products, take possession when producers ship goods such as grain, produce, and livestock to central markets for sale. Commission merchants act as producers' agents and receive agreed-upon fees when they make sales. Because customers inspect the products and prices fluctuate, commission merchants receive considerable latitude in marketing decisions. The owners of the goods may specify minimum prices,

table 14.2 Comparison of the Types of Merchant Wholesalers and Their Services

| Service | Full-Function | Limited-Function Wholesaler | | | |
		Cash-and-Carry	Truck	Drop Shipper	Mail-Order
Anticipates customer needs	Yes	Yes	Yes	No	Yes
Carries inventory	Yes	Yes	Yes	No	Yes
Delivers	Yes	No	Yes	No	No
Provides marketing information	Yes	Rarely	Yes	Yes	No
Provides credit	Yes	No	No	Yes	Sometimes
Assumes ownership risk by taking title	Yes	Yes	Yes	Yes	Yes

but the commission merchants sell these goods at the best possible prices. The commission merchants then deduct their fees from the sales' proceeds.

An *auction house* gathers buyers and sellers in one location and allows potential buyers to inspect merchandise before submitting competing purchase offers. Auction house commissions typically reflect specified percentages of the sales prices of the auctioned items. Auctions are common in the distribution of tobacco, used cars, artwork, livestock, furs, and fruit. The Internet has led to a new type of auction house that connects customers and sellers in the online world. A well-known example is eBay, which auctions a wide variety of products in all price ranges.

Auction house eBay offers a wide variety of products in all price ranges.

Brokers work mainly to bring together buyers and sellers. A broker represents either the buyer or the seller—but not both—in a given transaction, and the broker receives a fee from the client when the transaction is completed. Intermediaries that specialize in arranging buying and selling transactions between domestic producers and foreign buyers are called *export brokers*. Brokers operate in industries characterized by large numbers of small suppliers and purchasers such as real estate, frozen foods, and used machinery. Because they provide one-time services for sellers or buyers, they cannot serve as effective channels for manufacturers seeking regular, continuing service. A firm that seeks to develop a more permanent channel might choose instead to use a selling agent or manufacturer's agent.

A **selling agent** typically exerts full authority over pricing decisions and promotional outlays, and it often provides financial assistance for the manufacturer. Selling agents act as independent marketing departments because they can assume responsibility for the total marketing programs of client firms' product lines. Selling agents mainly operate in the coal, lumber, and textiles industries. For a small, weakly financed, production-oriented firm, such an intermediary might prove the ideal marketing channel.

While a manufacturer may deal with only one selling agent, a firm that hires **manufacturers' representatives** often delegates marketing tasks to many of these agents. Such an independent salesperson may work for a number of firms that produce related, noncompeting products. Manufacturers' reps are paid on a commission basis, such as 6 percent of sales. Unlike selling agents, who may contract for exclusive rights to market a product, manufacturers' agents operate in specific territories. They may develop new sales territories or represent relatively small firms and those firms with unrelated lines.

Robertson Heating Supply Company in Alliance, Ohio, serves the plumbing industry in Michigan, Ohio, and Pennsylvania. Recently named Wholesaler of the Year by *Supply House Times,* the company was one of the first plumbing wholesalers to computerize. And while online sales are growing—they currently represent about 3 percent of annual revenues—the company maintains a full-time salesforce that helps customers identify and meet their needs.[33]

broker Agent wholesaling intermediary that does not take title to or possession of goods in the course of its primary function, which is to bring together buyers and sellers.

selling agent Agent wholesaling intermediary for the entire marketing program of a firm's product line.

manufacturers' representative Agent wholesaling intermediary that represents manufacturers of related but noncompeting products and receives a commission on each sale.

table 14.3   Services Provided by Agents and Brokers

Service	Commission Merchant	Auction House	Broker	Manufacturers' Agent	Selling Agent
Anticipates customer needs	Yes	Sometimes	Sometimes	Yes	Yes
Carries inventory	Yes	Yes	No	No	No
Delivers	Yes	No	No	Sometimes	No
Provides marketing information	Yes	Yes	Yes	Yes	Yes
Provides credit	Sometimes	No	No	No	Sometimes
Assumes ownership risk by taking title	No	No	No	No	No

The importance of selling agents in many markets has declined because manufacturers want better control of their marketing programs than these intermediaries allow. In contrast, the volume of sales by manufacturers' agents has more than doubled and now accounts for 37 percent of all sales by agents and brokers. Table 14.3 compares the major types of agents and brokers on the basis of the services they perform.

assessment check

1. What is the difference between a merchant wholesaler and a rack jobber?
2. Differentiate between agents and brokers.

Retailer-Owned Cooperatives and Buying Offices

Retailers may assume numerous wholesaling functions in an attempt to reduce costs or provide special services. Independent retailers sometimes band together to form buying groups that can achieve cost savings through quantity purchases. Other groups of retailers establish retailer-owned wholesale facilities by forming cooperative chains. Large chain retailers often establish centralized buying offices to negotiate large-scale purchases directly with manufacturers.

Direct Marketing and Other Nonstore Retailing

7 Compare the basic types of direct marketing and nonstore retailing.

Although most retail transactions occur in stores, nonstore retailing is an important marketing channel for many products. Both consumer and business-to-business marketers rely on nonstore retailing to generate leads or requests for more information that may result in future orders.

Direct marketing is a broad concept that includes direct mail, direct selling, direct-response retailing, telemarketing, Internet retailing, and automatic merchandising. Direct and interactive marketing expenditures amount to hundreds of billions of dollars in yearly purchases. The last sections of this chapter consider each type of nonstore retailing.

direct marketing
Direct communications, other than personal sales contacts, between buyer and seller, designed to generate sales, information requests, or store or Web site visits.

Direct Mail

Direct mail is a major component of direct marketing. It comes in many forms: sales letters, postcards, brochures, booklets, catalogs, house organs (periodicals published by organizations to cover internal issues), and DVDs. Both not-for-profit and profit-seeking organizations make extensive use of this distribution channel.

Direct mail offers several advantages such as the ability to select a narrow target market, achieve intensive coverage, send messages quickly, choose from various formats, provide complete information, and personalize each mailing piece. Response rates are measurable and higher than other types of advertising. In addition, direct mailings stand alone and do not compete for attention with magazine articles and television programs. On the other hand, the per-reader cost of direct mail is high, effectiveness depends on the quality of the mailing list, and some consumers object to direct mail, considering it "junk mail."

Direct-mail marketing relies heavily on database technology in managing lists of names and in segmenting these lists according to the objectives of the campaign. Recipients get targeted materials, often personalized with their names within the ad's content.

Catalogs are a popular form of direct mail, with more than 10,000 different consumer specialty mail-order catalogs—and thousands more for business-to-business sales—finding their way to almost every mailbox in the United States. In a typical year, about 20 billion mail-order catalogs are mailed; about half of all American consumers buy from catalogs.[34] Catalog marketing continues to grow at a faster rate than brick-and-mortar retailers. Catalogs can be a company's only or primary sales method. Pajamagram, Fetch Dog, Popcorn Factory, and Improvements are well-known examples. Brick-and-mortar retailers such as Crate & Barrel, Coldwater Creek, Land of Nod, and Orvis also distribute catalogs.

Environmental concerns and new technologies are changing catalog marketing. More than 1.1 million American consumers have registered with Catalog Choice, a nonprofit organization, to have their names removed from catalog mailing lists. Most cite a desire to save natural resources for their decision to stop receiving a blizzard of paper catalogs by mail.[35] By moving a catalog online, a merchant can update content easily and quickly, providing consumers with the latest information and prices. Online technology also allows marketers to use video and other techniques to display their merchandise. For example, Nordstrom's online shoe store catalog allows browsers to zoom in and out and view a shoe from different angles and in different colors.

Direct Selling

Through direct selling, manufacturers completely bypass retailers and wholesalers. Instead, they set up their own channels to sell their products directly to consumers. Amway, Avon, Pampered Chef, and Tupperware are all direct sellers. This channel was discussed in detail in Chapter 13.

Direct-Response Retailing

Customers of a direct-response retailer can order merchandise by mail or telephone, by visiting a mail-order desk in a retail store, or by computer or fax machine. The retailer then ships the merchandise to the customer's home or to a local retail store for pickup.

Many direct-response retailers rely on direct mail, such as catalogs, to create telephone and mail-order sales and to promote in-store purchases of products featured in the catalogs. Some firms, such as Lillian Vernon, make almost all their sales through catalog orders. Mail-order sales have grown at about twice the rate of retail store sales in recent years.

Direct-response retailers are increasingly reaching buyers through the Internet and through unique catalogs that serve special market niches. Many catalogs sell specialty products, such as kitchenware for the professional cook, art supplies, or supplies for the home renovator.

Direct-response retailing also includes home shopping, which runs promotions on cable television networks to sell merchandise through telephone orders. One form of home shopping, the *infomercial,* has existed for years. Infomercials can be short—one to two minutes—or run up to 30 minutes. Both have demonstrated success at generating revenues. The "king of infomercials," the late Billy Mays, became famous for hawking such products as OxiClean, Orange Glo, and Mighty Putty. Mays created a "brand" that projected authority, no matter what he was selling. Industry observers say Mays was successful because he was likeable and managed to get consumers to buy products they didn't know they needed.[36]

 assessment check

1. What is direct marketing?
2. What is direct mail?

Telemarketing

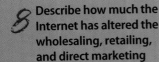

Describe how much the Internet has altered the wholesaling, retailing, and direct marketing environments.

Telemarketing refers to direct marketing conducted entirely by telephone. It is the most frequently used form of direct marketing. It provides marketers with a high return on their expenditures, an immediate response, and the opportunity for personalized two-way conversations. Telemarketing is discussed in further detail in Chapter 17.

Internet Retailing

Internet-based retailers sell directly to customers via virtual storefronts on the Web. They usually maintain little or no inventory, ordering directly from vendors to fill customer orders received via their Web sites. In recent years, conventional retailers have anxiously watched the rise—and then the demise—of many poorly planned, financed, and marketed Internet-based retailers. During the dot-com bust, 130 e-tailers failed. Even early successes such as Ezshop, an online home furnishings retailer, eventually ran aground. Traditional retailers, using the Web to support brick-and-mortar stores—the so-called *brick-and-click retailers*—have had much better staying power. The Gap, Best Buy, and Lands' End, for example, succeeded in extending their expertise to the Web. Office Max offers thousands of office supply products on its Web site, which also offers e-mail alerts, favorite-item lists, and a customer loyalty program. Chapter 4 discussed Internet retailing and other forms of e-business in more detail.

Automatic Merchandising

The world's first vending machines dispensed holy water for five-drachma coins in Egyptian temples around 215 B.C. This retailing method has grown rapidly ever since; today, nearly 5,000 vending machine operators sell about $6 billion in convenience goods annually to Americans.[37]

Although U.S. vending machines primarily sell items like snacks, soft drinks, or lottery tickets, Japanese consumers use automatic merchandising for everything, including fresh sushi and new underwear. Recently, U.S. marketers have begun to realize the potential of this underused marketing tool. Several vending-machine companies, like Illinois-based Healthy U and Ohio-based Healthy Vending, work with schools to replace traditional vending-machine offerings with fresh, healthy snacks.[38] The three major soft-drink companies recently agreed to remove sweetened drinks such as soda and iced tea from vending machines in elementary and high schools nationwide. The calorie-laden drinks will be replaced by bottled water, low-fat milk, and 100 percent fruit juice or sports drinks. The ability to accept credit cards has enabled vending machines to sell high-end items like iPods, headphones, and Sony PlayStation games. Technological advances such as touch screens, animation, and digital imagery make the buying experience fun—and even allow customers to read the back of the package before they buy.[39]

 assessment check

1. Describe Internet-based retailers.
2. Explain how the Internet has enhanced retailers' functions.

strategic implications of marketing in the 21st century

s the Internet revolution steadily becomes a way of life—both for consumers and for the businesses marketing goods and services to them—technology will continue to transform the ways in which retailers, wholesalers, and direct marketers connect with customers.

In the retail sector, the unstoppable march toward lower prices has forced retailers from Neiman Marcus to dollar stores to reevaluate everything, including their logistics and supply networks and their profit margins. Many have used the power of the Internet to strengthen such factors as store image, the merchandising mix, customer service, and the development of long-term relationships with customers.

Although manufacturers first anticipated that Internet technology would enable them to bypass such intermediaries as wholesalers and agents, bringing them closer to the customer, the reality is quite different. Successful wholesalers have established themselves as essential links in the supply, distribution, and customer service network. By leveraging technology, they have carved out new roles, providing such expert services as warehousing and fulfillment to multiple retail clients.

The Internet has empowered direct marketers by facilitating ever more sophisticated database segmentation. Traditional catalog and direct-mail marketers have integrated Internet sites, Web advertising, and e-mailing programs into a cohesive targeting, distribution, and repeat-buying strategy.

Review of Chapter Objectives

 Explain the wheel of retailing.

The wheel of retailing is the hypothesis that each new type of retailer gains a competitive foothold by offering lower prices than current suppliers and maintains profits by reducing or eliminating services. Once established, the innovator begins to add more services and its prices gradually rise, making it vulnerable to new low-price retailers. This turns the wheel again.

 Discuss how retailers select target markets.

A retailer starts to define its strategy by selecting a target market. The target market dictates, among other things, the product mix, pricing strategy, and location strategy. Retailers deal with consumer behavior at the most complicated level, and a clear understanding of the target market is critical. Strategies for selecting target markets include merchandising, customer services, pricing, location/ distribution, and promotional strategies.

 Show how the elements of the marketing mix apply to retailing strategy

A retailer must first identify a target market and then develop a product strategy. Next, it must establish a customer service strategy. Retail pricing strategy involves decisions on markups and markdowns. Location is often the determining factor in a retailer's success or failure. A retailer's promotional strategy and store atmosphere play important roles in establishing a store's image.

 Explain the concepts of retail convergence and scrambled merchandising.

Retail convergence is the coming together of shoppers, goods, and prices, resulting in the blurring of distinctions between types of retailers and the merchandise mix they offer. Similar selections are available from multiple sources and are differentiated mainly by price. Scrambled merchandising refers to retailers' practice of carrying dissimilar product lines in an attempt to generate additional sales volume. Retail convergence and scrambled merchandising have made it increasingly difficult to classify retailers.

 Identify the functions performed by wholesaling intermediaries.

The functions of wholesaling intermediaries include creating utility, providing services, and lowering costs by limiting contacts.

 Outline the major types of independent wholesaling intermediaries and the appropriate situations for using each.

Independent wholesaling intermediaries can be divided into two categories: merchant wholesalers and agents and brokers. The two major types of merchant wholesalers are full-function merchant wholesalers, such as rack jobbers, and limited-function merchant wholesalers, including cash-and-carry wholesalers, truck wholesalers, drop shippers, and mail-order wholesalers. Full-function wholesalers are common in the drug, grocery, and hardware industries.

Limited-function wholesalers are sometimes used in the food, coal, lumber, cosmetics, jewelry, sporting goods, and general-merchandise industries. Agents and brokers do not take title to the products they sell; this category includes commission merchants, auction houses, brokers, selling agents, and manufacturers' reps. Companies seeking to develop new sales territories, firms with unrelated lines, and smaller firms use manufacturers' reps. Commission merchants are common in the marketing of agricultural products. Auction houses are used to sell tobacco, used cars, livestock, furs, and fruit. Brokers are prevalent in the real estate, frozen foods, and used machinery industries.

 Compare the basic types of direct marketing and nonstore retailing.

Direct marketing is a distribution channel consisting of direct communication to a consumer or business recipient. It generates orders and sales leads that may result in future orders. Because direct marketing responds to fragmented media markets and audiences, growth of customized products, and shrinking network broadcast audiences, marketers consider it an important part of their planning efforts. While most U.S. retail sales take place in stores, such nonstore retailing activities as direct mail, direct selling, direct-response retailing, telemarketing, Internet retailing, and automatic merchandising are important in marketing many types of goods and services.

 Describe how much the Internet has altered the wholesaling, retailing, and direct marketing environments.

The Internet has affected everything, including how supply networks operate and how relationships are formed with customers. Successful wholesalers have carved out a niche as a source of expertise offering faster, more efficient, Web-enabled distribution and fulfillment. The Internet has allowed retailers to enhance their merchandising mix and their customer service by, among other things, giving them access to much broader selections of goods. Direct marketers have merged their traditional catalog or direct-mail programs with an Internet interface that allows for faster, more efficient, and more frequent contact with customers and prospects.

Assessment Check: Answers

1.1 What is retailing? Retailing refers to the activities involved in selling merchandise to ultimate consumers.

1.2 Explain the wheel-of-retailing concept. The wheel of retailing is the hypothesis that each new type of retailer gains a competitive foothold by offering lower prices than current suppliers and maintains profits by reducing or eliminating services.

2.1 How does a retailer develop a marketing strategy? A retailer develops a marketing strategy based on its goals and strategic plans.

2.2 How do retailers select target markets? Strategies for selecting target markets include merchandising, customer services, pricing, location/distribution, and promotional strategies.

3.1 What is an SKU? An SKU, or stock-keeping unit, is a specific product offering within a product line.

3.2 What are the two components of a markup? A markup consists of the product's cost and an amount added by the retailer to determine its selling price.

3.3 What are store atmospherics? Store atmospherics are physical characteristics and amenities that attract customers and satisfy their shopping needs.

4.1 How do we classify retailers by form of ownership? There are two types of retailers by form of ownership: chain stores and independent retailers.

4.2 Categorize retailers by shopping effort and by services provided. Convenience retailers and specialty retailers are classified by shopping effort; self-service, self-selection, and full-service describe retailers in terms of services provided.

4.3 List several ways to classify retailers by product line. Retailers classified by product line include specialty stores, limited-line retailers, and general merchandise retailers. General merchandise retailers include variety stores, department stores, and mass merchandisers.

5.1 What is a wholesaler? How does it differ from a wholesaling intermediary? A wholesaler is a channel intermediary that takes title to goods it handles and then distributes these goods to retailers, other distributors, or B2B customers. A wholesaling intermediary can be a wholesaler, an agent, or a broker and can perform wholesaling activities without taking title to the goods.

5.2 How do wholesaling intermediaries help sellers lower costs? Wholesaling intermediaries lower the number of transactions between manufacturers and retail outlets, thus lowering distribution costs.

6.1 What is the difference between a merchant wholesaler and a rack jobber? A merchant wholesaler takes title to the goods it handles. A rack jobber is a full-function merchant wholesaler that markets specialized lines of merchandise to retailers.

6.2 Differentiate between agents and brokers. Agents and brokers may or may not take possession of the goods they handle, but they never take title. Brokers work mainly to bring together buyers and sellers. A selling agent typically exerts full authority over pricing decisions and promotional outlays and often provides financial assistance for the manufacturer.

7.1 What is direct marketing? Direct marketing is a distribution channel consisting of direct communication to a consumer or business recipient. It generates orders and sales leads that may result in future orders.

7.2 What is direct mail? Direct mail is a form of direct marketing that includes sales letters, postcards, brochures, booklets, catalogs, house organs, and DVDs.

8.1 Describe Internet-based retailers. Internet-based retailers sell directly to customers via virtual storefronts on the Web. They usually maintain little or no inventory, ordering directly from vendors to fill customers' orders.

8.2 Explain how the Internet has enhanced retailers' functions. The Internet has allowed retailers to enhance their merchandising mix and their customer service by, among other things, giving them access to much broader selections of goods. Direct marketers have merged their traditional catalog or direct-mail programs with an Internet interface that allows for faster, more efficient, and more frequent contact with customers and prospects.

Marketing Terms You Need to Know

retailing 450
wheel of retailing 451
stock-keeping unit (SKU) 455
markup 457
markdown 457
planned shopping center 457
atmospherics 460
convenience retailer 461

specialty retailer 461
limited-line store 462
category killer 462
general merchandise retailer 463
department store 463
mass merchandiser 463
discount house 463
hypermarket 464

supercenter 464
retail convergence 465
scrambled merchandising 465
wholesaler 465
wholesaling intermediary 465
merchant wholesaler 469
rack jobber 469
truck wholesaler (truck jobber) 470

drop shipper 470
mail-order wholesaler 470
commission merchant 470
broker 471
selling agent 471
manufacturers' representative 471
direct marketing 473

Assurance of Learning Review

1. Find some examples of retailers that demonstrate the concept of the wheel of retailing. Explain the stages they went through and are in currently.

2. How do retailers identify target markets? Explain the major strategies by which retailers reach their target markets.

3. Explain the importance of a retailer's location to its strategy.

4. What is retail convergence?

5. Define *scrambled merchandising*. Why has this practice become so common in retailing?

6. What is a wholesaling intermediary? Describe the activities it performs.

7. Distinguish among the different types of manufacturer-owned wholesaling intermediaries. What conditions might suit each one?

8. Differentiate between direct selling and direct-response retailing. Cite examples of both.

9. In what ways has the Internet changed direct-response retailing?

10. Define *automatic merchandising,* and explain its role in U.S. retailing today and in the future.

Projects and Teamwork Exercises

1. Research and then classify each of the following retailers:
   a. Ace Hardware
   b. Petite Sophisticate
   c. Best Buy
   d. Ethan Allen Galleries
   e. Gymboree

2. Visit a local Walmart store and observe product placement, shelf placement, inventory levels on shelves, traffic patterns, customer service, and checkout efficiency. Discuss what makes Walmart the world's most successful retailer.

3. Target has become known for trendy clothes and stylish house-wares, all readily available in spacious stores at reasonable prices. Visit a local Target store or the company's Web site and compare its product selection to that of your local hardware store or a department store. Make a list of each store's advantages and disadvantages, including convenience, location, selection, service, and general prices. Do any of their product lines overlap? How are they different from each other?

4. Match each industry with the most appropriate type of whole-saling intermediary.
   ___hardware   a. drop shipper
   ___perishable foods b. truck wholesaler
   ___lumber   c. auction house
   ___wheat   d. full-function merchant wholesaler
   ___used cars   e. commission merchant

5. In teams, develop a retailing strategy for an Internet retailer. Identify a target market and then suggest a mix of merchandise, promotion, service, and pricing strategies that would help a retailer reach that market via the Internet. What issues must Internet retailers address that do not affect traditional store retailers?

6. With a classmate, visit two or three retail stores that compete with one another in your area and compare their customer service strategies. (You might wish to visit each store more than once to avoid making a snap judgment.) Select at least five criteria and use them to assess each store. How do you think each store sees its customer service strategy as fitting into its overall retailing strategy? Present your findings in detail to the class.

7. Visit a department store and compare at least two departments' pricing strategies based on the number of markdowns you find and the size of the discount. What, if anything, can you conclude about the success of each department's retailing strategy?

8. Think of a large purchase you make on a nonroutine basis, such as a new winter coat or expensive clothing for a special occasion. Where will you shop for such items? Will you travel out of your way? Will you go to the nearest shopping center? Will you look on the Internet? Once you have made your decision, describe any strategies used by the retailer that led you to this decision. What might make you change your mind about where to shop for this item?

9. Outlet malls are a growing segment of the retail market. Visit a local outlet mall or research one on the Internet. What types of stores are located there? How do the product selection and price compare with typical stores?

10. Torrid is a national chain of about 150 stores that feature clothing for plus-size women. Recommend an appropriate retailing strategy for this type of retailer.

Critical-Thinking Exercises

1. Retail chain Anthropologie sells a unique mix of women's clothing and home furnishings. Since its founding in 1992, Anthropologie has opened stores across the United States, in Canada, and in Great Britain. The retailer aims to create a shopping "experience" where its customers—independent-minded college-educated female professionals between ages 30 and 45—can find their own look. No two Anthropologie stores are exactly alike, and the chain does not use advertising. Visit the Web site at www.anthropologie.com. How does it differentiate itself from its competitors?

2. Several major retailers have begun to test the extreme markdown strategy that lies behind popular dollar stores such as Dollar General and Family Dollar Stores. Kroger, A&P, Walmart, and others have opened sections in selected stores that feature items from snacks to beauty supplies priced at $1. Is this experiment simply a test of pricing strategy? What else might motivate these retailers to offer such deep discounts?

3. When Tower Records filed for bankruptcy, it was only one symptom of the general decline of the retail music store. Industry watchers blame everything, including music downloading programs and changes in consumers' tastes. Most, however, feel that music stores will somehow remain viable. What are some changes these retailers could make in their merchandising, customer service, pricing, location, and other strategies to try to reinvent their business?

4. McDonald's has traditionally relied on a cookie-cutter approach to its restaurant design. One store looked essentially like every other—until recently. The chain has decided to loosen its corporate design mandate to fit within special markets and to update its image with customers. Research McDonald's makeover efforts. What types of changes has the company made and where? How have changes in atmospherics helped the chain with customers? Have the changes you researched modified your perception of McDonald's at all? If so, how?

Ethics Exercise

As the largest company in the world, with more than a million employees worldwide and more than $400 billion in sales in a recent year, Walmart has become big and powerful enough to influence the U.S. economy. It is responsible for 10 percent of total U.S. imports from China and for about 12 percent of U.S. productivity gains since the late 1990s. Some observers believe Walmart is also responsible for the low U.S. inflation rates of recent years. However, its unbeatable buying power and efficiency have sometimes forced local stores to close when Walmart opens a new store in their area

1. Some economists fear what might happen to the U.S. economy if Walmart has a bad year (so far, it has had more than four decades of nonstop growth). Should retailers have that much influence on the economy? Why or why not?

2. Walmart is selective about what it sells—refusing, for instance, to carry music or computer games with mature ratings, magazines with content it considers too adult, or, in some of its stores, handguns. Because of its sheer size, these decisions can become influential on the culture. Do you think this is a positive or negative effect of the growth of this retailer? Why?

Internet Exercises

1. **Shopping center trends.** Visit the Web site listed here. Click on "development" and then "trends." Review the material and then prepare a brief report on some of the major trends in shopping center development.
   http://retailtrafficmag.com/

2. **Online retailing strategy.** Go to the Web site of Kohl's (http://www.kohls.com). Using the material in the chapter on retailing strategy, answer the following questions:
   a. How does the design and layout of the Kohl's Web store appeal to the retailer's target market?
   b. In your opinion, what is the main strategic objective of Kohl's online store? Is it to generate revenue independently of its brick-and-mortar stores? Or, is the online store's main purpose to support so-called Web to store shoppers (shoppers who use the Web mainly to obtain product information and prices but make actual purchases at brick-and-mortar stores)?

3. **Wholesaling industry.** Visit the Web site of the Statistical Abstract of the U.S. (published by the Census Bureau). Click on "wholesale and retail trade." Review the data and prepare a brief report identifying five major facts about the U.S. wholesaling industry.
   http://www.census.gov/compendia/statab/

Note: Internet Web addresses change frequently. If you don't find the exact site listed, you may need to access the organization's home page and search from there or use a search engine such as Google or Bing.

Case 14.1   *Groupon: Finding Strength in Numbers*

Want a deep discount on a deep-dish pizza...a day at a health spa...Major League Baseball tickets? If you like a bargain, e-coupon site Groupon may be for you. Or suppose you're opening a gym: you need customers, and you need them fast. You can advertise your business

and hope to reach people with the desire and the cash to join. Or, using the power of social commerce offered by a site like Groupon, you gain exposure for your new business and attract interested shoppers through a discounted membership deal.

Founded in Chicago, Groupon uses the Internet to help business owners connect with prospective customers. The rules are simple: Groupon works with the business to create a deal offering a discount on goods or services. Owners set the terms of the deal: the minimum and maximum number of takers and the discount amount (usually around 50 percent but sometimes more). Groupon features the deal for one day. If a prescribed number of shoppers—typically 50—take the deal, it's a go. If not, the deal expires and no money changes hands. Meanwhile, Groupon makes money by pocketing a finder's fee on successful deals.

Groupon helps businesses reach target audiences without costly advertising and lets them mine a segment that doesn't respond to conventional appeals: young professionals ages 20 to 30 who are typically online constantly.

Subscribing is easy, and the site is fun: there's a new deal each day in each of the 45 U.S. cities where Groupon currently operates. The deals represent a broad array of products and services. Some of them are your everyday purchases, like a haircut, a Mexican dinner, or a supermarket trip. Other deals may come from a new business in your city or an experience you haven't tried, such as kayaking lessons, theatre tickets, or a museum membership. As Groupon knows, that the experience comes with a discount may be the push you need to buy. Subscribers have just a day to grab the deal.

But nothing is entirely risk free. A successful Groupon deal creates a surge of business that brings the owner little or no profit.

Where owners see profit is in follow-on business. Until then, a business can capsize under the surge if the owner didn't take care to set things up wisely, with minimum and maximum limits and the right discount amount.

Today, Groupon has more than 2 million subscribers and, in Chicago alone, a waiting list of business owners ready to make a deal.

Questions for Critical Thinking

1. Coupons are a tried-and-true promotion method, and the Internet includes other couponing sites. How does Groupon differentiate itself?

2. Groupon's business strategy harnesses what it calls "collective buying power." What facets of the marketing environment have enabled a business like Groupon to emerge and become successful?

Sources: Jesse Hempel, "Social Media Meets Retailing," *Fortune*, March 22, 2010, p. 30; Wailin Wong, "Groupon Spawns Rivals on Social Media Bargain-Hunting Scene," *Chicago Tribune*, February 22, 2010, http://www.chicagotribune.com; Heather Green, "Coaxing Shoppers of a Feather to Flock Together," *BusinessWeek*, December 14, 2009, http://www.businessweek.com; Taylor Buley, "The Best Discounts on the Web," *Forbes*, November 25, 2009, http://www.forbes.com; John Sviokla, "Groupon's Four Keys to Customer Interaction," *Harvard Business Review*, September 14, 2009, http://blogs.hbr.org; Mary Pilon, "Finding Group Discounts Online," *The Wall Street Journal*, August 11, 2009, http://blogs.wsj.com; Gabriella Boston, "Site Leverages Power of Group Purchases," *Washington Times*, July 8, 2009, http://www.washingtontimes.com; Brad Tuttle, "Q&A with Groupon.com Founder Andrew Mason," *Time*, June 24, 2009, http://money.blogs.time.com.

Video Case 14.2
Retailing at Flight 001

There's nothing like a lazy afternoon spent browsing Main Street or the mall, latte in hand, taking in the sights, sounds, and intoxicating smell of Cinnabon. You just can't get that online at iTunes, Amazon, or eBay. That's why Flight 001 founders John Sencion and Brad John take every detail in their retail stores very seriously.

Flight 001 is all about the experience. They care deeply about the experience you have in the store and carefully select every product, whether it be a $6.00 lime green luggage tag or a $600 designer carry-on, to ensure you feel just as great once you arrive at your destination.

The company gets its name from the famous Pan Am Flight 001. The flight originated in San Francisco and continued for 46 hours, stopping in Hawaii, Tokyo, Hong Kong, Bangkok, Calcutta, Delhi, Beirut, Istanbul, Frankfurt, London, and finally landing in New York. From the late 1940s through the 1980s, Flight 001 was the flight for the sophisticated world traveler. The founders set out to create a retail experience worthy of the name. Every store features a curved interior, mimicking the walls of an airplane fuselage. The sales desk looks like the ticket counter at an airport. It was important to Sencion that every aspect of the store design suggested First Class, from the walnut panels on the walls to the time zone clocks and top-notch customer service.

When the first store opened, one of the most unique features that came out of all of that attention to detail was a sense of intimacy, something you don't get in a large department store or discount retailer. The founders began to notice that people were exploring the store, rather than just running in and picking up what they came in for. This type of grazing is great for sales. When customers come in for a travel clock, they very often leave with something they didn't realize they needed—perhaps unique space-saving packing supplies, an interesting guide book, or a stylish document organizer.

In its tenth year, Flight 001 was rapidly opening new locations in selected cities in the United States. You definitely won't see them in a strip mall off the highway; that's something Brad John feels very strongly about. While there's something for everyone in the store, their customers tend to be young, trendy, and affluent. These people prefer to shop on secondary streets with clusters of boutiques and coffee shops. "Our stores that do the best seem to be in the most hip, cool places," remarks John. "It's been a bit difficult because these kind of streets don't exist in every city in America." John acknowledges that if they want to continue to grow the company, they will eventually need to be open to other types of locations, even upscale malls, but as a relatively young brand, staying consistent in design and venue is important.

While Flight 001 has made their products available on several airline Web sites, they have yet to set up shop at the airport. With airport layovers, delays, and early arrival times getting longer, airports are rethinking the way they look at retail and are asking retailers to consider opening in their "air malls." In recent years, many larger airports have added celebrity chef restaurants, Aveda spas, wine bars, and upscale clothing retailers. "I do think people are spending a lot more money in airports and not just picking up little items," says John. "We do want to open up in airports, but we want to open up in cool airports."

Questions

1. What are the key components to Flight 001's retailing strategy?

2. Flight 001 was started in the late 1990s because the founders couldn't find all their travel needs in one place. Do you think they face any impending threat from so-called category killers as these stores continue to raise the bar in terms of products offered and style? Explain.

Greensburg, Inc.

© CENGAGE LEARNING

A Little Hope for the Little Guy

John Miggins was 12 when Neil Armstrong took his first steps on the moon. It was on that day Miggins knew he wanted to be an astronaut. He spent all his free time reading and researching his future career. He thought one of the coolest things, aside from walking on the moon, was how they got electricity all the way up in space. As early as 1905, Einstein discussed harnessing the sun's energy in a paper on the photoelectric effect; and, by 1964, NASA's Nimbus spacecraft launch was powered by a solar array.

The astronaut thing didn't quite work out for Miggins, but all that research didn't go to waste.

Flash forward about 25 years. Miggins was at a turning point in his life. Recently laid off and with a family to support, Miggins decided to go off the grid and start his own business. He purchased a small 800-square-foot bungalow on a busy Tulsa street—for a song—and opened Harvest Solar & Wind Power.

Unfortunately, passion wasn't enough to keep Harvest Solar energized. Even though plenty of people were aware of solar and wind power, for many it was little more than a solution to heat your pool or a back-up battery for rural homeowners. Miggins and his partner took plenty of calls, but few jobs panned out. On the jobs that did, they were always under the gun—scrambling to get what they needed when they needed it, hiring extra hands and subcontractors, keeping just enough money in the bank to make it all happen while putting in 80-hour weeks. If a customer was late on payment, or didn't pay at all, it could be catastrophic for the business.

In January 2008, Miggins received a call from Studio 804, a design group made up of students from the University of Kansas School of Architecture and Urban Planning. The students were on a semester-long project to build an art and community center in Greensburg, Kansas. The 547 Art Center, aptly named for the date of the devastating tornado that struck the town on May 4, 2007, would be the town's first completed building. As with most projects in Greensburg, they were looking for donations. Lots of them. They were hoping Miggins, who was still operating as Harvest Solar at the time, would be able to do the solar and wind power systems for the building. Miggins was in no position to donate the $50,000 it would cost but submitted a bid and worked with the students on some plans, "just 'cause it was cool."

The frustrations were mounting. Miggins was doing his taxes one day and thought, "I show my income, but I don't know where it all goes." Around that same time, an old friend from his hometown of Houston called with an offer Miggins couldn't refuse. A new company called Standard Renewable Energy was looking to expand and needed experienced regional sales managers to cover the Oklahoma and Kansas territories. Miggins knew the area and definitely knew his stuff, so it was a perfect fit. Standard Renewable could provide the corporate infrastructure, financial backing, logistics, and purchasing power Miggins lacked while allowing him some of the freedoms he enjoyed while running his own show.

Although Miggins was confident in his decision to join Standard Renewable Energy, some of his customers didn't understand the need for him to be part of a larger organization. Solar homeowner Emily Priddy purchased her system from Harvest Solar in early 2007 and was very happy with the level of service received from Miggins on his own. Shortly after Priddy's system was installed, Miggins joined Standard. An ardent supporter of independent local businesses, Priddy has mixed feelings about the market share large companies have nowadays. "When the big guys catch on, at least it makes the technology more widely available," says Priddy. Miggins still provides customer support for Priddy's system, but now as Standard Renewable Energy.

On April 1, 2008, Studio 804 called again. They were ready to go and hoped Miggins was still interested in their project. The thing was, he had less than a month to engineer, take delivery of the necessary components, and install the system. May 4, 2008 was to be the grand opening, and everything had to be perfect. President George W. Bush was to be the guest of honor. Oh, and they still needed at least some of the installation for free.

The next call was to Standard Renewable Energy in Houston. They agreed that the Studio 804 project was a worthy cause and gave Miggins the green light to make it happen. A normal installation takes at least 60 days to turn around. They had half of that. The building, the first of its kind in Kansas, needed to be special, so last-minute changes and upgrades had them down to the wire. The three wind turbines were so new that they had to be special ordered from Australia and shipped via air to the rural Kansas town. None of it could have been done without the backing of the larger and more well-heeled Standard Renewable Energy.

Their participation in the project has paid off. Miggins has projects pending with several of the architecture firms he met while working in Greensburg. He's hopeful the referrals will keep coming—and isn't looking back to the old days at Harvest Solar.

Questions

1. Compare the logistics and supply chain systems of Harvest Solar with that of Standard Renewable Energy.

2. What kind of marketing channel is Standard Renewable Energy?

3. Do you prefer to shop at big box stores, like Costco and Walmart, or local independent merchants? What are the pros and cons of each?

4. Visit a local big-box store, ask for a meeting with a store manager, and write a report (3 to 5 pages) on the green initiatives they are involved in.

Promotional Decisions

PART 6

6

PART 6

Chapter 15
Integrated Marketing Communications

Chapter 16
Advertising and Public Relations

Chapter 17
Personal Selling and Sales Promotion

ch15 Integrated
Marketing Communications

1 Explain how integrated marketing communications relates to the development of an optimal promotional mix.

2 Describe the communication process and how it relates to the AIDA concept.

3 Explain how the promotional mix relates to the objectives of promotion.

4 Identify the different elements of the promotional mix, and explain how marketers develop an optimal promotional mix.

5 Describe the role of sponsorships and direct marketing in integrated marketing communications.

6 Discuss the factors that influence the effectiveness of a promotional mix.

7 Contrast pushing and pulling strategies.

8 Explain how marketers budget for and measure the effectiveness of promotion.

9 Discuss the value of marketing communications.

Denny's Gets the Word Out • • • Denny's, the casual dining chain, enjoys 95 percent brand recognition among consumers. It operates nearly 1,550 family restaurants worldwide, the majority of them in the United States, and boasts annual U.S. sales of about $2.3 billion.

Yet the chain, more than half a century old, was losing traction with customers, despite promotions, menu updates, and a new breakfast take-out option. The restaurant business in general was hurting, with people falling back on fast-food outlets or home cooking. "We realized we were in sort of a quagmire," said the company's executive vice president and chief marketing and concept innovation officer. Was more advertising the answer, or were consumers already familiar enough with the brand? "What does it mean if Denny's put a commercial out there?" the vice president asked. "People would say, 'Denny's, I already know about them.' Given what we were facing, we felt we really had to grab the consumer by the lapels and shake him."

So Denny's decided to do a massive breakfast giveaway, promising free "Grand Slam" breakfasts during an eight-hour period on one day. The promotion was simple, the plans were thorough, and store employees across the chain were prepared and energized. The most important piece now was getting the word out.

To publicize the promotion, Denny's went for broke, purchasing its first ever Super Bowl ad, generating a sharp jump in traffic to its Web site and what the firm estimates was about $50 million in free publicity. The giveaway, "like a big tailgate party," was such a huge success, with 2 million breakfasts given out, that the company repeated it the following year. This time it ran three 30-second Super Bowl spots promoting the one-day breakfast giveaway and other events throughout the year, including a contest to win a free Grand Slam every week for a year and free breakfast on a customer's birthday (with proof of date of birth).

Denny's also expanded its marketing communications to promote the free meals, including a humorous online campaign featuring exclusive Webisodes on the same chicken theme as the ads, in-store displays, a new rewards program, and a lot of Twitter traffic. (Denny's was one of Twitter's top ten trending topics during the recent Super Bowl.)

Welcome
YOUR FREE GRAND SLAM® HAS BEEN EXPECTING YOU.

GET A FREE GRAND SLAM®
Today, from 6 AM–2 PM
(DINE-IN ONLY)
WHILE SUPPLIES LAST

OFFER LIMITED TO TUESDAY, 2/3/09, 6 AM TO 2 PM. NO SUBSTITUTIONS.
LIMIT ONE PER CUSTOMER. ©2009 DNC, INC.

© MARK RIGHTMIRE, THE ORANGE COUNTY REGISTER/NEWSCOM

"We looked for every possible way to show [customers] what was new at Denny's," the vice president said. Denny's CEO called the response "an outpouring of the most genuine and heartwarming comments from our guests, servers, and managers." The giveaway might have been expensive, but the firm believes it's been worth it. "I look at our giveaways as just a big sample," said the vice president, "and that's why we didn't look at ROI [return on investment] necessarily. We didn't look for a payback right then."

Getting the word out about the promotion was a priority in-house too. Company managers met with franchisees around the country talking about the event, holding town-hall style meetings to brainstorm ideas, and pumping up enthusiasm among the staff. Here too, attention to communication paid off in the form of expert detailed planning that allowed for every contingency, including bad weather, long lines, and product shortages. "At the end of the day," said Denny's vice president of marketing, "you don't know what to expect."[1]

evolution of a brand

Denny's opened its first restaurant, a donut shop, in California in 1953. It started expanding almost immediately, adding stores and menu items at a rapid pace. By 1959, there were 20 Denny's, and, in 1977, the chain introduced the Grand Slam breakfast, still its most popular breakfast item. Now headquartered in South Carolina, the company is the largest family-service restaurant chain in the United States, with 21,000 employees in its company-owned and franchise outlets.

1. What do you think accounts for the success of Denny's attempts to revitalize its brand?

2. Do you think Denny's would benefit from more marketing communications via online channels like Twitter and Facebook? Why or why not?

chapter overview

promotion
Communication link between buyers and sellers; the function of informing, persuading, and influencing a consumer's purchase decision.

marketing communications
Messages that deal with buyer–seller relationships.

briefly speaking

" Y ou can say the right thing about a product and nobody will listen. You've got to say it in a way that people will feel it in their gut. Because if they don't feel it, nothing will happen."

—William Bernbach
(1911–1982)
Cofounder of DDB advertising agency

integrated marketing communications (IMC) Coordination of all promotional activities to produce a unified, customer-focused promotional message.

Two of the four components of the marketing mix—product and distribution strategies—were discussed in previous chapters. The three chapters in Part 6 analyze the third marketing mix variable—promotion. **Promotion** is the function of informing, persuading, and influencing the consumer's purchase decision.

This chapter introduces the concept of integrated marketing communications, briefly describes the elements of a firm's promotional mix—personal and nonpersonal selling—and explains the characteristics that determine the success of the mix. Next, we identify the objectives of promotion and describe the importance of developing promotional budgets and measuring the effectiveness of promotion. Finally, we discuss the importance of the business, economic, and social aspects of promotion. Chapter 16 covers advertising, public relations, and other nonpersonal selling elements of the promotional mix, including sponsorships and guerrilla advertising. Chapter 17 completes this part of the book by focusing on personal selling and sales promotion.

Throughout *Contemporary Marketing*, special emphasis has been given to new information that shows how technology is changing the way marketers approach *communication*, the transmission of a message from a sender to a receiver. Consumers receive **marketing communications**—messages that deal with buyer–seller relationships—from a variety of

media, including television, radio, magazines, direct mail, the Internet, and cell phones. Marketers can broadcast an ad on the Web to mass markets or design a customized appeal targeted to a small market segment. Each message the customer receives from any source represents the brand, company, or organization. A company needs to coordinate all these messages for maximum total impact and to reduce the likelihood that the consumer will completely tune them out.

To prevent this loss of attention, marketers are turning to **integrated marketing communications (IMC)**, which coordinates all promotional activities—media advertising, direct mail, personal selling, sales promotion, public relations, and sponsorships—to produce a unified, customer-focused promotional message, as shown in Figure 15.1. IMC is a broader concept than marketing communications and promotional strategy. It uses database technology to refine the marketer's understanding of the target audience, segment this audience, and select the best type of media for each segment.

This chapter shows that IMC involves not only the marketer but all other organizational units that interact with the consumer. Marketing managers set the goals and objectives of the firm's promotional strategy in accordance with overall organizational objectives and marketing goals. Based on these objectives, the various elements of the promotional strategy—personal selling, advertising, sales promotion, direct marketing, publicity, and public relations—are formulated into an integrated communications plan. This plan becomes a central part of the firm's total marketing strategy to reach its selected market segments. The feedback mechanism, including marketing research and field reports, completes the system by identifying any deviations from the plan and suggesting improvements.

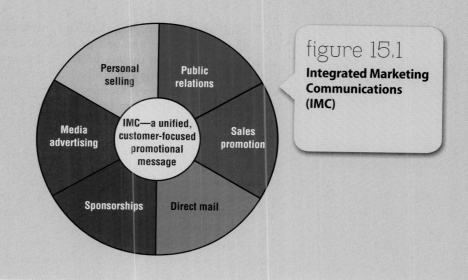

figure 15.1
Integrated Marketing Communications (IMC)

Integrated Marketing Communications

Stop and think for a moment about all the marketing messages you receive in a single day. You click on the television for the morning news, and you see commercials. Listen to the car radio on the way to work or school, and you can sing along with the jingles. You get catalogs, coupons, and flyers in the mail. People even leave promotional flyers under your car's windshield wiper while it sits in the parking lot. When you go online, you find banner and pop-up ads and even marketing-related e-mail. Marketers know you receive many types of communication. They know they need to compete for your attention, so they look for ways to reach you in a coordinated manner through integrated marketing communications.

Successful marketers use the marketing concept and relationship marketing to develop customer-oriented marketing programs. The customer is at the heart of integrated marketing communications. An IMC strategy begins not with the organization's goods and services but with consumer wants or needs and then works in reverse to the product, brand, or organization. It sends receiver-focused rather than product-focused messages.

Rather than separating the parts of the promotional mix and viewing them as isolated components, IMC looks at these elements from the consumer's viewpoint: as information about the brand, company, or organization. Even though the messages come from different sources—sales presentations, word of mouth, TV, radio, newspapers, billboards, direct mail, coupons, public relations, and online services—consumers may perceive them as "advertising" or a "sales pitch." IMC broadens promotion to include all the ways a customer has contact with an organization, adding to traditional media and direct mail such sources as package design, store displays, sales literature, and online and interactive media. Unless the organization takes an integrated approach to present a unified, consistent message, it may send conflicting information that confuses consumers.

Today's business environment is characterized by many diverse markets and media creating both opportunities and challenges. The success of any IMC program depends on identifying the members of an audience and understanding what they want. Without accurate, current information about existing and potential customers and their purchase histories, needs, and wants, marketers may send the wrong message. But they cannot succeed simply by improving the quality of the messages or by sending more of them. IMC must not only deliver messages to intended audiences but also gather responses from them. Databases and interactive marketing are important

1 Explain how integrated marketing communications relates to the development of an optimal promotional mix.

IMC tools that help marketers collect information from customers and then segment markets according to demographics and preferences. Marketers can then design specialized communications programs to meet the needs of each segment.

Young male consumers can be hard to pin down. That's why the U.S. Navy became a sponsor of the ESPN Winter X Games, a favorite of extreme sports fans—usually boys 13 to 17 years of age. The Navy signed on for the highest level of sponsorship rights and, with Jeep and Taco Bell, enjoys on-site signage and activation; rights to the X Games marks; and print, online, and TV exposure.[2]

The increase in media options provides more ways to give consumers product information; however, it can also create information overload. Marketers have to spread available dollars across fragmented media markets and a wider range of promotional activities to achieve their communication goals. Mass media such as TV ads, while still useful, are no longer the mainstays of marketing campaigns. In 1960, a marketer could reach about 90 percent of U.S. consumers by advertising on the three major TV networks—CBS, NBC, and ABC. Today, even though overall TV viewing is at an all-time high, consumers spend less than 20 percent of their viewing hours watching these stations. Basic cable, with channels such as ESPN, CNN, and the Food Network, now accounts for about 50 percent of viewing time, with additional networks such as the CW, and PBS (public broadcasting) eating up hours as well.[3] So to reach targeted groups of consumers, organizations must turn to niche marketing—advertising in special-interest magazines, purchasing time on cable TV channels, reaching out through telecommunications media such as cell phones and the Internet, and sponsoring events and activities. Without an IMC program, marketers frequently encounter problems within their own organizations because separate departments have authority and responsibility for planning and implementing specific promotional mix elements.

The coordination of an IMC program often produces a competitive advantage based on synergy and interdependence among the various elements of the promotional mix. With an IMC strategy, marketers can create a unified personality for the product or brand by choosing the right elements from the promotional mix to send the message. At the same time, they can develop more narrowly focused plans to reach specific market segments and choose the best form of communication to send a particular message to a specific target audience. IMC provides a more effective way to reach and serve target markets than less-coordinated strategies. Establishing an effective IMC program requires teamwork.

Importance of Teamwork

IMC requires a big-picture view of promotional planning, a total strategy that includes all marketing activities, not just promotion. Successful implementation of IMC requires that everyone involved in every aspect of promotion—public relations, advertising, personal selling, and sales promotion—function as a team. They must present a consistent, coordinated promotional effort at every point of customer contact with the organization. This way, they save time, money, and effort. They avoid duplication of efforts, increasing marketing effectiveness and reducing costs. Ultimately, it means that the result—the IMC program—is greater than the sum of its parts.

Teamwork involves both in-house resources and outside vendors. It involves marketing personnel; members of the sales force who deal with wholesalers, retailers, and organizational buyers; and customer service representatives. A firm gains nothing from a terrific advertisement featuring a great product, an informational Web site, and a toll-free number if unhelpful salespeople frustrate customers when they answer the phones. The company must train its representatives to send a single positive message to consumers and to solicit information for the firm's customer database.

IMC also challenges the traditional role of the outside advertising agency. A single agency may no longer fulfill all of a client's communications requirements, including traditional advertising and sales promotions, interactive marketing, database development, direct marketing, and public relations. To best serve client needs, an agency must often assemble a team with members from other companies.

Role of Databases in Effective IMC Programs

With the explosive growth of the Internet, marketers have the power to gather more information faster and to organize it more easily than ever before. By sharing this detailed knowledge appropriately among all relevant parties, a company can lay the foundation for a successful IMC program.

The move from mass marketing to a customer-specific marketing strategy—a characteristic of online marketing—requires not only a means of identifying and communicating with the firm's target market but also information regarding important characteristics of each prospective customer. As discussed in Chapter 10, organizations can compile different kinds of data into complete databases with customer information, including names and addresses, demographic data, lifestyle considerations, brand preferences, and buying behavior. This information provides critical guidance in designing an effective IMC strategy that achieves organizational goals and finds new opportunities for increased sales and profits. This increased ability to acquire huge amounts of data poses a new challenge: how to sift through it efficiently so it becomes useful information. Newer technology allows researchers to do exactly that—work with millions of sets of data to make very specific analyses.

Direct sampling is another method frequently used to quickly obtain customer opinions regarding a particular firm's goods and services. If you've ever received a free sample of laundry detergent, air freshener, breakfast cereal, or even a new magazine in your mailbox, you've been the recipient of direct sampling.

 assessment check

1. Define *promotion*.
2. What is the difference between marketing communications and integrated marketing communications (IMC)?

The Communication Process

When you have a conversation with someone, do you wonder whether the person understood your message? Do you worry that you might not have heard the person correctly? Marketers have the same concerns: when they send a message to an intended audience or market, they want to make sure it gets through clearly and persuasively. That is why the communication process is so important to marketing. The top portion of Table 15.1 shows a general model of the communication process and its application to promotional strategy.

The **sender** acts as the source in the communication system as he or she seeks to convey a **message** (a communication of information, advice, or a request) to a receiver. An effective message accomplishes three tasks:

1. It gains the receiver's attention.
2. It achieves understanding by both receiver and sender.
3. It stimulates the receiver's needs and suggests an appropriate method of satisfying them.

Table 15.1 also provides several examples of promotional messages. Although the types of promotion may vary from a highly personalized sales presentation to such nonpersonal promotions as television advertising and dollar-off coupons, each goes through every stage in the communications process.

The three tasks just listed are related to the **AIDA concept** (**a**ttention, **i**nterest, **d**esire, **a**ction), the steps consumers take in reaching a purchase decision. First, the promotional message must gain the potential consumer's attention. It then seeks to arouse interest in the good or service. At the next

> **2** Describe the communication process and how it relates to the AIDA concept.

sender Source of the message communicated to the receiver.

message Communication of information, advice, or a request by the sender to the receiver.

AIDA concept Steps through which an individual reaches a purchase decision: attention, interest, desire, and action.

table 15.1   Relating Promotion to the Communication Process

Type of Promotion	Sender	Encoding by Sender	Channel	Decoding by Receiver	Response	Feedback
Personal selling	SAP ERP system	Sales presentation on new applications of system	SAP sales representative	Office manager and employees discuss sales presentation and those of competing suppliers.	Order is placed for SAP system.	Customer asks about a second system for a subsidiary company.
Dollar-off coupon (sales promotion)	SC Johnson Wax	Coupon for Pledge Duster Plus	Coupon insert in Sunday newspaper	Newspaper reader sees coupon for Pledge Duster Plus.	Product is purchased by consumer using coupon.	SC Johnson Wax researchers see increase in market share.
Television advertising	Capital One	Advertisement featuring "What's in Your Wallet" slogan	Network television ads during program with high percentages of viewers 20–40 years old	Adults 20–40 see an ad and decide to try out the card.	Capital One cards are applied for.	Customers make purchases with Capital One cards.

stage, it stimulates desire by convincing the would-be buyer of the product's ability to satisfy his or her needs. Finally, the sales presentation, advertisement, or sales promotion technique attempts to produce action in the form of a purchase or a more favorable attitude that may lead to future purchases.

The message must be **encoded**, or translated into understandable terms, and transmitted through a communications channel. **Decoding** is the receiver's interpretation of the message. The receiver's response, known as **feedback**, completes the system. Throughout the process, **noise** (in such forms as ineffective promotional appeals, inappropriate advertising media, or poor radio or television reception) can interfere with the transmission of the message and reduce its effectiveness.

The marketer is the message sender in Table 15.1. He or she encodes the message in the form of sales presentations, advertising, displays, or publicity releases. The **channel** for delivering the message may be a salesperson, a public relations outlet, a Web site, or one of the numerous advertising media. Decoding is often the most troublesome step in marketing communications because consumers do not always interpret promotional messages in the same way that senders do. Because receivers usually decode messages according to their own frames of reference or experiences, a sender must carefully encode a message in a way that matches the frame of reference of the target audience. Consumers today are bombarded daily by hundreds of sales messages through many media channels. This communications traffic can create confusion as noise in the channel increases. Because the typical shopper will choose to process only a few messages, ignored messages are wasted communications expenditures.

The AIDA concept is also vital to online marketers. It is not enough to say a Web site has effective content or high response rates. Marketers must know just how many "eyeballs" are looking at the site, how often they come to view a message, and what they are examining. Most important, they must find out what consumers do besides just look. The bottom line is that if nobody is responding to a Web site, it might as well not exist. Experts advise attracting users' attention by including people in advertisements and other communications in addition to new content and formats. For the Winter Olympic Games in Vancouver, NBC offered programming on several different platforms, including its network channels, the cable channels of NBC Universal, the Web site NBCOlympics.com, and downloadable clips and mobile updates for smartphone users. Calling the estimated 185 million viewers of the Games "the world's biggest focus group," NBC planned to measure viewers' use of new and mobile media in particular, and it hired six market research companies to help track viewership as well as Olympics-related word-of-mouth on social networking sites.

encoding Translating a message into understandable terms.

decoding Receiver's interpretation of a message.

feedback Receiver's response to a message.

noise Any stimulus that distracts a receiver from receiving a message.

channel Medium through which a message is delivered.

briefly speaking

"History repeats itself because no one listens the first time."

—Anonymous

Among other research projects related to the Games, NBC gave about 2,000 viewers an Arbitron Portable People Meter to measure TV viewing and outfitted several dozen others with measuring devices for their BlackBerries and iPhones. "Like network advertisers, we all want to better understand how the new media environment works," said the network's head of research.[4]

Feedback, the receiver's response to the message, provides a way for marketers to evaluate the effectiveness of the message and tailor their responses accordingly. Feedback may take the form of attitude changes, purchases, or nonpurchases. In some instances, organizations use promotion to create favorable attitudes toward their goods or services in the hope of future purchases. Other promotional communications have the objective of directly stimulating consumer purchases. Marketers using infomercials that urge the viewer to call a toll-free number to place orders for music collections, the latest fitness fad, or other products can easily measure their success by counting the number of calls they receive that result in orders.

Even nonpurchases may serve as feedback to the sender. Failure to purchase may result from ineffective communication in which the receivers do not believe the message, don't remember it, or even associate it with another firm's products. Or receivers may remember it correctly, but the message may have failed to persuade them that the firm's products are better than those of the competition. So marketers need to be keenly aware of why messages fail. Interpersonal messages can fail, too, from lack of listening skills.

Noise represents interference at some stage in the communication process. It may result from disruptions such as transmissions of competing promotional messages over the same communications channel, misinterpretation of a sales presentation or advertising message, receipt of the promotional message by the wrong person, or random events such as people conversing or leaving the room during a television commercial. Noise can also result from distractions within an advertising message itself. Buzzwords and jargon can create a linguistic jungle for consumers who are just trying to find out more about a product. AARP, for instance, surveyed about 1,200 adults and found more than half were confused by the language of the investment industry, often saving too little or making costly mistakes because they didn't understand terms like *basis point* and *expense ratio*. "We learned that jargon is one of the key reasons for investor hesitation and missteps, and so off-putting for some, that it discourages investing altogether."[5]

Noise can be especially problematic in international communications. One problem is that there may be too many competing messages. Italian television channels broadcast all advertisements during a single half-hour slot each night. Or technology may be poor, and language translations inaccurate. Nonverbal cues, such as body language and tone of voice, are important parts of the communication process, and cultural differences may lead to noise and misunderstandings. For example, in the United States, the round *O* sign made with the thumb and first finger means "okay." But in Mediterranean countries, the same gesture means "zero" or "the worst." A Tunisian interprets this sign as "I'll kill you," and to a Japanese consumer, it means "money." It's easy to see how misunderstandings could arise from this single gesture. Perhaps the most misunderstood language for U.S. marketers is English. With 74 English-speaking nations, local terms can confuse anyone trying to communicate globally. The following examples illustrate how easy it can be for marketers to make mistakes in English-language promotional messages:

- *Police:* bobby (Britain), garda (Ireland), Mountie (Canada), police wallah (South Africa)

- *Porch:* stoep (South Africa), gallery (Caribbean)

- *Bar:* pub (Britain), hotel (Australia), boozer (Australia, Britain, New Zealand)

- *Swimsuit:* swimming costume (Britain), bathers (Australia)

- *Ghost or monster:* wendigo (Canada), duppy (Caribbean), taniwha (New Zealand)

- *Barbecue:* braai (South Africa), barbie (Australia)

- *Angry:* berko (Australia)

- *Festival:* feis (Ireland)

- *Sweater:* jumper (England)

briefly speaking

"England and America are two countries separated by a common language."

—George Bernard Shaw
(1856–1950)
Irish playwright

career *readiness* **B**ody Language: Watch What You "Say"

Communicating is much more than words. Gestures, posture, eye contact, facial expression, and distance from others all signal our thoughts and can allow us to gauge the thoughts of others. While nonverbal communications, often called body language, are not infallible guides to what people are feeling, some carry nearly universal meaning. In centuries past, for instance, a handshake indicated the absence of hidden weapons, and today it is still a signal of trust. Here are a few ideas about nonverbal communications and what they generally mean:

- "Open" body language signals a welcoming and attentive attitude. Posture is relaxed and easy, hands are visible, and eyes are making contact. The message is that the person is receptive to you and attentive to what you may say.

- Tensed shoulders, crossed arms and/or legs, and lack of eye contact can suggest the person feels threatened or hostile and is trying to protect himself or herself. Trust might be lacking, which will hamper open communication.

- Body language sometimes sends a different message than the speaker's words are sending. For instance, some people laugh when they are embarrassed, and in some cultures it is common to smile when disappointed. Be cautious about taking the verbal message at face value when it conflicts with the nonverbal one.

- Standing too close to someone is often perceived as a threatening gesture, one that violates the individual's "personal space." Be aware that personal space varies among cultures.

- Angry people sometimes lean forward in conversation, but this posture can also indicate high interest. Look for other clues before you interpret.

Finally, consider your own body language, and notice how a change of posture or the addition of a smile can change your message, and your mood.

Sources: Phillip Khan-Panni, "20 Essential International Body Language Tips," *ByteStart*, www.bytestart.co.uk, accessed March 31, 2010; "How to Read Body Language," *EHow*, www.ehow.com, accessed March 31, 2010; "Body Language—Top 10 Tips for Reading Client Posture and Gestures," *LanguagesMBlog*, http://languagesmblog.co.uk, February 28, 2010; James Borg, "10-Minute Body Language Tips," *The Daily Telegraph*, www.telegraph.co.uk, February 8, 2010.

- *Exact information:* good oil (Australia)
- *Soccer:* football (the rest of the world)
- *Tow truck:* breakdown van (Britain)

Faulty communications can be especially risky on a global level, where noise can lead to some interesting misinterpretations. Here are three international examples:

- *On a sign in a Bucharest hotel lobby*—The lift is being fixed for the next day. During that time, we regret that you will be unbearable.

- *From a Japanese information booklet about using a hotel air conditioner*—Cooles and Heates: If you want just condition of warm in your room, please control yourself.

- *In an Acapulco hotel*—The manager has personally passed all the water served here. Nonverbal language is also expressive. See the "Career Readiness" feature for some examples.

✓ assessment check

1. What are the three tasks accomplished by an effective message?
2. Identify the four steps of the AIDA concept.
3. What is noise?

Objectives of Promotion

What specific tasks should promotion accomplish? The answers to this question seem to vary as much as the sources consulted. Generally, however, marketers identify the following objectives of promotion:

1. Provide information to consumers and others.
2. Increase demand.
3. Differentiate a product.
4. Accentuate a product's value.
5. Stabilize sales.

Provide Information

The traditional function of promotion was to inform the market about the availability of a particular good or service. In fact, marketers still direct much of their current promotional efforts at providing information to potential customers. An advertisement for a concert typically provides information about the performer, time, and place. A commercial for a theme park offers information about rides, location, and admission price. Information can also help differentiate a product from its competitors by focusing on its features or benefits.

In addition to traditional print and broadcast advertising, marketers often distribute a number of high-tech, low-cost tools to give consumers product information. DVDs and online video clips are currently used for products such as cosmetics, automobiles, and exercise equipment, providing virtual demonstrations of the products. Political candidates even distribute them, packed with scenes from speeches, rallies, and the candidate on the job. Consumers still regard these media as a novelty, so they are less likely to throw them out or click elsewhere. Blogs are another channel for information. The "Solving an Ethical Controversy" feature discusses who controls customers' reviews and rankings of local businesses.

primary demand
Desire for a general product category.

General product category promotions, such as this one for cotton, aim at increasing primary demand.

a **natural** part of everyday life.
Spring showers? Cotton reigns.
Cotton. Naturally.

cotton
Natural
www.TheFabricofOurLives.com

© AP IMAGES/PRNEWSFOTO/COTTON INCORPORATED

Increase Demand

Most promotions pursue the objective of increasing demand for a product. Some promotions are aimed at increasing **primary demand**, the desire for a general product category such as smartphones or video game systems. Funding for the advertisement of agricultural commodities

solving an ethical controversy
Should Companies Filter Their Online Reviews?

"**G**etting Yelped," for business owners, is the experience of receiving negative Yelp reviews. Yelp.com allows users to review and rank local restaurants, hotels, and other businesses. It initially allowed advertisers to place a positive review at the top of the list, only subtly identified as a "sponsored result." But several firms around the country filed class-action suits against Yelp, claiming it routinely highlighted negative reviews unless firms agreed to become advertisers when it would substitute positive reviews it had systematically removed.

Should advertisers be able to manipulate the reviews potential customers see?

PRO

1. Businesses have the right to control their own message, whether it's a marketing campaign they pay for, a promotion they plan and run, or a sponsored search result on a Web site.

2. Yelp runs a spam filter to eliminate reviews by obviously biased sources such as a firm's competitors or friends and relatives. Letting the business owner make similar filtering choices is no different.

CON

1. One of the complaints from the Yelp suit was that "business listings on Yelp.com are in fact biased in favor of businesses that buy Yelp advertising."

2. Consumers' right to know is threatened when advertisers can literally buy reviews. Unlike impartial search results, reviews and rankings can influence consumers' buying decisions and should not be for sale.

Summary

Yelp recently agreed to provide a link allowing users to see all the reviews it has filtered out, and it will no longer allow advertisers to select the post that appears at the top of the page. "I hope that these changes will debunk some of the myths and conspiracy theories out there about Yelp and its advertising and whether those are linked," said the company's co-founder and CEO.

Sources: Claire Cain Miller, "Yelp Makes Changes in Response to Small-Business Owners," *The New York Times*, http://bits.glogs.nytimes.com, April 6, 2010; Jason Kincaid, "Yelp Hit with Second Extortion Lawsuit, CEO Calls It Meritless," *TechCrunch.com*, http://techcrunch.com, March 4, 2010; Peter Burrows and Joseph Galante, "Yelp: Advertise or Else?" *BusinessWeek*, www.businessweek.com, March 3, 2010; Caroline McCarthy, "Yelp CEO: This Lawsuit Is Bunk," *CNet News*, http://news.cnet.com, February 26, 2010.

such as milk, sorghum, and cotton comes from mandatory fees called *checkoffs* charged to farmers on the sale of their products—in order to stimulate primary demand for the entire category of products, not just one brand.[6] The fees, totaling $750 million a year, have generated some controversy. Supporters say it's good for everyone in the industry but critics say the program is unfair, pointing out that small farmers contribute to the advertising budgets of major firms such as Hormel and Smithfield. Still, these funds have generated such memorable slogans as these:

- "Beef. It's what's for dinner."
- "Pork. The other white meat."
- "The incredible edible egg."
- "Cotton. The fabric of our lives."

Primary-demand promotions are also typical for firms holding exclusive patents on significant product improvements and for marketers who decide to expand overseas, creating new markets for their products in other parts of the world. When Procter & Gamble first introduced its Pampers disposable diapers in Hungary, most parents were using overpants with paper inserts to diaper their babies. So early Pampers television ads focused on generating interest in the novel product.

More promotions, however, are aimed at increasing **selective demand**, the desire for a specific brand. Suzuki is implementing "a multi-faceted ad campaign designed to highlight the standout features and class-leading characteristics of its all-new sport sedan," the Kizashi. The campaign includes print ads, a 30-second television spot focusing on the car's styling, another promoting its all-wheel drive capability, reinforcing radio and online ads, and a Facebook game.[7]

selective demand
Desire for a specific brand within a product category.

Differentiate the Product

A frequent objective of the firm's promotional efforts is **product differentiation**. Homogeneous demand for many products results when consumers regard the firm's output as virtually identical to its competitors' products. In these cases, the individual firm has almost no control over marketing variables such as price. A differentiated demand schedule, in contrast, permits more flexibility in marketing strategy, such as price changes. As more companies try to reposition themselves as high-quality service providers, they are leaning heavily on the use of design—not only of the product but also of the consumer experience—to create emotional connections and make themselves unique and memorable. See how Redbox created a new movie-renting experience in the "Marketing Success" feature.

product differentiation Occurs when consumers regard a firm's products as different in some way from those of competitors.

Suzuki is trying to increase selective demand for its brand with ads highlighting standout features of its new sport sedan.

© JOHN DOOLEY/SIPA PRESS/AUTOSHOW.069/0912041652/NEWSCOM

Coffee sales generally follow a seasonal pattern, rising during colder months and dropping when the weather turns warm. Dunkin' Donuts recently catered to coffee lovers who buck the trend, promoting iced coffee in January.

© NEWSCOM

Accentuate the Product's Value

Promotion can explain the greater ownership utility of a product to buyers, thereby accentuating its value and justifying a higher price in the marketplace. This objective benefits both consumer and business products. A firm's promotional messages must build brand image and equity and at the same time deliver a "call to action." Advertising typically offers reasons why a product fits into the consumer's lifestyle. Today, consumers everywhere value their time; the challenge for marketers is to demonstrate how their merchandise will make their lives better.

Marketers must choose their words wisely when creating messages that accentuate their product's value. One expert advises staying away from five words: *quality, value, service, caring,* and *integrity.* These overused words are vague and tend to fall on deaf ears.[8]

Stabilize Sales

Sales of most goods and services fluctuate throughout the year. These fluctuations may result from cyclical, seasonal, or irregular demand. Ice cream, ski trips, and swimming pools have obvious fluctuations, as do snow shovels and lawn mowers. Sales of bottled water and flashlights might spike just before a forecasted storm, while vacation rentals might be canceled in the path of the same oncoming hurricane. Stabilizing these variations often is an objective of promotional strategy. Although it may seem less obvious than ice cream, coffee sales generally follow a seasonal pattern, rising during colder months and dropping when the weather turns warm. Dunkin' Donuts, however, recently catered to coffee lovers who buck the trend, promoting iced coffee in January with "Twitter Games" and a

mktg: *success*

Redbox Rules

Background. Facing increased competition for film lovers' loyalty from options like cable, satellite, smartphones, Wi-Fi, and even movie theaters, video-rental giants Blockbuster and Netflix saw their market shrinking fast. But some saw an opportunity.

The Challenge. To enter an industry with an uncertain future required a new business model. Video-rental kiosks, bright

red and instantly recognizable machines under the Redbox brand name, were the answer, sweetened with a low rental fee of $1 a night. Kiosks may lack the personal touch, but only the public library is cheaper.

The Strategy. Redbox operates about 22,400 rental kiosks around the country, near fast-food outlets and big discount chains, in malls and supermarkets. With a kiosk added

every hour around the clock, that number could soon top 60,000. Consumers rent more than 300 million Redbox DVDs a year, saving about $450 million in fees over Blockbuster and Netflix rentals, and Redbox's sales were expected to double in a year. The firm relies in part on viewers' existing awareness of what's hot. "We found that as we narrowed the selection, mostly things people are

special edition of its Facebook Fan of the Week competition. "Engaging our iced coffee fans on Twitter and Facebook is a great way to celebrate their passion for the coffee that keeps them running throughout the year," said the company's chief global customer and marketing officer.[9]

assessment check

1. What are the objectives of promotion?
2. Why is product differentiation important to marketers?

Elements of the Promotional Mix

Like the marketing mix, the promotional mix requires a carefully designed blend of variables to satisfy the needs of a company's customers and achieve organizational objectives. The **promotional mix** works like a subset of the marketing mix, with its product, distribution, promotion, and pricing elements. With the promotional mix, the marketers attempt to create an optimal blend of various elements to achieve promotional objectives. The components of the promotional mix are personal selling and nonpersonal selling, including advertising, sales promotion, direct marketing, public relations, and guerrilla marketing.

Personal selling, advertising, and sales promotion usually account for the bulk of a firm's promotional expenditures. However, direct marketing, guerrilla marketing, sponsorships, and public relations also contribute to integrated marketing communications. Later sections of this chapter examine the use of guerrilla marketing, sponsorships, and direct marketing, and Chapters 16 and 17 present detailed discussions of the other elements. This section defines the elements and reviews their advantages and disadvantages.

 Identify the different elements of the promotional mix, and explain how marketers develop an optimal promotional mix.

promotional mix
Subset of the marketing mix in which marketers attempt to achieve the optimal blending of the elements of personal and nonpersonal selling to achieve promotional objectives.

---

aware of from advertising and marketing campaigns—big celebrities, big box-office titles—that's what people wanted," said Redbox's president.

The Outcome. "Redbox created an incredibly efficient way to distribute movies, and we pass those savings on to customers," said its president. "Because of the dollar price point, people are watching movies they

wouldn't otherwise." Meanwhile, to appease major movie studios who felt the $1-a-night model threatened their business and tried to cut off Redbox's supply, the firm agreed not to rent new films until 28 days after release, when about 90 percent of DVD sales typically occur. Meanwhile, it added an online reservation service that lets customers reserve a film and pick it up wherever they like.

Sources: Brad Tuttle, "Movies for Cheap," *Time*, March 8, 2010, p. 50; Mike Duff, "Redbox New Year's Success Highlights Blockbuster Distress," *Industry Bnet.com*, http://industrybnet.com, January 7,.2010; Rob Fernandez, "Cheap Thrillers," *The Philadelphia Inquirer*, www.philly.com, October 25, 2009; Rob Walker, "Few Releases," *The New York Times*, www.nytimes.com, October 25, 2009.

Personal Selling

personal selling
Interpersonal influence
process involving a seller's
promotional presentation
conducted on a person-to-
person basis with the buyer.

Personal selling is the oldest form of promotion, dating back as far as the beginning of trading and commerce. Traders vastly expanded both market sizes and product varieties as they led horses and camels along the Silk Road from China to Europe roughly between 300 B.C.E. and A.D. 1600, conducting personal selling at both ends. Personal selling may be defined as a seller's promotional presentation conducted on a person-to-person basis with the buyer. This direct form of promotion may be conducted face-to-face, over the telephone, through videoconferencing, or through interactive computer links between the buyer and seller.

Today, almost 16 million people in the United States have careers in sales and related occupations. They may sell real estate, insurance, and financial investments or tractors, automobiles, and vacuum cleaners; they may work in retail or wholesaling; they may be regional managers or in the field. In other words, the range of jobs, as well as the products they represent, is huge.[10]

Nonpersonal Selling

nonpersonal selling
Promotion that includes
advertising, product
placement, sales promotion,
direct marketing, public
relations, and guerilla
marketing—all conducted
without being face-to-face
with the buyer.

Nonpersonal selling includes advertising, product placement, sales promotion, direct marketing, public relations, and guerrilla marketing. Advertising and sales promotion usually are regarded as the most important forms of nonpersonal selling. About one-third of marketing dollars spent on nonpersonal selling activities are allocated for media advertising; the other two-thirds fund trade and consumer sales promotions.

ADVERTISING

advertising Paid,
nonpersonal communication
through various media about
a business firm, not-for-profit
organization, product, or
idea by a sponsor identified
in a message intended to
inform or persuade members
of a particular audience.

Advertising is any paid, nonpersonal communication through various media about a business firm, not-for-profit organization, product, or idea by a sponsor identified in a message intended to inform, persuade, or remind members of a particular audience. It is a major promotional mix component for thousands of organizations—total ad spending in the United States remained above $115 billion in a recent year despite a slowing economy, and online ad spending was estimated to be $23 billion.[11] Mass consumption and geographically dispersed markets make advertising particularly appropriate for marketing goods and services aimed at large audiences likely to respond to the same promotional messages.

Advertising primarily involves the mass media, such as newspapers, television, radio, magazines, movie screens, and billboards, but it also includes electronic and computerized forms of promotion such as Web commercials, DVDs, and TV monitors at supermarkets. The rich potential of the Internet as an advertising channel to reach millions of people—one at a time—has attracted the attention of companies large and small, local and international. As consumers become increasingly savvy—and tune out messages that don't interest them—marketers are finding new ways to grab their attention. Ads on Web sites are commonplace, but now they also appear on cell phones. Consumers see them on taxis, in restroom stalls and elevators, on park benches, during sporting events, on gas pumps, at the movies, and pressed into sand on the beach. A Russian rocket carried a 30-foot Pizza Hut logo into space.[12]

PRODUCT PLACEMENT

product placement
Form of promotion in which
a marketer pays a motion
picture or television program
owner a fee to display a
product prominently in the
film or show.

Product placement is a form of nonpersonal selling in which the marketer pays a motion picture or television program a fee to display his or her product prominently in the film or show. The practice gained attention more than two decades ago in the movie *E.T.: The Extra-Terrestrial* when Elliott, the boy who befriends E.T., lays out a trail of Reese's Pieces for the extraterrestrial to follow, to draw the alien from his hiding place. Product sales for Reese's Pieces candies went through the roof. (Interestingly, this was not the moviemaker's first choice of candy; Mars turned down the opportunity to have its M&Ms appear in the film.) Today, hundreds of products, notably Coca-Cola as the drink of choice for "American Idol" judges, appear in movies and on television shows, and the fees charged for these placements have soared. Apple Computer had 12 exposures in a recent season-opener of the hit TV show "24," while Pontiac's brand was seen seven times and mentioned once. Nissan's Altima was featured in the premiere episode of "Parenthood," for which it was also the exclusive sponsor. And product placements are turning up on Twitter as well.[13]

Some firms have moved to the next generation of product placement, seeking new places for their merchandise. One popular venue for product placement is video games. Given that 75 percent of households with males between 8 and 34 have video game consoles, game placements can generate recognition and awareness, and they can also result in an immediate sale. Marketers need to be sure, however, that their product fits in the game environment, or at least doesn't interrupt the game experience.[14]

SALES PROMOTION

Sales promotion consists of marketing activities other than personal selling, advertising, guerrilla marketing, and public relations that stimulate consumer purchasing and dealer effectiveness. This broad category includes displays, trade shows, coupons, contests, samples, premiums, product demonstrations, and various nonrecurring, irregular selling efforts. Sales promotion provides a short-term incentive, usually in combination with other forms of promotion, to emphasize, assist, supplement, or otherwise support the objectives of the promotional program. Restaurants, including those serving fast food, often place certain items on the menu at a lower price "for a limited time only." Advertisements may contain coupons for free or discounted items for a specified period of time. Or companies may conduct sweepstakes for prizes such as new cars or vacations, which may even be completely unrelated to the products the companies are selling.

Movie promotional tie-ins are a classic example. Although this is still a popular—and profitable—type of promotion, some companies are discovering they aren't getting the return on their investment they had hoped for. If the movie flops, it may be bad news for the product as well. And some fast-food and snack companies are growing wary of tie-ins with films bearing G and PG ratings, due to past criticism that such deals help promote junk food to children. Creative control and quick results keep television advertising attractive to marketers, while the rising cost of airing spots on such high-profile broadcasts as the Super Bowl and the Olympics grabs an ever-larger share of their advertising budgets. A recent tie-in for the Warner Brothers movie "Valentine's Day" included an online sweepstakes hosted by Melting Pot, a national fondue franchise, to win a trip to Los Angeles for the film's premiere. Said the chain's vice president for brand development, the promotion for the romantic film "just made sense for our brand as a way to create memorable experiences for guests and incentivize them to return."[15]

Burger King planned a multifaceted promotion to tie in with "Eclipse," the third film in the popular "Twilight" series, including fan packs, limited-edition BK Crown Cards, and themed water bottles.[16]

Sales promotion geared to marketing intermediaries is called **trade promotion**. Companies spend about as much on trade promotion as on advertising and consumer-oriented sales promotion combined. Trade promotion strategies include offering free merchandise, buyback allowances, and merchandise allowances along with sponsorship of sales contests to encourage wholesalers and retailers to sell more of certain items or product lines.

DIRECT MARKETING

Another element in a firm's integrated promotional mix is **direct marketing**, the use of direct communication to a consumer or business recipient designed to generate a response in the form of an order, a request for further information (lead generation), or a visit to a place of business to purchase specific goods or services (traffic generation). While many people equate direct marketing with direct mail, this promotional category also includes telemarketing, direct-response advertising and infomercials on television, direct-response print advertising, and electronic media. Direct marketing is an important element of the promotional mix, and it is discussed in depth later in this chapter.

sales promotion
Marketing activities other than personal selling, advertising, guerrilla marketing, and public relations that stimulate consumer purchasing and dealer effectiveness.

trade promotion Sales promotion that appeals to marketing intermediaries rather than to consumers.

direct marketing
Direct communications, other than personal sales contacts, between buyer and seller, designed to generate sales, iformation requests, or store or Web site visits.

PUBLIC RELATIONS AND PUBLICITY

public relations Firm's communications and relationships with its various publics.

Public relations refer to a firm's communications and relationships with its various publics. These publics include customers, suppliers, stockholders, employees, the government, and the general public. Public relations programs can conduct either formal or informal contacts. The critical point is that every organization, whether or not it has a formally organized program, must be concerned about its public relations.

publicity Nonpersonal stimulation of demand for a good, service, place, idea, person, or organization by unpaid placement of significant news regarding the product in a print or broadcast medium.

Publicity is the marketing-oriented aspect of public relations. It can be defined as nonpersonal stimulation of demand for a good, service, person, cause, or organization through unpaid placement of significant news about it in a published medium or through a favorable presentation of it on the radio or television. Compared with personal selling, advertising, and even sales promotion, expenditures for public relations usually are low in most firms. Because companies do not pay for publicity, they have less control over the publication by the press or electronic media of good or bad company news. But this often means consumers find this type of news source more believable than if the information were disseminated directly by the company. Of course, bad publicity can damage a company's reputation and diminish brand equity. Organizations that enjoy good publicity generally try to make the most of it. Those who have suffered from bad publicity try to turn the situation around.

GUERRILLA MARKETING

guerrilla marketing Unconventional, innovative, and low-cost marketing techniques designed to get consumers' attention in unusual ways.

Guerrilla marketing uses unconventional, innovative, and low-cost techniques to attract consumers' attention. It is a relatively new approach used by marketers whose firms are underfunded for a full marketing program. Many of these firms can't afford the huge costs involved in the orthodox media of print and broadcasting, so they need to find an innovative, low-cost way to reach their market. But some large companies, such as PepsiCo and Toyota, engage in guerrilla marketing as well.

As mentioned in Chapter 10, *buzz marketing* can be part of guerrilla marketing. This type of marketing works well to reach college students and other young adults. Marketing firms may hire students to mingle among their own classmates and friends, creating buzz about a product. Often called *campus ambassadors,* they may wear logo-bearing T-shirts or caps, leave Post-it Notes with marketing messages around campus, and chat about the good or service with friends during class breaks or over meals.

Viral marketing, also mentioned in Chapter 10, is another form of guerrilla marketing that has rapidly caught on with large and small firms. The shoe retailer Steve Madden has partnered with online shoe and apparel store Zappos.com to create "Steve Madden's SOLE SEARCH powered by Zappos," to let consumers share their own shoe designs with their social networks and enter them in a contest. The winning design will be produced by Steve Madden and sold at Zappos.com. "It's amazing that through the Internet we're able to tap into so much creative energy for this exciting project," Steve Madden said.[17]

The results of guerrilla marketing can be funny and

> Steve Madden partnered with Zappos.com to create a contest to let consumers share their own shoe designs with their social networks.

outrageous—even offensive to some people. But they almost always get consumers' attention. Some guerrilla marketers stencil their company and product names anywhere graffiti might appear. Street artists are hired to plaster company and product logos on blank walls or billboards.

Advantages and Disadvantages of Types of Promotion

As Table 15.2 indicates, each type of promotion has both advantages and shortcomings. Although personal selling entails a relatively high per-contact cost, it involves less wasted effort than nonpersonal forms of promotion such as advertising. Personal selling often provides more flexible promotion than the other forms because the salesperson can tailor the sales message to meet the unique needs—or objections—of each potential customer.

The major advantages of advertising come from its ability to create instant awareness of a good, service, or idea; build brand equity; and deliver the marketer's message to mass audiences for a relatively low cost per contact. Major disadvantages include the difficulty of measuring advertising effectiveness and high media costs. Sales promotions, by contrast, can be more accurately monitored and measured than advertising, produce immediate consumer responses, and provide short-term

table 15.2 Comparison of the Six Promotional Mix Elements

	Personal Selling	Advertising	Sales Promotion	Direct Marketing	Public Relations	Guerrilla Marketing
Advantages	Permits measurement of effectiveness	Reaches a large group of potential consumers for a relatively low price per exposure	Produces an immediate consumer response	Generates an immediate response	Creates a positive attitude toward a product or company	Is low cost
	Elicits an immediate response	Allows strict control over the final message	Attracts attention and creates product awareness	Covers a wide audience wit h targeted advertising	Enhances credibility of a product or company	Attracts attention because it is innovative
	Tailors the message to fit the customer	Can be adapted to either mass audiences or specific audience segments	Allows easy measurement of results	Allows complete, customized, personal message		Is less cluttered with competitors trying the same thing
			Provides short-term sales increases	Produces measurable results		
Disadvantages	Relies almost exclusively on the ability of the salesperson	Does not permit totally accurate measurement of results	Is nonpersonal in nature	Suffers from image problem	May not permit accurate measurement of effect on sales	May not reach as many people
	Involves high cost per contact	Usually cannot close sales	Is difficult to differentiate from competitors' efforts	Involves a high cost per reader	Involves much effort directed toward non-marketing-oriented goals	If the tactics are too outrageous, they may offend some people
				Depends on quality and accuracy of mailing lists		
				May annoy consumers		

sales increases. Direct marketing gives potential customers an action-oriented choice, permits narrow audience segmentation and customization of communications, and produces measurable results. Public relations efforts such as publicity frequently offer substantially higher credibility than other promotional techniques. Guerrilla marketing efforts can be innovative and highly effective at a low cost to marketers with limited funds, as long as the tactics are not too outrageous, but it is more difficult to reach people. The marketer must determine the appropriate blend of these promotional mix elements to effectively market the firm's goods and services.

assessment check

1. Differentiate between personal and nonpersonal selling.
2. What are the six major categories of nonpersonal selling?

Sponsorships

5 Describe the role of sponsorships and direct marketing in integrated marketing communications.

One of the most significant trends in promotion offers marketers the ability to integrate several elements of the promotional mix. Commercial sponsorships of an event or activity involve personal selling, advertising, sales promotion, and public relations in achieving specific promotional goals. These sponsorships, which link events with sponsors and media ranging from TV and radio to print and the Internet, have become a multi-billion-dollar business in which sports is the largest category. Although two of the biggest participants, the automobile and financial industries, cut their sponsorship spending in the recent economic slowdown, sponsorship spending was still expected to grow slightly to more than $17 billion.[18]

sponsorship
Relationship in which an organization provides funds or in-kind resources to an event or activity in exchange for a direct association with that event or activity.

Sponsorship occurs when an organization provides money or in-kind resources to an event or activity in exchange for a direct association with that event or activity. The sponsor purchases two things: (1) access to the activity's audience and (2) the image associated with the activity. Sponsorships typically involve advertising, direct mail and sales promotion, publicity in the form of media coverage of the event, and personal selling at the event itself. They also involve relationship marketing, bringing together the event, its participants, the sponsoring firms, and their channel members and major customers. Marketers underwrite varying levels of sponsorships depending on the amount their companies wish to spend and the types of events.

Commercial sponsorship is not a new phenomenon. Aristocrats in ancient Rome sponsored gladiator competitions and chariot races featuring teams that often were supported financially by competing businesses. More than 2,000 years ago, wealthy Athenians underwrote drama, musical, and sporting festivals. Craft guilds in 14th-century England sponsored plays, occasionally insisting that the playwrights insert "plugs" for their lines of work in the scripts. During the 1880s, some local baseball teams in the United States were sponsored by streetcar companies.

Although they include both commercial and not-for-profit events, today's sponsorships are most prevalent in sports—LPGA and PGA golf, NASCAR races, the Olympics, the World Cup, the Super Bowl, the NCAA basketball championships, Major League Soccer, baseball farm teams, the Tour de France bicycle race, and thousands of smaller events as well. Local firms may sponsor soccer and softball teams.

Companies may also sponsor reading and child-care programs, concerts or art exhibits, programs that support small businesses and create new jobs, and humanitarian programs such as the Special Olympics and the American Cancer Society's Relay for Life.

How Sponsorship Differs from Advertising

Even though sponsorship spending and traditional advertising spending represent forms of nonpersonal selling, they differ in a number of ways. These differences include potential cost-effectiveness, the sponsor's degree of control versus that of advertising, the nature of the message, and audience reaction.

Escalating costs of traditional advertising media have made commercial sponsorships a cost-effective alternative. Except for the really large events, which often have multiple sponsors, most are less expensive than an advertising campaign that relies on television, print, and other advertising. In addition, sponsors often gain the benefit of media coverage anyway, because associated events are covered by the news. And in the case of naming rights of such venues as sports arenas, the name serves as a perpetual advertisement. Examples include the Safeco Field (Seattle), HP Pavilion (San Jose), and the United Center (Chicago). Even mass-transit systems are looking into sponsorship, which would take the form of naming station stops after sponsoring firms. Apple has first right of refusal if the Chicago Transit Authority ever decides to sell naming rights to the North/Clybourn Red Line station, recently refurbished with an almost $4 million investment by the technology firm. "Part of what we're doing is exploring every possibility for non-fare revenue," said a Chicago Metra spokesperson.[19]

Marketers have considerable control over the quantity and quality of market coverage when they advertise. But sponsors have little control of sponsored events beyond matching the audiences to profiles of their own target markets. Instead, event organizers control the coverage, which typically focuses on the event—not the sponsor. By contrast, a traditional advertisement allows the marketer to create an individual message containing an introduction, a theme, and a conclusion.

Audiences react differently to sponsorship as a communications medium than to other media. The sponsor's investment provides a recognizable benefit to the sponsored activity that the audience can appreciate. As a result, sponsorship often is viewed more positively than traditional advertising. Some marketers have tried to take advantage of this fact by practicing **ambush marketing**, in which a firm that is not an official sponsor tries to link itself to a major international event, such as the Olympics or a concert tour by a musical group. If a nonsponsor used the Olympic rings in an advertisement, however, the ad would be an illegal use of a trademark. Said one ambush marketer in anticipation of the recent World Cup, of which Adidas was the official sponsor, "Nike will definitely try and ambush Adidas, as will a number of other brands. It always happens at every sporting event because it's a cheap way to generate noise around your brand. The authorities can move you on, so you've got to create your activity so you're always on the move." One ad director warned, however, "Consumers know who have earned the association properly and those who are only trying to. This can result in major credibility issues for the ambusher."[20]

ambush marketing
Attempt by a firm that is not an official sponsor of an event or activity to link itself to the event or activity.

To assess the results of sponsorships, marketers use some of the same techniques by which they measure advertising effectiveness. However, the differences between the two promotional alternatives often necessitate some unique research techniques as well. A few corporate sponsors attempt to link expenditures to sales. Other sponsors measure improved brand awareness and image as effectiveness indicators; they conduct traditional surveys before and after the events to secure this information. Still other sponsors measure the impact of their event marketing in public relations terms.

Direct Marketing

Few promotional mix elements are growing as fast as direct marketing. Direct marketing advertising expenditures in the United States continued to account for more than half of all U.S. advertising spending and totaled more than $153 billion in one recent year.[21] Both business-to-consumer and business-to-business marketers rely on this promotional mix element to generate orders or sales leads—requests for more information that may result in future orders. Direct marketing also helps increase store traffic, improving the chances that consumers will evaluate and perhaps purchase the advertised goods or services.

Direct marketing opens new international markets of unprecedented size. Electronic marketing channels have become the focus of direct marketers, and Web marketing is international marketing. Even direct mail and telemarketing will grow outside the United States as commerce becomes more global. Consumers in Europe and Japan are responsive to direct marketing, but most global marketing systems remain undeveloped, and many are almost dormant. The growth of international direct marketing is spurred by marketing operations born in the United States.

Direct marketing communications pursue goals beyond creating product awareness. Marketers want direct marketing to persuade people to place an order, request more information, visit a store, call a toll-free number, or respond to an e-mail message. In other words, successful direct marketing should prompt consumers to take action. Because direct marketing is interactive, marketers can tailor individual responses to meet consumers' needs. They can also measure the effectiveness of their efforts more easily than with advertising and other forms of promotion. Direct marketing is a very powerful tool that helps organizations win new customers and enhance relationships with existing ones.

The growth of direct marketing parallels the move toward integrated marketing communications in many ways. Both respond to fragmented media markets and audiences, growth in customized products, shrinking network broadcast audiences, and the increasing use of databases to target specific markets. Lifestyles also play a role because today's busy consumers want convenience and shopping options that save them time.

Databases are an important part of direct marketing. Using the latest technology to create sophisticated databases, a company can select a narrow market segment and find good prospects within that segment based on desired characteristics. Marketers can cut costs and improve returns on dollars spent by identifying customers most likely to respond to messages and by eliminating others who are not likely to respond from their lists. In fact, mining information about customers is a trend boosted by the growth of e-marketing.

Direct Marketing Communications Channels

Direct marketing uses many different media forms: direct mailings such as brochures and catalogs; telecommunications initiated by companies or customers; television and radio through special offers, infomercials, or shopping channels; the Internet via e-mail and electronic messaging; print media such as newspapers and magazines; and specialized channels such as electronic kiosks. Each works best for certain purposes, although marketers often combine two or more media in one direct marketing program. As long as it complies with current "do not call" regulations, a company might start with telemarketing to screen potential customers and then follow up by sending more material by direct mail to those who are interested.

Direct Mail

As the amount of information about consumer lifestyles, buying habits, and wants continues to mount, direct mail has become a viable channel for identifying a firm's best prospects. Marketers gather information from internal and external databases, surveys, personalized coupons, and rebates that require responses. **Direct mail** is a critical tool in creating effective direct-marketing campaigns. It comes in many forms, including sales letters, postcards, brochures, booklets, catalogs, *house organs* (periodicals issued by organizations), and DVDs.

Direct mail offers advantages such as the ability to select a narrow target market, achieve intensive coverage, send messages quickly, choose from various formats, provide complete information, and personalize each mailing piece. Response rates are measurable and higher than other types of advertising. In addition, direct mailings stand alone and do not compete for attention with magazine ads and radio and TV commercials. On the other hand, the per-reader cost of direct mail is high, effectiveness depends on the quality of the mailing list, and some consumers object to what they consider "junk mail."

Recently, some firms have been trying a direct-mail tactic that has sparked some debate—sending marketing messages that appear to be from the government, banks, or even a personal friend. One envelope might bear a logo that looks like a government seal; inside is a solicitation for refinancing a loan. Another might have what looks like a handwritten note from a friend—but actually contains an ad for a fitness center. Some envelopes look like bank statements. All are intended to cut through the clutter that appears in consumers' mailboxes.

Catalogs

Catalogs have been a popular form of direct mail in the United States since the late 1800s. During the early 1900s, consumers could even order a house from the famous Sears, Roebuck catalog. More

direct mail Communications in the form of sales letters, postcards, brochures, catalogs, and the like conveying messages directly from the marketer to the customer.

than 10,000 different catalogs fill mailboxes every year. Catalogs fill so many segments that you could probably order just about anything you need for any facet of your life from a catalog. A recent survey found that "more than 8 in 10 households read or scan their advertising mail," and a study by the Rochester Institute of Technology's Printing Industry Center found that 67 percent of respondents "like getting direct mail from companies they do business with." The Print Council reported that paper catalogs generated 42 percent of sales, compared to 26 percent for Web sites.[22]

Pottery Barn, L.L.Bean, and Williams-Sonoma are well known for their catalogs. But these and other retailers have also added online catalogs to their direct marketing lineup. Women's clothing retailer J. Jill created an online catalog that replicated each page of its print catalog so that consumers could flip through both and find items on the same "page." Nordstrom has begun a "buy online, pick up in-store" program for shoes, apparel, and cosmetics and many other categories.[23]

The 21st-century consumer is time-pressed and overloaded with information. To help consumers escape the barrage of mail stuffed into their boxes, the Direct Marketing Association established its Mail Preference Service. This consumer service sends name-removal forms to people who do not wish to receive direct-mail advertising.

Catalogs have been a popular form of direct mail in the United States since the late 1800s. Many companies well known for their catalogs, including J. Jill, have created online catalogs as well.

Telemarketing

Although its use has been limited by a number of "do not call" restrictions enacted by the Federal Trade Commission, telemarketing remains the most frequently used form of direct marketing. It provides marketers with a high return on their expenditures, an immediate response, and the opportunity for personalized two-way conversations. In addition to business-to-consumer direct marketing, business-to-business telemarketing is another form of direct customer contact.

Telemarketing refers to direct marketing conducted entirely by telephone, and it can be classified as either outbound or inbound contacts. Outbound telemarketing involves a sales force that uses only the telephone to contact customers, reducing the cost of making personal visits. The customer initiates inbound telemarketing, typically by dialing a toll-free number firms provide for customers to use at their convenience to obtain information or make purchases.

New predictive dialer devices improve telemarketing's efficiency and reduce costs by automating the dialing process to skip busy signals and answering machines. When the dialer reaches a human voice, it instantaneously puts the call through to a salesperson. This technology is often combined with a print advertising campaign that features a toll-free number for inbound telemarketing.

Because recipients of both consumer and business-to-business telemarketing calls often find them annoying, the Federal Trade Commission passed a *Telemarketing Sales Rule* in 1996. The rule curtailed abusive telemarketing practices by establishing allowed calling hours (between 8 a.m. and 9 p.m.) and regulating call content. Companies must clearly disclose details of any exchange policies; maintain lists of people who do not want to receive calls; and keep records of telemarketing scripts, prize winners, customers, and employees for two years. This regulation was recently strengthened by the passage of amendments, creating the national Do Not Call Registry. These rules prohibit telemarketing calls to anyone who has registered his or her phone number, restrict the number and duration of telemarketing calls generating dead air space with use of automatic dialers, crack down on unauthorized billing, and require telemarketers to transmit their Caller ID information. Violators

telemarketing Promotional presentation involving the use of the telephone on an outbound basis by salespeople or on an inbound basis by customers who initiate calls to obtain information and place orders.

can be fined as much as $11,000 per occurrence. Exempt from these rules, however, are current customers, charities, opinion pollsters, and political candidates.

The Federal Trade Commission (FTC) recently levied penalties amounting to $7.7 million against several companies for violating the provisions of the Do Not Call Registry. A major new enforcement effort is under way to target firms that violate the do-not-call rule or make prerecorded calls to consumers.[24]

In further restrictions to telemarketing, after receiving many complaints about recorded sales messages left on consumers' answering machines, the FTC recently required those calls to have an "opt out" selection for recipients to stop getting those calls. Telemarketers also may send recorded messages only to consumers who have provided signed written or electronic consent to receive them.[25]

Direct Marketing via Broadcast Channels

Broadcast direct marketing can take three basic forms: brief direct-response ads on television or radio, home shopping channels, and infomercials. Direct-response spots typically run 30, 60, or 90 seconds and include product descriptions and toll-free telephone numbers for ordering. Often shown on cable television and independent stations and tied to special-interest programs, broadcast direct marketing usually encourages viewers to respond immediately by offering them a special price or a gift if they call within a few minutes of an ad's airing. Radio direct-response ads also provide product descriptions and addresses or phone numbers to contact the sellers. However, radio often proves expensive compared with other direct marketing media, and listeners may not pay close enough attention to catch the number or may not be able to write it down because they are driving a car, which accounts for a major portion of radio listening time.

home shopping channel Television direct marketing in which a variety of products are offered and consumers can order them directly by phone or online.

Home shopping channels, such as Quality Value Convenience (QVC), Home Shopping Network (HSN), and ShopNBC, represent another type of television direct marketing. Broadcasting around the clock, these channels offer consumers a variety of products, including jewelry, clothing, skin-care products, home furnishings, computers, cameras, kitchen appliances, and toys. In essence, home shopping channels function as on-air catalogs. The channels also have Web sites that consumers can browse through to make purchases. In both cases, customers place orders via toll-free telephone numbers and pay for their purchases by credit card.

infomercial Paid 30-minute or longer product commercial that resembles a regular television program.

Infomercials are 30-minute or longer product commercials that resemble regular television programs. Because of their length, infomercials do not get lost as easily as 30-second commercials can, and they permit marketers to present their products in more detail. But they are usually shown at odd hours, and people often watch only portions of them. Lavalife Voice, a telephone dating service, recently launched an infomercial campaign via direct response TV. "This is the third spot we've done…for Lavalife Voice," said the company's director. "With this new spot…we're heading toward a more branded direct response. Most people are aware of our online product, but we wanted to let people know that we have [the Lavalife Voice service] out there as well."[26]

Infomercials provide toll-free telephone numbers so that viewers can order products or request more information. Although infomercials may incur higher production costs than prime-time 30-second ads on national network TV, they generally air on less expensive cable channels and in late-night time slots on broadcast stations.

Electronic Direct Marketing Channels

Anyone who has ever visited the Web is abundantly aware of the growing number of commercial advertisements that now clutter their computer screen. Web advertising is a recurring theme throughout this text, corresponding to its importance as a component of the promotional mix. In fact, Chapter 4 explained the vital role e-business now plays in contemporary marketing practices. U.S. spending on online advertising now represents almost 8 percent of total advertising spending.[27] Companies that were once skeptical—or at least slow to adopt online advertising—now embrace it.

Web advertising, however, is only one component of electronic direct marketing. E-mail direct marketers have found that traditional practices used in print and broadcast media are easily adapted to electronic messaging. You might receive e-mail notices from retailers from whom you've made past purchases, telling you about special promotions or new products. Banner ads on your cell phone might offer "click to call" options for responding. You might see a billboard or commercial promoting a code you can text to enter a sweepstakes or get a discount coupon. Experts agree that the basic rules for online direct marketing mirror those of traditional practices. Any successful offline direct marketing campaign can be applied to e-mail promotions. Electronic media deliver data instantly to direct marketers and help them track customer buying cycles quickly. As a result, they can place customer acquisition programs online for less than the cost of traditional programs.

Other Direct Marketing Channels

Print media such as newspapers and magazines do not support direct marketing as effectively as Web marketing and telemarketing. However, print media and other traditional direct marketing channels are still critical to the success of all electronic media channels. Magazine ads with toll-free telephone numbers enhance inbound telemarketing campaigns. Companies can place ads in magazines or newspapers, include reader-response cards, or place special inserts targeted for certain market segments within the publications. Newspapers are savvy about the Internet, producing online versions of their content that naturally include online, interactive ads.

Kodak's in-store photo kiosks now provide customers with access to their Facebook and Picasa photos.

© CALE MEREGE/BLOOMBERG VIA GETTY IMAGES

Kiosks provide another outlet for electronic sales. In its drive to transform its business, Blockbuster adapted in-store kiosks so customers can download movies for digital delivery.[28] Kodak's in-store photo kiosks, the largest fleet of such retail kiosks in the world, now provide customers with access to their Facebook and Picasa photos, as well as to pictures stored on Kodak's Gallery.[29]

✓ assessment check

1. Define *sponsorship*.
2. How is sponsorship different from advertising?
3. Define *direct mail*.
4. What are the benefits of electronic direct marketing?

Developing an Optimal Promotional Mix

6 Discuss the factors that influence the effectiveness of a promotional mix.

By blending advertising, personal selling, sales promotion, and public relations to achieve marketing objectives, marketers create a promotional mix. Because quantitative measures are not available to determine the effectiveness of each mix component in a given market segment, the choice of an effective mix of promotional elements presents one of the marketer's most difficult tasks. Several factors influence the effectiveness of a promotional mix: (1) the nature of the market, (2) the nature of the product, (3) the stage in the product lifecycle, (4) the price, and (5) the funds available for promotion.

Nature of the Market

The marketer's target audience has a major impact on the choice of a promotion method. When a market includes a limited number of buyers, personal selling may prove a highly effective technique. However, markets characterized by large numbers of potential customers scattered over sizable geographic areas may make the cost of contact by personal salespeople prohibitive. In such instances, extensive use of advertising often makes sense. The type of customer also affects the promotional mix. Personal selling works better in high-priced, high-involvement purchases—for instance, a target market made up of industrial purchasers or retail and wholesale buyers—than in a target market consisting of ultimate consumers. Similarly, pharmaceuticals firms use large sales forces to sell prescription drugs directly to physicians and hospitals, but they also advertise to promote over-the-counter and prescription drugs for the consumer market. So the drug firm must switch its promotional strategy from personal selling to consumer advertising based on the market it is targeting.

Subway used direct marketing in the form of its popular spokesperson, Jared Fogle, who lost 245 pounds eating its sandwiches. The company had Fogle record inspirational messages on its Web site, where consumers could sign up for a time to receive them. Subway has faith that other ordinary people can also adopt healthier eating habits; it is one of the sponsors of the popular reality show "The Biggest Loser." Contestants and their trainers visit Subway during TV segments to learn healthful food selection, which consumers can view at the show's Web site, and the company also sponsors contests to win free trips to the filming of the show's season finale. Subway's newest spokesperson is Shay Sorrells, a recent Biggest Loser contestant.[30]

Nature of the Product

A second important factor in determining an effective promotional mix is the product itself. Highly standardized products with minimal servicing requirements usually depend less on personal selling than custom products with technically complex features or requirements for frequent maintenance. Marketers of consumer products are more likely to rely heavily on advertising than business products. For example, soft drinks lend themselves more readily to advertising than large pieces of business machinery.

Promotional mixes vary within each product category. In the B2B market, for example, installations typically rely more heavily on personal selling than marketing of operating supplies. In contrast, the promotional mix for a convenience product is likely to involve more emphasis on manufacturer advertising and less on personal selling. On the other hand, personal selling plays an important role in the promotion of shopping products, and both personal and nonpersonal selling are important in the promotion of specialty items. A personal-selling emphasis is also likely to prove more effective than other alternatives in promotions for products involving trade-ins.

Stage in the Product Lifecycle

The promotional mix must also be tailored to the product's stage in the product lifecycle. In the introductory stage, both nonpersonal and personal selling are used to acquaint marketing intermediaries and final consumers with the merits of the new product. Heavy emphasis on personal selling helps inform the marketplace of the merits of the new good or service. Salespeople contact marketing intermediaries to secure interest in and commitment to handling the newly introduced item. Trade shows are frequently used to inform and educate prospective dealers and ultimate consumers about its merits over current competitive offerings. Advertising and sales promotion are also used during this stage to create awareness, answer questions, and stimulate initial purchases.

As the product moves into the growth and maturity stages, advertising gains relative importance in persuading consumers to make purchases. Marketers continue to direct personal selling efforts at marketing intermediaries in an attempt to expand distribution. As more competitors enter the marketplace, advertising begins to stress product differences to persuade consumers to purchase the firm's brand. In the maturity and early decline stages, firms frequently reduce advertising and sales promotion expenditures as market saturation is reached and newer items with their own competitive strengths begin to enter the market.

Price

The price of an item is the fourth factor that affects the choice of a promotional mix. Advertising dominates the promotional mixes for low-unit-value products due to the high per-contact costs in personal selling. Advertising permits a low promotional expenditure per sales unit because it reaches mass audiences. For low-value consumer goods, such as chewing gum, soft drinks, and snack foods, advertising is the most feasible means of promotion. Even shopping products can be sold at least partly on the basis of price. On the other hand, consumers of high-priced items such as luxury cars expect lots of well-presented information from qualified salespeople. High-tech direct marketing promotions such as video presentations on a laptop PC or via cell phone, fancy brochures, and personal selling by informed, professional salespeople appeal to these potential customers. Denny's held a giveaway to promote its breakfasts, as the chapter-opening vignette discusses.

Funds Available for Promotion

A real barrier in implementing any promotional strategy is the size of the promotional budget. A single 30-second television commercial during the Super Bowl telecast costs an advertiser between $2.5 and $2.8 million.[31] While millions of viewers may see the commercial, making the cost per contact relatively low, such an expenditure exceeds the entire promotional budgets of thousands of firms, a dilemma that at least partially explains how guerrilla marketing got its start. And if a company wants to hire a celebrity to advertise its goods and services, the fee can run into millions of dollars a year. Snowboarding phenomenon and Olympic gold medalist Shaun White earns about $7.5 million a year from companies like Target, Red Bull, and snowboard maker Burton. Earning about the same amount is South Korean figure-skating star Kim Yu-Na, also an Olympic gold medalist, whose sponsors include Hyundai Motor, Nike, Procter & Gamble, and Kookim Bank. Yu-Na has her own branded Samsung phone.[32] Table 15.3 summarizes the factors that influence the determination of an appropriate promotional mix.

Olympic gold medalist Shaun White earns millions per year advertising for various companies.

© NEWSCOM

table 15.3 Factors Influencing Choice of Promotional Mix

	Emphasis	
	Personal Selling	**Advertising**
Nature of the market		
Number of buyers	Limited number	Large number
Geographic concentration	Concentrated	Dispersed
Type of customer	Business purchaser	Ultimate consumer
Nature of the product		
Complexity	Custom-made, complex	Standardized
Service requirements	Considerable	Minimal
Type of good or service	Business	Consumer
Use of trade-ins	Trade-ins common	Trade-ins uncommon
Stage in the product life cycle	Often emphasized at every stage; heavy emphasis in the introductory and early growth stages in acquainting marketing intermediaries and potential consumers with the new good or service	Often emphasized at every stage; heavy emphasis in the latter part of the growth stage, as well as the maturity and early decline stages, to persuade consumers to select specific brands
Price	High unit value	Low unit value

assessment check

1. What are the five factors that affect the choice of a promotional mix?
2. Why is the choice of a mix a difficult task for marketers?

7 Contrast pushing and pulling strategies.

Pulling and Pushing Promotional Strategies

pulling strategy
Promotional effort by the seller to stimulate final-user demand, which then exerts pressure on the distribution channel.

pushing strategy
Promotional effort by the seller directed to members of the marketing channel rather than final users.

Marketers may implement essentially two promotional alternatives: a pulling strategy or a pushing strategy. A **pulling strategy** is a promotional effort by the seller to stimulate final-user demand, which then exerts pressure on the distribution channel. When marketing intermediaries stock a large number of competing products and exhibit little interest in any one of them, a firm may have to implement a pulling strategy to motivate them to handle its product. In such instances, this strategy is implemented with the objective of building demand so consumers will request the product from retail stores. Advertising and sales promotion often contribute to a company's pulling strategy.

In contrast, a **pushing strategy** relies more heavily on personal selling. Here the objective is promoting the product to the members of the marketing channel rather than to final users. To achieve this goal, marketers employ cooperative-advertising allowances to channel members, trade discounts, personal-selling efforts by salespeople, and other dealer supports. Such a strategy is designed to gain marketing success for the firm's merchandise by motivating representatives of wholesalers and retailers to spend extra time and effort promoting the products to customers. About half of manufacturers' promotional budgets are allocated for cash incentives used to encourage retailers to stock their products.

Timing also affects the choice of promotional strategies. The relative importance of advertising and selling changes during the various phases of the purchase process. Prior to the actual sale, advertising is usually more important than personal selling. However, one of the primary advantages of a successful advertising program is the support it gives the salesperson who approaches the prospective buyer for the first time. Selling activities are more important than advertising at the time of purchase. Personal selling provides the actual mechanism for closing most sales. In the postpurchase period, advertising regains primacy in the promotional effort. It affirms the customer's decision to buy a particular good or service and, as pointed out in Chapter 5, reminds him or her of the product's favorable qualities by reducing any cognitive dissonance that might occur.

The promotional strategies used by auto marketers illustrate this timing factor. Car, truck, and SUV makers spend heavily on consumer advertising to create awareness before consumers begin the purchase process. At the time of their purchase decisions, however, the personal-selling skills of dealer salespeople provide the most important tools for closing sales. Finally, advertising is used frequently to maintain postpurchase satisfaction by citing awards such as *Motor Trend*'s Car of the Year and results of J. D. Power's customer satisfaction surveys to affirm buyer decisions.

 assessment check

1. What is a pulling strategy?
2. What is a pushing strategy?

Budgeting for Promotional Strategy

Promotional budgets may differ not only in amount but also in composition. Business-to-business marketers generally invest larger proportions of their budgets in personal selling than in advertising, while the reverse usually is true of most producers of consumer goods.

Evidence suggests that sales initially lag behind promotional expenses for structural reasons—funds spent filling up retail shelves, boosting low initial production, and supplying buyer information. This fact produces a threshold effect in which few sales may result from substantial initial investments in promotion. A second phase might produce sales proportionate to promotional expenditures—the most predictable range. Finally, promotion reaches the area of diminishing returns, in which an increase in promotional spending fails to produce a corresponding increase in sales.

For example, an initial expenditure of $40,000 may result in sales of 100,000 units for a consumer-goods manufacturer. See Figure 15.2 for a display of this example. An additional $10,000 expenditure during the second phase may generate sales of 40,000 more units, and another $10,000 may produce sales of an additional 30,000 units. The cumulative effect of the expenditures and repeat sales will have generated increasing returns from the promotional outlays. However, as the advertising budget moves from $60,000 to $70,000, the marginal productivity of the additional expenditure may fall to 25,000 units. At some later point, the return may actually become zero or negative as competition intensifies, markets become saturated, and marketers employ less expensive advertising media.

The ideal method of allocating promotional funds would increase the budget until the cost of each additional increment equals the additional incremental revenue received. In other words,

8 Explain how marketers budget for and measure the effectiveness of promotion.

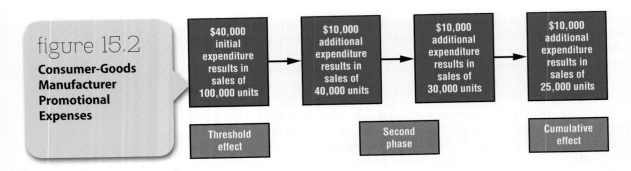

figure 15.2

Consumer-Goods Manufacturer Promotional Expenses

the most effective allocation procedure increases promotional expenditures until each dollar of promotional expense is matched by an additional dollar of profit. This procedure, referred to as *marginal analysis,* maximizes the input's productivity. The difficulty arises in identifying the optimal point, which requires a precise balance between marginal expenses for promotion and the resulting marginal receipts. In addition, as marketing communications become more integrated, it becomes harder to identify exact amounts that companies spend on individual elements of promotion.

Traditional methods used for creating a promotional budget include the percentage-of-sales and fixed-sum-per-unit methods, along with techniques for meeting the competition and achieving task objectives. Each method is briefly examined in Table 15.4.

The **percentage-of-sales method** is perhaps the most common way of establishing promotional budgets. The percentage can be based on sales either from some past period (such as the previous year) or forecasted for a future period (the current year). While this plan is appealingly simple, it does not effectively support the achievement of basic promotional objectives. Arbitrary percentage allocations can't provide needed flexibility. In addition, sales should depend on promotional allocation rather than vice versa.

The **fixed-sum-per-unit method** allocates a predetermined amount to each sales or production unit. This amount can also reflect either historical or forecasted figures. Producers of high-value consumer durable goods, such as automobiles, often use this budgeting method.

Another traditional budgeting approach, the **meeting competition method,** simply matches competitors' outlays, either in absolute amounts or relative to the firms' market shares. But this

percentage-of-sales method Method of promotional budgeting in which a dollar amount is based on a percentage of past or projected sales.

fixed-sum-per-unit method Method of promotional budgeting in which a predetermined amount is allocated to each sales or production unit.

meeting competition method Method of promotional budgeting that simply matches competitors' outlays.

table 15.4 Promotional Budget Determination

Method	Description	Example
Percentage-of-sales method	Promotional budget is set as a specified percentage of either past or forecasted sales.	"Last year we spent $1 million on promotion and had sales of $20 million. Next year we expect sales to grow to $30 million, so we are keeping our promotion allocation to 5 percent of expected sales, upping it to $1.5 million."
Fixed-sum-per-unit method	Promotional budget is set as a predetermined dollar amount for each unit sold or produced.	"Our forecast calls for sales of 14,000 units, and we allocate promotion at the rate of $65 per unit."
Meeting competition method	Promotional budget is set to match competitor's promotional outlays on either an absolute or relative basis.	"Promotional outlays average 4 percent of sales in our industry. We will match this percentage."
Task-objective method	Once marketers determine their specific promotional objectives, the amount (and type) of promotional spending needed to achieve them is determined.	"By the end of next year, we want 75 percent of the area high school students to be aware of our new, highly automated fast-food prototype outlet. How many promotional dollars will it take, and how should they be spent?"

method doesn't help a company gain a competitive edge. A budget appropriate for one company may not be appropriate for another.

The **task-objective method** develops a promotional budget based on a sound evaluation of the firm's promotional objectives. The method has two steps:

1. The firm's marketers must define realistic communication goals that they want the promotional mix to achieve. Say that a firm wants to achieve a 25 percent increase in brand awareness. This step quantifies the objectives that promotion should attain. These objectives in turn become integral parts of the promotional plan.

2. Then the company's marketers determine the amount and type of promotional activity required for each objective they have set. Combined, these units become the firm's promotional budget.

A crucial assumption underlies the task-objective approach: marketers can measure the productivity of each promotional dollar. That assumption explains why the objectives must be carefully chosen, quantified, and accomplished through promotional efforts. Generally, budgeters should avoid general marketing objectives such as, "We want to achieve a 5 percent increase in sales." A sale is a culmination of the effects of all elements of the marketing mix. A more appropriate promotional objective might be, "We want to achieve an 8 percent response rate from a targeted direct-mail advertisement."

Promotional budgeting always requires difficult decisions. Still, recent research studies and the spread of computer-based models have made it a more manageable problem than it used to be.

task-objective method
Development of a promotional budget based on evaluation of the firm's promotional objectives.

> **briefly speaking**

> "Half the money I spend on advertising is wasted; the trouble is, I don't know which half."
>
> —John Wanamaker
> *(1838–1922)*
> *U.S. retailer*

Measuring the Effectiveness of Promotion

Marketers know that part of a firm's promotional effort is ineffective. Evaluating the effectiveness of a promotion today is a far different exercise in marketing research than it was even a few decades ago. For years, marketers depended on store audits conducted by large organizations such as ACNielsen. Other research groups conducted warehouse withdrawal surveys of shipments to retail customers. These studies were designed to determine whether sales had risen as a direct result of a particular promotional campaign. During the 1980s, the introduction of scanners and automated checkout lanes completely changed marketing research. For the first time, retailers and manufacturers had a tool to obtain sales data quickly and efficiently. The problem was that the collected data were used for little else other than determining how much of which product was bought at what price and at what time.

By the 1990s, marketing research entered another evolutionary period with the advent of the Internet. Now marketing researchers can delve into each customer's purchase behavior, lifestyle, preferences, opinions, and buying habits. All this information can also be obtained in a matter of seconds. Consulting firm Accenture relies on computer modeling to perform "what if" analysis, helping its clients use *trade promotion management* to find out how best to spend their promotional budgets. The analysis breaks results down by customer segment, customer type, product brand, and type of promotion.[33] The next section explains the impact of electronic technologies on measuring promotional effectiveness. However, marketers today still depend on two basic measurement tools: direct sales results tests and indirect evaluations.

Most marketers would prefer to use a **direct sales results test** to measure the effectiveness of promotion. Such an approach would reveal the specific impact on sales revenues for each dollar of promotional spending. This type of technique has always eluded marketers, however, because of their inability to control other variables operating in the marketplace. A firm may receive $20 million in additional sales orders following a new $1.5 million advertising campaign, but the market success may really have resulted from the products' benefiting from more intensive distribution

direct sales results test Method for measuring promotional effectiveness based on the specific impact on sales revenues for each dollar of promotional spending.

as more stores decide to carry them or price increases for competing products rather than from the advertising outlays.

Marketers often encounter difficulty isolating the effects of promotion from those of other market elements and outside environmental variables. **Indirect evaluation** helps researchers concentrate on quantifiable indicators of effectiveness, such as recall—how much members of the target market remember about specific products or advertisements—and readership—size and composition of a message's audience. The basic problem with indirect measurement is the difficulty in relating these variables to sales. Will the fact that many people read an ad lead directly to increased sales?

Marketers need to ask the right questions and understand what they are measuring. Promotion to build sales volume produces measurable results in the form of short-term returns, but brand-building programs and efforts to generate or enhance consumers' perceptions of value in a product, brand, or organization cannot be measured over the short term.

Measuring Online Promotions

The latest challenge facing marketers is how to measure the effectiveness of electronic media. Early attempts at measuring online promotional effectiveness involved counting hits, user requests for a file, and visits, pages downloaded or read in one session. But as Chapter 4 explained, it takes more than counting "eyeballs" to measure online promotional success. What matters is not how many times a Web site is visited but how many people actually buy something. Traditional numbers that work for other media forms are not necessarily relevant indicators of effectiveness for a Web site. For one thing, the Web combines both advertising and direct marketing. Web pages effectively integrate advertising and other content, such as product information, that may often prove to be the page's main—and most effective—feature. For another consideration, consumers generally choose the advertisements they want to see on the Internet, whereas traditional broadcast or print media automatically expose consumers to ads.

One way marketers measure performance is by incorporating some form of direct response into their promotions. This technique also helps them compare different promotions for effectiveness and rely on facts rather than opinions. Consumers may say they will try a product when responding to a survey question yet not actually buy it. A firm may send out three different direct-mail offers in the same promotion and compare response rates from the groups of recipients receiving each alternative. An offer to send for a sample may generate a 75 percent response rate, coupons might show a 50 percent redemption rate, and rebates might appeal to only 10 percent of the targeted group.

The two major techniques for setting Internet advertising rates are cost per impression and cost per response. **Cost per impression** is a measurement technique that relates the cost of an ad to every thousand people who view it. In other words, anyone who sees the page containing the banner or other form of ad creates one impression. This measure assumes the site's principal purpose is to display the advertising message. **Cost per response** (or **click-throughs**) is a direct marketing technique that relates the cost of an ad to the number of people who click it. However, not everyone who clicks on an ad makes a purchase. So the **conversion rate** measurement was developed—the percentage of Web site visitors who actually make a purchase. All three rating techniques have merit. Site publishers point out that click-through rates are influenced by the creativity of the ad's message. Advertisers, on the other hand, point out that the Web ad has value to those who click it for additional information.

---

indirect evaluation
Method for measuring promotional effectiveness by concentrating on quantifiable indicators of effectiveness such as recall and readership.

cost per impression
Measurement technique that relates the cost of an ad to every thousand people who view it.

cost per response (or **click-through**) Direct marketing technique that relates the cost of an ad to the number of people who click it.

conversion rate
Percentage of visitors to a Web site who make a purchase.

---

 assessment check

1. What is the most common way of establishing a promotional budget?
2. What is the task-objective budgeting method? Describe its two steps.
3. What is the direct sales results test?
4. What is indirect evaluation?

The Value of Marketing Communications

The nature of marketing communications is changing as new formats transform the traditional idea of an advertisement or sales promotion. Sales messages are now placed subtly, or not so subtly, in movies and television shows, blurring the lines between promotion and entertainment and changing the traditional definition of advertising. Messages show up at the beach in the form of skywriting, in restrooms, on stadium turnstiles, on buses, and even on police cars.

Despite new tactics by advertisers, promotion often has been the target of criticism. Some people complain that it offers nothing of value to society and simply wastes resources. Others criticize promotion's role in encouraging consumers to buy unnecessary items they cannot afford. Many ads seem to insult people's intelligence or offend their sensibilities, and they criticize the ethics—or lack thereof—displayed by advertisers and salespeople.

New forms of promotion are considered even more insidious because marketers are designing promotions that bear little resemblance to paid advertisements. Many of these complaints cite issues that constitute real problems. Some salespeople use unethical sales tactics. Some product advertising hides its promotional nature or targets consumer groups that can least afford the advertised goods or services. Many television commercials contribute to the growing issue of cultural pollution. One area that has sparked both criticism and debate is promotion aimed at children.

While promotion can certainly be criticized on many counts, it also plays a crucial role in modern society. This point is best understood by examining the social, business, and economic importance of promotion.

Social Importance

We live in a diverse society characterized by consumer segments with differing needs, wants, and aspirations. What one group finds tasteless may be quite appealing to another. But diversity is one of the benefits of living in our society because it offers us many choices and opportunities. Promotional strategy faces an averaging problem that escapes many of its critics. The one generally accepted standard in a market society is freedom of choice for the consumer. Consumer buying decisions eventually determine acceptable practices in the marketplace.

Promotion has also become an important factor in campaigns aimed at achieving social objectives. Advertising agencies donate their expertise in creating **public service announcements (PSAs)** aimed at promoting such important causes as stopping drug abuse or supporting national parks.

9 Discuss the value of marketing communications.

public service announcement (PSA) Advertisement aimed at achieving socially oriented objectives by focusing on causes and charitable organizations that are included in print and electronic media without charge.

Marketing messages show up all over—in skywriting, in restrooms, and on buses.

40 MILLION NIKKOR LENSES ... AND COUNTING

RECORD BREAKER

D40X   D80   D300   D3   D90   D40

Nikon

© WALTER PIETSCH/ALAMY

The LetsMove initiative aims to raise awareness of childhood obesity and how to prevent it.

Let's raise a glass of milk to Michelle Obama's *Let's Move!* program.

First Lady Michelle Obama just unveiled the *Let's Move!* campaign to fight childhood obesity. The campaign aims to solve childhood obesity in a generation by helping families make healthier choices.

The program recommends small changes that add up. We were glad to hear that one of those changes includes drinking fat-free milk. Milk has nine essential nutrients to help kids be healthy. Eating right, drinking milk and being active for at least 60 minutes a day can help kids maintain a healthy weight. That's why we encourage kids to "fuel up to play 60."

Small changes like these, at home and in schools, can make a big difference.

So to the First Lady and First Mom, and to every mom, America's Milk Processors and Producers, together with the NFL, raise a glass to your efforts to build healthier, stronger families. Learn more at whymilk.com and fueluptoplay60.com

© AP IMAGES/PRNEWSFOTO/MILK PROCESSOR EDUCATION PROGRAM

The Ad Council coordinates a program to raise awareness of childhood obesity and how to prevent it, to complement the LetsMove initiative. The Council's public service announcements were created for free by Warner Bros. Consumer Products and Scholastic Media. They feature Looney Tunes' characters, pro quarterback Drew Brees (a Super Bowl MVP), two-time Olympic gold medalist Misty May Treanor, and skateboarder Tony Hawk, among others, and direct kids and families to the government Web site, www.letsmove.gov.[34]

Promotion performs an informative and educational task crucial to the functioning of modern society. As with everything else in life, what is important is how promotion is used rather than whether it is used.

Business Importance

Promotional strategy has become increasingly important to both large and small business enterprises. The well-documented, long-term increase in funds spent on promotion certainly attests to management's faith in the ability of promotional efforts to encourage attitude changes, brand loyalty, and additional sales. It is difficult to conceive of an enterprise that would not attempt to promote its offerings in some manner. Most modern institutions simply cannot survive in the long run without promotion. Business must communicate with its publics.

Nonbusiness enterprises also recognize the importance of promotional efforts. The U.S. Census helps determine the allocation of millions of dollars in federal funds and the distribution of seats in the House of Representatives, so it is not surprising that the Census Bureau budgeted $133 million (of a $340 million effort) to promote the most recent count. Ads in 28 languages urged citizens to mail back their Census questionnaires to avoid costly in-person follow-up.[35]

Economic Importance

Promotion has assumed a degree of economic importance because it provides employment for millions of people. More important, however, effective promotion has allowed society to derive benefits not otherwise available. For example, the criticism that promotion costs too much isolates an individual expense item and fails to consider its possible beneficial effects on other categories of expenditures.

Promotional strategies increase the number of units sold and permit economies of scale in the production process, thereby lowering the production costs for each unit of output. Lower unit costs allow lower consumer prices, which in turn make products available to more people. Similarly, advertising subsidizes the information content of newspapers and the broadcast media. In short, promotion pays for many of the enjoyable entertainment and educational opportunities in contemporary life as it lowers product costs.

briefly speaking

"Early to bed, early to rise, work like hell, and advertise."

—Laurence J. Peter
(1919–1990)
American author

 assessment check

1. Identify the three areas in which promotion exerts influence.

strategic implications
of marketing in the 21st century

With the incredible proliferation of promotional messages in the media, today's marketers—consumers themselves—must find new ways to reach customers without overloading them with unnecessary or unwanted communications. Guerrilla marketing has emerged as an effective strategy for large and small companies, but ambush marketing has raised ethical concerns. Product placement has gained popularity in movies, television shows, and video games.

In addition, it is difficult to overstate the impact of the Internet on the promotional mix of 21st-century marketers—for small and large companies alike. Even individual entrepreneurs find the

Internet to be a lucrative launchpad for their enterprises. But even though cyberspace marketing has been effective in business-to-business transactions and, to a lesser extent, for some types of consumer purchases, a major source of Internet revenues is advertising.

Integrating marketing communications into an overall consumer-focused strategy that meets a company's promotional and business objectives has become more and more critical in the busy global marketplace. Chapter 16 will examine specific ways marketers can use advertising and public relations to convey their messages; then Chapter 17 will discuss personal selling, sales force management, and sales promotion in the same manner.

Review of Chapter Objectives

 1 Explain how integrated marketing communications relates to the development of an optimal promotional mix

Integrated marketing communications (IMC) refers to the coordination of all promotional activities to produce a unified, customer-focused promotional message. Developing an optimal promotional mix involves selecting the personal and nonpersonal selling strategies that will work best to deliver the overall marketing message as defined by IMC.

 2 Describe the communication process and how it relates to the AIDA concept.

In the communication process, a message is encoded and transmitted through a communications channel; then it is decoded, or interpreted by the receiver; finally, the receiver provides feedback, which completes the system. The AIDA concept (attention, interest, desire, action) explains the steps through which a person reaches a purchase decision after being exposed to a promotional message. The marketer sends the promotional message, and the consumer receives and responds to it via the communication process. advances.

 3 Explain how the promotional mix relates to the objectives of promotion.

The objectives of promotion are to provide information, stimulate demand, differentiate a product, accentuate the value of a product, and stabilize sales. The promotional mix, which is the blend of numerous variables intended to satisfy the target market, must fulfill the overall objectives of promotion.

 4 Identify the different elements of the promotional mix, and explain how marketers develop an optimal promotional mix.

The different elements of the promotional mix are personal selling and nonpersonal selling (advertising, product placement, sales promotion, direct marketing, and public relations). Guerrilla marketing is frequently used by marketers with limited funds and firms attempting to attract attention for new-product offerings with innovative promotional approaches. Marketers develop the optimal mix by considering the nature of the market, the nature of the product, the stage in the product lifecycle, price, and funds available for promotion.

Describe the role of sponsorships and direct marketing in integrated marketing communications.

Sponsorship, which occurs when an organization provides money or in-kind resources to an event or activity in exchange for a direct association with the event or activity, has become a hot trend in promotion. The sponsor purchases access to an activity's audience and the image associated with the activity, both of which contribute to the overall promotional message delivered by a firm. Direct marketing involves direct communication between a seller and a B2B or final customer. It includes such promotional methods as telemarketing, direct mail, direct-response advertising and infomercials on TV and radio, direct-response print advertising, and electronic media.

 Discuss the factors that influence the effectiveness of a promotional mix.

Marketers face the challenge of determining the best mix of components for an overall promotional strategy. Several factors influence the effectiveness of the promotional mix: (1) the nature of the market, (2) the nature of the product, (3) the stage in the product lifecycle, (4) price, and (5) the funds available for promotion.

 Contrast pushing and pulling strategies.

In a pulling strategy, marketers attempt to stimulate final-user demand, which then exerts pressure on the distribution channel. In a pushing strategy, marketers attempt to promote the product to channel members rather than final users. To do this, they rely heavily on personal selling.

 Explain how marketers budget for and measure the effectiveness of promotion.

Marketers may choose among several methods for determining promotional budgets, including percentage-of-sales, fixed-sum-per-unit, meeting competition, or task-objective, which is considered the most flexible and most effective. Today, marketers use either direct sales results tests or indirect evaluation to measure effectiveness. Both methods have their benefits and drawbacks because of the difficulty of controlling variables.

 Discuss the value of marketing communications.

Despite a number of valid criticisms, marketing communications provide socially important messages, are important to businesses, and have economic importance. As with every communication in society, it is important to consider how promotion is used rather than whether it is used at all.

 ## Assessment Check: Answers

1.1 Define *promotion*. Promotion is the function of informing, persuading, and influencing the consumer's purchase decision.

1.2 What is the difference between marketing communications and integrated marketing communications (IMC)? Marketing communications are messages that deal with buyer–seller relationships, from a variety of media. IMC coordinates all promotional activities to produce a unified, customer-focused promotional message.

2.1 What are the three tasks accomplished by an effective message? An effective message gains the receiver's attention; it achieves understanding by both receiver and sender; and it stimulates the receiver's needs and suggests an appropriate method of satisfying them.

2.2 Identify the four steps of the AIDA concept. The four steps of the AIDA concept are attention, interest, desire, and action.

2.3 What is noise? Noise represents interference at some stage in the communication process.

3.1 What are the objectives of promotion? The objectives of promotion are to provide information to consumers and others, to increase demand, to differentiate a product, to accentuate a product's value, and to stabilize sales.

3.2 Why is product differentiation important to marketers? Product differentiation, distinguishing a good or service from its competitors, is important to marketers because they need to create a distinct image in consumers' minds. If they can do so, they can then exert more control over variables such as price.

4.1 Differentiate between personal selling and nonpersonal selling. Personal selling involves a promotional presentation conducted on a person-to-person basis with a buyer. Nonpersonal selling involves communication with a buyer in any way other than on a person-to-person basis.

4.2 What are the six major categories of nonpersonal selling? The six major categories of nonpersonal selling are advertising, product placement, sales promotion, direct marketing, public relations, and guerrilla marketing.

5.1 Define *sponsorship*. Sponsorship occurs when an organization pays money or in-kind resources to an event or activity in exchange for a direct association with that event or activity.

5.2 How is sponsorship different from advertising? Although sponsorship generates brand awareness, the sponsor has little control over the message or even the coverage, unlike advertising.

5.3 Define *direct mail*. Direct mail is communications in the form of letters, postcards, brochures, and catalogs containing marketing messages and sent directly to a customer or potential customer.

5.4 What are the benefits of electronic direct marketing? Electronic media deliver data instantly to direct marketers and help them track customer buying cycles quickly.

6.1 What are the five factors that affect the choice of a promotional mix? The five factors affecting the choice of a promotional mix are the nature of the market, the nature of the product, the stage in the product lifecycle, price, and the funds available for promotion.

6.2 Why is the choice of a mix a difficult task for marketers? The choice of a mix is difficult because no quantitative measures are available to determine the effectiveness of each component in a given market segment.

7.1 What is a pulling strategy? A pulling strategy is a promotional effort by the seller to stimulate final-user demand.

7.2 What is a pushing strategy? A pushing strategy is an effort to promote a product to the members of the marketing channel.

8.1 What is the most common way of establishing a promotional budget? The most common method of establishing a promotional budget is the percentage-of-sales method.

8.2 What is the task-objective budgeting method? Describe its two steps. The task-objective method develops a promotional budget based on an evaluation of the firm's promotional objectives. Its two steps are defining realistic communication goals and determining the amount and type of promotional activity required for each objective.

8.3 What is the direct sales results test? The direct sales results test reveals the specific impact on sales revenues for each dollar of promotional spending.

8.4 What is indirect evaluation? Indirect evaluation helps researchers concentrate on quantifiable indicators of effectiveness.

9.1 Identify the three areas in which promotion exerts influence. The three areas in which promotion exerts influence are society, business, and the economy.

Marketing Terms You Need to Know

promotion 488
marketing communications 488
integrated marketing
    communications (IMC) 488
sender 491
message 491
AIDA concept 491
encoding 492
decoding 492
feedback 492
noise 492
channel 492

primary demand 495
selective demand 497
product differentiation 497
promotional mix 499
personal selling 500
nonpersonal selling 500
advertising 500
product placement 500
sales promotion 501
trade promotion 501
direct marketing 501
public relations 502

publicity 502
guerrilla marketing 502
sponsorship 504
ambush marketing 505
direct mail 506
telemarketing 507
home shopping channel 508
infomercial 508
pulling strategy 512
pushing strategy 512
percentage-of-sales method 514
fixed-sum-per-unit method 514

meeting competition method 514
task-objective method 515
direct sales results test 515
indirect evaluation 516
cost per impression 516
cost per response (click-through)
    516
conversion rate 516
public service announcement
    (PSA) 517

Assurance of Learning Review

1. What is the role of integrated marketing communications (IMC) in a firm's overall marketing strategy? When executed well, what are its benefits?

2. Describe the five stages of communication.

3. What is the difference between primary demand and selective demand?

4. Differentiate between advertising and product placement. Which do you think is more effective, and why?

5. What are the benefits and drawbacks of publicity?

6. Why is sponsorship such an important part of a firm's IMC?

7. For each of the following goods and services, indicate which direct marketing channel or channels you think would be best:
   a. vacation time share
   b. denim jacket
   c. custom-made bracelet
   d. lawn-care service
   e. magazine subscription

8. How does the nature of the market for a firm's goods or services affect the choice of a promotion method?

9. What is the difference between a pushing strategy and a pulling strategy?

10. What are two major ways of setting Internet advertising rates, and how do they work?

Projects and Teamwork Exercises

1. Not-for-profit organizations rely on IMC just as much as for-profit firms do. The Egyptian government, which owns the remains and artifacts of boy pharaoh King Tutankhamun, has sent the King Tut collection on a worldwide tour of selected nations and museums. Many organizers—including *National Geographic* and museums such as the Los Angeles County Museum of Art—were involved in a multi-million-dollar marketing campaign promoting the exhibit, titled Tutankhamun and the Golden Age of the Pharaohs. On your own or with a classmate, conduct online research to learn how museums and other organizers have used IMC to promote this or other tours. Present your findings to the class.

2. On your own or with a classmate, select a print advertisement that catches your attention and analyze it according to the AIDA concept (attention, interest, desire, action). Identify features of the ad that catch your attention, pique your interest, make you desire the product, and spur you toward a purchase. Present your findings to the class.

3. Watch a television show and see how many products you can find placed within the show. Present your findings to the class.

4. With a classmate, choose a good or service you think could benefit from guerrilla marketing. Imagine you have a limited promotional budget, and come up with a plan for a guerrilla approach. Outline several ideas and explain how you plan to carry them out. Present your plan to the class.

5. Evaluate two or three pieces of direct mail you received recently. Which items caught your attention and perhaps made you save the mailing? Which items did you toss in the trash without even opening or considering beyond an initial glance? Why?

Critical-Thinking Exercises

1. Choose one of the following products and discuss what you think the objective(s) of promotion should be for the product:
   a. beef
   b. Kraft Macaroni & Cheese
   c. Ford Focus
   d. Verizon cell phone service

2. Identify a corporate sponsorship for a cause or program in your area, or find a local company that sponsors a local charity or other organization. What do you think the sponsor is gaining from its actions? Be specific. What does the sponsored organization receive? Do you think this sponsorship is good for your community? Explain.

3. What are some of the advantages and disadvantages of using a celebrity spokesperson to promote a good or service? How might this affect a firm's public relations efforts?

4. Take a careful look at a direct-mail catalog you have received recently. Who is the audience for the products? Did the firm target you correctly or not?

5. Describe a public service announcement you have seen recently. Do you believe the announcement will help the organization achieve its goals? Why or why not?

Ethics Exercise

Pop-up ads, those unsolicited messages that sometimes pop onto your computer screen and block the site or information you're looking for until you close or respond to them, are inexpensive to produce and cost nearly nothing to send. But they are so annoying to some computer users that dozens of special programs have been written to block them from appearing on the screen during Internet use.

1. Do you think that because they are unsolicited, pop-up ads are also intrusive? Are they an invasion of privacy? Explain your reasoning.

2. Do you consider the use of pop-up ads to be unethical? Why or why not?

Internet Exercises

1. **Pulling versus pushing strategies.** Review the material in the chapter on pulling and pushing strategies and go to the Web sites of Honda Motors and S.C. Johnson. Based on the Web sites, which firm appears to follow more of a pulling promotion strategy? Which firm follows more of a pushing promotional strategy? Be prepared to defend your answers.
   http://automobiles.honda.com
   http://www.scjohnson.com

2. **Product placements.** Visit the Web site listed here. It tracks product placements in movies. Review the material on the Web site and then answer the following questions:
   a. Which movies have had the largest number of product placements?

   b. Which brands have appeared most often?
   c. What are some of the benefits and risks to marketers of movie product placements?
   http://www.brandchannel.com/brandcameo_films.asp

3. **Public relations.** Visit the Web sites of at least three large, multinational corporations. Examples include Siemens, DuPont, and ExxonMobil. Review the material on the Web sites and prepare a brief report outlining how each firm includes public relations as part of its promotional strategy.

Note: Internet Web addresses change frequently. If you don't find the exact site listed, you may need to access the organization's home page and search from there or use a search engine such as Google or Bing.

Case 15.1 Google Wants to Dominate in Display Ads

While Google may be the premiere search engine of the Internet, it has lagged in its ability to earn revenue from display ads, a business that is expected to grow to almost $8 billion in the United States alone. Yahoo! has run in first place for some time, although

Google's acquisitions of ad-friendly YouTube and ad specialist DoubleClick were major investments the firm hoped would help it catch up in the display ad business.

Now, Google is drawing near its goal. Its display advertising business should soon be generating $1 billion in sales each year, according to industry analysts and the company's CEO. That will represent a 40 percent increase and will account for about 4 percent of Google's total annual sales. The revenue is expected to come mostly from about $700 million raised from video and banner ads on YouTube. "Display is now a key business for us," said Google's vice president of product management. "Our goal is to bring the science of search to the art of display," agrees the firm's executive in charge of display advertising.

The U.S. search advertising marketing is worth more than $11 billion a year, but its growth is slowing and Google already dominates this area. Online search ads have generally been cheaper than display ads, and their messages often inspire specific customer responses, such as clicking on a Web link or making a purchase. These concrete results make the effects of search advertising easy to measure and have sometimes kept advertisers away from the more expensive display business, which is typically effective for more general purposes such as raising brand awareness. But Internet firms that rely on ad revenue may be seeing a shift in that trend, as advertisers begin to switch their branding campaigns online from print and TV. "There's a lot of money to be tapped that otherwise would be allocated to TV that will be moved online," says one technology analyst.

That migration will be good news for Google in its drive to increase display advertising. The search firm is setting up new tools to attract more advertisers and offer concrete benefits for their ad dollars. It has purchased Teracent, for instance, a firm that customizes color, language, and other advertising elements according to the viewer's identity. Google hopes to leverage this capability with DoubleClick's skill in ad placement to help target messages better. Google will also use a tool called Campaign Insights to combine its own user database with advertisers' server logs and help advertisers better measure the effectiveness of their ads. "The consensus is the click is the wrong metric in display," says one digital ad agency CEO. One reason is that 8 percent of Web users account for about 85 percent of all clicks. Google hopes to help solve that problem. "This should help advertisers get the balance between search and display right because they will have a better understanding of any lift that results from their display campaigns," said Google's advertising product director.

Google will also expand the DoubleClick Ad Exchange, which it created to offer advertisers more options for buying and trading online ad display space. And it has purchased AdMob, a mobile ad network that could help it consolidate mobile display advertising, as it did for search. With this purchase, said Google's vice president of product management, "we see an opportunity to be able to work together to deliver faster and more innovative experiences to users and advertisers."

Questions for Critical Thinking

1. How do you think Google's expected dominance of the online display advertising market will affect marketers who already use the Internet for marketing communications? Will its push into this market attract any marketers who aren't currently using online marketing messages?

2. Do you think Google is investing enough in efforts to measure the effectiveness of online display ads? Are you ever influenced by these ads?

Sources: Douglas MacMilan, "Google's New Billion-Dollar Baby," *Bloomberg BusinessWeek,* February 22, 2010, p. 22; Douglas MacMilan, "Google's Display-Ad Sales Should Top $1 Billion," *BusinessWeek,* www.businessweek.com, February 8, 2010; Rita Chang, "Google Goes Buy-over-Build with AdMob," *Advertising Age,* www.adage.com, November 16, 2009; Michael Learmonth, "Search-Titan Google Makes Display Play with ROI Tool," *Advertising Age,* www.adage.com, October 19, 2009.

Video Case 15.2
Integrated Marketing Communications at Ogden Publications

Integrated marketing communications is all about consistency. For some companies, that's pretty simple—slap your logo on the press kit and you're good to go. For Ogden Publications of Tulsa, Oklahoma, it's a little more complicated. The small publishing house has 13 titles,

ranging from *Mother Earth News* and *Natural Home* to *Cappers,* a magazine about traditional American values and rural lifestyles, and everything from *Motorcycle Classics* to *Utne Reader,* a collection of articles about art, politics, and everything in between. In addition to its magazines, the company also offers merchandise and electronic companions to its titles.

It has been difficult to present an Ogden Publications "look," although brand manager Brandy Ernzen and Cherilyn Olmsted, Ogden's circulation and marketing director, consider this one of their many priorities as they take marketing at the company to the next level. "Each of the titles is so unique that they have their own brand identity," says Ernzen, but the common thread throughout all of Ogden's offerings is that "we tell people how to do really cool things." For Ernzen and Olmsted, the focus is on raising the bar on promotions, events, and ad sales as well as driving traffic to their

Web properties and increasing circulation and awareness for each magazine.

As brand manager, Ernzen leads the charge to help maintain the integrity of all the public relations and marketing efforts at Ogden. It has actually become a pretty big job in recent years. The do-it-yourself trend started about ten years ago and has been energized by the increasing interest in environmentally and socially conscious consumerism and green living. These trends have sparked tons of interest with the company's core audiences as well as a new, more mainstream, demographic, but Ernzen is cautious. "I work really closely with all the different editorial staffs as well as advertising and the media," she says. "You're making sure everyone on the different [marketing] teams is aware of what's going on." She is constantly running between the circulation department at *Herb Companion* and the book warehouse to ask about a new cookbook or gardening guide to identify opportunities for tie-ins. She might then look for a green event or seminar on exotic heirloom tomatoes to raise awareness for their magazines, books, and products. That triggers a press release and, before you know it, "you can really maximize what you're doing to get the most results," says Ernzen. "There are higher newsstand sales and people are buying that product because it is a full campaign."

Communicating with consumers is really only one part of Ernzen's job. "Internal communications is also a big part that a lot of people don't think about," she says. The company recently developed an electronic newsletter to let people know what's going on in the company. "That way, everybody's on the same page." Ogden is not publicly traded, yet, like publicly traded companies listed on the stock market, it must extend the same consistency in communications and messaging to investors and the regulatory agencies watching over the market.

As Ogden continues to develop each magazine's Web site, a whole new series of challenges await. The Web sites are really another product rather than a Web version of the print counterpart, and finding an appropriate mix of content, editorial voice, and design style consistent with the branding of the print magazine can be challenging. "We're trying to have fairly loose standards, right now," says Ernzen. "Start small and evolve." The first plan of attack is to nail down the design standards, including colors, fonts, and use of buttons, icons, and layout. A larger Ogden style manual and training session is in the works for the ad sales department, production, the rest of the marketing, and PR team so everyone will be working from the same standard. "Right now, I'm that person," says Ernzen, "who takes care of everything and makes sure everything is lined up like it should be in terms of what logos we're using and colors and the whole nine yards."

Questions

1. Come up with a single marketing and PR campaign to promote three or four of Ogden's magazines. Visit www.ogdenpubs.com to learn more about each title.

2. What are the challenges of maintaining a consistent look and feel across different media? What are the editorial and design differences between a Web magazine and a print one?

ch16

Advertising
and Public Relations

1 Identify the three major advertising objectives and the two basic categories of advertising.

2 List the major advertising strategies.

3 Describe the process of creating an advertisement.

4 Identify the major types of advertising appeals, and discuss their uses.

5 List and compare the major advertising media.

6 Outline the organization of the advertising function and the role of an advertising agency.

7 Explain the roles of cross-promotion, public relations, publicity, and ethics in an organization's promotional strategy.

8 Explain how marketers assess promotional effectiveness.

Snickers: "You're Not You When You're Hungry" ...

Snickers—the iconic nougat-, caramel-, and nut-laden candy bar—has a great "life story." Despite being introduced in America during the Great Depression, it rose to become the world's best-selling chocolate candy

bar. Today, it's a brand worth more than $2 billion.

And Snickers owes it all to a young man named Frank Mars who, during his convalescence from polio, learned the fine points of candy making from his mother in her Seattle kitchen. Mars began selling candy for a living, experiencing commercial success in 1923 with a candy bar he named Milky Way. In 1929, Mars moved the family business to Chicago to take advantage of the more central location and Chicago's excellent proximity to rail shipping. The following year, Mars introduced the Snickers bar—a treat named after the family's favorite horse—and priced it at five cents.

Perhaps because Snickers contained peanuts, advertising

initially positioned it as more of a food item than candy bar: a nutritious, high-quality snack that satisfies your hunger. Snickers' sales soon outpaced Milky Way's and, in spite of desperate economic times in the United States, Snickers became a runaway hit. Throughout the 1930s and into the 1940s, Snickers advertising continued to emphasize the peanuts. From 1949 to 1952, as the sponsor of "The Howdy Doody Show," one of early television's most popular children's programs, Snickers' popularity grew.

Mars concentrated on building market share for Snickers with advertising. Its most famous and longest-running campaign, "Packed with Peanuts, Snickers Satisfies," was created by the ad agency Ted Bates Worldwide and ran from 1979 to 1995.

As American consumers became more health-conscious and turned their focus to healthier food choices like granola and energy bars, Snickers has faced some challenges. However, the brand countered by reaching back to the market segment that viewed its first television commercials: baby boomers. Another campaign, "Snacklish," featured the highly recognizable Snickers logo and packaging, but with a play on the word "Snickers"—for example, a sign with the image of a Snickers bar atop a taxicab with the word "Snaxi" in place of "Snickers."

But Snickers' most famous advertising to date aired during Super Bowl XLIV. A spot titled "Game" showcases the talents of octogenarians Betty White and

© AP IMAGES/PRNEWSFOTO/MARS CHOCOLATE NORTH AMERICA

Abe Vigoda, two TV sitcom stars from the 1970s. Under the tagline "You're not you when you're hungry," White scrimmages with a group of 20-something guys before being tackled and landing on her back in a mud puddle. After taking a quick break to wolf down a Snickers bar, White morphs into a young man, his energy restored, who's ready to get back into the game. With a score of 8.68, the commercial won the *USA Today* Super Bowl Ad Meter competition, one of the most influential gauges of an ad's popularity.

For advertisers, the Super Bowl represents an annual sink-or-swim opportunity to showcase creative talent before a global audience recently estimated at more than 106 million viewers.

The Snickers commercial did not disappoint. Within only days after the Super Bowl, the ad went viral, then became a global sensation. Fans subsequently launched a Facebook campaign to persuade Lorne Michaels, producer of "Saturday Night Live," to engage Betty White as a guest host—an episode that garnered the show's highest ratings since 2008.[1]

evolution of a brand

From its introduction during an economic depression, the Snickers bar captured the hearts of consumers. Decades later, it endures—the world's most popular candy bar. Mars, Incorporated, used advertising to promote Snickers, making it a fixture in the everyday life of the American consumer. Now the company's flagship brand, Snickers is one of the most recognizable products around the globe.

- How did the original advertising—positioning Snickers as a food item rather than a candy— help build its popularity? Would that type of positioning be possible today? Why?

The recent Snickers commercial featured two elderly senior citizens playing football with a group of young men. In your opinion, did marketers take a risk with this humorous portrayal?

chapter overview

From the last chapter, you already know the nonpersonal elements of promotion include advertising and public relations. Thousands of organizations rely on nonpersonal selling to develop their promotional mixes and integrated marketing communications strategies. Advertising is the most visible form of nonpersonal promotion, as witnessed by the success of the Snickers bar, and marketers often use it together with sales promotion (discussed in the next chapter) to create effective promotional campaigns. Television is probably the most obvious medium for nonpersonal selling dollars. But marketers are becoming increasingly creative in identifying new or unusual media through which to deliver their messages. California-based Brand in the Hand enables advertisers to deliver their promotional messages on the beverage cups, cocktail napkins, and other consumables used aboard the flights of commercial airlines, where the ads will be seen by air travelers—an audience numbering 600 million in the United States alone.[2]

Other firms are banking on reaching consumers by beaming ads directly to their Bluetooth-enabled cell phones. Marketers hope the popularity of cell phones will help them reach younger consumers, who are spending less time with traditional advertising media such as television, newspapers, and magazines. RainedOut, the Virginia company that delivers text messaging to sports enthusiasts, includes advertising along with its alerts about game cancellations, field changes, and other related issues.[3] Still others are moving away from creating promotional Web sites for products and instead establishing communities for their products on Facebook and YouTube.[4]

Marketers seeking excitement for new-product launches—and the rejuvenation of older products—pay millions for celebrities to promote their products. MasterCard, Target, and T-Mobile feature celebrities like Eric Clapton and Nick Jonas and groups like the Black Eyed Peas and Pearl Jam in their recent ads. Cover Girl signed actress Drew Barrymore as its glamour spokesperson.[5]

This chapter begins with a discussion of the types of advertising and explains how advertising is used to achieve a firm's objectives. It then considers alternative advertising strategies and the process of creating an advertisement. Next, we provide a detailed look at various advertising media channels: television, radio, print advertising, direct mail, and outdoor and interactive media. The chapter then focuses on the importance of public relations, publicity, and cross-promotions. Alternative methods of measuring the effectiveness of both online and offline nonpersonal selling are examined. We conclude the chapter by exploring current ethical issues relating to nonpersonal selling.

Advertising

Advertising in the 21st century is closely linked to integrated marketing communications (IMC) in many respects. While IMC involves a message dealing with buyer–seller relationships, **advertising** consists of paid nonpersonal communication through various media with the purpose of informing or persuading members of a particular audience. Advertising is used by marketers to reach target markets with messages designed to appeal to business firms, not-for-profit organizations, or ultimate consumers.

The United States is home to many of the world's leading advertisers. AT&T, Procter & Gamble, and Verizon Communications top the list, each spending more than $3 billion annually on advertising.[6] Advertising spending varies among industries as well as companies. Automotive, personal care, food, and pharmaceuticals make up the top four industries, each spending more than $10 billion on advertising in a recent year.[7]

As discussed in previous chapters, the emergence of the marketing concept, with its emphasis on a companywide consumer orientation, boosted the importance of integrated marketing communications. This change, in turn, expanded the role of advertising. Today, a typical consumer is exposed to hundreds of advertising messages each day. Advertising provides an efficient, inexpensive, and fast method of reaching the ever-elusive, increasingly segmented consumer market.

Types of Advertising

Advertisements fall into two broad categories: product advertising and institutional advertising. **Product advertising** is nonpersonal selling of a particular good or service. This is the type of advertising the average person usually thinks of when talking about most promotional activities.

Institutional advertising, in contrast, promotes a concept, an idea, a philosophy, or the goodwill of an industry, company, organization, person, geographic location, or government agency. This term has a broader meaning than *corporate advertising* that typically is limited to advertising sponsored by a specific profit-seeking firm. Institutional advertising often is closely related to the public relations function.

Objectives of Advertising

Marketers use advertising messages to accomplish three primary objectives: to inform, to persuade, and to remind. These objectives may be used individually or, more typically, in conjunction with each other. For example, an ad for a not-for-profit agency may inform the public of the existence of the organization and at the same time persuade the audience to make a donation, join the organization, or attend a function.

Informative advertising seeks to develop initial demand for a good, service, organization, person, place, idea, or cause. The promotion of any new market entry tends to pursue this objective because marketing success at this stage often depends simply on announcing availability. Therefore,

advertising
Paid, nonpersonal communication through various media about a business firm, not-for-profit organization, product, or idea by a sponsor identified in a message intended to inform or persuade members of a particular audience.

product advertising
Nonpersonal selling of a particular good or service.

institutional advertising Promotion of a concept, an idea, a philosophy, or the goodwill of an industry, company, organization, person, geographic location, or government agency.

informative advertising Promotion that seeks to develop initial demand for a good, service, organization, person, place, idea, or cause.

YOU WORK ALL OVER. SHOULDN'T YOUR 3G?
PUT YOUR BUSINESS ON THE MAP.

verizon

© VERIZON WIRELESS

Verizon Communications tops the list of leading advertisers, spending more than $3 billion annually on advertising.

Product advertising, like this Aquafresh ad, is non-personal selling of a good or service.

COURTESY OF AQUAFRESH/GLAXOSMITHKLINE

informative advertising is common in the introductory stage of the product lifecycle, for Ford's new F-Series Super Duty trucks or for Sprint's money-back guarantee on service plans.[8]

Persuasive advertising attempts to increase demand for an existing good, service, organization, person, place, idea, or cause. Persuasive advertising is a competitive type of promotion suited to the growth stage and the early part of the maturity stage of the product lifecycle. In a change of pace, Procter & Gamble launched a persuasive campaign for Tide. Unlike previous ads that focused on Tide's ability to keep clothes clean, the new ads suggest that keeping your existing wardrobe clean is preferable to spending money on new clothes.[9]

Reminder advertising strives to reinforce previous promotional activity by keeping the name of a good, service, organization, person, place, idea, or cause before the public. It is common in the latter part of the maturity stage and throughout the decline stage of the product lifecycle. Striving, like other financial institutions, to rebound from the recent recession, Bank of America has partnered with the History Channel to sponsor "America: The Story of Us." Mini-documentaries about the bank will run during commercial breaks, showcasing its role in helping to build America over the years.[10]

Figure 16.1 illustrates the relationship between advertising objectives and the stages of the product lifecycle. Informative advertising tends to work best during the early stages, while reminder advertising is effective later on. Persuasive advertising, if done well, can be effective through the entire lifecycle.

Traditionally, marketers stated their advertising objectives as direct sales goals. A more current and realistic standard, however, views advertising as a way to achieve communications objectives—including informing, persuading, and reminding potential customers of the product. Advertising attempts to condition consumers to adopt favorable viewpoints toward a promotional message. The goal of an ad is to improve the likelihood that a customer will buy a particular good or service. In this sense, advertising illustrates the close relationship between marketing communications and promotional strategy.

persuasive advertising
Promotion that attempts to increase demand for an existing good, service, organization, person, place, idea, or cause.

reminder advertising
Advertising that reinforces previous promotional activity by keeping the name of a good, service, organization, person, place, idea, or cause before the public.

To get the best value for a firm's advertising investment, marketers must first determine a firm's advertising objectives. Effective advertising can enhance consumer perceptions of quality in a good or service, leading to increased customer loyalty, repeat purchases, and protection against price wars. In addition, perceptions of superiority pay off in the firm's ability to raise prices without losing market share.

figure 16.1

Advertising Objectives in Relation to Stage in the Product Lifecycle

Advertising Strategies

If the primary function of marketing is to bring buyers and sellers together, then advertising is the means to an end. Effective advertising strategies accomplish at least one of three tasks: informing, persuading, or reminding consumers. The secret to choosing the best strategy is developing a message that best positions a firm's product in the audience's mind. Among the advertising strategies available for use by 21st-century marketers are comparative advertising and celebrity advertising as well as decisions about global and interactive ads. Channel-oriented decisions, such as retail and cooperative advertising, can also be devised.

Marketers often combine several of these advertising strategies to ensure the advertisement accomplishes set objectives. As markets become more segmented, the need for personalized advertising increases. The next sections describe strategies that contemporary marketers may use to reach their target markets.

> **2** List the major advertising strategies.

Comparative Advertising

Firms whose products are not the leaders in their markets often favor **comparative advertising**, a promotional strategy that emphasizes advertising messages with direct or indirect comparisons to dominant brands in the industry. By contrast, advertising by market leaders seldom acknowledges that competing products even exist, and when they do, they do not point out any benefits of the competing brands.

Wireless telecommunications carriers have been battling it out in media advertising, promoting their calling plans and inviting comparison to competitors. Some offer "in" calling, free text messaging, no roaming charges, or extended hours at reduced rates to compete against similar offers from other companies.

A generation ago, comparative advertising was not the norm; in fact, it was frowned on. But the Federal Trade Commission now encourages comparative advertising. Regulators believe such ads keep marketers competitive and consumers better informed about their choices. Generally speaking, when competition through advertising exists, prices tend to go down because people can shop around. This benefit has proved increasingly true for online consumers, who now use shopping bots to help find the best prices on goods and services.

> **comparative advertising** strategy that emphasizes messages with direct or indirect promotional comparisons between competing brands.

Celebrity Testimonials

A popular technique for increasing advertising readership in a cluttered promotional environment and improving overall effectiveness of a marketing message involves the use of celebrity spokespeople, such as New York Giants quarterback Eli Manning. This type of advertising is also popular in foreign countries. In Japan, a majority of ads use celebrities, both local and international stars. Since the Winter Olympics in Vancouver, ads using medal winners, such as snowboarder Shaun White, have become popular.[11] However, it is important for companies to be sure their brand's tie to a celebrity makes sense and is genuine.

Both the number of celebrity ads and the dollars spent on those ads have increased in recent years. Professional athletes such as NBA star LeBron James are among the highest-paid product endorsers, raking in millions each year. In a recent year, James reportedly had about $170 million

> **briefly speaking**
>
> "As a profession advertising is young; as a force it is as old as the world. The first four words ever uttered, 'Let there be light,' constitute its charter. All nature is vibrant with its impulse."
>
> —Bruce Barton
> *(1886–1967)*
> *American author and advertising executive*

A popular technique for increasing advertising readership involves the use of celebrity spokespeople. Julia Roberts is a glamour spokesperson for Lancome.

IMAGE COURTESY OF THE ADVERTISING ARCHIVES

JULIA ROBERTS *for* LANCÔME PARIS

in endorsement deals with such firms as The Coca-Cola Company, McDonald's, Nike, and State Farm. With the exception of Nike, none of the others have anything to do with basketball.[12] In the top six superstars—in recent annual earnings from endorsements—are golfer Phil Mickelson, $53 million; racecar driver Dale Earnhardt Jr., $22 million; and NBA player Shaquille O'Neal, $15 million.[13]

One advantage of associations with big-name personalities is improved product recognition in a promotional environment filled with hundreds of competing 15- and 30-second commercials. Advertisers use the term *clutter* to describe this situation. As e-marketing continues to soar, one inevitable result has been the increase in advertising clutter as companies rush to market their goods and services online. But marketers need to remember that an effective online site must have meaningful content and helpful service.

Another advantage to using celebrities occurs when marketers try to reach consumers of various ethnic groups. Blockbuster Video and McDonald's have hired Hispanic stars to attract Hispanic consumers to their stores. Actress Daisy Fuentes appeared in ads for McDonald's, while John Leguizamo and Hector Elizondo advertised for Blockbuster.

A celebrity testimonial generally succeeds when the celebrity is a credible source of information for the promoted product. The most effective ads of this type establish relevant links between the celebrities and the advertised goods or services. Several studies of consumer responses show that celebrities improve the product's believability, recall of the product, and brand recognition. Celebrity endorsements also create positive attitudes, leading to greater brand equity. Olympic speedskater Apolo Ohno, the most decorated winter athlete in U.S. history, scored endorsement deals from a number of advertisers, including Alaska Airlines, The Coca-Cola Company, Omega watches, Vick's, and the Washington State Potato Commission.

Similarly, downhill skier Lindsey Vonn boasts a roster of sponsors that include Procter & Gamble, Red Bull, and Under Armour.[14]

However, a celebrity who endorses too many products may create marketplace confusion. Customers may remember the celebrity but not the product or brand; worse, they might connect the celebrity to a competing brand. Another problem arises if a celebrity is linked with scandal or encounters legal problems. After Tiger Woods' recent marital problems, several sponsors, including Accenture, AT&T, and Gatorade, severed their ties with him.[15]

Some advertisers try to avoid problems with celebrity endorsers by using cartoon characters as endorsers. The GEICO gecko, the cocky reptile with a Cockney accent, has been appearing in GEICO ads for years.[16] Some advertisers may actually prefer cartoon characters because the characters can never say anything negative about the product, they do exactly what the marketers want them to do, and they cannot get involved in scandals. The only drawback is high licensing fees; popular animated characters often cost more than live celebrities. Companies may create their own cartoon characters or talking animals, which eventually become celebrities in their own right as a result of many appearances in advertisements, as is the case with Duke the dog, who appears in ads for Bush's Baked Beans.

In recent years, marketers have begun to consider celebrities as marketing partners rather than pretty or famous faces who can sell goods and services. NHL star Sidney Crosby has marketing deals with Reebok, restaurant chain Tim Horton's, and Verizon, to name a few.[17] Former supermodel Claudia Schiffer not only agreed to endorse a signature line of Palm Pilots but also helped position the handheld computers in the electronics market by selecting fashionable colors and her own favorite software programs.

Retail Advertising

Most consumers are confronted daily with **retail advertising**, which includes all advertising by retail stores that sell goods or services directly to the consuming public.

Advertisers might avoid problems with celebrity endorsers by using cartoon characters as endorsers, such as the GEICO gecko.

© JEFF GREENBERG/ALAMY

While this activity accounts for a sizable portion of total annual advertising expenditures, retail advertising varies widely in its effectiveness. One study showed that consumers often respond with suspicion to retail price advertisements. Source, message, and shopping experience seem to affect consumer attitudes toward these advertisements.

An advertiser once quipped that the two most powerful words to use in an ad are "New" and "Free"—and these terms often are capitalized on in retail ads. Although "Free" may be featured only in discussions of customer services, the next best term—"Sale"—is often the centerpiece of retail promotions. And "New" typically describes new-product lines. However, many retail stores continue to view advertising as a secondary activity, although that is changing. Local independent retailers rarely use advertising agencies, probably because of the expense involved. Instead, store managers may accept responsibility for advertising in addition to their other duties. Management can begin to correct this problem by assigning one individual the sole responsibility and authority for developing an effective retail advertising program.

A retailer often shares advertising costs with a manufacturer or wholesaler in a technique called **cooperative advertising**. For example, an apparel marketer may pay a percentage of the cost of a retail store's newspaper advertisement featuring its product lines. Cooperative advertising campaigns originated to take advantage of the media's practice of offering lower rates to local advertisers than to national ones. Later, cooperative advertising became part of programs to improve dealer relations. The retailer likes the chance to secure advertising that it might not be able to afford otherwise. Cooperative advertising can strengthen vertical links in the marketing channel, as when a manufacturer and retailer coordinate their resources. It can also involve firms at the same level of the supply chain. In a horizontal arrangement, a group of retailers—for example, all the Ford dealers in a state—might pool their resources.

retail advertising Advertising by stores that sell goods or services directly to the consuming public.

cooperative advertising Strategy in which a retailer shares advertising costs with a manufacturer or wholesaler.

Interactive Advertising

interactive advertising Two-way promotional messages transmitted through communication channels that induce message recipients to participate actively in the promotional effort.

Millions of advertising messages float across idle—and active—computer screens in homes and offices around the country every day. Net surfers play games embedded with ads from the site sponsors. Companies offer free e-mail service to people willing to receive ads with their personal messages. Video screens on grocery carts display ads for shoppers to see as they wheel down the aisles of grocery stores.

Because marketers realize that two-way communications provide more effective methods for achieving promotional objectives, they are interested in interactive media. **Interactive advertising** involves two-way promotional messages transmitted through communication channels that induce message recipients to participate actively in the promotional effort. Achieving this involvement is the difficult task facing contemporary marketers. Although interactive advertising has become nearly synonymous with e-marketing and the Web, it also includes other formats such as kiosks in shopping malls and text messages on cell phones. Multimedia technology, the Internet, and commercial online services are changing the nature of advertising from a one-way, passive communication technique to more effective, two-way marketing communications. Interactive advertising creates dialogue between marketers and individual shoppers, providing more materials at the user's request. The advertiser's challenge is to gain and hold consumer interest in an environment where these individuals control what they want to see.

Interactive advertising changes the balance between marketers and consumers. Unlike the traditional role of advertising—providing brief, entertaining, attention-catching messages—interactive media provide information to help consumers throughout the purchase and consumption processes. In a sense, it becomes closer to personal selling as consumers receive immediate responses to questions or requests for more information about goods and services. Interactive advertising provides consumers with more information in less time to help them make necessary comparisons between available products.

Successful interactive advertising adds value by offering the viewer more than just product-related information. A Web site can do more than display an ad to promote a brand; it can create a company store, provide customer service, and offer additional content. And many marketers, at companies both large and small, hope such ads will soon be so finely targeted that they can cut through increasing advertising clutter and reach only consumers ready to hear their messages. In one survey, marketers learned that online video ads scored a 65 percent general recall with viewers, as compared with 46 percent for TV ads. Marketers theorize that the video ads scored better because there are fewer of them than TV ads—and viewers are more inclined to sit through online ads than TV commercials.[18]

Most firms deliver their interactive advertising messages through proprietary online services and through the Web. And online ad spending is climbing. At about $120 billion, spending for online advertised recently outpaced the total reportedly spent on print—$112 billion.[19]

 assessment check

1. What is comparative advertising?
2. What makes a successful celebrity testimonial?
3. What is cooperative advertising?

Creating an Advertisement

3 Describe the process of creating an advertisement.

Marketers spend an estimated $368 billion on advertising campaigns in the United States alone.[20] With so much money at stake, they must create effective, memorable ads that increase sales and enhance their organizations' images. They cannot afford to waste resources on mediocre messages that fail to capture consumers' attention; communicate their sales message effectively; or lead to a purchase, donation, or other positive action for the organization.

Research helps marketers create better ads by pinpointing goals an ad needs to accomplish, such as educating consumers about product features, enhancing brand loyalty, or improving consumer perception of the brand. These objectives should guide the design of the ad. Marketers can also discover what appeals to consumers and can test ads with potential buyers before committing funds for a campaign.

Marketers sometimes face specific challenges as they develop advertising objectives for services. They must find a creative way to fill out the intangible images of most services and successfully convey the benefits consumers receive. The "You're in Good Hands" message of Allstate Insurance is a classic example of how advertising can make the intangible nature of services tangible.

Translating Advertising Objectives into Advertising Plans

Once a company defines its objectives for an advertising campaign, it can develop its advertising plan. Marketing research helps managers make strategic decisions that guide choices in technical areas such as budgeting, copywriting, scheduling, and media selection. Posttests, discussed in greater detail later in the chapter, measure the effectiveness of advertising and form the basis for feedback concerning possible adjustments. The elements of advertising planning are shown in Figure 16.2. Experienced marketers know the importance of following even the most basic steps in the process, such as market analysis.

As Chapter 9 explained, positioning involves developing a marketing strategy that aims to achieve a desired position in a prospective buyer's mind. Marketers use a positioning strategy that distinguishes their good or service from those of competitors. Effective advertising then communicates the desired position by emphasizing certain product characteristics, such as performance attributes, price/quality, competitors' shortcomings, applications, user needs, and product classes.

advertising campaign Series of different but related ads that use a single theme and appear in different media within a specified time period.

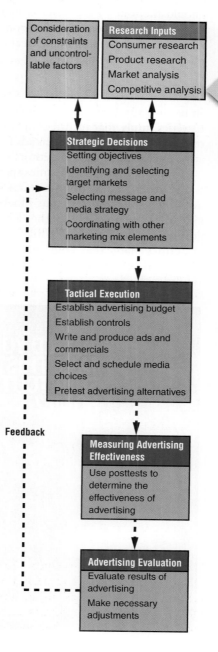

figure 16.2

Elements of the Advertising Planning Process

Advertising Messages

The strategy for creating a message starts with the benefits a product offers to potential customers and moves to the creative concept phase, in which marketers strive to bring an appropriate message to consumers using both visual and verbal components. Marketers work to create an ad with meaningful, believable, and distinctive appeals—one that stands out from the clutter and is more likely to escape "zapping" by the television remote control or clicking by a mouse.

Ads usually are created not individually, but as part of specific campaigns. An **advertising campaign** is a series of different but related ads that use a single theme and appear in different media within a specified time period. Retail chain Target's "Hello . . . Good Buy" ads featuring the Beatles' music is one example. Different products flash across the screen in the spots, but all have the catchy song playing in the background while the familiar red bull's-eye logo appears. In developing a creative strategy, advertisers must decide how to communicate their marketing message. They must balance message characteristics—such as the tone of the appeal, the extent of information provided, and the conclusion to which it leads the consumer—the side of the story the ad tells, and its emphasis on verbal or visual primary elements.

assessment check

1. What is an advertising campaign?
2. What are an advertisement's three main goals?

Advertising Appeals

Identify the major types of advertising appeals, and discuss their uses.

Should the tone of the advertisement focus on a practical appeal such as price or gas mileage, or should it evoke an emotional response by appealing to, say, fear, humor, sex, guilt, or fantasy? This is another critical decision in the creation of memorable ads that possess the strengths needed to accomplish promotional objectives.

FEAR APPEALS

In recent years, marketers have relied increasingly on fear appeals. Ads for insurance, autos, and even batteries imply that incorrect buying decisions could lead to property loss, injury, kidnapping, or other bad consequences. Even ads for business services imply that if a company doesn't purchase the advertised services, its competitors will move ahead or valuable information may be lost.[21]

Pharmaceutical companies spend several billion dollars a year on advertising, much of which is directed toward consumer fears—whether it's a fear of hair loss, allergic attacks, or heart attacks and other potentially serious illnesses. These drug advertisements have flourished in both print and broadcast media after the Food and Drug Administration lifted a ban on prescription drug advertising on television. While drug firms insist these advertisements are informative to consumers, critics charge that a high percentage use fear appeals and very few provide enough details about causes and risk factors for medical conditions or lifestyle changes that might bring about the same results as the drug.

In recent years, marketers have relied increasingly on fear appeals.

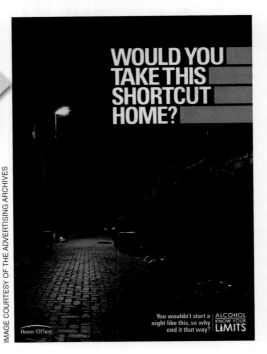

IMAGE COURTESY OF THE ADVERTISING ARCHIVES

Fear appeals can backfire, however. Viewers are likely to practice selective perception and tune out statements they perceive as too strong or not credible. Some consumer researchers believe viewer or reader backlash will eventually occur due to the amount of prescription drug advertising based on fear appeals.

HUMOR IN ADVERTISING MESSAGES

A humorous ad seeks to create a positive mood related to a firm's goods or services, but advertising professionals differ in their opinions of the ads' effectiveness. Some believe humor distracts attention from brand and product features; consumers remember the humor but not the product. Humorous ads, because they are so memorable, may lose their effectiveness sooner than ads with other kinds of appeals. In addition, humor can be tricky because what one group of consumers finds funny may not be funny at all to another group. Men and women sometimes have a different sense of humor, as do people of different ages. This distinction may become even greater across cultures.

ADS BASED ON SEX

Ads with sex-based appeals immediately attract the consumer's attention. Advertisements for Victoria's Secret lingerie and clothing are designed this way. While many people accept these and other ads, they do not appeal to everyone. And marketers using sex-based appeals know they walk a fine line between what is acceptable to the consumers they want to reach—and what is not. Sometimes, in fact, a firm's image can be hurt by its advertising approach. A recent ad campaign for Brazilian beer Debassa Bem Loura starring Paris Hilton has attracted the attention of the country's regulatory body, Conar, which is investigating reports that the ads are sexually provocative—even by Brazil's standards.[22]

Developing and Preparing Ads

The final step in the advertising process—the development and preparation of an advertisement—should flow logically from the promotional theme selected. This process should create an ad that becomes a complementary part of the marketing mix with a carefully determined role in the total marketing strategy. Preparation of an advertisement should emphasize features such as its creativity, its continuity with past advertisements, and possibly its association with other company products.

What immediate tasks should an advertisement accomplish? Regardless of the chosen target, an advertisement should (1) gain attention and interest, (2) inform or persuade, and (3) eventually lead to a purchase or other desired action. It should gain attention in a productive way; that is, it should instill some recall of the good or service. Otherwise, it will not lead to buying action.

Gaining attention and generating interest—cutting through the clutter—can be formidable tasks. Stimulating buying action is often difficult because an advertisement cannot actually close a sale. Nevertheless, if an ad gains attention and informs or persuades, it probably represents a worthwhile investment of marketing resources. Too many advertisers fail to suggest how audience members can purchase their products if they desire to do so. Creative design should eliminate this shortcoming.

The Cesar ad in Figure 16.3 shows the four major elements of this print advertisement: headline, illustration, body copy, and signature. *Headlines* and *illustrations* (photographs, drawings, or other artwork) should work together to generate interest and attention. *Body copy* informs, persuades, and stimulates buying action. The *signature,* which may include the company name, address, phone number, Web address, slogan, trademark, or simply a product photo, names the sponsoring organization. An ad may also have one or more headings subordinate to the main headline that either link the main headline to the body copy or subdivide sections of the body copy.

After advertisers conceive an idea for an ad that gains attention, informs and persuades, and stimulates purchases, their next step involves refining the thought sketch into a rough layout. Continued refinements of the rough layout eventually produce the final version of the advertisement design ready to be executed, printed, or recorded.

The creation of each advertisement in a campaign requires an evolutionary process that begins with an idea and ultimately results in a finished ad ready for distribution through print or electronic media. The idea itself must first be converted into a thought sketch—a tangible summary of the intended message. Advances in technology allow

Headline

Illustration

Body Copy

Signature

© IMAGE COURTESY OF THE ADVERTISING ARCHIVES

figure 16.3

Elements of a Typical Ad

advertisers to create novel, eye-catching advertisements. Innovative computer software packages allow artists to merge multiple images to create a single image with a natural, seamless appearance.

Creating Interactive Ads

Web surfers want engaging, lively content that takes advantage of the medium's capabilities and goes beyond what they find elsewhere. The Web's major advantages make it possible for advertisers to provide that, offering speed, information, two-way communications, self-directed entertainment, and personal choice. Web ads are also vibrant in their visual appeal, and some believe they will not experience the swings in spending that traditional ad media do.

Web ads have grown from information-based home pages to innovative, interactive channels for transmitting messages to cyberaudiences, including banners, pop-ups, keyword ads, advertorials, and interstitials. *Advergames* are either online games created by marketers to promote their products to targeted audiences in an interactive way or ads or product placements inserted into online video games. Automakers use these product placements to reach younger audiences—those who may not watch their TV commercials as often. To capitalize on the significant interest in World Cup soccer, PepsiCo International and Microsoft partnered to create an advergame campaign in which users move their avatars along a "game board" to unlock reward videos that they can share through instant messaging, e-mail, and social networks. The campaign, called "Football Hero" (outside the United States, soccer is known as football), is expected to run in 14 international markets, including Europe, South America, and the Middle East.[23]

Banners, advertisements on a Web page that link to an advertiser's site, are the most common type of advertising on the Web. They can be free of charge or cost thousands of dollars per month, depending on the amount of hits the site receives. Online advertisers often describe their Internet ads in terms of "richness," referring to the degree to which such technologies as streaming video, 3-D animation, JavaScript, video layers, and interactive capabilities are implemented in the banners.[24]

Banners have evolved into a more target-specific technique for Internet advertising with the advent of *missiles:* messages that appear on the screen at exactly the right moment. When a customer visits the site of Company A's competitor, a missile can be programmed to appear on the customer's monitor, allowing the customer to click a direct link to Company A's site. However, many people feel the use of such missiles is a questionable practice.

Keyword ads are an outcropping of banner ads. Used in search engines, keyword ads appear on the results page of a search and are specific to the searched term. Advertisers pay search engines to target their ads and display the banners only when users search for relevant keywords, allowing marketers to target specific audiences. For example, if a user searched for the term "digital camera," keyword ads might appear for electronic boutiques or camera shops that sell digital cameras and film.

Banner designs that have also evolved into larger advertising squares that closely resemble advertisements in the telephone book's Yellow Pages are called *advertorials.* Advertisers quickly expanded on these advertorials with *interstitials*—ads that appear between Web pages of related content. Interstitials appear in a separate browser window while the user waits for a Web page to download.

Then there are pop-ups—little advertising windows appearing in front of the top window of a user's computer screen—and "pop-unders" that appear under the top window. Many users complain that interstitials, like pop-ups and missiles, are intrusive and unwanted. Interstitials are more likely to contain large graphics and streaming presentations than banner ads and therefore are more difficult to ignore than typical banner ads. But despite complaints, some studies show that users are more likely to click interstitials than banners.

Perhaps the most intrusive form of online advertising is *adware,* which allows ads to be shown on users' screens via software downloaded to their computers without their consent or through trickery. Such software can be difficult to remove, and some industry experts believe that marketers should avoid dealing with Internet marketing firms that promote the use of adware.

Revenues for *social network advertising* on sites such as Facebook and MySpace are skyrocketing. In a recent year, firms spent an estimated $2.2 billion worldwide on this type of advertising—and the number is expected to grow. However, the very nature of the advertising makes it difficult to evaluate and measure its effectiveness. For example, if a virtual bottle of Coca-Cola appears on Facebook or in an online game, how likely is it that consumers will actually purchase Coke the next time they want something to drink?[25]

banner ads Strip messages placed in high-visibility areas of frequently visited Web sites.

✓ **assessment check**

1. What are some common emotional appeals used in advertising?

2. What are the main types of interactive ads?

Media Selection

One of the most important decisions in developing an advertising strategy is the selection of appropriate media to carry a firm's message to its audience. The media selected must be capable of accomplishing the communications objectives of informing, persuading, and reminding potential customers of the good, service, person, or idea advertised.

Research identifies the ad's target market to determine its size and characteristics. Advertisers then match the target characteristics with the media best able to reach that particular audience. The objective of media selection is to achieve adequate media coverage without advertising beyond the identifiable limits of the potential market. Finally, cost comparisons between alternatives should determine the best possible media purchase.

Table 16.1 compares the major advertising media by noting their shares of overall advertising expenditures. It also compares the advantages and disadvantages of each media alternative. *Broadcast media* include television (network and cable) and radio. Newspapers, magazines, outdoor advertising, and direct mail represent the major types of print media. Electronic media include the Internet and kiosks. A recent study projected that many firms will shift away from traditional advertising and more toward direct marketing—especially Internet and mobile media—in the next few years.

5 List and compare the major advertising media.

Television

Television—network and cable combined—still accounts for more than one of every three advertising dollars spent in the world.[27] The attractiveness of television advertising is that marketers can reach local and national markets. Whereas most newspaper advertising revenues come from local advertisers, the greatest share of television advertising revenues comes from organizations that advertise nationally. A newer trend in television advertising is virtual ads—banner-type logos and brief messages superimposed onto television coverage of sporting events so they seem to be a part of the arena's signage but cannot be seen by anyone attending the game. Then there are streaming headlines run by some news stations and paid for by corporate sponsors whose names and logos appear within the news stream.

Other trends in television advertising include the abbreviated spot—a 15- or 30-second ad that costs less to make and buy and is too quick for most viewers to zap with their remote control—and single-advertiser shows. These advertisements work well when viewers are watching live, but as more consumers record programs with DVRs, as many as 70 percent fast-forward through even the briefest commercials.[28]

Web sites that aggregate TV programming, like Hulu and Clicker, have become top video destinations on the Internet. There, viewers can watch complete, high-resolution episodes of current TV programs on their computers. The sites are free and do not require any additional wires or boxes for access. Instead, viewers see brief ads they seem to tolerate in order to watch their favorite shows. Hulu has added a new feature called Hulu Plus that, for a monthly fee, will allow viewers to watch a complete season of shows. In addition to episodes from more than 10,000 TV shows, Clicker's archive includes 20,000 movies and 80,000 music videos from 20,000 artists.[29]

In the past decade, cable television's share of ad spending and revenues has grown tremendously. Satellite television has contributed to increased cable penetration; almost three-fourths of all Americans now have cable installed in their homes. In response to declining ratings and soaring costs, network television companies such as NBC, CBS, ABC, FOX, and the CW (a network formed by the merger of the WB and UPN) are refocusing their advertising strategies with a heavy emphasis on moving onto the Internet to capture younger audiences.

table 16.1 Comparison of Advertising Media Alternatives

Media Outlet	Percentage of Total Spending*	Advantages	Disadvantages
Broadcast			
Broadcast television networks	18.8	Extensive coverage; repetition; flexibility; prestige	High cost; brief message; limited segmentation
Cable television networks	13.3	Same strengths as network TV; less market coverage because not every viewer is a cable subscriber	Same disadvantages as network TV, although cable TV ads are targeted to more-specific viewer segments
Radio	6.7	Immediacy; low cost; flexibility; segmented audience; mobility	Brief message; highly fragmented audience
Print			
Newspapers	17.7	Tailored to individual communities; ability to refer back to ads	Limited life
Direct mail	NA	Selectivity; intense coverage; speed; flexibility; opportunity to convey complete information; personalization	High cost; consumer resistance; dependence on effective mailing list
Magazines (consumer and business)	20.1	Selectivity; quality image reproduction; long life; prestige	Flexibility is limited
Outdoor (out of home)	2.8	Quick, visual communication of simple ideas; link to local goods and services; repetition	Brief exposure; environmental concerns
Electronic			
Internet	6.9	Two-way communications; flexibility; link to self-directed entertainment	Poor image reproduction; limited scheduling options; difficult to measure effectivenes

*Direct mail was not included in the data. In addition to broadcast network and cable TV advertising, syndicated TV totaled 3.1 percent and spot TV 10.7 percent of ad spending.

Source: Data from "U.S. Ad Spend Trends: 2008," *Advertising Age*'s Data Center, June 22, 2008, www.adage.com. Reprinted with permission from the June 22, 2008, issue of *Advertising Age*. Copyright © Crain Communications, Inc., 2010.

Because cable audiences have grown, programming has improved, and ratings risen, advertisers have earmarked more of their advertising budgets for this medium. Cable advertising offers marketers access to more narrowly defined target audiences than other broadcast media can provide—a characteristic referred to as *narrowcasting*. The great variety of special-interest channels devoted to subjects such as cooking, golf, history, home and garden, health, fitness, and various shopping channels attract specialized audiences and permit niche marketing.

Television advertising offers the advantages of mass coverage, powerful impact on viewers, repetition of messages, flexibility, and prestige. Its disadvantages include loss of control of the promotional message to the telecaster, which can influence its impact; high costs; and some public distrust. Compared with other media, television can suffer from lack of selectivity because specific TV programs may not reach consumers in a precisely defined target market without a significant degree

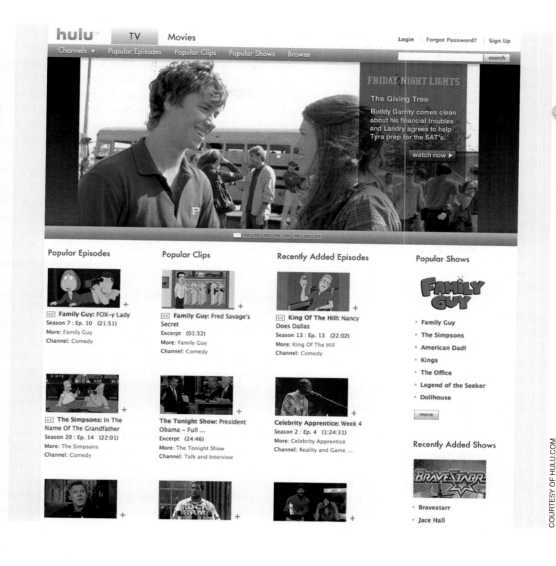

Hulu viewers can watch complete, high-resolution episodes of current TV programs. The only cost is time—to get to the show, they must watch brief ads. There is a charge for the new Hulu Plus. Hulu also has more than 40 distribution partnerships with video sites like Yahoo!, MSN, and Facebook, so people can watch Hulu videos in a number of places that are not Hulu.com.

of wasted coverage. However, the growing specialization of cable TV channels can help resolve the problem. Finally, some types of products are banned from television advertising. Tobacco goods, such as cigarettes, cigars, and smokeless tobacco, fall into this category.

With the high cost of television advertising, some companies seek cheaper alternatives, such as online blogs and print ads, for launch campaigns. When Kimberly-Clark recently introduced its Huggies Pure & Natural disposable diapers, it did so not on TV but on "mom blogs," where new parents research pregnancy and parenting topics. The campaign included ads in parenting magazines, along with offers for a free sample of the diapers.[30]

Television commercials can promote more than a firm's products; they can highlight the organization's efforts to address a crisis, repair a corporate reputation, and attempt to solidify customer loyalty. Toyota used TV commercials for all these reasons in the midst of its massive U.S. product recall, as described in the "Marketing Failure" feature.

Radio

Radio advertising has always been a popular media choice for up-to-the-minute newscasts and for targeting advertising messages to local audiences. But in recent years, radio has become one of the fastest-growing media alternatives. As more and more people find they have less and less time, radio provides immediate information and entertainment at work, at play, and in the car. In addition, as e-business continues to grow globally, more people are traveling abroad to seek out new markets. For these travelers, radio stations, including those aired over the Internet, are a means of staying in touch with home—wherever that may be. Marketers frequently use radio advertising to reach local audiences. But in recent years, it plays an increasingly important role as a national—and even global—listening favorite. Thousands of online listeners use the Internet to tune in to radio stations from almost every city—an easy-listening station in London, a top 40 Hong Kong broadcaster, or a chat show from Toronto. Other listeners equip their vehicles with satellite radio to maintain contact with hometown or destination stations during long trips.

Satellite radio offers much higher-quality digital signals than regular radio stations, with many more channels mostly free of Federal Communications Commission oversight as well as commercials. XM Radio, the first such service to be licensed, began airing commercials on a few of its nearly 200 music, sports, and talk channels. XM and its competitor, Sirius, both charged an annual subscription fee. When the two merged, they agreed initially to offer à la carte pricing, under which subscribers could select the programming they preferred. Fans of Blue Collar Comedy, Major League Baseball, the National Football League, and other popular programming could still get the shows they wanted.[31]

Advertisers like radio for its ability to reach people while they drive because they are a captive audience. Other benefits include low cost, flexibility, and mobility. Stations can adapt to local preferences by changing format, such as going from country and western to an all-news or sports station. The variety of stations allows advertisers to easily target audiences and tailor their messages to those listeners. Clear Channel Radio recently debuted a first-of-its-kind contextual ad platform, which permits national advertisers to match their ad to programming on Clear Channel stations. The platform enabled national advertiser Walmart to run a spot for the AC/DC "Black Ice" album, carried exclusively at Walmart stores, immediately after 106 Clear Channel rock stations across the country played an AC/DC song.[32]

Disadvantages to radio advertising include highly segmented audiences (reaching most people in a market may require ads placed on multiple stations), the temporary nature of messages (unlike print ads, radio and TV ads are instantaneous and must be broadcast again to reach consumers a second time), and a minimum of research information compared with television.

While most radio listening is often done in cars or with headset-equipped portables, technology has given birth to Internet radio. Webcast radio allows customers to widen their listening times

mktg: *failure*

Toyota Takes a Wrong Turn

Background. With its reputation for quality, Toyota Motor Corp. rose to become the world's largest automaker. Then came a growing rash of reports of jammed accelerator pedals, causing drivers of some Toyotas to lose control of their car and resulting in numerous injuries and 34 deaths.

The Challenge. For several days, Toyota leadership issued denials, claiming the

incidents were anecdotal, insisting there was nothing wrong with the cars, and blaming the problem on improperly installed floor mats. However, evidence piled up—some of it dating back to 2002—until what had first appeared to be a series of isolated car problems became the threat of a massive problem. The National Highway Traffic Safety Administration launched an investigation, and Toyota issued a recall.

The Outcome. Toyota recalled more than 9 million cars in four months, including some Prius and Lexus models for an unrelated brake problem, and suspended the sale of eight Toyota models. It ran full-page ads in major U.S. newspapers, alerting readers to the recall. CEO Akio Toyoda, grandson of the founder, testified before a U.S. Senate panel. Since then, Toyoda has issued an apology and the company has run

and choices through their computers. With an estimated weekly audience of 42 million people, online radio listenership continues to grow, and the potential for selling on this new channel is great. The HD Digital Radio Alliance, formed by Clear Channel Radio, CBS Radio, Citadel Broadcasting's ABC Radio, and seven other firms, offers a mobile marketing campaign.[33]

Newspapers

Newspaper advertising continues to dominate local markets, accounting for nearly 18 percent, or slightly more than $25 billion, of annual advertising expenditures.[34] In addition to retail advertisements, classified advertising is an important part of newspaper revenues. Although some predict the decline of newspaper audiences, when online readers are included in circulation figures, newspapers are as popular as ever. Most dailies and many weeklies have their own Web sites, which attract a monthly average of 74 million visitors, or 37 percent of all Internet users. Although newspaper advertising as a whole has decreased, activity on newspaper Web sites has increased, creating new opportunities for marketers.[35]

Newspapers' primary advantages start with flexibility because advertising can vary from one locality to the next. Newspapers also allow intensive coverage for ads. Readers sometimes keep the printed advertising message, unlike television or radio advertising messages, and can refer back to newspaper ads. Newspaper advertising does have some disadvantages: hasty reading and relatively poor reproduction quality, although that is changing as technology improves. The high quality of ads in *USA Today* is an example of the strides in newspaper ad quality made possible by new technologies.

Newspapers have also begun to struggle to "get through the noise" of other advertisers. To retain big advertisers such as trendy designers and national retailers, some have launched their own annual or semiannual fashion magazines, taking advantage of their finely tuned distribution capabilities.

Magazines

Advertisers divide magazines into two broad categories: consumer magazines and business magazines. These categories are also subdivided into monthly and weekly publications. The top five magazines in terms of circulation are *AARP The Magazine, AARP Bulletin, Reader's Digest, Better Homes and Gardens,* and *Good Housekeeping.*[36] The primary advantages of magazine advertising include the ability to reach precise target markets, quality reproduction, long life, and the prestige associated with some magazines, such as *National Geographic.* The primary disadvantage is that magazines lack the flexibility of newspapers, radio, and television.

TV ads with American employees, alluding indirectly to the problems without accepting blame, and asking consumers to trust Toyota again. To many, it's a case of "too little, too late."

Lesson Learned. It took Toyota decades to build its reputation as one of the world's most admired companies—but just a few months to come close to losing it. Ironically, the lean manufacturing process

that competitors emulated may have played a role in spreading the problem to other Toyota models, since the process typically involves using the same part in many models rather than a different part for each model. Meanwhile, only time will tell whether Toyota can fix the car problems—and regain the public's trust.

Sources: Bill Saporito, "Toyota Tangled," *Time,* February 22, 2010, 26–30; Tim Webb, Robert Booth, Justin McCurry, and Paul Harris, "How Did Toyota Veer So Far off Course?" *Guardian,* February 7, 2010, http://www.guardian.co.uk; Mayumi Negishi, "Toyota Grapples with PR Bungles, Tarnished Brand," *Reuters,* February 4, 2010, http://www.reuters.com; John Reed and Bernard Simon, "Toyota Recall Spreads to Europe," *CNN.com,* January 28, 2010, http://cnn.com.

Media buyers study circulation numbers and demographic information for various publications before choosing optimal placement opportunities and negotiating rates. The same advertising categories have claimed the title for big spenders for several years running. Automotive, retail, and movies and media advertising have held their first, second, and third places, respectively, each year and have continued to show strong growth percentages. Advertisers seeking to promote their products to target markets can reach them by advertising in the appropriate magazines.

Direct Mail

As discussed in Chapter 14, direct-mail advertising includes sales letters, postcards, leaflets, folders, booklets, catalogs, and house organs—periodicals published by organizations to cover internal issues. Its advantages come from direct mail's ability to segment large numbers of prospective customers into narrow market niches, speed, flexibility, detailed information, and personalization. Disadvantages of direct mail include high cost per reader, reliance on the quality of mailing lists, and some consumers' resistance to it.

The advantages of direct mail explain its widespread use. Data are available on previous purchase patterns and preferred payment methods as well as household characteristics such as number of children or seniors. Direct mail accounts for more than $45 billion of advertising spending annually.[37] The downside to direct mail is clutter, otherwise known as *junk mail*. So much advertising material is stuffed into people's mailboxes every day that the task of grabbing consumers' attention and evoking some interest is daunting to direct mail advertisers. Also, some consumers find direct mail annoying.

Outdoor Advertising

Outdoor advertising, sometimes called *out-of-home advertising,* is perhaps the oldest and simplest media business around. It represents 2.8 percent of total advertising spending.[38] Traditional outdoor advertising takes the form of billboards, painted displays such as those that appear on the walls of buildings, and electronic displays. Transit advertising includes ads placed both inside and outside buses, subway trains and stations, and commuter trains. Some firms place ads on the roofs of taxicabs, on bus stop shelters and benches, on entertainment and sporting event turnstiles, in public restrooms, and even on parking meters. A section of highway might be cleaned up by a local real estate company or restaurant, with a nearby sign indicating the firm's contribution. All these are forms of outdoor advertising.

Outdoor advertising quickly communicates simple ideas. It also offers repeated exposure to a message and strong promotion for locally available products. Outdoor advertising is particularly effective along metropolitan streets and in other high-traffic areas.

But outdoor advertising, just like every other type, is subject to clutter. It also suffers from the brevity of exposure to its messages by passing motorists. Driver concerns about rush-hour safety and limited time also combine to limit the length of exposure to outdoor messages. As a result, most of these ads use striking, simple illustrations, short selling points, and humor to attract people interested in products such as beverages, vacations, local entertainment, and lodging.

A third problem relates to public concerns over aesthetics. The Highway Beautification Act, for example, regulates the placement of outdoor advertising near interstate highways. In addition, many cities have local ordinances that set regulations on the size and placement of outdoor advertising messages, and Hawaii prohibits them altogether.

New technologies are helping revive outdoor advertising. Technology livens up the billboards themselves with animation, large sculptures, and laser images. Digital message signboards can display winning lottery numbers or other timely messages such as weather and traffic reports. Of the 450,000 billboards in the United States, about 2,000 are digitized and their numbers are growing. While safety advocates express concern that such billboards constitute a driving hazard, studies are under way to confirm that the high-tech signage poses no risk.[39]

Outdoor advertising, like electronic billboards, is particularly effective in high-traffic areas.

New uses are also helping to revive outdoor advertising. Organizations are using billboards to promote social causes. A recent national campaign used outdoor advertising to raise awareness of the H1N1 virus, promote proper hygiene, and encourage the public to get vaccinated.[40]

Interactive Media

Interactive media—especially the Internet—are growing up. Keyword ads dominate online advertising, accounting for more than 47 percent of annual online ad spending around the world.[41] Not surprisingly, interactive advertising budgets are beefing up at a growing number of companies.

As video and broadcast capabilities expand, advertising comes to cell phones in interesting ways. Mobile advertising revenues in the United States recently hit an estimated $2.6 billion and are expected to continue their explosive growth. Through an emerging technology known as *augmented reality*, virtual imaging can be incorporated into real-time video on a mobile phone, creating an exciting new experience for cell phone users.[42]

Other Advertising Media

As consumers filter out appeals from traditional and Internet ads, marketers need new ways to catch their attention. In addition to the major media, firms use a vast number of other vehicles to communicate their messages. One such device is Total Immersion's D'Fusion system, consisting of a kiosk, Web cameras, and software that can recognize, track, and render images on the screen. At the kiosk, customers can see themselves on a screen through the Webcam while holding up a two-dimensional brochure of an advertiser's product. The system transforms the picture into a three-dimensional image of the consumer with the product. Marketers believe this type of system increases an advertiser's engagement with the consumer in a new way.[43]

Ads also appear on T-shirts, inlaid in store flooring, in printed programs of live theater productions, and as previews on movie DVDs. Directory advertising includes the familiar Yellow Pages in telephone books, along with thousands of business directories. Some firms pay to have their

© TOTAL IMMERSION U.S.A. (DFUSION SOFTWARE, INC.)

Total Immersion's D'Fusion system allows customers to see themselves on a screen through a Webcam while holding up a two-dimensional brochure of an advertiser's product or a three-dimensional product.

advertising messages placed on hot-air balloons, blimps, banners behind airplanes, and scoreboards at sporting events. Individuals sometimes agree to paint their own vehicles with advertising messages or tattoo them onto their bodies—for a fee. Hot Jobs.com, Yahoo!, and Nokia are just some of the advertisers who pay to have their logos and company messages placed on autos via Autowrapped (www.autowrapped.com). The drivers are chosen based on their driving habits, routes, occupations, and living and working locations and are paid a monthly fee for the use of the outside of their vehicles as advertising space.[44]

Media Scheduling

media scheduling
Setting the timing and sequence for a series of advertisements.

Once advertisers have selected the media that best matches their advertising objectives and promotional budget, attention shifts to **media scheduling**—setting the timing and sequence for a series of advertisements. A variety of factors influence this decision—sales patterns, repurchase cycles, and competitors' activities are the most important variables.

Seasonal sales patterns are common in many industries. An airline might reduce advertising during peak travel periods and boost its media schedule during low travel months. Repurchase cycles may also play a role in media scheduling—products with shorter repurchase cycles will more likely require consistent media schedules throughout the year. Competitors' activities are still other influences on media scheduling. A small firm may avoid advertising during periods of heavy advertising by its rivals.

Advertisers use the concepts of reach, frequency, and gross rating points to measure the effectiveness of media scheduling plans. *Reach* refers to the number of different people or households exposed to an advertisement at least once during a certain time period, typically four weeks. *Frequency* refers to the number of times an individual is exposed to an advertisement during a certain time period. By multiplying reach times frequency, advertisers quantitatively describe the total weight of a media effort, which is called the campaign's *gross rating point (GRP)*.

Recently, marketers have questioned the effectiveness of reach and frequency to measure ad success online. The theory behind frequency is that the average advertising viewer needs a minimum of three exposures to a message to understand it and connect it to a specific brand. For Web surfers, the "wear-out" is much quicker—hence, the greater importance of building customer relationships through advertisements.

A media schedule is typically created in the following way. Say an auto manufacturer wants to advertise a new model designed primarily to appeal to professional consumers in their 30s. The model would be introduced in November with a direct-mail piece offering test drives. Outdoor, newspaper, and magazine advertising would support the direct-mail campaign but also follow through the winter and into the spring and summer. Early television commercials might air during a holiday television special in mid-December, and then one or more expensively produced, highly creative spots would be first aired during the Super Bowl in late January. Another television commercial—along with new print ads—might be scheduled for fall clearance sales as the manufacturer gets ready to introduce next year's models. This example illustrates how marketers might plan their advertising year for just one product.

assessment check

1. What types of products are banned from advertising on television?
2. What are some advantages radio offers to advertisers? What about newspapers?
3. Define *media scheduling,* and identify the most important factors influencing the scheduling decision.

Organization of the Advertising Function

Although the ultimate responsibility for advertising decision making often rests with top market-ing management, organizational arrangements for the advertising function vary among companies. A producer of a technical industrial product may operate with a one-person department within the company who primarily writes copy for submission to trade publications. A consumer-goods company, on the other hand, may staff a large department with advertising specialists.

The advertising function is usually organized as a staff department reporting to the vice president (or director) of marketing. The director of advertising is an executive position with the responsibility for the functional activity of advertising. This position requires not only a skilled and experienced advertiser but also an individual who communicates effectively within the organization. The success of a firm's promotional strategy depends on the advertising director's willingness and ability to commu-nicate both vertically and horizontally. The major tasks typically organized under advertising include advertising research, design, copywriting, media analysis, and, in some cases, sales and trade promotion.

6 Outline the organization of the advertising function and the role of an advertising agency.

Advertising Agencies

Most large companies in industries characterized by sizable advertising expenditures hire an inde-pendent **advertising agency,** a firm whose marketing specialists help businesses plan and prepare advertisements. Advertising is a huge, global industry. Ranked by worldwide revenue, the top five ad agencies are Dublin-based WPP, followed by Omnicom (New York), Publicis (Paris), Interpublic (New York), and Tokyo-based Dentsu.[45]

Most large advertisers cite several reasons for relying on agencies for at least some aspects of their advertising. Agencies typically employ highly qualified specialists who provide a degree of creativity and objectivity difficult to sustain in a corporate advertising department. Smaller firms find they can benefit from the knowledge and experience of specialists as well. In the extremely competitive advertising industry, Portland, Oregon–based Leopold Ketel & Partners (LKP) has emerged as one of the hottest agencies of this decade. In addition to creative services, LKP provides media planning and buying, interactive services, and public relations. Through its creative and strategic skills, it frequently edges out larger agencies for client business. LKP serves a wide-ranging clientele that includes Benchmade Knife, Friedrich Air Conditioning, KHMD-Radio, Oregon Coast Aquarium, Oregon Public Broadcasting, and Tillamook Cheese, among others.[46]

Figure 16.4 shows a hypothetical organization chart for a large advertising agency. Although job titles may vary among agencies, the major functions may be classified as creative services; account services; marketing services, including media services, marketing research, and sales pro-motion; and finance and management. Whatever organization structure it selects, an agency often stands or falls on its relationships with its clients. The fast pace and pressure of ad agencies are legendary, but good communication remains paramount to maintaining that relationship.

advertising agency Firm whose marketing specialists help advertisers plan and prepare advertisements.

assessment check

1. What is the role of an advertising agency?
2. What are some advantages of using an agency?

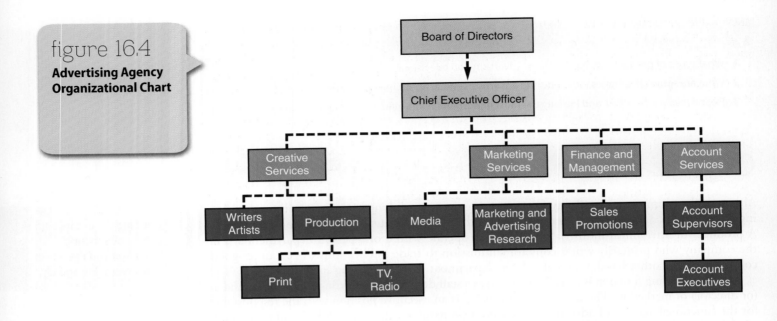

figure 16.4
Advertising Agency Organizational Chart

Public Relations

7 **Explain the roles of cross-promotion, public relations, publicity, and ethics in an organization's promotional strategy.**

In Chapter 15, we defined public relations as the firm's communications and relationships with its various publics, including customers, employees, stockholders, suppliers, government agencies, and the society in which it operates. Organizational public relations efforts date back to 1889, when George Westinghouse hired two people to publicize the advantages of alternating-current electricity and to refute arguments originally championed by Thomas Edison for direct-current systems.

Public relations is an efficient, indirect communications channel through which a firm can promote products, although it serves broader objectives than those of other components of promotional strategy. It is concerned with the prestige and image of all parts of the organization. Today, public relations plays a larger role than ever within the promotional mix, and it may emphasize more marketing-oriented information. In addition to its traditional activities, such as surveying public attitudes and creating a good corporate image, PR also supports advertising in promoting the organization's goods and services.

Although there are about 57,000 public relations managers in the United States, nearly 200,000 people actually work in the public relations field for both profit-centered and not-for-profit organizations.[47] Public relations is in a period of major growth as a result of increased public pressure on industries regarding corporate ethical conduct and environmental and international issues. International expenditures on public relations are growing more rapidly than those for advertising and sales promotion. Many top executives are becoming more involved in public relations as well. The public expects top managers to take greater responsibility for company actions than they have accepted in the past. Those who refuse are widely criticized.

The PR department is the link between the firm and the media. It provides press releases and holds news conferences to announce new products, the formation of strategic alliances, management changes, financial results, or similar developments. The PR department may also issue its own publications, including newsletters, brochures, and reports. The PR staff at the Four Seasons Hotel in Las Vegas promoted its Daycation Spa with online press releases describing the spa's services and encouraging visitors to use the services.[48]

A PR plan begins much like an advertising plan, with research to define the role and scope of the firm's overall public relations and current challenges. Next come strategic decisions on short-term and long-term goals and markets, analysis of product features, and choices of messages and media channels—or other PR strategies such as speaking engagements or contests—for each market. Plan execution involves developing messages highlighting the benefits the firm brings to each market. The final step is to measure results. The Internet has changed some PR planning, as PR representatives now have more direct access to the public instead of having their messages filtered through journalists and the news media. This direct access gives them greater control over their messages.

PR professionals at Frito-Lay North America recently created a full-scale campaign to help its SunChips multigrain snacks brand introduce the world's first 100 percent compostable chip bag. The multifaceted campaign included details of a national education effort to help consumers lead a greener, more eco-friendly lifestyle. SunChips revealed its new bag in the form of a 25- by 40-foot billboard representation, crafted of hundreds of compostable tiles during a presentation in Los Angeles. The demonstration to show how the chip bags are compostable was recorded to be included with the online nationwide education campaign. The rollout of the new SunChips bag was designed to coincide with the 40th anniversary of Earth Day, April 22.[49]

Marketing and Nonmarketing Public Relations

Nonmarketing public relations refers to a company's messages about general management issues. When a company makes a decision that affects any of its publics, input from public relations specialists can help smooth its dealings with those publics. A company that decides to close a plant would need advice on how to deal with the local community, while a firm dealing with a long strike might try to achieve a favorable attitude from the public. Either of these situations might be considered a crisis, as would a massive product recall. Companies that have a plan of action and can effectively handle a crisis by generating positive public relations generally can survive these types of crises, as discussed in the "Career Readiness" feature. Although companies typically organize their public relations departments separately from their marketing divisions, PR activities invariably affect promotional strategies.

In contrast, **marketing public relations (MPR)** refers to narrowly focused public relations activities that directly support marketing goals. MPR involves an organization's relationships with consumers or other groups about marketing concerns and can be either proactive or reactive.

With proactive MPR, the marketer takes the initiative and seeks out opportunities for promoting the firm's products, often including distribution of press releases and feature articles. For example, companies send press releases about new products to newspapers; television stations; and relevant consumer, business, and trade publications. It is a powerful marketing tool because it adds news coverage that reinforces direct promotion activities.

Reactive MPR responds to an external situation that has potential negative consequences for an organization. As Toyota's reputation began to slide in the wake of serious accelerator problems and subsequent massive car recalls, the automaker directed its advertising agency, Saatchi & Saatchi LA, to pull its national "Portfolio" campaign from the media. The campaign had emphasized quality. In addition, Toyota hired the PR firm of Robinson Lerer & Montgomery to help deal with the growing crisis.[50]

Publicity

The aspect of public relations most directly related to promoting a firm's products is **publicity**: nonpersonal stimulation of demand for a good, service, place, idea, person, or organization by unpaid placement of significant news regarding the product in a print or broadcast medium. It has been said that if advertising is the hammer, publicity is the nail. It creates credibility for the advertising to follow. Firms generate publicity by creating special events, holding press conferences, and preparing news releases and media kits. Many firms, such as Starbucks and Sam's Club, built their brands with virtually no advertising. Primary Wave Music, one of the largest

nonmarketing public relations Organizational messages about general management issues.

marketing public relations (MPR) Narrowly focused public relations activities that directly support marketing goals.

publicity Nonpersonal stimulation of demand for a good, service, place, idea, person, or organization by unpaid placement of significant news regarding the product in a print or broadcast medium.

Primary Wave Music has teamed up with Motel 6 on their "Rock Yourself to Sleep" campaign, providing touring bands the chance to win six week of free lodgings.

music publishing and marketing companies in the United States, has teamed up with Motel 6 on their "Rock Yourself to Sleep" campaign. Targeting touring bands, the campaign offers a chance to win six weeks of free lodging at more than 1,000 Motel 6 locations while groups are on the road. Bands compete for the freebie by submitting a song. Contestants' songs are posted online, and six winners are chosen by fans' online voting. Providing publicity for both the advertisers and the competing bands, the campaign generated so much buzz that Primary Wave and Motel 6 relaunched it a second year.[51]

While publicity generates minimal costs compared with other forms of promotion, it does not deliver its message entirely for free. Publicity-related expenses include the costs of employing marketing personnel assigned to create and submit publicity releases, printing and mailing costs, and related expenses.

Firms often pursue publicity to promote their images or viewpoints. Other publicity efforts involve organizational activities such as plant expansions, mergers and acquisitions, management changes, and research breakthroughs. A significant amount of publicity, however, provides information about goods and services, particularly new products.

Because many consumers consider news stories to be more credible than advertisements as sources of information, publicity releases often are sent to media editors for possible inclusion in news stories. The media audiences perceive the news as coming from the communications media, not the sponsors. The information in a publicity release about a new good or service can provide valuable assistance for a television, newspaper, or magazine writer, leading to eventual broadcast or publication. Publicity releases sometimes fill voids in publications, and at other times, they become part of regular features. In either case, they offer firms valuable supplements to paid advertising messages.

Unfortunately, not every item of publicity is positive for a firm. Because a company cannot control the news that surrounds its decisions and actions, sometimes negative publicity creates poor images in consumers' minds. Airline travel, once regarded as an exciting adventure, has now become more of a chore. And as the airline industry struggles to survive increased costs, many carriers have cut flights, raised fares, and added all sorts of fees. The result has been much bad publicity.

How to Handle a Business Crisis

All organizations face crises during their lifetime. While most crises are relatively small—missing a deadline, arriving late to a client meeting—some are genuinely massive in scale. Recalls of food and products—like spinach with salmonella or Shrek drinking glasses with toxic paint—or revelations of unethical investment practices create real public relations crises for individual firms as well as entire industries. But crises can be managed effectively. Here are a few tips for handling a business crisis:

- *Have a plan.* Establish a plan for dealing with crises before one ever arises. Appoint key people to communicate and lead.

- *Pay attention.* If a bad situation seems to be unfolding, don't ignore it. Get the facts and implement your plan.

- *Move promptly.* A crisis is not like a storm that will blow over if you wait. Letting too much time elapse causes the public to think you're stonewalling.

- *Communicate.* You will probably have to communicate several times during the crisis and afterward. Be direct and concise. Provide necessary information and show concern and empathy for those affected. Do not point fingers or speculate. Reassure listeners that communication will continue.

- *Apologize if appropriate.* If you or your firm has made a mistake, acknowledge it. Apologize and then focus on solutions.

- *Find solutions.* Work with colleagues, customers, or others in the industry, if necessary, to correct the problem. This may mean devising both an immediate and a long-term solution.

- *Follow through.* Any promises made during this time must be kept. If your firm says it will replace all defective products with new ones, for example, do so.

- *Learn from your mistakes.* A business crisis is costly. Once it's passed, it's important for your organization to reflect on what happened and take steps to assure it doesn't recur.

Sources: "Business Crisis Management: Handling a Work-Place Crisis," *MoneyInstructor.com*, http://www.moneyinsructor.com, accessed June 9, 2010; "Crisis Management," *Encyclopedia of Small Business*, http://www.enotes.com, accessed June 9, 2010; "Some Simple Advice on Crisis Management," *Value Based Management.net*, http://www.valuebasedmanagement.net, accessed June 9, 2010; William Neuman, "McDonald's Offers Cash in Recall of Shrek Glasses," *The New York Times*, June 8, 2010, http://www.nytimes.com; "Produce Co. Issues Voluntary Spinach Recall," *KSBW.com*, June 4, 2010, http://www.ksbw.com.

Cross-Promotion

In recent years, marketers have begun to combine their promotional efforts for related products using a technique called **cross-promotion**, in which marketing partners share the cost of a promotional campaign that meets their mutual needs—an important benefit in an environment of rising media costs. Relationship marketing strategies such as comarketing and cobranding, discussed in Chapter 10, are forms of cross-promotion. Marketers realize these joint efforts between established brands provide greater benefits in return for both organizations; investments of time and money on such promotions will become increasingly important to many partners' growth prospects. Recently, Coldplay's "Viva la Vida" album was cross-promoted with Apple's iTunes Web site.

cross-promotion
Promotional technique in which marketing partners share the cost of a promotional campaign that meets their mutual needs.

assessment check

1. Distinguish between marketing public relations and nonmarketing public relations.

2. What is publicity?

3. What are the advantages of cross-promotion?

Measuring Promotional Effectiveness

Each element of the promotional mix represents a major expenditure for a firm. Although promotional prices vary widely, advertisers typically pay a fee based on the cost to deliver the message to viewers, listeners, or readers—the so-called *cost per thousand impressions (CPM)*. Billboards are the cheapest way to spend advertising dollars, with television and some newspapers the most expensive. But while price is an important factor in media selection, it is by no means the only one—or all ads would appear on billboards.

Because promotion represents such a major expenditure for many firms, they need to determine whether their campaigns accomplish appropriate promotional objectives. Companies want their advertising agencies and in-house marketing personnel to demonstrate how promotional programs contribute to increased sales and profits. Marketers are well aware of the number of advertising messages and sales promotions consumers encounter daily, and they know these people practice selective perception and simply screen out many messages.

By measuring promotional effectiveness, organizations can evaluate different strategies, prevent mistakes before spending money on specific programs, and improve their promotional programs. As the earlier discussion of promotional planning explained, any evaluation program starts with objectives and goals; otherwise, marketers have no yardstick against which to measure effectiveness. However, determining whether an advertising message has achieved its intended objective is one of the most difficult undertakings in marketing. Sales promotions and direct marketing are somewhat easier to evaluate because they evoke measurable consumer responses. Like advertising, public relations is also difficult to assess on purely objective terms.

Measuring Advertising Effectiveness

Measures to evaluate the effectiveness of advertising, although difficult and costly, are essential parts of any marketing plan. Without an assessment strategy, marketers will not know whether their advertising achieves the objectives of the marketing plan or whether the dollars in the advertising budget are well spent. To answer these questions, marketers can conduct two types of research. **Media research** assesses how well a particular medium delivers the advertiser's message, where and when to place the advertisement, and the size of the audience. Buyers of broadcast time base their purchases on estimated Nielsen rating points, and the networks have to make good if ratings do not reach promised levels. Buyers of print advertising space pay fees based on circulation. Circulation figures are independently certified by specialized research firms.

The other major category, **message research**, tests consumer reactions to an advertisement's creative message. Pretesting and posttesting, the two methods for performing message research, are discussed in the following sections.

As the role of marketing expands in many organizations, marketers are employing increasingly sophisticated techniques to measure marketing effectiveness not only throughout the company but through the entire marketing channel. As more firms also conduct multichannel promotional efforts, keeping track of the data is a challenge. However, when they do so, they can better track which channels are most effective.[52]

PRETESTING

To assess an advertisement's likely effectiveness before it actually appears in the chosen medium, marketers often conduct **pretesting**. The obvious advantage of this technique is the opportunity to evaluate ads when they are being developed. Marketers can conduct a number of different pretests, beginning during the concept phase in the campaign's earliest stages, when they have only rough copy of the ad, and continuing until the ad layout and design are almost completed.

Pretesting employs a variety of evaluation methods. For example, focus groups can discuss their reactions to mock-ups of ads using different themes, headlines, or illustrations. To screen potential radio and television advertisements, marketers often recruit consumers to sit in a studio and indicate their preferences by pressing two buttons, one for a positive reaction to the commercial and the other for a negative reaction. Sometimes proposed ad copy is printed on a postcard that also offers a free

media research Advertising research that assesses how well a particular medium delivers an advertiser's message, where and when to place the advertisement, and the size of the audience.

message research Advertising research that tests consumer reactions to an advertisement's creative message.

pretesting Research that evaluates an ad during its development stage.

product; the number of cards returned represents an indication of the copy's effectiveness. *Blind product tests* are also frequently used. In these tests, people are asked to select unidentified products on the basis of available advertising copy.

Mechanical and electronic devices offer yet another method of assessing how people read advertising copy. One mechanical test uses a hidden camera to photograph eye movements of readers. The results help advertisers determine headline placement and copy length. Another mechanical approach measures the galvanic skin response—changes in the electrical resistance of the skin produced by emotional reactions. Audiobrain creates unique sounds that helps advertisers brand their products; when consumers hear the sound—whether it's a tune, a voice, a bird call, a drop of rain, or another sound—they automatically think of the brand. McDonald's tests some of Audiobrain's created sounds in different restaurants to evoke different moods, then evaluates how those sound-created moods affect customers. If they are successful, the sounds become a part of in-store advertising.[53]

POSTTESTING

Posttesting assesses advertising copy after it has appeared in the appropriate medium. Pretesting generally is a more desirable measurement method than posttesting because it can save the cost of placing ineffective ads. However, posttesting can help in planning future advertisements and in adjusting current advertising programs.

In one of the most popular posttests, the *Starch Readership Report* interviews people who have read selected magazines to determine whether they observed various ads in them. A copy of the magazine is used as an interviewing aid, and each interviewer starts at a different point in the magazine. For larger ads, respondents are also asked about specifics, such as headlines and copy. Figure 16.5 shows a magazine advertisement with its Starch scores. All such *readership tests*, also called recognition tests, assume that future sales are related to advertising readership.

Unaided recall tests are another method of posttesting the effectiveness of advertisements. Respondents do not see copies of the magazine after their initial reading but are asked to recall the ads from memory. Podcasts are fast becoming a popular medium for advertisers because posttests reveal that unaided recall among respondents is high. A recent Edison Research survey of consumer attitudes toward podcast advertising revealed that nearly 80 percent of respondents prefer to buy products advertised on podcasts and hold a positive opinion of companies that advertise on podcasts.[54]

posttesting   Research that assesses advertising effectiveness after it has appeared in a print or broadcast medium.

"Noted %" indicates the percentage of readers interviewed who saw any part of the advertisement. 64% noted this ad.

"Associated %" indicates the percentage of readers interviewed who saw any part of the ad that indicates the brand or advertiser. 62% associated this ad with Chevrolet.

"Read Most %" indicates the percentage of readers interviewed who read more than half of the body copy. 22% read most of this ad.

"Read Some %" indicates the percentage of readers interviewed who read any amount of the body copy. 61% read some of this ad.

© GENERAL MOTORS CORP. USED WITH PERMISSION, GM MEDIA ARCHIVES.

figure 16.5

Magazine Advertisement with Starch Scores

554

Inquiry tests are another popular form of posttest. Advertisements sometimes offer gifts—generally product samples—to people who respond to them. The number of inquiries relative to the advertisement's cost forms a measure of its effectiveness.

Split runs allow advertisers to test two or more ads at the same time. Although advertisers traditionally place different versions in newspapers and magazines, split runs on cable television systems frequently test the effectiveness of TV ads. With this method, advertisers divide the cable TV audience or a publication's subscribers in two; half view advertisement A and the other half view advertisement B. The relative effectiveness of the alternatives is then determined through inquiries or recall and recognition tests.

Regardless of the exact method they choose, marketers must realize that pretesting and posttesting are expensive efforts. As a result, they must plan to use these techniques as effectively as possible.

split runs Methods of testing alternate ads by dividing a cable TV audience or a publication's subscribers in two, using two different ads, and then evaluating the relative effectiveness of each.

Measuring Public Relations Effectiveness

As with other forms of marketing communications, organizations must measure PR results based on their objectives both for the PR program as a whole and for specific activities. In the next step, marketers must decide what they want to measure. This choice includes determining whether the message was heard by the target audience and whether it had the desired influence on public opinion.

The simplest and least costly level of assessment measures outputs of the PR program: whether the target audience received, paid attention to, understood, and retained the messages directed to them. To make this judgment, the staff could count the number of media placements and gauge the extent of media coverage. They could count attendees at any press conference, evaluate the quality of brochures and other materials, and pursue similar activities. Formal techniques include tracking publicity placements, analyzing how favorably their contents portrayed the company, and conducting public-opinion polls.

To analyze PR effectiveness more deeply, a firm could conduct focus groups, interviews with opinion leaders, and more detailed and extensive opinion polls. The highest level of effectiveness measurement looks at outcomes: did the PR program change people's opinions, attitudes, and behavior? PR professionals measure these outcomes through before-and-after polls (similar to pretesting and posttesting) and more advanced techniques such as psychographic analysis (discussed in Chapter 5).

Evaluating Interactive Media

Marketers employ several methods to measure how many users view Web advertisements: *hits* (user requests for a file), *impressions* (the number of times a viewer sees an ad), and *click-throughs* (when the user clicks the ad to get more information). *View-through* rates measure responses over time. However, some of these measures can be misleading. Because each page, graphic, or multimedia file equals one hit, simple interactions can easily inflate the hit count, making it less accurate. To increase effectiveness, advertisers must give viewers who click through their site something good to see. Successful Web campaigns use demonstrations, promotions, coupons, and interactive features.

Internet marketers price ad banners based on cost per thousand (CPM). Web sites that sell advertising typically guarantee a certain number of impressions—the number of times an ad banner is downloaded and presumably seen by visitors. Marketers then set a rate based on that guarantee times the CPM rate.

assessment check

1. What is CPM, and how is it measured?

2. Distinguish between media research and message research.

3. Describe several research techniques used in posttesting.

Ethics in Nonpersonal Selling

Chapter 3 introduced the topic of marketing ethics and noted that promotion is the element in the marketing mix that raises the most ethical questions. People actively debate the question of whether marketing communications contribute to better lives. The final section of this chapter takes a closer look at ethical concerns in advertising and public relations.

Advertising Ethics

Even though ads promoting alcohol, targeting children, and touting prescription drugs are technically legal, these types of promotions raise ethical issues. In the case of advertising aimed at children, when it comes to influencing parents' purchase decisions, nothing beats influencing kids. By promoting goods and services directly to children, firms can sell not only to them but to the rest of the household, too. However, as the feature "Solving an Ethical Controversy" points out, many parents and consumer advocates question the ethics of promoting directly to children. Their argument: at a time when kids need to learn how to consume thoughtfully, they are inundated with promotional messages teaching the opposite.

Another issue is the insertion of product messages in media programs without full disclosure of the marketing relationship to audiences. To woo younger consumers, especially teens and those in their 20s, advertisers attempt to make these messages appear as different from advertisements as possible; they design ads that seem more like entertainment.

The Food and Drug Administration recently cited an ad campaign for pain and anxiety relief drug Cymbalta as misleading. The agency accused the drug's manufacturer, Eli Lilly & Co., of omitting and minimizing risk information about the drug in the ads. In fact, says the FDA, the company also overstated the drug's ability to treat fibromyalgia, a chronic pain condition. They implied in the ad that more than half of the treated patients would find a 30 percent improvement, but the FDA insists there are no data to support those statements. [55]

In cyberspace ads, it is often difficult to separate advertising from editorial content because many sites resemble magazine and newspaper ads or television infomercials. Another ethical issue surrounding advertising online is the use of **cookies**, small text files automatically downloaded to a user's computer whenever a site is visited. Each time the user returns to that site, the site's server accesses the cookie and gathers information: What site was visited last? How long did the user stay? What was the next site visited? Marketers claim this device helps them determine consumer preferences and argue that cookies are stored in the user's PC, not the company's Web site. The problem is that cookies can and do collect personal information without the user's knowledge.

PUFFERY AND DECEPTION

Puffery refers to exaggerated claims of a product's superiority or the use of subjective or vague statements that may not be literally true. A company might advertise the "most advanced system" or claim that its product is "most effective" in accomplishing its purpose.

Exaggeration in ads is not new. Consumers seem to accept advertisers' tendencies to stretch the truth in their efforts to distinguish their products and get consumers to buy. This inclination may provide one reason that advertising does not encourage purchase behavior as successfully as sales promotions do. A tendency toward puffery does raise some ethical questions, though: Where is the line between claims that attract attention and those that provide implied guarantees? To what degree do advertisers deliberately make misleading statements?

The *Uniform Commercial Code* standardizes sales and business practices throughout the United States. It makes a distinction between puffery and any specific or quantifiable statement about product quality or performance that constitutes an "express warranty," which obligates the company to stand behind its claim. Boasts of product superiority and vague claims are puffery, not warranties. They are considered so self-praising or exaggerated that the average consumer would not rely on them to make a buying decision.

cookies Techniques for collecting information about online Web site visitors in which small text files are automatically downloaded to a user's computer to gather such data as length of visit and the site visited next.

puffery Exaggerated claims of a product's superiority, or the use of subjective or vague statements that may not be literally true.

Should the Government Curb Advertising That Targets Children?

Marketers of goods and services designed for children have always targeted at least some of their advertising to the end users. However, once television programming began to be developed for children, the amount and intensity grew. In addition, over the years, the practice of using TV as a "babysitter" became increasingly common, with TV advertising to children even more pervasive. Child advocacy groups, the Better Business Bureau, and the Federal Trade Commission have prevailed on marketers and the advertising industry to be more responsible for their activities. In 2006, marketers who accounted for 80 percent of TV food ads agreed not to market to children under 12 unless their product met a minimum nutritional standard. To some observers, that commitment to self-regulate has failed.

Should the government curb advertising that targets children?

PRO

1. Because of their age, children are easily manipulated and unduly influenced by advertising and need to be protected.

2. Research on advertising to children reveals that children who watch TV ads consume more calories, particularly those of the low-nutrient foods typically advertised on TV. The link to childhood obesity is clear.

CON

1. Government regulation of TV advertising to children is a freedom of speech issue and goes to the heart of our free-enterprise system.

2. Only parents can parent—and that includes monitoring their children's TV viewing.

Summary

Historically, the FTC has been reluctant to impose measures on companies that advertise to children. However, it recently observed that advertisers could do much more to self-regulate. Continuing pressure from consumer groups will likely have some influence on the FTC, who says it intends to "continue to monitor" the issue.

Sources: Jane E. Brody, "Risks for Youths Who Eat What They Watch," *The New York Times,* April 19, 2010, http://www.nytimes.com; John Eggerton, "FTC Asks for More Media Self-Regulation on Children's TV Protections," *Broadcasting & Cable,* April 12, 2010, http://www.broadcstingcable.com; Stephanie Clifford, "A Fine Line When Ads and Children Mix," *The New York Times,* February 15, 2010, http://www.nytimes.com.

A quantifiable statement, on the other hand, implies a certain level of performance. For example, tests can establish the validity of a claim that a brand of long-life light bulbs outlasts three regular light bulbs.

Ethics in Public Relations

Several public relations issues open organizations to criticism. Various PR firms perform services for the tobacco industry; publicity campaigns defend unsafe products. Also, marketers must weigh ethics before they respond to negative publicity. For example, do firms admit to problems or product deficiencies, or do they try to cover them up? It should be noted that PR practitioners violate the Public Relations Society of America's Code of Professional Standards if they promote products or causes widely known to be harmful to others.

strategic
implications → f t 🛒
of marketing in the 21st century

s greater portions of corporate ad budgets continue to migrate to the Web, marketers must be increasingly aware of the benefits and pitfalls of Internet advertising. But they should not forget the benefits of other types of advertising as well.

Promotion industry experts agree that e-business broadens marketers' job tasks, though many promotional objectives still remain the same. Today, advertisers need 75 different ways to market their products in 75 countries in the world and innumerable market segments. In years to come, advertisers also agree that channels will become more homogeneous while markets become more fragmented.

Review of Chapter Objectives

 Identify the three major advertising objectives and the two basic categories of advertising.

The three major objectives of advertising are to inform, to persuade, and to remind. The two major categories of advertising are product advertising and institutional advertising. Product advertising involves the nonpersonal selling of a good or service. Institutional advertising is the nonpersonal promotion of a concept, idea, or philosophy of a company or organization.

2 List the major advertising strategies.

The major strategies are comparative advertising, which makes extensive use of messages with direct comparisons between competing brands; celebrity, which uses famous spokespeople to boost an advertising message; retail, which includes all advertising by retail stores selling products directly to consumers; and interactive, which encourages two-way communication either via the Internet or kiosks.

 Describe the process of creating an advertisement.

An advertisement evolves from pinpointing goals, such as educating consumers, enhancing brand loyalty, or improving a

product's image. From those goals, marketers move to the next stages: creating a plan, developing a message, developing and preparing the ad, and selecting the appropriate medium (or media). Advertisements often appeal to consumers' emotions, such as fear or humor.

 Identify the major types of advertising appeals, and discuss their uses.

Sometimes, emotional appeals to fear, humor, sex, guilt, or fantasy can be effective. However, marketers need to recognize that fear appeals can backfire; people's sense of humor can differ according to sex, age, and other factors; and use of sexual imagery must not overstep the bounds of taste.

 List and compare the major advertising media.

The major media include broadcast (television and radio), newspapers and magazines, direct mail, outdoor, and interactive. Each medium has benefits and drawbacks. Newspapers are flexible and dominate local markets. Magazines can target niche markets. Interactive media encourage two-way communication. Outdoor advertising in a high-traffic location reaches many people every day; television and radio reach even more. Direct mail allows effective segmentation.

Outline the organization of the advertising function and the role of an advertising agency.

Within a firm, the advertising department is usually a group that reports to a marketing executive. Advertising departments generally include research, art and design, copywriting, and media analysis. Outside advertising agencies assist and support the advertising efforts of firms. These specialists are usually organized by creative services, account services, marketing services, and finance.

Explain the roles of cross-promotion, public relations, publicity, and ethics in an organization's promotional strategy.

Cross-promotion, illustrated by tie-ins between popular movies and fast-food restaurants, permits marketing partners to share the cost of a promotional campaign that meets their mutual needs. Public relations consists of the firm's communications and relationships with its various publics, including customers, employees, stockholders, suppliers, government, and the society

in which it operates. Publicity is the dissemination of newsworthy information about a product or organization. This information activity is frequently used in new-product introductions. Although publicity is welcomed by firms, negative publicity is easily created when a company enters a gray ethical area with the use of its promotional efforts. Therefore, marketers should be careful to construct ethically sound promotional campaigns, avoiding such practices as puffery and deceit. In addition, negative publicity may occur as a result of some action a firm takes—or fails to take, such as a product recall.

Explain how marketers assess promotional effectiveness.

The effectiveness of advertising can be measured by both pretesting and posttesting. Pretesting is the assessment of an ad's effectiveness before it is actually used. It includes such methods as sales conviction tests and blind product tests. Posttesting is the assessment of the ad's effectiveness after it has been used. Commonly used posttests include readership tests, unaided recall tests, inquiry tests, and split runs.

 ## Assessment Check: Answers

1.1 What are the goals of institutional advertising? Institutional advertising promotes a concept, an idea, a philosophy, or the goodwill of an industry, company, organization, person, geographic location, or government agency.

1.2 At what stage in the product lifecycle are informative ads used? Informative ads are common in the introductory stage of the product lifecycle.

1.3 What is reminder advertising? Reminder advertising strives to reinforce previous promotional activity by keeping the name of a good, service, organization, person, place, idea, or cause before the public.

2.1 What is comparative advertising? Comparative advertising makes extensive use of messages with direct comparisons between competing brands.

2.2 What makes a successful celebrity testimonial? Successful celebrity ads feature figures who are credible sources of information for the promoted product.

2.3 What is cooperative advertising? Cooperative advertising is advertising whose costs a retailer shares with a manufacturer or wholesaler.

3.1 What is an advertising campaign? An advertising campaign is a series of different but related ads that use a single theme and appear in different media within a specified time period.

3.2 What are an advertisement's three main goals? Advertising's three main goals are to educate consumers about product features, enhance brand loyalty, and improve consumer perception of the brand.

4.1 What are some common emotional appeals used in advertising? Advertisers often focus on making emotional appeals to fear, humor, sex, guilt, or fantasy.

4.2 What are the main types of interactive ads? Interactive ads include Internet banners, pop-ups, keyword ads, advertorials, advergames, and interstitials.

5.1 What types of products are banned from advertising on television? Tobacco goods such as cigarettes, cigars, and smokeless tobacco are banned from television advertising.

5.2 What are some advantages radio offers to advertisers? What about newspapers? Radio ads allow marketers to target a captive audience and offer low cost, flexibility, and mobility. Newspaper ads are flexible and provide nearly complete coverage of the market. Readers can also refer back to newspaper ads.

5.3 Define *media scheduling*, and identify the most important factors influencing the scheduling decision. Media scheduling sets the timing and sequence for a series of advertisements. Sales patterns, repurchase cycles, and competitors' activities are the most important variables in the scheduling decision.

6.1 What is the role of an advertising agency? An advertising agency's role is to help businesses plan and prepare advertisements.

6.2 What are some advantages of using an agency? Using an ad agency offers the advantages of highly qualified specialists who provide creativity and objectivity and sometimes cost savings.

7.1 Distinguish between marketing public relations and nonmarketing public relations. Marketing public relations refers to narrowly focused public relations activities that directly support marketing goals. Nonmarketing public relations refers to a company's messages about general issues.

7.2 What is publicity? Publicity is nonpersonal stimulation of demand for a good, service, place, idea, person, or organization by unpaid placement of significant news regarding the subject in a print or broadcast medium.

7.3 What are the advantages of cross-promotion? Cross-promotion divides the cost of a promotional campaign that meets the mutual needs of marketing partners and provides greater benefits for both in return.

8.1 What is CPM, and how is it measured? CPM is cost per thousand, a fee based on cost to deliver the advertisers' message to viewers, listeners, or readers.

8.2 Distinguish between media research and message research. Media research assesses how well a particular medium delivers the advertiser's message, where and when to place the ad, and the size of the audience. Message research tests consumer reactions to an advertisement's creative message.

8.3 Describe several research techniques used in posttesting. Commonly used posttests include readership tests, unaided recall tests, inquiry tests, and split runs.

Marketing Terms You Need to Know

advertising 529
product advertising 529
institutional advertising 529
informative advertising 529
persuasive advertising 530
reminder advertising 530
comparative advertising 531

retail advertising 533
cooperative advertising 533
interactive advertising 534
advertising campaign 535
banner ads 538
media scheduling 546
advertising agency 547

nonmarketing public relations 549
marketing public
  relations (MPR) 549
publicity 549
cross-promotion 551
media research 552
message research 552

pretesting 552
posttesting 553
split runs 554
cookies 555
puffery 555

Assurance of Learning Review

1. Identify and define the two broad categories of advertising. Give an example of each.

2. What are the three primary objectives of advertising? Give an example of when each one might be used.

3. Describe each of the four major advertising strategies.

4. Identify the different types of emotional appeals in advertising. What are the benefits and pitfalls of each?

5. How are interactive ads different from traditional ads? How are they similar?

6. Identify and describe the different advertising media. Which are on the rise? Which are facing possible decline?

7. What is the role of an advertising agency?

8. How can firms use marketing public relations (MPR) to their advantage?

9. Describe the ways in which marketers assess promotional effectiveness.

10. What is puffery? Where does it cross the line from ethical to unethical?

Projects and Teamwork Exercises

1. Choose a print ad to cut out and place on a poster board. With a marker, identify all the elements of the ad. Then identify what you believe is the objective of the ad—to inform, persuade, or remind. Finally, identify the strategy used—comparative, celebrity, or retail. If there is an interactive component offered, note that, too.

2. According to *Advertising Age,* some of the top advertising campaigns of all time include Nike's "Just do it" (1988), McDonald's "You deserve a break today" (1971), and Burger King's "Have it your way" (1973).[56] With a classmate, choose an ad campaign you think is effective—based on its slogan, images, storyline, or whatever strikes you. Present the ad and your evaluation of it to the class.

3. With a classmate, create your own plan for cross-promoting two products you think would be good candidates for cross-promotion.

4. Access the Internet and surf around to some sites that interest you. How many banner ads or pop-ups do you see? Do you like to view these ads, or do you find them intrusive? Which are most appealing?

5. With a classmate, choose a product you have purchased in the past and come up with a plan for using a nontraditional advertising medium—such as balloons, T-shirts, water bottles, anything you imagine will grab people's attention and promote the product effectively. If possible, create a prototype for your ad. If not, create a sketch of your ad. Present your new ad to the class.

Critical-Thinking Exercises

1. What are some of the benefits and drawbacks of using celebrity testimonials in advertising? Identify an ad you believe makes effective use of a celebrity's endorsement, and explain why.

2. Choose one of the following products and outline a possible media schedule for advertising.
   a. toy
   b. line of bathing suits
   c. line of candles

3. Select two different advertisers' television or print ads for the same product category (cars or soft drinks, for instance) and decide what emotion each appeals to. Which ad is more effective and why?

4. Do outdoor ads and pop-up ads have any characteristics in common? What are they?

5. Think back to any good or bad publicity you have heard about a company or its products recently. If it was good publicity, how was it generated and what media were used? If it was bad publicity, where did you find out about it and how did the firm try to control or eliminate the situation?

6. Imagine that a writer says that children exposed to puffery in ads grow into teens who are healthily skeptical of advertising claims. Find several print ads aimed at children, and identify what you think might be puffery in these ads. Select one ad you think children would be influenced by and rewrite the ad without the puffery.

Ethics Exercise

In an effort to target the youngest of consumers, some firms have begun to advertise tiny mobile phones sized to fit the hands of children. The MO1, developed by toy firm Imaginarium and the Spanish communications firm Telefonica, is designed specifically for the younger set—it's a real cell phone, not a toy. In Europe, where the phone is marketed, some parents and consumer groups are objecting to the marketing of the product, noting that long-term health effects of cell phone use are unknown, and young children are quickly impressed by advertising. "The mobile telephone industry is acting like the tobacco industry by designing products that addict the very young," argues one environmental advocacy group for children.[57]

1. Do you believe that Imaginarium and Telefonica are acting in an ethical manner? Why or why not? Be sure to use concepts from this chapter to build your argument.

2. What steps might Imaginarium and Telefonica take to develop good public relations and generate positive publicity surrounding their product?

Internet Exercises

1. **Future of newspaper advertising.** Using a news source, such as Google news (http://news.google.com) or Yahoo! news (http://news.yahoo.com), research the current status of newspaper advertising. How much has ad revenue declined in recent years? Do you agree or disagree that the future of news-paper advertising lies online?

2. **Super Bowl advertising.** Visit the Web sites listed here. How many different organizations ran ads during the most recent Super Bowl? Which organizations have run the most ads in Super Bowls? During the most recent Super Bowl, which ads were the highest rated? The lowest rated? How much has the cost of a 30-second Super Bowl ad changed since the first game was played?

    http://www.superbowl-commercials.org

    http://www.cbssports.com/video/player/superbowlcommercials

3. **Not-for-profit advertising.** Review the material in the chapter on creating an advertisement and then go to the Web site listed here. It outlines the basic steps involved in creating an advertisement for a not-for-profit organization. Review the material and prepare a brief report comparing and contrasting the process of creating an advertisement for a for-profit and a not-for-profit organization.

    http://marketing.about.com/cs/nonprofitmrktg/a/8stepnonprofit.htm

    Note: Internet Web addresses change frequently. If you don't find the exact site listed, you may need to access the organization's home page and search from there or use a search engine such as Google or Bing.

Case 16.1   *Politicians and "Their" Music*

As political advertising becomes increasingly big business, the branding that accompanies a campaign has come to rely heavily on music. This is not surprising, according to neuro-scientists, whose research on the brain reveals that music has the power to infuse itself into our nervous system, triggering feelings and responses and, hence, our behavior.

While the earliest political marketers may not have known the scientific benefits of music, they recognized that music has power. Presidential candidate Franklin D. Roosevelt used the song "Happy Days Are Here Again" during his 1932 campaign, when America was caught in the grip of the Great Depression and the nation's mood was desperate. The song's message enabled voters to envision a better day on the horizon and transfer that emotional response to their feelings about the candidate. After Roosevelt won the election, he reinforced the song's message in his inaugural address with the famous words, "The only thing we have to fear is fear itself."

Years after his presidency, strains of Fleetwood Mac's "Don't Stop" still conjure up memories of Bill Clinton's 1992 campaign. Pairing a candidate with a wildly popular song—sparked fervor among followers. However, when it came to a campaign song choice for Hillary Clinton's run for president, she picked a less well-known song by Celine Dion called, "You and I." The song lyrics were criticized for being about "dreams" instead of her opponent's song lyrics about having "plans."

The use of music in political campaigns can have its pitfalls. Consider the glitch during Ronald Reagan's 1984 presidential run, when the Bruce Springsteen hit "Born in the USA" was selected as a campaign theme. Had Reagan or his handlers listened to the lyrics first, they would have recognized them not as the words of a patriotic song but the bitter memoir of a Vietnam veteran.

Of course, part of the issue stems from the unauthorized use of artists' copyrighted work. But that, apparently, is not all: musicians work hard to build their brand, and many are offended by the idea of a candidate they don't support glomming on to that brand. For example, the rock duo Heart was reportedly irritated when vice presidential candidate Sarah Palin used their 1970s hit "Barracuda" as her theme song, playing off a nickname from her high-school basketball days. As it turned out, however, the Republican National Committee had purchased the rights to the song.

Rand Paul, a candidate for the U.S. Senate from Kentucky, recently heard from the attorney for Canadian rockers Rush after Paul co-opted their music for his Web ads, a fund-raising video, and public appearances. Talking Heads co-founder David Byrne sued then Florida governor Charlie Crist for using "Road to Nowhere" in his campaign advertising for a Senate seat. In a letter posted on his Web site, Byrne claimed that while he licenses his work for dance companies and student filmmakers, he has never permitted its use in advertising. Rock guitarist Steve Miller got riled up when Crist's opponent, Mark Rubio, used the Steve Miller Band tune "Take the Money and Run" to underscore Crist's move from Republican to independent after accepting GOP money.

Questions for Critical Thinking

1. How does the use of music in a political campaign play a role in establishing a candidate's brand?

2. Does a candidate's use of a song you like (or dislike) affect your overall impression of the candidate? Why?

Sources: James R. Carroll, "Rock Band Rush Says Rand Paul's Campaign Can't Use Its Songs," *Courier-Journal.com*, June 2, 2010, http://www.courier-journal.com; Bruce Edwin, "David Byrne of Talking Heads Sues Florida Governor for $1 Million," *News Blaze*, May 26, 2010, http://newsblaze.com; "Miller to Rubio: Hands Off My Song," *UPI.com*, May 23, 2010, http://www.upi.com; Aman Batheja, "Using Popular Songs, YouTube in Political Campaigns an Issue for Some," *McClatchy Washington Bureau*, March 1, 2010, http://www.mcclatchydc.com; Jeffrey Kluger, "Now Hear This," *Time*, March 1, 2010, 43; "Rico Blanco Cries Foul over Gibo's Use of His Song," *Manila Times*, January 12, 2010, http://www.manilatimes.com.

Video Case 16.2
Advertising and Public Relations at Ogden Publications

Ogden Publications of Topeka, Kansas, has been working in the green space for decades. Its most popular magazine, *Mother Earth News*, reaches about 1.85 million readers annually. It was started in 1970 around the time of the very first Earth Day and features

projects you can do to reduce your impact on the environment. The company's second most popular magazine, *Natural Home*, debuted in 1999. *Natural Home* is for those interested in "greening up" their suburban home. The key difference between the two magazines is that *Natural Home* is more focused on things one might buy—heating systems, cleaning products, appliances, and décor. *Mother Earth*'s readers tend to be a bit more hands-on with their projects. Ogden also publishes nine other magazines, including *Motorcycle Classics* for collectors and *Utne Reader*, for alternative media junkies.

Ogden Publications and *Mother Earth News* enjoy a reputation as an authority on sustainable living. This gives them a lot of credibility with their readers, but to potential advertisers, it's pretty scary. Welch admits it has been a challenge explaining to advertisers and partners that we're not "a bunch of holier than thou old hippies" ready to rip their product's greenness to shreds. On the upside, according to a study by leading advertising and marketing research firm, Signet Research Inc., *Mother Earth* readers are on average 80 to 90 percent more likely to pay more money or go out of their way to purchase organic and earth-friendly products. Few publications, even mainstream magazines, could offer such a great advertising proposition.

Natural Home is an easier sell to more mainstream advertisers breaking into the green marketplace. On their pages, you are likely to see Toyota Prius and Home Depot ads alongside a beautiful gourmet kitchen photo spread. A solid 95 percent of readers are willing to pay more for green products. They are almost exclusively female with a median age of 45. Many of them are married with children and own their own homes. Add to that a $90,000 average household income, and an advertiser can feel pretty good about presenting their bamboo flooring and European high-efficiency washer/dryer unit.

According to publisher Bryan Welch, Ogden's main types of advertisers are either endemic or consumer. An endemic advertiser sells a product directly related to the editorial content of the magazine or Web site. Because the demographic for each of Ogden's magazines is pretty specific, the bulk of its ads are endemic. Endemic ads are fairly easy to sell, usually featuring a specific product—a low-flow showerhead, for instance. Advertisers know that 75 percent of the magazine's readership consists of building contractors who will likely purchase this product in the next six months. There is little gamble on the part of the showerhead manufacturer. Consumer advertising is more for products that know no specific demographic. You can sell soft drinks to pretty much anyone around the world, so it doesn't matter where you place the ad. Or does it? Do health-conscious readers with organic gardens and compost heaps in their backyards drink soft drinks? Not likely. If they do, they probably don't want to talk about it too much. The very sight of a soft-drink ad in their favorite publication may cause them to stop purchasing the magazine. This puts publishers like Welch in a difficult position. Magazines are funded by ad sales, and companies like PepsiCo, Ford, or GE can afford big ad buys. All of these companies are looking to magazines like *Natural Home* for an "in" to their very desirable readers. And some of these large companies may be able to make inroads. "A lot of big consumer advertisers have a great authentic message. [They] have new products that are genuinely more enlightened," says Welch. He names Honda, Toyota, and Owens Corning as companies that have demonstrated a true commitment to improving the sustainability of

their products. "Those are the folks we are trying to connect with," he says, "and our readers want to know about those products and bring them into their lives and the lives of their friends. That's the perfect formula."

Questions

1. Given that most of a magazine's revenue comes from ads, would you be willing to turn down a large consumer advertiser because your readers may disagree with their product or business practices? Discuss the ethical, PR, and financial implications of your decision.

2. What challenges do specialized magazines such as *Mother Earth News* face when trying to entice advertisers? Create a pitch to a potential green-product advertiser stating the benefits of advertising in *Mother Earth News*.

ch17 Personal
Selling and Sales Promotion

1. Describe the role of today's salesperson.

2. Describe the four sales channels.

3. Describe the major trends in personal selling.

4. Identify and briefly describe the three basic sales tasks.

5. Outline the seven steps in the sales process.

6. Identify the seven basic functions of a sales manager.

7. Explain the role of ethical behavior in personal selling.

8. Describe the role of sales promotion in the promotional mix, and identify the different types of sales promotions.

Salesforce.com: Living It Up on a Cloud • • • In the digital age, successful salespeople have a system—that is, a software platform that helps them track customers and prospects, monitor their progress with key accounts, oversee their billing and collection

activity—in short, to help them keep tabs on the myriad of details surrounding a job in sales.

However, few employers have the time or resources to develop a truly customized system for their sales force. Instead, firms typically license a software package from a company like SAP or Oracle, then pay to have the software customized and purchase monthly for maintenance, tech support, and other services.

This costly arrangement puzzled Marc Benioff, an Oracle executive at the time. He pondered whether there was a way to develop a more affordable option. Benioff came up with the answer—Salesforce.com. In a modest San Francisco apartment, he launched this fledgling company, and the "End of Software" era began.

Using Salesforce CRM, businesses can leverage the capabilities of the Internet to create their own customized customer relationship management (CRM) system. And they do it with a software product that's not a product at all.

That is, Salesforce CRM doesn't sit in a box on a shelf, waiting to be ordered, delivered, and installed on your computer. Rather, CRM resides on an Internet "cloud," available at an affordable price. Business customers access CRM from the cloud, then easily customize it to their unique requirements.

Salesforce CRM is an example of what is known as "on-demand software," which customers can access and use at their convenience. Salesforce.com is a pioneer in cloud computing and one of the

most successful players in the SaaS ("software as a service") category in the rapidly growing technology marketplace. As Benioff discovered, using the Internet to develop, market, and distribute products makes it highly affordable and exceedingly efficient.

For large organizations, Salesforce.com developed an "enterprise edition" of CRM. Clients can begin using CRM even before it is fully integrated into the organization's existing systems. Once integration is complete, the transition to the new platform is swift and relatively uncomplicated. Salesforce.com's clientele continues to grow, currently including such giants as Alltel, Dell, *The Wall Street Journal,* Sprint, and Time Warner Cable among its more than 78,000 customers.

Since the success of Salesforce.com, other on-demand software providers have emerged, automating a variety of corporate activities, such as travel-budget and personnel management. Meanwhile, the company has built a global presence and recently opened its third data center, in Singapore, to take advantage of the burgeoning Asia-Pacific market for enterprise cloud computing.

One of Salesforce.com's latest innovations is Force.com, a hosting site for data centers and platform technologies. Force.com can even be used as a platform for launching new SaaS companies. FinancialForce.com, one of the programs, offers the systems and services needed by finance and accounting departments, such as ledgers, budgeting, spreadsheets, accounts payable and receivable, and more.

Industry observers predict that FinancialForce.com will do for the finance and accounting world what Salesforce.com has done for customer relationship management.

Salesforce.com may have looked and operated like a typical dot-com of the 1990s. However, unlike thousands of those businesses, it succeeded because it saw—and satisfied—a valid need in the marketplace.[1]

evolution of a brand

Barely ten years in operation, Salesforce.com quickly moved to the forefront of the tech economy, harnessing the power of the Internet and cloud computing for businesses large and small. From its humble beginnings in a San Francisco apartment, Salesforce.com quickly went global and today serves an ever-growing international clientele.

Regularly acknowledged by such organizations as *BusinessWeek*, Forrester, Gartner, *InfoWorld*, *PC* magazine, *Wired*, and others for

its success and its advancement of the industry, Salesforce.com has changed how sales professionals operate.

- The introduction of Salesforce CRM changed the way sales professionals do business. How does on-demand software present a threat to the traditional means of marketing technology goods and services?

- Salesforce.com became successful by identifying an unmet need in the marketplace and filling it. Where should the company's management look to locate the next unmet need?

chapter overview

The Salesforce.com story illustrates how important it is for marketers to not simply sell products but to understand their customers and connect with them through product innovations that make life easier. In exploring personal selling strategies, this chapter gives special attention to the relationship-building opportunities that the selling situation presents.

personal selling
Interpersonal influence process involving a seller's promotional presentation conducted on a person-to-person basis with the buyer.

Personal selling is the process of a seller's person-to-person promotional presentation to a buyer. The sales process essentially is interpersonal, and it is basic to any enterprise. Accounting, engineering, human resource management, production, and other organizational activities produce no benefits unless a seller matches the needs of a client or customer. The more than 15 million people employed in sales occupations in the United States testify to the importance of selling.[2] Personal selling is much more costly and time-consuming than other types of promotion because of its direct contact with customers. This makes personal selling the single largest marketing expense in many firms.

Personal selling is a primary component of a firm's promotional mix when one or more of several well-defined factors are present:

1. customers are geographically concentrated;
2. individual orders account for large amounts of revenue;
3. the firm markets goods and services that are expensive, are technically complex, or require special handling;
4. trade-ins are involved;
5. products move through short channels; or
6. the firm markets to relatively few potential customers.

For example, personal selling is an important component of the promotional mix for a car dealer, although both dealers and manufacturers also rely heavily on advertising. Because cars and trucks are expensive, customers usually like to go to a dealership to compare models, discuss a purchase, or obtain service, and trade-ins often are involved. So, a dealer's salespeople provide valuable assistance to the customer.

Table 17.1 summarizes the factors that influence the importance of personal selling in the overall promotional mix based on four variables: consumer, product, price, and marketing channels. This chapter also explores *sales promotion*, which includes all marketing activities—other than personal selling, advertising, and publicity—that enhance promotional effectiveness.

table 17.1 **Factors Affecting the Importance of Personal Selling in the Promotional Mix**

Variable	Conditions That Favor Personal Selling	Conditions That Favor Advertising
Consumer	Geographically concentrated	Geographically dispersed
	Relatively low numbers	Relatively high numbers
Product	Expensive	Inexpensive
	Technically complex	Simple to understand
	Custom made	Standardized
	Special handling requirements	No special handling requirements
	Transactions frequently involve trade-ins	Transactions seldom involve trade-ins
Price	Relatively high	Relatively low
Channels	Relatively short	Relatively long

The Evolution of Personal Selling

Selling has been a standard business activity for thousands of years. As long ago as 2000 B.C., the Code of Hammurabi protected the rights of the Babylonian salesman, who was referred to as a *peddler.* Throughout U.S. history, selling has been a major factor in economic growth. Even during the 1700s, Yankee peddlers pulled their carts full of goods from village to village and farm to farm, helping expand trade among the colonies. Today, professional salespeople are problem solvers who focus on satisfying the needs of customers before, during, and after sales are made. Armed with knowledge about their firm's goods or services, those of competitors, and their customers' business needs, salespeople pursue a common goal of creating mutually beneficial long-term relationships with customers.

> **1** Describe the role of today's salesperson.

Personal selling is a vital, vibrant, dynamic process. As domestic and foreign competition increases the emphasis on productivity, personal selling is taking on a more prominent role in the marketing mix. Salespeople must communicate the advantages of their firms' goods and services over those of competitors. They must be able to do the following:

- Focus on a customer's situation and needs and create solutions that meet those needs.

- Follow through and stay in touch before, during, and after a sale.

- Know the industry and have a firm grasp, not only of their own firm's capabilities but also of their competitors' abilities.

- Work hard to exceed their customers' expectations, even if it means going above and beyond the call of duty.

Relationship marketing affects all aspects of an organization's marketing function, including personal selling. This means marketers in both internal and external relationships must develop different sales skills. Instead of working alone, many salespeople now unite their efforts in sales teams. The customer-focused firm wants its salespeople to form long-lasting relationships with buyers by providing high levels of customer service rather than going for quick sales. Even the way salespeople perform their jobs is constantly changing. Growing numbers of companies have integrated communications and computer technologies into the sales routine. These trends are covered in more detail later in the chapter.

Personal selling is an attractive career choice for today's college students. According to the Bureau of Labor Statistics, jobs in sales and related fields are expected to grow by about 8 percent over the next decade.[3] Company executives usually recognize a good salesperson as a hard worker who can solve problems, communicate clearly, and be consistent. In fact, many corporations are headed by executives who began their careers in sales.

assessment check

1. What is personal selling?
2. What is the main focus of today's salespeople?

The Four Sales Channels

2 Describe the four sales channels.

Personal selling occurs through several types of communication channels: over-the-counter selling, including online selling; field selling; telemarketing; and inside selling. Each of these channels includes business-to-business and direct-to-customer selling. Although telemarketing and online selling are lower-cost alternatives, their lack of personal interaction with existing or prospective customers often makes them less effective than personalized, one-to-one field selling and over-the-counter channels. In fact, many organizations use a number of different channels.

Over-the-Counter Selling

over-the-counter selling Personal selling conducted in retail and some wholesale locations in which customers come to the seller's place of business.

The most frequently used sales channel, **over-the-counter selling**, typically describes selling in retail and some wholesale locations. Most over-the-counter sales are direct-to-customer, although business customers are frequently served by wholesalers with over-the-counter sales reps. Customers typically visit the seller's location on their own initiative to purchase desired items. Some visit their favorite stores because they enjoy shopping. Others respond to many kinds of appeals including direct mail; personal letters of invitation from store personnel; and advertisements for sales, special events, and new-product introductions.

Marketers are getting increasingly creative in their approach to over-the-counter selling. When marketers at Orchard Supply Hardware, a chain of nearly 90 stores based in San Jose, California, discovered that customers enjoy browsing, it reworked store layouts and design to return to the feel of an old-time hardware store. Creating four distinct "neighborhoods" of related merchandise—Indoors, Outdoors, Hardware, and Tools—and signage that draws shoppers in, Orchard made stores accessible and inviting.[4]

Electronics giant Best Buy continues to outsell its competitors; with more than 1,000 stores, the firm's annual sales total more than $45 billion.[5] Perhaps Best Buy's success comes from the training its salespeople receive. Training focuses on the firm's mantra: CARE Plus. *C* stands for contact with the customer. *A* means asking questions to learn what the customer needs. *R* represents making recommendations to the customer. *E* stands for encouragement, praising the customer for a wise purchase.

Clothing retailers have begun to enhance the shopping experience by expanding the capabilities of the fitting room. Some Gap and Banana Republic stores added call buttons and delivery doors to their fitting rooms so that salespeople can offer more service. Bloomingdale's has piloted an interactive mirror and Webcam system in fitting rooms that enables shoppers to e-mail or text-message their friends with information on items they are trying on. By logging on to a special Web site, the friends can view the items and offer comments. What's more, shoppers can use the system to learn about other merchandise in the store, click on an item, and have it superimposed on their image—in short, trying on a garment virtually.[6]

Regardless of a retailer's innovation, a few things remain the same in selling. For example, customers never like hearing salespeople say the following:

- "That's not my department."
- "If it's not out (on the rack or shelf), we don't have it."
- "I don't know/I'm new."
- "I'm closing" or "I'm on a break."
- "The computer is down."

While these quotes may seem humorous, they also ring true. You've probably heard them, and you may have said them yourself if you've worked in a retail environment. But each statement conveys the message that the salesperson is not willing or able to serve the customer—exactly the opposite of what every marketer wants to convey.

Some Gap and Banana Republic stores added call buttons and delivery doors to their fitting rooms so that salespeople can offer more service.

© TERRI MILLER/ E-VISUAL COMMUNICATIONS, INC.

Field Selling

Field selling involves making sales calls on prospective and existing customers at their businesses or homes. Some situations involve considerable creative effort, such as the sale of major computer installations. Often, the salesperson must convince customers first that they need the good or service and then that they need the particular brand the salesperson is selling. Field sales of large industrial installations such as Boeing's 787 Dreamliner jet also often require considerable technical expertise.

field selling Sales presentations made at prospective customers' locations on a face-to-face basis.

Largely because it involves travel, field selling is considerably more expensive than other selling options. Rising prices of fuel, air fares, car rentals, and hotel rates have forced up the cost of business trips. Needing to find ways to trim costs while increasing productivity, some firms have replaced certain travel with conference calls, while others require salespeople to stay in less expensive hotels and spend less on meals. Some firms have simply shortened the time allowed for trips.

In fairly routine field selling situations, such as calling on established customers in industries like food, textiles, or wholesaling, the salesperson basically acts as an order taker who processes regular customers' orders. But more complex situations may involve weeks of preparation, formal presentations, and many hours of postsales call work. Field selling is a lifestyle that many people enjoy; they also cite some of the negatives, such as travel delays, impact on family life, and high costs of fuel. The "Solving an Ethical Controversy" feature describes a controversial type of field selling: schools' and organizations' use of children as salespeople.

Panasonic manufactures the Toughbook series with field sales reps in mind, building a strong case for rugged handling.

© YOSHIKAZU TSUNO/AFP/GETTY IMAGES/NEWSCOM

solving an ethical controversy

Under-Age Sales Force: Using Kids to Sell?

Whether you attended public or private elementary school, most likely at some time in your childhood you sold merchandise to help your school raise funds. Whether it's drumming up financial support for worthy causes or selling merchandise like pizzas, raffle tickets, or magazine subscriptions, most schools regard their student population as a ready-made sales force, expected to go door to door to sell.

Should schools use children as salespersons?

PRO

1. Helping your school raise funds is a rite of passage for kids. And the money raised through such initiatives provide items that a school might not otherwise be able to afford, such as playground equipment, a public-address system, computers, band uniforms, and more.

2. The behaviors involved in selling are important skills for children to learn. Selling to friends and neighbors can help children build confidence and communication skills.

CON

1. Children are in school to learn, not to be mini-salespeople; they should not be responsible for filling their school's coffers. Schools—not their students—are wholly responsible for their financial management.

2. There are safety concerns involved in having children go door to door. If schools need to raise funds, let them hire a professional fund-raising firm.

Summary

Although most schools claim fund-raising is voluntary, it's a fact of life that children feel some pressure to participate in it, if only not to appear "different" from their peers. Many schools are taking a closer look at the nature and number of fund-raisers they sponsor, and some are creating new parameters. For example, many institutions are making the fund-raising task voluntary. But one thing is certain: most people find it hard to say no to a pint-sized salesperson.

Sources: Monica Patrick, "Crafts for Kids to Sell," www.ehow.com, accessed August 2, 2010; Daniel Austin, "Schools End Lucrative Casino Fundraisers; Catholic Ban," *National Post*, December 10, 2009, http://www.nationalpost.com; Innocent Madawo, "Why Are Our Schools Using Children As Fundraisers?" *Toronto Sun*, November 9, 2009, http://www.torontosun.com; Sharon Kennedy Wynne, "Run! School Fundraisers Are Coming," *St. Petersburg Times*, September 20, 2009, http://www.tampabay.com; Marilyn Sokol, "Boosters Make Huge Difference at Schools," *St. Petersburg Times*, September 11, 2009, http://www.tampabay.com.

network marketing
Personal selling that relies on lists of family members and friends of the salesperson, who organizes a gathering of potential customers for a demonstration of products.

Some firms view field selling as a market in itself and have developed goods and services designed to help salespeople do their jobs. Panasonic manufactures the Toughbook series—a line of tablet computers loaded with Microsoft Office software and designed with field sales reps in mind. The computer has a magnesium alloy case—significantly stronger than the plastic cases of standard computers—and is built for rugged handling. The Toughbook can withstand a six-foot drop and is rain-, dust-, and vibration-resistant.[7]

Taking their cue from the successes of businesses such as Avon, Pampered Chef, and Tupperware, thousands of smaller businesses now rely on field selling in customers' homes. Often called **network marketing**, this type of personal selling relies on lists of family members and friends of the salesperson or "party host," who organizes a gathering of potential customers for an in-home demonstration of products. The Girl Scouts organization has been selling cookies for decades. Despite being a largely inexperienced sales team that offers its product seasonally, annual revenues typically total as much as $700 million.[8] Mary Kay Cosmetics, with more than 36,000 sales consultants, enjoyed global sales of $2.6 billion in a recent year.[9]

Telemarketing

Telemarketing, a channel in which the selling process is conducted by phone, serves two general purposes— sales and service—and two general markets—business-to-business and direct-to-customer. Both inbound and outbound telemarketing are forms of direct marketing.

Outbound telemarketing involves sales personnel who rely on the telephone to contact potential buyers, reducing the substantial costs of personal visits to customers' homes or businesses. Technologies such as predictive dialers, autodialing, and random-digit dialing increase chances that telemarketers will reach people at home. *Predictive dialers* weed out busy signals and answering machines, nearly doubling the number of calls made per hour. *Autodialing* allows telemarketers to dial numbers continually; when a customer answers the phone, the call is automatically routed to a sales representative. However, the Telephone Consumer Protection Act of 1991 prohibits the use of autodialers to contact (or leave messages) on telephone devices such as answering machines.[10] *Random-digit dialing* allows telemarketers to reach unlisted numbers and block Caller ID.

A major drawback of telemarketing is that most consumers dislike the practice, and more than 191 million have signed up for the national Do Not Call Registry.[11] If an unauthorized telemarketer does call any of these numbers, the marketer is subject to a fine of up to $16,000.[12] Organizations exempt from the fine include not-for-profits, political candidates, companies that have obtained the customer's permission, marketing researchers, and firms that have an existing business relationship with the customer.

Why do some firms still use telemarketing? The average call cost is low, and companies point to a significant rate of success. In a recent year, total sales from telemarketing exceeded $660 billion. According to the Direct Marketing Association, about 6 million people are employed in telemarketing jobs.[13]

Inbound telemarketing typically involves a toll-free number that customers can call to obtain information, make reservations, and purchase goods and services. When a customer calls a toll-free number, the caller can be identified and routed to the representatives with whom he or she has done business before, creating a human touch not possible before. This form of selling provides maximum convenience for customers who initiate the sales process. Many large catalog merchants, such as Pottery Barn, L.L. Bean, Lands' End, and Performance Bike, keep their inbound telemarketing lines open 24 hours a day, seven days a week.

Some firms are taking dramatic steps to incorporate inbound telemarketing into their overall marketing strategy. JetBlue Airlines, for example, keeps operating costs low by employing 900 reservation agents who work from home.[14]

The Girl Scouts have been successfully field selling their cookies for decades, despite an inexperienced sales force and short selling season.

© JEFF GREENBERG/PHOTOEDIT

telemarketing
Promotional presentation involving the use of the telephone on an outbound basis by salespeople or on an inbound basis by customers who initiate calls to obtain information and place orders.

outbound telemarketing Sales method in which sales personnel place phone calls to prospects and try to conclude the sale over the phone.

inbound telemarketing Sales method in which prospects call a seller to obtain information, make reservations, and purchase goods and services.

© SEAN PRIOR/SHUTTERSTOCK.COM

Inside Selling

The role of many of today's telemarketers is a combination of field selling techniques applied through inbound and outbound telemarketing channels with a strong customer orientation, called **inside selling**. Inside sales reps perform two primary jobs: they turn opportunities into actual sales, and they support technicians and purchasers with current solutions. Inside sales reps do far more than read a canned script to unwilling prospects. Their role goes beyond taking orders to solving problems, providing customer service, and selling. A successful inside sales force relies on close working relationships with field representatives to solidify customer relationships.

The ten-member inside sales force of the NBA's Detroit Pistons supports the team's marketing efforts, such as special events for season ticket holders, including backstage tours, scavenger hunts, and privileges such as getting into games 30 minutes early. Pistons sales reps use online chat, telephone, and e-mail to stay connected.[15]

Integrating the Various Selling Channels

Figure 17.1 illustrates how firms are likely to blend alternative sales channels, from over-the-counter selling and field selling to telemarketing and inside selling, to create a successful cost-effective sales organization. Existing customers whose business problems require complex solutions are likely best served by the traditional field sales force. Other current customers who need answers but not the same attention as the first group can be served by inside sales reps who contact them as needed. Over-the-counter sales reps serve existing customers by supplying information and advice and completing sales transactions. Telemarketers may be used to strengthen communication with customers or to reestablish relationships with customers that may have lapsed over a few months.

inside selling Selling by phone, mail, and electronic commerce.

assessment check

1. What is over-the-counter selling?
2. What is field selling?
3. Distinguish between outbound and inbound telemarketing.

Trends in Personal Selling

3 Describe the major trends in personal selling.

In today's complex marketing environment, effective personal selling requires different strategies from those used by salespeople in the past. As pointed out in the discussion of *buying centers* in Chapter 6, rather than selling one-on-one, in B2B settings it is now customary to sell to teams of corporate representatives who participate in the client firm's decision-making process. In

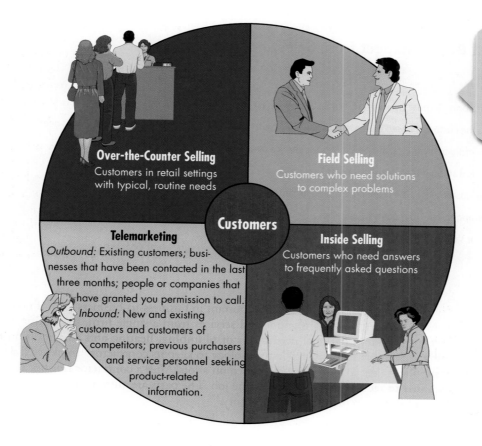

figure 17.1

Alternative Sales Channels for Serving Customers

business-to-business sales situations involving technical products, customers expect salespeople to answer technical questions—or bring along someone who can. They also want representatives who understand technical jargon and can communicate using sophisticated technological tools. Patience is also a requirement because the B2B sales cycle, from initial contact to closing, may take months or even years. To address all of these concerns, companies rely on three major personal selling approaches: relationship selling, consultative selling, and team selling. Regardless of the approach, however, experts agree on a few basic guidelines for conducting successful personal selling.

Relationship Selling

Most firms now emphasize **relationship selling**, a technique for building a mutually beneficial partnership with a customer through regular contacts over an extended period. Such buyer–seller bonds become increasingly important as companies cut back on the number of suppliers and look for companies that provide high levels of customer service and satisfaction. Salespeople must also find ways to distinguish themselves and their products from competitors. To create strong, long-lasting relationships with customers, salespeople must meet buyers' expectations. Table 17.2 summarizes the results of several surveys that indicate what buyers expect of professional salespeople.

The success of tomorrow's marketers depends on the relationships they build today in both the business-to-consumer and business-to-business markets. Sovereign Bank, located throughout the Northeast, knew that first impressions are particularly important in relationship selling, and for this reason it decided to automate its sales activity. A software application helped the bank standardize many sales processes and implement sales effectiveness tools to help it become more customer focused.[16]

relationship selling
Regular contacts between sales representatives and customers over an extended period to establish a sustained buyer–seller relationship.

table 17.2 What Buyers Expect from Salespeople

Buyers prefer to do business with salespeople who:

- Orchestrate events and bring to bear whatever resources are necessary to satisfy the customer
- Provide counseling to the customer based on in-depth knowledge of the product, the market, and the customer's needs
- Solve problems proficiently to ensure satisfactory customer service over extended time periods
- Demonstrate high ethical standards and communicate honestly at all times
- Willingly advocate the customer's cause within the selling organization
- Create imaginative arrangements to meet buyers' needs
- Arrive well prepared for sales calls

Relationship selling is equally important in business-to-business sales, if not more so. Firms may invest millions of dollars in goods and services from a single firm, so creating relationships is vital. Barnett, a leading national distributor of plumbing, heating and air conditioning, electrical, and hardware products, uses barcode technology to keep its contractors' trucks well stocked with all sorts of supplies—just in case they are needed on a job. After a contractor finishes at a site, he or she uses a scanner to record the parts used in the job. The parts are automatically reordered at the end of the day, and Barnett replenishes the inventory.[17]

Consultative Selling

consultative selling
Meeting customer needs by listening to them, understanding their problems, paying attention to details, and following through after the sale.

Field representatives and inside sales reps require sales methods that satisfy today's cost–conscious, knowledgeable buyers. One such method, **consultative selling**, involves meeting customer needs by listening to customers, understanding—and caring about—their problems, paying attention to details, and following through after the sale. It works hand in hand with relationship selling in building customer loyalty. Richardson, a sales consulting firm based in Philadelphia, recently trained sales staff at Fireman's Fund Insurance in consultative selling techniques. Earlier, Fireman's had adopted a new customer-focused sales strategy, and the sales force needed to sharpen its skills to better align with the new strategy. During the training, participants learned how to prepare for sales meetings, position the company's products to meet needs, close deals, and build relationships, and they received coaching and feedback. As a result of the training, the sales representatives were able to adapt to the new strategy and win business.[18] One important aspect of consultative selling is being prepared for a sales call, including dressing professionally. The "Career Readiness" feature provides tips on dressing for a successful call.

Online companies have instituted consultative selling models to create long-term customers. Particularly for complicated, high-priced products that require installation or specialized service, Web sellers must quickly communicate the benefits and features of their products. They accomplish this through consultative selling.

cross-selling Selling multiple, often unrelated, goods and services to the same customer based on knowledge of that customer's needs.

Cross-selling—offering multiple goods or services to the same customer—is another technique that capitalizes on a firm's strengths. It costs a bank five times as much to acquire a new customer as to cross-sell to an existing one. Moreover, research shows that the more a customer buys from an institution, the less likely that person is to leave. So, a customer who opens a checking account at a local bank may follow with a safe-deposit box, retirement savings account, and a mortgage loan.

Team Selling

team selling Selling situation in which several sales associates or other members of the organization are employed to help the lead sales representative reach all those who influence the purchase decision.

Another development in the evolution of personal selling is **team selling**, in which a salesperson joins with specialists from other functional areas of the firm to complete the selling process. Teams can be

career readiness Dressing Like a Sales Professional

While people say you can't tell a book by its cover, it's human nature to form impressions about others from their appearance. If you want a career in sales, pay attention to your appearance. Successful salespeople know the first hurdle is dressing in a way that makes others feel comfortable. In industries where it's important that customers feel confident about the service rendered, such as airlines and hospitals, employees often wear uniforms. Other employers may specify a general dress code so their employees are easily distinguishable—for example, Target's red shirt and khaki pants.

Unfortunately, some firms don't give their employees much guidance on dressing for sales calls. But a prospective customer will notice your appearance and form an impression about you. Although great latitude exists in industries like entertainment, here's what's safe to wear in most other settings:

- Men: Two-piece suit and dress shirt. Shirt and tie can be plain or patterned, as long as they complement each other. Shoes may be oxfords or loafers, and remember to shine them.

- Women: Skirt suit or pantsuit, with a shirt or shell under the jacket, or a dress with a jacket. Low- to medium-heeled shoes with stockings. In some settings, women can wear contrasting jacket-skirt or jacket-pants combinations.

- For both genders: A blazer or sport coat and dress pants, or even a golf shirt and khakis, are acceptable in some industries. Just make sure everything is clean and pressed. Watch your personal hygiene and don't go overboard with fragrances.

- What's *never* appropriate on a sales call: Denim, T-shirts, bare feet, athletic shoes, or flip-flops. Anything tight fitting, low cut, or midriff baring. Avoid visible tattoos and piercings, other than a couple in the earlobe.

- A rule of thumb: If in doubt, it's better to be a bit overdressed rather than underdressed. It shows respect for your customer.

Sources: Thad Peterson, "Dress Appropriately for Interviews," *Monster.com,* http://career-advice.monster.com, accessed May 6, 2010; "Dress for Success No Matter What Your Job," *St. Petersburg Times,* March 13, 2010, http://www.tampabay.com; Walethia Aquil, "Dress for Success in 2010," *SelfGrowth.com,* January 14, 2010, http://www.selfgrowth.com.

formal and ongoing or created for a specific, short-term selling situation. Although some salespeople have hesitated to embrace the idea of team selling, preferring to work alone, a growing number believe team selling brings better results. Customers often prefer the team approach, which makes them feel well served. Consider a restaurant meal. If the host, servers, wine steward, chef, and kitchen crew are all working well together as a team, your experience at the restaurant is likely to be positive. But if the service stops and starts, your order is recorded wrong, the food is cold, the silverware is dirty, and the staff seems grouchy, you probably won't eat at that restaurant again. In fact, you may not even finish the meal.

Another advantage of team selling is the formation of relationships between companies rather than between individuals. In sales situations that call for detailed knowledge of new, complex, and ever-changing technologies, team selling offers a distinct competitive edge in meeting customers' needs. In most computer software B2B departments, a third of the sales force is made up of technically trained, nonmarketing experts such as engineers or programmers. A salesperson continues to play the lead role in most sales situations, but technical experts bring added value to the sales process. Some companies establish permanent sales-and-tech teams that conduct all sales presentations together; others have a pool of engineers or other professionals who are on call for different client visits.

Some resourceful entrepreneurs are building a **virtual sales team**—a network of strategic partners, suppliers, and others qualified and willing to recommend a firm's goods or services. GMAC Mortgage recently launched a virtual sales network to sell its residential mortgage products. The Fort Washington, Pennsylvania–based firm believes its virtual network will be able to attract more home buyers. The first of its kind among larger lenders, the virtual sales network launched initially across a five-state area, with plans for expansion.[19]

briefly speaking

" Your most unhappy customers are your greatest source of learning."

—Bill Gates
(b. 1955)
Co-founder and chairman of Microsoft

virtual sales team
Network of strategic partners, suppliers, and others who recommend a firm's goods or services.

Sales Tasks

4 Identify and briefly describe the three basic sales tasks.

Today's salesperson is more concerned with establishing long-term buyer–seller relationships and helping customers select the correct products for meeting their needs than with simply selling whatever is available. Where repeat purchases are common, the salesperson must be certain that the buyer's purchases are in his or her best interest; otherwise, no future relationship will be possible. The seller's interests are tied to the buyer's in a mutually beneficial relationship.

While all sales activities help the customer in some manner, they are not all alike. Three basic sales tasks can be identified: (1) order processing, (2) creative selling, and (3) missionary sales. Most of today's salespeople are not limited to performing tasks in a single category. Instead, they often perform all three tasks to some extent. A sales engineer for a computer firm may do 50 percent missionary sales, 45 percent creative selling, and 5 percent order processing. Most sales positions are classified on the basis of the primary selling task performed.

Then there's the philosophy that *everyone* in the organization, regardless of what his or her job description is, should be engaged in selling. Southwest Airlines believes delivering great customer service is paramount for every employee, from the reservations agent to the baggage handler to the flight attendant. All Southwest employees are trained to put the customer's needs first, and the airline relies heavily on technology to coordinate the effort.[20]

Order Processing

order processing
Selling, mostly at the wholesale and retail levels, that involves identifying customer needs, pointing them out to customers, and completing orders.

Order processing, which can involve both field selling and telemarketing, most often is typified by selling at the wholesale and retail levels. For instance, a Pepsi-Cola route salesperson who performs this task must take the following steps:

1. *Identify customer needs.* The route salesperson determines that a store has only seven cases of Mountain Dew left in stock when it normally carries an inventory of 40.

2. *Point out the need to the customer.* The route salesperson informs the store manager of the inventory situation.

3. *Complete (write up) the order.* The store manager acknowledges the need for more of the product. The driver unloads 33 cases of Mountain Dew, and the manager signs the delivery slip.

Order processing is part of most selling positions. It becomes the primary task in situations in which needs can be readily identified and are acknowledged by the customer. Even in such instances, however, salespeople whose primary responsibility involves order processing will devote some time persuading their wholesale or retail customers to carry more complete inventories of their firms' merchandise or to handle additional product lines. They are also likely to try to motivate purchasers to feature some of their firms' products, increase the amount of shelf space devoted to these items, and improve product location in the stores.

Technology now streamlines order-processing tasks. Interactive store kiosks, a recent innovation by California-based Escalate Retail, provide a touch screen that lets customers browse a store's catalog, compare brands and product features, and even place their order—all from a single user-friendly device, putting an end to endlessly cruising the store aisles.[21]

Creative Selling

When a considerable amount of decision making is involved in purchasing a good or service, an effective salesperson uses **creative selling** techniques to solicit an order. In contrast to the order-processing task, which deals mainly with maintaining existing business, creative selling is generally used to develop new business either by adding new customers or by introducing new goods and services. New products or upgrades to more expensive items often require creative selling. The salesperson must first identify the customer's problems and needs and then propose a solution in the form of the item offered. When attempting to expand an existing business relationship, creative selling techniques are used in over-the-counter selling, field selling, inside selling, and telemarketing.

Creative selling can generate "buzz" for a product. When Ford wanted to create excitement around its new small car, the Fiesta, it launched an imaginative campaign that involved offering 100 consumers the opportunity to drive a Fiesta at no charge for six months. The only condition: each individual was to drive the car someplace different each month, then report the results on such social media as Facebook, Twitter, and YouTube. As a result, Fiesta garnered 6.5 million YouTube views, and Ford received 50,000 requests for more information about the Fiesta. In the first six days of the campaign, the company sold 10,000 cars.[22]

creative selling
Personal selling in which a considerable degree of analytical decision making on the buyer's part results in the need for skillful proposals of solutions for the customer's needs.

Missionary Selling

Missionary selling is an indirect approach to sales. Salespeople sell the firm's goodwill and educate their customers, often providing technical or operational assistance. A cosmetics company salesperson may call on retailers to demonstrate how a new product is used or to check on special promotions and overall product movement, while a wholesaler takes orders and delivers merchandise. For years, large pharmaceutical companies operated the most aggressive missionary selling, courting doctors (the indirect customer) by providing lavish restaurant meals, educational seminars, and other incentives in the hope of persuading them to prescribe a particular brand to patients. While the doctor is clearly the decision maker, the transaction is not complete until the patient hands the prescription over to a pharmacist. But recent changes in the industry code of conduct now prohibit missionary salespeople from offering any incentives of value to their customers. Instead, the Pharmaceutical Research and Manufacturers of America decreed that meetings with doctors must focus exclusively on education, not freebies.[23]

Some missionary sales may offer **sales incentives** such as trips, gas cards, free product upgrades, and other inducements. Missionary sales may involve both field selling and telemarketing. Many aspects of team selling can also be seen as missionary sales, as when technical support salespeople help design, install, and maintain equipment; when they train customers' employees; and when they provide information or operational assistance.

missionary selling
Indirect selling method in which salespeople promote goodwill for the firm by educating customers and providing technical or operational assistance.

sales incentives
Programs that reward salespeople for superior performance.

When Ford wanted to create excitement around its new Fiesta, it launched a campaign that involved offering 100 consumers the opportunity to drive a Fiesta at no charge for six months.

© TERRI MILLER/E-VISUAL COMMUNICATIONS, INC.

The Sales Process

5 Outline the seven steps in the sales process.

If you have worked in a retail store, or if you've sold magazine subscriptions or candy to raise money for your school or sports team, you will recognize many of the activities involved in the following list of steps in the sales process. Personal selling encompasses the following sequence of activities: (1) prospecting and qualifying, (2) approach, (3) presentation, (4) demonstration, (5) handling objections, (6) closing, and (7) follow-up.

As Figure 17.2 indicates, these steps follow the AIDA concept (attention, interest, desire, action). Once a sales prospect has been qualified, an attempt is made to secure his or her attention. The presentation and demonstration steps are designed to generate interest and desire. Successful handling of buyer objections should arouse further desire. Action occurs at the close of the sale.

Salespeople modify the steps in this process to match their customers' buying processes. A neighbor who eagerly looks forward to the local symphony orchestra's new concert season each year needs no presentation except for details about scheduled performances and perhaps whether any famous musicians will be on the bill. But the same neighbor would expect a demonstration from an auto dealer when looking for a new car or might appreciate a presentation of dinner specials by the server prior to ordering a meal at a restaurant.

Prospecting and Qualifying

prospecting Personal selling function of identifying potential customers.

Prospecting—the process of identifying potential customers—may involve hours, days, or weeks of effort, but it is a necessary step. Leads about prospects come from many sources: the Internet, computerized databases, trade show exhibits, previous customers, friends and neighbors, other vendors, nonsales employees in the firm, suppliers, and social and professional contacts. Although a firm may emphasize personal selling as the primary component of its overall promotional strategy, direct mail and advertising campaigns are also effective in identifying prospective customers.

Before salespeople begin their prospecting effort, they must be clear about what their firm is selling and create a "brand story," that is, define their product in terms of what it can do for a customer. Because customers are generally looking for solutions to problems or ways to make their lives better or businesses more successful, this focus on the customer is critical. Once they develop

figure 17.2

The AIDA Concept and the Personal Selling Process

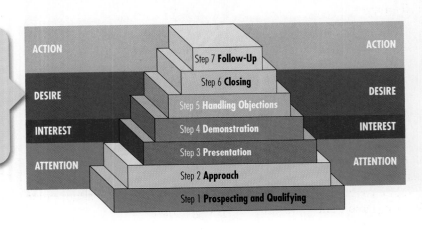

a brand story, the sales team must be consistent about telling it at every possible point of contact, whether in a face-to-face conversation with a prospect, in advertising, or in promoting the product to the media.[24]

In addition, salespeople must be well informed about the goods and services of the industry in general. They need to find out how other goods are marketed and packaged. They can try out a service themselves to understand how the industry operates. In these ways, they will understand what prospective customers need and want—and how they can serve them.

Qualifying—determining that the prospect really is a potential customer—is another important sales task. Not all prospects are qualified to make purchase decisions. Even though an employee in a firm might like your products, he or she might not be authorized to make the purchase. A consumer who test-drives a Porsche might fall in love with it but not be able to cover the $100,000+ price tag. Qualifying can be a two-way street. As a sales representative, you might determine that a certain prospect is qualified to make a purchase. But the prospect must agree in order for the process to go forward. If either you or the prospect determine at the outset that there's no chance for a purchase, then it's best to move on.

Approach

Once you have identified a qualified prospect, you need to collect all relevant information and plan an **approach**—your initial contact with the prospective customer. If your firm already has a relationship with the customer or has permission to contact the person, you may use telemarketing. But before you do so, gather as much information as you can.

Information gathering makes **precall planning** possible. As mentioned earlier, educate yourself about the industry in general, as well as goods and services offered by competitors. Read any marketing research available. Go to trade shows—you can learn a lot about many companies and their products at one location, usually in one day. Learn as much as you can about the firm you plan to approach: browse the company's Web site; find online news articles and press releases about the company; talk with other people in the industry. Know its product offerings well. If possible, buy at least one of the firm's products and use it yourself. Identify ways you can help the firm do better. Without invading an individual customer's privacy, see if you have anything in common—perhaps you grew up in the same state, or you both like to play tennis. All of this planning will help you make an effective approach.

As you plan your approach, try to answer the following questions:

- Who am I approaching, and what are their jobs within the company?

- What is their level of knowledge? Are they already informed about the idea I am going to present?

- What do they want or need? Should I speak in technical terms or provide general information?

- What do they need to hear? Do they need to know more about specific products or how those products can serve them? Do they need to know how the product works? Do they need to know about cost and availability?

If you are a retail salesperson, you can ask a shopper questions to learn more about his or her needs and preferences. Say you work at a large sporting goods store. You might ask a young male shopper whether he works out at home, what equipment he already has, what his fitness goals are. The answers to these questions should lead you in the direction of a sale.

Presentation

In a **presentation**, you convey your marketing message to the potential customer. You describe the product's major features, point out its strengths, and cite other customers' successes with the product. One popular form of presentation is a "features-benefits" framework, wherein you talk about the good or service in terms meaningful to the buyer. If you work for a car dealership, you might point out safety features such as side airbags and built-in car seats to a young couple.

qualifying Determining a prospect's needs, income, and purchase authority as a potential customer.

approach Salesperson's initial contact with a prospective customer.

precall planning Use of information collected during the prospecting and qualifying stages of the sales process and during previous contacts with the prospect to tailor the approach and presentation to match the customer's needs.

presentation Personal selling function of describing a product's major features and relating them to a customer's problems or needs.

cold calling Contacting a prospect without a prior appointment.

Your presentation should be well organized, clear, and concise. If appropriate, use visual sales support materials such as a chart, a brochure, a DVD, or even streaming video from your laptop. If this is your first presentation to a potential customer, it will likely be more detailed than a routine call to give an existing customer some updates. Regardless of the situation, though, be attuned to your audience's response so you can modify your presentation—even on the spur of the moment—to meet their needs.

Many presentations now use computer-based multimedia, which can offer everything from interactivity to current pricing information. Companies like SlideShare and BrainShark, which enable users to share their presentations online, are now offering video capabilities. Users can embed video into their presentations along with traditional PowerPoint slides and other images.[25]

However, technology must be used efficiently to be effective. For example, a company's Web site can be an excellent selling tool if it is easy for salespeople to present and buyers to use. A salesperson can actually use the site during a presentation by showing a potential customer how to use it to learn about and purchase products.

In a **cold calling** situation, the approach and presentation often take place at the same time. Cold calling means phoning or visiting the customer without a prior appointment and making a sales pitch on the spot. Cold calling requires nerve, skill, and creativity, but salespeople who are successful at it still point to the importance of preparation. During economic downturns, the ability to make cold calls becomes even more essential, as Zafar Shaikh discovered recently. Shaikh is founder and CEO of SoftNice, a provider of programming, Web development, and business intelligence services in Allentown, Pennsylvania. When SoftNice and its competitors struggled financially during the recent recession, Shaikh decided to invest in his sales force, adding another person and turning the team loose. Through Web research and cold calling, the three-person team brought in project work for the company, managing to double its monthly workload.[26]

Demonstration

demonstration Stage in the personal selling process in which the customer has the opportunity to try out or otherwise see how a good or service works before purchase.

One of the most important advantages of personal selling is the opportunity to demonstrate a product. During a **demonstration**, the buyer gets a chance to try the product or at least see how it works. A demonstration might involve a test-drive of the latest hybrid car or an in-store cooking class using pots and pans that are for sale.

Visual sales support materials may be used in a sales presentation.

© AP IMAGES/STEVE HELBER

Many firms use new technologies to make their demonstrations more outstanding than those of their competitors. Multimedia interactive demonstrations are now common. Visitors to the Black & Decker Web site can click on video demonstrations of such products as the Alligator Lopper (an electric branch clipper) and the Scumbuster Extreme power floor scrubber.[27] The key to an outstanding demonstration—one that gains the customer's attention, keeps his or her interest, is convincing, and stays in the customer's memory—is planning. But planning should also include time and space for free exchanges of information. During your demonstration, you should be prepared to stop and answer questions, redemonstrate a certain feature, or even let the customer try the product firsthand.

Handling Objections

Potential customers often have legitimate questions and concerns about a good or service they are considering. **Objections** are expressions of resistance by the prospect, and it is reasonable to expect them. Objections might appear in the form of stalling or indecisiveness. "Let me call you back," your prospect might say, or "I just don't know about this." Or your buyer might focus on something negative such as high price.

You can answer objections without being aggressive or rude. Use an objection as an opportunity to reassure your buyer about price, features, durability, availability, and the like. If the objection involves price, you might be able to suggest a less-expensive model or a payment plan. If the objection involves a comparison to competitive products, point out the obvious—and not so obvious— benefits of your own. If the objection involves a question about availability, a few clicks on your laptop should show how many items are in stock and when they can be shipped.

objection Expression of sales resistance by the prospect.

Closing

The moment of truth in selling is the **closing**—the point at which the salesperson asks the prospect for an order. If your presentation has been effective and you have handled all objections, a closing would be the natural conclusion to the meeting. But you may still find it difficult to close the sale. Closing does not have to be thought of in terms of a "hard sell." Instead, you can ask your customer, "Would you like to give this a try?" or, "Do I have your approval to proceed?"

Other methods of closing include the following:

1. Addressing the prospect's major concern about a purchase and then offering a convincing argument. *"If I can show you how the new heating system will reduce your energy costs by 25 percent, would you be willing to let us install it?"*

2. Posing choices for the prospect in which either alternative represents a sale. *"Would you prefer the pink sweater or the green one?"*

3. Advising the buyer that a product is about to be discontinued or will go up in price soon. (But be completely honest about this—you don't want a customer to learn later that this was not true.)

4. Remaining silent so the buyer can make a decision on his or her own.

5. Offering an extra inducement designed to motivate a favorable buyer response, such as a quantity discount, an extended service contract, or a low-interest payment plan.

Even if the meeting or phone call ends without a sale, the effort is not over. You can use a written note or an e-mail to keep communication open, letting the buyer know you are ready and waiting to be of service.

closing Stage of the personal selling process in which the salesperson asks the customer to make a purchase decision.

Follow-Up

The word *close* can be misleading because the point at which the prospect accepts the seller's offer is where much of the real work of selling begins. In today's competitive environment, the most successful salespeople make sure that today's customers will also be tomorrow's.

briefly speaking

"Just do what you do best."

—Red Auerbach
*(1917–2006)
Coach and president, NBA's
Boston Celtics*

It is not enough to close the sale and move on. Relationship selling involves reinforcing the purchase decision and ensuring the company delivers the highest-quality merchandise. As a salesperson, you must also ensure that customer service needs are met and that satisfaction results from all of a customer's dealings with your company. Otherwise, some other company may get the next order.

These postsale activities, which often determine whether a person will become a repeat customer, constitute the sales **follow-up**. Sales experts believe in a wide array of follow-up techniques, ranging from expensive information folders to holiday cards to online greetings. Some suggest phone calls at regular intervals. Others prefer automatic e-mail reminders when it is time to renew or reorder. At the very least, however, you should contact customers to find out if they are satisfied with their purchases. This step allows you to psychologically reinforce the customer's original decision to buy. It also gives you an opportunity to correct any problems and ensure the next sale. Follow-up helps strengthen the bond you are trying to build with customers in relationship selling. You have probably experienced follow-up as a customer—if your auto dealership called to see if you were satisfied with recent service or if your doctor's office phoned to find out if you were feeling better.

follow-up Postsale activities that often determine whether an individual who has made a recent purchase will become a repeat customer.

---

 assessment check

1. Identify the seven steps of the sales process.
2. Why is follow-up important to the sales effort?

Managing the Sales Effort

6 Identify the seven basic functions of a sales manager.

The overall direction and control of the personal selling effort are in the hands of a firm's sales managers. In a typical geographic sales structure, a district or divisional sales manager might report to a regional or zone manager. This manager in turn reports to a national sales manager or vice president of sales.

Currently, there are about 347,000 sales managers in the United States.[28] The sales manager's job requires a unique blend of administrative and sales skills, depending on the specific level in the sales hierarchy. Sales skills are particularly important for first-level sales managers because they are involved daily in the continuing process of training and directly leading the sales force. But as people rise in the sales management hierarchy, they require more managerial skills and fewer sales skills to perform well. Madison L. "Buddy" Cox Jr. recently became sales director for North Carolina–based TwinVision, marketers of transportation and transit industry software, such as the Talking Bus voice announcement system. Cox started his career in sales, working for various bus companies, and gradually ascended to progressively more responsible sales and executive positions.[29]

Sales force management links individual salespeople to general management. The sales manager performs seven basic managerial functions: (1) recruitment and selection, (2) training, (3) organization, (4) supervision, (5) motivation, (6) compensation, and (7) evaluation and control. Sales managers perform these tasks in a demanding and complex environment. They must manage an increasingly diverse sales force that includes more women and minorities. Women account for nearly half of U.S. professional salespeople, and their numbers are growing at a faster rate than that for men. As the workforce composition continues to change, an even more diverse blend of people will be needed to fill a growing number of sales positions.[30]

Recruitment and Selection

Recruiting and selecting successful salespeople are among the sales manager's greatest challenges. After all, these workers will collectively determine just how successful the sales manager is. New salespeople—like you—might come from colleges and universities, trade and business schools, the military, other companies, and even the firm's current nonsales staff. A successful sales career offers satisfaction in all of the following five areas a person generally considers when deciding on a profession:

1. *Opportunity for advancement.* Studies have shown that successful sales representatives advance rapidly in most companies.

2. *Potential for high earnings.* Salespeople have the opportunity to earn a very comfortable living.

3. *Personal satisfaction.* A salesperson derives satisfaction from achieving success in a competitive environment and from helping customers satisfy their wants and needs.

4. *Job security.* Selling provides a high degree of job security because there is always a need for good salespeople.

5. *Independence and variety.* Salespeople often work independently, calling on customers in their territory. They have the freedom to make important decisions about meeting their customers' needs and frequently report that no two workdays are the same.

During an interview, a sales manager looks for enthusiasm, organizational skills, sociability, and other traits.

Careful selection of salespeople is important for two reasons. First, a company invests a substantial amount of time and money in the selection process. Second, hiring mistakes can damage relationships with customers and overall performance and are costly to correct.

Most large firms use a specific seven-step process in selecting sales personnel: application screening, initial interview, in-depth interview, testing, reference checks, physical examination, and hiring decision. An application screening typically is followed by an initial interview. If the applicant looks promising, an in-depth interview takes place. During the interview, a sales manager looks for the person's enthusiasm, organizational skills, ambition, persuasiveness, ability to follow instructions, and sociability.

Next, the company may administer aptitude, interest, and knowledge tests. One popular testing approach is the assessment center. This technique uses situational exercises, group discussions, and various job simulations, allowing the sales manager to measure a candidate's skills, knowledge, and ability. Assessment centers enable managers to see what potential salespeople can do rather than what they say they can do. Before hiring a candidate, the firm checks references, reviews company policies, and may request a physical examination.

Training

To shape new sales recruits into an efficient sales organization, managers must conduct an effective training program. The principal methods used in sales training are on-the-job training, individual instruction, in-house classes, and external seminars.

Popular training techniques include instructional videos or DVDs, lectures, role-playing exercises, and interactive computer programs. Simulations can help salespeople improve their selling techniques. Many firms supplement their training by enrolling salespeople in executive development programs at local colleges and by hiring specialists to teach customized training programs. In other instances, sales reps attend courses and workshops developed by outside companies.

While sales meetings often are packed with a variety of topics, they can be an excellent vehicle for sales training. Happauge, New York-based Santinelli International, the manufacturer of lens edging equipment to the optical industry, uses its national sales meeting as a platform for training. The practical advice and give-and-take in such sessions motivates colleagues to reassess their own skills and try new techniques.[31]

Ongoing sales training is important for all salespeople, even veterans. Sales managers often conduct this type of training informally, traveling with field reps and then offering constructive criticism or suggestions. Like sales meetings, classes and workshops are other ways to reinforce training. Mentoring is also a key tool in training new salespeople.

Organization

Sales managers are responsible for the organization of the field sales force. General organizational alignments—usually made by top marketing management—may be based on geography, products, types of customers, or some combination of these factors. Figure 17.3 presents a streamlined organizational chart illustrating each of these alignments.

A product sales organization is likely to have a specialized sales force for each major category of the firm's products. This approach is common among B2B companies that market large numbers of highly technical, complex products sold through different marketing channels.

Firms that market similar products throughout large territories often use geographic specialization. Multinational corporations may have different sales divisions on different continents and in different countries. A geographic organization may also be combined with one of the other organizational methods.

However, many companies are moving away from using territorial sales reps as they adopt customer-focused sales forces. For example, a single territory that contains two major customers might be redefined so that the same sales rep covers both customers. Customer-oriented organizations use different sales force strategies for each major type of customer served. Some firms assign separate sales forces for their consumer and organizational customers. Others have sales forces for specific industries, such as financial services, educational, and automotive. Sales forces can also be organized by customer size, with a separate sales force assigned to large, medium, and small accounts.

national accounts organization
Promotional effort in which a dedicated sales team is assigned to a firm's major customers to provide sales and service needs.

Many firms using a customer-oriented structure adopt a **national accounts organization**. This format strengthens a firm's relationship with its largest customers by assigning senior sales personnel or sales teams to major accounts. Organizing by national accounts helps sales representatives develop cooperation among departments to meet special needs of the firm's most important customers. An example of national account selling is the relationship between Walmart and its major vendors. SC Johnson, Unilever, H. J. Heinz, Johnson & Johnson, Kimberly-Clark, Kraft, Nestlé, Hormel, and Colgate Palmolive are just some of the companies that have sales offices near Walmart's headquarters in Bentonville, Arkansas.

As companies expand their market coverage across national borders, they may use a variant of national account sales teams. These global account teams may be staffed by local sales representatives in the countries in which a company is operating. In other instances, the firm selects highly trained sales executives from its domestic operations. In either case, specialized training is critical to the success of a company's global sales force.

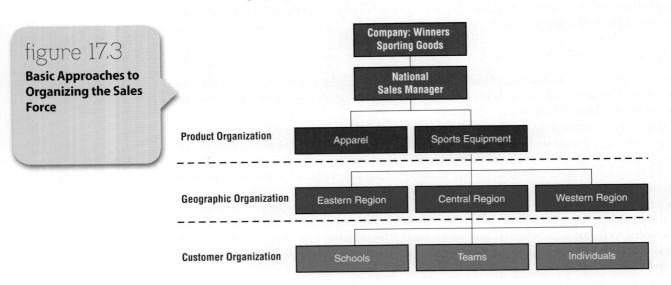

figure 17.3

Basic Approaches to Organizing the Sales Force

The individual sales manager also must organize the sales territories within his or her area of responsibility. Factors such as sales potential, strengths and weaknesses of available personnel, and workloads are considered in territory allocation decisions.

Supervision

Sales managers have differing opinions about the supervision of a sales force. Individuals and situations vary, so it is impossible to write a recipe for the exact amount of supervision needed in all cases. However, a concept known as **span of control** helps provide some general guidelines. Span of control refers to the number of sales representatives who report to first-level sales managers. The optimal span of control is affected by such factors as complexity of work activities, ability of the individual sales manager, degree of interdependence among individual salespeople, and the extent of training each salesperson receives. A 6-to-1 ratio has been suggested as the optimal span of control for first-level sales managers supervising technical or industrial salespeople. In contrast, a 10-to-1 ratio is recommended if sales representatives are calling on wholesale and retail accounts.

span of control
Number of representatives who report to first-level sales managers.

Motivation

What motivates salespeople to perform their best? The sales manager is responsible for finding the answer to this question. The sales process involves problem solving, which sometimes includes frustration—particularly when a sale is delayed or falls through. Information sharing, recognition, bonuses, incentives, and benefits can all be used to help defray frustration and motivate a sales staff. Developing an enthusiastic sales staff who are happy at their jobs is the goal of the sales manager. Motivation is an important part of a company's success.

Creating a positive, motivating environment doesn't necessarily mean instituting complex or expensive incentive programs. Monetary rewards—cash—often is considered king. But sometimes simple recognition—a thank-you, a dinner, a year-end award—can go a long way. It is important for the sales manager to figure out what types of incentives will be most effective with his or her particular group of employees. Some firms go all out, dangling luxury items such as computers, digital cameras, or trips in front of the sales force as rewards. A Caribbean cruise, a trip to Disney World, or a weekend in Las Vegas could be the carrot that works, particularly if family members are included. Some firms purchase gift cards from retailers such as L.L.Bean or Lowe's to distribute to sales staff who perform well.

But not all incentive programs are effective at motivating employees. A program with targets set too high, that isn't publicized, or that allows only certain sales personnel to participate can actually backfire. So it is important for sales management to plan carefully for an incentive program to succeed.

Sales managers can also gain insight into the subject of motivation by studying the various theories of motivation developed over the years. One theory that has been applied effectively to sales force motivation is **expectancy theory**, which states that motivation depends on the expectations an individual has of his or her ability to perform the job and on how performance relates to attaining rewards the individual values.

Sales managers can apply the expectancy theory of motivation by following a five-step process:

expectancy theory
Theory that motivation depends on an individual's expectations of his or her ability to perform a job and how that performance relates to attaining a desired reward.

1. Let each salesperson know in detail what is expected in terms of selling goals, service standards, and other areas of performance. Rather than setting goals just once a year, many firms do so on a semiannual, quarterly, or even monthly basis.

2. Make the work valuable by assessing the needs, values, and abilities of each salesperson and then assigning appropriate tasks.

3. Make the work achievable. As leaders, sales managers must inspire self-confidence in their salespeople and offer training and coaching to reassure them.

4. Provide immediate and specific feedback, guiding those who need improvement and giving positive feedback to those who do well.

5. Offer rewards each salesperson values, whether it is an incentive as described previously, opportunity for advancement, or a bonus.

Compensation

Money is an important part of any person's job, and the salesperson is no exception. So deciding how best to compensate the sales force can be a critical factor in motivation. Sales compensation can be based on a commission, a straight salary, or a combination of both. Bonuses based on end-of-year results are another popular form of compensation. The increasing popularity of team selling has also forced companies to set up reward programs to recognize performance of business units and teams. Today, about 25 percent of firms rewards business-unit performance.

A **commission** is a payment tied directly to the sales or profits a salesperson achieves. A salesperson might receive a 5 percent commission on all sales up to a specified quota and a 7 percent commission on sales beyond that point. This approach to sales compensation is increasingly popular. But while commissions reinforce selling incentives, they may cause some sales force members to overlook nonselling activities such as completing sales reports, delivering promotion materials, and servicing existing accounts. In addition, salespeople who operate entirely on commission may become too aggressive in their approach to potential customers, which could backfire.

A **salary** is a fixed payment made periodically to an employee. A firm that bases compensation on salaries rather than commissions might pay a salesperson a set amount every week, twice a month, or once a month. A company must balance benefits and disadvantages in paying predetermined salaries to compensate managers and sales personnel. A straight salary plan gives management more control over how sales personnel allocate their efforts, but it may reduce the incentive to find new markets and land new accounts.

Many firms find it's best to develop compensation programs that combine features of both salary and commission plans. A new salesperson often receives a base salary while in training, even if he or she moves to full commission later on. If the salesperson does a lot of driving as part of the job, he or she may receive a vehicle. If the person works from home, there might be an allowance toward setting up an office there.

Total compensation packages vary according to industry, with the finance, insurance, and real estate industries coming out on top, followed closely by general services. They also vary according to years of experience in sales. Figure 17.4 reflects the findings of a recent pay survey of *account managers*—another name for a salesperson responsible for one or more customers, or *accounts*. The data show how account managers' median base pay, bonus, and commissions vary by years of experience.

commission Incentive compensation directly related to the sales or profits achieved by a salesperson.

salary Fixed compensation payment made periodically to an employee.

sales quota Level of expected sales for a territory, product, customer, or salesperson against which actual results are compared.

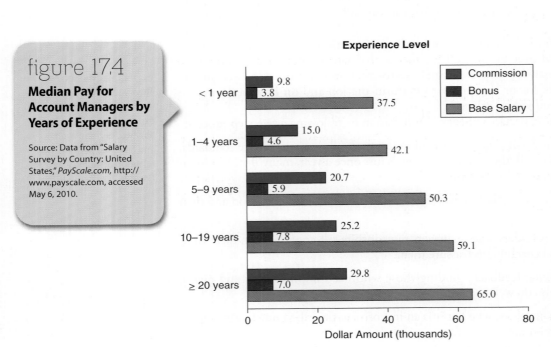

figure 17.4

Median Pay for Account Managers by Years of Experience

Source: Data from "Salary Survey by Country: United States," *PayScale.com*, http://www.payscale.com, accessed May 6, 2010.

Evaluation and Control

Perhaps the most difficult tasks required of sales managers are evaluation and control. Sales managers are responsible for setting standards and choosing the best methods for measuring sales performance. Sales volume, profitability, and changes in market share are the usual means of evaluating sales effectiveness. They typically involve the use of **sales quotas**—specified sales or profit targets that the firm expects salespeople to achieve. A particular sales representative might be expected to generate sales of $2.25 million in his or her territory during a given year. In many cases, the quota is tied to the compensation system. Technology has greatly improved the ability of sales managers to monitor the effectiveness of their sales staffs. Databases help sales managers to quickly divide revenues by salesperson, account, and geographic area.

In today's marketing environment, other measures such as customer satisfaction, profit contribution, share of product-category sales, and customer retention also come into play. This is the result of three factors:

1. A long-term orientation that results from emphasis on building customer relationships.

2. The fact that evaluations based on sales volume alone may lead to overselling and inventory problems that may damage customer relationships.

3. The need to encourage sales representatives to develop new accounts, provide customer service, and emphasize new products. Sales quotas tend to put focus on short-term selling goals rather than long-term relationships.

The sales manager must follow a formal system that includes a consistent series of decisions. This way, the manager can make fair and accurate evaluations. The system helps the sales manager answer three general questions:

1. *Where does each salesperson's performance rank relative to predetermined standards?* This comparison takes into consideration any uncontrollable variables on sales performance, such as a natural disaster or unforeseen change in the industry. Each adjusted rank is stated as a percentage of the standard.

2. *What are the salesperson's strong points?* The manager might list areas of the salesperson's performance in which he or she has performed above the standard. Or strong points could be placed in such categories as technical ability, processes, and end results.

3. *What are the salesperson's weak points?* No one likes to hear criticism, but when it is offered constructively, it can be motivation to improve performance. The manager and employee should establish specific objectives for improvement and set a timetable for judging the employee's improvement.

In completing the evaluation summary, the sales manager follows a set procedure so all employees are treated equally:

- Each aspect of sales performance for which a standard exists should be measured separately. This helps prevent the so-called halo effect, in which the rating given on one factor influences those on other performance variables.

- Each salesperson should be judged on the basis of actual sales performance rather than potential ability. This is why rankings are important in the evaluation.

- Sales managers must judge each salesperson on the basis of sales performance for the entire period under consideration, rather than for a few particular incidents.

- The evaluation should be reviewed by a third party, such as the manager's boss or a human resources manager, for completeness and objectivity.

Once the evaluation is complete, both manager and salesperson should focus on positive action—whether it is a drive toward new goals or correcting a negative situation. An evaluation should be motivation for improved performance.

 assessment check

1. What are the seven basic functions performed by a sales manager?

2. Define *span of control.*

3. What are the three main questions a sales manager must address as part of a salesperson's evaluation?

Ethical Issues in Sales

7 Explain the role of ethical behavior in personal selling.

Promotional activities can raise ethical questions, and personal selling is no exception. A difficult economy or highly competitive environment may tempt some salespeople—particularly those new to the business—to behave in ways they might later regret. They might use the company car for a family trip. They might give personal or expensive gifts to customers. They might try to sell a product they know is not right for a particular customer's needs. But today's experienced, highly professional salespeople know long-term success requires a strong code of ethics. They also know a single breach of ethics could have a devastating effect on their careers.

Some people believe ethical problems are inevitable because of the very nature of the sales function. And in the wake of corporate scandals in which top executives have benefited at the expense of customers, employees, and shareholders, ethical managers are working harder than ever to build trust.

Sales managers and top executives can do a lot to foster a corporate culture that encourages honesty and ethical behavior. Here are some characteristics of such a culture:

- *Employees understand what is expected of them.* A written code of ethics—which should be reviewed by all employees—in addition to ethics training helps educate employees in how to conduct ethical business.

- *Open communication.* Employees who feel comfortable talking with their supervisors are more apt to ask questions if they are uncertain about situations or decisions and to report any violations they come across.

- *Managers lead by example.* Workers naturally emulate the ethical behavior of managers. A sales manager who is honest with customers, doesn't accept inappropriate gifts, and leaves the company car at home during vacation is likely to be imitated by his or her sales staff.

Regardless of corporate culture, every salesperson is responsible for his or her own behavior and relationship with customers. If, as a new salesperson, you find yourself uncertain about a decision, ask yourself these questions. The answers should help you make the ethical choice.

sales promotion
Marketing activities other than personal selling, advertising, and publicity that enhance consumer purchasing and dealer effectiveness.

1. Does my decision affect anyone other than myself and the bottom line?

2. Is my success based on making the sale or creating a loyal customer?

3. Is my dealings with a customer in their best interest and not exploiting their trust?

4. What price will I pay for this decision?

assessment check

1. Why is it important for salespeople to maintain ethical behavior?

2. What are the characteristics of companies that foster corporate cultures that encourage ethical behavior?

Sales Promotion

8 Describe the role of sales promotion in the promotional mix, and identify the different types of sales promotions.

Sales promotion includes marketing activities other than personal selling, advertising, and publicity designed to enhance consumer purchasing and dealer effectiveness. Sales promotion can be traced back as far as the ruins of Pompeii and Ephesus. In the United States, companies have been giving away trinkets and premiums for more than 100 years.

Sales promotion techniques were originally intended as short-term incentives aimed at producing an immediate response: a purchase. Today, however, marketers recognize sales promotion as an integral part of the overall marketing plan, and the focus has shifted from short-term goals to long-term objectives of building brand equity and maintaining continuing purchases. A frequent-flyer program enables a new airline to build a base of loyal customers. A frequent-stay program allows a hotel chain to attract regular guests.

Both retailers and manufacturers use sales promotions to offer consumers extra incentives to buy. These promotions are likely to stress price advantages, giveaways, or special offerings. The general objectives of sales promotion are to speed up the sales process and increase sales volume. Promotions can also help build loyalty. Through a consumer promotion, a marketer encourages consumers to try the product, use more of it, and buy it again. The firm also hopes to foster sales of related items and increase impulse purchases. Back-to-school sales are one type of sales promotion. Retailers run them each fall to attract shoppers who need clothing and supplies for the new academic year. In recent campaigns, Office Max and Staples sold a different school item, like pencils or pocket folders, for a penny each week, as well as offering 50 percent off big-ticket items such as electronics and furniture.[32]

Retailers use sales promotions to offer consumers extra incentives to buy.

Today, consumers have many more choices among products than in the past, and for this reason many marketers create special programs to build loyalty among their customers. However, with loyalty programs no longer unique, marketing and sales professionals work to build loyalty among their customers by managing customer relationships and regularly evaluating those relationships to determine how they can enhance them.[33]

Because sales promotion is so important to a marketing effort, an entire promotion industry exists to offer expert assistance in its use and to design unique promotions, just as the entire advertising industry offers similar services for advertisers. These companies, like advertising agencies, provide other firms with assistance in promoting their goods and services. Figure 17.5 shows current spending by companies for different types of sales promotions, many of which are conducted by these firms.

Sales promotions often produce their best results when combined with other marketing activities. Ads create awareness, while sales promotions lead to trial or purchase. After a presentation, a salesperson may offer a potential customer a discount coupon for the good or service. Promotions

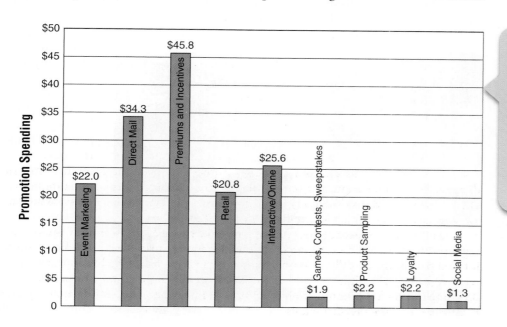

figure 17.5

Current Spending by Companies for Different Sales Promotions (in billions)

Source: Data from *Promo*, December 1, 2009, http://promomagazine.com.

encourage immediate action because they impose limited time frames. Discount coupons and rebates usually have expiration dates. In addition, sales promotions produce measurable results, making it relatively easy for marketers to evaluate their effectiveness. If more people buy shoes during a buy-one-get-one-free promotion at a shoe store, its owners know the promotion was successful.

It is important to understand what sales promotions can and cannot do. They can encourage interest in both new and mature products, help introduce new products, encourage trial and repeat purchases, increase usage rates, neutralize competition, and reinforce advertising and personal selling efforts. On the other hand, sales promotions cannot overcome poor brand images, product deficiencies, or poor training for salespeople. While sales promotions increase volume in the short term, they may not lead to sales and profit growth in the long run.

Sales promotion techniques may serve all members of a marketing channel. In addition, manufacturers may use trade promotion methods to promote their products to resellers. Promotions are usually employed selectively. Sales promotion techniques include the following consumer-oriented promotions: coupons, refunds, samples, bonus packs, premiums, contests, sweepstakes, and specialty advertising. Trade-oriented promotions include trade allowances, point-of-purchase advertising, trade shows, dealer incentives, contests, and training programs.

Consumer-Oriented Sales Promotions

In the promotion industry, marketers use all types of sales promotions, including games, contests, sweepstakes, and coupons to persuade new and existing customers to try their products. Consumer-oriented sales promotions encourage repurchases by rewarding current users, boosting sales of complementary products, and increasing impulse purchases. These promotions also attract consumer attention in the midst of advertising clutter.

It's important for marketers to use sales promotions selectively; if they are overused, consumers begin to expect price discounts at all times, which ultimately diminishes brand equity. The following sections describe the various forms of consumer-oriented sales promotions.

COUPONS AND REFUNDS

coupon Sales promotion technique that offers a discount on the purchase price of goods or services.

Coupons, the most widely used form of sales promotion, offer discounts on the purchase price of goods and services. Consumers can redeem the coupons at retail outlets, which receive the face value of the coupon plus a handling fee from the manufacturer. The coupon industry has been somewhat "clipped" in recent years due to the growing clout of retailers and more complex accounting rules that make couponing less attractive to some marketers. In addition, consumers receive so many coupons that they cannot possibly redeem them all. In a recent year, an estimated 311 billion coupons were offered in the United States, and only 3.2 billion were redeemed. Still, consumers saved nearly $3.5 billion.[34]

Mail, magazines, newspapers, package inserts and, increasingly, the Internet are the standard methods of distributing coupons. But another distribution channel for coupons has emerged: cell phones. Thanks to advances in barcode technology, retailers can distribute coupons digitally to cell phone users, who can also redeem the coupons digitally when they shop. Target is one of the first national retailers to adopt the practice, which Target.com president Steve Eastman characterizes as "a competitive advantage" for the company.[35]

> Coupons, which offer discounts on goods and services, can be redeemed at retail outlets.

© SUSAN VAN ETTEN/PHOTOEDIT

Refunds, or rebates, offer cash back to consumers who send in proof of purchasing one or more products. Refunds help packaged-goods companies increase purchase rates, promote multiple purchases, and reward product users. Although many consumers find the refund forms too bothersome to complete, plenty still do.

refund Cash given back to consumers who send in proof of purchase for one or more products.

SAMPLES, BONUS PACKS, AND PREMIUMS

Marketers are increasingly adopting the "try it, you'll like it" approach as an effective means of getting consumers to try and then purchase their goods and services. **Sampling** refers to the free distribution of a product in an attempt to obtain future sales. Samples may be distributed door-to-door, by mail, online, via demonstrations in stores or at events, or by including them in packages with other products.

Sampling produces a higher response rate than most other promotions. In supermarkets, an estimated 70 million consumers receive samples of some kind each quarter, with one-third making a product purchase during the same shopping trip. Total annual spending on this sales promotion technique has topped $2.2 billion.[36]

With sampling, marketers can target potential customers and be certain the product reaches them. Sampling provides an especially useful way to promote new or unusual products because it gives the consumer a direct product experience. It also has a "Wow!" factor. Recently, a group of architects, designers, and contractors in New York City got together under one roof to host a ten-day event they called Pop Up Design Clinic, offering free half-hour design consultations. The professionals scheduled the event during what is normally a slow period in their industry: a useful time to concentrate on business development. Hundreds of business cards were exchanged and contacts made during the unique sampling opportunity.[37]

A major disadvantage of sampling is the high cost involved. Not only must the marketer give away small quantities of a product that might otherwise have generated revenues through regular sales, but the market is also in effect closed for the time it takes consumers to use up the samples. In addition, the marketer may encounter problems in distributing the samples. Hellman's marketers once annoyed consumers instead of pleasing them when the firm distributed sample packets of Italian and French salad dressing in home-delivered copies of *The New York Times*. Many of the packets burst when the papers hit the driveways.

A **bonus pack** is a specially packaged item that gives the purchaser a larger quantity at the regular price. For instance, Camay soap recently offered three bars for the price of two, and Salon Selectives is known to increase the size of its shampoos and conditioners for the same price as regular sizes. **Premiums** are items given free or at reduced cost with purchases of other products. For example, Pantene frequently attaches a purse-size bottle of hairspray to the sides of its other hair-care products. Premiums have proven effective in motivating consumers to try new products or different brands. A premium should have some relationship with the product or brand it accompanies, though. For example, a home improvement center might offer free measuring tapes to its customers.

sampling Free distribution of a product in an attempt to obtain future sales; process of selecting survey respondents or research participants.

bonus pack Specially packaged item that gives the purchaser a larger quantity at the regular price.

premium Item given free or at a reduced cost with purchases of other products.

CONTESTS AND SWEEPSTAKES

Firms often sponsor contests and sweepstakes to introduce new goods and services and to attract additional customers. **Contests** require entrants to complete a task such as solving a puzzle or answering questions in a trivia quiz, and they may also require proofs of purchase. **Sweepstakes,** on the other hand, choose winners by chance, so no product purchase is necessary. They are more popular with consumers than contests because they do not take as much effort for consumers to enter. Marketers like them, too, because they are inexpensive to run and the number of winners is predetermined. With some contests, the sponsors cannot predict the number of people who will correctly complete the puzzles or gather the right number of symbols from scratch-off cards.

Marketers are increasingly turning to the Internet for contests and sweepstakes because of its relatively low cost and ability to provide data immediately. Interactivity is also a key part of the online experience: as consumers become more engaged in the contest or sweepstakes event, they also build a relationship with the firm's products. With its first-ever online sweepstakes, Long John Silver's promoted the introduction of Crispy Breaded Pollock to its seafood menu. By entering the "Spin & Win Fish Fry," players could print a coupon for a free serving of the new fish dish and stood to win $20,000.[38] With a number of recent court rulings and legal restrictions, the use of contests requires careful administration. A firm contemplating this promotional technique might consider the services of online promotion specialists such as WebStakes or NetStakes.

contest Sales promotion technique that requires entrants to complete a task, such as solving a puzzle or answering questions on a quiz, for the chance to win a prize.

sweepstakes Sales promotion technique in which prize winners are selected by chance.

SPECIALTY ADVERTISING

The origin of specialty advertising has been traced to the Middle Ages, when artisans gave wooden pegs bearing their names to prospects, who drove them into the walls at home to serve as convenient hangers for armor. Corporations began putting their names on a variety of products in the late 1800s, as newspapers and print shops explored new methods to earn additional revenues from their expensive printing presses. Today, just about everyone owns a cap or T-shirt with the name or logo of a company, organization, or product displayed on it.

specialty advertising
Sales promotion technique that places the advertiser's name, address, and advertising message on useful articles that are then distributed to target consumers.

Specialty advertising is a sales promotion technique that places the advertiser's name, address, and advertising message on useful articles that are then distributed to target consumers. Wearable products are the most popular, accounting for nearly a third of specialty advertising sales. Pens, mugs, glassware, and calendars are other popular forms.

Advertising specialties help reinforce previous or future advertising and sales messages. Consumers like these giveaways, which generate stronger responses to direct mail, resulting in three times the dollar volume of sales compared with direct mail alone. Companies use this form of promotion to highlight store openings and new products, motivate salespeople, increase visits to trade show booths, and remind customers about their products.

Trade-Oriented Promotions

trade promotion Sales promotion that appeals to marketing intermediaries rather than to consumers.

Sales promotion techniques can also contribute effectively to campaigns aimed at retailers and wholesalers. **Trade promotion** is sales promotion that appeals to marketing intermediaries rather than to final consumers. Marketers use trade promotions in push strategies by encouraging resellers to stock new products, continue to carry existing ones, and promote both effectively to consumers. The typical firm spends about half of its promotional budget on trade promotion—as much money as it spends on advertising and consumer-oriented sales promotions combined. Successful trade promotions offer financial incentives. They require careful timing and attention to costs and are easy to implement by retailers. These promotions should bring quick results and improve retail sales.

TRADE ALLOWANCES

trade allowance
Financial incentive offered to wholesalers and retailers that purchase or promote specific products.

Among the most common trade promotion methods are **trade allowances**—special financial incentives offered to wholesalers and retailers that purchase or promote specific products. These offers take various forms. A buying allowance gives retailers a discount on goods. They include off-invoice allowances through which retailers deduct specified amounts from their invoices or receive free goods, such as one free case for every ten ordered. When a manufacturer offers a promotional

mktg: *success*

Toy Fair: Betting on Tinseltown

Background. The American International Toy Fair is one of the industry's oldest and largest trade shows. With more than 1,100 exhibitors displaying more than 100,000 products, the four-day event attracts 32,000 attendees each year. Buyers for toy retailers come for a glimpse of toy manufacturers' latest product lines and to place their orders for the upcoming holiday season—eight months in advance.

The Challenge. With nearly 40 percent of toy sales coming during the last two months of the year, the toy business is full of risk taking. Fortunes rise and fall on the decisions toy manufacturers and retailers must make nearly a year earlier. For toy manufacturers, it's guessing what will appeal to consumers during the holidays. Toy buyers have an additional problem: the possibility of their store getting

stuck with unwanted inventory. As industry observers point out, the key is to have the *right* inventory, not necessarily the most inventory.

The Strategy. In recent years, toys based on characters from TV, movies, and books accounted for 25 percent of all U.S. sales—close to $5.4 billion in a recent year. The industry knew that toys from the movies *Toy Story* and

allowance, it agrees to pay the reseller a certain amount to cover the costs of special promotional displays or extensive advertising that features the manufacturer's product. The goal is to increase sales to consumers by encouraging resellers to promote their products effectively.

As mentioned in previous chapters, some retailers require vendors to pay a special slotting allowance before they agree to take on new products. These fees guarantee slots, or shelf space, for newly introduced items in the stores. This practice is common in large supermarket chains. Retailers defend these fees as essential to cover the added costs of carrying the products, such as redesigning display space and shelves, setting up and administering control systems, managing inventory, and taking the risks inherent in stocking new products. The fees can be sizable, from several hundred dollars per store to many thousands of dollars for a retail chain and millions of dollars for nationally distributed products.

POINT-OF-PURCHASE ADVERTISING

A display or other promotion located near the site of the actual buying decision is known as **point-of-purchase (POP) advertising**. This method of sales promotion capitalizes on the fact that nearly two-thirds of shoppers make their purchase decisions as they walk through a store, so it encourages retailers to improve on-site merchandising.[39] Product suppliers assist the retailer by creating special displays designed to stimulate sales of the promoted item.

Freestanding POP promotions often appear at the ends of shopping aisles. On a typical trip to the supermarket, you might see a POP display for Disney videos, Coppertone sunscreen, or Duracell batteries. Warehouse-style retailers such as Home Depot and Sam's Club, along with Staples and Kmart, all use POP advertising displays frequently. Electronic kiosks, which allow consumers to place orders for items not available in the store, have begun to transform the POP display industry, as creators of these displays look for ways to involve consumers more actively as well as entertain them.

point-of-purchase (POP) advertising Display or other promotion placed near the site of the actual buying decision.

TRADE SHOWS

To influence resellers and other members of the distribution channel, many marketers participate in **trade shows**. These shows often are organized by industry trade associations; frequently, they are part of these associations' annual meetings or conventions. Vendors who serve the industries display and demonstrate their products for attendees. Industries that hold trade shows include manufacturers of sporting goods, medical equipment, electronics, automobiles, clothing, and home furnishings. Service industries include hair styling, health care, travel, and restaurant franchises. The "Marketing Success" feature discusses the Toy Fair, a popular trade show that has stood the test of time.

Because of the expense involved in trade shows, a company must assess the value of these shows on several criteria such as direct sales, any increase in product awareness, image building, and any contribution to the firm's marketing communications efforts. Trade shows give especially effective opportunities to introduce new products and to generate sales leads. Some types of shows reach ultimate consumers as well as channel members. Home, recreation, and automobile shows, for

trade show Product exhibition organized by industry trade associations to showcase goods and services.

Toy Story 2 had sold well. Relying on Hollywood again might help the industry hedge its bets.

The Outcome. Manufacturers flooded the most recent Toy Fair with toys related to the film *Toy Story 3*. Items included Mr. and Mrs. Potato Head dressed like characters Buzz, Woody, and Jessie; the Buzz Lightyear Wing Pack with movable light-up airfoils; a

Lego Western train set; and Barbie and Ken dolls in *Toy Story 3* costuming. As expected, the film rocked the box office, grossing more than $100 million in its first weekend—a sign that this could be a profitable year for the toy industry.

Sources: Nicole Sperling, "Box Office Update: Toy Story '3' on Fire; 'Jonah Hex' Bombs," *Hollywood Insider*, June 19, 2010, http://hollywoodinsider.com; Association Web site, http://www.toyassociation.org, accessed April 12, 2010; Andrea

Chang "Merchandising: It's Not All Fun and Games," *Los Angeles Times*, February 16, 2010, http://www.latimes.com; Dawn C. Chmielewski, "Company Town: Woody and Friends Wait in the Wings at Toy Fair; Facing Fickle Buyers, Industry Pins Hopes on Hollywood," *Los Angeles Times*, February 16, 2010, http://www.latimes.com; Andrea Chang, "Giant Toy Fair Gives a Preview of Christmas," *Los Angeles Times*, February 15, 2010, http://www.latimes.com; Mae Anderson, "A Good Time for Toys That Go 'Cheap!'" *Washington Post*, February 15, 2010, http://www.washingtonpost.com; Company Web site, "American International Toy Fair and Engage! Expo to Co-Locate in New York City," press release, June 22, 2009, http://www.engagedigitalmedia.com.

instance, allow businesses to display and demonstrate home improvement, recreation, and other consumer products to entire communities.

DEALER INCENTIVES, CONTESTS, AND TRAINING PROGRAMS

Manufacturers run dealer incentive programs and contests to reward retailers and their salespeople who increase sales and, more generally, to promote specific products. These channel members receive incentives for performing promotion-related tasks and can win contests by reaching sales goals. Manufacturers may offer major prizes to resellers such as trips to exotic places. **Push money**—which retailers commonly refer to as *spiffs*—is another incentive that gives retail salespeople cash rewards for every unit of a product they sell. This benefit increases the likelihood that the salesperson will try to persuade a customer to buy the product rather than a competing brand.

For more expensive and highly complex products, manufacturers often provide specialized training for retail salespeople. This background helps sales personnel explain features, competitive advantages, and other information to consumers. Training can be provided in several ways: a manufacturer's sales representative can conduct training sessions during regular sales calls, or the firm can distribute sales literature and DVDs.

push money Cash reward paid to retail salespeople for every unit of a product they sell.

 assessment check

1. Define *sales promotion*.
2. Identify at least four types of consumer-oriented sales promotions.
3. Identify at least three types of trade-oriented sales promotions.

strategic implications of marketing in the 21st century

Today's salespeople are a new breed. Richly nourished in a tradition of sales, their roles are strengthened even further through technology. However, as many companies are discovering, nothing can replace the power of personal selling in generating sales and in building strong, loyal customer relationships.

Salespeople today are a critical link in developing relationships between the customer and the company. They communicate customer needs and wants to coworkers in various units within an organization, enabling a cooperative, companywide effort in improving product offerings and in better satisfying individuals within the target market. For salespeople, the greatest benefit of electronic technologies is the ability to share knowledge when it is needed with those who need to know, including customers, suppliers, and employees.

Because buyers are now more sophisticated, demanding more rapid and lower-cost transactions, salespeople must be quick and creative as they find solutions to their customers' problems. Product lifecycles are accelerating, and customers who demand more are likely to switch from one product to another. Recognizing the long-term impact of keeping satisfied buyers—those who make repeat and cross-purchases and provide referrals—versus dissatisfied buyers, organizations are increasingly training their sales forces to provide superior customer service and rewarding them for increasing satisfaction levels.

The traditional skills of a salesperson included persuasion, selling ability, and product knowledge. But today's sales professionals are also likely to possess strong communication and problem-solving skills. Earlier generations of sales personnel tended to be self-driven; today's sales professional is more likely to be a team player as well as a customer advocate who serves his or her buyers by solving problems.

The modern professional salesperson is greatly assisted by the judicious use of both consumer- and trade-oriented sales promotions. Sales promotion often is overlooked in discussions of high-profile advertising; the typical firm allocates more promotional dollars for sales promotion than for advertising. The proven effectiveness of sales promotion makes it a widely used promotional mix component for most marketers.

Review of Chapter Objectives

 Describe the role of today's salesperson.

Today's salesperson seeks to form long-lasting relationships with customers by providing high levels of customer service rather than going for the quick sale. Firms have begun to integrate their computer and communications technologies into the sales function, so people involved in personal selling have an expanded role.

 Describe the four sales channels.

Over-the-counter (retail) selling takes place in a retail location and usually involves providing product information and completing a sale. Field selling involves making personal sales calls on customers. Under certain circumstances, telemarketing is used to provide product information and answer questions from customers who call. Inside selling relies on phone, mail, and e-marketing to provide sales and product services for customers on a continuing basis.

 Describe the major trends in personal selling.

Companies are turning to relationship selling, consultative selling, and team selling. Relationship selling occurs when a salesperson builds a mutually beneficial relationship with a customer on a regular basis over an extended period. Consultative selling involves meeting customer needs by listening to customers, understanding and caring about their problems, paying attention to the details, and following through after the sale. Team selling occurs when the salesperson joins with specialists from other functional areas of the firm to complete the selling process.

 Identify and briefly describe the three basic sales tasks.

Order processing is the routine handling of an order. It characterizes a sales setting in which the need is made known and is acknowledged by the customer. Creative selling is persuasion aimed at making the prospect see the value of the good or service presented. Missionary selling is indirect selling, such as making goodwill calls and providing technical or operational assistance.

 Outline the seven steps in the sales process.

The basic steps in the sales process are prospecting and qualifying, approach, presentation, demonstration, handling objections, closing, and follow-up.

 Identify the seven basic functions of a sales manager.

A sales manager links the sales force to other aspects of the internal and external environments. The manager's functions are recruitment and selection, training, organization, supervision, motivation, compensation, and evaluation and control.

 Explain the role of ethical behavior in personal selling.

Ethical behavior is vital to building positive, long-term relationships with customers. Although some people believe ethical problems are inevitable, employers can do much to foster a corporate culture that encourages honesty and ethical behavior. In addition, each salesperson is responsible for his or her own behavior and relationship with customers.

 Describe the role of sales promotion in the promotional mix, and identify the different types of sales promotions.

Sales promotion includes activities other than personal selling, advertising, and publicity designed to enhance consumer purchasing and dealer effectiveness. Sales promotion is an integral part of the overall marketing plan, intended to increase sales and build brand equity. Promotions often produce their best results when combined with other marketing activities. Consumer-oriented sales promotions include coupons, refunds, samples, bonus packs, premiums, contests and sweepstakes, and specialty advertising. Trade-oriented promotions include trade allowances, point-of-purchase (POP) advertising, trade shows, dealer incentives, contests, and training programs.

Assessment Check: Answers

1.1 What is personal selling? Personal selling is the process of a seller's person-to-person promotional presentation to a buyer.

1.2 What is the main focus of today's salespeople? The main focus of today's salespeople is to build long-lasting relationships with customers.

2.1 What is over-the-counter selling? Over-the-counter selling describes selling in retail and some wholesale locations. Most of these transactions take place directly with customers.

2.2 What is field selling? Field selling involves making sales calls on prospective and existing customers at their businesses or homes.

2.3 Distinguish between outbound and inbound telemarketing. Outbound telemarketing takes place when a salesperson phones customers; inbound telemarketing takes place when customers call the firm.

3.1 Identify the three major personal selling approaches. The three major personal selling approaches are relationship selling, consultative selling, and team selling.

3.2 Distinguish between relationship selling and consultative selling. Relationship selling is a technique for building a mutually beneficial partnership with a customer. Consultative selling involves meeting customer needs by listening to, understanding, and paying attention to their problems, then following up after a sale.

4.1 What are the three major tasks performed by salespeople? The three major tasks are order processing, creative selling, and team selling.

4.2 What are the three steps of order processing? The three steps of order processing are identifying customer needs, pointing out the need to the customer, and completing the order.

5.1 Identify the seven steps of the sales process. The seven steps of the sales process are prospecting and qualifying, approach, presentation, demonstration, handling objections, closing, and follow-up.

5.2 Why is follow-up important to the sales effort? Follow-up allows the salesperson to reinforce the customer's purchase decision, strengthen the bond, and correct any problems.

6.1 What are the seven basic functions performed by a sales manager? The seven basic functions of a sales manager are recruitment and selection, training, organization, supervision, motivation, compensation, and evaluation and control.

6.2 Define *span of control*. Span of control refers to the number of sales representatives who report to first-level sales managers.

6.3 What are the three main questions a sales manager must address as part of a salesperson's evaluation? The three main questions a sales manager must address are the following: Where does each salesperson's performance rank relative to predetermined standards? What are the salesperson's strong points? What are the salesperson's weak points?

7.1 Why is it important for salespeople to maintain ethical behavior? Salespeople need to maintain ethical behavior because it is vital to their firm's relationships with customers and because they are representing their company. A breach of ethics could also be detrimental to an individual's career.

7.2 What are the characteristics of companies that foster corporate cultures that encourage ethical behavior? Characteristics of corporations fostering ethical behavior include the following: employees who understand what is expected of them, open communication, and managers who lead by example.

8.1 Define *sales promotion*. Sales promotion includes marketing activities other than personal selling, advertising, and publicity designed to enhance consumer purchasing and dealer effectiveness.

8.2 Identify at least four types of consumer-oriented sales promotions. Consumer-oriented sales promotions include coupons, refunds, samples, bonus packs, premiums, contests, sweepstakes, and specialty advertising.

8.3 Identify at least three types of trade-oriented sales promotions. Trade-oriented sales promotions include trade allowances, POP advertising, trade shows, dealer incentives, contests, and training programs.

Marketing Terms You Need to Know

personal selling 566
over-the-counter selling 568
field selling 569
network marketing 570
telemarketing 571
outbound telemarketing 571
inbound telemarketing 571
inside selling 572
relationship selling 573
consultative selling 574
cross-selling 574
team selling 574

virtual sales team 575
order processing 576
creative selling 577
missionary selling 577
sales incentives 577
prospecting 578
qualifying 579
approach 579
precall planning 579
presentation 579
cold calling 580
demonstration 580

objection 581
closing 581
follow-up 582
national accounts organization 584
span of control 585
expectancy theory 585
commission 586
salary 586
sales quota 586
sales promotion 588
coupon 590
refund 591

sampling 591
bonus pack 591
premium 591
contest 591
sweepstakes 591
specialty advertising 592
trade promotion 592
trade allowance 592
point-of-purchase (POP)
    advertising 593
trade show 593
push money 594

Assurance of Learning Review

1. How does each of the following factors affect the decision to emphasize personal selling or nonpersonal advertising and sales promotion?
   a. geographic market concentration
   b. length of marketing channels
   c. degree of product technical complexity

2. Which of the four sales channels is each of the following salespeople most likely to use?
   a. salesperson in a Macy's store
   b. Coldwell Banker real estate agent
   c. route driver for Keebler snack foods (sells and delivers to local food retailers)
   d. technical support for HP

3. What is team selling? Describe a situation in which you think it would be effective.

4. Why is it important for a salesperson to understand order processing—regardless of the type of selling he or she is engaged in?

5. What is the role of a sales incentive?

6. Suppose you are hired as a salesperson for a firm that offers prep courses for standardized tests. Where might you find some leads?

7. What is expectancy theory? How do sales managers use it?

8. What is the role of sales promotion in the marketing effort?

9. What are the benefits of sampling? What are the drawbacks?

10. What is trade promotion? What are its objectives?

Projects and Teamwork Exercises

1. Cross-selling can be an effective way for a firm to expand. Locate an advertisement for a firm you believe could benefit from cross-selling. List ways it could offer multiple goods or services to the same customer. Then create a new ad illustrating the multiple offerings.

2. With a partner, choose one of the following sales situations. Then take turns coming up with creative ways to close the deal—one of you plays the customer and the other plays the salesperson. Present your closing scenarios to the class.
   a. You are a sales associate at a car dealership, and a potential customer has just test-driven one of your newest models. You have handled all the customer's objections and settled on a price. You don't want the customer to leave without agreeing to purchase the car.
   b. You operate a lawn-care business and have visited several homeowners in a new development. Three of them have already agreed to give your service a try. You are meeting with the fourth and want to close that sale, too.

3. As sales representatives for a cooperative of organic farmers, you are about to make a sales presentation to a national supermarket chain. List the most important messages you wish to relate and then role-play the sales presentation.

4. On your own or with a classmate, go online and research a firm such as Kraft, General Mills, Ford, or Burger King to find out what kinds of consumer-oriented promotions the company is conducting for its various brands or individual products. Which promotions seem the most appealing to you as a consumer? Why? Present your findings to the class.

5. With a classmate, design a specialty advertising item for one of the following companies or its products, or choose one of your own. Present your design sketches to the class.
   a. SeaWorld or Busch Gardens
   b. Dunkin' Donuts
   c. Verizon Wireless
   d. Equal Exchange coffee
   e. Apple iPad

Critical-Thinking Exercises

1. Since the implementation of the national Do Not Call Registry, some Americans have noticed an increase in door-to-door selling as well as e-mails containing sales messages. As a marketer, do you think this type of selling is effective? Why or why not?

2. Green Mountain Coffee Roasters is well known for its specialty coffees, available in many retail outlets such as supermarkets and convenience stores. But visit a medical office or a car dealership, and you might find it there as well—in one-cup dispensers, ready for individuals to brew while waiting. This requires personal selling to office managers, doctors, and the like. What role does relationship selling play in this situation? What kind of training might Green Mountain sales reps receive?

3. Assume that a friend asks you to solicit donations for a local charity. (You pick the charity.) Outline your approach and presentation as a salesperson would.

4. Why is the recruitment and selection stage of the hiring process one of a sales manager's greatest challenges?

5. Food manufacturers often set up tables in supermarkets and offer free samples to shoppers, along with coupons for the promoted items. Sometimes restaurants offer free coffee or drink refills. What other products might lend themselves to sampling? Make a list. Pick one of the items and come up with a sampling plan for it. Where and when would you sample? To whom would you offer samples?

Ethics Exercise

You have been hired by a discount sporting-goods retailer in an over-the-counter sales position. You have completed a training course that includes learning about the products, assisting customers, and cross-selling. You have made several good friends in the training course and sometimes get together after work to go running, play golf, or have dinner. You've noticed that one of your friends has really taken the training course to heart and has adopted a very aggressive attitude toward customers in the store, pushing them to buy just about anything, whether they need it or not.

1. Do you agree with your friend's actions? Why or why not?

2. Should you discuss the situation with your friend? Should you discuss it with your supervisor? Explain your response.

Internet Exercises

1. **Sales careers.** Visit the three Web sites listed here and review the material on careers in sales. Make a list of five interesting facts about sales careers. Did this exercise make you more or less interested in a sales career? Explain your answer.
   http://www.collegegrad.com/careers/marke.shtml
   http://www.wetfeet.com/Careers-and-Industries/Careers/Sales.aspx
   http://www.bls.gov/oco/ocos020.htm

2. **Compensation systems.** Go to the Web sites shown here and review the material on compensation systems. Prepare a report outlining the major issues associated with designing a sales compensation system.
   http://www.evancarmichael.com/Sales/414/Compensation-systems-in-sales-organizations.html

   http://resources.bnet.com/topic/sales+compensation+system.html
   http://www.davekahle.com/compfeature.html

3. **CES.** The Consumer Electronics Show (CES) is one of the largest trade shows in the world. Visit the CES Web site (http://www.cesweb.org/) and answer the following questions:
   a. When and where is the CES held?
   b. How many attended the most recent CES? How many firms and organizations had exhibits?
   c. What were the major new products introduced at the most recent CES?

Note: Internet Web addresses change frequently. If you don't find the exact site listed, you may need to access the organization's home page and search from there or use a search engine such as Google or Bing.

Case 17.1 *Private Jets: In Rarefied Air*

Welcome to the world of the rich and famous—where people relax in luxury on their own small jet planes rather than climb aboard a commercial airliner and fold themselves into a cramped cabin along with 100 or more fellow passengers. Billionaires, CEOs, and companies—

particularly those overseas—constitute a lively, growing marketplace for small jets. One of the leading manufacturers of business aircraft, Brazil-based Embraer, markets its Phenom line that includes the entry-level 100 (valued at $3.6 million) and the 300 (an upgraded model particularly appealing to jet owners who want to trade up). Phenoms can accommodate four passengers and can fly at 41,000 feet fully loaded.

Embraer is seeing its product line beginning to take off—pardon the pun—in Asia, a region that already accounts for 12 percent of the world's business jets. Embraer recently opened a plant in Harbin, China, to help meet market need. In a recent year, Embraer took orders for more than 800 of its Phenom 100s and 300s.

Embraer has recently penetrated the India market, where its prospects include training schools, charter companies, businesses, and individuals interested in fractional ownership. In prospecting, the company considers such factors as a company's economic growth, corporate profits, and stock performance. After just a few months in India, Embraer's orders have topped 30. Planning for the future, Embraer has partnered with Mumbai-based Indamer as its authorized service center and has begun training mechanics and engineers to work on its planes. Embraer isn't the only player in this niche market. Italian aircraft manufacturer Piaggio Aero Industrie is building business jets for customers in India and the Middle East.

According to some industry analysts, the market for private jets enjoyed a brief boom period before declining in the wake of widespread global criticism over companies' extravagant spending and corporate waste. Today, however, analysts see an uptick in the sale of used jets—a harbinger of better days ahead for new aircraft—with prospective markets for private jets including Russia, Mexico, and China.

Suppose you had the financial means and the desire to buy a private jet. How would you locate a dealer? Some turn to salespeople like George Rependa, a Canadian, whose company—Executive Aircraft Services—brokers the sale of private airplanes. Rependa, a professional pilot, says there are only a few people in his business. They travel the globe inspecting and evaluating planes, setting up deals, arranging financing, and doing due diligence on buyers and sellers (as well as the planes). Their expenses, he says, are "huge"—but commissions from such technical, specialized sales are even higher. And, as Rependa points out, he's selling a complicated product: "Selling an airplane is not like selling a washing machine."

But if you lack the cash to buy a jet of your own, take heart. You can still enjoy a luxury ride by booking a flight with Los Angeles–based Spectrum Air, a player in the luxury private jet industry. Passengers fly on one of the Gulfstream IVs or Falcon 2000 jets in Spectrum's fleet and enjoy the same amenities as, say, a Hollywood producer or Oscar-winning actor on the way to the Sundance film festival.

Questions for Critical Thinking

1. Who might be a good prospect for a private jet? If you were a salesperson for such aircraft, how would you go about qualifying a prospect?

2. In your opinion, what would be the advantages and disadvantages of working as a salesperson in a niche industry like private or business jets? For someone interested in that kind of job, what would be the barriers to entry?

Sources: Embraer, www.embraer.com, accessed August 2, 2010; Piaggio Aero, www.piaggioaero.com, accessed August 2, 2010. Bruce Edwin, "Airline to the Stars — Spectrum Air Flies A-List to Sundance," *News Blaze*, January 6, 2010, http://newsblaze.com; Neelam Mathews, "Embraer Executive Jets Strike Gold in India," *Aviation Daily*, December 2, 2009, http://www.aviationweek.com; "Private Jets Are Back! (Or Not)," *The Wall Street Journal*, October 9, 2009, http://blogs.wsj.com; Sean Silcoff, "George Rependa Circles the Globe as Plane Salesman to the Stars," *Globe and Mail*, March 5, 2009, http://www.theglobeandmail.com; Andy Nativi Andy, "Italian Company Piaggio Aero Continues with New Biz Jet Plans," *Aviation Daily*, February 6, 2009, http://www.aviationweek.com.

Video Case 17.2
Personal Selling and Sales Promotion at Scholfield Honda

"We want our customer to have a long-term relationship with us," explains Vinnie Koc, a sales consultant with Scholfield Honda, "by providing them the service that Scholfield Honda has always provided." Scholfield Honda of Wichita, Kansas, is the largest Honda dealer in the

state, and for good reason. The *Wichita Business Journal* voted them one of the Best Places to Work. Roger Scholfield, owner and general manager of the dealership, attributes their company's success, both internally and with its customers, to the simple fact that "we can train anybody to do anything, but we can't train you to be a happy person." To ensure that those on the front line of every sale are the best in the business, Scholfield takes the new hire process very seriously. Every interview is vetted by at least three senior people, and Scholfield meets each potential hire before a final decision is made. The result is a staff of sales and service people who actually want to come to work every day and who believe in the product they are selling. In sales, where trust and attitude is everything, that's a pretty big deal. Scholfield's policy of "hiring good attitudes" is simple. Lose your good attitude, and the door is just a few feet away.

"I love my job," says Koc. "I love Hondas, and my whole family drives a Honda. I love the product, and I love to help people." He also loves his generous commissions and bonuses from Scholfield and extra incentives provided by Honda. As anyone who has bought a car knows, bargaining is just part of the game, and at Scholfield, they try to make it less of a contest and more of a conversation. Koc estimates that about 75 percent of his customers know what they want and know what they want to pay. They've done research, checked Blue Book values, and looked at prices in different parts of the country. They don't want to mess around. Koc understands this and treats each customer with the same respect he would want. The dealership gives its sales consultants a reasonable amount of freedom to work with customers on price. Koc keeps a spreadsheet of prices of the different models and

features for customers to compare and make a reasonable offer. He takes every offer to his managers and negotiates with them to find a price each party can live with. Sometimes, that may mean less commission for him, but he's making an investment in repeat customers and referrals.

A close second to the personal sales experience customers receive at Scholfield Honda is advertising. If you've ever been in the Wichita area, you've probably seen or heard a Scholfield Honda advertisement in print, on the radio, on television, or on a billboard. The company has its own on-site advertising agency, Scholfield Creative, dedicated to keeping every man, woman, and child abreast of sales, rebates, and incentives available at the dealership.

As soon as he sits down with a client, Koc reviews all the sales. A large part of his business is driven by ads, but for those who may not be up on the latest deals, taking the time can make all the difference because "it might trigger something in their mind and we can go ahead and do the deal that day," he says.

While most walk into Scholfield Honda because of its reputation, they come back because of the experience. From test drive to trade in, every customer is treated like family, and Scholfield wouldn't have it any other way.

Questions

1. How important is sales force management in Scholfield Honda's overall success? Why?

2. Which step in the sales process is most important in a consumer's decision to purchase a car?

Greensburg, Inc.

© CENGAGE LEARNING

A Town Rebounds

The January 2008 press release from Greensburg GreenTown read as follows:

TOWN REBOUNDING FROM TORNADO TO BECOME ECO-TOURISM DESTINATION

Greensburg, Kansas—*Greensburg is the small Kansas town that was decimated by a powerful EF-5 tornado last May, the result of which 12 residents died and the community experienced the loss of 95% of its structures. It is rebuilding as a model green community, focusing on energy self-sufficiency and other principles of sustainability, with the aim to become the greenest community in America.*

As a component of this Green Initiative, the nonprofit organization Greensburg GreenTown launched a project to oversee the building of a dozen demonstration homes in the community. Each home will showcase different designs, technologies, and products and will serve as a "living science museum" both for residents and visitors. In addition to the educational aspects of this project, these models of sustainable living will also provide bed-and-breakfast type lodging to give people the opportunity to experience green living first-hand, in true eco-tourism fashion. Homes will be constructed of a variety of wall systems including straw bale, insulated concrete forms, structural insulated panels, and traditional wood built with "advanced framing" techniques. Each home will be equipped with monitoring devices to measure the performance of green design under real-world conditions. There are plans for homes incorporating passive solar elements, photovoltaic cells, wind generated power, and myriad other technologies of sustainable design.

Cool idea, sure, but the 12 high-tech, low-impact homes were not going to build themselves. At an estimated cost of $50,000 to $300,000 per structure, GreenTown's Catherine Hart and Daniel Wallach have had to hit the pavement and the phones in search of outside help. AT&T; Caroma USA, which manufactures low-flow, dual-flush toilets; Harvest Solar Energy; university architecture departments; and green building experts have committed time, expertise, product, and generous cash infusions to the project.

Eco-building guru and educator Dan Chiras of EverGreen Design-Build Partnership plans to build two 1,200-square-foot wind and solar "eco lodges." He and his team of green architects, designers, and builders alone have donated approximately $50,000. "Businesses are showing an outpouring of generosity," Chiras said in a press release. He has received donations ranging from wind and solar systems to discount energy rating and LEED certification for his project.

Despite all the generous donations of product and labor the project has received, the folks at GreenTown must work hard to keep this and other Greensburg projects moving forward. Executive Director Dan Wallach is always on the lookout for like-minded organizations to help him keep Greensburg on the map.

Ogden Publications of Topeka, Kansas, has been working in the greenspace for decades. Their most popular magazine, *Mother Earth News*, was started in 1970 around the time of the very first Earth Day and features projects you can do to reduce your impact on the environment. They also publish *Natural Home*, a popular decorating and lifestyle magazine for those interested in greening up their homes.

One day, not long after the tornado hit, publisher and editorial director Bryan Welch received a call from Daniel Wallach at GreenTown. Wallach was looking for a partner on the model homes project. *Natural Home* had recently begun work on a model green home in Brooklyn, New York, and Ogden had experience working on similar projects in the past offering advertisers priority product placement in exchange for donations and sponsorship. "We got involved because we thought it was cool," says Welch of the Greensburg project. "If it hadn't attracted all this attention, it would still be cool, so it was a safe bet."

It may have been safe, but it hasn't been easy.

Ogden Publications and *Mother Earth News* in particular enjoy a reputation for being an authority on sustainable living. This gives them a lot of credibility with their readers, but to potential advertisers, it's pretty scary. Welch admits it has been a challenge explaining to advertisers and partners that we're not "a bunch of holier than thou old hippies" ready to rip their product's greenness to shreds. For the Greensburg project, he is up against another hurdle. The whole point of the demonstration homes is for them to become a destination for visitors, a resource for builders and consumers, and potentially a home for residents. If an advertiser is placing a donated product for the purposes of advertising, in six months that product is outdated and they've moved on to another promotion. If the buildings are going to be living examples of a sustainable lifestyle, it's pretty impractical to replace the toilets or bamboo flooring every few months. Welch recognizes this is a tricky proposition and one that will take some time to work out completely.

In the meantime, *Mother Earth News* and *Natural Home* will continue to reach out to their million-plus Web visitors urging them to help keep the greenest town in America moving forward.

Questions

1. What are the challenges in soliciting product placements and donations for the Model Homes Project?

2. To which sales channels does Greensburg GreenTown market the Model Homes Project?

3. Why is personal selling an important aspect of Ogden Publications' approach to advertisers?

4. Why is advertising more advantageous for Ogden's ad clients?

5. Put yourself in the role of a product manager for a company (like low-flush toilets or solar panels) interested in donating some of their products to the Greenburg project. Your manager has asked you to comment on whether they should concentrate on the promotion opportunities this initiative provides for the consumer, business-to-business customers, or a combination of both. Write a memo (3 to 5 pages) on the approach you suggest, along with some creative ideas.

Pricing
Decisions

PART 7

Chapter 18
Pricing Concepts

Chapter 19
Pricing Strategies

Pricing
Concepts

Microsoft Priced to Win • • • With its near-monopoly on PC software, especially its flagship Windows products, Microsoft has long been able to maintain premium prices for its products no matter how the economy or the computer industry has fared. Now, however, in what

1. Outline the legal constraints on pricing.

2. Identify the major categories of pricing objectives.

3. Explain price elasticity and its determinants.

4. List the practical problems involved in applying price theory concepts to actual pricing decisions.

5. Explain the major cost-plus approaches to price setting.

6. List the chief advantages and shortcomings of using breakeven analysis in pricing decisions.

7. Explain the use of yield management in pricing decisions.

8. Identify the major pricing challenges facing online and international marketers.

BusinessWeek calls "a risky experiment in price elasticity," the company is shifting to a new pricing strategy. Microsoft is reducing the prices of some of its most popular software products worldwide, and even giving some away free, to try to grow market share in selected business and consumer market segments.

For instance, Windows customers upgrading to Windows 7 could purchase it at retail for $40 less than Microsoft charged for its last new operating system, Vista. That's a bigger discount than the firm has offered on a new Windows version in a long time. Microsoft hopes customers will be persuaded to upgrade Windows 7 more often, especially those who opt for the

cheaper Starter edition, which they can later enhance by adding premium features. Customers who bought a new PC during Windows 7's introduction got an even better deal. They were offered either a 50 percent discount on the software or a free upgrade from the older Vista operating system. "We definitely saw the results of aggressive pricing," said one software industry analyst.

While sales of upgrades and new versions were relatively strong, helped by favorable reviews, Windows 7 didn't appear to be creating much new demand for PCs in its early months on the market, which could mean the company will have to support its predecessor operating systems Vista and

Windows XP longer than it had planned. Many suppliers still had inventory of less-expensive laptops and notebooks that were running on these systems. But home users and students buying the discounted Home Premium version of Windows 7 were expected to make up in volume for lower sales of the Ultimate version, which sells for more. The company also hopes to attract more corporate buyers with new prices for both software and Internet services. "We're focusing on gaining share in those areas that are most critical," says the head of Microsoft's business division.

Microsoft is also discounting its Office software package, with promotions that amount to a 33 percent price reduction (even

Windows live mail

lower abroad), and to compete with Google and others, it offered free versions of two component Office programs, Word and Excel. Sales of Office were up 415 percent following the promotions.

In another price innovation, customers willing to install less powerful Office 2010 software were able to download it free (though with advertising) from the Internet. And in addition to selling its e-mail program Exchange for download on CD, Microsoft will sell it online for a monthly fee, which is cheaper for the customer though only about a third as profitable for the company. "I'm not saying it will be easy," said Microsoft's CEO Steven Ballmer. "But we have great opportunities to grow total profit dollars."

One further price cut was made to try to discourage piracy. In China, it cut the price to $29 as a test and watched sales climb more than 800 percent. It was "like taking firewood from under [piracy's] cauldron," according to one Chinese software distributor's vice president. Microsoft agrees and plans to make the price cut permanent.[1]

evolution of a brand

Microsoft's Windows 7 operating system has gotten off to a more successful start than the company's previous new release, the Vista operating system, which debuted to intense criticism from the media and users alike. Measured in terms of how many computers are using it to access the Internet, it appears that Windows 7 has already captured a 10 percent market share. By contrast, it took Vista over 16 months to reach this level.

1. Which do you think has been more influential in the success of Microsoft's introduction of

evolution of a

Windows 7: the perceived quality of the product or the reduced price and other promotions? Why?

2. Consider the fact that most consumer and
business PC users wait to get the latest version of Windows until they are ready to buy

a new computer, rather than installing new
software to upgrade a computer they already
have. That means that new sales of operating
systems are dependent on new sales of PCs.
How do you think this link affects Microsoft's
pricing strategy?

chapter overview

One of the first questions shoppers ask is, "How much does it cost?" Marketers understand the critical role price plays in the consumer's decision-making process. For products as varied as lipstick and perfume, automobiles and gasoline, and doughnuts and coffee, marketers must develop strategies that price products to achieve their firms' objectives.

As a starting point for examining pricing strategies, consider the meaning of the term *price*. A **price** is the exchange value of a good or service; in other words, it represents whatever that product can be exchanged for in the marketplace. Price does not necessarily denote money. In earlier times, the price of an acre of land might have been 20 bushels of wheat, three head of cattle, or one boat. Even though the barter process continues to be used in some transactions, in the 21st century, price typically refers to the amount of funds required to purchase a product. Prices are both difficult to set and dynamic;

they shift in response to a number of variables. A higher-than-average price can convey an image of prestige, while a lower-than-average price may connote good value, as the trend toward consumers' purchases of private-label store brands shows. In other instances, though, a price much lower than average may be interpreted as an indicator of inferior quality, and a higher price—like the increasing price of gasoline—may reflect both high demand and scarce supply. And pricing can also be used to modify consumer behavior.

This chapter discusses the process of determining a profitable but justifiable (or fair) price. The focus is on management of the pricing function, including pricing strategies, price–quality relationships, and pricing in various sectors of the economy. The chapter also looks at the effects of environmental conditions on price determination, including legal constraints, competitive pressures, and changes in global and online markets.

price Exchange value of a good or service.

Pricing and the Law

Pricing decisions are influenced by a variety of legal constraints imposed by federal, state, and local governments. Included in the price of products are not only the cost of the raw materials, processing and packaging, and profit for the business, but also various taxes. For instance, excise taxes are levied on a variety of products, including real estate transfers, alcoholic beverages, and motor fuels. Sales taxes can be charged on food, clothing, furniture, and many other purchases.

In the global marketplace, prices are directly affected by special types of taxes called *tariffs*. These taxes—levied on the sale of imported goods and services—often make it possible for firms to protect their local markets while still setting prices on domestically produced goods well above world market levels. The average tariff on fruits and vegetables around the world is more than 50 percent, although it varies considerably from country to country. The United States levies tariffs of less than 5 percent on more than half its fruit and vegetable imports, and in transactions with its largest trading partners in the produce market—Mexico and Canada—tariffs for both imports and exports are minimal or zero.[2] In other instances, tariffs are levied to prevent foreign producers from engaging in a practice described in Chapter 7: *dumping* foreign-produced products in international markets at prices lower than those set in their domestic market.

The United States is not the only country to use tariffs to protect domestic suppliers. For example, China, which now surpasses Canada as the leading source of U.S. imports, recently agreed to repeal tariffs on energy services and technologies that sometimes ran as high as 16 percent. Yet the United States and other countries still contend that Chinese trade policies put them at a disadvantage. For instance, China, rapidly becoming the world's largest market for cars, taxes imported auto parts at 10 percent. But beyond a certain quantity, those same parts are taxed at the 25 percent rate that normally applies only to completed vehicles.[3] These tariffs raise the prices overseas consumers must pay to purchase U.S. goods.

Not every "regulatory" price increase is a tax, however. Rate increases to cover costly government regulations imposed on the telecommunications industry have been appearing on Internet and cell phone bills as "regulatory cost recovery fees" or similarly named costs. But these charges are not taxes, because the companies keep all the income from the fees and apply only some of it to complying with the regulations. In essence, such "recovery fees" are a source of additional revenues in an industry so price-sensitive that any announced price increase is likely to send some customers fleeing to competitors.

1 Outline the legal constraints on pricing.

China, rapidly becoming the world's largest market for cars, taxes imported auto parts at 10 percent and completed vehicles at an even higher rate, raising the price of U.S. cars in China.

© IMAGINECHINA VIA AP IMAGES

Many people looking for a ticket to a high-demand sporting or concert event have encountered an expensive, often illegal, form of pricing called *ticket scalping*. Scalpers camp out in ticket lines—or hire someone else to stand in line—to purchase tickets they expect to resell at a higher price. Although some cities and states have enacted laws prohibiting the practice, it continues to occur in many locations.

But the ticket reselling market is both highly fragmented and susceptible to fraud and distorted pricing. In response, buyers and sellers are finding that the Internet is helping create a market in which both buyers and sellers can compare prices and seat locations. Web firms such as StubHub.com and TicketsNow.com, the latter owned by Ticketmaster, act as ticket clearinghouses for this secondary market. These firms have signed deals with several professional sports teams that allow season ticket holders to sell unwanted tickets and buyers to purchase them with a guarantee. Its partnership with StubHub has been a success for the University of Southern California, among others.[4]

Pricing is also regulated by the general constraints of U.S. antitrust legislation, as outlined in Chapter 3. The following sections review some of the most important pricing laws for contemporary marketers.

Robinson-Patman Act

Robinson-Patman Act Federal legislation prohibiting price discrimination not based on a cost differential; also prohibits selling at an unreasonably low price to eliminate competition.

The **Robinson-Patman Act** (1936) typifies Depression-era legislation. Known as the Anti-A&P Act, it was inspired by price competition triggered by the rise of grocery store chains; it is said that the original draft was suggested by the U.S. Wholesale Grocers Association. Enacted in the midst of the Great Depression, when legislators viewed chain stores as a threat to employment in the traditional retail sector, the Act was intended primarily to save jobs.

The Robinson-Patman Act was an amendment to the Clayton Act, enacted 22 years earlier, which had applied only to price discrimination between geographic areas, injuring local sellers. Broader in scope, Robinson-Patman prohibits price discrimination in sales to wholesalers, retailers, and other producers. It rules that differences in price must reflect cost differentials and prohibits selling at unreasonably low prices to drive competitors out of business. Supporters justified the amendment by arguing that the rapidly expanding chain stores of that era might be able to attract substantial discounts from suppliers anxious to secure their business, while small, independent stores would continue to pay regular prices.

Price discrimination, in which some customers pay more than others for the same product, dates back to the very beginnings of trade and commerce. Today, however, technology has added to the frequency and complexity of price discrimination as well as the strategies marketers adopt to get around it. For example, marketers may encourage repeat business by inviting purchasers to become "preferred customers," entitling them to average discounts of 10 percent. As long as companies can demonstrate that their price discounts and promotional allowances do not restrict competition, they avoid penalties under the Robinson-Patman Act. Direct-mail marketers frequently send out catalogs of identical goods but with differing prices for different catalogs. Zip code areas that traditionally consist of high spenders get the higher-price catalogs, while price-sensitive Zip code customers receive catalogs with lower prices. Firms accused of price discrimination often argue that they set price differentials to meet competitors' prices and that cost differences justify variations in prices. When a firm asserts it maintains price differentials as good-faith methods of competing with rivals, a logical question arises: What constitutes good-faith pricing behavior? The answer depends on the particular situation.

A defense based on cost differentials works only if the price differences do not exceed the cost differences resulting from selling to various classes of buyers. Marketers must then be prepared to justify the cost differences. Many authorities consider this provision one of the most confusing areas in the Robinson-Patman Act. Courts handle most charges brought under the act as individual cases. Therefore, domestic marketers must continually evaluate their pricing actions to avoid potential Robinson-Patman violations.

Unfair-Trade Laws

unfair-trade laws State laws requiring sellers to maintain minimum prices for comparable merchandise.

Most states supplement federal legislation with their own **unfair-trade laws**, which require sellers to maintain minimum prices for comparable merchandise. Enacted in the 1930s, these laws were intended to protect small specialty shops, such as dairy stores, from so-called loss-leader pricing tactics in which chain stores might sell certain products below cost to attract customers. Typical state laws set retail price floors at cost plus some modest markup. Although most unfair-trade laws have remained on the books for decades, marketers had all but forgotten them until recently, when several lawsuits were brought against different warehouse clubs over their practice of loss-leader gasoline pricing. Most were found to violate no laws.

Fair-Trade Laws

The concept of fair trade has affected pricing decisions for decades. **Fair-trade laws** allow manufacturers to stipulate minimum retail prices for their products and to require dealers to sign contracts agreeing to abide by these prices.

Fair-trade laws assert that a product's image, determined in part by its price, is a property right of the manufacturer. Therefore, the manufacturer should have the authority to protect its asset by requiring retailers to maintain a minimum price. Exclusivity is one method manufacturers use to achieve this. By severely restricting the number of retail outlets that carry their upscale clothing and accessories, designers can exert more control over their prices and avoid discounting, which might adversely affect their image.

Like the Robinson-Patman Act, fair-trade legislation has its roots in the Depression era. In 1931, California became the first state to enact fair-trade legislation. Most other states soon followed; only Missouri, the District of Columbia, Vermont, and Texas failed to adopt such laws. A U.S. Supreme Court decision invalidated fair-trade contracts in interstate commerce, and Congress responded by passing the Miller-Tydings Resale Price Maintenance Act (1937). This law exempted interstate fair-trade contracts from compliance with antitrust requirements, thus freeing states to keep these laws on their books if they so desired.

Over the years, fair-trade laws declined in importance as discounters emerged and price competition gained strength as a marketing strategy component. These laws became invalid with the passage of the Consumer Goods Pricing Act (1975), which halted all interstate enforcement of resale price maintenance provisions, an objective long sought by consumer groups.

fair-trade laws Statutes enacted in most states that once permitted manufacturers to stipulate a minimum retail price for their product.

assessment check

1. What was the purpose of the Robinson-Patman Act?
2. What laws require sellers to maintain minimum prices for comparable merchandise?
3. What laws allow manufacturers to set minimum retail prices for their products?

Pricing Objectives and the Marketing Mix

The extent to which any or all of the factors of production—natural resources, capital, human resources, and entrepreneurship—are employed depends on the prices those factors command. A firm's prices and the resulting purchases by its customers determine the company's revenue, influencing the profits it earns. Overall organizational objectives and more specific marketing objectives guide the development of pricing objectives, which in turn lead to the development and implementation of more specific pricing policies and procedures.

A firm might, for instance, set an overall goal of becoming the dominant producer in its domestic market. It might then develop a marketing objective of achieving maximum sales penetration in each region, followed by a related pricing objective of setting prices at levels that maximize sales. These objectives might lead to the adoption of a low-price policy implemented by offering substantial price discounts to channel members.

Price affects and is affected by the other elements of the marketing mix. Product decisions, promotional plans, and distribution choices all affect the price of a good or service. For example,

2 Identify the major categories of pricing objectives.

table 18.1 Pricing Objectives

Objective	Purpose	Example
Profitability objectives	Profit maximization Target return	Samsung's initially high price for the Blu-ray disc player
Volume objectives	Sales maximization Market share	Delta's low fares in new markets
Meeting competition objectives	Value pricing	Target's lower prices on private house brands
Prestige objectives	Lifestyle Image	High-priced luxury autos such as BMW and stereo equipment by Bose
Not-for-profit objectives	Profit maximization Cost recovery Market incentives Market suppression	Reduced or zero tolls for high-occupancy vehicles to encourage carpooling

products distributed through complex channels involving several intermediaries must be priced high enough to cover the markups needed to compensate wholesalers and retailers for services they provide. Basic so-called fighting brands are intended to capture market share from higher-priced, options-laden competitors by offering relatively low prices. Those cheaper products are intended to entice customers to give up some options in return for a cost savings.

Pricing objectives vary from firm to firm, and they can be classified into four major groups: (1) profitability objectives, (2) volume objectives, (3) meeting competition objectives, and (4) prestige objectives. Not-for-profit organizations as well as for-profit companies must consider objectives of one kind or another when developing pricing strategies. Table 18.1 outlines the pricing objectives marketers rely on to meet their overall goals.

Profitability Objectives

Marketers at for-profit firms must set prices with profits in mind. Even not-for-profit organizations realize the importance of setting prices high enough to cover expenses and provide a financial cushion to cover unforeseen needs and expenses. As the Russian proverb says, "There are two fools in every market: one asks too little, one asks too much." For consumers to pay prices either above or below what they consider the going rate, they must be convinced they are receiving fair value for their money.

Economic theory is based on two major assumptions. It assumes, first, that firms will behave rationally and, second, that this rational behavior will result in an effort to maximize gains and minimize losses. Some marketers estimate profits by looking at historical sales data; others use elaborate calculations based on predicted future sales. It has been said that setting prices is an art, not a science. The talent lies in a marketer's ability to strike a balance between desired profits and the customer's perception of a product's value.

Marketers should evaluate and adjust prices continually to accommodate changes in the environment. The technological environment, for example, forces Internet marketers to respond quickly to competitors' pricing strategies. Search capabilities performed by shopping bots (described in Chapter 4) allow customers to compare prices locally, nationally, and globally in a matter of seconds.

Intense price competition, sometimes conducted even when it means forgoing profits altogether or reducing services, often results when rivals battle for leadership positions. For some years, passenger airlines cut costs to compete on pricing. Computer

Computer technology allowed airlines to automate many services and put passengers in charge of others, like checking in at electronic kiosks.

technology allowed them to automate many services and put passengers in charge of others, such as making reservations online and checking in at electronic kiosks. Now, thanks to increased industry concentration and the rising price of jet fuel, which climbed 71 percent in a recent year, airlines are struggling to cover their costs. As a result, passengers now pay sharply higher fares and find amenities, like in-flight meals, have all but disappeared. American Airlines charges $8 for a pillow and blanket for domestic trips and some international flights and will join Delta in also charging most passengers to fly standby. Nearly all airlines now charge for checking baggage and for buying tickets other than online.[5]

Profits are a function of revenue and expenses:

$$\text{Profits} = \text{Revenue} - \text{Expenses}$$

Revenue is determined by the product's selling price and number of units sold:

$$\text{Total revenue} = \text{Price} \times \text{Quantity sold}$$

Therefore, a profit-maximizing price rises to the point at which further increases will cause disproportionate decreases in the number of units sold. A 10 percent price increase that results in only an 8 percent cut in volume will add to the firm's revenue. However, a 10 percent price hike that results in an 11 percent sales decline will reduce revenue.

Economists refer to this approach as **marginal analysis**. They identify **profit maximization** as the point at which the addition to total revenue is just balanced by the increase in total cost. Marketers must resolve a basic problem of how to achieve this delicate balance when they set prices. Relatively few firms actually hit this elusive target. A significantly larger number prefer to direct their effort toward more realistic goals.

Consequently, marketers commonly set **target-return objectives**—short-run or long-run goals usually stated as percentages of sales or investment. The practice has become particularly popular among large firms in which other pressures interfere with profit-maximization objectives. In addition to resolving pricing questions, target-return objectives offer several benefits for marketers. For example, these objectives serve as tools for evaluating performance; they also satisfy desires to generate "fair" profits as judged by management, stockholders, and the public.

marginal analysis
Method of analyzing the relationship among costs, sales price, and increased sales volume.

profit maximization
Point at which the additional revenue gained by increasing the price of a product equals the increase in total costs.

target-return objective Short-run or long-run pricing objectives of achieving a specified return on either sales or investment.

Volume Objectives

Some economists and business executives argue that pricing behavior actually seeks to maximize sales within a given profit constraint. In other words, they set a minimum acceptable profit level and then seek to maximize sales (subject to this profit constraint) in the belief that the increased sales are more important in the long-run competitive picture than immediate high profits. As a result, companies should continue to expand sales as long as their total profits do not drop below the minimum return acceptable to management.

Sales maximization can also result from nonprice factors such as service and quality. Marketers succeeded in increasing sales for Dr. Scholl's new shoe insert, Dynastep, by advertising heavily in magazines. The ads explained how the Dynastep insert would help relieve leg and back pain. Priced around $14 for two inserts—twice as much as comparable offerings—Dynastep ran over its competitors to become number one in its category.

Another volume-related pricing objective is the **market-share objective**—the goal of controlling a specified minimum share of the market for a firm's good or service. Apple applied this strategy to its iPhone price reduction. The company introduced annual updates for three years, dropping the top price each time from the original $399 to $99, but a new model may soon be marketed for even less. One analyst said, "The cost of device and service plan is currently the biggest barrier to incremental demand in both mature markets like the U.S. and emerging markets like China."[6]

THE PIMS STUDIES

Market-share objectives may prove critical to the achievement of other organizational objectives. High sales, for example, often mean more profits. The **Profit Impact of Market Strategies (PIMS) project**, an extensive study conducted by the Marketing Science Institute, analyzed more than 2,000 firms and revealed that two of the most important factors influencing profitability were product quality and market share. Companies such as outdoor gear maker REI and Best Buy, the electronics giant, introduced their loyalty programs as a means of retaining customers and protecting their market share. Faced with a slowing economy, other retailers are joining them, hoping to boost sluggish sales. Among them are Starbucks and Red Lion Hotels. Companies as diverse as Zpizza, American Airlines, and Kroger offer rewards to frequent or loyal customers. When consumer spending slowed in the recent recession, "many chains...lost customers they wished they could have retained," said the global retail director of Accenture, the consultancy firm. "Retailers now feel the pressure to constantly work on creating additional services that will keep shoppers loyal."[7]

The relationship between market share and profitability is evident in PIMS data that reveal an average 32 percent return on investment (ROI) for firms with market shares above 40 percent. In contrast, average ROI decreases to 24 percent for firms whose market shares are between 20 and 40 percent. Firms with a minor market share (less than 10 percent) generate average pretax investment returns of under 10 percent.[8] The relationship also applies to a firm's individual brands. PIMS researchers compared the top four brands in each market segment they studied. Their data revealed the leading brand typically generates after-tax ROI of 18 percent, considerably higher than the second-ranked brand. Weaker brands, on average, fail to earn adequate returns.

Marketers have developed an underlying explanation of the positive relationship between profitability and market share. Firms with large shares accumulate greater operating experience and lower overall costs relative to competitors with smaller market shares. Accordingly, effective segmentation strategies might focus on obtaining larger shares of smaller markets and on avoiding smaller shares of larger ones. A firm might achieve higher financial returns by becoming a major competitor in several smaller market segments than by remaining a relatively minor player in a larger market.

MEETING COMPETITION OBJECTIVES

A third set of pricing objectives seeks simply to meet competitors' prices. In many lines of business, firms set their own prices to match those of established industry price leaders. Price is a pivotal factor in the ongoing competition between long-distance telephone services and wireless carriers. In addition to unlimited calls to the United States and Canada for $2.95 a month, Skype, the Internet calling company owned by eBay, allows unlimited calls to overseas landline phones in 40

---

market-share objective Volume-related pricing objective in which the goal is to achieve control of a portion of the market for a firm's good or service.

Profit Impact of Market Strategies (PIMS) project Research that discovered a strong positive relationship between a firm's market share and product quality and its return on investment.

briefly speaking

"Price is what you pay. Value is what you get."

—Warren Buffett
(b. 1930)
U.S. investor

other countries for $12.95 a month. The countries include most of Europe as well as Australia, New Zealand, China, Japan, Korea, and Malaysia.[9]

Pricing objectives tied directly to meeting prices charged by major competitors deemphasize the price element of the marketing mix and focus more strongly on nonprice variables. Pricing is a highly visible component of a firm's marketing mix and an easy and effective tool for obtaining a differential advantage over competitors. It is, however, a tool other firms can easily duplicate through price reductions of their own. Because price changes directly affect overall profitability in an industry, many firms attempt to promote stable prices by meeting competitors' prices and competing for market share by focusing on product strategies, promotional decisions, and distribution—the nonprice elements of the marketing mix.

VALUE PRICING

When discounts become normal elements of a competitive marketplace, other marketing mix elements gain importance in purchase decisions. In such instances, overall product value—not just price—determines product choice. In recent years, a new strategy, **value pricing**, has emerged that emphasizes the benefits a product provides in comparison to the price and quality levels of competing offerings. This strategy typically works best for relatively low-priced goods and services. Kroger, a major player in the grocery industry, offers more than 10,000 product discounts, marked by yellow tags, in the over 200 stores in its Southwest Division. Reduced-price products include meat, produce, and health and beauty aids. Seniors receive a regular 10 percent discount on store-brand products including cereal, bread, and skin-care products.[10]

Value-priced products generally cost less than premium brands, but marketers point out that value does not necessarily mean *inexpensive*. The challenge for those who compete on value is to convince customers that low-priced brands offer quality comparable to that of a higher-priced product. An increasing number of alternative products and private-label brands has resulted in a more competitive marketplace in recent years. Trader Joe's—a rapidly growing grocery chain that began in the Los Angeles area and has since expanded throughout the West, Midwest, and mid-Atlantic states—stands out from other specialty food stores with its cedar plank walls, nautical décor, and a captain (the store manager), first mate (the assistant manager), and the other employees (known as crew members) all attired in colorful Hawaiian shirts. The chain uses value pricing for the more than 2,000 upscale food

value pricing
Pricing strategy emphasizing benefits derived from a product in comparison to the price and quality levels of competing offerings.

Kroger offers more than 10,000 product discounts, marked by yellow tags, in the more than 200 stores in its Southwest Division.

© AP IMAGES/AL BEHRMAN

Trader Joe's uses value pricing to sell upscale food products.

© MICHAEL NAGLE/GETTY IMAGES

products it develops or imports. It sells wines, cheeses, meats, fish, and other unique gourmet items at everyday closeout prices, mostly under its own brand names. If the high quality doesn't persuade customers at its 280 stores to buy, they can also take comfort from the fact that Trader Joe's tuna are caught without environmentally dangerous nets, its dried apricots contain no sulfur preservatives, and its peanut butter is organic.[11]

Value pricing is perhaps best seen in the personal computer industry. In the past few years, PC prices have collapsed, reducing the effectiveness of traditional pricing strategies intended to meet competition. Falling prices have helped sales grow as much as 15 percent worldwide in a recent quarter, and about 4 percent in the United States. Worldwide PC sales were expected to rise as economic recovery strengthened, but some observers think prices might begin to inch up as well as the cost of components rise.[12]

Prestige Objectives

The final category of pricing objectives, unrelated to either profitability or sales volume, is prestige objectives. Prestige pricing establishes a relatively high price to develop and maintain an image of quality and exclusiveness that appeals to status-conscious consumers. Such objectives reflect marketers' recognition of the role of price in creating an overall image of the firm and its product offerings.

Prestige objectives affect the price tags of such products as David Yurman jewelry, Tag Heuer watches, Baccarat crystal, and Lenox china. When a perfume marketer sets a price of $400 or more

mktg: *success*

Super Bowl Ads Are a Win–Win

Background. The Super Bowl has long been one of the most-watched programs on television, and memorable and inventive spots during the game have launched many new products. "The potential payoff of a great ad here for an advertiser is incalculable," says a marketing consultant from Canada. "The ads have become part of the event." They are also expensive.

The Challenge. While most of Super Bowl XLIV's 62 commercial spots were quickly sold, a slowing economy kept some big advertisers, like PepsiCo and General Motors, from buying slots at prices that in past years have topped $3 million.

The Strategy. CBS, which aired Super Bowl XLIV, revealed there was

some flexibility in ad pricing. "There's not one price for ads in the game," said the network's executive vice president for sales. Ad prices, which dropped that year for only the second time in Super Bowl history, ranged from $2 million (for a very few) to $3 million, with the first quarter costing the most and the fourth quarter the least. "In a way," said one observer, "Super

per ounce, this choice reflects an emphasis on image far more than the cost of ingredients. Analyses have shown that ingredients account for less than 5 percent of a perfume's cost. Thus, advertisements for Joy that promote the fragrance as the "costliest perfume in the world" use price to promote product prestige. Diamond jewelry also uses prestige pricing to convey an image of quality and timelessness.

In the business world, private jet ownership imparts an image of prestige, power, and high price tags—too high for most business travelers to consider. Most owners are worth $10 million or more, according to one industry researcher, and include those who see private ownership enabling them to visit three cities in a day as a business need, not a luxury. Recognizing that cost is the primary factor that makes jet ownership prohibitive, companies such as NetJets have created an alternative: fractional ownership. Corporate boards of directors pressed to cut costs in a weak economy are much more willing to pay for a share in a jet than to purchase a whole new aircraft.[13] In the world of advertising, the Super Bowl's expensive advertising slots carry a certain kind of prestige. See the "Marketing Success" feature for a discussion of pricing these ads.

IN LIFE AS IN MUSIC, CHOOSE YOUR INSTRUMENTS WISELY.

JAGUARUSA.COM

Jaguar Cars is proud to sponsor the 2010 Platinum Series concerts at the famed Hollywood Bowl. For tickets and information, log on to hollywoodbowl.com.

JAGUAR
PLATINUM SERIES

© AP IMAGES/PRNEWSFOTO/JAGUAR

Prestige objectives help market exclusive products, like Jaguar automobiles.

Bowl advertisers are acting like people are acting in the economy, which is they'll buy only if there's a deal. If the price is right, people will step up."

The Outcome. Super Bowl XLIV's ad spots sold out in advance, as always. Attracted by the price flexibility, a vacation rental company called HomeAway became a first-time buyer, taking a spot in the third quarter. "We certainly had a hunch that it wasn't going to be massively overpriced versus last year," said the company's CEO. The game drew a record television audience.

Sources: Hollie Shaw, "Super Bowl Spots Sell Out in Advance; U.S. and Canada," *Financial Post and FP Investing* (Canada), www.nationalpost.com, February 3, 2010; Emily Fredrix, "Super Bowl Commercial Prices Fall for Second Time Every," *Huffington Post*, www.huffingtonpost.com, January 11, 2010; Bruce Horovitz, "Super Bowl Commercial Slots Selling Fast, CBS Says," *USA Today*, www.usatoday.com, January 4, 2010.

assessment check

1. What are target-return objectives?
2. What is value pricing?
3. How do prestige objectives affect a seller's pricing strategy?

Pricing Objectives of Not-for-Profit Organizations

Pricing is also a key element of the marketing mix for not-for-profit organizations. Pricing strategy can help these groups achieve a variety of organizational goals:

1. *Profit maximization.* While not-for-profit organizations by definition do not cite profitability as a primary goal, numerous instances exist in which they try to maximize their returns on single events or a series of events. A $1,000-a-plate political fund-raiser is a classic example.

2. *Cost recovery.* Some not-for-profit organizations attempt to recover only the actual cost of operating the unit. Mass transit, toll roads and bridges, and most private colleges and universities are common examples. The amount of recovered costs often is dictated by tradition, competition, or public opinion. A more original solution is Indiana's decision to lease its 157-mile toll road to a team of Australian and Spanish companies for the next 75 years, creating almost $4 billion in revenue to fund needed transportation projects in the state. Many drivers, especially truckers, have been surprised by early toll increases, but price hikes after 2016 will proceed on a schedule worked out with the state.[14]

3. *Market incentives.* Other not-for-profit groups follow a lower-than-average pricing policy or offer a free service to encourage increased usage of the good or service. Seattle's bus system offers free service in the downtown area in an attempt to reduce traffic congestion and pollution, encourage retail sales, and minimize the effort required to access downtown public services.[15]

4. *Market suppression.* Price can also discourage consumption. High prices help accomplish social objectives independent of the costs of providing goods or services. Illustrations include tobacco and alcohol taxes—the so-called sin taxes—parking fines, tolls, and gasoline excise taxes. A new report promoting raising tobacco taxes proposes that states like Arkansas and Texas could raise hundreds of millions of dollars by increasing their current tax rates for cigarettes, and deter more than 200,000 children from taking up smoking.[16] Another way to curb consumption—of gasoline and roadways—is congestion pricing. See the "Solving an Ethical Controversy" feature for answers to some questions about who bears the burden of such pricing strategies.

Methods for Determining Prices

Marketers determine prices in two basic ways: by applying the theoretical concepts of supply and demand and by completing cost-oriented analyses. During the first part of the 20th century, most discussions of price determination emphasized the classical concepts of supply and demand. During the last half of the century, however, the emphasis began to shift to a cost-oriented approach. Hindsight reveals certain flaws in both concepts.

Treatments of this subject often overlook another concept of price determination—one based on the impact of custom and tradition. **Customary prices** are retail prices consumers expect as a result of tradition and social habit. Candy makers have attempted to maintain traditional price

customary prices
Traditional prices that customers expect to pay for certain goods and services.

solving an ethical controversy

Revisiting Congestion Pricing

London, Milan, Singapore, Rome, and Stockholm all impose congestion pricing, charging drivers extra tolls to enter the city center during peak hours. The payment system is relatively easy to administer with today's technology; London drivers pay online, by mail, in person, or via cell phone. A congestion pricing proposal was defeated in New York City, but the idea isn't going away. New South Wales, the most heavily populated Australian state, is considering road-use charges to reduce traffic that's estimated to cost the nation $3.5 billion a year and climbing. Congestion pricing has even been proposed for heavily trafficked airport runways.

Is congestion pricing really fair to those who must bear the cost?

PRO

1. Everyone benefits from reduced traffic and less pollution, as observed in London and Stockholm. Traffic jams reappeared in Stockholm the first day after a trial run of congestion pricing ended.

2. Variable pricing can generate substantial revenues for improving mass transit, which further reduces congestion and pollution.

CON

1. Congestion pricing adds another layer of tax on working-class commuters. Because it is a flat rate per car, the less you make, the bigger a percentage of your income it represents.

2. Few people benefit from the policy. Because congestion pricing is so costly to operate, the British government abandoned plans to implement London's system nationwide.

Summary

The number of cars in Singapore continues to grow despite congestion pricing, but New York City's Metropolitan Transit Authority faces budget deficits and possible service cuts that prompt some analysts to call for revisiting the idea. The original plan would have imposed $8 per vehicle on cars entering the business district during peak weekday hours. One new proposal says such a pricing system would "create a permanent revenue source for long-term maintenance, repair, and expansion of the mass transit system, the backbone of the regional economy."

Sources: John Petro, "The Urgency of Resurrecting Congestion Pricing in New York," Drum Major Institute for Public Policy, www.drummajorinstitute.org, accessed March 9, 2010; Ong Soh Chin, "Curb Global Warming, Make Car Owners Sweat," *The Straits Times* (Singapore), www.straitstimes.com, January 10, 2010; Robert W. Poole, Jr., "Flight Delays this Christmas?" *Christian Science Monitor*, December 23, 2009; Andrew West, "Transport Plan Backs Peak-Hour Driver Fees," *Sydney Morning Herald*, www.smh.com.au, December 12, 2009.

---

levels by greatly reducing overall product size. Similar practices have prevailed in the marketing of soft drinks, chips, mayonnaise, soap, and ice cream as manufacturers attempt to balance consumer expectations of customary prices with the realities of rising costs. Sometimes customary prices hide a real price increase, however, when the quantity of the product has been imperceptibly reduced. Northern brand toilet paper shrank the size of each sheet on its rolls by a fraction of an inch and reduced the number of sheets from 300 to 286. The price remains the same and was intended to prevent a price increase, according to a customer service rep for Georgia Pacific. The Coca-Cola Company has introduced a "90-calorie portion-control mini-can" and offers eight-packs of the smaller-size cans for prices that range from 50 percent more to double the per-ounce price of regular size cans.[17] Housing prices have suffered in the recent real estate bubble. See the "Career Readiness" feature for some ideas about how to fairly price a house in a down market.

The Coca-Cola Company has introduced a "90-calorie portion-control mini-can" and offers 8 packs of the smaller-size cans for prices that range from 50 percent more to double the per-ounce price of regular size cans.

© RICHARD B. LEVINE/NEWSCOM

7.5 FL OZ (222 mL)

The changing price of U.S. gasoline presents another example of supply and demand. When average prices for a gallon of gas near the $3.50-a-gallon mark, frustrated drivers begin demanding to know who, if anyone, is cashing in on the price spike. Even though the United States is the world's largest refiner of gasoline, strong demand leads to an increase in oil imports. Higher gas prices have effects on other consumer costs as well. The U.S. Department of Energy counts 57 different major uses of petroleum in addition to gasoline, in products ranging from cosmetics to chewing gum. Consumer product giant Procter & Gamble recently introduced price increases on several bath soaps due to increased prices for raw materials, and Dow Chemical raised the price of its emulsion polymer-based products in North America, also due to raw materials hikes.[18]

With fuel at record highs, hybrid cars are in greater demand than ever before, and some dealers have had months-long waiting lists even at premium prices. Toyota recently unveiled a

career readiness Housing: Pricing to Sell in a Slow Economy

t's easy to sell a house in a seller's market. But when the economy slows and buyers grow bearish (retreating to more conservative spending policies), closing a sale can be a challenge in which price plays a big role. While a realtor can give you a professional appraisal of your house, here are some tips for arriving at your own estimate of the price that's right:

- Stake out an area within a half mile of your home and note the selling price of every similar home that's sold in the last few months. Make sure you're looking at houses that are truly comparable to yours in age, size, and character of the neighborhood.

- Recognize that every real estate market is different. Some have seen rising prices even in years when other areas have suffered. Know which type of area you are in.

- Get to know the type of buyers who are looking at homes in your area. Are they young families who will love your backyard, or professional couples who'll want your extra bedrooms for home office space?

- Go to open houses and study current and recent home sales in your area, using newspapers and the Internet. Those sellers are your competition. You won't find out what last-minute concessions they might make to close their deals, but you can find out what they're generally offering for the money.

- Be aware that buyers no longer make the same big allowances for upgrades like new kitchens or finished basements as in the past when the real estate market was stronger.

- Make sure you've taken care of all the cosmetic details you can, such as putting on a fresh coat of paint, removing clutter and personal belongings, and making necessary repairs to house and property. It's all part of what one broker calls "find[ing] the point between, 'Hey, that's interesting,' and 'It's too good to pass up.'"

Sources: Melanie Speed, " Strategies for Selling Real Estate in a Tough Market," *Street Directory.com*, www.streetdirectory.com, accessed March 10, 2010; "8 Tips for Pricing Your Home in a Buyer's Market," *MSN.com*, http://realestate.msn.com, accessed March 9, 2010; Elizabeth Weintraug, "Home Selling in a Market Dominated by Foreclosures and Short Sales," *About.com*, http://homebuying.about.com, accessed March 9, 2010; Matthew C. Keegan, "7 Tips for Pricing Your Home in Today's Economy," *Say Educate.com*, www.sayeducate.com, October 23, 2009.

new model of its fuel-efficient Prius hybrid, which promises an average of 50 miles per gallon. "It's a core model for us," said the president of Toyota Motor Sales USA. The company's group vice president and general manager said, "Since Prius was first introduced, the consumer demographics has shifted from an early adopter to a mainstream shopper." The company hopes to keep the auto in the number-one spot among hybrids in the U.S. market.[19]

assessment check

1. What goals does pricing strategy help a not-for-profit organization achieve?
2. What are the two basic ways in which marketers determine prices?

Price Determination in Economic Theory

Microeconomics suggests a way of determining prices that assumes a profit-maximization objective. This technique attempts to derive correct equilibrium prices in the marketplace by comparing supply and demand. It also requires more complete analysis than actual business firms typically conduct.

Demand refers to a schedule of the amounts of a firm's product that consumers will purchase at different prices during a specified time period. **Supply** refers to a schedule of the amounts of a good or service that will be offered for sale at different prices during a specified period. These schedules may vary for different types of market structures. Businesses operate and set prices in four types of market structures: pure competition, monopolistic competition, oligopoly, and monopoly.

Pure competition is a market structure with so many buyers and sellers that no single participant can significantly influence price. Pure competition presupposes other market conditions as well: homogeneous products and ease of entry for sellers due to low start-up costs. The agricultural sector exhibits many characteristics of a purely competitive market, making it the closest actual example. But many U.S. ranchers have switched their beef herds to an all-grass diet in an attempt to differentiate their product from those raised in feedlots.

Monopolistic competition typifies most retailing and features large numbers of buyers and sellers. These diverse parties exchange heterogeneous, relatively well-differentiated products, giving marketers some control over prices.

Relatively few sellers compete in an **oligopoly**. Pricing decisions by each seller are likely to affect the market, but no single seller controls it. High start-up costs form significant barriers to entry for new competitors. Each firm's demand curve in an oligopolistic market displays a unique kink at the current market price. Because of the impact of a single competitor on total industry sales, competitors usually quickly match any attempt by one firm to generate additional sales by reducing prices. Price cutting in such industry structures is likely to reduce total industry revenues. Oligopolies operate in the petroleum refining, automobile, tobacco, and airline industries.

Rising fuel prices and a slowing economy have led the leading U.S. airlines not only to raise prices but also to cut capacity, limiting flights to major cities and eliminating service to some less-profitable or heavily discounted locations. "Being angry at the airlines is misplaced," said US Airways president. "You have to look at what happened," including overexpansion by airlines in earlier years, cutbacks in business travel, and too few passengers paying full fare.[20]

A **monopoly** is a market structure in which only one seller of a product exists and for which there are no close substitutes. Antitrust legislation has nearly eliminated all but temporary monopolies such as those created through patent protection. Regulated industries constitute another form of monopoly. The government allows regulated monopolies in markets in which competition would lead to an uneconomical duplication of services. In return for such a license, government reserves the right to regulate the monopoly's rate of return.

The four types of market structures are compared in Table 18.2 on the following bases: number of competitors, ease of entry into the industry by new firms, similarity of competing products, degree of control over price by individual firms, and the elasticity or inelasticity of the demand curve facing the individual firm. Elasticity—the degree of consumer responsiveness to changes in price—is discussed in more detail in a later section.

demand Schedule of the amounts of a firm's product that consumers will purchase at different prices during a specified time period.

supply Schedule of the amounts of a good or service that firms will offer for sale at different prices during a specified time period.

pure competition Market structure characterized by homogeneous products in which there are so many buyers and sellers that none has a significant influence on price.

monopolistic competition Market structure involving a heterogeneous product and product differentiation among competing suppliers, allowing the marketer some degree of control over prices.

oligopoly Market structure in which relatively few sellers compete and where high start-up costs form barriers to keep out new competitors.

monopoly Market structure in which a single seller dominates trade in a good or service for which buyers can find no close substitutes.

table 18.2 Distinguishing Features of the Four Market Structures

Characteristics	Type of Market Structure			
	Pure Competition	Monopolistic Competition	Oligopoly	Monopoly
Number of competitors	Many	Few to many	Few	No direct competitors
Ease of entry into industry by new firms	Easy	Somewhat difficult	Difficult	Regulated by government
Similarity of goods or services offered by competing firms	Similar	Different	Can be either similar or different	No directly competing goods or services
Control over prices by individual firms	None	Some	Some	Considerable
Demand curves facing individual firms	Totally elastic	Can be either elastic or inelastic	Kinked; inelastic below kink; more elastic above	Can be either elastic or inelastic
Examples	Indiana soybean farm	Best Buy stores	Verizon Wireless	Waste Management

variable costs Costs that change with the level of production (such as labor and raw materials costs).

fixed costs Costs that remain stable at any production level within a certain range (such as lease payments or insurance costs).

average total costs Costs calculated by dividing the sum of the variable and fixed costs by the number of units produced.

Cost and Revenue Curves

Marketers must set a price for a product that generates sufficient revenue to cover the costs of producing and marketing it. A product's total cost is composed of total variable costs and total fixed costs. **Variable costs**, such as raw materials and labor costs, change with the level of production, and **fixed costs**, such as lease payments or insurance costs, remain stable at any production level within a certain range. **Average total costs** are calculated by dividing the sum of the variable and fixed costs by the number of units produced. Finally, **marginal cost** is the change in total cost that results from producing an additional unit of output.

The demand side of the pricing equation focuses on revenue curves. Average revenue is calculated by dividing total revenue by the quantity associated with these revenues. Average revenue is actually the demand curve facing the firm. Marginal revenue is the change in total revenue that results from selling an additional unit of output. Figure 18.1 shows the relationships of various cost and revenue measures; the firm maximizes its profits when marginal costs equal marginal revenues.

figure 18.1

Determining Price by Relating Marginal Revenue to Marginal Cost

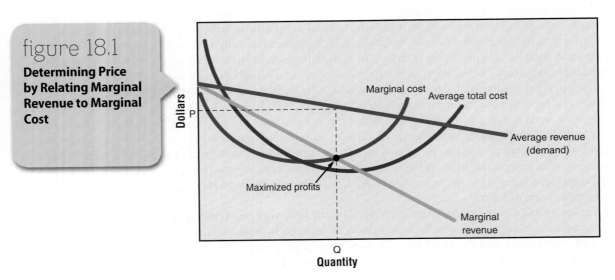

table 18.3 Price Determination Using Marginal Analysis

Price	Number Sold	Total Revenue	Marginal Revenue	Total Costs	Marginal Costs	Profits (Total Revenue Minus Total Costs)
—	—	—	—	—	—	($50)
$34	1	$34	$34	$57	$7	(23)
32	2	64	30	62	5	2
30	3	90	26	66	4	24
28	4	112	22	69	3	43
26	5	130	18	73	4	57
24	6	144	14	78	5	66
22	7	154	10	84	6	70
20	8	160	6	91	7	69
18	9	162	2	100	9	62
16	10	160	(2)	101	11	50

Table 18.3 illustrates why the intersection of the marginal cost and marginal revenue curves is the logical point at which to maximize revenue for the organization. Although the firm can earn a profit at several different prices, the price at which it earns maximum profits is $22. At a price of $24, $66 in profits is earned—$4 less than the $70 profit at the $22 price. If a price of $20 is set to attract additional sales, the marginal costs of the extra sales ($7) are greater than the marginal revenues received ($6), and total profits decline.

marginal cost Change in total cost that results from producing an additional unit of output.

 assessment check

1. What are the four types of market structures?
2. Identify the two types of costs that make up a product's total cost.

The Concept of Elasticity in Pricing Strategy

Although the intersection of the marginal cost and marginal revenue curves determines the level of output, the impact of changes in price on sales varies greatly. To understand why it fluctuates, one must understand the concept of elasticity.

3 Explain price elasticity and its determinants.

Elasticity is the measure of the responsiveness of purchasers and suppliers to price changes. The price elasticity of demand (or elasticity of demand) is the percentage change in the quantity of a good or service demanded divided by the percentage change in its price. A 10 percent increase in the price of eggs that results in a 5 percent decrease in the quantity of eggs demanded yields a price elasticity of demand for eggs of 0.5. The price elasticity of supply of a product is the percentage change in the quantity of a good or service supplied divided by the percentage change in its price. A 10 percent increase in the price of shampoo that results in a 25 percent increase in the quantity supplied yields a price elasticity of supply for shampoo of 2.5.

elasticity Measure of responsiveness of purchasers and suppliers to a change in price.

Consider a case in which a 1 percent change in price causes more than a 1 percent change in the quantity supplied or demanded. Numerically, that means an elasticity measurement greater than 1.0. When the elasticity of demand or supply is greater than 1.0, that demand or supply is said to be elastic. If a 1 percent change in price results in less than a

© NATALIYA HORA/SHUTTERSTOCK.COM

A 10 percent increase in the price of eggs that results in a 5 percent decrease in the quantity of eggs demanded yields a price elasticity of demand for eggs of 0.5.

1 percent change in quantity, a product's elasticity of demand or supply will be less than 1.0. In that case, the demand or supply is called *inelastic*. For example, the demand for cigarettes is relatively inelastic; research studies have shown that a 10 percent increase in cigarette prices results in only a 4 percent sales decline.

In some countries whose economies are in shambles, price levels bear little resemblance to the laws of elasticity or supply and demand. Prices in Zimbabwe once rose at unheard-of rates, the result of hyperinflation that rose to more 7,600 percent in a *month*— estimated to be as high as 12.5 million percent a year. More recently, however, changes in the country's monetary policies, including the abandonment of its local currency, began to bring prices down and it appeared that inflation in Zimbabwe might soon be a thing of the past.[21]

DETERMINANTS OF ELASTICITY

Why is the elasticity of supply or demand high for some products and low for others? What determines demand elasticity? One major factor influencing the elasticity of demand is the availability of substitutes or complements. If consumers can easily find close substitutes for a good or service, the product's demand tends to be elastic. A product's role as a complement to the use of another product also affects its degree of price elasticity. For example, the relatively inelastic demand for motor oil reflects its role as a complement to a more important product, gasoline. High prices for gasoline, in turn, are fueling a search for alternative fuels.[22]

As increasing numbers of buyers and sellers complete their business transactions online, the elasticity of a product's demand is drastically affected. Take major discounters and other price-competitive stores, for example. Small businesses and individual do-it-yourselfers shop Lowe's for tools, such as wheelbarrows; parents look for birthday gifts at Walmart; and homeowners go to Home Depot for new refrigerators or stoves. Today, however, the Internet lets consumers contact many more providers directly, often giving them better selections and prices for their efforts with service sites such as Shopzilla.com for consumer goods and electronics, Net-à-Porter.com for high fashion clothing, Kayak.com for travel bargains, and Shoebuy.com for shoes from dozens of different manufacturers. The increased options available to shoppers combine to create a market characterized by demand elasticity.

Elasticity of demand also depends on whether a product is perceived as a necessity or a luxury. The Four Seasons chain of luxury hotels and resorts enjoys a strong reputation for service, comfort, and exclusiveness and is a favorite among affluent individual travelers and business professionals.

Most people regard high-fashion clothes, such as a $1,300 Escada embroidered dress at Neiman Marcus, as luxuries. If prices for designer outfits increase dramatically, people can respond by purchasing lower-priced substitutes instead. In contrast, medical and dental care are considered necessities, so price changes have little effect on the frequency of visits to the doctor or dentist.

Elasticity also depends on the portion of a person's budget spent on a good or service. For example, people no longer really need matches; they can easily find good substitutes. Nonetheless, the demand for matches remains very inelastic because people spend so little on them that they hardly notice a price change. In contrast, the demand for housing or transportation is not totally inelastic, even though they are necessities, because both consume large parts of a consumer's budget.

Elasticity of demand also responds to consumers' time perspectives. Demand often shows less elasticity in the short run than in the long run. Consider the demand for home air conditioning.

In the short run, people pay rising energy prices because they find it difficult to cut back on the quantities they use. Accustomed to living with specific temperature settings and dressing in certain ways, they prefer to pay more during a few months of the year than to explore other possibilities. Over the long term, though, they may consider insulating their homes and planting shade trees to reduce cooling costs.

San Francisco's Bay Area Rapid Transit (BART) officials seem to believe the demand for rapid rail transit is inelastic. They raise fares when they need more money.

ELASTICITY AND REVENUE

The elasticity of demand exerts an important influence on variations in total revenue as a result of changes in the price of a good or service. Assume, for example, that San Francisco's Bay Area Rapid Transit (BART) officials are considering alternative methods of raising more money for their budget. One possible method for increasing revenues would be to change rail pass fares for commuters. But should BART raise or lower the price of a pass? The correct answer depends on the elasticity of demand for subway rides. A 10 percent decrease in fares should attract more riders, but unless it stimulates more than a 10 percent increase in riders, total revenue will fall. A 10 percent increase in fares will bring in more money per rider, but if more than 10 percent of the riders stop using the subway, total revenue will fall. A price cut will increase revenue only for a product with elastic demand, and a price increase will raise revenue only for a product with inelastic demand. BART officials seem to believe the demand for rapid rail transit is inelastic; they raise fares when they need more money.

 assessment check

1. What are the determinants of elasticity?
2. What is the usual relationship between elasticity and revenue?

Practical Problems of Price Theory

Marketers may thoroughly understand price theory concepts but still encounter difficulty applying them in practice. What practical limitations interfere with setting prices? First, many firms do not attempt to maximize profits. Economic analysis is subject to the same limitations as the assumptions on which it is based—for example, the proposition that all firms attempt to maximize profits. Second, it is difficult to estimate demand curves. Modern accounting procedures provide managers with a clear understanding of cost structures, so managers can readily comprehend the supply side of the pricing equation. But they find it difficult to estimate demand at various price levels. Demand curves must be based on marketing research estimates that may be less exact than cost figures. Although the demand element can be identified, it is often difficult to measure in real-world settings.

> *4* **List the practical problems involved in applying price theory concepts to actual pricing decisions.**

 assessment check

1. List the three reasons it is difficult to put price theory into practice.

Price Determination in Practice

5 Explain the major cost-plus approaches to price setting.

The practical limitations inherent in price theory have forced practitioners to turn to other techniques. **Cost-plus pricing**, the most popular method, uses a base-cost figure per unit and adds a markup to cover unassigned costs and to provide a profit. The only real difference among the multitude of cost-plus techniques is the relative sophistication of the costing procedures employed. For example, a local apparel shop may set prices by adding a 45 percent markup to the invoice price charged by the supplier. The markup is expected to cover all other expenses and permit the owner to earn a reasonable return on the sale of clothes.

In contrast to this rather simple pricing mechanism, a large manufacturer may employ a complex pricing formula requiring computer calculations. However, this method merely adds a more complicated procedure to the simpler, traditional method for calculating costs. In the end, someone still must make a decision about the markup. The apparel shop and the large manufacturer may figure costs differently, but they are remarkably similar in completing the markup side of the equation.

Cost-plus pricing often works well for a business that keeps its costs low, allowing it to set its prices lower than those of competitors and still make a profit. Walmart keeps costs low by buying most of its inventory directly from manufacturers, using a supply chain that slashes inventory costs by quickly replenishing inventory as items are sold and relying on other intermediaries only in special instances such as localized items. This strategy has played a major role in the discounter's becoming the world's largest retailer.

cost-plus pricing Practice of adding a percentage of specified dollar amount—or markup—to the base cost of a product to cover unassigned costs and to provide a profit.

Alternative Pricing Procedures

The two most common cost-oriented pricing procedures are the full-cost method and the incremental-cost method. **Full-cost pricing** uses all relevant variable costs in setting a product's price. In addition, it allocates fixed costs that cannot be directly attributed to the production of the specific priced item. Under the full-cost method, if job order 515 in a printing plant amounts to 0.000127 percent of the plant's total output, then 0.000127 percent of the firm's overhead expenses are charged to that job. This approach allows the marketer to recover all costs plus the amount added as a profit margin.

The full-cost approach has two basic deficiencies. First, no consideration of competition or demand exists for the item; perhaps no one wants to pay the price the firm has calculated. Second, any method for allocating overhead (fixed expenses) is arbitrary and may be unrealistic—in manufacturing, overhead allocations often are tied to direct labor hours; in retailing, the square footage of each profit center is sometimes the factor used in computations. Regardless of the technique employed, it is difficult to show a cause–effect relationship between the allocated cost and most products.

One way to overcome the arbitrary allocation of fixed expenses is with **incremental-cost pricing**, which attempts to use only costs directly attributable to a specific output in setting prices. Consider a very small-scale manufacturer with the following income statement:

full-cost pricing Pricing method that uses all relevant variable costs in setting a product's price and allocates those fixed costs not directly attributed to the production of the priced item.

incremental-cost pricing Pricing method that attempts to use only costs directly attributable to a specific output in setting prices.

Sales (10,000 units at $10)		$ 100,000
Expenses:		
Variable	$50,000	
Fixed	40,000	90,000
Net profit		$ 10,000

Suppose the firm is offered a contract for an additional 5,000 units. Because the peak season is over, these items can be produced at the same average variable cost. Assume the labor force would otherwise be working on maintenance projects. How low should the firm price its product to get the contract?

Under the full-cost approach, the lowest price would be $9 per unit. This figure is obtained by dividing the $90,000 in expenses by an output of 10,000 units. The incremental approach, on the other hand, could permit any price above $5, which would significantly increase the possibility of securing the additional contract. This price would be composed of the $5 variable cost associated with each unit of production plus a $0.10-per-unit contribution to fixed expenses and overhead. With a $5.10 proposed price, the income statement now looks like this:

Sales (10,000 at $10; 5,000 at $5.10)		$ 125,500
Expenses:		
Variable	$75,000	
Fixed	40,000	115,000
Net profit		$ 10,500

Profits thus increase under the incremental approach.

assessment check

1. What is full-cost pricing?

2. What is incremental-cost pricing?

Admittedly, the illustration is based on two assumptions: (1) the ability to isolate markets such that selling at the lower price will not affect the price received in other markets and (2) the absence of legal restrictions on the firm. The example, however, does illustrate that profits can sometimes be enhanced by using the incremental approach.

Breakeven Analysis

Breakeven analysis is a means of determining the number of goods or services that must be sold at a given price to generate sufficient revenue to cover total costs. Figure 18.2 graphically depicts this process. The total cost curve includes both fixed and variable segments, and total fixed cost is represented by a horizontal line. Average variable cost is assumed to be constant per unit as it was in the example for incremental pricing.

The breakeven point is the point at which total revenue equals total cost. In the example in Figure 18.2, a selling price of $10 and an average variable cost of $5 result in a per-unit contribution to fixed cost of $5. The breakeven point in terms of units is found by using the following formula, in which the per-unit contribution equals the product's price less the variable cost per unit:

$$\text{Breakeven point (in units)} = \frac{\text{Total fixed cost}}{\text{Per-unit contribution to fixed cost}}$$

$$\text{Breakeven point (in units)} = \frac{\$40,000}{\$5} = 8,000 \text{ units}$$

The breakeven point in dollars is found with the following formula:

$$\text{Breakeven point (in dollars)} = \frac{\text{Total fixed cost}}{1 - \text{Variable cost per unit price}}$$

$$\text{Breakeven point (in dollars)} = \frac{\$40,000}{1 - (\$5/\$10)} = \frac{\$40,000}{0.5} = \$80,000$$

Sometimes breakeven is reached by reducing costs. Faced with declining sales and revenues, Ford Motor Co. recently beat its own goals for cost reductions by reducing costs, as well as restructuring debt.[23]

Once the breakeven point has been reached, sufficient revenues will have been obtained from sales to cover all fixed costs. Any additional sales will generate per-unit profits equal to the difference between the product's selling price and the variable cost of each unit. As Figure 18.2 reveals, sales of 8,001 units (1 unit above the breakeven point) will produce net profits of $5 ($10 sales price less

List the chief advantages and shortcomings of using breakeven analysis in pricing decisions.

breakeven analysis
Pricing technique used to determine the number of products that must be sold at a specified price to generate enough revenue to cover total cost.

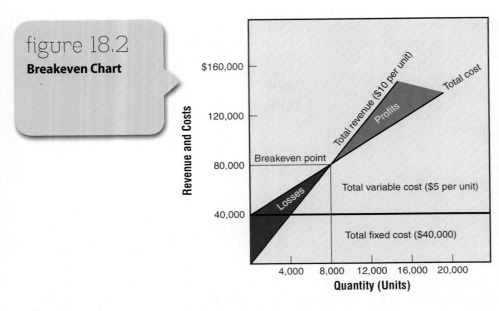

figure 18.2

Breakeven Chart

per-unit variable cost of $5). Once all fixed costs have been covered, the per-unit contribution will become the per-unit profit.

TARGET RETURNS

Although breakeven analysis indicates the sales level at which the firm will incur neither profits nor losses, most marketers include a targeted profit in their analyses. In some instances, management sets a desired dollar return when considering a proposed new product or other marketing strategy. A retailer may set a desired profit of $250,000 in considering whether to expand to a second location. In other instances, the target return may be expressed in percentages, such as a 15 percent return on sales. These target returns can be calculated as follows:

$$\text{Breakeven point (including specific dollar target return)} = \frac{\text{Total fixed cost} + \text{Profit objective}}{\text{Per-unit contribution}}$$

$$\text{Breakeven point (in units)} = \frac{\$40,000 + \$15,000}{\$5} = 11,000 \text{ units}$$

If the target return is expressed as a percentage of sales, it can be included in the breakeven formula as a variable cost. Suppose the marketer in the preceding example seeks a 10 percent return on sales. The desired return is $1 for each product sold (the $10 per-unit selling price multiplied by the 10 percent return on sales). In this case, the basic breakeven formula will remain unchanged, although the variable cost per unit will be increased to reflect the target return, and the per-unit contribution to fixed cost will be reduced to $4. As a result, the breakeven point will increase from 8,000 to 10,000 units:

$$\text{Breakeven point} = \frac{\$40,000}{\$4} = 10,000 \text{ units}$$

 assessment check

1. What is the formula for finding the breakeven point in units and in dollars?
2. What adjustments to the basic breakeven calculation must be made to include target returns?

EVALUATION OF BREAKEVEN ANALYSIS

Breakeven analysis is an effective tool for marketers in assessing the sales required for covering costs and achieving specified profit levels. It is easily understood by both marketing and nonmarketing executives and may help them decide whether required sales levels for a certain price are realistic goals. However, it has its shortcomings.

First, the model assumes costs can be divided into fixed and variable categories. Some costs, such as salaries and advertising outlays, may be either fixed or variable depending on the particular situation. In addition, the model assumes per-unit variable costs do not change at different levels of operation. However, these may vary because of quantity discounts, more efficient use of the workforce, or other economies resulting from increased levels of production and sales. Finally, the basic breakeven model does not consider demand. It is a cost-based model and does not directly address the crucial question of whether consumers will purchase the product at the specified price and in the quantities required for breaking even or generating profits. The marketer's challenge is to modify the breakeven analysis and the other cost-oriented pricing approaches to incorporate demand analysis. Pricing must be examined from the buyer's perspective. Such decisions cannot be made by only considering cost factors.

 assessment check

1. What are the advantages of breakeven analysis?
2. What are the disadvantages of breakeven analysis?

The Modified Breakeven Concept

Traditional economic theory considers both costs and demand in determining an equilibrium price. The dual elements of supply and demand are balanced at the point of equilibrium. In actual practice, however, most pricing approaches are largely cost oriented. Because purely cost-oriented approaches to pricing violate the marketing concept, modifications that add demand analysis to the pricing decision are required.

Consumer research on such issues as degree of price elasticity, consumer price expectations, existence and size of specific market segments, and buyer perceptions of strengths and weaknesses of substitute products is necessary for developing sales estimates at different prices. Because much of the resulting data involves perceptions, attitudes, and future expectations of present and potential customers, such estimates are likely to be less precise than cost estimates. The breakeven analysis method illustrated in Figure 18.2 assumes a constant $10 retail price, regardless of quantity. But what happens at different retail prices? As Figure 18.3 shows, a more sophisticated approach, **modified breakeven analysis**, combines the traditional breakeven analysis model with an evaluation of consumer demand.

Table 18.4 summarizes both the cost and revenue aspects of a number of alternative retail prices. The $5 per-unit variable cost and the $40,000 total fixed cost are based on the costs used in the basic breakeven model. The expected unit sales for each specified retail price are obtained from marketing research. The table contains the information necessary for calculating the breakeven point for each of the five retail price alternatives. These points are shown in Figure 18.3(a).

modified breakeven analysis Pricing technique used to evaluate consumer demand by comparing the number of products that must be sold at a variety of prices to cover total cost with estimates of expected sales at the various prices.

figure 18.3

Modified Breakeven Chart: Parts A and B

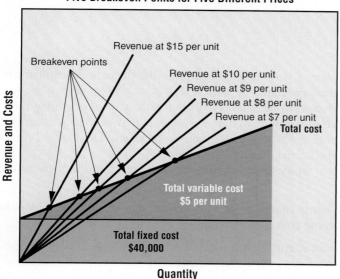

(a)
Five Breakeven Points for Five Different Prices

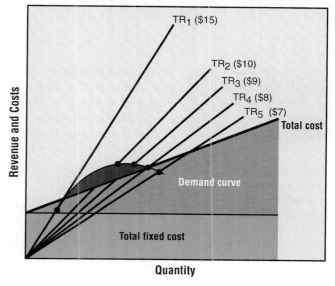

(b)
Superimposing a Demand Curve on the Breakeven Chart

table 18.4 Revenue and Cost Data for Modified Breakeven Analysis

	Revenues		Costs			Breakeven Point (Number of Sales Required to Break Even)	Total Profit (or Loss)
Price	Quantity Demanded	Total Revenue	Total Fixed Cost	Total Variable Cost	Total Cost		
$15	2,500	$37,500	$40,000	$12,500	$52,000	4,000	$(15,000)
10	10,000	100,000	40,000	50,000	90,000	8,000	10,000
9	13,000	117,000	40,000	65,000	105,000	10,000	12,000
8	14,000	112,000	40,000	70,000	110,000	13,334	2,000
7	15,000	105,000	40,000	75,000	115,000	20,000	(10,000)

The data shown in the first two columns of Table 18.4 represent a demand schedule that indicates the number of units consumers are expected to purchase at each of a series of retail prices. As Figure 18.3(b) shows, these data can be superimposed onto a breakeven chart to identify the range of feasible prices for the marketer to charge.

Figure 18.3 reveals that the range of profitable prices exists from a low of approximately $8 (TR4) to a high of $10 (TR2), with a price of $9 (TR3) generating the greatest projected profits. Changing the retail price produces a new breakeven point. At a relatively high $15 retail price (TR1), the breakeven point is 4,000 units; at a $10 retail price, it is 8,000 units; and at the lowest price considered, $7 (TR5), it is 20,000 units.

The contribution of modified breakeven analysis is that it forces the marketer to consider whether the consumer is likely to purchase the number of units required for achieving breakeven at a given price. It demonstrates that a large number of units sold does not necessarily produce added profits, because—other things equal—lower prices are necessary for stimulating additional sales. Consequently, it is important to consider both costs and consumer demand in determining the most appropriate price.

 assessment check

1. What is modified breakeven analysis?

Yield Management

Explain the use of yield management in pricing decisions.

When most of a firm's costs are fixed over a wide range of outputs, the primary determinant of profitability will be the amount of revenue generated by sales. **Yield management** strategies allow marketers to vary prices based on such factors as demand, even though the cost of providing those goods or services remains the same. Hotels use software to track customer patterns and help determine attractive discounts that fill their spas during off-peak hours such as weekdays. The lowered prices also reduce unprofitable downtime for specialized spa employees.[24]

Similar yield management strategies typify the marketing of such goods and services as the following:

yield management
Pricing strategy that allows marketers to vary prices based on such factors as demand, even though the cost of providing those goods or services remains the same.

- *sports teams*—the San Francisco Giants charge more for weekend games, and the Colorado Rockies raise ticket prices based on the crowd-pleasing power of visiting teams

- *lodging*—lower prices in the off-season and higher prices during peak-season periods; low-priced weekend rates (except in locations such as Las Vegas, New Orleans, and Charleston, with high weekend tourist visits)

- *auto rental*—lower prices on weekends when business demand is low and higher prices during the week when business demand is higher

- *airfares*—lower prices on nonrefundable tickets with travel restrictions such as advance purchase and Saturday-night stay requirements and penalties for flight changes and higher prices on refundable tickets that can be changed without penalty.

The following example from the airline industry demonstrates how yield management maximizes revenues in situations in which costs are fixed.[25] Airlines constantly monitor reservations on every flight. Beginning approximately 330 days before the flight, space is allocated between full-fare, discount-fare, and free tickets for frequent flyers who qualify for complimentary tickets. This allocation is monitored and adjusted at regular intervals until the flight departs.

Assume, for example, that American Airlines has scheduled a 136-seat plane as Flight 2332 with a 9:15 a.m. departure from Dallas–Fort Worth to Chicago's O'Hare Airport on October 23. When Flight 2332 leaves its gate, all costs associated with the flight (fuel, crew, and other operating expenses) are fixed. The pricing that maximizes revenues on this flight will also maximize profits. An examination of past sales indicates that American could sell 30 to 40 round-trip, full-fare tickets at $500 per passenger and 100 to 110 round-trip restricted-fare tickets at $200 per passenger. Demand for frequent-flyer space should be at least 10 seats.

If American reserves 40 seats for full-fare passengers and accepts reservations for 86 restricted-fare tickets but sells only 30 full-fare tickets (leaving 20 vacant seats), total revenues will be as follows:

$$\text{Revenues} = (30 \times \$500) + (86 \times \$200) = \$32,200$$

On the other hand, if American's pricing decision makers want to reduce vacancies, they might decide to reduce the number of full-fare tickets to 15 and increase the restricted-fare tickets to 111. If the plane leaves the gate at full capacity, the flight will generate the following total revenues:

$$\text{Revenues} = (15 \times \$500) + (111 \times \$200) = \$29,700$$

Instead of rigidly maintaining the allocations established nearly a year before the flight, though, American will use yield management to maximize the revenue per flight. In this example, the airline initially holds 40 full-fare seats and accepts reservations for up to 86 restricted-fare seats. Thirty days before the October 23 departure, updated computer projections indicate that 27 full-fare seats are likely to be sold. The allocation is now revised to 27 full-fare and 99 restricted-fare tickets. A full flight leaves the gate and revenues are as follows:

$$\text{Revenues} = (27 \times \$500) + (99 \times \$200) = \$33,300$$

Applying yield management for the Dallas–Chicago flight increases revenues by at least $1,100 over the inflexible approach of making advance allocations and failing to adjust them based on passenger reservations and other data.

 assessment check

1. Explain the goal of yield management.

Global Issues in Price Determination

It is equally important for a firm engaging in global marketing to use a pricing strategy that reflects its overall marketing strategy. Prices must support the company's broader goals, including product development, advertising and sales, customer support, competitive plans, and financial objectives.

In general, firms can use five pricing objectives to set prices in global marketing. Four of them are the same pricing objectives we discussed earlier in the chapter: profitability, volume, meeting competition, and prestige. In addition, international marketers work to achieve a fifth objective: price stability.

 Identify the major pricing challenges facing online and international marketers.

In the global arena, marketers may choose profitability objectives if their company is a price leader that tends to establish international prices. Profitability objectives also make sense if a firm is a low-cost supplier that can make a good profit on sales.

Volume objectives become especially important on the global stage. Ralph Lauren was chosen as the official outfitter of the U.S. Olympic Team in Vancouver and will reprise the role for the London Games in 2012. The spectacularly choreographed Opening Ceremonies and Closing Ceremonies at the Games, which drew a worldwide audience of about 2 billion people for the Beijing Summer Olympics, provide a runway as large as any clothing designer could desire. Replicas of the Lauren U.S. Team apparel line sold at Ralph Lauren retail stores, at the designer's Web site, via the Hudson Bay Company, and through U.S. Olympic and Team USA shops.[26]

Increased competition in Europe has spurred firms to work toward the third pricing objective of meeting competitors' prices. The widespread adoption of the euro, the currency of the European Union, has become a driving force in price convergence. Now nearly 330 million people in 16 EU countries use it, and the European Commission believes this adoption of a single currency promotes stability, low inflation, low interest rates, and increased price transparency, all of which help facilitate international trade.[27]

Prestige is a valid pricing objective in international marketing when products are associated with intangible benefits, such as high quality, exclusiveness, or attractive design. The greater a product's perceived benefits, the higher its price can be. Marketers must be aware, however, that cultural perceptions of quality can differ from one country to the next. Sometimes items that command prestige prices in the United States are considered run-of-the-mill in other nations; sometimes products that are anything but prestigious in America seem exotic to overseas consumers. American patrons, for instance, view McDonald's restaurants as affordable fast-food eateries, but in China, they are seen as fashionable and relatively expensive.

The fifth pricing objective, price stability, is desirable in international markets, although it is difficult to achieve. Wars, terrorism, economic downturns, changing governments and political parties, and shifting trade policies can alter prices. A retailer can even be the victim of its own success at managing prices. British international supermarket giant Tesco faces fierce competition at home and abroad, as well as a backlash among UK consumers against its growing dominance in so-called Tesco towns. After Tesco announced plans to open a store in Bristol, England, where it

Ralph Lauren was chosen as the official outfitter of the U.S. Olympic Team in Vancouver and will repeat the role for the London Games in 2012.

© AP IMAGES/MATT SAYLES

already owns 17 supermarkets and other stores in a 2.5–mile radius, consumers and local trades-people were alarmed. Said the leader of the local traders' association, "We are very concerned. Tesco is using its financial muscle to take over everything in Bristol. Tesco Expresses are so small they can describe themselves as a local shop and they look wonderful because they are cheap."[28]

Price stability can be especially important for producers of commodities—goods and services that have easily accessible substitutes that other nations can supply quickly. Countries that export international commodities, such as wood, chemicals, and agricultural crops, suffer economically when their prices fluctuate. A nation such as Nicaragua, which exports sugarcane, can find that its balance of payments changes drastically when the international price for sugar shifts. This makes it vulnerable to stiff price competition from other sugarcane producers. In contrast, countries that export value-oriented products, rather than commodities, tend to enjoy more stable prices. Prices of electronic equipment and automobiles tend to fluctuate far less than prices of crops such as sugarcane and bananas.

strategic implications
of marketing in the 21st century

his chapter has focused on traditional pricing concepts and methods—principles critical to all marketing strategies, especially in e-business. Consumers can now compare prices quickly, heightening the already intense competitive pricing environment. The Web allows for prices to be negotiated on the spot, and nearly anything can be auctioned. For products as varied as sports tickets and automobiles, the Web allows consumers to name their price.

While Internet shopping has not resulted in massive price cutting, it has increased the options available for consumers. Online price comparison engines, known as *shopping bots*, promise to help consumers find the lowest price for any good or service. Reverse auctions offered by sites such as Priceline.com, which allow cus-

tomers to submit the highest price they are willing to pay for airline tickets, could conceivably be extended to other types of goods and are already gaining in popularity in business-to-business purchasing.

Electronic delivery of music, books, and other goods and services will only lead to further price reductions. E-business has smoothed out the friction of time, which kept pricing relatively static. The current obsession with time and the ability to measure it will change the perceptions and pricing of tangible goods. A growing number of products are not made until they are ordered, and increasingly, their prices are no longer fixed; instead, prices can shift up and down in response to changing market conditions.

assessment check

1. What are five pricing objectives in global and online marketing?

2. Why is price stability difficult to achieve in online and global marketing?

Review of Chapter Objectives

 Outline the legal constraints on pricing.

A variety of laws affect pricing decisions. Antitrust legislation provides a general set of constraints. The Robinson-Patman Act amended the Clayton Act to prohibit price discrimination in sales to other producers, wholesalers, or retailers not based on a cost differential. This law does not cover export markets or sales to the ultimate consumer. At the state level, unfair-trade laws require sellers to maintain minimum prices for comparable merchandise. These laws have become less frequently enforced in recent years. Fair-trade laws represented one legal barrier to competition that was removed in the face of growing price competition. These laws permitted manufacturers to set minimum retail prices for products and to require their dealers to sign contracts agreeing to abide by such prices. The Consumer Goods Pricing Act banned interstate use of fair-trade laws.

 Identify the major categories of pricing objectives.

Pricing objectives are the natural consequence of overall organizational goals and more specific marketing goals. They can be classified into four major groups: (1) profitability objectives, including profit maximization and target returns; (2) volume objectives, including sales maximization and market share; (3) meeting competition objectives; and (4) prestige objectives.

 Explain price elasticity and its determinants.

Elasticity is an important element in price determination. The degree of consumer responsiveness to price changes is affected by such factors as (1) availability of substitute or complementary goods, (2) the classification of a good or service as a luxury or a necessity, (3) the portion of a person's budget spent on an item, and (4) the time perspective.

 List the practical problems involved in applying price theory concepts to actual pricing decisions.

Three problems are present in using price theory in actual practice. First, many firms do not attempt to maximize profits, a basic assumption of price theory. Second, it is difficult to accurately estimate demand curves. Finally, inadequate training of managers and poor communication between economists and managers make it difficult to apply price theory in the real world.

 Explain the major cost-plus approaches to price setting.

Cost-plus pricing uses a base-cost figure per unit and adds a markup to cover unassigned costs and to provide a profit. It is the most commonly used method of setting prices today. There are two primary cost-oriented pricing procedures. Full-cost pricing uses all relevant variable costs in setting a product's price and allocates those fixed costs that cannot be directly attributed to the production of the priced item. Incremental-cost pricing attempts to use only those costs directly attributable to a specific output in setting prices to overcome the arbitrary allocation of fixed expenses. The basic limitation of cost-oriented pricing is that it does not adequately account for product demand.

 List the chief advantages and shortcomings of using breakeven analysis in pricing decisions.

Breakeven analysis is a means of determining the number of goods or services that must be sold at a given price to generate revenue sufficient for covering total costs. It is easily understood by managers and may help them decide whether required sales levels for a certain price are realistic goals. Its shortcomings are as follows. First, the model assumes cost can be divided into fixed and variable categories and ignores the problems of arbitrarily making some allocations. Second, it assumes that per-unit variable costs do not change at different levels of operation, ignoring the possibility of quantity discounts, more efficient use of the workforce, and other possible economies. Third, the basic breakeven model does not consider demand. It is a cost-based model and fails to directly address the crucial question of whether consumers will actually purchase the product at the specified price and in the quantities required for breaking even or generating profits. The modified breakeven concept combines traditional breakeven analysis with an evaluation of consumer demand. It directly addresses the key question of whether consumers will actually purchase the product at different prices and in what quantities.

 Explain the use of yield management in pricing decisions.

Yield management pricing strategies are designed to maximize revenues in situations in which costs are fixed, such as airfares, auto rentals, and theater tickets.

 Identify the major pricing challenges facing online and international marketers.

In general, firms can choose from among five pricing objectives to set prices in global marketing. Four of these objectives are the same pricing objectives discussed earlier: profitability, volume, meeting competition, and prestige. The fifth objective is price stability, which is difficult to achieve because wars, border conflicts, terrorism, economic trends, changing governments and political parties, and shifting trade policies can alter prices. The same types of changes can alter pricing in online marketing.

Assessment Check: Answers

1.1 What was the purpose of the Robinson-Patman Act?
The Robinson-Patman Act amended the Clayton Act to prohibit price discrimination in sales to other producers, wholesalers, or retailers that are not based on a cost differential.

1.2 What laws require sellers to maintain minimum prices for comparable merchandise? At the state level, unfair-trade laws require sellers to maintain minimum prices for comparable merchandise.

1.3 What laws allow manufacturers to set minimum retail prices for their products? Fair-trade laws permitted manufacturers to set minimum retail prices for products and to require their dealers to sign contracts agreeing to abide by such prices.

2.1 What are target-return objectives? Target-return objectives are short-run or long-run goals usually stated as percentages of sales or investment.

2.2 What is value pricing? Value pricing emphasizes the benefits a product provides in comparison to the price and quality levels of competing offerings.

2.3 How do prestige objectives affect a seller's pricing strategy? Prestige pricing establishes a relatively high price to develop and maintain an image of quality that appeals to status-conscious customers. The seller uses price to create an overall image of the firm.

2.4 What goals does pricing strategy help a not-for-profit organization achieve? Pricing strategy helps not-for-profit organizations achieve a variety of goals: profit maximization, cost recovery, market incentives, and market suppression.

2.5 What are the two basic ways in which marketers determine prices? Marketers determine prices by applying the theoretical concepts of supply and demand and by completing cost-oriented analysis.

2.6 What are the four types of market structures? The four types of market structures are pure competition, monopolistic competition, oligopoly, and monopoly.

2.7 Identify the two types of costs that make up a product's total cost. A product's total cost is composed of total variable costs and total fixed costs.

3.1 What are the determinants of elasticity? The degree of consumer responsiveness to price changes—elasticity—is affected by such factors as (1) availability of substitute or complementary goods, (2) the classification of a good or service as a luxury or a necessity, (3) the portion of a person's budget spent on an item, and (4) the time perspective.

3.2 What is the usual relationship between elasticity and revenue? A price cut increases revenue only for a product with elastic demand, and a price increase raises revenue only for a product with inelastic demand.

4.1 List the three reasons it is difficult to put price theory into practice. A basic assumption of price theory is all firms attempt to maximize profits. This does not always happen in

practice. A second reason is demand curves can be extremely difficult to estimate. Finally, there is poor communication between economists and managers, making it difficult to apply price theory in the real world.

5.1 What is full-cost pricing? Full-cost pricing uses all relevant variable costs in setting a product's price.

5.2 What is incremental-cost pricing? Incremental-cost pricing attempts to use only costs directly attributable to a specific output in setting prices to overcome the arbitrary allocation of fixed expenses.

6.1 What is the formula for finding the breakeven point, in units and in dollars? Breakeven point in units = Total fixed cost/Per-unit contribution to fixed cost. Breakeven point in dollars = Total fixed cost/(1 − Variable cost per unit price).

6.2 What adjustments to the basic breakeven calculation must be made to include target returns? Breakeven point (including specific dollar target return) = (Total fixed cost + Profit objective)/Per-unit contribution.

6.3 What are the advantages of breakeven analysis? Breakeven analysis is easily understood by managers and may help them decide whether required sales levels for a certain price are realistic goals.

6.4 What are the disadvantages of breakeven analysis? First, the model assumes cost can be divided into fixed and variable categories and ignores the problems of arbitrarily making some allocations. Second, it assumes per-unit variable costs do not change at different levels of operation, ignoring the possibility of quantity discounts, more efficient use of the workforce, and other possible economies. Third, the basic breakeven model does not consider demand.

6.5 What is modified breakeven analysis? The modified breakeven concept combines traditional breakeven analysis with an evaluation of consumer demand. It directly addresses the key question of whether consumers will actually purchase the product at different prices and in what quantities.

7.1 Explain the goal of yield management. Yield management pricing strategies are designed to maximize revenues in situations in which costs are fixed such as airfares, auto rentals, and theater tickets.

8.1 What are five pricing objectives in global and online marketing? Five pricing objectives in global and online marketing are profitability, volume, meeting competition, prestige, and price stability.

8.2 Why is price stability difficult to achieve in online and global marketing? Price stability is difficult to achieve because wars, border conflicts, terrorism, economic trends, changing governments and political parties, and shifting trade policies can alter prices.

Marketing Terms You Need to Know

price 606
Robinson-Patman Act 608
unfair-trade laws 608
fair-trade laws 609
marginal analysis 611
profit maximization 611
target-return objective 611
market-share objective 612

Profit Impact of Market Strategies (PIMS) project 612
value pricing 613
customary prices 616
demand 619
supply 619
pure competition 619
monopolistic competition 619

oligopoly 619
monopoly 619
variable costs 620
fixed costs 620
average total costs 620
marginal cost 621
elasticity 621
cost-plus pricing 624

full-cost pricing 624
incremental-cost pricing 624
breakeven analysis 625
modified breakeven analysis 627
yield management 628

Assurance of Learning Review

1. Distinguish between fair-trade and unfair-trade laws. As a consumer, would you support either fair-trade or unfair-trade laws? Would your answer change if you were the owner of a small store?

2. Give an example of each of the major categories of pricing objectives.

3. What are the major price implications of the PIMS studies? Suggest possible explanations for the relationships the PIMS studies reveal.

4. Identify each factor influencing elasticity and give a specific example of how it affects the degree of elasticity in a good or service.

5. What are the practical problems in applying price theory concepts to actual pricing decisions?

6. Explain the advantages and drawbacks of using incremental-cost pricing rather than full-cost pricing.

7. How can locating the breakeven point assist in price determination?

8. Explain the advantage of modified breakeven analysis over the basic breakeven formula.

9. Explain how the use of yield management can result in greater revenue than other pricing strategies.

10. How do pricing objectives for a global firm differ from those used generally?

Projects and Teamwork Exercises

1. In small teams, categorize each of the following as a specific type of pricing objective. Suggest a company or product likely to use each pricing objective. Compare your findings.
   a. 5 percent increase in profits over the previous year
   b. prices no more than 6 percent higher than prices quoted by independent dealers
   c. 5 percent increase in market share
   d. 25 percent return on investment (before taxes)
   e. setting the highest prices in the product category to maintain favorable brand image

2. How are the following prices determined and what do they have in common?
   a. ticket to a local museum
   b. college tuition
   c. local sales tax rate
   d. printing of business cards
   e. lawn mowers

3. WebTech Development of Nashville, Tennessee, is considering the possible introduction of a new product proposed by its research and development staff. The firm's marketing director estimates the product can be marketed at a price of $70. Total fixed cost is $278,000, and average variable cost is calculated at $48.
   a. What is the breakeven point in units for the proposed product?
   b. The firm's CEO has suggested a target profit return of $214,000 for the proposed product. How many units must be sold to both break even and achieve this target return?

4. Research the price schedule at your local movie theater multiplex. What pricing strategy accounts for any price differentials you discover? Why don't matinee prices constitute price discrimination against those who don't qualify for the discounts?

5. How do cell phone companies make money by charging a flat rate per month for a set number of minutes, such as $35 for 300 minutes? Can you think of a more profitable plan? Would it appeal to consumers?

Critical-Thinking Exercises

1. Prices at amusement parks are expected to rise because operators such as Disney and Universal Studios are adding new rides and coping with the rising cost of fuel. List as many things as you can think of that parks like these offer patrons in return for their money. Which of these do you think are directly reflected in the price of admission?

2. Music artists earn only about 9 percent in royalties per CD, using a royalty base of retail price less 25 percent for packaging costs. The rest goes to the producer and to cover recording costs, promotion, copies given away to radio stations and reviewers, and other costs such as videos. What do you think happens to the artist's royalties when a CD is marked down to sell faster? Consider two cases: (a) the marked-down CD sells more copies, and (b) it sells the same number of copies as before.

3. Some finance experts advise consumers not to worry about rising gasoline prices, the cost of which can easily be covered by forgoing one takeout meal a month, but to worry about how high energy prices will affect the rest of the economy. For example, each dollar-a-barrel price increase is equivalent to a $20 million-a-day "tax" on the economy. Explain what this means.

4. Ajax Motor Company recently announced that it will rely less on high-volume strategies such as discounts and rebates to improve its profitability. Another strategy it will employ is to sell fewer cars to rental fleets, which eventually return the cars to Ajax for sale at low auction prices. How do these types of sales affect Ajax's profitability?

Ethics Exercise

You work for a major restaurant in your town. The manager is facing cost pressures from rising food prices and says she needs to raise revenues. She decides to reduce the size of the meal portions and use cheaper cuts of meat and fish in some entrées while holding the menu prices constant. She tells you and other staff members not to mention the changes to customers and to deflect any questions or complaints you hear. The descriptions in the menu will not be changed, she says, "because the printing costs would be too high."

1. You know the restaurant advertises the quality of its ingredients in the local media. But the menu changes are not advertised, and it bothers you. What course of action would you take?

2. A customer mentions the beef in the dish he ordered is "tough and dry" and the order seems smaller than before. What would you do?

Internet Exercises

1. **Price competition**. Using a popular travel site—such as Expedia.com or Kayak.com—look up airfares for each of the following pairs of cities:

   New York to Los Angeles

   Atlanta to Boston

   Jacksonville, Florida to Dallas

   Chicago to Omaha

   Denver to Albuquerque

   Do some fares appear higher (on a per mile basis) than others? Do these differences reflect how many airlines provide nonstop service between each city pair? What about the impact on fares of so-called discount airlines (such as JetBlue and Southwest)?

2. **Yield management**. Say you'd like to visit Walt Disney World. Visit the Web site (http://disneyworld.disney.go.com/vacation-packages/) to price week-long stays at various times of the year. Be sure to choose similar hotels. Which weeks are the most and least expensive? Do the days of arrival and departure make any difference? Prepare a summary of your findings and bring it to class so you can participate in a discussion on yield management.

3. **Airbus and Boeing subsidies.** The U.S. and European Union have had a long-running dispute over allegations of improper government subsidies to commercial aircraft manufacturers (the U.S. about Airbus and the EU about Boeing). Government subsidies may give the manufacturer a price advantage over its competition. Both sides have filed complaints with the World Trade Organization. Go to the Web site of the WTO (http://www.wto.org) and write a report outlining the trade dispute and its current status.

Note: Internet Web addresses change frequently. If you don't find the exact site listed, you may need to access the organization's home page and search from there or use a search engine such as Google or Bing.

Case 18.1 *The Cash for Clunkers Program*

During a recent summer, the federal government undertook the temporary Car Allowance Rebate System, abbreviated CARS but popularly known as the Cash for Clunkers program. Under the plan, drivers of qualifying cars from the years 1984 through 2002 with an

EPA-rated efficiency of 18 miles per gallon or less received a voucher worth $3,500 to $4,500 for trading those cars in to purchase a new car with an EPA rating of 22 miles per gallon or better. (The voucher amount varied depending on the difference in miles per gallon between the trade-in and the new purchase.) In other words, the government wanted to encourage the purchase of efficient new cars by, in effect, temporarily reducing the price to qualified buyers.

The purpose of the plan was twofold: one goal, motivated by the recession-weakened economy, was to "shift expenditures by households, businesses, and governments from future periods when the economy is likely to be stronger, to the present when the economy has an abundance of unemployed resources that can be put to work at low net economic cost," as stated by Christopher Carroll. The second goal was to reduce harmful emissions by getting a large number of older, gas-guzzling vehicles off the road.

While some critics said the plan would simply pull future sales into the rebate period, resulting in no net increase in sales, several studies have shown that Cash for Clunkers was a success. More than 130,000 cars were traded in, and the budgeted allocation of $1 billion for the rebates was gone within a week. Congress had to quickly authorize the release of an additional $2 billion to keep the program going for the announced time period. More than half the cars traded in were at least ten years old and about eight in ten had been driven more than 100,000 miles.

In an even more striking result, another quarter-million cars were sold during the Clunkers period to buyers who wanted to cash in, didn't qualify, and decided to purchase a new car anyway. Many of these "halo sales" were of fuel-efficient hybrids, further contributing to what the U.S. Department of Transportation says was a mileage gain of nearly ten miles per gallon overall on vehicles purchased

during the plan, compared to the goal of increasing efficiency by four miles per gallon.

"Our findings not only provide strong evidence that many more vehicles were sold as a direct result of the incentive program than were previously estimated," said the vice president of an auto industry research group. "They also largely debunk the myth that 'cash for clunkers' mortgaged future car and truck sales. In fact, the program resulted in sales of vehicles to people who don't normally buy them."

Some estimate that more than 540,000 of the purchases made during the plan were to buyers and lessees who wouldn't have made a purchase without the cash incentive. And with car sales continuing to rise, the research group concludes, "the program did not [mortgage] the future of the industry by stealing sales that would have occurred otherwise."

And according to the National Highway Traffic Safety Administration, the CARS program saved or created nearly 60,000 jobs.

Questions for Critical Thinking

1. Who really pays the cost of a government price-incentive plan like Cash for Clunkers? Why? What other ways can you think of to distribute such costs?

2. The cash incentive in the CARS plan appears to have succeeded in its goal of reducing harmful emissions. What lessons do you think that success offers for other efforts to safeguard the environment?

Sources: Christina Romer and Christopher Carroll, "Did 'Cash-for-Clunkers' Work as Intended?" Council of Economic Advisors, www.whitehouse.gov/blog/, April 5, 2010; John Voelcker, "Clunkers Program Worked, Didn't Hurt Car Sales, Study Says," *Green Car Reports.com*, www.greencarreports.com/blog/, March 12, 2010; "Study: 'Cash for Clunkers' a Success," *The Detroit News*, www.detnews.com, March 10, 2010.

Video Case 18.2
Pricing Concepts at Evogear.com

n a recent year, Evo, the Seattle-based snow and water sports equipment e-tailer, made nc. magazine's list of the 500 fastest-growing private companies. Founder Bryce Phillips tarted the company in 2001 out of his garage as a way to support his expensive ski habit.

e rounded up and sold closeout and used skis in hopes that other nthusiasts would be looking for a good deal on good stuff. Four ears later, Phillips had added snowboards, skateboards, wakeoards, and all the apparel and accessories one could need. He mped up the Web site and opened an 8,000-square-foot retail ore in the funky Freemont neighborhood for those who want to y before they buy. The Seattle store also offered all the fashions you ould need to look awesome in the lodge or bar after a long day n the slopes. His original three employees now numbered around) and, in addition to the bargains, he added top-of-the-line new uff, too. The success of Evo and Evogear.com has been incredible, it Phillips isn't going back on what got him there in the first place: od stuff at a great price, hassle-free.

The online shopper is a different kind of shopper, and the nline retailer is different as well. The low overhead enjoyed by nline retailers allows them to stock more inventory in a lower-rent arehouse. Larger orders translate into better discounts from the anufacturer or wholesaler. Evo is able to pass these savings on to e consumer.

While the hard-core rider or skier is more likely to want the latest d greatest models every year, most are happy with replacing their uipment every few years with a gently used or last year's model an average savings of 30 to 75 percent off the original price. Evo aintains buying relationships with all the best brands—Burton, K2, uicksilver, Rossignol, Powell, and many more—but also looks to sorts and pro shops for used rental and demo gear. They even hit their own brick-and-mortar store for last year's unsold merchanse. The big brands see Evo as a preferred customer and often give em first crack at their closeout and "sale" merchandise as well. This ying strategy puts Evo and Evogear.com right in front of both the o and weekend warrior, while maintaining credibility with both.

One of the reasons Evo enjoys such great relationships with its customers is its famous price match policy. Shop around—if you find a lower price anywhere, Evo will beat it by 5 percent. Just send customer service an e-mail and as soon as they can verify the competitor's price, they'll lock in that lower price. Five percent might not sound like a lot, but as explained on Evo's Web site, if you see a product that lists on Evogear.com for $400 offered elsewhere for $350, Evo will sell it to you for $332.50. That $67.50 could pay for your lift ticket.

What sets Evo's policy apart from many competitors is that the company will match *any* lower price (except eBay auctions), including promotions, rebates, and end-of-season blowout sales. The price guarantee doesn't stop with the competition. If Evo offers a lower price within 20 days of your purchase, they'll give you a store credit for the difference. If something goes on sale at a competitor within a week of your purchase, you get the difference, too. The way they see it, if you're that committed to finding a bargain, you deserve the break. It takes a little more effort on Evo's side, but "it's a small price to pay for a lifetime customer," says Molly Hawkins, affiliate program manager at Evo. "Maybe we'll sacrifice a little bit of margin, but in the end, hopefully, they'll be coming back for the rest of their life to buy their gear from us."

Questions

1. Do you believe Evo's pricing strategy for evogear.com meets the five pricing objectives outlined in the text? Provide examples for each objective.

2. Do you think the opening of the 8,000-square-foot brick-and-mortar store in Seattle distracts from their pricing strategy or enhances it? Why? To learn more about the brick-and-mortar store, visit culture.evogear.com/category/seattle/.

Pricing
Strategies

1 Compare the alternative pricing strategies, and explain when each strategy is most appropriate.

2 Describe how prices are quoted.

3 Identify the various pricing policy decisions marketers must make.

4 Relate price to consumer perceptions of quality.

5 Contrast competitive bidding and negotiated prices.

6 Explain the importance of transfer pricing.

7 Compare the three alternative global pricing strategies.

8 Relate the concepts of cannibalization, bundle pricing, and bots to online pricing strategies.

JoS. A. Bank Tackles the Recession • • • Recent college graduates likely regard earning their degree as their most significant accomplishment. However, many of them are discovering that an even greater challenge lies before them: finding a job. With unemployment in

the United States at a record high, landing a job is no small feat. And before they can do that, many new grads must make an upfront investment in interview clothing.

JoS. A. Bank Clothiers to the rescue.

To help customers navigate the tight job market in sartorial splendor, the Hampstead, Maryland–based company instituted the "JoS. A. Bank Risk Free Suit Program." Under this special promotion, customers buy a suit, sport coat, or separate coat and pants during the store's $199 sale. If they subsequently lose their job, they can apply for a refund on their clothing purchase. What's more, they get to keep the merchandise— presumably to wear during the next round of interviews.

It's a form of "altruism marketing" that has served this national retailer well. JoS. A. Bank's risk-free promotion is marketing designed to take advantage of the current downturn in the U.S. economy. Through this strategy, the national chain—founded in 1905 and now numbering more than 4,000 employees—hopes to reinforce customer loyalty and win some new customers as well.

Said company CEO R. Neal Black: "We believe that our customers will appreciate another opportunity to look great at work and at the same time be assured that their purchase will be free if they lose their job." In addition to the 473 retail stores operating in 42 states and the District of

Columbia, JoS. A. Bank maintains a nationwide catalog, a Web site, and Facebook and Twitter pages. All selling channels are integrated in an effort to minimize fixed costs. Photography for the catalog is repurposed for use in retail store signage and on the Web. The same "value" message is delivered across all channels. An in-house staff maintains a single, integrated database that contains customers from all selling channels, segmenting and analyzing the data to optimize the company's marketing efforts and enable the same promotions to be offered across all channels. The company e-mails promotional messages to its constituents weekly, and mobile messaging is under consideration.

© TERRI MILLER/ E-VISUAL COMMUNICATIONS, INC.

JoS. A. Bank's promotions have increased sales and built customer loyalty. Annual sales in a recent year approached $700 million, with record-high net income of more than $58 million. During a recent period, the firm posted year-over-year growth for 32 of 33 quarters.

The risk-free promotion signaled a change in philosophy that arose when management examined the marketplace and addressed the challenges with new, creative promotions designed to build customer confidence. A business suit represents an investment; with a promotion that offers a refund in case of job loss, the investment becomes significantly less risky. It's a strategy and an angle that few, if any, of the company's competitors have exploited: Remarked CEO Black: "We think our 5.2 million customers and potential new customers deserve our support in these uncertain times."[1]

evolution of a brand

Through its innovative Risk Free Suit Program, JoS. A. Bank Clothiers carefully reviewed the cards it was dealt—that is, having to do business in the midst of a cautious consumer mood spawned by an economic downturn—and played them to its advantage.

- One industry observer takes this view of JoS. A. Bank's strategy: "If tactics aren't approached in a branded way, brands risk becoming genericized." Do you believe JoS. A. Bank could damage its brand with periodic promotions like "buy one, get one free"? In your opinion, would store management be wise

to research whether its customers appear to have shifted their spending habits to buy only during the sale periods?

- Currently, JoS. A. Bank's retail sales account for about 90 percent of its business, and many of those customers require tailoring services. Before the customer leaves the store, the sales

clerk secures all of his pertinent information, including the e-mail address, which is fed into the customer database. This practice helps encourage customers to shop more than one selling channel. How do you think this activity benefits the company? Do you think it results in new-channel sales?

chapter overview

Setting prices is neither a one-time decision nor a standard routine.

As illustrated by the promotions JoS. A. Banks Clothiers has undertaken, pricing is just one aspect of the overall marketing effort. Pricing is a dynamic function of the marketing mix. While about half of all companies change prices once a year or less frequently, one in ten does so every month. Online companies may adjust prices more often, depending on what they are selling. Some firms negotiate prices on the spot, as in the case of a car dealership or an antique shop.

Companies translate pricing objectives into pricing decisions in two major steps. First, someone takes responsibility for making pricing decisions and administering the resulting pricing structure. Second, someone sets the overall pricing structure—that is, basic prices and appropriate discounts for channel members, quantity purchases, and geographic and promotional considerations.

The decision to make price adjustments is directly related to demand. Most businesses slowly change the amounts they charge customers, even when they clearly recognize strong demand. Instead of raising prices, they may scale down customer service or add fees. They may also wait to raise prices until they see what their competitors do.

Few businesses want the distinction of being the first to charge higher prices. Because many firms base their prices on manufacturing costs rather than consumer demand, they may wait for increases in their own costs before responding with price changes. These increases generally emerge more slowly than changes in consumer demand. Finally, because many business executives believe steady prices help preserve long-term relationships with customers, they are reluctant to raise prices even when strong demand probably justifies the change.

Chapter 18 introduced the concept of price and its role in the economic system and marketing strategy. This chapter examines various pricing strategies and price structures, such as reductions from list prices and geographic considerations. It then looks at the primary pricing policies, including psychological pricing, price flexibility, product-line pricing, and promotional pricing, as well as price–quality relationships. Competitive and negotiated prices are discussed, and one section focuses entirely on transfer pricing. Finally, the chapter concludes by describing important factors in pricing goods and services for online and global markets.

Pricing Strategies

The specific strategies firms use to price goods and services grow out of the marketing strategies they formulate to accomplish overall organizational objectives. One firm's marketers may price their products to attract customers across a wide range; another group of marketers may set prices to appeal to a small segment of a larger market; still another group may simply try to match competitors' price tags. In general, firms can choose from three pricing strategies: skimming, penetration, and competitive pricing. The following sections look at these choices in more detail.

> **1** Compare the alternative pricing strategies, and explain when each strategy is most appropriate.

Skimming Pricing Strategy

Derived from the expression "skimming the cream," **skimming pricing strategies** are also known as **market-plus pricing**. They involve intentionally setting a relatively high price compared with the prices of competing products. Although some firms continue to use a skimming strategy throughout most stages of the product lifecycle, it is more commonly used as a market-entry price for distinctive goods or services with little or no initial competition. When the supply begins to exceed demand, or when competition catches up, the initial high price is dropped.

Such was the case with high-definition televisions (HDTVs), whose average price was $19,000, including installation, when they were first introduced. The resulting sticker shock kept them out of the range of most household budgets. But nearly a decade later, price cuts have brought LCD models into the reach of mainstream consumers. At Best Buy, shoppers can pick up a Toshiba 19-inch flat-panel LCD model for $229.99. On the higher end, they can purchase a Sony Bravia 60-inch flat-panel LCD model for $2,699.99.[2]

A company may practice a skimming strategy in setting a market-entry price when it introduces a distinctive good or service with little or no competition. Or it may use this strategy to market higher-end goods. British vacuum cleaner manufacturer Dyson has used this practice. Offering an entirely new design and engineering, Dyson sells several of its vacuum cleaner models for between $400 and $600, significantly more than the average vacuum. Even the various models of iRobot's Roomba vacuum sell for $200 and up, and the company claims it does all the work for you.[3]

In some cases, a firm may maintain a skimming strategy throughout most stages of a product's lifecycle. The jewelry category is a good example. Although discounters such as Costco and Home Shopping Network (HSN) offer heavier gold pieces for a few hundred dollars, firms such as Tiffany and Cartier command prices ten times that amount just for the brand name. Exclusivity justifies the pricing—and the price, once set, rarely falls.

Sometimes maintaining a high price through the product's lifecycle works, but sometimes it does not. High prices can drive away otherwise loyal customers. Baseball fans may shift from attending major league games to minor league games—if available—because of ticket, parking, and food prices. Amusement park visitors may shy away from high admission prices and head to the beach instead. If an industry or firm has been known to cut prices at certain points in the past, consumers—and retailers—will expect it. If the price cut doesn't come, consumers must decide whether to pay the higher tab or try a competitor's products.

skimming pricing strategy Pricing strategy involving the use of a high price relative to competitive offerings.

market-plus pricing Intentionally setting a relatively high price compared with the prices of competing products; also known as *skimming pricing*.

British vacuum cleaner Dyson uses a skimming strategy, pricing its vacuum cleaner models significantly higher than the average vacuum, and even higher than iRobot's Roomba vacuum, which iRobot claims does all of the work for the consumer.

step out Pricing practice
in which one firm raises
prices and then waits to see
if others follow suit.

Significant price changes in the retail gasoline and airline industries occur in the form of a **step out**, in which one firm raises prices and then waits to see if others follow suit. If competitors fail to respond by increasing their prices, the company making the step out usually reduces prices to the original level. Although airlines are prohibited by law from collectively setting prices, they can follow each other's example.

Despite the risk of backlash, a skimming strategy does offer benefits. It allows a manufacturer to quickly recover its research and development (R&D) costs. Pharmaceutical companies, fiercely protective of their patents on new drugs, justify high prices because of astronomical R&D costs: an average of 16 cents of every sales dollar, compared with 8 cents for computer makers and 4 cents in the aerospace industry. To protect their brand names from competition from lower-cost generics, drug makers frequently make small changes to their products—such as combining the original product with a complementary prescription drug that treats different aspects of the ailment.

A skimming strategy also permits marketers to control demand in the introductory stages of a product's lifecycle and then adjust productive capacity to match changing demand. A low initial price for a new product could lead to fulfillment problems and loss of shopper goodwill if demand outstrips the firm's production capacity. The result will likely be consumer and retailer complaints and possibly permanent damage to the product's image. Excess demand occasionally leads to quality issues, as the firm strives to satisfy consumer desires for the product with inadequate production facilities.

During the late growth and early maturity stages of its lifecycle, a product's price typically falls for two reasons: (1) the pressure of competition and (2) the desire to expand its market. Figure 19.1 shows that 10 percent of the market may buy Product X at $10.00, and another 20 percent could be added to its customer base at a price of $8.75. Successive price declines may expand the firm's market size and meet challenges posed by new competitors.

A skimming strategy has one major chief disadvantage: it attracts competition. Potential competitors see innovative firms reaping large financial returns and may decide to enter the market. This new supply may force the price of the original product even lower than its eventual level under a sequential skimming procedure. However, if patent protection or some unique proprietary ability allows a firm to exclude competitors from its market, it may extend a skimming strategy.

Penetration Pricing Strategy

**penetration pricing
strategy** Pricing strategy
involving the use of a
relatively low entry price
compared with competitive
offerings, based on the
theory that this initial low
price will help secure market
acceptance.

A **penetration pricing strategy** sets a low price as a major marketing weapon. Marketers often price products noticeably lower than competing offerings when they enter new industries characterized by dozens of competing brands. Once the product achieves some market recognition through consumer trial purchases stimulated by its low price, marketers may increase the price to the level of competing products. Marketers of consumer products such as detergents often use this strategy. A penetration pricing strategy may also extend over several stages of the product lifecycle as the firm seeks to maintain a reputation as a low-price competitor.

**figure 19.1
Price Reductions
to Increase Market
Share**

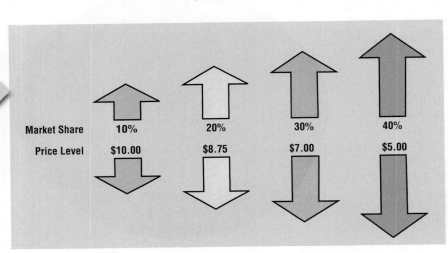

| Market Share | 10% | 20% | 30% | 40% |
| Price Level | $10.00 | $8.75 | $7.00 | $5.00 |

A penetration pricing strategy is sometimes called *market-minus pricing* when it implements the premise that a lower-than-market price will attract buyers and move a brand from an unknown newcomer to at least the brand-recognition stage or even to the brand-preference stage. Because many firms begin penetration pricing with the intention of increasing prices in the future, success depends on generating many trial purchases. Penetration pricing is common among credit card firms, which typically offer low or zero interest rates for a specified introductory period, then raise the rates. If competitors view the new product as a threat, marketers attempting to use a penetration strategy often discover that rivals will simply match their prices.

Because the market already contains so many competing brands, detergent marketers often use a penetration pricing strategy when they enter the market, pricing products noticeably lower than the competition.

© JEFF GREENBERG/ALAMY

Retailers may use penetration pricing to lure shoppers to new stores. Strategies might take such forms as zero interest charges for credit purchases at a new furniture store, two-for-one offers for dinner at a new restaurant, or an extremely low price on a single product purchase for first-time customers to get them to come in and shop.

Penetration pricing works best for goods or services characterized by highly elastic demand. Large numbers of highly price-sensitive consumers pay close attention to this type of appeal. The strategy also suits situations in which large-scale operations and long production runs result in low production and marketing costs. Finally, penetration pricing may be appropriate in market situations in which introduction of a new product will likely attract strong competitors. Such a strategy may allow a new product to reach the mass market quickly and capture a large share prior to entry by competitors.

Some auto manufacturers have been using penetration pricing for some new models to attract customers who might not otherwise consider purchasing a vehicle during a given year or who might be looking at a more expensive competitor. India's Tata Motors launched the world's cheapest car: the Nano, which carries a price tag of $2,500 in India. Tata has unveiled plans to sell the Nano in Europe, too, for about $8,000, but it has yet to confirm when the Nano will be available in the United States. Company spokespersons indicate its price tag would be similar to that of the European model—considerably less than the Hyundai Accent which, at a sticker price of $9,970, is the lowest-priced car in the United States.[4]

EVERYDAY LOW PRICING

Closely related to penetration pricing is **everyday low pricing (EDLP)**, a strategy devoted to continuous low prices as opposed to relying on short-term price-cutting tactics such as cents-off coupons, rebates, and special sales. EDLP can take two forms. In the first, retailers such as Walmart and Lowe's compete by consistently offering consumers low prices on a broad range of items. Through its EDLP policy, Lowe's pledges not only to match any price the consumer sees elsewhere but also to take off an additional percentage in some cases. Walmart states that it achieves EDLP by negotiating better prices from suppliers and by cutting its own costs. In addition, Walmart holds suppliers to a strict four-day delivery window. Goods that arrive at the regional distribution center before or after the window are assessed a 3 percent penalty.[5]

The second form of the EDLP pricing strategy involves its use by the manufacturer in dealing with channel members. Manufacturers may seek to set stable wholesale prices that undercut offers competitors make to retailers, offers that typically rise and fall with the latest trade promotion deals. Many marketers reduce list prices on a number of products while simultaneously reducing promotion allowances to retailers. While reductions in allowances mean retailers may not fund

briefly speaking

" There is scarcely anything in this world that some man cannot make a little worse and sell a little cheaper, and the buyers who consider price only are this man's lawful prey."

—John Ruskin
(1819–1900)
English art and social critic

everyday low pricing (EDLP) Pricing strategy of continuously offering low prices rather than relying on such short-term price cuts as cents-off coupons, rebates, and special sales.

Walmart employs everyday low pricing, a strategy devoted to continuous low prices instead of special sales and other short-term pricing tactics.

such in-store promotions as shelf merchandising and end-aisle displays, the manufacturers hope stable low prices will stimulate sales instead.

Some retailers oppose EDLP strategies. Many grocery stores, for instance, operate on "high–low" strategies that set profitable regular prices to offset losses of frequent specials and promotions. Other retailers believe EDLP will ultimately benefit both sellers and buyers. Supporters of EDLP in the grocery industry point out that it already succeeds at two of the biggest competitors: Walmart and warehouse clubs such as Costco.

One popular pricing myth is that a low price is a sure sell. Low prices are an easy means of distinguishing the offerings of one marketer from other sellers, but such moves are easy to counter by competitors. Unless overall demand is price elastic, overall price cuts will mean less revenue for all firms in the industry. In addition, low prices may generate an image of questionable quality.

Competitive Pricing Strategy

competitive pricing strategy Pricing strategy designed to deemphasize price as a competitive variable by pricing a good or service at the level of comparable offerings.

opening price point Setting an opening price below that of the competition, usually on a high-quality private-label item.

Although many organizations rely heavily on price as a competitive weapon, even more implement **competitive pricing strategies**. These organizations try to reduce the emphasis on price competition by matching other firms' prices and concentrating their own marketing efforts on the product, distribution, and promotion elements of the marketing mix. As pointed out earlier, while price offers a dramatic means of achieving competitive advantage, it is also the easiest marketing variable for competitors to match. In fact, in industries with relatively homogeneous products, competitors must match each other's price reductions to maintain market share and remain competitive.

Retailers such as The Home Depot and Lowe's both use price-matching strategies, assuring consumers that they will meet—and beat—competitors' prices. Grocery chains such as Kroger's and Stop & Shop may compete with seasonal items: soft drinks and hot dogs in the summer, hot chocolate and turkeys in the winter. As soon as one store lowers the price of an item, the rest follow suit.

Another form of competitive pricing is setting an **opening price point** within a category. Retailers often achieve this by pricing a quality private-label product below the competition. Grocery giants Publix and Kroger have begun actively advertising their private-label goods, most of which are priced below those of manufacturers' brands. In a turbulent economy, more consumers are giving private-label products a try, and many say the quality is comparable to that of national brands.[6]

Prices can really drop when companies continually match each other's prices, as evident in the airline and computer industries. But competitive pricing can be tricky; a price reduction affects not only the first company but also the entire industry as other firms match the reduction. Unless lower prices can attract new customers and expand the overall market enough to offset the loss of per-unit revenue, the price cut will leave all competitors with less revenue. Research shows that nearly two-thirds of all firms set prices using competitive pricing as their primary pricing strategy.

What happens when one discounter undercuts another? Although many retailers fear competition from Walmart, one type of store seems well positioned against the powerful chain: the so-called dollar stores. Today's equivalent of the five-and-dime variety stores of the 20th century, dollar stores sell inexpensive items such as cleaning supplies, paper plates, toothpaste, greeting cards, and other household products—and compete on price and convenience, especially nearby parking and easy access to the goods.

Once competitors are routinely matching each other on price, marketers must turn away from price as a marketing strategy, emphasizing other variables to develop areas of distinctive competence and to attract customers. That might mean offering personalized services such as gift wrapping or a sales associate who knows the type of clothing or books you like.

assessment check

1. What are the three major pricing strategies?
2. What is EDLP?

Price Quotations

The choice of the best method for quoting prices depends on many industry conditions, including competitive trends, cost structures, and traditional practices, along with the policies of individual firms. This section examines the reasoning and methodology behind price quotation practices.

> **2** Describe how prices are quoted.

Most price structures are built around **list prices**—the rates normally quoted to potential buyers. Marketers usually determine list prices by one or a combination of the methods discussed in Chapter 18. The sticker price on a new automobile is a good example: it shows the list price for the basic model and then adds the prices of options. The sticker price for a new Kia Spectra sedan is $16,146. But you can add such features as keyless entry, a six-speaker CD system, full power accessories—all at additional cost. Most car manufacturers bundle features into packages for one price. So if you order trim level EX on the Spectra, you'll automatically get those features, among other add-ons.[7]

list price Established price normally quoted to potential buyers.

market price Price a consumer or marketing intermediary actually pays for a product after subtracting any discounts, allowances, or rebates from the list price.

The price of oil is equally important to consumers—particularly those who drive cars—because it directly affects the list price of gasoline. Disruptions such as hurricanes and wars affect the price of oil, and ultimately the price that drivers pay at the pump. Prices may also fluctuate seasonally, as demand for gasoline rises and falls. Figure 19.2 illustrates where the money from a gallon of gas goes on its journey from the oil field to your gas tank.

Reductions from List Price

The amount a consumer pays for a product—its **market price**—may or may not equal the list price. Discounts and allowances sometimes reduce list prices. A list price often defines a starting point from which discounts set a lower market price. Marketers offer discounts in several classifications: cash, trade, and quantity discounts.

CASH DISCOUNTS

Consumers, industrial purchasers, or channel members sometimes receive reductions in price in exchange for

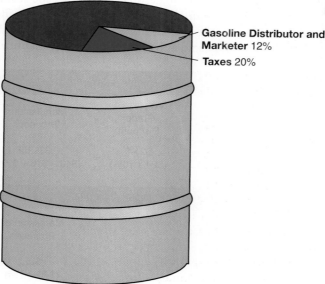

Who gets the money from retail gas sales?

Oil Wholesaler (includes crude oil price and refinery costs) 68%

Gasoline Distributor and Marketer 12%

Taxes 20%

Note: Percentages are rounded to nearest percent.

figure 19.2

Components of Retail Gasoline Prices

Source: Data from U.S. Energy Information Administration, "Gasoline and Diesel Fuel Update," March 15, 2010, http://tonto.eia.doe.gov.

cash discount Price reduction offered to a consumer, business user, or marketing intermediary in return for prompt payment of a bill.

prompt payment of bills; these price cuts are known as **cash discounts**. Discount terms usually specify exact time periods, such as 2/10, net 30. This notation means the customer must pay within 30 days, but payment within 10 days entitles the customer to subtract 2 percent from the amount due. Consumers may receive a cash discount for immediate payment, say, paying with cash instead of a credit card at the gas pump or paying the full cash amount up front for elective healthcare services such as orthodontia. Cash discounts represent a traditional pricing practice in many industries. They fulfill legal requirements provided that all customers can take the same reductions on the same terms.

In recent years, sellers have increasingly attempted to improve their own liquidity positions, reduce their bad-debt losses, and cut collection expenses by moving to a form of *negative cash discount*. Confronted with purchasers who may defer paying their bills as long as possible, another notice has begun to appear on customer statements:

> **Due on Receipt.** A FINANCE CHARGE of 1.5% per month (18% A.P.R.) is computed on and added to the unpaid balance as of the statement date.

Past-due accounts may be turned over to collection agencies.

TRADE DISCOUNTS

trade discount Payment to a channel member or buyer for performing marketing functions; also known as a *functional discount*.

Payments to channel members for performing marketing functions are known as **trade discounts**, or functional discounts. Services performed by various channel members and the related costs were discussed in Chapters 13 and 14. A manufacturer's list price must incorporate the costs incurred by channel members in performing required marketing functions and expected profit margins for each member.

Trade discounts initially reflected the operating expenses of each category, but they have become more or less customary practices in some industries. The Robinson-Patman Act allows trade discounts as long as all buyers in the same category, such as all wholesalers or all retailers, receive the same discounts.

Figure 19.3 shows how a chain of trade discounts works. In the first instance, the trade discount is "40 percent, 10 percent off list price" for wholesalers. In other words, the 40 percent discount on the $40 product is the trade discount the retailer receives to cover operating expenses and earn a profit. The wholesaler receives 10 percent of the $24 price to retailers to cover expenses and earn a profit. The manufacturer receives $21.60 from the wholesaler for each order.

In the second example, the manufacturer and retailer decide to bypass the wholesaler. The producer offers a trade discount of 45 percent to the retailer. In this instance, the retailer receives $18 for each product sold at its list price, and the manufacturer receives the remaining $22. Either the retailer or the manufacturer must assume responsibility for the services previously performed by the wholesaler, or they can share these duties between them.

quantity discount Price reduction granted for a large-volume purchase.

figure 19.3
Chain of Trade Discounts

"40 PERCENT, 10 PERCENT OFF" TRADE DISCOUNT			
List Price	− Retail Trade Discount	− Wholesale Trade Discount	= Manufacturer Proceeds
$40	− $16 ($40 x 40%)	− $2.40 ($24 x 10%)	= $21.60 ($40 − $16 − $2.40)

"45 PERCENT" TRADE DISCOUNT		
List Price	− Retail Trade Discount	= Manufacturer Proceeds
$40	− $18 ($40 x 45%)	= $22 ($40 − $18)

QUANTITY DISCOUNTS

Price reductions granted for large-volume purchases are known as **quantity discounts**. Sellers justify these discounts on the grounds that large orders reduce selling expenses and may shift some costs for storage, transportation, and financing to buyers. The law allows quantity discounts provided they are applied on the same basis to all customers.

Quantity discounts may specify either cumulative or noncumulative terms. **Cumulative quantity discounts** reduce prices in amounts determined by purchases over stated time periods. Annual purchases of at least $25,000 might entitle a buyer to a 3 percent rebate, and purchases exceeding $50,000 would increase the refund to 5 percent. These reductions are really patronage discounts because they tend to bind customers to a single supply source.

Noncumulative quantity discounts provide onetime reductions in the list price. For example, a firm might offer the following discount schedule for a product priced at $1,000 per unit:

1 unit	List: $1,000
2–5 units	List less 10 percent
6–10 units	List less 20 percent
More than 10 units	List less 25 percent

Many businesses have come to expect quantity discounts from suppliers. Online photo supply retailer Shutterfly offers volume discounts for photo books and discounts of as much as 47 percent on prepaid orders.[8] Marketers typically favor combinations of cash, trade, and quantity discounts. See's Candies offers a quantity discount for a minimum purchase of $615, plus continued savings throughout the year.[9]

ALLOWANCES

Allowances resemble discounts by specifying deductions from list price. The major categories of allowances are trade-ins and promotional allowances. **Trade-ins** are often used in sales of durable goods such as automobiles. The new product's basic list price remains unchanged, but the seller accepts less money from the customer along with a used product—usually the same kind of product as the buyer purchases.

Promotional allowances reduce prices as part of an attempt to integrate promotional strategies within distribution channels. Manufacturers often return part of the prices buyers pay in the form of advertising and sales-support allowances for channel members. Automobile manufacturers frequently offer allowances to retail dealers to induce them to lower prices and stimulate sales. In an effort to alert consumers to the difference between a car's sticker price and the price the dealer actually pays to the manufacturer, *Consumer Reports* sells car and truck buyers a breakdown on dealers' wholesale costs. The information reveals undisclosed dealer profits such as manufacturers' incentives, rebates from the dealer-invoice price, and "holdbacks"—amounts refunded to the dealer after sales are completed.[10] Dealers dislike the move to reveal their markups, arguing that no other retail sector is forced to give consumers details of their promotional allowances.

Minimum advertised pricing (MAP) occurs when a manufacturer pays a retailer not to advertise a product below a certain price. Recently, the U.S. Supreme Court ruled that retailers are required to stick to their MAPs on items. However, some retailers invite shoppers to call or e-mail for lower—unpublished—prices on items ranging from espresso machines to desktop computers.[11]

REBATES

In still another way to reduce prices, marketers may offer a **rebate**—a refund of a portion of the purchase price. Rebates appear everywhere—

cumulative quantity discount Price discount determined by amounts of purchases over stated time periods.

noncumulative quantity discount Price reduction granted on a one-time-only basis.

allowance Specified deduction from list price, including a trade-in or promotional allowance.

trade-in Credit allowance given for a used item when a customer purchases a new item.

promotional allowance Promotional incentive in which the manufacturer agrees to pay the reseller a certain amount to cover the costs of special promotional displays or extensive advertising.

minimum advertised pricing (MAP) Fees paid to retailers who agree not to advertise products below set prices.

rebate Refund of a portion of the purchase price, usually granted by the product's manufacturer.

Rebates refund a portion of the purchase price for items such as mattresses. Marketers offer rebates as a way to reduce the price paid by customers.

on appliances, electronics, and auto promotions—by manufacturers eager to get consumers to try their merchandise or to move products during periods of slow sales. Mattress manufacturer Sealy has successfully used rebates to move consumers up to more expensive models in its product line, offering the biggest rebates for its top-priced mattresses.

Rebates can have their problems. Many consumers complain about the paperwork they have to fill out to get a rebate, particularly on larger items such as computers and kitchen appliances. Some say they fill out the paperwork only to be denied the claim on a technicality. Others report never receiving the rebate—or even a response—at all. The Better Business Bureau notes that the number of complaints filed relating to rebates has grown significantly in the past few years. Some state legislators have moved to require companies to fulfill rebate requests within a certain period of time while also requiring consumers to file their request promptly. Yet companies argue that many consumers never even apply for their legitimate rebates.[12]

Geographic Considerations

In industries dominated by catalog and online marketers, geographic considerations weigh heavily on the firm's ability to deliver orders in a cost-effective manner at the right time and place. In other instances, geographic factors affect the marketer's ability to receive additional inventory quickly in response to demand fluctuations. And although geographic considerations strongly influence prices when costs include shipping heavy, bulky, low-unit-value products, they can also affect lightweight, lower-cost products.

Buyers and sellers can handle transportation expenses in several ways: (1) the buyer pays all transportation charges, (2) the seller pays all transportation charges, or (3) the buyer and the seller share the charges. This decision has major effects on a firm's efforts to expand its geographic coverage to distant markets. How can marketers compete with local suppliers in distant markets who are able to avoid the considerable shipping costs that their firms must pay? Sellers can implement several alternatives for handling transportation costs in their pricing policies.

FOB PRICING

FOB (free on board) plant (FOB origin) Price quotation that does not include shipping charges.

FOB (free on board) plant, or **FOB origin**, prices include no shipping charges. The buyer must pay all freight charges to transport the product from the manufacturer's loading dock. The seller pays only to load the merchandise aboard the carrier selected by the buyer. Legal title and responsibility pass to the buyer after the seller's employees load the purchase and get a receipt from the representative of the common carrier. Firms such as Walmart often handle freight charges over the entire supply chain. Because Walmart sources so many products from China, "FOB China" is now becoming common.

Many marketing intermediaries sell only on FOB plant terms to downstream channel members. These distributors believe their customers have more clout than they do in negotiating with carriers. They prefer to assign transportation costs to the channel members in the best positions to secure the most cost-effective shipping terms.

FOB origin-freight allowed (freight absorbed) Price quotation system that allows the buyer to deduct shipping expenses from the cost of purchases.

Sellers may also quote prices as **FOB origin-freight allowed**, or **freight absorbed**. These terms permit buyers to subtract transportation expenses from their bills. The amount such a seller receives for its product varies with the freight charged against the invoice. This alternative is popular among firms with high fixed costs because it helps them expand their markets by quoting the same prices regardless of shipping expenses.

UNIFORM-DELIVERED PRICING

uniform-delivered pricing Pricing system for handling transportation costs under which all buyers are quoted the same price, including transportation expenses. Sometimes known as *postage-stamp pricing*.

When a firm quotes the same price, including transportation expenses, to all buyers, it adopts a **uniform-delivered pricing** policy. This method of handling transportation expenses is the exact opposite of FOB origin pricing. The uniform-delivered system resembles the pricing structure for mail service, so it is sometimes called **postage-stamp pricing**. The price quote includes a transportation charge averaged over all of the firm's customers, meaning that distant customers actually pay a smaller share of shipping costs while nearby customers pay what is known as *phantom freight*—the amount by which the average transportation charge exceeds the actual cost of shipping.

ZONE PRICING

Zone pricing modifies a uniform-delivered pricing system by dividing the overall market into different zones and establishing a single price within each zone. This pricing structure incorporates average transportation costs for shipments within each zone as part of the delivered price of goods sold there; by narrowing distances, it greatly reduces but does not completely eliminate phantom freight. The primary advantage of zone pricing comes from its simplified administration that helps a seller compete in distant markets. The U.S. Postal Service's parcel rates depend on the system of pricing.

Zone pricing helps explain why gasoline can cost more in one suburb than in a neighborhood just two or three miles down the road. One way in which gasoline marketers boost profits is by mapping out areas based on formulas that factor in location, affluence, or simply what the local market will bear. Dealers are then charged different wholesale prices, which are reflected in the prices paid at the pump by customers. Some dealers argue that zone pricing should be prohibited. When drivers shop around for cheaper gas in other zones, stations in high-price zones are unable to compete.

BASING-POINT PRICING

In **basing-point pricing**, the price of a product includes the list price at the factory plus freight charges from the basing-point city nearest the buyer. The basing point specifies a location from which freight charges are calculated—not necessarily the point from which the goods are actually shipped. In either case, the actual shipping point does not affect the price quotation. Such a system seeks to equalize competition between distant marketers because all competitors quote identical transportation rates. Few buyers would accept a basing-point system today, however.

For many years, the best-known basing-point system was the Pittsburgh-plus pricing structure common in the steel industry. Steel buyers paid freight charges from Pittsburgh regardless of where the steel was produced. As the industry matured, manufacturing centers emerged in Chicago; Gary, Indiana; Cleveland; and Birmingham. Still, Pittsburgh remained the basing point for steel pricing, forcing a buyer in Atlanta who purchased steel from a Birmingham mill to pay phantom freight from Pittsburgh.

> **postage-stamp pricing** System for handling transportation costs under which all buyers are quoted the same price, including transportation expenses; also known as *uniform-delivered price.*

> **zone pricing** Pricing system for handling transportation costs under which the market is divided into geographic regions and a different price is set in each region.

> **basing-point pricing** System used in some industries during the early 20th century in which the buyer paid the factory price plus freight charges from the basing-point city nearest the buyer.

 assessment check

1. What are the three major types of discounts?
2. Identify the four alternatives for handling transportation costs in pricing policies.

Pricing Policies

Pricing policies contribute important information to buyers as they assess the firm's total image. A coherent policy provides an overall framework and consistency that guide day-to-day pricing decisions. Formally, a **pricing policy** is a general guideline that reflects marketing objectives and influences specific pricing decisions.

Decisions concerning price structure generally tend to focus on technical, detailed questions, but decisions concerning pricing policies cover broader issues. Price-structure decisions take the firm's pricing policy as a given, from which they specify applicable discounts. Pricing policies have important strategic effects, particularly in guiding competitive efforts. They form the basis for more practical price-structure decisions.

Firms implement variations of four basic types of pricing policies: psychological pricing, price flexibility, product-line pricing, and promotional pricing. Specific policies deal effectively with

> **3** Identify the various pricing policy decisions marketers must make.

> **pricing policy** General guideline that reflects marketing objectives and influences specific pricing decisions.

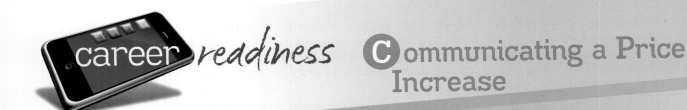

career readiness — Communicating a Price Increase

no marketer likes to deliver bad news to a customer, but sometimes—as in the case of a price increase—it's unavoidable. When you find yourself in this situation, here are some tips for softening the blow:

- *Slow down.* When you're delivering bad news, speak slowly and in a lowered tone of voice. You'll sound calm and rational rather than excited and emotional.

- *Explain what the price increase is and why.* Be honest. Tell them which products—if only a few—will increase in price and why. Without revealing every detail of your business, explain which of your costs has increased; perhaps it's the price of lumber or the cost of shipping.

- *Give advance warning.* If possible, notify customers well before the increase takes place so they can make budget adjustments. If a product is being phased out and replaced by a new product at a higher price, notify customers of this as well.

- *Help customers find alternatives.* Perhaps your firm has similar products comparable to the ones a particular customer has been using and will not be increasing in price.

- *Create new pricing packages, bundles, or product groupings.* By regrouping certain products—or separating products if they were previously grouped—you might be able to offer a better price despite the increase.

- *Emphasize value.* If the price increases because of your commitment to quality, say so. Perhaps your firm provides a better value overall. A product might be more concentrated to last longer, or packages might contain more items.

- *Use promotions.* Offer a promotional price, discount coupon, or rebate for a short period of time prior to the increase.

Sources: Devra Gartenstein, "The Best Way to Announce a Price Increase," *eHow*, http://www.ehow.com, accessed March 22, 2010; Jeff Mowatt, "10 Ways to Break It to Them Gently," *Business Know-how*, http://www.businessknowhow.com, accessed March 19, 2010; Mark Hunter, "Selling a Price Increase in a Soft Market," *Business Know-how*, http://www.businessknowhow.com, accessed March 18, 2010; Beth Jinks, "Carnival Jumps after Announcing 5% Price Increase," *BusinessWeek*, February 24, 2010, http://www.businessweek.com; "Propex Announces Price Increase in Its Furnishing Solutions Business Unit," *PR Newswire*, February 10, 2010, http://www.prnewswire.com; Kevin Daley, "How to Deliver Bad News to a Group," *Harvard Business Review*, October 16, 2009, http://blogs.hbr.org.

various competitive situations; the final choice depends on the environment within which marketers must make their pricing decisions. Regardless of the strategy selected, however, marketers sometimes must raise prices. Although it is never easy to deliver this decision to customers, if it is accomplished with honesty and tact, customers are likely to remain loyal. The "Career Readiness" feature provides some pointers on communicating price increases.

Psychological Pricing

psychological pricing
Pricing policy based on the belief that certain prices or price ranges make a good or service more appealing than others to buyers.

odd pricing Pricing policy based on the belief that a price ending with an odd number just under a round number is more appealing, for instance, $9.97 rather than $10.

Psychological pricing applies the belief that certain prices or price ranges make products more appealing than others to buyers. No research offers a consistent foundation for such thinking, however, and studies often report mixed findings. Nevertheless, marketers practice several forms of psychological pricing. Prestige pricing, discussed in Chapter 18, sets a relatively high price to convey an image of quality and exclusiveness. Two more psychological pricing techniques are odd pricing and unit pricing.

In **odd pricing**, marketers set prices at odd numbers just under round numbers. Many people assume that a price of $9.95 appeals more strongly to consumers than $10.00, supposedly because buyers interpret it as $9.00 plus change. Odd pricing originated as a way to force clerks to make change, thus serving as a cash-control device, and it remains a common feature of contemporary price quotations.

Some producers and retailers practice odd pricing but avoid prices ending in 5, 9, or 0. These marketers believe customers view price tags of $5.95, $5.99, or $6.00 as regular retail prices, but they think of an amount such as $5.97 as a discount price. Walmart, for example, avoids using 9s as ending prices for their merchandise.

Unit pricing states prices in terms of some recognized unit of measurement (such as grams and liters) or a standard numerical count. Unit pricing began to be widely used during the late 1960s to make price comparisons more convenient following complaints by consumer advocates about the difficulty of comparing the true prices of products packaged in different sizes. These advocates thought posting prices in terms of standard units would help shoppers make better-informed purchases. However, unit pricing has not improved consumers' shopping habits as much as supporters originally envisioned. Instead, research shows standard price quotes most often affect purchases only by relatively well-educated consumers with high earnings.

unit pricing Pricing policy in which prices are stated in terms of a recognized unit of measurement or a standard numerical count.

Price Flexibility

Marketing executives must also set company policies that determine whether their firm will permit price flexibility—that is, whether or not to set one price that applies to every buyer or to permit variable prices for different customers. Generally, one-price policies suit mass-marketing programs, whereas variable pricing is more likely to be applied in marketing programs based on individual bargaining. In a large department store, customers do not expect to haggle over prices with retail salespeople. Instead, they expect to pay the amounts shown on the price tags. Usually, customers pay less only when the retailer replaces regular prices with sale prices or offers discounts on damaged merchandise. Variable pricing usually applies to larger purchases such as automobiles, real estate, and hotel room rates. While variable pricing adds some flexibility to selling situations, it may conflict with provisions of the Robinson-Patman Act. It may also lead to retaliatory pricing by competitors, and it may stir complaints among customers who find they paid higher prices than necessary.

price flexibility Pricing policy permitting variable prices for goods and services.

Recently, some Internet service providers began setting usage caps on their customers and requiring subscribers who download the most content to pay the most. To help subscribers in the Panama Beach, Florida, area gauge how many gigabytes they're using, Comcast introduced a free online usage meter. Comcast's monthly limit—250 gigabytes—has been in place for some years; thus far, only about 1 percent of its residential customers have exceeded it. The first time customers exceed the limit, they receive a warning; thereafter, they can have their service suspended.[13]

Product-Line Pricing

Because most firms market multiple product lines, an effective pricing strategy must consider the relationships among all of these items instead of viewing each in isolation. Product-line pricing is the practice of setting a limited number of prices for a selection of merchandise. For example, one well-known clothier might offer three lines of men's suits: one priced at $500, a second at $795, and the most expensive at $1,395. These price points help the retailer define important product characteristics that differentiate the three product lines and help the customer decide on whether to trade up or down.

product-line pricing Practice of setting a limited number of prices for a selection of merchandise and marketing different product lines at each of these price levels.

Retailers practice extensive product-line pricing. In earlier days, five-and-dime variety stores exemplified this technique. It remains popular, however, because it offers advantages to both retailers and customers. Shoppers can choose desired price ranges and then concentrate on other product variables such as colors, styles, and materials. Retailers can purchase and offer specific lines in limited price categories instead of more general assortments with dozens of different prices.

Sunglasses have become a hot fashion item in recent years, and prices for designer glasses have jumped from an average of $250 per pair to as much as $900 for Thornhill Aviators at Bergdorf Goodman in New York. While sales of other luxury goods have softened, sunglass sales are getting long looks from retailers. Younger consumers—teens and young women—seem to be snapping up designer shades most often. Bvlgari, Dolce & Gabbana, Prada, Stella McCartney, and Versace all offer high-end glasses carried by luxury retailers. And for those who want their shades studded with diamonds, they can grab a pair from Gold & Wood's Bling-Bling collection, which features a jeweled nose bridge and earpieces. A pair with 264 diamonds retailed at $55,000.[14]

The price for designer sunglasses has jumped in recent years as consumer demand has increased.

PRADA
eyewear

IMAGE COURTESY OF THE ADVERTISING ARCHIVES

A potential problem with product-line pricing is that once marketers decide on a limited number of prices to use as their price lines, they may have difficulty making price changes on individual items. Rising costs, therefore, force sellers to either change the entire price-line structure, which results in confusion, or cut costs through production adjustments. The second option opens the firm to customer complaints that its merchandise is not what it used to be.

Promotional Pricing

promotional pricing Pricing policy in which a lower-than-normal price is used as a temporary ingredient in a firm's marketing strategy.

In **promotional pricing**, a lower-than-normal price is used as a temporary ingredient in a firm's marketing strategy. Some promotional pricing arrangements form part of recurrent marketing initiatives, such as a shoe store's annual "buy one pair, get the second pair for one cent" sale. Another example would be "7 CDs for 1 cent." This artificially low price attracts customers who must then agree to purchase a set number of CDs at regular prices within a specified time limit. Another firm may introduce a promotional model or brand with a special price to begin competing in a new market.

Managing promotional pricing efforts requires marketing skill. Customers may get hooked on sales and other promotional pricing events. If they know their favorite department store has a one-day sale every month, they will likely wait to make their purchases on that day. Car shoppers have been offered so many price incentives that it is becoming harder and harder for manufacturers and dealers to take them away—or to come up with new ones. Several restaurants in Ridgewood, New Jersey, teamed up to offer wintertime promotional pricing on fixed-price three-course dinners at their establishments, all to combat a seasonal downturn in business and to attract new customers.[15]

In an effort to preserve customer traffic despite a tough economy, fast-food restaurants are trying a variety of promotions designed to attract business. However, where franchisees operate the fast-food restaurants, they oftentimes bear the brunt of those value-priced promotions, as discussed in the "Solving an Ethical Controversy" feature.

LOSS LEADERS AND LEADER PRICING

loss leader Product offered to consumers at less than cost to attract them to stores in the hope that they will buy other merchandise at regular prices.

Retailers rely most heavily on promotional pricing. In one type of technique, stores offer **loss leaders**: goods priced below cost to attract customers who, the retailer hopes, will also buy regularly priced merchandise. Loss leaders can form part of an effective marketing program, but states with unfair-trade laws limit the practice. The milk at your grocery store is likely a loss leader, as is fruit in season. A casino near Minneapolis recently offered lobster dinners as a loss leader to entice would-be gamblers. For $20, guests could order two lobster dinners, each consisting of a whole Canadian lobster, baked potato, corn on the cob, roll, and house salad.[16] See the "Marketing Success" feature for an approach to loss leaders.

leader pricing Variant of loss-leader pricing in which marketers offer prices slightly above cost to avoid violating minimum-markup regulations and earn a minimal return on promotional sales.

Retailers frequently use a variant of loss-leader pricing called **leader pricing**. To avoid violating minimum-markup regulations and to earn some return on promotional sales, they offer so-called leader merchandise at prices slightly above cost. Among the most frequent practitioners of this combination pricing/promotion strategy are supermarkets and mass merchandisers such as Walmart, Target, and Kmart. Retailers sometimes treat private-label products, such as Sam's Choice colas at Walmart stores, as leader merchandise because the store brands cost, on average, about 27 percent less than those of comparable national brands. While store

solving **an ethical controversy**

Ⓕast-Food Prices: Who Gets to Set Them?

The rising cost of food and a struggling economy have combined to create the perfect storm in the fast-food industry, causing many companies, including McDonald's, Burger King, KFC, and Taco Bell, to tinker with their pricing strategy. By introducing new menu items and pricing promotions geared to draw consumers back into their restaurants, companies are raising the ire of their franchisees, who find their already slim profit margins shaved to the bone.

Should fast-food companies unilaterally set pricing policies?

PRO

1. Pricing policy cannot be left to the discretion of individual franchisees: uniformity from store to store is an important facet of the company's brand.

2. Fast-food restaurants have to be creative in trying new things to stay competitive. What's more, in devising promotions, marketers must consider every possibility as they attempt to pull customers away from their competition. For example, promoting $1 fountain drinks during the summer months creates an opportunity to woo customers away from minimarts and convenience stores; introducing specialty coffees puts them head to head with coffee houses.

CON

1. Franchise operators are at the mercy of the parent company because they have little say over corporate decisions like pricing policy and must pay a percentage of their sales to the parent. Some recent promotions—such as Burger King's introduction of the $1 double cheeseburger—actually lost money for franchisees because the item cost more than $1 to prepare and serve.

2. Because franchises represent the lifeblood of companies like McDonald's and Burger King, it is important for the parent company to maintain a good relationship with its franchisees. If franchisees perceive they have little power in influencing their store's future, they may decide their investment was a poor one—and the company would be in trouble.

Summary

Some sense of balance needs to be achieved between the parent company and franchisees if they are to coexist peacefully—and profitably.

Sources: "McDonald's Eyeing $1 Drinks for Summer," *Chicago Breaking Business*, March 17, 2010, http://www.chicagobreakingbusiness.com; Lisa Baertlein, "Burger King Pulling Slice from Double Cheeseburger," *Reuters*, February 17, 2010, http://www.reuters.com; Dionne Rose, "Fast Food Price Hike — Customers Paying More at KFC, Burger, King, Island Grill," *Jamaica Gleaner Online*, January 10, 2010, http://www.jamaica-gleaner.com, David Sterrett, "Price Hikes on Menu at McD's; Bigger Boosts Would Ease Pressure on Franchisee Profit But Risk Irking Customers," *Crain's Chicago Business*, April 13, 2009, http://www.chicagobusiness.com.

brand items generate lower per-unit revenues than national brands, higher sales volume will probably offset some of the difference as will related sales of high-margin products such as toiletries and cosmetics.

Digital cameras are a good example. While a digital point-and-shoot camera once ranged from $400 to $600, today, for the same money, shoppers can get a more technologically advanced digital SLR camera. Meanwhile, prices on the point-and-shoot models have dropped. A Canon PowerShot SD850 IS—once priced at $400—is now about $240, and many models are available for under $200.[17]

But marketers should anticipate two potential pitfalls when making a promotional pricing decision:

1. Some buyers are not attracted by promotional pricing.

2. By maintaining an artificially low price for a period of time, marketers may lead customers to expect it as a customary feature of the product. That is the situation currently faced by U.S. car manufacturers: sales of their models lag when they do not offer price incentives.

assessment check

1. Define *pricing policy*.
2. Describe the two types of psychological pricing other than prestige pricing.
3. What is promotional pricing?

Price–Quality Relationships

4   **Relate price to consumer perceptions of quality.**

One of the most thoroughly researched aspects of pricing is its relationship to consumer perceptions of product quality. In the absence of other cues, price serves as an important indicator of a product's quality to prospective purchasers. Many buyers interpret high prices as signals of high-quality products. Prestige is also often associated with high prices. However, a recent study at Cornell University found that while consumers may form more positive impressions about higher-priced products, those perceptions don't translate to heightened demand.[18]

A new type of prestige surrounds ecofriendly products. Many consumers are willing to pay more for green goods and services—those made with environmentally friendly materials and processes. These purchases make consumers feel good about themselves and convey status among others.

Despite the appeal of prestige, nearly every consumer loves a good deal. Marketers work hard to convince consumers they are offering high-quality products at the lowest possible price.

mktg: *success*

Restaurants Serve Up Tasty Discounts

Background. For years, the full-service casual dining industry has enjoyed consistent growth and expansion. This category, which represents an estimated $183 billion in revenues, includes such chains as Applebee's, Chili's, Olive Garden, Outback Steakhouse, Ruby Tuesday, Texas Roadhouse, and T.G.I. Friday's.

The Challenge. The recent economic downturn in the United States has taken a serious toll on the industry, as consumers became more price-sensitive and increasingly cautious about their discretionary spending. Some chains reported same-store sales falling for 15 consecutive months during a recent period.

The Strategy. In an effort to attract customers, virtually every restaurant chain has instituted some type of meal deal or other promotion. For example, Chili's offered entrees for under $7; at Texas Roadhouse, it was $7.99, and T.G.I. Friday's and Outback Steakhouse featured a selection of special entrees priced at under $10. Behind this strategy is the hope

Motels were once considered both cheap and seedy. The Motel 6 chain, for example, was so named because when it opened in 1962, a room cost $6 a night, plus tax. Today, a night at Motel 6 is still low-priced—about $40 plus tax—and the chain is renovating its properties to convey a chic yet efficient look, with pedestal beds, 32-inch flat-screen TVs, granite countertops, wood-look laminate floors, and more.[19]

Probably the best statement of the price–quality connection is the idea of price limits. Consumers define certain limits within which their product-quality perceptions vary directly with price. A potential buyer regards a price below the lower limit as too cheap, and a price above the higher limit seems too expensive. This perception holds true for both national brands and private-label products.

 assessment check

1. Describe the price–quality connection.
2. What are price limits?

Competitive Bidding and Negotiated Prices

Many government and organizational procurement departments do not pay set prices for their purchases, particularly for large purchases. Instead, they determine the lowest prices available for items that meet specifications through **competitive bidding**. This process consists of inviting potential suppliers to quote prices on proposed purchases or contracts. Detailed specifications describe the good or service the government agency or business organization wishes to acquire. One of the most important procurement tasks is to develop accurate descriptions of products the organization seeks to buy. This process generally requires the assistance of the firm's technical personnel such as engineers, designers, and chemists.

In competing for students, colleges and universities differentiate themselves on many dimensions, including price. In order to keep operating costs down, institutions routinely

5 Contrast competitive bidding and negotiated prices.

competitive bidding
Inviting potential suppliers to quote prices on proposed purchases or contracts.

---

that once customers come in the door, they will be inclined to spend over and above the promotional special, on drinks, appetizers, side dishes, and desserts.

The Outcome. Using an entrée as a loss leader seems to be working. In fact, some chains—like Chili's, for example—have

actually discontinued some of their more eye-popping meal deals and recently began raising prices on some menu items, such as side dishes and desserts, in an attempt to recoup their losses.

Sources: Lisa Jennings, "To Deal or Not to Deal: Chains Reconsider Discounting," *Nation's Restaurant News*, February 8, 2010 pp. 1–2; Elissa Elan, "Casual-Dining Prices Jump Even as Brands Tout Deals," *Nation's Restaurant News*, November 2, 2009, pp. 3–5; Bruce Horovitz, "Restaurants Resort to Mouth-Watering Deals," *USA Today*, March 25, 2009, p. B1.

Goods made with environmentally friendly materials and processes have a new prestige. Many consumers are willing to pay more for these eco-friendly products.

© HELEN SESSIONS/ALAMY

invite competitive bids in many areas of operation, including building maintenance and janitorial services, landscaping, and food service. With costs soaring for everything related to academic life, schools look for ways to economize without diminishing their appeal in the eyes of prospective students and their parents.

A select group of state troopers test potential police cars every year to determine the best model—and price—for their organization. While Ford's Crown Victoria police interceptor has come out on top for many years, it has been increasingly challenged by the Dodge Charger and Chevy Caprice models. Recently, Ford also announced a new-generation interceptor based on the Taurus.[20]

In some cases, business and government purchasers negotiate contracts with favored suppliers instead of inviting competitive bids from all interested parties. The terms of such a contract emerge through offers and counteroffers between the buyer and the seller. When only one supplier offers a desired product, or when projects require extensive research and development, buyers and sellers often set purchase terms through negotiated contracts. In addition, some state and local governments permit their agencies to skip the formal bid process and negotiate product purchases under certain dollar limits—say, $500 or $1,000. This policy seeks to eliminate economic waste that would result from obtaining and processing bids for relatively minor purchases. By contrast, Massachusetts requires that any services totaling $50,000 or more be subject to competitive bidding. However, with rising prices for most services, it is easy for proposals to exceed that ceiling.[21]

Negotiating Prices Online

Many people see the Internet as one big auction site. Whether it's toys, furniture, or automobiles, an online auction site seems to be waiting to serve every person's needs—buyer and seller alike. Auctions are the purest form of negotiated pricing.

Ticket sales are an online auction favorite. Consumers can bid on tickets for all sorts of events: Broadway shows, professional sports, and rock concerts. Razor Gator and Ticket

Liquidator are two such online ticket sellers. Razor Gator specializes in finding tickets to sold-out events and providing a "VIP experience." Ticket Liquidator offers low prices on tickets for more than 80,000 events daily.[22]

Online auctions also take place at sites such as eBay and uBid.com, where consumers can snap up items as varied as Italian gold cufflinks and a home in upstate New York. Recently, eBay reported that more than half of its transactions now take place through its "Buy It Now" option, suggesting that the novelty of online bidding may have worn off or that consumers prefer to secure an item by paying a set price for it. Regardless of how it is purchased, merchandise on eBay continues to move at astonishing speed: a cell phone reportedly sells every seven seconds, while a car sells every 56 seconds.[23]

Many people see the Internet as one big auction site. Auctions can occur at many places, including sites like eBay.

© IMAGEBROKER/ALAMY

 assessment check

1. What is competitive bidding?
2. Describe the benefits of an auction—to the buyer and the seller.

The Transfer Pricing Dilemma

A pricing problem peculiar to large-scale enterprises is the determination of an internal **transfer price**—the price for moving goods between **profit centers**, which are any part of the organization to which revenue and controllable costs can be assigned, such as a department. As companies expand, they tend to decentralize management and set up profit centers as a control device in the newly decentralized operation.

In a large company, profit centers might secure many needed resources from sellers within their own organization. The pricing problem thus poses several questions: What rate should profit center A (maintenance department) charge profit center B (production department) for the cleaning compound used on B's floors? Should the price be the same as it would be if A did the work for an outside party? Should B receive a discount? The answers to these questions depend on the philosophy of the firm involved.

Transfer pricing can be complicated, especially for multinational organizations. The government closely monitors transfer pricing practices because these exchanges offer easy ways for companies to avoid paying taxes on profits. For example, Congress passed a bill outlawing federal

 Explain the importance of transfer pricing.

transfer price Cost assessed when a product is moved from one profit center in a firm to another.

profit center Any part of an organization to which revenue and controllable costs can be assigned.

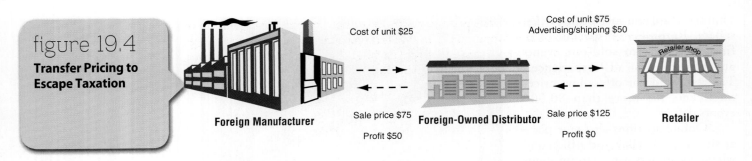

figure 19.4
Transfer Pricing to Escape Taxation

Cost of unit $25

Cost of unit $75
Advertising/shipping $50

Foreign Manufacturer

Sale price $75
Profit $50

Foreign-Owned Distributor

Sale price $125
Profit $0

Retailer

contractors from hiring workers through offshore "shell"—nonexistent—companies and thus avoiding having to pay Social Security and Medicare taxes.

Figure 19.4 shows how this type of pricing manipulation might work. Suppose a South Korean manufacturer of DVD players sells its machines to its Irish subsidiary for distribution to dealers throughout the United Kingdom. Although each unit costs $25 to build, the manufacturer charges the distributor $75. In turn, the distributor sells the DVD players to retailers for $125 each. This arrangement gives the South Korean manufacturer a $50 profit on each machine, on which it pays taxes only in South Korea. Meanwhile, the Irish distributor writes off $50 for advertising and shipping costs, leaving it with no profits—and no tax liability.

assessment check

1. Define *transfer price*.
2. What is a profit center?

Global Considerations and Online Pricing

Compare the three alternative global pricing strategies.

Throughout this course, we have seen the impact of the Internet on every component of the marketing mix. This chapter has touched on the outer edges of the Internet's influence on pricing practices. Remember: every online marketer is inherently a global marketer that must understand the wide variety of internal and external conditions affecting global pricing strategies. Internal influences include the firm's goals and marketing strategies; the costs of developing, producing, and marketing its output; the nature of the products; and the firm's competitive strengths.

External influences include general conditions in international markets, especially those in the firm's target markets; regulatory limitations; trade restrictions; competitors' actions; economic events; and the global status of the industry.

Traditional Global Pricing Strategies

In general, a company can implement one of three export pricing strategies: a standard worldwide price, dual pricing, or market-differentiated pricing. Exporters often set standard worldwide prices, regardless of their target markets. This strategy can succeed if foreign marketing costs remain low enough that they do not affect overall costs or if their prices reflect average unit costs. A company that implements a standard pricing program must monitor the international marketplace carefully, however, to make sure domestic competitors do not undercut its prices.

The dual pricing strategy distinguishes prices for domestic and export sales. Some exporters practice cost-plus pricing to establish dual prices that fully allocate their true domestic and foreign costs to product sales in those markets. These prices ensure an exporter makes a profit on any product it sells, but final prices may exceed those of competitors. Other companies opt for flexible cost-plus pricing schemes that allow marketers to grant discounts or change prices according to shifts in the competitive environment or fluctuations in the international exchange rate.

The third strategy, market-differentiated pricing, makes even more flexible arrangements to set prices according to local marketplace conditions. The dynamic global marketplace often requires frequent price changes by exporters who choose this approach. Effective market-differentiated pricing depends on access to quick, accurate market information.

assessment check

1. What are the three traditional global pricing strategies?
2. Which is the most flexible global pricing strategy?

Characteristics of Online Pricing

To deal with the influences of the Internet on pricing policies and practices, marketers are applying old strategies in new ways, and companies are updating operations to compete with electronic technologies. Some firms offer online specials that do not appear in their stores or mail-order catalogs. These may take such forms as limited-time discounts, free shipping offers, or coupons that are good only online.

> 8 Relate the concepts of cannibalization, bundle pricing, and bots to online pricing strategies.

THE CANNIBALIZATION DILEMMA

By pricing the same products differently online, companies run the risk of **cannibalization**. The new twist on an old tactic is companies self-inflicting price cuts by creating competition among their own products. During the first decade of e-business, marketers debated whether it was worth taking the risk of alienating customers and channel members by offering lower prices for their products online—then an unproven retail outlet. But today, marketers are more savvy about integrating marketing channels, including online sites and affiliated stores—different stores owned by the same company. The trend is moving toward standardizing pricing across channels.

cannibalization Loss of sales of an existing product due to competition from a new product in the same line.

Walmart was one of the first brick-and-mortar retailers to introduce a "Site to Store" feature to its Web site so shoppers could choose how and where they want to make purchases, all at the

> Walmart was one of the first brick-and-mortar retailers to introduce a "Site to Store" feature on its Web site so shoppers could choose how and where they want to make purchases.

© MARC F. HENNING/ALAMY

same price. Retailers are adopting this convenience feature in increasing numbers: the Container Store's "Click & Pickup" and Lowe's "In-Store Pickup" features are two such examples. As consumers become *multichannel shoppers*, shopping their preferred retailers both online and off, they are embracing this feature and expect the retailer to recognize them as regular shoppers, regardless of the channel they choose. Research shows that multichannel shoppers are more profitable than those who stick to one channel.[24]

USE OF SHOPBOTS

bot (shopbot) Software program that allows online shoppers to compare the price of a particular product offered by several online retailers.

A second characteristic of online pricing is the use of search programs called **bots** or **shopbots**—derived from the word *robots*—that act as comparison shopping agents. Bots search the Web for a specific product and print a list of sites offering the best prices. In online selling, bots force marketers to keep prices low. However, marketing researchers report that the majority of online shoppers check out several sites before buying, and price is not the only variable they consider when making a purchase decision. Service quality and support information are powerful motivators in the decision process. Also, while price is an important factor with products such as books and DVDs, it is not as important with complex or highly differentiated products such as real estate or investment banking. Brand image and customer service may outweigh price in these purchase decisions.

Bundle Pricing

bundle pricing Offering two or more complementary products and selling them for a single price.

As marketers have watched e-business weaken their control over prices, they have modified their use of the price variable in the marketing mix. Whenever possible, they have moved to an approach called **bundle pricing**, in which customers acquire a host of goods and services in addition to the tangible products they purchase.

Nowhere is bundle pricing more prevalent than in the telecommunications industry. Consumers are bombarded daily by advertisements for all kinds of Internet, cell phone, and cable TV packages. Verizon recently debuted three fiber-optic service bundles: Prime HD, Extreme HD, and Ultimate HD. Signing up for a "triple-play" bundle also provides access to thousands of wi-fi hot spots in the United States—a plus for sales representatives whose work takes them on the road.[25]

But sometimes consumers resist the practice of bundling, claiming they are forced to pay for services they don't want in order to receive the ones they do. This is particularly the case with cable television. Cable companies insist they have spent billions of dollars to expand their networks and technology and would be left with unused capacity if they sold only a few channels at a time to each customer. Consumer advocates argue that customers are not only forced to pay for unwanted services but also wind up paying inflated prices. The solution seems to be à la carte pricing—allowing consumers to pick and choose the shows or channels they want. While in the past some industry observers believed bundling kept prices low, today the market shows signs of change. Some cable companies believe offerings should be required to stand on their own merits. "We are very happy to compete in a market where networks are paid commensurate with the value they bring," said John Lansing, president of Scripps Networks Interactive, the cable company that owns HGTV and the Food Network.[26]

 assessment check

1. What is cannibalization?
2. What is bundle pricing?

strategic implications → f t 🛒
of marketing in the 21st century

Price has historically been the marketing variable least likely to be used as a source of competitive advantage. However, using price as part of a marketing program designed to meet a firm's overall organizational objectives can be a powerful strategy.

Technology has forever changed the marketplace, which affects the pricing function. Traditional geographic boundaries that allowed some businesses to operate have been broken by the Internet as well as mass merchandisers who offer a larger selection and lower prices. A customer in Wyoming might want to purchase a hand-carved walking cane from Kenya or an ornamental fan from Kyoto. Not a problem—the Web connects buyers and sellers around the globe.

Similarly, the cost of shipping an overnight FedEx package from New York to California is no more than shipping it to a nearby city.

Not only is it possible to escape the boundaries of time and space on the Internet, but price is no longer a constant in the marketing process. With the increasing number of auction sites and search technologies such as bots, customers now have more power to control the prices of goods and services. Consumers can find the lowest prices on the market, and they can also negotiate prices for many of the products they buy. To succeed, marketers will continue to offer value—fair prices for quality goods and services—and superior customer service. Those traditions will always be in style.

Review of Chapter Objectives

 Compare the alternative pricing strategies, and explain when each strategy is most appropriate.

The alternative pricing strategies are skimming pricing strategy, penetration pricing strategy, and competitive pricing strategy. Skimming pricing is commonly used as a market-entry price for distinctive products with little or no initial competition. Penetration pricing is used when a wide array of competing brands exists. Everyday low pricing (EDLP), a variant of penetration pricing, is used by discounters attempting to hold the line on prices without having to rely heavily on coupons, rebates, and other price concessions. Competitive pricing is employed when marketers wish to concentrate their competitive efforts on marketing variables other than price.

 Describe how prices are quoted.

Methods for quoting prices depend on such factors as cost structures, traditional practices in the particular industry, and policies of individual firms. Price quotes can involve list prices, market prices, cash discounts, trade discounts, quantity discounts, and allowances such as trade-ins, promotional allowances, and rebates. Shipping costs often figure heavily into the pricing of goods. A number of alternatives for dealing with these costs exist: FOB plant pricing, in which the price includes no shipping charges; FOB origin-freight allowed, or freight absorbed, which allows the buyer to deduct transportation expenses from the bill; uniform-delivered price, in which the same price, including shipping expenses, is charged to all buyers; and zone pricing, in which a set price exists within each region.

Identify the various pricing policy decisions marketers must make.

A pricing policy is a general guideline based on pricing objectives and is intended for use in specific pricing decisions. Pricing policies include psychological pricing, unit pricing, price flexibility, product-line pricing, and promotional pricing.

 Relate price to consumer perceptions of quality.

The relationship between price and consumer perceptions of quality has been the subject of considerable research. In the absence of other cues, price is an important influence on how the consumer perceives the product's quality. A well-known and accepted concept is that of price limits—limits within which the perception of product quality varies directly with price. The concept of price limits suggests that extremely low prices may be considered too cheap, thus indicating inferior quality.

 Contrast competitive bidding and negotiated prices.

Competitive bidding and negotiated prices are pricing techniques used primarily in the B2B sector and in government and organizational markets. Sometimes prices are negotiated through competitive bidding, in which several buyers quote prices on the same service or good. Buyer specifications describe the item the government or B2B firm wishes to acquire. Negotiated contracts are another possibility in many procurement situations. The terms of the contract are set through negotiations between buyer and seller.

 Explain the importance of transfer pricing.

A phenomenon in large corporations is transfer pricing, in which a company sets prices for transferring goods or services from one company profit center to another. The term *profit center* refers to any part of the organization to which revenue and controllable costs can be assigned. In large companies whose profit centers acquire resources from other parts of the firm, the prices charged by one profit center to another will directly affect both the cost and profitability of the output of both profit centers.

 Compare the three alternative global pricing strategies.

Companies can choose from three export pricing strategies: a standard worldwide price, dual pricing, or market-differentiated pricing. A standard worldwide price may be possible if foreign marketing costs are so low that they do not affect overall costs or if the price is based on an average unit cost. The dual pricing approach establishes separate price strategies for domestic and exported products. Some exporters use cost-plus pricing methods to establish dual prices that fully allocate their true domestic and foreign costs to their product; others choose flexible cost-plus pricing. Market-differentiated pricing is the most flexible export pricing strategy because it allows firms to price their products according to marketplace conditions. It requires easy access to quick, accurate market information.

 Relate the concepts of cannibalization, bundle pricing, and bots to online pricing strategies.

To deal with the influences of the Internet on pricing policies and practices, marketers are applying old strategies in new ways, and companies are updating operations to compete with electronic technologies. Cannibalization secures additional sales through lower prices that take sales away from the marketer's other products. Bots, also known as shopbots, act as comparison-shopping agents. Bundle pricing is offering two or more complementary products and selling them for a single price.

Assessment Check: Answers

1.1 What are the three major pricing strategies? The three major pricing strategies are skimming, penetration, and competitive.

1.2 What is EDLP? EDLP stands for everyday low pricing. It is a variation of penetration pricing often used by discounters.

2.1 What are the three major types of discounts? The three major types of discounts are cash discounts, trade discounts, and quantity discounts.

2.2 Identify the four alternatives for handling transportation costs in pricing policies. The four alternatives for handling transportation costs are FOB pricing, uniform-delivered pricing, zone pricing, and basing-point pricing.

3.1 Define *pricing policy*. A pricing policy is a general guideline that reflects marketing objectives and influences specific pricing decisions.

3.2 Describe the two types of psychological pricing other than prestige pricing. The two additional types of psychological pricing are odd pricing, in which marketers set prices at odd numbers just under round numbers, and unit pricing, which states prices in terms of a recognized unit of measurement.

3.3 What is promotional pricing? Promotional pricing is a lower-than-normal price for a set period of time.

4.1 Describe the price–quality connection. Price serves as an important indicator of a product's quality. However, many marketers now work hard to convince consumers they are offering high-quality products at the lowest possible price.

4.2 What are price limits? Price limits indicate certain boundaries within which consumers' product-quality perceptions vary directly with price. A price set lower than expected seems too cheap, and one set above the expected limit is seen as too expensive.

5.1 What is competitive bidding? Competitive bidding consists of inviting potential suppliers to quote prices on proposed purchases or contracts.

5.2 Describe the benefits of an auction—to the buyer and the seller. An auction can provide buyers with opportunities to buy goods and services at very low prices. It can also offer the seller an opportunity to sell to a wider audience (online), perhaps at a higher price than otherwise would be possible, if the item is particularly popular.

6.1 Define *transfer price*. A transfer price is the price for moving goods between profit centers.

6.2 What is a profit center? A profit center is any part of the organization to which revenue and controllable costs can be assigned.

7.1 What are the three traditional global pricing strategies? The three global pricing strategies are standard worldwide pricing, dual pricing, and market-differentiated pricing.

7.2 Which is the most flexible global pricing strategy? The most flexible global pricing strategy is market-differentiated pricing, which allows firms to set prices according to actual conditions.

8.1 What is cannibalization? Cannibalization involves cutting prices in one selling channel, which creates direct competition with a firm's own products.

8.2 What is bundle pricing? Bundle pricing involves combining a number of goods or services together and offering them at a set price.

Marketing Terms You Need to Know

skimming pricing strategy 641
market-plus pricing 641
step out 642
penetration pricing strategy 642
everyday low pricing (EDLP) 643
competitive pricing strategy 644
opening price point 644
list price 645
market price 645
cash discount 646
trade discount 646
quantity discount 646

cumulative quantity discount 647
noncumulative quantity
    discount 647
allowance 647
trade-in 647
promotional allowance 647
minimum advertised pricing
    (MAP) 647
rebate 647
FOB (free on board) plant (FOB
    origin) 648

FOB origin-freight allowed (freight
    absorbed) 648
uniform-delivered pricing 648
postage-stamp pricing 649
zone pricing 649
basing-point pricing 649
pricing policy 649
psychological pricing 650
odd pricing 650
unit pricing 651
price flexibility 651

product-line pricing 651
promotional pricing 652
loss leader 652
leader pricing 652
competitive bidding 655
transfer price 657
profit center 657
cannibalization 659
bot (shopbot) 660
bundle pricing 660

Assurance of Learning Review

1. What is the difference between a skimming price strategy and a penetration pricing strategy? Under which circumstances is each most likely to be used?

2. Why is competitive pricing risky for marketers?

3. What is the difference between a list price and a market price?

4. What are allowances? How do they work?

5. Describe the three ways buyers and sellers handle transportation expenses.

6. How is product-line pricing helpful to both retailers and their customers?

7. What is the difference between loss-leader and leader pricing? When do retailers use each?

8. What is the difference between a competitive bid and a negotiated price?

9. Describe briefly the three traditional global pricing strategies. Give an example of a firm or product that would be likely to adopt one of the three approaches, and explain why.

10. Although cannibalization generally forces price cuts, in what ways can it actually benefit a firm?

Projects and Teamwork Exercises

1. With a classmate, create two advertisements for the same product. One advertisement should feature a high price, the other advertisement should feature a low price. Present your advertisements to students in your class. Record students' perceptions of the price–quality relationship.

2. Figure out how much it will cost to buy and own one of the following new cars from a dealership, or select another model. What is the list price? What price could you negotiate?
   a. Ford Escape hybrid
   b. Mercedes E350
   c. Hyundai Santa Fe
   d. Scion tC

3. Assume a product sells for $100 per ton and Pittsburgh is the basing-point city for calculating transportation charges. Shipping from Pittsburgh to a potential customer in Cincinnati costs $10 per ton. The actual shipping costs of suppliers in three other cities are $8 per ton for Supplier A, $11 per ton for Supplier B, and $10 per ton for Supplier C. Using this information, answer the following questions:
   a. What delivered price would a salesperson for Supplier A quote to the Cincinnati customer?
   b. What delivered price would a salesperson for Supplier B quote to the Cincinnati customer?
   c. What delivered price would a salesperson for Supplier C quote to the Cincinnati customer?
   d. How much would each supplier net (after subtracting actual shipping costs) per ton on the sale?

4. On your own or with a classmate, visit a local supermarket to find examples of promotional pricing and loss leaders. Note instances of both. Does the promotional pricing make you more apt to purchase a product? Does knowing the store uses loss-leader pricing of bananas or apples make you more inclined to buy them? Present your findings and opinions to the class.

5. Decide on a trip you'd really like to take. Then go online to several of the travel sites—Orbitz, Travelocity, Priceline.com, or others—and compare prices for your trip, including airfares, hotels, car rental, and so forth. Does bundling the different components give a price break? Note any coupons or promotions for restaurants and attractions as well. Decide which trip is the best deal, and explain why.

Critical-Thinking Exercises

1. When Dell recently launched its Mini3 smartphone, it targeted consumers not in the United States but in Brazil and China. Its strategy: to create loyal customers as those markets emerge. A few years ago, when Dell introduced computers in the emerging markets of China and India, it used a penetration pricing strategy. That is, it priced the new computers under $500, significantly less than its computers sell for in the United States.[27] Why do you think Dell chose that pricing strategy? Do you think it was successful? Do you predict Dell will use the same pricing strategy for its smartphone? Why or why not?

2. As a consumer, would you rather shop at a store that features a sale once a month or a store that practices everyday low pricing (EDLP)? Why?

3. Under Staples' Easy Rebates program, customers can submit most of their rebate applications online for products purchased over the Internet, through the catalog, and in Staples stores. Customers may also submit several rebates at once and receive e-mails about the status of their rebates at every stage.[28] Staples claims the rebates are processed much faster than those of other companies. Do you think the Easy Rebates program will increase the number of rebates customers actually submit? Why or why not? Do you think other firms will follow with similar programs?

4. Go online to a shopping site you use regularly and note the prices for different types of products. Does the firm use psychological pricing? Product line pricing? Note any pricing strategies you can identify. Do any of these strategies make you prefer the site over a competitor's site?

5. Why is competitive bidding an important factor in major purchase decisions like vehicles for a police force, the construction of a bridge, or the manufacture of military uniforms?

Ethics Exercise

The law allows companies in a variety of industries to add what many refer to as "hidden" charges to customers' bills. Phone bills, airline tickets, and hotel receipts often contain charges that are difficult to identify. A visitor who stays in a hotel might be hit with a "hospitality fee," a "resort fee," and an "automatic gratuity" to name just a few. These charges are not taxes, and although they are itemized, it is difficult for the average traveler to make sense of them. Most people either don't check their bills thoroughly or are in a hurry to check out and don't bother to dispute the charges, which may be only a few dollars. But these charges add up over the course of hundreds or thousands of visitors each year, and hotels are pocketing them—legitimately.[29]

1. Do you think adding hidden charges to hotel visitors' bills is a smart marketing strategy? Why or why not?

2. Visit the Web site of a hotel chain with which you are familiar to learn if it gives any information about additional surcharges. If consumers were informed about the charges ahead of time, would you feel differently about them? Why or why not?

Internet Exercises

1. **Price competition.** Using a popular travel site—such as Expedia.com or Kyack.com—look up airfares for each of the following pairs of cities:

   New York to Los Angeles

   Atlanta to Boston

   Jacksonville, Florida to Dallas

   Chicago to Omaha

   Denver to Phoenix

   Do some fares appear higher (on a per mile basis) than others? Do these differences reflect how many airlines provide nonstop service between each city pair? What about the impact of fares of so-called discount airlines (such as Jet Blue and Southwest)?

2. **Yield management.** Say you'd like to visit Walt Disney World. Visit the WDW Web site (http://disneyworld.disney.go.com/vacation-packages/) to price week-long stays at various times of the year. Be sure to choose similar hotels. Which weeks are the most and least expensive? Do the days of arrival and departure make any difference? Prepare a summary of your findings and bring it to class so you can participate in a discussion on yield management.

3. **Airbus and Boeing subsidies.** The U.S. and European Union have had a long-running dispute over allegations of improper government subsidies to commercial aircraft manufacturers (the U.S. about Airbus and the EU about Boeing). Government subsidies may give the manufacturer a price advantage over its competition. Both sides filed complaints with the World Trade Organization. Go to the Web site of the WTO (http://www.wto.org) and write a report outlining the trade dispute and its current status.

Note: Internet Web addresses change frequently. If you don't find the exact site listed, you may need to access the organization's home page and search from there or use a search engine such as Google or Bing.

Case 19.1 *Holding the (Price) Line on Luxury Goods*

In a tough economy, the market for luxury goods and services faces unique challenges. Many people who at one time might have splurged on a Rolex watch or a Lexus sedan are now unemployed and, possibly, facing foreclosure on their home. Even those with high

net worth felt the pinch when their investments—affected by a stock market in free-fall—took a hit, some losing as much as 50 percent of value. Thus, even the wealthy had less disposable income for high-priced vacations and weekly spa treatments.

The luxury goods market experienced a several-quarter drought during which sales fell 8 percent—about $227 billion. As the stock market began to stabilize, however, sales in the sector have begun to pick up: high-fashion house Hermes posted a 19 percent spike in sales for a recent quarter, and LVMH Moet Hennessy Louis Vuitton reported an 11 percent increase.

Still, luxury retailers aren't out of the woods yet, and they resist applying the same promotional strategies to bring in business that more mainstream retailers might try. Tiffany's—widely regarded as a premier jeweler—would risk damaging its carefully tended image if it were to advertise, for instance, a "buy one, get one free" sale or discounts on its crystal or sterling patterns. Interestingly, such promotions by retailers like JCPenney or Lord & Taylor seemingly have no adverse effect on shoppers' perception of value.

Recently, Tiffany's quietly discounted its prime line, diamond engagement rings, by about 10 percent, but did it without hoopla. Only those shopping for an engagement ring would have known about the reduced prices, having been informed by the salesperson. Discounting merchandise without making it widely known allows retailers like Tiffany's to maintain their traditional pricing policy—outwardly, at least.

But what can a luxury retailer do to increase traffic during a recession if it doesn't advertise a sale? Many retailers choose to be discreet and communicate sales only through emails to regular customers. Others communicate more publicly, positioning the sale as "clearing inventory" while bolstering revenues. During a recent holiday season, Saks Fifth Avenue announced savings of as much as 70 percent, through print and Web ads, store signage, and e-mails. Saks management said the sales didn't hurt the store's image at all.

When spas and beauty salons discount the cost of services to encourage business, they run the risk that customers will think the service was initially overpriced. Instead, spas and salons have found success in bundling services: for example, a customer who gets a manicure can, for a reduced price, get a facial at the same time. For some reason, the notion of bundled services does not diminish their value in the customer's mind. Another tactic that works is the incentive plus special offer: for example, by referring a customer to your spa or salon, you'll receive a coupon good for 10 percent off on your next appointment. Such a promotion can also encourage the purchase of multiple services.

Questions for Critical Thinking

1. What other pricing promotions could a luxury retailer offer to build sales? Should a retailer use different strategies when targeting existing customers and new customers? Why?

2. How do you think the price–quality relationship affects the marketing of luxury goods?

Sources: David Eisen, "Luxury Good Sales Show Improvement," *Luxury Travel Advisor*, May 7, 2010, http://www.luxuryta.com; Astrid Wendlandt, "Bain Sees 2010 Global Luxury Goods Sales up 4 Percent," *Reuters*, April 15, 2010, http://www.reuters.com; Vanessa O'Connell, "Luxury-Goods Sales Still Soft, Recovery Unlikely before 2011," *The Wall Street Journal*, October 20, 2009, http://online.wsj.com; Brian Burnsed, "Where Discounting Can Be Dangerous," *BusinessWeek*, August 3, 2009, http://www.businessweek.com; "Restrained Indulgence: As More Clients Refrain from Spending, Luxury Service Providers Redouble Efforts to Entice Business," *Crain's Cleveland Business*, March 9, 2009, http://www.crainscleveland.com.

Video Case 19.2
Pricing Strategy at Standard Renewable Energy

Green is hot, there's no doubt about it. Visit any large retailer such as Walmart, and you can fill your reusable shopping bag with hormone-free dairy products, organic cotton T-shirts, and environmentally friendly bathroom cleaner. Demand is so high that some chains have

leveraged their purchasing power to offer store-brand organics and earth-friendly products at prices just a few cents higher than conventional products.

When the average consumer makes the decision to pay more for organic or earth-friendly products, several things should be considered. Will you get more enjoyment out of the free-range chicken or the frozen chicken nuggets? Would it be better for your health to use the bleach-free detergent? Speaking of towels, could you skip the Brawny and invest in real dishtowels to save a tree or two?

"Return on investment, that's one of our main points," says John Miggins, a Tulsa-based regional sales rep for Standard Renewable Energy (SRE). "It's on the front page of our proposal." For some customers, the return comes in the form of actual cash savings on electric bills. For others, it's more about doing good.

Headquartered in Houston, SRE specializes in providing alternative energy systems for residential, corporate, and government architects and builders. In addition to solar panels and inverters, the company designs geothermal and wind systems and performs energy audits at each customer site. The energy audit not only surveys the site and takes measurements, it also shows customers other areas in which they can improve their energy usage. SRE often asks its customers to consider new foam insulation and to update lighting and inefficient heating and air conditioning units. By providing customers with the big picture, SRE can help justify the initial expense of a new system and show how it can pay off in the long run.

"The people call me and say, 'I have a 2,000-square-foot house. What do I need?'" laments Miggins. It's just not that simple, unfortunately. Many factors must be considered—location and weather as well as expectations and energy needs, to name a few. Pricing on solar or wind systems is based on a per-watt number—use 900 kilowatts per month, and a solar system will probably cost about $40,000. Miggins understands that number can hit most consumers pretty hard, so he often helps soften the blow by offering a wind generator for about $17,500. The initial investment on wind is lower, but it can only provide about half the power. The decision then becomes pay now or pay later.

Emily Priddy and her husband own a modest, 900-square-foot home in Tulsa, Oklahoma. A teacher, writer, beekeeper, and self-described hippie child, protecting the environment has always been important to Priddy. When she and her husband purchased their home, they knew they wanted to look for ways to reduce their impact on the earth, but solar seemed financially out of reach. "The last figure I had heard quoted fifteen years earlier was that a solar panel would cost you about eight hundred bucks," she says. "And I knew we were going to need quite a few solar panels!"

Concerned about the cost and what they could expect back in the form or lower energy bills, the couple figured they'd have to go at it one panel at a time. Working with Miggins at SRE, they learned that they could take a home improvement loan to get started and still come out on budget at the end of the month. Sure, it will take them 15 years to pay off the loan, but after that, they will be free of an electric bill. The biggest selling point for Priddy is that she is well insulated from rising energy costs; her loan is fixed at $150 each month, and her electric bill went down by almost 90 percent in the first month. "It's a lot less whim-based and a lot more predictable," she says.

For customers like Priddy who are in it for the long haul, return on investment is a definite selling point. "If that's the only reason they [homeowners] are talking to me, I usually pack up and go, because solar is 15, 17, even 20 years away, but on the commercial, solar is very lucrative," says Miggins. For corporate customers, long-term financial planning is key, so a 15-year payback is really tempting. Because they can afford more elaborate systems to begin with, they can actually start profiting off their own energy generation earlier. Other incentives, like tax credits and bragging rights, only sweeten the deal.

Questions

1. How does Miggins quote prices for SRE's solar systems?

2. How does SRE engage in psychological pricing?

© CENGAGE LEARNING

Watt's the Deal?

Pricing on most items isn't all that mysterious. Fast food lunch: $5.37. Hamburger: $2.49; fries: $1.89; drink: $.99. Those prices pretty much break down into operating expenses, food cost, and profit. It is what it is. When it comes to pricing an alternative energy system for your home, it's a different story.

The first thing you have to understand is what you're buying. First, you pay for the materials and labor, and you can count on a 20 percent mark-up for the company's profit and operations. Next comes the idea of watts, the electric company's unit of measure for how much electricity you use. Then there are the intangibles. When pricing an energy-saving system like wind or solar, you have to look at your initial investment and what you can expect to save when the electric bill comes. If you are really good about limiting your energy use, you may be able to sell some of your extra power back to the "grid." But what if it takes ten years to pay off the home improvement loan you took out to finance the system? What will the interest be? Is that adjusted for inflation? Is the cost of electricity always going to go up, or will it stabilize or even go down in two years? What are the maintenance and repair costs? Get through all these questions and you're still faced with the choice of wind or solar. Wind is cheaper to start, but less predictable on the return on investment—solar is the opposite.

That's just for residential. Add an Inc. after your name and there's a whole bunch of other considerations. What is the depreciation on the equipment? Can it be accelerated? Are there state, local, or federal tax credits?

John Miggins of Standard Renewable Energy in Tulsa, Oklahoma, can do these calculations in his sleep but is quick to admit they are complicated. "The people call me and say, 'I have a 2,000-square-foot house. What do I need?'" There's no way to answer that, but what he does tell them is what the average customer *might* want. From there, all bets are off until he can do a custom quote designed for the customer's home—the location, type of construction, exposure, zoning, energy needs, what the customer realistically expects to get out of a wind or solar system and, most importantly, what the customer is willing to give up to get the most out of the system he or she wants.

When the students at the the University of Kansas School of Architecture and Urban Planning's Studio 804 called Miggins looking for a solar and wind system for their 547 Art Center design-build in Greensburg, Kansas, the needs versus wants equation really came into play. The building, a community and art museum in the heart of Greensburg, was a unique project. 547 Art Center was the first building to be completed in the devastated town and is definitely one of, if not the greenest, buildings in Kansas. Like all projects in Greensburg, money was an issue, but building a truly sustainable, green LEED Platinum building was just as important. Add to that the fact that the building was going to be a showpiece for the town, so aesthetics couldn't suffer either. Miggins quoted the project at about $50,000. Although he would have loved to give it all away for free, the studio needed to cover his costs. As they were completing the plans for the project, the design team threw him a curveball. They wanted three smaller wind turbines to power the building rather than the one larger one Miggins recommended. "It was a ten thousand dollar difference, easily," recalls Miggins. A frugal guy himself, he couldn't understand why they would spend the extra money on an already strapped project. "A friend of mine told me architects like threes," said Miggins. "And you gotta admit, it looks really cool!" In the end, he got what they were going for and donated some of the extra labor involved in installing the three turbines so they could achieve their vision.

"We can't treat everybody like that," says Miggins. As a sales rep for the Oklahoma/Kansas region, Miggins has some wiggle room in pricing jobs. Every project is carefully reviewed, and he knows he'll get a talking to if he gives too much away. The return on investment in cool projects like Greensburg isn't lost on the finance department at Standard Renewable. Miggins was recently called by Make it Right, Brad Pitt's foundation dedicated to the sustainable rebuilding of the 9th Ward of New Orleans, the area hardest hit by Hurricane Katrina. He is now involved in designing a solar system for a neighborhood playground. Standard knows they won't make a killing on the project, but the exposure will more than make up for it.

Questions

1. Why is it important for Standard Renewable Energy to allow Miggins flexibility in pricing?

2. Why is return on investment such an important factor for the consumer choosing an alternative energy system?

3. While one can probably find a better price for the components online, what is the value of choosing Miggins for your solar or wind system?

4. Which pricing objective best fits Standard Renewable Energy?

5. Perform a breakeven analysis for the owner of an average 2000-square-foot home. Prepare a presentation using a spreadsheet, powerpoint slides, and handouts that Miggins could use when discussing solar with potential customers.

Your Career in Marketing

One Marketer's Career • • • Imagine being in charge of marketing for a company that is a giant in the global consumer products market and the world's second-largest advertiser. That's the job of Keith Weed, the chief marketing and communications officer for Unilever.

Think of all the major brands produced by Unilever—from Dove to Lifebuoy, from Knorr to Lipton, from Degree to Vaseline. Unilever products are used by hundreds of millions of consumers in the United States and around the world. Weed—former executive vice president of Unilever's home care, oral care, and water brands—now gets to test his marketing expertise in the largest arena.

Weed is the first marketing chief at Unilever to also have responsibility for the company's communication function—a further blurring of the line between public relations and conventional advertising. He will oversee Unilever's media services, consumer insights, research, agency relationships, and its internal marketing academy. Weed presided over the home care division at a critical time in Unilever's history, when it battled chief competitor Procter & Gamble for dominance in many developing markets. Also, for the first time in Unilever history, the marketing chief will be part of the firm's executive committee, signifying the importance of this role.

Whether you relax with Lipton tea, shower with Dove soap, or spread Hellmann's mayonnaise on your sandwich, Unilever chief marketing and communications officer Keith Weed intends to use every resource and strategy he can possibly muster to ensure that you continue to rely on Unilever products in the future.

© TERRI MILLER/E-VISUAL COMMUNICATIONS, INC.

Weed succeeds Simon Clift, a 28-year Unilever veteran who served as the company's first chief marketing officer. During his tenure, Clift introduced some new, formerly untried advertising agencies to Unilever and directed the company's global advertising, including the award-winning Dove "Real Beauty" and Persil "Dirt Is Good" campaigns. Clift was also responsible for the global launch of the popular Axe line of men's personal care products (a brand known as "Lynx" in some parts of the world).

CEO Paul Polman says Weed's appointment signals a new direction for Unilever. "This is the first time Unilever has had a CMO at its top table and is a key step to having a sharper consumer focus in the company."

In his new role piloting both marketing and communication functions at Unilever, Weed faces many challenges. In a recent year, his company spent more than $5.7 billion on measured media. Unilever products touch the lives of people in the more than 170 countries in which they are marketed. Also, like its competitors, Unilever must learn how to leverage social media for optimal results.

Whether you satisfy your thirst with a bottle of Lipton iced tea, shower with Lifebuoy soap, or wash your clothes using Surf detergent, you're likely to come into contact with a Unilever product today. Weed knows this, and he intends to use every resource and strategy he can possibly muster to ensure that you continue to rely on Unilever products in the future.[1]

overview

> Congratulations on your decision to take this course.

briefly speaking

"People are definitely a company's greatest asset. It doesn't make any difference whether the product is cars or cosmetics. A company is only as good as the people it keeps."

—Mary Kay Ash
(1915–2001)
Founder, Mary Kay Cosmetics

As a consumer, you already know marketing is a pervasive element in our lives. In one form or another, it reaches every person. This course informed you about the different types of marketing messages, showed you how they are created, and helped you understand the impact they have.

As you have seen throughout this course, marketing activities are interwoven in daily business processes, helping develop useful products consumers need, pricing them for a fair profit, promoting them so consumers are aware of their availability, and bringing them to market. But marketing also has a huge impact on society and the economy in general.

A large portion of the total cost consumers pay for Wii gaming consoles goes to marketing costs.

© ROBYN BECK/AFP/GETTY IMAGES

Marketing Costs are a Big Component of a Product's Total Budget

Up to half of the $199 you pay for a Wii gaming console may go to marketing costs—making sure you are aware of Wii's existence and its capabilities and persuading you to buy it. Yes, the cost of the high-tech features is an important component, as is the plastic console, the remote, and interactive games. But marketing expenses also figure into the total cost of the product. The same is true of that Mini Cooper you have your eye on.

But costs alone do not indicate the value of marketing to the success of a product. Marketing sends important messages to consumers and businesses, usually expanding overall sales and spreading production costs over more items sold, reducing the total cost to bring the product to market.

Marketers Contribute to Society as Well as to Individual Employers

Marketing decisions affect everyone's welfare. How much quality should be built into a product? Will people buy a safer product if it costs twice as much as the current version? Should every community adopt recycling programs? Because ethics and social responsibility are critical factors in creating long-term relationships with consumers, business customers, and the community, marketers must strive to exceed customer and government expectations of ethical behavior. The "Solving an Ethical Controversy" features included in every chapter of this book got you thinking about ethical issues in marketing and increased your awareness of the importance of maintaining high ethical standards in every dimension of marketing. These features allowed you to examine such current issues as airport scanners, behavioral targeting, stuffing cookies, spending on advertising, taking advantage of seniors, social networking sites, shelf-space wars, and hiring a contingent workforce, to name a few. The topics also made good springboards for discussion between you and your classmates.

Not only does marketing influence numerous facets of our daily lives, but decisions regarding marketing activities also affect everyone's welfare. Opportunities to advance to more responsible decision-making positions often come sooner in marketing than in most occupations. This combination of challenges and opportunities has made marketing one of the most popular fields of academic study.

Although many paths can lead to the top of the corporate ladder, marketing remains one of the strongest and most popular. The growing global economy depends on proven market leaders in winning the fight to increase a firm's worldwide market shares. Marketing provides a solid background for developing the long-term, loyal relationships with customers that are necessary for success in the global marketplace.

You May Choose a Career in Marketing

Even if you aren't sure about a career now, this course could have helped you decide on a path in marketing. In fact, of the many career paths chosen by business graduates, marketing is the largest employment category in the U.S. labor force, and job growth in the field is expected to accelerate. All firms must somehow get their goods and services into the hands of customers profitably, and doing so is becoming increasingly challenging. So marketing plays a significant role in the survival and growth of all companies—which means that, as a field, it will continue to grow.

The U.S. Bureau of Labor Statistics anticipates stiff competition for desirable jobs. College graduates having "related experience, a high level of creativity, strong communication skills, and computer skills" stand the best chance of landing these jobs. These job candidates can expect high earnings along with travel and long working hours, including evenings and weekends.[2]

Your Quest for a Successful, Rewarding Career

Selecting a career is an important life decision—your career will determine such things as where you live, how much money you make, and for what kind of company you work. That's why *Contemporary Marketing* discusses the best ways to approach career decisions and to prepare for an *entry-level*

briefly speaking

"If I had my life to live over again, I would be a trader of goods rather than a student of science. I think barter is a noble thing."

—Albert Einstein
(1879–1955)
American Physicist

position—your first permanent employment after leaving school. We also look at a range of marketing careers and describe employment opportunities in fields related to each major part of the text.

The average starting salary for marketing graduates is about $42,700.[3] As mentioned earlier, the field of marketing is the largest area of employment in the United States—and employers are continuing to hire. This positive outlook does *not* mean competition isn't tough or you can be casual in your approach to your first job. You are not guaranteed anything. But if you are creative, hardworking, and determined—and if you learn everything you can about business and marketing before you begin your search—you are likely to land a good entry-level position at a company that suits you. In your coursework, you have been introduced to all the key functional areas of marketing. Armed with this knowledge, you should be able to identify areas of employment you may wish to pursue.

Education improves your prospects of finding and keeping the right job. Recent college graduates can earn nearly twice what workers with high school diplomas earn. Better-educated graduates also find jobs more quickly than others, and they have lower unemployment rates.[4] Applying yourself in class and expanding your experiences through career-directed volunteer efforts, part-time and summer jobs, and high-quality internships—and selecting the right major—are significant steps on your way toward improving these salary statistics when you launch your career.

In addition to taking classes, try to gain related experience either through a job or by participating in campus organizations. Internships, summer and part-time jobs, and volunteer activities on campus and in your community can also give you valuable hands-on experience while you pursue your education. Work-related experience, whether paid or volunteer, lets a potential employer know you are serious about pursuing your career. It also helps you decide on your own path.

This guide to planning your career provides you with a brief look at the trends and opportunities available for future marketers in an increasingly diversified, professional field. It describes essential elements of an effective résumé and discusses the latest trends in electronic job searches. Finally, it includes a listing of primary marketing information sources that contain answers to many of the questions typically asked by applicants. This information will provide valuable career-planning assistance in this and other future courses, whether your career plans involve marketing or you decide to major in another field.

Many of the marketing positions you read about throughout this text are described here. Specifically, the job summaries outline the responsibilities and duties typically required as well as the usual career path for each of these marketing-related positions. You might follow a traditional career path, or you might wind up in one of the new types of marketing jobs emerging such as blogging for a particular company or organization. Richard Brewer-Hay spent years working for a media company and in public relations before eBay recruited him to write an unedited blog to help improve the company's image among buyers and sellers. As eBay's "blogger in chief," Brewer-Hay serves as a conduit for news and analysis of the company while also providing a personal touch because the blog emanates from an independent server, not eBay's official one. Brewer-Hay likens his role to that of a bartender: just as a bartender represents the "face" of the bar, he says, his blog represents the eBay brand and the people behind it.[5]

Marketing your skills to a prospective employer is much the same as marketing a product to a consumer. Increasingly, job seekers are selling their skills online, bypassing intermediaries such as employment agencies and leveling the playing field between applicant and potential employer. The greatest challenge for online job seekers is learning how to market themselves.

Despite the vast databases and fancy tools of giant career sites like Monster.com, Yahoo!HotJobs, and CareerBuilder.com, which may receive hundreds of thousands of visits each day, savvy job seekers also zero in on niche boards offering more focused listings. You can find sites that focus specifically on sales, such as SalesJobs.com, and those that emphasize sports industry positions for female professionals, such as WomenSportsJobs.com.[6] Regardless of which type of online job board you use—general or specific—be aware that this medium is the most often used recruiting tool among employers for hiring managers at smaller and mid-sized companies.[7]

In many instances, students seeking interviews with specific employers or in certain geographic locations go directly to the employer's or region's Web site to learn of available positions. Most employers include an employment site as part of their home page. Some offer virtual tours of what it is like to work for the firm. For example, the Enterprise Rent-A-Car Web site features profiles of young assistant managers as they perform daily work activities. The employees answer several questions about their jobs and the abilities candidates need to be a successful employee at Enterprise. The site also outlines the skills employees gain while working there, the friendships formed among workers, opportunities for involvement in the community, the management training program, and available internships.[8]

Huge career sites, including Yahoo! HotJobs, receive hundreds of thousands of visits each day.

© RICHARD B. LEVINE/NEWSCOM

The key to finding the job you want is letting the market know who you are and what you can do. While few college graduates are hired directly based on their response to an online listing, this approach often is an important first step in zeroing in on specific employers of interest and then soliciting interviews that may lead to job offers. So you should familiarize yourself with the way online job sites work, including those of specific companies.

As you begin your career, you will apply many of the principles and concepts discussed in this text, including how to target a market, capitalize on brand equity, position a product, and use marketing research techniques. Even in jobs that seem remote from the marketing discipline, this knowledge will help you stay focused on the most important aspect of business: the consumer.

briefly speaking

"Anyone who keeps learning stays young."

—Henry Ford
(1863–1947)
American automobile manufacturer

Standing Out from the Crowd of Job Seekers

Because high-quality employees provide companies the edge they need in competitive markets, employers need to be choosy in deciding which applicants will make the cut, be interviewed, and possibly be offered a position. And often the applicant's accumulated job and leadership experiences will be key criteria in determining whether he or she is given serious consideration as a potential employee.

Some students continue their studies following graduation and pursue an MBA degree or enter a master's program specially suited to their career goals. But many enter the job market right away, perhaps pursuing an advanced degree later. Experience is one factor in a prospective employee's favor, and some activities that enhance a candidate's profile are internships and volunteering.

Internships Provide Valuable Work Experience

Internships have been described as a critical link in bridging the theory–practice educational gap. They help carry students between the academic present and the professional future. They provide students with an opportunity for learning how classroom theory is applied in real-world business environments.

Internships are popular for both employers and students or recent grads. In fact, interning is now the number-one recruiting technique among employers, and many students are hired for full-time jobs from their internships. Some internships include a salary, which may be as high as

"Ambition is the path to success. Persistence is the vehicle you arrive in."

—Bill Bradley
(b. 1943)
Former U.S. Senator, NBA player, and U.S. Olympian

$15 to $25 per hour, depending on the industry and the level of education reached by the student. Other internships are unpaid, which means students must find other ways of earning money. But the majority of students who participate in unpaid internships still believe the experience gained is much more important than a salary would have been. They cite the actual work experience, along with references and contacts in the industry, as more valuable than pay. A recent study by the National Association of Colleges and Employers revealed that 50 percent of college grads had held an internship.[9]

Start your search for an internship at your college placement office or library. Some college Web sites have catalogs of internships available through organizations such as the American Association of Advertising Agencies, the Inroads Minority Internship Program, and the Washington Center for Internships and Academic Seminars.[10] Also check with the alumni office, which may have a listing of alumni willing to talk with seniors or recent grads about their fields. You can talk with your instructors, visit the Web sites of companies that interest you, and check your local bookstore for career and internship reference guides.

Your Résumé

Writing a résumé is a vital task, but it doesn't need to be daunting. Your résumé is like a verbal snapshot of you. It tells a potential employer about you, your credentials, and your goals. It provides an all-important first impression of you and may be the only written record available with which an employer can make a decision about you. Your résumé is a concise summary of your academic, professional, and personal accomplishments; it makes focused statements about you as a student and potential employee.

Résumé Miscues

Here are some tips on writing your résumé—and what to avoid:

- *Stick to the truth.* It's easy for a prospective employer to check facts like previous job experience and graduation dates. Don't lie about or even embellish your accomplishments. It can catch up with you and you may lose a promising job as a result.

- *Stick to the point.* Don't begin your résumé with the overused "career objective." Who *doesn't* want to be thought of as a career-oriented person looking for challenging work that will help you grow? Instead, try writing a "snapshot" of yourself as a candidate. Perhaps you're an honors graduate of your university with experience running charitable events, or you are a native Spanish speaker who has lived on more than one continent. Or maybe as an undergrad you took on increasingly responsible roles on your college newspaper. Giving recruiters an idea of who you are sparks their interest and improves your chances as a candidate.

- *Obsess about accuracy.* Don't rely on spell-check to catch typos, inconsistencies, or other errors in your document. With employers finding huge responses for most jobs, they can afford to eliminate outright any candidates who present a résumé that's carelessly written. It's easy to miss errors in a document you've spent a lot of time preparing. A friend or relative can read your document with fresh eyes.

- *Zero in on the right stuff.* Many employers use technology to manage résumés, so it's important to insert keywords that will ensure that your résumé is pulled up during searches. Consider the words and phrases most relevant to your job search.

- *Monitor your reputation.* With recruiters increasingly looking to social media, you'll want to be discreet about what you put on Facebook, YouTube, and other sites. Photos and text that position you in an unprofessional light may hurt your chances in many organizations.

Sources: Kim Isaacs, "Common Résumé Blunders," *Monster Career Advice*, career-advice. monster.com, accessed May 11, 2010; Lisa Vaas, "13 Ways Your Résumé Can Say 'I'm Unprofessional,' " *The Ladders*, http://www.theladders.com, accessed May 11, 2010; "Résumé Mistakes: What Should NOT Be on Your Résumé," *Job-hunt.org*, http://www. job-hunt.org, accessed May 10, 2010.

Three basic formats are used in preparing a résumé. A *chronological résumé* arranges information in reverse chronological order, emphasizing job titles and organizations and describing responsibilities held and duties performed. This format highlights continuity and career growth. A *functional résumé* accents accomplishments and strengths, placing less emphasis on job titles and work history, and often omits job descriptions. A functional résumé prepared by a recent graduate is shown in Figure A.1. Some applicants use a *combined résumé* format, which emphasizes skills first, followed by employment history. This format highlights a candidate's potential and suits students who often have little experience directly related to their desired positions.

Regardless of which format you choose, all résumés contain certain information. And they all have the same goal: to interest an employer enough to invite you to apply formally for a job and conduct an interview. A résumé should be concise—for recent grads, no more than a single page. Before writing your résumé, take the time to outline your goals, skills, abilities, education,

figure A.1
Functional Résumé

Roberto Chavez
Two Seaside Drive, Apt. 3A
Los Angeles, CA 90026
215-555-7092
RCHAVEZ@hotmail.com

Marketing honors grad with merchandising experience. Strong analytical and organizational skills. Creative problem solver, team player.

Professional Experience
Administration
Management responsibilities in a major retail buying office included coordinating vendor relation efforts. Supervised assistant buyers.

Category Management
Experience in buying home improvement and sport, recreation, and fitness categories.

Planning
Leader of a team charged with reviewing the company's annual vendor evaluation program.

Problem Solving
Successfully developed a program to improve margins in the tennis, golf, and fishing product categories.

Work Experience
Senior Buyer
Southern California Department Stores   2010–Present

Merchandiser
Pacific Discount Stores, a division of Southern California
Department Stores   2008–2010

Education
Bachelor of Science degree in business
Double major in marketing and retailing
California State University–San Bernardino   2006–2010

Computer Skills
Proficient with IBM-compatible computers and related software, including spreadsheets, graphics, desktop publishing, and word processing.
Packages: Microsoft Word, Excel, PowerPoint, Adobe PageMaker, CorelDRAW

Familiar with Adobe Photoshop and the Macintosh.

Language Skills
Fluent in speaking and writing Spanish.

"A résumé is a balance sheet without any liabilities."

—Robert Half
*(1918–2001)
American personnel
agency executive*

and work experience and list any relevant volunteer or extracurricular activities. You can pare these down later, but having them in front of you will make it easier to build your final résumé.

Your contact information should appear at the top of the page: full name, address, phone number, and e-mail address. If your e-mail username is "MachoDude" or "SnowboardDoll," replace it with one related to your real name or location to persuade employers to take you seriously. Likewise, avoid using a nickname. Even if all of your friends call you Sully, cite your name as Jason E. Sullivan.

Next, include a brief personal summary of two or three statements that describes you as a job candidate. This summary helps set the context for your readers, piques their interest, and may help them remember you in a field of candidates. For example, in your personal summary you might use such phrases as "honors student with campus leadership experience," "fluent in three languages," "creative team player," or "strong analytical and organizational skills."

Your education information generally comes next. State your most recent level of education first. There is no need to list high school unless you attended a specialized school or received particular honors. Include your degree, academic honors, and grade point average if it is above 3.0.

State your work history, including employment, internships, and related volunteer work. Include the name of the organization, the dates you worked there, your job title, and your responsibilities on the job. Provide a statement of your skills, such as leadership, managing others, computer software knowledge, and the like. At the end of your résumé, add a note that you will furnish references on request—do *not* include your references' names and contact information on your résumé.

Whether yours is a traditional résumé on paper or posted on an Internet résumé listing, the important point to remember in creating an effective résumé is to present the most relevant information in a clear, concise manner that emphasizes your best attributes.

Cover Letter

Typically, your potential employer "meets" you through a cover letter. Like gift wrap on a present, a cover letter should attract attention and interest about what is inside. Your letter should be addressed to a specific person, not "To Whom It May Concern." It should include information about the job for which you are applying, why you are interested in it, a brief summary of your top accomplishments or skills, and a note that you are available for an interview. Close your letter by thanking the person for his or her time and consideration.

Here are a few additional tips to guide you.

Do

- Keep your letter to a single page.
- Customize the letter to the company or person for whom it is intended, even though you may be writing 20 such letters. Send an original letter, not a photocopy.
- Proofread it several times, making sure there are no typos.
- Remember to sign your letter.
- Include your contact information, including cell phone number and e-mail address.

Don't

- Use slang or rude language.
- Rehash your résumé.
- Address the letter "Gentlemen" or "Dear Sirs." The person reading the letter might be a woman. Instead, take the time to find out exactly to whom you should send your materials.
- Challenge the reader to hire you. And avoid appearing desperate. Instead, briefly state what you can contribute to the workplace.[11]

Letters of Recommendation

Letters of recommendation serve as testimonials to your performance in academic and work settings. The best references provide information relevant to the desired industry or marketing specialty as well as opinions of your skills, abilities, and character. You can obtain references from former or current employers, supervisors from volunteer experiences, instructors, and others who can attest to your academic and professional competencies.

An effective letter of recommendation typically contains the following elements:

1. Statement of the length and nature of the relationship between the writer and the job candidate

2. Description of the candidate's academic and career growth potential

3. Review of important achievements

4. Evaluation of personal characteristics (what kind of colleague the candidate will make)

5. Summary of the candidate's outstanding strengths and abilities

Because letters of recommendation take time and effort, it helps to provide a résumé and any other information relevant to the recommendation, along with a stamped, addressed (typed) envelope. When requesting letters of recommendation, allow ample time for your references to compose them—as long as a month is not unusual.

In addition to including a cover letter, résumé, and letters of recommendation, you should include photocopies of transcripts, writing samples, or other examples of work completed. For instance, if you are applying for a position in public relations, advertising, or sports marketing, you may want to include examples of professional writing, graphics, and audiovisual media to support written evidence of your credentials. Research and service projects that resulted in published or unpublished articles may also enhance your portfolio.

Using Paperless Systems

Most large firms have moved toward electronic (paperless) résumé processing and applicant-tracking systems. In fact, some human resource experts say outright that the fastest way to get your résumé to the correct person is to use the firm's own online application system. So it's best to prepare a résumé compatible with these systems. Figure A.2 contains a number of tips for preparing an effective, readable, technology-compatible résumé.

In addition, keep in mind a few overall rules. First, read the directions for completing and transmitting your résumé or application carefully—and follow them to the letter. If you try to stand out by doing something different, your application will probably be lost or ignored, or you may be viewed as someone who might not follow instructions on the job. Second, complete all possible fields, even those not required. Third, if the firm offers an optional online assessment test, take it. An employer will appreciate your initiative and can evaluate some of your skills immediately.

Finally, choose effective keywords for your résumé. Employers who review electronic résumés posted on their sites and on big boards save time by using computers to search for

figure A.2

Tips for Preparing an Electronic Résumé

- Use a standard typeface like Times, Courier, or Arial. Stick with 12-point to 14-point type size. Single space the text, but double space where appropriate between sections. The text should be clean and easy to read.

- Use punctuation where necessary, but avoid graphics, shading, underlines, or other visual distractions.

- Use white paper and black type; avoid the temptation to include color.

- Use keywords that will attract the reader's attention whether the résumé is scanned into a electronic system, indexed for an online search, or printed on paper to be distributed to the appropriate people. Examples might include *marketing, entry-level, Web-based training (WBT), or Microsoft Office.*

- Follow the format required by the employer or job site. Most online forms are submitted in chronological format, which pinpoints recent work history.

- A plain text file that is ready to copy and paste onto an online form or to print out is the easiest for most recipients to handle. However, if you are applying for a position in the visual arts or programming field, you may create an HTML version of your résumé.

Source: "Prepare Your Résumé for Email and Online Posting," *The Riley Guide: Résumés & Cover Letters,* http://www.rileyguide.com, accessed May 11, 2010; "Scannable Résumés," *Proven Resumes.com,* http://provenresumes.com, accessed May 11,2010; "Scannable Résumé Design," *Technical Job Search.com,* http://technicaljobsearch.com, accessed May 11, 2010.

keywords in job titles, job descriptions, or résumés to narrow the search. In fact, *manager* is the number one word for which companies search. Regardless of the position you seek, one key to an effective electronic résumé is to use exact words and phrases, emphasizing nouns rather than the action verbs you are likely to use in a print-only résumé. For example, a company looking for a marketing account manager with experience in Microsoft Office applications such as Word and Excel may conduct computer searches only for résumés that include the job title and the three software programs.

Learning More about Job Opportunities

As you continue with your application and selection process, study the various employment opportunities you have identified. Obviously, you will like some more than others, but keep an open mind; remember, this is the beginning of a long career. Examine a number of factors when assessing each job possibility:

1. Actual job responsibilities
2. Industry characteristics
3. Nature of the company
4. Geographic location
5. Salary and opportunities for advancement
6. The contribution the job is likely to make to your long-range career opportunities

Many job applicants consider only the most striking features of a job, perhaps its location, or the salary offered. However, a comprehensive review of job openings will give you a more balanced perspective of the overall employment opportunity, including both long- and short-run factors.

Job Interviews

Your first goal in your job search is to land an interview with a prospective employer. If the experience is new to you and you feel uncertain or nervous, you can do a lot to turn those feelings into confidence.

PREPARING FOR THE INTERVIEW

Do your homework. Learn as much as you can about the company, the industry in which it operates, the goods or services it offers, the working environment, and the like. If you are well prepared for the questions you are asked—and prepared to ask educated questions—you are much more likely to have a positive interview experience. You can prepare by researching the following basic information about the firm:

How long has the firm been in business?

In what industry does the firm operate? What is its role within the industry?

Who are the firm's customers? Who are its competitors?

How is the firm organized? How many people work there? Where are its headquarters? Does it have other offices and production facilities located around the nation or around the world?

What is the company's mission? Does the company have a written code of ethics?

This information is useful in several ways. Not only will it increase your confidence about the interview, but it may also help you weed out any firms that might not be a good fit for you. You've also shown the interviewer you are motivated enough to come to the discussion prepared.

You can find this information in many of the same places you looked initially for information about companies at the beginning of your job search. Your school's career center, library, and, most important, the company's own Web site will have much of the information you need. In addition, you can find brief company profiles on business sites like Hoovers.com, and don't forget to check the various business magazines.

When you prepare for an interview, think about questions you will likely be asked.

© CHABRUKEN/TAXI/GETTY IMAGES

WHAT TO EXPECT IN AN INTERVIEW

You've made the interview appointment, done your research on the company, and chosen the right attire for the occasion according to suggestions provided in the "Career Readiness" feature. What's next?

Prepare yourself for the questions you will likely be asked. As you gain experience in interviewing, you will recognize variations of similar questions and be able to answer them comfortably. An interviewer needs to get to know you in a short period of time, so he or she will ask questions that deal with your personality, your life and work experience, and decision-making or problem-solving style. Here are a few examples:

- Why did you apply for this job? Why do you want this job?
- What are the requirements of the job as you understand them?
- What are your key strengths? What are your weaknesses?
- Are you an organized person? How do you manage your time?
- What were your responsibilities on your last job or internship? How would they apply here?
- What were your biggest successes or failures—in school or work?
- How do you make important decisions? How do you function under pressure?
- What do you know about this company?
- What are your most important long-term goals?[12]

To prepare effective answers, ask a friend or family member to role-play the interview with you, asking questions so you have an opportunity to hear yourself respond out loud before the actual interview.

When you arrive for your interview, be sure to confirm the name of the person (or people) who will conduct the interview. If this person is with the human resources department and your interview goes well, he or she will probably recommend you to a manager or supervisor for further interviewing. Some hiring decisions are made by a single supervisor, while others result from joint interviews conducted by both human resources personnel and the immediate supervisor of the prospective employee.

During a typical interview, the interviewer usually talks little. This approach, referred to as an *open-ended interview,* forces you to talk about yourself and your career goals. This is a major reason it is important to arrive prepared. If you appear uncertain or disorganized in your thinking, the interviewer may surmise that you have not prepared or aren't serious about the job. Keep the conversation on target; don't ramble on and on. You may also ask questions of the interviewer, so be sure to listen carefully to the responses. Appropriate questions include those about job responsibilities, training, and long-range opportunities for advancement. Don't ask when you will get a raise or promotion or how many vacation days you will receive. In the end, a successful interview represents a mutual exchange of information.

briefly speaking

" T he best way to get what you want is to help other people get what they want."

—Zig Ziglar
(b. 1927)
American motivational speaker

career readiness How to Dress for Your Job Interview

Landing a job interview is a big step on the road to starting your chosen career. You can make the most of the opportunity to create a good impression by presenting yourself in a professional way. You need to be prepared with knowledge about the company, project confidence and a willingness to learn, and convey that you will be a reliable employee. You also need to look the part. After all, you will be representing your company even if you do not deal directly with its customers.

Unless you are applying for a job that requires certain clothing—say, a uniform or outdoor work clothes—on most days you will be wearing business attire. So you should arrive at your interview in the clothing you would likely wear to work. The following suggestions will serve you well:

- *Dress conservatively.* A conservative suit is best for both men and women, with a long-sleeved shirt or blouse. Men should choose a traditional tie with a simple pattern and muted colors. If you wear jewelry, keep it unobtrusive. Cover any tattoos and limit pierced jewelry to ears.

- *Your clothes should be clean and pressed.* Be sure you have no runs in stockings or threadbare socks. Shoes should be clean and polished. Avoid open-toed shoes, sandals, or wild colors.

- *Be sure your hair is trimmed, washed, and well groomed.* Wear your hair in a neat, professional style—a sleek, simple cut or combed into place. Men should be clean-shaven or at least have trimmed mustaches or beards.

- *Make sure your overall appearance is clean and classic.* Be sure your fingernails are clean and short. If you wear polish, use a conservative color or clear. Any makeup should be understated, and not attract attention.

- *Avoid cologne or perfume.* Some people are allergic to scents, particularly in closed areas such as offices and conference rooms.

- *Empty your pockets.* Don't jingle coins, keys, or a cell phone. In addition, turn off any cell phones or pagers before your interview.

- *Carry a lightweight portfolio, briefcase, or tote.* You'll want to be able to supply an extra copy of your résumé, a sample of your writing, or copies of ads you've created.

Overall, you want to present a neat, clean, professional, and appealing appearance. Looking professional is one of the first steps to conducting a successful interview and landing a job. So think about how professionals conduct themselves—and dress accordingly. No one expects you to splurge on an expensive suit or briefcase as you start your career. But you can convey yourself as the professional you know you're going to be.

Sources: "How to Dress for a Job Interview," *University Language Services,* http://www.universitylanguage.com, accessed May 12, 2010; "Dressing for Success for the Job Interview," *Employment News,* April 29, 2010, http://www.employmentdigest.net; Tatiana Varenik, "Job Interview: Dressing for Success," *Resumark.com,* March 1, 2010, http://www.resumark.com; Marva Goldsmith, "How to Dress for Your Next Job Interview," *More,* December 2009, http://www.more.com.

A successful first interview may result in an invitation to return to take a skills test, tour the building, or even meet other managers and coworkers. All of these experiences point toward getting the right fit between a company and its potential employees. On the other hand, even after a good interview, you may not be asked back. Do not consider this a personal rejection—the job market is competitive, and companies must make their selections carefully to achieve the best match. It might not have been the right firm or job for you in the long run, and the interviewer realized this. Treat each job application and interview as a chance to build confidence and experience—and eventually, the right job will be yours.

Employment Decisions

By now, a firm that is still considering you as a strong candidate knows quite a bit about you. You should also know a lot about the company and whether you want to work there. When the interview process is complete, you may be offered a position with the firm. Your decision to accept the offer should depend on a variety of factors, including the following:

- Do you want to work in this industry?

- Do you want to be part of the company's mission? Would you be proud to work for this company?

- Could this particular job lead to other opportunities within the company?

- Will you be able to work well with your coworkers and supervisors?

- Can you already see ways you can learn and contribute your best efforts to the company?

If you are offered the job and decide to accept it, congratulations! Approach your new job with professionalism, creativity, and a willingness to learn. You are on your way to a successful career in marketing.

Marketing Positions

To survive and grow, an organization must market its goods or services. Marketing responsibilities vary among organizations and industries. In a small firm, the owner or president may assume many of the company's marketing responsibilities. A large firm needs experienced sales, marketing, and advertising managers, as well as staff, to coordinate these activities. The "Career Path" features that follow outline major marketing positions, providing job descriptions and projected career paths for each. Each position is also cross-referenced to the chapter in this text that discusses the marketing area in detail.

Career Path 1: Marketing, Advertising, Product, and Public Relations Managers

Related Chapters: Chapters 1 and 2 (marketing); Chapters 11 and 12 (product); Chapters 15 and 16 (advertising and public relations)

Marketing management spans a range of positions, including vice president of marketing, marketing manager, sales manager, product or category manager, advertising manager, promotion manager, and public relations manager. The vice president directs the firm's overall marketing policy, and all other managers report through channels to this person. Sales managers direct the efforts of sales professionals by assigning territories, establishing goals, developing training programs, and supervising local sales managers and their personnel. Advertising managers oversee account services, creative services, and media services departments. Promotion managers direct promotional programs that combine advertising with purchase incentives designed to increase the sales of the firm's goods or services. Public relations managers communicate with the firm's various publics, conduct publicity programs, and supervise the specialists who implement these programs.

Job Description

As with senior management positions in production, finance, and other areas, top marketing management positions often involve long hours and regular travel. Work under pressure is also common to solve problems and meet deadlines. For sales managers, job transfers between headquarters and regional offices may disrupt one's personal life. Nearly 624,000 marketing, advertising, promotions, public relations, and sales managers are currently employed in the United States. The Bureau of Labor Statistics estimates the number of these jobs will increase through the year 2018.

Career Path

A degree in business administration, preferably with a concentration in marketing, usually is preferred for these positions, but for advertising positions, some employers want a bachelor's degree in advertising or journalism. Those looking for jobs in public relations should have a bachelor's degree in public relations or journalism. In highly technical industries, such as computers, chemicals, and electronics, employers may look for bachelor's degrees in science or engineering combined with business courses or a master's degree in business administration. Liberal arts students can also find many opportunities, especially if they

have business minors. Most managers are promoted from positions such as sales representatives, product or brand specialists, and advertising specialists within their organizations. Skills or traits most desirable for these jobs include high motivation levels, maturity, creativity, resistance to stress, flexibility, and the ability to communicate persuasively. In addition, these candidates must be willing to work long hours, manage their time well, and handle meetings with clients and media representatives when necessary.

Source: "Advertising, Marketing, Promotions, Public Relations, and Sales Managers," *Occupational Outlook Handbook, 2010–2011 Edition*, Bureau of Labor Statistics, http://data.bls.gov, accessed May 12, 2010.

Career Path 2: Sales Representatives and Sales Managers

Related Chapter: Chapter 17

Millions of items are bought and sold every day. The people who carry out this activity may have a variety of titles—sales representative, account manager, manufacturer's representative, sales engineer, sales agent, retail salesperson, wholesale sales representative, and service sales representative. Sales managers typically are selected from people in the current sales force who have demonstrated they possess the managerial skills needed to lead teams of sales representatives. In addition, many organizations require all marketing professionals to spend some time in the field to experience the market firsthand and to understand the challenges faced by front-line personnel.

Job Description

Salespeople usually develop prospective client lists, meet with current and prospective customers to discuss the firm's products, and then follow up to answer questions and supply additional information. By knowing the business needs of each customer, the sales representative can identify products that best satisfy these needs. After a purchase, sales personnel are likely to revisit their customers to ensure the products are

meeting the customers' needs and to explore further business opportunities or referrals provided by satisfied buyers. Some sales of technical products involve lengthy interactions. In these cases, a salesperson may work with several clients simultaneously over a large geographic area. Those responsible for large territories may spend most of their workdays on the phone, receiving and sending e-mail messages or traveling to customers' locations. Sales managers direct a firm's sales program. They manage the sales force by assigning territories, setting goals, and implementing training programs for sales staff. Managers also review the performance of sales representatives and guide them toward improvement. The Bureau of Labor Statistics projects average job growth in this category, with keen competition for top jobs through the year 2018. Currently, there are about 347,000 sales managers in the United States.

Work as a sales representative or sales manager can be rewarding for those who enjoy interacting with people, are invigorated by competition, and feel energized by the challenge of expanding sales in their territories. Successful sales professionals—both individual sales reps and sales managers—should be goal oriented, persuasive, self-motivated, and independent. In addition, patience and perseverance are important qualities.

Career Path

The background needed for a position in sales varies according to the product line and market. Most professional sales jobs require a college degree, preferably with a major in business administration or marketing. Creativity and strong communications skills are a plus. Many companies run their own formal training programs that can last up to two years for sales representatives in technical industries. This training may take place in a classroom, in the field with a mentor, or most often using a combination of both methods. Sales managers usually are promoted from the field; they are likely to include successful sales representatives who exhibit managerial skills and promise. Sales management positions begin at a local or district level, then advance to positions of increased authority and responsibility, such as area, regional, national, and international sales manager.

Source: "Advertising, Marketing, Promotions, Public Relations, and Sales Managers," *Occupational Outlook Handbook, 2010–2011 Edition,* Bureau of Labor Statistics, http://data.bls.gov, accessed May 12, 2010.

Career Path 3: Advertising Specialists

Related Chapters: Chapters 15 and 16

Most companies, especially firms serving consumer markets, maintain groups of advertising specialists who serve as liaisons between the marketer and its outside advertising agencies. The leader of this liaison function is sometimes called a *marketing communications manager.* Advertising agencies also employ specialists in account services, creative services, and media services. Account services functions are performed by account executives, who work directly with clients. An agency's creative services department develops the themes and presentations of the advertisements. This department is supervised by a creative director, who oversees the copy chief, the art director, and their staff members. The media services department is managed by a media director, who oversees the planning group that selects media outlets for ads. In a recent year, more than 50,000 firms provided advertising and public relations services in the United States.

Job Description

Advertising can be one of the most glamorous and creative fields in marketing. Because the field combines the best of both worlds—that is, the tangible and scientific aspects of marketing along with creative artistry—advertising attracts people with a broad array of abilities.

As exciting as it may seem, advertising is also stressful. Those in the creative field often have to come up with innovative plans on a tight schedule. Long hours are also common. Advertising professionals must be able to manage their time wisely, be willing to travel, and deal with a wide range of clients. Typical tasks in the advertising field include writing copy, preparing artwork and graphics, and placing ads in the media.

Career Path

Most new hires begin as assistants or associates for the position they hope to acquire, such as copywriter, art director, and media buyer. Often, a newly hired employee must receive two to four promotions before becoming manager of these functions. A bachelor's degree with a broad education in courses, such as graphic arts, communications, psychology, and marketing, usually is required for an entry-level position in advertising. Superior communications skills, creativity, and a willingness to work long hours to complete the job are important traits for advertising candidates.

Source: "Advertising and Public Relations Services," *Occupational Outlook Handbook, 2010–2011 Edition,* Bureau of Labor Statistics, http://data.bls.gov, accessed May 12, 2010.

Career Path 4: Public Relations Specialists

Related Chapters: Chapters 15 and 16

Specialists in public relations strive to build and maintain positive relationships with various publics. They may assist management in drafting speeches, arranging interviews, overseeing company archives, responding to information requests, and handling special events, such as sponsorships and trade shows, that generate promotional benefits for the firm.

Job Description

Public relations specialists may work hectic schedules to help a firm respond to and manage a crisis or to meet the deadline for a special event. Although public relations positions tend to be concentrated in large cities near major press services and communications facilities, this is changing as communications technologies allow more freedom of movement. Most public relations consulting firms are concentrated in New York, Los Angeles, Chicago, and Washington, DC, and they range in size from hundreds of employees to just a handful. Nearly 57,000 professionals serve as public relations managers in the United States.

Essential characteristics for a public relations specialist include creativity, initiative, good judgment, and the ability to express thoughts clearly and simply—both verbally and in writing. An outgoing personality, self-confidence, and enthusiasm are also important traits.

Career Path

A college degree combined with public relations experience, usually gained through one or more internships, is considered excellent preparation for public relations. Many entry-level public relations specialists hold degrees with majors in public relations, advertising, marketing, or communications. New employees in larger organizations are likely to participate in formal training programs; those who begin their careers at smaller firms typically work under the guidance of experienced staff members. Entry-level positions carry such titles as *research assistant* or *account assistant*. A potential career path includes a promotion to account executive, account supervisor, vice president, and eventually senior vice president.

Source: "Advertising, Marketing, Promotions, Public Relations, and Sales Managers," *Occupational Outlook Handbook, 2010–2011 Edition,* Bureau of Labor Statistics, http://data.bls.gov, accessed May 12, 2010; "Advertising and Public Relations Services," *Occupational Outlook Handbook, 2010–2011 Edition,* Bureau of Labor Statistics, http://data.bls.gov, accessed May 12, 2010.

Career Path 5: Purchasing Agents and Managers

Related Chapter: Chapter 6

In today's competitive business environment, the two key marketing functions of buying and selling are performed by trained specialists. Just as every organization is involved in selling its output to meet the needs of customers, so too must all companies purchase goods and services to operate their businesses and turn out items for sale. Purchasing agents and managers represent a vital component of a company's supply chain.

Job Description

About 457,000 people work as purchasing agents and buyers for firms in the United States (excluding farms), and the Bureau of Labor Statistics projects employment to remain steady in this field over the next several years. Technological advances have transformed the role of the purchasing agent. Moving routine tasks to computers allows contract specialists, or procurement officers, to focus on products, suppliers, and contract negotiations. The primary function of this position is to purchase the goods, materials, component parts, supplies, and services required by the organization. These buyers ensure that suppliers deliver quality and quantity levels that match the firm's needs; they also secure these inputs at reasonable prices and make them available when needed.

Purchasing agents must develop good working relationships both with colleagues in their own organizations and with vendors. As the popularity of outsourcing has increased, the selection and management of suppliers have become critical functions of the purchasing department. In the government sector, this role is dominated by laws and regulations that change frequently.

Most purchasing agents and their managers work in comfortable environments, but they work more than the standard 40-hour week to meet production deadlines or to be ready for special sales, conferences, or other events. Depending on the industry, these specialists may have to work extra hours prior to holidays or certain seasons, such as back-to-school, in order to have enough merchandise to meet demand. Many buyers do at least some travel. Those who work for firms with manufacturing or sources overseas—such as clothing manufacturers—may travel outside the United States.

Career Path

Organizations prefer college-educated candidates for entry-level jobs in purchasing. Strong analytical and communication skills are required for these positions. New hires often begin their careers in extensive company training programs in which they learn procedures and operations. Training may include assignments dealing with production planning. Professional certification is becoming an essential criterion for advancement in both the private and the public sectors. A variety of associations serving the different categories of purchasing confer certifications on agents, including Certified Professional in Supply Management, Certified Professional Public Buyer, Certified Public Purchasing Officer, Certified Purchasing Professional, and Certified Professional Purchasing Manager.

Source: "Purchasing Managers, Buyers, and Purchasing Agents," *Occupational Outlook Handbook, 2010–2011 Edition,* Bureau of Labor Statistics, http://data.bls.gov, accessed May 12, 2010.

Career Path 6: Retail and Wholesale Buyers and Merchandise Managers

Related Chapter: Chapter 14

Buyers working for retailers and wholesale businesses purchase goods for resale. Their goal is to find the best possible merchandise at the lowest prices. They also influence the distribution and marketing of this merchandise. Successful buyers must understand what appeals to consumers and what their establishments can sell. Product bar codes and point-of-purchase terminals allow organizations to accurately track goods that are selling and those that are not; buyers frequently analyze this data to improve their understanding of consumer demand. Buyers also check competitors' prices and sales activities and watch general economic conditions to anticipate consumer buying patterns.

Job Description

Approximately 148,000 people in the United States work as retail and wholesale buyers. These jobs often require substantial travel, as many orders are placed during buying trips to shows and exhibitions. Effective planning and decision-making skills are strong assets in this career. In addition, the job involves anticipating consumer preferences and ensuring the firm keeps needed goods in stock. Consequently, the people filling these positions must possess such qualities as resourcefulness, good judgment, and self-confidence.

Career Path

Most retail and wholesale buyers begin their careers as assistant buyers or trainees. Larger retailers seek college-educated candidates, and extensive training includes job experience in a variety of positions. Advancement often comes when buyers move to departments or new locations with larger volumes—or become merchandise managers who coordinate or oversee the work of several buyers.

Source: "Advertising, Marketing, Promotions, Public Relations, and Sales Managers," *Occupational Outlook Handbook, 2010–2011 Edition,* Bureau of Labor Statistics, http://data.bls.gov, accessed May 12, 2010.

Career Path 7: Marketing Research Analysts

Related Chapter: Chapter 8

These marketing specialists provide information that helps marketers identify and define opportunities. They generate, refine, and evaluate marketing actions and monitor marketing performance. Marketing research analysts devise methods and procedures for obtaining needed decision-oriented data. Once they compile data, analysts evaluate it and then make recommendations to management.

Job Description

Firms that specialize in marketing research and management consulting employ most of the nation's marketing research analysts. Those who pursue careers in marketing research must be able to work accurately with detail, display patience and persistence, work effectively both independently and with others, and operate objectively and systematically. Significant computer and analytical skills are essential for success in this field. Deadlines are typical in this field, but these specialists tend to have fairly regular work hours compared with other marketing professionals. Marketing and survey researchers hold about 273,000 jobs in the United States, and employment opportunities are expected to grow faster than average through 2018.

Marketing research analysts create methods and procedures for gathering the necessary data to serve their clients. They develop ways to find out what consumers are thinking and buying, as well as who they are and how they live. Marketing researchers may design telephone, mail, or Internet surveys to evaluate consumer preferences. They may also conduct in-person interviews or lead focus group discussions. Once they have compiled data, they evaluate information to make recommendations based on their research.

Career Path

A bachelor's degree with an emphasis in marketing provides sufficient qualifications for many entry-level jobs in marketing research. Because of the importance of quantitative skills and the need for competence in using analytical software packages, this professional's education should include courses in computer science and information systems. Students should try to gain experience in conducting interviews or surveys while still in college. A master's degree in business administration or a related discipline are typically required for improving advancement opportunities.

Source: "Market and Survey Researchers," *Occupational Outlook Handbook, 2010–2011 Edition*, Bureau of Labor Statistics, http://data.bls.gov, accessed May 12, 2010.

Career Path 8: Logistics: Materials Receiving, Scheduling, Dispatching, and Distributing Occupations

Related Chapter: Chapter 13

Logistics offers a myriad of career positions. Job titles under this broad heading include materials receiving, scheduling, dispatching, materials management executive, distribution operations coordinator, distribution center manager, and transportation manager. The logistics function includes responsibilities for production and inventory planning and control, distribution, and transportation.

Job Description

About 86,000 people are employed as cargo and freight agents in the United States, along with more than 750,000 shipping, receiving, and traffic clerks. In addition, U.S. firms employ thousands of production and planning specialists, dispatchers, stock clerks, and order fillers. These positions demand good communication skills and the ability to work effectively under pressure. Depending on the job, these workers are involved in planning, directing, and coordinating storage or distribution activities according to laws and regulations. A logistician analyzes and coordinates the logistical functions of a firm or organization.

Career Path

Computer skills are highly valued in these jobs. Employers look for candidates with degrees in logistics and transportation. However, graduates in marketing and other business disciplines may succeed in this field.

Sources: "Cargo and Freight Agents," *Occupational Outlook Handbook, 2010–2011 Edition*, Bureau of Labor Statistics, http://data.bls.gov, accessed May 12, 2010; "Shipping, Receiving, and Traffic Clerks," *Occupational Outlook Handbook, 2010–2011 Edition*, Bureau of Labor Statistics, http://data.bls.gov, accessed May 12, 2010.

Developing an Effective
Marketing Plan

overview

These are some of the questions addressed by a **marketing plan**—a detailed description of the resources and actions needed to achieve stated marketing objectives. Chapter 2 discussed **strategic planning**—the process of anticipating events and market conditions and deciding how a firm can best achieve its organizational objectives. Marketing planning encompasses all the activities devoted to achieving marketing objectives, establishing a basis for designing a marketing strategy. This appendix deals in depth with the formal marketing plan, which is part of an organization's overall business plan. At the end of this appendix, you'll see what an actual marketing plan looks like. Each plan component for a hypothetical firm called Blue Sky Clothing is presented.

briefly
speaking

"Knowing your destination is half the journey."

—Anonymous

marketing plan
Detailed description of the resources and actions needed to achieve stated marketing objectives.

strategic planning
Process of anticipating events and market conditions and deciding how a firm can best achieve its organizational objectives.

Components of a Business Plan

business plan Formal document that outlines what a company's objectives are, how they will be met, how the business will obtain financing, and how much money the company expects to earn.

A company's **business plan** is one of its most important documents. The business plan puts in writing what all of the company's objectives are, how they will be met, how the business will obtain financing, and how much money the company expects to earn over a specified time period. Although business plans vary in length and format, most contain at least some form of the following components:

- An *executive summary* briefly answers the *who, what, when, where, how,* and *why* questions for the plan. Although the summary appears early in the plan, it typically is written last, after the firm's executives have worked out the details of all the other sections.

- A *competitive analysis* section focuses on the environment in which the marketing plan is to be implemented. Although this section is more closely associated with the comprehensive business plan, factors specifically influencing marketing are likely to be included here.

- The *mission statement* summarizes the organization's purpose, vision, and overall goals. This statement provides the foundation on which further planning is based.

- The overall business plan includes a series of *component* plans that present goals and strategies for each functional area of the enterprise. They typically include the following:

  o The *marketing plan*, which describes strategies for informing potential customers about the goods and services offered by the firm as well as strategies for developing long-term relationships. At the end of this appendix, a sample marketing plan for Blue Sky Clothing is presented.

  o The *financing plan*, which presents a realistic approach for securing needed funds and managing debt and cash flows.

  o The *production plan*, which describes how the organization will develop its products in the most efficient, cost-effective manner possible.

  o The *facilities plan*, which describes the physical environment and equipment required to implement the production plan.

  o The *human resources plan*, which estimates the firm's employment needs and the skills necessary to achieve organizational goals, including a comparison of current employees with the needs of the firm, and which establishes processes for securing adequately trained personnel if a gap exists between current employee skills and future needs.

This basic format encompasses the planning process used by nearly every successful organization. Whether a company operates in the manufacturing, wholesaling, retailing, or service sector—or a combination—the components described here are likely to appear in its overall business plan. Regardless of the size or longevity of a company, a business plan is an essential tool for a firm's owners because it helps them focus on the key elements of their business. Even small firms just starting out need a business plan to obtain financing. Figure B.1 shows the outline of a business plan for Blue Sky Clothing.

briefly speaking

"You don't win on emotion. You win on execution."

—Tony Dungy
(b. 1954)
Former professional football coach

Creating a Marketing Plan

Keep in mind that a marketing plan should be created in conjunction with the other elements of a firm's business plan. In addition, a marketing plan often draws from the business plan, restating the executive summary, competitive analysis, and mission statement to give its readers an overall view of the firm. The marketing plan is needed for a variety of reasons:

figure B.1
Outline of a Business Plan

The Blue Sky Clothing Business Plan

I. Executive Summary
  • Who, What, When, Where, How, and Why

II. Table of Contents

III. Introduction
  • Mission Statement
  • Concept and Company
  • Management Team
  • Product

IV. Marketing Strategy
  • Demographics
  • Trends
  • Market Penetration
  • Potential Sales Revenue

V. Financing the Business
  • Cash Flow Analysis
  • Pro Forma Balance Sheet
  • Income Statement

VI. Facilities Plan
  • Physical Environment
  • Equipment

VII. Human Resources Plan
  • Employment Needs and Skills
  • Current Employees

VIII. Résumés of Principals

• To obtain financing, because banks and most private investors require a detailed business plan—including a marketing plan component—before they will even consider a loan application or a venture capital investment

• To provide direction for the firm's overall business and marketing strategies

• To support the development of long- and short-term organizational objectives

• To guide employees in achieving these objectives

• To serve as a standard against which the firm's progress can be measured and evaluated

In addition, the marketing plan is where a firm puts into writing its commitment to its customers and to building long-lasting relationships. After creating and implementing the plan, marketers must reevaluate it periodically to gauge its success in moving the organization toward its goals. If changes are needed, they should be made as soon as possible.

Formulating an Overall Marketing Strategy

Before writing a marketing plan, a firm's marketers formulate an overall marketing strategy. A firm may use a number of tools in marketing planning, including business portfolio analysis and the BCG matrix. Its executives may conduct a SWOT analysis, take advantage of a strategic window, study Porter's Five Forces model as it relates to their business, or consider adopting a first or second mover strategy, all of which are described in Chapter 2.

spreadsheet analysis
Grid that organizes numerical information in a standardized, easily understood format.

In addition to the planning strategies discussed in Chapter 2, marketers are likely to use **spreadsheet analysis**, which lays out a grid of columns and rows that organize numerical information in a standardized, easily understood format. Spreadsheet analysis helps planners answer various "what if" questions related to the firm's financing and operations. The most popular spreadsheet software is Microsoft Excel. A spreadsheet analysis helps planners anticipate marketing performance given specified sets of circumstances. For example, a spreadsheet might project the outcomes of various pricing decisions for a new product, as shown in Figure B.2.

Once general planning strategies are determined, marketers begin to flesh out the details of the marketing strategy. The elements of a marketing strategy include identifying the target market, studying the marketing environment, and creating a marketing mix. When marketers have identified the target market, they can develop the optimal marketing mix to reach their potential customers:

- *Product strategy*. Which goods and services should the company offer to meet its customers' needs?

- *Distribution strategy*. Through which channel(s) and physical facilities will the firm distribute its products?

- *Promotional strategy*. What mix of advertising, sales promotion, and personal selling activities will the firm use to reach its customers initially and then develop long-term relationships?

- *Pricing strategy*. At what level should the company set its prices?

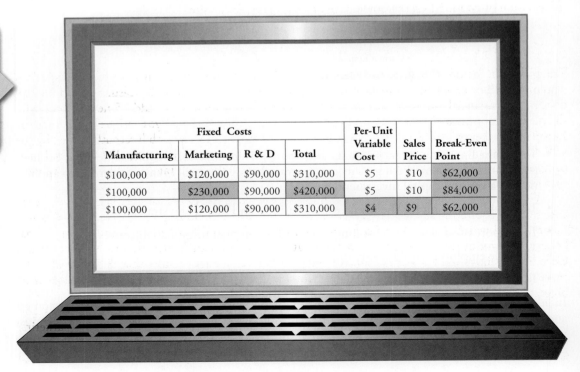

figure B.2
How Spreadsheet Analysis Works

Fixed Costs				Per-Unit Variable Cost	Sales Price	Break-Even Point
Manufacturing	Marketing	R & D	Total			
$100,000	$120,000	$90,000	$310,000	$5	$10	$62,000
$100,000	$230,000	$90,000	$420,000	$5	$10	$84,000
$100,000	$120,000	$90,000	$310,000	$4	$9	$62,000

The Executive Summary, Competitive Analysis, and Mission Statement

Because these three elements of the business plan often reappear in the marketing plan, it is useful to describe them here. Recall that the executive summary answers the *who, what, when, where, how,* and *why* questions for the business. The executive summary for Google includes references to its current strategic planning process for its search services, which involves "developing the perfect search engine . . . [one that] understands exactly what you mean and gives you back exactly what you want."[1] It goes on to answer such questions as who is involved (key people and organizations), what length of time the plan represents, and how the goals will be met.

The competitive analysis focuses on the environment in which the marketing plan is to be implemented. Trenton, New Jersey–based TerraCycle manufactures a wide variety of products, all made from recycled materials. Believing the green movement will eventually hold sway in consumer products, TerraCycle's business goal is to become the leading ecofriendly organic brand in each of the product categories in which it competes. It doesn't attempt to overpower the category leader; instead, it aims to beat other ecofriendly competitors. For example, TerraCycle wants its window cleaner to outsell green competitors Mrs. Meyers and Seventh Generation, but it is less concerned about beating Windex, the category leader.[2]

The mission statement puts into words an organization's overall purpose and reason for being. According to Nintendo's corporate mission, the company is "strongly committed to producing and marketing the best products and support services available." Not only does Nintendo strive to manufacture the highest-quality video products, but it also attempts "to treat every customer with attention, consideration and respect." Nintendo is similarly committed to its employees and believes in treating them "with the same consideration and respect that we, as a company, show our customers."[3]

Description of the Company

Near the beginning of the marketing plan—typically following the executive summary and before the mission statement—a description of the company is included. The company description may include a brief history or background of the firm, the types of products it offers or plans to introduce, recent successes or achievements—in short, it consists of a few paragraphs containing the kind of information often found on the home page of a company's Web site.

Statement of Goals and Core Competencies

The plan then includes a statement of the firm's goals and its core competencies—the things it does extremely well or better than anyone else. The goals should be specific and measurable and may be divided into financial and nonfinancial aims. A financial goal might be to add 75 new franchises in the next 12 months or to reach $10 million in revenues. A nonfinancial goal might be to enter the European market or to add a new product line every other year. An energy bill recently passed by the U.S. Congress mandates growth in the use of ethanol in the United States: by 2022, ethanol consumption must triple. So ethanol producers are setting specific goals to ramp up production to meet that requirement.[4]

Core competencies make a firm stand out from everyone else in the marketplace. Costco's core competency is offering a wide variety of goods at low prices, including unexpected bargains like luxury-brand watches and Dom Perignon champagne. Costco CEO and co-founder Jim Sinegal believes his workforce is a significant differentiator in the company's success, and for that reason, Costco pays above-market wages. The average Costco hourly wage is more than $17—double the current minimum wage in the United States and significantly higher than the hourly wage at its biggest competitor, Walmart.[5]

Small businesses often begin with a single core competency and build their business and reputation on it. It is important for a new firm to identify its core competency in the marketing plan so investors or banks understand why they should lend the firm money to get started or to grow to the next stage. As a college student, David Kim found he enjoyed tutoring children. When he discovered a real demand for skilled tutoring, he decided to launch a tutoring business, which he named C2 Education. Because C2's core competency is helping children to excel, employees are hired and trained according to rigorous standards. Today, C2 Education operates in more than 110 U.S. locations, with annual revenues estimated at more than $50 million.[6]

Outline of the Marketing Environment (Situation Analysis)

Every successful marketing plan considers the marketing environment—the competitive, economic, political-legal, technological, and social-cultural factors that affect the way a firm formulates and implements its marketing strategy. Marketing plans may address these issues in different ways, but the goal is to present information that describes the company's position or situation within the marketing environment. J. Crew, for instance, has a well-known brand name and a CEO with an impressive track record, Mickey Drexler, who previously headed The Gap. The retail environment for stores like J. Crew is highly competitive. Merchandise that doesn't appeal to enough customers ends up on a clearance rack and hurts the bottom line. According to Drexler, the key to J. Crew's success is that it sells merchandise that "cannot be sold anywhere else." Drexler pushes his buyers to "out-product" their competitors.[7] A marketing plan for J. Crew would include an evaluation of competing stores such as The Gap and Urban Outfitters; any technological advances that would affect such factors as merchandise distribution or inventory; social-cultural issues such as fashion preferences and spending habits of customers; and economic issues affecting a pricing strategy.

One such method for outlining the marketing environment in the marketing plan is to include a SWOT analysis, described in Chapter 2. SWOT analysis identifies the firm's strengths, weaknesses, opportunities, and threats within the marketing environment. A SWOT analysis for J. Crew might include strengths such as its corporate leadership, brand name, and upscale target market. Weaknesses might include the risks inherent in the business of correctly spotting fashion trends. A major opportunity lies in the fact that J. Crew can expand almost anywhere. In fact, the company recently acquired Madewell, a retailer that sells hip, casual clothes to an upscale clientele, and expanded the chain to 18 U.S. cities. Threats for Madewell could include competition from other trendy stores, sudden changes in customer preferences, and financial crises that affect spending.[8] A SWOT analysis can be presented in chart format so that it is easy to read as part of the marketing plan. The sample marketing plan in this appendix includes a SWOT analysis for Blue Sky Clothing.

The Target Market and Marketing Mix

The marketing plan identifies the target market for the firm's products. In marketing its new Head & Shoulders Hair Endurance for Men, Procter & Gamble targeted males with thinning hair. The reason? The company's research revealed that more than 44 percent of males in the United States who experience hair loss also report dandruff in the months prior to the hair loss. The new shampoo reportedly reduces hair breakage by eliminating dandruff.[9] In another example of targeting, the Cute Overload Web site (www.cuteoverload.com) contains photos and videos of animals that visitors can share and about which they can post comments. But the site also offers a page-a-day desk calendar of the same name featuring images of puppies, kittens, birds, and chipmunks with humorous captions. Cute Overload targets women ages 18 to 34 who need a laugh and a brief escape from the real world. The calendars are also offered for sale on Amazon.com, and the retailer's inventory sold out in one day, which astonished the developer.[10]

The marketing plan also discusses the marketing mix the firm has selected for its products. Hollywood studios are known for implementing lavish strategies for promoting their films. Not only did Columbia Pictures use all the traditional means for launching *The Karate Kid,* a remake of the 1984 hit, it also partnered with other organizations and products to promote the movie. Little Caesars Pizza and PepsiCo co-sponsored a scratch-off game promotion featuring the film. Before the film's debut, Six Flags amusement parks held on-site competitions to identify the most talented karate students. And Apple's recently launched iPad included a free mobile game that promoted the film's opening. *The Karate Kid* raked in $56 million in revenues in its first weekend.[11]

Budget, Schedule, and Monitoring

Every marketing plan requires a budget, a time schedule for implementation, and a system for monitoring the plan's success or failure. At age 21, entrepreneur Joe Cirulli of Gainesville, Florida, made a to-do list of ten life goals, which included "Own a health club" and "Make it respected in the community." By age 33, Cirulli had achieved all ten of his life goals, including the opening of his Gainesville Health & Fitness Center. As Cirulli's business grew, however, he discovered a larger mission: to make Gainesville the healthiest community in America. Today, Gainesville is the first and only city to win the Gold Well City award from the Wellness Councils of America, and Cirulli's fitness center is widely regarded as one of the best in the industry. Whether or not he realized it at the time, Cirulli's life and business plan at age 21 had the makings of a marketing plan, with goals and budgets, setting a timeline, and measuring progress—a formula for business success.[12]

Most long-range marketing plans encompass a two- to five-year period, although companies that do business in industries such as auto manufacturing, pharmaceuticals, or lumber may extend their marketing plans further into the future because it typically takes longer to develop these products. However, marketers in most industries will have difficulty making estimates and predictions beyond five years because of the many uncertainties in the marketplace. Firms also may opt to develop short-term plans to cover marketing activities for a single year.

The marketing plan, whether it is long term or short term, predicts how long it will take to achieve the goals set out by the plan. A goal may be opening a certain number of new stores, increasing market share, or achieving an expansion of the product line. Finally, the marketing program is monitored and evaluated for its performance. Monthly, quarterly, and annual sales targets are usually tracked; the efficiency with which certain tasks are completed is determined; customer satisfaction is measured; and so forth. All of these factors contribute to the overall review of the program.

At some point, a firm may implement an *exit strategy*, a plan for the firm to leave the market. A common way for a large company to do this is to sell off a business unit. A number of these strategies have been implemented recently: for example, GMAC Financial Services exited the European mortgage market by selling its UK financial unit, GMAC-RFC, to Fortress Investment Group. The move is expected to help improve GMAC's financial performance.[13]

Another example of an exit strategy involves insurance giant American International Group (AIG). After receiving a $182 billion bailout from the U.S. government, AIG was 80 percent government owned. To begin paying back the loan, AIG sold two of its larger insurance groups, AIA and American Life, for about $50 billion, exiting those markets.[14]

Sample Marketing Plan

The following pages contain an annotated sample marketing plan for Blue Sky Clothing. At some point in your career, you will likely be involved in writing—or at least contributing to—a marketing plan. And you'll certainly read many marketing plans throughout your business career. Keep in mind that the plan for Blue Sky is a single example; no one format is used by all companies. Also, the Blue Sky plan has been somewhat condensed to make it easier to annotate and illustrate the most vital features. The important point to remember is that the marketing plan is a document designed to present concise, cohesive information about a company's marketing objectives to managers, lending institutions, and others involved in creating and carrying out the firm's overall business strategy.

Five-Year Marketing Plan
Blue Sky Clothing, Inc.

Table of Contents

The executive summary outlines the *who, what, where, when, how,* and *why* of the marketing plan. Blue Sky is only three years old and is successful enough that it now needs a formal marketing plan to obtain additional financing from a bank or private investors for expansion and the launch of new products.

Executive Summary

This five-year marketing plan for Blue Sky Clothing has been created by its two founders to secure additional funding for growth and to inform employees of the company's current status and direction. Although Blue Sky was launched only three years ago, the firm has experienced greater-than-anticipated demand for its products, and research has shown that the target market of sports-minded consumers and sports retailers would like to buy more casual clothing than Blue Sky currently offers. As a result, Blue Sky wants to extend its current product line as well as add new product lines. In addition, the firm plans to explore opportunities for online sales. The marketing environment has been very receptive to the firm's high-quality goods—casual clothing in trendy colors with logos and slogans that reflect the interests of outdoor enthusiasts around the country. Over the next five years, Blue Sky can increase its distribution, offer new products, and win new customers.

The company description summarizes the history of Blue Sky—how it was founded and by whom, what its products are, and why they are unique. It begins to "sell" the reader on the growth possibilities for Blue Sky.

Company Description

Blue Sky Clothing was founded three years ago by entrepreneurs Lucy Neuman and Nick Russell. Neuman has an undergraduate degree in marketing and worked for several years in the retail clothing industry. Russell operated an adventure business called Go West!, which arranges group trips to locations in Wyoming, Montana, and Idaho, before selling the enterprise to a partner. Neuman and Russell, who have been friends since college, decided to develop and market a line of clothing with a unique—yet universal—appeal to outdoor enthusiasts.

Blue Sky Clothing reflects Neuman's and Russell's passion for the outdoors. The company's original cotton T-shirts, baseball caps, and fleece jackets and vests bear logos of different sports, such as kayaking, mountain climbing, bicycling, skating, surfing, and horseback riding. But every item shows off the company's slogan: "Go Play Outside." Blue Sky sells clothing for both men and women, in the hottest colors with the coolest names—sunrise pink, sunset red, twilight purple, desert rose, cactus green, ocean blue, mountaintop white, and river rock gray.

Blue Sky attire is currently carried by small retail stores that specialize in outdoor clothing and gear. Most of these stores are concentrated in northern New England, California, the Northwest, and the South. The high quality, trendy colors, and unique message of the clothing have gained Blue Sky a following among consumers between ages 25 and 45. Sales have tripled in the last year alone, and Blue Sky is currently working to expand its manufacturing capabilities.

Blue Sky is also committed to giving back to the community by contributing to local conservation programs. Ultimately, the company would like to develop and fund its own environmental programs. This plan will outline how Blue Sky intends to introduce new products, expand its distribution, enter new markets, and give back to the community.

It is important to state a firm's mission and goals, including financial and nonfinancial goals. Blue Sky's goals include growth and profits for the company as well as the ability to contribute to society through conservation programs.

Blue Sky's Mission and Goals

Blue Sky's mission is to be a leading producer and marketer of personalized, casual clothing for consumers who love the outdoors. Blue Sky wants to inspire people to get outdoors more often and enjoy family and friends while doing so. In addition, Blue Sky strives to design programs for preserving the natural environment.

During the next five years, Blue Sky seeks to achieve the following financial and nonfinancial goals:

Financial goals

1. Obtain financing to expand manufacturing capabilities, increase distribution, and introduce two new product lines

2. Increase revenues by at least 50 percent each year

3. Donate at least $25,000 a year to conservation organizations

Nonfinancial goals

4. Introduce two new product lines—customized logo clothing and lightweight luggage

5. Enter new geographic markets, including southwestern and mid-Atlantic states

6. Develop a successful Internet site, while maintaining strong relationships with retailers

7. Develop its own conservation program aimed at helping communities raise money to purchase open space

Core Competencies

Blue Sky seeks to use its core competencies to achieve a sustainable competitive advantage, in which competitors cannot provide the same value to consumers that Blue Sky does. Already Blue Sky has developed core competencies in (1) offering a high-quality, branded product whose image is recognizable among consumers; (2) creating a sense of community among consumers who purchase the products; and (3) developing a reputation among retailers as a reliable manufacturer, delivering their orders on schedule. The firm intends to build on these competencies through marketing efforts that increase the number of products offered as well as distribution outlets.

By forming strong relationships with consumers, retailers, and suppliers of fabric and other goods and services, Blue Sky believes it can create a sustainable competitive advantage over its rivals. No other clothing company can say to its customers with as much conviction, "Go Play Outside"!

Situation Analysis

The marketing environment for Blue Sky represents overwhelming opportunities. It also contains some challenges the firm believes it can meet successfully. Table A illustrates a SWOT analysis of the company conducted by its marketers to highlight Blue Sky's strengths, weaknesses, opportunities, and threats.

The SWOT analysis presents a thumbnail sketch of the company's position in the marketplace. In just three years, Blue Sky has built some impressive strengths while looking forward to new opportunities. Its dedicated founders, the growing number of brand-loyal customers, and sound financial management place the company in a good position to grow. However, as Blue Sky considers expansion of its product line and entry into new markets, the firm will have to guard against marketing myopia (the failure to recognize the scope of its business) and quality slippages. As the company finalizes plans for new products and expanded Internet sales, its management will also have to guard against competitors who attempt to duplicate the products. However, building strong relationships with consumers, retailers, and suppliers should help thwart competitors.

This section reminds employees and those outside the company (such as potential lenders) exactly what Blue Sky does so well and how it plans to achieve a sustainable competitive advantage over rivals. Note here and throughout the plan: Blue Sky focuses on relationships.

The situation analysis provides an outline of the marketing environment. A SWOT analysis helps marketers and others identify clearly a firm's strengths, weaknesses, opportunities, and threats. Again, relationships are a focus. Blue Sky has also conducted research on the outdoor clothing market, competitors, and consumers to determine how best to attract and keep customers.

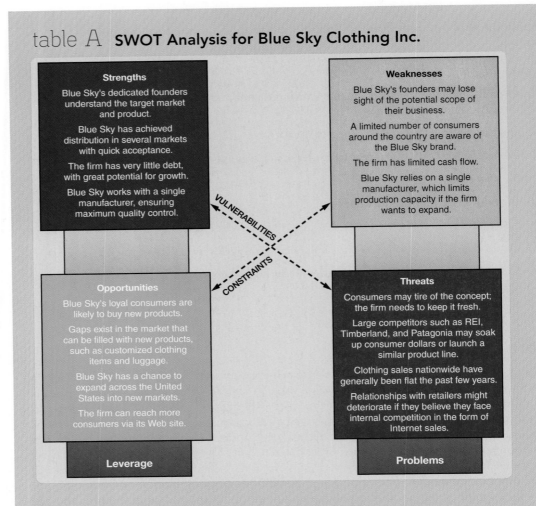

table A   SWOT Analysis for Blue Sky Clothing Inc.

Strengths

Blue Sky's dedicated founders understand the target market and product.

Blue Sky has achieved distribution in several markets with quick acceptance.

The firm has very little debt, with great potential for growth.

Blue Sky works with a single manufacturer, ensuring maximum quality control.

Weaknesses

Blue Sky's founders may lose sight of the potential scope of their business.

A limited number of consumers around the country are aware of the Blue Sky brand.

The firm has limited cash flow.

Blue Sky relies on a single manufacturer, which limits production capacity if the firm wants to expand.

VULNERABILITIES

CONSTRAINTS

Opportunities

Blue Sky's loyal consumers are likely to buy new products.

Gaps exist in the market that can be filled with new products, such as customized clothing items and luggage.

Blue Sky has a chance to expand across the United States into new markets.

The firm can reach more consumers via its Web site.

Threats

Consumers may tire of the concept; the firm needs to keep it fresh.

Large competitors such as REI, Timberland, and Patagonia may soak up consumer dollars or launch a similar product line.

Clothing sales nationwide have generally been flat the past few years.

Relationships with retailers might deteriorate if they believe they face internal competition in the form of Internet sales.

Leverage

Problems

Competitors in the Outdoor Clothing Market

The outdoor retail sales industry sells about $5 billion worth of goods annually, ranging from clothing to equipment. The outdoor apparel market has many entries. L.L. Bean, Dick's Sporting Goods, REI, Timberland, Bass Pro Shops, Cabela's, The North Face, and Patagonia are among the most recognizable companies offering these products. Smaller competitors such as Title IX, which offers athletic clothing for women, and Ragged Mountain, which sells fleece clothing for skiers and hikers, also capture some of the market. The outlook for the industry in general—and Blue Sky in particular—is positive for several reasons. First, consumers are participating in and investing in recreational activities near their homes. Second, consumers are looking for ways to enjoy their leisure time with friends and family without overspending. Third, consumers tend to be advancing in their careers and are able to spend more.

While all of the companies listed earlier can be considered competitors, none offers the kind of trendy, yet practical products provided by Blue Sky—and none carries the customized logos and slogans that Blue Sky plans to offer in the near future. In addition, most of these competitors sell performance apparel in high-tech manufactured fabrics. With the exception of the fleece vests and jackets, Blue Sky's clothing is made of strictly the highest-quality cotton, so it may be worn both on the hiking trail and around town. Finally, Blue Sky products are offered at moderate prices, making them affordable in multiple quantities. For instance, a Blue Sky T-shirt sells for $15.99, compared with a competing high-performance T-shirt that sells for $29.99. Consumers can easily replace a set of shirts from one season to the next, picking up the newest colors, without agonizing over the purchase.

A survey conducted by Blue Sky revealed that 67 percent of responding consumers prefer to replace their casual and active wear more often than other clothing, so they are attracted by the moderate pricing of Blue Sky products. In addition, as the trend toward health-conscious activities and concerns about the natural environment continue, consumers increasingly relate to the Blue Sky philosophy as well as the firm's future contributions to socially responsible programs.

The Target Market

The target market for Blue Sky products is active consumers between ages 25 and 45—people who like to hike, rock climb, bicycle, surf, figure skate, in-line skate, ride horses, snowboard or ski, kayak, and other such activities. In short, they like to "Go Play Outside." They might not be experts at the sports they engage in, but they enjoy themselves outdoors.

These active consumers represent a demographic group of well-educated and successful individuals; they are single or married and raising families. Household incomes generally range between $60,000 and $120,000 annually. Despite their comfortable incomes, these consumers are price conscious and consistently seek value in their purchases. Regardless of their age (whether they fall at the upper or lower end of the target range), they lead active lifestyles. They are somewhat status oriented but not overly so. They like to be associated with high-quality products but are not willing to pay a premium price for a certain brand. Current Blue Sky customers tend to live in northern New England, the South, California, and the Northwest. However, one future goal is to target consumers in the Mid-Atlantic states and Southwest as well.

> Blue Sky has identified its customers as active people between ages 25 and 45. However, that doesn't mean someone who is older or prefers to read about the outdoors isn't a potential customer as well. By pinpointing where existing customers live, Blue Sky can plan for growth into new outlets.

The Marketing Mix

The following discussion outlines some of the details of the proposed marketing mix for Blue Sky products.

PRODUCT STRATEGY

Blue Sky currently offers a line of high-quality outdoor apparel items including cotton T-shirts, baseball caps, and fleece vests and jackets. All bear the company logo and slogan, "Go Play Outside." The firm has researched the most popular colors for its items and given them names that consumers enjoy—sunset red, sunrise pink, cactus green, desert rose, and river rock gray, among others. Over the next five years, Blue Sky plans to expand the product line to include customized clothing items. Customers may select a logo that represents their sport, say, rock climbing. Then they can add a slogan to match the logo, such as "Get Over It." A baseball cap with a bicyclist might bear the slogan, "Take a Ride." At the beginning, there would be ten new logos and five new slogans; more would be added later. Eventually, some slogans and logos would be retired, and new ones introduced. This strategy will keep the concept fresh and prevent it from becoming diluted with too many variations.

The second way in which Blue Sky plans to expand its product line is to offer items of lightweight luggage—two sizes of duffel bags, two sizes of tote bags, and a daypack. These items would also come in trendy and basic colors, with a choice of logos and slogans. In addition, every product would bear the Blue Sky logo.

> The strongest part of the marketing mix for Blue Sky involves sales promotions, public relations, and nontraditional marketing strategies such as attending outdoor events and organizing activities such as day hikes and bike rides.

DISTRIBUTION STRATEGY

Currently, Blue Sky is marketed through regional and local specialty shops scattered along the California coast, into the Northwest, across the South, and in northern New England. So far, Blue Sky has not been distributed through national sporting goods and apparel chains. Climate and season tend to dictate the sales at specialty shops, which sell more T-shirts and baseball caps during warm weather and more fleece vests and jackets during colder months. Blue Sky obtains much of its information about overall industry trends in different geographic areas and at different types of retail outlets from its trade organization, Outdoor Industry Association.

Over the next three years, Blue Sky seeks to expand distribution to retail specialty shops throughout the nation, focusing next on the Southwest and mid-Atlantic regions. The firm has not yet determined whether it would be beneficial to sell through a major national chain, as these outlets could be considered competitors.

In addition, Blue Sky plans to expand online sales by offering the customized product line via the Internet only, thus distinguishing between Internet offerings and specialty shop offerings. Eventually, the firm may be able to place Internet kiosks at some of the more profitable store outlets so consumers could order customized products from the stores. Regardless of its expansion plans, Blue Sky fully intends to monitor and maintain strong relationships with distribution channel members.

PROMOTION STRATEGY

Blue Sky communicates with consumers and retailers about its products in a variety of ways. Information about Blue Sky—the company as well as its products—is available via the Internet, through direct mailings, and in person. The firm's promotional efforts also seek to differentiate its products from those of its competitors.

The company relies on personal contact with retailers to establish the products in their stores. This contact, whether in person or by phone, helps convey the Blue Sky message, demonstrate the products' unique qualities, and build relationships. Blue Sky sales representatives visit each store two or three times a year and offer in-store training on the features of the products for new retailers or for those who want a refresher session. As distribution expands, Blue Sky will adjust to meet greater demand by increasing sales staff to make sure its stores are visited more frequently.

Sales promotions and public relations currently make up the bulk of Blue Sky's promotional strategy. Blue Sky staff works with retailers to offer short-term sales promotions tied to events and contests. In addition, Nick Russell is currently working with several trip outfitters to offer Blue Sky items on a promotional basis. Because Blue Sky also engages in cause marketing through its contribution to environmental programs, good public relations have followed.

Nontraditional marketing methods that require little cash and a lot of creativity also lend themselves perfectly to Blue Sky. Because Blue Sky is a small, flexible organization, the firm can easily implement ideas, such as distributing free water, stickers, and discount coupons at outdoor sporting events. During the next year, the company plans to engage in the following marketing efforts:

- Create a Blue Sky Tour, in which several employees take turns driving around the country to campgrounds to distribute promotional items, such as Blue Sky stickers and discount coupons.

- Attend canoe and kayak races, bicycling events, and rock climbing competitions with our Blue Sky truck to distribute free water, stickers, and discount coupons for Blue Sky shirts or hats.

- Organize Blue Sky hikes departing from participating retailers.
- Hold a Blue Sky design contest, selecting a winning slogan and logo to be added to the customized line.

PRICING STRATEGY

As discussed earlier in this plan, Blue Sky products are priced with the competition in mind. The firm is not concerned with setting high prices to signal luxury or prestige, nor is it attempting to achieve the goals of offsetting low prices by selling large quantities of products. Instead, value pricing is practiced so customers feel comfortable purchasing new clothing to replace the old, even if it is just because they like the new colors. The pricing strategy also makes Blue Sky products good gifts—for birthdays, graduations, or "just because." The customized clothing will sell for $2 to $4 more than the regular Blue Sky logo clothing. The luggage will be priced competitively, offering a good value against its competition.

Budget, Schedule, and Monitoring

Though its history is short, Blue Sky has enjoyed a steady increase in sales since its introduction three years ago. Figure A shows these three years, plus projected sales for the next three years, including the introduction of the two new product lines. Additional financial data are included in the overall business plan for the company.

The timeline for expansion of outlets and introduction of the two new product lines is shown in Figure B. The implementation of each of these tasks will be monitored closely and evaluated for its performance.

An actual plan will include more specific financial details, which will be folded into the overall business plan. For more information, see Appendix C, "Financial Analysis in Marketing." In addition, Blue Sky states that at this stage, it does not have plans to exit the market by merging with another firm or making a public stock offering.

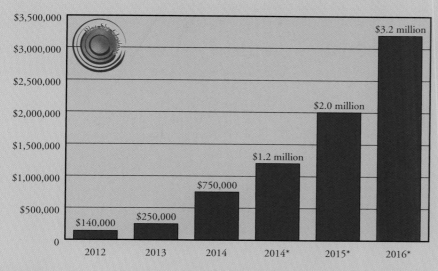

*Projected sales

figure A
Annual Sales for Blue Sky Clothing: 2012–2016

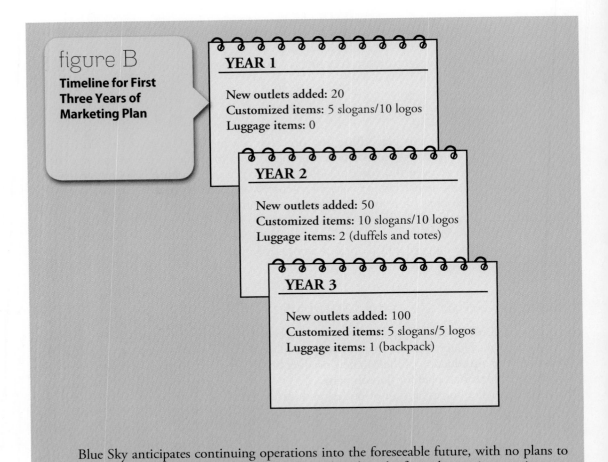

figure B
**Timeline for First
Three Years of
Marketing Plan**

YEAR 1

New outlets added: 20
Customized items: 5 slogans/10 logos
Luggage items: 0

YEAR 2

New outlets added: 50
Customized items: 10 slogans/10 logos
Luggage items: 2 (duffels and totes)

YEAR 3

New outlets added: 100
Customized items: 5 slogans/5 logos
Luggage items: 1 (backpack)

Blue Sky anticipates continuing operations into the foreseeable future, with no plans to exit this market. Instead, as discussed throughout this plan, the firm plans to increase its presence in the market. At present, there are no plans to merge with another company or to make a public stock offering.

Financial Analysis in Marketing

A number of basic concepts from accounting and finance offer invaluable tools to marketers. Understanding the contributions made by these concepts can improve the quality of marketing decisions. In addition, marketers often must be able to explain and defend their decisions in

financial terms. These accounting and financial tools can be used to supply quantitative data to justify decisions made by marketing managers. In this appendix, we describe the major accounting and finance concepts that have marketing implications and explain how they help managers make informed marketing decisions.

Financial Statements

All companies prepare a set of financial statements on a regular basis. Two of the most important financial statements are the income statement and balance sheet. The analogy of a movie often is used to describe an *income statement* because it presents a financial record of a company's revenues, expenses, and profits over a period of time, such as a month, quarter, or year. By contrast, the *balance sheet* is a snapshot of what a company owns (called *assets*) and what it owes (called *liabilities*) at a point in time, such as at the end of the month, quarter, or year. The difference between assets and liabilities is referred to as *owner's, partners', or shareholders' equity*—the amount of funds the firm's owners have invested in its formation and continued operations. Of the two financial statements, the income statement contains more marketing-related information.

A sample income statement for Composite Technology is shown in Figure C.1. Headquartered in a Boston suburb, Composite Technology is a B2B producer and marketer. The firm designs and manufactures a variety of composite components for manufacturers of consumer, industrial, and government products. Total sales revenues for 2012 amounted to $675.0 million. Total expenses, including taxes, for the year were $583.1 million. The year 2012 proved profitable for Composite Technology—the firm reported a profit, referred to as net income, of $91.9 million. While total revenue is a fairly straightforward number, several of the expenses shown on the income statement require additional explanation.

For any company that makes its own products (a manufacturer) or simply markets one or more items produced by others (an importer, retailer, or wholesaler), the largest single expense usually is a category called *cost of goods sold*. This reflects the cost, to the firm, of the goods it markets to its customers. In the case of Composite Technology, the cost of goods sold represents the cost of

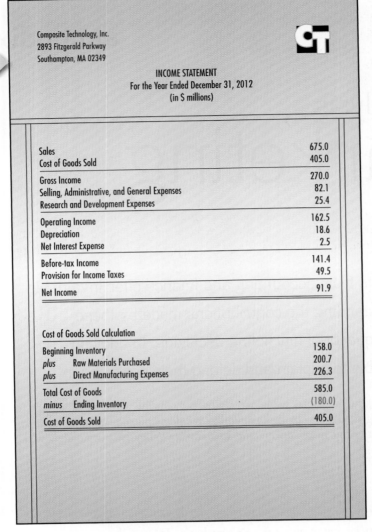

figure C.1

Composite Technology 2012 Income Statement

Composite Technology, Inc.
2893 Fitzgerald Parkway
Southampton, MA 02349

INCOME STATEMENT
For the Year Ended December 31, 2012
(in $ millions)

Sales	675.0
Cost of Goods Sold	405.0
Gross Income	270.0
Selling, Administrative, and General Expenses	82.1
Research and Development Expenses	25.4
Operating Income	162.5
Depreciation	18.6
Net Interest Expense	2.5
Before-tax Income	141.4
Provision for Income Taxes	49.5
Net Income	91.9

Cost of Goods Sold Calculation

Beginning Inventory		158.0
plus	Raw Materials Purchased	200.7
plus	Direct Manufacturing Expenses	226.3
Total Cost of Goods		585.0
minus	Ending Inventory	(180.0)
Cost of Goods Sold		405.0

components and raw materials as well as the cost of designing and manufacturing the composite panels the firm produces and markets to its business customers.

The income statement illustrates how cost of goods sold is calculated. The calculation begins with the value of the firm's inventory at the beginning of 2012. Inventory is the value of raw materials, partially completed products, and finished products held by the firm at the end of some time period, say the end of the year. The cost of materials Composite Technology purchased during the year and the direct cost of manufacturing the finished products are then added to the beginning inventory figure. The result is the cost of goods the firm has available for sale during the year. Once the firm's accountants subtract the value of inventory held by the firm at the end of 2012, they know the cost of goods sold. By simply subtracting cost of goods sold from total sales revenues generated during the year, they determine that Composite achieved gross profits of $270.0 million in 2012.

Operating expenses are another significant cost for most firms. This broad category includes such marketing outlays as sales compensation and expenses, advertising and other promotions, and the expenses involved in implementing marketing plans. Accountants typically combine these financial outlays into a single category with the label *Selling, Administrative, and General Expenses*. Other expense items included in the operating expenses section of the income statement are administrative salaries, utilities, and insurance.

Another significant expense for Composite Technology is research and development (R&D). This category includes the cost of developing new products and modifying existing ones. Firms such as pharmaceuticals, biotechnology, and computer companies spend significant amounts of money each year on R&D. Subtracting selling, administrative, and general expenses and R&D expenses from the gross profit equals the firm's operating income. For 2012, Composite had operating income of $162.5 million.

Depreciation represents the systematic reduction over time in the value of certain company assets, such as production machinery, office furniture, or laptops provided for the firm's sales representatives. Depreciation is an unusual expense because it does not involve an actual cash expense. However, it does reflect the reality that equipment owned by the company is physically wearing out over time from use and/or from technological obsolescence. Also, charging a portion of the total cost of these long-lived items to each of the years in which they are used results in a more accurate determination of the total costs involved in the firm's operation each year.

Net interest expense is the difference between what a firm paid in interest on various loans and what it collected in interest on investments it might have made during the time period involved.

Subtracting depreciation and net interest expense from the firm's operating profit reveals the firm's taxable income. Composite had depreciation of $18.6 million and a net interest expense of $2.5 million for the year, so its 2012 taxable income was $141.4 million.

Profit-seeking firms pay taxes calculated as a percentage of their taxable income to the federal government as well as state income taxes in most states. Composite paid $49.5 million in taxes in 2012. Subtracting taxes from taxable income gives us the firm's *net income*, $91.9 million.

Performance Ratios

Managers often compute a variety of financial ratios to assess the performance of their firm. These ratios are calculated using data found on both the income statement and the balance sheet. Ratios are then compared with industry standards and with data from previous years. Several ratios are of particular interest to marketers.

A number of commonly used financial ratios focus on *profitability measures.* They are used to assess the firm's ability to generate revenues in excess of expenses and earn an adequate rate of return. Profitability measures include gross profit margin, net profit margin, and return on investment (or sales).

GROSS PROFIT MARGIN

The gross profit margin equals the firm's gross profit divided by its sales revenues. In 2012, Composite had a gross profit margin of

$$\frac{\text{Gross profit}}{\text{Sales}} = \frac{\$270.0 \text{ million}}{\$675.0 \text{ million}} = 40\%$$

The gross profit margin is the percentage of each sales dollar that can be used to pay other expenses and meet the firm's profit objectives. Ideally, businesses would like to see gross profit margins equal to or higher than those of other firms in their industry. A declining gross profit margin may indicate the firm is under some competitive price pressure.

NET PROFIT MARGIN

The net profit margin equals net income divided by sales. For 2012, Composite had a net profit margin of

$$\frac{\text{Net income}}{\text{Sales}} = \frac{\$91.9 \text{ million}}{\$675.0 \text{ million}} = 13.6\%$$

The net profit margin is the percentage of each sales dollar the firm earns in profit or keeps after all expenses have been paid. Companies generally want to see rising, or at least stable, net profit margins.

RETURN ON ASSETS (ROA)

A third profitability ratio, return on assets, measures the firm's efficiency in generating sales and profits from the total amount invested in the company. For 2012, Composite's ROA is calculated as follows:

$$\frac{\text{Sales}}{\text{Average assets}} \times \frac{\text{Net income}}{\text{Sales}} = \frac{\text{Net income}}{\text{Average assets}}$$

$$\frac{\$675.0 \text{ million}}{\$595.0 \text{ million}} \times \frac{\$91.9 \text{ million}}{\$675.0 \text{ million}} = 1.13 \times 13.6\% = 15.4\%$$

The ROA ratio actually consists of two components. The first component, *asset turnover,* is the amount of sales generated for each dollar invested. The second component is *net profit margin.* Data for total assets are found on the firm's balance sheet.

Assume Composite began 2012 with $560 million in assets and ended the year with $630 million in assets. Its average assets for the year would be $595 million. As in the other profitability ratios, Composite's ROI should be compared with other firms in the industry and with its own previous performance to be meaningful.

INVENTORY TURNOVER

Inventory turnover typically is categorized as an activity ratio because it evaluates the effectiveness of the firm's resource use. Specifically, it measures the number of times a firm "turns" its inventory each year. The ratio can help answer the question of whether the firm has the appropriate level of inventory. Inventory turnover equals sales divided by average inventory. From the income statement, we see Composite Technology began 2012 with $158 million in inventory and ended the year with $180 million in inventory. Therefore, the firm's average inventory was $169 million. The firm's inventory turnover ratio equals:

$$\frac{\text{Sales}}{\text{Average inventory}} = \frac{\$675.0 \text{ million}}{\$169.0 \text{ million}} = 3.99$$

For 2012, Composite Technology turned its inventory almost four times a year. While a faster inventory turn usually is a sign of greater efficiency, to be really meaningful the inventory turnover ratio must be compared with historical data and appropriate peer firm averages. Different organizations can have very different inventory turnover ratios, depending on the types of products they sell. For instance, a supermarket might turn its inventory every three weeks for an annual rate of roughly 16 times per year. By contrast, a large furniture retailer is likely to average only about two turns per year. Again, the determination of a "good" or "inadequate" inventory turnover rate depends on typical rates in the industry and the firm's performance in previous years.

ACCOUNTS RECEIVABLE TURNOVER

Another activity ratio that may be of interest to marketers is accounts receivable turnover. This ratio measures the number of times per year a company "turns" its receivables. Dividing accounts receivable turnover into 365 gives us the average age of the company's receivables.

Companies make sales on the basis of either cash or credit. Credit sales allow the buyer to obtain a product now and pay for it at a specified later date. In essence, the seller is providing credit to the buyer. Credit sales are common in B2B transactions. It should be noted that sales to buyers using credit cards like MasterCard and Visa are counted as cash sales because the issuer of the credit card, rather than the seller, is providing credit to the buyer. Consequently, most B2C sales are counted as cash sales.

Receivables are uncollected credit sales. Measuring accounts receivable turnover and the average age of receivables are important for firms in which credit sales make up a high proportion of total sales. Accounts receivable turnover is defined as follows:

$$\text{Accounts receivable turnover} = \frac{\text{Credit sales}}{\text{Average accounts receivable}}$$

Assume all of Composite Technology's sales are credit sales. Also assume the firm began 2012 with $50 million in receivables and ended the year with $60 million in receivables (both numbers can be found on the balance sheet). Therefore, it had an average of $55 million in receivables. The firm's receivables turnover and average age equal:

$$\frac{\$675.0 \text{ million}}{\$55.0 \text{ million}} = 12.3 \text{ times}$$

$$\frac{365}{12.3} = 29.7 \text{ days}$$

Composite turned its receivables slightly more than 12 times per year. The average age of its receivables was slightly less than 30 days. Because Composite expects its customers to pay outstanding invoices within 30 days, these numbers appear appropriate. As with other ratios, however, receivables turnover and average age of receivables should also be compared with peer firms and historical data.

Markups and Markdowns

The importance of pricing decisions was discussed earlier. This section expands on the prior comments by introducing two important pricing concepts: markups and markdowns. They can help establish selling prices and evaluate various pricing strategies, and they are closely tied to a firm's income statement.

MARKUPS

The amount a marketer adds to a product's cost to set the final selling price is the markup. The amount of the markup typically results from two marketing decisions:

1. The services performed by the marketer. Other things being equal, retailers who offer more services charge larger markups to cover their costs.

2. The inventory turnover rate. Other things being equal, retailers with a higher turnover rate can cover their costs and earn a profit while charging a smaller markup.

A marketer's markup exerts an important influence on its image among present and potential customers. In addition, the markup affects the retailer's ability to attract shoppers. An excessive markup may drive away customers; an inadequate markup may fail to generate sufficient income to cover costs and return a profit.

Markups typically are stated as percentages of either the selling prices or the costs of the products. The formulas for calculating markups are as follows:

$$\text{Markup percentage of selling price} = \frac{\text{Amount added to cost (markup)}}{\text{Selling price}}$$

$$\text{Markup percentage on cost} = \frac{\text{Amount added to cost (markup)}}{\text{Cost}}$$

Consider a product with an invoice of 60 cents and a selling price of $1. The total markup (selling price less cost) is 40 cents. The two markup percentages are calculated as follows:

$$\text{Markup percentage on selling price} = \frac{\$0.40}{\$1.00} = 40\%$$

$$\text{Markup percentage on cost} = \frac{\$0.40}{\$0.60} = 66.7\%$$

To determine the selling price knowing only the cost and markup percentage on selling price, a marketer applies the following formula:

$$\text{Price} = \frac{\text{Cost in dollars}}{(100\% - \text{Markup percentage on selling price})}$$

In the previous example, to determine the correct selling price of $1, the marketer would calculate as follows:

$$\text{Price} = \frac{\$0.60}{(100\% - 40\%)} = \$1.00$$

Similarly, you can convert the markup percentage from a specific item based on the selling price to one based on cost and the reverse using the following formulas:

$$\text{Markup percentage on selling price} = \frac{\text{Markup percentage on cost}}{(100\% + \text{Markup percentage on cost})}$$

$$\text{Markup percentage on cost} = \frac{\text{Markup percentage on selling price}}{(100\% - \text{Markup percentage on selling price})}$$

Again, data from the previous example give the following conversions:

$$\text{Markup percentage on selling price} = \frac{66.7\%}{(100\% + 66.7\%)} = 40\%$$

$$\text{Markup percentage on cost} = \frac{40\%}{(100\% - 40\%)} = 66.7\%$$

Marketers determine markups based partly on their judgments of the amounts consumers will pay for a given product. When buyers refuse to pay a product's stated price, however, or when improvements in other products or fashion changes reduce the appeal of the current merchandise, a producer or retailer must take a markdown.

MARKDOWNS

A markdown is a price reduction a firm makes on an item. Reasons for markdowns include sales promotions featuring price reductions or a decision that the initial price was too high. Unlike markups, markdowns cannot be determined from the income statement because the price reduction takes place before the sale occurs. The markdown percentage equals dollar markdowns divided by sales. For example, a retailer may decide to reduce the price of an item by $10, from $50 to $40, and sells 1,000 units. The markdown percentage equals:

$$\frac{(1{,}000 \times \$10)}{(1{,}000 \times \$40)} = \frac{\$10{,}000}{\$40{,}000} = 25\%$$

Chapter 1

1. Company Web site, investors.walmartstores.com, accessed February 23, 2010; Barbara Farfan, "U.S. Green Retailing: Will Wal-Mart Profit from Sustainability Labeling," *About.com*, retailindustry.about.com, accessed February 10, 2010; Kate Rockwood, "Attention, Walmart Shoppers: Clean-up in Aisle Nine," *Fast Company*, February 2010, pp. 30, 32; Catherine Greener, "Quality Expert Says Walmart's Sustainability Journey Is the Real Deal," *GreenBiz.com*, www.greenbiz.com, July 16, 2009; Marc Gunther, "Wal-Mart to Become Green Umpire," *The Big Money*, www.thebigmoney.com, July 13, 2009.

2. Roy Furchgott, "AT&T and Apple Allow Cheap VoIP Calls on 3G," *The New York Times*, www.nytimes.com, January 28, 2010.

3. Vince Knightley, "Electronic Reading Devices Reviews—3 Different Ebook Readers to Compare Before You Buy," *Artipot*, artipot.com, January 2, 2010.

4. Eileen Reslen, "BU Chosen to Host Video Game Kiosk," *The Daily Free Press*, www.dailyfreepress.com, April 2, 2009.

5. Mark Anderson, "A New Spin on an Old Toy," *IEEE Spectrum*, spectrum.ieee.org, November 2009.

6. Joseph P. Guiltinan and Gordon W. Paul, *Marketing Management*, 6th ed., (New York: McGraw-Hill), 1996, pp. 3–4.

7. American Marketing Association, "Resource Library," www.marketingpower.com, accessed February 5, 2010.

8. Bill Saporito, "Airline Baggage Charges: It's Customer Abuse," *Time*, www.time.com, January 13, 2010.

9. "Automobiles and Trucks Overview," Plunkett Research, Ltd., www.plunkettresearch.com, accessed February 5, 2010.

10. U.S. Census Bureau, Foreign Trade Statistics, www.census.gov, accessed February 5, 2010.

11. Emily-Sue Sloane, "U.S. Manufacturing Slides in Cost-Competitiveness Study," *Managing Automation*, www.managingautomation.com, February 3, 2010.

12. Jack Ewing, "Telecom's Last Great Growth Markets," *BusinessWeek*, May 22, 2008, www.businessweek.com.

13. Steve Lohr, "Steve Jobs and the Economics of Elitism," *The New York Times*, www.nytimes.com, January 29, 2010.

14. Gregory Polek, "UAL Finalizes Boeing 787 Order," *AINonline*, www.ainonline.com, February 25, 2010; Boeing Web site, "Boeing 787 Dreamliner Will Provide New Solutions for Airlines, Passengers," www.boeing.com, accessed March 3, 2010.

15. "Wirefly's Top 10 Best Selling Phones of '09 and Wireless Trends '10," *Wirefly*, www.wirefly.com, January 26, 2010.

16. Brennon Slattery, "Apple's Future Is in Solar-Powered Devices," *PC World*, www.pcworld.com, January 22, 2010.

17. Catherine Rampell, "Volunteer Rate Budged in 2009," *The New York Times*, www.nytimes.com, January 27, 2010.

18. Organization Web site, www.connerprairie.org, accessed February 20, 2010.

19. Company press release, "Target House Celebrates 10 Years with a Celebrity-Studded Big Top Party," pressroom.target.com, September 14, 2009.

20. Organization Web site, feedingamerica.org, accessed February 4, 2010.

21. Blake Ellis, "Haiti Donations Exceed $220 Million," *CNNMoney.com*, money.cnn.com, January 19, 2010.

22. Rafe Needleman, "Piryz Raises Money for Your Cause," *CNET News*, news.cnet.com, September 22, 2009.

23. "Cause Awareness Calls for Promo Products," Virgo Publishing, www.corporatelogo.com, October 13, 2009.

24. Elena Malykhina, "Michael Phelps in Subway Return," *Adweek*, www.adweek.com, December 29, 2009; "Manning Brothers and 'Double Trump' Face-off for the Future of the Oreo Double Stuf Racing League," *Market Watch*, www.marketwatch.com, January 12, 2010; press release, "GreenLight Ad Grammys Finds . . ." *Shoot Publicity Wire*, www.shootonline.com, February 4, 2010; "Burger King Puts Celebrity Endorsement to the Test, *Adweek*, www.adweek.com, September 8, 2009; Barry Janoff, "Eli Manning Already Scoring off MVP Showing," *BrandWeek*, February 6, 2008, www.brandweek.com; Tim Arango, "Top 10 Endorsement Superstars," *Fortune*, November 2007, money.cnn.com, accessed September 29, 2008; Tim Arango, "LeBron Inc.," *Fortune*, November 28, 2007, money.cnn.com, accessed September 29, 2008; Sarah Jane Gilbert, "Marketing Maria: Managing the Athlete Endorsement," *Working Knowledge* (Harvard Business School), October 29, 2007, www.hbswk.hbs.edu.

25. Neal Karlinsky and Eloise Harper, "Law Vegas Gambles on $8.5 Billion CityCenter," *ABC News*, abcnews.com, December 16, 2009.

26. Dennis J. Carroll, "Spaceport America Pushes Legislation Protecting Space Travel Firms from Lawsuits," *The New Mexican*, www.santafenewmexican.com, January 31, 2010.

27. Organization Web site, industry.exploreminnesota.com, accessed February 6, 2010.

28. T. K. Moyer, "Timberline Ski Resort in West Virginia: A Review," *Associated Content*, www.associatedcontent.com, accessed February 5, 2010; "Skiing at Davis, West Virginia's Timberline Resort," *Ski NC*, www.skinorthcarolina.com, accessed May 30, 2008.

29. "Staples/Do Something 101 National School Supply Drive Raises More than $750,000 for Underserved Youth," *Money*, news.moneycentral.msn.com, September 22, 2009.

30. Emily Fredrix, "Super Bowl Ad Prices Drop But Still Cost Millions," *The Detroit News*, detnews.com, January 12, 2010.

31. Thomas Alan Gray, "Official Suppliers at Vancouver 2010," *Marketing PR*, marketingpr.suite101.com, September 30, 2009.

32. Press release, "The Collegiate Licensing Company Names Top Selling Universities and Manufacturers," www.clc.com, November 11, 2009.

33. John H. Ostdick, "Embracing Social Media," *Success*, March 2010, pp. 65–69.

34. Spencer E. Ante, "The Real Value of Tweets," *Bloomberg Businessweek*, January 18, 2010, p. 31.

35. John Moore, "Four Big Ideas Influencing Marketing in 2010," *Promo*, www.promomagazine.com, December 17, 2009.

36. Ostdick, "Embracing Social Media."

37. Jefferson Graham, "Cake Decorator Finds Twitter a Tweet Recipe for Success," *USA Today*, April 1, 2009, p. 5B.

38. Ostdick, "Embracing Social Media."

39. Moore, "Four Big Ideas."

40. Peter J. Schwartz, "Hook 'Em Horns," *Forbes*, January 18, 2010, p. 51.

41. Organization Web site, Susan G. Komen for the Cure, ww5.komen.org, accessed February 5, 2010.

42. Geoff Colvin, "Interview with Linda Fisher," *Fortune*, November 23, 2009, pp. 45–50.

43. Ibid.

44. Dean Krehmeyer, Michael Lenox, and Brian Moriarty, "Sustainability Strategy and Corporate Strategy," *Ethisphere*, ethisphere.com, November 2, 2009.

45. Ibid.

46. Matt Ford, "Green Electronics: The Good, the Bad and the Better," *CNN.com*, cnn.com, January 15, 2010.

47. Justin Fox, "Cash for Clunkers," *Time*, August 17, 2009, p. 14.

Chapter 2

1. Ford Motor Company Web site, www.ford.com, accessed February 1, 2010; "Ford's Strong Hybrid Sales Buck Industry Trend," Ford Motor Company, www.ford.com, accessed February 1, 2010; "Ford Cites Energy Policy as Critical Factor in Shaping Future Vehicle Fleet," Ford Motor Company, www.ford.com, accessed February 1, 2010; "Welcome to Your Ford SMPRs," Ford Motor Company, ford.digitalsnippets.com, accessed February 1, 2010; "Ford Motor Co. Is In Express Lane," *NY Daily News*, January 28, 2010, www.nydailynews.com; Keith Naughton, "Ford's Comeback Makes Mulally a Star at Detroit Show," *Bloomberg.com*, January 14, 2010, www.bloomberg.com; Bill Vlasic, "Ford's Bet: It's a Small World After All," *The New York Times*, January 10, 2010, www.nytimes.com.

2. Alicia Chang, "Virgin Galactic Unveils Commercial Spaceship," *Associated Press*, December 7, 2009, news.yahoo.com.

3. "New Solar Panel Conveyor Displayed at Photovoltaic Technology Show," January 7, 2010, www.shuttleworth.com.

4. Procter & Gamble Web site, www.pg.com, accessed January 12, 2010.

5. Yuri Kageyama, "Toyota Pedal Fix Too Late to Prevent Backlash," *Associated Press*, February 2, 2010, news.yahoo.com.

6. Tanya Irwin, "Study: 2/3 of Marketers Invest in Social Media," *MediaPost Publications*, January 21, 2010, www.mediapost.com.
7. "Owners: $5.4B NY Housing Complexes Go to Creditors," *Associated Press*, January 25, 2010, finance.yahoo.com.
8. "Microsoft Explores Ad Business," *MediaPost News*, February 2, 2010, www.mediapost.com.
9. Sean Gregory, "Latte with Fries? McDonald's Takes Aim at Starbucks," *Time*, May 7, 2009, www.time.com.
10. Nanette Byrnes, "Why Dr. Pepper Is in the Pink of Health," *BusinessWeek*, October 26, 2009, p. 59.
11. Ibid.
12. Derek F. Abell, "Strategic Windows," *Journal of Marketing*, 42, no. 3 (July 1978), pp. 21–26.
13. Walmart Web site, www.walmart.com, accessed February 3, 2010.
14. Stacy Perman, "For Some Small Businesses, Recession Is Good News," *BusinessWeek*, February 6, 2009, www.businessweek.com.
15. Julie Jargon, "Kraft Reformulates Oreo, Scores in China," *The Wall Street Journal*, wsj.com, accessed February 3, 2010.
16. Maria Ermakova and Duane D. Stanford, "Kraft Beats Russian Recession with Bolshevik Biscuits," *Bloomberg.com*, www.bloomberg.com, accessed February 11, 2010.
17. "Hispanic Population in the United States: 1970 to 2050," U.S. Census Bureau, www.census.gov, accessed February 3, 2010.
18. S. Ramesh Kumar, "Addressing Diversity: The Marketing Challenge in India," *The Wall Street Journal*, wsj.com, accessed February 3, 2010.
19. Michael Liedtke, "Want to Read All About It Online? It May Cost You," *Associated Press*, September 20, 2009, tech.yahoo.com.
20. Dunkin' Donuts Web site, www.dunkindonuts.com, accessed February 3, 2010; Jerry Hirsch, "Profiting Off Value Meals," *Chicago Tribune*, May 4, 2009, p. 17.
21. Ylan Q. Mui, "A Race to Keep Up With the Tightwads," *The Washington Post*, June 5, 2009, www.washingtonpost.com.
22. "Our Services for U.S. Companies," U.S. Department of Commerce, www.buyusa.gov/mexico, accessed February 4, 2010.
23. Brian Quinton, "On the Move," *Promo Magazine*, December 1, 2009, promomagazine.com.
24. EBay, www.ebay.com, accessed February 4, 2010.
25. "About IBM," www.ibm.com, accessed February 4, 2010.
26. BlackBerry Web site, www.blackberry.com, accessed February 4, 2010.
27. Microsoft Web site, www.microsoft.com, accessed February 4, 2010.
28. Blair Candy Web site, www.blaircandy.com, accessed February 4, 2010.
29. Moon Ihlwan, "Sony and Samsung's Strategic Split," *Bloomberg Businessweek*, January 18, 2010, p. 52.
30. "Diet Shocker: Food Calorie Counts Are Often Off," *Associated Press*, as reported by *MSNBC.com*, January 7, 2010, www.msnbc.com.

Chapter 3

1. Leora Broydo Vestel, "Nike Makes Environmental Strides and Abandons Carbon Offsets," *The New York Times*, February 2, 2010, greeninc.blogs.nytimes.com; "Nike Outlines Global Strategy for Creating a More Sustainable Business," company press release, January 22, 2010, www.nikebiz.com/media/pr; company Web site, "Corporate Responsibility Report," www.nikebiz.com/responsibility/reporting.html, accessed January 13, 2010; Reena Jana, "Nike Goes Green, Very Quietly," *BusinessWeek*, June 22, 2009, p. 56.
2. Terry Maxon, "High Fuel Costs, Recession Prompt U.S. Airlines to Cut Capacity," *Dallas Morning News*, January 19, 2010, www.dallasnews.com.
3. Nicole Howley, "CPSC Recall: Papyrus Brand Greeting Cards with Bracelets Contain Lead," *Justice News Flash*, February 4, 2010, www.justicenewsflash.com; Associated Press, "'Princess and Frog' Children's Necklaces Recalled for Cadmium," *USA Today*, January 29, 2010, www.usatoday.com.
4. Jennifer Liberto, "Consumers Score a Win on Credit Card Rules," *CNNMoney.com*, January 14, 2010, money.cnn.com.
5. Ken Belson and Alan Schwarz, "Antitrust Case Has Implications Far Beyond N.F.L.," *The New York Times*, January 7, 2010, www.nytimes.com.
6. Calum MacLeod, "China Wants to Rival Boeing, Airbus with Its C919 'Big Plane,'" *USA Today*, October 12, 2009, www.usatoday.com.
7. Company Web site, www.costco.com, accessed February 15, 2010.
8. ENERGY STAR Web site, www.energystar.gov, accessed February 15, 2010; Nathan Rothman, Achieving New Heights in Energy Efficiency," *Xconomy Seattle*, January 13, 2010, www.xconomy.com.
9. "WiFi Hotspot Market Stages Revival in 2009," *Microwave Journal*, January 1, 2010, www.mwjournal.com.
10. Matt Hamblen, "Verizon Wireless Flexes LTE Muscle at CES," *Computerworld*, January 7, 2010, www.computerworld.com.
11. "Accor to Split into 2 Companies," *Hotels*, December 15, 2009, www.hotelsmag.com; Adrian Kerr, "Cable & Wireless Aims to Demerge by March 31, 2010," *Dow Jones Newswires*, November 17, 2009, www.wsj.com.
12. Matthew Herper, "What J&J's Cougar Buy Means," *Forbes*, May 22, 2009, www.forbes.com.
13. Ted Mininni, "What Stonyfield, Method, and Green Mountain Roasters Know (and You Should, Too)," *MarketingProfs*, January 26, 2010, www.marketingprofs.com.
14. Brad Tuttle, "Flight Innovations You'll Love," *CNN.com*, February 9, 2010, www.cnn.com.
15. Tom Field, "ID Theft Threats to Watch in 2010," *Bank Info Security*, December 29, 2009, www.bankinfosecurity.com; "Can the Law Protect You from Identity Theft?" *IdentityTheftFixes.com*, accessed February 17, 2010, www.identitytheftfixes.com.
16. Federal Trade Commission, "DIRECTV, Comcast to Pay Total of $3.21 Million for Entity-Specific Do Not Call Violations," press release, April 16, 2009, www.ftc.gov.
17. Ken Thomas, "Inside Washington: Missed Signs in Toyota Recalls," *Yahoo! News*, February 6, 2010, news.yahoo.com.
18. "TransUnion Shifts to Consumer-Friendly VantageScore," company press release, January 11, 2010, www.marketwire.com.
19. Coalition for Fire-Safe Cigarettes Web site, www.firesafecigarettes.org, accessed February 18, 2010.
20. "AARP Foundation Announces 4th Annual Women's Scholarship Program," AARP press release, February 1, 2010, www.prnewswire.com.
21. Direct Marketing Association Web site, www.the-dma.org, accessed February 18, 2010.
22. "Fourth Quarter GDP Growth Surprises at 5.7%," *InvestorCentric Blog*, February 1, 2010, www.nuwireinvestor.com.
23. J. David Goodman, "An Electric Boost for Bicyclists," *The New York Times*, February 1, 2010, www.nytimes.com.
24. Financial Forecast Center Web site, forecasts.org, accessed February 9, 2010.
25. Damien Cave, "In Recession, Americans Doing More, Buying Less," *The New York Times*, January 3, 2010, www.nytimes.com.
26. "Personal Income and Outlays: December 2009," Bureau of Economic Analysis, February 1, 2010, www.bea.gov.
27. "Food Shortages Coming, Buy Commodities: Jim Rogers," *CNBC.com*, January 15, 2010, www.cnbc.com; "Government Cover-up of Food Shortage Feared," *WorldNetDaily*, January 10, 2010, www.wnd.com.
28. Martha T. Moore, "Cities Promote Scooter Commuting," *USA Today*, December 3, 2009, www.usatoday.com.
29. Sam Abuelsamid, "CNG-Fueled Honda Civic GX Ranked #1 on ACEEE Greenest Vehicle List. Again," *Autoblog*, January 22, 2010, green.autoblog.com.
30. Michael Wines, "As China Rises, Fears Grow on Whether Boom Can Endure," *The New York Times*, January 12, 2010, www.nytimes.com.
31. Zoltan Simon, "Hungary's Budget Deficit May Overshoot 2010 Target, OECD Says," *BusinessWeek*, February 11, 2010, www.businessweek.com; "EC Extends Deadline for Hungary's Budget Deficit Cut to 2011," *RealDeal*, June 25, 2009, www.realdeal.hu.
32. Dean A. Ayers, "Implant 'RFID' Chips in Your Dogs, Cats or Pets? No Way!," *Associated Content*, November 12, 2009, www.associatedcontent.com; Mary Catherine O'Connor, "Students to Develop RFID-Enabled Robotic Guide Dog," *RFID Journal*, September 14, 2009, www.rfidjournal.com.
33. David Barker, "MSU Researches Nonfood Biofuel," *State News*, February 2. 2010, www.statenews.com; Jim Lane, "Algae, Algae, Algae," *World Biofuels Markets News*, October 19, 2009, www.worldbiofuelsmarkets.com.
34. Sue Moncure, "Solar Panels Latest in Green Technology at UD Dairy Farm," *UDaily*, February 10, 2010, www.udel.edu.
35. Joanna Stern, "Cheap Mobile Calls, Even Overseas," *The New York Times*, January 7, 2010, www.nytimes.com.
36. Continuum Crew, "Baby Boomers Emerging as New Social Media Mavens, Continuum Crew Survey Finds," press release, January 20, 2010, www.newsguide.us.
37. "Hispanic Media Facts," *Hispanic PR Wire*, www.hispanicprwire.com, accessed February 21, 2010.
38. Envirosax Web site, "Dangers of Plastic Bags," www.envirosax.com, accessed February 21, 2010; David Krough and Associated Press, "Plastic Grocery Ban Proposal back on the Table," *KGW.com*, February 1, 2010, www.kgw.com; Brian Shrader, "Stores Pay Customers to Shop with Reusable Bags," *WRAL.com*, November 16, 2009, www.wral.com.
39. Susan K. Livio, "N.J. Chain Restaurants Are Required to Add Calorie Counts to Menus," *Star-Ledger*, January 18, 2010, www.nj.com; Drucilla Dyess, "Calorie Count Labels on Restaurant Menus Are Helping Consumers Make Better Choices," *HealthNews*, October 28, 2009, www.healthnews.com.
40. Todd Slaughter, "Now We're Getting It—Recalls.gov—What More Can Be Done?" *InjuryBoard.com*, January 18, 2010, www.injuryboard.com.
41. Corporate Ethics-US Web site, www.corporate-ethics.us, accessed February 21, 2010.
42. Jane Porter, "Using Ex-Cons to Scare MBAs Straight," *BusinessWeek*, May 5, 2008, p. 58.
43. Campaign for Tobacco Free Kids, "New Report: States Cut Funding for Tobacco Prevention Programs Despite Receiving Record Amounts of Tobacco Revenue," press release, December 9, 2009, www.tobaccofreekids.org.

44. Larry Barrett, "TJX Hacker Pleads Guilty to Ripping off Millions," *InternetNews,* September 11, 2009, www.internetnews.com.
45. Lucas Mearian, "Health Net Says 1.5M Medical Records Lost in Data Breach," *Computerworld,* November 19, 2009, www.computerworld.com.
46. Company Web site, www.kelloggcompany.com, accessed February 21, 2010.
47. Mike Adams, "Food Industry Continues to Market Junk Food to Children," *NaturalNews,* January 27, 2010, www.sott.net; Julie Deardorff, "Pact to Limit Sugary Cereals to Kids Not Worth Its Salt," *Chicago Tribune,* January 20, 2010, www.chicagotribune.com.
48. "FTC Childhood Obesity Forum: Working Group Announces Tentative Proposed Nutritional Guidelines for Food Marketed to Children," *Consumer Advertising Law Blog,* December 18, 2009, www.consumeradvertisinglawblog.com.
49. John Hechinger, "Team-Color Bud Cans Leave Colleges Flat," *The Wall Street Journal,* August 21, 2009, online.wsj.com.
50. Jeremy M. Simon, "Credit Card Interest Rates Soar; Bad-Credit Borrowers Hit Hardest," *CreditCards.com,* February 3, 2010, www.foxbusiness.com.
51. Connie Prater and Tyler Metzger, "A Guide to the Credit CARD Act of 2009," *CreditCards.com,* www.creditcards.com, accessed February 22, 2010; Liberto, "Consumers Score a Win on Credit Card Rules."
52. International Labor Rights Forum, "2010 Sweatshop Hall of Shame," November 17, 2009, www.laborrights.org.
53. "834 Certified Community Development Financial Institutions As of 12/31/2009," CDFI Fund, January 7, 2010, www.cdfifund.gov.
54. Lori Brown, "Best Buy's Recycling Program Is Expensive, But Worth It,"*Earth911.com,* December 17, 2009, www.earth911.com.
55. "Electronics Companies, Retailers Team to Simplify Green Electronics Purchasing for Consumers," *PR Newswire,* January 21, 2010, www.prnewswire.com.
56. "As Green Hotels Proliferate, So Do Eco-Rating Systems," *Environmental Leader,* January 19, 2010, www.environmentalleader.com.
57. Mark Hyman, "Green Grow the Ballparks," *BusinessWeek,* April 20, 2009, www.businessweek.com.

Chapter 4

1. Company Web site, www.net-a-porter.com, accessed March 3, 2010; Eric Pfanner, "Luxury Firms Move to Make Web Work for Them," *The New York Times,* www.nytimes.com, November 18, 2009; Stephanie Rosenbloom, "Costly, Yes, But for You . . ." *The New York Times,* www.nytimes.com, August 1, 2009; Claire Cain Miller, "Luxury Shopping, via iPhone," *The International Herald Tribune,* www.global.nytimes.com, July 21, 2009; Lindsay Chappell, "Luxury Car Shoppers on Web Want Instant Info," *Automotive News,* March 16, 2009.
2. "E-stats," U.S. Census Bureau, www.census.gov/estats, accessed March 2, 2010.
3. "Stats—Web Worldwide," www.clickz.com, accessed March 2, 2010.
4. "Top 20 Countries with the Highest Number of Internet Users," www.internetworldstats.com, accessed March 2, 2010.
5. Ibid.
6. "S. Korea, Japan, Have World's Fastest Internet Links: Survey," *Physorg.com,* www.physorg.com, February 2, 2010.
7. "Top Online Activities of North American Internet Users," *BitBriefs.com,* www.bitbriefs.com, July 28, 2009.
8. Christine L. Hohlbaum, "7 Signs You're an Internet Addict," *Women on the Web,* www.wowowow.com, accessed February 12, 2010.
9. Tate Law, "Chinese Internet Users: A Brief Overview," *Ezine Articles,* ezinearticles.com, February 3, 2010.
10. Cameron French, "Filmmakers Eye Web, TV as Alternate to Theaters," *Business & Financial News,* www.reuters.com, January 23, 2010.
11. "Get Lean, Get Green, Get a Great Bike for a Good Cause," Good Men Project, www.goodmenproject.org, January 1, 2010.
12. Nick Bilton, "Foursquare Teams with Bravo TV," *The New York Times,* bits.blogs.nytimes.com, January 31, 2010.
13. Logan Tod, "Online Shopping to Increase in 2010, Survey Shows," *Marketing Week,* www.marketingservicetalk.com, January 28, 2010.
14. "Bleak Friday: Retail v. E-Tail in America," *The Economist,* www.economist.com, November 28, 2009.
15. Company Web site, www.burgerking.com, accessed March 2, 2010.
16. Company Web site, www.usa.canon.com, accessed March 2, 2010.
17. "E-commerce 2008," U.S. Census Bureau, www.census.gov/estats, May 27, 2010.
18. Malia Spencer, "Schneider Downs Opens Line of Communication with Intranet," Pittsburgh Business Times, pittsburg.bizjournals.com, January 15, 2010.
19. Company Web site, "SAP Customer Success Story: Royal Dutch/Shell Group," www.sap.com, accessed March 2010.
20. Company Web site, "The City of Edinburgh Council Saves US$8 Million in 2007–08 through Intelligent, Automated Procurement," www.oracle.com, June 2008.
21. Organization Web site, www.eva.state.va.us, accessed January 31, 2010.
22. "Online Retail Sales Set a Single-Day Record by Topping $900 Million," *Internet Retailer,* www.internetretailer.com, December 21, 2009.
23. Jayne O'Donnell, "When Shopping, They'll Phone It In," *USA Today,* www.usatoday.com, November 27, 2009.
24. Company Web site, www.ae.com, accessed March 2, 2010.
25. Jamie Lendino, "Study: Smartphones Used Increasingly to Make Purchases," *PC Magazine,* www.pcmag.com, January 5, 2010; "2010 Prediction No. 3: Mobile Commerce Will Finally Go Mainstream," FierceMobileContent, www.fiercemobilecontent.com, January 4, 2010.
26. Nick Moley, "Best Online Travel Deals 2009 and 2010," *Digital Trends,* www.digitaltrends.com, September 28, 2009.
27. Brad Tuttle, "What's Next for Airline Baggage Fees?" *Newsweek.com,* current.newsweek.com, January 13, 2010.
28. Company Web site, www.barnesandnoble.com, accessed March 2, 2010.
29. Leena Rao, "Like.Com Acquires Street Style Fashion Community Weardrobe," *TechCrunch.com,* techcrunch.com, November 18, 2009.
30. "30 Top Online-Shopping Trends," Smart-products, smart-products.tmcnet.com, December 28, 2009.
31. Amy Nutt, "Most Common Items Sold Online," *Articlesbase.com,* www.articlesbase.com, September 18, 2009.
32. "Facebook Top Spot in Social Media for Retailers," *Home Textiles Today,* www.hometextilestoday.com, February 11, 2010.
33. Company Web site, www.verisign.com, accessed February 14, 2010.
34. Bruce Cundiff, "Alternative Payments Vendors That Embrace Triangle of Value Are in the Driver's Seat," *BankTech.com,* www.banktech.com, October 20, 2009.
35. Bob Sullivan, "Online Privacy Fears Are Real," *MSNBC,* www.msnbc.com, December 6, 2009.
36. "Top 5 Security Breaches of 2009," *NetworkWorld.com* Community, www.networkworld.com, December 24, 2009; Byron Acohido, "Hackers Breach Heartland Payment Credit Card System," *USA Today,* www.usatoday.com, January 20, 2009.
37. Organization Web site, www.ic3.gov, accessed March 2, 2010.
38. "2010 CyberSecurity Watch Survey: Cybercrime Increasing Faster than Some Company Defenses," opensource.sys-con.com, accessed February 14, 2010.
39. "Twitter Explains Recent Phishing Attack," Mashable.com, mashable.com, February 3, 2010.
40. Linda McGlasson, "Vishing Scam: Four More States Struck," *BankInfoSecurity.com,* www.bankinfosecurity.com, February 1, 2010.
41. Kristina Peterson, "Overstock.com, Liz Claiborne Gain," *The Wall Street Journal,* December 31, 2009, p. C5.
42. "Nielsen Reports 875 Million Consumers Have Shopped Online," *Nielsen Media Research,* January 28, 2008, www.nielsenmedia.com.
43. Tom Krazil, "Authors Guild: We Don't Want to Be the RIAA," *CNET News,* news.cnet.com, February 5, 2010.
44. "More Than 95 Percent of All Email Is Spam," *Softpedia,* news.softpedia.com, accessed February 14, 2010.
45. Company Web site, www.facebook.com/chasecommunity giving, accessed March 2, 2010.
46. Jeremiah Owyang, "2010: Marketers Get Serious about Social Media," *Forbes.com,* www.forbes.com, January 22, 2010.
47. Heather Green and Robert D. Hof, "Six Million Users: Nothing to Twitter At," *BusinessWeek,* March 16, 2009, p. 51–52.
48. Ibid.
49. Ibid.
50. Owyang, "2010: Marketers Get Serious about Social Media."
51. Jefferson Graham, "Facebook's a Great Friend to Businesses," *USA Today,* www.usatoday.com, August 5, 2009.
52. Ibid.
53. Ibid.
54. Ibid.
55. "Quickoffice® Launches Corporate Blog," *Market Wire,* marketwire.com, January 2010.
56. "General Motors Case Study," e20portal.com, e20portal.com, accessed February 15, 2010.
57. Michael Learmonth, "For Some Consumers, Online Video Ads Still Grate," *Advertising Age,* adage.com, February 2, 2010.
58. Aliza Sherman, "Which Widgets to Use to Enhance Your Site," *The Digital Marketer,* digitalmarketer.quickanddirtytips.com, January 14, 2010.
59. Ian Paul, "Facebook Homepage Redesign: A Feature Breakdown," *PCWorld,* www.pcworld.com, February 5, 2010.
60. "GoDaddy Hosting," Web Site Hosting Review, www.review-web-hosting.com, February 2010.
61. "10 Tips to Boosting Your Web site Traffic," *Response Targeted Marketing.com,* www.responsetargetedmarketing.com, January 14, 2010.
62. "5 Easy & Free Tools to Measure Website Performance," *Webmastershouse.com,* www.webmastershouse.com, January 20, 2010.
63. Chris Harnick, "Webtrends Mobile Analytics Gives Insights into App, WAP performance," *Mobile Marketer,* www.mobilemarketer.com, February 2, 2010.

Chapter 5

1. Envirosell Web site, www.envirosell.com, accessed February 10, 2010; Gary McCartney, "It's a Woman's World," *Inside Retailing*, February 10, 2010, www.envirosell.com; "RichRelevance and Envirosell's Paco Underhill to Present New Findings on Consumer Retailing at NRF Big Show," *BusinessWire*, January 8, 2010, www.businesswire.com; Damien Cave, "In Recession, Americans Doing More, Buying Less," *The New York Times*, January 2, 1020, www.nytimes.com; Paco Underhill, "Drop How You Shop," *The Washington Post*, November 29, 2009, www.washingtonpost.com.
2. "Utah Real Estate Builder Focuses on Green Houses," *PRLog*, February 11, 2010, www.prlog.org.
3. "Stouggers, CASA Urge Families to Eat Dinner Together," *Brandweek*, February 11, 2010, www.mediapost.com.
4. Sarah Mahoney, "Target Makes its Gift Cards Mobile, Scannable," *MediaPost News*, February 10, 2010, www.mediapost.com.
5. Susan L. Nasr. "10 Unusual Items from McDonald's International Menu," *How Stuff Works*, money.howstuffworks.com, accessed February 11, 2010.
6. "An Older and More Diverse Nation by Midcentury," *U.S. Census Bureau News*, www.census.gov, accessed February 25, 2010.
7. U.S. Census Bureau, Table 1a, "Projected Population of the United States, by Race and Hispanic Origin: 2000 to 2050," www.census.gov, accessed February 11, 2010.
8. Les Christie, "Americans Tame Their Wanderlust," *CNNMoney.com*, September 25, 2009, realestate.yahoo.com.
9. Pew Hispanic Center, pewhispanic.org, accessed February 12, 2010.
10. Ibid.
11. "Marketing to Hispanics," *Real Estate Radio USA*, December 28, 2009, www.realestateradiousa.com.
12. Ibid; Gretchen Livingston, "Latinos Online: Narrowing the Gap," Pew Research Center, December 22, 2009, prewresearch.org.
13. "Hispanic Buying Power: Will It Continue in 2009?" *Transpanish*, February 25, 2009, transpanish.biz.
14. "People QuickFacts," U.S. Census Bureau, quickfacts.census.gov, accessed February 12, 2010.
15. Thomas Umsted, "African-Americans Grow in Numbers, Buying Power," *Multichannel News*, January 26, 2010, www.multichannel.com.
16. Ibid.
17. "People QuickFacts."
18. "Asian American Consumers by Lead Me Media," *Direct Marketing News*, January 10, 2010, www.dmnews.com.
19. Sorabol Web site, www.sorabolrestaurants.com, accessed February 12, 2010.
20. "The DogSmith National Dog Training and Pet Care Franchise Adds Pet Waste Cleanup to Services," *PRLog*, February 11, 2010, www.prlog.org.
21. Jason Notte, "Apple Fans Pay Thousands for Cool Factor," *The Street.com*, February 9, 2010, finance.yahoo.com/news.
22. "CPG Shopping Habits: 5 Key Predicitons for 2010," *Marketing Charts.com*, January 6, 2010, www.marketingcharts.com.
23. "Gap Unveils Premium Denim Line for Babies Zero to 2," *Retailing Today*, February 11, 2010, www.mediapost.com.
24. Amanda Lenhart, Kristen Purcell, Aaron Smith and Kathryn Zickuhr, "Social Media & Mobile Internet Use Among Teens and Adults," *Pew Research Center Publications*, February 3, 2010, pewrsearch.org.
25. "Saving Saks," *Forbes*, August 24, 2009, p. 31.
26. Ads from *The Wall Street Journal*, Fall 2009.
27. "Oprah's No Phone Zone Pledge," *The Oprah Winfrey Show*, January 18, 2010, www.oprah.com.
28. "Hottest Retail Trends in 2010," *Food Product Design*, January 4, 2010, www.foodproductdesign.com.
29. Laura Sullivan, "Boys Gone Shopping Wild," *Mint.com*, January 27, 2009, www.mint.com.
30. "The Youth Network: Teens," Alloy Marketing, www.alloymarketing.com, accessed February 15, 2010.
31. Kevin Davis, "Teens, Parents Face Special Issues When Buying Cars," *Crain's Chicago*, February 8, 2010, www.chicagobusiness.com.
32. "The Internet as an Information and Economic Appliance in the Lives of Teens and Young Adults," Pew Internet and American Life Project, www.pewinternet.org, accessed February 15, 2010.
33. "Billboard with Mannequin Spurs 911 Calls," *Associated Press*, January 18, 2010, www.azcentral.com.
34. Aaron Baar, "ANA: Fewer Foresee Death of TV Spot in Decade," *MediaPost News*, February 8, 2010, www.mediapost.com.
35. "Michigan's Travel Campaign Shows ROI," *MediaPost News*, February 6, 2010, www.mediapost.com.
36. Laurie Burkitt, "Neuromarketing: Companies Use Neuroscience for Consumer Insights," *Forbes*, November 16, 2009, www.forbes.com.
37. Connie Thompson, "Predicting Consumer Trends for 2010," *KOMO News*, January 14, 2010, www.komonews.com.
38. Chase Web site, www.chasesapphire.com, accessed February 17, 2010.
39. "A Blossoming Flower in the Fashion Field—Ed Hardy," *Ed Hardy Class*, January 16, 2010, www.edhardyclass.com; "Ed Hardy Clothing, the Ultimate Fashion Statement," *Business News Blog*, May 5, 2009, www.noplc.co.cc.
40. Gord Hotchkiss, "Decisiveness and Search: Two Different Strategies," *MediaPost Publications*, February 11, 2010, www.mediapost.com.
41. Biz Rate Web site, www.bizrate.com, accessed February 17, 2010.
42. Lee Eisenberg, "The American Shopper: Down but Not Out," *BusinessWeek*, October 26, 2009, www.businessweek.com.
43. Gavin O'Malley, "Nielsen: Consumers Will Spend Money Online on Certain Content, But News Has Become a Commodity," *MediaPost News*, February 17, 2010, www.mediapost.com.

Chapter 6

1. Stuart Elliott, "Tireless Employees Get Their Tribute, Even if It's in Felt and Polyester," *The New York Times*, www.nytimes.com, March 4, 2010; Christopher Palmeri, "Now for Sale, The Zappos Culture," *Bloomberg Businessweek*, January 11, 2010, p. 57; Ed Frauenheim, "Sharing 'Insights' on Happiness," *Workforce Management*, www.workforce.com, September 14, 2009; Ed Frauenheim, "Jungle Survival: The Fun-yet-Focused Culture at Online Retailer Zappos," *Workforce Management*, www.workforce.com, September 14, 2009.
2. "Department of Defense Releases Fiscal 2010 Budget Proposal," U.S. Department of Defense news release, May 7, 2009, www.defense.gov.
3. "E-Stats," U.S. Census Bureau, May 16, 2008, www.census.gov.
4. "AT&T OneNet Service," Company Web site, AT&T, www.business.att.com, accessed February 17, 2010.
5. Company Web site, Jan-Pro, www.jan-pro.com, accessed February 17, 2010.
6. "ACCO Brands Corporation—Investing," www.blogged.com, accessed February 17, 2010.
7. "Agencies in Ohio Use Web to Auction Unused Items," *Associated Press*, www.wfmj.com, January 15, 2010.
8. "E-Stats."
9. "B2B Online Marketing Holds Strong Growth Potential," *Marketing Charts.com*, www.marketingcharts.com, February 4, 2010.
10. Company Web site, The Seam, www.theseam.com, accessed February 17, 2010.
11. "Kirtsy.com and Microsoft Office Live Team to Present Free 'Hands On Small Business' Sessions Across the Country," *Market Wire*, www.marketwire.com, October 2009.
12. Company Web site, Tetra Tech, www.tetratech.com, accessed February 17, 2010.
13. "North American Industry Classification System (NAICS)," *Encyclopedia of Business*, www.enotes.com, accessed February 17, 2010.
14. "Military Cell Phone Discounts," *Military Discounts & Coupons*, www.bascops.net, accessed February 17, 2010.
15. "Manufacturing," *How Stuff Works.com*, geography.howstuffworks.com, accessed February 17, 2010.
16. "Volkswagen to Add 500 Jobs at Supplier Park," www.thechattanoogan.com, February 5, 2010.
17. Company Web site, CDW, www.cdw.com, accessed February 18, 2010.
18. "Wal-Mart Stores, Inc.," Organization Web site, Children's Miracle Network, www.childrensmiraclenetwork.org, accessed February 18, 2010.
19. "OPK, Indiana Jones and 4.6 Billion Other People," Company blog, conversations.nokia.com, January 8, 2010.
20. Ramanathan Nagasamy, "Top Outsourcing Destination—India," *Article Alley*, www.articlealley.com, February 12, 2010.
21. "Brand Name Companies Go Bankrupt," *CNNMoney.com*, cnnmoney.com, September 25, 2009.
22. "Walmart Reports Fourth Quarter and Fiscal Year 2010 Results," *Forbes.com*, www.forbes.com, February 28, 2010.
23. "Xerox at a Glance," Company Web site, www.xerox.com, accessed February 21, 2010.
24. Debbie Kline, "Hugo Boss Threatens to Move Overseas If Workers Refuse $4/Hr Pay Cut," Jobs with Justice blog, www.jwjblog.org, February 3, 2010.
25. "Outsourcing and Offshoring Overview," Plunkett Research Ltd., www.plunkettresearch.com, accessed February 19, 2010.
26. "Florida Freeze Damages as Much as 5% of Orange Crop," *BusinessWeek*, www.businessweek.com, January 11, 2010.
27. "The Keurig Story," Company Web site, Keurig, www.keurig.com, accessed March 9, 2010.

28. "Keurig Introduces First Single-Cup Commercial Brewers with Touch Screen User Interface," *Business Wire*, www.thestreet.com, February 2, 2010.

29. "FedEx Couriers Play Cupid This Valentine's Day," *Business Wire*, www.businesswire.com, February 11, 2010.

30. "Indiana University," Company Web site, Hewlett-Packard, www.hp.com, accessed April 16, 2010.

31. "Table 416. Number of Governmental Units by Type, 2007," U.S. Census Bureau, www.census.gov, accessed February 18, 2010.

32. "Supplier Diversity Program," Company Web site, United States Postal Service, www.usps.com, accessed February 18, 2010.

33. "GSA Advantage," Company Web site, Sybase, www.sybase.com, accessed February 21, 2010.

Chapter 7

1. Company Web site, www.pollocampero.com, accessed March 26, 2010; Michael Arndt, "At Pollo Campero, Growth Is on the Menu," *BusinessWeek*, March 9, 2010, www.businessweek.com; "Pollo Campero India to Launch 50 Stores by 2012," *Thai Indian*, February 10, 2010, www.thaindian.com; Heather McPherson, "Pollo Campero Will Replace McDonald's in Downtown Disney in Late 2010," *Orlando Sentinel*, February 3, 2010, thedailydisney.com; "Pollo Campero Makes Healthy Eating Fast, Affordable with New Menu of Three Complete Meals under 505 Calories," *News Guide*, January 11, 2010, www.newsguide.us; "Pollo Campero Opens Restaurant in India," *Prensalibre.com*, January 7, 2010, en.centralamericadata.com; "Global Fast Food Comes to America," *Fortune*, August 26, 2009, www.fortune.com.

2. Tom Moeller, "U.S. Foreign Trade Activity: Recently a Smaller Share of U.S. GDP," *Haver.com*, July 13, 2009, www.haver.com.

3. United Nations Conference on Trade and Development, *World Investment Report 2009*, www.unctad.org, page xxi.

4. U.S. Department of Commerce, "U.S. Goods Trade: Imports and Exports by Related-Parties," *U.S. Census Bureau News*, May 12, 2009, www.census.gov.

5. James T. Areddy, "In China: More 'Made in America,'" *The Wall Street Journal*, February 11, 2010, blogs.wsj.com.

6. International Trade Administration, "U.S. Export Fact Sheet," February 11, 2009, www.trade.gov; U.S. Department of Commerce, "United States Exports," www.4uth.gov.ua, accessed February 25, 2010.

7. Chris Isidore, "Who Needs Consumer Spending?" *CNNMoney.com*, January 21, 2010, money.cnn.com.

8. Andrew Clark, "Wal-Mart, the U.S. Retailer Taking over the World by Stealth," *Guardian.co.uk*, January 12, 2010, www.guardian.co.uk.

9. Jack M. Germain, "Brutally Honest Fault-Finding Pays off for Coverity," *E-Commerce Times*, February 19, 2010, www.ecommercetimes.com.

10. Daniel Workman, "Top U.S. Exports & Imports 2009," *International Trade*, February 20, 2010, import-export.suite.101.com.

11. U.S. Bureau of Economic Analysis, "Gross Domestic Product in Current and Chained Dollars by Industry," *Survey of Current Business*, May 2009, www.bea.gov.

12. Jin Jing and Patricia Jiayi Ho, "Ford's 2009 China Sales from JVs, Imports Jump 44%," NASDAQ, www.nasdaq.com, accessed March 1, 2010; Procter & Gamble Web site, www.pg.com.cn, accessed March 1, 2010.

13. U.S. Department of Commerce, "U.S. International Trade in Goods and Services," *U.S. Census Bureau News*, December 2009, www.census.gov.

14. COTTM Web site, "China Outbound Travel and Tourism Market," www.cottm.com, accessed February 26, 2010.

15. "Nearly 70 Million U.S. Households Now Use Internet Banking," *Internet Banking*, July 10, 2009, www.internet-banking.com.

16. "Strikeforce Goes Global with New TV Deal," *ProWrestling.com*, February 2, 2010, www.pro-wrestling.com.

17. Tim Feran, "Retailer Counting on Sales Overseas," *Columbus Dispatch*, February 17, 2010, www.dispatch.com.

18. "Yum Brands Sets Sights on Indian Market," *2point6billion.com*, December 17, 2009, www.2point6billion.com.

19. Chris Kenning and Alex Davis, "Pizza Chain Plans 120 Stores This Year," *Business Opportunities Journal*, www.boj.com, accessed February 19, 2010; Company Web site, "Papa John's Takes the Field as Official Pizza Sponsor of the NFL and Super Bowl XLIV," press release, January 12, 2010, www.papajohns.com.

20. "China GDP Per Capita (PPP), US Dollars Statistics," *Economy Watch*, February 23, 2010, www.economywatch.com; "India GDP Per Capita (PPP), US Dollars Statistics," *Economy Watch*, February 23, 2010, www.economywatch.com; "United States GDP Per Capita (PPP), US Dollars Statistics," *Economy Watch*, February 23, 2010, www.economywatch.com.

21. Ibid.

22. "Will India's Population Rise to 2 Billion?" *Earthsky Blogs*, February 7, 2009, www.earthsky.org.

23. Alex Carrick, "U.S. Foreign Trade Position Becomes More Familiar: Canada's Remains an Anomaly," *Reed Construction Data*, January 13, 2010, www.reedconstructiondata.com.

24. Desire Athow, "IBM to Create 5000 New Jobs in India," *ITProPortal.com*, January 11, 2010, www.itproportal.com.

25. "Internet Usage Statistics," *Internet World Stats*, September 30, 2009, www.internetworldstats.com.

26. "'Frankenstein'—Food Fears Keep GMOs out of Europe," *Global News Journal*, February 5, 2010, blogs.reuters.com.

27. Robert J. Rosoff, "Addressing Labor Rights Problems in China," *China Business Review*, www.chinabusinessreview.com, accessed February 22, 2010.

28. International Organization for Standardization Web site, "ISO Members," www.iso.org, accessed February 22, 2010.

29. Mike Masnick, "How China's Attempts to Censor the Internet Are Failing," *Techdirt*, January 4, 2010, www.techdirt.com; Charles Arthur, "China's Internet Users Surpass US Population," *The Guardian*, July 16, 2009, www.guardian.co.uk.

30. "Despite Uncertainties, Asian Economies Heading towards Full Recovery in 2010," *Philstar.com*, February 13, 2010, www.philstar.com.

31. Christopher Conkey, Jose de Cordoba, and Jim Carlton, "Mexico Issues Tariff List in U.S. Trucking Dispute," *The Wall Street Journal*, March 19, 2009, online.wsj.com.

32. "Europe Strikes 'Banana Wars' Deal," *BBC News*, December 15, 2009, news.bbc.co.uk.

33. Leonie Barrie, "Apparel Industry Issues to Watch in 2010," *Just-Style.com*, February 9, 2010, www.just-style.com.

34. "S.Korea–EU FTA Indicates European Beef Imports May Resume," *Hankyoreh*, October 29, 2009, english.hani.co.kr.

35. "Subsidies to Boost China's 3G Handset Market in 2010," *EDN Asia*, February 8, 2010, www.ednasia.com.

36. Elise Owen, "Standards in China: Behind the Headlines," *China Business Review*, January–February 2010, chinabusinessreview.com.

37. Lucy Hornby and Niu Shuping, "China to Levy Anti-Dumping Duties on U.S. Chicken," *Reuters*, February 5, 2010, www.reuters.com.

38. World Trade Organization Web site, www.wto.org, accessed March 1, 2010.

39. Ibid.

40. Thomas L. Gallagher, "NAFTA Trade Grew for Fifth Month in October," *Journal of Commerce*, January 6, 2010, www.joc.com.

41. "Best Countries for Business," *Forbes*, March 18, 2009, www.forbes.com.

42. Central Intelligence Agency, *The World Factbook*, www.cia.gov, page last updated May 18, 2010.

43. Jason Burke, "Vaclav Klaus Sets Seal on Lisbon Treaty Ratification," *Guardian*, November 3, 2009, www.guardian.co.uk.

44. "Adidas and the Italian Tennis Player Flavia Pennetta Team up until 2012," press release, February 5, 2010, www.press.adidas.com; "Adidas JABULANI Official Match Ball of the 2010 FIFA World Cup—Grip'n'Groove Profile for Football 'Celebration' in South Africa," press release, December 4, 2009, www.press.adidas.com.

45. Company Web site, www.ikea.com, accessed March 3, 2010.

46. "EA SPORTS to Expand Brand with Launch of New Peripherals," press release, January 7, 2010, investor.ea.com.

47. "Working Conditions in Sports Shoe Factories in China," *AF1STAR.com*, January 2, 2010, www.af1star.com.

48. "International Investment Activity Collapses in 2009, Major Emerging Economies Suffer Their First Sharp Declines," *OECD Investment News*, December 2009, www.oecd.org; David Hunkar, "What's Greater, U.S. Direct Investments Aborad or Foreign Directo Investments in the U.S.?" *Seeking Alpha*, November 18, 2009, seekingalpha.com.

49. Kathy Chu, "Chinese Buy More U.S. Assets Than U.S. Buys in China," *USA Today*, January 17, 2010, www.usatoday.com.

50. "AREVA to Acquire the U.S. Solar Company Ausra," press release, February 8, 2010, www.ausra.com.

51. Christian Fea, "Follow Wal-Mart's Joint Venture Example," *ChristianFea.com*, October 21, 2009, www.christianfea.com.

52. "A. T. Kearney Report Finds Multinational Companies Turning to Chile for Global Services," press release, February 2, 2010, www.redorbit.com; "Chile Selected for ABB's First Remote Services Center in Latin America," press release, October 26, 2009, www.prnewswire.com.

53. "Innovating from the Outside In," *P&G Views*, December 16, 2009, www.pg.com.

54. "DIRECTV Now the Exclusive Satellite TV Provider of RTVi Russian Television Network in the U.S.," press release, December 22, 2009, www.directv.com.

55. "Is Singapore Ready for a Renewed Domino's Pizza Effect?" *Media*, February 22, 2010, www.media.asia.

56. "UPS Rival FedEx Launches International Ad Campaign," *Business First*, December 22, 2009, www.louisville.bizjournals.com.

57. "Avoiding Culture Clash," *Global Communicator,* December 2009, www.globallanguages.com.

58. U.S. Census Bureau Web site, "State & County QuickFacts," quickfacts.census.gov, accessed February 23, 2010.

59. "LG's Promoting New Blu-Ray Players in US," *Korea IT Times,* January 10, 2010, www.digitaltrends.com.

60. Company Web site, www.nissanusa.com, accessed March 4, 2010; Mallory Factor, "The (Successful) U.S. Auto Industry," *FOXnews.com,* June 9, 2009, www.foxnews.com.

31. Government Web site, *Export.gov,* www.export.gov, accessed March 2, 2010.

32. Government Web site, STAT-USA®, www.stat-usa.gov, accessed March 2, 2010.

33. Peter Sims, "How Google and P&G Approach New Customers, New Markets," *The Conversation,* blogs.hbr.org, March 2, 2009.

34. Marc Brenner, "Ethnography App Debuts on iTunes Store," *Research,* www.research-live.com, December 21, 2009.

35. "Toyota-Led Quality 'Evolution' Inspires Volkswagen, Ford 'Revolution,' Says Strategic Vision's Total Value Index™ Report," press release, November 23, 2009.

36. Company Web site, SmartOrg, www.smartorg.com, accessed March 2, 2010.

Chapter 8

1. Company Web site, Polaris Marketing Research, www.polarimr.com, accessed February 16, 2010; "Atlanta Marketing Research Company Celebrates 20 Years of Quality," *PRWeb,* instantbrand.com, November 1, 2009; "Customer Satisfaction Research Company Introduces White Paper Series," *PRWeb,* www.prweb.com, July 19, 2009; "Atlanta Marketing Research Company, Polaris Marketing Research, Revamps Website," *PRWeb,* consumerrants.com, February 15, 2009.

2. Company Web site, J.D. Power and Associates, www.jdpower.com, accessed February 26, 2010.

3. Company Web site, BRAIN, www.brain-research.com, accessed February 26, 2010.

4. Company Web site, The Nielsen Company, cn-us.nielsen.com, accessed February 26, 2010.

5. Company Web site, BazaarVoice, www.bazaarvoice.com, accessed February 26, 2010.

6. "2009 AQR Results Show Airline Performance Improvement for First Time in Five Years," Wichita University, www.wichita.edu, April 21, 2009.

7. Company Web site, California Pizza Kitchen, www.cpksurvey.com, accessed February 26, 2010.

8. Cristel Mohrman, "Target Field Report," *In-Store Marketer,* www.instoremarketer.org, February 22, 2010; "Grocery Format Freshens Target Sales," *Retailer Daily,* www.retailerdaily.com, January 22, 2010.

9. "SuperPharm Transforms the Pharmacy Business in Trinidad with Help from an ERP/POS Solution from VAI and IBM," Company website, IBM Corporation, www.ibm.com, January 28, 2010.

10. Leonor Vivanco, "Mac Snack Wrap, Other Items Dreamed Up in McDonald's Test Kitchen," *Chicago Tribune.com,* www.chicagotribune.com, February 21, 2010.

11. Company Web site, Synovate, www.synovate.com, accessed March 1, 2010.

12. Tami Lubby, "Can GPS make the Census Better?" www.money.com, July 21, 2009.

13. Haya El Nasser, "Count Starts with No. 1 in Alaska," *USA Today,* January 25, 2010, p. 3A.

14. Government Web site, 2010census.gov, accessed March 1, 2010; Alexandra Silver, "Brief History: The U.S. Census," *Time,* February 8, 2010, p. 16.

15. "2009 TIGER/Line® Shapefiles," www.census.gov, accessed March 1, 2010.

16. "American Apparel Finds the Right Fit with Motorola RFID," *Retail Technology Review,* www.retailtechnologyreview.com, November 5, 2009.

17. "Who We Are," company Web site, Datamonitor Group, datamonitor.com, accessed March 1, 2010.

18. Company Web site, Google Analytics, www.google.com, accessed March 12, 2010; Brian Kraemer, "Facebook Partners with Neilsen on Ad Tracking," *ChannelWeb,* www.crn.com, September 22, 2009; Evan Gerber, "Making Twitter Success Measurable," *Marketing Profs.com,* www.marketingprofs.com, September 8, 2009.

19. Company Web site, YouTube, help.youtube.com, accessed March 1, 2010.

20. David McMillin, "4 Tips to Lowering Survey Abandonment," survey.cvent.com, March 1, 2010.

21. Mark Guarino, "Four Ways Technology Will Change Advertising in 2010," *The Christian Science Monitor,* www.csmonitor.com, December 29, 2009.

22. Company Web site, TRU, www.teenresearch.com, accessed March 1, 2010.

23. Company Web site, Dorland Health, www.dorlandhealth.com, accessed March 1, 2010.

24. "Q&A for Telemarketers and Sellers About the Do Not Call Provisions of the FTC's Telemarketing Sales Rule," Federal Trade Commission, www.ftc.gov, accessed March 1, 2010.

25. "Definition of Focus Groups," *EHow,* www.ehow.com, accessed March 1, 2010.

26. "Fax Advertising: What You Need to Know," Federal Communications Commission, www.fcc.gov, accessed March 10, 2010.

27. "Led by Facebook, Twitter, Global Time Spent on Social Media Sites Up 82% over Year," *NielsenWire,* blog.nielsen.com, January 22, 2010.

28. Mary K. Pratt, "What's Your Twitter ROI? How to Measure Social Media Payoff," *Computerworld,* www.computerworld.com, September 21, 2009.

29. Brian Solis, "The Maturation of Social Media ROI," *Mashable,* mashable.com, January 26, 2010; Dana Oshira, "Experts Predict 2010 the Year for Social Media ROI," *ReadWriteWeb,* www.readwriteweb.com, December 22, 2009.

30. Mike Shields, "Coke, P&G Test MySpace 'In-Stream' Ads," *Brandweek,* www.brandweek.com, February 23, 2010.

Chapter 9

1. Company Web site, www.shopjustice.com, accessed April 15, 2010; "Dress Barn Completes Merger with Tween Brands," press release, November 25, 2009, phx.corporate-ir.net; "Tween Brands Reports Third Quarter 2009 Results," *Business Wire,* November 16, 2009, www.businesswire.com; Ian Ritter, "Dress Barn–Tween Brands Marriage Not As Weird As You Think," *BNET.com,* June 26, 2009, industry.bnet.com.

2. U.S. Census Bureau, "U.S. & World Population Clock," www.census.gov, accessed April 16, 2010.

3. Joanna L. Krotz, "Women Power: How to Market to 51% of Americans," Microsoft Small Business Center, www.microsoft.com, accessed March 21, 2010.

4. "Marketing to Women Requires a Different Mindset," *The Economic Times,* March 10, 2010, economictimes.indiatimes.com.

5. Organization Web site, www.askpatty.com, accessed March 21, 2010.

6. Company Web site, www.designbasics.com, accessed April 16, 2010; Melissa Dittmann Tracey, "Designing for Women: See It from Her Perspective," *Realtor,* March 2010, www.realtor.org.

7. "H-D and Jillian Michaels Encourage Women to Ride," Harley-Davidson press release, March 5, 2010, www.motorcycle-usa.com.

8. "Top 10 Biggest and Fastest-Growing Areas in the US," *Marketing Charts,* www.marketingcharts.com, accessed March 21, 2010; "New Orleans Was Nation's Fastest-Growing City in 2008," *U.S. Census Bureau News,* July 1, 2009, www.census.gov.

9. U.S. Census Bureau, "State Resident Population—Projections: 2010 to 2030," www.census.gov, accessed March 21, 2010.

10. "Country Comparison: Population," *CIA World FactBook,* www.cia.gov, accessed March 21, 2010.

11. "World: Largest Cities" and "World: Metropolitan Areas," *World Gazetteer,* world-gazetteer.com, accessed March 21, 2010.

12. Michael Barone, "How the Recession Has Changed American Migration," *The American,* February 17, 2010, www.american.com.

13. U.S. Census Bureau, "Metropolitan and Micropolitan Statistical Areas," www.census.gov, accessed March 21, 2010.

14. Ibid.

15. "Ice Cream Consumption," *MakeIceCream.com,* www.makeicecream.com, accessed April 17, 2010; "The Top 5 Cities with Highest Caffeine Consumption in America," *Healia.com,* February 17, 2009, blog.healia.com.

16. Corporate Web site, www.dominos.com, accessed April 18, 2010; Roslyn Anderson, "Highest Number of Pizzas Delivered on Super Bowl Sunday," *WLBT.com,* February 7, 2010, www.wlbt.com..

17. Shine Web site, "About Us," shine.yahoo.com, accessed March 22, 2010.

18. Courtney Perkes, "Study Finds Junk Food Ads, Not TV, Make Kids Fat," *Orange County Republican,* February 9, 2010, healthyliving.freedomblogging.com.

19. Bea Fields, "Marketing to Gen Y: What You Can't Afford Not to Know," *Startup Nation,* www.startupnation.com, accessed March 22, 2010.

20. Company Web site, "About PBteen," www.pbteen.com, accessed April 18, 2010.

21. "Baby Boomer Statistics," *BusinessWeek,* September 26, 2009, bx.businessweek.com.

22. Jack Johnson Web site, www.jackjohnsonmusic.com, accessed April 18, 2010.

23. "Baby Boomer Statistics."

24. "Baby Boomers Are Flocking to Social Media – Is Your Brand?" Baby Boomer Knowledge Center, February 13, 2010, www.babyboomerknowledgecenter.com.

25. "Boomer Demographics and Media Usage," *Research and Markets,* www.researchandmarkets.com, accessed March 23, 2010; Mark Briggs, "Targeting Baby Boomers, the 'Forwarding Generation,'" *LostRemote.com,* March 1, 2010, www.lostremote.com.

26. Daisy Nguyen, "Beefing Up: Aging Bikers Are Turning to Trikes to Stay on the Road," *Associated Press,* February 26, 2010, blog.marketplace.nwsource.com; "Motorized Trikes Are Great Alternative for Baby Boomers," *TRIKE.US,* February 15, 2010, www.trike.us.

27. U.S. Census Bureau, "Resident Population by Sex and Age: 1980 to 2008," www.census.gov, accessed April 18, 2010; Company Web site, "Marketing to Seniors," comingofage.com, accessed March 23, 2010.

28. Company Web site, "About Us," www.oattravel.com, accessed April 18, 2010.

29. Fields, "Marketing to Gen Y."

30. U.S. Census Bureau, "Population Projections," www.census.gov, accessed March 23, 2010.

31. Ibid.

32. "Orange County, Fla., Joins the Growing List of 'Majority-Minority' Counties," *U.S. Census Bureau News*, May 14, 2009, www.census.gov.

33. U.S. Census Bureau, "Money Income of Families—Number and Distribution by Race and Hispanic Origin: 2007," www.census.gov, accessed March 23, 2010; Betty Beard, "Latino Purchasing Power Grows," *Arizona Republic*, November 18, 2009, www.azcentral.com.

34. Company Web site, "Case Studies," www.consortemedia.com, accessed April 19, 2010; Helen Leggatt, "Report: Internet Use among U.S. Hispanics Continues to Rise," *BizReport*, March 24, 2009, www.bizreport.com.

35. "Facts for Features: Black (African American) History Month: February 2010," *Fox Business*, January 26, 2010, www.foxbusiness.com.

36. Hardy Green, "Books@Daily Finance: Marketing to Well-Heeled African Americans," *Daily Finance*, March 20, 2010, www.dailyfinance.com; Todd Wasserman, "Report Shows a Shifting African-American Population," *Brandweek*, January 12, 2010, www.brandweek.com.

37. Kenneth Hein, "Pepsi Program Targets African-American Moms," *Brandweek*, September 19, 2009, www.brandweek.com.

38. U.S. Census Bureau, "Population Projections."

39. U.S. Census Bureau, "Facts for Features: Asian/Pacific American Heritage Month: May 2010," March 2, 2010, www.census.gov.

40. U.S. Census Bureau, "Facts for Features: American Indian and Alaska Native Heritage Month: November 2009," October 15, 2009, www.census.gov.

41. Ibid.

42. Organization Web site, www.native-american-bus.org, accessed March 23, 2010.

43. Company Web site, www.rez-biz.com, accessed March 23, 2010.

44. Haya El Nasser, "Multiracial No Longer Boxed In by the Census," *USA Today*, March 15, 2010, www.usatoday.com; Jennifer Modenessi, "Framing Mixed Race: The Face of America Is Changing," *InsideBayArea.com*, February 7, 2010, www.insidebayarea.com.

45. U.S. Census Bureau, "Resident Population Projections by Race, Hispanic Origin Status, and Age: 2010 and 2015," www.census.gov, accessed March 13, 2010.

46. Sarah Kershaw, "Ready for Life's Encore Performances," *The New York Times*, March 19, 2009, nytimes.com.

47. "Boomerang Kids: How to Handle Them Returning to the Nest," *The Christian Science Monitor*, March 19, 2010, www.csmonitor.com.

48. Judy Caprez, "Grandparents Raising Grandchildren Face Obstacles in U.S.," *HD News*, www.hdnews.net, accessed March 23, 2010.

49. U.S. Census Bureau, "Average Household Size," www.factfinder.census.gov, accessed March 23, 2010.

50. Sam Roberts, "Birth Rate Is Said to Fall as a Result of Recession," *The New York Times*, August 7, 2009, www.nytimes.com.

51. Steve Rothaus, "Marketing Pitches Aimed to Gay, Lesbian Consumers," *SunSentinel.com*, March 5, 2010, articles.sun-sentinel.com.

52. Jo-Ann Heslin, "Grocer Shopping Forecasts 2010—What to Expect," *HealthNewsDigest.com*, January 10, 2010, healthnewsdigest.com.

53. U.S. Department of Agriculture, "Food CPI and Expenditures: Table 7," ers.usda.gov, accessed March 23, 2010.

54. Sara Clemence, "What Are We Still Spending On?" *RecessionWire*, July 31, 2009, www.recessionwire.com; Mamie Hunter, "Upscale Restaurants Rolling Out Dining Deals," *CNN*, March 27, 2009, www.cnn.com.

55. Joe Rauch, "World Wealth Down 11 Percent, Fewer Millionaires," *Reuters*, September 15, 2009, www.reuters.com; "Japan Ranks Globally #2 at Number of Millionaires," *Japan Retail News*, September 15, 2009, www.japanretailnews.com; Boston Consulting Group, "North America Overtaken by Europe as the World's Richest Region, As Equity-Heavy U.S. Investors Are Hit with Steep Losses, Says Report by The Boston Consulting Group," press release, September 15, 2009, www.bcg.com.

56. Company Web site, "Japan—VALS™," www.strategicbusinessinsights.com, accessed March 23, 2010.

57. Company Web site, "LifeMatrix," www.gfkamerica.com, accessed March 23, 2010.

58. Company Web site, "MRI and Media Behavior Institute Partner on New Consumer-Centric, Multimedia Measurement Offering," press release, March 1, 2010, www.gfk.com.

59. Helen Leggatt, "Experian Segments Mobile Users by Behavior/Attitudes," *BizReport*, March 18, 2010, www.bizreport.com.

60. Reebok Web site, www.shiekhshoes.com, accessed April 20, 2010; K-Swiss Web site, www.kswiss.com, accessed April 20, 2010.

61. Ashley M. Heher, "Burger King to Upgrade Its Coffee with Starbucks Line," *Detroit News*, February 17, 2010, detnews.com.

62. Philip Elmer-DeWitt, "Day 1 Estimate: 120,000 iPads Sold," *Brainstorm Tech*, March 13, 2010, brainstormtech.blogs.fortune.cnn.com.

63. Cathy Jett, "Extreme Makeover for McDonald's," *AllBusiness*, February 26, 2010, www.allbusiness.com.

64. Organization Web site, "About Mount Vernon,," www.mountvernon.org, accessed March 23, 2010.

65. Organization Web site, "Welcome to the Sierra Club!" www.sierraclub.org, accessed March 23, 2010.

66. Organization Web site, "About Tauck Bridges," www.tauckbridges.com, accessed March 23, 2010.

67. Company Web site, "Welcome!" ilovepeanutbutter.com, accessed March 23, 2010.

68. Robin Van Tan, "From Fast Food to Fast Casual," *ASR Magazine*, November 2009, www.qsrmagazine.com.

69. Frank Filipponio, "Spyker Releases More Details on Saab Purchase, Promises New 9-3 for 2012," *Autoblog*, February 2, 2010, www.autoblog.com.

Chapter 10

1. "British Airways, Iberia Sign Merger Deal," *Arkansas Democrat Gazette*, April 9, 2010; Nicola Clark, "Air Alliance, Approved by U.S., Is Now Up to E.U.," *The International Herald Tribune*, www.iht.com, February 15, 2010; Matt O'Sullivan, "Qantas Relieved as Japan Airlines Decides to Stay in Oneworld Camp," *Sydney Morning Herald*, www.smh.com.au, February 11, 2010; John Wright, "Big Is Not Always Better," *The Courier Mail*, www.news.com.au, February 1, 2010.

2. Scott Reeves, "Why Petsmart Looks Like a Smart Buy," www.minyanville.com, November 17, 2009.

3. "Top 10 Hall of Fame," *Training*, www.trainingmag.com, February 2010.

4. News release, "Four Seasons Hotels and Resorts Named to FORTUNE List of the "100 Best Companies to Work for," press.fourseasons.com, January 21, 2010.

5. Bruce Horovitz, "McDonald's, Burger King, Taco Bell Add to Fast Food Value Deals," *USA Today*, www.usatoday.com, December 10, 2009.

6. Company Web site, www.verizonwireless.com, accessed March 6, 2010.

7. Mike Pearson, "TiVo Brings Web, TV One Step Closer to Tying the Knot," *TechNewsWorld*, www.technewsworld.com, March 4, 2010.

8. Jessica Sebor, "The 2010 CRM Service Awards: The Service Elite—Southwest Airlines," *Destination CRM*, www.destinationcrm.com, March 11, 2010.

9. Organization Web site, American Customer Satisfaction Index, www.theacsi.org, accessed March 6, 2010.

10. Roko Nastic, "Using Social Media for Better Customer Management," *Quick Online Tips*, www.quickonlinetips.com, February 19, 2010.

11. Brad Stone, "Ding! Mail. OMG! It's Steve Jobs," *The New York Times*, www.nytimes.com, March 24, 2010.

12. Company Web site, www.sportstrackernokia.com, accessed March 25, 2010.

13. Christine Durkin, "The Cost of Customer Churn," The Marketing Executives Group International, www.marketingexecutives.biz, accessed March 4, 2010.

14. Jessica Scarpati, "Fighting Wireless Churn with Trendy Smartphones and Fast Data Networks," *Search Telecom.com*, searchtelecom.techtarget.com, March 4, 2010.

15. Company Web site, "Marriott Rewards," www.marriott.com, accessed March 7, 2010.

16. "Credit Card Statistics, Industry Facts, Debt Statistics," *CreditCards.com*, www.creditcards.com, accessed March 7, 2010.

17. Stephanie Rice, "Can I Live on Campus Forever," *The Collegian* (University of Richmond), www.thecollegianur.com, February 18, 2010.

18. Organization Web site, "Team USA Fans, Support Your Team Through MyTeamUSA Rewards," www.teamusa.org, February 9, 2010.

19. Organization Web site, "Membership & Benefits," www.thirteen.org, accessed March 7, 2010.

20. Arthur Middleton Hughes, "The 24 Essential Database Marketing Techniques," Database Marketing Institute, dbmarketing.com, March 7, 2010.

21. Douglas MacMillan, "Google Gets Real-Time, Personalized Search," *BusinessWeek*, blogs.businessweek.com, December 7, 2009; Tom Krazit, "Google Extends Personalized Search to All," *CNET News*, news.cnet.com, December 4, 2009.

22. David Bauder, "Super Bowl Is Most-Watched TV Show Ever," *Yahoo! Sports*, sports.yahoo.com, February 8, 2010.

23. "Net Connected TV Could Approach Half a Billion Homes," *Informitv*, informitv.com, January 18, 2010.

24. Company Web site, Ning, www.ning.com, accessed March 25, 2010.

25. Company Web site, Convio, www.convio.com, accessed March 7, 2010.

26. Company Web site, www.refresheverything.com, accessed March 25, 2010; Scott Moir, "Pepsi Refresh Project: Huge Potential Viral Marketing Success," *Online PR News*, www.onlineprnews.com, February 13, 2010.

27. Company Web site, "P&G Tremor," Procter & Gamble, www.pg.com, accessed March 7, 2010.

28. Organization Web site, "A Brief History of WOMMA," Word of Mouth Marketing Associaton, womma.org, accessed March 7, 2010.

29. "Spy Optic-Microsoft Dynamics CRM Case Study," CRM Software, www.crmsoftwareblog.com, January 2010.

30. Company Web site, "Kimberly-Clark," www.us.capgemini.com, accessed March 7, 2010.

31. "Benefits of a CRM System," Customer Service Point, www.customerservice.point.com, accessed March 7, 2010; "Benefits of CRM," Systems2Business, www.systems2business.com, accessed March 7, 2010; Gene Gander, "10 Ways an Integrated CRM Tool Can Improve the Forwarding Process," The Journal of Commerce, www.joc.com, accessed March 7, 2010.

32. "How to Avoid CRM Implementation Failures," Market for Cause, marketforcause.com, February 8, 2010.

33. Jane Ridley, "Toyota, Jet Blue, Other Big Companies Say They're Sorry in Major Ads, Spotlighting Shortcomings," The Daily News, www.nydailynews.com, February 10, 2010.

34. Peter S. Goodman, "In Case of Emergency: What Not to Do," The New York Times, August 22, 2010, p. BU1 and BU6.

35. Leena Rao, "AT&T Already Has One Million eReaders on Its Network, Without the iPad," TechCrunch.com, techcrunch.com, January 28, 2010.

36. Ibid.

37. "The Tasty Appeal of Co-Branding," ChicagoNow.com, www.chicagonow.com, January 6, 2010.

38. News release, "Body Shaping Companies Announce Co-Marketing and Sales Alliance at American Academy of Dermatology," PR Newswire, finance.yahoo.com, March 3, 2010.

39. Company Web site, Intermec, "Case Studies: Blue C. Shusi Tracks Food Quality and Orders with RFID Technology," www.intermec.com, accessed March 7, 2010.

40. "Velvac Chooses Datalliance's Vendor Managed Inventory Program," TruckingInfo, www.truckinginfo.com, February 1, 2010.

41. Company Web site, "Nailing the Supply Chain: True Value," JDA Software Group Inc., www.jda.com, accessed March 7, 2010.

42. Joe Drape, "NBC Will Televise Major Triple Crown Prep Races," The New York Times, www.nytimes.com, January 11, 2010.

43. Arthur Middleton Hughes, "The Loyalty Effect: A New Look at Lifetime Value," Database Marketing Institute, dbmarketing.com, accessed March 7, 2010.

Chapter 11

1. Company Web site, www.massageenvy.com, accessed April 30, 2010; "Massage Envy Performs 20 Millionth Massage," Drug Week, April 2, 2010, www.newsrx.com; "Massage Envy Receives Official World Record for Most Simultaneous Massagers," Drug Week, March 19, 2010, www.newsrx.com.

2. "World's Most Admired Companies 2010," CNNMoney.com, March 22, 2010, money.cnn.com.

3. U.S. Bureau of Labor Statistics, "Overview of the 2008–18 Projections," Occupational Outlook Handbook, 2010–2011 ed., www.data.bls.gov, accessed April 2, 2010.

4. Bureau of Economic Analysis, 'U.S. International Trade in Goods and Services," International Economic Account, February 10, 2010, www.bea.gov.

5. Penny Crosman, "Transamerica Finds Back-Office Efficiency, Accuracy through Insourcing," Wall Street Technology, January 25, 2010, www.wallstreetandtech.com; Kathleen Goolsby, "Enabling Offshored Call Centers to Move Back on Shore," Outsourcing Journal, September 2009, www.outsourcing-journal.com.

6. Jeremy Caplan, "Phonesourcing: Bringing Call Centers back to the U.S." Time, April 5, 2010, www.time.com.

7. Toluse Olorunnipa, "CEO Conquers Job Loss with 'Homeshoring,' " Miami Herald, February 22, 2010, www.miamiherald.com.

8. Bill Peters, "A Truly Green Work Environment Solution—Goodbye Brick and Mortar," Hospitality Net, November 9, 2009, www.hospitalitynet.org.

9. Matthew Arnold, "DTC Report: Flat Is the New Up," Medical Marketing and Media, March 15, 2010, www.mmm-online.com.

10. Company Web site, www.arttowngifts.com, accessed April 2, 2010.

11. This concept was introduced in Christopher H. Lovelock, "Classifying Services to Gain Strategic Marketing Insights," Journal of Marketing, Summer 1983, 9.

12. "Car Rankings," U.S. News & World Report, March 2010, usnews.rankingsandreviews.com; "Aston Martin Rumored to Launch a One-77 Roadster," Car Buyers' Notebook, www.carbuyersnotebook.com, accessed April 5, 2010.

13. David Robertson, "Airbus Order Brings $2 Billion in Sales for Rolls-Royce," Times Online, December 9, 2009, www.business.timesonline.com.

14. Company Web site, www.bose.com, accessed April 5, 2010.

15. Company Web site, www.cargill.com, accessed April 5, 2010.

16. Company Web site, www.officemax.com, accessed April 5, 2010.

17. Company Web site, www.cisco.com, accessed April 5, 2010.

18. Company Web site, www.regus.com, accessed April 5, 2010.

19. Company Web site, "ISO 9001: Frequently Asked Questions," www.praxiom.com, accessed April 30, 2010; "Quality Portal," www.nist.gov, accessed April 30, 2010.

20. Public Broadcasting System, "Who Made America?" www.pbs.org, accessed April 5, 2010.

21. "Improving the Quality Function: Driving Organizational Impact and Efficiency," Research and Markets, www.researchandmarkets.com, accessed April 5, 2010.

22. "Zappos' Customer Service Draws Raves in a New Report," Internet Retailer, March 22, 2010, www.internetretailer.com; Matt Mickiewicz, "How Zappos Does Customer Service and Company Culture," Sitepoint, March 30, 2009, www.sitepoint.com.

23. "Salesforce.com Outage Has Customers Tweeting," Network World, March 11, 2010, www.networkworld.com.

24. Company Web site, www.llbean.com, accessed April 5, 2010.

25. Ibid.

26. Company Web site, www.jnj.com, accessed April 5, 2010.

27. Company Web site, www.geoxusa.com, accessed May 1, 2010; Marie-Louise Gumuchian and Cristina Carlevaro, "Geox's H1 Revenue Up, Sees Year Sales Flat," Reuters, July 28, 2009, www.reuters.com.

28. "Prime Line Acquires Leeman New York Product Line," Promo Marketing, January 11, 2010, magazine.promomarketing.com.

29. "SunnyRidge Farm Launches New Product Line Extension," FreshPlaza, February 23, 2010, www.freshplaza.com.

30. Chris Foresman, "Years Late, Universal Cuts CD Prices to Combat Poor Sales," Ars Technica, arstechnica.com, accessed April 5, 2010.

31. "GPS Guide," Consumer Reports, www.consumerreports.com, accessed April 5, 2010.

32. Company Web site, www.bestbuy.com, accessed May 1, 2010.

33. "Nike Launches Mercurial Vapor SuperFly II, Delivering Greater Speed and Exclusive Insider Access to the World's Top Players," press release, February 24, 2010, www.nikebiz.com.

34. Jacqui Cheng, "Digital Albums, Vinyls Made a Comeback in '09 while CDs Slide," Ars Technica, January 7, 2010, arstechnica.com.

35. "ABC to Launch New 24 Hour Free News Channel," eBroadcast, January 21, 2010, www.ebroadcast.com.

36. Company Web site, www.armhammer.com, accessed April 6, 2010.

37. "P&G Launches U.S. Campaign to Highlight 'Future Friendly' Products," GreenBiz.com, March 15, 2010, www.greenbiz.com.

38. "Packaging Change for ALDI's Carlini Olive Oil," The Crafty Dollar, January 3, 2010, thecraftydollar.com.

39. "Holiday Inn Relaunches 1000th Hotel," press release, July 24, 2009, www.ihgplc.com.

40. Deepa Seetharaman, "Spirit Air to Experiment with Carry-On Bag Fees," Reuters, April 6, 2010, www.reuters.com.

Chapter 12

1. Company Web site, "Liz Claiborne at J.C.Penney," www.lizclaiborne.com, accessed May 21, 2010; Anne D'Innocenzio, "Big Brands Trade Names for Exposure," Arkansas Democrat-Gazette, November 8, 2009, G1; Mark Albright, "Designer Landscape in Midst of Makeover," St. Petersburg Times, October 13, 2009, www.sptimes.com; Stephanie Rosenbloom, "Liz Claiborne to Be Sold Only at J.C. Penney Stores," The New York Times, October 9, 2009, www.nytimes.com.

2. Allison Ross, "Private Label Sales Hurting Branded Labels," Palm Beach Post, May 11, 2010, blogs.palmbeachpost.com.

3. Company Web site, "Here's Your Guide to Buying Green," www.officedepot.com, accessed April 9, 2010.

4. Company Web site, pressroom.target.com, accessed April 9, 2010.

5. "World's Most Valuable Brands: Brand Finance," Huffington Post, February 18, 2010, www.huffingtonpost.com.

6. "BrandAsset Valuator," Consult Brand Strategy, www.consultbrandstrategy.com, accessed April 9, 2010.

7. Category Management Association Web site, "What Is Category Management?" www.cpgcatnet.org, accessed May 11, 2010.

8. Ibid.

9. Company Web site, www.igd.com, accessed April 12, 2010.

10. Company Web site, wwwhersheys.com, accessed April 9, 2010.

11. "Laser Etching Safe Alternative for Labeling Grapefruit," PhysOrg.com, November 3, 2009, www.physorg.com.

12. Bryan Davis Keith, "The Struggles of a NASCAR Underdog—How Clements Perseveres," Front Stretch, February 24, 2010, www.frontstretch.com.

13. Ariel Cheung, "Naked Cowboy: EXPOSED," News Record, April 9, 2010, www.newsrecord.org.

14. Stuart J. Johnston, "Bing Dinged for Trademark Infringement," *Internet News,* December 17, 2009, www.internetnews.com.

15. Milord & Associates, Inc., "Marc Jacobs Sues Christian Audigier's Company for Trade Dress and Trademark Infringement," press release, February 7, 2010, www.iptrademarkattorney.com.

16. "Beverage Packaging: Maker's Mark Wins Lawsuit Against Cuervo," *Packaging Digest,* April 6, 2010, www.packagingdigest.com.

17. Linda Lisanti, "Sara Lee Sees Daypart Traffic Shift at C-Stores," *Convenience Store News,* December 6, 2009, www.conveniencestorenews.com.

18. Company Web site, "ClearRX/Pharmacy," pressroom.target.com, accessed April 9, 2010.

19. Dan Sewell, "Procter & Gamble, Kraft Settle Lawsuit Over Folgers Packaging," *Huffington Post,* January 16, 2009, www.huffingtonpost.com.

20. Alissa Walker, "What's the Square Root of Sustainability? This Coke Bottle," *Fast Company,* March 30, 2010, www.fastcompany.com.

21. "Food Allergies: Watch Food Labels for These Top Eight Allergens," *MayoClinic.com,* www.mayoclinic.com, accessed April 11, 2010.

22. Company Web site, wiifit.com, accessed April 12, 2010.

23. Company Web site, barbieshanghai.com, accessed May 12, 2010; "Thanks to a Big Mattel Move, Toys and Movies Come One Step Closer to Being the Same Exact Thing," *New York Magazine,* March 24, 2010, www.nymag.com.

24. "Licensing Royalty Rates," *InventionStatistics.com,* www.inventionstatistics.com, accessed April 12, 2010.

25. Mario Marsicano, "Cheetos Lip Balm and More Bizarre Brand Extensions," *The Wall Street Journal,* July 15, 2009, online.wsj.com.

26. Greg Beato, "Starbucks' Midlife Crisis," *Reason,* March 2010, reason.com; Susan Berfield, "Steaming over Via Instant Coffee at Starbucks," *BusinessWeek,* November 11, 2009, www.businessweek.com; Ted Mininni, "Starbucks: Undercutting Its Own Brand?" *MarketingProfsDailyFix.com,* October 8, 2009, www.mpdailyfix.com; "Starbucks Extension Tempts Failure," *Branding Strategy Insider,* May 7, 2009, www.brandingstrategyinsider.com.

27. Karl Greenberg, "ABC: Hyundai Coalesces Its Marketing Plan," *MarketingDaily,* February 19, 2010, www.mediapost.com.

28. Company Web site, www.asianfoodmarkets.com, accessed May 21, 2010; Andy Lagomarsino, "Jersey Trend: Asian Food Markets Reaches out to the Everyday Consumer," *NewJerseyNewsroom.com,* December 29, 2009, www.newjerseynewsroom.com.

29. Erik Gruenwedel, "Panasonic Sells World's First 3D TV System," *Hollywood Reporter,* March 10, 2010, hollywoodreporter.com.

30. Company Web site, www.stetsoncologne.com, accessed April 12, 2010.

31. "Pepsi Gets a Makeover," *Economist.com,* March 25, 2010, www.economist.com.

32. Patricia Odell, "Cinnabon Gives away Cupcakes on Tax Day," *Promo Magazine,* April 7, 2010, www.promomagazine.com.

33. Company Web site, www.bose.com, accessed May 12, 2010.

34. Dev Patnaik, "The Fundamentals of Innovation," *BusinessWeek,* February 10, 2010, www.businessweek.com.

35. Company Web site, www.thescottsmiraclegrocompany.com, accessed April 12, 2010.

36. Company Web site, www.eclipseaerospace.com, accessed May 12, 2010.

37. "Louisiana Gets $20 Million in Eli Lilly Settlement," *Indianapolis Star,* April 8, 2010, www.indystar.com.

38. Jess Bravin, "High Court Eases Way to Liability Lawsuits," *The Wall Street Journal,* March 5, 2009, online.wsj.com.

Chapter 13

1. "Panama Canal Expansion Will Loosen LNG Trade," *Oil & Gas Journal,* March 15, 2010, ogj.com; Rick Jervis, "Ports Get in Shipshape for Wider Panama Canal; More Traffic in 2014 Could Channel Profits," *USA Today,* February 16, 2010, www.usatoday.com; "Panama Canal Expansion Moving Forward as Planned," *BBC,* January 27, 2010, news.bbc.co.uk; A Plan to Unlock Prosperity," *The Economist,* December 5, 2009, www.economist.com; Sean Mattson, "Panama Canal Bulks Up; Mega-Ship Capability Expected to Boost Trade with U.S. and Caribbean," *National Post,* November 19, 2009, www.nationalpost.com; Brad Reagan, "The Panama Canal's Ultimate Upgrade," *Popular Mechanics,* October 1, 2009, www.popularmechanics.com.

2. Zach Kaplan, "Here Comes the Fun," *Nintendo Life,* May 27, 2010, wii.nintendolife.com; Company Web site, www.nintendo.com, accessed April 13, 2010.

3. "Want to Make Money on Twitter? Take a Look at How Dell Does It," *Open Forum,* January 7, 2010, www.openforum.com; Matthew Yeomans, "How Dell Got Out of Hell," *The Big Money,* December 14, 2009, www.thebigmoney.com.

4. "American Airlines Takes on GDS Charges with a New Distribution Model–and Intermediaries Fight Back," *Centre for Aviation,* April 9, 2010, www.centreforaviation.com.

5. "Sales Representatives, Wholesale and Manufacturing," *Occupational Outlook Handbook, 2010–2011,* Bureau of Labor Statistics, U.S. Department of Labor, www.bls.gov.

6. Company Web site, home.stelladot.com, accessed April 18, 2010; Grace L. Williams, "How I … Scaled Quickly to Handle Rapid Growth," *The Wall Street Journal,* October 30, 2009, online.wsj.com.

7. Company Web site, www.bagborroworsteal.com, accessed April 18, 2010.

8. Alexandru Nistor, "Netflix Brings All of Their Movie Content on the Nintendo Wii Console," *Softpedia,* April 12, 2010, gadgets.softpedia.com.

9. Battery Council International, www.batterycouncil.org, accessed May 28, 2010; Organization Web site, www.aaaexchange.com, accessed May 28, 2010.

10. Company Web site, www.nikereuseashoe.com, accessed May 28, 2010; "Staples Expands Ink Cartridge Recycling Program," *Small Business Trends,* January 27, 2009, www.smallbiztrends.com.

11. Colin Moynihan, "24-Hour Bike Shop (Bring Plenty of Quarters)," *The New York Times,* March 25, 2010, cityroom.blogs.nytimes.com.

12. Company Web site, press.spanx.com, accessed April 18, 2010.

13. Brian Stelter, "Networks Wary of Apple's Push to Cut Show Prices," *The New York Times,* February 22, 2010, www.nytimes.com.

14. "The Changing World of Industrial Distribution," *B2B International,* www.b2binternational.com, accessed April 18, 2010.

15. Mark Hamstra and Elliot Zwiebach, "What Will the Next Decade Bring in Food Retailing?" *Supermarket News,* March 1, 2010, supermarketnews.com.

16. Bruce Blythe, "Wal-Mart Makes Few Food Price Changes—So Far," *The Packer,* April 16, 2010, thepacker.com.

17. John Hughes, "American, British Airways Accord Accepted by U.S.," *Bloomberg BusinessWeek,* February 13, 2010, www.businessweek.com.

18. Company Web site, www.tru2way.com, accessed April 18, 2010.

19. Kevin Voigt, "iPad Hits Hong Kong—Before Global Release," *CNN.com,* April 8, 2010, cnn.com; Owen Fletcher, "Amazon Kindle Hits China's Grey Market," *Macworld UK,* March 30, 2010, www.macworld.co.uk.

20. Brian Stelter, "Discovery, Imax and Sony Form 30D Television Channel," *The New York Times,* January 5, 2010, mediadecoder.blogs.nytimes.com.

21. "Quick Franchise Facts, Franchising Industry Statistics," *AZFranchises.com,* www.azfranchises.com, accessed April 18, 2010.

22. Company Web site, www.pier1.com, accessed April 18, 2010.

23. Company Web site, www.jda.com, accessed May 30, 2010.

24. "Boeing RFID Progress," presentation, May 18, 2010, www.ataebiz.org.

25. Richard MacManus, "iPhone as RFID Tag and Reader: Coming Soon," *ReadWriteWeb.com,* January 13, 2010, www.readwriteweb.com.

26. "2010 Prediction: The Year ERP (SAP, Oracle, and Infor) Get Spend Management Right," *SpendMatters.com,* January 10, 2010, www.spendmatters.com.

27. "100 Percent Screening 'Still Two Years Away,' " *Air Cargo World,* March 2010, www.aircargoworld.com.

28. Eric Snyder, "Logistics Industry Grows into Economic Giant," *Nashville Business Journal,* March 5, 2010, www.bizjournals.com.

29. Organization Web site, www.1800flowers.com, accessed April 18, 2010.

30. "Trucking Statistics," *Truckinfo.net,* truckinfo.net, accessed April 18, 2010.

31. "Warren Buffett's $5Billion Railroad Stake … And How to Profit by Following in His 'Tracks,' " *Investment U,* www.investmentu.com, accessed April 18, 2010.

32. FedEx Small Business Center, "Holtkamp Greenhouses," fedex.com, accessed April 19, 2010.

33. Yonah Freemark, "High-Speed Rail Grants Announced; California, Florida, and Illinois Are Lucky Recipients," *The Transport Politic,* January 28, 2010, www.thetransportpolitic.com.

34. American Trucking Associations, "ATA Truck Tonnage Index Fell 0.5 Percent in February," press release, March 25, 2010, www.truckline.com.

35. Brandi Kruse, "Truckers Worries about the Long-Haul," *ABC News,* February 26, 2010, abcnews.com.

36. Patrick Burnson, "Ocean Cargo/Global Logistics: Carriers Are Now in Position to Make Rate Hikes Stick," *Logistics Management,* February 8, 2010, www.logisticsmgmt.com.

37. Jeff Berman, "Global Logistics: FedEx Trade Networks Expands Presence in Asia and Europe," *Logistics Management,* November 16, 2009, www.logisticsmgmt.com.

38. U.S. Department of Transportation Pipeline and Hazardous Materials Safety Administration, "Pipeline Basics," *PHMSA Stakeholder Communications,* phmsa.dot.gov, accessed April 19, 2010.

39. Company Web site, www.ups.com, accessed April 19, 2010.

40. "Clayco to Build $65M Caterpillar Distribution Center," *St. Louis Business Journal,* March 24, 2010, www.bizjournals.com.

41. Wayne Risher, "Nike's $135 Million Distribution Center Saves Energy as It Ships Shoes," *Commercial Appeal,* November 19, 2009, www.commercialappeal.com.

42. "Hubbell Managed Vendor Inventory (VMI) Program Wins Progressive Manufacturing Award," *Marketwire,* April 9, 2010, www.marketwire.com.

43. Company Web site, "At Port Wentworth, a More Efficient Way to Make a Pallet," www.iscnewsroom.com, accessed April 19, 2010.

44. Jennifer Levitz, "Heists Targeting Truckers on Rise," *The Wall Street Journal,* February 1, 2010, online.wsj.com.

Chapter 14

1. Bernard J. Scally, "Celebrating New Partnerships," *Montgomery News,* February 16, 2010, montgomerynews.com; Company Web site, www.wawa.com, accessed February 9, 2010; "Wawa, Inc.," *Answers.com,* www.answers.com, accessed February 9, 2010; "At Wawa Food Stores, a Personalized Web Site Supports Multichannel Sales," *Internet Retailer,* February 4, 2010, www.internetretailer.com; "America's Largest Private Companies," *Forbes,* October 28, 2009, www.forbes.com.
2. "The End of the Sam Walton Era," *Wal-Mart Watch,* walmartwatch.com, accessed February 25, 2010.
3. Ian Ritter, "Wild Oats Founder Looks to Grow Sunflower Markets," *BNET,* January 3, 2010, industry.bnet.com; Max Jarman, "Sunflower Chain Plans to Grow," *Arizona Republic,* December 24, 2009, www.azcentral.com.
4. Anne D'Innocenzio, "Target's 4Q Profit Rises 53.7%," *USA Today,* February 23, 2010, www.usatoday.com.
5. Company Web site, "Women, Men Debunk D-I-Y Gender Myths; Survey Shows Both Sexes Envision Level Playing Field in Home Improvement Abilities," press release, August 20, 2009, lowes.mediaroom.com.
6. Company Web site, www.dswinc.com, accessed February 26, 2010.
7. Alan Wolf, "Best Buy Picks NYC for Its First 24-Hour Store," *TWICE,* October 15, 2009, www.twice.com.
8. "Specialty Foods," *Entrepreneur,* www.entrepreneur.com, accessed March 3, 2010.
9. Company Web site, www.callwave.com, accessed February 25, 2010.
10. Company Web site, www.lapalmera.com, accessed March 7, 2010.
11. Katherine Field, "Lifestyle Centers 2010: Still Viable?" *Chain Store Age,* January 4, 2010, www.chainstoreage.com.
12. Randy White, "Retail-tainment: The Next Big Thing for Retail and Shopping Centers?" white paper, White Hutchinson Leisure & Learning Group, www.whitehutchinson.com, January 16, 2010.
13. Todd Wasserman, "Guerrilla Marketing's Newest Revolution," *Brandweek,* January 9, 2010, www.brandweek.com.
14. Barney Beal, "Smartphones Changing the Face of Web Analytics," *Enterprise Innovation,* February 1, 2010, www.enterpriseinnovation.net.
15. Janet L. Hoffman and Renee V. Sang, "The 'Me-Tail' Revolution," *Accenture Outlook,* February 2010, www.accenture.com.
16. Kristen Fritz, "The Sephora Experience: Shopping Simplified," *The Next Great Generation,* February 1, 2010, www.thenextgreatgeneration.com.
17. Phil Lempert, "Setting the Mood for Higher Sales," *Supermarket Guru,* January 28, 2010, www.supermarketguru.com; Joanna Douglas, "Sneaky Scents: Fragrances Really Are Pumped into Stores to Make You Buy Them," *Shine,* November 2, 2009, shine.yahoo.com.
18. M. S. Enkoji, "Stores within Bigger Stores Seem to Pump up Sales," *Sacramento Bee,* January 17, 2010, www.sacbee.com.
19. "Consumer Connection," *TVAed.com,* www.tvaed.com, accessed March 9, 2010; Barbara Farfan, "Retail Industry Information: Overview of Facts, Research, Data & Trivia," *About.com,* retailindustry.about.com, accessed February 25, 2010.
20. Company Web site, www.gloriajeans.com, accessed March 9, 2010.
21. Company Web site, news.walgreens.com, accessed February 25, 2010.
22. Michelle Chapman, "Macy's Focuses on Localization, Sees 4Q Profit," *ABC News,* February 23, 2010, abcnews.go.com.
23. Company Web site, sale.vente-privee.com, accessed March 10, 2010.
24. Company Web site, www.meijer.com, accessed May 26, 2010.
25. Rich Whittle, "Wal-Mart Tests Drive-Thru Window," *Business Opportunities,* December 21, 2009, www.business-opportunities.com.
26. Nikki Finke, "Wal-Mart Is Buying Digital Entertainment Provider VUDU," *Deadline Hollywood,* February 22, 2010, www.deadline.com.
27. Leslie Barrie, "When It's OK to Skip the Doc," *Health,* January 4, 2010, living.health.com.
28. Company Web site, "Ingram Micro Fact Sheet," www.ingrammicro.com, accessed February 25, 2010.
29. Company Web site, www.unitedstationers.com, accessed February 25, 2010.
30. Organization Web site, "About CES, " www.cesweb.org, accessed February 25, 2010; "CES Officially North America's Largest Trade Show," *Skyline Trade Show Tips,* June 14, 2009, www.skylinetradeshowtips.com.
31. "Merchandising Service Companies," *Product Profitability,* www.productprofitability.com, accessed February 25, 2010.
32. "New Leaf Brands Expands Ohio Distribution with S. Abraham & Sons and United Dairy Farmers," *Market Wire,* February 17, 2010, www.marketwire.com.
33. Jim Olsztynski, "2009 Wholesaler of the Year: Robertson Heating Supply Co," *Supply House Times,* December 1, 2009, www.supplyht.com.
34. Association Web site, "Catalog Industry Fact Sheet," American Catalog Mailers Association, www.catalogmailers.org, accessed February 27, 2010.
35. Catalog Choice, www.catalogchoice.org, accessed March 15, 2010.
36. "Milestones," *Time,* July 13, 2009, p. 21; David Hinckley, "Billy Mays: Pitch Perfect," *New York Daily News,* June 29, 2009, www.nydailynews.com.
37. "Vending Machine Operators," *First Research,* www.bvmarketdata.com, accessed March 15, 2010.
38. "McHenry Company Offers Healthier Vending Machines," *Chicago Tribune,* February 4, 2010, archives.chicagotribune.com; Tammy Wairo, "Vending Machines Offer Students Healthy Snack Options," *Press Publications,* January 21, 2010, www.presspublications.com.
39. Monica Hesse, "Vending Machine Food: Just a Touch-Screen Away," *Washington Post,* February 4, 2010, www.washingtonpost.com.

Chapter 15

1. Alan J. Liddle, "Denny's Details Results of Second Giveaway," *Nation's Restaurant News,* www.nrn.com, February 10, 2010; "Denny's Free Breakfast Today," *Huffington Post,* www.huffingtonpost.com, February 9, 2010; Eleftheria Parpis, "Denny's in Super Bowl Giveaway Return," *Ad Week,* www.adweek.com, January 28, 2010; "How to Hold an Orderly Giveaway," *Advertising Age,* www.adage.com, May 11, 2009; Emily Bryson York, "CMO Boosts Awareness with Free-Meal Promo," *Advertising Age,* www.adage.com, March 23, 2009.
2. Tripp Mickle, "Sponsors Have More Flexibility at X Games," *SportsBusiness Journal,* www.sportsbusinessjournal.com, January 25, 2010.
3. Bill Gorman, "Broadcast Network TV Ratings Season to Date Through Week 25," *TVBytheNumbers.com,* .tvbythenumbers.com, March 18, 2010.
4. Amy Chozick, "NBC Rallies for the Count," *The Wall Street Journal,* online.wsj.com, February 16, 2010.
5. Organization Web site, "Money Smarts," *AARP Financial,* www.moneysmarts.com, accessed March 31, 2010.
6. Ron Smith, "Sorghum Checkoff Funds Research, Marketing," *Southwest Farm Press,* www.southwestfarmpress.com, March 26, 2010.
7. "Suzuki Launches Integrated Marketing Campaign for All-New 1010 Kizashi," *Autochannel.com,* www.theautochannel.com, February 25, 2010.
8. "Five Words to Never Use in an Ad," *Intermarketing Matric,* intermarketing.matrix-e.com, accessed March 31, 2010.
9. Company press release, "Dunkin' Donuts Launches "Twitter Games" and "Yeddi of the Week" to Celebrate Winter Iced Coffee Drinkers," www.dunkindonuts.com, January 11, 2010.
10. "Table 5, Employment by Major Occupational Groups, 2008 and Projected 2018," Bureau of Labor Statistics, www.bls.gov, accessed March 31, 2010.
11. Ken Doctor, "The Newsonomics of Online Ad Spending, and Its Costs," *Nieman Journalism Lab,* www.niemanlab.org, March 2010; Rob Golum, "U.S. Ad Spending Shrank 9% to $117 Billion in 2009, Nielsen," *BusinessWeek,* www.businessweek.com, February 24, 2010.
12. "Advertising: It's Everywhere," *Media Awareness Network,* www.media-awareness.ca, accessed March 31, 2010.
13. "Product Placement Is Now on Twitter," *Product Placement,* www.productplacement.biz, March 25, 2010; Wayne Friedman, "Nissan Drives 'Parenthood' Premiere," *Media Daily News,* www.mediapost.com, March 2, 2010; Wayne Friedman, "TV Product Placement Delivers for '24,' " *Media Daily News,* www.mediapost.com, January 19, 2010; Wayne Friedman, " 'Idol' Gives Coke Millions in Media Value," *Media Daily News,* www.mediapost.com, January 14, 2010.
14. "10 Reasons Why Video Games Are Ideal for Product Placement," *Bid and Brand,* bidandbrand.com, accessed March 31, 2010.
15. Karlene Lukovitz, "Melting Pot, Skyy Vodka Tie In with Movie," *Marketing Daily,* www.mediapost.com, January 5, 2010.
16. "Burger King Readies for Next Twilight Film Promo," www.wsrweb.com, February 23, 2010.
17. Press Release, "Zappos.com and Steve Madden Team Up for a Brickfish Powered 'Sole Search," *Business Wire,* www.your-story.org, December 11, 2009.
18. Patricia Odell, "Sponsorship Spending Struggles to Recover," *Promo magazine,* www.promomagazine.com, January 28, 2010.
19. "Metra Exploring Sale of Naming Rights to Stations, Routes," *Chicago Breaking News,* www.chicagobreakingnews.com, February 12, 2010.
20. "Ambush Marketing to Be Expected at This Year's Football Events," *Bet on World Cup 2010.com,* www.betonworldcup2010.com, accessed March 31, 2010.
21. "DMA's Power of Direct Marketing Report Finds DM Ad Expenditures Climb to Over 54% of All Advertising Expenditures," Direct Marketing Association, www.the-dma.org, October 19, 2009.
22. "Direct Mail vs. Email," *Service Printers,* www.serviceprinters.com, January 15, 2010.
23. Company Web site, J. Jill, www.jjill.com, accessed April 7, 2010; company Web site, Nordstrom, shop.nordstrom.com, accessed April 1, 2010.
24. "DNC Regulatory Information: January 2010," *DNCListManager,* www.dnclistmanager.com, accessed April 1, 2010.
25. William B. Baker, "FCC Proposes to Adopt Stricter Rules Governing Prerecorded Sales Messages," Wiley Rein, LLP, www.wileyrein.com, February 2010.
26. Nathan Golia, "Lavalife Begins DRTV Campaign," *DMNews,* www.dmnews.com, January 11, 2010.

27. Doctor, "The Newsonomics of Online Ad Spending, and Its Costs."
28. Victor Godinez, "Blockbuster Fighting Back with New Technologies," *Philly.com,* www.philly.com, February 17, 2010.
29. "Kodak Connects Comprehensive Ecosystem to the World's Largest Retail Photo Kiosk Feel to Drive More In-Store Printing," *PR Newswire,* www.prnewsire.com, February 20, 2010.
30. "Biggest Loser Contestant Is New Subway Spokeswoman," *QSRWeb,* www.qsrweb.com, December 9, 2009.
31. "Super Bowl Ad Prices Fall; Still Cost Millions," *Crain's New York Business.com,* www.crainsnewyork.com, January 11, 2010.
32. "Top-Earning Athletes of the 2010 Winter Olympics," *Forbes,* www.forbes.com, February 9, 2010.
33. Company Web site, Accenture, www.accenture.com, accessed April 1, 2010.
34. Ad Council, "Childhood Obesity Prevention," www.adcouncil.org, accessed April 1, 2010.
35. Carol Morello, "$133 Million Ad Campaign Promotes Census Participation," *The Washington Post,* www.washingtonpost.com, January 15, 2010.

Chapter 16

1. Company Web site, www.mars.com, accessed June 4, 2010; "Betty White's Golden Touch Keeps Her Red-Hot," *Los Angeles Times,* April 12, 2010, www.latimes.com; Emily Bryson York, "Snickers Uses Humor to Satisfy Generations of Hunger," *Advertising Age,* March 29, 2010, https://adage.com; David Gianatasio, "Snickers' 'Celebrity Sack' Tops 'USA Today' Ad Meter," *Adweek.com,* February 8, 2010, www.adweek.com; Bruce Horovitz, "Betty White and Snickers Score Top Ad Honors," *USA Today,* February 8, 2010, www.usatoday.com; Rick Kissell, "Super Bowl Breaks Ratings Records," *Variety,* February 8, 2010, www.variety.com; "Snickers Debuts Campy, Celeb-Filled Ad Campaign during Super Bowl," *Progressive Grocer,* February 7, 2010, www.progressivegrocer.com.
2. Sarah LeTrent, "Brand-Placement Marketing Targets Huge Airline Traveler Audience," *CNN.com,* March 26, 2010, www.cnn.com.
3. "Rained Out Paves Way for New Mobile Advertising Medium for Sports Industry," *Sportstechy,* February 26, 2010, sports.tmcnet.com.
4. "Cover Story: Coke Drops Campaign Sites in Favour of Social Media," *NewMediaAge,* January 14, 2010, www.nma.co.uk.
5. "GreenLight Ad Gauge of the Grammys Finds That Black Eyed Peas, Eric Clapton, Drew Barrymore and Luke Wilson among Celebs Pitching Target, T-Mobile, Olay, AT&T and Other Brands," *PR Newswire,* February 1, 2010, www.prnewswire.com.
6. "Marketer Database from Abbott to Yum," *Advertising Age,* December 28, 2009, www.adage.com.
7. "Total U.S. Measured Advertising Spending by Category," *Advertising Age,* June 22, 2009, www.adage.com.
8. "2011 Ford Super Duty Marketing Demonstrates Truck's Class-Leading Capability, Fuel Economy," *Auto Channel,* April 7, 2010, www.theautochannel.com; "New Sprint Ad Campaign Highlights Sprint Free Guarantee," *MarketWatch.com,* April 1, 2010, www.marketwatch.com.
9. Stuart Elliott, "A Campaign Linking Clean Clothes with Stylish Living," *The New York Times,* January 8, 2010, www.nytimes.com.
10. Andrew Hampp, "BofA Tries to Remind People of Rosier Era," *AdvertisingAge,* April 19, 2010, adage.com.
11. Michael McCarthy, "Safe-Bet Winter Olympics Stars Could See Endorsement Spikes," *USA Today,* March 1, 2010, www.usatoday.com.
12. Jeremy Mullman, "Why Market Size Won't Matter for LeBron James' Endorsements," *Advertising Age,* May 24, 2010, adage.com.
13. Jonah Freedman, "The 50 Highest-Earning American Athletes," *SportsIllustrated.com,* sportsillustrated.cnn.com, accessed June 6, 2010.
14. McCarthy, "Safe-Bet Winter Olympics Stars Could See Endorsement Spikes"; Kristi Heim, "Ohno Turns Olympic Medals into Endorsement Gold," *Seattle Times,* February 22, 2010, seattletimes.com.
15. McCarthy, "Safe-Bet Winter Olympics Stars Could See Endorsement Spikes."
16. Company Web site, "GEICO Gecko Hits the New York Fashion Show Scene," press release, February 16, 2010, www.geico.com.
17. Darren Rovell, "Wanted: Sidney Crosby's Signature," *CNBC,* March 4, 2010, www.cnbc.com.
18. Meghan Keane, "Online Video Ads Are More Effective Than TV—Because Viewers Are Forced to Watch Them," *eConsultancy.com,* April 23, 2010, econsultancy.com.
19. "Outsell Forecasts Advertising/Marketing Spending to Grow, But Only 1.2 Percent," *Outsell,* March 8, 2010, www.outsellinc.com.
20. Eliot Van Buskirk, "Is 2010 the Year Digital Will Eclipse Print Ad Spending?" *Wired,* March 8, 2010, www.wired.com.
21. "The Four-Letter Word in Advertising: Fear," *Insite,* January 27, 2010, insite.artinstitutes.edu.
22. Laurel Wentz, "Is Paris Hilton Too Sexy for Brazil?" *Advertising Age,* February 25, 2010, adage.com.
23. Aaron Baar, "PepsiCo, Microsoft Team for Soccer Advergame," *MediaPostNews,* April 16, 2010, www.mediapost.com.

24. "Deliver Your Message with Impactful Banner Ads," *OrgMarketing.com,* April 1, 2010, www.orgmarketing.com.
25. "Facebook to Surpass MySpace in Ad Revenue," *Adweek,* December 23, 2009, www.adweek.com.
26. Deborah Yao, "Forecaster Raises 2010 Ad Spending Forecast," *Boston.com,* April 8, 2010, www.boston.com.
27. Rupert Neate, "TV Advertising Growing for the First Time in Five Years," *Telegraph,* April 7, 2010, www.telegraph.co.uk; "U.S. Ad Spend Trends: 2008," *Advertising Age,* June 22, 2009, adage.com.
28. James Gallagher, "Duke Study: TiVo Doesn't Hurt TV Advertising," *Triangle Business Journal,* May 3, 2010, www.bizjournals.com.
29. Company Web site, www.hulu.com, accessed July 19, 2010; Company Web site, www.clicker.com, accessed April 27, 2010; Harry McCracken, "Five Ways to Get More out of Internet TV," *FOXNews.com,* April 6, 2010, www.foxnews.com.
30. Burt Helm, "TV Commercials: Who Needs Them?" *BusinessWeek,* May 25, 2009, p. 24.
31. Company Web site, www.sirius.com, accessed April 29, 2010.
32. Andrew Hampp, "Contextual Radio Ads: Clear Channel's New Pitch to National Marketers," *Advertising Age,* January 15, 2010, adage.com.
33. "Internet Radio Advertising Effectiveness," *ATouchofBusiness.com,* www.atouchofbusiness.com, accessed April 29, 2010; "HD Radio Alliance Launches 2Q2010 HD Radio Campaign," *Radio Magazine,* March 24, 2010, www.radiomagonlinecom.
34. "U.S. Ad Spend Trends: 2008," *Advertising Age,* June 22, 2008, adage.com.
35. Nat Ives, "Newspapers' Paid Circulation Losses Shrink," *Advertising Age,* April 26, 2010, adage.com.
36. Magazine Publishers of America, "Average Total Paid and Verified Circulation for Top 100 ABC Magazines," www.magazine.org, accessed April 29, 2010.
37. Julie Preston, "Mail Spend to Rise," *The Magazine,* January 7, 2010, www.delivermagazine.com.
38. "U.S. Ad Spend Trends: 2008," *Advertising Age,* June 22, 2008, adage.com.
39. Matt Richtel, "Digital Billboards, Diversions Drivers Can't Escape," *The New York Times,* March 1, 2010, www.nytimes.com.
40. "Outdoor Advertising Extends Reach Beyond Products to out of Home Media," *MB.com,* April 26, 2010, www.mb.com.ph.
41. Interactive Advertising Bureau, "Internet Ad Revenues Reach Record Quarterly High of $6.3 Billion in Q4 '09," www.iab.net, April 7, 2010.
42. Rimma Kats, "Augmented Reality Is Next Big Thing in Mobile Advertising: CTIA Panel," *Mobile Marketer,* March 26, 2010, www.mobilemarketer.com; "Mobile Advertising to Grow 45% in 2010 to $3.8 Billion," *MobileMarketingWatch,* January 5, 2010, www.mobilemarketingwatch.com.
43. Company Web site, www.t-immersion.com, accessed April 29, 2010.
44. Company Web site, autowrapped.com, accessed April 29, 2010.
45. "World's Top 50 Agency Companies," *Advertising Age,* April 26, 2010, adage.com.
46. Laura Gunderson, "Portland's Leopold Ketel Ad Agency Makes Pivotal Pitch to Friedrich Air Conditioning," *OregonLive.com,* April 24, 2010, blog.oregonlive.com; "Leopold Ketel & Partners Recruits New President and Partner with Extensive Experience Building National Brands," *BusinessWire,* February 26, 2010, www.marketwatch.com.
47. Public Relations Society of America, "Industry Facts and Figures, " media.prsa.org, accessed June 9, 2010; "Advertising, Marketing, Promotions, Public Relations, and Sales Managers," *Occupational Outlook Handbook, 2010–11 Edition,* U.S. Bureau of Labor Statistics, data.bls.gov.
48. Company Web site, "Escape for the Day: The Daycation Now Available at Four Seasons Hotel Las Vegas," press release, April 29, 2010, press.fourseasons.com.
49. "SunChips Kicks off Earth Month with Introduction of World's First 100 Percent Compostable Chip Bag," *PRNewswire,* March 31, 2010, www.prnewswire.com.
50. Suzanne Vranica, "Toyota Pulls Ads, Hires PR Firm," *The Wall Street Journal,* January 27, 2010, online.wsj.com.
51. "Primary Wave Music and Motel 6 Launch Second Run of the 'Rock Yourself to Sleep' Campaign Giving Touring Bands Free Rooms," *Billboard Publicity Wire,* March 15, 2010, www.billboardpublicitywire.com.
52. Bruce Rogers, "Advertising Accountability: Every CMO Wants It, But Few Know How to Get It," *iMediaConnection.com,* March 12, 2010, ad-tech.blogs.imediaconnection.com.
53. Company Web site, www.audiobrain.com, accessed April 30, 2010.
54. Company Web site, "The Edison/ADM Consumer Attitudes to Podcast Advertising Study," January 29, 2010, www.edisonresearch.com.

55. Brandon Glenn, "FDA Slaps Eli Lilly for 'False or Misleading Claims' in Ads for Cymbalta,'" *Med City News,* January 14, 2010, www.medcitynews.com.
56. "Move over 2010 Super Bowl Ads! *Ad Age* Ranks the Best Ad Campaigns of All Time," *New York Daily News,* February 7, 2010, www.nydailynews.com.
57. Company Web site, www.telefonica.com, accessed June 10, 2010.

Chapter 17

1. Company Web site, www.salesforce.com, accessed June 16, 2010; Cliff Saran, "Clovd Infantes Salesforce Revenues," Computerweekly.com, February 25, 2010; associated Press, "Salesforce.com IQ Profit Soars on Big Sales Jump," The Boston Globe, www.boston.com, February 24, 2010; Jessica Hodgson, "Selling and Software," *The Wall Street Journal,* December 16, 2009, online.wsj.com; "Finance Firm Partners with Salesforce.com," *BusinessWorld,* October 5, 2009, www.businessworld.com; Mary Hayes Weier, "Salesforce.com Helps Launch SaaS Company," *InformationWeek,* September 30, 2009, www.informationweek.com; Jack Loo, "Salesforce.com Opens Its First International Data Centre," *Network World,* July 16, 2009, www.networkworld.com.
2. U.S. Bureau of Labor Statistics, *Occupational Outlook Handbook, 2010–2011 Edition,* data.bls.gov, accessed May 4, 2010.
3. Ibid.
4. Marianne Wilson, "Orchard Supply Hardware Reinvents Its Box," *Chain Store Age,* April 19, 2010, www.chainstoreage.com.
5. Company Web site, "Best Buy Plans to Open 22 New Stores for Third Fiscal Quarter," press release, accessed May 4, 2010, www.bby.com.
6. Emily Torres, "The Future of Shopping," *Young Money,* February 17, 2010, www.youngmoney.com.
7. Eric Lai, "Panasonic's Toughbook Tablet Takes Swing at Rugged Rivals," *PCWorld,* February 10, 2010, www.pcworld.com.
8. Rachel Dornhelm, "Enabling Cookies: Girl Scouts Take Sales Online," *VOA News.com,* March 5, 2010, www1.voanews.com.
9. Company Web site, "Company Quick Facts," www.marykay.com, accessed May 4, 2010.
10. Federal Communications Commission, "Unwanted Telephone Marketing Calls," www.fcc.gov, accessed May 4, 2010.
11. Federal Communications Commission, "Additional Report to Congress Pursuant to the Do Not Call Registry Fee Extension Act of 2007," December 2009, www.ftc.gov.
12. Federal Trade Commission, "FTC Business Alert," www.ftc.gov, accessed May 4, 2010.
13. Direct Marketing Association Web site, "Telemarketing Resource Center," www.the-dma.org, accessed May 4, 2010.
14. Company Web site, "Work from Home Technology," www.databasesystemscorp.com, accessed May 4, 2010.
15. Company Web site, www.nba.com, accessed June 18, 2010.
16. Company Web site, "Clients & Awards," www.rightnow.com, accessed May 6, 2010.
17. Adam J. Fein, "Demand-Driven Customer Relationships," in *Facing the Forces of Change: Lead the Way in the Supply Chain,* www.naw.org, accessed May 6, 2010.
18. Company Web site, "Fireman's Fund Insurance Company," www.richardson.com, accessed May 6, 2010.
19. Jeff Blumenthal, "ResCap Subsidiary GMAC Mortgage Launches Virtual Sales Network," *Philadelphia Business Journal,* April 19, 2010, www.bizjournals.com.
20. Company Web site, "A Brief History," www.southwest.com, accessed May 6, 2010.
21. "New Interactive Store Kiosk with Microsoft Silverlight Technology at NRF 2010 from Escalate Retail," *TechArena,* January 12, 2010, www.techarena.com.
22. Grant McCracken, "How Ford Got Social Marketing Right," *Harvard Business Review,* January 7, 2010, blogs.hbr.org.
23. Lee Howard, "Pharma Opposes Bill to Limit Perks for Doctors," *The Day,* April 22, 2010, www.theday.com.
24. "Five Proven Tools and Techniques to Generate Sales Leads," *Cake Marketing,* March 12, 2010, cakemarketing.com.
25. "SlideShare Goes beyond PowerPoint and Adds Video," *ReadWriteWeb,* May 5, 2010, www.readwriteweb.com.
26. Josh Spiro, "One Company's Budget: Cold Calling Saved My Company," *Inc.com,* March 18, 2010, www.inc.com.
27. Company Web site, www.blackanddecker.com, accessed May 6, 2010.
28. U.S. Bureau of Labor Statistics, *Occupational Outlook Handbook, 2010–2011 Edition,* www.bls.gov, accessed June 18, 2010.
29. "DRI Corporation Announces New Sales Director for U.S. Subsidiary," *BusinessWire,* May 5, 2010, www.businesswire.com.
30. U.S. Department of Labor, "20 Leading Occupations of Employed Women," March 2010, www.dol.gov.
31. Company Web site, www.santinelli.com, accessed June 18, 2010; "Santinelli Sales Meeting in Florida," *The Optical Vision Site,* February 3, 2010, theopticalvisionsite.com.

32. Tanya Batallas, "Back-to-School Shoppers Get Their Penny's Worth," *Star-Ledger,* August 21, 2009, www.nj.com.
33. "CRM Best Practices," *CRM Trends,* www.crmtrends.com, accessed May 6, 2010.
34. Bill Shea, "Consumers Saved $3.5 Billion with Coupons in 2009, Valassis Reports," *Crain's Detroit Business,* January 29, 2010, www.crainsdetroit.com.
35. Edward C. Baig, "Target Puts Mobile Coupons on Customers' Cellphones," *USA Today,* March 11, 2010, www.usatoday.com.
36. Patricia Odell, "Steady Growth," *Promo,* December 1, 2009, www.promomagazine.com.
37. Barbara Findley Schenck, "Pique Interests with a Sample," *Entrepreneur,* March 9, 2010, www.entrepreneur.com.
38. "Long John Silver's Launches Spin & Win Fish Fry Online Sweepstakes," *Enhanced Online News,* February 2, 2010, eon.businesswire.com.
39. Carroll Trosclair, "Point-of-Purchase Advertising Trends," *Advertising,* January 21, 2010, advertising.suite101.com.

Chapter 18

1. "Windows 7 Service Pack 1 Beta Leaks Online," *EWeek,* www.pcmag.com, April 8, 2010; Gavin Clarke, "Discounts Damage for Microsoft Windows 7 PC Boost?" *The Register,* www.theregister.co.uk, January 16, 2010; Alex Pham, "Win 7 Beats Vista in Sales; Aggressive Pricing and Positive Reviews Boost Microsoft's New Operating System," *Los Angeles Times,* www.latimes.com, November 7, 2009; Byron Acohido, "PC Prices Should Stay Low with Windows 7," *USA Today,* www.usatoday.com, October 13, 2009; Peter Burrows, "Microsoft's Aggressive New Pricing Strategy," *BusinessWeek,* July 27, 2009, p. 51.
2. Renée Johnson, "The U.S. Trade Situation for Fruit and Vegetable Products," *Congressional Research Service,* December 15, 2009.
3. "Change to Auto Parts Imports Regulation Has Limited Market Impact," *Xinhua News Agency,* www.china.org.cn, September 2, 2009.
4. "StubHub Is the Fan's Ticket Marketplace," company Web site, www.stubhub.com, accessed March 8, 2010.
5. "American Airlines Blankets Will Cost 8 Dollars," *Huffington Post,* www.huffingtonpost.com, February 8, 2010; Charlie Leocha, "American Airlines Institutes a $50 Coach Standby Fee," *ConsumerTraveler.com,* www.comsumertraveler.com, February 11, 2010.
6. Andy Patrizio, "Could a Cheaper iPhone Be on the Way?" *Enterprise Mobile Today,* www.enterprisemobiletoday.com, February 26, 2010.
7. Deena M. Amato-McCoy, "Focus on Loyalty Programs," *Chain Store Age,* www.chainstoreage.com, February 1, 2010.
8. Robert D. Buzzell, Bradley T. Gale, and Ralph G. M. Sultan, "Market Share, A Key to Profitability, *Harvard Business Review,* hbr.org, accessed March 3, 2010.
9. Company Web site, Skype, www.skype.com, accessed March 3, 2010.
10. "The Kroger Southwest Division Launches New Marketing Campaign: Low Prices Plus More," *Fox Business,* www.foxbusiness.com, March 8, 2010.
11. Company Web site, Trader Joe's, traderjoes.com, accessed March 8, 2010.
12. David Coursey, "PC Sales Up, Prices May Follow. Buy Now?" *PC World,* www.pcworld.com, January 14, 2010.
13. Company Web site, NetJets, www.netjets.com, accessed March 8, 2010; Thomas Flohr, "Luxury Private Jets Taking Off in Asia," *Business Times,* www.businesstimes.com, February 1, 2010.
14. Keith Benman, "Bumpy Indiana Toll Road Ride Far from Over," *Northwest Indiana Times,* nwitimes.com, January 3, 2010.
15. Organization Web site, *Seattle.gov,* www.cityofseattle.net, accessed March 9, 2010.
16. "Sin Taxes Aren't the Whole Solution," *Tobacco Issues.com,* www.tobaccoissues,com, February 10, 2010.
17. Brad Tuttle, "Your Butt's Not Getting Bigger," *Time,* money.blogs.time.com, February 1, 2010.
18. "Procter & Gamble Hikes Soap Prices," *GMA News,* www.gmanews.tv, February 4, 2010; Company press release, "Dow Increases Prices for Emulsion Polymer Based Products in North America," news.dow.com, January 12, 2010.
19. "Toyota Unveils 2010 Fuel-Sipper Prius in Detroit," *Japan Today,* www.japantoday.com, January 13, 2010.
20. "Fewer Flights, Rising Fares Plague Some Big Airports," *Allbusiness.com,* December 20, 2009, www.allbusiness.com.
21. "Zimbabwe Inflation at –4.8% in January," *The Harare Tribune,* www.hararetribune.com, February 18, 2010; "Zimbabwe Inflation Rising as Disinflationary Effect of Hard-Currency Move Fades," *VOANews.com,* www1.voanews.com, February 18, 2010.
22. "Alternative Fuel Sources—Moving Away from Gas," *Clean Diesel,* cleandieselgeorgia.org, February 16, 2010.
23. John Neff, "Ford Earned $2.7B Profit in 2009, Predicts Repeat in 2010," *AutoBlog,* www.autoblog.com, January 28, 2010.
24. "Revenue Management Is Coming to the Spa Industry," *SpaFinder,* blog.spafinder.com, accessed March 9, 2010.
25. James L. McKenney, "Stouffer Yield Management System," Harvard Business School Case 9-190-193, Boston: Harvard Business School, 1994; Anirudh Dhebar and Adam

Brandenburger, "American Airlines, Inc.: Revenue Management," Harvard Business School Case 9-190-029, Boston: Harvard Business School, 1992.

26. Robin Givhan, "Olympic Games' Tortured Relationship with Fashion Won't Change in Vancouver," *The Washington Post,* www.washingtonpost.com, January 31, 2010; Hudson Bay company press release, "Polo Ralph Lauren US Olympic Team Clothing to Be the First of Foreign 2010 Uniforms Available Exclusively at the Bay," www.tradingmarkets.com, December 8, 2009.

27. "The Euro," The European Commission, ec.europa.eu, accessed April 16, 2010.

28. Richard Smith, "Small Shopkeepers Hit Out as Tesco Plans to Open 18th Store in Bristol," *The Mirror,* www.mirror.co.uk, January 30, 2010.

Chapter 19

1. Bruce Horovitz, "Marketers Target Job-Loss Fears," *USA Today,* March 31, 2010, P. 1A; Company Web site, www.josbank.com, accessed March 17, 2010; Ryan Sharrow, "Jos. A. Bank Brings Back Suit Promotion for Laid-off Customers," *Dayton Business Journal,* March 8, 2010, www.daytonbizjournals.com; "JoS. A. Bank Clothiers Announces Its Popular 'Risk Free' Promotion," *Yahoo! Finance,* March 8, 2010, finance.yahoo.com; "JoS. A. Bank Clothiers Reports 26% Increase in Profits," press release, December 2, 2009, newsblaze.com; Andrew Ortlieb, "Flurry of Promotions Weakens JoS. A. Bank Brand," *Anxiety Index,* November 5, 2009, anxietyindex.com; Joe Keenan, "Tailored Deals Bank Sales," *All About ROI,* September 2009, www.allaboutroimag.com.

2. Company Web site, www.bestbuy.com, accessed March 17, 2010.

3. Ibid.

4. Chris Gaylord, "World's Cheapest Car, Tata Nano, Revs toward US," *Christian Science Monitor,* January 15, 2010, www.csmonitor.com.

5. Steve Painter and Laurie Whalen, "Wal-Mart Sets Late-Delivery Fee," *Arkansas Democrat Gazette,* February 14, 2010, G1.

6. Jenn Abelson, "Seeking Savings, Some Ditch Brand Loyalty," *Boston.com,* January 29, 2010, www.boston.com.

7. "Kia Spectra Review," *Edmunds.com,* www.edmunds.com, accessed March 17, 2010.

8. Company Web site, www.shutterfly.com, accessed March 17, 2010.

9. Company Web site, qd.sees.com, accessed March 17, 2010.

10. Organization Web site, www.consumerreports.com, accessed March 17, 2010.

11. Brad Stone, "The Fight over Who Sets Prices at the Online Mall," *The New York Times,* February 8, 2010, www.nytimes.com.

12. Paula Ebben, "Are Rebates Worth Your Time and Effort?" *WBZTV.com,* February 24, 2010, wbztv.com; Mark Huffman, "Consumers Continue to Fall into the Rebate Trap," *ConsumerAffairs.com,* January 5, 2010, www.consumeraffairs.com.

13. Scarlet Sims, "Comcast Unveils Internet Usage Meter," *NewsHerald.com,* March 16, 2010, www.newsherald.com.

14. Company Web site, www.bergdorfgoodman.com, accessed June 27, 2010; company Web site, www.sunglasshut.com, accessed June 27, 2010; company Web site, www.gold-and-wood.com, accessed June 27, 2010; "$55,000 Diamond Eyeglasses from Gold and Wood," *Optical Vision Site,* theopticalvisionsite.com, accessed June 27, 2010.

15. Kelly Ebbels, "Restaurants Offer $20.10 Menu for 2010," *Ridgewood Patch,* January 15, 2010, ridgewood.patch.com.

16. Brad Tuttle, "Where's the Cheapest Milk? And the Cheapest Caffeine Fix?" *Time,* March 16, 2010, money.blogs.time.com; John Ewoldt, "Mystic Lake Offers Lobster Loss Leader," *StarTribune.com,* February 17, 2010, www.startribune.com.

17. "Price Drops," *CNET.com,* shopper.cnet.com, accessed March 17, 2010; Lori Grunin, "Digital SLR Cameras on a Shoestring," *CNET.com,* March 12, 2010, reviews.cnet.com.

18. "Consumers Don't Always Equate Higher Prices with Quality," *PhysOrg.com,* October 14, 2009, www.physorg.com.

19. Helen Anders, "Cheap Chic: Motel 6 Steps up Its Style," *Statesman.com,* January 29, 2010, www.statesman.com.

20. Sam Abuelsamid, "Officially Official: 2012 Ford Police Interceptor Unveiled, Second Utility Model Announced," *Autoblog,* March 12, 2010, www.autoblog.com; Jeremy Korzeniewski, "Chicago 2010: Chevrolet Rolls out Caprice Police Car," *Autoblog,* February 12, 2010, www.autoblog.com.

21. John J. Monahan, "State Auditor Says Sheriff's Office Violated Bidding Policy," *Worcester Telegram and Gazette,* March 2, 2010, www.telegram.com.

22. Company Web site, www.razorgator.com, accessed March 17, 2010; company Web site, www.ticketliquidator.com, accessed March 17, 2010.

23. Company Web site, www.pageonce.com, accessed March 18, 2010; company Web site, www.ubid.com, accessed March 18, 2010; Murad Ahmed, "eBay's Fixed-Price Sales Overtake Profits from Web Auctions," *Times Online,* December 10, 2009, technology.timesonline.co.uk.

24. Company Web site, www.containerstore.com, accessed March 18, 2010; company Web site, www.lowes.com, accessed March 18, 2010; Steve Banker, "Multichannel Logistics: Walmart.com's Site-to-Store Strategy," *Logistics Viewpoints,* January 27, 2010, logisticsviewpoints.com.

25. Todd Spangler, "Verizon Sets New FiOS Bundles, Hikes Early Termination Fee," *Multichannel News,* January 15, 2010, www.multichannel.com.

26. James Surowiecki, "Bundles of Cables," *New Yorker,* January 25, 2010, www.newyorker.com; Yinka Adegoke, "Cable Fee Battles Point to Smaller TV Bundles," *Reuters,* January 12, 2010, www.reuters.com.

27. Colin Gibbs, "Dell Wisely Chooses Emerging Markets for Smartphone Play," *GigaOM,* November 13, 2009, gigaom.com.

28. Company Web site, www.stapleseasyrebates.com, accessed June 28, 2010.

29. Liz Pulliam Weston, "How to Fight All Those Hidden Charges," *MSN Money,* articles.moneycentral.com, accessed June 28, 2010.

Appendix A

1. "Unilever Appoints New Chief Marketing & Communications Officer," press release, May 3, 2010, www.unilever.com; Tim Bradshaw, "Warning over 'Lost Generation' of Marketeers," *Financial Times,* April 5, 2010, www.ft.com; Andrew McMains, "Unilever Names Keith Weed CMO," *Adweek,* March 5, 2010, adweek.com; Jack Neff, "Unilever Names Keith Weed as New CMO," *Advertising Age,* March 5, 2010, adage.com; Andrew McMains, "Unilever Shops Face Life without Simon," *Adweek,* February 15, 2010, adweek.com; Jack Neff, "Unilever CMO Simon Clift Announces Retirement,"*Advertising Age,* February 9, 2010, adage.com.

2. "Advertising, Marketing, Promotions, Public Relations, and Sales Managers," *Occupational Outlook Handbook, 2010–2011 Edition,* Bureau of Labor Statistics, data.bls.gov, accessed May 11, 2010.

3. "Starting Salary Offers to College Class of 2010 Decline," National Association of Colleges and Employers, April 8, 2010, www.naceweb.org.

4. "Employment Projections: 2008-2018 Summary," *Occupational Outlook Handbook, 2010–2011 Edition,* Bureau of Labor Statistics, data.bls.gov, accessed May 11, 2010.

5. Steve Rosenbush, "The Bartender of eBay," *Portfolio.com,* June 21, 2010, www.portfolio.com.

6. Company Web site, salesjobs.com, accessed May 11, 2010; company Web site, womensportsjobs.com, accessed May 11, 2010.

7. Mike O'Brien, "To Find a Job, Go Where the Recruiters Are," *Yahoo!HotJobs,* hotjobs.com, accessed May 11, 2010.

8. Company Web site, www.erac.com, accessed May 11, 2010.

9. Steven Greenhouse, "The Unpaid Intern, Legal or Not," *The New York Times,* April 2, 2010, www.nytimes.com.

10. Association Web site, www2.aaaa.org, accessed May 11, 2010; organization Web site, www.twc.edu, accessed May 11, 2010; organization Web site, ext1.inroads.org, accessed May 11, 2010.

11. Kim Isaacs, "10 Cover Letter Don'ts," *Monster.com,* career-advice.monster.com, accessed May 11, 2010; Katie Lorenz, "Cover Letter Dos and Don'ts," *CareerBuilder.com,* msn.careerbuilder.com, accessed May 11, 2010; Tim Bearden, "Cover Letter Do's and Don'ts," *Philly.com,* May 4, 2010, www.philly.com.

12. Carole Martin, "Prep for the Top 10 Interview Questions," *Monster.com,* career-advice. monster.com, accessed May 12, 2010.

Appendix B

1. Corporate Web site, www.google.com, accessed May 12, 2010.

2. Ariel Schwartz, "TerraCycle's Next Venture: Turning Trash into Trash Cans," *Fast Company,* February 16, 2010, www.fastcompany.com.

3. Corporate Web site, www.nintendo.com, accessed May 12, 2010.

4. Lisa Gibson, "RFS2 Reduces 2010 Cellulosic Ethanol Requirement," *Biomass,* February 2010, www.biomassmagazine.com.

5. John Hollon, "How Costco Does Succession Planning," *Workforce Management,* February 3, 2010, www.workforce.com.

6. Company Web site, www.c2educate.com, accessed July 2, 2010.

7. Christina Cheddar Berk, "J. Crew CEO: Retailers Have Come Back, Not Consumers," *CNBC,* April 8, 2010, www.cnbc.com; Elizabeth Holmes, "J Crew Swings to 4Q Profit on Higher Margins," *The Wall Street Journal,* March 10, 2010, online.wsj.com.

8. Company Web site, www.madewell.com, accessed July 2, 2010.

9. Elaine Wong, "P&G Growing Hair Growth Biz," *Brandweek,* January 23, 2010, www.brandweek.com.

10. Company Web site, cuteoverload.com, accessed May 12, 2010.

11. Richard Corliss, "Box Office Weekend: *Karate Kid* Whups *A Team," Time,* June 13, 2010, www.time.com; "Little Caesars Pizza Teams with PepsiCo and Columbia Pictures' 'The Karate Kid' to Kick off 'Your Ticket to Kick It' National Promotion," *Restaurant News,* April 26, 2010, www.restaurantnews.com; Jason Ankeny, "How the iPad Could Revolutionize the Marketing Mix," *Fierce Mobile Content,* April 20, 2010, www.fiercemobilecontent.com; Stuart Elliott, "Now in the Movie Marketing Mix: Six Flags," *The New York Times,* March 31, 2010, www.nytimes.com.

12. Company Web site, www.ghfc.com, accessed May 12, 2010.

13. Natalie Martin, "GMAC Sells Its UK Financial Arm as Part of European Exit Strategy," *Mortgage Strategy,* April 19, 2010, www.mortgagestrategy.com.

14. Paul Tharp, "AIG Eyes Easing U.S. Out," *New York Post,* March 4, 2010, www.nypost.com.

glossary

80/20 principle Generally accepted rule that 80 percent of a product's revenues come from 20 percent of its customers.

A

accessory equipment Capital items such as desktop computers and printers that typically cost less and last for shorter periods than installations.

administered marketing system VMS that achieves channel coordination when a dominant channel member exercises its power.

adoption process Stages consumers go through in learning about a new product, trying it, and deciding whether to purchase it again.

advertising Paid, nonpersonal communication through various media about a business firm, not-for-profit organization, product, or idea by a sponsor identified in a message intended to inform or persuade members of a particular audience.

advertising agency Firm whose marketing specialists help advertisers plan and prepare advertisements.

advertising campaign Series of different but related ads that use a single theme and appear in different media within a specified time period.

affinity marketing Marketing effort sponsored by an organization that solicits responses from individuals who share common interests and activities.

AIDA concept Steps through which an individual reaches a purchase decision: attention, interest, desire, and action.

AIO statements Items on lifestyle surveys that describe various activities, interests, and respondents' opinions.

allowance Specified deduction from list price, including a trade-in or promotional allowance.

ambush marketing Attempt by a firm that is not an official sponsor of an event or activity to link itself to the event or activity.

antitrust Laws designed to prevent restraints on trade such as business monopolies.

application service providers (ASPs) Outside companies that specialize in providing both the computers and the application support for managing information systems of business clients.

approach Salesperson's initial contact with a prospective customer.

atmospherics Combination of physical characteristics and amenities that contribute to a store's image.

attitudes Person's enduring favorable or unfavorable evaluations, emotions, or action tendencies toward some object or idea.

average total costs Costs calculated by dividing the sum of the variable and fixed costs by the number of units produced.

B

backward integration Process through which a manufacturer attempts to gain greater control over inputs in its production process, such as raw materials.

banner ad Strip message placed in high-visibility areas of frequently visited Web sites.

basing-point pricing System used in some industries during the early 20th century in which the buyer paid the factory price plus freight charges from the basing-point city nearest the buyer.

benchmarking Method of measuring quality by comparing performance against industry leaders.

blog Short for *Web log*—an online journal for an individual or organization.

bonus pack Specially packaged item that gives the purchaser a larger quantity at the regular price.

bot (shopbot) Software program that allows online shoppers to compare the price of a particular product offered by several online retailers.

bottom line Reference to over all company profitability.

brand Name, term, sign, symbol, design, or some combination that identifies the products of one firm while differentiating them from that of the competition.

brand equity Added value that a respected, well-known brand name gives to a product in the marketplace.

brand extension Strategy of attaching a popular brand name to a new product in an unrelated product category.

brand insistence Consumer refusal of alternatives and extensive search for desired merchandise.

brand licensing Practice that expands a firm's exposure in the marketplace.

brand manager Marketer responsible for a single brand.

brand mark Symbol or pictorial design that distinguishes a product.

brand name Part of a brand, consisting of letters, numbers, or words, that can be spoken and that identifies and distinguishes a firm's offerings from those of its competitors.

brand preference Consumer reliance on previous experiences with a product to choose that item again.

brand recognition Consumer awareness and identification of a brand.

breakeven analysis Pricing technique used to determine the number of products that must be sold at a specified price to generate enough revenue to cover total cost.

broker Agent wholesaling intermediary that does not take title to or possession of goods in the course of its primary function, which is to bring together buyers and sellers.

bundle pricing Offering two or more complementary products and selling them for a single price.

business cycle Pattern of stages in the level of economic activity: prosperity, recession, depression, and recovery.

business plan Formal document that outlines what a company's objectives are, how they will be met, how the business will obtain financing, and how much money the company expects to earn.

business products Goods and services purchased for use either directly or indirectly in the production of other goods and services for resale.

business services Intangible products firms buy to facilitate their production and operating processes.

business-to-business (B2B) e-marketing Use of the Internet for business transactions between organizations.

business-to-business (B2B) marketing Organizational sales and purchases of goods and services to support production of other products, to facilitate daily company operations, or for resale.

business-to-business (B2B) product Product that contributes directly or indirectly to the output of other products for resale; also called industrial or organizational product.

business-to-consumer (B2C) e-marketing Selling directly to consumers over the Internet.

buyer Person who has the formal authority to select a supplier and to implement the procedures for securing a good or service.

buyer partnership Relationship in which a firm purchases goods or services from one or more providers.

buyer's market A market in which there are more goods and services than people willing to buy them.

buying center Participants in an organizational buying action.

buzz marketing Marketing that gathers volunteers to try products and then relies on them to talk about their experiences with their friends and colleagues.

C

cannibalization Loss of sales of an existing product due to competition from a new product in the same line.

captive brand National brand sold exclusively by a retail chain.

cash discount Price reduction offered to a consumer, business user, or marketing intermediary in return for prompt payment of a bill.

category advisor (category captain) Trade industry vendor who develops a comprehensive procurement plan for a retail buyer.

category killer Store offering huge selections and low prices in single product lines.

category management Product management system in which a category manager—with profit and loss responsibility—oversees a product line.

cause marketing Identification and marketing of a social issue, cause, or idea to selected target markets.

Central American Free Trade Agreement-DR (CAFTA-DR) Trade agreement among the United States, Central American nations, and the Dominican Republic.

channel Medium through which a message is delivered.

channel captain Dominant and controlling member of a marketing channel.

channel conflicts Conflicts between manufacturers, wholesalers, and retailers.

click-through rate Percentage of people presented with a banner ad who click on it.

closed sales territory Exclusive geographic selling region of a distributor.

closing Stage of the personal selling process in which the salesperson asks the customer to make a purchase decision.

cluster sample Probability sample in which researchers select a sample of subgroups (or clusters) from which they draw respondents; each cluster reflects the diversity of the whole population sampled.

cobranding Cooperative arrangement in which two or more businesses team up to closely link their names on a single product.

cognitive dissonance Imbalance among knowledge, beliefs, and attitudes that occurs after an action or decision, such as a purchase.

cohort effect Tendency of members of a generation to be influenced and bound together by events occurring during their key formative years—roughly ages 17 to 22.

cold calling Contacting a prospect without a prior appointment.

collaborative planning, forecasting, and replenishment (CPFaR) Planning and forecasting approach based on collaboration between buyers and sellers.

comarketing Cooperative arrangement in which two businesses jointly market each other's products.

commercial market Individuals and firms that acquire products to support, directly or indirectly, production of other goods and services.

commission Incentive compensation directly related to the sales or profits achieved by a salesperson.

commission merchant Agent wholesaling intermediary who takes possession of goods shipped to a central market for sale, acts as the producer's agent, and collects an agreed-upon fee at the time of the sale.

common carriers Businesses that provide transportation services as for-hire carriers to the general public.

common market Extension of a customs union by seeking to reconcile all government regulations affecting trade.

comparative advertising Advertising strategy that emphasizes messages with direct or indirect promotional comparisons between competing brands.

competitive bidding Inviting potential suppliers to quote prices on proposed purchases or contracts.

competitive environment Interactive process that occurs in the marketplace among marketers of directly competitive products, marketers of products that can be substituted for one another, and marketers competing for the consumer's purchasing power.

competitive pricing strategy Pricing strategy designed to deemphasize price as a competitive variable by pricing a good or service at the general level of comparable offerings.

competitive strategy Methods through which a firm deals with its competitive environment.

component parts and materials Finished business products of one producer that become part of the final products of another producer.

concentrated (or niche) marketing Focusing marketing efforts on satisfying a single market segment.

concept testing Method for subjecting a product idea to additional study before actual development by involving consumers through focus groups, surveys, in-store polling, and the like.

consolidated metropolitan statistical area (CMSA) Urban area that includes two or more PMSAs.

consultative selling Meeting customer needs by listening to them, understanding their problems, paying attention to details, and following through after the sale.

consumer behavior Process through which buyers make purchase decisions.

consumer innovators People who purchase new products almost as soon as the products reach the market.

consumer orientation Business philosophy incorporating the marketing concept that emphasizes first determining unmet consumer needs and then designing a system for satisfying them.

consumer (B2C) product Product destined for use by ultimate consumers.

consumer products Products bought by ultimate consumers for personal use.

consumer rights List of legitimate consumer expectations suggested by President John F. Kennedy.

consumerism Social force within the environment that aids and protects the consumer by exerting legal, moral, and economic pressures on business and government.

containerization Process of combining several unitized loads into a single, well-protected load for shipment.

contest Sales promotion technique that requires entrants to complete a task, such as solving a puzzle or answering questions on a quiz, for the chance to win a prize.

contract carriers For-hire transporters that do not offer their services to the general public.

contractual marketing system VMS that coordinates channel activities through formal agreements among participants.

controlled experiment Scientific investigation in which a researcher manipulates a test group (or groups) and compares the results with those of a control group that did not receive the experimental controls or manipulations.

convenience products Goods and services consumers want to purchase frequently, immediately, and with minimal effort.

convenience retailer Store that appeals to customers on accessible location, long hours, rapid checkout, and adequate parking.

convenience sample Nonprobability sample selected from among readily available respondents.

conversion rate Percentage of visitors to a Web site who make a purchase.

cookies Techniques for collecting information about online Web site visitors in which small text files are automatically downloaded to a user's computer to gather such data as length of visit and the site visited next.

cooperative advertising Strategy in which a retailer shares advertising costs with a manufacturer or wholesaler.

core based statistical area (CBSA) Collective term for metropolitan and micropolitan statistical areas.

core region Region from which most major brands get 40 to 80 percent of their sales.

corporate marketing system VMS in which a single owner operates the entire marketing channel.

corporate Web site Site designed to increase a firm's visibility, promote its offerings, and provide information to interested parties.

cost per impression Measurement technique that relates the cost of an ad to every thousand people who view it.

cost per response (or click-through) Direct marketing technique that relates the cost of an ad to the number of people who click it.

cost-plus pricing Practice of adding a percentage of specified dollar amount—or markup—to the base cost of a product to cover unassigned costs and to provide a profit.

countertrade Form of exporting whereby goods and services are bartered rather than sold for cash.

coupon Sales promotion technique that offers a discount on the purchase price of goods or services.

creative selling Personal selling in which a considerable degree of analytical decision making on the buyer's part results in the need for skillful proposals of solutions for the customer's needs.

cross-promotion Promotional technique in which marketing partners share the cost of a promotional campaign that meets their mutual needs.

cross-selling Selling multiple, often unrelated, goods and services to the same customer based on knowledge of that customer's needs.

culture Values, beliefs, preferences, and tastes handed down from one generation to the next.

cumulative quantity discount Price discount determined by amounts of purchases over stated time periods.

customary prices Traditional prices that customers expect to pay for certain goods and services.

customer churn Turnover in a company's customer base.

customer relationship management (CRM) Combination of strategies and tools that drives relationship programs, reorienting the entire organization to a concentrated focus on satisfying customers.

customer satisfaction Extent to which customers are satisfied with their purchases.

customer win-back Process of rejuvenating lost relationships with customers.

customer-based segmentation Dividing a business-to-business market into homogeneous groups based on buyers' product specifications.

customs union Establishment of a free-trade area plus a uniform tariff for trade with nonmember unions.

D

data mining Process of searching through customer databases to detect patterns that guide marketing decision making.

database marketing Use of software to analyze marketing information, identifying and targeting messages toward specific groups of potential customers.

decider Person who chooses a good or service, although another person may have the formal authority to complete the sale.

decline stage Final stage of the product lifecycle, in which a decline in total industry sales occurs.

decoding Receiver's interpretation of a message.

Delphi technique Qualitative sales forecasting method that gathers and redistributes several rounds of anonymous forecasts until the participants reach a consensus.

demand Schedule of the amounts of a firm's product that consumers will purchase at different prices during a specified time period.

demarketing Process of reducing consumer demand for a good or service to a level that the firm can supply.

demographic segmentation Division of an overall market into homogeneous groups based on variables such as gender, age, income, occupation, education, sexual orientation, household size, and stage in the family life cycle; also called *socioeconomic segmentation*.

demonstration Stage in the personal selling process in which the customer has the opportunity to try out or otherwise see how a good or service works before purchase.

department store Large store that handles a variety of merchandise, including clothing, household goods, appliances, and furniture.

derived demand Demand for a resource that results from demand for the goods and services produced by that resource.

differentiated marketing Strategy that focuses on producing several products and pricing, promoting, and distributing them with different marketing mixes designed to satisfy smaller segments.

diffusion process Process by which new goods or services are accepted in the marketplace.

direct channel Marketing channel that moves goods directly from a producer to the business purchaser or ultimate user.

direct mail Communications in the form of sales letters, postcards, brochures, catalogs, and the like conveying messages directly from the marketer to the customer.

direct marketing Direct communications, other than personal sales contacts, between buyer and seller, designed to generate sales, information requests, or store or Web site visits.

direct sales results test Method for measuring promotional effectiveness based on the specific impact on sales revenues for each dollar of promotional spending.

direct selling Strategy designed to establish direct sales contact between producer and final user.

discount house Store that charges low prices but may not offer services such as credit.

discretionary income Money available to spend after buying necessities such as food, clothing, and housing.

distribution Movement of goods and services from producers to customers.

downstream management Controlling part of the supply chain that involves finished product storage, outbound logistics, marketing and sales, and customer service.

drop shipper Limited-function merchant wholesaler that accepts orders from customers and forwards these orders to producers, which then ship directly to the customers who placed the orders.

dual distribution Network that moves products to a firm's target market through more than one marketing channel.

dumping Controversial practice of selling a product in a foreign market at a price lower than what it receives in the producer's domestic market.

E

e-business Conducting online transactions with customers by collecting and analyzing business information, carrying out the exchanges, and maintaining online relationships with customers.

economic environment Factors that influence consumer buying power and marketing strategies, including stage of the business cycle, inflation and deflation, unemployment, income, and resource availability.

elasticity Measure of responsiveness of purchasers and suppliers to a change in price.

electronic bulletin board Internet forum that allows users to post and read messages on a specific topic.

electronic data interchange (EDI) Computer-to-computer exchanges of invoices, orders, and other business documents.

electronic shopping cart File that holds items the online shopper has chosen to buy.

electronic signatures Electronic identification that allows legal contracts such as home mortgages and insurance policies to be executed online.

electronic storefronts Company Web site that sells products to customers.

e-marketing Strategic process of creating, distributing, promoting, and pricing goods and services to a target market over the Internet or through digital tools.

embargo Complete ban on the import of specified products.

emergency goods and services Products bought in response to unexpected and urgent needs.

employee satisfaction Employee's level of satisfaction in his or her company and the extent to which that loyalty—or lack thereof—is communicated to external customers.

encoding Translating a message into understandable terms.

encryption The process of encoding data for security purposes.

end-use application segmentation Segmenting a business-to-business market based on how industrial purchasers will use the product.

engagement Amount of time users spend on sites.

Engel's laws Three general statements about the impact of household income on consumer spending behavior: as household income increases, a smaller percentage of expenditures goes for food; the percentage spent on housing, household operations, and clothing remains constant; and the percentage spent on other items (such as recreation and education) increases.

enterprise resource planning (ERP) system Software system that consolidates data from among a firm's various business units.

environmental management Attainment of organizational objectives by predicting and influencing the competitive, political-legal, economic, technological, and social-cultural environments.

environmental scanning Process of collecting information about the external marketing environment to identify and interpret potential trends.

e-procurement Use of the Internet by organizations to solicit bids and purchase goods and services from suppliers.

ethics Moral standards of behavior expected by a society.

European Union (EU) Customs union that is moving in the direction of an economic union by adopting a common currency, removing trade restrictions, and permitting free flow of goods and workers throughout the member nations.

evaluative criteria Features a consumer considers in choosing among alternatives.

event marketing Marketing of sporting, cultural, and charitable activities to selected target markets.

everyday low pricing (EDLP) Pricing strategy of continuously offering low prices rather than relying on such short-term price cuts as cents-off coupons, rebates, and special sales.

evoked set Number of alternatives a consumer actually considers in making a purchase decision.

exchange control Method used to regulate international trade among importing organizations by controlling access to foreign currencies.

exchange functions Buying and selling.

exchange process Activity in which two or more parties give something of value to each other to satisfy perceived needs.

exchange rate Price of one nation's currency in terms of another country's currency.

exclusive distribution Distribution of a product through a single wholesaler or retailer in a specific geographic region.

expectancy theory Theory that motivation depends on an individual's expectations of his or her ability to perform a job and how that performance relates to attaining a desired reward.

exploratory research Process of discussing a marketing problem with informed sources both within and outside the firm and examining information from secondary sources.

exponential smoothing Quantitative forecasting technique that assigns weights to historical sales data, giving the greatest weight to the most recent data.

exporting Marketing domestically produced goods and services in foreign countries.

external customers People or organizations that buy or use a firm's goods or services.

F

fair-trade laws Statutes enacted in most states that once permitted manufacturers to stipulate a minimum retail price for their product.

family brand Single brand name that identifies several related products.

family lifecycle Process of family formation and dissolution.

feedback Receiver's response to a message.

field selling Sales presentations made at prospective customers' locations on a face-to-face basis.

firewall Electronic barrier between a company's internal network and the Internet that limits access into and out of the network.

first mover strategy Theory advocating that the company first to offer a product in a marketplace will be the long-term market winner.

fixed costs Costs that remain stable at any production level within a certain range (such as lease payments or insurance costs).

fixed-sum-per-unit method Method of promotional budgeting in which a predetermined amount is allocated to each sales or production unit.

FOB origin-freight allowed (freight absorbed) Price quotation system that allows the buyer to deduct shipping expenses from the cost of purchases.

FOB (free on board) plant (FOB origin) Price quotation that does not include shipping charges.

focus group Simultaneous personal interview of a small group of individuals that relies on group discussion about a certain topic.

follow-up Postsale activities that often determine whether an individual who has made a recent purchase will become a repeat customer.

foreign licensing Agreement that grants foreign marketers the right to distribute a firm's merchandise or to use its trademark, patent, or process in a specified geographic area.

forward integration Process through which a firm attempts to control downstream distribution.

franchise Contractual arrangement in which a wholesaler or retailer agrees to meet the operating requirements of a manufacturer or other franchiser.

free-trade area Region in which participating nations agree to the free trade of goods among themselves, abolishing tariffs and trade restrictions.

Free Trade Area of the Americas (FTAA) Proposed free-trade area stretching the length of the entire Western Hemisphere and designed to extend free trade benefits to additional nations in North, Central, and South America.

frequency marketing Frequent-buyer or -user marketing programs that reward customers with cash, rebates, merchandise, or other premiums.

friendship, commerce, and navigation (FCN) treaties International agreements that deal with many aspects of commercial relations among nations.

full-cost pricing Pricing method that uses all relevant variable costs in setting a product's price and allocates those fixed costs not directly attributed to the production of the priced item.

full-service research supplier Marketing research organization that offers all aspects of the marketing research process.

G

gatekeeper Person who controls the information that all buying center members will review.

General Agreement on Tariffs and Trade (GATT) International trade accord that has helped reduce world tariffs.

general merchandise retailer Store that carries a wide variety of product lines, stocking all of them in some depth.

generic products Products characterized by plain labels, no advertising, and the absence of brand names.

geographic information systems (GISs) Software packages that assemble, store, manipulate, and display data by their location.

geographic segmentation Division of an overall market into homogeneous groups based on their locations.

global marketing strategy Standardized marketing mix with minimal modifications that a firm uses in all of its domestic and foreign markets.

global sourcing Purchasing goods and services from suppliers worldwide.

goods Tangible products customers can see, hear, smell, taste, or touch.

goods–services continuum Spectrum along which goods and services fall according to their attributes, from pure good to pure service.

grassroots marketing Efforts that connect directly with existing and potential customers through nonmainstream channels.

gray goods Products manufactured abroad under license from a U.S. firm and then sold in the U.S. market in competition with that firm's own domestic output.

green marketing Production, promotion, and reclamation of environmentally sensitive products.

gross domestic product (GDP) Sum of all goods and services produced by a nation in a year.

growth stage Second stage of the product lifecycle that begins when a firm starts to realize substantial profits from its investment in a product.

guerrilla marketing Unconventional, innovative, and low-cost marketing techniques designed to get consumers' attention in unusual ways.

H

high-involvement purchase decisions Purchases with high levels of potential social or economic consequences.

home shopping channel Television direct marketing in which a variety of products are offered and consumers can order them directly by phone or online.

homeshoring Hiring workers to do jobs from their homes.

hypermarket Giant one-stop shopping facility offering wide selections of grocery items and general merchandise at discount prices, typically filling up 200,000 or more square feet of selling space.

hypothesis Tentative explanation for a specific event.

I

import quotas Trade restrictions limiting the number of units of certain goods that can enter a country for resale.

importing Purchasing foreign goods and services.

impulse goods and services Products purchased on the spur of the moment.

inbound telemarketing Sales method in which prospects call a seller to obtain information, make reservations, and purchase goods and services.

incremental-cost pricing Pricing method that attempts to use only costs directly attributable to a specific output in setting prices.

indirect evaluation Method for measuring promotional effectiveness by concentrating on quantifiable indicators of effectiveness such as recall and readership.

individual brand Single brand that uniquely identifies a product.

industrial distributor Channel intermediary that takes title to goods it handles and then distributes these goods to retailers, other distributors, or business or B2B customers; also called a, *wholesaler*.

inelastic demand Demand that, throughout an industry, will not change significantly due to a price change.

inflation Rising prices caused by some combination of excess consumer demand and increases in the costs of one or more factors of production.

influencer Typically, technical staff such as engineers who affect the buying decision by supplying information to guide evaluation of alternatives or by setting buying specifications.

infomercial Paid 30-minute or longer product commercial that resembles a regular television program.

informative advertising Promotion that seeks to develop initial demand for a good, service, organization, person, place, idea, or cause.

infrastructure A nation's basic system of transportation networks, communications systems, and energy facilities.

inside selling Selling by phone, mail, and electronic commerce.

installations Major capital investments in the B2B market.

institutional advertising Promotion of a concept, an idea, a philosophy, or the goodwill of an industry, company, organization, person, geographic location, or government agency.

integrated marketing communications (IMC) Coordination of all promotional activities to produce a unified, customer-focused promotional message.

intensive distribution Distribution of a product through all available channels.

interactive advertising Two-way promotional messages transmitted through communication channels that induce message recipients to participate actively in the promotional effort.

interactive marketing Buyer–seller communications in which the customer controls the amount and type of information received from a marketer through such channels as the Internet and virtual reality kiosks.

interactive television Television service package that includes a return path for viewers to interact with programs or commercials by clicking their remote controls.

intermodal operations Combination of transport modes, such as rail and highway carriers (piggyback), air and highway carriers (birdyback), and water and air carriers (fishyback), to improve customer service and achieve cost advantages.

internal customers Employees or departments within an organization that depend on the work of another employee or department to perform tasks.

internal marketing Managerial actions that help all members of the organization understand, accept, and fulfill their respective roles in implementing a marketing strategy.

internal partnership Relationship involving customers within an organization.

interpretative research Observational research method developed by social anthropologists in which customers are observed in their natural setting and their behavior is interpreted based on an understanding of social and cultural characteristics; also known as *ethnography*, or "going native."

introductory stage First stage of the product lifecycle, in which a firm works to stimulate sales of a new-market entry.

ISO 9001:2000 Standards developed by the International Organization for Standardization in Switzerland to ensure consistent quality management and quality assurance for goods and services throughout the European Union (EU).

ISO (International Organization for Standardization) certification Internationally recognized standards that ensure a company's goods, services, and operations meet established quality levels and its operations minimize harm to the environment.

J

joint demand Demand for a product that depends on the demand for another product used in combination with it.

jury of executive opinion Qualitative sales forecasting method that assesses the sales expectations of various executives.

just-in-time (JIT)/II (JIT II) Inventory practices that seek to boost efficiency by cutting inventories to absolute minimum levels. With JIT II, suppliers' representatives work at the customer's facility.

L

label Branding component that carries an item's brand name or symbol, the name and address of the manufacturer or distributor, information about the product, and recommended uses.

lateral partnership Strategic relationship that extends to external entities but involves no direct buyer–seller interactions.

leader pricing Variant of loss-leader pricing in which marketers offer prices slightly above cost to avoid violating minimum-markup regulations and earn a minimal return on promotional sales.

learning Knowledge or skill acquired as a result of experience, which changes consumer behavior.

lifetime value of a customer Revenues and intangible benefits such as referrals and customer feedback a customer brings to the seller over an average lifetime of the relationship, less the amount the company must spend to acquire, market to, and service the customer.

limited-line store Retailer that offers a large assortment within a single product line or within a few related product lines.

limited-service research supplier Marketing research firm that specializes in a limited number of research activities such as conducting field interviews or performing data processing.

line extension Development of individual offerings that appeal to different market segments while remaining closely related to the existing product line.

list price Established price normally quoted to potential buyers.

logistics Process of coordinating the flow of information, goods, and services among members of the distribution channel.

loss leader Product offered to consumers at less than cost to attract them to stores in the hope that they will buy other merchandise at regular prices.

low-involvement purchase decisions Routine purchases that pose little risk to the consumer.

M

mail-order wholesaler Limited-function merchant wholesaler that distributes catalogs instead of sending sales personnel to contact customers.

mall intercepts Interviews conducted inside retail shopping centers.

manufacturer's brand Brand name owned by a manufacturer or other producer.

manufacturers' representative Agent wholesaling intermediary that represents manufacturers of related but noncompeting products and receives a commission on each sale.

marginal analysis Method of analyzing the relationship between costs, sales price, and increased sales volume.

marginal cost Change in total cost that results from producing an additional unit of output.

markdown Amount by which a retailer reduces the original selling price of a product.

market Group of people with sufficient purchasing power, authority, and willingness to buy.

market development strategy Strategy that concentrates on finding new markets for existing products.

market penetration strategy Strategy that seeks to increase sales of existing products in existing markets.

market price Price a consumer or marketing intermediary actually pays for a product after subtracting any discounts, allowances, or rebates from the list price.

market segmentation Division of the total market into smaller, relatively homogeneous groups.

marketing Organizational function and a set of processes for creating, communicating, and delivering value to customers and for managing customer relationships in ways that benefit the organization and its stakeholders.

marketing (distribution) channel System of marketing institutions that enhances the physical flow of goods and services, along with ownership title, from producer to consumer or business user.

marketing communications Messages that deal with buyer–seller relationships.

marketing concept Companywide consumer orientation with the objective of achieving long-run success.

marketing decision support system (MDSS) Marketing information system component that links a decision maker with relevant databases and analysis tools.

marketing ethics Marketers' standards of conduct and moral values.

marketing information system (MIS) Planned, computer-based system designed to provide managers with a continuous flow of information relevant to their specific decisions and areas of responsibility.

marketing intermediary (or middleman) Wholesaler or retailer that operates between producers and consumers or business users.

marketing mix Blending of the four strategy elements—product, distribution, promotion, and pricing—to fit the needs and preferences of a specific target market.

marketing myopia Management's failure to recognize the scope of its business.

marketing plan Detailed description of the resources and actions needed to achieve stated marketing objectives.

marketing planning Implementing planning activities devoted to achieving marketing objectves.

marketing public relations (MPR) Narrowly focused public relations activities that directly support marketing goals.

marketing research Process of collecting and using information for marketing decision making.

marketing strategy Overall, company-wide program for selecting a particular target market and then satisfying consumers in that market through the marketing mix.

marketing Web site Site whose main purpose is to increase purchases by visitors.

market-plus pricing Intentionally setting a relatively high price compared with the prices of competing products; also known as *skimming pricing*.

market-share objective Volumes related pricing objective in which the goal is to achieve control of a portion of the market for a firms road or service.

markup Amount a retailer adds to the cost of a product to determine its selling price.

mass merchandiser Store that stocks a wider line of goods than a department store, usually without the same depth of assortment within each line.

materials handling system Set of activities that move production inputs and other goods within plants, warehouses, and transportation terminals.

maturity stage Third stage of the product lifecycle, in which industry sales level out.

media research Advertising research that assesses how well a particular medium delivers an advertiser's message, where and when to place the advertisement, and the size of the audience.

media scheduling Setting the timing and sequence for a series of advertisements.

meeting competition method Method of promotional budgeting that simply matches competitors' outlays.

merchandisers Trade sector buyers who secure needed products at the best possible prices.

merchant wholesaler Independently-owned wholesaling intermediary that takes title to the goods it handles; also known as an industrial distributor in the business goods market.

message Communication of information, advice, or a request by the sender to the receiver.

message research Advertising research that tests consumer reactions to an advertisement's creative message.

metropolitan statistical area (MSA) Freestanding urban area with a population in the urban center of at least 50,000 and a total MSA population of 100,000 or more.

micromarketing Targeting potential customers at very narrow, basic levels such as by Zip code, specific occupation, or lifestyle—possibly even individuals themselves.

micropolitan statistical area Area with at least one town of 10,000 to 49,999 people with proportionally few of its residents commuting to outside the area.

minimum advertised pricing (MAP) Fees paid to retailers who agree not to advertise products below set prices.

mission Essential purpose that differentiates one company from others.

missionary selling Indirect selling method in which salespeople promote goodwill for the firm by educating customers and providing technical or operational assistance.

mobile marketing Marketing messages transmitted via wireless technology.

modified breakeven analysis Pricing technique used to evaluate consumer demand by comparing the number of products that must be sold at a variety of prices to cover total cost with estimates of expected sales at the various prices.

modified rebuy Situation in which a purchaser is willing to reevaluate available options for repurchasing a good or service.

monopolistic competition Market structure involving a heterogeneous product and product differentiation among competing suppliers, allowing the marketer some degree of control over prices.

monopoly Market structure in which a single seller dominates trade in a good or service for which buyers can find no close substitutes.

motive Inner state that directs a person toward the goal of satisfying a need.

MRO items Business supplies that include maintenance items, repair items, and operating supplies.

multidomestic marketing strategy Application of market segmentation to foreign markets by tailoring the firm's marketing mix to match specific target markets in each nation.

multiple sourcing Purchasing from several vendors.

N

national account selling Promotional effort in which a dedicated sales team is assigned to a firm's major customers to provide sales and service.

national accounts organization Promotional effort in which a dedicated sales team is assigned to a firm's major customers to provide sales and service needs.

nearshoring Moving jobs to vendors in countries close to the business's home country.

need Imbalance between a consumer's actual and desired states.

network marketing Personal selling that relies on lists of family members and friends of the salesperson, who organizes a gathering of potential customers for a demonstration of products.

new-task buying First-time or unique purchase situation that requires considerable effort by decision makers.

noise Any stimulus that distracts a receiver from receiving a message.

noncumulative quantity discount Price reduction granted on a one-time-only basis.

nonmarketing public relations Organizational messages about general management issues.

nonpersonal selling Promotion that includes advertising, product placement, sales promotion, direct marketing, public relations, and guerilla marketing—all conducted without being face-to-face with the buyer.

nonprobability sample Sample that involves personal judgment somewhere in the selection process.

North American Free Trade Agreement (NAFTA) Accord removing trade barriers among Canada, Mexico, and the United States.

North American Industry Classification System (NAICS) Classification used by NAFTA countries to categorize the business marketplace into detailed market segments.

O

objection Expression of sales resistance by the prospect.

odd pricing Pricing policy based on the belief that a price ending with an odd number just under a round number is more appealing, for instance, $9.97 rather than $10.

offshoring Movement of high-wage jobs from one country to lower-cost overseas locations.

oligopoly Market structure in which relatively few sellers compete and where high start-up costs form barriers to keep out new competitors.

opening price point Setting an opening price below that of the competition, usually on a high-quality private-label item.

opinion leaders Trendsetters who purchase new products before others in a group and then influence others in their purchases.

order processing Selling, mostly at the wholesale and retail levels, that involves identifying customer needs, pointing them out to customers, and completing orders.

organization marketing Marketing by mutual-benefit organizations, service organizations, and government organizations intended to persuade others to accept their goals, receive their services, or contribute to them in some way.

outbound telemarketing Sales method in which sales personnel place phone calls to prospects and try to conclude the sale over the phone.

outsourcing Using outside vendors to provide goods and services formerly produced in-house.

over-the-counter selling Personal selling conducted in retail and some wholesale locations in which customers come to the seller's place of business.

P

partnership Affiliation of two or more companies that help each other achieve common goals.

penetration pricing strategy Pricing strategy involving the use of a relatively low entry price compared with competitive offerings, based on the theory that this initial low price will help secure market acceptance.

percentage-of-sales method Method of promotional budgeting in which a dollar amount is based on a percentage of past or projected sales.

perception Meaning that a person attributes to incoming stimuli gathered through the five senses.

perceptual screens The mental filtering processes though which all inputs must pass.

person marketing Marketing efforts designed to cultivate the attention, interest, and preferences of a target market toward a person (perhaps a political candidate or celebrity).

personal selling Interpersonal influence process involving a seller's promotional presentation conducted on a person-to-person basis with the buyer.

persuasive advertising Promotion that attempts to increase demand for an existing good, service, organization, person, place, idea, or cause.

phishing High-tech scam that uses authentic-looking e-mail or pop-up messages to get unsuspecting victims to reveal personal information.

physical distribution Broad range of activities aimed at efficient movement of finished goods from the end of the production line to the consumer.

place marketing Marketing efforts to attract people and organizations to a particular geographic area.

planned shopping center Group of retail stores planned, coordinated, and marketed as a unit.

planning Process of anticipating future events and conditions and of determining the best way to achieve organizational objectives.

podcast Online audio or video file that can be downloaded to other digital devices.

point-of-purchase (POP) advertising Display or other promotion placed near the site of the actual buying decision.

political risk assessment (PRA) Units within a firm that evaluate the political risks of the marketplaces in which they operate as well as proposed new marketplaces.

political-legal environment Component of the marketing environment consisting of laws and their interpretations that require firms to operate under competitive conditions and to protect consumer rights.

population (universe) Total group that researchers want to study.

pop-up ad Separate window that pops up with an advertising message.

Porter's Five Forces Model developed by strategy expert Michael Porter that identifies five competitive forces that influence planning strategies: the threat of new entrants, the bargaining power of buyers, the bargaining power of suppliers, the threat of substitute products, and rivalry among competitors.

positioning Placing a product at a certain point or location within a market in the minds of prospective buyers.

positioning map Tool that helps marketers place products in a market by graphically illustrating consumers' perceptions of competing products within an industry.

postage-stamp pricing System for handling transportation costs under which all buyers are quoted the same price, including transportation expenses; also known as *uniform-delivered price.*

posttesting Research that assesses advertising effectiveness after it has appeared in a print or broadcast medium.

precall planning Use of information collected during the prospecting and qualifying stages of the sales process and during previous contacts with the prospect to tailor the approach and presentation to match the customer's needs.

premium Item given free or at a reduced cost with purchases of other products.

preroll video ad Brief marketing message that appears before expected video content.

presentation Personal selling function of describing a product's major features and relating them to a customer's problems or needs.

pretesting Research that evaluates an ad during its development stage.

price Exchange value of a good or service.

price flexibility Pricing policy permitting variable prices for goods and services.

pricing policy General guideline that reflects marketing objectives and influences specific pricing decisions.

primary data Information collected for a specific investigation.

primary demand Desire for a general product category.

primary metropolitan statistical area (PMSA) Urbanized county or set of counties with social and economic ties to nearby areas.

private brand Brand offered by a wholesaler or retailer.

private carriers Transporters that provide service solely for internally generated freight.

probability sample Sample that gives every member of the population a chance of being selected.

product Bundle of physical, service, and symbolic attributes designed to satisfy a customer's wants and needs.

product advertising Nonpersonal selling of a particular good or service.

product development Introduction of new products into identifiable or established markets.

product differentiation Occurs when consumers regard a firm's products as different in some way from those of competitors.

product diversification strategy Developing entirely new products for new markets.

product liability Responsibility of manufacturers and marketers for injuries and damages caused by their products.

product lifecycle Progression of a product through introduction, growth, maturity, and decline stages.

product line Series of related products offered by one company.

product manager Marketer responsible for an individual product or product line; also called a brand manager.

product mix Assortment of product lines and individual product offerings a company sells.

product placement Form of promotion in which a marketer pays a motion picture or television program owner a fee to display a product prominently in the film or show.

product positioning Consumers' perceptions of a product's attributes, uses, quality, and advantages and disadvantages relative to competing brands.

production orientation Business philosophy stressing efficiency in producing a quality product, with the attitude toward marketing that "a good product will sell itself."

product-line pricing Practice of setting a limited number of prices for a selection of merchandise and marketing different product lines at each of these price levels.

product-related segmentation Division of a population into homogeneous groups based on their relationships to a product.

profit center Any part of an organization to which revenue and controllable costs can be assigned.

Profit Impact of Market Strategies (PIMS) project Research that discovered a strong positive relationship between a firm's market share and product quality and its return on investment.

profit maximization Point at which the additional revenue gained by increasing the price of a product equals the increase in total costs.

promotion Communication link between buyers and sellers; the function of informing, persuading, and influencing a consumer's purchase decision.

promotional allowance Promotional incentive in which the manufacturer agrees to pay the reseller a certain amount to cover the costs of special promotional displays or extensive advertising.

promotional mix Subset of the marketing mix in which marketers attempt to achieve the optimal blending of the elements of personal and nonpersonal selling to achieve promotional objectives.

promotional pricing Pricing policy in which a lower-than-normal price is used as a temporary ingredient in a firm's marketing strategy.

prospecting Personal selling function of identifying potential customers.

protective tariffs Taxes designed to raise the retail price of an imported product to match or exceed that of a similar domestic product.

psychographic segmentation Division of a population into groups having similar attitudes, values, and lifestyles.

psychological pricing Pricing policy based on the belief that certain prices or price ranges make a good or service more appealing than others to buyers.

public relations Firm's communications and relationships with its various publics.

public service announcement (PSA) Advertisement aimed at achieving socially oriented objectives by focusing on causes and charitable organizations that are included in print and electronic media without charge.

publicity Nonpersonal stimulation of demand for a good, service, place, idea, person, or organization by unpaid placement of significant news regarding the product in a print or broadcast medium.

puffery Exaggerated claims of a product's superiority, or the use of subjective or vague statements that may not be literally true.

pulling strategy Promotional effort by the seller to stimulate final-user demand, which then exerts pressure on the distribution channel.

pure competition Market structure characterized by homogeneous products in which there are so many buyers and sellers that none has a significant influence on price.

push money Cash reward paid to retail salespeople for every unit of a product they sell.

pushing strategy Promotional effort by the seller directed to members of the marketing channel rather than final users.

Q

qualifying Determining a prospect's needs, income, and purchase authority as a potential customer.

qualitative forecasting Use of subjective techniques to forecast sales, such as the jury of executive opinion, Delphi technique, sales force composite, and surveys of buyer intentions.

quantitative forecasting Use of statistical forecasting techniques such as trend analysis and exponential smoothing.

quantity discount Price reduction granted for a large-volume purchase.

quick-response merchandising Just-in-time strategy that reduces the time a retailer must hold merchandise in inventory, resulting in substantial cost savings.

quota sample Nonprobability sample divided to maintain the proportion of certain characteristics among different segments or groups seen in the population as a whole.

R

rack jobber Full-function merchant wholesaler that markets specialized lines of merchandise to retail stores.

radio frequency identification (RFID) Technology that uses a tiny chip with identification information that can be read by a scanner using radio waves from a distance.

raw materials Natural resources such as farm products, coal, copper, or lumber that become part of a final product.

rebate Refund of a portion of the purchase price, usually granted by the product's manufacturer.

reciprocity Buying from suppliers who are also customers.

reference groups People or institutions whose opinions are valued and to whom a person looks for guidance in his or her own behavior, values, and conduct, such as a spouse, family, friends, or celebrities.

refund Cash given back to consumers who send in proof of purchase for one or more products.

related party trade Trade by U.S. companies with their subsidiaries overseas as well as trade by U.S. subsidiaries of foreign-owned firms with their parent companies.

relationship marketing Development and maintenance of long-term, cost-effective relationships with individual customers, suppliers, employees, and other partners for mutual benefit.

relationship selling Regular contacts between sales representatives and customers over an extended period to establish a sustained buyer–seller relationship.

remanufacturing Efforts to restore older products to like-new condition.

reminder advertising Advertising that reinforces previous promotional activity by keeping the name of a good, service, organization, person, place, idea, or cause before the public.

repositioning Changing the position of a product within the minds of prospective buyers relative to the positions of competing products.

research design Master plan for conducting marketing research.

resellers Marketing intermediaries that operate in the trade sector.

retail advertising Advertising by stores that sell goods or services directly to the consuming public.

retail convergence Situation in which similar merchandise is available from multiple retail outlets, resulting in the blurring of distinctions between types of retailers and merchandise offered.

retail cooperative Group of retailers that establish a shared wholesaling operation to help them compete with chains.

retailing Activities involved in selling merchandise to ultimate consumers.

revenue tariffs Taxes designed to raise funds for the importing government.

reverse channel Channel designed to return goods to their producers.

Robinson-Patman Act Federal legislation prohibiting price discrimination not based on a cost differential; also prohibits selling at an unreasonably low price to eliminate competition.

S

salary Fixed compensation payment made periodically to an employee.

sales analysis In-depth evaluation of a firm's sales.

sales force composite Qualitative sales forecasting method based on the combined sales estimates of the firm's salespeople.

sales forecast Estimate of a firm's revenue for a specified future period.

sales incentives Programs that reward salespeople for superior performance.

sales orientation Belief that consumers will resist purchasing nonessential goods and services, with the attitude toward marketing that only creative advertising and personal selling can overcome consumers' resistance and persuade them to buy.

sales promotion Marketing activities other than personal selling, advertising, guerrilla marketing, and public relations that stimulate consumer purchasing and dealer effectiveness.

sales quota Level of expected sales for a territory, product, customer, or salesperson against which actual results are compared.

sampling Process of selecting survey respondents or research participants.

scrambled merchandising Retailing practice of combining dissimilar product lines to boost sales volume.

search marketing Paying search engines, such as Google, a fee to make sure the company's listing appears toward the top of the search results.

second mover strategy Theory that advocates observing closely the innovations of first movers and then improving on them to gain advantage in the marketplace.

secondary data Previously published information.

Secure Sockets Layer (SSL) Technology that secures a Web site by encrypting information and providing authentication.

selective demand Desire for a specific brand within a product category.

selective distribution Distribution of a product through a limited number of channels.

self-concept Person's multifaceted picture of himself or herself.

seller partnership Relationship involving long-term exchanges of goods or services in return for cash or other valuable consideration.

seller's market A market in which there are more buyers for fewer goods and services.

selling agent Agent wholesaling intermediary for the entire marketing program of a firm's product line.

sender Source of the message communicated to the receiver.

service encounter Point at which the customer and service provider interact.

service quality Expected and perceived quality of a service offering.

services Intangible tasks that satisfy the needs of consumer and business users.

shaping The process of applying a series of rewards and reinforcements to permit more complex behavior to evolve.

shopping products Products consumers purchase after comparing competing offerings.

simple random sample Basic type of probability sample in which every individual in the relevant universe has an equal opportunity of being selected.

skimming pricing strategy Pricing strategy involving the use of a high price relative to competitive offerings.

social marketing The use of online social media as a communications channel for marketing messages.

social responsibility Marketing philosophies, policies, procedures, and actions that have the enhancement of society's welfare as a primary objective.

social-cultural environment Component of the marketing environment consisting of the relationship between the marketer, society, and culture.

sole sourcing Purchasing a firm's entire stock of an item from just one vendor.

spam Popular name for junk e-mail.

span of control Number of representatives who report to first-level sales managers.

specialty advertising Sales promotion technique that places the advertiser's name, address, and advertising message on useful articles that are then distributed to target consumers.

specialty products Products with unique characteristics that cause buyers to prize those particular brands.

specialty retailer Store that combines carefully defined product lines, services, and reputation to persuade shoppers to spend considerable shopping effort there.

split runs Methods of testing alternate ads by dividing a cable TV audience or a publication's subscribers in two, using two different ads, and then evaluating the relative effectiveness of each.

sponsorship Relationship in which an organization provides funds or in-kind resources to an event or activity in exchange for a direct association with that event or activity.

spreadsheet analysis Grid that organizes numerical information in a standardized, easily understood format.

staples Convenience goods and services consumers constantly replenish to maintain a ready inventory.

step out Pricing practice in which one firm raises prices and then waits to see if others follow suit.

stock-keeping unit (SKU) Offering within a product line such as a specific size of liquid detergent.

straight rebuy Recurring purchase decision in which a customer repurchases a good or service that has performed satisfactorily in the past.

strategic alliances Partnerships in which two or more companies combine resources and capital to create competitive advantages in a new market.

strategic business units (SBUs) Key business units within diversified firms.

strategic planning Process of determining an organization primary objectives and adopting courses of action that will achieve these objectives.

strategic window Limited periods when key requirements of a market and a firm's particular competencies best fit together.

stratified sample Probability sample constructed to represent randomly selected subsamples of different groups within the total sample; each subgroup is relatively homogeneous for a certain characteristic.

subcontracting Contractual agreements that assign the production of goods or services to local or smaller firms.

subcultures Groups with their own distinct modes of behavior.

subliminal perception The subconscious receipt of incoming information.

suboptimization Condition that results when individual operations achieve their objectives but interfere with progress toward broader organizational goals.

subsidies Government financial support of a private industry.

supercenter Large store, usually smaller than a hypermarket, that combines groceries with discount store merchandise.

supplies Regular expenses a firm incurs in its daily operations.

supply Schedule of the amounts of a good or service that firms will offer for sale at different prices during a specified time period.

supply chain Sequence of suppliers that contribute to the creation and delivery of a product.

supply chain management Control of the activities of purchasing, processing, and delivery through which raw materials are transformed into products and made available to final consumers.

survey of buyer intentions Qualitative sales forecasting method that samples opinions among groups of present and potential customers concerning their purchase intentions.

sustainable products Products that can be produced, used, and disposed of with minimal impact on the environment.

sweepstakes Sales promotion technique in which prize winners are selected by chance.

SWOT analysis Review that helps planners compare internal organizational strengths and weaknesses with external opportunities and threats.

syndicated service Organization that provides standardized data on a periodic basis to its subscribers.

systems integration Centralization of the procurement function within an internal division or as a service of an external supplier.

T

tactical planning Planning that guides the implementation of activities specified in the strategic plan.

target market Group of people to whom a firm decides to direct its marketing efforts and ultimately its goods and services.

target-return objective Short-run or long-run pricing objectives of achieving a specified return on either sales or investment.

tariff Tax levied against imported goods.

task-objective method Development of a promotional budget based on evaluation of the firm's promotional objectives.

team selling Selling situation in which several sales associates or other members of the organization are employed to help the lead sales representative reach all those who influence the purchase decision.

technological environment Application to marketing of knowledge based on discoveries in science, inventions, and innovations.

telemarketing Promotional presentation involving the use of the telephone on an outbound basis by salespeople or on an inbound basis by customers who initiate calls to obtain information and place orders.

test marketing Marketing research technique that involves introducing a new product in a specific area and then measuring its degree of success.

third-party (contract) logistics firm Company that specializes in handling logistics activities for other firms.

time-based competition Strategy of developing and distributing goods and services more quickly than competitors.

total quality management (TQM) Continuous effort to improve products and work processes with the goal of achieving customer satisfaction and world-class performance.

trade allowance Financial incentive offered to wholesalers and retailers that purchase or promote specific products.

trade discount Payment to a channel member or buyer for performing marketing functions; also known as a *functional discount*.

trade dress Visual components that contribute to the overall look of a brand.

trade industries Retailers or wholesalers that purchase products for resale to others.

trade promotion Sales promotion that appeals to marketing intermediaries rather than to consumers.

trade show Product exhibition organized by industry trade associations to showcase goods and services.

trade-in Credit allowance given for a used item when a customer purchases a new item.

trademark Brand for which the owner claims exclusive legal protection.

transaction-based marketing Buyer and seller exchanges characterized by limited communications and little or no ongoing relationships between the parties.

transfer price Cost assessed when a product is moved from one profit center in a firm to another.

trend analysis Quantitative sales forecasting method that estimates future sales through statistical analyses of historical sales patterns.

truck wholesaler (or truck jobber) Limited-function merchant wholesaler that markets perishable food items.

tying agreement Arrangement that requires a marketing intermediary to carry items other than those they want to sell.

U

undifferentiated marketing Strategy that focuses on producing a single product and marketing it to all customers; also called *mass marketing*.

unemployment Proportion of people in the economy actively seeking work that do not have jobs.

unfair-trade laws State laws requiring sellers to maintain minimum prices for comparable merchandise.

uniform-delivered pricing Pricing system for handling transportation costs under which all buyers are quoted the same price, including transportation expenses. Sometimes known as *postage-stamp pricing*.

unit pricing Pricing policy in which prices are stated in terms of a recognized unit of measurement or a standard numerical count.

Universal Product Code (UPC) Numerical bar code system used to record product and price information.

unsought products Products marketed to consumers who may not yet recognize a need for them.

upstream management Controlling part of the supply chain that involves raw materials, inbound logistics, and warehouse and storage facilities.

user Individual or group that actually uses a business good or service.

utility Want-satisfying power of a good or service.

V

VALS Segmentation system that divides consumers into eight psychographic categories: innovators, thinkers, achievers, experiencers, believers, strivers, makers, and survivors.

value analysis Systematic study of the components of a purchase to determine the most cost-effective approach.

value pricing Pricing strategy emphasizing benefits derived from a product in comparison to the price and quality levels of competing offerings.

variable costs Costs that change with the level of production (such as labor and raw materials costs).

vendor analysis Assessment of supplier performance such as price, back orders, timely delivery, and attention to special requests.

vendor-managed inventory (VMI) Inventory management system in which the seller—based on an existing agreement with a buyer—determines how much of a product is needed.

venture team Associates from different areas of an organization who work together in developing new products.

vertical marketing system (VMS) Planned channel system designed to improve distribution efficiency and cost-effectiveness by integrating various functions throughout the distribution chain.

Video Game Generation During this cohort's formative years, while their preferences and behaviors were being shaped, so too were video games.

viral marketing Efforts that allow satisfied customers to spread the word about products to other consumers.

virtual sales team Network of strategic partners, suppliers, and others who recommend a firm's goods or services.

vishing Scam that collects personal information through voice response systems; stands for *voice phishing*.

VoIP (Voice over Internet protocol) A phone connection through a personal computer with any type of broadband Internet connection.

W

Web services Platform-independent information exchange systems that use the Internet to allow interaction between the firms.

Web-to-store shoppers Consumers who use the Internet as a tool to aid them at brick-and-mortar retailers.

wheel of retailing Hypothesis that each new type of retailer gains a competitive foothold by offering lower prices than current suppliers charge; the result of reducing or eliminating services.

wholesaler Channel intermediary that takes title to goods it handles and then distributes these goods to retailers, other distributors, or business or B2B customers.

wholesaling intermediary Comprehensive term that describes wholesalers as well as agents and brokers.

widgets Tiny interactive applications that Internet users can copy and add to their own pages to play music, video, or slide shows.

wiki Web page anyone can edit.

World Trade Organization (WTO) Organization that replaces GATT, overseeing GATT agreements, making binding decisions in mediating disputes, and reducing trade barriers.

Y

yield management Pricing strategy that allows marketers to vary prices based on such factors as demand, even though the cost of providing those goods or services remains the same.

Z

zone pricing Pricing system for handling transportation costs under which the market is divided into geographic regions and a different price is set in each region.

name & company index

A

AARP, 74, 493
AARP Bulletin, 543
AARP Magazine, 543
ABB, 223
ABC Radio, 543
ABC Television Network, 490, 539
Abell, Derek, 46
Abercrombie & Fitch, 13, 50, 207
ABM, 353
Accenture, 43, 532, 612
Acco, 173
Accor North America, 92
Accor SA, 69
AC/DC, 542
Ace Hardware, 478
ACNielsen, 242, 250, 269, 515
ACT!, 336
Activision, 287
Adams, Anthony, 247
Adams, Scott, 265
Ad Council, 517
AdECN, 44
Adidas, 19, 118, 219, 505
AdMob, 524
Advertising Age, 560
Advertising Initiative, 115
Adweek, 253
A&E, 139
Airbus Industries, 67, 171, 178, 199, 354, 635, 665
Air Canada, 308
Air France, 308
Air New Zealand, 308
Ajax Motor Company, 635
Alaska Airlines, 532
ALDI, 368, 425
Aleve, 17
Alitalia, 308
All At Once, 284
AllBusiness.com, 343
Allegra, 14
Allen, Robert G., 177
Allen Family Foods, 80
Allison, Farrell, 234–235
Allstate Insurance, 206, 535
Alltell Corporation, 564
Altschul, Charles, 407–408
Amazon.com, 31, 45, 49–50, 90, 110, 112–114, 116, 168, 193, 242, 317, 325, 347, 358, 427, 430–431, A-24
"America: The Story of Us," 530
American Airlines, 64, 290, 308–310, 426, 611–612, 629
American Apparel, 250
American Association of Advertising Agencies, A-6
American Automobile Association (AAA), 420

American Cancer Society, 31, 41, 504
American Chamber of Commerce, 8
American Council for an Energy Efficient Economy (ACEEE), 79
American Customer Satisfaction Index (ACSI), 316–317
American Diabetes Association, 16, 320
American Eagle Outfitters, 6, 31, 110, 465
American Express, 31, 114, 183, 207, 299, 336, 431
American Girl dolls, 117
American Heart Association, 14
"American Idol," 124, 284
American International Group (AIG), A-25
American International Toy Fair, 592
American Kennel Club, 14
American Marketing Association, 385
American Massage Therapy Association, 342
American Medical Association (AMA), 143, 270
American Needle, 67
American Red Cross, 15–16
American Trucking Association (ATA), 435
America Online (AOL), 71, 317
ampm Mini Market, 429, 462
Amway, 473
Anago Cleaning Systems, 429
Anderson, Mae, 593
Anderson Merchandisers, 469
Android, 110, 328–329
Anheuser-Busch, 88
Ann Taylor, 458
Anthropologie, 137, 479
Anytime Fitness, 429
A&P, 479
Applebee's, 654
Apple Inc., 4, 6–7, 11, 13, 26–27, 31, 45, 57, 64, 144, 148, 230, 298, 315, 317, 328, 337, 347, 407, 422, 431, 461, 501, 505, 551, 597, A-24
Aquafina, 381
Aquil, Walethia, 575
Aravon, 373
Arbitron, 242, 493
AREVA, 222
Aria Resort & Casino, 146
Arise Virtual Solutions, 347
Arm & Hammer, 296, 367, 373
Armstrong, Lance, 22
Armstrong Rubber, 380
ArtTownGifts.com, 349
Ash, Mary Kay, 579, A-2
Asian Food Markets, 393
Ask.com, 122
AskPatty.com, 278
Associated Druggists, 428
Association of National Advertisers, 151
Aston-Martin, 34, 54, 352
Atari, 287

Atlanta Braves, 92, 319
AT&T, 4, 43, 67–68, 171, 207, 325, 328, 529, 532, 601
Audi, 14, 354, 372
Audigier, Christian, 156
Audiobrain, 553
Auerbach, Red, 581
Aunt Jemima, 381
Ausra, 222
Austin, Daniel, 570
Australian Broadcasting Company, 367
Authors Guild, 117
Autowrapped, 546
Aveeno, 361
Avelle, 418
Avis Rental Cars, 288
Avon, 149, 389, 417, 473, 570
Avril, Tom, 81
A&W, 379
Ayer, N. W., 240

B

Baby Bells, 74
BabyGap, 145–146
Baccarat, 614
Baertlein, Lisa, 653
Baig, Edward C., 157
Baker, Stephen, 253
Balenciaga, 379
Ballmer, Steve, 325, 605
Bally, 101
Banana Republic, 445, 458, 568–569
Band-Aid, 361, 382, 383
Bandy, Filip, 59
Bank of America, 53, 283, 358
Banks, Tyra, 422
Bannon, Lisa, 145
Barbie dolls, 117, 274, 593
Barbie Girls, 390–391, 405
Barbie Store, 390–391
Barilla, 305
Barnes-Jewish Hospital, 20
Barnes & Noble, 6, 111, 114, 272, 325, 445
Barnett, 574
"Barracuda," 561
Barret, Victoria, 98
Barrymore, Drew, 528
Barton, Bruce, 531
Baskin Robbins, 48
Bass Pro Shops, A-28
Batheja, Aman, 562
Bay Area Rapid Transit (BART), 623
Baylor College of Medicine, 20
B&B Lumber, 234–235
Bean, Leon Leonwood, 360
Bear Stearns, 96
Beatles, 535

Becker, Boris, 294
Beckham, David, 219
Bed, Bath & Beyond, 458, 462
Behar, Yves, 33
Belzer, Richard, 458
Benchmade Knife, 547
Benioff, Marc, 564
Ben & Jerry's, 379
Bergdorf Goodman, 461, 651
Berkshire Hathaway, 347
Berkus, Nate, 147
Bernback, William, 488
Berra, Yogi, 264
Berry, Leonard L., 314
Berry Chill, 326
Bertolli, 283, 381
Best Buy, 91–92, 106, 110, 136–138, 288,
    290, 300, 415–416, 444, 454, 462,
    474, 478, 568, 612, 641
BestPrice Modern Wholesale, 222
Best Western, 461
Better Business Bureau, 149, 556, 648
Better Homes and Gardens, 543
Beverly, Greg, 383
Bezos, Jeff, 242, 430
B.F. Goodrich, 277
Bharti Enterprises, 222
Bic, 391
Biewald, Lukas, 98
Big Apple Circus, 445
"The Biggest Loser," 510
Bill and Melinda Gates Foundation, 31
Bill Me Later, 114
Bing, 32, 59, 97, 130, 165, 200, 231, 270,
    306, 336–337, 373, 387, 406, 445,
    479, 523, 561, 598, 635, 665
Biz Rate, 159
BJ's, 463
Black, Neal, 638–639
BlackBerry, 54, 60, 252, 260, 278, 353,
    372, 493
Black & Decker, 581
Black Eyed Peas, 17, 528
BlackRock Reality, 42
Blackwell, Roger, 158
Blair Candy, 54
Blakely, Sara, 422
Blasingame, Jim, 323
Blockbuster Video, 6, 498, 532
Bloomberg, Michael, 17
Bloomingdale's, 100, 146, 463
Blu Dot, 458–459
Blue Collar Comedy, 542
Blue Cross Blue Shield, 301
Blue C Sushi, 327
Bluefly, 57
Blue Singapore, 157
Blue Skies Solar and Wind Power, 80
Bluetooth, 528
BMW, 151, 227, 301, 331
BN.com, 106
Bock, Fred, 200
Boeing, 12, 47, 67, 171, 178, 199, 205,
    353–354, 431, 569, 635, 665
Bolshevik Biscuits, 47
Bondy, Filip, 59
Bon Ton, 376

Bonus Building Care, 429
Booth, Robert, 543
Borg, James, 495
"Born in the USA," 561
Bosch, 353
Bose, 399
Boston, Gabriella, 480
Boston Consulting Group (BCG), 53–54, 292
Boucheron, 379
Boudreaux, George, 385
Boudreaux Butt Paste, 385
Bounty, 130, 385
Bowerman, Bill, 63
Boyles, Mike, 234–235
Bradley, Bill, A-6
Brain Research Group, 243
Brand Finance, 406
Brand in the Hand, 528
Branson, Richard, 37–38, 309–310
Bravo, 106, 139
Brees, Drew, 517–518
Brewer-Hay, Richard, A-4
Brin, Sergey, 57
Brine, 373
Bristol-Myers Squibb, 51
British Airways, 178, 308–310, 426
British Petroleum (BP), 71, 206
Broad, Eli, 610
Brody, Jane E., 556
Brooks Brothers, 15
Brussels Airlines, 308
Bryan, Paul W. ("Bear"), 506
Budweiser, 386
Buffett, Jimmy, 159
Buffett, Warren, 434, 612
Buley, Taylor, 480
Buls, Bruce, 446
Burberry, 101–102
Burck, Robert, 386
Bureau of Economic Analysis, 78
Bureau of Justice Assistance, 115
Bureau of Labor Statistics, A-3, A-13
Buress, Tim, 386–387
Burger King, 17, 48, 107, 230, 297, 306,
    560, 653
Burnett, Leo, 490
Burns, George, 296
Burnsed, Brian, 666
Burritt, Chris, 364
Burrows, Peter, 496
Burstyn, Paris, 467
Burton, 511, 637
Busch Gardens, 305, 597
Bush's Baked Beans, 533
Business Horizons, 90
BusinessWeek, 49, 406, 604
Buskirk, Richard H., 399
Buzz, 315
Bvlgari, 651
Byrne, David, 561–562

C

Cabbage Patch dolls, 117
Cabela's, A-28
Cablevision, 82
Cable & Wireless, 69

Cadillac, 231, 331, 354
California Pizza Kitchen, 243
CallWave, 455
Calmarc Construction, 234–235
Camay Soap, 397, 591
Campbell Soup Company, 241–242,
    305, 423
Canada Dry Green Tea Ginger Ale, 45
Canon.com, 107
Canon products, 407–408, 653
Canyon Ranch, 149
Capgemini, 322
Cap'n Crunch cereal, 381
Cappers, 524
CareerBuilder.com, A-4
Caribou Coffee, 138
Carlini Olive Oil, 368
Carolyn Dorothy, 446
Carroll, Christopher, 636
Carroll, James R., 562
Carrols Restaurant Group, 306–307
Cascade, 382
Cash for Clunkers program, 636
Castro, Fidel, 214
Caterpillar, 172, 205, 306
Cathay Pacific, 308
Caverly, Doug, 337
CBS Radio, 543
CBS Television Network, 249, 320, 490, 539
CDW, 359
Census of Manufacturers, 178
Census of Retailing and Wholesaling, 178
Centers for Disease Control, 85
Central Michigan University, 80
Cesar, 537
Chalk, Peter, 437
Chalmers, Edward, 211
Chambers, John, 474
Champion, 372
Chanel, 418
Chang, Andrea, 593
Chang, Rita, 524
Charles Schwab, 110, 317
Charmin, 130
Chase, 118
Cheer, 382
Cheetos, 391, 406
Chevrolet, 9, 149, 231, 352, 656
Chevron, 206
Chicago Transit Authority, 505
Children Now, 88
Children's Advertising Review Unit
    (CARU), 165
Children's Miracle Network, 180
Chili's, 96, 654–655
China Southern, 308
Chiras, Dan, 601
Chmielewski, Dawn C., 593
Choi, Roy, 406–407
Choice Hotels International, 429
Chrysler, 34
Cinnabon, 394–395, 481
Cioffi, Ralph, 96
Circuit City, 451
Cirque du Soleil, 445
Cirulli, Joe, A-25
Cisco Systems, 355–356, 474

Citadel Broadcasting, 543
Citibank, 359
Citigroup, 206
Citizen Watch, 17, 222
Clapton, Eric, 528
CleanNet USA Inc., 429
Clear Channel Radio, 542–543
Cleveland Cavaliers, 17
Clicker, 539
Clif Bar, 307
Clifford, Stephanie, 556
Clift, Simon, A-1–A-2
Clinton, Bill, 561
Clinton, Hillary, 561
Clinton Presidential Library, 20
Clorox, 327, 379
ClubMed, 14, 31
CNBC, 223
CNET.com, 104
CNN, 223, 490
Coach, 146, 351
Coalition for Fire-Safe Cigarettes, 74
Coca-Cola Company, 4, 17, 23, 92, 118,
    152, 165, 258, 287, 317, 347, 386,
    388–389, 431, 501, 532, 538, 617–618
Code of Professional Standards, 556
Coldplay, 551
Coldwater Creek, 473
Colgate, 149, 378
Colgate-Palmolive, 584
Colorado Rockies, 628
Comcast, 74, 82, 317, 651
Commercial Aircraft Company, 67
Commodore, 287
Composite Technology, A-33–A-38
ConAgra Foods, 385
Conar, 537
Condé Nast, 58, 372
Conner Prairie, 14
Conservation International, 69
Consorte Media, 287–288
Consumer Product Safety Commission
    (CPSC), 65–66, 73, 84, 400–401
Consumer Reports, 647
Continental Airways, 8, 308, 319
Convio, 320
Coors, 389
Coppertone, 593
Corner Bakery, 301
Corporate Angel Network, 15
Cosby, Bill, 555
Costco, 2, 67, 116–117, 205, 207, 425, 428,
    441, 463, 465, 483, 641, 643, A-23
Cott Beverages, 15
Coty, 394
Council of Better Business Bureaus, 74–75
Cover Girl, 528
Coverity, 206
Cox, Madison L. ("Buddy"), 582
Craftsman, 379
Craiglist, 110–111, 160
Crane's, 301
Crate & Barrel, 374, 429, 447, 473
Crawford, Tiffany, 216
Crayola, 536
Crest, 130, 207
Crist, Charlie, 561–562

Crosby, Sidney, 533
CrowdFlower, 98
Crystal Cruises, 6
CSX, 353
Cuban, Mark, 152, 188
Cuisinart, 374
Cummins, 353
Curtis Publishing, 241
Curves, 296
Cute Overload, A-24
CVS, 82, 364, 465
CW Television, 539
Cymbalta, 555

D

Daimler AG, 225
Daley, Kevin, 650
Dallas Cowboys, 59
Dallas Mavericks, 152, 188
Dana Buchman, 378
Dannon Company, 69
Dasani, 421
Dave & Buster's, 458
David, Mark, 115
David Yurman jewelry, 614
Davis, Bob, 145
DDB Worldwide, 405, 488
Deal$, 453
Dealix, 288
Debassa Bem Loura, 537
DeBeers, 224
Defense Logistics Agency (DLA), 193
Defotis, Dimitra, 179
Degree, A-1
Dell, Michael, 415, 431
Dell Computers, 4, 92, 105, 172, 183, 317,
    353, 380, 415–416, 431, 664
Del Monte Foods Company, 15
Delta Airlines, 8, 64, 308, 336, 611
DeMint, James, 16
Democratic Party, 20
Denny's, 288, 486–488
Dentsu, 547
DePaul University, 20
DePuy, 361
Design Basics, 278
DHL, 14
Dickler, Jessica, 456
Dick's Sporting Goods, A-28
Didley, Bo, 646
Dillard's, 376, 461
Dillon, Nancy, 43
Dione, Celine, 561
Direct Marketing Association (DMA), 74,
    87, 507, 571
DIRECTV, 74, 82, 223
Discovery Channel, 99
Discovery Communications, 427
Dish Network, 74, 82
Disney, 2, 207, 382, 593
Disney World, 67, 276, 585, 635
DKNY, 377
Dodge, 9, 656
DogSmith, 143–144
Dolan, Darla, 286
Dolan, Ken, 286

Dolce & Gabbana, 101, 349, 651
Dollar General, 301, 453, 479
Dollar Stores, 164
Dollar Tree, 58, 453
Dolores Labs, 98
Domino, Fats, 373
Domino's Pizza, 31, 221, 223–224, 230,
    281–282, 325
Dom Perignon champagne, A-23
Donald Trump steaks, 391
Donna Karan, 351
Do Not Call Registry, 71, 74, 87, 254,
    506–508, 571, 598
"Don't Stop," 561
Doostang, 320
Doritos, 381
Dorland Healthcare Information, 254
DoSomething.org, 19
DoubleClick, 54
Dove (ice cream), 379
Dove (soap), 305, 381, 431, A-1
Dow Chemical, 8, 618
Dr. Pepper Snapple Group (DPSG),
    45–46, 379
Dr. Scholls, 612
Drake, Isobel, 216
Dress Barn, 275–276
Drexler, Mickey, A-24
Drucker, Peter, 7, 41, 119
Drysdale, Rhea, 43
DSW, 454
Duggan, Bill, 151
Duke the dog, 533
Duke University, 313
Dun & Bradstreet, 178, 262, 343
Dungy, Tony, A-20
Dunham, 373
Dunkin' Donuts, 44, 50, 107, 429,
    498–499, 597
DuPont, 26, 172, 358
Duracell, 130, 593
Durocher, Leo, 22
Dyson, 641

E

Earnhardt, Dale, Jr., 532
Earp, Wyatt, 358
Earth Day, 549, 563
Eastern Michigan University, 319
Eastman, Steve, 590
Eaton, Kit, 315
eBay, 4, 52, 57, 110–111, 114, 116, 160,
    173–174, 301, 432, 471, 481, 612,
    657, A-4
eBillme, 114
Eclipse Aviation, 399
Ed Hardy brand, 155–156
Edison, Thomas A., 548
Edison Research, 553
Edwin, Bruce, 562
Edy's ice cream, 305
Eggerton, John, 556
Einstein, Albert, 240, 482, A-5
Eisen, David, 666
Eisenhower, Dwight D., 39
Elan, Elissa, 655

Electronic Arts, 221
Electronic Privacy Information Center, 157
Elemé Medical Inc., 326
Eli Lilly, 400, 555
Elizondo, Hector, 532
Elle magazine, 112
Ellis, Tim, 51
Elsevier, 90
Embraer, 599
Emerson, Ralph Waldo, 462
Emerson Electric, 245
Emery, Albert W., A-23
Emilio Pucci, 101
Emirates Airlines, 178
ENERGY STAR, 67, 139
Engel, James F., 158
English, Tony, 45
Enron, 24
Enterprise Rent-A-Car, A-4
Entrepreneur magazine, 343
Environmental Defense Fund, 3
Environmental Protection Agency (EPA), 2,
    26, 67, 71, 73, 96, 193, 199, 339, 636
Envirosell, 136–138, 164
Equal Exchange, 597
Equaline, 380
Equifax, 74
Ericsson, 190
Ernzen, Brandy, 524–525
Erzhop, 474
Escalate Retail, 576
ESPN, 122, 490
Estupinian, Robert, 418
Ethan Allen Galleries, 478
Ethics Officer Association, 86
E*Trade, 31, 57, 283
eVay, 109
EverGreen Design-Build Partnership, 601
Everly Brothers, 373
Everyday Lives, 260
"Everyday with Rachel Ray," 447
Evo, 131–132, 232–233, 374, 637
Evogear.com, 637
Executive Aircraft Services, 599
Expedia.com, 76, 104–105, 111, 635
Experian, 74
Experience Stores, 373
Export.gov, 259
Exxon Mobil, 206
E-Z Washing Machines, 387

F

Facebook, 15, 19, 21–22, 45, 82, 103,
    113, 118–119, 121, 130, 140, 151,
    156–157, 249, 253, 256, 287, 301,
    315–316, 320, 393, 449, 497, 509,
    528, 538, 577, 638, A-6
Family Dollar Stores, 301, 453, 479
FAO Schwartz, 171
FastLane, 120
Federal Acquisition Regulation (FAR), 193
Federal Bureau of Investigation (FBI), 115
Federal Communications Commission
    (FCC), 542
Federal Power Commission, 73

Federal Railroad Administration, 435
Federal Trade Commission (FTC), 14, 71,
    73–75, 87–88, 95, 157, 190, 298, 350,
    507–508, 531, 556
FedEx, 96, 178, 188, 224–225, 346, 434,
    436, 438, 661
Feeding America, 15, 320
Feltelberg, Rosemary, 373
Fendi, 67
Ferrari, 354, 406
Fetch Dog, 473
Fidelity Investments, 149
FiguAktiv instant drinks, 295
Fila USA, 51
FinancialForce.com, 565
Finer, Suzi, 21–22
Finnegan, David, 36
Fireman's Fund Insurance, 574
Fisher, Linda, 26
Fiskar's, 305
Fitzgerald, F. Scott, 100
547 Art Center, 482
Five Guys Burgers, 452–453
Fleetwood Mac, 561
Flex shampoo, 454
Flickr, 31
Flight 001, 33, 201, 481
flightOptions, 164
Flywire, 365
Fogle, Jared, 510
Food and Drug Administration (FDA), 73,
    84, 390, 401, 536, 555
Food Network, 490, 660
Food & Wine magazine, 407
"Football Hero," 538
Foot Locker, 207
Ford, Henry, 9, 10, 277, 358, A-5
Ford Motor Company, 13, 34–36, 45, 54,
    77, 149, 181, 186, 207, 223, 277, 357,
    385, 522, 533, 563, 577, 625, 656, 664
Forecast Pro, 263, 271
Fortune 100 corporations, 21, 466
Fortune 500 corporations, 114, 175, 178,
    247, 377
Fortune magazine, 313
Fortune's Best American Companies to
    Work For, 168, 346
Fortune's Most Admired American
    Companies, 346–347
Foss Maritime, 446
Foster, Dave, 98
Four Seasons Hotels and Resorts, 150, 164,
    313, 548, 622
Foursquare, 106, 315
Fox Network, 124, 223, 539
Fox Sports Net, 139
Fredrix, Emily, 615
Freeman & Liedtka, 90
The Free Press, 44
French's, 380
Friedmann, Susan, 180
Friedrich Air Conditioning, 547
Frisbees, 396
Frito-Lay, 2, 152, 381, 549
Frost, David, 210
Fuentes, Daisy, 532

Fujitsu, 31
Fusion, 130

G

Gad, Sham, 179
Gainesville Health & Fitness Center, A-25
Galante, Joseph, 496
Gale, Thomson, 248–249
Gamefly, 6
Gap, 136, 207, 276, 465, 474, 568–569, A-24
Garbett Homes, 139
Garden State tourism, 19
Garmin, 363
Gartenstein, Devra, 650
Garza, G., 337
Gates, Bill, 106, 451, 575
Gatorade, 305, 532
Geely, 230
GEICO Insurance, 379, 532–533
General Electric (GE), 8, 31, 58, 178, 183,
    222, 563
General Mills, 2–3, 51, 88, 166, 230, 313,
    349, 353, 358, 383, 405, 597
General Motors, 34, 120, 181, 231–232, 302
General Services Administration (GSA),
    192–193, 200
George, Mike, 4
Georgia Aquarium, 256–257
Georgia Pacific, 617
Geox, 361–362
Geranios, Nicholas K., 81
Gerstner, Lou, A-25
GfK NOW, 294–295
GfK Roper Consulting, 293
Gibson, William, 122
Gillette, 43, 130, 382, 447
Gingrich, Newt, 80
Ginsburg, Steve, 453
Giorgio Armani, 146
Girl Scouts, 168, 570–571
Girls Gone Wild, 391
Glad, 379–380
Gloria Jean's Coffees, 462
GMAC Financial Services, 575, A-25
GNC, 149
GoDaddy, 123
Goddard, Jacqui, 384
Godiva, 150
Goldman Sachs, 347
Goldsmith, Marva, A-12
Gold & Wood, 651
Gomez, Armando, 211
Good Housekeeping, 543
Goodman, Gail, 323
Goodyear, 14, 427
Google, 12, 32, 44, 57, 59, 97, 114, 117,
    121–122, 130, 165, 174, 200, 213,
    250, 270, 306, 320, 328–329, 336,
    346–347, 373, 382, 386, 406, 445,
    459, 479, 523–524, 561, 598, 605,
    635, 665, A-23
Google Checkout, 114
Google Earth, 282
Gore, Al, 99
Gottschalks, 451

Gourmet, 60
Graham, Nicholas, 386
Grand Circle Travel Company, 286
Grant, Amy, 15
Grapevine Mills Mall, 458
Great Depression, 10, 71, 77, 287, 526, 609
Green, Heather, 431, 480
Green Acres Bed & Breakfast, 234
Greene, Kate, 253
Green Mountain Coffee Roasters, 598
Greenpeace, 13, 27
Greensburg, Inc., 133–134, 234–235, 339–340, 409, 482–483, 601–602, 668–669
GreenStop, 461
GreenTown, 339, 601
Greenyer, Andrew, 324
Grove, Andrew, 108
Groves, Robert, 249
Grupon, 480
Gucci Group, 379, 418, 423
Guinness Book of World Records, 342–343
Gutiérrez, Juan Bautista, 202–203
Gymboree, 478

H

Habitat for Humanity, 9, 31
Hagen, Kevin, 27
Haley, Bill, 373
Half, Robert, A-8
Hallmark, 305, 319, 383, 399
Hallock, Betty, 407
Hamilton, Scott, 15
Haney, Janice, 234–235
Haney, John, 234–235
Hannaford's, 447
Hansen's Cakes, 21–22
Happauge, 583
"Happy Days Are Here Again," 561
Hard, Rob, 180
Hardy, Don Ed, 156
Harley-Davidson, 278
Harley Owners Group (HOG), 143
Harold's and Levitz Furniture, 451
Harper, Kate, 38
Harris, Michael, 323
Harris, Paul, 543
Hart, Catherine, 133, 601
Harvard University, 117
Harvest Solar & Wind Power, 482–483, 601
Harvey, Mike, 337
Hawaiian Airlines, 243
Hawk, Tony, 518
Hawkins, Molly, 131–132, 232–233, 637
Hayden, C. J., 12
HBO, 346
HCA Healthcare, 194
HD Digital Radio Alliance, 543
HDNet, 152, 188
Head & Shoulders, A-24
Healthy Choice, 58, 305, 385
Healthy U, 475
Healthy Vending, 475
Heart, 561
Heartland Payment Systems, 114–115

Heath Net, 87
Heine, Christopher, 271
Heinz, 15, 378, 380, 405, 584
Heller, Walter, 624
Herman Miller, 172, 353
Hermès, 350, 422, 665
Herrin, Jessica, 417
Hershey Foods, 149, 367, 383, 432
Hertz, 318
Hewitt, Steve, 133
Hewlett-Packard (HP), 27, 32–33, 91–92, 190, 290, 372, 380
HGTV, 660
Hicks, Todd, 386
Highway Beautification Act, 544
Hilton, Paris, 537
Hilton Hotels, 306
Hindustan Lever, 226
History Channel, 530
Hite, Morris, 538
Ho, Patricia Jiayi, 232
Holiday Inns, 368
Holland America Line, 5
Holtkamp Greenhouses, 434
Home Depot, 125, 434, 453, 455–456, 458, 562, 593, 622, 644
Homelife, 380
Home Shopping Network (HSN), 444, 508, 641
Honda, 36, 50, 68, 79, 99, 167, 227, 339–340, 383, 409, 523, 563, 600
Hool, Joyce, 157
Hoover, 385–386
Hopkins, Claude C., 383
Hopkins, Michael S., 431
Hormel, 496, 584
Horovitz, Bruce, 393, 453, 615, 655
Hotel Nikko San Francisco, 359
Hot Jobs.com, 546, A-4
Houpt, Simon, 145
"The Howdy Doody Show," 526
HP Pavilion, 505
Hsieh, Anthony, 168–169
HTC, 328
Hubbel Inc., 440
Hudson, Eric, 60, 374
Hudson Bay Company, 630
Huggies, 382, 541
Hugo Boss, 101, 183
Hulu, 539, 541
Humane Society, 31
Humphrey, Hubert, 503
Hunter, Mark, 650
Hutt, Michael D., 187
Huxley, Thomas H., 246
Hyundai, 5, 77, 96, 144, 152, 227, 385, 393, 511, 643, 664

I

Iams, 130, 384
Iberia Airlines, 309
IBM, 41, 45, 53, 166, 210
Icebreaker, 366–367
IDA Software Group, 430
IKEA, 220

iMac, 298
Imaginarium, 560
Imax, 427
IMG Sports Management, 425
Improvements, 473
Indamer, 599
Independent Grocery Alliance (IGA), 428
Indianapolis Colts, 16–17, 320, 384
Infiniti, 41, 331, 349, 354, 381
Information Resources, 242, 250
ING Group, 206
Ingram Micro, 466
In-N-Out Burgers, 48–49
Inroads Minority Internship Program, A-6
Intel, 92, 108, 172, 205, 353
Interactive Services Association, 75
Interbrand, 382
InterContinental Hotels Group, 368, 429
International Airline Passengers Association (IAPA), 308–309
International Consumer Electronics Show (CES), 469
International Monetary Fund, 79
International Organization for Standardization, 358
International Programs Center (IPC), 292
International Social Media Association, 21
Internet Crime Complaint Center (IC3), 116
internetworldstats.com, 104
Interpublic, 547
Interstate Commerce Commission (ICC), 435
iPad, 11, 597, A-24
iPhone, 4, 51, 64, 100, 110, 252, 260, 298, 315, 328, 337, 493
iPod, 6, 19, 33, 64, 221, 298, 385, 396, 475
iPod touch, 64
Irving gas stations, 50
Isaac Mizrahi, 381
Isaacs, Kim, A-6
Isabelle de Borchgrave, 481
iTunes, 422, 481, 551

J

J. Crew, A-24
J. D. Power and Associates, 189, 242
Jackson, Phil, 17
Jaguar, 34, 54, 331, 405, 615
JAL, 308–309
Jamal, Nadia, 216
James, Geoffrey, 418
James, LeBron, 17, 531
Jan-Pro, 171–172, 428–429
Jazzercise Inc., 31, 429
JCPenney, 119, 301, 376–378, 455, 460, 666
JC Watts Companies, 87
Jeep, 9, 490
Jell-O, 383, 385
Jennings, Lisa, 655
Jet Blue Airways, 201, 347, 571
JetPass Select, 146
Jewish National Fund, 320
Jindal, Bobby, 384
Jinks, Beth, 650
J.Jill, 507
Jobs, Steven, 11, 317

Joe Boxer Inc., 386
John, Brad, 33, 201, 481
Johnson, H. F., 68
Johnson, Jack, 284–285
Johnson & Johnson, 58, 69, 347, 361, 381, 584
Jonas, Nick, 528
Jones, Jerry, 59
Jones, LeRoi, 140
Jones soda, 138
JoS. A. Bank Clothiers, 638–639
Jose Cuervo, 388
JPMorgan, 118
Juicy Couture, 377, 379
Junkbusters, 87

K

K2, 637
Kansas City Chiefs, 57
The Karate Kid, A-24
Kate Spade, 350, 377
Kavilanz, Parija, 364
Kayak.com, 622, 635
KB Toys, 451
Keegan, Matthew C., 618
Keith, Toby, 16
Kellogg Company, 15, 48, 51, 88, 288, 349, 353
Ken dolls, 593
Kennedy, John F., 36, 83
Kentucky Derby, 330
Kenya Airways, 353–354
Kerry, John F., 217
Keurig, 187–188
KFC, 22, 49, 207, 379, 653
Khan, Panni, Phillip, 495
Kharif, Olga, 111
KHMD-Radio, 547
Kia, 14, 227, 352, 372, 645
Kiel, George, III, 373
Kierland Commons, 458
Kim, David, A-23
Kimberley-Clark, 322, 374, 381, 541, 584
Kincaid, Jason, 496
Kindle, 49–50, 325, 427
King, Stephen, 119
Kirtsy.com, 175
KitchenAid, 381
Kleenex, 379, 385, 454
KLM, 308
Kluger, Jeffrey, 562
Klum, Heidi, 294
Kmart, 96, 205, 380, 453, 593, 652
Knight, Charles F., 245
Knorr, 381, A-1
Koc, Vinnie, 167, 600
Kodak, 21, 119, 385, 388, 509
Kogi BBQ, 406–407
Kohl's, 47, 301, 372, 378, 452, 465, 479
Komen, Susan G., 15, 23
Kookim Bank, 511
Korean Air, 308
Kraft Foods, 47, 53, 58, 88, 317, 358, 383, 385, 389, 522, 584, 597
Kramer, Andrew E., 209
Kravets, David, 174
Krispy Kreme, 154

Kroger, 2, 50–51, 178, 425, 462, 479, 612–613, 644
Krzyzewski, Mike, 313
K-Swiss, 296
Kupcinet, Irv, 92
Kurtenbach, Elaine, 232
Kyle, Dennis, 153

L

Lady Foot Locker, 462
Lady Gaga, 31, 276
Lagasse, Emeril, 406
Lamborghini, 111, 352
Lancôme, 532
Land of Nod, 473
Land Rover, 34
Lands' End, 474, 571
Lansing, John, 144, 660
Lao Tzu, A-3
Las Vegas Convention and Visitors Authority, 139
Laura Ashley, 453
Lavalife Voice, 508
Lay's, 378, 381
Lazarus, Shelly, 344
Leadership Group, 86
Leadership in Energy and Environmental Design (LEED), 133
Lean Cuisine, 58
Lear Corporation, 181
Learmonth, Michael, 524
Le Cirque, 346
Lee jeans, 149
Leeman Designs, 361
Lego, 6, 458, 593
Leguizamo, John, 532
Lenox, 614
LensCrafters, 6, 346
Leo Burnett advertising agency, 490
Leonard's Bakery, 326
Leopold Ketel & Partners (LKP), 547
LetsMove Initiative, 517–518
Leukemia and Lymphoma Society, 7
Leung, Alison, 232
Leventhal, Ben, 407
Levi Strauss, 317
Levitt, Theodore, 10, 13
Levitz, Jennifer, 286, 384
Lewin, Kurt, 138
Lewis, Blake, 15
Lewis, Jerry Lee, 373
Lewis, Leona, 294
LexisNexis, 104
Lexus, 73, 331, 349–350, 351, 380–381, 665
LG Electronics, 226–227
Liberty Tax Service, 429
Lifebuoy, 381, A-1
Life cereal, 381
LifeMatrix, 293–294
Likins, Cheryl Waters, 38
Lillian Vernon, 473
Limited, 274
Limited Too, 275
Lindeman, Teresa F., 81
Lindquist, Lee, 99, 339
Linens 'n Things, 451

LinkedIn, 151
Lipton, 381, A-1
Little Caesars Pizza, A-24
Little Richard, 373
Liu, Lucy, 288
Live Nation, 57
Live Strong, 22
Liz Claiborne, 376–378
Liz Lang, 381
L.L. Bean, 58, 110, 166, 360, 465, 507, 571, 585, A-28
Loehmann's, 464
Logo, 139
Long, Sharon, 257
Long John Silver's, 429, 591
Loopt, 315
Lord & Taylor, 666
L'Oreal Paris, 149, 350
Los Angeles Angels, 288
Los Angeles County Museum of Art, 522
Los Angeles Lakers, 17
Los Angeles Times, 122
Louis Vuitton, 48, 164, 665
Love, Elaine, 166
Lowe's, 149, 327, 434, 453, 585, 644
LPGA, 504
LR Health and Beauty Systems, 294–295
Lubold, Gordon, 437
Lucky Brand Jeans, 13, 372, 377
Lucky magazine, 33
Lucy.com, 106
Lufthansa, 308, 310
Lux, 381
Lysol, 149

M

M01, 560
MacDougall, Alice Foote, 365
MacMillan, Douglas, 524
MACTEC, 193
Macy's, 4, 301, 376, 457, 460, 462, 597
Madawo, Innocent, 570
Madewell, A-24
Maersk Line, 436
Magellan, 363
Magnavox, 287
Maine Media Workshops, 407–408
Major League Baseball (MBL), 92, 176, 288, 444, 480, 542
Major League Soccer, 504
Maker's Mark, 388
Malcom Baldrige National Quality Award, 358
Mallo Cups, 54
Mango ministores, 460
Manning, Eli, 17, 531
Manning, Peyton, 16–17
Marathon, 67
Marchetti, Federico, 101
March of Dimes, 16
Marc Jacobs, 387
Marcus, Stanley, 280
Marketing Science Institute, 612
Marks, Kathy, 216
Marriott, 92, 276, 317–319
Mars, Frank, 526
Marshall, Matt, 253

Marshall, Trevor, 467
Marshall Field, 376
Marshall's, 86, 464
Mars Inc., 387, 501, 526–528
Martin, Holly, 81
Mary, Rob, 12
Mary Kay Cosmetics, 571
Maslow, Abraham H., 149–150, 164
Massage Envy, 342–344
MasterCard, 14, 31, 96, 109, 114, 129, 431, 528
Matchbox cars, 117
Mattel, 117, 230, 390–391, 405
Maurices, 275
Mays, Billy, 474
Mazda, 96
MCA, 9
McCain, John, 249
McCormack, Mark, 425
McCurry, Justin, 543
McDonald's, 4, 14, 44–45, 48, 77, 88, 140,
    166, 178, 203, 207–209, 221, 223,
    246, 269, 297, 299, 387, 389, 429,
    460, 479, 532, 553, 560, 630, 653
McGinn, Daniel, 33
McKesson, 428
McLuhan Marshall, 255
McQueen, Jeff D., 174
Mechanical Turk, 98
Media Behavior Institute, 295
Mediamark Research, 242, 295
Mega Toys, 182
Memorex, 353
Mercedes-Benz, 5, 164, 225, 227, 291,
    331, 664
Merck, 51
Merrill Lynch, 347, 387
Merritt, Lynn, 532
Merry Maids, 345
Metro AG, 431
Meyer, Adele, 47
MGM, 17
Michael Graves, 381
Michaels, Lorne, 527
Michigan.org, 151
Michelin Tires, 385
Mickelson, Phil, 532
Microsoft, 22, 31, 41, 44, 54, 71, 105, 113,
    121–122, 152, 166, 175, 223, 287,
    325, 336–337, 383, 451, 538, 570,
    604–605, A-10, A-22
Miggins, John, 482, 666–669
Mighty Putty, 474
Milk & Honey Granola, 326
Milky Way, 526
Millan, Cesar, 393
Miller, Claire Cain, 496
Miller, Steve, 562
Millicom International, 9
Mini Cooper, 13, 33, 372, A-3
Minlard, Paul W., 158
Minnesota Tourism, 18
Mio, 363
Mitsubishi, 222
M&Ms, 150
Mobile World Congress, 329
Mohan, Anne Marie, 27
Monsanto, 2, 24

Monster.com, A-4
Moon, Jeremy, 366
Moreno, Arturo ("Arte"), 288
Morga, Alicia, 288
Mossimo Giannulli, 381
Motel 6, 92, 549–550
Mother Earth News, 272, 524, 562–563,
    601–602
Motorola, 205, 353, 357
Motor Trend, 513
Mott's apple juice, 45–46
Mountain Dew, 381, 576
MP3 players, 4, 227, 336, 390
Mr. and Mrs. Potato Head, 296
Mrs. Meyers, A-23
MTN, 9
MTV, 223
Mui, Ylan Q., 216
Mulally, Alan R., 34–35
Mulcahy, Anne, 317
Mullin, Jennifer, 307, 337
Murad Inc., 343
Murdoch, Rupert, 102
Murrell, Janie, 452–453
Murrell, Jerry, 452–453
Myerson, Alan, 407
MyMap, Inc., 185
MySpace.com, 15, 45, 121, 157, 249, 256,
    258, 287, 315, 320, 538

N

Nabisco, 17
Naisbitt, John, 76
Nakao, Kevin, 315
Narayanan, Lakshmi, 223
NASCAR, 17, 385, 445, 504
National Advertising Division (NAD), 74
National Advertising Review Board, 74
National Aeronautics and Space
    Administration (NASA), 199, 482
National Association for Resale and Thrift
    Shops, 47
National Association of Colleges and
    Employers, A-6
National Basketball Association (NBA), 17,
    239, 531–532
National Breast Cancer Awareness, 15
National Business Aviation Association, 15
National Center for Addiction and
    Substance Abuse (CASA), 140
National Cristina Foundation, 32–33
National Football League (NFL), 59, 67,
    168, 171, 384, 542
National Geographic, 522, 543
National Highway Traffic Safety
    Administration (NHTSA), 73, 542
National Hockey League (NHL), 533
National Institute of Standards and
    Technology (NIST), 358
National Marrow Donor Program, 306
National Retail Federation, 115, 323
National White Collar Crime Center, 115
Native American Business Alliance Fund
    (NABA), 288
Natural Home, 272, 524, 562–563, 601–602
Natural Resources Defense Council, 92

The Nature Conservancy, 41
Nautica, 390
NBC Sports, 330
NBC Television Network, 422, 490, 493, 539
NCAA basketball, 504
NCR Corp., 6
Necco Wafers, 54
Neff, Jack, 131
Negishi, Mayumi, 543
Neiman Marcus, 100, 301, 422, 461, 475, 622
Nelson, Charles, 119
Nelson, Melanie, 120
Nestlé, 109, 183, 584
Net-a-Porter, 100–101, 622
Netflix, 58, 317, 372, 420, 444, 498
NetJets, 615
Netscape, 71
NetStakes, 591
Network for Business Sustainability, 26
Neuman, William, 551
Neutrogena, 361
Newark Police Department, 20
New Balance, 373
Newegg.com, 104
New England Patriots, 57
Newman, Andrew Adam, 393
New Mexico Spaceport Authority, 17–18
New Orleans Saints, 59, 319, 320, 384
Newsweek, 32
New York City Metropolitan Transit
    Authority, 617
New York Giants, 17, 59, 531
New York Jets, 59
New York Metropolitan Opera, 386
New York Public Library, 117
New York Stock Exchange, 207
New York Times, 591
New York Times Magazine, 60, 447
Next Net, 253
Nexus One, 328–329
Nicole, Chelsea, 383
Niedt, Bob, 307
Nielsen Company, 130, 250, 270, 320
Nielsen Media Research, 21, 64, 243
Nielsen/Net Ratings, 124
Nielsen Online, 113
Nike, 17, 19, 22–23, 43, 51, 62–63, 112,
    219, 365, 385, 420, 439, 505, 511, 532
Nikon, 5, 517
Nimoy, Leonard, 17
99¢ Only, 453
Nintendo, 31, 221, 287, 390, 415, 420, A-23
Nissan, 4, 9, 51, 227, 317, 385, 501
Nivea, 283
Nokia, 9, 27, 180–181, 190, 252, 317, 546
Nonni's Food Company, 23
Nooyi, Indra, 394
Nordstrom, 58, 112, 116, 186, 301, 422,
    461, 473, 507
North Face, A-28
Northwest Airlines, 201
Northwestern Mutual, 359
Norwegian Cruise Lines, 68
Notre Dame, 319
Notte, Jason, 364
Novak, Kim, 152
Numi Tea, 307, 337–338

O

Oak Brook Promenade, 458
Oakley, 399
Oberto Sausage, 271
O'Connell, Vanessa, 666
O'Donnell, Jayne, 115
Office Depot, 173, 207, 380
OfficeMax, 355, 474, 589
Ogden Publications, 272, 524–525,
    562–563, 601
Ogilvy, David, 501, 553
Ogilvy & Mather, 344, 553
Ohno, Apolo, 542
O'Keefe, Ed, 249
Olay, 130, 207
Old London, 23
Old Navy, 57
Old Spice, 130
Olive Garden, 654
Olmsted, Cherilyn, 272, 524–525
Olympic Games, 17, 19, 319, 367, 493,
    501, 504–505, 511, 518, 531, 630
Omega watches, 301, 532
Omnicom, 547
ONE, Inc., 470
O'neal, Shaquille, 532
1-800-FLOWERS, 317, 433–434
OneNet Service, 171
Oneworld, 308–310
Ong Soh Chin, 617
Oracle, 322, 564
Oral-B, 130
Orange Glo, 474
Orascom Telecom Holding, 9
Orbitz.com, 201
Orchard Supply Hardware, 568
Oregon Coast Aquarium, 547
Oregon Public Broadcasting, 547
Orman, Suze, 17
Orville Redenbacher, 378
Orvis, 444, 473
Oscar Mayer, 299
Osyris Medical USA, 326
Outback Steakhouse, 317, 445, 654
Overseas Adventure Travel (OAT), 286
Overstock.com, 7, 116, 317
Owens Corning, 387, 563
Oxfam, 31
Oxford University, 117
OxiClean, 474

P

Pacific Gas & Electric, 92
Page, Larry, 57
Pajamagram, 473
Palin, Sarah, 561
Palmer, Alex, 27
Palm Pilot, 533
Paltrow, Gwyneth, 422
Pampered Chef, 417, 473, 570
Pampers, 130
Panama Canal, 412–414
Pan Am Airlines, 45, 481
Panasonic, 365, 372, 393, 569, 570

Pandey, Kundan, 174
Pandora, 150
Pantene, 130
Papa John's, 138, 208
Papyrus, 65
Parkway Imaging and Graphics, 182
Parlin, Charles C., 241
Patagonia, A-28
Patrick, Monica, 570
Paul, Ian, 157
Paul, Rand, 561
Payless shoes, 149
PBS, 490
PBteen, 284
Peabody Coal, 437
Peanut Butter & Company, 300
Pearl Jam, 528
Peerless Pump Co., 200
Peet's Coffee & Tea, 460
Pekala, Nancy, 166
Pepperidge Farm, 15, 381
PepsiCo, 4, 23, 43, 152, 226, 306, 321,
    380–381, 394, 405, 502, 538, 563,
    576, A-24
Performance Bike, 571
Perman, Stacy, 49
Peter, Laurence J., 518
Peterson, Thad, 575
Petite Sophisticate, 478
Petro, John, 617
PetroChina, 206
PetSmart, 311, 391
Pew Research Center, 285, 290
PF Flyers, 373
Pfizer, 51, 190
PGA, 504
Phelps, Michael, 17
Philadelphia Eagles, 4
Philips, 231
Phillips, Bryce, 131, 233, 637
Phillips Auctioneers, 427
Phoenix Opportunity System, 193
Piaggio Aero Industrie, 599
Picasa, 509
Pier 1, 429–430
Pillsbury, 9
Pilon, Mary, 480
Pinkerton, 353
Piryx, 15
Pizza Hut, 51–52, 119, 207, 221, 346, 429, 500
Pizzeria Uno, 13
Planet Green, 99
PlayStation, 287, 475
PNC Financial Services Group, 110
Polaris Marketing Research, 238–239
Pollo Campero, 202–204
Pollo Tropical, 306
Pond's, 381
Pontiac, 501
Poole, Robert W., 617
Popcorn Factory, 473
Porsche, 381, 382
Porter, Kristen, 12
Porter, Michael E., 43–45, 644
Post Cereal, 51
Pottery Barn, 284, 429, 458, 507, 571

Powell, 637
Prada, 5, 418, 651–652
Praxair, 176
Precious Moments, 391
Preserve, 60–61, 374, 447
President's Choice, 380
PriceGrabber.com, 110–111
Priceline.com, 17, 631
Priddy, Emily, 482, 667
Primary Wave Music, 549–550
Prime Line, 362
The Princess and the Frog pendants, 65
Pringles, 130, 223
Print Council, 507
Privacy Commission of Canada, 157
Procter & Gamble (P&G), 26–27, 39, 109,
    121, 130–131, 182, 190, 207, 223,
    258, 260, 287, 321, 327, 347, 368,
    381, 383, 389, 392–393, 397, 431,
    497, 511, 529, 532, 618, A-1, A-24
ProFlowers, 188
Progressive Insurance, 149
Progresso, 379
ProQuest Direct, 249
Prudential Financial, 384
Publicis, 547
Publilius Syrus, 616
Publix, 644
Pulitzer, Joseph, A-10
Pull-Ups, 382
Pur, 149
Purex, 379
Purina, 149

Q

Qantas, 308–309, 353–354
Quaker Foods, 88, 317, 381
Quality Value Convenience (QVC), 508
Quickoffice Inc., 119
Quicksilver, 637
Quizno's, 58

R

Raghavan, Anita, 153
Rahim, Ahmed, 307, 337–338
Rahim, Reem, 307, 337–338
RAID, 379
RainedOut, 528
Raley's supermarkets, 460
Ralph Lauren, 630
Ramsey, Lydia, 211
Rao, Leena, 98
Ray, Rachel, 17, 33
Razor Gator, 657
Reader's Digest, 543
Reagan, Ronald, 561
Real Good chairs, 458–459
Really Simple Syndication (RSS), 119
Real Time Search, 320
Redbox, 498–499
Red Bull, 511, 532
Red Cross, 7
Red Lion Hotels, 612
Red Lobster, 6

Reebok, 17, 51, 67, 296, 533
Reed, John, 543
Reese's Pieces, 500–501
Regus Group, 356
Reich, Robert, 207
REI.com, 106, 117, 440, 612, A-28
Rein, Irving, 43
Reinberg, Steven, 25
Rependa, George, 599
Republican National Committee, 561
Republican Party, 20
Restoration Hardware, 458
Reynolds, George W., 431
Rez-Biz, 289
Ricadela, Aaron, 25
Rice-a-Roni, 381
Richardson, Hayley, 407
Richardson consulting firm, 574
Rickenbacker, Edward, V., 179
Rigby, Bill, 337
Right90, 263
Ritchie, Rene, 315
Ritz-Carlton, 350
"Road to Nowhere," 561–562
Roberto Coin, 150
Roberts, Julia, 532
Robertson Heating Supply Company, 471
Robinson Lerer & Montgomery, 549
Rochester Institute of Technology, 507
"Rock Yourself to Sleep," 549–550
Rogers, Will, 516
Rolex, 149, 213, 223, 380, 422, 665
Rolls-Royce, 178, 381
Romano's Macaroni Grill, 245
Romeo, Peter, 307
Romer, Christina, 636
Roosevelt, Eleanor, A-7
Roosevelt, Franklin D., 561
RoperASW, 250, 294–295
Rose, Dionne, 653
Rosenfeld, Irene, 47
Ross, 464
Rossignol, 233, 637
Rotenberg, Marc, 157
Royal Dutch/Shell Group, 109, 206
RTVi, 223
Rubbermaid, 374, 447
Rubenstein's of New Orleans, 462
Rubio, Mark, 562
Ruby Tuesday, 58, 654
Ruffles, 381
Ruiz Foods, 182
Ruskin, John, 643
Ryder, 353

S

S. Abraham & Sons, 470
Saab, 302
Saatchi & Saatchi LA, 549
Sacramento Fire Department, 20
Safeco Field, 505
Safeguard, 207
Safeway, 425, 462
Saint Louis University, 243
St. John's Town Center, 458

St. Joseph's baby aspirin, 283
St. Jude Children's Research Hospital, 14, 16
Saks Fifth Avenue, 50, 146, 378, 460, 666
Salesforce.com, 322, 359, 564–566
SalesJobs.com, A-4
Salon Selectives, 591
Saltsman, Peter, 453
Salvation Army, 47
Sam's Club, 425, 441, 463, 465, 549, 593
Samsung, 5, 31, 57–58, 231, 328, 365, 511
Sandals, 6
San Francisco Giants, 92, 628
Santana Row, 458
Santinelli International, 583
SAP, 322, 432, 564
SAP America, 172
Saporito, Bill, 367, 543
Sarah's Candies, 326
Sara Lee, 172, 349
SAS, 263
"Saturday Night Live," 527
The Saturday Evening Post, 241–242
Save-A-Lot, 425
S.C. Johnson, 68–69, 523, 584
Schick, 374
Schiffer, Claudia, 533
Schneider Downs & Co., 108
Scholastic Media, 517
Scholfield, Roger, 99, 167, 339, 409
Scholfield Honda, 99, 167, 339–340,
    409, 600
Schumacher, Michael, 294
Schwarzenegger, Arnold, 146
Science Diet, 296
Scott, Lee, 10
ScottsMiracle-Gro, 399
Scripps Networks Interactive, 144, 660
Sealy, 648
The Seam, 173–174
Sean Conway, 381
Sears, 58, 110, 205, 379, 423, 506
Seattle bus system, 616
Seattle's Best Coffee, 297
SeaWorld, 96, 597
Secret, 130
Sega, 287
Seidman, Dan, 418
Seiko, 222
Sencion, John, 33, 481
Sense Networks, 253
Sentry Hardware, 428
Sephora, 41, 372, 459
Service Employees International Union, 20
7-Eleven, 45
Seven Cycles, 106
Seventh Generation, 2, A-23
Shah, Agam, 33
Shaikh, Zafar, 580
Sharper Image, 451
Shatner, William, 17
Shaw, George Bernard, 493
Shaw, Hollie, 615
Shaw's Supermarket, 49, 447
Shell, 67, 387
Shingler, Dan, 43
Shirouzu, Norihiko, 232

Shoebuy.com, 622
ShopNBC, 508
Shopzilla.com, 622
Shuttleworth, 38
Siemens, 222
Sierra Club, 299, 339
Sierra Mist, 381
Signet Research, Inc., 562
Simon, Bernard, 543
Sinegal, James, 463, A-23
Singapore Airlines, 178, 308
Sinopec-China Petroleum, 206
Six Flags, 67, A-24
Skittles, 421
Skype, 80, 372, 612
SkyTeam, 308–310
Slim-Fast, 381
Slotnick, Herbert N., 306
Smartfood popcorn, 381
Smart fortwo car, 305
SmartOrg, 262
Smith, Aaron, 249
Smith, Ed, 43
Smith, Greg, 407
Smithfield, 496
Snap Fitness, 429
Snickers, 526–528
Snyder, Esther, 48
Snyder, Harry, 48
Sobe juices, 381
Sofitel, 92
SoftNice, 580
Sokol, Marilyn, 570
Song airlines, 33, 201
Sonic Drive-In Restaurants, 429
Sony, 9, 57–58, 105, 231, 305, 365, 368,
    380, 407, 427, 475, 641
Sony Ericsson, 27
Sony Reader Daily Edition, 325
Sorabol Korean BBQ & Asian Noodles, 143
Sorrells, Shay, 510
Southwest Airlines, 8, 105, 116–117, 123,
    316, 336, 346
Sovereign Bank, 573
Spaceport America, 17–18
Spanx, 422
Special Olympics, 504
Spector, Sean, 6
Spectrum Air, 599
Speed, Melanie, 618
Speh, Thomas W., 187
Sperling, Nicole, 593
Spors, Kelly, 78
Sports Authority, 458
Sports Illustrated, 445
Sportsman's Warehouse, 451
Sports Tracker, 317
Springsteen, Bruce, 561
Sprinkles, 119
Sprint, 13, 68, 325, 564
Spyker, 302
Spy Optic, 322
SRI Consulting Business Intelligence
    (SRIC-BI), 293
SRI International, 293
Stair, Ralph M., 431

Standard Renewable Energy (SRE), 482–483, 666–668
Staples, 19, 270, 420, 589, 593, 664
Star Alliance, 308–310
Starbucks, 44, 118, 124, 166, 296, 391, 465, 549, 612
Starch Readership Report, 553
Starwood Hotels & Resorts Worldwide, 288, 336, 353
State Farm, 532
Stein, Ben, 42
Stein, Joel, 407
Stein Mart, 464
Stella & Dot, 417
Stella McCartney, 379, 651
Sterrett, David, 653
Stetson, 393–394
Steve Madden, 379, 502–503
Steve Miller Band, 562
Stewart, Tony, 17
Stolichnaya vodka, 226
Stoll, Clifford, 114
Stone, Andrea, 437
Stone, Biz, 118
Stone, Susan, 295
Stone, W. Clement, 87
Stonyfield Farms, 60, 69
Stop and Shop, 447, 644
Stouffer's, 140
Strategic Vision, 262
Stratus Building Solutions, 428–429
Strauss, Marina, 145
StubHub.com, 31
Studio 6, 92
Studio 804, 482
Subway, 17, 23, 428–429, 510
Sun Chips, 421, 549
Sunflower Farmers Market, 452
Sunglass Hut, 460
Sunkist Growers, 384
Sun Life of Canada, 9
Sunny Ridge Farm, 362
Sunsilk, 381
Super Bowl, 19, 249, 281, 320, 384, 486, 501, 504, 511, 518, 526–527, 546, 561, 614–615
SuperValu, 31, 51, 380, 425
Supply House Times, 471
Surowiecki, James, 43
Sustainability Consortium, 91
Suzuki, 67, 497
Sviolka, John, 480
Sweeney, Kelly, 437
Swiffer, 392–393
Swinmurn, Nick, 169
Synovate, 246
Sysco, 178
System4, 429
Szczesny, Joseph, 232

T

Taco Bell, 57, 490, 653
Taco Cabana, 306
Tag Heuer, 614
"Take the Money and Run," 562

Tampa Bay Rays, 92
Tan, Zona Marie, 120
Tannin, Matthew, 96
Target, 2, 14, 17, 45, 58, 82, 96, 116, 140, 205, 244, 301, 327, 338, 374, 380, 388, 425, 444, 447, 453, 457, 465, 478, 511, 528, 535, 590, 652
Tastefully Simple, 417
Tata Motors, 643
Tauck Bridge, 299
Tauck Tours, 299
Tay, Dary, 157
Team Earth, 69
Ted Bates Worldwide, 526
Teenage Research Unlimited (TRU), 253
Teleflora.com, 372
Telemundo, 82
Telfonica, 560
TerraCycle, A-23
Tesco, 630–631
Tessler, Joelle, 25
Tetra Tech, 175, 180, 193
Texaco, 388
Texas Instruments, 223
Texas Roadhouse, 654
T.G.I. Friday's, 96, 654
Thai Airways, 308
Thompson, Don, 44
Thornhill Aviators, 651
3M, 358
Ticket Liquidator, 657
Ticketmaster, 57, 608
TicketsNow.com, 608
Tide, 130, 207, 382
Tiffany, 145–146, 164, 291, 350, 665–666
Tillamook Cheese, 547
Timberland, 91, 144–145, A-28
Timberline Four Seasons Ski Resort, 18
Time Warner, 82, 426, 564
Timex, 222
Tim Horton's, 533
Tishman Speyer Properties, 42
TiVo, 315
T.J. Maxx, 86, 464
TJX, 86
T-Mobile, 17, 67, 96, 278, 328, 528
"The Today Show," 60, 447
Tomlinson, Henry M., 295
Tony Robbins, 149
Torrid, 478
Toshiba, 31, 92, 368, 641
Tostitos, 381
Total, 206
Total Immersion, 545
Tour de Cure, 16
Tour de France, 504
Tower Records, 479
Toyoda, Akio, 542
Toyota, 23, 36, 39, 73, 75, 124, 148, 206, 227, 347, 353, 405, 502, 541, 542–543, 549, 562–563, 618–619
Toys "R" Us, 110, 117
Toy Story, 592
Toy Story 2, 593
Toy Story 3, 593
Trader Joe's, 13, 58, 347, 379, 425, 447,

613–614
Traif Bike Gesheft, 421
Training magazine, 313
Transamerica Asset Management, 347
Transportation Security Administration (TSA), 25, 70
TransUnion, 74
Travel Michigan, 151–152
Travelocity, 76
Treanor, Misty May, 518
Treffinger, Stephen, 393
Tripsas, Mary, 78
Tropicana Products, 15, 48
tru2way, 426
Trump, Donald J., 17, 579
TruServ, 328
TRUSTe, 114
Tucker, Neely, 384
Tudge, Niki, 143
Tupperware, 374, 417, 473, 570
Turcotte, Jon, 447
Turner, Robin, 431
Tutankhamun, 522
Tween Brands, 274–275
Twitter, 21–22, 102–103, 113, 116, 118, 130, 140, 151, 168, 249, 301, 315–316, 406, 416, 459, 486, 499, 501, 577, 638
Tyco, 24
Tyson Foods, 405

U

uBid.com, 657
Ugg, 97
U-Haul, 346
Under Armour, 532
Underhill, Paco, 136–138, 164
UNICEF, 15
Uniform Commercial Code, 555
Unilever, 2, 182, 190, 226, 381, 584, A-1–A-2
Union Pacific, 437
United Airlines, 64, 308, 354
United Center, 505
United Stationers, 467–468
United Technology, 178
United Way, 16
Universal Studios Amusement Park, 67, 96, 635
University of Delaware, 80
University of Findlay, 149
University of Florida, 319
University of Kansas, 482, 668
University of Massachusetts, 374
University of North Carolina-Chapel Hill, 319
University of Richmond, 319
University of Southern California, 608
University of Texas, 20, 23
University of Virginia, 319
Univision, 82
Unlistme.com, 87
Upper Deck, 17
UPS, 6, 31, 96, 178, 289, 437–438
Urban Outfitters, A-24

U.S. Airways, 243
U.S. Census Bureau, 48, 97, 102, 108,
    141–142, 147, 205, 247–249, 270,
    282, 287–290, 292, 518
U.S. Coast Guard, 20, 437
U.S. Congress, 80, 358, 518, A-23
U.S. Department of Agriculture (USDA),
    396
U.S. Department of Commerce, 51, 78,
    193, 259, 290
U.S. Department of Defense, 170, 176, 193
U.S. Department of Energy (DOE), 67,
    193, 618
U.S. Department of Health and Human
    Services, 199
U.S. Department of Justice, 71, 74, 114, 190
U.S. Department of Labor, 347, 417
U.S. Department of Transportation,
    308, 636
U.S. Federal Sentencing Guidelines for
    Organizations, 85
U.S. Food and Drug Administration (FDA), 66
U.S. Green Building Council, 92, 133
U.S. Navy, 437, 490
U.S. Patent and Trademark Office, 406
U.S. Pentagon, 193
U.S. Postal Service, 20, 96, 192, 207,
    438, 649
U.S. Secret Service, 114
U.S. Supreme Court, 67, 387, 401,
    609, 647
U.S. Transportation Security Administration
    (TSA), 432
U.S. Treasury Department, 91
U.S. Wholesale Grocers Association, 608
US Airways, 354
USA Today, 122, 527, 543
Utne Reader, 272, 562–563

V

Vaas, Lisa, A-6
Valentino, 101
Valu-Rite Pharmacies, 461
Vanguard, Danny J., 467
Vanguard Cleaning Systems, 429
Varenik, Tatiana, A-12
Varsa, 70
Vaseline, A-1
Vasilyeva, Nataliya, 209
Veeck, Bill, 656
Velvac, 328
Vente-privée.com, 464
VeriSign, 114
Verizon, 13, 57, 67–68, 96, 177, 285, 314,
    328, 522, 529, 533, 597, 660
Versace, 651
Vick's, 532
Victoria's Secret, 51, 110, 382, 537
Vigoda, Abe, 527
Villareal, Phil, 456
Vincent, Laurence, 378
Virgin Atlantic, 309, 426
Virgin Galactic, 18, 37–38, 45
Virtuosity, 455

Visa, 31, 96, 114, 129, 149
Vista, 605
Vodafone, 328
Voelcker, John, 636
Volkswagen, 5, 51, 405
Volunteers of America, 143
Volvo, 34, 401
Von Maur, 450
Vonn, Lindsey, 532

W

Walgreens, 110, 463, 465
Wallach, Daniel, 133–134, 339, 601
Wall Street Journal, 49–50, 564
Walmart, 2–4, 10, 25, 45–48, 51, 65, 77, 92,
    109, 116, 125, 136–138, 144–145, 182,
    205–206, 222, 287, 289–290, 301, 327,
    347, 359, 364, 374, 380, 382, 401, 425,
    431, 434, 451, 453, 455, 462, 464–465,
    469, 479, 483, 542, 584, 622, 643–644,
    648, 651–652, 659–660, 666, A-23
Walmsley, Andrew, 329
Walt Disney World, 31, 203
Walton, Sam, 451
Wanamaker, John, 515
Waring, 374
Warner Brothers, 517
Warner Music, 459
Warrior, 373
Washington Center for Internships and
    Academic Seminars, A-6
Washington State Potato Commission, 532
Watts, J. C., Jr., 87
Wawa, 448–450
Webb, C. A., 60, 447
Webb, Tim, 543
Webkinz, 6, 366
WebStakes, 591
WebTech Development, 634
Webtrends' Mobile Analytics, 124
Weed, Keith, A-1
Weight Watchers, 58
Weintraug, Elizabeth, 618
Welch, Bryan, 272, 562–563, 601–602
Welch, John F., Jr., 8, 42
Wellness Councils of America, A-25
Wendlandt, Astrid, 666
Wendy's, 58, 166, 178, 374
West, Andrew, 617
Western Auto, 428
Westinghouse, 380
Westinghouse, George, 548
Weston Solutions, 193
Weyerhaeuser, 353
White, Betty, 526–527
White, Shaun, 15, 511, 531
White Flint Mall, 458
Whiting, Susan, 64
Whole Foods Market, 82–83, 374, 425, 447
Whoriskey, Peter, 232
Wichita Business Journal, 600
Wichita State University, 243
Wii, 221, 287, 390, 415, A-2
Wilde, Oscar, 615

Wilder, Gene, 407
Wild Oats, 447
Williams-Derry, Clark, 446
Williams-Sonoma, 118, 122, 458, 465, 507
Wilson Sporting Goods, 171
Windows 7, 604–605
Winfrey, Oprah, 147
WomenSportsJobs.com, A-4
Wong, Wailin, 480
Wood, Zoe, 364
Wood family, 448
Woods, Tiger, 43, 532
Word of Mouth Marketing Association, 321
Working Group on Food Marketed to
    Children, 88
World Cup, 19, 505, 538
Wortham, Jenna, 315
WPP, 547
Wright Investors, 250
Wyndham Hotels, 372
Wynne, Sharon Kennedy, 570

X

Xanadu, 458
Xerox, 183, 317, 357, 386
XM Satellite Radio, 542

Y

Yahoo!, 15, 122–123, 152, 283, 336–337,
    523, 546, A-4–A-5
Yale University, 88
Yang, Jia Lynne, 179
Yellow Pages, 538, 545
Yelp.com, 496
Yen, Hope, 249
Yoox, 101
Yoplait, 69
York, Emily Bryson, 453
"You and I," 561
Young, Scott, 120
Young & Rubicam (Y&R), 382
YourCause.com, 15
YouTube, 104, 121, 249, 250, 256–257,
    314, 523, 528, 577, A-6
Yu, Roger, 453
Yum! Brands, 207
Yu-Na, Kim, 511
Yves Behar, 33
Yves Saint Laurent, 379

Z

Zagnut Candy Bars, 54
Zahorsky, Darrell, 166
Zappone, Chris, 456
Zappos.com, 116, 168–170, 358, 502–503
Zara stores, 459
Ziglar, Zig, 20, A-11
Zippo, 230
Zogby, John, 145
Zpizza, 612
Zsigmond, Vilmos, 407
Zumba, 31

subject index

A

accessory equipment, **354**
accidental sample, **251**
accounting data, 245
account managers, 586
acquisitions/mergers, 69
activities, interests, opinions (AOI), 292
administered marketing systems, **427**–428
adoption process, **394**–395
advertising, 171, 489, 495, **500**, **529**. *See also*
   marketing
   accessory equipment and, 354
   ad elements, 537
   banned television advertising, 541
   banner ad, 120, 538
   campaigns, 141
   clutter, 532
   comparative, 531
   cooperative, 423, 533
   corporate, 529
   creating ads, 534–535
   deception, 555–556
   developing ads, 537–538
   directory, 545–546
   ethics, 555–556
   fear appeals, 536
   function organization, 547
   humor, 536–537
   informative, 529
   institutional, 529
   interactive, 534, 538
   Internet, 500, 538
   keyword ads, 538, 545
   location-based, 315
   measuring effectiveness, 552–554
   media scheduling, 546
   media selection, 539–546
   messages, 535–539
   mobile, 545
   nonpersonal selling, 500
   objectives, 529–530
   outdoor, 544–545
   out-of-home, 544
   persuasive, 530
   planning, 535
   political, 561–562
   POP, 593
   pop-up ad, 120
   preroll video ad, 121
   product, 529–530
   product lifecycle and, 530
   reminder, 530
   retail, 534
   sex-based appeals, 537
   social networking, 538
   soft drink, 87
   specialty, 592

   sponsorship *vs.*, 504–505
   television, 151, 539–541
   truth in, 87
   t-shirts, 545
   2010 U.S. Census, 249
   types, 529
   words to use, 533
advertising agency, **547**–548
advertising campaign, **535**
advertising strategy, 531–534
advertorials, 538
advocates, 20–21, 320–321
adware, 538
affiliate marketing, 174
affinity marketing, **319**
African Americans, 48, 141–142, 287–288
age
   baby boomers, 48, 82, 277, 285, 526
   demographic segmentation, 283–287
   Generation X, 284–285
   school-age children, 283–284
   seniors, 285–286
   tweens/teens, 284
agents, 470, **471**, 472
aggregators, 250, 262
AIDA. *See* attention interest, desire, action
AIDA concept, **491**, 578
AIO statements, **292**
Airline Deregulation Act, 73
Airline Quality Rating survey, 243
airlines, 70, 73, 113, 243, 308–310, 426
airplanes, 12, 67
airport scanners, 25
Alaska Natives, 141
alcohol, 73, 88
allowances, **647**
alternative energy, 80, 622
alternative pricing procedures, 624–625
altruists, 294
ambush marketing, **505**
Anti-A&P Act, 608
Anticybersquatting Consumer Protection Act, 72
antitrust, **67**, 71, 213
anxiety, 159–160
AOI. *See* activities, interests, opinions
application service providers (ASPs), **320**
approach, **579**
Asch phenomenon, 144–145
Asian Americans, 142–143, 288
ASPs. *See* application service providers
assembly line, 358
assurances, 359
ATM, 140
atmospherics, **460**
attention interest, desire, action (AIDA), **492**, 578
attitudes, **152**
   affective components, 153–154
   behavioral components, 153–154

   body language, 153
   changing, 153–154
   cognitive components, 153–154
   in consumer behavior, 152–154, 161
   favorable/unfavorable, 152–153
   modifying components, 154
auction houses, 471
augmented reality, 545
autodialing, 571
automatic merchandising, 474–475
automobile industry, 5, 10, 34–36, 167, 173–
   174, 206, 277, 339–340, 529, 607, 643
   clunkers program, 27
   emissions laws, 73
   exclusive distribution, 424
   green score, 79
   hybrid cars, 51, 75, 80, 619
   plant locations, 177
   recalls, 73
   smart cars, 225
   teenagers purchasing autos, 148
   women purchasing autos, 148
average total costs, **620**

B

B2B. *See* business-to-business
B2B databases, 327
B2B e-marketing, **108**
B2B marketing, **170**, **324**
   business buying process, 185–191
   business market demand, 181–183
   buyer-seller relationships, 179–180, 324–327
   buyer sizes/numbers, 178
   buying centers, 191–192
   characteristics, 177–181
   components, 172–173
   customer-based segmentation, 175
   defined, 170
   demographic segmentation, 175
   diversity, 172
   e-business, 108–109
   end-use application segmentation, 176
   e-procurement, 108, 109
   evaluating international, 180–181
   in foreign business markets, 173–174
   geographic market concentration, 177–178
   government, 173, 192–193
   improving buyer-seller relationships, 326–327
   institutions, 173, 194
   international market challenges, 194
   Internet connection, 173
   make/buy/lease decision, 183–185
   marketing compared to, 171
   NAICS, 176
   nature of market, 171–175
   offshoring, 183–185
   online, 103

outsourcing, 183–185
proprietary B2B transactions, 104, 108–109
purchase categories segmentation, 177
purchase decision process, 178–179
relationships, 22
resource-producing industries, 172
trade industries, 173
B2B marketing strategy, 192–195
B2C. *See* business-to-consumer
B2C e-marketing, 103, **109**. *See also* e-tailing
access/convenience, 111–112
benefits, 111–112
competitive pricing, 111
e-business, 109–113
electronic storefronts, 110–111
online buyers/sellers, 112–113
personalized marketing, 112
baby boomers, 48, 82, 277, 285, 526
backshoring, 347
backward integration, **427**
banner ad, **120**, **538**
bar codes, 250. *See also* Universal Product Code
basing-point pricing, **649**
basis point, 493
BCG matrix, 53–54
behavioral targeting, 115
believers, 293
benchmarking, **358**
BFRs. *See* brominated flame retardants
big-box retailers, 468
billboards, 151, 544–545, 552
birdyback, 439
blind product tests, 553
blogs, 4, 21, 81, 104, **119**, 173, 317, 321, 495, A-4
career readiness, 120
Internet communications, 119–120
"mom," 541
news/information, 103
shopping, 102
body copy, 537
body language, 153, 493, 495. *See also* gestures
bonus packs, **591**
bots. *See* shopbots
bottom line, **15**
boycotts, 75
brainstorming, 238
brand(s), **379**, 402, 474
captive, 381
category management, 378, 383
cobranding, 326
evolution of, 3–4, 35, 63–64, 101–102,
137–138, 169–170, 203–204, 239–240,
275–276, 309–310, 343–344, 377–378,
413–414, 449–450, 487–488, 527–528,
565–566, 605–606, 639–640
family, 381–382
fighting, 610
flanker, 393–394
generic, 145
house, 364
individual, 381–382
loyalty, 152, 296–297, 379–380
managing for competitive advantage, 378–383
manufacturer's *vs.* private, 380
national, 380
overextension, 391

private, 380
research, 238
role, 378
shelf space for product, 364
types of, 380–382
brand equity, **382**–383, 532
brand extensions, **390**–391
brand insistence, **380**
brand licensing, **391**
brand manager, **383**
brand marks, **385**–386
brand names, 49, **385**–388
brand personality, 382–383
brand preference, **379**
brand recognition, 19, **379**
breakeven analysis, **625**–627
brick-and-click retailers, 474
brick-and-mortar banks, 110
brick-and-mortar stores, 117, 430–431
broadcast media, 539
brochureware, 123
brokers, 110, 470, **471**, 472. *See also* agents
brominated flame retardants (BFRs), 27
budgets, 15, 76, 513–515
bundle pricing, **660**
business buying process
analysis tools, 190
in B2B marketing, 185–191
classifying buying situations, 189–190
environmental influences, 185–186
interpersonal influences, 186
merchandisers/category advisors in, 186–187
model of organizational, 187–189
organizational factors, 185–186
business cycle, **76**, 93
business market demand
in B2B marketing, 181–183
categories, 181
derived demand, 181–182
inelastic demand, 182, 622
inventory adjustments, 182–183
joint demand, 182
volatile demand, 182
business models, 106, 187–189
business plan, **A-20**–A-21. *See also* marketing
plan; marketing planning
business products, **277**
accessory equipment, 354
benchmarking, 358
business services, 355–356
classification, 353
classification impact, 356
component parts/materials, 354
installations, 353–354
raw materials, 355
supplies, 355
types, 353–356
business (B2B) products, **348**
business services, **355**–356
business-to-business (B2B), 22
business-to-consumer (B2C), 103
buyer, **191**. *See also* B2B marketing; B2C
e-marketing
buyer's market, 11
expectations, 7
expectations of salespeople, 574

online, 112–113
partnerships, 325
sizes/numbers, 178
survey of buyer intentions, 264
buyer partnerships, **325**
buyer-seller relationships, 179–180, 311–312
in B2B marketing, 179–180, 324–327
building, 318–321
buyer's market, **11**
buying, 23–24, 64, 138–139
buying centers, **191**–192
buzz marketing, **22**, **321**, 502, 577
buzzwords, 493

C

cable television, 74, 82, 539–541, 660
CAD/CAM. *See* computer-aided design
and manufacturing
CAFTA. *See* China-ASEAN Free Trade Area
CAFTA-DR. *See* Central American Free Trade
Agreement-DR
call centers, 347
Caller ID, 254
campus ambassadors, 502
cannibalization, **394**, **659**–660
captive brands, **381**
carbon footprint, 69
career readiness. *See also* marketing careers
blogs, 120
body language, 153, 495
communicating price increase, 650
culture tips, 211
dressing for job interview, A-12
dressing professionally, 575
establishing CRM relationships, 323
feedback, 357
going green, 98
handling business crisis, 551
housing pricing, 618
jargon, 386
networking, 12
online surveys, 257
sales calls, 418
suppliers, 467
target market, 283
trade shows, 180
virtual conferences, 38
caring, 498
carload (CL), 438
carriers, 73, 435–436, 438
cash-and-carry wholesalers, 469
cash cows, 54
cash discounts, 645–**646**
*Catalog of U.S. Government Publications
(CGP)*, 248
catalogs, 10, 50, 248, 473, 506–507
category advisors, **186**–187
category killer, **462**
category management, 378, **383**, 402, 454
category promotions, 497
cause marketing, 16, **18**–19
caveat emptor, 251
CBSA. *See* core based statistical area
CDs, 49
cease-and-desist orders, 73

celebrity endorsements, 17, 42, 43, 531–533
cell phones, 9, 13, 17, 66–67, 80, 252, 317, 490, 528, 545
    Do Not Call Registry, 71
    video options, 69
cellulosic ethanol, 80
Central American Free Trade Agreement-DR (CAFTA-DR), **217**
CEOs. *See* chief executive officers
CGP. See Catalog of U.S. Government Publications
chain stores, 380, 461
channel, **492**–493
channel captain, **425**
channel conflicts, **117**
    e-business, 117
    gray goods, 426–427
    horizontal, 426
    marketing channels, 426–427
    vertical, 426
chat rooms, 321
checkoffs, 496
chief executive officers (CEOs), 40, 89
chief operating officers (COOs), 40
child protection, 71
children, 48, 161. *See also* teenagers
    ethics in advertising, 556
    in family purchases, 148
    family purchasing, 148
    Internet and, 71, 72
    marketing to, 88
    reference groups and, 145–146
    salespeople, 569–570
    school-age, in age segmentation, 283–284
    smart phones, 146
    social networking, 146
Children's Online Privacy Protection Act, 71, 72
China-ASEAN Free Trade Area (CAFTA), 213
chlorofluorocarbons, 68
cigarette industry, 72, 85
CL. *See* carload
Clayton Act, 72, 424, 608
click-through rate, **124**, **516**, 554
click-to-call, 509
closed sales territory, **424**
closing, **581**
cluster sample, **251**
CMSA. *See* consolidated metropolitan statistical area
cobranding, **326**
Code of Hammurabi, 567
cognitive dissonance, **160**
cohort effect, **287**
cold calling, **580**
cold storage, 439
Cold War, 287
collaborative planning, forecasting, and replenishment (CPFaR), **328**
colleges, 16, 20, 80, 102
    logos, 88
    marketing to students, 88
    selecting, 139
color, 151, 166
comarketing, **326**
commercialization, 400
commercial market, **172**
commercial organizations. *See* for-profit organizations
commission, **586**

commission merchants, **470**–471
common carriers, **434**
common market, **215**
communications, 488. *See also* integrated marketing communications; Internet communications; marketing communications; telecommunications
    consumer, 13
    direct marketing channels, 506
    process, 491–494, 492
    promotions and, 492
    technology, 4–5
community shopping center, 457–458
Community Trademark (CTM), 218
comparative advertising, **531**
compatibility, 396
compensation, 586
competition, 50
    direct, 67
    indirect, 67–68
    Internet, 462
    laws regulating, 72
    monopolistic, 619
    objectives, 612–613
    protecting competitors, 71
    pure, 619
    time-based, 69–70
    types, 67–68
competitive advantage, 34, 42, 55, 81, 262, 302, 358, 378–383
competitive bidding, **655**–657
competitive environment, **66**. *See also* competition
    competitive strategy development, 68–69
    laws maintaining, 72
    in marketing environment, 66–70
    time-based competition, 69–70
competitive pricing strategy, **644**–645
competitive strategy, **68**–69
component parts/materials, **354**
computer-aided design and manufacturing (CAD/CAM), 399
computer industry, 7, 32, 50, 60, 206, 261–262
concentrated (or niche) marketing, **299**–300
concept testing, **399**
conflict, 311
congestion pricing, 616–617
consignment shops, 144
consolidated metropolitan statistical area (CMSA), **281**
conspicuous consumption, 137
consultative selling, **574**
consumer(s), 8, 9, 64, 72, 390, 400, 571, 609. *See also* B2C e-marketing; shoppers
    African Americans, 142
    Asian Americans, 142–143
    communications, 13
    elastic, 145
    empowering, 125
    groups, 65–66
    habits, 136
    Hispanic Americans, 142
    laws protecting, 72
    middle-class, 146
    on-the-go, 116
    protection, 71
    sales promotion, 590–592
    spending, 76

    value-conscious, 144–145
consumer awareness, 50–51
consumer behavior, **138**
    attitudes, 152–154, 161
    cultural influences, 139–143, 161
    family influences, 147–148
    interpersonal determinants, 139–148
    learning in, 154–155
    Lewin's proposition, 138–139
    motives, 148
    needs, 148–150
    perceptions, 150–152
    personal determinants, 148–156
    repeat, 155
    research, 136–138
    self-concept theory, 155–156
    social influences, 143–147
consumer decision process
    classifying, 160–161
    evaluation of alternatives, 159
    extended problem solving, 161
    high involvement purchase decisions, 156, 161
    integrated model, 158
    limited problem solving, 161
    low involvement purchase decisions, 156
    postpurchase evaluation, 160
    problem/opportunity recognition, 158
    purchase decision/act, 159–160
    routinized response behavior, 160–161
    search, 158–159
    steps in, 156–161
Consumer Goods Pricing Act (1975), 609
consumer innovators, **395**
consumerism, **82**–84
consumer orientation, **11**
consumer-oriented sales promotion, 590–592
consumer packaged goods (CPG), 374
consumer products, **277**
    applying classification system, 352
    classification, 349
    convenience, 348–350, 352
    shopping, 350, 352
    specialty, 350–352
    types, 348–351
    unsought, 348
consumer (B2C) products, **348**
Consumer Product Safety Act, 72, 400
consumer rights, **83**
Consumer Telephone Records Act, 72
contacts, 467–468
containerization, **441**
contests, **591**, 594
contract carriers, **435**
contractual agreements, 221
contractual systems, **428**
contract workers, 456
controlled experiment, **258**
convenience products, 348–350, 352
convenience retailers, **461**
convenience sample, **251**
conventions, 212
conversion rate, **124**, **516**
cookies, 114–115, 174, 257, **555**
cooperation, 311
cooperative advertising, 423, 533
COOs. *See* chief operating officers
copyright disputes, 117
core based statistical area (CBSA), **280**

core competencies, 45–46
core region, **281**
core values, 140
corporate advertising, 529
corporate criminals, 85
corporate marketing systems, **427**–428
corporate responsibility, 62–64
corporate Web sites, **107**, 124
cost per impression, **516**
cost per response, **516**
cost per thousand impressions (CPM), 552, 554
cost/revenue curves, 620–621
costs. *See also* price; pricing
  average total, 620
  control, 432
  cost/revenue curves, 620–621
  fixed, 620
  full-cost pricing, 624
  incremental-cost pricing, 624
  lowering, 467–468
  marginal, 621
  marketing, 23–24, 28
  marketing cost analysis, 245
  packaging, 389
  regulatory cost recovery fees, 607
  variable, 620
  wholesaling intermediaries lowering, 467–468
countertrade, **226**
County and City Data Book, 248
coupons, 50, **590**–591
CPFaR. *See* collaborative planning, forecasting, and replenishment
CPG. *See* consumer packaged goods
CPM. *See* cost per thousand impressions; critical path method
craft guilds, 504
creatives, 295
creative selling, **577**
Credit Card Accountability, Responsibility and Disclosure Act, 72, 89
credit cards, 74
  applications, 319
  chargebacks, 116
  industry, 65–66, 72, 88–89
  memory chips, 223
  record stealing, 114
credit-reporting agencies, 74
critical path method (CPM), 398
CRM. *See* customer relationship management
cross-promotion, **551**
cross-selling, **574**
CTM. *See* Community Trademark
cues, 154–155
cultural influences
  in consumer behavior, 139–143, 161
  core values, 140
  international perspective, 140–141
  subcultures, 141–143
cultural preferences, 174
culture, **139**, 211, 223. *See also* subcultures
cumulative quantity discount, **647**
customary prices, **616**–617
customer(s)
  as advocates, 20–21, 320–321
  complex, 227
  creation, 6
  defection rates, 324
  defined, 325

expectations, 116
  external, 312
  feedback, 243, 317
  identifying, 302
  internal, 312
  keeping, 318–319
  lifetime value, 330–331
  lost, 323–324
  loyalty, 4, 85, 112, 113, 144, 170, 238
  needs, 316–317
  preferences, 7, 114
  relationships, 5, 7, 19
  repeat, 20, 22, 28
  retention, 238
  wholesaling services, 466
customer-based segmentation, **175**
customer churn, **318**
customer-oriented management, 13
customer relationship management (CRM), **177**, 312, **321**
  benefits, 321–322
  career readiness, 323
  defined, 321
  lost customers, 323–324
  problems, 322–323
customer satisfaction, 7, 170, 238, **316**, 369
  as art/science, 5
  customer needs, 316–317
  enhancing, 69, 316–318
  ensuring, 317
  marketing research, 243
  measuring, 316
customer service
  e-business, 116–117
  retailing strategy, 455–456
  standards, in physical distribution, 433
customer win-back, **324**
customization, 154–155
customs union, **215**
cybercrime, 71
cyberfraud, 116
cybermalls, 110, 390
cyberspace, 71, 125, 250, 555

D

database marketing, **319**–320
databases, 81, 261, 327, 491
data collection, 246
data interpretation/presentation, 246–247. *See also* primary data; secondary data
data mining, **261**–262
data warehouse, 261
dealer incentives, **594**
decider, **191**
decline stage, **365**–366
decoding, **492**–493
deflation, 77
Delphi technique, **264**
demand, 77, **619**. *See also* business market demand
  derived, 181–182
  inelastic, 182, 622
  joint, 182
  primary, 495–496
  promotion increasing, 496–497
  selective, 497
  volatile, 182

demarketing, **79**
demographic segmentation, 175, **282**
  abroad, 291–292
  age, 283–286
  cohort effect, 287
  ethnic groups, 287–289
  family lifecycle, 289–290
  gender, 282–283
  household type, 290
  income/expenditure patterns, 291
  video game generation, 287
demonstration, **580**–581
department stores, **463**
depreciation, 181
deregulation, 74
derived demand, **181**–182
devouts, 294
differentiated marketing, **299**
diffusion process, **395**
Digital Millennium Copyright Act, 72
Digital Snippets, 36
digital world, 103–104
direct channel, **416**
direct competition, 67
direct investment, 222
direct mail, 473, **503**, 544, 608
direct marketing, 6, 105, **473**, **501**, 505–506
  automatic merchandising, 474–475
  broadcast channels *vs.*, 508
  catalogs, 506–507
  communications channels, 506
  direct mail, 473, 503, 544, 608
  direct-response retailing, 473–474
  direct selling, 473
  electronic channels, 508–509
  Internet, 474
  kiosks, 6, 105, 498, 509, 545, 576, 611
  as nonpersonal selling, 501–502
  nonstore retailing and, 472–475
  print media, 509
  telemarketing, 474, 507–508
directory advertising, 545–546
direct-response retailing, 473–474
direct sales results test, **515**
direct sampling, 491
direct selling, 416, **417**–418
discount houses, **463**–464
discount stores, 50, 144
discretionary income, **77**–78
distribution, 7, 65, 69, **414**. *See also* physical distribution
  dual, 419–420
  ethics, 87
  exclusive, 424
  global marketing strategy, 225
  intensity, in marketing channels, 422–424
  intensive, 423
  Internet and, 49
  marketing ethics, 87
  physical, 414
  retailing strategy, 457–458
  selective, 423
  strategy, in marketing mix, 49
distribution channels, **414**
diversity, 48
dollar, 79, 210
dollar stores, 50
domain name, 122

Do-Not-Call Improvement Act, 73
Do Not Call Registry, 71, 74, 87, 254,
    506–508, 571, 598
dot.com companies, 266
downstream management, **430**–431
dressing professionally, 575
drop shipper, **470**
dual distribution, **419**–420
dumping, **215**
DVD technology, 365, 368

E

early adopters, 396
early majority, 395
e-business, **102**, 441. *See also* e-marketing;
    Internet; Web sites
    B2B marketing, 108–109
    B2C e-marketing, 109–113
    categories, 104
    channel conflicts, 117
    copyright disputes, 117
    customer service, 116–117
    defined, 102
    digital world, 103–104
    e-marketing and, 104–107
    merchandise delivery, 116
    online payment safety, 113–114
    potential, 125
    privacy issues, 114–115
    reverse logistics, 116
    scope, 102–103
    site design, 116–117
    Web business models, 106
eco-friendly products, 656
eco-labels, 218
ecology, 90–91
economic environment, **76**, 209–210
    business cycle stages, 76
    deflation, 77
    global economic crisis, 77
    income, 77–78
    inflation, 77
    international, 79
    resource availability, 78–79
    unemployment, 77
economics, 5
    economic downturn, 26–78, 654
    global economy, 79
economic theory
    cost/revenue curves, 620–621
    elasticity, 621–623
    practical problems, 623–624
    price determination, 619–627
EDIs. *See* electronic data interchanges
EDLP. *See* everyday low pricing
education, 140, 390. *See also* colleges
efficiency, 140
80/20 principle, **296**
elastic consumers, 145
elasticity, **621**. *See also* inelastic demand
    determinants, 622–623
    revenue and, 623
electric bicycle industry, 76
electronic bulletin boards, **118**
electronic businesses, 7

electronic conversations, 21
electronic data interchanges (EDIs), 104, 108,
    182, 190, **327**, 355, 455
electronic delivery, 631
electronic exchanges, 108
electronic reading devices, 4
electronic shopping bag, 110
electronic shopping cart, **110**
Electronic Signature Act, 72
electronic signatures, 72, **114**
electronic storefronts, **110**–111
e-mail, 21, 47, 50, 79, 104, 116–117, 173,
    257, 326
    spam, 118
    for tracking, 112
e-marketing, **104**. *See also* B2B e-marketing;
    B2C e-marketing; e-business; Internet;
    online marketing; Web sites
    activities, 104
    capabilities, 105
    defined, 104
    e-business and, 104–107
    global reach, 105
    integrated marketing, 105–106
    interactive marketing, 105–106
    opportunities, 105–107
    personalized marketing, 105–106
    potential, 125
    right-time marketing, 105–106
embargo, **214**
EMC. *See* export management company
emergency goods/services, **349**
empathy, 359
employee research, 238
employee satisfaction, **313**
employment, 204
encoding, **492**–493
encryption, 87, **113**–114
Encyclopedia of Associations, 249
end-use application segmentation, **176**
energy conservation, 4, 67, 92
engagement, **124**
Engel's laws, **291**
enterprise resource planning (ERP), **432**
entertainment industry, 207
entrepreneurs, 33, 122, 342, 519
environment, 72. *See also* competitive environment;
    ecology; economic environment; greenhouse-
    gas emissions; marketing environment;
    political-legal environment; recycling;
    social-cultural environment; sustainability;
    technological environment
    competitive, 72
    evaluating environmental risks/
        opportunities, 42
    external marketing, 50
    global warming, 91
    issues, 69, 90
    LEED, 133
    risks/opportunities, in marketing
        planning, 42
    social responsibility, 90
environmental influences, 185–186
environmental management, **65**–66
environmental scanning, **65**
e-procurement, 108, **109**

ERP. *See* enterprise resource planning
esteem, 150, 383
e-tailing, 104, 109, 111
ETC. *See* export trading company
ethanol, 80
ethics, **24**, 28, 93, 588. *See also* marketing ethics
    advertising, 555
    advertising to children, 556
    arms on ocean-going vessels, 437
    behavioral targeting, 115
    bottled water sales, 216
    business, 85
    celebrity accountability, 43
    children as salespeople, 570
    contract workers, 456
    cookie stuffing, 174
    defined, 24
    fast-food prices, 653
    full body scanning, 25
    location-based advertising, 315
    marketing abuses against seniors, 286
    marketing research, 86–87
    in nonpersonal selling, 555–556
    officers, 85
    online reviews, 496
    phosphates, 81
    pricing, 88–89
    privacy settings, 157
    product brands shelf space, 364
    product strategy, 87
    promotions, 86–87
    in public relations, 556
    social responsibility and, 24–26
    steps for improving, 85
    2010 U.S. Census advertising, 249
    "Who Dat?" slogan, 384
ethnic groups, 287–289. *See also specific groups*
ethnographic studies, 260
EU. *See* European Union (EU)
euro, 8, 140, 210, 218
European Union (EU), 8, 79, 140, 192, 210,
    212, 214–215, **218**
evaluation, 394
evaluative criteria, **159**
event marketing, 16, **19**
everyday low pricing (EDLP), **643**–644
Every Day with Rachel Ray, 17
evoked set, **159**
e-waste, 91–92
exaggeration, 555
exchange control, **215**
exchange functions, **24**
exchange process, **9**
exchange rate, **210**
exclusive distribution, **424**
expectancy theory, **585**
expense items, 182
expense ratio, 493
experiencers, 293
exploratory research, **245**
exponential smoothing, **265**
exporting, 8, **204**, 205, 213
    EMC, 220
    ETC, 220
    in global marketing, 220–221
    service/retail, 206–207

export management company (EMC), 220
export trading company (ETC), 220
Export Trading Company Act (1982), 213
express warranty, 555
extended problem solving, 161
Extensible Markup Language (XML), 102, 108
external customers, **312**
external marketing environment, 50
extranets, 108

F

fads, 366
Fair Packaging and Labeling Act (1966), 389–390, 400
fair-trade laws, **609**
family, 140, 147–148
family brands, **381**–382
family lifecycle, **289**–290
fast food restaurants, 83
fax machines, 79
fax surveys, 256
FCN. *See* friendship, commerce and navigation treaties
fear-based advertising appeals, 536
"features-benefits" framework, 579
Federal Food and Drug Act, 71, 72
Federal Trade Commission Act, 71, 72, 424
Federal Trademark Dilution Act (1995), 387
feedback, 188–189, **492**–493
    career readiness, 357
    customer, 243, 317
field selling, **569**–571
financial analysis, A-33–A-38
financial services industry, 207
financing, 23–24
FindEx: The Directory of Market Research Reports, Studies, and Surveys, 250
firewall, **115**
first mover strategy, **45**
fishyback, 439
fixed costs, **620**
fixed-sum-per-unit method, **514**
Flammable Fabrics Act (1953), 400
flanker brands, 393–394
FOB. *See* free on board
FOB origin, **648**
FOB origin-freight allowed (freight absorbed), **648**
FOB plant, **648**
focus groups, 238, **255**, 552, 554
follow-up, 581–**582**
Food Allergen Labeling and Consumer Protection Act, 390, 400
food industry, 355, 529
    genetic engineering, 211–212
    labels, 390
    single-serving foods, 290
    test kitchens, 246
foreign business markets, 173–174
Foreign Corrupt Practices Act, 213
foreign licensing, **221**
form utility, 5–6
for-profit organizations, 175, 180, 277, 325
    broadening scope, 28
    Internet and, 102
    not-for-profit organizations *vs.*, 15–16

objectives/goals, 15
    traditional boundaries, 16
forward integration, **427**
franchises, 202–203, **221**, 421, **428**–429
fraud, 72, 85, 116
Fraud Enforcement And Recovery Act, 72
freedom, 140
Free Extension Act, 73
free on board (FOB), 648
free trade area, **215**
Free Trade Area of the Americas (FTAA), **217**
freight forwarders, 438
frequency, 546
frequency marketing, **319**
friendship, commerce and navigation treaties (FCN), **212**
full body scanning, 25
full-service research suppliers, **243**
fun seekers, 294

G

gatekeepers, **191**
GATT. *See* General Agreement on Tariffs and Trade
GDP. *See* gross domestic product
gender, 282–283
General Agreement on Tariffs and Trade (GATT), 213, **216**–217, 230
general merchandise retailers, **463**–464
Generation Next, 287
Generation X, 284–285
Generation Y, 287
generic products, 145, **380**
genetically modified organisms (GMOs), 212
genetic engineering, 212–213
geographic information systems (GISs), 281–**282**
geographic market concentration, 177–178
geographic segmentation, **279**
    migration, 280
    population, 279–280
    urbanization, 280–281
GeoVALS, 293
gestures, 493
gift cards, 140
GISs. *See* geographic information systems
global economic crisis, 77
global economy, 79
globalization, 219
global marketing, 5, 48. *See also* international marketing
    benefits, 207–209
    categories, 204
    contractual agreements, 221
    developing global marketing strategy, 223–226
    direct investment, 222
    dumping, 215
    economic environment, 209–210
    employment and, 204
    exporting, 220–221
    globalization and, 219
    importing, 220–221
    laws in, 212–213
    levels of involvement, 220
    marketing mix, 223–226
    from multinational corporations, 222–223

multinational economic integration, 215–219
    new era, 227
    political-legal environment, 212–213
    role of, 205–209
    service/retail exports, 206–207
    social-cultural environment, 210
    technological environment, 211–212
    trade barriers, 213–215
    world's largest marketers, 206
global marketing strategy, 9, 220–222, **223**
    countertrade, 226
    developing, 223–226
    distribution strategy, 225
    multidomestic marketing strategy, 224
    pricing strategy, 226
    product/promotion strategy, 225
global marketplace, 7–9
global positioning system (GPS), 171, 185, 285, 315, 329, 346, 363–364, 459
global reach, 105
global sourcing, **181**
global warming, 91
GMOs. *See* genetically modified organisms
going green, 98
goods, 187, 344, **345**. *See also* products
    classifying, 348–356
    CPG, 374
    defined, 345–346
    emergency, 349
    impulse, 349
    services *vs.*, 345–346
goods-services continuum, **345**
goodwill, 577
government, 248
    B2B marketing, 173, 192–193
    data, 247
    Internet spending, 178
    online, 193
    purchasing procedures, 192–193
    technology sources, 80
government regulation
    antimonopoly period, 71
    child protection, 71
    consumer protection, 71
    cyberspace, 71
    industry deregulation, 71
    in political-legal environment, 71–73
    privacy, 71–72
    protecting competitors, 71
GPS. *See* global positioning system
grandparents, 82, 145–146
grassroots marketing, **320**–321
gray goods, **426**–427
Great Depression, 10, 71, 77, 287, 526, 609
Green Book, 79
greenhouse-gas emissions, 4, 32, 69, 80
green living, 133
green marketing, **91**–92
green products, 60, 380
green washing, 2–4
gross domestic product (GDP), **76**, 204, 217, 226
    China, 77, 79, 209–210
    growth, 77
    India, 77, 79, 209–210
    United States, 77, 79, 209–210
gross rating point (GRP), 546

growth stage, **364**–365
GRP. *See* gross rating point
guanxi, 215
guerrilla marketing, **502**–503, 511, 519
Gulf oil spill, 71

H

hackers, 114
hand shaking, 211
hard sell, 581
headlines, 537
health, 140, 144, 147–149
Helms-Burton Act (1996), 213
Helping Families Save Their Homes Act, 72
high involvement purchase decisions, **156**, 161
Hispanic Americans, 48, 82, 141–142, 277, 287–288, 532
holdbacks, 647
home shopping channels, **508**
homeshoring, **347**
hot spots, 67–68
house brands, 364
household types, 290
humor, 211, 536–537
hyperinflation, 622
hypermarkets, **464**
hypothesis, **245**–246

I

identity theft, 87
Identity Theft Enforcement and Restitution Act, 71, 72
ID theft, 71
illustrations, 537
image, 19
IMC. *See* integrated marketing communications
IMF. *See* International Monetary Fund
importing, 8, **204**, 206, 214
   global marketing, 220–221
   tariffs, 215
import quotas, **214**
impulse goods/services, **349**
IMS. *See* Internet Protocol Multimedia Subsystem
inbound telemarketing, **571**
income, 77–78, 146
income/expenditure patterns, 291
incremental-cost pricing, **624**
independent retailers, 461
indirect competition, 67–68
indirect evaluation, **516**
individual brands, **381**–382
individualism, 140
industrial distributor, **354**, 469
Industrial Revolution, 310
industry deregulation, 71
inelastic demand, **182**, 622
inflation, **77**, 622
influencer, 40, **191**
infomercials, 474, **508**
information investigation, 245
information technology (IT), 5, 22, 184
informative advertising, **529**
infrastructure, **210**
ingenuity, 17
innovators, 293

inquiry tests, 554
inside selling, **572**
installations, **353**–354, 510
instant messaging, 104, 118, 287, 321. *See also* e-mail
institutional advertising, **529**
institutions, 173, 194
integrated marketing, 105–106
integrated marketing communications (IMC), 50, **488**
   components, 489
   databases in, 491
   overview, 489–490
   teamwork, 490–491
integrity, 498
intensive distribution, **423**
interactive advertising, **534**, 538
interactive marketing, **21**, 81
   in e-marketing, 105–106
   relationship marketing and, 21–22
interactive media, 545, 554
interactive television, **320**
interdependent partnership, 316
interest groups, 74–75
intermodal coordination, 439
intermodal operations, **435**
internal customers, **312**
internal data, 245
internal marketing, **312**–313
internal partnerships, **325**
international business markets, 180–181
international marketing, 66, 194. *See also* global marketing
international marketing research, 259
International Monetary Fund (IMF), 213
International Organization for Standardization (ISO), **213**
International Trade Commission (ITC), 215
Internet, 9, 13, 38, 54–55, 80–81, 93, 145, 146, 171, 213, 300, 326, 415, 490, 519, 631. *See also* blogs; cookies; e-business; e-marketing; online marketing; Web sites
   advertising, 500, 538
   aggregators, 250
   as attractive option, 108
   auction houses, 471
   availability, 67–68
   B2B marketing connection, 173
   children and, 71, 72
   competition, 462
   crime, 116
   development, 80, 103
   direct marketing, 474
   direct-response retailing, 474
   direct selling and, 417–418
   distribution and, 49
   financial services industry, 207
   for-profit organizations and, 102
   forums, 118
   functions, 117
   government spending, 178, 193
   Hispanic Americans on, 142
   improving technology, 178
   as interactive media, 545
   music downloads, 64
   nature of, 206
   privacy, 86, 114

reducing marketing barriers, 43–44
regulating, 75
retailers, 439
revolution, 102, 475
search, 328
search engines, 336–337
"stickiness," 257
supplier networks, 187
technology, 211
trademarks and, 387
user characteristics, 113
worldwide use, 103–104
Internet communications. *See also* blogs
   marketing and, 117–121
   online communities, 118–119
   podcasts, 119–120
   promotions, 120–121
   social networking, 118–119
Internet Protocol Multimedia Subsystem (IMS), 80–81
Internet service providers (ISPs), 66, 116, 123
internships, A-4–A-6
interpersonal determinants, in consumer behavior, 139–148
interpersonal influences, 186
interpretative research, **254**, 260
interstitials, 538
intimates, 294
intranets, 108
introductory stage, **363**–364
inventory adjustments, 182–183
inventory control systems, 49, 440
ISO. *See* International Organization for Standardization
ISO 9001:2000, **358**
ISPs. *See* Internet service providers
IT. *See* information technology
ITC. *See* International Trade Commission

J

jargon, 386, 493
JavaScript, 538
JIT. *See* just-in-time
JITII, **182**
job interview, A-12
jobs, 79, A-12. *See also* employment; marketing careers; marketing positions
joint demand, **182**
joint ventures, 222
junk fax law, 256
jury of executive opinion, **264**
just-in-time (JIT), **182**

K

keyword ads, 538, 545
kiosks, 6, 105, 498, 509, 545, 576, 611
kirana-style markets, 48
knowledge, 383
knuckle cracking, 211
Korean War, 287

L

labeling, 2
labels, **389**–390

laggards, 395
language, 146, 210, 212, 223, 387, 493–494.
    See also body copy; buzzwords; Extensible
    Markup Language; jargon
Lanham Act (1946), 385
laptop computers, 32, 60
lateral partnerships, **325**
laws. *See also* government regulation; *specific laws*
    alcohol sales, 73, 88
    antitrust, 213
    automobile emissions, 73
    competition regulated, 72
    competitive environment maintained, 72
    consumers protected, 72
    deregulation, 73
    enforcing, 73
    Engel's laws, 291
    in global marketing, 212–213
    international, 212
    junk fax, 256
    marketing affected, 72
    Praedo's law, 296
LCL. *See* less-than-carload
lead, 65
leader pricing, **652**–653
Leadership in Energy and Environmental
    Design (LEED), 133
learning, **154**–155
LEED. *See* Leadership in Energy and
    Environmental Design
less-than-carload (LCL), 438
less-than-truckload (LTL), 438
letter writing, 79
leverage, 45
life-cycle, 3
life expectancy, 82
lifestyles, 292, 458
lifetime value of a customer, **330**–331
limited-function wholesalers, 469
limited line retailers, 462
limited line store, **462**
limited problem solving, 161
limited-service research supplier, **243**
line extension, **362**, **390**
list price, **645**
lobbying, 75
location
    location-based advertising, 315
    in planned shopping centers, 457–458
    plant, in automobile industry, 177
    retailers by, 465
    retailing strategy, 457–458
    store, 349
location-based advertising, 315
logistics, **414**, 441, 475. *See also* physical
    distribution
    cost control, 432
    ERP, 432
    reverse, 116
    RFID, 430–431
    supply chain management and, 429–432
    third-party, 432
logos, 19, 34, 88
long-distance telephone services, 612
long-term evolution (LTE), 68
loss leaders, **652**
low involvement purchase decisions, **156**

loyalty
    brand, 152, 296–297, 379–380
    customer, 4, 85, 112, 113, 144, 170, 238
    ladder, 20–21
LTE. *See* long-term evolution
LTL. *See* less-than-truckload
luxury goods, 146, 223–224, 262, 291, 380
luxury retailers, 67
luxury shopping, 100–101

M

mad cow disease, 214
magazines, 543–544
mail-order, 49
mail-order wholesaler, **470**
mail surveys, 255–256
maintenance, repair, operating supplies
    (MRO), 355
makers, 293
mall intercept, **255**
malls, 125, 255
    cybermalls, 110, 390
    surveys, 238
manufacturers, 24, 380
manufacturers' brands, **380**. *See also* national
    brands
manufacturers' representative, **419**, **471**
manufacturing, 67, 79. *See also* remanufacturing
MAP. *See* minimum-advertised pricing
mapping, 252–253
marginal analysis, 514, **611**
marginal costs, **621**
markdown, **457**, A-37–A-38
market(s), 249, **276**. *See also* target markets
    factors, in marketing channels, 421, 423
    foreign business, 173–174
    geographic market concentration, 177–178
    international business, 180–181
    kirana-style, 48
    nature, in promotional mix, 510
    orientation, 11
    segments, 69
    share, 45
    supermarkets, 151
    types, 277
market development strategy, **393**
marketing, **7**. *See also* B2B marketing; direct
    marketing; e-marketing; global marketing;
    online marketing; relationship marketing
    affiliate, 174
    affinity, 319
    ambush, 505
    B2B marketing compared to, 171
    buzz, 22, 321, 502
    cause, 16, 18–19
    to children, 88
    to college students, 88
    comarketing, 326
    concentrated (or niche), 299–300
    costs, 23–24, 28
    database, 319–320
    defined, 7
    differentiated, 299
    ecology and, 90–91
    event, 16, 19
    financial analysis, A-33–A-38

frequency, 319
functions, 23–24
global marketplace, 7–9
grassroots, 320–321
green, 91–92
guerrilla, 502–503, 511, 519
integrated, 105–106
interactive, 21–22, 81, 105–106
internal, 312–313
Internet communications and, 117–121
Internet reducing barriers, 43–44
mass, 299
messages, 517–519
mobile, 21
network, 570
neuromarketing, 152
nontraditional, 16–20
in not-for-profit organizations, 14–15
one-to-one, 22
organization, 16, 20
origins, 5–6
person, 16–17
personalized, 105–106, 112
place, 16–18
relationship-based, 20–23
right-time, 105–106
search, 121
selling and, 11
social responsibility, 25–26, 89–92
sports, 18
success, 26–27, 48–49, 68–69, 111–112,
    144–145, 178–179, 208–209, 252–253,
    294–295, 328–329, 366–367, 392–393,
    592–593, 614–615, 654–655
transaction-based, 20–23
undifferentiated, 299
viral, 321, 502
marketing careers, A-1–A-18. *See also* career
    readiness; marketing positions
marketing channels, 49, **414**
    alternative, 417
    channel conflict, 426–427
    communications, 506
    cooperation, 427
    direct selling, 416–418
    distribution intensity, 422–424
    dual distribution, 419–420
    exchange process, 415
    intermediaries, 418–419
    management/leadership, 425–427
    market factors, 421, 423
    in marketing strategy, 415–416
    organizational/competitive factors,
        421–423
    performing functions, 424–425
    product factors, 421, 423
    reverse, 420
    searches, 415
    selection, 421–422
    sorting, 415
    standardizing, 415
    strategies, 421–425
    types, 416–421
    VMS, 427–429
marketing communications, **488**. *See also*
    integrated marketing communications
    business importance, 518

marketing communications (*continued*)
　economic importance, 518
　integration, 519
　social importance, 517–518
　value, 517
marketing concept, 10, **11**, 12
marketing cost analysis, 245
marketing decision support systems (MDSSs), **261**
marketing environment
　competitive environment, 66–70
　economic environment, 76–79
　environmental management, 65–66
　environmental scanning, 65
　marketing mix, 65
　in marketing strategy, 50–52
　political-legal environment, 70–75
　shaping, 64
　social-cultural environment, 52, 82–84
　strategic alliances, 66
　technological environment, 79–80
　technology and, 51
marketing ethics, **84**
　creating program, 85
　defined, 84
　distribution, 87
　ethics officers, 85
　marketing research, 86–87
　pricing, 88–89
　product strategy, 87
　promotions, 86–87
　questions/issues in, 84
　standards, 85
　"stick-and-carrot approach," 85
　workplace test, 86
marketing history
　converting wants to needs, 13
　historical eras, 9–13
　marketing era, 10–12
　production era, 9–10
　relationship era, 10, 12
　sales era, 10
marketing information systems (MISs), **261**
marketing intermediary (or middleman), **416**
marketing mix, **48**, **344**, 488, A-24–A-25
　accessory equipment and, 354
　distribution strategy, 49
　global marketing, 223–226
　in marketing environment, 65
　in marketing strategy, 48–50
　pricing objectives and, 609–616
　pricing strategy, 50
　product strategy, 48–49
　promotion strategy, 49–50
marketing myopia, **13**–14
marketing plan, **A-19**
marketing planning, **38**. *See also* marketing strategy
　assessing organization resources, 42
　BCG matrix, 53–54
　creating marketing plan, A-19–A-32
　defined, 38
　defining mission, 41
　determining objectives, 41
　evaluating environmental risks/
　　opportunities, 42
　formulating strategy, 42

implementing strategy, 42
methods, 52–54
monitoring strategy, 42
overview, 36–37
portfolio analysis, 53
process steps, 41
tactics, 37–41
tools/techniques, 42–47
trends, 39
marketing positions, A-13–A-18
marketing public relations (MPR), **549**
marketing research, **240**
　answers from, 238–240
　computer technology, 261–262
　customer satisfaction, 243
　data collection, 246
　data interpretation/presentation, 246–247
　defined, 240
　defining problem, 244–245
　development, 240–242
　ethics, 86–87
　exploratory research, 245
　hypothesis, 245–246
　international, 259
　interpretative, 260
　marketing ethics, 86–87
　methods, 247–258
　process, 244–247
　research design, 246
　who conducts, 242–243
marketing rules, 4
marketing strategy, **42**, 138, 140. *See also*
　　advertising strategy; B2B marketing
　　strategy; marketing planning
　backfiring, 42
　business practices and, 139
　defined, 42
　elements, 47–52
　first mover strategy, 45
　formulating, A-22
　marketing channels in, 415–416
　marketing environment, 50–52
　marketing mix, 48–50
　Porter's Five Forces, 43–44
　second mover strategy, 45
　selecting/executing, 300–302
　strategic window, 46–47
　SWOT analysis, 45–46, 60
　target market, 47–48
marketing Web site, **107**
market-minus pricing, 643
market penetration strategy, **392**
market-plus pricing, **641**
market potential forecast, 298
market price, **645**
market segmentation, **277**
　climate, 281
　demographic segmentation, 282–292
　effective, 278
　geographic segmentation, 279–282
　GISs, 281–282
　market potential forecast, 298
　multiple variables, 281
　practice, 277
　probable market share, 298
　process, 297–298

product-related segmentation, 296–297
psychographic segmentation, 292–295
regional preferences, 281
relevant profile development, 297–298
selecting segments, 298
strategies, 298–300
understanding, 279
market-share objective, **612**
market structures, 619–620
markup, **457**, A-37–A-38
Maslow's hierarchy of needs, 149–150
mass marketing, 299
mass media, 500
mass merchandisers, **463**
mass-production line, 9
materials handling system, 440–441
mathematics, 5
maturity stage, **365**
MDSSs. *See* marketing decision support systems
meals ready to eat (MRE), 171
media. *See also* radio; television
　advertising selection, 539–546
　broadcast, 539
　comparing alternatives, 540
　direct mail, 473, 503, 544, 608
　interactive, 545
　magazines, 543–544
　newspapers, 4, 543
　outdoor, 544–545
　radio, 541–543
　technologies, 21
media research, **552**
media scheduling, **546**
meeting competition method, **514**
merchandise delivery, 116
merchandise marts, 469
merchandisers, **186**–187
merchandising
　automatic, 474–475
　quick-response, 327
　retailing strategy, 454–455
　scrambled, 465
merchant wholesalers, **469**, 470
message, **491**–492
message boards, 317
message research, **552**
metropolitan statistical area (MSA), **280**
micromarketing, **300**
micropolitan statistical area, **280**
microwave ovens, 80
middle-class consumers, 146
middleman, **416**
Millennial Generation, 287
Miller-Tydings Resale Price Maintenance Act
　(1937), 609
minimum-advertised pricing (MAP), **647**
minorities, 74, 141. *See also specific minorities*
MISs. *See* marketing information systems
mission, **41**, 55
missionary selling, **577**
mobile advertising, 545
mobile marketing, **21**, 111
modified breakeven analysis, **627**–628
modified rebuy, **189**–190
"mom" blogs, 541
monopolistic competition, **619**

monopoly, **66**, **619**. *See also* antitrust
  antimonopoly period, 71
  oligopoly, 67
  operating as, 67
  temporary, 66
motivation, 585
motives, **148**
Motor Carrier Act and Staggers Rail Act, 73
movies, 152
MPR. *See* marketing public relations
MRE. *See* meals ready to eat
MRO. *See* maintenance, repair, operating supplies
MRO items, **355**
MSA. *See* metropolitan statistical area
multidomestic marketing strategy, **224**
multinational corporations, 222–223
multinational economic integration, 215–219
multiple sourcing, **186**
mutual-benefit organizations, 20
mystery shoppers, 238, 243, 317

N

NAFTA. *See* North American Free Trade
    Agreement
NAICS. *See* North American Industry
    Classification System
narrowcasting, 540
national account selling, **327**
national accounts organization, **584**
national brands, 380
National Environmental Policy Act, 72
Native Americans, 141, 288–289
Native Hawaiians, 141
nearshoring, **184**
needs, **148**
  converting to wants, 13
  esteem, 150
  immediate, 159
  Maslow's hierarchy, 149–150
  physiological, 149
  safety, 149
  self-actualization, 150
  social/belongingness, 149–150
negotiated prices, 655–657
neighborhood shopping center, 457
networking, 12
network marketing, **570**
neuromarketing, 152
newsgroups, 118
newsletters, 50
newspapers, 4, 543
new-task buying, **190**
9–11 Generation, 287
noise, **492**–494
nonbusiness enterprises, 518
noncumulative quantity discount, **647**
nonmarketing public relations, **549**
nonpersonal selling, **500**
  advertising, 500
  direct marketing, 501–502
  ethics in, 555–556
  guerrilla marketing, 502–503
  product placement, 500–501
  publicity, 502
  public relations, 502

sales promotion, 501
  television and, 526
nonprobability sample, **251**
nonpurchases, 493
nonstore retailing, 472–475
nontraditional marketing
  categories, 16
  cause marketing, 16, 18–19
  event marketing, 16, 19
  organization marketing, 16, 20
  person marketing, 16–17
  place marketing, 16–18
"No Phone Zone" campaign, 147
North American Free Trade Agreement
    (NAFTA), 8, 72, 176, **217**
North American Industry Classification System
    (NAICS), **176**, 178, 180
not-for-profit organizations, 47, 150, 173,
    180, 194, 277, 325
  broadening scope, 28
  budgets, 15
  clients/sponsors, 15–16
  for-profit organizations *vs.*, 15–16
  marketing, 14–15
  marketing characteristics, 15–16
  objectives/goals, 15
  partnerships, 14–15
  pricing objectives, 616
  promotional items, 15
  strategic alliances and, 23
  technology development, 80
Nutrition Labeling and Education Act
    (1990), 390

O

obesity, 83, 87
objections, **581**
observation, 253, 396
Occupational Outlook Handbook, 417
odd pricing, **650**–651
off-price retailers, 464
offset agreements, 221
offshoring, **183**, 347
  in B2B marketing, 183–185
  problems, 184
  rise of, 183–184
oil industry, 206
  gasoline prices, 618
  oil prices, 8, 654
  OPEC, 226
  pipelines, 436–437
  turmoil affecting, 79
oligopoly, **67**, **619**
Omnibus Trade and Competitiveness Act,
    213–214
one-to-one marketing, 22
online buyers/sellers, 112–113
online catalog, 110
online classified ads, 110–111
online communities, 118–119
online companies, 574
online marketing, 100, 103, 105, 115.
    See also e-marketing
online negotiated prices, 656–657
online payment safety, 113–114

online photos, 112
online pricing
  bundle, 660
  characteristics, 659–660
  global considerations, 658–660
  traditional strategies, 658–659
online promotion, 516
online shopping, 71, 111
online surveys, 256–258
OPEC. *See* Organization of Petroleum
    Exporting Countries
opening price point, **644**
opinion leaders, **146**–147. *See also* trendsetters
order processing, 49, **576**
organic foods, 69
organizational model of buying process
  1: anticipate problem/need/opportunity/
      solution, 187
  2: determine characteristics/quantity of
      good/service, 187
  3: describe characteristics/quantity of goods/
      service, 187
  4: search/qualify sources, 188
  5: acquire/analyze proposals, 188
  6: evaluate proposals/select suppliers, 188
  7: select order routine, 188–189
  8: feedback/evaluation, 188–189
organization marketing, 16, **20**
Organization of Petroleum Exporting
    Countries (OPEC), 226
Orthodox Jews, 141
outbound telemarketing, **571**
outdoor advertising, 544–545
out-of-home advertising, 544
outsourcing, **184**, 210, 215. *See also*
    nearshoring; offshoring
  in B2B marketing, 183–185
  · problems, 184
overstocks, 441
over-the-counter selling, **568**–569
ownership utility, 6

P

Pacific Islanders, 141
packaging, 2
  cost-effective, 389
  CPG, 389
  damage, spoilage, pilferage protection,
      388–389
  design, 49
  Fair Packaging and Labeling Act (1966),
      389–390, 400
  labels, 389–390
  pharmaceutical industry, 388–389
  Poison Prevention Packaging Act (1970), 400
  in product identification, 385–388
  protective, in physical distribution,
      440–441
partnerships, **324**, 332
  buyer, 325
  choosing partners, 325
  interdependent, 316
  internal, 325
  lateral, 325
  not-for-profit organizations, 14–15

partnerships (*continued*)
  product development, 23
  relationship marketing and, 22–23, 316
  seller, 325
  types, 325
party plan, 417
patents, 49, 66
pawn shops, 47
payback, 330–331
payment fraud, 116
pay-per-click, 132
PDA. *See* personal digital assistant
peddlers, 567
penetration pricing strategy, **642**–644. *See also*
    market-minus pricing
people of mixed race, 289
percentage-of-sales method, **514**
perceptions, **150**
  in consumer behavior, 150–152
  individual factors, 150
  perceptual screens, 151–152
  stimulus factors, 150
  subliminal, 152
perceptual screens, **151**–152
personal care industry, 529
personal digital assistant (PDA), 70
personal interviews, 254–255
personalized marketing, 105–106, 112
personal selling, **500, 566**
  AIDA concept, 491, 578
  consultative selling, 574
  ethical issues, 588
  evolution of, 567–568
  field selling, 569–571
  inside selling, 572
  integration among channels, 572–573
  over-the-counter selling, 568–569
  in promotional mix, 500, 567
  relationship selling, 573–574
  sales channels, 568–572
  sales force, 582–587, 594
  sales process, 578–582
  sales tasks, 576–578
  team selling, 574–575
  telemarketing, 571
  trends, 572–576
person marketing, 16–**17**
persuasive advertising, **530**
PERT. *See* program evaluation and review
    technique
pets, 80
phantom freight, 649
pharmaceutical industry, 206, 388–389, 529
philanthropy, 25–26
phishing, 71, **116**
phosphates, 81
physical distribution, **414**
  customer service standards, 433
  elements, 432–433
  freight forwarders/supplemental carriers, 438
  intermodal coordination, 439
  inventory control systems, 440
  materials handling system, 440–441
  protective packaging, 440–441
  suboptimization, 433
  transportation in, 434–438
  warehousing, 49, 261, 439–440, 464, 475

physiological needs, 149
piggyback, 439
PIMS. *See* Profit Impact of Market Strategies
PIMS studies, 612
pipelines, 436–437
place marketing, 16, **17**–18
place utility, 6
planning, **37**, 328. *See also* marketing planning;
    strategic planning
  advertising, 535
  classifications, 39–40
  ERP, 432
  "influencers," 40
  input, 40
  levels, 40–41
  precall, 579
  tactical, 39–40
PLU. *See* price look-up
PMSA. *See* primary metropolitan statistical area
podcasts, 104, **119**, 120, 173
point-of-purchase (POP) advertising, **593**
Poison Prevention Packaging Act (1970), 400
political advertising, 561–562
political-legal environment, **70**
  controlling, 75
  government regulation, 71–73
  interest groups, 74–75
  in marketing environment, 70–75
  regulatory agencies, 73–74
  regulatory forces, 74–75
  self-regulation, 74–75
political risk assessment (PRA), **212**
politics, 79
pollution, 4, 91
polyvinyl chloride (PVC), 27
POP adverting. *See* point-of-purchase advertising
population, 48, 161, **251**
  China, 210, 280
  geographic segmentation, 279–280
  India, 210, 280
  Mexico, 280
  shifts, 141
  United States, 48, 161, 277, 280, 287–288
pop-unders, 538
pop-up ad, **120**
Pop Up Design Clinic, 591
pop-up messages, 116
Porter's Five Forces, **43**–44
portfolio analysis, 53
positioning, **301**. *See also* product positioning
positioning map, **301**
possibility of trial use, 396
postage-stamp pricing, **649**
postpurchase evaluation, 160
posttesting, **553**
power center, 458
PRA. *See* political risk assessment
Praedo's law, 296
precall planning, **579**
predatory practices, 71
predictive dialers, 571
premiums, **591**
preroll video ad, **121**
prescription drugs, 348, 380
presentation, **579**–580
prestige objectives, 614–615
pretesting, **552**–553

price, **606**, 609. *See also* costs
  communicating increase, 650
  customary, 616–617
  determination in economic theory, 619–627
  determination in practice, 624–627
  determination methods, 616–619
  discrimination, 608
  fast-food, 653
  gasoline, 618
  list, 645–648
  marginal costs, 621
  market, 645
  negotiated, 655–657
  off-price retailers, 464
  oil, 8, 654
  online negotiated, 656–657
  opening price point, 644
  price-quality relationships, 654–655
  reductions, 642
  regulatory, 607
  relationship marketing price level, 314
  transfer, 657–658
price flexibility, **651**
price look-up (PLU), 385
price quotations
  allowances, 647
  basing-point pricing, 649
  cash discounts, 645–646
  FOB pricing, 648
  geographic considerations, 648–649
  leader pricing, 652–653
  list price, 645–648
  loss leaders, 652
  price flexibility, 651
  price-quality relationships, 654–655
  product-line pricing, 651–652
  promotional pricing, 652
  quantity discounts, 646–647
  rebates, 331, 647–648
  trade discounts, 646
  uniform-delivered pricing, 648–649
  zone pricing, 649
pricing, 7, 65, 69, 661. *See also* online pricing
  alternative procedures, 624–625
  basing-point, 649
  breakeven analysis, 625–627
  bundle, 660
  competitive, in B2C e-marketing, 111
  concepts, 631
  congestion, 616–617
  decisions, 640
  EDLP, 643–644
  ethics, 88–89
  fixing, 85
  full-cost, 624
  global issues, 629–631
  global marketing strategy, 226
  housing, 618
  increase, 67
  incremental-cost, 624
  law and, 607–609
  leader, 652–653
  luxury, 145
  MAP, 647
  marketing ethics, 88–89
  market-minus, 643
  market-plus, 641

modified breakeven analysis, 627–628
objectives, marketing mix and, 609–616
objectives, not-for-profit organizations, 616
odd, 650–651
postage-stamp, 649
prestige objectives, 614–615
product-line, 651–652
profitability objectives, 610–611
promotional, 652
in promotional mix, 511
psychological, 650–651
retailing strategy, 456–457
strategy, in marketing mix, 50
uniform-delivered, 648–649
unit, 651
value, 613–614
volume objectives, 612–614
Web sites, 123
yield management, 628–629
zone, 649
pricing policies, **649**–651
pricing strategies
competitive, 644–645
penetration, 642–644
skimming, 641–642
primary data, **246**
collection methods, 252–254
controlled experiment, 258
observation method, 252
primary demand, **495**–496
primary metropolitan statistical area (PMSA), **281**
print media, 509
privacy, 252
Children's Online Privacy Protection Act, 71, 72
e-business, 114–115
government regulation, 71–72
Internet, 86, 114
settings, 157
private brands, **380**. *See also* private labels
private carriers, **435**
private data, 248–250
private exchanges, 108
private labels, 380
probability sample, **251**
probable market share, 298
problem/opportunity recognition, 158
product(s), 7, 65, **345**. *See also* business
    products; consumer products; goods
advertising, 529–530
alternative, 159, 160
attributes, 67
banned television advertising, 541
business (B2B), 348
consumer (B2C), 348
defined, 48–49, 344–345
differentiation, 497
eco-friendly, 656
factors, in marketing channels, 421, 423
functional, 76
generic, 145, 380
green, 60, 380
invention, 225
lines, 53
nature, in promotional mix, 510
new, 10–11, 13, 238
new, on Web sites, 103
obsolete, with technology, 79–80

placement, 500–501
recalls, 65
single-product firms, 422
substitute, 67
sustainable, 26–27
types of consumer, 348–351
product advertising, **529**–530
product deletion, 344, 368–369
product development, 49, 392, **393**
adopter categories, 395
adoption process, 394–395
commercialization, 400
development, 399
idea generation, 399
new-product committees, 397
new product departments, 397
organizing for, 396–398
partnerships, 23
process, 398–400
product managers, 397
screening, 399
strategies, 392–395
test marketing, 400
venture teams, 397–398
product differentiation, **497**
product diversification strategy, **394**
product identification, 384–385
brand extensions, 390–391
brand licensing, 391
brand marks, 385–386
brand names, 385–388
packaging, 385–390
trademarks, 386–388
production orientation, **9**
product liability, **400**–402
product lifecycle, 49, 344, **362**
advertising and, 530
decline stage, 365–366
extending, 366–368
fads, 366
finding new uses, 367
growth stage, 364–365
increasing use frequency, 366–367
increasing users, 367
introductory stage, 363–364
making physical changes, 368
maturity stage, 365
in promotional mix, 510–511
stages, 363–366
product-line pricing, **651**–652
product lines, **359**, 651–652
growing, 360
market position, 360
resources and, 360
retailers, 462–464
product managers, **397**
product mix, 344, **360**, 369
decisions, 361–362
depth, 361
length, 361
width, 361
product-oriented management, 13
product placement, **500**–501
product positioning, **392**
product-related segmentation, **296**
benefits sought, 296
brand loyalty, 152, 296–297, 379–380

multiple bases, 297
usage, 296
product strategy
alternative, 225
ethics, 87
international, 224–225
in marketing mix, 48–49
quality as, 356–359
profitability objectives, 610–611
profit center, **657**–658
Profit Impact of Market Strategies (PIMS), **612**
profit maximization, **611**
program evaluation and review technique
    (PERT), 398
promotion, 7, 65, 69, 314, **488**. *See also*
    cross-promotion; sales promotion; trade
    promotions
accentuating value, 498
category, 497
communication process and, 492
consumer sales, 590–592
cross-, 551
defined, 49
demand increasing, 496–497
effectiveness, 515–516
ethics, 86–87
global marketing strategy, 224–225
increasing demand, 496–497
industry, 557
Internet communications, 120–121
measuring effectiveness, 552–554
nonpersonal selling, 501
not-for-profit organizations, 15
objectives, 495
online, 516
pricing, 652
product differentiation, 497
providing information, 495–496
retailing strategy, 458–459
stabilizing sales, 498–499
strategy, in marketing mix, 49–50
promotional allowance, **647**
promotional items, 15
promotional mix, **499**
advantages/disadvantages, 503–504
elements, 499–504
factors influencing, 512
funding, 512
nature of market, 510
nature of product, 510
nonpersonal selling, 500–503
optimal, 509–510
personal selling, 500, 567
pricing, 511
product lifecycle, 510–511
promotional pricing, **652**
promotion strategy
alternative, 225
budgeting, 513–515
international, 224–225
marketing mix, 49–50
pulling, 512–513
pushing, 512–513
retailing, 458–459
timing, 513
proprietary B2B transactions, 104, 108–109
prospecting, **578**–579

prosperity, 76
protective packaging, 440–441
protective tariffs, **213**
PSAs. *See* public service announcements
psychographic segmentation, **292**
    advantages, 295
    global, 294–295
    VALS™, 293–294
psychological pricing, **650**–651
psychology, 5, 138
Public Health Cigarette Smoking Act, 72
publicity, **502, 549**. *See also* advertising
    nonpersonal selling, 502
    public relations and, 549–551
public relations, **502**, 548–549
    ethics in, 556
    marketing, 549
    measuring effectiveness, 554
    nonmarketing, 549
    nonpersonal selling, 502
    publicity and, 549–551
public service announcements (PSAs), **517**
puffery, **555**–556
pulling strategy, **512**–513
purchase categories segmentation, 177
purchase decision/act, 159–160
purchase decision process, 178–179
purchase volume, 19
pure competition, **619**
"pure-play" dot-com retailers, 116–117
pushing strategy, **512**–513
push money, **594**
PVC. *See* polyvinyl chloride

Q

qualifying, **579**
qualitative forecasting, **263**–264, 266
quality, 243, 498
    price-quality relationships, 654–655
    as product strategy, 356–359
    service, 358–359
    TQM, 357
    worldwide programs, 357–358
quantitative forecasting, 258, **263**–266
quantity discounts, **646**
    cumulative, 647
    noncumulative, 647
    price quotations, 646–647
question marks, 54
quick-response merchandising, **327**
quota sample, **251**

R

rack jobber, **469**
radio, 541–543
radio-frequency identification (RFID), 80,
    250, 320, 327, 390, **430**, 440
    logistics, 430–431
railroads, 73, 435
random-digit-dialing, 571
raw materials, **355**
R&D. *See* research and development (R&D)
reach, 546
readership tests, 553
Read ID Act, 72

rebates, 331, **647**–648
recalls, 65, 73, 83, 553
recession, 76–77, 144, 179, 456
reciprocal tax treaties, 212
reciprocity, **190**
recovery, 76
recycling, 27, 32, 78, 91, 374
reference groups, **145**–146
refunds, 590–**591**
regional shopping center, 458
regulatory agencies, 73–74
regulatory cost recovery fees, 607
reinforcement, 154–155
rejection, 394
related party trade, **204**
relationship marketing, **12**, 39, 194, **310**, 567
    airlines, 308–310
    beginning early, 21
    continuum, 314–316
    elements, 312
    emphasis, 311–312
    evaluating, 330–332
    focus, 332
    interactive marketing and, 21–22
    interdependent partnership level, 316
    internal marketing, 312–313
    IT and, 22
    levels, 314–316
    loyalty ladder and, 20–21
    partnerships and, 22–23, 316
    price level, 314
    social interactions level, 314–315
    social marketing and, 21–22
    strategic alliances and, 22–23
    transaction-based marketing shift, 20–23,
        310–314
relationship selling, **573**–574
relative advantage, 396
relevance, 383
relevant profile development, 297–298
reliability, 359
remanufacturing, **194**
reminder advertising, **530**
repeat buying, 475
repositioning, **302**
research, 69, 250. *See also* marketing research
    brands, 238
    computer, 80, 261–262
    consumer behavior, 136–138
    employee, 238
    exploratory, 245
    full-service research suppliers, 243
    international marketing, 259
    interpretative, 254, 260
    limited-service research supplier, 243
    media, 552
    message, 552
    research, 246
    technology, 80
research and development (R&D), 642
research design, **246**
resellers, **173**
resource-producing industries, 172
Responsibility and Disclosure (CARD) Act, 72
responsiveness, 359
restrained spending, 144–145
résumés, A-4, A-6–A-10

retail advertising, **534**
retail cooperative, **428**
retailer convergence, **465**
retailers
    big-box, 468
    brick-and-click, 474
    categorizing, 460
    chain stores, 461
    convenience, 461
    by form of ownership, 461
    general merchandise, 463–464
    independent, 461
    Internet, 439
    limited line, 462
    by location, 465
    luxury retailers, 67
    off-price, 464
    by product lines, 462–464
    "pure-play" dot-com, 116–117
    retailer convergence, 465
    retailer-owned cooperatives/buying offices, 472
    scrambled merchandising, 465
    showroom/warehouse retailers, 464
    specialty, 461
    types, 460
retailing, **450**
    direct-response, 473–474
    nonstore, 472–475
    promotion strategy, 458–459
    wheel of, 451
retailing strategy
    atmospherics, 460
    components, 452
    customer service, 455–456
    fundamental steps, 451
    location/distribution, 457–458
    merchandising strategy, 454–455
    pricing, 456–457
    promotional, 458–459
return on investment (ROI), 21, 258, 612
revenue, 213
    cost/revenue curves, 620–621
    elasticity and, 623
revenue tariffs, **213**
reverse channels, **420**
reverse logistics, 116
RFID. *See* radio-frequency identification
right-time marketing, 105–106
risk taking, 23–24
rivalry, 44
Robinson-Patman Act, 71, 72, **608**, 609, 651.
    See also Anti-A&P Act
robotics, 80
ROI. *See* return on investment
routinized response behavior, 160–161
RSS, 102
rule of three, 51

S

safety needs, 149
salary, **586**
sales analysis, **245**
sales attire, 575
sales branches, 468–469
sales calls, 418

sales force, 594
 compensation, 586
 evaluation/control, 586–587
 motivation, 585
 organization, 584–585
 recruitment/selection, 582–583
 supervision, 585
 training programs, 583–584
sales force composite, **264**
sales forecasting, **263**
 benefits/limitations, **263**
 in marketing plan, 262–263
 qualitative forecasting, 263, 266
 quantitative forecasting, 263, 266
 software, 263
sales incentives, **577**
sales managers, 581–582, 585, 587
sales offices, 469
sales orientation, **10**
salespeople, 594
 buyers' expectations, 574
 children, 569–570
 distinguishing themselves, 573
 selling goodwill, 577
sales pitch, 489
sales process
 approach, 579
 closing, 581
 demonstration, 580–581
 follow-up, 581–**582**
 objections, 581
 in personal selling, 578–582
 presentation, 579–580
 prospecting, 578–579
 qualifying, 579
sales promotion, **501**, 566, **588**, 594
 consumer-oriented, 590–592
 incentives to buy, 589
 spending for, 589
 trade, 592–594
sales quota, **586**
sales tasks
 creative selling, 577
 missionary selling, 577
 order processing, 576
 in personal selling, 576–578
sampling, **251**, **591**
satellite television, 74, 82, 539
scanning technology, 250
scoreboards, 546
scrambled merchandising, **465**
screening, 399
sculptural physics, 399
search marketing, **121**
secondary data, **246**
 caveat emptor, 251
 collection, 247–251
 government data, 247
 online sources, 250–251
 private data, 248–250
 2010 U.S. Census, 247–248
second mover strategy, **45**
Secure Sockets Layer (SSL), **114**
selective demand, **497**
selective distribution, **423**
self-concept, **155**–156

self-regulation, 74–75
seller partnerships, **325**
seller's market, **10**
selling agents, **471**
selling up, 459
sender, **491**
seniors, 48, 74, 161, 285–286
service encounter, **358**
service quality, **358**–359
services, 187, 344, **345**, 498. *See also* customer
  service; Internet service providers
 agents, 470–472
 ASPs, 320
 brokers, 110, 470–472
 classifying, 348–356
 defined, 345–346
 emergency, 349
 exporting, 206–207
 financial services industry, 207
 full-service research suppliers, 243
 goods *vs.*, 345–346
 impulse, 349
 limited-service research supplier, 243
 merchant wholesalers, 470
 quality of, 358–359
 service sector role, 346–348
 syndicated, 242–243
 Web services, 108, 327
 wholesaling, for customers/producer-
  suppliers, 466
 wholesaling intermediaries, 466
 wireless, 13
service sector, 346–348
sex-based advertising appeals, 537
shaping, **155**
shelf space, 454–455
Sherman Antitrust Act, 71, 72, 424
shopbots (bots), **111**, 631, **660**, 661
shoppers, 123, 136, 137. *See also* consumers
shopping. *See also* online shopping
 blogs, 102
 comparisons, 111
 cybershopping, 111
 electronic shopping bag, 110
 electronic shopping cart, 110
 luxury, 100–101
shopping centers. *See also* malls
 community, 457–458
 lifestyle center, 458
 locations in planned, 457–458
 neighborhood, 457
 power center, 458
 regional, 458
shopping products, **350**, 352
shortages, 78–79
showroom/warehouse retailers, 464
SIC. *See* Standard Industrial Classification
signature, 537
simple random sample, **251**
single-product firms, 422
skimming pricing strategy, **641**–642. *See also*
  market-plus pricing
SKU. *See* stock-keeping unit
slogans, 384
slotting allowances, 349–350, 455. *See also*
  slotting fees

slotting fees, 349–350
smart phones, 27, 51, 54, 110–111, 140, 223,
  252, 315, 328–329
 reaching children, 146
SMPRs. *See* Social Media Press Releases
snail mail, 117
social/belongingness needs, 149–150
social causes, 19
social classes, 146
social-cultural environment, 52, **82**, 210
 consumerism, 82–84
 in marketing environment, 82–84
social influences
 Asch phenomenon, 144–145
 in consumer behavior, 143–147
 opinion leaders, 146–147
 reference groups, 145–146
social marketing, **21**–22
social media, 21, 36, 151, 175, 287
Social Media Press Releases (SMPRs), 36
social networking, 19, 36, 82, 101–102, 250, 256
 advertising, 538
 African Americans, 142
 Internet communications, 118–119
 reaching children, 146
 social classes, 146
social responsibility, **25**, **89**, 93
 defined, 89
 ecology, 90–91
 environmental issues, 90
 ethics and, 24–26
 global effect, 90
 long-term effects, 90
 in marketing, 25–26, 89–92
 pyramid, 90
socioeconomic segmentation, 282. *See also*
  demographic segmentation
sociology, 5, 138
soft currencies, 210
soft drink advertising, 87
solar panels, 80
sole sourcing, **182**
sorting, 23–24, 415
spam, 71, **118**
span of control, **585**
special rates, 434
specialty advertising, **592**
specialty products, **350**–352
specialty retailers, **461**
specialty stores, 462
spiffs, 594
split runs, **554**
sponsorship, **504**–505
sports marketing, 18
sports sponsorships, 19
spreadsheet analysis, **A-22**
spyware, 114
SSL. *See* Secure Sockets Layer
Standard Industrial Classification (SIC), 176
standardizing/grading, 23–24
staples, **349**–350
start-up companies, 80
"staycations," 36
step-out, **642**
"stick-and-carrot approach," 85
stock-keeping unit (SKU), **455**
store location, 349

straight rebuy, **189**
strategic alliances, **23**, **66**, 119, **329**–339
    in marketing environment, 66
    not-for-profit organizations and, 23
    relationship marketing and, 22–23
    vertical alliances, 23
strategic business units (SBUs), **53**–54
strategic planning, **39**–40, **A-19**
strategic window, **46**–47
strategy. *See also* advertising strategy; global
        marketing strategy; marketing strategy;
        pricing strategies; product strategy; pro-
        motion strategy; retailing strategy
    advertising, 531–534
    B2B marketing, 192–195
    competitive, 68–69
    competitive pricing, 644–645
    distribution, 49, 225, 457–458
    distribution, in marketing mix, 49
    first mover, 45
    market development, 393
    marketing channels, 421–425
    in marketing mix, 50
    marketing planning, 37–42
    market penetration, 392
    market segmentation, 298–300
    multidomestic marketing, 224
    origin, 39
    penetration pricing, 642–644
    product, 87
    product development, 392–395
    product diversification, 394
    pulling, 512–513
    pushing, 512–513
    second mover, 45
    skimming pricing, 641–642
stratified sample, **251**
"street fashion," 155
strengths, weaknesses, opportunities, and
        threats (SWOT), 45
stress, 159. *See also* anxiety
strivers, 293–294
subcontracting, **221**
subcultures, **141**
    African Americans as, 141–142
    Asian Americans as, 141–143
    Hispanic Americans as, 141–142
subliminal perceptions, **152**
suboptimization, **433**
subsidies, **214**–215
substitute products, 67
suggestions selling, 459
supercenters, **464**
supermarkets, 151
superstores, 125
supplemental carriers, 438
suppliers, 188, 466–467
supplies, 79, **355**
supply, **619**
supply chain management, **414**, **429**,
        429–432, 441
supply chains, 2, 62, **328**–329. *See also*
        value chain
supply networks, 475
support teams, 327
surfer, 102
survey of buyer intentions, **264**

Survey of Current Business, 248
Survey of Media Markets, 249
surveys, 243, 248–250, 264
    fax, 256
    focus groups, 238, 255
    mail, 255–256
    malls, 238
    online, 256–258
    personal interviews, 254–255
    telephone interviews, 254
survivors, 293
sustainability, 50, 68–69, 91–92
sustainability index, 2–4
sustainable products, **26**–28
sweatshops, 62–64
sweepstakes, **591**
SWOT. *See* strengths, weaknesses, opportuni-
        ties, and threats
SWOT analysis, **46**, 60, A-24
syndicated services, **242**–243
systems integration, **186**

T

tactical planning, **39**–40
tag lines, 160, 167
tangibles, 359
target markets, 19, 49, 65, **276**, A-24–A-25
    career readiness, 283
    marketing strategy, 47–48
target-return objective, **611**
target returns, 626
tariffs, **213**, 607. *See also* General Agreement
        on Tariffs and Trade; North American
        Free Trade Agreement
    defined, 213
    import, 215
    protective, 213–214
    revenue, 213
task-objective method, **515**
taxes, 212, 658
teams, 327
team selling, **574**–575
teamwork, 490–491
technological environment, **79**, 211–212
    applying technology, 80–81
    in marketing environment, 79–80
technology, 49–50, 64, 93, 227, 576, 661
    advances, 55
    applying in technological environment, 80–81
    computer, in marketing research, 261–262
    government sources, 80
    green, 80
    Internet, 178, 211
    leveraging, 332
    marketing environment and, 51
    media, 21
    not-for-profit organizations developing, 80
    obsolete products and, 79–80
    research, 80
    revolution, 4
    social concerns addressed, 80
teenagers, 274–276
    in age segmentation, 284
    auto purchasing, 148
    in family purchases, 148
    social networking, 146

telecommunications, 4, 9, 73, 74, 212, 490
Telecommunications Act, 73, 74
teleconferencing, 76
telemarketing, 71, 73, **507**–508, **571**
Telemarketing Sales Rule Amendments, 73
Telephone Consumer Protection Act of
        1991, 571
telephone interviews, 254
television, 27, 146, 253, 490, 493
    advertising, 151, 539–541
    banned products, 541
    cable, 74, 82, 539–541, 660
    commercials, 151, 495
    interactive, 320
    nonpersonal selling and, 526
    satellite, 74, 82, 539
temporary monopoly, 66
terrorist attacks, 76
test marketing, **258**, 265, 400
texting, 287, 386
thinkers, 293
third generation (3G), 214
third party (contract) logistics firms (3PL
        firms), **432**
3-D players, 393, 427
3G. *See* third generation
3G networks, 4
3PL firms. *See* third party (contract) logistics
        firms
thrift stores, 47
ticket scalping, 608
TIGER. *See* Topographically Integrated Geographic
        Encoding and Referencing system
time-based competition, **69**–70
time utility, 6
TL. *See* truckload
tobacco industry, 72, 74, 85. *See also* cigarette
        industry
Topographically Integrated Geographic Encoding
        and Referencing system (TIGER), 248
total quality management (TQM), **357**
tourism, 17–18, 67, 207
toy fairs, 592–593
toys, 6
TQM. *See* total quality management
trade, 7
    agreements, 8
    associations, 178
    controlling, 215
    countertrade, 226
    deficit, 347
    gap, 79
    regulation, 212
Trade Act (1998), 213
trade allowances, **592**–593
trade barriers
    embargo, 214
    exchange control, 215
    global marketing, 213–215
    import quotas, 214
    subsidies, 214–215
trade discounts, **646**
trade dress, **387**
trade fairs, 469
trade-in, **647**
trade industries, **173**, 195
trademarks, 49, **386**

CTM, 218
global, 387–388
Internet and, 387
for product identification, 386–388
protecting, 386–387
trade dress, 387
trade promotions, **501**, **592**
dealer incentives/contests/training programs, 591, 594
management, 515
POP advertising, 593
trade allowances, 592–593
trade shows, 180, 579, 593–594
trade shows, 180, 579, **593–594**
training programs, 583–584, 594
transaction-based marketing, **20**, **310**
closing deals, 20
goals, 311
relationship marketing shift, 20–23, 310–314
transaction economies, 467
transfer price, **657**–658
transparency, 62
transportation, 23–24, 49
air freight, 437–438
carriers, 73, 434–435
comparing modes, 438
major modes, 435–438
motor carriers, 435–436
in physical distribution, 434–438
pipelines, 436–437
railroads, 73, 435
water carriers, 436
trend analysis, **265**
trendsetters, 146, 156
trial, 394
truck jobber, 470
truckload (TL), 438
truck wholesaler, **470**. *See also* truck jobber
trunk shows, 417
truth in advertising, 87
t-shirts, 545
2010 U.S. Census, 247–249
tying agreement, **424**

U

unaided recall tests, 553
undifferentiated marketing, **299**. *See also* mass marketing
unemployment, **77**
unfair trade laws, **608**–609
uniform-delivered pricing, **648**–649
unitized pallets, 441
unit pricing, **651**
universal product code (UPC), 250, **390**
unsought products, **348**
UPC. *See* universal product code
upstream management, **430**–431
users, **191**
utility, **5**, 66, 74
defined, 5
form, 5–6
ownership, 6
place, 6
time, 6
types, 5–6

V

vacationing, 67
VALS™, **293**–294
value, 292, 498
value-added service, 430
value analysis, **190**
value chain, 328, 429
value pricing, **613**–614
variable costs, **620**
variety stores, 463
vending machines, 421
vendor analysis, **190**
vendor-managed inventory (VMI), **327**–328, **440**
vendors, 353
venture teams, **397**–398
vertical alliances, 23
vertical marketing systems (VMS), **427**–429
videoconferencing, 76
video game generation, **287**
Vietnam War, 287
view-through, 554
viral marketing, **321**, 502
virtual conferences, 38
virtual reality, 151
virtual sales support, 580
virtual sales team, **575**
virtual storefronts, 104
vishing, **116**
visual buzz, 22
VMI. *See* vendor-managed inventory
VMS. *See* vertical marketing systems
voice over Internet Protocol (VoIP), 4, **80**–81, 102, 116
VoIP. *See* voice over Internet Protocol
volatile demand, 182
volume objectives, 612–614
volunteerism, 140

W

WAP. *See* Wireless Application Protocol
warehouse clubs, 67, 144, 463
warehousing, 49, 261, 439–440, 464, 475
warranties, 49
Webcams, 545–546
Web contacts, 104
Web services, 108, **327**
Web sites, 71, 82, 83, 87, 102. *See also* Internet
assessing, 123–124
business models, 106
click-through rate, 124
conversion rate, 124
corporate, 107, 124
domain name, 122
effective Web presence, 121–123
engagement, 124
exclusives, 110
goals, 121
implementation/interest, 121–123
maintaining, 122–123
marketing, 107
navigation, 123
new product information, 103

pricing, 123
profitability, 123
revamping, 123
for shopping comparisons, 111
site design, 116–117
standards, 123
successful development, 121
Web-to-store shoppers, **123**
Wheeler-Lea Act, 72
wheel of retailing, **451**
"Who Dat?" slogan, 384
wholesalers, **24**, **416**, **465**, 475
cash-and-carry, 469
limited-function, 469
mail-order, 470
merchant, 469–470
services, for customers/producer-suppliers, 466
truck, 470
wholesaler-sponsored voluntary chain, 428
wholesaling intermediaries, **465**
creating utility, 465–466
functions, 465–468
independent, 469–471
lowering costs, 467–468
services, 466
transaction economies through, 467
types, 468–469
widget, **121**, 320
Wi-Fi. *See* wireless fidelity
wikis, **119**
Wi-Max, 68
win-back, 238
wind energy, 69
Wireless Application Protocol (WAP), 459
wireless fidelity (Wi-Fi), 67–68, 80, 252, 431
women, 48, 161
auto purchasing, 148
in family purchases, 147–148
purchase influence, 278, 283
shoppers, 137
women's movement, 287
wool, 366–367
word of mouth, 151
world's economies, 7
World Trade Organization (WTO), 8, 213, 214, **217**, 230
World War II, 10, 287
Wow! factor, 591
WTO. *See* World Trade Organization

X

XML. *See* Extensible Markup Language

Y

yield management, **628**–629
youth, 140
yo-yos, 6

Z

zapping, 535
Zip codes, 608
zone pricing, **649**

international index

A

Africa, 8, 104, 150, 204, 211, 294
Americas, 246
Andorra, 202
Argentina, 217
Asia, 8, 62–64, 101, 204, 208, 223–224, 246, 393
  developing, 294
  economy, 204
  Internet use, 103–104, 211
  outsourcing, 184
  relationship marketing, 194
  technology research, 80
  workers, 79
Association of Southeast Asian Nations (ASEAN), 213
Australia, 141, 173, 232, 295, 367, 385
  airline travel, 309
  bottled water, 216
  congestion pricing, 617
  Internet use, 104, 211
  language, 494
  TV networks, 207
Austria, 212, 218, 269

B

backshoring, 347
Bahamas, 306
Bahrain, 202
Belgium, 211, 218, 269
Brazil, 68, 141, 181, 217, 225, 599
Bulgaria, 212, 218

C

Canada, 4, 9, 26, 27, 157, 172, 175–176, 208, 217, 222, 233, 291, 542, 630
  airline travel, 309
  battery roundup, 420
  bottled water, 216
  economy, 204
  fire-safe cigarettes, 74
  FTAA, 217
  labels, 391
  language, 494
  NAFTA, 217
  nearshoring, 184
  plastic shopping bags, 82
  sports marketing, 18
  tariffs, 607
  U.S. trading partner, 205
  wireless service, 612
Caribbean, 69, 104, 211, 306, 494
Central America, 184, 203, 206, 217
Central American Free Trade Agreement-DR (CAFTA-DR), **217**

Chile, 216–217, 223
China
  aircraft manufacture, 67
  auto market, 607
  CAFTA, 213
  cell phone satellites, 181
  electric bicycle industry, 76
  emerging markets, 612
  exports to United States, 8
  fast-food, 207
  GDP, 77, 79, 209–210
  global sourcing, 181
  gray market, 427
  import quotas, 214
  Internet use, 103, 213
  investments, 222
  millionaires, 292
  offshoring destination, 183–184
  oil/gas operations, 206
  outsourcing, 215
  pizza, 208
  population, 210, 280
  private jets, 599
  sports marketing, 18
  tourism, 207
  trade controls, 215
  U.S. imports, 207
  U.S. trading partner, 205
China-ASEAN Free Trade Area (CAFTA), 213
Colombia, 217
common market, **215**
Costa Rica, 202
countertrade, **226**
Croatia, 218
Cuba, 214, 227
customs union, **215**
Cyprus, 218
Czech Republic, 218

D

Denmark, 207, 218
Dominican Republic, 217
dumping, **215**

E

Ecuador, 202, 217, 306
Egypt, 9, 181, 208
El Salvador, 202
Estonia, 218
euro, 8, 140, 210, 218
Europe, 8, 9, 33, 101, 223, 233, 246, 295, 382, 432, 500, 505, 538
  auto industry, 225, 643
  bananas, 214
  cell phones, 560
  economy, 204

  electric bicycle industry, 76
  generic products, 380
  GMOs, 212
  Internet use, 104, 211
  intimates, 294
  investors, 222
  ISO standardization, 213
  open skies agreement, 426
  outsourcing, 184
  product preferences, 140
  recession, 79
  technology research, 80
  TV networks, 207
  wireless service, 318
European Court of Justice, 212
European Union (EU), 79, 140, 192, 214, 358
  airline travel, 309
  bananas, 214
  benefits, 219
  euro, 210, 218
  GMOs, 212
  members, 218
exchange control, **215**
exchange rate, **210**
exporting, 8, **204**–205, 213, 220
  China to U.S., 8
  in global marketing, 220–221
  service/retail, 206–207

F

Finland, 9, 218, 269
France, 166, 218, 269, 291, 464
  debate, 210
  GMOs, 212
  handshaking, 211
  income data, 292
  investments, 222
  oil/gas operations, 206
  U.S. trading partner, 205
free trade area, **215**
Free Trade Area of the Americas (FTAA), **217**
friendship, commerce and navigation treaties (FCN), **212**

G

General Agreement on Tariffs and Trade (GATT), 213, **216**–217, 230
Germany, 18, 141, 194, 218–219, 222, 225, 232, 269, 294–295, 481
  census, 291
  GMOs, 212
  handshaking, 211
  humor, 211
  millionaires, 292

private brands, 380
  U.S. trading partner, 205
global marketing, 5, 48
  benefits, 207–209
  contractual agreements, 221
  developing global marketing strategy,
    223–226
  direct investment, 221–222
  dumping, 215
  economic environment, 209–210
  employment and, 204
  exporting, 220–221
  globalization and, 219
  laws in, 212–213
  levels of involvement, 220
  marketing mix, 223–226
  from multinational corporations,
    222–223
  multinational economic integration,
    215–219
  new era, 227
  political-legal environment, 212–213
  role of, 205–209
  service/retail exports, 206–207
  social-cultural environment, 210
  technological environment, 211–212
  trade barriers, 213–215
  world's largest marketers, 206
global marketing strategy, 9, 220–226, **223**
Great Britain, 292, 494, 542
Greece, 166, 218
Guatemala, 202, 217
Gulf of Aden, 437

H

Haiti, 15
homeshoring, **347**
Honduras, 202, 306
Hong Kong, 4, 205, 207, 211, 223–224,
    427, 481, 542
Hungary, 79, 212, 218, 497

I

importing, 8, **204**, 206, 214–215, 220–221
import quotas, **214**
India, 8, 101, 202, 206, 225–226, 230, 393,
    481, 599
  auto industry, 643
  cell phone satellites, 181
  electric bicycle industry, 76
  fast-food, 207
  franchises, 221
  GDP, 77, 209–210
  global sourcing, 181
  Internet use, 103
  investments, 222
  kirana-style markets, 48
  offshoring destination, 183
  outsourcing, 210
  pizza, 208
  population, 210, 280
  Western influences, 48
Indonesia, 202, 205, 224, 233, 280
International Monetary Fund (IMF), 213

International Organization for
    Standardization (ISO), **213**, **358**
Ireland, 208, 218, 292, 494
Italy, 101, 141, 218, 269, 599, 617

J

Jamaica, 217
Japan, 9, 33, 141, 173, 206, 222, 225, 233,
    382, 393, 481, 505, 613, 661
  airline travel, 309
  census, 291
  consumer durable industry, 206
  handshaking, 211
  income data, 292
  Internet use, 103
  investors, 222
  language, 494
  millionaires, 292
  population, 280
  recession, 79
  signs/gestures, 493
  sports marketing, 18
  technology research, 80
  U.S. trading partner, 205
Jordan, 181

K

Korea, 232, 393, 613
Kuwait, 292

L

Latin America, 202, 204, 260, 412
  bananas, 214
  consumers, 259
  Internet use, 211
  TV networks, 207
Latvia, 218
Lebanon, 481
Lithuania, 218
Luxembourg, 9, 218

M

Macau, 69
Macedonia, 218
Malaysia, 181, 613
Malta, 218
Mediterranean, 493
Mexico, 4–5, 8, 51, 176, 202, 217, 225,
    230, 243, 463
  airline travel, 309
  FTAA, 217
  language, 494
  NAFTA, 217
  nearshoring, 184
  outsourcing, 215
  pizza, 208
  population, 280
  private jets, 599
  tariffs, 214, 607
  U.S. trading partner, 205
Middle East, 8, 104, 204, 211, 246, 274,
    294, 538

multidomestic marketing strategy, **224**
multinational corporations,
    222–223

N

nearshoring, **184**
Netherlands, 5, 206, 218, 222, 269, 302
New Zealand, 295, 366–367, 494, 613
Nicaragua, 202, 631
North America, 9, 131, 203, 359, 434
  foreign trade, 204
  Internet use, 104, 211
  outsourcing, 184
North American Free Trade Agreement
    (NAFTA), 8, 72, 176, **217**
North American Industry Classification
    System (NAICS), **176**, 178, 180
Norway, 309

O

Oceania, 211
offshoring, **183**–185, 347
Oman, 295
Organization of Petroleum Exporting
    Countries (OPEC), 226

P

Panama, 69, 412–414
Peru, 217
Philippines, 295, 393
Poland, 218
Portugal, 141, 218
Puerto Rico, 274, 306

R

related party trade, **204**
revenue tariffs, **213**
Romania, 218, 494
Russia, 47, 79, 208–209, 217, 223,
    274, 610
  humor, 211
  pizza, 208
  private jets, 599

S

Saudi Arabia, 205, 295, 441
Scandinavia, 18
Scotland, 109
Singapore, 211, 224, 292, 565, 617
Slovakia, 218
Slovenia, 218
soft currencies, 210
South Africa, 9, 494
South America, 206, 233, 306, 538
South Korea, 5, 205, 208, 214,
    225–226, 658
Soviet Union, 226
Spain, 194, 202, 218, 292, 459, 463
subcontracting, **221**
subsides, **214**–215
Sweden, 210–211, 218, 617
Switzerland, 211, 233, 292, 309, 358

T

Taiwan, 393
tariffs, **213**–215, 607
Thailand, 210, 224, 481
Trinidad and Tobago, 217, 245, 306
Tunisia, 493
Turkey, 218, 481

U

United Arab Emirates, 292, 481
United Kingdom, 18, 27, 69, 101, 112,
     173, 206, 218, 222, 225, 230, 232,
     269, 385, 387, 469, 481, 658
  congestion pricing, 617
  investments, 222
  investors, 222
  oil/gas operations, 206
  plastic shopping bags, 82
  private brands, 380
  Tesco towns, 630–631
  TV networks, 207
  U.S. trading partner, 205
  wireless service, 328
United Nations, 204
United States, 27, 33, 69, 101, 116, 140–141,
     157, 166, 172, 175–176, 202, 204, 214,
     217, 222, 230, 232, 244–245, 274, 306,
     314, 358, 367, 379–380, 412, 435, 469,
     486, 500, 612, 630
  advertising, 500, 528–529
  airline travel, 309
  auto industry, 148, 167, 173, 225, 643
  baseball teams, 504
  battery roundup, 420
  billboards, 544
  blogs, 103, 119
  bottled water, 216
  CAFTA-DR, 217
  cell phone market, 69, 70
  China exports to, 8
  congestion pricing, 617
  consumers, 144, 291
  culture, 139, 142

defense programs, 195
department stores, 463
direct marketing, 505
discretionary income, 78
dumping, 215
e-business, 102
economy, 204, 221–222, 654
electricity industry, 74
ethnic populations, 287–288
exports, 205, 207
fire-safe cigarettes, 74
foreign markets attracted to, 9
franchises, 428
FTAA, 217
GDP, 79, 209–210
geographic segmentation, 279–280
global market research, 259
GMOs, 212
goods/services, 347
government customer group, 192
gray market, 426–427
handshaking, 211
Hispanic consumers, 82, 142
humor, 211
import quotas, 214
inflation, 77
international marketers target,
     226–227
Internet development, 80
Internet users, 103, 113
intimates, 294
investments, 222
labels, 390–391
legal environment, 70, 212–213
manufacturing concentration, 177
market dominance, 223
Mexico markets and, 51
millionaires, 292
mobile advertising, 545
NAFTA, 217
offshoring, 183
oil/gas operations, 206
open skies agreement, 426
PC sales, 614
pipelines, 436

plastic shopping bags, 82
population, 48, 161, 277, 280
private brands, 380
product recalls, 65
raw materials purchases, 206
recession, 79
retailing, 206
sales managers, 582
sales promotion, 588
search advertising, 523
service firms, 346
signs/gestures, 493
soda consumption, 45
spending, 78, 137
sports leagues, 219
sports marketing, 18
subcultures, 141
tariffs, 213–215, 607
technology research, 80
third-party logistics, 432
toy industry, 6
trademark protection, 387
trading partners, 205
trucking, 434
2010 Census, 247–249
unemployment, 77
vacationers, 67
VoIP business, 80
volunteers, 14
wireless service, 318, 328, 612
Uruguay, 216–217

V

Venezuela, 79, 205, 217
Vietnam, 8, 181, 214

W

World Trade Organization (WTO), 8, 213,
     214, 217, 230

Z

Zimbabwe, 622